The Detective Novels
of Agatha Christie

The Detective Novels of Agatha Christie

A Reader's Guide

JAMES ZEMBOY

McFarland & Company, Inc., Publishers
Jefferson, North Carolina

The present work is a reprint of the illustrated case bound edition of The Detective Novels of Agatha Christie: A Reader's Guide, *first published in 2008 by McFarland.*

LIBRARY OF CONGRESS CATALOGUING-IN-PUBLICATION DATA

Zemboy, James.
The detective novels of Agatha Christie : a reader's guide / James Zemboy.
p.   cm.
Includes index.
softcover : acid free paper ∞
1. Christie, Agatha, 1890–1976—Stories, plots, etc.—Handbooks, manuals, etc.
2. Christie, Agatha, 1890–1976—Characters—Handbooks, manuals, etc.
3. Detective and mystery stories, English—Handbooks, manuals, etc.   I. Title.
PR6005.H66Z98   2016   823'.912—dc22   2008004078

BRITISH LIBRARY CATALOGUING DATA ARE AVAILABLE

ISBN (print) 978-1-4766-6595-5
ISBN (ebook) 978-0-7864-5168-5

©2008 James Zemboy. All rights reserved

No part of this book may be reproduced or transmitted in any form or by any means, electronic or mechanical, including photocopying or recording, or by any information storage and retrieval system, without permission in writing from the publisher.

Printed in the United States of America

On the cover: Agatha Christie ca. 1950s (Photofest); typewriter © 2016 Shutterstock

McFarland & Company, Inc., Publishers
Box 611, Jefferson, North Carolina 28640
www.mcfarlandpub.com

Table of Contents

Preface 1
Introduction 3

The Mysterious Affair at Styles (1920)	15	Death Comes as the End (1945)	215
The Secret Adversary (1922)	20	Remembered Death (1945)	218
Murder on the Links (1923)	24	Murder After Hours (1946)	224
The Man in the Brown Suit (1924)	30	There Is a Tide (1948)	231
The Secret of Chimneys (1925)	34	Crooked House (1949)	239
The Murder of Roger Ackroyd (1926)	39	**Summary for the 1940s**	243
The Big Four (1927)	43	A Murder Is Announced (1950)	245
The Mystery of the Blue Train (1928)	48	They Came to Baghdad (1951)	253
The Seven Dials Mystery (1929)	53	Mrs. McGinty's Dead (1952)	257
Summary for the 1920s	57	Murder with Mirrors (1952)	266
Murder at the Vicarage (1930)	57	A Pocket Full of Rye (1953)	270
Murder at Hazelmoor (1931)	62	Funerals Are Fatal (1953)	275
Peril at End House (1932)	69	So Many Steps to Death (1954)	282
Thirteen at Dinner (1933)	74	Hickory, Dickory, Death (1955)	288
The Boomerang Clue (1934)	80	Dead Man's Folly (1956)	293
Murder in the Calais Coach (1934)	86	What Mrs. McGillicuddy Saw (1957)	303
Murder in Three Acts (1935)	92	Ordeal by Innocence (1958)	311
Death in the Air (1935)	97	Cat Among the Pigeons (1959)	315
The A.B.C. Murders (1935)	105	**Summary for the 1950s**	323
Murder in Mesopotamia (1936)	111	The Pale Horse (1961)	327
Cards on the Table (1936)	117	The Mirror Crack'd (1962)	333
Death on the Nile (1937)	125	The Clocks (1963)	342
Poirot Loses a Client (1937)	131	A Caribbean Mystery (1964)	348
Appointment with Death (1938)	144	At Bertram's Hotel (1965)	353
A Holiday for Murder (1938)	149	Third Girl (1966)	360
Easy to Kill (1939)	155	Endless Night (1967)	367
And Then There Were None (1939)	162	By the Pricking of My Thumbs (1968)	369
Summary for the 1930s	166	Hallowe'en Party (1969)	375
Sad Cypress (1940)	167	**Summary for the 1960s**	382
The Patriotic Murders (1940)	174	Passenger to Frankfurt (1970)	382
Evil Under the Sun (1941)	181	Nemesis (1971)	387
N or M? (1941)	187	Elephants Can Remember (1972)	393
The Body in the Library (1942)	192	Postern of Fate (1974)	398
The Moving Finger (1942)	200	Curtain (1975)	403
Murder in Retrospect (1943)	204	Sleeping Murder (1976)	407
Towards Zero (1944)	209	**Summary for the 1970s**	414

Appendix: British Expressions 417
Title and Character Index 425
Subject Index 441

Preface

The most widely read author of the English language in the world is William Shakespeare. The second most widely read author of the English language in the world is Agatha Christie. With the exception of the Bible, Christie's detective novels have been translated into more foreign languages than any other books in the world.

In her amusing essay, "Cornwallis's Revenge," Emma Lathen makes the following statements in an effort to express the sheer numbers of copies of Christie's detective novels that exist:

1. A column composed of all US editions of *Peril at End House* would stretch from Peoria, Illinois, to the moon.

2. Merely keeping *What Mrs. McGillicuddy Saw* in print in the United States deforests five thousand woodland acres in Maine every year.

3. Of all departing passengers on United Airlines—going anywhere—58.6 percent carry hand luggage and 47.2 percent carry an Agatha Christie.

4. The more Americans there are, the more people there are reading *The Body in the Library*.

These tongue-in-cheek remarks were made in approximately 1977. It is now 2007 and there can be no doubt that the column of US editions of *Peril at End House* would now stretch from Peoria to Mars and that Maine and several neighboring states must now be totally deforested. As to specific percentages of airline passengers carrying an Agatha Christie, we may now add the fact that for every one thousand DVD players in American homes, there are four hundred thirty-three boxed sets of the Hercule Poirot films and three hundred seventy-six boxed sets of the Miss Marple films on DVD reposing in shelves near them.

There must be a reason for all of this, and in my opinion the reason is that, for pure fun and relaxation, nothing beats Agatha Christie's detective novels, no matter how many times one rereads them. The characters sparkle with life, whether they are stereotypical English housemaids, stereotypical American tourists at an English seaside resort, stereotypical boring old ex–Anglo-Indian colonels, or stereotypical aging English-village spinsters. The stories themselves are sometimes engaging, sometimes forgettable. One unkind critic once wrote, "Who cares who killed Roger Ackroyd?" The fact is, Agatha Christie fans know perfectly well who killed Roger Ackroyd, but that doesn't prevent them from having an awfully good time reading about it again and again.

Just the right combination of gentle, inoffensive humor along with recognizable, not-very-seriously-threatening situations and characters, and universal types who are portrayed never with animosity or bitterness but with gentle pen strokes and with a smile, make Christie a special joy to her fans. That word "gentle" comes up often in my thoughts about Christie. There is never anger or bitterness or disgust hidden beneath Christie's storylines or character portrayals. The Christie experience is always a pleasant experience.

Christie invites the reader to enjoy an amusing, fairly interesting and even exciting story that's populated by amusing, fairly interesting and even exciting characters, and she does it in a gentle, friendly, chatty way that never draws attention to her own genius. If a serious flower gardener invites you to inspect his garden, you know by the way he gives his tour whether he hopes you will love the flowers or if he hopes you will be impressed by his gardening skill. Reading Christie is like being taken for a pleasant garden tour by a gardener who really loves flowers and wants you to love them, too.

In this book I have attempted to show the uniqueness of each of Christie's sixty-six detective novels *and* the uniqueness of every one of the characters who populate them by tracing Christie's developing skill in characterization. In order to increase the reader's enjoyment of Christie's works, I have pointed out some interesting facts about the geographical and historical backgrounds for each of the novels. For the benefit of readers who are unfamiliar with the French language and Christie's nuanced use of it, I have provided English translations of all of the French that occurs in the novels. There is also an Appendix that explains some of the peculiarly British terms with which some readers may be unfamiliar and which occur in Christie's novels. My goal is to create, for fans of Agatha Christie's detective novels, even more enjoyment of and appreciation for the novels than they may already feel.

What follows is the product of countless hours enjoying Christie's detective novels, complemented by her 1977 autobiography. Many excellent books have already been written about Christie's works, and most of them deal with her detective novels *and* her short stories, her plays and her six non-detective novels that were published under the Mary Westmacott pseudonym. Christie's popularity largely rests, however, on the sixty-six detective novels because it is in those that her ingenious storytelling and character portrayals are most clearly expressed. Therefore I leave to other writers the pleasure of commenting on Christie's "other" works, and I dedicate this book to the legions of Agatha Christie fans who, like me, never tire of rereading our favorite not-very-serious author.

Introduction

A Few Facts about Agatha Christie's Life (1890–1976)

Agatha Christie was born Agatha Mary Clarissa Miller in Torquay, a resort town on the south coast of Devon in southwestern England. Her family was "upper middle class" and her father was an American whose investment income permitted him to support his family without working.

Christie's childhood was apparently a happy one and she got along well with her parents and siblings. She had no formal schooling, but her mother taught her to read at an early age and young Agatha was an avid reader, although the reading materials available to her may have been of doubtful literary value. Adventure novels such as *Treasure Island* and *The Prisoner of Zenda* seem to figure prominently among the books she read and reread as a youngster. Christie's father taught her basic arithmetic but Christie never made any systematic study of history, geography, or any of the sciences or mathematics. She was provided with piano lessons and, for a year or two, with a monolingual French governess for the purpose of forcing her to acquire fluency in spoken French. At that time, a familiarity with conversational French was a very useful skill among the upper middle class in Britain, as vacationing in France was extremely common among them. While she was a teenager, Christie spent a year or two at a *pensionnat*, or "finishing school," in Paris where she continued her music studies, improved her reading and writing of French, and briefly contemplated a career as an opera singer.

Christie had two marriages. The first, to Archibald Christie, began in 1914 and ended in divorce in 1928. Christie gave birth to her only child, Rosalind, in 1919. Her second marriage, to archeologist Max Mallowan, began in 1930 and lasted until Christie's death in 1976. Christie's daughter Rosalind married in 1941 and gave birth to a child, Christie's only grandchild, in 1943. Rosalind's husband was killed in action toward the end of World War Two, and she remarried in 1949.

Christie's second husband, Max Mallowan, outlived her by two years, marrying his longtime mistress, Barbara Parker, in 1977.

A Few Facts about Her England (1890–1976)

In 1890 Great Britain was the richest nation in the world and had the world's highest standard of living. The British Empire was at its fullest extent. England had been the first country in the world to industrialize, vast numbers of British working-class people earned their livings by working in grim industrial towns, and thousands of middle class families became wealthy as a result of industrial production. The vast British Empire provided enormous amounts of additional wealth for Britain. Because Britain's living standard was so much higher than that of any other country, it became common for affluent Britons to travel abroad, usually to France, when "on holiday." It was even customary for British families, if they happened to find themselves in financial difficulty, to "go abroad for a time" since living expenses were so much lower in other countries. Any British family who owned a home, or even rented an apartment, could let their home or sublet their apartment, go abroad for a year or two, and live cheaply enough to pay off their debts with the rent money they received for their home or flat in England. Christie's own family lived in France for that very purpose, for a short time, when she was a child.

World War One (1914–1918) was a disaster for all of Europe, of course, but in different ways for different countries. In France, the war resulted in underpopulation for the next generation, since approximately one half of the young men in France who would have married and produced families died in battle before marrying. For a full generation France was largely a nation of "old maids." For England, the consequences of World War One were different. Before the War, a good deal of England's wealth had been attributable to international trade alliances and shipping, and all of that was disrupted by the War and it was never fully reestablished. During the decade of the 1920s, which Americans remember as the wildly prosperous "Roaring Twenties," England grew steadily poorer and unemployment was rampant. There was constant fear, among the British middle and upper classes, of a "general strike" and there was intense fear of Bolshevism, which had brought about revolution in Russia just a few years earlier. There was, in fact, a General Strike in England in 1926, which brought the nation's already ailing economy to a standstill.

Economic conditions in England became even worse during the 1930s when America's "Great Depression" spread to Europe.

The Second World War (1939–1945) impoverished Britain still further, and then the British Empire came apart rapidly. One by one, British colonial holdings in Africa, the Middle East and Asia became independent. The loss of India in 1947 effectively marked the death of the British Empire and after 1947 England, once the richest country in the world, was just another struggling post-war European nation. The rationing of food, clothing and other essential goods in Britain continued well into the 1950s. By the middle of the 1950s it became clear that England's living standard was falling behind the living standards of the rest of Western Europe. The few Britons who could still afford to travel abroad were forced to accept a "travel allowance" which limited the amount of British currency that could be taken out of England. By the time Agatha Christie died, in 1976, England was being characterized as the "poor boy" of Europe.

Loss of wealth, loss of power and loss of international prestige was the fate of Britain as the twentieth century progressed, and all of this is chronicled in Agatha Christie's detective stories, although not deliberately or directly. The changes are often simply *felt* by the reader through the conversations, thoughts and attitudes of Christie's characters, especially in the novels that she wrote during the 1950s and 1960s.

Some Facts about Her Writing Career

Agatha Christie has been quoted as saying, "Nothing in my life surprised me more than success as a writer," and as late as the 1950s she was reluctant to call herself a professional author. Her "writing career" began as a bet that her sister made with her in 1912. The sister bet that Agatha could not write a detective story.

As children, Agatha and her siblings had been encouraged to use their imaginations freely in creating games and play activities. They often wrote and acted their own plays, and they wrote poems and stories. Agatha had already written several poems and stories, and even a complete novel, before her sister made her the bet about writing a detective novel, although none of those had ever been published.

During World War One, while her young husband was away at war (he was an air force pilot) Christie worked for the war effort, first as a nurse and then as a medical dispenser. It should be remembered that, at that time, "nursing" was not the sophisticated profession that it is today. Christie's "nursing" consisted primarily of doing emergency bandaging for wounded soldiers who were brought back daily in large numbers from the front, and her "training" for this probably took no more than a few days. At the dispensary Christie learned a good deal about poisons, and while not at work, she had plenty of time to herself. She wrote her first detective novel, *The Mysterious Affair at Styles*, at that time, and an interesting chemical phenomenon, which Christie learned about while working in the dispensary, is a part of the solution of the mystery. It was in that book that the eccentric foreign detective Hercule Poirot and his sidekick Hastings made their first appearances. The book was finished in 1916 and between 1916 and 1918 Christie sent the manuscript to three different publishers, each one returning it to her as "not acceptable." In 1918, she sent it to a fourth publisher, The Bodley Head, and then soon forgot about it because the War ended suddenly, her husband returned home, and the young couple moved to London where Christie's husband was lucky enough to find a job in some financial capacity.

Agatha soon found herself pregnant and her daughter Rosalind was born in 1919. Christie had been discouraged by the rejection of her book by three successive publishers but had "quite forgotten about it" until one day, in 1920, she received a letter from The Bodley Head expressing some interest in the book and suggesting that "something might be done with it."

The publishing editor explained to Christie that the book had possibilities, but that the final chapter, a courtroom scene, was all wrong and could not have happened in the way Christie had written it. He offered her the choice of rewriting the chapter completely, without the courtroom scene, or obtaining the assistance of a lawyer who could guide her in courtroom procedures. Christie chose to rewrite the final chapter differently, and thus was born the famous "Poirot reveals all" ending which characterized most of her future detective novels.

In her excitement about the prospect of having her detective novel published, Christie accepted all of the terms of the contract The Bodley Head offered her. She was to receive no author's royalties unless more than two thousand copies were sold; she would have to split with The Bodley Head any money offered by periodicals for serial rights to the book; and The Bodley Head was to have "publication rights" for her next five books.

Christie had no intention of ever writing another book. The only reason she had written *The Mysterious Affair at Styles* in the first place was the bet that her sister had made with her. She eagerly agreed to the terms of the contract simply to have her book published. The book sold just under two thousand copies, and so she received no author's royalties. A magazine offered fifty pounds for serialization rights, and so she received half of the fifty pounds for that. It may seem that twenty-five pounds was a paltry sum, but we should remember that inflation has, over the decades, vastly diminished the value of all currencies, and as we read Christie's early detective novels, we must be careful not to undervalue the "murder motive" of inheritances and legacies. During the 1930s, for example, Britons commonly supported families on three digit annual incomes, and in a 1939 Christie detective novel the skilled private secretary of a millionaire earns six pounds a week. In a 1946 Christie novel, a woman works as a saleslady in a London dress shop for four pounds a week. Therefore the twenty-five pounds that Christie received for serial rights to her first book in 1920 was not nearly as little as it may appear to have been.

In any case, Christie had no intention of ever writing another book. However, in 1921 Christie's mother found it necessary to contemplate selling the family home, Ashfield, in Torquay. Christie had a sentimental attachment to the family home and was very upset by the prospect of its having to be sold. It was her husband, Archibald Christie, who suggested to her, "Why don't you do something about it? You could write another book." Christie gave some thought to this and soon completed her second book, *The Secret Adversary*, an adventure story which she later said was "much easier to write" than the earlier book. The Bodley Head was not very impressed by this second book but agreed to publish it in 1922. *Murder on the Links* soon followed, and this third novel was more to the publishers' liking, being a true detective story, and again featuring Hercule Poirot and his friend Hastings. It appeared in print in 1923.

Christie had experienced at least two disputes with The Bodley Head by this time. In the publishing of *The Mysterious Affair at Styles,* the person in charge of spelling at The Bodley Head insisted on spelling the word "cocoa" as "coco," which was of course incorrect. Christie went to The Bodley Head offices with at least two dictionaries and some tins of cocoa to prove that her spelling of the word was correct, but to no avail. The word is still spelled "coco" in modern printings of that novel. A second dispute occurred when *Murder on the Links* was published. Without consulting with Christie and obtaining her approval, the publisher had the jacket of the book designed with a painting of a scene that did not take place in the story. This angered Christie very much, and by now she had formed the opinion that the terms of her contract with The Bodley Head were unfair to her. She resolved to seek another publisher as soon as she had complied with her contractual obligations, which meant that The Bodley Head had publication rights for three more books.

In 1922, a friend of Christie's husband, who worked in some capacity for the Government, was about to sail around the world, visiting all of the countries of the British Empire in preparation for an Imperial Exposition scheduled to take place in 1923. Archibald Christie had some expertise in financial matters, and the friend asked him to come along on the trip as a "financial adviser." He told Archibald that his job in London would probably be held for him, which was wishful thinking. The Christies agreed enthusiastically to the plan, eager for a chance to sail around the world, and they left their daughter Rosalind, then aged about three, in the care of Christie's mother and sister in Torquay.

During the trip, which Christie enjoyed immensely despite a severe bout with seasickness early in the trip, the couple visited South Africa and traveled northwards in Africa as far as Rhodesia and the famous Victoria Falls. They then proceeded eastwards to India and China, and then to Australia and across the Pacific to Canada, finally returning to England across the Atlantic via New York. The trip took the better part of a year.

When the Christies arrived in London they found that Archibald's job had *not* been saved for him but had been given to another man, and the employment situation in England was extremely bad and getting worse. It took some time for Archibald to find another job, and so for the second time Christie turned to writing a book simply to earn some money. She disliked writing this fourth book very much and found it very difficult. It was *The Man in the Brown Suit* and Christie was not fond of it, although she made good use of her experiences in Africa in writing the story. The Bodley Head was not any fonder of the book than they had been of *The Secret Adversary*, but they accepted it and published it in 1924. Christie then wrote another novel for The Bodley Head, which they refused to publish, but since Christie had in fact written it, it had to be counted as one of the "next five books" to which they had "publication rights." And so although that book was never published, it left just one more book for Christie to write for The Bodley Head before she was allowed to seek another publisher. She quickly produced *The Secret of Chimneys,* another book that did not please The Bodley Head very much, but they published it in 1925, and that ended Christie's relationship with them.

Christie chose Collins as her new publisher. The first manuscript that she presented to them was *The Murder of Roger Ackroyd,* her first masterpiece, and they published it in 1926. The book was hugely successful and made the name "Agatha Christie" a household word. Unfortunately, 1926 was an unhappy year for Christie because it was then that her husband announced his desire for a divorce in order to marry another woman. Christie may have suffered a nervous breakdown as a result of this situation. She disappeared one day and a nationwide search for her was made. There was enormous publicity and some newspapers suggested that her "disappearance" was nothing but a publicity stunt to promote her latest book. Christie's car was found abandoned somewhere and she was found registered at a country hotel under the name of her husband's girlfriend. The true facts about this incident have never been made clear and Christie herself does not mention the incident at all in her *Autobiography*. As a consequence of the incident, Christie developed an extremely negative attitude toward the press and reporters, and in all of her future novels, reporters and newspapers in general are very negatively portrayed.

As to the divorce requested by her husband, Christie resisted the idea for two years but finally accepted the inevitable and agreed to it in 1928. During this time she wrote *The Big Four*, published in 1927, and *The Mystery of the Blue Train*, published in 1928. She later characterized *The Mystery of the Blue Train* as her all time worst book, probably because of the extreme personal depression she undoubtedly felt while writing it, and while writing *The Big Four,* which has never been popular among readers. Her next book, the 1929 *The Seven Dials Mystery*, was a sequel to the 1925 *The Secret of Chimneys.*

Christie's feelings of personal depression about her failed marriage caused her to follow friends' advice "to take a long trip abroad." Christie had often crossed the English Channel when traveling to France, and at the French port of Calais she had often noticed the Orient Express train waiting for British passengers bound for Baghdad. The idea of traveling to Baghdad on the Orient Express train had always been a source of romantic excitement to her, and so she decided to travel to Baghdad herself just for fun, aboard the Orient Express, late in 1928.

In Iraq (which was then still called Mesopotamia and was a British "protectorate") Christie met an archeologist and his family, and a family friend of theirs, a younger archeologist named Max Mallowan. Christie was then thirty-eight years old and Max was just twenty-three. A friendship developed between them and they married after about a year and a half, after considerable resistance on Christie's part because of the age difference. Why Max Mallowan wanted to marry Agatha Christie remains a bit of a mystery. According to her *Autobiography,* Max explained his interest in her by pointing out that she had never "made a fuss" about inconveniences of travel and daily living in the Middle East, and would therefore make a good wife for an archeologist. It seems to be a rather weak reason for wanting to marry a woman, but be that as it may, the couple married in 1930.

It should be mentioned that, during 1926, Agatha Christie and her daughter Rosalind had spent a good deal of time in Torquay attending to family matters—the sale of the family home, for one thing—and for an extended time her first husband Archibald lived alone in London. It was during this "time alone" that he met and fell in love with his new girlfriend. Christie—and probably a lot of women in those days—felt strongly that if a woman is away from her husband, she is "neglecting" him, and therefore she should not be surprised if he seeks the company of other women. And so when Christie married her second husband, she was bound and determined that she would never "neglect" *him*. From the beginning of their marriage, she never left his side, spending six months of every year with him in the Middle East as he studied history and pre-history in the buried ruins of ancient peoples, leaving her daughter in the care of boarding schools in England. She made herself as useful as possible at the digging sites, acquiring considerable knowledge and skill in photography among other things. She was, at first, so involved with her husband and his work that, in later years, she confessed that she had no recollection of the books she had written between 1929 and 1932. Those were *Murder at the Vicarage,* in which the famous Jane Marple character was introduced, *Murder at Hazelmoor,* and *Peril at End House.*

Christie was apparently very happy in her marriage to Max Mallowan and the 1930s are a magnificent decade in her writing. She wrote and published seventeen detective novels during those years, nearly every one a masterpiece, ending the decade with the 1939 *And Then There Were None,* which may be her best known mystery story.

Because of the threat of a new war in the late 1930s, Max Mallowan's archeological work in the Middle East was suspended in 1938 and did not resume until about ten years later. During the war years, both Christie and her husband worked in war-related activities, but she continued her writing, producing additional masterpieces and salting two of them away to be published after her death. Those were the Hercule Poirot adventure *Curtain* and the Miss Marple novel *Sleeping Murder.*

Christie's detective novels of the 1940s had a more serious atmosphere than the books she had written during her first two decades, and her skill in characterization advanced to a remarkable degree. Christie had actually wished to write more "serious" fiction for quite a long time, and had written a "serious," non-detective novel during the late 1920s, which Collins reluctantly published in 1930 under the pseudonym Mary Westmacott. Over the next couple of decades, Christie wrote and published five more novels under that pseudonym. As a group they are not memorable, although one that she published during the 1940s, *Absent in the Spring,* is a fascinating study of a woman's thoughts about her marriage when she finds herself forced to do nothing but think. Married women who have always "known" that their husbands are devoted to them will not sleep well the first night after reading it.

Because of her interest in creating more "serious" fiction and in creating characters of more substance and complexity than the ones that usually populate detective stories and other "light fiction," several of Christie's detective novels of the 1940s seem more like serious works of fiction than recreational reading. Examples are the 1943 *Murder in Retrospect,* the 1945 *Remembered Death,* the 1946 *Murder After Hours* and the 1948 *There Is a Tide.* These books lack the lightness, humor and "sparkle" of Christie's earlier detective novels and were probably disappointing to her readers. Christie also took a strong interest in writing plays during the 1940s and at least one of them, *The Mousetrap,* was hugely successful, becoming the longest-running British play in history, opening in London in 1952 and still running as of this writing (October 2007).

Regarding the "serious tone" of a few of Christie's detective novels of the 1940s, there are at least three possible origins for that new direction, in addition to Christie's desire to write "more serious" fiction. World War Two was a very frightening and depressing experience for all Britons. Christie had lived through the First World War, of course, but she was a much younger person and she was "in love" and probably very happy despite the events of the War. When the Second World War began Christie was a mature woman of nearly fifty, and as early as 1940 Germany had already defeated or formed an alliance with every country in Continental Europe except the Soviet Union, leaving Britain the only Western European country still at war with her. There were undoubtedly large numbers of Britons who fully expected a German conquest of Britain. Life in postwar England was extremely grim, despite the defeat of Germany, and the whole decade of the 1940s was a period of psychological depression for most thinking Britons. By contrast, the post-war years in America were filled with optimism, energy and material prosperity.

A second event of the 1940s—in Christie's personal life—was the marriage of her daughter Rosalind in 1941. Announcing her intention of getting married, Rosalind then casually asked her mother "Do you want to be at the wedding?" The question shocked Christie very much. Her response was "Of course I want to be at the wedding," but the question must have caused Christie to begin a thorough self-examination in the matter of her relationship with her daughter. From a modern point of view, Christie had been an extremely uninterested, probably even "neglectful" parent to Rosalind. We recall that when Rosalind was about three years old, Christie and her first husband cheerfully left her in the care of relatives and sailed around the world for a year, returning to find that their daughter scarcely remembered them. Then, from 1930 through 1938, when the child was aged eleven through nineteen, Christie and her second husband spent half of each year in the Middle East, leaving Rosalind in the care of boarding schools in England. There was probably no closeness or "bonding" between the mother and daughter at any time. In Christie's detective novels of the 1940s, and well into the 1950s, we can see evidence that "mothering" and "parenting" became a major preoccupation to her.

A third *possible* event in Christie's life during the 1940s—only *possible* because there is no hard documentation of it—is that Christie *may* have become aware of her second husband's marital infidelities during that decade. The subject of marital fidelity receives rather more serious treatment in Christie's detective novels during that period, most notably in the 1945 *Remembered Death* and the 1946 *Murder After Hours*. See the *Characters* sections for those novels—in particular the characterizations of John and Gerda Christow in *Murder After Hours*, and those of Stephen and Sandra Farraday in *Remembered Death*. The Christie novel *Absent in the Spring*, published under her Mary Westmacott pseudonym, was also clearly a product of Christie's intense preoccupation, at that time, with a husband's infidelity and a wife's reaction to it.

During the 1950s Christie returned to a lighter touch in her detective novels, a change that her fans undoubtedly welcomed. Her books of the 1950s are also noteworthy as chronicles, for it was during the 1950s that Christie clearly became aware of major changes in society and, in particular, English society. In general it is the increasing impoverishment of the British middle class to which almost constant references are made, but there are also interesting references to the Cold War, the threat of nuclear war, improvements in medical care and education for the lower-income classes, an increase in senseless, violent crime and, most of all, the disappearance of the "servant class" in England.

With the beginning of the 1960s, the quality of Christie's detective novels began to decline, and several of her books of that period are remembered more for the nostalgic musings of the older characters than for the "mystery stories" that they were supposed to be. Only one of Christie's detective novels of the 1960s—*A Caribbean Mystery*—measures up to most of her previous books. The others should be avoided by all readers except devoted Christie fans who have read most of her previous works.

During the 1970s Christie wrote only four additional detective novels and they are embarrassingly poor, although the 1970 *Passenger to Frankfurt* may be amusing to persons who are, as Christie herself must have been, disgusted with the path the modern world, especially politics, seems to be taking.

The Geography of Christie's Detective Novels

In Christie's detective novels there are always references to counties, cities, towns and villages in England. Sometimes they are real places and sometimes they are fictitious. When they are fictitious, however, there is usually something in the story that indicates in which part of England they are located. For example, in an early novel the fictitious town of Market Basing is mentioned. Although there is no mention of the county in which Market Basing is located, characters in the story travel by train from London to Market Basing by boarding trains at London's Paddington Railway Station. Because it is well known that Paddington Station serves only points west of London, we know that Market Basing must be "somewhere west of London." In one story the actual number of miles by train from Paddington Station to a certain fictitious town is stated. These remarks give the reader a good idea of the locations of even the "fictitious" places mentioned in the stories.

The following remarks may be useful to American readers unfamiliar with English geography.

English Counties

England is divided into a large number of counties of widely varying sizes. Over the years boundaries between counties have been adjusted several times, and major changes occurred especially during the early 1970s. During that period certain counties, such as Worcestershire for example, disappeared from the administrative map of England and their territories were absorbed by neighboring counties. Later, however, Worcestershire in particular regained its official status. Incidentally, the "-shire" ending of county names is pronounced "-sher," not "-shire." The counties whose names end in "-shire" nearly always have a city within them after which the county was named. Examples: Nottingham (in Nottinghamshire), York (in Yorkshire), Gloucester (in Gloucestershire), Worcester (in Worcestershire), etc. The county of Berkshire is an exception, as there is no town in that county called "Berk."

The recent adjustments of county boundaries are of no importance to a reader of Agatha Christie's stories, however, and in the following paragraphs—as well as throughout this book—the *present tense* is used in references to the "historical" counties of England, since their existence is "present" with respect Christie's writing.

The borders of the counties usually have more to do with historical events than administrative convenience. Rutland is a tiny county with a tiny population; Yorkshire is a huge county filled with large industrial cities and a population numbering in the millions. Not all of England's counties are settings in Christie novels and most are not even mentioned. Those that are settings, or are at least favored with "mentions," are the following, beginning with the North and working towards the South:

Northumberland. This is England's northernmost county, sharing a border with Scotland, and it is sparsely populated. Northumberland is a minor setting in just one Christie novel, the 1976 *Sleeping Murder* (written during the 1940s.) A brief scene in that story takes place at country home in Northumberland.

Yorkshire. This is England's largest and most populous county. Because of its large size, it is divided for administrative purposes into three regions called "Ridings." "Riding" is a linguistic descendent of the older term "thriding" which meant "one third part." There are a West Riding, a North Riding and an East Riding, these last two having coastlines on the North Sea. The geography of the North and East Ridings is wild and picturesque and includes a vast area of beautiful wasteland known as "the Yorkshire moors," the setting for Emily Brontë's romantic novel *Wuthering Heights*.

The West Riding of Yorkshire, however, is the largest of the three. It is densely populated and includes a large number of drab industrial cities which may be relatively pleasant places to inhabit nowadays but which were, during the nineteenth century—and during most of Christie's lifetime—grimy, inhospitable places. The West Riding of Yorkshire is in fact part of an area known as "The Industrial Midlands" which include the counties of Nottinghamshire, Derbyshire, Staffordshire, Lancashire and Leicestershire. Sheffield, Manchester, Leeds, Mansfield, Doncaster, Nottingham, Wolverhampton, Birmingham and other grim industrial cities are crowded together in "The Midlands."

The Midlands are rarely settings for Christie stories and are rarely mentioned. Two early exceptions are the 1935 *Murder in Three Acts,* in which a sanatorium in Yorkshire is the setting of some scenes late in the story, and the 1935 *The A.B.C. Murders,* in which a murder takes place in the city of Doncaster, in Yorkshire. A character in the 1946 *Murder After Hours,* Midge Hardcastle, is described has having spent her childhood in an unspecified "grim northern industrial town."

Because of their industrial history, the "Midlands" are associated with the great wealth that Victorian industrialists accumulated. Two of Christie's novels of the 1950s have as their settings "vast Victorian mansions" in the Midlands. Both are negatively described with terms such as "temples to wealth" or "temples to Plutocracy." The two novels are the 1952 *Murder with Mirrors* and the 1953 *Funerals Are Fatal*. The 1938 *A Holiday for Murder* is set in the fictitious county of "Middleshire"—which suggests by its name "the Midlands," and the house in which the crime takes place is an "ugly" Victorian mansion that was built by an industrialist. A male character in that story wonders why a young Spanish girl of exotic beauty would be traveling by train from London to "the grimy industrial Midlands of England." In the 1950 novel *A Murder Is Announced,* Middleshire is said to be the county in which the village of Chipping Cleghorn is located. Supposedly it is the same "Middleshire" as in the earlier novel, although in *A Murder Is Announced,* the large fictitious city of Milchester is said to be only forty minutes by bus from Chipping Cleghorn. However, in many of Christie's novels, the fictitious Milchester is said to be near the village of St. Mary Mead, which is generally thought of as being located much further south (see below.)

Lincolnshire and Norfolk. These two counties are in the East and have coastlines on the North Sea. Each one has but one brief reference in a Christie novel and neither county is ever a major setting. In one story, the 1968 *By the Pricking of My Thumbs,* Tommy and Tuppence Beresford attend a funeral in Lincolnshire.

Berkshire (pronounced "Bark'sher"). This county is located a few miles west of London, and it borders the county of Oxfordshire just to its north. During the 1970s it lost some of its area to Oxfordshire. Berkshire was a favorite area for Christie. In the early 1930s, Christie and her second husband, the archeologist Max Mallowan, purchased a Queen Anne period home in the town of Wallingford, Berkshire and kept this home as one of their main residences for the rest of their lives.

A large number of Christie's stories take place either in Berkshire or in fictitious counties (for example, Downshire, Radfordshire and Melfordshire) which can be thought of as simply fictitious names for Berkshire. An early mention of the fictitious town of Market Basing (in the 1929 *The Seven Dials Mystery*) places that town in the general area of Berkshire, although "Berkshire" is never mentioned. We simply know that Market Basing must be in that area since passengers in an earlier novel, *The Secret of Chimneys*, travel to that town from London by train from Paddington Station, which is known to serve points west of London. Market Basing is the main setting for the 1937 *Poirot Loses a Client*, and in that novel, the real county of Berkshire is named as its location.

The village of St. Mary Mead, which over the years will become famous as the home of Christie's sleuth Miss Jane Marple, is first mentioned in the 1928 *The Mystery of the Blue Train*, although Miss Marple will not be introduced until the 1930 *Murder at the Vicarage*. Over the years, St. Mary Mead will be located in "Downshire," "Radfordshire" and "Melfordshire" but it will not move from its generally "west of London" location until a late novel in which it will be placed "fifteen miles south of London," therefore in the county of Surrey. Christie took great liberties with the locations of St. Mary Mead for convenience. In one novel it is "just a half-hour's drive" from an English Channel resort town, an important fact in that story.

Somerset, Worcestershire, Hertfordshire (pronounced "HARTferdsher,") and **Middlesex**. These four counties are mentioned only once each in Christie novels. Worcestershire is mentioned in the 1927 *The Big Four*. An unnamed village in Hertfordshire is the setting of a brief scene in the 1940 *The Patriotic Murders*, and in that same story a character visits an aunt who lives in Somerset. A community in Middlesex is the setting for one or two scenes in the 1933 *Thirteen at Dinner*. Worcestershire is in the picturesque Cotswold Hills region northwest of London, and Hertfordshire is just north of London and quite close to it. Middlesex is right next to London, just to the west and north of it. Somerset has a long coastline on the Bristol Channel and shares a border with the county of Devon (see below).

Surrey. This county is located just south of London. It is mentioned in the 1941 *Evil Under the Sun* as the setting for several past murders that resemble the one committed in the story. The village of St. Mary Mead, the home of the Christie sleuth Miss Marple, will be located in Surrey in one or two novels, although that fictitious village is usually thought of as being somewhere west of London, either in Berkshire or in a fictitious county modeled after it. An important scene in the 1970 *Passenger to Frankfurt* takes place at a house near Godalming in Surrey.

Essex. This is the county just northeast of London, on the north bank of the river Thames. Christie's first novel, the 1920 *The Mysterious Affair at Styles*, takes place at a country house in Essex, and the final adventure of Hercule Poirot, the 1975 *Curtain*, (written during the 1940s) takes place at the same house in Essex. The port of Tilbury is located on the river Thames just east of London in Essex. It is at this port that Joan Sutcliffe and her daughter Jennifer arrive by ocean liner "by the long sea route"—a five-week trip around Africa—from the Middle East in the 1959 *Cat Among the Pigeons*.

Devon and Cornwall. These two neighboring counties are located in the extreme southwest of England, Cornwall being the narrow peninsula at England's southwestern tip. The two counties are often spoken of together as "Devon and Cornwall" as they share a reputation for being pleasant vacation spots and have England's warmest weather in the summer. Resorts dot the southern coastlines of both of these counties, and Devon was another county very much loved by Christie, as she was born and grew up in the Devonshire resort of Torquay on the Channel coast. In the late 1930s, Christie and her husband Max Mallowan purchased a large country estate called Greenway House not far from Torquay and, along with Winterbrook House in Wallingford, Berkshire, maintained Greenway House as their second principal residence for the rest of their lives.

Because of Christie's fondness for Devon, she placed the action of a great many of her novels in Devon and at least two in Cornwall. The 1931 *Murder at Hazelmoor* takes place on the edge of Dartmoor in Devon. Dartmoor is an area of picturesque wasteland similar to the Yorkshire moors mentioned above, although it is much smaller. The action in the 1935 *Murder in Three Acts* begins at a modern home perched on a cliff on the south coast of Cornwall. The 1932 *Peril at End House* takes place in the fictitious resort town of St. Loo, also on the south coast of Cornwall. In a later novel, the 1941 *Evil Under the Sun*, "St. Loo" is placed on the south coast of Devon. The action in the 1944 *Towards Zero* takes place at an English Channel resort "near St. Loo," therefore probably in Devon or Cornwall. There will be many other Christie novels in which, although the county of Devon is not specifically named, Devon is clearly implied to be the setting, such as the 1943 *Murder in Retrospect,* the 1956 *Dead Man's Folly* and the 1958 *Ordeal by Innocence.*

Devon is also the county in which the important port city of Plymouth is located. It is at Plymouth that Gwenda Reed, the protagonist in the 1976 *Sleeping Murder,* arrives by ocean liner from her native New Zealand. She soon purchases a home not far from Plymouth and this home becomes the setting for the remainder of the story. Plymouth was, of course, the English port from which the Pilgrims sailed for America in 1620. The county of Devon is sometimes referred to as "Devonshire," but this usage of the word is not correct. The word "Devonshire" is correctly used as an adjective, however, as when speaking of "a Devonshire village," etc.

Dorset, Hampshire, Sussex and Kent. These four southern counties all have coastlines on the English Channel, and they are to the east of Cornwall and Devon. They occur as minor settings from time to time in Christie novels. In the 1935 *Death in the Air* one of the major characters is an aristocrat whose family home is in Sussex and one or two scenes take place at that estate. A scene in the 1945 *Remembered Death* also takes place at a home in Sussex, and the county is a major setting for the 1946 *Murder After Hours,* although in that story the county is called "Wieldshire." Kent is the county in which Dover, Canterbury, Folkstone and Maidstone are located. A few Christie novels feature brief settings in the county of Kent, most importantly the 1941 *The Patriotic Murders,* the 1944 *Towards Zero,* and the 1948 *There Is a Tide.* In this last novel, the fictitious county "Oastshire" can be assumed to be Kent, since travelers from a village in "Oastshire" travel by train to London and arrive at Victoria Station. Trains from London's Victoria station carried huge numbers of passengers to Dover for the "Channel Crossing" to France, and so there are numerous references to Dover and to Victoria Station whenever British characters are traveling to and from France.

Hampshire is the county in which the important port of Southampton is located. Hampshire is a major setting for the 1934 *The Boomerang Clue* and the 1935 *The A.B.C. Murders.* It is also a major setting in the 1942 *The Body in the Library* but in that story it is called "Glenshire."

To clarify and summarize: the following are *fictitious* county names used by Christie in some of her novels: Downshire, Middlishire, Radfordshire, Glenshire, Wieldshire, Oastshire, and Melfordshire.

Wales is not a county; in fact it is considered to be, like Scotland, a separate country with its own laws and a measure of self-government, although like Scotland, it is part of Great Britain, uses British currency, recognizes the British monarch as its head of state, etc. One novel, the 1934 *The Boomerang Clue,* has for its opening setting a village on the north coast of Wales. Wales is attached to the western edge of England and is across the Irish Sea from Ireland.

London

Many pages could be written about London, of course, but the following few specific remarks may be helpful to American readers of Christie's novels.

Railway Stations. London has had, for a long time, numerous railway stations that were built to serve railway lines to various parts of England. The stations most commonly mentioned in Christie's novels are Paddington, Victoria, Waterloo, Charing Cross, Kings Cross and Euston. By far the most important is Paddington Station, as it serves all of western and southwestern England. In Christie novels, travelers to Devon or Cornwall, and travelers to the area of the fictitious Market Basing and St. Mary Mead, always leave London by train at Paddington Station. As a matter of fact, the original British title of the 1957 *What Mrs. McGillicuddy Saw* was *4:50 from Paddington.* As the story opens an old friend of Miss Jane Marple boards a train at Paddington Station with the purpose of traveling to Milchester, a town near St. Mary Mead where Miss Marple lives.

Victoria Station, as mentioned above, serves the port cities of Folkstone and Dover in the County of Kent and is mentioned several times in Christie novels whenever travelers are departing for or returning from France. Nowadays Victoria Station has lost its importance in international travel, as there is much more travel to the Continent by air than formerly, and there is the new railway tunnel linking England with France. Tunnel trains from London to France leave London nowadays from Waterloo Station and not Victoria. This fact is not important in Christie's stories, however, since the tunnel was built long after her death. During her lifetime, and especially during her earlier years, all travel from England to France took place by means of a "Channel Crossing." One traveled by train from London's Victoria Station to Dover or Folkstone in Kent, and then boarded a ferry which crossed the twenty-one mile Strait of Dover to Calais or Boulogne-Sur-Mer in France, where one boarded another train for Paris.

Waterloo Station is mentioned in a couple of earlier novels as the place to board trains for the port of Southampton, as do Hercule Poirot and his friend Hastings at the beginning of the 1927 *The Big Four*. Charing Cross station also served trains to Southampton, and "boat trains" from Southampton generally arrived in London at Charing Cross. On the subject of "boat trains," these were special trains scheduled to be waiting at the ports of Plymouth, Southampton, Dover and perhaps others, ready to receive the "boat passengers" leaving ships and destined for London. One's steamship fare usually included the fare for the "boat train," and as soon as the ship was in the harbor, the passengers passed through customs and then directly onto the train, which departed as soon as the last traveler was aboard.

The remaining two stations mentioned above—Kings Cross and Euston—serve points north of London. Trains to Scotland have traditionally departed from Kings Cross. In the 1935 *The A.B.C. Murders* a character's statement that he plans to go to Cheltenham, which is west of London, is later shown to be false by another character who happened to see him at Euston Station instead of Paddington. The man's real destination was Doncaster, in Yorkshire.

There are other railway stations in London but the six mentioned above are the only important ones mentioned in Christie's novels.

Districts of London. Certain "neighborhoods" or "boroughs" of London are mentioned from time to time in Christie's novels, and it may be useful to know something about their associations. Chelsea is a district traditionally known for artists and theater people. In the 1946 *Murder After Hours* a talented sculptress has her studio in Chelsea, and in the 1953 *Funerals Are Fatal*, a young married couple, both stage actors, have a shabby apartment there. In the 1976 *Sleeping Murder* (written during the 1940s) Raymond West, a writer, and his artist wife Joan, live in Chelsea. Chelsea is also the setting of one or two scenes in the 1961 *The Pale Horse*, and it is home to the "beatniks" of the period. The neighborhood known as "Soho" is not often mentioned in Christie, but it plays an important part in the 1922 *The Secret Adversary* and the 1929 *The Seven Dials Mystery*. Soho is generally thought of as being filled with unsavory types, foreigners of all kinds, and the underworld in general. Sinister expressions such as "the house in Soho" are expected to send chills down the reader's spine. Soho has been the center of London's sex and drug trade for at least a century and probably longer. But in that disreputable district, in the 1952 *Mrs. McGinty's Dead,* Hercule Poirot finds a "dingy little restaurant" called *La Vieille Grand'Mère* where the food is wonderful.

Mayfair, Kensington, and Grosvenor Square are very high-class residential neighborhoods. If a character lives in one of those neighborhoods, he or she is extremely rich. Brook Street is in Mayfair and is reputed to be a very fashionable residential street. In the 1929 *The Seven Dials Mystery,* Lord Caterham maintains a London residence in Brook Street, as do Lord Marchington in the 1934 *The Boomerang Clue* and Lord Dittisham in the 1943 *Murder in Retrospect.*

Jermyn Street is mentioned in just two Christie novels. In the 1928 *The Mystery of the Blue Train,* Ruth Kettering's philandering husband Derek has "rooms" in Jermyn Street, probably for extramarital encounters. In the 1929 *The Seven Dials Mystery,* Jimmy Thesiger, who is an independently wealthy young man who does not work and "just tools around," also has "rooms" in Jermyn Street. Jermyn Street is home to a large number of expensive, custom shirt makers and is just off Piccadilly Circus.

Bond Street in Mayfair is famous for expensive jewelry, leather goods and clothing shops for both women and men, and stylish shops in Bond Street are frequent settings for minor scenes in Christie novels. Savile Row is a street that is famous for expensive custom made clothing for men and there are scenes at a jewelry shop in Bond Street and a tailor shop in Savile Row in the 1951 *They Came to Baghdad*. In the 1935 *Murder in Three Acts* there is an amusing scene at the shop of an expensive dressmaker in Bond Street.

Harley Street is famous for its medical doctors, all of whom are fashionable specialists, at least in Christie novels. Numerous "Harley Street specialists" are minor characters in Christie, and one major character, Dr. John Christow in the 1946 *Murder After Hours*, has his residence and office there. The comic figure, Mrs. Ariadne Oliver, a writer of detective stories whom Christie superficially modeled after herself, and who makes her first appearance in a novel in the 1936 *Cards on the Table*, lives in Harley Street "among all the doctors." She will move from Harley Street to a succession of other residences during the 1960s, however.

"The City" is a term applied to central London and it is the seat of the financial district. "The City" is to the English what "Wall Street" is to Americans. In Christie novels, the term "The City" is usually used in a negative sense, as Christie was not fond of financiers and, in general, anyone who devoted a good deal of energy to making money, her favorite kind of people being those who already *had* money. And so when a Christie character declares his intention of "going into The City" he is telling us that he intends to make money instead of spending his life doing something "nice." A character in the 1943 *Murder in Retrospect,* Philip Blake, is very negatively portrayed by certain other characters as being a "nasty money grubber" who "went into the City" instead of remaining at the family's country home and pursuing a more "genteel" career. In the 1953 *A Pocket Full of Rye,* the murder victim Rex Fortescue is an unpleasant, somewhat shady but wealthy businessman with an office "in The City." His home is in an expensive London suburb that features three golf courses catering to the local residents, most of whom are men "of The City."

Certain other London landmarks are occasionally mentioned in Christie, but not very often. The American Embassy in stylish Grosvenor Square plays a role in the 1970 *Passenger to Frankfurt.* Luxury hotels such as The Ritz (referred to satirically as "The Blitz" in the 1925 *The Secret of Chimneys,*) as well as Claridge's, the Savoy, the Piccadilly Palace and others are occasionally mentioned and are sometimes settings. The "Lyon's Tea Shops" are often mentioned, as well as Logan's Corner House Restaurant. The well-known London department store Debenham's is mentioned in the 1936 *Cards on the Table,* the 1949 *Crooked House,* and the 1965 *At Bertram's Hotel.*

Hyde Park and Regent's Park are mentioned fairly frequently. Piccadilly Circus (or simply "Piccadilly") is a busy intersection that is normally snarled with pedestrian and automobile traffic, and it is mentioned once or twice. In the 1948 *There Is a Tide* a "spiritualistic" woman, Katherine Cloade, speaks to Hercule Poirot of "Africa, a place where a person could disappear and never be heard from again," to which Poirot satirically replies, "Yes, but the same thing could happen in Piccadilly." Off Piccadilly Circus runs fashionable Shaftesbury Avenue with its expensive shops; it is at a garage near Shaftesbury Avenue that Magda Leonides, in the 1949 *Crooked House,* obtains her illegal clothing ration coupons.

Other Settings

Although most of Christie's detective novels take place in England, there are a few exceptions. The 1923 *Murder on the Links* takes place almost entirely at a village on the north coast of France between the Channel ports of Boulogne and Calais. The 1924 *The Man in the Brown Suit* takes place mostly aboard a steamer bound for South Africa, and then within Africa itself, as far north as Rhodesia. The 1925 *The Secret of Chimneys* has a brief early scene in Rhodesia, but the remainder of the action takes place in England. The 1928 *The Mystery of the Blue Train* begins in England but most of the action takes place aboard a train bound for the South of France and then on the French Riviera. There are also, in that novel, early scenes at the home of a prostitute in a seedy district of Paris, and at the shop of an antique dealer in a finer district. The action in the 1934 *Murder in the Calais Coach* begins at Aleppo in Syria, then moves to Istanbul, and finally to a train which becomes stranded in snow banks in Yugoslavia. In the 1935 *Death in the Air,* a murder takes place in a plane traveling from Paris to London; most of the further action in that novel occurs about equally in England and in France.

The 1936 *Murder in Mesopotamia* is Christie's earliest novel that is set entirely in the Middle East; it is at an archeological digging site not far from Baghdad that the murder takes place and is investigated. At that time all of modern-day Iraq was a British protectorate still known as "Mesopotamia."

The 1937 *Death on the Nile* takes place aboard a Nile steamer in Egypt. The 1938 *Appointment with Death* takes place in Jerusalem and at the ruins of an ancient city in Jordan (then called Transjordan.)

The 1945 *Death Comes as the End* is a novelty. The story takes place in ancient Egypt.

The 1951 *They Came to Baghdad* begins in London but most of the story takes place in Baghdad, in the immediate area around it, and in Basrah. By the middle 1940s the area formerly known as Mesopotamia had assumed its present name, Iraq. The action in the 1954 *So Many Steps to Death* begins at the airport in London, then moves to Casablanca and Fez in Morocco and finally to a mysterious location in the Atlas Mountains.

The 1964 *A Caribbean Mystery,* as its title implies, takes place in the Caribbean, on the fictitious island of St. Honoré. Finally, the 1970 *Passenger to Frankfurt* takes place mostly in England but there are some important scenes at the airport in Frankfurt, at a castle in Bavaria, and at a government office in Paris.

The only scenes in Christie novels that take place in America are in the 1937 *Death on the Nile* (one brief scene in a luxury apartment overlooking Central Park, and another at the office of a lawyer further downtown) and in the 1951 *They Came to Baghdad* (one brief scene at the office of an international banker in New York.)

The Mysterious Affair at Styles (1920)

Setting

Styles Court is a large country estate near the fictitious village of Styles St. Mary, in the county of Essex, just east of London. The year is 1916 and World War I is still in progress. The lady of the house is active in charitable and patriotic activities and, because of that, some gasoline is permitted for their automobiles, although it is rationed. There is a reference to one character's avoiding the use of scarce sugar in her coffee, and the family takes its evening meal before dusk in order to save candles, gas lighting and kerosene lighting because of war shortages. One character works in a hospital dispensary to assist in the war effort. As the property includes a farm, another character "works the land," rising at 5:00 in the morning to milk cows, etc., again as part of the war effort. In addition to the rationing of gasoline and the scarceness of sugar, we learn that every scrap of waste paper at Styles is saved and bundled for some war use, and that there are vases containing "spills"—scraps of paper rolled into sticks for the purpose of carrying flame from the fireplace to a lamp or a man's pipe, etc. in order to save matches.

There is no electricity at Styles, not because of the war but because of the early date, and so clearly electricity for private homes—even homes of the rich—was not yet standard, at least not in the country. There are numerous references to candles and, at night, when the murder victim screams in her room, one character carries a candle for light and once inside the room, another person "goes across the room and lights the gas," presumably a gas lighting fixture on the wall. In the room a "reading lamp" has fallen to the floor, breaking the "chimney" in two places; therefore it is a kerosene lamp. There is also a "spirit lamp" in the room where the murder victim had been in the habit of warming a saucepan of cocoa late in the evening. In addition to gas for lighting there is a gas stove in the kitchen. There is no telephone. In order to summon the doctor upon the victim's convulsions and death, the chauffeur is sent to fetch him by car. Automobiles are referred to either as "car" or "motor." The family also has a pony trap that is used for short trips, to Tadminster, for example, which is seven miles distant.

The house itself is very large. It should be mentioned here, in case it should be useful to the reader, that in Britain and in Continental Europe as well, the entry level of a house or other building is called the "ground floor," not the "first floor" as it is in America. If there is just one upper floor, that floor is called the "first floor," and if there are three levels, the uppermost is the "second floor." In Chapter III of the novel there is a plan of the "first floor" (actually the "second" from the American point of view) of the house. It contains two wings joined by a gallery and large open stairway, and there are eleven bedrooms and one bathroom; these are for the use of the family. A doorway in the hall leads to a passage to the servants' quarters which are on the same floor but not shown in the plan.

The ground floor rooms are not specified in detail but a drawing room, a dining room, a boudoir, and a smoking room are mentioned, and there must certainly be other rooms—a kitchen, a pantry and a library for sure, and probably also a study, a music room and a conservatory.

The household consists of six adults and at least nine servants. There are no children. The servants referred to in the story are a parlormaid, two housemaids, a chauffeur, and three gardeners. There must also be a cook and a kitchen maid, although they are never mentioned. The gardeners are two older men and a woman, the parlormaid declaring that properly there should be five men working as gardeners but the "times being what they are...." Presumably all young, able bodied men who might be domestic servants are in the armed forces. The work of the gardeners is all manual labor, of course, since there are not yet such devices as motorized lawn mowers. The property is very large and, as mentioned earlier, includes a working farm.

The neighboring village of Styles St. Mary has a tiny railway station. There is also a chemist's shop (pharmacy), a post office, an inn called "The Stylites Arms" and probably other establishments as well, but in this novel, scenes in the village are few and nearly all of the action and conversations take place at Styles Court itself.

The story takes place during a warm spell in June or July of 1916.

Story

It is 1916 and World War I is in progress. John Cavendish and his wife Mary live with his stepmother, Emily Inglethorpe, at the family home, Styles Court, near the village of Styles St. Mary in Essex. Also living at the home are Emily's new husband Alfred, who is twenty years her junior; John's younger brother Lawrence; Mrs. Inglethorpe's protégée, Cynthia Murdoch, who is a penniless orphan; and Mrs. Inglethorpe's good friend and paid companion, Evelyn Howard. The family and servants alike resent Alfred Inglethorpe and suspect that he married Mrs. Inglethorpe only for her money.

Mr. Hastings, a member of the armed forces, is at a convalescent home because of a recent war injury. As he is an old friend of John Cavendish, John invites him to Styles Court for a few weeks' rest. Installing himself as a houseguest at Styles Court, Mr. Hastings also has the pleasure of renewing the acquaintance of an old friend, Hercule Poirot, who is living in the nearby village, Styles St. Mary, with some of his Belgian compatriots who are war refugees.

About two weeks later, in the middle of the night, Mrs. Inglethorpe is seized by violent convulsions. The sound of her screams awakens most of the household who, finding her bedroom door locked, break in just in time to witness her death. It is soon discovered that her death was caused by strychnine poisoning.

Inspector Japp of Scotland Yard conducts the official investigation. Poirot and Hastings assist Inspector Japp marginally, providing facts but not sharing ideas with him. Inspector Japp's investigation results in the arrest and trial of one of the suspects, but it is Hercule Poirot who, in the end, reveals the true identity of the murderer.

CHARACTERS

Mr. Hastings, the narrator, age thirty and wounded in the War, who is living in a convalescent home not far from Styles St. Mary. His rank in the military service is not specified and he is referred to as Mr. Hastings or simply as "Hastings." He enjoys telling of his adventures in the war and especially appreciates a "good listener." He is susceptible to the charms of beautiful women and, fortunately for him, there are two of these in the story, one of whom proves to be "a very good listener." The other has beautiful auburn hair, which he finds enchanting.

Mr. Hastings is an old friend of Hercule Poirot and becomes Poirot's sidekick during the investigation of the mystery. According to Poirot, Hastings has "a nature so honest and a countenance so transparent that—*enfin*—to conceal your feelings is impossible." Therefore Poirot is careful not to reveal to Hastings any idea that, if made public, might jeopardize the successful unmasking of the criminal. Hastings often complains that Poirot never tells him anything and never explains anything, but Poirot reminds him that he has provided facts and "hints" which should lead Hastings to the same conclusions as Poirot's.

Hercule Poirot, the sleuth. Poirot is a retired detective from the Belgian police force who is temporarily residing in the village of Styles St. Mary along with other Belgian refugees. He is a little man, no more than five feet five inches tall, with a "perfectly egg-shaped head" and a stiff military moustache. His eccentricities include an obsession with neatness and symmetry, and "order and method." He is always dressed impeccably. His English is punctuated with French expressions and is often flawed by direct but incorrect English translations of French. For example, he says "What magnificent chance!" (Quelle chance magnifique—What magnificent luck!); "Ah, the brave Dorcas!" (Ah, la brave Dorcas—Ah, good old Dorcas!) His "fractured English" is only mildly noticeable in this novel but in later novels it will be much more apparent and eventually he will use it deliberately in order to stress his "foreignness" when speaking with people he feels will be more candid in the presence of "a mere foreigner." As to his obsession for neatness, in this novel he "buries neatly" a match stick, which another character has casually tossed into a flower bed; he straightens Hastings's necktie, he readjusts the alignment of a young girl's broach, he rearranges the ornaments on a mantel, and he flicks microscopic bits of dust from his sleeve.

Poirot refers to his "little grey cells" just once in this novel but will refer to them more often in later novels. His other trademark eccentricities—an aversion for cold weather, his dislike for water and air travel, his disgust for whiskey, beer and English cooking, have not yet made their appearance, nor have the trademark patent leather shoes or his gloating pride respecting his "glorious mustaches" and his "suspiciously black hair." These all come later.

Note: Because Agatha Christie, when writing *The Mysterious Affair at Styles,* had no idea she would ever write another novel, she of course had no idea that Poirot would ever appear in print again. She soon regretted that she had made him so old in *The Mysterious Affair at Styles* because, as the years and decades rolled by, with Poirot's popularity among readers never diminishing, she realized that he must be aging inordinately.

Emily Inglethorpe, age seventy, the stepmother of John and Lawrence Cavendish. She is an energetic, autocratic woman inclined to charitable and social notoriety with a fondness for opening bazaars and playing the Lady Bountiful. Generous, wealthy and civic-minded, Emily provides "adequately" for her two grown stepsons and a young protégée but not so generously as to make them independent of her. One character in the story states that Emily was generous but that she was the kind of person who never lets people forget what she has done for them. Emily's two stepsons resent their dependent position, and they are especially resentful of her recent marriage, but she is oblivious to their feelings.

John Cavendish, age forty-five and **Lawrence Cavendish**, a few years younger, stepsons of Emily Inglethorpe. John has chosen the life of a country squire despite qualifying as a barrister; Lawrence has qualified as a doctor but chooses to live at home and spend his time writing poetry, "publishing rotten verses in fancy bindings" in the derisive words of his brother. Both live with their stepmother and await their inheritance; both resent their father's Will, which left the family home, Styles Court—plus a substantial income—to their stepmother for the duration of her lifetime. John, in particular, is hard up for cash and he admits this to his friend, Mr. Hastings.

Mary Cavendish, John's young wife, with whom he lives at Styles Court. Hastings finds her to be a thoroughly fascinating woman with a wild, untame spirit in an exquisitely civilized body.

Mary Cavendish is jealous because she suspects her husband John of carrying on an affair with the wife of a nearby farmer, but she herself appears to be altogether too attracted to a newly arrived visitor to Styles St Mary, the black-bearded toxicology expert, Dr. Baurstein. She had married John not for love but in order to escape from a dull existence living with an aging aunt.

Alfred Inglethorpe, Emily's new husband, twenty years younger than she, bitterly resented by the entire household, including the servants. According to John Cavendish, he is "an absolute outsider, anyone can see that," and if that were not enough, he "wears a beard and pince-nez and patent leather boots in all weather." He is suspected by everyone of being interested only in Emily's money.

Evelyn Howard refers to Alfred as "that devil."

Evelyn Howard, Emily Inglethorpe's close friend and paid companion ("factotum" in the affectionate words of John Cavendish.) She has the strongest personality of anyone in the household and is very outspoken. She uses an amusing "telegraphic style" of speech, omitting pronouns and other unnecessary words. She is especially resentful and suspicious of Alfred and actually confronts Emily on that subject, calling her an old fool for trusting him and implying that Alfred wants nothing but her money and would stop at nothing to get it.

Cynthia Murdoch, the daughter of an old friend of Emily Inglethorpe, a penniless orphan whom Emily has taken in as a protégée. Employed for the duration of the War at a dispensary in Tadminster, seven miles distant, she too is financially dependent on Emily Inglethorpe. There is no provision in Emily's will for Cynthia, and this tearful revelation, coming from "...a fresh-looking young creature full of life and vigour, with great loose waves of auburn hair and small, white hands..."—Hastings's words—provoke Hastings to propose marriage to her, causing her to forget her troubles instantly and to laugh hysterically.

For the remainder of Hastings's career as Poirot's sidekick, Poirot will periodically tease him about "the girl with auburn hair," and each time Hastings tells Poirot about an attractive woman he has met, Poirot will ask "Does she have auburn hair?"

Dr. Bauerstein, a world expert on toxicology, residing in the nearby village of Styles St. Mary for a rest cure after a nervous breakdown. He has "the longest and blackest beard" Hastings has ever seen, causing Hastings to take an instant dislike to him. Mary Cavendish is mysteriously attracted to him.

Farmer Raike's Wife, a "pretty young woman of gypsy type" who smiles with "a vivid, wicked little face," according to Hastings. Evelyn Howard insinuates that Alfred spends altogether too much time at the Raikes's home.

Dorcas, the parlormaid, who is described by Hastings as the very model and picture of a good old-fashioned servant.

Annie, a housemaid. She is a fine, strapping girl, laboring under intense excitement mingled with a certain ghoulish enjoyment of the tragedy.

Elizabeth Wells, second housemaid. She is not described but she provides evidence at the trial which the defense attorney shows to be worthless and probably a fabrication.

Manning, the head gardener at Styles Court. When addressed by Hercule Poirot, Manning's eye "swept over him with a faint contempt."

William Earl, undergardener

Baily, the family chauffeur

Mr. Mace, an employee at the chemist's shop

Amy Hill, a shop assistant at the post office

Mr. Wells, Emily Inglethorpe's personal lawyer and the Coroner, a pleasant man of middle age, with keen eyes, and "the typical lawyer's mouth." This last must be a reference to "discretion" unless there is some physical peculiarity of the mouths of lawyers.

Mr. Phillips, K.C., attorney for the prosecution

Sir Ernest Heavywether, attorney for the defense.

FRENCH INTO ENGLISH

Chapter 4
Voyons—Let's see.
À merveille!—Perfectly
Ça y est!—There!
En voilà une table!—Some table!
Eh bien, eh bien!—Not so fast, wait a minute.
Bien!—Good!
Voilà!—Here it is!

Chapter 5
Oh, là là!—Oh, for goodness sake!
Ne vous fâchez pas!—Don't get upset!
Bien!—Well, all right!
Mal de tête—Headache
Sacré!—Damn!
Chut!—Hush!
Hein!—Ahah!
Mille tonnerres!—Oh, my God!
En voilà une affaire!—This is bad news!
Là-bas—Back there
Tiens!—I'll be darned!

Chapter 6 *Sacré!*—Damn!

Chapter 7
Comme ça!—Just like that!
Mon dieu!—God!
Sympathique—Nice
Soit!—So be it!
Mesdames and *messieurs*—Ladies and gentlemen

Chapter 8
Voilà!—Here! *Allons!*—Let's go!
Oho!—Hmm!

Chapter 10
Bon jour, mon ami!—Good morning!
Un moment, s'il vous plaît!—Come here for a minute, please!

Chapter 11
En règle—Natural
Ma foi—Heavens

Chapter 12
Réunion—Gathering
Salon—Drawing room, living room
Messieurs, mesdames—Ladies and gentlemen
Carte blanche—Full permission

Bien!—Very good!
Mauvais quart d'heure—Attack of guilt

Chapter 13
Enfin—Well, frankly
Bon jour—Good bye
Eh bien!—All right, then. *Bon!*—Fine!
Dénouement—Outcome
La pauvre petite!—Poor thing!
Les femmes!—Women

COMMENTS

The plot and detection in *The Mysterious Affair at Styles* are carefully worked out and, as a detective novel, it is a great success. The characters, however, are rather dull compared with those in later Christie novels. Perhaps the only memorable character is Evelyn Howard, because of her strong personality and her amusingly laconic style of speaking, and the novel contains very little humor, youthfulness or "sparkle." Christie recognized this herself and made up for it in her second novel, *The Secret Adversary*, which stars two bright, "sparkling" young people who have the most exciting adventures imaginable tracking down a master criminal.

There are a few things in *The Mysterious Affair at Styles* that some modern readers may find at least mildly annoying: a certain attitude toward servants, a certain attitude toward "work" and at least one suggestion of anti–Semitism.

About half way through the novel, in a conversation with Hastings, the parlormaid Dorcas has this to say about Hercule Poirot:

> "A very nice gentleman he is, sir. And quite a different class from them two detectives from London what goes prying about. I don't hold with foreigners as a rule, but from what the newspapers say, I make out as how these brave Belges isn't the ordinary run of foreigners ... and certainly he's a most polite spoken gentleman."

Hastings's thoughts:

> Dear old Dorcas! As she stood there, with her honest face upturned to mine, I thought what a fine specimen she was of the old-fashioned servant that is fast dying out.

Aside from the ignorant provincialism expressed by Dorcas who "doesn't hold by foreigners as a rule" and her generous admission that Poirot and his Belgian compatriots are "not the ordinary run of foreigners"—this woman has probably never set foot out of England, or even outside the county of Essex, but she feels qualified to have a negative attitude towards "foreigners"—just what is it that Hastings means by "a fine specimen of the old-fashioned servant that is fast dying out?" Undoubtedly it is the old-fashioned servant who knew his or her place, was satisfied with a position of subservience and saw no reason to expect more from life than to be at the beck and call of persons of a higher social class.

Agatha Christie makes it amply clear in her *Autobiography* that, in the happy days of her childhood and earlier, servants were very happy in their subservience. If a girl's name was Muriel, and she was your parlormaid, she was only too happy to have you say to her, "Muriel is not a suitable name for a servant. In this house you will be called Ellen," just as you would name a dog or a cat or some other piece of chattel. Christie felt that her mother was extremely kind and gracious in her attitude toward servants. On one occasion a visiting child had said to a servant, "You're only a servant," and Agatha's mother reprimanded the child, saying "you must not be rude to servants because their position forbids them to be rude to you in return."

That was certainly true. If you were a housemaid, and the mistress of the house was an ornery person, or a cruel person, or a mentally-ill person, or a person with a "textbook" inferiority complex who took pleasure in belittling people and performing character assassination whenever possible in order to feel good about herself, then you were just unlucky and you had no choice but to endure her insults and belittling. If you talked back, you were sacked without a reference, and without a reference there would never be another job for you, except perhaps in prostitution, since you had no skills of any kind except housework. If the master of the house was one of those men who enjoy leering at women just to make them feel uncomfortable, or even demanded sex below stairs, you didn't have much choice but to provide him with it, since it was just your word against his. House servants were truly "owned" by their masters. They were, in fact, paid slaves.

Christie also states, in her *Autobiography*:

> ...servants were, I think, actively happy, mainly because they knew they were appreciated as experts, doing expert work. As such, they had that mysterious thing, prestige; they looked down with scorn on shop assistants and their like. One of the things I think I should miss most, if I were a child nowadays, would be the presence of servants. To a child they were the most colourful part of daily life. Nurses supplied platitudes; servants supplied drama, entertainment and all kinds of unspecified but interesting knowledge.... They "knew their place," as was said, but knowing their place meant not subservience but pride, the pride of the professional.

As to servants being "actively happy and appreciated," if that were true there would be plenty of people interested in being house servants today. In Christie's future detective novels there will be numerous examples of "good, old-fashioned servants" for a long time, because Christie will never change her mind on this subject. In her novels of the 1950s, in particular, the demise of the "servant class" will be viewed by all middle-class characters as a definite loss for society. See the *Setting* section for the 1950 *A Murder Is Announced*, the *Setting* and *Comments* sections for the 1953 *Funerals Are Fatal*, and the *Summary for the 1950s* for further remarks on the "sad" subject of the demise of the servant class in Britain.

A second item of interest is the attitude toward "work" that is exhibited by John and Lawrence Cavendish and of which Christie clearly does not disapprove. Both are highly educated men—one has qualified as a barrister and the other as a medical doctor, but both choose to sit around and relax, living in their mother's home (John is actually married and his wife lives with him there in his mother's home) as they await their mother's death and their inheritance. In other words, there is no "work ethic" in them, but Agatha Christie had no problem with that. The following is a quotation from P. 121 of her *Autobiography*:

> There seems to me to be an odd assumption that there is something meritorious about working. Why? In early times man went out to hunt animals in order to feed himself and keep alive. Later, he toiled over crops, and sowed and ploughed for the same reason. Nowadays, he rises early, catches the 8:15, and sits in an office all day—still for the same reason. He does it to feed himself and have a roof over his head—and, if skilled and lucky, to go a bit further and have comfort and entertainment as well. It's economic and necessary. But why is it meritorious?

The pride of earning one's own living—"pulling one's weight," so to speak, was alien to Christie's schema. She loved her "lazy" father very much. She actually used the word "lazy" in fondness to describe him. His family had made money in America and he had inherited investments which produced an income sufficient to support him and his family. He spent most of his days at his club playing card games and he never worked at anything. He was "lazy" but always very agreeable, charming, friendly and kind. Therefore there is no reason for Christie not to present these two loafers, John and Lawrence Cavendish, as honorable people.

The third item is anti–Semitism. At one point in the story, John Cavendish has a row with his wife Mary because of her unusual attachment to Dr. Baurstein.

> "It will be the talk of the village! My mother was only buried on Saturday, and here you are gadding about with the fellow…. I've had enough of the fellow hanging about. He's a Polish Jew, anyway."

Later Poirot himself makes this statement about Bauerstein, after the man is arrested for being a German spy. "He is, of course, a German by birth," said Poirot thoughtfully, "though he has practised so long in this country that nobody thinks of him as anything but an Englishman. He was naturalized about fifteen years ago. A very clever man—a Jew, of course."

There are anti–Semitic comments in a good number of Christie's novels until approximately the late 1930s, but nearly all of them were edited out of the American editions. It would be a silly mistake, however, to attribute *strong* feelings of anti–Semitism to Christie, because anti–Semitism is a collective sin that has *always* afflicted the so-called Christian world. It would be very easy, but irresponsible, for modern-day Americans to point the politically correct finger of guilt at a woman born in England in 1890, when here in America five or six decades *later,* films and television programs were still painting the false picture of a purely white, Gentile America.

The Secret Adversary (1922)

Setting

The year is 1919 or 1920, but there are important references to the sinking of the passenger liner *Lusitania* which occurred four or five years earlier. The action takes place primarily in London except for brief excursions to a lonely house near the North Sea coast in Yorkshire, to the home of a doctor in Manchester, to a nursing home in Bournemouth and to a house in a fictitious town in the county of Kent.

In London, action and conversation take place in Lyons' teashops, at the Ritz, Savoy and Claridge's hotels, at two or three luxury flats, at the office of a businessman, and at a sinister, shabby building in London's Soho district.

Communications are sometimes by telephone but more often by telegram, which costs only nine pence within London. Transportation in London takes place by tube (subway), bus, private car and taxi and on foot. At the building in Soho, interior lighting is by gas; elsewhere it is probably electrical, although there is no specific mention of electric lighting.

Post-war unemployment, labor unrest and the Bolshevist threat are the historical backgrounds to this adventure novel.

Story

It is approximately 1919 or 1920 and England is plagued with post-war unemployment and labor unrest. The Bolshevists, having succeeded in overthrowing the government in Russia, are behind the labor unrest in England with funding and propaganda and seek to incite revolution there also. Behind the Bolshevists is a mysterious "master criminal" known as "Mr. Brown."

A certain secret draft treaty, written in America, was on its way to England aboard the ill-fated liner *Lusitania* when she was torpedoed and sunk in 1915. It is believed that the man bearing the secret document had entrusted it to a young American girl, Jane Finn, just before the liner sank, knowing that, being a woman, she would have a better chance than he of reaching shore and delivering the document to the American Embassy in London. The girl was rescued but, after her landing in Ireland, nothing was heard of her again, and so she and the draft treaty were forgotten.

But now, with the labor unrest and the Bolshevist threat, if the draft treaty were to be made public, it would be disastrous to certain persons important in the British government. That disgrace, coupled with the present labor unrest, might turn the population against the government and trigger revolution in England. Therefore the British government must prevent the draft treaty—if it still exists—from falling into the hands of the Bolshevists who hope to publish it to further their aims.

Two personable young people, Prudence Cowley (Tuppence) and Thomas Beresford (Tommy) meet by chance in a London park and confide to each other that they are both "broke" with no prospects for work in the depressed post-war economy. They had been childhood friends and had renewed their acquaintance during the war when Tommy was in hospital with an injury and Tuppence was working as a nurse. Together they dream of finding work, hopefully *exciting* work, and they decide to advertise themselves as "Two Young Adventurers, Willing to Do Anything, Go Anywhere" in a newspaper.

Our "Young Adventurers" are commissioned by an important officer in the Secret Service (who uses the false name of A. Carter for unofficial business—and Tommy and Tuppence's work will be entirely unofficial and therefore without protection) to find Jane Finn and the draft treaty. This quest leads them into the midst of a criminal organization, the head of which is the mysterious "Mr. Brown" whom nobody has ever seen but whom all fear.

One exciting adventure after another lead to the finding of Jane Finn and the draft treaty, and to the destruction of Mr. Brown, "the finest criminal mind of the age."

CHARACTERS

Mr. Danvers, entrusted to carry a secret draft treaty from America to England aboard the ill-fated liner *Lusitania* in 1915. It is believed that, before the ship sank, he passed the document to an American girl with instructions to take it to the American Ambassador in London unless she heard from him by newspaper advertisement within two days. He is not rescued and goes down with the ship.

Jane Finn, the young American girl whom Danvers meets on the ship. An American nurse who has studied French, she is en route to France to aid the Allied cause by working in a hospital there. After she lands safely by rescue boat in Ireland, all traces of her disappear.

Thomas Beresford (Tommy), a personable young Englishman, wounded in the Great War, desperately seeking work in the grim post-War labor market. He has a "pleasantly ugly" face and exquisitely slicked-back red hair. According to one character in the story, it is impossible to lead Tommy astray through his imagination, since he hasn't any.

Prudence Cowley (Tuppence), one of five children of a country archdeacon, having served as a hospital nurse in the Great War, now also desperately seeking work, her only alternative being to return to her village and to a dull existence with her family.

Tuppence is impulsive, restless and creative. She seems to come up with most of the ideas and Tommy provides the practical objections. They constantly spar but always agree in the end about what to do. They complement each other perfectly as a team and their mutual affection grows.

Mr. Edward Whittington, a member of the criminal organization headed by the mysterious "Mr. Brown." He approaches Tuppence in St. James Park with a job offer.

"Mr. A. Carter," the alias of an important figure in the Secret Service, recognized by Tommy who had met him in France during the war. It is "Mr. Carter" who sends Tommy and Tuppence on their search for Jane Finn and the secret draft treaty, providing them with "funds within reason" but "no official recognition."

Julius P. Hersheimer, an American millionaire who has come to England in search of Jane Finn, a cousin with whom he wishes to share his inherited wealth, feeling that his father had treated her family unfairly during his lifetime.

Julius's speech is filled with Agatha Christie's idea of American slang. Hardly an utterance escapes his lips without including "shucks!" "put me wise!" "sure thing!" "so long!" "let's get a move on!" "I better hustle," "that tickles me to death!" "nothing doing!" "sure enough!" "mighty pretty," "mighty uncertain," "mighty politely," etc., "for a spell," "pretty dark," "pretty near," "I sort of got it into my head that..." and the list could go on for pages.

Julius becomes an ally of Tommy and Tuppence. He is willing to spend any amount of money to find his cousin Jane and announces that he will guarantee one million dollars for the search.

Marguerite Vandemeyer (Rita), a member of the criminal gang who takes orders only from Mr. Brown. Tuppence succeeds in being hired as house-parlormaid at Rita's home in order to spy on her. Rita is the first person in the story who inspires genuine fear in Tuppence.

Count Boris Ivanovitch Stepanov, another member of the gang. He is fair, with a weak, unpleasant face, and his small, crafty eyes shift unceasingly.

Albert, the "small lift boy" at the luxury apartment building South Audley Mansions, where Rita Vandemeyer lives. He is probably no more than eleven or twelve years old, reads threepenny detective and spy novels and believes all of Tuppence's fibs. She flashes at him a small enameled badge (nothing but a device of a local training corps originated by her archdeacon father early in the war, and which she had happened to use to pin some flowers to her coat a day or two before) to prove her status, and hisses "American Detective Force!" Telling him she's after "Ready Rita" (Mrs. Vandemeyer,) Tuppence obtains Albert's full cooperation and, through him, obtains a position as Rita's house-parlormaid. Albert is ecstatic to be working with a "real" detective, repeating deliriously, "Oh, ain't it just like the pictures!" Later he assists Tommy in the investigation of a house in Kent where they believe Tuppence and Jane are imprisoned, and while Tommy anticipates a fierce watchdog, Albert's fancy runs to a puma or a tame cobra.

Annie, Rita Vandemeyer's house-parlormaid who is just about to leave her job, providing Tuppence with an opportunity to obtain her job as a means of spying upon Rita.

Sir James Peel Edgerton, a famous criminal lawyer and MP to a small Scotch constituency. He radiates magnetism and force far beyond the ordinary. He becomes an ally of Tommy, Tuppence and Julius in their search for Jane Finn, the draft treaty, and "Mr. Brown."

Conrad, a hate-filled brute of a fanatic and a member of the criminal gang who coshes Tommy on the head and, later during questioning, says to Tommy, "Speak, swine of an Englishman!"

Annette, a beautiful young French girl and member of the criminal gang who, when Tommy is their prisoner at the sinister house in Soho, brings him his daily ration. After Tommy escapes, he tells another man that he cannot believe that Annette is really one of the gang because "she seems so different." The other man smiles and says, "Good looking, I suppose." This causes Tommy to blush profusely.

Dr. Hall, who keeps a nursing home at Bournemouth, on the southern coast of England.

Dr. Roylance, a friend of Peel Edgerton, living in Manchester

Dr. Adams, no longer practicing regularly, but occasionally receiving "balmy" patients at his home, Astley Priors in Gatehouse, Kent

Archdeacon Cowley, Tuppence's father

The American Ambassador

The Prime Minister of Great Britain

Sir William Beresford, Tommy's wealthy, estranged uncle

Inspector James Japp of Scotland Yard, not an active character in this novel, but who responds to an inquiry by Julius Hersheimer about his cousin Jane Finn. Japp was introduced in *The Mysterious Affair at Styles* and will appear in a few other Hercule Poirot novels until 1940.

Various unnamed members of a criminal organization seen and heard by Tommy as he spies on their meeting at the sinister house in Soho. One is an Irish Sinn Feiner, one is from the "working classes," one is "from the dregs of society," one has the appearance of a "city clerk," and there are others.

"Mr. Brown," the "finest criminal mind of the century," a fictitious name for one character.

COMMENTS

The Secret Adversary is an action-packed thriller and, unlike *The Mysterious Affair at Styles,* its characters are interesting and fun to read about, and there is humor. As mentioned earlier, the only really "interesting" character in *The Mysterious Affair at Styles* was Evelyn Howard, and her part in the story was minimal except at the very beginning and then at the end. In *The Secret Adversary,* the reader is treated right from the beginning to two loveable young people full of life and spirit who "take on the world" and find excitement and adventure. Their conversations are filled with youthful vigor. Agatha Christie herself observed that the characters in *The Mysterious Affair at Styles* had been rather dull, and the "love interest" between John Cavendish and his wife was uninteresting. She must have decided right away that there would be no dull characters in *The Secret Adversary,* and indeed there are none.

In addition to the "fun" characters of Tommy and Tuppence, there is the rather outlandishly exaggerated "American millionaire," Julius, with his picturesque speech and endless wealth. Then there's loveable Albert, the lift boy, who reads three-penny adventure novels and joins forces with Master Detective Tuppence, deliriously rhapsodizing, "Oh, ain't it just like the pictures!" There is the intensely serious Mr. A. Carter (not his real name but an alias he uses for such unofficial purposes as this) who explains the "secret draft treaty" and its deadly importance. There is the powerful and magnetic Sir James Peel Edgerton. Then there are the frightening criminals: the hard and menacing Rita Vandemeyer, the strong-armed, hate-filled Conrad ("Speak, swine of an Englishman!"); the sinister Count Boris Ivanovitch Stepanov, the Bolshevist "venomous snake" Kramenin and his secretary Ivan Grieber, and the shadowy master criminal, "Mr. Brown" whom nobody has ever seen but whom all fear.

It is important not to judge the "realism" of this book against modern novels with similar subjects. After all, it was published in 1922 as "light fiction" and purchased and read by the same people who read wildly improbable science fiction stories that presented mammals, birds and reptiles living on oxygenless planets and outer-space humanoids who spoke English, as well as detective novels featuring untraceable poisons and snakes that could be trained to climb a rope over a wall, attack a human victim and then return via the same rope. The fact that *The Secret Adversary* contains situations that are at best "improbable" is something Christie was well aware of. Hence Albert's repeated, delirious outpouring, "Oh, ain't it just like the pictures!" and Julius Hersheimer's remark, "...reads like a dime novel" after hearing a recitation of Tuppence's adventure with Rita Vandemeyer. And at one point Tommy is "shadowing" two crooks and it occurs to him that they may hail a taxi. Tommy's thoughts about what to do if that should happen:

> In books, you simply leapt into another, promised the driver a sovereign—or its modern equivalent—and there you were. In actual fact, Tommy foresaw that it was extremely likely there would be no second taxi. Therefore he would have to run.

Christie knew that she was writing a book for nothing but "fun and entertainment" and she succeeded splendidly with it.

It is important, too, to remember that the "political correctness" of today did not exist in those early days. In addition to the "postwar unemployment" background, there was at that time a desperate fear of Bolshevism, which was quite new. It was just three or four years after the Russian Revolution and most Europeans, especially those from the upper classes, were very nervous about it, and probably the British were as nervous as anybody because of the vast working class population and the "menace" of the powerful labor unions.

In *The Secret Adversary* there are negative or hostile suggestions about several nationalities. Germans, for example, are referred to as "Bosches" or "Huns." At the sinister house in Soho, Tommy spies on the meeting of the criminal gang and thinks of one of them,

> "If that isn't a Hun, I'm a Dutchman! And running the show darned systematically too—as they always do."

Germans, evidently, had already acquired a reputation for being "systematic" or "organized."

Another participant of the meeting is described thus:

> He was a small man, very pale, with a gentle almost womanish air. The angle of the cheek-bones hinted at his Slavonic ancestry, otherwise there was nothing to indicate his nationality. As he passed the recess, he turned his head slowly. The strange light eyes seemed to burn through the curtain; Tommy could hardly believe that the man did not know he was there and in spite of himself he shivered. He was no more fanciful than the majority of young Englishmen, but he could not rid himself of the impression that some unusually potent force emanated from the man. The creature reminded him of a venomous snake.

Attitudes of British people towards "foreigners," at least as portrayed by Agatha Christie in this book, also include the view that they are cowardly. When Julius points a gun at a Russian named Kramenin, the latter shoots his hands up into the air instantly, indicating to Julius that "The man was an abject physical coward..." Fear of being shot by a man pointing a gun directly at you and threatening you is evidently "cowardice" that an Englishman would not be guilty of.

At the house in Soho, Tommy recognizes one of the criminals as a well-known Sinn Feiner. The Sinn Feiners were Irish proponents of "home rule" for Ireland, which in 1920 was still a part of Great Britain. There had been an insurrection in Belfast during the Great War, and finally in 1922 Ireland became a separate country within the British Commonwealth, and in 1937 even withdrew from the Commonwealth. So the Sinn Feiners were "bad guys" and, not surprisingly, one of them is a member of the Bolshevist gang.

There is plenty of social stereotyping, too, in *The Secret Adversary*:

> The man who came up the staircase with a furtive, soft-footed tread was quite unknown to Tommy. He was obviously of the very dregs of society. The low beetling brows, and the criminal jaw, the bestiality of the whole countenance were new to the young man, though he was a type that Scotland Yard would have recognized at a glance.

"...the criminal jaw, the bestiality of the whole countenance..." One might wonder what a "criminal jaw" looks like. This kind of characterization is typical in Christie's early novels. One of her favorite phrases is "a determined chin," whatever that may be; in this story Tuppence Cowley actually has one of those.

Let us note, however, that this "criminal gang" also includes respectable-looking Englishmen and early in the novel, when Mr. Carter is discussing the arch-criminal "Mr. Brown," Tommy suggests that he may be a naturalized German. Mr. Carter responds,

> "On the contrary, I have every reason to believe he is an Englishman. He was pro–German, as he would have been pro–Boer."

And so despite the outlandish ethnic and social stereotyping that is expressed in the novel, and the portrayals of foreigners as cowardly or serpent-like, we have "every reason to believe" that the Master Criminal we are up against is not a foreigner but an Englishman.

Note: Christie's next novel will be a "detective story," again featuring Hercule Poirot, and eventually she will be thought of primarily as a writer of "detective stories." But from time to time she will produce other "adventure stories" often including the idea of a "master criminal bent on world control." In the 1920s there are *The Man in the Brown Suit, The Secret of Chimneys, The Seven Dials Mystery* and *The Big Four.*

Tommy and Tuppence will return in 1941 in the espionage thriller *N or M?* During the 1950s there will be *They Came to Baghdad* and *So Many Steps to Death* and, in the 1970s, *Passenger to Frankfurt.*

Murder on the Links (1923)

Setting

The principal setting is a large country home, the Villa Geneviève, on the outskirts of a fictitious village, Merlinville-sur-Mer, on the north coast of France half way between Calais and Boulogne-sur-Mer. The area was a popular vacation spot catering mainly to British vacationers seeking sun. The crime occurs near the Villa Geneviève, which is occupied by the wealthy Paul and Eloise Renauld and their adult son Jack along with at least three servants. Poirot and Hastings stay at the Hôtel des Bains in the village itself. Adjoining the villa is another, smaller home, the Villa Marguerite, which is occupied by a beautiful, mysterious woman, Madame Daubreuil, her even more beautiful daughter Marthe and at least one servant. Because the area is a vacation spot, a large golf course is nearby and its recently expanded grounds abut one or both of the villa properties, hence the title *Murder on the Links,* for it is on the newly-developed grounds of the golf course that the crime takes place.

The Renaulds have an automobile but it is always driven by a chauffeur, as neither Paul nor Eloise drives. There is no indication of whether the two villas have electricity or telephones, nor is there any mention of those in London at Poirot's flat. As a matter of fact, when Poirot and Hastings return briefly to London and stay overnight at their flat, they have to do legwork to find Poirot's old friend Mr. Aarons and this takes until after midnight. They ask him for certain information which he promises to bring them before 11:00 a.m. the following day. The next morning, that information arrives in the form of a "scribbled note" and not by telephone. At the villas and at the hotel in Merlinville there is never a phone call or a reference to one.

There is little description of the village, the hotel or the two villas, except for the study in the Villa Geneviève, which is a comfortable room with large leather-covered armchairs, a writing desk with pigeonholes, bookshelves lining two walls, curtains in a soft, dull green and a carpet matching them in tone.

The time is June of 1922 or thereabouts. The weather is warm and there are one or two references to Poirot and Hastings walking along "the hot, white road" as they go from the village to one of the villas and back.

The story actually begins on a train in which Hastings is traveling from Paris to Calais on a trip back to London where he has been sharing rooms with Poirot, possibly since the *Styles* case of about five or six years earlier. Once Hastings arrives in London the setting is the apartment he shares with Poirot. But the two leave immediately for France, taking a train from Victoria Station to Dover, then a ferry across the English Channel, and then a short train trip from Calais to Merlinville, where the rest of the story takes place except for a brief trip by the two friends back to London and to Coventry in search of a certain person.

There is little "local color" in the novel other than, perhaps, the amusing personalities of the French servants. There is the grumbling old housekeeper Françoise, who swears "by the holy saints" that she is truthful, and the grumbling old gardener Auguste, who resents questions but softens when complimented on his magnificent geraniums, and the hysterical and imaginative Denise, who fears the Mafia has killed her master.

There are occasional remarks from these servants suggesting the cultural differences between the French and the English. The cynical Françoise suggests that a certain extramarital love affair, because it lacks reticence and discretion, is "*style anglais,*" thus angering Hastings. A police officer, when asked if Françoise did not find it odd that the front door was open in the morning after she had sworn "by all the saints" that she had locked it the preceding evening, states,

> "Françoise is of the opinion that the English are mad and apt to do all kinds of unaccountable things at any time…"

and so she did not question it. Otherwise there is nothing particularly "French" about the setting.

Story

In the summer of approximately 1922, Hercule Poirot receives a letter from Paul Renauld, a wealthy British businessman living near a village on the northern coast of France. The letter is a frantic appeal entreating Poirot to come at once, as Paul knows that his life is in danger. Poirot and his friend Hastings depart at once for France, but arriving at Paul's home they are informed that he was murdered the preceding evening.

Monsieur Giraud of the Sûreté in Paris soon

arrives and begins to investigate the case in his own way, treating Poirot and Hastings with contempt because of their "old fashioned and unscientific" methods. Several unpleasant encounters lead Poirot and Giraud to wager 500 francs between them, the prize going to the one who solves the case first.

The body of Paul Renauld had been found, with a knife in his back, lying face down in an open grave on a new golf course adjoining his estate. A servant had discovered Eloise Renauld, Paul's wife, bound and gagged in her bedroom. Poirot notices that there is a resemblance between this case and another case of some twenty years earlier—a famous murder case in which a wife was found bound and gagged and the husband had been abducted. The wife was later accused and tried for murder but was acquitted. Suspecting a connection with the present case, Poirot makes a quick trip to Paris to research the matter and returns convinced that there is indeed a connection between the two crimes.

Poirot and Hastings solve the mystery, their adventures taking them briefly back to England, first to London and then to Coventry. All ends happily with Poirot winning his 500 franc bet with Giraud. With the money, he purchases a fine model of a foxhound to grace his mantelpiece forever under the name of "Giraud." It is suggested, at the end, that Hastings will soon be going to South America to live.

CHARACTERS

Captain Hastings: It was "Mr. Hastings" or simply "Hastings" in *The Mysterious Affair at Styles* but in *Murder on the Links* he is called Captain Hastings. He is now a sort of private secretary to an MP, but this job only takes about two hours a day of his time and sometimes there are periods of several days during which he has nothing to do. He confides that he feels fortunate to be a sort of "assistant" to a great detective, Hercule Poirot, who has set up as a private investigator in London and is doing very well at it. Hastings's personality has not changed since *The Mysterious Affair at Styles*, although he must now be about thirty-six years old, since he was thirty in the earlier novel. He is still very much fascinated by beautiful women; first by a cute young dancer he meets on a train who refuses to tell him her real name, and then by a beautiful French girl. He eventually proposes to a young woman he has only seen three times, and on that occasion he performs the hilarious stunt of pinning Hercule Poirot against the wall in a hotel room in order to allow this young woman to escape, since he's madly in love with her despite the fact that Hercule Poirot suspects her of murder. Poirot is angered but also highly amused by this bit of silliness.

As in *The Mysterious Affair at Styles* Hastings is Poirot's "sidekick," his "Dr. Watson" who assumes all the wrong things and never uses his "little gray cells" sufficiently. Hastings is constantly exasperated by Poirot's refusal to explain things to him, insisting on only "hinting" at things. It is mostly through conversations between Hastings and Poirot that we are treated to Poirot's theories about human psychology and in particular the psychology of criminals and, in this novel, his answer to the question "When does a woman lie?"

At the end of the novel we understand that Hastings may go to South America to live. This will be a useful device for Christie when she ultimately tires of the Hastings character and banishes him in 1937, reviving him only once again for the 1975 *Curtain*.

Hercule Poirot, the sleuth. The eccentricities noted in *The Mysterious Affair at Styles* are magnified and expanded in *Murder on the Links*. Poirot's atrocious fracturing of English with incorrect direct translations of French expressions are apparent in his very first utterances, as well as his obsession with neatness and symmetry, and there is a new eccentricity—an exaggerated horror of seasickness. At the breakfast table he addresses Hastings thus:

> "You have slept well, yes? You have recovered from the crossing so terrible? It is a marvel, almost you are exact this morning. *Pardon,* but your tie is not symmetrical. Permit that I rearrange him."

Also at the breakfast table, Poirot complains of toast made from asymmetrical slices of bread.

The "crossing" refers to the British expression "channel crossing," a boat trip across the English Channel. On the same page Hastings summarizes Poirot's obsession with order and method, his habit of mechanically straightening things, and his conviction that one solves mysteries "not by sniffing the ground for clues but by using the 'little gray cells.'"

French expressions that Poirot translates directly into English include "se moquer" (to make fun); he often remarks "You mock yourself at me," meaning "You're making fun of me." And the French expressions *enfin, pas du tout, mais oui, ah non!, je m'en fiche, quelle idée,* and others punctuate his speech with regularity.

In the story Hastings and Poirot cross the Channel on a ferry twice and Poirot has confidence in combating seasickness with a form of exercises known as "la méthode Laverguier" which Hastings laughs at, since on the day of their crossing to England the Channel happens to be unusually smooth.

Incidentally, the waters of the English Channel are notoriously rough in general and the one-hour crossing in a large ferry carrying scores of automobiles and hundreds of passengers does produce seasickness in a lot of people. When Poirot speaks of the "crossing so terrible," therefore, he really is referring to rough seas.

Occasionally Poirot will comment in dismay about what he sees as "no order and method" in the English way of life. At one point, conversing with Hastings on the subject of the latter's susceptibility to the charms of women, he says,

> "Ah, my friend, have faith in Papa Poirot. Some day I will arrange you a marriage of great suitability."

Hastings responds with "Thank you, but the prospect leaves me cold." Poirot sighs and shakes his head and says,

> "*Les Anglais!* No method—absolutely none whatever. They leave all to chance!"

This kind of banter between Hastings and Poirot touching on the cultural differences between the English and the French (and by extension between the English and all Continental Europeans) will come frequently in future novels and will be a source of amusement and diversion. English cooking will soon be a special butt of Poirot's criticism, but fortunately he will be able to find special little *bistrots* in London to which he will escape from time to time for a delicious meal.

At least three times in this novel Poirot embraces someone because of enthusiasm about one thing or another, "with Gallic fervor" in the words of Hastings. On one occasion he catches himself in time to remember that Hastings is embarrassed at being hugged and kissed on both cheeks by a man, and replaces it by a simple *"poignée de main"* (handshake.) In this novel, since the characters are either French or are English people living in France and accustomed to French ways, there are not many instances of people reacting negatively to Poirot's "foreignness" but in future novels with settings in England, especially in villages, he will be viewed with contempt for his "foreign" mannerisms and bizarre appearance.

Regarding Poirot's insistence that mysteries are solved by studying the "psychology" of the crime rather than "sniffing the ground for tangible clues," we may observe that in *The Mysterious Affair at Styles,* Poirot certainly made full use of such trivia as "tangible clues." We recall the broken coffee cup which was "crushed to a powder" while the lamp chimney was only broken in two places; the fingerprints on the poison bottle; the fragment of a Will found in the ashes of the fireplace; a fire in the fireplace on a day when the temperature was eighty degrees; a costume wig hidden in a trunk in the attic; samples taken in test tubes from every coffee cup and the saucepan containing the chocolate; the color of the spilled candle wax; the empty sleeping-powder box without the name of a pharmacy printed on it; a fragment torn from a garment of a certain color, a fresh coffee stain on a carpet, the shininess of a new key—the list could go on. But in *Murder on the Links,* whenever Hastings mentions "tangible clues," Poirot ridicules them, leaving them to the "human foxhounds" as he refers to lesser detectives, including the famous Monsieur Giraud of the Paris Sûreté.

"**Cinderella,**" the name given to Hastings by a girl he meets in Chapter One while riding in a train towards England. She shocks Hastings by using the word "hell." American born, she has been an acrobat/dancer since age six and works with her sister doing song and dance, "a bit of patter, etc." in traveling shows.

Paul Renauld, a wealthy English businessman with financial interests in South America, who had lived for about a month at the Villa Geneviève with his wife and adult son and at least three servants. He is the murder victim. He was suspected by certain persons—in particular by his housekeeper—of conducting an extramarital affair with a beautiful woman living nearby, but his secretary insists that Paul was devoted to his wife and would have been the last man in the world to have an extramarital affair. He had a temper, too, according to another of the servants who claims that when he had a row with his son, their voices could be heard as far away as the village.

Eloise Renauld, Paul's wife. When called upon to identify her dead husband's body, she faints upon viewing the corpse, leaving no room for doubt that her grief is genuine.

Jack Renauld, their adult son, who lives with them. Somewhat taller than his father, with dark hair and good looks, he is in love with a French girl who lives with her mother in a neighboring villa. He would have inherited half of his father's fortune had his father not altered his Will, a few days before dying, leaving everything to his wife. About two weeks before the crime Jack and his father had a violent quarrel on the subject of his romance with the French girl.

Madame Daubreuil, a beautiful and mysterious Frenchwoman who lives with her equally beautiful daughter at the Villa Marguerite, just a few steps away from the Villa Geneviève. She is "a woman with a past," and certain characters suspect that Madame Daubreuil and Paul Renauld were lovers.

Marthe Daubreuil, Madame Daubreuil's beautiful daughter. Hastings, who is always enchanted by beautiful women, finds Marthe to be one of the most beautiful girls he has ever seen. Poirot, however, who sees Marthe at the same moment, comments, "I saw only a girl with anxious eyes."

Françoise Arrichet, "old Françoise," the Renaulds' housekeeper, who remained at the Villa Geneviève after the former owner sold the villa to them a month earlier. When pressed for certainty that she had indeed locked the front door on the evening of the tragedy, she says, "I swear it by the blessed saints, Monsieur."

Léonie and **Denise Oulard**, sisters, housemaids to the Renaulds. Denise, who speaks English well and is very proud of it, reports the content of a conversation in that language that she overheard between Paul Renauld and a certain lady in his study, who she insists was *not* Madame Daubreuil. Denise is convinced that it was the Mafia that killed Paul Renauld.

Masters, chauffeur to the Renaulds. He had been sent away on holiday the day before the tragedy and so is not in the story at all. Old Françoise asserts that only Masters used the automobile, as Monsieur Renauld did not drive.

Auguste, the aging gardener at the Villa Geneviève. He grumbles constantly at being questioned by the police, but Poirot, applying the principle that one catches more flies with honey than with vinegar, flatters Auguste by first admiring his magnificent geraniums and then proceeding with questions.

Gabriel Stonor, private secretary to Paul Renauld.

> The man who entered the room was a striking figure. Very tall, with a well-knit athletic frame, and a deeply bronzed face and neck, he dominated the assembly. Even Giraud seemed anemic beside him. When I knew him better I realized that Gabriel Stonor was quite an unusual personality. English by birth, he had knocked about all over the world. He had shot big game in Africa, ranched in California, and traded in the South Sea Islands. He had been secretary to a New York railway magnate, and had spent a year encamped in the desert with a friendly tribe of Arabs.

Christie supplies this long description of a character of little importance perhaps just for the pleasure of describing a type of "manly man" for which she must have had a special fondness. One such "bronzed, strong, silent man," Colonel Race, will soon appear in *The Man in the Brown Suit*, her next book.

Monsieur Lucien Bex, Commissary of Police at Merlinville, who announces the death of Paul Renauld to Poirot and Hastings.

Monsieur Hautet, the examining magistrate or "Juge d'Instruction." He is a tall, gaunt man with piercing dark eyes and a neatly cut gray beard, which he has a habit of caressing as he speaks.

Marchand, one of two "sergents de ville" (ordinary police officers).

Monsieur Giraud, of the Sûreté in Paris (the French equivalent of Scotland Yard), officially in charge of the case. He is tall, perhaps about thirty years of age, with auburn hair, a mustache and a military carriage. There is also a trace of arrogance in his manner.

From the moment that Giraud meets Poirot he derides Poirot's "old fashioned" methods and he makes much of clues such as cigarette stubs, match ends and footprints. He ignores Poirot for the most part and Poirot soon despises him.

Joseph Aarons, a theatrical agent in London who owes Poirot a favor (Poirot had once assisted him in the matter of a Japanese wrestler). He assists Poirot in locating the "Dulcibella Kids."

The Dulcibella Kids, twin sisters who sing and dance and do acrobatic routines for provincial audiences. One of them is the aforementioned "Cinderella" and one of them receives the amorous attentions of Hastings.

Note: In the course of the investigation, Poirot recalls a murder case of about twenty years earlier which he suspects may have a connection with the present crime. He goes to Paris to research it, bringing back the following names as central figures in that case:

Mr. Hiram Trapp, an extremely wealthy American

Monsieur Arnold Béroldy, an unremarkable wine merchant of Lyons

Madame Béroldy, his wife, a woman who never denied rumors of having been at the center of sensational intrigues related to crown jewels, secret papers of international political importance, illegitimate royal birth, etc.

Georges Conneau, a young lawyer rumored by many to be Madame Béroldy's lover, and not the only one

The story of these four people is discussed by Poirot and Hastings and may have a bearing on the present mystery.

FRENCH INTO ENGLISH

Chapter 2
Pardon—Excuse me
Du tout!—Nonsense!
Nous Autres—The rest of us
Par Example, C'est Trop Fort!—Damn it, this is the limit!
Banal—Boring
Carte Blanche—A free hand, full permission
Mon Dieu, for Pete's sake!
Parbleu—Good grief
Je m'en Fche—To Hell with it
Quelle Idée—What an idea!
Eh Bien—Well
Je Ne Sais Quoi—I don't know what it is
Ça Commence!—It's starting!
Sergent De Ville—Policeman

Chapter 3
sergent de ville—policeman
Voilà!—here
Sacré tonnerre—Good grief!
cette dame—that lady
celle-là—that one
voilà—There you are
milord anglais, très riche—an English gentleman, very rich
très chic—well dressed
ma foi!—good grief
Style anglais—English style
voilà tout—that's all

Chapter 4
hein?—right?
Bien—all right, then
Tiens!—Well, look at this
Ma foi!—wow!

Chapter 5
une maîtresse femme—an imposing, masterful woman
pardon—excuse me
Mon Dieu!—Good heavens!
pardon—excuse me
Eh bien—all right, then

Chapter 6
Pauvre femme—the poor woman

Chapter 7
Eh bien—All right
Mon dieu!—My God!
maman—mom
dossier—file
Sacré!—Damn!

Chapter 8
la pauvre dame—the poor lady
par example—really!
ma foi—good heavens
Quelle idée—What a silly idea
Au revoir—Good bye [Note: the use of "*au revoir*" implies that the two people will see each other again. A permanent "good bye" is expressed by "*adieu.*"]
empressement—warmth

Chapter 9
parbleu—For Pete's sake!
pardon—excuse me
sac à papier!—For Christ's sake! (euphemism for *sacristi*—"holy Christ!"
bien entendu—of course
eh bien—so!
Comment?—What's that you're saying?
D'accord—Agreed
eh bien—all right

Chapter 10
mon Dieu!—goodness!
voilà une idée!—there's a thought!

Chapter 11
M. le juge—your honor
comment?—What!
par example—[difficult to translate in words—the phrase expresses annoyance and outrage]
O jeunesse, jeunesse!—Ah, to be young again!
Ils sont mal renseignés, les accomplices!—these "accomplices" don't have much sense

Chapter 12
Parbleu—Obviously
c'est entendu?—is that quite clear?
C'est bien!—All right, then!
là, là—c'mon, now
cette histoire-là—that silly story
cause célèbre—famous case
À la bonne heure!—Finally! It's about time! [Note—in some editions this may be incorrectly spelled "*à la bonheur*"]
eh bien, méfiez-vous!—Better be careful!

Chapter 13
Eh bien—well, now!
Tiens!—Humph!
empressement—warmth
Les anglais!—The English!
Une poignée de main, alors.—A handshake, then.
Chéri—Darling
petit déjeuner—breakfast

Chapter 14
c'est l'Anglais—it's the Englishman

Chapter 15
Mon cher ami—my good friend

Chapter 16
crime passionnel—unpremeditated murder committed while in extreme anger

Chapter 18
un moment, s'il vous plaît—please come here for a moment
maman—mom, mama
Sacré tonnerre—God damn it!
jeune homme—young man

Chapter 19
Bien!—Very well, then.

Chapter 20
Enfin!—Finally!
Aucunement!—None whatever!
De mieux en mieux!—Better and better!
Quelle idée!—What an idea!
Précisément!—Precisely!
Mon Dieu!—My goodness
triste—sad
ne vous impatientez pas!—Don't be impatient!

Chapter 21
la mauvaise chance—bad luck
comme ça—like this
Ah! voilà une femme!—now there's a great woman!
soupçon—subtle hint

Chapter 22
Vive l'amour!—Hooray for love!

Chapter 24
c'est entendu—that's understood
empressement—enthusiasm
Enfin!—frankly
Toqué!—nutty, crazy
Sapristi—God damn! (Euphemism for "*Sacristi*"—"*Holy Christ*")
petite—dear

Chapter 25
greffier—clerk

Chapter 27
Eh, ma foi—And to be sure...
Vous voilà—Ah, there you are...
Sacré tonnerre—Good heavens (literally "holy thunder")

entrecôte—a cut of meat; steak, chop, etc.
café noir—black coffee
mes enfants—kids, youngsters
Très bien, mon enfant—Very good, my child
Mille tonnerres—Oh my God! (Literally: a thousand thunderbolts)

Chapter 28
garde-malade—nurse
enfin—at last
la petite acrobate—the little acrobat
crise of the nerves—nervous breakdown
les femmes—women

COMMENTS

The characters in *The Mysterious Affair at Styles*, written in 1916, are, with the exception of young Cynthia Murdoch, mature adults of at least age thirty-five. Their conversation is staid and their outlooks on life are conventional. Cynthia herself, though young, has no particular individuality or vitality and is no more memorable than the rest of the characters, who are a rather dull lot. Christie admitted this herself. She was dissatisfied with the "love aspect" (John and Mary) in *The Mysterious Affair at Styles* but did not know how to make it more interesting. The detection of the mystery, consisting mostly of conversations between Poirot and Hastings, is interesting enough but the characters themselves, with the possible exception of Evelyn Howard, with her special laconic, telegraphic speech and her outspokenness, are for the most part not memorable. There is little "sparkle" and practically no humor in the book, unless you count Hastings's absurd marriage proposal to Cynthia.

It was not until a year or two after the publication of *The Mysterious Affair at Styles* in 1920 that Christie thought about writing a second book for publication, and in that novel, *The Secret Adversary,* she made up for all of the earlier book's shortcomings. "No dull people in this one!" she must have promised herself, "And nobody just sitting around awaiting an inheritance!" Two charming young people, penniless but full of "pluck," take on the world and find excitement and adventure through their own courage and initiative.

In *Murder on the Links,* her third published novel, Christie returns to the straight detective genre but, right from the beginning, with "Cinderella" shocking Hastings with her exclamation "Hell!" in the railway compartment, this detective novel has more youthfulness and freshness than *The Mysterious Affair at Styles*. And there are more varied personalities—ones that are more easily remembered. The characters are "sexier," so to speak. There is gorgeous Marthe Daubreuil, and Madame Daubreuil with her real or imagined scandalous past. There is bronzed, game-hunting Stonor, and the handsome young ex-aviator Jack Renauld. There is bold-as-brass "Cinderella" who tumbles and dances in show-biz for a living and flirts with strangers in railway compartments. There is dapper, self-confident (and a bit arrogant) Monsieur Giraud of the French police. There are masked intruders demanding to know "the secret." There is an abduction, a love affair between two lovable young people, an entreating letter from a girl abandoned by her lover, the amusingly cynical pronouncements of the very French servant "old Françoise" plus the relatively exotic location of France instead of England. There is rivalry between Poirot and Giraud and more of Hastings' childish amorous behaviors. Christie's writing has advanced a bit; not to the full, but in the right direction. Reading *Murder on the Links* is much more "fun" than reading *The Mysterious Affair at Styles*, even though as a detective novel, *The Mysterious Affair at Styles* is equally good.

In *The Mysterious Affair at Styles*, there had been one or two "lucky guesses" that Poirot relied upon to help him in his deduction, (the matter of the lost key to the dispatch case, for example.) In *Murder on the Links* there is simply pure, intelligent reasoning that brings the solution. There are no footprints on the second flowerbed but Auguste replenished both beds yesterday, therefore someone must have had a reason for raking the second flowerbed smooth and not the first one, therefore there must have been incriminating footprints, therefore somebody must have entered or left the house through the window above the flowerbed, therefore the door must have been left open simply to delude us, therefore Madame must be lying, but when does a woman lie? To protect herself, or the man she loves, or her child, etc.; she has no lover, her husband is dead, therefore she must be protecting her child, etc....

The Man in the Brown Suit (1924)

Setting

The dressing room of a famous dancer in Paris, the cottage of an anthropologist in an English village, a luxury flat in the Kensington district of London, a London tube station, a real estate office in London, a lonely house on the river near London, an office at London's Scotland Yard, a steamship booking office in London and a hotel in the southern French city of Cannes provide the settings in the first eight chapters of *The Man in the Brown Suit*.

Next, there is a long ocean voyage, taking several days. Several important events occur on the steamer and conversations occur in various cabins, on deck and in the restaurant. The ship travels from Southampton, England to the island of Madeira where it makes a brief stop, then goes on to Capetown, South Africa where the characters in the story disembark and the steamer leaves for a further destination.

The setting is now Capetown and its environs, followed by a train trip lasting several days north to Rhodesia and the town of Livingstone near the famous Victoria Falls, and eventually to a semi-inhabited island a few miles further north.

The final setting is Johannesburg during a popular uprising.

Britain's interests in Africa, in particular her interests in diamond mining at Kimberley, and the political unrest in South Africa during the early 1920s are the historical backgrounds. The action takes place in the early months of 1922.

The excitement of an ocean voyage, the unique beauties of the sea, of the Grand Peak of Tenerife, of Table Mountain, and Victoria Falls and their surrounding forests are enthusiastically and romantically described by the author who had visited them only a few months earlier during a similar ocean voyage. The descriptions are brief, however, as the narrators focus most of their attention on the exciting adventure story they are relating. There are no important interactions between the main characters and natives of these foreign places. Nearly all of the characters are English; a few are Dutch or South African British.

Story

The story revolves around a master criminal known as "the Colonel." His crimes have included jewel theft, forgery, espionage, sabotage, discreet assassination, and so on. He has always been careful to commit the crimes through other people and therefore he has always been free of suspicion.

Anne Beddingfeld, the daughter of anthropologist Professor Beddingfeld, is left a penniless orphan when he dies suddenly of pneumonia at his home in a village in England. Anne is a bright young woman who has always longed for adventures and romance. In London one day Anne witnesses an accident in a subway station: a man falls onto the electrically-charged track and is electrocuted. A "doctor" steps out from the crowd to "examine" the man and to pronounce him dead, but the "doctor" then disappears into the crowd and he does not appear at the inquest the next day.

Suspecting that the "doctor" was not a real doctor, Anne decides to investigate the matter herself and succeeds in being hired as a newspaper reporter. Her adventures, which lead her on an ocean voyage to South Africa and to the interior of Africa, are all she could ask for. A handsome man with a scar and a stab wound stumbles into her cabin aboard the ship one night; on another night someone tries to strangle her and throw her overboard. In South Africa she is lured into "the Colonel's" camp and held prisoner but escapes by her own ingenuity. Later, at a tourist hotel near Victoria Falls in Rhodesia she is lured outside at night and chased over a cliff. She eventually swims with her "man with the scar" across a crocodile-infested river, and uses a rifle for the first time in her life, handles a revolver and is surrounded by explosions during a revolt in Johannesburg. Through all of this, Anne receives three marriage proposals, two of them from men she actually loves.

CHARACTERS

Nadina, a "Russian" dancer, one of a gang of criminals headed by a mysterious man known as The Colonel. Not really Russian, her true nationality is South African.

Count Sergius Paulovitch, another member of the gang of criminals, and who is no more Russian than Nadina is. Nor is he really a count.

The Colonel, a master criminal who remains at a safe distance from his crimes, using others as his instruments and scapegoats

Jeanne, Nadina's dresser

Anne Beddingfeld, the daughter of Professor Beddingfeld, a famous anthropologist. She dutifully assists her father in his work at Hampsley Cavern where he catalogs the remains of prehistoric humans and animals. She yearns for a life filled with thrills, adventure and love but contents herself with well-worn copies of adventure and romance novels from the local library, dreaming of "stern, silent Rhodesians." After her father's death, all of her dreams come true—with a vengeance.

Professor Beddingfeld, an anthropologist. He is completely absorbed in his work and is incompetent in money matters. He dies early the story, leaving Anne a penniless orphan.

Emily, the Beddingfelds' maid, who later encourages Anne to write about her adventures.

The Doctor who, in an effort to rescue Anne from her fate as a penniless orphan, suggests that she marry him.

Mr. Henry Flemming, Professor Beddingfeld's London solicitor, an ardent anthropologist himself. He kindly offers a temporary home to Anne after her father's death while she looks for a job.

Mrs. Flemming, who is surprised and rather annoyed by her husband's interest in Anne's welfare, and by his bringing the girl home to London to live with them without consulting with her first.

Several Boring Housewives, friends of Mrs. Flemming, who annoy Anne by the fact that, despite great wealth (most of them) they have no interest in travel of any kind. In fact, they dislike travel because every place is so different from England, "except the Riviera, of course, because one meets all one's friends there."

Mr. L. B. Carton of Kimberley, South Africa, the unfortunate accident victim in London's Hyde Park tube station. He was heavily tanned and wore a long overcoat smelling of mothballs. Suddenly startled by something he saw in the station, he stepped backwards and fell onto the electrically charged track and was killed instantly. In his pocket was an Order to View for a house—the Mill House—on the river near Marlow.

"The Doctor," who happened to be in the crowd on the platform when the accident in the tube station occurred. He examined the victim and, pronouncing him dead, he quickly disappeared back into the crowd. He did not appear at the inquest.

The Coroner, who found it puzzling that "the doctor" did not come forward later or appear at the inquest

Sir Eustace Pedlar, M.P., hopefully not your average Member of Parliament. He has an intense dislike for work and considers his dedicated secretary to be a slave driver. His extensive *Diary* forms many of the chapters of the book. Wintering at Cannes when the murder of an unknown foreign woman occurs at his house in January, he grudgingly returns to England to deal with the "annoying problem of someone getting herself murdered in my house, and a foreign woman, which is worse!"

Guy Pagett, Sir Eustace's devoted, hardworking secretary of eight years.

Mrs. de Castina, address unknown but staying at the Hyde Park Hotel. It was she who was strangled at the Mill House

Caroline James, the wife of Sir Eustace's gardener. The couple lives in the lodge at the Mill House. James himself, according to Sir Eustace, is a bad gardener, but Sir Eustace keeps them both on because Mrs. James is such a good cook. It is Mrs. James who gives evidence that Mrs. de Castina came to see the house and that a bearded young man in a brown suit soon followed.

Mr. Augustus Milray, a political friend of Sir Eustace who is worried about labor unrest and talk of a general strike in South Africa. He begs Sir Eustace to take an important message to General Smuts in South Africa and, since Sir Eustace is planning to go there soon anyway, why not go at once?

Jarvis, Sir Eustace's butler

Harry Rayburn, sent by Mr. Milray to be a "second secretary" (implication: a bodyguard) to Sir Eustace for the voyage to South Africa because of the dangerous and important nature of a certain document that is in Sir Eustace's possession. Rayburn is a well-built young fellow with a deeply tanned face. A scar runs diagonally from the corner of his eye to the jaw, disfiguring what would otherwise have been a handsome though somewhat reckless countenance.

The Purser, who settles the dispute over who shall have cabin number seventeen, responding warmly to Anne's feminine charms

The Rev. Chichester, an unpleasant missionary who "talked a lot about 'our poor black brothers.'" Anne disliked him. "He had false teeth that clicked when he ate. Many men have been hated for less." He was determined to have cabin number seventeen, but the Purser gave it to Anne.

The Honorable Mrs. Clarence Blair (Suzanne), a passenger aboard the *Kilmorden Castle*. She is about thirty and has a round dimpled face and very blue eyes. She is one of those people who know what they want, see that they get it, and manage to do so without being offensive to anyone. She is devoted to her husband Clarence and, because everyone knows it, she can enjoy the attentions of other men without provoking gossip.

Anne and Suzanne form a kind of partnership which proves to be very useful to Anne. As soon as Anne tells Suzanne about her adventures, Suzanne sends a cable to her husband: "Involved in the most thrilling mystery please send a thousand pounds at once Suzanne."

Colonel Race, described thus by Anne:

> ...a tall, soldierly-looking man with dark hair and a bronzed face whom I had noticed striding up and down the deck earlier in the day. I put him down at once as one of the strong, silent men of Rhodesia. He was about forty, with a touch of graying hair at either temple, and was easily the best-looking man on board.

Sir Eustace describes Colonel Race as "that long-legged taciturn ass." Anne is attracted to Colonel Race but is always a little afraid of him.

The Ship Captain, who dines with Mrs. Blair, Colonel Race and Sir Eustace one evening.

Mr. Reeves, another passenger on the liner, a member of the South African Labour Party, a "horrible little man," according to Sir Eustace, "but useful in providing information about labour activities in South Africa."

Miss Pettigrew, a temporary shorthand-typist obtained by Guy Pagett for Sir Eustace's railway trip to Rhodesia. Sir Eustace describes her as a forty-year-old slab-faced woman with pince-nez and sensible boots and an air of brisk efficiency that will be the death of him.

John Eardsley, a young man who had done prospecting with a partner in South America and discovered diamond fields there. He had been wild at Cambridge and his father had paid his debts more than once.

Lucas, John Eardsley's prospecting partner in South America. The two were later implicated in a jewel theft in South Africa.

Anita Grünberg, the real name of the dancer Nadina, with whom both John Eardsley and Lucas fell in love. She participated in the jewel robbery and effected a substitution in order to implicate the two men as jewel thieves.

Sir Lawrence Eardsley, John's wealthy father, who disowned his son after learning of his son's involvement in the jewel robbery

A Small Man with a Big Nose, a member of the gang, who follows Anne about Capetown, on and off trams, finally summoning a police officer to help him chase her to the railway station.

A Tall Man with a Flaming Orange Beard, Anne's captor at the Villa Medgee in Muizenberg. Anne's description: "Obviously a Dutchman."

A Short Black-bearded Dutchman who meets Anne at the railway station in Johannesburg

Minks, a member of the Colonel's gang who is a master of disguises

Various stewards, stewardesses, waiters, etc.

COMMENTS

The settings for *The Man in the Brown Suit* had an interesting origin. As mentioned in the *Introduction*, Agatha Christie and her husband Archibald made a trip around the world, in 1922 or 1923, at the invitation of one of Archibald's friends, a certain Major Belcher. This trip included South Africa as well as a trip by railway as far north as Victoria Falls in Rhodesia. Upon their return to England, Archibald found that his job in London had not been held for him, and it took quite a long time for him to secure employment again. Agatha wrote *The Man in the Brown Suit* at that time simply to earn some money. She found the book very difficult to write and she did not like it, but she made good use of her travel experiences in writing it.

Regarding the Christies' world tour, the first leg of the trip was on a liner called the *Kildonan Castle*, from England to Capetown, South Africa, stopping at the island of Madeira. As the liner left England, Agatha became enormously seasick at once, and lay "prostrate in her cabin for four days." Her husband said, "Oh I expect you'll feel better soon." "No," she said, "I shall never feel better. I must get off this boat. I must get on dry land." "You'll still have to get back to England," he pointed out, "even if you did get off in Madeira." "I needn't," said Agatha, "I could stay there. I could do some work there.... I could be a parlourmaid. I would quite *like* to be a parlourmaid."

Whether or not Agatha was being serious about the idea of staying on in Madeira and being a parlourmaid, she recovered from seasickness as soon as the seas calmed, and the voyage proceeded as scheduled—first to South Africa, then up into Rhodesia by train, then back to South Africa and by liner to Australia and finally to Canada (stopping for a week in Hawaii) and then back home to England via New York.

Meanwhile Major Belcher proved to be a very irritating traveling companion. Even before the trip began, he had suggested to Agatha that she write a mystery story about his home, which was called "Mill House," and he insisted on being one of the characters in the book. During the trip he often brought up the subject and it was difficult for Agatha to politely dismiss this "pest" and his ideas since he was, more or less, their host.

Christie had never liked the idea of writing about a real person. She always conceived the characters in her books in her own mind, only in small ways allowing herself to be "inspired" by the appearance or words of real people. As an example, she once noticed an older woman talking ceaselessly with a younger man in a tram and thus conceived of the couple Emily and Alfred Inglethorpe for *The Mysterious Affair at Styles*. On another occasion she overheard some people discussing a certain "Jane Fish" and came up with the "Jane Finn" name for a character in *The Secret Adversary*.

When Christie began writing *The Man in the Brown Suit* she intended to call it *The Mystery of the Mill House,* and she did try to model the owner of the house, Sir Eustace Pedlar, after Major Belcher, even narrating some of his antics in it. At Capetown, for example, Major Belcher had become angry about the food at the hotel, especially the unripe peaches, and he rudely bounced a peach off the floor to express his disgust. In the book Sir Eustace bounces a peach on the floor but it squashes, being less hard than he had imagined.

Christie's experience with seasickness and her not-very-serious idea of leaving the ship at Madeira to become a parlourmaid are replicated in the book with the sufferer being Anne Beddingfeld. In the novel, Anne buys a first class ticket for an ocean voyage to South Africa and rushes home, full of enthusiasm for the trip. As she arrives there, her hostess, Mrs. Flemming, generously offers to provide Anne with a permanent home with them. Anne thanks her but explains that it's unnecessary, as she is leaving in a few days for South Africa. Mrs. Flemming says, "To South Africa? My dear Anne. We would have to look into anything of that kind very carefully."

> That was the last thing I wanted. I explained that I had already taken my passage, and that upon arrival I proposed to take up the duties of a parlormaid. It was the only thing I could think of on the spur of the moment. There was, I said, a great demand for parlormaids in South Africa...

As soon as the ship sails out of Southampton, of course, Anne becomes seasick and is confined to her cabin for four days:

> It was on the fourth day that the stewardess finally urged me up on deck. Under the impression that I should die quicker below, I had steadfastly refused to leave my bunk. She now tempted me with the advent of Madeira. Hope rose in my breast. I could leave the boat and go ashore and be a parlormaid there. Anything for dry land.

Once in Africa, Anne's adventures occur in many of the places that Christie and her husband had visited the year before—Capetown, Kimberley, Muizenberg, Livingstone, Victoria Falls, Johannesburg, etc.

The Man in the Brown Suit is an "adventure" story but it also has the flavor of a "romance novel" which might make it appeal more to feminine readers than to macho types. Readers who are able to forget their modern concepts of male-female relationships and to try to see the world through the eyes of a naïve twenty-year-old girl from rural England eighty years ago, will be delighted with the book, if for nothing more than its humor. It would be difficult to bring this story to the screen, however, because no modern audience is likely to relate to the motivations and feelings of Anne Beddingfeld.

The story is filled with dangerous adventures. A handsome man with a stab wound stumbles into Anne's cabin on the ship one night; soon someone attempts to throw her overboard, also at night, but she is rescued by "her man." She is lured into a den of criminals, bound and gagged and imprisoned in an attic. She is lured outside and chased over a cliff where some fortunately positioned branches catch her, preserving her life; she swims with her lover across a stream infested with crocodiles; she is passionately embraced and kissed by a man she worships for his strength. Through all this she receives three marriage proposals (two from men she actually loves).

As with *The Secret Adversary,* Agatha Christie knew that she was writing "light fiction" of a very entertaining and improbable kind and she probably smiled often as she wrote. At many points in the story the heroine has thoughts such as "if this were happening in a book...."

The characters in *The Man in the Brown Suit* are just as entertaining—and as memorable—as those in *The Secret Adversary.* One of the most amusing passages is Anne's visit to the office of Lord Nasby, the owner of *The Daily Budget.* She has just arrived and handed the footman the calling card of the Marquis of Loamsley, upon which *she* had written "Please give Miss Beddingfeld a few moments of your time."

> The thing worked. A footman received the card and bore it away. Presently a pale secretary appeared. I fenced with him successfully. He retired defeated. He again reappeared and begged me to follow him. I did so. I entered a large room. A frightened-looking shorthand-typist fled past me like a visitant from the spirit-world. Then the door shut and I was face to face with Lord Nasby.
> A big man. Big head. Big face. Big mustache. Big stomach. I pulled myself together. I had not come here to comment on Lord Nasby's stomach. He was already roaring at me...

The book sparkles with such humorous touches, plenty of action and thrills, colorful characters and exotic settings, and the story is complex and challenging to follow, as it is related by Anne Beddingfeld, in some chapters, and by Sir Eustace Pedlar in others.

Note: One character in *The Man in the Brown Suit,* one of the "suspects," in fact, will prove to be guilt-free and will reappear in three Christie detective novels of later years. Be warned that this person's name is mentioned in the chapters on the following novels: *Cards on the Table, Death on the Nile,* and *Remembered Death.* If you have read any of them, then you know who the person is. But if you have not, and you want to read *The Man in the Brown Suit* with full enjoyment, avoid for now the chapters on those other three novels.

The Secret of Chimneys (1925)

SETTING

The story begins at Bulawayo, a town in the African country then called Rhodesia. Then it moves briefly to London, then to a fictitious country mansion called Chimneys near the town of Market Basing. The English county in which Market Basing is located is not specified in this novel, but we know that it must be somewhere west of London, since trains from London to that town leave from Paddington Station. Twelve years later, in the 1937 novel *Poirot Loses a Client,* the action will take place in Market Basing, and in that novel Market Basing will be located in the real county of Berkshire, which is just a short distance west of London.

In London there are scenes in a guest room at the fictitious Blitz Hotel, probably a tongue-in-cheek reference to the Ritz Hotel. Another scene takes place in the office of the hotel manager. The luxurious London home of a wealthy young widow is also a setting early in the novel. Her small drawing room is described as "all pale and mauve and green and yellow, like crocuses surprised in a meadow." The home also has a library and it is in this room that the young woman discovers the dead body of a man who had threatened to blackmail her. The bedrooms are on an upper floor.

A brief scene takes place in London's Paddington railway station where a character boards a train for Market Basing on her way to Chimneys, and where a trunk containing the blackmailer's dead body is left at the baggage claim and then picked up later and taken out into the country north of London and left by the side of the road. Towards the end of the story there is a brief scene at a house in a village just outside of Dover, in the county of Kent.

Chimneys is described as "one of the great, old, historic houses" of England, one of those that are open to the public periodically. It is immense and is probably at least three centuries old. There are several sitting rooms, including one called "the white drawing room." One room on the ground floor is called the "council chamber;" another room is "the blue morning room."

Several of the ground floor rooms, including the dining room and the "council chamber" have French windows which can serve as entrances from the outside, as the windows are tall, the sills are near the floor and the windows open inward on hinges. In America they would be called "French doors." In the story people often enter these two rooms directly from the outside through the French windows.

There are terraces running along the perimeter of parts of the house; these are uncovered porches that are paved in some way. The grounds include a goldfish pond, a double row of yews, a large rose garden with a sundial, and a boat house with row boats to be used on the river that runs along the property.

The house has three "hidden features" within: a "priest's hole" and two secret passages, one accessed inside the "white drawing room" on the upper floor and one accessed in the "council chamber."

There is electric lighting in the house (a wall switch controls a large chandelier in the council chamber) and there is a telephone. This is the first direct reference to electric lighting in a Christie novel; the telephone had made its first appearance in the 1922 *The Secret Adversary*.

The story takes place in 1924 or thereabouts, but there are references to fictitious events that occurred seven years earlier in England and France, and in Herzoslovakia, a fictitious Balkan republic. Most of the characters are British, some are French and others are "Herzoslovakian." All of the action, however, takes place in Rhodesia and England.

The historical background to the story, of course, includes Britain's nineteenth and early twentieth-century imperialism. Vast areas of Africa were made part of the British Empire and for a time all of eastern Africa, from Egypt south to South Africa, was a part of it. A "Cape to Cairo" railway was contemplated but never built.

The idea of "The Comrades of the Red Hand" may sound melodramatic today, but if we look at the history of World War I we recall that the immediate cause of the War was the assassination of Archduke Francis Ferdinand, the heir to the throne of the Austro-Hungarian Empire. In June of 1914 he visited Bosnia-Herzogovina, an area in which nationalistic resentment of the Vienna government was strong. A secret organization known as The Black Hand sent three men to Sarajevo to assassinate him. The Hapsburg family had never accepted Francis Ferdinand's marriage to his wife Sophie, considering Sophie to be of an inappropriate rank to marry the heir to the throne, and the two were forced to have a morganatic marriage. On June 28 both the Archduke and his pregnant wife were assassinated as they passed through the streets of Sarajevo in an open automobile. The incident aroused international outrage and precipitated World War I with Austria's invasion of Serbia and a system of alliances that brought several nations into the conflict.

There is no doubt that the memory of "The Black Hand" inspired Agatha Christie to conceive the idea of "The Comrades of the Red Hand" and that her name for the fictitious country Herzoslovakia was derived from Herzogovina. The fact of Sophie's "inappropriate rank to marry the heir to the throne of the Austro-Hungarian Empire" was the inspiration for the rejection of "Queen Varaga" by the populace of Herzoslovakia in *The Secret of Chimneys* which, of course, was written only ten years after these historical events.

STORY

The year is 1924. In a fictitious Balkan country, Herzoslovakia, the following events occurred about seven years ago:

King Nicholas IV, of the Obolovitch dynasty, chose for his bride a certain Angele Mory, "a little guttersnipe of a music-hall artiste in Paris," presenting her to the population of Herzoslovakia as "Countess Popoffsky," and installing her on the throne as "Queen Varaga." The King and Queen soon made a royal visit to England and were welcomed at Chimneys, a grand old residence that was frequently used to host such international visits. Also present on this occasion was a certain Count Stylptitch, the "Grand Old Man of the Balkans," then Prime Minister of Herzoslovakia. A fabulous jewel owned by the royal family, the Kohinoor Diamond, was in the possession of the Queen during the visit to Chimneys and it disappeared there, apparently stolen. The royal couple returned to Herzoslovakia and very soon a bloody revolution took place and the King and Queen were murdered by a mob on the steps of the royal palace. The country then became a republic.

Count Stylptitch had been writing his *Memoirs,* and it was suspected that the *Memoirs* contained various embarrassing secrets, one of them being the location of the stolen diamond, in addition to indiscreet comments about the Herzoslovakian royal family.

At present (1924) the population of Herzoslovakia has grown weary of its republic and is disposed to welcome a restoration of the monarchy. The late King Nicholas IV is being portrayed in the press as "half saint-half hero" and not the "stupid little man besotted by a common music hall artiste that he was," in the words of one of the characters. The British government would like to see the Herzoslovakian monarchy restored because the heir to the throne, Prince Michael, who had been educated in England in the tradition of Herzoslovakian nobility, is pro-British and he has promised that if the monarchy is restored, he will grant important oil concessions to Britain. Herzoslovakia has recently been found to be rich in oil deposits.

Furthermore, Count Stylptitch, the author of the notorious *Memoirs,* has died. A few weeks before he died, he secretly entrusted the manuscript of the *Memoirs* to an unknown person with instructions to take them to a certain publisher in England for immediate publication upon his death. If published, these *Memoirs* might re-ignite negative feelings in Herzoslovakia towards the royal family, preventing the restoration of the monarchy and also bringing to light the disappearance of the Kohinoor Diamond, which would embarrass the British Government. People would ask "Why was the disappearance of the jewel 'hushed up'?" Therefore the British government wishes at all costs to prevent the publication of the *Memoirs.*

Chimneys is scheduled to be the scene of a second visit by Herzoslovakian royalty. The heir to the throne, Prince Michael, will be there, along with a certain Mr. Isaacstein, who heads the British oil syndicate, and the purpose of the event will be to cement the relationship between the British government, the oil syndicate and the Prince. On the first night of this royal visit, however, Prince Michael is murdered at Chimneys.

The murder is investigated by Superintendent Battle of Scotland Yard, and a group of loveable young people—Anthony Cade, Virginia Revel, Lady Eileen Brent and Bill Eversleigh—watch the proceedings and "assist" Superintendent Battle, who solves the murder case and restores the Kohinoor Diamond. Lady Eileen and Bill Eversleigh, along with Lady Eileen's father and a few other friends, will rejoin Superintendent Battle in a later novel, the 1929 *The Seven Dials Mystery.*

CHARACTERS

Anthony Cade, a young Englishman, age thirty-two, tall, lean and suntanned, educated at Eton and Cambridge but preferring a life of adventures. He has an instinct for "rows" and the nine lives of a cat. He has been away from England since age eighteen. An adventurer at heart, he is "keen on revolutions" and would love to be involved in one. Currently he is short of cash and bored silly by his job as a tour guide in Rhodesia.

James (Jimmy) McGrath, from "the backwoods of Canada," tall, thickset, and not as good looking as Anthony. He has prospected for gold in many places and is now prospecting for it in the interior of Africa. He has saved the lives of at least two people: one Count Stylptitch of Herzoslovakia and a certain Herzoslovakian scoundrel known as Dutch Pedro.

Count Stylptitch of Herzoslovakia, the "grand old man of the Balkans." Depending on which newspaper you read, he's "the greatest statesman of modern times," or "the biggest villain unhung." He's been a dictator and a patriot and a statesman—a perfect king of intrigue. His *Memoirs,* not yet published, may cause embarrassment to more than one government. A while ago, Jimmy saved his life as he was being attacked in Paris by a group of street thugs. The grateful Count entrusted the manuscript of the *Memoirs* to Jimmy to ensure their publication in England upon his death, arranging for him to be paid a thousand pounds for the service. His *Memoirs* may also reveal the location of the Kohinoor Diamond, a fabulous jewel belonging to the royal family of Herzoslovakia which disappeared during the royal family's visit to England seven years ago.

King Nicholas IV of Herzoslovakia who was murdered by the mob in a revolution seven years ago, mainly because of his taste in wives. He had married a third-rate French actress and set her up as Queen Varaga, thereby infuriating the barbaric populace and inciting them to revolt.

Queen Varaga of Herzoslovakia, alias Countess Popoffsky, alias Angèle Mory, the third-rate actress installed on the throne of Herzoslovakia and then murdered by an outraged public along with her husband.

"King Victor" alias Captain O'Neill, a notorious jewel thief, the son of an Irish father and a French mother, fluent in five languages and a master of disguise. He has worked mostly in Paris and has recently been released from prison in France, having served seven years on a minor charge. The French police have lost his trail but believe he is in England, traveling in disguise, in an attempt to locate the Kohinoor Diamond, as he is believed to have been the brains behind the theft seven years earlier. Fact: though a master criminal of international repute, King Victor has never been known to take a human life.

"Dutch Pedro," a Herzoslovakian scoundrel whose life Jimmy McGrath had once saved in Africa. Six months later he died of fever, but not before passing a "gold mine" to Jimmy in the form of a packet of love letters from a married woman to her lover, excellent material for blackmail.

Sir Clement Edward Alistair Brent, Ninth Marquis of Caterham, lord of the manor at Chimneys. He is uninterested in politics. The only things that bore him more than politics are politicians themselves. Lord Caterham was expected to follow in the footsteps of his predecessor and older brother Henry, who had been Secretary of State for Foreign Affairs and used the family home, Chimneys to host numerous gatherings of international importance. The current Lord Caterham's greatest needs are comfort and peace and quiet.

Lady Eileen Brent, familiarly called "Bundle," Lord Caterham's eldest daughter, approximately age twenty. She shares her father's boredom with politics. She is a very modern young woman who terrifies her father, and even much younger men, with her reckless driving.

The Honorable George Lomax (derisively called "Codders" by his friends), a person of high rank within the British Foreign Office who is constantly worried about state secrets being made public. His favorite expression is "utmost discretion." He is nervous and tense at all times. He is terrified that the notorious *Memoirs* may be published and that the theft of Kohinoor Diamond, a few years earlier, may become public knowledge. He lives at Wyvern Abbey, seven miles from Chimneys. Lady Eileen cannot stand him and neither can her father, Lord Caterham.

Prince Michael Obolovitch, the heir to the throne of Herzoslovakia, educated in England and sympathetic to British interests. He is murdered in the council chamber at Chimneys.

Mr. Herman Isaacstein, a representative of the British Oil Syndicate who hopes to be favored with oil exploitation rights by a restored Herzoslovakian monarchy.

Bill Eversleigh, George Lomax's assistant, age about twenty-five. He is big and rather ungainly in his movements and has a "pleasurably ugly face." A good sportsman with pleasant manners, he obtained his position at the Foreign Office not because of his intelligence or knowledge but through connections. His work consists of being "George's dog" and requires no brainwork.

Miss Oscar, George Lomax's secretary

Richardson, another person employed at George Lomax's office.

The Honorable Virginia Revel, the supposed writer of some incriminating love letters, a beautiful young English widow of twenty-seven. Her husband had been the British Ambassador to Herzoslovakia at the time of the jewel theft and revolution. She is a cousin of George Lomax of the Foreign Office.

Elise, Virginia Revel's French maid. When Virginia finds the dead body of Giuseppe in her study, she does not tell Elise, because "she's French and would go into hysterics."

Chilvers, Virginia's butler

Walton, Virginia's chauffeur

Dorothy Kirkpatrick, a stage actress, and another love interest of Bill Eversleigh

Baron Lolopretjzyl, a representative of the Loyalist Party in Herzoslovakia. He is a big man with an immense fan-like black beard and a high, bald forehead. Extremely formal and serious in disposition, (he often bows and clicks his heels together in the Prussian manner) the Baron is determined that Count Stylptitch's *Memoirs* shall *not* be published, as they might ruin the chances of the restoration of the Herzoslovakian monarchy.

An Unnamed Representative of the Comrades of the Red Hand, the kind of man whom Anthony had fondly imagined existed only in the chorus of a comic opera: a sinister-looking figure, with a squat brutal head and lips drawn back in an evil grin.

Giuseppe Manelli, a waiter at the Blitz Hotel who serves Anthony a meal in his room, attempts to steal Count Stylptitch's *Memoirs* and then later attempts to blackmail Virginia Revel.

The Manager of the Blitz Hotel, a Frenchman with an exquisitely suave manner, and "an expression of superhuman discretion, only to be achieved by a Frenchman."

Mr. Holmes, employed by the publishing firm of Balderson, Balderson and Hodgkins, a small, fair man with a quiet manner, who picks up the manuscript from Anthony at the Blitz Hotel in exchange for a check for one thousand pounds.

Inspector Badgworthy, of Market Basing, a tall portly man with a heavy regulation tread. He is inclined to breathe hard in moments of professional strain.

Constable Johnson, very new to the Force, with a downy unfledged look about him, like a human chicken. At first thrilled by the excitement of a murder at Chimneys, he is disappointed when he learns that the murder victim is only a foreigner since, after all, "foreigners are *liable* to be shot."

Dr. Cartwright, a youngish man, the local physician who examines the body of Prince Michael

Tredwell, the unimpeachable butler at Chimneys.

Sir Abner Willis, Lord Caterham's Harley Street doctor

Colonel Melrose, the chief constable of Market Basing

Superintendent Battle of Scotland Yard, a squarely built middle-aged man with a face so singularly devoid of expression as to be quite remarkable. He makes a point of never displaying emotion. His technique for catching a crook is to give him plenty of rope with which to hang himself.

Boris Anchoukoff, Prince Michael's valet, a big fair man, squarely built, with high Slavonic cheekbones, and dreamy fanatic eyes.

Captain Andrassy, Prince Michael's equerry

Mr. Hiram Fish, an American enthusiast of first editions, and a houseguest of Lord Caterham who is also a collector of first editions. He is a tall man with black hair neatly parted in the middle, china blue eyes with a particularly innocent expression, and a large placid face.

Dulcie and Daisy, aged twelve and ten, younger sisters of Lady Eileen. Their behavior is more like that of four or five year olds.

Prince Nicholas Obolovitch, thought to have died in Africa, the younger brother of Prince Michael.

Mademoiselle Genevieve Brun, the French governess of the two children at Chimneys, a small, middle-aged woman with a sallow face, pepper and salt hair, and a budding mustache. She often suffers from migraine.

A Mysterious Frenchman, registered at the Jolly Cricketers Inn in Market Basing as "Monsieur Chilles," a silk merchant. Later introduced as Monsieur LeMoine of the French Sûreté, he is obsessed with the idea of capturing King Victor in the act of stealing.

Professor Wynward, an expert in decoding, a small red-haired man of middle age.

A Sentry at Hurstmere, near Dover, a short, square thickset man, foreign in appearance.

Six Foreign Men at Hurstmere, in Langley Road, in a village near Dover:

> Half a dozen men were sprawling around a table. Four of them were big, thickset men, with high cheekbones, and eyes set in Magyar slanting fashion. The other two were ratlike little men with quick gestures. The language that was being spoken was French, but the four big men spoke it with uncertainty and a hoarse gutteral intonation.

A Man being kept prisoner at Hurstmere

COMMENTS

The story in *The Secret of Chimneys* is carefully worked out, the characters are enormously amusing and the novel is extremely entertaining. There is nothing "realistic" about the story or the characters, except for what seems to be an eternal determination of Western nations to exploit Eastern ones; the "oil interests" that Britain is determined to pursue in the tiny central European nation of Herzoslovakia do not seem much different from America's oil interests in the Middle East today, nor does the British government's determination to set up a government in Herzoslovakia which is favorable to British interests seem to be unthinkable today considering America's behavior in the Middle East, Latin America and elsewhere.

Agatha Christie, in her *Autobiography*, makes just a passing reference to this novel, not even bothering to mention its title, describing it only as an adventure story similar to *The Secret Adversary* and "much easier to write" than a detective story. The fact that Christie does not mention the book by its title suggests that she did not consider it to be one of her better efforts, or that she did not have clear memories of it. In her *Autobiography* she notes that she had, in later years, no recollection of writing *Peril at End House,* which is certainly one of her best books, and the writing of *The Secret of Chimneys* was probably a small, forgettable event in Christie's life. In reading her *Autobiography* one develops the impression, too, that writing books was a very secondary thing in her life, even much later when she became famous. As late as the 1950s, she notes, she was tempted to give "housewife" as her status on Inland Revenue forms, still not considering herself to be a professional writer.

There is also the possibility that Christie was not very proud of *The Secret of Chimneys* for certain reasons. The mythical "Slavonic" people of Herzoslovakia are portrayed as a practically subhuman species. The Boris Anchoukoff character, for example, once his master dies, knows "instinctively, like a dog" to which person he must transfer his devotion. "High, Slavonic cheekbones," and "eyes slanted in the Magyar fashion" evidently suggested to Christie a menacing evil in a person, as in a later chapter a group of "ratlike men"—foreigners, of course—are discovered plotting revolution.

Even the language of the Herzoslovakians is ridiculed; Baron Lolopretjzyl's name cannot be pronounced by people with normal human mouths, according to Anthony Cade, who says "my throat's not made that way—sounds like a cross between a dog's bark and gargling." Lady Eileen Brent comments that pronouncing the name over the telephone had done damage to the instrument.

In one of the final chapters, a certain character who is briefly suspected of having married a "black woman of Africa," reassures everyone with, "Come, come, it's not so bad as all that. She's white enough—white all through, bless her," to everyone's relief.

Cowardice is, in much of Christie's writing, at least at this period, a very foreign trait. In this novel, the muscular, macho, heroic Jimmy McGrath rescues an old gentleman from no fewer than six thugs in Paris by simply beating the tar out of all six, causing them to scatter. Anthony Cade deals easily with the cowardly representative of the Comrades of the Red Hand (a Herzoslovakian, of course) by giving him a good, swift kick which sends him flying out of the hotel room into the hall.

> Anthony stepped out after him, but the doughty Comrade of the Red Hand had had enough. He got nimbly to his feet and fled down the passage. "So much for the Comrades of the Red Hand," he remarked. "Picturesque appearance, but easily routed by direct action."

They are "foreign wimps," in other words, unlike brave Englishmen. Virginia Revel explains that she did not tell her maid, Elise, about the dead body in the library because, "She's French and would go into hysterics." Virginia is, of course, a level-headed, clear thinking, upper-middle-class Brit who can easily deal with dead bodies found in libraries. In the 1942 *The Body in the Library,* a British female will "go into hysterics" and scream her bloody head off when she finds a dead body in the library, but of course she's not upper-middle-class. She's nothing but a housemaid, and so in her case, *that's* why she's such a wimp.

Englishmen are moral bastions concerning women, at least *English* women, and British women are morally superior to women of other places, especially immoral places like France. An amusing portrayal of an Englishman and his French mistress is found in *The Mystery of the Blue Train,* published a couple of years after *The Secret of Chimneys.* In the first chapter of *The Secret of Chimneys,* Jimmy and Anthony are discussing the packet of letters Dutch Pedro had given to Jimmy, calling them a "gold mine" as blackmail material. The morally outraged Anglo-Saxon Jimmy says that, upon reading them,

> "I was never so disgusted in my life. Gold mine, indeed. I dare say it may have been a gold mine to him, the dirty dog. Do you know what it was? A woman's letters—yes, a woman's letters, *and an Englishwoman at that.* The skunk had been blackmailing her."

It's bad enough to blackmail a woman, but it's *doubly* bad if she's English, evidently.

Immoral, sub-human, violent, Slavonic, Magyar, dog-like, rat-like; such are the adjectives used to describe many of the foreigners in this novel. It's possible that Christie in later years regretted the ethnocentricity that is so brazenly displayed in *The Secret of Chimneys.*

Despite all of this, *The Secret of Chimneys* is an enormously entertaining novel.

The Murder of Roger Ackroyd (1926)

SETTING

The story takes place in the fictitious village of King's Abbot, nine miles from the fictitious town of Cranchester, somewhere in England. There is no indication of what part of England this may be. The village is small but it has a large, busy railway station because it is a major junction of several lines and large numbers of travelers change trains there. Hercule Poirot has taken up residence in King's Abbot for his retirement, living in a cottage named The Larches and pursuing gardening as a hobby, and the growing of vegetable marrows in particular. (For the benefit of Americans unfamiliar with the term, "vegetable marrow" is the British name for one or more varieties of garden squash.) Poirot's only servant mentioned in the book is an "old woman with an enormous Breton cap," evidently his French-speaking housekeeper.

Next door to The Larches is the home of Dr. James Sheppard, his slightly older sister Caroline Sheppard and their maid, Annie.

There are only two "important" houses in the village, that is to say, homes of wealthy persons. One is Fernly Park, occupied by Mr. Roger Ackroyd, a wealthy industrialist, his sister-in-law and niece, and Mr. Ackroyd's male secretary. The servants include a butler, a housekeeper, a cook, a parlormaid, a kitchenmaid and two housemaids. The property is large and includes a lodge occupied by at least one tenant. (For a discussion of the term "lodge," see the *Appendix.*)

The interior of Fernly Park is not described in very much detail, but a sketch of the right-hand wing of the ground floor is shown in an early chapter and this wing includes the billiard room, the drawing room, the dining room and the pantry plus a central hall. Off the central hall is a door leading to a narrow passage to the study and a smaller stairway leading to a private bedroom on the upper floor. A veranda wraps around two sides of this wing, and from one end of the veranda a path leads directly to the lodge and gate, passing a small summer house on the way. It is in the study that the crime occurs. A sketch of the study is also included and shows a fireplace, three armchairs, two occasional tables and a desk and chair. One of the armchairs is described as a "grandfather chair" with an extra-high back. There is one window, not of the hinged French type but the vertically-sliding type.

The drawing room has two windows of the long French type, through which one may step out onto the veranda. In that room there is a "silver table" the lid of which lifts and through whose glass panels curios and artifacts can be displayed. In this silver table are stored some Chinese jade figures, some African curios, some pieces of old silver and one or two other items which normally include a unique dagger with which the victim is murdered.

Conversations take place in all three of these houses—Fernly Park and the cottages of Hercule Poirot and of Dr. Sheppard—and in the "summer house" of Fernly Park, as well as in a nearby wooded area which includes a goldfish pond and rustic seats positioned to offer pleasant views of the countryside. Additionally, Poirot and two other characters make a brief railway trip to Liverpool and conversations take place in the train and at the police headquarters in that city. One brief scene takes place at the office of a lawyer in the village of King's Abbot.

The other "house of importance" in the village is King's Paddock, the home a wealthy widow, Mrs. Ferrars. No scene in the novel takes place at that house, however, and the house is not described, as the story begins just after Mrs. Ferrars dies.

The story takes place in the month of September, probably in 1925 since the novel was published in 1926.

This is the first novel in the Poirot series in which electric lighting and telephones are specifically mentioned. There is a reference to an electric light in the study at Fernly Park and the butler there takes a phone call on the evening of the crime. There is also a telephone at the home of Dr. Sheppard, and Hercule Poirot is the proud owner of "one of those new vacuum cleaners;" therefore his cottage must have electrical service. There is probably no central heating in any of the houses, as there are references to fires in the fireplaces of all three. There is no mention of automobiles in the novel.

No contemporary historical events are mentioned in this story.

Story

Dr. James Sheppard, the narrator of the story, lives in the village of King's Abbot and is a neighbor of Hercule Poirot, who has "retired" and decided spend his retirement years living in an English village, growing vegetable marrows as a hobby.

The wealthiest man in the village, industrialist Roger Ackroyd, is stabbed to death one evening in his study. His stepson Ralph Paton is suspected of the crime because he disappears immediately after the crime and because there has been a recent estrangement between him and his stepfather for reasons unknown. Also suspected of the crime, or at least of complicity, is Ralph's fiancée Flora Ackroyd, Roger's niece.

The police accomplish nothing in their investigations, but Dr. Sheppard assists Hercule Poirot in solving this mystery.

Characters

Dr. James Sheppard, the narrator, a country doctor living in the village of King's Abbot with his sister Caroline who is eight years older. He is one of Roger Ackroyd's closest friends and one of the last to see him alive. He is also a neighbor of detective Hercule Poirot and assists Poirot in the unraveling of the mystery. Over the years he has formed the habit of withholding as much private information about his patients as possible, largely due to the fact that his sister Caroline is insatiably curious and an established link in the local grapevine. His comments about Poirot, about his sister and everyone else in the novel are often highly amusing.

Caroline Sheppard, Dr. Sheppard's sister who relies on the local grapevine for the receiving and disseminating of all information of local interest, however private it may be. When she is excited about any new piece of information, her long, thin nose quivers at the tip. In the very first chapter, early in the morning, her brother diagnoses the death of Mrs. Ferrars, and then goes straight home to breakfast. At the table he tells Caroline that Mrs. Ferrars has died. Caroline says, "I know." "How can you possibly know?" he asks. "Mrs. Ferrars' maid told the milkman who told our Annie." Such is the local grapevine in the village of King's Abbot.

Note: This is the first of Christie's detective novels set in an English village. The "local village gossip grapevine" will be a fixture in many Christie novels to come, particularly those featuring aging spinster **Jane Marple** as the sleuth. Christie was extremely fond of the Caroline Sheppard character and may have modeled Miss Marple on Caroline's busy-body personality when introducing her in the 1930 novel *Murder at the Vicarage*.

Hercule Poirot, a retiree who has recently purchased a cottage next to the home of Dr. Sheppard. He is as skilled at withholding information as Caroline Sheppard is at extracting it, much to Dr. Sheppard's amusement, and one item of information with which he refuses to part is his former occupation. Dr. Sheppard decides that, with his flamboyant mustache, Poirot must be a retired hairdresser, but Caroline dismisses that outlandish idea citing the fact that all hairdressers have wavy hair while Poirot's hair is straight. Soon, however, the entire village knows that Poirot is a famous retired detective from London.

Note: Poirot's characteristic eccentricities, developed in the first two novels in which he appeared, now include an aversion to the cold and a fondness for sweet liqueurs or "sirops" as he calls them. He keeps his cottage stiflingly hot with a large fire in the fireplace and all windows closed; he offers Irish whiskey to Dr. Sheppard while partaking of hot cocoa himself. In later novels his favorite drink will be "sirop de cassis" (black currant liqueur) and he will be wrapped in wool mufflers whenever the weather in England turns chilly. His outlandish egocentricity is now fully developed. As we may recall, at the end of the novel *Murder on the Links*, his sidekick Captain Hastings had hinted at a plan to move to South America to pursue business ventures. That has indeed come to pass and Poirot makes several references to his dear friend Hastings who was "so helpful—usually arriving at the truth quite by accident." Poirot also makes references to his friend Inspector James Japp of Scotland Yard, whom we met in *The Mysterious Affair at Styles*. Both Hastings and Japp will reappear in future novels but in this story, Poirot works alone, aided only marginally by the local police and by Dr. Sheppard.

Roger Ackroyd, a wealthy industrialist, the murder victim.

Captain Ralph Paton, Roger Ackroyd's stepson, a handsome, dark-haired, charming young man of twenty-five. He is rather self-indulgent and extravagant but very much liked by his friends. Currently he is estranged from his stepfather for reasons not publicly known.

Miss Russell, Roger Ackroyd's housekeeper for the past five years. Roger has been widowed for eighteen years and there has been a succession of housekeepers. The Village Intelligence Corps (the local grapevine of servants and tradespeople and general gossip) has always expected that he would one day marry one of his housekeepers, and Miss Russell has remained at Fernly Park longer than any of the others. If in fact Miss Russell has ever entertained thoughts of marrying Roger, however, those hopes were crushed when Roger's sister-in-law arrived from Canada and took up permanent residence with her daughter at Fernly Park. Mrs. Cecil Ackroyd, in fact, has "quite succeeded," according to Caroline, "in putting Miss Russell in her proper place."

Mrs. Cecil Ackroyd, widow of Roger Ackroyd's ne'er-do-well younger brother. She has recently come to live at Fernly Park and is entirely dependent on her brother-in-law's generosity. She is "all chains and teeth and bones. A most unpleasant woman," according to Dr. Sheppard.

Flora Ackroyd, daughter of the above, recently engaged to handsome Ralph Paton. When Ralph is suspected of murdering her uncle, she is the only person who feels certain that he is innocent.

Major Hector Blunt, a big game hunter, an old friend of Roger Ackroyd and a houseguest at Fernly Park at the time of the murder.

Parker, the butler at Fernly Park who discovers the body of Roger Ackroyd when he and Dr. Sheppard break into the locked study. On the evening of the murder, he had been noticed, at least twice, lurking at the locked study door and apparently eavesdropping.

Geoffrey Raymond, Ackroyd's efficient secretary, debonair and charming, and hard up for money. A five-hundred pound legacy from Roger Ackroyd came to him just in time.

Charles Kent, a stranger who asked his way to Fernly Park on the evening of the murder. He is traced to Liverpool and detained there for questioning.

Miss Ganett, a spinster living in the village and an unabashed gossip.

Colonel Carter, a retired military man and resident of the village. During a conversation at a Mah Jong party, the colonel tells a story about India which is "one of interminable length, and of curiously little interest."

Note: Colonel Carter is the first in a long line of "retired military men with interminable, boring stories of Africa, India or China" in Christie's novels who will recur again and again, adding a touch of humor. England must have been filled with boring, retired military types who had served in the outposts of the Empire, and Christie clearly felt little respect for them. For a full inventory of *The Boring Retired Military Man from the Colonies* see the *Comments* section for the 1937 *Poirot Loses a Client*.

Ursula Bourne, a parlormaid at Fernly Park, discharged early on the day of the crime by Roger Ackroyd because of the trivial matter of "disarranging some papers on his table." Or was there a more important reason for her being fired?

Annie, housemaid to Dr. Sheppard and his sister Caroline

Mary Black, tenant of the lodge of Fernly Park

Clara, Miss Ganett's maid

Elsie Dale, a housemaid at Fernly Park, a big, fair girl, with a pleasant but slightly stupid face.

Mrs. Cooper, the cook at Fernly Park

Gladys Jones, second housemaid at Fernly Park

Mary Thripp, kitchenmaid at Fernly Park

Colonel Melrose, the Chief Constable at the village of King's Abbot

Inspector Raglan, the officer of the Cranchester Police who is in charge of the case. In the words of Flora Ackroyd, he is "a horrid, weaselly man," who suspects her fiancé of murder.

Superintendent Hayes of the Liverpool Police who has heard of Poirot and has great respect for him. He is also a friend of Inspector James Japp of Scotland Yard in London.

An Old Woman in an Enormous Breton Cap, Poirot's only servant at his cottage in King's Abbot.

Note: There are references to Poirot's good friend and former colleague **Captain Hastings,** who now lives in the Argentine, and to **Inspector James Japp** of Scotland Yard who was in charge of the "Styles Case" and later worked closely with Poirot in many cases in London. Neither of these individuals appears in *The Murder of Roger Ackroyd,* except in Hercule Poirot's thoughts and conversations, but they will reappear in future novels.

FRENCH INTO ENGLISH

Chapter 7
Voilà ce qui est curieux—That's strange

Chapter 8
Ou tous les deux—Or both of them

Chapter 9
Une belle propriété—a beautiful estate
Inutile!—Useless!

Chapter 10
C'est compris?—Understand?
Eh bien?—Well?

Chapter 12
comment dire?—how do you say it?
bien entendu—of course
amour propre—pride
pas de blagues—no games, no tricks
messieurs et mesdames—ladies and gentlemen
c'est dommage—that's a pity

Chapter 13
c'est possible—It's possible
les femmes—women
précisément—exactly

Chapter 15
En vérité?—Really?
allez—go ahead

Chapter 17
Précisément—Exactly
Je ne pense pas—I doubt it
c'est tout—that's all
métier—job, expertise
bien entendu—of course

Chapter 20
bien entendu—of course
complot—scheme
précisément—exactly
pour ça, oui!—That's for sure!

Chapter 22
bagatelle—trifle
rien du tout—trifle

Chapter 23
bien entendu—of course
épatant!—terrific!

Chapter 25
très bien—very good

Chapter 26
ça va sans dire—that goes without saying

COMMENTS

The Murder of Roger Ackroyd was Agatha Christie's sixth published book and her first with a new publisher, Collins, which remained her publisher forever. Its sensational *dénouement* brought it to the attention of millions and made Agatha Christie's name a household word. Her first five novels had been moderately successful but were soon more or less forgotten, only to be revived much later when it became obvious that Christie had become the undisputed "queen of crime."

In addition to the famous and shocking ending to this detective story, there are a few "firsts" to be noted in it. As the years went on, Christie became famous for her "quiet English village" settings, especially after introducing Miss Marple in 1930 with *Murder at the Vicarage*. *The Murder of Roger Ackroyd* was her first novel set in a country village where, supposedly, "nothing exciting ever happens."

Two stock character types, which will reappear again and again in Christie novels, are introduced in the novel: the village busy-body, usually a spinster who relishes village gossip (Miss Gannett and Caroline Sheppard in this novel in particular) and the ex-colonial military type who is oppressively boring at all times with his stories about India, Africa and China that nobody wants to hear. In this novel it is Colonel Carter who tells a story of "interminable length and curiously little interest" about something that happened in India several years earlier.

Agatha Christie relates, in her *Autobiography*, that it may have been her fondness for the Caroline Sheppard character in *The Murder of Roger Ackroyd* that inspired her to create Miss Marple a few years later—with her cynical views of the "very wicked world," her ubiquitous binoculars (so useful for viewing interesting birds and, accidentally of course, whatever village activities may be going on at some distance).

We are also treated, in *The Murder of Roger Ackroyd*, to some observations about new developments in society, as in the discussion between Dr. Sheppard and Miss Russell about drug use, cocaine in particular. Miss Russell observes, "Drugs do a lot of harm. Look at the cocaine habit. It's very prevalent in high society." And the "breathless and interrogatory" Miss Gannett suggests that Mrs. Ferrars "had been a drug addict." We generally think of widespread drug use as an innovation of the late 1960s with LSD, pep pills, and marijuana use among the young, but during the 1920s and 1930s, drug use among the affluent in America, and evidently in Europe also, was a fad of major renown.

In the summer house at Fernly Park, Poirot finds a "goose quill," which suggests to him that a heroin user has been in the summer house recently, and that the heroin user was probably from the United States or Canada. Showing the quill to Dr. Sheppard, he states, "Yes, heroin 'snow.' Drug-takers carry it like this, and sniff it up the nose. This method of taking the drug is very common on the other side. Another proof, if we wanted one, that the man came from Canada or the States."

Most of us have forgotten the "Mah Jong craze" of the 1920s. Mah Jong was a popular parlor game using little square tiles marked with Chinese symbols. Monopoly, Scrabble and Touring were other popular games that lasted much longer, but the "Mah Jong" craze was intense for a very short time. Dr. Sheppard and his sister host a little Mah Jong party at their cottage where local gossip, the progress of the investigation of the murder and the Mah Jong play compete for the players' attention in an amusing way.

As the years go on, observations of social phenomena such as the above will be another aspect of Christie's novels and cause her fans to observe that her books are almost a chronicle of the development of British society over several decades.

Agatha Christie developed a special knack for presenting amusing characters—usually minor ones—which will develop further over the years and provide her readers with plenty of laughs. Her introduction of Mrs. Cecil Ackroyd—"all chains and teeth and bones—she gave me a handful of assorted knuckles and rings to squeeze and began talking volubly..."—is amusingly memorable and there will be many equally memorable characters in the future.

A final remark: it was noted in *The Mysterious Affair at Styles* that Christie did not hesitate to refer to Jewish people in a negative way. In *The Murder of Roger Ackroyd* Mrs. Cecil Ackroyd tells the narrator, Dr. Sheppard, that financial problems had necessitated her borrowing money from lenders.

"I couldn't sleep at nights. And a dreadful fluttering round the heart. And then I got a letter from a Scotch gentleman—as a matter of fact there were two letters—both Scotch gentlemen. Mr. Bruce MacPherson was one, and the other was Colin MacDonald. Quite a coincidence."

"Hardly that," I said dryly. "They are usually Scotch gentlemen, but I suspect a Semitic strain in their ancestry."

In other words, Jewish money lenders.

The Big Four (1927)

SETTING

The first setting is Hercule Poirot's flat in London. Then there is an aborted railway trip to

Southampton and a return to London. Soon there are visits to a village in Devon at the edge of Dartmoor, to the village of Chobham in Surrey, then to a luxury home and hotel in the fashionable Passy district of Paris, then to Hatton Chase, the seat of the Duke of Loamshire, then a private home in Market Hanford in Worcestershire, then a private flat in London, then an expensive restaurant in London, a sinister house in London's Chinatown, a small restaurant in Soho, a private home in Belgium, brief trips on two ocean-going vessels, and a railway trip from London to the Tyrol in Italy via Paris.

Story

Captain Hastings who, at the end of the 1923 *Murder on the Links,* had spoken of marrying "Cinderella," the girl he met on the train at the beginning of that novel, did marry her and he took her to Argentina where he prospered in ranching. It is now eighteen months later and he has returned to London to spend a couple of months taking care of some business, and to visit his dear friend, Hercule Poirot.

Hastening at once to Poirot's flat, he finds that his friend is about to depart for Rio! Poirot explains that a certain American "Soap King," Abe Ryland, the richest man in the world, has offered him an enormous sum to go and investigate some trouble at a business of his in South America. Poirot is all packed and ready to go to Waterloo Station when a sound is heard coming from his bedroom. There, he and Hastings find a dirty-looking man who speaks in a disoriented way as if dazed. He suddenly makes a very strange speech describing a criminal organization called The Big Four, naming a Chinaman as being Number One, a wealthy American as Number Two, a Frenchwoman as Number Three and, in an expression of extreme horror, he names Number Four as "The Destroyer." Then he faints.

Poirot and Hastings have no idea how the man entered the room, except perhaps by the window, quite a feat since the flat is on an upper floor. They summon a doctor who is puzzled by the man's condition and prescribes rest. Leaving the man in the custody of Poirot's housekeeper, Hastings and Poirot go to Waterloo Station and board a train bound for Southampton, but suddenly Poirot realizes that he "is being gotten out of the way." When the train stops for a signal in open country, Poirot and Hastings leave the train and return to London by car. In Poirot's flat they find the man dead. A doctor is summoned, and soon a man claiming to be from an asylum arrives in search of a recent escapee, identifying the dead man as he. However, a phone call by Poirot to the asylum reveals that there has been no "escape."

Hastings and Poirot visit a Mr. Ingles, an expert on China who knows something about The Big Four, an international criminal organization seeking to destroy all governments and turn the world to chaos. He mentions a letter he received from a man in Devon pleading for money to escape from "The Big Four." Poirot and Hastings go to Devon only to find that the man has been murdered. A manservant has been arrested, based on very incriminating evidence, but Poirot succeeds in proving his innocence, suspecting that the true murderer is "Number Four."

The disappearance of an English scientist in Paris leads to a brush with death for Hastings and Poirot and the discovery that a brilliant French scientist, Madame Olivier, is "Number Three." Further dangerous encounters prove that the American millionaire, Abe Ryland, is in fact Number Two. Several other unexplained deaths are investigated and in each case a different person exhibiting a particular nervous habit is present.

Eventually, with the cooperation of three governments, The Big Four are destroyed. Hastings returns to Argentina and Poirot decides to retire to the country and grow vegetable marrows.

Characters

Captain Hastings, Hercule Poirot's sidekick in two earlier novels and a group of short stories, who went with his bride to live in Argentina after his adventures in the 1923 *Murder on the Links.* He now returns to England "for a few months to settle some business," and rejoins Poirot for a new adventure.

Hercule Poirot, the famous private investigator. Having tired of his life in England investigating trivial matters, he is about to travel to Brazil in response to a monetary offer that is too good to refuse.

Abe Ryland, the "American Soap King," the richest man in the world, who achieves the feat of convincing Poirot to undertake a sea voyage considerably longer than a Channel Crossing. Money talks, evidently, when there's enough of it, even to Poirot. Ryland is one of four Master Criminals (Master Criminal #2, to be exact) who have joined forces to gain control of the world and turn it to chaos.

Mrs. Pearson, Poirot's landlady, who opens

the door, hands letters to Poirot, relays phone messages and otherwise does not speak.

Meyerling, a former Secret Service agent, a victim of The Big Four who dies in Poirot's flat

An Unnamed Doctor who pronounces Meyerling dead.

A Man from Hanwell Asylum who visits Poirot and declares the dead man to be a recently-escaped inmate of the asylum

Inspector James Japp of Scotland Yard, a good friend of Poirot's who identifies Meyerling

Mr. John Ingles, a retired civil servant "of mediocre intellect," according to Poirot, but an expert on all things Chinese and having a certain knowledge of Li Chang Yen, Master Criminal #1.

Mr. Halsey, a person who achieved Poirot's interview with the knowledgeable Mr. Ingles.

An Impassive-faced Chinese Servant of Mr. Ingles

Li Chang Yen, Master Criminal #1 who never leaves his palace in Pekin, but pulls strings that influence events around the world. He is "the finest brain in the world."

Johnathan Whalley, another victim of The Big Four. He is murdered at his home, Granite Bungalow, in the lonely village of Hoppaton on the edge of Dartmoor. He had written to Mr. Ingles pleading for money to help him escape from The Big Four.

An Old Rustic at the village of Hoppaton who, giving Poirot and Hastings directions to Granite Bungalow, informs them of the murder

Inspector Meadows, of the Moretonhampstead police, a friend of Inspector Japp and therefore willing to involve Poirot in the case

Betsy Andrews, Johnathan Walley's housekeeper who discovered his dead body in a pool of blood and screamed and screamed

Robert Grant (alias Abraham Biggs,) a "rough kind of man-servant" to Johnathan Walley, questioned and arrested on suspicion of murder

Mr. Saunders, a man "looking like a preacher," with a broken front tooth and a mincing way of speaking, who arranged the job as man-servant for Robert Grant upon his release from jail

Captain Kent of the United States Secret Service, who provides some assistance in the matter of the scientist Mr. Halliday, and who appreciates the sound legislation in Britain regarding alcoholic beverages. That is, he is fed up with Prohibition in America.

John Halliday, a scientist who went to Paris to confer with other scientists and then disappeared

Mrs. Halliday who is mystified by her husband's disappearance

Professor Borgonneau, one of the scientists in Paris whom Mr. Halliday visited

Madame Olivier, a famous French scientist who worked first with her husband and then alone after his death. She is Master Criminal #3, the "brains" of the group.

Mademoiselle Claude and Monsieur Henri, assistants to Madame Olivier

Inez Véroneau, a.k.a. Countess Vera Rossakoff, an old friend-adversary of Poirot, currently employed as secretary to Madame Olivier

Félix Laon, a tall, thin man who visits Hastings in his hotel room in Paris and scuffles with him, then "accidentally" drops his wallet for Hastings to find.

Pierre Combeau, an obliging friend of Poirot who, owing him a favor, pulls the emergency cord in the Paris-Calais train, permitting Poirot and Hastings to leave the train unobserved in open country.

The Right Honourable Sydney Crowther, Home Secretary, another useful friend who also owes Poirot a favor and will recommend Hastings to Abe Ryland as secretary while Ryland is working in England He will later introduce Poirot to Monsieur Desjardeaux, the French Premier, for the purpose of discussing The Big Four

Arthur Nevill, Hastings' alias while working for Abe Ryland

Mr. Appleby, Mr. Ryland's American secretary

Miss Martin, Mr. Ryland's "auburn-haired" stenographer who captivates Hastings and tells him of a mysterious letter to Mr. Ryland she inadvertently opened. She is the second "auburn-haired" young woman who captivates Hastings, the first having been Cynthia Murdoch in *The Mysterious Affair at Styles,* to whom Hastings proposed. Over the years, Poirot will never let Hastings forget his weakness for auburn-haired girls and, whenever Hastings suggests the innocence of a beautiful young murder suspect, Poirot will slyly ask "Does she have auburn hair?" and Hastings will blush.

Arthur Leversham, author of the aforementioned letter

Deans, Mr. Ryland's English valet, brought to England from America

James, Mr. Ryland's footman

Mr. Paynter, age fifty-five, who invited a young artist nephew to live with him at his home, then died in a terrible accident in his room

Gerald Paynter, the aforementioned artist, a "wild and extravagant type," like all artists, according to Inspector Japp. He inherited upon Mr. Paynter's death.

Dr. Quentin, who was blamed for Mr. Paynter's unfortunate accident

Ah Ling, a Chinese servant of Mr. Paynter, suspected by Inspector Japp of murder

Dr. Savaronoff, the world's second best chess player, who lives in London and who was challenged to a chess game by an American champion.

Gilmour Wilson, the young American chess champion who died while playing chess with Dr. Savaronoff, apparently from poison

Sonia Daviloff, Dr. Savaronoff's niece who shares his London flat. She was left a fortune by Madame Gospoja, whose husband was a sugar profiteer under the Old Regime in Russia.

Mr. Bronson, Hastings' ranch manager in Argentina who cables bad news to Hastings

Mr. Joseph Aarons, another obliging friend of Poirot, a theatrical agent who helps Poirot identify Claud Darrell. We met him in the 1923 *Murder on the Links,* and we will meet him from time to time in the future.

Claud Darrell, a minor stage actor fitting Poirot's description of Master Criminal #4.

Flossie Monro, a former friend of Claud Darrell, who provides an important clue about Darrell while being wined and dined by Poirot. She has bleached blonde hair and keeps Max Factor in monogrammed shirts.

Numerous Extraordinary-looking Slavs and other Repulsive-looking Foreigners who visit Poirot mysteriously at his flat.

Achille Poirot, Hercule Poirot's equally brilliant but singularly indolent and not nearly as handsome twin brother (description provided by Poirot himself)

Miss Mabel Palmer, a hospital nurse who approaches Poirot with suspicions of foul play at the home of a Mr. and Mrs. Templeton

Mr. Templeton, an older gentleman who has been taken mysteriously ill at meal time

Mrs. Templeton, wife of the above who becomes dreadfully nervous upon hearing Poirot relate a story of a wife who poisoned her husband

Dr. Treves, who hosts a dinner at the home of the Templetons, during which Poirot becomes suddenly ill

Mickey, Mrs. Templeton's mentally-deficient son by a previous marriage who blurts out unpleasant suggestions about his mother. He has a nervous habit that reminds Poirot of Claud Darrell

Dr. Ridgeway, Poirot's medical doctor

A Thin, Dark Man of Middle Age, who seats himself at Hastings's table in a small restaurant in Soho and strongly advises Hastings to return to South America

An Unnamed Chinaman, a former servant of Mr. Ingles, who dies at St. Giles Hospital in London after delivering a cryptic message to Hastings

An Unnamed Officer aboard the steamer *Ansonia,* bound for South America, who rouses Hastings from sleep to transfer him to another ship bound for Belgium

An Elderly Belgian Manservant who receives Hastings at the villa of Achille Poirot at Spa in Belgium

Captain Harvey, a young member of the British Intelligence Service who brings the news that China is politically isolated, that there is soon to be a meeting of The Big Four in Italy, and that the English, French and Italian governments are apprised and in support of Poirot's efforts

An Unnamed Diner at the restaurant of a hotel in Bolzano, Italy, who has a nervous habit reminiscent of Claud Darrell; upon viewing Hercule Poirot, he is violently startled and springs up suddenly from his seat.

An Unfortunate Waiter in the above hotel restaurant who, colliding with the aforementioned springing diner, upsets a platter of perfectly good *haricots verts.*

FRENCH INTO ENGLISH

Chapter 1
chance épouvantable—awful luck
ma foi—good grief
Sacré mille tonnerres—God in Heaven! (rough translation)

Chapter 2
Ah, parfaitement—very good

Chapter 3
Je vous remercie—Thank you
à l'heure même—immediately
par example—(not translatable—it expresses annoyance, such as "for Pete's sake!"

Chapter 5
au grand sérieux—very seriously
petit déjeuner—breakfast
Cherchez la femme—"find the woman" (implication: "A woman is behind this.")

Chapter 6
salon—drawing room, living room, lounge
Pas tout à fait—not quite, not really
Cela va sans dire—That goes without saying

Chapter 7
Cela va sans dire—That goes without saying
le boxe—boxing (the sport)

petit bleu—a short message on blue paper delivered by courier

signale d'arrêt—emergency stop signal (cord or button used in emergencies by passengers to stop a train, etc.)

Chapter 8
épatant—amazing

Chapter 11
bouleversé—upset, disoriented
parbleu—for Pete's sake (mild annoyance is expressed)

Chapter 13
chez vous—at home (literally: at "your" home)
beaux yeux—pretty eyes

Chapter 14
tant mieux—so much the better
déjeuner—lunch
ça ne fait rien—that doesn't matter

Chapter 15 *Pas si mal!*—Not bad!

Chapter 16 *ruse de guerre*—war trick

Chapter 17 *haricots verts*—green beans

Chapter 18 *coup de théâtre*—surprise

COMMENTS

The Big Four does not have the unity of plot that a novel should have, the only unifying trait being Hercule Poirot's wish to discover the identity of one of the criminals. The only characters of consequence in *The Big Four* are unique—each one is evil personified—but there is nothing amusing, engaging, or even personally interesting about them. The minor characters can hardly even be thought of as characters—they are usually just messengers, or information providers, like Mr. Ingles who provides several pages of information about arch-criminal #1, or Flossie Monro who provides Poirot with one clue, or Sonia Daviloff who shows Poirot the position of the chess table.

A reader whose first experience with Agatha Christie is *The Big Four* may not bother to ever read another of her novels. Not only does the book lack unity of plot, it lacks unity of characters. We move from one dangerous encounter to another, from one failure to catch the criminals to another and the book could have been twice as long—or only half as long—without making any difference. Poirot lays traps for the enemy, and the enemy learns of the traps by some means that is never explained. The enemy lays traps for Poirot, who cleverly recognizes the traps and avoids them, only to find later that the enemy knew he would recognize and avoid the traps, only to fall into others as a consequence.

It is doubtful that this novel is often favored by a rereading even by the most devoted of Christie's fans. As a stage in Christie's development as a writer, it is a puzzle. It does give us confirmation, however, that Captain Hastings married "Cinderella," as it was hinted at the end of *Murder on the Links,* and that he went away to South America, which was also suggested. At the end of *The Big Four* we learn that Poirot has decided to retire once and for all, to move to the country, and to pursue the growing of vegetable marrows as a hobby.

What is interesting is that, at the beginning of the 1926 novel *The Murder of Roger Ackroyd,* Poirot has already retired and has taken a cottage in the country and is growing vegetable marrows as a hobby. This strongly suggests that Christie wrote *The Big Four before* she wrote *The Murder of Roger Ackroyd*. Christie states in her *Autobiography* that she wrote "another novel" for The Bodley Head, after the 1924 *The Man in the Brown Suit,* and that The Bodley Head refused to publish it. She does not name the novel, but it is just possible that it was *The Big Four*. The next manuscript that Christie submitted to The Bodley Head was *The Secret of Chimneys* which they reluctantly published in 1925, and that ended the unpleasant relationship that Christie had with The Bodley Head and allowed her to select another publisher.

The new publisher was Collins, and Christie may have realized that *The Big Four* was an inferior book and presented to Collins, as her first book to be published with them, the much better *The Murder of Roger Ackroyd,* which appeared in 1926. Then, during 1926 Christie's husband announced his desire for a divorce and she suffered a good deal of emotional stress as a result. It is possible that, rather than attempt to write another book while in a state of depression, she submitted *The Big Four* to Collins at that time, since it was already written, and that Collins agreed to publish it because of the enormous success of *The Murder of Roger Ackroyd*.

The Mystery of the Blue Train (1928)

SETTING

There are many physical settings in this novel, including an English village, London, Paris, Nice and Antibes. The crime takes place in a special luxury train used primarily by British travelers destined for the French Riviera (explained below.)

In the opening scene a man purchases some fabulously expensive jewels at the sordid apartment of a prostitute in a seedy district of Paris. The scene includes the sinister, darkened streets of the surrounding area and the shop of an antique dealer in a finer district on the other side of the river Seine.

In London we visit the Savoy, a luxury hotel, the offices of a firm of solicitors, two luxury residential flats, and Victoria Railway Station.

An early scene takes place in the fictitious English village of St. Mary Mead in the fictitious county of Downshire, evidently somewhere west of London, since it is served by London's Paddington Railway Station. In 1930 Christie will introduce the Miss Marple character for the first time, and she will be a resident of St. Mary Mead. Over the next several decades, Miss Marple will reappear with increasing frequency, and the village of St. Mary Mead will be a setting in several books. Its location within England will be adjusted, however, for the needs of the story. It will be placed "fifteen miles south of London" in one book, for example, but usually it will be located at some distance west of London, as it is in the 1957 *What Mrs. McGillicuddy Saw*.

There is no important historical background for this novel, except for a few references to World War I (referred to simply as "the War" since World War II is yet to come.) One of the wealthy characters operated a hospital at Nice during the War, and another character had been a patient at that hospital. The year is approximately 1927.

A WORD ABOUT THE "BLUE TRAIN" (*TRAIN BLEU*)

For the benefit of readers unfamiliar with the *Train Bleu* (Blue Train), the following information may be useful. Paris, like London, has numerous railway stations serving various destinations around the country. Trains going from Paris to points northwest of the city such as Rouen, Le Havre and other towns in Normandy leave from the Gare St. Lazare (St. Lazare Station). Trains going west to Chartres and to towns in Brittany leave from the Gare Montparnasse. There are also the Gare du Nord, the Gare de l'Est, the Gare de Lyon and the Gare d'Austerlitz depending on the destinations of the trains. When going from one part of France to another by train, it is quite often necessary to go first to Paris and board another train there—at another station.

Early in the twentieth century the French Riviera became an extremely popular travel destination of wealthy Britons seeking warmth and sun during the winter months. Travel from London to the French Riviera meant a train from London's Victoria Station to the port of Dover, then a "channel crossing" by passenger ferry to Calais. At Calais, passengers boarded a second train terminating in Paris at the Gare du Nord. Then there was a taxi ride, with luggage, across Paris to the Gare de Lyon and onto a third train, which went to points south of Paris, including Cannes and Nice.

Since so many British travelers, especially in wintertime, were traveling to these Mediterranean places, the French railway system offered an arrangement whereby such travelers could avoid the inconvenience of changing trains in Paris, the taxi ride, etc. At Calais, there were special passenger cars marked "*Train Bleu.*" British travelers destined for the Riviera and *not* Paris could board these special cars. The special cars were detached from the train somewhere in the north suburbs of Paris and then pulled by a second engine *around* the city of Paris to the Gare de Lyon station. There, they were attached to the *Train Bleu*, which sped to the south of France, stopping only at Lyons, Cannes and Nice. This was a major convenience for which well-heeled travelers were quite willing to pay extra, and there were enough wealthy British travelers to make these special arrangements practical for the railway company. Today, of course, quick air travel and the tunnel beneath the English Channel make all of this unnecessary.

In *The Mystery of the Blue Train*, certain characters travel from London to Nice by train and there are references to "going around the *ceinture*" at Paris. This is the semi-circular route used by the locomotive pulling the special cars around Paris to be attached to the second train at the Gare de Lyon.

There will also be a mention of the Blue Train in the 1935 *Murder in Three Acts*.

Story

The year is 1927. Ruth Kettering is the twenty-eight-year-old daughter of Rufus Van Aldin, a rich American businessman. Unfortunately Ruth has made an unhappy marriage with Derek Kettering, an English aristocrat who is soon to inherit the title of Lord Leconbury. The couple is estranged and while Derek amuses himself with a French mistress, Ruth has taken up again with a former lover, a scoundrel known as the Comte Armand de la Roche.

Through underworld connections in Paris, Rufus purchases a set of fabulous rubies as a gift for Ruth. One of these jewels is the famous "Heart of Fire," once owned by Catherine the Great of Russia. In criminal circles there has been plenty of talk about the secret sale of these historic jewels, so it is just a matter of time before a theft is attempted.

Meanwhile, in an obscure village in England, young Katherine Grey, age thirty-three, has devoted the past ten years of her life caring for an ailing old woman, Mrs. Harfield, who has finally succumbed, leaving all her worldly wealth and possessions to the devoted Katherine who then becomes, very unexpectedly, a very rich woman. She decides at once that she will begin enjoying her new wealth with a trip to the Riviera, escaping for the very first time from a dreary English winter.

In order to meet her lover in secret, Ruth Kettering travels to the French Riviera aboard the Blue Train, taking the "Heart of Fire" jewel with her. Unknown to her, her husband Derek and his mistress are also aboard the train, as well as the famous Belgian sleuth Hercule Poirot and Katherine Grey.

One of these characters is murdered aboard the train. Hercule Poirot solves the murder in the South of France.

Characters

Boris Ivanovitch Krassnine, an important underworld middleman in the traffic of stolen jewels. He is "a little man with the face of a rat."

Olga Vassilovna Demiroff, a Paris prostitute and an agent of Boris Ivanovitch. She receives stolen jewels and provides a venue for their sale.

Rufus Van Aldin, an American millionaire, "almost" the richest man in the world. Through underworld connections, he purchases a set of fabulous rubies as a gift for his daughter, Ruth.

Two "Apaches," or Paris thugs of the underworld, stationed outside Olga Vassilovna's home awaiting the chance to attack and rob the purchaser of the jewels.

"Monsieur le Marquis," a white-haired man with the movements of a young man. He wears a small black satin mask to hide his features and is the employer of the above-referenced Apaches. A failed attempt, by means of the two Apaches, to steal the jewels from the American does not distress him, as he has further plans which will not fail.

Demetrius Papapolous, a wealthy dealer in antiques whose shop is in a fashionable district of Paris and whose residence overlooks the Champs-Élysées.

Zia Papapolous, the daughter of Demetrius. She is a handsome young woman, with dark flashing eyes.

A Servant at the Papapolous establishment. He wears gold rings in his ears and is of a swarthy cast of countenance.

Major Knighton, Rufus Van Aldin's English secretary for the ten-month duration of his stay in England.

Ruth Kettering, age twenty-eight, the only child of Rufus Van Aldin. Though not beautiful, or even pretty, she is striking because of her coloring, her hair being almost pure auburn. As to her character, she has inherited her millionaire father's hardness and determination.

Mr. Goby, a kind of private detective whose ability to gather information is unsurpassed. "Give him twenty-four hours and he would lay the private life of the Archbishop of Canterbury bare for you." In future novels, Hercule Poirot will occasionally avail himself of Mr. Goby's services.

Derek Kettering, who will inherit the title of his ailing father, Lord Leconbury, upon his father's death. He harbors no illusions that his wife has ever loved him, as she married him only for his title, and consequently he sees no reason to deprive himself of a mistress.

Pavett, Derek Kettering's manservant at his rooms in Jermyn Street.

Annie, one of the housemaids at the Kettering home

Mirelle, a well-known Parisian dancer, Derek's mistress, "a rich man's luxury," in Derek's words. She is a beautifully-made woman whose face, if somewhat haggard, has a bizarre charm of its own.

Mirelle's Servant, a trim Frenchwoman

Claud Ambrose, the composer of an operatic setting for Ibsen's *Peer Gynt*. He has just left Mirelle's apartment where he has been playing the new music for her when Derek comes to visit her.

Katherine Grey, age thirty-three, an intelligent, perceptive and selfless young Englishwoman who for ten years had served as a devoted companion to old Mrs. Jane Harfield until her recent death, and who inherits Mrs. Harfield's savings, "such as they are." Nobody remembered that Mrs. Harfield had been one of the original shareholders in Mortaulds, and over a forty-year period her investment had accumulated at compound interest. Katherine, therefore, has suddenly and unexpectedly become a fabulously rich woman.

Mrs. Samuel (Mary Anne) Harfield, a distant relative of the deceased Jane Harfield, who writes to Katherine in an attempt to bluff her into believing that old Mrs. Harfield's Will can be successfully contested in favor of "family."

Old Miss Viner, a resident of the village of St. Mary Mead, two years older than the deceased Mrs. Harfield. She attributes her good health to a slice of brown bread with every supper, and a little "stimulant." She cautions Katherine against abusing her new wealth, assuring her that she will probably never marry, not being the kind to attract the men.

Alice, Old Mrs. Harfield's maid, an admirer of the kind and selfless Katherine Grey

Dr. Harrison, old Mrs. Harfield's middle-aged physician who advises Katherine to disregard the letter from Mrs. Harfield's greedy distant relatives.

Mrs. Polly Harrison, his kindly wife who describes Katherine as a saint with a sense of humor.

Johnnie, the Harrisons' adenoidal youngest son

Viscountess Rosalie Tamplin, a resident of the Villa Marguerite on the French Riviera, a very distant relative of Katherine, who reads of Katherine's newly acquired wealth and suddenly takes an interest in her. Her idea: invite Katherine to the Riviera in order to introduce her to "Society" in exchange for some of that lovely money. Lady Tamplin has been a social climber all her life and is currently in her fourth marriage.

Charles Evans (Chubby), age twenty-seven, handsome, sporting, and poor. He is Lady Tamplin's current husband.

The Honorable Lenox Tamplin, Rosalie's teen-age daughter, who looks older than her age. Lenox is unusually perceptive and sees through all her mother's motives. "How much do you think you would get her to cough up?" she sneers when her mother suggests that they invite Katherine for a stay with them in exchange for being introduced into Society. She feels no respect for her social-climbing mother and sees no reason to be delicate on the subject. She becomes a friend and confidante of Katherine Grey.

Marie, a servant at the Villa Marguerite

A Well-known Dressmaker in London, a slim, elderly Frenchwoman.

Pierre Michel, a conductor on the train who discovers the dead body of Ruth Kettering

Ada Beatrice Mason, Ruth Kettering's personal maid

Count Armand de la Roche, a resident of Antibes who is loved by all women, especially by Ruth Kettering. He is writing a book about historic jewels and asks Ruth to bring her newly-acquired $400,000 worth of jewels to the Riviera to show them to him.

Hercule Poirot, the recently-retired private investigator, who travels to the Riviera on holiday

George, Hercule Poirot's English valet (his first appearance in a Poirot novel)

Hippolyte and Marie Flavelle, servants of the Comte de la Roche at his home, the Villa Marina, in Antibes.

Antonio Pirezzio, a person in Zia Papapolous' past, the memory of whom Poirot finds it useful to evoke.

French into English

Chapter 6
chérie—darling
un beau garçon—a good-looking guy
ce n'est pas pratique—it's not practical
Parbleu!—For heaven's sake!

Chapter 8
très anglaise—very English
Une belle Anglaise—a pretty English girl
tailleur gris clair—light gray tailored dress
robe de soirée 'soupir d'automne'—evening dress "Autumn Sigh"
goût—taste

Chapter 10
ceinture—literally "belt"; railway track encircling the city to connect stations
roman policier—detective novel

Chapter 11
billet de bagages—luggage claim ticket
bon—good
très bien—very good
roman policier à nous—our private detective novel

Chapter 14 *Chère Amie*—My Darling

Chapter 15
à fond—thoroughly, to the core
Ah, ça par example—(no real translation—mild annoyance is expressed.)

Chapter 16
très bien—Very good!
La Vie—Life

Chapter 17
un morceau—a bit (in this context, a bit of food)
très bien!—Very nice!
empressement—warmth, enthusiasm
train de luxe—luxury train

Chapter 18
mais c'est inouï!—that's ridiculous!

Chapter 19
déjeuner—lunch
objets d'art—art objects
mise en scène—stage set

Chapter 20
mauvais sujet—literally "bad subject"; in this context, a "bad lot" (disreputable or untrustworthy man)
les femmes—women

Chapter 21
empressement—enthusiasm
bon jour—good morning (more correctly written "bonjour" as one word)
poseur—pretender, phony
Ça n'est pas pratique—That's impractical
voilà!—look at this!

Chapter 22
Faites monter ce monsieur—Have that gentleman come up
Voilà—OK!
je me sauve—I'm outta here

Chapter 24
sympathique—nice, congenial
Ça y est!—Very good!
chez moi—home (chez moi=to my home, chez vous=to your home, etc.) In this context, Poirot is returning to his room at the hotel.

Chapter 25
chasseur—messenger
peignoir—dressing gown
ce type-là—that guy
chéri—darling

Chapter 26
métier—line of work, area of expertise
Ah, mais c'est anglais ça—Boy, that's really English!
les femmes—women

Chapter 27
chère amie—mistress
On m'a dit—I've been told
au pied de la lettre—literally, word for word
diablement chic—damned good-looking
grand seigneur—aristocrat

Chapter 28
tête à tête—private conversation
l'amour—love
distraite—preoccupied

Chapter 29
le bon Dieu—God
distraite—preoccupied
ce type-là—that guy
voilà—Here I am
déjeuner—lunch
Ah, sacré!—Bullshit!

Chapter 33 *pas la guerre*—not the war

Chapter 35
bien entendu—of course
mille tonnerres—a strong expression of surprise such as "Incredible!" or "Fantastic!"
les femmes—women

Chapter 36 *le bon Dieu*—God

COMMENTS

The Mystery of the Blue Train is Agatha Christie's eighth published novel and the fifth detective novel featuring Hercule Poirot. The four earlier detective novels were *The Mysterious Affair at Styles, Murder on the Links, The Murder of Roger Ackroyd* and *The Big Four*.

In some ways *The Mystery of the Blue Train* shows a remarkable advancement in Christie's abilities, notably in the development of interesting characters and the relationships between them. In the earlier Poirot novels, there was a narrator (Hastings in three of them and Dr. Sheppard in *The Murder of Roger Ackroyd,*) and so all knowledge about the characters came to the readers through the thoughts of that narrator, or through the spoken words of the characters themselves. *The Mystery of the Blue Train* has no narrator—the story is told in the omniscient third person, making it possible for Christie to express the *thoughts of various characters*. Naturally that technique brings those characters much more clearly to life than the thoughts of even the most observant and perceptive of narrators can.

The Mystery of the Blue Train contains a superior cast of distinctly individual characters whose private motivations could have been used more creatively by the author in the plotting of the investigation and solution of the crime. There is, for example, Rufus Van Aldin, who is probably ruthless in business but is genuinely loving towards his daughter, trying to exercise fatherly influence to help guide her but at the same time knowing that too much force will alienate her from him.

There is Ruth herself who, while knowing that her father sincerely wishes for her happiness, resents his control and wants to exercise her independence, while at the same time knowing that pursuing her private wishes has led to unhappiness more than once. There is Derek, whom some people would view as just another of the world's philandering husbands, but who knows that he and his wife married simply for convenience—he for money and she for a title—and therefore he feels no need to deprive himself of the favors of another woman.

There is Mirelle, whom some people might describe as "nothing but a home-wrecking tramp," but who sees, in her realistic French way, the above realities and feels no guilt about her relationship with "Dereek" since it brings happiness to both of them.

There is the social climbing Viscountess Tamplin and her less-than-tactful daughter Lenox who "calls a spade a spade," openly despising her mother's exploitation of social possibilities. There is the kind, intelligent and perceptive Katherine Grey who, more amused than gratified by her newly-acquired status of "very wealthy woman," is disgusted by the silliness that surrounds her—in particular the distant relatives who suddenly notice her for the very first time, now that she is rich.

There is Armand, the Comte de la Roche, despised by all men but loved by all women for his charms, using those charms—and the scandalous secrets of women—to blackmail them but who, according to authorities, would never stoop to murder.

An example of the kind of character analysis found in *The Mystery of the Blue Train* and not in previous Christie novels are the following paragraphs, which record Ruth Kettering's *thoughts* while riding in the train from London to Dover:

Ruth sat very still, biting her under lip and trying hard to keep the unaccustomed tears from her eyes. She felt a sudden sense of horrible desolation. There was a wild longing upon her to jump out of the train and to go back before it was too late. She, so calm, so self-assured, for the first time in her life felt like a leaf swept by the wind. If her father knew—what would he say?

Madness! Yes, just that, madness! For the first time in her life she was swept away by emotion, swept away to the point of doing a thing which even she knew to be incredibly foolish and reckless. She was enough Van Aldin's daughter to realize her own folly, and level headed enough to condemn her own action. But she was his daughter in another sense also. She had that same iron determination that would have what it wanted, and once it had made up its mind would not be balked. From her cradle she had been self-willed; the very circumstances of her life had developed that self-will in her. It drove her now remorselessly. Well, the die was cast. She must go through with it now.

Ruth found an increasing difficulty in fixing her mind on the printed page in front of her. In spite of herself, a thousand apprehensions preyed on her mind. What a fool she had been! What a fool she was! Like all cool and self-sufficient people, when she did lose her self-control she lost it thoroughly. It was too late.... Was it too late? Oh, for some one to speak to, for someone to advise her. She had never before had such a wish; she would have scorned the idea of relying on any judgment other than her own, but now—what was the matter with her? Panic. Yes, that would describe it best—panic. She, Ruth Kettering, was completely and utterly panic stricken.

In addition to the large number of interesting characters, there is "atmosphere" in *The Mystery of the Blue Train*. The opening chapters, in particular, have a sinister, frightening feel, being set in the darkened streets of Paris with visions of mysterious figures:

Two shadows stole from a doorway and followed noiselessly. Pursuers and pursued vanished into the night.

The fragrance of perfume in the apartment of Mirelle, the blue sky and water of the Mediterranean coast, the profusion of yellow jasmine growing everywhere in the South of France; the fresh excitement of a long train journey for Katherine; the charming scene in the dressmaker's shop in London; all of these are touches of a kind that will characterize future Christie novels. Though unrelated to each other, these are "extras" that make Agatha Christie so much fun to read—and to remember—and they are quite new in *The Mystery of the Blue Train*.

As it was mentioned earlier, the characters in Christie's first novel, *The Mysterious Affair at Styles*, were rather dull but it was quite a good detective novel. In the case of *The Mystery of the*

Blue Train, the opposite is true. The characters in this novel are interesting and memorable, but as a detective novel it is a disappointment. The detection and eventual solution of the mystery have little if anything to do with the interesting interpersonal relationships of the characters. Poirot has "ideas" and "hunches" which he verifies through private inquiries not revealed to us until the final chapter. Therefore even with careful reading we cannot have all of the information necessary to solve the crime. This will not be the case in most of Christie's later novels, although from time to time Poirot will do some rather fortunate guessing, as in the 1938 *A Holiday for Murder* and the 1955 *Hickory, Dickory, Death*.

The early chapters of *The Mystery of the Blue Train* seem to hold great promise but once the characters are established on the Riviera and Poirot is pursuing his investigations there, the conversations seem sometimes to "go nowhere" and to be labored. The solution is not very interesting and the guilty parties are not among the more memorable characters.

Agatha Christie stated in her *Autobiography* that *The Mystery of the Blue Train* was her all-time worst book. In terms of interesting, memorable characters, it is equal to some of her best books, but as a detective novel it is not one of her successes. Christie wrote this novel while at a low point in her personal life. Her husband had just announced his desire for a divorce in order to marry another woman, and Christie took it hard. Personal depression probably took its toll in this case.

The Seven Dials Mystery (1929)

Setting

The story takes place in September and October of 1928. The action begins at Chimneys—one of the "great houses of England"—an immense fictitious residence of historical importance, which was the setting for the 1925 novel *The Secret of Chimneys,* near the fictitious town of Market Basing in Berkshire. The name of the county is not specified in either novel, but the action of a later novel—the 1937 *Poirot Loses a Client*—takes place in Market Basing and in that novel Berkshire is named as the county in which it is located. There is a brief scene in Market Basing itself when a group of young people visit a department store, Murgatroyd's, to buy eight alarm clocks.

Soon most of the action moves to Wyvern Abbey, another impressive but less grand residence, seven miles distant. A very brief scene occurs at Dean Priory, a still smaller country house twenty minutes by car from Chimneys. One scene occurs at Letherbury, another impressive country house, owned by the Duke of Alton, forty miles from Chimneys.

The London settings include Lord Caterham's house in Brook Street, the "rooms" in Jermyn Street occupied by Jimmy Thesiger; the home of Bundle's Aunt Marcia, the Marchioness of Caterham, which "smells of sealing wax, bird seed and slightly decaying flowers." More importantly, there is a seedy nightclub called Seven Dials where underworld types mix with the gentry. An upstairs room at the club is a meeting room for a mysterious society calling itself "The Seven Dials."

There is no special historical background to the novel other than the lingering fear of potential war, in particular with Germany. World War I had ended only ten years earlier, and there was general fear of advanced technological secrets becoming the property of one government or the other, potentially to be used in warfare. The specific "advancement" spoken of in this novel is a new way to strengthen wire so that it can replace heavier substances in airplane construction, a valuable asset to any nation's air force.

Electric lighting is mentioned as existing at Chimneys and Wyvern Abbey, and telephone use is an everyday occurrence. For the first time in an Agatha Christie novel, an automobile make is mentioned: Hispano, a luxury car for the rich. The automobile horn on that car is called the Klaxon, spelled with the capital K; it was a patented electrically operated auto horn emitting the "Ooo-gah" sound characteristic of that period. Radio (known in England as "the wireless") is mentioned for the first time in an Agatha Christie novel. It is specifically mentioned that Wyvern Abbey is "old fashioned" and has no central heating, relying on fireplaces in each room; one character notes that fireplaces are inefficient, sending more heat up the chimney than into the room. Probably Chimneys, Dean Priory and Letherbury are equally antiquated in this respect.

There is a passing reference to the "great houses of England" being sold to developers and made into "desirable flats with pleasant recreational grounds," something that must have been happening as a result of the impoverishment of the aristocracy. There are deprecating remarks about immense wealth being made by persons in industry who, despite having ability in business and certain specific knowledge, lack general education and the enjoyment and appreciation of the finer aspects of life.

Story

Lord Caterham has let Chimneys, his vast ancestral home, to Sir Oswald and Lady Maria Coote for a two-year period while he travels abroad. As the story begins, several young people have been enjoying the hospitality of the Cootes as houseguests at Chimneys. One of the young men, Gerald Wade, dies in his sleep, apparently from an accidental overdose of a sleeping preparation. A few days later another of the young men is shot to death in the open country near Chimneys. Before dying he murmurs the phrase "Seven Dials" and the name "Jimmy Thesiger." Jimmy Thesiger was one of the young guests at Chimneys a few days earlier.

Lord Caterham's daughter Lady Eileen, together with Bill Eversleigh, Jimmy Thesiger and Gerald Wade's half-sister Elaine, suspect that the Seven Dials is a secret organization bent on stealing a valuable formula for strengthening wire used in airplane construction in order to sell it to an enemy government. Through a series of thrilling adventures the young people, together with Superintendent Battle, recover the formula and bring the murderer to justice.

Characters

Jimmy Thesiger, a pleasant young man of independent means who does not need to work and "just tools around." He has "rooms" in Jermyn Street in London and a husband and wife team of servants. He is a friend of several young men who work at the Foreign Office, and was a schoolmate of Rupert Bateman, Sir Oswald Coote's private secretary.

Tredwell, the butler at Chimneys who is "accustomed to the ways of Young Gentlemen," and is therefore not the least bit annoyed by their arriving for breakfast at noon or even later. He is the perfect butler, according to Lord Caterham.

Sir Oswald Coote, in the words of Lord Caterham, "the kind of man that would result if suddenly a steam roller turned into a human being." He is an immensely successful steel magnate. He believes in early rising and "regular methods."

Lady Maria Coote, the melancholy middle-aged wife of the immensely, but only materially, successful Sir Oswald Coote. She fondly recalls the early days of their marriage when he was "just plain Mr. Coote" when they lived in a cozy little house instead of the grandiose, servant-staffed mansions that Sir Oswald has lately been in the habit of renting in order to convince himself of his success. She never feels quite "at home" in them, and the well-trained servants intimidate her. She wonders if life wouldn't have been much more pleasant for the two of them if Sir Oswald had *not* had "regular methods."

MacDonald, the head gardener at Chimneys who "surveys the domain he rules with an autocratic eye."

William, undergardener at Chimneys

Rupert Bateman, who is called "Pongo" by his old school chum Jimmy Thesiger. Pongo is "brainy," according to all the other young people, but humorless. Jimmy recalls Pongo at school as being "a serious, spectacled boy ... and very much the same sort of ass now that he had been then. The words 'Life is real, life is earnest' might have been written specially for him." Pongo is Sir Oswald Coote's private secretary and Sir Oswald thinks the world of him.

Vera "Socks" Daventry, a young houseguest of the Cootes, and a niece of Lady Coote. Her favorite word is "subtle."

Nancy and **Helen**, two other young guests of the Cootes' at Chimneys

George Lomax, the owner of a fine estate, Wyvern Abbey, seven miles from Chimneys. We met him in the 1925 *The Secret of Chimneys*. George is a public-spirited Cabinet Minster, His Majesty's permanent Under Secretary of State for Foreign Affairs, and he is shunned by many because of his inveterate habit of quoting from his own public speeches in private. In allusion to his bulging eyeballs, he is known to many—Bill Eversleigh among others—as "Codders." He is in a constant state of anxiety about "state secrets" and his favorite term is "utmost discretion."

Bill Eversleigh, who is employed in a purely ornamental capacity at the Foreign Office and is a young man of very mediocre intellect. Physically he is big and clumsy. He doesn't enter a room; he "bustles in," reminding Bundle of an enthusiastic dog wagging its tail. He is, in fact, George Lomax's "dog," running odd errands for him and making himself useful in a general way but clearly despising Lomax, to whom he refers as "Codders."

Gerald Wade, another young man at the foreign office, fluent in German, described by some of his friends as "rather an ass" but in the opinion of Jimmy Thesiger, perhaps much less of an ass than most people think, and possibly an important figure in espionage. Gerald dies of an overdose of a sleeping preparation at Chimneys.

Ronny Devereux, still another young man who works at the foreign office with Gerald and Bill. Ronny strongly suspects that Gerald's death was neither accident nor suicide. Ronny is murdered in open country not far from Chimneys a few days after Gerald's death. His mysterious dying words to Bundle include "Seven Dials" and the name "Jimmy Thesiger."

Mr. Murgatroyd, the owner of Murgatroyd's Stores, who is mystified by the simultaneous sale of eight alarm clocks at his Market Basing store.

Sir Clement Edward Alistair Brent, Ninth Marquis of Caterham, usually called "Lord Caterham." He loves the peace and comfort of the countryside and enjoys first editions, golf, and relaxation. He dislikes politics and politicians, in particular his sister-in-law Marcia, the widow of his deceased older brother Henry. Marcia had pushed Henry into politics, turning Chimneys into practically a convention center during her years in residence there. Lord Caterham's reaction to Gerald Wade's dying at Chimneys: "Damned inconsiderate." He enjoys an affectionate relationship with his daughter, Lady Eileen (known to everyone as "Bundle") and he has a surprisingly modern attitude toward young people and their right to choose their friends and spouses. At one point he states that if Bundle had announced to him her intention to marry the chauffeur, he would not have put up the least objection. Though a dyed-in-the-wool aristocrat himself with no interest in doing anything productive, other than enjoying life, he sees nothing special about social position.

Lady Eileen Brent, familiarly known as "Bundle," the eldest of three daughters of Lord Caterham. She is about twenty-four years old, finds country life boring, and loves excitement and action. She dislikes politics and politicians—and George Lomax, in particular—even more than her father does. She has a close relationship with her father—close enough to tell him "You haven't the brains of a rabbit," with no fear of offending him—and she feels much more respect for him than for all of the world's politicians and industrial magnates combined.

Bundle is fearless and action prone: "To think was to act with Bundle." No grass grows under her feet. She works together with Jimmy Thesiger, Elaine Wade and Bill Eversleigh to get to the bottom of the deaths of Gerald Wade and Ronny Devereux. She is also a notoriously reckless driver.

Mrs. Howell, the housekeeper at Chimneys who brings Bundle up to date on changes in the staff during Bundle's and her father's two-year absence.

Williams, a male servant at Chimneys who discovers the death of Gerald Wade

Alfred, formerly a footman at Chimneys who was paid one hundred pounds by Mr. Mosgorovsky to leave Chimneys "this instant moment" and go to look after the Seven Dials Club in London at triple his usual wages. He later helps Bundle to spy on the Seven Dials secret society.

John Bauer, who is hired by Tredwell to replace the suddenly-departing Alfred. John was recommended by Mr. Musgorovksy and just happened to be available to start work immediately.

Elaine Wade, half-sister of Gerald Wade. Devastated by her half-brother's sudden death, she is determined to assist Bundle and Jimmy in tracking down his killer.

Mrs. Coker, in Jimmy Thesiger's words, "the old trout who lives with Elaine."

Inspector Raglan, the local police officer in charge of the investigation of Gerry Wade's death and who believes it may have been murder, despite a preponderance of evidence that it was suicide or an accident.

Katie, a little girl, the daughter of the lodge keepers at Chimneys, who flies out to open the gates for Bundle who is "in a mortal hurry as always."

Dr. Cassell, a kindly, middle-aged doctor to whom Bundle takes the body of Ronny Devereux who died in the road after apparently being struck by Bundle's car.

A Police Inspector, a slow-speaking man who is somewhat overawed by Bundle's name and address. He surmises that the shooting of Ronny Devereux was an accident by "lads practising marksmanship."

Stevens, Jimmy Thesiger's manservant, an intelligent fellow who is studying French by correspondence courses and who is well enough trained *not* to ask why his master wants him to go out and buy a blue-nosed revolver.

Mrs. Stevens, wife of the above who cooks an excellent meal consisting of an omelet, quails and the lightest thing in soufflés for Jimmy and two unexpected guests.

Superintendent Battle of Scotland Yard, a big man who works almost entirely on cases of a political nature. He never displays emotion and he never gives up once he is determined to catch his man. We met him in the 1925 *The Secret of Chimneys.*

Colonel Melrose, the coroner who presides at the inquest on the death of Ronny Devereux.

Mrs. Macatta, M.P., invited to Wyvern Abbey for the conference but unable to attend. She is "always going off the deep end about Welfare and Pure Milk and Save the Children," according to Bill Eversleigh. To Bundle's Aunt Marcia, Mrs. Macatta is "a most estimable woman with a brilliant brain, whose work is of truly national importance, and of the utmost value to all women."

Countess Radsky, a Hungarian aristocrat, who is passionate about infant mortality in her homeland.

> Leaning very far back on a sofa, with her legs crossed in a daring manner, she was smoking a cigarette in an incredibly long turquoise studded holder.... Bundle thought she was one of the most beautiful women she had ever seen. Her eyes were very large and blue, her hair was coal black, she had a matte skin, the slightly flattened nose of the Slav, and a sinuous, slender body. Her lips were reddened to a degree with which Bundle was sure Wyvern Abbey was totally unacquainted.

Sir Stanley Digby, the British Air Minister, "a little round man with a cheerful smile."

Terence O'Rourke, Sir Stanley's secretary, a tall young man with laughing blue eyes and a typical Irish face. He is "rather a lad," according to Bill Eversleigh, and an ex-pilot from the war days. He later entertains Socks Daventry with exaggerated accounts of his adventures at Wyvern Abbey.

Herr Eberhard, who has developed a formula for strengthening wire for use in the manufacture of lighter aircraft.

Marcia, Marchioness of Caterham, Bundle's aunt and Lord Caterham's sister-in-law. She lives in a large gloomy house in one of London's higher-class squares. "Inside it smelt of sealing wax, bird seed and slightly decayed flowers."

Marcia is devoted to party politics (Conservative, of course) and rather despises her brother-in-law for not following in her husband's footsteps and taking an interest in politics as she and her husband had for many years when *he* was the Marquis of Caterham. Marcia is delighted to hear that Bundle has suddenly "grown up" and that she now feels that politics are "the most fascinating study there is." Bundle had made this "extravagantly untruthful statement of her feelings without even a blush," for the purpose of achieving an invitation to Wyvern Abbey in order to do some sleuthing with Jimmy Thesiger. Marcia swallows the bait and invites Bundle, sending her home with an armful of boring political literature. Bundle, in fact, detests Marcia and all politicians, as does her father, Lord Caterham.

Five Observed Members of the Seven Dials Secret Society, All Sinister (#2 and #7 not in story):
#1, Anna, a Foreign Woman of Unknown Nationality
#3, An Unnamed Englishman
#4, An Unnamed American Man
#5, An Unnamed Foreign Man of Unknown Nationality
#6, Mr. Mosgorovsky, a Russian

COMMENTS

The Seven Dials Mystery is a lot of fun largely because of its youthful and likeable cast of characters. It's almost a picture of a silly grown-up world seen through the eyes of children who are more sensible than their elders.

The Secret of Chimneys, published four years earlier, was very similar. The silliest grown-up in that book was George Lomax, the dedicated politician who ran his ridiculous little butt off gasping "utmost discretion" at every opportunity while Anthony Cade and Virginia Revel took pot-shots at him and his ilk under the benevolent and smiling watch of the fun-loving Lord Caterham. All that silly business of "vital oil interests" and "the Kohinoor Diamond" was just laughed at by the young people. Of course it was middle-aged, wooden-faced, never-expressing-emotion Superintendent Battle who solved the mystery and not really the young folks, but it was mainly the young folks who were his friends.

In *The Seven Dials Mystery,* it is again Superintendent Battle who solves the mystery while certain "bright young people" spin their wheels earnestly, but it is the young people again who are his friends in even bigger ways. And again there is more grown-up silliness—this time a new invention that greedy nations would like to use to make more efficient warfare.

Our friend George Lomax again runs around in a panic gasping "utmost discretion" while Lord Caterham shakes his head in befuddlement, joined by his daughter Lady Eileen who despises Lomax even more than her father does. Politicians take a special beating in *The Seven Dials Mystery*. The scene in which Bundle causes her Aunt Marcia to believe that she has finally "grown up" and taken an interest in politics is superb. "How nice to see that you have grown up at last," says Aunt Marcia, as Bundle gags, bites her tongue and does everything possible not to roar with hysterical laughter at this asinine woman who sees a bright future for Bundle as "the foremost political hostess in England—provided that she marries suitably."

Agatha Christie must have absolutely detested politics and politicians as a group. We recall Sir Eustace Pedlar in the 1924 *The Man in the Brown Suit*. He was a lazy loafer who resented his secretary because the secretary actually worked and expected him to do the same. In the future there will be other politicians who are ineffectual and incompetent, and there will be another lady politician—Lady Westholme in the 1938 *Appointment with Death*—who will flare her nostrils and lecture on any one of her subjects of interest at a moment's notice. Christie will only leave off ridiculing politicians once in her career. In the 1945 *Remembered Death*, one of her all-time masterpieces of sensitive characterization, she will portray the political Kidderminster family and Stephen and Sandra Farraday as real human beings with psychological complexity. But that will be the *only* time. Towards the end of her life, in her 1970 *Passenger to Frankfurt*, she will trash all politicians, including presidents and prime ministers.

Christie wasted no affection on the "working rich," either. Bundle's assessment of Sir Oswald and his meaningless gathering of wealth will be repeated again and again by the "younger and wiser" in future Christie novels. There will be numerous negative references to "Victorian ironmongers" and other industrialists of the 19th century who accumulated vast wealth, built ridiculous "mini-castles" for themselves to live in (and to advertise their success), had no education or appreciation for the fine things of life, and despised their children for thinking there was more to life than money.

Meanwhile, in *The Seven Dials Mystery*, the kids have fun and their favorite uncle treats them to some bubbly at the end.

Summary for the 1920s

The first decade of Agatha Christie's writing career—the 1920s—is characterized by variety, and there is of course "growth and development" in some aspects of Christie's writing skill. The most notable advancement is in character development, as evidenced in Christie's portrayals of Katherine Grey and Ruth Kettering in *The Mystery of the Blue Train*. Although Christie later became famous for writing classic detective novels in which one or more murders occur and the main focus is on crime detection, only four of the nine novels that she published during her first decade fall into that category. They are *The Mysterious Affair at Styles*, *Murder on the Links*, *The Murder of Roger Ackroyd*, and *The Mystery of the Blue Train*. *The Murder of Roger Ackroyd* is, of course, a unique masterpiece. *The Secret Adversary*, *The Man in the Brown Suit*, *The Secret of Chimneys* and *The Seven Dials Mystery* are light-hearted adventure stories that probably do not score high points among detective story connoisseurs but they are certainly highly amusing and entertaining. *The Big Four* reads more like a series of loosely connected short stories than a novel.

Murder at the Vicarage (1930)

Setting

The year is 1929 or 1930. The entire story takes place in a fictitious village, St. Mary Mead, in the fictitious county of Downshire. Its location in England is not specified, but the village name was used in *The Mystery of the Blue Train*, in which railway passengers from St. Mary Mead arrived at London's Paddington Station; therefore the reader may assume that "Downshire" is somewhere west of London. In two earlier novels, *The Secret of Chimneys* and *The Seven Dials Mystery*, the town of Market Basing is also mentioned as being in the area served by train from Paddington. Then, in 1937, Market Basing becomes the setting for *Poirot Loses a Client* and in that novel it is said to be in the real county of Berkshire. A road leading out of Market Basing is named "The Much Benham Road," suggesting that Much Benham and Market Basing are not far apart, and are probably in the same county. Therefore we can assume that "Downshire" is actually Berkshire and that all three places—St. Mary Mead, Much Benham and Market Basing—are in that county.

Despite the fact that St. Mary Mead was mentioned in *The Mystery of the Blue Train*, no character from that novel appears in *Murder at the Vicarage* or is even mentioned.

There are no references to any historical events—other than one mention of The War (World War One) having adversely affected the mental health of some of the returning soldiers. There are one or two references to "modern" women's clothing being close fitting and "hiding none of the creator's intentions,"—this to explain why a female character could not have had a firearm concealed on her person. In one scene a young woman is described as wearing extremely shiny pink stockings and sitting with her legs crossed, a "modern" and supposedly "unladylike" act.

There appears to have been scientific research on the effects of certain diseases on the personalities of the sufferers, specifically *encephalitis lethargica*, leading some researchers to suggest that criminal tendencies may in the future be viewed more as "health" than "moral" issues. This leads to a difference of opinion between the modern-thinking Doctor Haydock and the more traditional thinking police officer, Colonel Melchett.

The telephone and electricity now appear to be universal, even in this old-world village, as electric lighting is mentioned several times and telephone calls are constantly being made between residences in the village. The telephone numbers are picturesquely "village like"—Miss Marple's phone number is 35; Dr. Haydock's is 39. There are a couple of references to "gramophone" records; in a previous Christie novel the "Victrola" was already mentioned as a term meaning "record player," derived from a trade name of the period.

The village has a medieval church with some worthwhile stained glass and a screen surviving. There is also an inn, The Blue Boar, which serves meals ("a good lunch of the joint and two vegetable type,") and there are several shops and terraced houses in addition to several "cottages," which are actually substantial detached homes with gardens and surrounding walls, etc. The large home owned by the murder victim, Colonel Lucius Protheroe, is called Old Hall and is somewhat removed from the village, reached by the road or by a shorter footpath. Two miles away there is a market town called Much Benham where there is a hospital.

Automobiles are owned by Dr. Haydock and Colonel Protheroe; the Colonel actually owns at least two—a closed car driven mostly by the family chauffeur and a Fiat two-seater sometimes driven by the teen-age daughter. No other automobiles are mentioned and the vicar, who is a main character and the narrator, does not own a car or even a bicycle. One character uses a "motor bicycle," which must be an old term for "motorcycle" or a lighter-weight "moped" type vehicle, but no other character in the story owns an automobile.

The crime takes place in the study of the vicarage, the residence of the village clergyman. In the book there are plans showing that room, the ground floor of the house and its relationship to the road and connecting paths and lanes and one or two neighboring houses. There is also a plan of part of the village showing several houses, shops, the church and the inn and their relative positions with respect to the vicarage.

Within the walls of the vicarage grounds, in a corner at some distance from the house, is small building described as a "shed" with an entrance door but no windows. There is a skylight, however, which must provide adequate light for painting, for the vicar permits an artist to use it as a painting studio. The ground floor of the vicarage consists of a kitchen and adjoining pantry, a dining room, drawing room, study and a central hall with stairs.

The room where the crime occurs is described as being furnished rather shabbily with two or three chairs clustered at the fireplace, a writing desk in a corner, a book case, one or two small tables and a stand with a large plant. The upstairs rooms are not mentioned.

Old Hall, the residence of the Protheroe family, is much grander and has a small drawing room on the upper floor (in European terms, the "first floor"). There is an additional floor above where there is an attic "lumber" room containing the usual cast-offs—old pictures, broken furniture, etc. The grounds must be substantial, as there are at least two "lodges," one of them temporarily vacant but equipped with a telephone of its own.

Brief scenes occur at two or three of the other homes in the village; the house of Mrs. Lestrange is described as being tastefully decorated, an improvement over its former condition when it was occupied by an Anglo-Indian colonel who had furnished it with numerous "brass tables and Burmese idols." The house of one of the village spinsters is described as having a "tiny, crowded drawing room;" that of another spinster has a drawing room filled with "quite good stuff," in the vicar's opinion—probably tastefully chosen furniture and art objects.

One of the police officers, Colonel Melchett, observes that there are "too many women in this part of the world," and indeed there is an abundance of older women living in the village, most of them spinsters with time on their hands and other people's private lives on their minds.

It can be assumed that we are in early summertime, since the windows of the vicarage and other houses are open most of the time and on one occasion a character admires the roses of another character who is busy working in her garden. Many of the ground floor windows of the vicarage and of other houses are of the French type, and so the characters are as likely to enter and leave the houses through those as through the entrance doors.

STORY

It is early summer of 1929 or 1930. The most prominent citizen living in the village of St. Mary Mead is Colonel Lucius Protheroe. He is the local magistrate and churchwarden and in both of these capacities he has been a source of annoyance to a large number of people. He is unbending, unforgiving, suspicious and extremely self-righteous. A small deficit in the church collection basket, noticed by a certain busy-body, causes him to initiate an investigation into the church funds and he insinuates that either the vicar or the curate or both have been engaging in embezzling. He prosecutes and persecutes local poachers relentlessly and takes acute pleasure in sentencing three of them in one day. His attitude—and his crude words—have made him a very unpopular person in the village. He is murdered in the vicarage library one evening.

Because he is such an unpleasant person there are a large number of suspects for whom substantial motives can be imagined. The police do their best to solve this mystery, but an elderly spinster living in the village, Miss Jane Marple, solves the mystery in her special way.

Characters

Leonard Clement, aged about forty-five, the narrator. He is the vicar of the village of St. Mary Mead. Five years ago he married a woman aged only twenty. He considers himself to be a "modern" person. In an early chapter, in a conversation with persons who are expressing disapproval of a young woman's working as secretary to an unmarried man, he states, "But surely in these days a girl can take a post the same as a man." He is compassionate and forgiving and prefers to give a person the benefit of doubt when there is a question of wrongdoing. When another character extols "justice," Leonard replies that there is also a virtue called "mercy." He is exasperated by the amount of vicious gossip that is practiced in the village.

Leonard says that he favors celibacy for the clergy and has never quite understood why he suddenly fell in love with a young woman of twenty and proposed to her after knowing her for only twenty-four hours.

Griselda Clement, the vicar's young wife, now aged twenty-five. She is a loving and supportive wife to the vicar, has an excellent sense of humor, and loves reading detective stories. As to her sense of humor, she tends to go a bit too far in her jesting, especially when in the presence of persons who do *not* have a sense of humor.

Dennis, age sixteen, a nephew of the vicar who lives in their home. We may assume that he is an orphan but no actual explanation is given for his living in the household. He is an ordinary, pleasant teenager who, having failed at entry to the Navy, is looking forward to a life in the Merchant Marine.

Mary Hill, the Clements' housemaid and cook. She is absolutely incompetent, careless and even insolent. The Clements employ her because they cannot afford to pay someone who is better and they know that if her work were ever to improve, she would move on to a better-paid position. She is rude, never using the words "Sir" or "Ma'am" and simply entering the room and beginning to speak; her housework is mediocre and her cooking is pitiful, even by English standards. According to the vicar, she "takes a perverse pleasure in how best to alternate overcooking and undercooking." Thus Griselda: "Mary's blancmange is so depressing ... it's like something from a mortuary." Mary produces boiled beef which is tough, moist and unpleasant dumplings, and undercooked rice pudding. She drops cracked dishes of greens with a "bang" on the dinner table.

Mary has a boyfriend, young Archer, who has recently been jailed by Colonel Protheroe for poaching, and so she resents the Colonel for that. When the Colonel is murdered, Mary is one of the suspects along with Archer.

Mr. Hawes, the young curate of the parish, who has "High Anglican" views which are at variance with the vicar's and even more at variance with Colonel Protheroe's. The Colonel, in addition to being the local magistrate, is the churchwarden and suspects that either the vicar or the curate has been pilfering church funds. Mr. Hawes is chronically ill, extremely nervous at all times and seems to have emotional problems. He lives alone in two rented rooms in the village. The vicar finds him to be a very tiresome young man.

In a surprising, inappropriate outburst, Mr. Hawes describes young Archer, the convicted poacher, as "a godless, irreligious ruffian. A drunken blackguard. A poacher, in and out of prison, capable of anything." The vicar suggests that this portrayal is a bit harsh.

Colonel Lucius Protheroe, an unbelievably unpleasant middle aged man who knows no compromise. As the churchwarden he is actively investigating possible petty peculations of church funds, openly accusing Hawes. He is found to be "in high good humor," one afternoon, "having sentenced three poachers in his capacity as magistrate." He has a beautiful young second wife, Anne, who detests him and who is pursuing a clandestine affair with a handsome man who is even younger than she. He has a daughter, Lettice, aged about eighteen, by his first marriage, who resents him bitterly for all of the reasons for which children resent uncompromising, unreasonable parents. He is murdered near the beginning of the story, and nearly all of the characters feel that the world is better off without him, even the vicar. Naturally, there are numerous suspects, since nearly everyone in the village has had at least one unpleasant experience with him, including the vicar himself.

Anne Protheroe, the young wife of Lucius Protheroe. She hates her cruel husband and is in love with a handsome young painter, Lawrence Redding. She is not fond of her stepdaughter Lettice but has tried to be a good mother to her. The vicar describes her as "a remarkably handsome woman in a rather unusual style."

Lettice Protheroe, daughter of Lucius by his first marriage, aged about eighteen. She resents her father and also her stepmother and openly declares to the vicar, one day, that if she had any money she would go away. She has a very "vague" manner—her conversation is disconnected and rather puzzling and she "drifts" in and out of people's houses unexpectedly. She cannot keep track of time—or even days—and constantly misplaces things and forgets appointments. The vicar believes that most of this vagueness is shammed and that Lettice is much brighter than she pretends to be. She is quite pleased to learn of her father's murder and refuses to wear black, declaring that "mourning is an archaic idea." She has a "crush" on handsome Lawrence Redding, of course, who is currently painting her portrait—that is, *was* painting her portrait, until banished from the Protheroe home for painting Lettice in her bathing suit.

Lawrence Redding, an unusually handsome young man aged about thirty, an artist, who lives in a rented cottage in the village and uses a shed on the vicarage property as a studio for painting. He has been painting portraits of Griselda and, until recently, of Lettice. Colonel Protheroe's death is a godsend to him, naturally, since he is in love with Mrs. Protheroe, but of course he is the prime murder suspect as a consequence.

Dr. Stone, a well-known archeologist who is currently staying at the Blue Boar. He is supervising the excavation of a barrow on the Protheroe property. He is "a little man, head round and bald, face round and rosy, he beams at you through very strong glasses." Colonel Protheroe thinks that Dr. Stone is a "fake" and Dr. Stone has called Protheroe an "ignoramus."

Miss Gladys Cram, "a healthy young woman of twenty-five, noisy in manner, with a high color, fine animal spirits, and a mouth that always seems to have more than its full share of teeth," according to the vicar. She is Dr. Stone's secretary and assistant, and is also staying at the Blue Boar. She describes St. Mary Mead as "a one-horse village without so much as a picture house." She is viewed locally as "common" and her working for an unmarried man—and staying at the same hotel as he—arouses suspicion in the minds of the local spinsters. She is described by Griselda thus: "...terribly common, but one of those big, bouncing, good-humoured girls you can't dislike."

Archer, a local young man who is Mary Hill's sweetheart. He is a murder suspect because Colonel Protheroe, as the village magistrate, had recently jailed him for poaching.

Mrs. Price Ridley, Miss Wetherby, Miss Hartnell and Miss Jane Marple, village ladies of advanced but indeterminate age who have time on their hands and whose chief occupation seems to be minding other people's business. In a word, they are incurable gossips and the vicar seems to have no Christianizing influence over them—they do not seem to regard vicious gossip as sinful. They gather for tea—at the vicarage, no less—and discuss Redding's painting of Lettice in her bathing suit and the possible sexual relationship he may have with her, or possibly with her mother. They also discuss a new arrival in the village, Mrs. Lestrange, and the possible nature of Dr. Haydock's visits to her home *without his doctor's bag*. And of course they discuss the fact that Miss Cram works for the unmarried Dr. Stone *and* stays at the same hotel where all the bedrooms are on the same floor!

All of these ladies are referred to as "cats," "old cats," and "old pussies" by the men and the younger women of the village. The police tend to disregard their opinions and observations with comments such as "just the kind of thing women always think."

Miss Jane Marple, of course, deserves much more attention, as it will be she who solves the mystery. Unlike the other ladies, who merely guess and suggest unsavory acts in other people's lives, Miss Marple has method. Her view of the world is that human nature is generally quite bad and that the worst is usually true. She realizes that young people, inexperienced in life, prefer to take optimistic views of their fellow humans, but that always leads to disappointment, because "the world is a very wicked place." The vicar holds the same opinion as the police do regarding the "old cats" of the village, but for Miss Marple he feels considerable respect, having noticed that she is nearly always right. He also appreciates the fact that she has a sense of humor. Per Griselda, "that kind of old cat is always right."

Although Miss Marple will reappear in a

1933 book of short stories entitled *The Tuesday Club Murders*, she will not appear in another novel until the 1942 *The Body in the Library*. After that, she will appear more frequently in Christie detective novels and will eventually rival Hercule Poirot in popularity among Christie fans.

Mrs. Lestrange, a middle-aged woman of refinement who has recently taken a house, Little Gates, in the village and keeps to herself. Because she is clearly a well-educated "woman of the world," the villagers wonder why she has chosen to bury herself "out of the world" in St. Mary Mead.

Dr. Haydock, "a big, fine, strapping fellow, with an honest, rugged face." He has "modern" ideas about some connection between criminal tendencies and physical health. He tends to excuse anti-social and even criminal behaviors when there appears to be a possible medical cause for them, and he suggests that criminal tendencies may one day be shown to be nothing more than a glandular dysfunction. Upon being called upon to examine the dead man, "like a true doctor he showed no signs of emotion."

Note: Dr. Haydock's "modern notions" about criminality will be repeated by other characters in future Christie novels, first in *Thirteen at Dinner*, published three years later in which an efficient secretary declares murderers to be mentally deficient due to a "glandular dysfunction." Christie was clearly unimpressed by "the excuses" that were being provided for criminals by well-meaning professionals, especially the psychologists who, during the 1940s made much of "environment." The 1952 *Murder with Mirrors* ridicules the notion of reforming juvenile delinquents through "art and theatre experiences" instead of simply punishing them and showing them that society will not tolerate destructive behaviors.

Dr. Haydock will reappear in several Miss Marple stories in the future, but his notions about "glandular dysfunction and criminality" will never be mentioned again. Perhaps he will have changed his mind on that subject.

Constable Hurst, a local police officer

Inspector Slack, one of the detectives in charge of the case, an overbearing, rude person. Among his faults is a tendency to generalize about women. Explaining why he does not suspect a woman of the murder, he says, "Women never like fiddling about with firearms. Arsenic's more in their line."

Colonel Melchett, "...a dapper little man with a habit of snorting suddenly and unexpectedly. He has red hair and rather keen, bright-blue eyes." He is a more pleasant police officer than Inspector Slack, but is equally prone to generalize about women. "Too many women in this part of the world," he comments. When finding it necessary to interview one of the "old cats," he "puts on his bluff, military manner, which he has an idea is attractive to elderly ladies." He strongly disagrees with Dr. Haydock's "modern" ideas about criminality and its supposed relationship to physical health.

Raymond West, Miss Marple's generous nephew, a proud, successful writer of "clever books" and poems without capital letters. He is sophisticated, urbane and condescending and he describes the village of St. Mary Mead as "a stagnant pool." To this Miss Marple responds,

"That is really not a very good simile, dear Raymond. Nothing, I believe, is so full of life under the microscope as a drop of water from a stagnant pool."

Raymond has a tolerant affection for "Aunt Jane," to whom he alludes as a "survival." She listens to his talk with a flattering interest, and if there is sometimes an amused twinkle in her eye, he never notices it. In a future novel, the 1964 *A Caribbean Mystery*, she will describe him—in her thoughts—as "ignorant," but she will always be grateful for his generosity, and in four future stories he will provide her with luxuries such as a holiday on a Caribbean island, another holiday at an expensive seaside resort in England, still another at an inland city known for its health spas, and a two-week stay at an expensive London hotel.

The Hartley Napiers, a family in Much Benham, friends of the Protheroes, with whom Lettice plays tennis on the day of the murder.

Dr. Roberts, a physician living at Much Benham, the neighboring market town. He is also the coroner.

Mr. Cherubim, the local chemist

Emily, Miss Marple's "tiny" maid

Dr. Haydock's Servant, a person of unspecified gender

Old Mrs. Archer, who does light housekeeping for Lawrence Redding. She is the mother of Archer, the young poacher recently released from jail who is Mary Hill's boyfriend

Clara, Mrs. Price Ridley's maid

Hilda, Mrs. Lestrange's maid

Reeves, the "perfect" butler at Old Hall, the Protheroe residence, who is sacked by the Colonel simply for allowing Mrs. Lestrange to enter the house

Manning, age about twenty-five, the chauffeur at Old Hall, who is very much intimidated by Inspector Slack

Rose, a parlourmaid at Old Hall, putty in the hands of handsome Lawrence Redding

Mrs. Simmons, the housekeeper at Old Hall

Gladdie, the kitchenmaid at Old Hall. She overhears a frightening conversation between Colonel Protheroe and Mrs. Lestrange and only reluctantly relates it to Lawrence Redding. She is terrified that it will come to the attention of the tyrannical Mrs. Pratt that she was taking an unauthorized leave to visit a boyfriend when she overheard the conversation through an open window.

Mrs. Pratt, the tyrannical cook at Old Hall.

Colonel Protheroe's valet, "...a thin, cadaverous looking man..."

Mrs. Sadler, Mr. Hawes's landlady

COMMENTS

In her *Autobiography,* Agatha Christie wrote that she had very unclear memories of her writings between 1929 and 1932. It was the period when she met and married her second husband, the archeologist Max Mallowan, and they were very happy times for her. She said that she could not remember where, when or how she wrote *Murder at the Vicarage,* although she felt that the Caroline Sheppard character from the 1926 *The Murder of Roger Ackroyd* may have inspired her in her creation of the Miss Marple character in 1930 for *Murder at the Vicarage.*

In any case, the Miss Marple character must not have been a favorite of Christie's at first, because although she did appear in a group of short stories published in 1933 as *The Tuesday Club Murders,* it was not until 1942 that Miss Marple again appeared in a novel. In the meantime, Hercule Poirot made fifteen more appearances in novels and many more in short stories, apparently without protests from Christie fans.

One of the things that make Agatha Christie enjoyable to many readers is her humor. Unfortunately, *Murder at the Vicarage* is quite a humorless book. The murder victim, a detestable person, fortunately dies early but the other characters are nearly as unpleasant as he is, each in his or her own way. The narrator, Leonard Clement, is a compassionate, Christian person but not very interesting otherwise. The issue of his young wife's being an incompetent household manager dealing with an insolent, incompetent housemaid is a rather silly, trivial subject, only mildly amusing and actually more tiresome than amusing. There are no "sparkling," memorable characters, not even the two youngsters, Lettice Protheroe and the vicar's nephew Dennis. Dennis, in particular, could have been developed into a "fun" character, perhaps a kind of "sidekick" to Miss Marple, which might have produced some amusing incidents and conversations with the old lady. As it is, both Dennis and Lettice just sort of "hang around," being there for no very good reason, and so does Griselda, the vicar's young wife, who also could have had a more active role. As a matter of fact, the Griselda character—an outspoken, unpredictable embarrassment to a relatively staid, older husband-clergyman—might have been made into an amusing sleuth herself in a separate book or even a series.

The army of serpent-tongued spinsters may be rather disgusting to some readers. The constant negative generalizations of the police officer, Colonel Melchett, about "women" and the rude behaviors of Inspector Slack are also unpleasant. The character of Mr. Hawes, the curate, is a curious mixture of physical illness and emotional illness; he's a pathetic figure. There is not one really attractive or interesting character in this book, possibly because, as Christie points out herself, having reread the book in later years, there are simply too many characters for any of them to be developed in a very interesting way.

Despite all of this, the Miss Marple character is unique and well developed as she presents the vicar with an explanation of her interest in solving the crime. She tells him that her hobby has always been Human Nature and that she has formed the habit of classifying people just as one would classify birds or flowers into group so and so, genus this, and species that. Thus equipped, she has conducted small experiments in order to solve minor mysteries, and she has always wondered if some day a really big mystery could be solved in the same way. In *Murder at the Vicarage* she answers that question in the affirmative.

Murder at Hazelmoor (1931)

(Alternate title: *The Sittaford Mystery*)

SETTING

Apart from one or two brief scenes at flats in London and Wimbledon, the entire story takes place in the county of Devon, mostly at a fictitious town called Exhampton and a tiny fictitious village called Sittaford on the edge of the large area of moorland called Dartmoor. There are a couple of scenes in a private home called The Laurels in the city of Exeter. The Laurels is described as having a sagging front gate and a drawing room badly needing attention but having a certain charm. It is a run-down house of moderate size.

Exhampton is a much smaller place about one-half hour by train from Exeter. It is a market town with at least one small inn, The Three Crowns. Since the action takes place in December there are only three or four people staying at the inn; presumably there are more during the warm season. Close to the inn is a police station, the home of the local doctor, and Hazelmoor, the house where the crime is committed.

Six miles from Exhampton is the tiny, isolated village of Sittaford, formerly consisting only of three dilapidated old cottages, a forge or "smithy," and a combination post-office/sweet shop. Ten years ago a vast granite house called Sittaford House was built close to the village by a rather eccentric wealthy man upon his retirement, along with six small, identical granite bungalows which he built as an investment. The occupant of one of the dilapidated old cottages owns an old Ford car which he rents, at a very high rate, to anyone in the village needing to go to Exhampton. It is the only car in the village.

The huge Sittaford House is not described in great detail but it is known that it has at least eight bedrooms. It has its own electricity generating plant but how this operates is not specified. Electric lighting in the large house is mentioned and it is possible that the six new bungalows receive electric service from the large house, but nothing is specified about that.

An unusually severe snowfall, resulting in drifts eight to ten feet deep in the area of Sittaford, prevents travel between there and Exhampton for three days, and news of the crime, which occurs in Exhampton, does not reach Sittaford until mail and newspapers can finally be taken there by car. Therefore we can assume that there are no telephones or radios in Sittaford by which the villagers would have received the news earlier.

In Exhampton the crime takes place in a moderately-sized house called Hazelmoor, which has three bedrooms and a bathroom on the "first floor" (in American terminology, the "second floor.") There is some confusion as to the names of the rooms on the ground floor. The murder victim is discovered in a room that is at first called the "study," but later that room is referred to as the "drawing room" and still later, as the "sitting room." It is possible that Christie wrote this book without her usual care and that she forgot what she had named the room in the earlier chapter. Unfortunately, one of the characters gestures towards "the drawing room" to indicate to another character where the crime took place. A careful reader might deduce from this that he had private knowledge that the crime took place in the "drawing room" and then the body was moved to the "study." But in fact it is the same room that is referred to. The house also has a dining room and a large storage closet off the dining room.

The story takes place in one week—from December 14 to December 21 in 1929 or 1930. There are no historical backgrounds of importance other than the usual references to "The War," (meaning World War I) by certain characters. One of the older men, for example, makes demeaning remarks about younger men who have had "an easy life" because they were not old enough to fight in "The War."

Regarding "the moors," England has at least two areas of picturesque wilderness known as "the moors" or "the moorlands." The largest is in the county of Yorkshire in the north; it is the area in which the novelists Emily and Charlotte Brontë grew up and is the setting for the famous novel *Wuthering Heights*. The Yorkshire moors are a desolate wilderness that is practically uninhabited. Evidently the soil will not sustain any kind of agriculture and there are practically no trees and only certain forms of vegetation, notably the purple-flowered plant heather, which thrives there. The area has a kind of wild beauty when the heather is in bloom.

Much smaller than the moors of Yorkshire are the moors of Devon in southwestern England; there are Exmoor in north Devon and Dartmoor in the south; Dartmoor is the larger of the two. The area has always been popular with travelers because of its wild, desolate kind of beauty and its desolateness has caused it to be a romantic setting for poems and stories such as Conan Doyle's frightening *The Hound of the Baskervilles* and others. The infamous Dartmoor Prison was established there because of the uninhabited surroundings.

In this novel a few real towns of the area, in addition to the large city of Exeter, are mentioned: the small towns of Moretonhampstead, Chagford, Dulverton and one or two others.

STORY

Captain Trevelyan is a wealthy, retired naval officer who, having inherited a large fortune, built Sittaford House, a huge granite residence in the tiny, remote village of Sittaford on the edge of Dartmoor, about ten years ago. Currently two ladies from Australia are renting Sittaford House and the Captain is renting a small house in Exhampton, which is six miles distant, for the duration of the ladies' tenancy.

At the tiny village of Sittaford, in addition to the large modern home, are several old, dilapidated cottages and six identical modern bungalows, which the Captain had built on speculation. All six of the bungalows are occupied, one of the occupants being the Captain's very good friend, Major Burnaby, with whom he has always shared enthusiasm for such athletic pursuits as mountain climbing and skiing. They are in the habit of spending two evenings a week together playing chess, on Tuesday evenings at the home of Major Burnaby and on Fridays at the home of the Captain. The fact that the Captain has moved temporarily to a home six miles away does not prevent the two friends from visiting each other twice a week, despite the fact that neither man owns an automobile, as both regard a six-mile walk as a healthful pleasure.

On a snowy Friday afternoon Major Burnaby, because of the weather, decides not to make his usual Friday visit to his friend, and instead he joins a few other villagers and the two ladies at Sittaford House for tea and conversation. One of the ladies suggests "table turning" as an amusement. For a while it is an amusing game with the usual "messages from the spirit world" but then the table spells the words "Trevelyan," "dead," and "murdered."

Everyone is shocked and angered, and accusations and denials go all around. The Major is very upset and, despite the urgings of his friends not to go out on this snowy evening, he resolves to walk the six miles to Exhampton to make sure that his friend is safe. There are no telephones in Sittaford, and so Major Burnaby walks the six miles to Exhampton, finding his friend dead, apparently killed by a burglar who was discovered in the act of stealing.

A London nephew of Captain Trevelyan is suspected of murder and is arrested, but his fiancée, Emily Trefusis, is convinced of his innocence. Working together with a young newspaper reporter, Charles Enderby, she assists the police in solving the mystery.

CHARACTERS

Captain Joseph Trevelyan, R.N., age about sixty, the owner of a huge granite mansion called "Sittaford House" which he built, upon retirement, near the tiny remote village of Sittaford. He is a retired naval man and an old friend of Major Burnaby. Both are allegedly "woman haters," although one or two characters remark that many older men appear to be "woman haters" but are simply shy, perhaps because of a bad experience with a girl during their youth. Both the Captain and the Major are reclusive. They have a shared enthusiasm for all athletics, and have often traveled together to Switzerland for mountain climbing and skiing. Although they are now much older, both are very fit for their ages.

Despite being wealthy, the Captain has a reputation for stinginess. His sister Jennifer had asked him for a loan, several years ago, in order to pay for a special medical treatment for her husband who had lost the use of his limbs during the War, but the Captain refused. Since then, he and his sister have rarely spoken to each other. The Captain is also on bad terms with his niece Sylvia Dering, whose husband he once insulted, but in spite of this, in his Will he generously divided his inheritance among all of his living relatives.

Miss Larpent, a middle aged lady who is the owner of Hazelmoor, a small house in Exhampton which Captain Trevelyan is renting temporarily while his own house is being let to others.

Robert Henry Evans, another retired naval man, and Captain Trevelyan's manservant. He married one month ago, to the annoyance of Captain Trevelyan who did not wish to have any female living in his house. Now, Mr. Evans and his new wife must live in a home of their own, though he continues to serve the Captain by going to his house each day for a few hours.

Rebecca Evans, the wife of Robert Evans and the daughter of Mrs. Bellings, who owns the Three Crowns Inn in Exhampton. She is a buxom young woman with dark hair and red cheeks. Fearing that her husband may be suspected of the murder, she states, "Cruel stupid the police are. Don't mind who they take up as long as they get hold of someone."

Major John Burnaby, age about sixty-two, who lives in Bungalow #1 at Sittaford. He has always been very athletic, practicing such sports as mountain climbing and winter sports with his old friend, Captain Trevelyan, with whom he often traveled to Switzerland. He is described by a neighbor as a typical retired army officer, narrow-minded and limited in outlook, and credulous in money matters.

Mrs. Willett who, with her daughter Violet, is currently renting Sittaford House for the winter. They claim to be from South Africa but one character notes that they use Australian expressions in their speech, so there is doubt about their past. Mrs. Willett has a powerful personality and a very hospitable nature, which is mildly annoying to the locals, who describe her as being "too hospitable" in the manner of "colonials."

Violet Willett, daughter of Mrs. Willett, age about twenty, described by one of the older males as pretty but scraggy, as he prefers women to have curves and notes with pleasure that, according to the papers, "curves are coming back. About time!"

Captain Wyatt, retired from military service in India, who lives in Bungalow #2. He is extremely surly and inhospitable, resenting visitors. He keeps his bungalow extremely warm because he is accustomed to the heat of India, and also for the benefit of his native servant. According to his neighbor, Miss Percehouse, "He smokes opium, and he's easily the worst-tempered man in England."

Abdul, the native Indian servant of Captain Wyatt. "Yes, sahib," is all he knows how to say in English, and all he needs to know.

Mr. Rycroft, a very old man who is enthusiastic about criminology, ornithology, and psychic phenomena. He lives in Bungalow #3, which is filled mostly with books.

Miss Caroline Percehouse, an elderly, invalid spinster who lives in Bungalow #4. She is very sharp-witted and very interested in her neighbors. In fact, she is very nosy and some of her neighbors resent her for that. She bullies her subservient nephew, Ronald, saying that she would feel more respect for him if he "stood up to her a little." She came to this remote spot "to die" because of her invalid state, but the pure air of this country place has caused her health to rebound and she feels very healthy despite being confined indoors.

Ronald Garfield, Miss Percehouse's nephew who is living with her temporarily. He tolerates his aunt's bullying because he hopes to inherit her fortune upon her death. According to Mr. Rycroft, he is "stony broke." He is a young man with "boyish" looks.

Mrs. Amelia Curtis, who lives in Bungalow #5 with her husband. According to one character, talking is "almost a disease" with Mrs. Curtis. She is an excellent source of all information about Sittaford. Another character observes that her talking is like water flowing from a hydrant and that all you need to do, if you are interested in hearing about another subject, is to change the subject and the direction of the "water" automatically changes with no interruption in the flow. She is a pathological blabber-mouth, worse than a mother-in-law, but extremely useful to the information-seeking Emily Trefusis and Charles Enderby.

Mr. Curtis, Mrs. Curtis's husband, who rarely speaks, since he rarely has a chance to speak. "Ah," he comments now and then, shifting his pipe from one corner of his mouth to the other. On one occasion he does speak (when Mrs. Curtis leaves the room briefly to get the tea things) and observes, "Women talk a lot."

Mr. Duke, a middle-aged man whose past life is not known. The most recent arrival to the village, he lives in #6 of the six small bungalows. The other residents of Sittaford are curious about his past but he does not reveal any facts to them. He appears to be interested primarily in gardening and is friendly but "close."

Mary Hibbert, the occupant of the post office and sweet shop in Sittaford. She has six children and a sister-in-law living with her.

Elmer, the occupant of one of the dilapidated cottages in Sittaford. He owns the only automobile in Sittaford and rents it, at a high rate, to anyone in Sittaford who needs to go to Exhampton.

Mr. and Mrs. Pound, the blacksmith and his wife, who live at the forge in Sittaford. They are expecting their eighth child.

Mrs. Bellings, the middle-aged owner of the Three Crowns Inn in Exhampton. She is the mother of Rebecca Evans, the young bride of Robert Evans.

Mary Pearson, the deceased sister of Captain Joseph Trevelyan

Jennifer Gardner, a middle-aged sister of Captain Trevelyan. She lives in poverty with her invalid husband in Exeter. She feels no sorrow upon learning of her brother's death, because in the past her brother refused her a loan that would have made a special medical treatment possible for her husband. She receives 20,000 pounds by the Captain's Will, however.

Robert Gardner, the invalid husband of Jennifer. He lost the use of his limbs during the War, evidently because of "shell shock." There is hope that he may recover and his wife plans to use her inheritance for medical treatment. He is a big, blue-eyed, fair-haired man. He is also a bitter, negative old man who, according to Emily Trefusis, "would take a malicious joy in giving you sharp digs in painful places."

Beatrice the "slatternly" housemaid at The Laurels who has the typical "Christie housemaid" ghoulish curiosity about the details of the crime.

Nurse Davis, Robert Gardner's live-in nurse.

James Pearson, a young nephew of Captain Trevelyan. He lives in London but was in Exhampton on the evening of the murder, returning to London by the first morning train. He is strongly suspected, arrested and held. He is Emily

Trefusis's fiancé. According to Emily, he's weak, he's an idiot, but he's *not* a murderer because he "hasn't got the guts."

Sylvia Dering, niece of Captain Trevelyan. She lives in Wimbledon with her writer husband and feels no more grief about the Captain's death than Jennifer Gardner does, saying that the Captain had insulted her husband at their last meeting.

Martin Dering, Sylvia's husband. His alibi for the evening of the murder is easily broken by Inspector Narracott, thanks to a tip from Charles Enderby. A moderately successful novelist, he is of middle height with thick, heavy chestnut hair. He is good-looking in a somewhat heavy fashion, with lips that are rather full and red. Emily Trefusis describes him as "...what I call a nasty sort of brute ... good-looking in a bold sort of way. Women talk about sex with him in corners. Real men hate him."

Brian Pearson, a young nephew of Captain Trevelyan, due to inherit 20,000 pounds upon his uncle's death. For several years he has lived in Australia and he is thought to be there now, although he is not. He has in fact been in England for two months without informing his sister Sylvia or his brother James.

Constable Graves of Exhampton. Together with Dr. Warren and Major Burnaby, he discovers the body of Captain Trevelyan.

Dr. Warren of Exhampton, who determines the time and cause of Captain Trevelyan's death.

Inspector Narracott from the Exeter police, a thoroughgoing, methodical man. He welcomes the assistance of Emily Trefusis and Charles Enderby and the three of them solve the mystery together.

Superintendent Maxwell, Inspector Narracott's superior

Sergeant Pollack of the Exhampton Police, Constable Graves's superior

Mr. Morseby and Mr. Jones, Commercial travelers staying at The Three Crowns

Mr. Kirkwood of Exhampton, Captain Trevelyan's solicitor

A Young Man at Messrs Williamson, house agents at Exhampton. It was he who received an appeal from Mrs. Willett seeking to rent a large home on the edge of Dartmoor and who arranged for her to meet Captain Trevelyan.

Emily Trefusis, who works as a model at a chic clothing establishment in London and who knows how to handle men in a male dominated work world. She is intelligent, assertive and determined. Her fiancé is weak and, in her words, "an idiot but not a murderer." She sets out to find the murderer, using all of her talents to gather the needed information. One of her tricks is to approach someone with "You won't tell anyone, will you..." and to approach others, especially men, with "It's so wonderful to find someone I feel I can really rely on...." A handy trick, she finds, is to leave a glove behind, in order to have an excuse to return soon after (hopefully unobserved.)

She is the heroine of the piece and the final chapter of the novel is entitled "Emily Explains," for it is she who goes to the trouble to thoroughly examine the murder scene after the police have concluded their own examination, finding a major clue that leads her to the solution of the mystery.

Mr. Dacres, Emily Trefusis's lawyer who is defending James Pearson

Charles Enderby, a reporter for *The Daily Wire* who, together with Emily (and actually, under her direction, although he doesn't realize it) helps gather information to solve the mystery. Emily has him firmly under her control with her reminders of "how nice it is to have someone that one can *rely* on."

A Housemaid at The Three Crowns, a sister of Constable Graves's wife. She helps keep Emily informed of facts in Exhampton, through Mrs. Bellings, the owner of the inn, while Emily is at Sittaford.

Tom, another employee of The Three Crowns

Fred, a boyfriend of the above housemaid

Amos Parker, a grocery tradesman in Exhampton

Numerous Unnamed Servants of the Willets' at Sittaford House

"Freemantle Freddie," a convict who escapes from Princetown Prison a few days after the murder

Edgar Rosenkraun, Martin Dering's American publisher who confirms his alibi (at Martin's request,) then later denies it when informed by Inspector Narracott that a murder case is being investigated. Mr. Rosenkraun had assumed it was just one of those cases of, well, you know, a woman.

Comments

Although *Murder at Hazelmoor* is not one of Christie's better-known detective novels, it would be a "good first Christie experience" since it presents a large cast of interesting and varied, sometimes very amusing characters ranging from the vigorous and youthful Emily Trefusis and Charles Enderby through middle-aged and older people, each one with a distinct personality whose conversation is consistent with that personality.

Some writers have suggested that the murder motive in this novel is an unacceptably weak one. Amounts of money mentioned in the early Christie novels, however, should be considered within the context of the value of the pound during that remote period. In this novel we must remember that the year is probably 1930. One of the characters in the novel rents a two-story, three-bedroom house at the rate of two guineas (two pounds and two shillings) per week. Therefore all money amounts mentioned in the novel should be considered in those terms of value.

Murder at Hazelmoor shows Agatha Christie to have reached her highest level of skill in character portrayals to date. Among the most interesting and amusing characters are Emily Trefusis, Caroline Percehouse, Old Captain Wyatt, the unforgettable Mrs. Amelia Curtis, and the reporter Charles Enderby.

Emily Trefusis is a strong willed, assertive, intelligent young woman who understands men and knows how to motivate them. With consummate success she declares, on several occasions to several different men, "It's so wonderful to find someone I can really rely on..." She does not hesitate to use an occasional small, inconsequential fib to further her goals but generally "comes straight to the point" and uses frankness, knowing that honesty is generally the best policy. In a way some people might describe her as "manipulative," but a more charitable way to express it would be to say that she has tact and skill in handling people. She is never offensive.

Emily is in love with James Pearson and fully admits that he is a man of considerable weakness but *not* of a criminal nature. A memorable quotation of hers is her comment about her fiancé's brother-in-law, Martin Dering, a moderately successful writer. "Women talk about sex with him in corners. Real men hate him."

Emily handles women very well also. Realizing that Mrs. Curtis, with whom she stays at the village of Sittaford, is an inveterate talker, she invites as much talk as Mrs. Curtis is willing and able to produce and is amply rewarded with information. She charms old Miss Percehouse, who declares, "I hate a slobbering female. I like one who gets up and does things." Miss Percehouse achieves an entrée for Emily at Sittaford house by finding out from her nephew that a coffee cake was served there a few days ago and writing a note to the Willetts asking for "the recipe for your delicious coffee cake" and giving the note to Emily to deliver.

Old Miss Percehouse is an interesting character in her own right. Having come to remote Sittaford "to die," she has revived, largely because of the fresh, clean air of this moorland region and is vitally interested in her surroundings. She bullies her nephew Ronald, although she is genuinely fond of him, and confides to Emily that she would like him much better if he would stand up to her a little. She knows that his main reason for coddling her is his concern about inheriting her money and she wishes it were not so, but that does not prevent her from being fond of him.

Old Captain Wyatt, who has spent many years in India and now lives in a bungalow in Sittaford with his Indian servant, overheating the bungalow because of his—and the servant's—being accustomed to a warmer climate, is described by Miss Percehouse in these terms: "He smokes opium, I believe. And he's easily the worst-tempered man in England." When we meet Captain Wyatt we find that this is probably true. Even sour-tempered old Major Burnaby finds Captain Wyatt to be obnoxious and insulting. Interestingly, Captain Wyatt recognizes his fault and, in his way, apologizes for it. He is a stereotypical "ex-military" type who sees no reason for young girls to prefer handsome young men.

Mrs. Curtis and her husband are hilarious together, he emitting only an occasional "Ah!" and she talking incessantly on any subject her listener will encourage. First Emily and Charles together, and later Charles alone, are regaled by Mrs. Curtis's endless flow of information:

> To familiarize himself with life as lived in Sittaford village he had only to turn on Mrs. Curtis much as you would turn on the tap of a hydrant. Listening slightly dazed to a stream of anecdote, reminiscence, rumours, surmise and meticulous detail he endeavored valiantly to sift the grain from the chaff. He then mentioned another name and immediately the force of the water was directed in that direction. He heard all about Captain Wyatt, his tropical temper, his rudeness, his quarrels with his neighbours, his occasional amazing graciousness, usually to personable young women. The life he led his Indian servant, the peculiar times he had his meals and the exact diet that composed them. He heard about Mr. Rycroft's library, his hair tonics, his insistence on strict tidiness and punctuality, his inordinate curiosity over other people's doings, his recent selling of a few old prized personal possessions, his inexplicable fondness for birds, and the prevalent idea that Mrs. Willett was setting her cap at him. He heard about Miss Percehouse and her tongue and the way she bullied her nephew, and of the rumours of the gay life that same nephew led in London. He heard all over again of Major Burnaby's friendship with Captain Trevelyan, their reminiscences of the past and their fondness for chess.

He heard everything that was known about the Willetts, including the belief that Miss Violet Willett was leading on Mr. Ronnie Garfield and that she didn't really mean to have him. It was hinted that she made mysterious excursions to the moor and that she had been seen walking there with a young man. And it was doubtless for that reason, so Mrs. Curtis had surmised, that they had come to this desolate spot. Her mother had taken her right away, "to get right over it like." But there—"girls can be far more artful than ladies ever dream of." About Mr. Duke, there was curiously little to hear. He had been there only a short time and his activities seemed to be solely horticultural.

It was half past three, and, with his head spinning from the effects of Mrs. Curtis's conversation, Mr. Enderby went out for a stroll.

In the words of Mrs. Willett, "It's almost a disease the way that woman talks." Major Burnaby refers to Mrs. Curtis as a "chattering magpie."

Note: The above remark about "rumours about the *gay* life he led in London" (in Mrs. Curtis's reference to Miss Percehouse's nephew Ronald Garfield) should be understood within the context of that word's meaning in 1930. There is no suggestion of homosexuality. "Rumours of a gay life" are simply "rumours about a lot of partying, probably a good deal of drinking, and possibly drug use." The word "gay" did not acquire its homosexual connotation until several decades later, at least in mainstream speech.

Charles Enderby, the reporter from *The Daily Wire* has "people skills" equal to those of Emily Trefusis. Seeing a good "scoop" for his paper in his contact with Major Burnaby, he correctly reasons that he will be able to ingratiate himself with Major Burnaby by expressing a strong interest in the Major's past military exploits, a plan that succeeds admirably.

As always in Christie novels, we have the usual assortment of housemaids who are generally presented as half-witted creatures likely to take a perverse pleasure in the crimes. Inspector Narracott visits the Gardners in Exeter, speaking first with their maid, Beatrice, whose eyes express a mixture of horror and intense enjoyment as she asks "Did they bash his head in or shoot him or what?" Later, Inspector Narracott speaks with Mrs. Gardner, and this higher-class lady asks him to "spare her the revolting details."

Inspector Narracott of the Exeter Police deserves at least a passing comment. Unlike the police officers of some other Christie novels, such as two officers in *Murder at the Vicarage*, Inspector Slack who refuses to listen to the vicar's explanation about the clock being set in advance one quarter hour, and Colonel Melchett who generalizes about women and refers to old ladies as "old cats" and "old pussies," Inspector Narracott does not bully people. He listens to them and gives consideration to what they have said. He is very much liked by his subordinates. Knowing that Emily Trefusis and Charles Enderby are doing their best to uncover facts surrounding the crime, he feels respect for them and values their efforts.

In Christie's preceding novel, *Murder at the Vicarage,* the characters were for the most part rather unpleasant and the book lacked Christie's usual humor. In *Murder at Hazelmoor* there are a couple of aged persons who are cantankerous and crotchety, but generally they are very amusing in their eccentricities, and for the most part the characters in this novel are much more appealing people. This novel is a pleasure to read and reread, although it is one whose solution, like that of *The Murder of Roger Ackroyd*, can never be forgotten.

There are a couple of "loose ends" in this story that Christie may have thrown in as false clues. While in a café in Exeter, Emily Trefusis notices one of the characters not previously associated with Exeter having tea at another table with another character who lives there. Previously it had not been known that these two people knew each other. The reader expects this to be explained but it never is. Then in a later chapter, one character mentions expecting a visit from another of the characters, describing her as his niece. We wait for something to come of this but nothing ever does.

Murder at Hazelmoor is one novel of which Christie makes no mention at all in her *Autobiography*. She does say that she has poor memories of her work between 1929 and 1932, and cannot remember how or where or why or exactly when she wrote *Murder at the Vicarage,* which preceded this one, or *Peril at End House* which followed it. She does state in her *Autobiography* that by this period, writing was becoming very easy for her and that she often wrote her stories "just for money." If her house needed something like a new roof, she would find out how much it would cost, and she would calculate how much a group of short stories or a novel would bring, and then set about writing them.

One final note: As stated in the *Introduction,* in 1926 Christie's first husband announced to her that he wanted a divorce in order to marry another woman. Christie took this very hard and tried unsuccessfully to dissuade him. Before the divorce actually took place, she disappeared one day and her car was found in a lonely spot. There was some story of "amnesia" and there were stories of a "nervous breakdown." The Press made the most of these sensational happenings, publishing a photograph of Christie, altering it to suggest various imaginable disguises and at least one newspaper suggested that Christie had planned the disappearance as a publicity stunt to promote her latest book. The incident was extremely distasteful to Christie in later years and she does not mention it in her *Autobiography*. One lasting result of the incident, however, was that she thoroughly detested reporters and the press in general for the rest of her life.

Even as early as the writing of *The Man in the Brown Suit*, the subject of newspapers and reporters was not a pleasant one to Agatha Christie, judging from her portrayal of the newspaper that distorted Professor Beddingfeld's theories on the natural history of the human race, and the tone of the newspaper office that Anne Beddingfeld later visits. In *Murder at the Vicarage*, after the inquest the vicar notices "a small army of young men with bright, alert faces, and a kind of superficial resemblance to each other.... Several of them were already known to me by sight, as having haunted the Vicarage the last few days..."

In *Murder at Hazelmoor* the reporter Charles Enderby, for all his supposed sincerity in wishing to help Emily to track down the real criminal, is largely motivated by bringing fame to himself in the form of a "good story" and he does not hesitate to send numerous packs of lies to the paper to be published as "truth," such as his invented "interviews with the prisoner's girlfriend" and "interviews with the murdered man's best friend."

The Press and reporters will receive equally poor treatment in *all* of Christie's future novels. Notable examples are the inquest scene in the 1935 *Death in the Air*, the personality of newspaper owner Gordon Easterfield in the 1939 *Easy to Kill*, and especially the obnoxious personality of reporter Pamela Horsefall in the 1952 *Mrs. McGinty's Dead*, who waves cigarettes while speaking, laughs loudly in a way that suggests the neighing of a horse, sits astride chairs, and says to Hercule Poirot, "My dear man! No point in accuracy!"

Peril at End House (1932)

SETTING

This story takes place at the fictitious pleasant resort town of St. Loo on the south coast of Cornwall at a resort hotel, The Majestic, and at a large private home not far from the hotel.

The historical background events include the general public's interest in new achievements in aviation. Charles Lindbergh had been the first pilot to fly across the Atlantic Ocean (in 1927) and other daring aviators were attempting still greater feats. Amelia Earhart had been active since the early 1920s, and in the novel a reference is made to "a woman pilot's achievements," presumably hers. Attempts were being made to circumnavigate the globe by airplane and in the novel that is the goal of Michael Seton.

A social development of the 1920s and early 1930s was the widespread use of drugs among the young people of the upper classes. There was an allusion to this in *The Murder of Roger Ackroyd* when a housekeeper asked about it in a conversation with Dr. Sheppard. Later Hercule Poirot found a goose quill in the summer house at Fernly Park, explaining that in America the goose quill is used by cocaine users in order to inhale the drug. In *Peril at End House* several of the main characters are cocaine users, one is discovered to be a cocaine dealer, and the spouse of one of the characters is a hopeless cocaine addict. For further discussion of this subject in this novel, please see the *Comments* section.

One of the settings, End House, is a very old private home which has been in the family of Magdala Buckley for generations. The house and grounds are extremely run down and the drawing room furniture is described as a mixture of solid Victorian and ultra-modern cheap, littered with "gramophone" records and containing a "gramophone" (record player) and a "wireless" (a radio.) Cocktails, including the dry martini, are fashionable drinks.

There is a reference to "the Talkies," an early term for motion pictures with sound. Sound films were introduced in approximately 1927 and were standard by about 1929, at least in America. When Poirot pays a visit to Nick Buckley, she notes his solemnity and asks derisively if he is a movie producer looking for a new heroine for "the Talkies."

There is no mention of the political situation of the time and no reference to World War One or its aftermath. The story takes place in the summer of approximately 1930 or 1931.

A point of passing interest is that the town of St. Loo occurs in a later Christie novel, the 1941 *Evil Under the Sun*, and so does the character Colonel Weston, the chief constable. In the later novel St. Loo is described as being in Devon, not Cornwall. Christie must have forgotten having placed it in Cornwall in *Peril at End House*.

Story

It is summer of 1930 or 1931. Hercule Poirot and his old friend Captain Hastings are spending one week's holiday at a luxurious hotel in the pleasant resort town St. Loo, on the southern coast of Cornwall.

In the garden of the hotel one day, Poirot and Hastings meet a young local resident of St. Loo, Magdala Buckley, who is also known as "Nick." She mentions to them that she has had three near escapes from sudden death in the last few days, and while seated with Poirot and Hastings a bullet flies past her face and makes a hole in her wide brimmed hat. The following evening, during a fireworks display arranged for the hotel guests, someone shoots and kills Nick's young cousin Maggie, who is visiting from Yorkshire. Maggie had just put on a brightly colored cloak that Nick had discarded in favor of a warmer wrap. The murderer must have mistaken Maggie for Nick in the darkness because of the cloak.

Who has been trying to kill Nick Buckley and why? Poirot and Hastings answer this baffling question through very careful questioning of suspects and by using methodical reasoning. There are no clues other than statements made by characters in the story.

Characters

Hercule Poirot, the retired Belgian private investigator. He is staying at the Majestic Hotel at St. Loo for a week's holiday. He is a little man with an egg-shaped head, very black hair (almost too black to be natural), and an enormous moustache. He solves the mystery by searching for motives and listening carefully to what everyone tells him. He is a realist and has no illusions about people.

Poirot is enormously proud of his past achievements, considering himself to be the world's greatest detective.

Captain Hastings, Poirot's assistant and an old friend. He has been living in Argentina since about 1923. Now and then he returns to England for visits and, on those occasions, he "assists" Poirot in his cases. While Poirot is a realist with no illusions about people, Hastings is an incurable romantic who believes that a beautiful woman cannot be a murderess and any man who is "one of the good old boys" from an English public school—specifically from Eton or Harrow—cannot be a murderer, or any kind of criminal. He is repeatedly scandalized by Hercule Poirot's practice of peeping through keyholes, eavesdropping, and especially reading a woman's love letters, accusing Poirot of "not playing the game," to which Poirot always replies, "I am not playing a game, I am solving a murder."

Sir Matthew Seton, the second richest man in England, an eccentric who buys islands and establishes bird sanctuaries. He is a woman hater owing to a bad experience with a girl who jilted him in his youth and therefore he will not countenance his nephew Michael's marrying.

Michael Seton, nephew of Sir Matthew and the future heir of a vast fortune. He is a famous aviator, known to the public as "Mad Seton," and is currently attempting to fly around the world in a new aircraft named "The Albatross." His wealthy uncle has financed Michael's flying projects, as well as the design and construction of the new aircraft. Because of his uncle's eccentric attitude toward women (he considers women to be destructive to men) Michael does not dare to make public his engagement to Nick Buckley.

Magdala Buckley ("Nick"), a young woman who is the last survivor of her family, living in the run-down family home, End House in St. Loo. According to her closest friend, she is an incurable liar. Nick is a sophisticated young woman who surrounds herself with other "bright young people," using all the latest fad expressions in her speech ("just too marvellous, too thrilling") while expressing boredom about everything. She is practically penniless and finds it necessary to let the lodge of her property to a married couple in order to have money to pay a mortgage on the main house. She is secretly engaged to Michael Seton.

She is called "Nick" because she has always had qualities similar to those of her grandfather, who was familiarly known as "Old Nick." She adored him and they went everywhere together.

Commander George Challenger, an ex-naval man aged about forty who is in love with Magdala (Nick) and hopes to marry her. He is not aware of her engagement to Michael Seton, of course. Because of his "hearty good fellow" manner and his military past, Hastings rules him out at once as a suspect, but Poirot does not.

Mr. Albert Croft, the tenant at the lodge of End House, an Australian aged about sixty. He's about six feet tall, with a powerful frame and a weatherbeaten face, almost completely bald, with "eyes that were a vivid blue and twinkled, and a genial manner."

Mrs. Millie Croft, his invalid wife. The two of them have always wanted to see "the old country," and so here they are. They seem just a bit "too" Australian to be real, calling "Cooee" loudly to each other and showing photographs of Australia to all guests. According to Nick, they are "simply oppressively kind ... too terribly friendly for words."

Edith, a nurse attendant to Mrs. Croft.

Ellen Wilson, a housemaid at End House. She is middle-aged, intelligent and observant. Typical of "her class," she is suspicious of foreigners and, when Poirot and Hastings call on Nick, it is Hastings whom Ellen addresses rather than the "foreigner," Hercule Poirot.

William Wilson, the gardener at End house, Ellen's husband. According to Magdala Buckley, he is stupid and lazy and spends a good deal of time in the shed pretending that he is sharpening shears.

Alfred Wilson, the son of Mr. and Mrs. Wilson, aged about ten, who takes a gruesome interest in the crime, wishing that the victim had had her throat cut rather than just being shot, as he once saw pigs being killed, and liked it.

James Lazarus, a friend and a guest of Nick at End House. He is the owner of a Bond Street art gallery and is "simply rolling in money," according to Nick. He is in love with Fredericka Rice.

Fredericka Rice (Freddie), a friend of Nick's who is married but seeking a divorce from her cocaine-addicted husband. Hastings describes her as having "fair, almost colourless hair, parted in the middle and drawn straight down over her ears to a knot in the neck. Her face was dead white and emaciated—yet curiously attractive. Her eyes were very light grey with large pupils. She had a curious look of detachment."

According to Nick Buckley, Fredericka is "married to a beast of a man who drank and drugged and was altogether a queer of the worst description. She had to leave him a year or two ago."

Charles Vyse, family attorney to Nick Buckley and also one of her suitors. According to Nick, he is "quite good and worthy but very dull. He gives me good advice and tries to restrain my extravagant tastes."

Maggie Buckley, a cousin of Nick Buckley, who lives in Yorkshire with her parents but visits Nick in St. Loo about once a year. Nick describes her as "one of those painfully pure girls, with the kind of hair that has just become fashionable by accident."

The Rev. Giles Buckley and Mrs. Buckley from Yorkshire, parents of the murdered girl.

Dr. Graham, who is summoned when Maggie is murdered and who tries to calm Nick

Colonel Weston, the Chief Constable, who is summoned when Maggie is murdered

Mr. Whitfield, Michael Seton's and Sir Matthew Seton's solicitor

Inspector James Japp of Scotland Yard, an old friend of Hercule Poirot, not personally involved in the case but who gathers some information at Poirot's request and appears in the final chapters to assist him.

Dr. MacAllister, the physician in charge at the nursing home where Nick is sent to be safely guarded

A Matron, An Orderly and A Nurse at the nursing home

FRENCH INTO ENGLISH

Chapter 1

bagatelle—a trifle, something of no importance
là—là—là—et là—here, here, here and here
tendresse—warm feeling, romantic attraction
Pas encore. Ça m'amuse—Not yet. This is interesting (or "I'm having fun with this")
Jeunesse—Youth

Chapter 2

Ça y est!—So that's that!
Mais dis donc!—For Pete's sake! (Expression of impatience.)
Sacré tonnerre!—For God's sake! (Stronger than the above but similar)
Revenons à nos moutons.—Let's get back to the subject.

Chapter 3

bon—all right, then
hein?—isn't it?
évidement—incorrect spelling of *évidemment*—obviously
Qu'est-ce que vous dîtes?—What's that you're saying?
Au revoir—Good-bye

Chapter 4

Tiens! C'est intéressant, ça.—Hmm ... that's interesting.
gauche—awkward, inappropriate
c'est tout simple—that's quite easy
C'est gentille, ça!—That sure was nice. (He is speaking sarcastically. In fact it was *not* nice. The spelling is also incorrect. It should have been *C'est gentil, ça!*)
une petite comme ça—a young girl like that
Je me demande ça sans cesse. Qu'est-ce que c'est?—I keep asking myself that question. What is it?

Chapter 5

allumeuse—instigator (from the verb *allumer,* "to ignite," as in the case of a woman who

deliberately arouses sexual desire in men for the sake of amusement or some malicious intent rather than any personal romantic feeling of her own)
maladroit—clumsy, awkward
Ah, c'est malin.—Oh, that was naughty of you!
voilà ce qu'il nous faut!—that's what we need!

Chapter 6
Bon jour—Good morning (correct spelling: *Bonjour*)
mon enfant—dear
Pauvre enfant—Poor child, poor thing, etc.

Chapter 7
la toilette—clothes, dressing up
enrhumer—to catch a cold
fluxion de poitrine—chest cold, lower respiratory infection
Les feus d'Artifices—fireworks (correctly spelled *feux d'artifice*)
mais qu'est-ce que vous avez?—but what's wrong?

Chapter 8
mon enfant—dear

Chapter 9
Pour les autres, eh bien!—As to the others, well...
Parbleu—(expression of impatience with Hastings' not seeing for himself the facts)
Voilà—there

Chapter 10
à la bonheur—It's about time! (correctly spelled *à la bonne heure*)
Mais oui, mais oui!—Absolutely!
Enchanté!—Delighted to see you!
aimable—kind
quelle idée!—Such an idea!

Chapter 11
Ah! ce n'est pas raisonable!—That doesn't make much sense!

Chapter 12
Ah!—c'est bien plus difficile.—That's a lot more difficult.
Attendez.—Wait.
Ce que femme veut, Dieu veut. French proverb, "What woman wants, God wants," or perhaps better translated, "The will of woman becomes the will of God."
le bon Dieu—God
métier—specialty, special expertise
Mais oui, mais oui—Yes, of course, of course

Chapter 13
Non—c'est idiot!—No, that's absurd!
C'est bien, ça.—That's very satisfactory.
Écoutez—Listen
mon cher—similar to *mon ami*—"friend, pal"

Chapter 14
C'est assez—That's quite enough.
Il me semble—It seems to me
C'est curieux—It's strange
Très correct, ce bon M. Croft.—Mr. Croft was absolutely right.
Comment?—What?
Au revoir—Good bye
Comment?—What?
Cette petite—That silly little girl
Parbleu—(expression of impatience)
Et voilà!—So much for that!
Le déjeuner—lunch

Chapter 15
Ah! je le sais bien.—Oh, I'm quite aware of that.
Parbleu—(expression of annoyance or impatience)
en reculant—backwards
Entre nous—Just between you and me
Inutile!—Useless!

Chapter 16
Parfaitement—Excellent
Comment?—What's that you are saying?
Mon dieu, mon dieu—Oh My God!

Chapter 17
Ah! Cette petite!—Oh, that dumb little girl.
Ah, c'est inouï!—God, that was stupid!
Pauvre petite!—Poor little thing!
Sacré tonnerre—Oh my god!
Comment?—What?
Diable!—Damn!
C'est tout à fait bien.—That's perfect!
spirituel—clever, witty
bien entendu—of course

Chapter 18
Comment ça va, mon ami?—How are you feeling?
Du tout—Not at all!
Et vous?—How about yourself?
A la bonheur!—It's about time! (Correct spelling: *À la bonne heure.*)
Tiens,—Hmm...
Très bien. Je vous remercie.—Very good. Thanks very much.

Chapter 21
quelle idée—what an idea
écoutez—listen

Chapter 22

Sapristi—God Damn! (euphemism for Sacristi—Holy Christ)
C'est épatant!—It's astounding!

COMMENTS

If a new Christie reader were to ask for a list of ten "typical" Christie novels that would make a good "first Christie experience," *Peril at End House* could be on that list, and it would be Christie's earliest novel on the list. All of Christie's important characteristic elements are in it. The murder is a very simple one—that is, the murderer has a solid motive, the murder plan is simple, the murderer does not take reckless chances, and the mystery is baffling yet the solution is logical. The characters, while not as much "fun" as in some other books, are believable and their conversations are consistent with their personalities. Even though the book was written in the early 1930s there is nothing especially "dated" about anything in it. Christie must have made a special effort not to load this book with too many characters, realizing that in a few of her earlier books there were too many characters, in particular *Murder at the Vicarage*.

In *The Murder of Roger Ackroyd*, published in 1926, Christie introduced the subject of drug addiction and the "recreational" use of drugs among the "upper classes" during a conversation between Dr. Sheppard and Miss Russell, the housekeeper at Fernly Park. Poirot later comments on the use of cocaine in America and on the American custom of using a goose quill to inhale it. In *The Mystery of the Blue Train*, when Ruth Kettering expresses a reluctance to seek a divorce from her husband, her father says, "You say that word, Ruth, as though you'd never heard it before. And yet your friends are doing it all round you every day."

Both drug use and divorce were becoming commonplace during the 1920s in America and in England as well. In *Peril at End House* those subjects occur as major factors for the first time in a Christie novel. The husband of Fredericka Rice is a hopeless drug addict and she, a cocaine user herself, is desperate to be rid of him. The main characters in the book, in fact, are a group of young people who, unlike the cheerful, energetic, adventure-seeking youngsters of earlier novels—Bundle Brent, Bill Eversleigh, Tommy and Tuppence, Anthony Cade and Virginia Revel—are generally depressed, world-weary and pessimistic. The main character, Nick Buckley, mechanically tosses around currently popular phrases such as "isn't it just too, too marvellous" without enthusiasm in a way that suggests a vague kind of preoccupation or unrest, and so do her friends Freddie Rice and Jim Lazarus. Hastings finds these young people unpleasant. He likes Nick's friend George Challenger much more, as he is one of the "good old boys," an ex-navy man, etc. (and considerably older—he's forty.) Hastings will have an unpleasant surprise about George Challenger before the story ends, however.

Despite the rather unpleasant personalities of the principal characters, the book must have been very much welcomed by Christie readers who had been deprived of Hercule Poirot since *The Mystery of the Blue Train* and of Hastings since *The Big Four*. Poirot's comical egotism is beautifully expressed right on the first page when Poirot says of his retirement,

> "This passive life suits me admirably, my friend. To sit in the sun—what could be more charming? To step from your pedestal at the zenith of your fame—what could be a grander gesture? They say of me—'That is Hercule Poirot!—The great—the unique!—There was never anyone like him, there never will be!' Eh bien—I am satisfied. I ask no more. I am modest."

Poirot is in rare form in this novel and so is Hastings. They spar constantly. Poirot wishes Hastings would part his hair in the middle instead of on one side in order to respect the laws of symmetry; Hastings is scandalized by Poirot's cheerful use of lies—so terribly un-English (or so he thinks)—to achieve greater purposes. He is shown to be incredibly stupid on the subject of whole-heartedly trusting any Englishman who has the "good-old-boy, old school" manner, and of course Poirot has to remind him constantly that beautiful women are not necessarily above suspicion. Their best scene is in the bedroom of Nick Buckley, when Poirot rifles through her underwear drawer with Hastings reddening and saying things like "Really, Poirot!" And when Poirot finds Nick's love letters, that's the limit, as far as Hastings is concerned.

> He [Poirot] held up a packet of letters tied with a faded pink ribbon.
> "The love letters of M. Michael Seton, if I mistake not."
> Quite calmly, he untied the ribbon and began to open out the letters.
> "Poirot," I cried scandalized. "You really can't do that. It isn't playing the game."
> "I am not playing a game, *mon ami*." His voice rang out suddenly harsh and stern. "I am hunting down a murderer."
> "Yes, but private letters—"

As usual, there are the Christie-world servants: the lazy gardener and his ghoulish son who once saw pigs being killed and "liked it," but the child's housemaid mother is a person of normal intelligence, although, being a person of "that class" she naturally distrusts foreigners and looks upon Poirot with distaste when he arrives to visit Nick Buckley. And we have another taste of the British view of "colonials" being "too friendly" or "too familiar." In *Murder at Hazelmoor* it was the overly hospitable South African Willets and in *Peril at End House* it is the overly hospitable Australian Crofts who, in turn, describe the British as "stuck up."

In this novel Poirot and Hastings have much more of a partnership in the solving of the mystery than in their earlier adventures. It is true that nearly all of the reasoning that leads to the solution is Poirot's and not Hastings's, and that Hastings's judgments are, as usual, proven to be foolish ones, but in this novel Poirot shares most of his ideas with Hastings. In the three earlier Poirot/Hastings novels—and especially in *The Big Four*—Poirot is generally secretive and Hastings complains bitterly and justifiably that Poirot "never tells him anything." In *Peril at End House* Hastings cannot complain of that, nor can we, the readers, say that we did not have all of the information needed to solve the mystery ourselves.

Thirteen at Dinner (1933)

(Alternate Title: *Lord Edgware Dies*)

SETTING

It is summer of 1931 or 1932. Nearly all of the action takes place in London but there are two scenes at the home of a wealthy family in Chiswick, a suburb just west of London in the county of Middlesex.

The London settings include private homes in the upper-class districts of Kensington, Regent Gate, Grosvenor Square and perhaps others, plus rooms and restaurants at fine hotels, the Savoy and the Piccadilly Palace in particular. There are also scenes at an exclusive ladies' millinery shop off Bond Street, at a small restaurant in Dover Street, at a little bistrot in Soho and at the private residence of Hercule Poirot. This residence is not described, but we know that it is *not* Whitehaven Mansions because Poirot will not move to that apartment building until 1935, when it will be mentioned and described for the first time at the beginning of the *The A.B.C. Murders*.

The luxurious home of the murder victim, Lord Edgware, has a very large drawing room on the "first floor" (second floor in American terms) and on the ground floor there is a room which is called the "library" in some references and the "study" in others. This is the room where the first murder takes place. The house is generally described as "gloomy" with no frivolities such as window boxes, and with blinds half-closed, causing a dim atmosphere in daytime. The home is richly but not very comfortably furnished.

Another luxury home, in Chiswick, has a huge dining room illuminated only by candles for an evening dinner party, and another large room on an upper floor filled with artworks and having windows overlooking the Thames.

Motion pictures are mentioned in Christie novels as early as the 1922 *The Secret Adversary* as Albert, the "small lift boy" who assists Tuppence, deliriously repeats "Oh, ain't it just like the pictures!" In the 1924 *The Man in the Brown Suit,* Anne Beddingfeld longs for the kind of adventures she has seen in *The Perils of Pamela* on the flickering screen while munching chocolate bars. Miss Cramm in the 1930 *Murder at the Vicarage* complains that St. Mary Mead is strictly a one-horse place with not so much as a "picture house." In the 1932 *Peril at End House* Nick Buckley at first thinks that Hercule Poirot is a film director searching for a new star for "the Talkies."

In *Thirteen at Dinner* two of the main characters are American-born film stars and they are portrayed as stereotypical film stars of the early 1930s. The male star is tall, dark and handsome; the female is gorgeous, blonde, and totally self-indulgent.

The prevalence of drug use among the "upper classes" was mentioned in two earlier Christie novels. In this novel there are references to cocaine and veronal addiction among movie stars, especially among "young actresses," ("Sunday-paper romantic stuff," in the words of Inspector Japp) and for a time it seems indicated that one of the young female characters is a drug addict.

There are Christie's usual negative references to "the Press," one newspaper being called "The Evening Shriek."

There is a remark about the prevalence of multiple divorces among American film stars, and as this novel begins, a film actress appeals to Hercule Poirot not to solve a murder case but to persuade her husband to consent to a divorce.

There are also two references to Chicago, which had developed a world-wide reputation for gangland crime. Jane Wilkinson mentions that, in Chicago, she could have her husband "bumped off" quite easily, but as she is in London, that can't be so easily arranged. When the American actress Carlotta Adams dies, her maid Alice mentions that she has heard all about "Chicago and them gunmen and all that. It must be a wicked country; and what the police can be about, I can't think. Not like our policemen."

The Daimler is the only make of automobile mentioned; Jane Wilkinson rents one.

A reference is made to the feminine millinery fashions of the early 1930s, in particular the plate-shaped hats that were worn at an "outrageous" angle hiding one eye and most of the face on that side. This point is made in order to explain why it must have been impossible for a female murder suspect to have been recognized when seen from her left and above.

Story

It is summer of 1931 or 1932. An American film actress, Jane Wilkinson, has been married for three years to a wealthy English aristocrat, Lord Edgware. She is an outlandishly and stereotypically self-centered "glamorous, blonde movie star." She wants to divorce her husband, Lord Edgware, in order to marry a wealthy duke, and she appeals to Hercule Poirot to reason with Lord Edgware, who has refused to discuss a divorce. She jokingly tells Poirot that, unless he agrees to help her to divorce her husband, she may be forced to "go round in a taxi and bump him off."

A couple of mornings later, the body of Lord Edgware is found in his library, where he has been stabbed to death. A butler and a secretary at the home state that Lady Edgware (Jane Wilkinson) had come to the house the preceding evening, entered the library and then left a short time later. However, twelve witnesses claim that Lady Edgware was with them at a dinner party in a London suburb for the whole evening.

An estranged nephew of Lord Edgware is suspected, as well as his butler, who disappears the day after the murder along with a large quantity of cash. A young American actress, Carlotta Adams, whose specialty was "imitations" of celebrities, is found dead in her apartment, apparently of a drug overdose. In her apartment the police find a blonde wig, a new black dress and new hat similar to the ones described by the butler and secretary at the Edgware home. Did Carlotta impersonate Lady Edgware with the purpose of entering the home and murdering Lord Edgware?

Soon a young actor telephones to Hercule Poirot, wishing to reveal some important facts, but during the call he excuses himself in order to answer the doorbell and he never returns to the telephone. Rushing to the young man's apartment, Poirot and Hastings find him dead, stabbed in the back of the neck just as Lord Edgware had been.

Inspector Japp works closely with Hercule Poirot in this baffling mystery but it is, of course, Poirot who "reveals all."

Characters

Hercule Poirot, the Belgian private investigator living in London, whom we have met before. He is a short little man with an egg-shaped head and eyes that turn "as green as a cat's" when he is especially excited about some new insight or an important new fact. He feels justified in describing himself the greatest detective in the world. He generally treats his sidekick, Captain Hastings, with kindness and repeatedly reminds him that he appreciates Hastings' "beautiful nature." This "beautiful nature" prevents Hastings from seeing evil in beautiful women, and especially beautiful women with auburn hair. (Hastings had fallen hopelessly in love with an auburn-haired girl during his first adventure with Poirot, and was again captivated by an auburn-haired girl in a later adventure.) In this novel, as in *Peril at End House,* there is a good deal of serious conversation between Poirot and Hastings about the case. In some of their earlier adventures Poirot withheld information routinely from Hastings, fearing that because of his "beautiful nature" he could not possibly keep those facts to himself.

In *The Mysterious Affair at Styles,* Poirot made the most of tangible clues in solving the mystery. Gradually in the later novels and stories he speaks more and more of "the psychology of the murderer" and also of the victim. In this novel there is much talk about psychology, and Poirot affirms more than once that he can come nearer to the solution of any problem by lying back in an armchair and using the little grey cells than by sniffing the ground in search of tangible clues.

Captain Hastings, Poirot's assistant. Since about 1923 he has lived in Argentina but he has returned to England on at least two occasions and has fallen in with his old friend each time, as he has now. They are currently sharing rooms in London. Hastings has grown weary of hearing Poirot pontificate on the subject of "the little grey cells" and he tends to "drift" once Poirot goes off on that subject. In this novel he has occasions to feel genuine sympathy for Poirot, who he truly believes is getting old and is losing his former abilities. Poirot becomes very depressed on one or two occasions because things are not going well in this investigation.

Hastings is the quintessential "good old school, fair play" Englishman and he is scandalized by many of Poirot's methods which sometimes include reading other people's private correspondence. In *Peril at End House* he objected to Poirot's rummaging through Magdala Buckley's underwear drawer and then reading her love letters. "It's not playing the game," he insisted. In *Thirteen at Dinner,* a similar scene occurs when Poirot shocks Hastings by reading, upside down, a love letter that is lying on the desk of a man he is interviewing in his office. Hastings sputters something about Poirot "not playing the game," to which Poirot replies, once again, that he is not playing a game but solving a murder.

Inspector James Japp of Scotland Yard. Poirot and Japp have worked together on several occasions and Japp feels great respect for Poirot's abilities, although he is often quite rude to Poirot, calling him "pigheaded" and other things. When Poirot makes a suggestion, Japp usually follows it up, often saying something like, "Not that it's likely to lead anywhere," then later telephoning Poirot with comments such as, "You're the goods, Poirot! You were right!"

Inspector Japp was introduced in the 1920 *The Mysterious Affair at Styles* and was in charge of the case of Mrs. Inglethorpe's murder, but he and Hercule Poirot did not work together in any way. Japp appeared briefly in several subsequent stories, but *Thirteen at Dinner* is the first novel in which Inspector Japp and Hercule Poirot work closely together to solve the case. They will work closely together again in just two future novels, the 1935 *Death in the Air* and the 1940 *The Patriotic Murders,* although Japp will make a brief appearance in the 1935 *The A.B.C. Murders* before turning the case over to Inspector Crome.

George Alfred St. Vincent Marsh, fourth Baron Edgware (Lord Edgware) His wife, Lady Edgware (screen actress Jane Wilkinson) wants desperately to be rid of him, describing him as "a queer man—not like other people—a kind of fanatic." When Poirot and Hastings visit Lord Edgware at his home, they notice that the shelves in his library are lined with books such as the *Memoirs of Casanova*, a volume on the Comte de Sade and one on medieval tortures. They also notice that Lord Edgware's butler, instead of being the usual older, conservative-looking gentleman, is an "unnaturally handsome young man with an effeminate sound in his voice." As readers we are left to form our own conclusions about what all of this suggests about Lord Edgware. At one point Hercule Poirot describes Lord Edgware as a man "on the very edge of madness."

Carlotta Adams, a talented, young American actress whose specialty is solo "sketches" without makeup, costumes or props, using only her gestures, facial expressions and voice to create a wide range of character types, imagined or real. Because Carlotta dies of an overdose of veronal, there is speculation that she may have been a regular drug user, although both her maid and her friend Miss Driver deny that.

Jane Wilkinson, (Lady Edgware), an American film star of incredible egotism. It does not occur to her that anyone else's needs or wishes even exist when she wants something. Her "friend," the young American film star Bryan Martin, describes her as not "immoral" but "amoral. Right or wrong just don't exist for her..."

In a conversation in which Hercule Poirot and Hastings discuss Jane's acting talent, Poirot comments that she is the kind of actress who could never play a minor role or a "character part." The play or film would have to be written "for her and about her."

Lady Edgware exhibits no curiosity about who killed her husband. To her, the fact that her husband has been murdered simply means that she is free to marry the Duke of Merton. She grudgingly spends half a day trying on black hats for mourning in an effort to find one in which she can look "stunning."

Bryan Martin, noticed sitting with Jane Wilkinson behind Hastings and Poirot at the theater, is described by Hastings in his narration as "a tall, extremely good-looking man, of the Greek-god type, whose face I recognized as one better known on the screen than on the stage. It was Bryan Martin, the hero of the screen most popular at the moment."

Captain Ronald Marsh, the young, estranged nephew of Lord Edgware. Upon Lord Edgware's death, he inherits his fortune and title; therefore he has the best motive for the murder. Inspector Japp describes Ronald Marsh as "a bit of a waster."

Mr. and Mrs. Dortheimer and their daughter Rachel, with whom Ronald Marsh attended the opera on the evening of the murder. This provided him with an alibi.

The Duke of Merton, one of the richest men in England, whom Jane Wilkinson plans to marry. Hastings describes him as "...hardly prepossessing in appearance, being thin and weakly. He had nondescript hair, going bald at the temples, a small, bitter mouth and vague, dreamy eyes." The Duke lives in London with his domineering mother.

Mr. Moxon, the attorney who advises Jane Wilkinson while she is questioned by the police

Mr. and Mrs. Archie Widburn, acquaintances of Jane Wilkinson who are part of the party of eight who have supper in her suite at the Savoy on the evening of Carlotta Adams's performance. They are wealthy patrons of art and the stage and are, according to Hastings, unwilling to talk on any other subject.

Man with A Gold Tooth who shadowed Bryan Martin all over America for some mysterious reason

Alton, Lord Edgware's butler. Poirot and Hastings pay a visit to Lord Edgware one morning, noting that the butler is not the "aged, white-haired butler" that would be expected, but instead an almost "unnaturally" handsome young man with an effeminate, soft voice. Later, Inspector Japp comments that Alton is mixed up with a couple of disreputable night clubs. "Not the usual thing. Something a great deal more recherché and nasty."

Miss Carroll, Lord Edgware's private secretary, a pleasant, efficient-looking woman of about forty-five with fair hair that is turning gray and shrewd blue eyes gleaming through a pince-nez.

Poirot has occasion to cite Miss Carroll as an example of a "bad witness." She is so certain of the identity of a person she saw entering the house that she bends facts to conform to that certainty. "I saw her face," she says of the woman she saw, which Poirot proves to be impossible from where Miss Carroll had been standing.

Geraldine Marsh, Lord Edgware's teen-age daughter. After her father is murdered, Poirot asks her if she was fond of him. Geraldine's reaction is to laugh hysterically and to declare that she hated him and that she is glad he is dead.

Ellis, Jane Wilkinson's (Lady Edgware's) maid, a neat middle-aged woman, with glasses and primly arranged gray hair.

Sir Montagu Corner and Lady Corner, wealthy art enthusiasts and patrons of young artists and actors. Sir Montagu is the kind of person to whom intelligence in another person consists of the faculty of listening to his own remarks with suitable attention.

Mrs. Van Dusen, an American friend of Jane Wilkinson whom she meets at the Piccadilly Palace Hotel

Alice Bennett, Carlotta Adams's maid, a neat, middle-aged woman with hair drawn tightly back from her face. Alice proves to be an excellent witness, describing with accuracy Carlotta Adams's movements of the preceding evening and her general habits, supplementing and complementing the facts provided later by Carlotta's friend, Jenny Driver.

Dr. Heath, who is called to the bedside of the dead Carlotta Adams. He is a fussy elderly man somewhat vague in manner. He knows Poirot by repute and expresses a lively pleasure at meeting him in the flesh. Knowing that Carlotta's handbag might contain important material needed at the inquest, he confiscates it before the maid can tamper with it and later shows its contents, including the gold box containing veronal, to Poirot.

Miss Jenny Driver, a close friend of Carlotta Adams. She owns a fashionable millinery shop, *Genevieve*, where women's hats are custommade. She is "a pugilistic little creature" who reminds Hastings in some ways of a fox terrier. Hercule Poirot is favorably impressed by her ability to give clear answers to his questions about Carlotta Adams.

Dorothy, "an imposing blonde creature" who greets Poirot and Hastings at the millinery shop *Genevieve* and who is not sure "modom" (the owner, Jenny Driver) can see them

Donald Ross, a young stage actor who has met with critical acclaim among critics but is, as yet, quite unknown to the public. He is a young fellow of about twenty-two, with a pleasant face and fair hair. During a conversation about Carlotta Adams and her performances, Poirot notices that Donald exhibits little interest in anyone's performances but his own.

A Butler at the home of Sir Montagu Corner. "He was a tall, middle-aged man of ecclesiastical appearance."

The Carthew West Family, with whom Geraldine Marsh has dinner and attends an opera performance on the evening of the murder

A Little Maid Servant at the home of Hercule Poirot

A Footman at the home of the Duke of Merton

The Dowager Duchess of Merton, the tyrannical mother of the young Duke of Merton. She condescends to pay a personal visit to Hercule Poirot and Hastings at their rooms. Hastings describes her as "every inch a *grande dame* with an almost ruthless personality."

Lady Yardly, who recommends Hercule Poirot to the Dowager Duchess of Merton. Though not a character in this novel, in a previous story Poirot had assisted her in a private matter.

Mr. Jobson, a taxi driver who took two fares from Covent Garden to Regent Gate and back on the evening of the murder.

French into English

Chapter 1
belle femme—a beautiful woman
mon cher—my friend, about the same as "mon ami"
mais oui, c'est vrai—Yes, it's true.
Elle est artiste!—She's an artist!

Chapter 2
Comment?—What's that you're saying?
genre—style
ce métier-là—that kind of work
merci—thank you

Chapter 3
Pourquoi pas?—Why not?
Dieu merci—Thank God!
En effet—in fact
Continuez—continue
Ah! Parfaitement!—Naturally!

Chapter 4
Comment?—What's that you're saying?
Écoutez—Listen

Chapter 5
Ah! Ce bon Japp!—Good old Japp!
bagatelle—a trifle, a trivial matter
amour propre—self-esteem, pride

Chapter 6
Mais oui, mais oui—Yes, certainly, certainly.

Chapter 7
Mais continuez—But do go on.

Chapter 8
Ah! C'est un peu trop, ça!—That's a bit much! (That's going a little too far!)
Mais oui, mais oui!—Yes, yes, of course!
mon Dieu—God!

Chapter 9
J'ai fait un serment—I've made a vow

Chapter 11
Vous avez parfaitement raison—You're absolutely right
Épatant—Amazing

Chapter 12
sans doute—without a doubt
maison de couture—dress shop
nous voici—here we are (we've arrived)
métier—trade, area of expertise

Chapter 13
En vérité?—Really?
Tout de même—All the same

Chapter 14
volte face—turnaround
aucune, aucune—none at all
les dames—ladies
la dame—the lady
Une petite omelette, n'est-ce pas?—A small omelet, how does that sound?
Baba au Rhum—a desert cake laced with rum
Mais non, ce n'est pas ça.—No, that's not what I meant
Ce cher—Dear old
Je me pose des questions—I'm asking myself questions (I'm wondering about things)
un peu vif—rather vivid
amour propre—pride

Chapter 15
C'est toujours possible—It's always possible

Chapter 16
Mais oui, c'est possible—Yes, that's possible

Chapter 17
Tout de même—all the same
En vérité?—Really?
Du tout, du tout—Not at all, not at all
Pas un sou—Not one penny
Il vous ressemble un peu.—He looks a bit like you.

Chapter 18
Pour que mon chien de chasse me rapporte le gibier—for my hunting dog to bring the catch to me
Ah! C'est très bien ça!—Oh, that's very good!
Je vous demande pardon—Please forgive me

Chapter 19
grande dame—great lady, aristocrat
Comment, Madame la Duchesse?—What's that you're saying, Duchess?
Mais non, mais non!—No, that's not it at all!
C'est une idée, ça!—Now *there's* an idea!

Chapter 22
Écoutez—Listen

Cela ce peut—That may be. (The correct spelling is *Cela se peut*)
C'est fini—That's the end of it.
Dieu, que je suis bête!—God, how stupid I've been!

Chapter 23
C'est épatant—It's uncanny
confiture—jam, preserves, extras. In this context, "jam money" is a metaphor for the "unexpected windfall" of the letter's allowing the murder to be pinned on someone else.

Chapter 24
Évidement—Obviously (correct spelling: *évidemment*)
Bonjour—Good morning
Comment?—What's that you're saying?
Tout de même—All the same

Chapter 25
gaffe—clumsy mistake

Chapter 28
Très bien—Very good

COMMENTS

Thirteen at Dinner is absolutely filled with characters, every one of which is memorably depicted, carefully developed through his or her own dialogue or by observations made by other characters—which we are able to evaluate because of our own understanding of *those* characters and their motivations—and through the objective though often distorted views of Captain Hastings and finally through the finer perceptions of Hercule Poirot.

A fault in *Murder at the Vicarage,* at least in Agatha Christie's opinion later in life, was that there were too many characters, and that not many of them were developed very thoroughly. A novel soon following it was *Peril at End House* in which the characters were much more developed, and that was made possible in part by the fact that there were so few of them. Now, in *Thirteen at Dinner* we have many more characters, all very different from each other and all memorable. A chronological listing of ten Agatha Christie "masterworks" would have to begin with *The Murder of Roger Ackroyd* and the second title would be *Thirteen at Dinner.*

An amusing character type is introduced in *Thirteen at Dinner*: the person who judges other people's intelligence by their willingness to listen attentively with appropriate murmurs of appreciation and agreement. In this book it is the cultured "show off" Sir Montagu Corner who characterizes an intellectually impoverished actress as having made some very intelligent remarks about Greek culture. In fact she had probably simply nodded and agreed with everything Sir Montagu had said.

In addition to very well developed characters specific to this novel, the characters we already know well—Inspector Japp, Hercule Poirot, and Captain Hastings—now become much more human. Poirot experiences depression now and then. He is depressed by Japp's constant certainty despite the "five unanswered questions." Hastings reveals to us his embarrassment about his own poor judgment. Japp goes through mood swings; this is the first Christie novel in which he and Poirot actually confer seriously and frequently about the case. It was in *Peril at End House* that Poirot and Hastings almost became "partners" in the discussions; that relationship continues in *Thirteen at Dinner* with the addition of Inspector Japp. In earlier novels both Japp and Hastings had been simply "foils" to Poirot's eloquence. Now they are active participants. It is, as always, Hercule Poirot who solves the case, but the three men are partners and not antagonists despite the sarcastic banter that is exchanged among them nearly all the time.

One little incident illustrates the new "humanness" of these three characters. At one point in the story, Japp is very depressed. Poirot in his "typical way" utters "sympathetic murmurs," sounding like a hen who is about to lay an egg. Hastings, with more understanding of the Englishman's needs, offers whisky and soda and Japp improves immediately.

There is, in *Thirteen at Dinner,* a magnificent illustration of how the relationship between Poirot and Hastings has developed since their first adventure together, *The Mysterious Affair at Styles,* at least fifteen years earlier. It must be read in full in order to be appreciated.

About half way through the story the two are dining at a little restaurant in Soho, one of Poirot's favorite haunts. On that occasion Poirot tells Hastings that he has come to depend on Hastings more than he ever realized. Hastings's response:

> I could hardly believe my ears. "Really, Poirot," I stammered, "I'm awfully glad. I suppose I've learned a good deal from you one way or another—"
> He shook his head.
> "*Mais non, ce n'est pas ça.* You have learned nothing."
> "Oh!" I said, rather taken aback.
> "That is as it should be. No human being should

learn from another. Each individual should develop his own powers to the uttermost, not try to imitate those of someone else. I do not wish you to be a second and inferior Poirot. I wish you to be the supreme Hastings. And you are the supreme Hastings. In you, Hastings, I find the normal mind almost perfectly illustrated."

"I'm not abnormal, I hope," I said.

"No, no. You are beautifully and perfectly balanced. In you sanity is personified. Do you realize what that means to me? When the criminal sets out to do a crime his first effort is to deceive. Whom does he seek to deceive? The image in his mind is that of the normal man. There is probably no such thing actually—it is a mathematical abstraction. But you come as near to realizing it as is possible. There are moments when you have flashes of brilliance, when you rise above the average, moments (I hope you will pardon me) when you descend to curious depths of obtuseness, but, take it all for all, you are amazingly normal. *Eh bien*, how does this profit me? Simply in this way. As in a mirror I see reflected in your mind exactly what the criminal wishes me to believe. That is terrifically helpful and suggestive."

I did not quite understand. It seemed to me that what Poirot was saying was hardly complimentary. However, he quickly disabused me of that impression.

"I have expressed myself badly," he said quickly. "You have an insight into the criminal mind, which I myself lack. You show me what the criminal wishes me to believe. It is a great gift."

"Insight," I said thoughtfully. "Yes, perhaps I have got insight."

I looked across the table at him. He was smoking one of his tiny cigarettes and regarding me with great kindliness.

"*Ce cher* Hastings," he murmured. "I have indeed much affection for you."

The Boomerang Clue (1934)

(Alternate Title: *Why Didn't They Ask Evans?*)

SETTING

There are four main settings in *The Boomerang Clue:*

The story begins on the northern coast of Wales near and in the fictitious village of Marchbolt, which is too small to have a railway station of its own, the nearest station being in the town of Sileham, three miles distant by road, and two miles by a shorter footpath. The principal setting in Marchbolt is the vicarage, as one of the main characters is the son of the vicar. In Marchbolt there is a café grandly named "The Orient Café" but whose interior "does not live up to its name;" a scene near the end of the novel takes place there. At the vicarage, there is a husband-and-wife servant team.

A second setting is London, in particular an auto garage "with three rooms above" that has been left to one of the characters by a loving aunt; he and another character plan to set up an auto repair/used auto sales business there. In addition to the auto garage, there is a scene at the London flat that an aging Welsh aristocrat maintains in Brook Street for his times in London. There are also two other London residences: a luxurious home in Tite Street, Chelsea, and a run-down house in St. Leonards Gardens, which is described as "a gloomy collection of houses, most of them in a somewhat dilapidated condition." Paddington Railway Station is mentioned early in the novel, as two of the main characters meet in a train just departing from there, bound for Wales.

A third setting is somewhere in the county of Hampshire, southwest of London. One character registers for a room at the Station Hotel in the "bustling little town" of Ambledever. Ten miles away, the small village of Staverly has an inn called The Angler's Arms. The most important settings in Hampshire, however, are a luxurious home called Merroway Court and, a short distance away, another large home, The Grange, which is currently being used by a doctor as a kind of sanatorium for nerve patients and drug addicts.

A fourth setting is a village called Chipping Somerton which has a combination general store and post office; a dilapidated house there called Tudor Cottage is the scene of some later action in the novel. There is no indication of the county in which this village is located. There is a reference to its being "not far, as the crow flies" from Staverly, which is in Hampshire, but one character makes a circuitous journey from Staverly to Chipping Somerton by local trains, changing trains three times, and the trip occupies the better part of a day because of all of the delays.

The only reference in the story to historical events are two comments by characters on the subject of the current "hard times," a reference to England's continued unemployment problems resulting from World War One coupled with the world-wide Depression of the 1930s. It is October of 1932 or 1933, when the Great Depression was at its lowest depths.

A profusion of automobile makes are mentioned in the novel: one aristocratic character drives "a large green Bentley," a luxury make; her father owns a Chrysler, also a luxury make.

One character owns a Daimler and another has a "dark blue Talbot." Other makes named are Austin, Morris, Rover, Standard, Essex and Fiat.

Airplanes are mentioned twice: an airplane is noticed flying overhead at approximately the moment that a crime takes place at Merroway Court, and towards the end of the story the two young sleuths charter a small private plane to take them quickly from somewhere in Hampshire to their village of Marchbolt in Wales.

On several occasions certain amounts of money are mentioned, and it is important for modern readers to remember that numbers of "dollars" or "pounds" quoted by characters in a novel written in the early 1930s have no relevance today. In this novel one character purchases a dilapidated but functional used car for ten pounds. When the character Bobby Jones receives a letter offering him a job in South America paying "a thousand a year," and his father feels it is ridiculous for him not to accept the offer, we need to remember that a thousand pounds in 1932-33 had the value of at least a hundred thousand dollars today. A character in a Christie novel published three years later will "survive" on an annual income of just under two hundred pounds and in a 1939 novel, a private secretary to a rich businessman will earn six pounds a week.

Story

On a misty afternoon in the autumn of 1932 or 1933, Bobby Jones, a son of the vicar of Marchbolt in Wales, is playing golf with a friend near the seaside in an area of high cliffs and deep chasms. Searching for a lost golf ball, they find an unconscious man at the bottom of a fifty or sixty foot chasm. He has broken his back and soon dies, but just before dying he asks the cryptic question, "Why didn't they ask Evans?"

A photograph found by the police in the dead man's pocket proves to be that of a sister, who goes to Marchbolt to identify him. A few days later, someone attempts to poison Bobby by lacing his beer with morphia. Bobby's imaginative childhood friend, Lady Frances Derwent, forms the conviction that the man must have been pushed over the cliff and that someone feared that, before dying, he must have told Bobby something that might lead to an identification of the murderer.

Bobby and Lady Frances (familiarly called "Frankie"), solve the mystery together. Their investigation takes them to a country house in Hampshire and to the establishment of a sinister doctor who maintains a treatment center for drug addicts. Together they have one exciting adventure after another, but their investigations eventually lead them back to Marchbolt, hence the title *The Boomerang Clue*.

Characters

Bobby Jones, "...an amiable-looking young man of about eight-and-twenty. His best friend could not have said that he was handsome, but his face was an eminently likable one, and his eyes had the honest brown friendliness of a dog's."

Bobby is one of four sons of Reverend Thomas Jones, the vicar of Marchbolt, a village in Wales. He has been discharged from the Navy because of poor vision and, because of the poor economic conditions of the times, he has no job prospects. He is extremely honorable in the matter of promises made, and as he has promised his friend, Badger Beadon, that he will help him get established with his auto repair/sales business, Bobby keeps that promise despite a surprising offer of a lucrative job abroad.

Bobby cherishes an old friendship with Lady Frances Derwent, a girl of the old aristocracy who was a childhood playmate, but now that they are adults he resists her social invitations, feeling strongly that because of the difference in class, they should not be social companions. Lady Frances responds to this by expressing the view that all of that "class" business is nonsense and she tells him that if he will consent to coming to one of her parties, she will serve sausage and beer, if it will please him. She adds that he may even bring Badger. "There's friendship for you," she adds, to which Bobby replies, "Look here, Frankie, it's no good and you know it."

Among Bobby's other conservative ideas is a belief that the quality of a person can be correctly judged by physical appearance. When he contemplates, in Chapter One, the man who has fallen from the cliff and is dying before his eyes, he knows—somehow—that this is a "pukka sahib" and in a later chapter he apologizes for that notion, saying:

> "The dead man was—well, it sounds a most awful thing to say and just like some deadly old retired Anglo-Indian—but the dead man was a pukka sahib."

[Note: For an explanation of the term "pukka sahib," see the *Appendix*.]

Reverend Thomas Jones, the Vicar of Marchbolt and the father of Bobby. Everything that he says to or about Bobby is negative. Bobby is never serious enough, never reverent enough, never *anything* enough. When Bobby is away in London, Rev. Jones writes letters to him, not with a feeling of affection for his son but out of a "spirit of duty" and they breathe "an atmosphere of Christian forbearance which was highly depressing."

Mr. and Mrs. Roberts, servants at the vicarage who are said "to run the vicarage."

Dr. Thomas, a middle aged friend of Bobby's who is a fine golfer and wishes Bobby were a better golfer than he is. The doctor is playing golf with Bobby when the two of them discover a dying man at the bottom of a chasm.

Alexander Pritchard, the cliff accident victim, described thus in the thoughts of Bobby Jones:

> Fine, healthy-looking fellow, too—probably never known a day's illness in his life. The pallor of approaching death couldn't disguise the deep tan of the skin. A man who had lived an out-of-door life—abroad perhaps. Bobby studied him more closely—the crisp curling chestnut hair just touched with gray at the temples, the big nose, the strong jaw, the white teeth just showing through the parted lips. Then the broad shoulders and the fine sinewy hands. The legs were twisted at a curious angle. Bobby shuddered and brought his eyes up again to the face. An attractive face, humorous, determined, resourceful. The eyes, he thought, were probably blue—And just as he reached that point in his thoughts, the eyes suddenly opened. They *were* blue, a clear deep blue. They looked straight at Bobby. There was nothing uncertain or hazy about them. They seemed completely conscious. They were watchful and at the same time they seemed to be asking a question..."

From all of this, Bobby concludes that the man is a "pukka sahib." Perhaps the obvious racially "Englishness" of the man (blue eyes) and the history of living abroad makes him a part of the "honorable" British tradition of serving the Empire—the "White Man's Burden," etc. This idea of "pukka sahib" has already been ridiculed by Hercule Poirot in *Peril at End House,* when one of the "Good Old Boys from the Good Old School" turned out to be a drug pusher. Later, in *Murder in the Calais Coach,* Poirot will ridicule the idea of "pukka sahib" with a brief and amusing comment. We should note that even Bobby realizes the silliness of the "pukka sahib" idea, frankly admitting that his use of the term makes him sound "like some deadly old Anglo-Indian Colonel."

Roger Bassington-ffrench, "a man of about thirty-five. He had a rather indecisive face which seemed to be calling for a monocle and a little mustache," according to Bobby Jones's first impression. His later recollection: "A sort of nondescript fellow. Pleasant voice. A gentleman and all that. I really didn't notice him particularly."

Lady Frances Derwent (Frankie), a young aristocrat, the daughter of Lord Marchington. They live at Derwent Castle close to Marchbolt in Wales, although Frankie spends most of her time in London at the family town house in Brook Street, for she is a modern girl who loves parties, cocktails and fun and finds life in the Welsh countryside to be boring. She admits to Bobby, however, that all of this partying becomes boring after a time, and that all of her money and the things it buys really don't bring her much happiness.

Frankie is not in the least impressed by the "class system," and she doesn't give a "hoot" about her title. However, she does not hesitate to *use* her title when it "comes in handy," as it does several times in this story.

It can be deduced that Frankie enjoys an easy relationship with her father, Lord Marchington. She comes and goes as she pleases, she does not hesitate to tell Bobby, "get a chauffeur's uniform, charge it to my father," and later she promises to have her father buy Badger out and hire him as manager of the auto repair shop. She also chooses her own future husband, at the end of the story, without consulting with her father. Frankie is, in fact, very similar to Lady Eileen Brent (Bundle) of *The Secret of Chimneys* and *The Seven Dials Mystery:* an energetic, modern-spirited, independent young woman.

Lord Marchington, Frankie's father. He plays a very small part in the story—conversing only once with Frankie on the subject of various branches of the Bassington-ffrench family. He is probably very much like Lord Caterham, the father of Lady Eileen Brent in two earlier novels—treating his grown daughter with respect and as a friend.

Mrs. Amelia Cayman, a sister of the man who died when he fell from the cliff near Marchbolt. She was identified by her photograph, which the police found in the dead man's pocket.

Mr. Leo Cayman, husband of Amelia Cayman, "a big florid man with a would-be hearty manner and a cold and somewhat shifty eye that rather belied the manner."

Badger Beadon, a life-long friend of Bobby Jones, having known both Bobby and Frankie since childhood. He stammers and has a peculiar laugh. He has recently inherited a garage with three rooms above, in London, and hopes to turn it into an auto repair/used car business, although he has had a poor record of success in work. He failed at chicken farming, was fired from a job with a company in the City, was finally sent to Australia (where young Englishmen are sent by their families when they have lost hope for them at home) "and then came back again." Bad enough to be sent to Australia, but "to come back again" is the worst! He is cheerful and optimistic about the prospects of the car business.

Aunt Carrie, Badger's recently-deceased aunt, who has left him the garage with three rooms above.

"Edward Hawkins," the alias used by Bobby Jones while posing as Frankie's chauffeur.

Mr. Owen of Wheeler and Owen, House Agents in Marchbolt, who confirms Roger Bassington-ffrench's statement that he had been visiting the Marchbolt area in view of purchasing a house there. Mr. Owen is well acquainted with Lady Frances and her family.

Frank, a lower-ranking employee of Wheeler and Owen

Inspector Williams of the Marchbolt Police, also well known to Lady Frances. By means of her title, and clever manipulation of the conversation, Frankie learns from Inspector Williams the exact contents of the pockets of the "accident victim."

George Arbuthnot, a medical doctor and friend of Lady Frances. He agrees to help her stage a sham auto accident outside a country home where she hopes to spend time investigating the occupants. The only description provided of him is that he has a "deep, melancholy voice."

Young Reeves, a messenger boy, age seventeen, who happens to be riding his bicycle past Merroway Court just after Frankie's "accident" and is delighted with the pleasurable spectacle. He helps Dr. Arbuthnot carry Frankie into the house and, later, spreads the word of the "accident," to Frankie and Bobby's advantage.

Sylvia Bassington-ffrench, Roger's sister-in-law, aged about thirty. She is tall, with red hair, and light, clear blue eyes. She has a cool, impersonal voice with a slight American accent.

Sylvia is an American heiress who married into the Bassington-ffrench family. She unsuspectingly welcomes the "injured" Lady Frances into her home and provides a bedroom for her. She becomes friends with Frankie and expresses certain fears to her, in particular an unexplained fear of Dr. Nicholson, a neighbor, and some anxiety about her husband who has been experiencing violent mood changes for the past few months.

Henry Bassington-ffrench, Roger's brother and Sylvia's husband, "a big man, heavy-jowled, with a kindly but rather abstracted air." Frankie correctly suspects Henry of being a drug addict.

Tommy Bassington-ffrench, the seven-year-old son of Henry and Sylvia.

Dr. Jasper Nicholson, a Canadian doctor and nerve specialist who operates a sanatorium in an old converted country house, The Grange, not far from Merroway Court. Sylvia experiences an unexplained fear of Dr. Nicholson and, when he expresses a kind of curious amusement about Frankie's "accident," probing for details and commenting about certain puzzling aspects of it, he inspires fear in Frankie as well. Dr. Nicholson's wife is also afraid of him.

Moira Nicholson, wife of Dr. Jasper Nicholson. She is terrified of her husband and is sure that he plans to murder her, and then to find a way to dispose of Henry Bassington-ffrench for the purpose of marrying Sylvia.

Alan Carstairs, a Canadian who had lived in Africa for many years and had just arrived in England for a visit. He recently visited Merroway Court with his London friends, Mr. and Mrs. Rivington.

Colonel H. Rivington, D.S.O. and Mrs. Rivington, his wife, London friends of Alan Carstairs and of Henry and Sylvia Bassington-ffrench. Mrs. Rivington is easily fooled by Bobby Jones's impersonation of Mr. Spragge, the solicitor, and she describes to Bobby the visit she and her husband made with Alan Carstairs to the Bassington-ffrenches at Merroway Court.

John Savage, a very rich Englishman who made the newspapers by committing suicide because of a certainty that he had cancer, despite his doctor's assertions that he did not. He wrote an uncharacteristic Will the day before he died, leaving small legacies to certain charities but the bulk of his wealth to a certain Mrs. Templeton, whom he had only recently met during an ocean voyage.

Frankie's Maid

"A Tall, Stooping Gentleman with a Pince-Nez," who claims to be a friend of Bobby Jones and who visits the vicarage after Bobby goes to live with Badger in London, inquiring about his whereabouts.

Thomas Askew, a stout genial person, the landlord of the Angler's Arms, the inn at Staverly where Bobby Jones poses as Edward Hawkins, chauffeur to Lady Frances. He enjoys conversation and allows information—and impressions—to leak from him about The Grange and the kinds of "goings-on" at The Grange that the locals suspect. "There's them as don't want to be there...shrieks in the night," etc.

Mr. Frederick Spragge, the aging senior partner of the firm of solicitors used by Lord Marchington, and the man whom Bobby Jones impersonates when he visits Mrs. Rivington in London. He loves titles, dukes, lords, etc. and "eats out of Frankie's hand."

Rose Emily Templeton, a young woman

whom John Savage met on an ocean voyage, soon falling under her fatal influence. During one of his visits to her home in England after the voyage, he committed suicide after creating a Will that left her his vast fortune.

Edgar Templeton, husband of Rose

The Boots at the Station Hotel, Ambledever, an employee who frightens Lady Frances with the fact of Bobby's disappearance.

A Young Lady in the Reception Office, another employee of the Station Hotel

Doctor Davidson, the coroner at Staverly who examines Henry Bassington-ffrench and conducts the inquest into his death.

Inspector Hammond of the Chipping Somerton police

A Doctor at Chipping Somerton who examines Moira Nicholson when she is found drugged with morphia

Rose Chudleigh Pratt, formerly the cook at Tudor Cottage, Chipping Somerton. She witnessed the signing of John Savage's Will the day before he died.

Alfred Mere, who died at age seventy-two, the former gardener at Tudor Cottage and the other witness to the signing of John Savage's Will.

Mr. Elford, the lawyer who presided at the signing and witnessing of John Savage's Will

Gladys, a former parlormaid at Tudor Cottage

The Post Mistress at Chipping Somerton who had been a friend of Gladys, and who continues to receive post cards from her.

Donald King, an airplane pilot and a friend of Frankie's

A Waitress at the Orient Café in Marchbolt, the first in the history of the café who actually hurried.

COMMENTS

With its two youthful and engaging amateur detectives who suspect foul play and solve a complex mystery without the aid of the police, *The Boomerang Clue* has much in common with *The Secret of Chimneys, The Seven Dials Mystery, The Secret Adversary,* and even *The Man in the Brown Suit*. All five novels are filled with fun characters and fun dialogue.

There is some interesting social commentary in this novel. The subject of drug use had been touched upon in several earlier Christie novels. As early as 1926, in *The Murder of Roger Ackroyd,* Hercule Poirot explained that, at least in America, cocaine users inhaled the drug through a goose quill. One of the characters in that novel is in fact a drug user, although not an addict. Then, in *Peril at End House* several characters, all members of the "idle rich" set, are regular cocaine users, and the husband of one of them is a hopeless addict, although the issue is very secondary in those novels and unrelated to the important crimes in the story. In *Thirteen at Dinner* there had been a suggestion but no clear evidence that one character, a young actress, might have been addicted to veronal, but again the issue was minimal.

In *The Boomerang Clue* one of the main characters is a morphia addict and there is morphia everywhere you turn; Bobby Jones is poisoned with morphia, there are morphia addicts being treated at Dr. Nicholson's sanatorium and one character is found drugged with morphia toward the end of the story.

There are also some amusing comments and anecdotes touching on the British class system. In an early conversation between Bobby Jones and Lady Frances Derwent, Bobby expresses the traditional view that it is not a good idea for "classes" to mix. Although a life-long friend of Lady Frances, and still calling her "Frankie" as he did during childhood, he resists her invitations to visit her in London when she has parties for her friends, citing class differences. Lady Frances, for her part, is far more advanced in her thinking and waves these comments—and their concepts—away. She is impatiently annoyed by Bobby's attitude and tries to persuade him that "titles" mean nothing. To her, they do not, and it's likely that to her father, Lord Marchington, they do not either. In two earlier novels, Lord Caterham and his daughter Lady Eileen Brent held similar views. "Bundle" Brent, in fact, marries the untitled Bill Eversleigh at the end of *The Seven Dials Mystery,* and in *The Boomerang Clue,* Bobby and Frankie decide to marry and it is understood that Frankie feels no need to obtain her father's permission for it.

There are, of course, characters such as Mr. Spragge, the lawyer, who is terribly impressed by "titles"—and Frankie takes full advantage of that weakness when seeking certain information which Mr. Spragge would never reveal to someone "common." And there is the amusing observation by Badger Beadon, when Frankie opens her bag and hands him ten pounds for a dilapidated car she is buying from him: "First time I ever knew anyone with a title who could pay cash!"

It is rather clear that Agatha Christie herself was not impressed with "aristocracy," although it is equally clear that she was one of those people who believe that personality and character traits are inherited. In other words, "blood" mattered to her. Just as one "inherits" blue eyes, a square chin and Caucasian skin and hair color, one also "inherits" talents such as musical or artistic creativity, or business acumen. For a person to have inherited "aristocratic" blood was of no particular importance, but to have inherited "servant class" blood was not a nice thing. In Agatha Christie novels, servants *never* stray from their class. Housekeepers, housemaids and cooks generally remain unmarried or they marry footmen, chauffeurs and gardeners, or perhaps junior shop assistants—young men who work for the greengrocer or the butcher. The servants are sometimes, but not very often, credited with powers of accurate observation and reporting (a housekeeper in the 1935 *Murder in Three Acts* will be one of those) but most often they are dull-witted, adenoidal, fearful, suspicious gossips who resist contact of any kind with the police. In *The Boomerang Clue*, the cook Rose Chudleigh is extremely stupid. In the 1930 *Murder at the Vicarage*, the vicarage cook Mary Hill is absolutely incompetent as well as insolent, and in the same novel a kitchenmaid trembles with fear lest the cook discover she has made an unauthorized visit to a male friend.

All of this stupidity, fearfulness and general lowness of spirit and intellect is, of course, portrayed as being natural to "that class." The phrase "that class" is common in Christie novels of every period, and is even used by the far-above-average thinker Hercule Poirot.

In the future, Christie will become rather "preachy" on the subject of inherited character traits. "Foolish" characters will dare to suggest that a child's education and environment will be a strong influence on the development of his character, but the "wise" characters will affirm that whatever the child "inherited" by blood is the true determiner of his character. It is known that Christie did not like the idea of children being adopted by other families. In her *Autobiography* she goes to great lengths to describe a true incident of a child who was sent away to live with friends or relatives by her mother, and who was extremely unhappy with the other family. Watch for this subject in the 1949 *Crooked House,* the 1952 *Mrs. McGinty's Dead,* the 1952 *Murder with Mirrors* and the 1958 *Ordeal by Innocence,* in particular.

The idea of character traits being easily identified by an observation of physical ones is rather annoyingly omnipresent in Christie's earlier novels. In this one, it is Bobby Jones's assessment of the dying man at the beginning of the story. Bobby seems to be able to know, simply by observing "tanned Caucasian skin" and "blue eyes" and "chestnut colored hair slightly graying at the temples" that this man is a "gentleman" and not one of some inferior class to which Mr. and Mrs. Caymen clearly belong.

On the subject of "class," the multitudes of British industrial workers inhabiting such unappetizing places as Nottingham, Doncaster, Leicester, Sheffield, Mansfield, Liverpool, Wolverhampton, Birmingham—the list could go on—are never Christie characters. They simply do not exist. The Christie world consists primarily of people who "inherit." If they have inherited "titles," they are usually impoverished aristocrats unless their recent ancestors have dirtied their hands by investing a portion of their money in industries or trade. If they have inherited "money but no title," then one of their recent ancestors actually stooped to the level of working and earning money, which has since become "family money." Christie herself was one of that class. Her own father and mother never stooped to "working" because someone in her father's family in America had dirtied his hands with work and produced money for her father to inherit.

So it's rather clear that, to Dame Agatha, one needs to "have" money but one must not "earn" it—it must be inherited. One must have a good character, but one cannot develop it—it also must be inherited. And to "adopt" a child and provide him or her with a more favorable environment is folly. If the child has "bad blood" he or she will be bad. In the 1949 novel *Crooked House* there are some amusing conversations—which Christie did not intend to be amusing—on the subject of two families, the Leonides and the de Havilands. The de Havilands are characterized as being "ruthless" and the Leonides are characterized as being "unscrupulous." The "unscrupulousness" of this family, however, is tempered with "kindliness." But what if a descendent of both families inherits the de Haviland "ruthlessness" and the Leonides "unscrupulousness" *without* the tempering trait of "kindliness?" The resulting offspring might then grow up to be a murderer! This is actually a serious discussion between two intelligent characters in the story.

Agatha Christie does not bring religion into her novels very often. She was probably not at all religious herself, or if she was, it was in a quiet, private way. She learned at an early age that the petty conflicts between religious sects were a silly, trivial item not worthy of her attention. For one thing, during her early childhood her mother was intensely interested in churchgoing and bounced around from one sect to another, trying to find one that satisfied her—and dragging her children around to the different churches with her. At one time, the family attended Roman Catholic services for a while. Christie's mother became disenchanted with Roman Catholicism and made her next stop the Unitarians, and there were others following that one. Her mother was always "into" one fad or another. For a time she had the family served fish at every meal because she had read that it was very good food for the brain. Christie's father found it necessary to put his foot down and insist on more variety in meals. Then at one time it was eggs that were being served at every single meal.

Christie must have realized at an early age that many of her mother's notions were just plain silly, and all of her intensity about different religious sects was nonsense. And so in her writing, there is never a judgmental or derogatory remark that is intended to be taken seriously about any religious sect, although there are plenty of characters who profess Christianity but clearly do not practice it, such as the father of Bobby Jones in *The Boomerang Clue,* the aunt of Nurse Leatheran in *Murder in Mesopotamia,* the spinster Emily Brent in *And Then There Were None,* the widow of Canon Leadbetter in *There Is a Tide,* Aunt Effie in *A Pocket Full of Rye,* and many others.

There are a couple of amusing comments about lawyers in *The Boomerang Clue* that have never occurred before: the maddening slowness and meticulous deliberation of lawyers, their round-about communication style and their verbosity, at least in the view of one or two of the characters. Regarding the Will of Mr. Savage, the lawyer Mr. Elford had objected to its being drawn up quickly "then and there"—he wanted to go away and "do it properly—you know how they do—sheets and sheets all about nothing—," in the words of Lady Frances.

And when Bobby Jones impersonates Mr. Spragge, the lawyer, and visits Mrs. Rivington at her home,

> "I must apologize for troubling you, Mrs. Rivington," said Bobby. "But the matter was rather urgent and we wished to avoid the delay of letters."
>
> That any solicitor could ever wish to avoid delay seemed so transparently impossible that Bobby for a moment wondered anxiously whether Mrs. Rivington would see through the pretense. Mrs. Rivington, however, was clearly a woman of more looks than brains, who accepted things as they were presented to her.

Newspapers were a favorite target for satire in Christie novels, and in this one Frankie, in her conversation with Inspector Williams, invents wildly contradictory reports in the press to explain her need for clarification of the facts:

> "He only had *one* photograph on him, didn't he? Someone told me he had *three!*"
>
> "One's right," said the inspector. "Photograph of a sister, it was. She came down and identified him."
>
> "How absurd to say there were three!"
>
> "Oh, that's easy, your ladyship. These newspaper reporters don't mind how much they exaggerate, and as often as not they get the whole thing wrong."
>
> "I know," said Frankie. "I've heard the wildest stories." She paused for a moment, then drew freely on her imagination. "I've heard that his pockets were full of dope, and there's another story about his having pockets full of counterfeit banknotes."
>
> The inspector laughed heartily. "That's a good one."

Frankie's ability to make use of her title—with the above police officer, with her father's lawyer and with the Bassington-ffrench family—is part of the humor of this book, making it a joy to read and reread.

Murder in the Calais Coach (1934)

(Alternate title: *Murder on the Orient Express*)

SETTING

Because this novel was first published in 1934, readers of the first edition were able to reasonably imagine that the action must be taking place as late as the winter of 1933–34. However, in the 1936 novel *Murder in Mesopotamia,* it is in 1935 that the narrator, Amy Leatheran, writes her account of that story which she states took place "four years ago," therefore in 1931. In that story, Hercule Poirot solves the mystery and then immediately returns to Europe via the Orient Express and becomes involved in "another mystery" aboard that train. Therefore if we are splitting hairs we must place the action of *Murder in the Calais Coach* in the winter of 1931–32.

In the first scene, Hercule Poirot boards a train at Aleppo in Syria, on his way to Istanbul where he boards the Orient Express train on his way to England. There is a brief scene at a hotel in Istanbul where Poirot has dinner before boarding the evening train.

The original name for Istanbul was Constantinople, and certain characters in the novel use that name in speaking about the city. The French name "Stamboul" is also used by certain characters, but all three words refer to the same city. In an early conversation there is a reference to the Church of Sainte Sophie, an important work of Byzantine architecture in Istanbul. It was a Christian church when constructed during the sixth century, and then was converted to an Islamic mosque during the fifteenth century.

The rest of the story takes place in the Calais coach, the railway car occupied by passengers traveling as far as the northern French port of Calais and destined for England. A snowstorm causes the train to be stranded in Yugoslavia between Belgrade and the Italian border. The murder takes place in the stalled train and Hercule Poirot conducts the entire investigation on the train, without the assistance of police, solving the mystery before the train resumes its journey.

As a matter of information, the "Orient Express" was a special train that began service in 1883 to provide convenience to travelers between western Europe and the Middle East. Operated by the Compagnie Internationale des Wagons Lits (International Sleeping Car Company), the original route was from Paris to Istanbul via Munich and Vienna to Giurgiu in Romania. Passengers were then ferried across the Danube to Ruse in Bulgaria, then traveled by train to Varna, from which they were again ferried across a portion of the Black Sea to Istanbul. Various alternate routes were added over the next few years, and in 1919 a railway tunnel was built at the Simplon Pass in Switzerland near the Italian border. This made a more southerly route possible, passing through Milan, Venice, Trieste and Belgrade and all the way to Istanbul. It then became possible to board a train in Paris and travel all the way to Istanbul in the same railway car. In addition, Orient Express cars could be boarded by British travelers at Calais. These were taken to Paris and attached to the Orient Express train, making it possible for British travelers to avoid the nuisance of a change in Paris.

It is this route—called the Simplon Orient Express—that is referred to in the novel. The passengers board the train in Istanbul. Poirot is on his way to London, and so it is his intention to remain on board all the way to Calais, where he will have to take a ferry across the English Channel to Dover and then a British train to Victoria Station in London. At least one passenger will leave the train in Paris and two are bound only for Lausanne in Switzerland. The cast of characters traveling in the coach includes several nationalities, which was typical for that line.

The Orient Express was an ordinary passenger train with both first and second class service but it was heavily used during the 1920s and 1930s by large numbers of wealthy people traveling between Europe and the Middle East, especially by the British who had colonial interests in the region. For this reason the "Orient Express" became associated with luxury travel, since most of the travelers were first-class passengers.

Because modern air travel has largely replaced long-distance passenger travel by train in all parts of the world, the Orient Express line was discontinued in 1977, although a nostalgic and probably very expensive "revival" of the Orient Express train later materialized as a tourist amusement.

There are no important historical backgrounds to the story, but in the conversations of some passengers there are passing references to the "Wall Street crisis" in America (the 1929 crash and the Depression that followed), prohibition and crime in America, and Stalin's "Five Year Plans" in Russia. In the story, the murder victim had been responsible for the kidnapping and murder of the baby daughter of a famous American pilot and his wife. This idea was inspired by the infamous Lindbergh baby kidnapping and murder of a few years earlier. The Bolshevist Revolution of 1917 had resulted in the scattering of the old Russian aristocracy throughout the capitals of Europe, and one of the characters in the novel is an old Russian princess who now lives in a fashionable district of Paris.

There is one reference to a stylish female passenger on the train who wears a hat at the fashionable "outrageous angle" that was mentioned in the 1933 *Thirteen at Dinner*, but there are no other references to contemporary fashions, fads, conditions or events.

STORY

It is the winter of 1931–32. Hercule Poirot has just assisted the French government in Syria in a matter of international importance and is now returning to England. One evening he boards the Orient Express train at Istanbul.

During lunch the following day, Poirot notes with interest the unusual number of passengers for this time of year and he observes the various nationalities. There is a very old Russian princess who now lives in Paris, traveling with her German maid. There are a Hungarian count and countess, an elderly American gentleman traveling with his American male secretary and British valet, a Swedish missionary nurse, a boisterous elderly American lady tourist, an American traveling salesman, an Italo-American automobile salesman, a British colonel from India and a British nursery governess.

After lunch, the elderly American gentleman, Mr. Ratchett, having recognized Poirot, approaches him with a "job." He is a stereotypical "rich American" who is accustomed to the idea that "money talks." It appears that he has personal enemies and that his life has been threatened. He offers Poirot twenty thousand dollars to "protect" him from danger during the trip. Poirot explains that he has retired and has no need for money. The American feels insulted and demands the real reason for Poirot's refusal and Poirot tells him "I do not like your face."

The following morning, Mr. Ratchett does not appear in the dining car for breakfast. He is found dead in his compartment, with twelve stab wounds in his torso. During the night the train had become stranded in snow banks because of an unusually heavy snowfall. It is clear that nobody could have left the train after the murder was committed, and therefore the murderer must still be on the train.

By late afternoon, Poirot has solved the mystery.

CHARACTERS

Hercule Poirot, the famous Belgian detective. His usual eccentricities—an obsession for order and method, for neatness and symmetry, and his pride in his magnificent mustache are not nearly so apparent in this book as in previous ones because he does not have Hastings to comment on them, this story being told in the third person. His "citizen of the world" quality is apparent, however, as he dismisses the national prejudices of his Belgian colleague Monsieur Bouc, who is convinced that the crime must have been committed by the Italian passenger, since the victim was stabbed and, according to Monsieur Bouc, "Italians stab." Poirot has occasion to laugh at the British term "pukka sahib," used by a British passenger to describe another British passenger in order to "prove" her innocence.

In a previous Poirot novel, *Peril at End House,* Captain Hastings uses the term "pukka sahib" to describe George Challenger who is a "good old boy" of the "old school loyalty" type and whom Hastings therefore declares repeatedly to be "above suspicion," to Poirot's extreme annoyance. Poirot is unimpressed by what he sees as a ridiculous British belief that the "good old boys of Eaton or Harrow" can do no wrong and is gratified by Hastings's embarrassment when Challenger and his Harley Street specialist father are shown to be partners in the cocaine racket. Later, in *Thirteen at Dinner* Hastings invokes his "British fair play" and "playing the game" notions when he criticizes Poirot for reading someone else's private love letter, and Poirot again has occasion to scold him for that nonsense, repeating that he is not "playing a game" but tracking down a killer.

Lieutenant Dubosc, a young French soldier who is given the task of seeing Poirot off at the station in Aleppo, desperately trying to make conversation as they both suffer in the cold awaiting the departure time of the train.

Monsieur Bouc, a short, stout, elderly man, his hair cut *en brosse*. A Belgian and an old friend of Poirot's, he is the director of the Compagnie Internationale des Wagons Lits and happens to be traveling on the train along with Poirot.

In his discussions with Poirot about the case he repeats continually that, because the victim was stabbed, the killer cannot be anyone but the one Italian passenger. Of that passenger, M. Bouc states, "He has been a long time in America and he is an Italian, and Italians use the knife! And they are great liars! I do not like Italians." It is to no avail that Poirot points out that there is no evidence against that particular passenger.

Pierre Michel, the conductor of the Calais coach, a Frenchman living near Calais who has worked for the company for more than fifteen years. According to Monsieur Bouc, he is respectable and honest, though perhaps not remarkable for his intelligence.

Colonel Arbuthnot, a British colonel returning home from India. He is the stereotypical British colonial military type who despises foreigners and speaks French in the "British Correct" way, that is to say, probably with grammatical correctness but with purely British vowels, syllable stress and intonation and not that "greasy foreigner" sound that the French use when speaking their own language.

Entering the restaurant car and seating himself at a table for breakfast,

> His eyes rested for a moment on Hercule Poirot, but they passed on indifferently. Poirot, reading the English mind correctly, knew that he had said to himself: "Only some damned foreigner."

Poirot asks the Colonel his opinion of Miss Debenham, a passenger with whom Poirot has reason to believe the Colonel has some intimacy, and the Colonel is annoyed by the question. Poirot presses the point, saying that in a murder investigation all facts are important. The Colonel replies angrily that "Miss Debenham is a lady!" He ends the conversation with the following reminder to Poirot and M. Bouc:

> "About Miss Debenham," he said rather awkwardly. "You can take it from me that she's all right. She's a *pukka sahib*." Then, flushing a little, he withdrew.
> "What," asked Dr. Constantine with interest, "does a *pukka sahib* mean?"
> "It means," said Poirot, "that Miss Debenham's father and brothers were at the same kind of school as Colonel Arbuthnot was."
> "Oh!" said Dr. Constantine, disappointed. "Then it has nothing to do with the crime at all."
> "Exactly," said Poirot.

Mary Hermione Debenham, a young English lady returning to London from Baghdad where she had been governess to two children. She is about twenty-eight years old, tall, slim and dark. Hercule Poirot is impressed by the cool efficiency in the way she orders breakfast and speaks with the train personnel, indicating a knowledge of the world and of traveling. But, he decides, she is just a little too efficient to be what he calls *jolie femme*.

Hector Willard MacQueen of New York City, age about thirty, secretary to Mr. Ratchett, the murder victim. He had worked for Mr. Ratchett for just over a year, not so much as a secretary but as a "courier." Mr. Ratchett knew no foreign languages and Hector was able to "get by" in several. His French is halting, however. "*Je crois que vous avez un erreur*," he says to Poirot instead of the more idiomatic "*Je crois que vous vous trompez*." After the murder, Hector confides to Poirot that he had disliked and distrusted Mr. Ratchett but for reasons he could not put into words. He was aware of threatening letters that Mr. Ratchett had received.

Samuel Edward Ratchett, a wealthy American between age sixty and seventy, traveling with a valet, a secretary and a "bodyguard." Poirot soon discovers that Mr. Ratchett is none other than the infamous criminal Cassetti who had engineered the kidnapping and murder of an American child, the three-year-old daughter of a famous aviator. Through the leverage of his money and connections he was found innocent of the crime on technicalities, but his guilt was well established. Since his trial he has been traveling abroad. He is found dead, one morning, in his first-class compartment, with twelve stab wounds in his body.

Hector MacQueen, his secretary, remarked that he felt Mr. Ratchett was "a cruel and dangerous man" even before learning of his true identity. Poirot, also, had formed a "wild animal" first impression of Ratchett. As the investigation proceeds, the other passengers learn of Mr. Ratchett's true identity and all agree that he deserved to be murdered.

Antonio Foscarelli, a loquacious Italo-American automobile salesman. He "was not a man who had to have information dragged from him. It gushed out." He is very proud of his knowledge of salesmanship and his favorite subject seems to be American-style salesmanship. In addition to Italian and English, he speaks French fluently with only a slight accent. According to Mr. Masterman, Mr. Ratchett's English valet, Foscarelli speaks "a kind of English ... he's been in America—Chicago, I understand." Mr. Foscarelli is not fond of the English, describing them as "a miserable race—the English, not sympathetic," and referring specifically to Mr. Masterman as "that miserable John Bull" who refuses to speak to him and acts superior.

Cyrus Bethman Hardman, age forty-one, an American posing as a traveling salesman of typewriter ribbons, but who is actually a private investigator hired by Mr. Ratchett as a bodyguard for the railway trip. Monsieur Bouc describes him as "a common-looking man with terrible clothes. He chews the gum, which I believe is not done in good circles."

Mr. Hardman is the stereotypically loud, crude, gum-chewing American traveling abroad. He uses American slang such as "Put me wise," "Sure," "That's so," "Guess I'd better come clean," etc. He refers to Italians as "Wops" during a conversation about the murder of the Armstrong baby. He refers to Mrs. Hubbard as "that American dame raising hell."

Mr. Masterman, age thirty-nine, who has the expressionless and disapproving face of the well-trained servant. He has been Mr. Ratchett's British valet for the past nine months. He is just as ethnocentric as Colonel Arbuthnot, having "a low opinion of Americans and no opinion of other foreigners," according to Hector MacQueen.

Princess Natalia Dragomiroff, an aged, wealthy Russian expatriate who lives on the prestigious Avenue Kléber in Paris. Despite her rank, the Princess has no objection to being questioned and to having her luggage searched, expressing the view that since there is a murder case at hand, these things are necessary.

Mrs. Caroline Martha Hubbard, another loquacious American, described as "elderly." She is as ethnocentric as anyone in the train, referring to the people in charge of the train accident as "just a pack of useless foreigners." When the train is stranded in the snow, she asks,

"What *is* this country anyway?"

On being told it is Jugo-Slavia, she says:

"Oh! One of these Balkan things. What can you expect?"

Mrs. Hubbard is the stereotypically uncouth, ignorant, self-centered, ethnocentric American traveler of that period.

Greta Ohlsson, age forty-nine, the matron in a missionary school near Istanbul and a trained nurse. Unlike the other European passengers, she is fond of American people, citing their generosity in the matter of building schools and hospitals abroad. She sheds a good many tears about the train delay, repeating that her sister in Lausanne will fear she has had an accident. Her English is poor and so Poirot interviews her in French.

Hildegarde Schmidt, the German ladies' maid to Princess Dragomiroff, for whom she has worked for the past fifteen years. Poirot interviews her in German as her English and French are minimal.

Count and Countess Andrenyi, young Hungarian aristocrats. The Count is very tall with broad shoulders and slender hips, and could be taken for an Englishman were it not for the length of his moustache and something in the line of the cheekbone. The Countess is a beautiful, stylishly-dressed young woman of twenty with beautiful, almond-shaped eyes and very long black lashes.

Both the Count and the Countess answer questions minimally and insist that they "heard nothing and saw nothing" related to the crime.

The "Chef de Train," in charge of all of the conductors of the individual cars, a big man in a blue uniform. When shown the twelve stab wounds in the body of the victim, he declares

"It is a woman. Depend upon it, it was a woman. Only a woman would stab like that."

Conductor for the Athens-Paris coach, a big, fair man

Dr. Constantine, a small, dark man who is the only passenger in the Athens-Paris coach, aside from Monsieur Bouc. He agrees to participate in the investigation of the crime along with Hercule Poirot and Monsieur Bouc.

FRENCH INTO ENGLISH

Part One

Chapter 1
Mon cher—My dear friend
comme ça—just like that
En voiture—All aboard
Enfin!—At last!
Voilà—Here you are
Merci—Thank you
jolie femme—a pretty lady

Chapter 2
Voilà ce qui est embêtant—This is very annoying
Très bien—very good
en brosse—brush cut (style of haircut)
Les affaires—les affaires—Business—business
Tout à fait au bout—all the way to the end
Je crois que vous avez un erreur.—(The American Mr. MacQueen is speaking and trying to express "I think you're making a mistake." The correct French would be *Je crois que vous vous trompez*. The line is supposed to indicate to the reader that Mr. MacQueen's French is not very idiomatic and is probably that of a non–French speaker translating awkwardly from his own language.)
Voilà, Monsieur—There you are, sir.
En voiture!—All aboard!

Chapter 3
mon cher—my friend, similar to *mon ami*
Elle est jolie—et chic—She's pretty—and stylishly-dressed

Chapter 4
Ce n'est rien. Je me suis trompé.—It's nothing. I made a mistake. (The line is a clue because it shows that the person speaks correct, idiomatic French whereas certain other characters do not.)

Chapter 5
Bonne nuit—Good night
De l'eau minérale, s'il vous plaît—Some mineral water, please
La dame américaine—The American lady
Bon soir—Good evening (correct spelling: *Bonsoir*)
Vous êtes un directeur de la ligne, je crois, Monsieur. Vous pouvez nous dire—I think you're one of the directors of the line, sir. Can you tell us....
déjeuner—lunch
Ah! c'était terrible!—Oh, it was awful!
C'est une femme—It's a woman
C'est entendu—It's agreed

Chapter 6
le docteur—the doctor
Qu'est-ce qu'il y a ... Pourquoi...?—What's going on ... why...?

Chapter 7

Que pensez-vous de ça?—What do you think of that?
Ah! c'est rigolo, tout ça!—This is just too ridiculous!

Chapter 8

Ah! quel animal!—What an animal!
Tout de même—all the same
Après vous, Monsieur—After you, sir.
Mais non, après vous—No, after you.

Part Two

Chapter 1

Ce n'est rien. Je me suis trompé.—It's nothing. I made a mistake.
cauchemar—nightmare

Chapter 5

pardon—excuse me
mon cher—my friend (similar to *mon ami*)
Ce n'est rien. Je me suis trompé.—It's nothing. I made a mistake.

Chapter 6

Voilà une grande dame—Now there's a great lady!

Chapter 7

Elle est jolie femme—She's a pretty woman

Chapter 8

en permission—on leave from work

Chapter 14

Encore un peu, Madame?—Would you like a little more, ma'am?
Mais il n'y a rien à voir—But there is nothing to see.

Chapter 15

Tout de même—All the same, in any case
dans son caractère—consistent with his personality
Entrez—Come in
chic—stylish, sharp-looking
c'est impayable—it cannot be bought
canaille—scoundrel, rotter
Vous êtes bien aimable, Madame—That's very good of you, ma'am.
Diable!—Damn!
grande dame—great lady
Qui s'excuse s'accuse—French proverb: "He who apologizes, accuses himself," that is, "If you apologize for something, then you must have done it."

Part Three

Chapter 1

Le voilà—Here he is.
Ce n'est rien. Je me suis trompé.—It's nothing. I made a mistake.

Chapter 3

objet de luxe—luxury article
Premier service. Le diner est servi. Premier diner—Dinner is being served, first sitting.

Chapter 5

hors de combat—out of the picture
grande seigneur—aristocrat (correct spelling: *grand seigneur*)

Chapter 7

Mon cher, vous êtes épatant!—My friend, you're astounding!
Comment?—What's that you say?

Chapter 8

roman policier—detective novel
c'est rigolo—it's crazy, ridiculous

Chapter 9

Messieurs et mesdames—Ladies and gentlemen
Comment?—What?
C'est possible—It's possible

COMMENTS

The characters in *Murder in the Calais Coach* are, for the most part, stereotypes. These include a loud, egocentric and ethnocentric American woman who complains incessantly about conditions abroad and the "uselessness of foreigners;" an equally obnoxious American man who wears loud clothing, chews gum and refers to Italians as "Wops;" an autocratic Russian expatriate aristocrat; a haughty Hungarian count and countess; a motor-mouthed Italo-American who talks about nothing but business (*his* business); a snobbish English manservant; a narrow-minded, foreigner-despising British colonel; an earnest missionary nurse from Sweden; a rather stupid German ladies' maid; a young American man who is a secretary without very much personality; and a young English nursery governess with considerable strength of character.

Since most of these people are stereotypes, their conversation has a certain amusing, picturesque quality but as individual human beings, their characterizations are without complexity.

A special feature of the novel is that there is

no way for Hercule Poirot to verify the statements that the characters make about themselves, since the murder occurs on a train that is stranded in a snow storm and there is no possibility of communication with the outside world. Poirot must listen to what the passengers say, and what the other passengers say about them, knowing that most of the passengers are substantially strangers to each other, and he must solve the mystery without any assistance from outside.

There is little in the way of useful clues. Poirot immediately recognizes at least two of the clues as "false clues" left by the murderer to mislead, and at least two more clues are later shown to be false also.

The story is intriguing and the solution is unique and unforgettable. Unfortunately a well-known filming of the story was made in the mid-1970s, making it impossible for anyone to fully enjoy reading the novel after seeing the film, since the reader cannot have the experience of sifting the evidence and suspecting first one character and then another. However, even if one has seen the film, the novel can be a fun reading experience because of the amusing characters and dialogue.

Because of the great variety of nationalities of the characters, and their comments about each other, Christie is able to make a very clear statement about ethnocentricity: it is a widespread and foolish attitude.

Murder in Three Acts (1935)

(Alternate Title: *Three Act Tragedy*)

Setting

The time is August through October of 1933 or 1934. The principal setting is a fictitious town called Loomouth in the real county of Cornwall. Cornwall is the narrow peninsula at the southwest corner of England. The setting for *Peril at End House*, the fictitious resort village of St. Loo, had also been in Cornwall.

The first murder occurs at Crow's Nest, the modern luxury home of one of the principal characters. It is perched high up on a cliff and reached quickly by a steep footpath from Loomouth, although by car the distance is a full mile, since the road curves inland for a considerable distance. The house is ultra modern with all the latest conveniences, including several bathrooms. One room is expensively decorated to resemble the captain's cabin of a ship.

A second setting is the home of a wealthy doctor in Yorkshire, in the north of England. Near the home is a modern nursing home for the doctor's "nerve patients." A second murder takes place at the doctor's home and subsequent scenes occur there and also at the nursing home. A third murder takes place at the nursing home itself.

In addition, there are a few scenes in London. These include several flats occupied by various characters, a luxury suite at the Ritz Hotel where Poirot happens to be staying late in the story, an expensive restaurant and the Bond Street shop of one of the characters, a fashionable dressmaker.

There are scenes at a place called Tooting, a London suburb, and at a cottage in a fictitious town called Gilling. The location of Gilling is not stated, but as two characters travel there by car from London via "the Folkstone Road," Gilling must be somewhere in the county of Kent. Kent is the county southeast of London, in which Canterbury and the ports of Dover and Folkstone are located.

There is one brief scene at Monte Carlo where Hercule Poirot and two other characters are vacationing and learn of the second murder through the newspapers.

There are no references to contemporary historical events in the novel. One of the characters, the lady who owns the dressmaking business, uses the latest "fashionable" forms of speech, which include a sort of drawling, lazy or weary style of delivery and over-use of the word "penetrating." The women's dress fashions that she conceives include deliberately useless features such as fabric knots and fringes or ruffles placed at locations specifically intended to be more "amusing" than functional.

Cocktails are the latest fashion in drinks and dry martinis are served in one or two scenes.

There is a mention of the "Blue Train," as a couple of the characters vacationing in Monte Carlo decide "to return to England by the next Blue Train." The Blue Train was a special train connecting the French Riviera with Paris and there were special conveniences arranged for travelers from England to the Riviera and back. For details, see the *Setting* section for the 1928 *The Mystery of the Blue Train*.

Story

It is late August of 1933 or 1934. Retired stage actor Sir Charles Cartwright hosts a dinner party at his luxurious modern house perched on a cliff on the south coast of Cornwall. Among his guests are a distinguished Harley Street physician, Dr. Strange; a benignly snobbish patron of the arts and theatre, Mr. Satterthwaite; and the famous Belgian detective Hercule Poirot. Also present are an aging but still beautiful stage actress, a playwright, a well-known dress designer and her husband, and a few local people, including the vicar and his wife.

After dinner, cocktails are served and the vicar, Reverend Babbington, suddenly experiences some kind of seizure and dies. The local people return to their homes and most of the London guests retire to their rooms, but Hercule Poirot, Sir Charles, Mr. Satterthwaite and Dr. Strange remain together to discuss the vicar's death. Sir Charles suggests that the vicar may have been murdered, but the other men express doubt about that. Who would want to murder a kindly old clergyman?

However, a few weeks later Dr. Strange dies at his home in Yorkshire in a similar way—after a dinner party just as he is sipping a glass of port. Hercule Poirot, Sir Charles and Mr. Satterthwaite wonder if Rev. Babbington could have been killed accidentally by someone who had intended to murder Dr. Strange—a murderer who then struck later with accuracy. It is known that Dr. Strange died of nicotine poisoning, and then an exhumation of Rev. Babbington's body proves that he died of the same poison.

Mr. Satterthwaite, Sir Charles, and one of the local dinner guests of the first party, young Hermione Lytton Gore, form a trio of amateur sleuths, consulting minimally with Hercule Poirot, who remains comfortably housed at a luxury hotel in London and offers assistance to the three amateurs only when asked. It is he, of course, who solves the mystery by the use of his "little gray cells," but not in time to prevent a third killing.

CHARACTERS

Hercule Poirot, the retired Belgian private investigator, whose characteristic eccentricities are not very apparent in this novel, although he does have occasion to ask for a "a glance of *sirop*," (which is not included in his English host's conception of drinkable fluids) and he does have opportunities to smoke quantities of his "tiny Russian cigarettes." He remains comfortably housed at the Ritz Hotel in London, using only his "gray cells" and offering his opinions and advice to three amateur sleuths only when asked.

Mr. Satterthwaite, an elderly patron of the arts and theatre, and a houseguest of Sir Charles Cartwright. His principal interest in life is "people," more women than men, and he knows far too much about women to be considered a "manly man." To him life is a fascinating drama in which he has never participated directly but which he enjoys "observing." He has never been married. At one time, he had a financial interest in one of Sir Charles Cartwright's plays and, since then, they have been friends. His house on Chelsea Embankment in London is filled with art works. Among his perceptions about women: "Young girls are always attracted to middle aged men with pasts."

Sir Charles Cartwright, a retired stage actor now in his fifties. He keeps a luxury flat in London, and two years ago he built "Crow's Nest," a good-sized, ultra-modern luxury home—big, square and white—high upon a cliff overlooking a picturesque Cornish village. He describes this house—which has three bathrooms and all the latest gadgets, and which features an entertainment room expensively decorated to resemble the cabin of a ship's captain—as his "simple shanty to come home to." He is such a consummate actor that his own "real life" is also an act—that is, a series of acts. As the story opens, his role of the moment is that of a retired seaman—he dresses appropriately in old gray flannel trousers and white sweaters. (He has acted parts of seamen on the stage many times.) When a murder occurs in his Ship Room, he speculates on the subject of possible suspects and motives, using exaggerated shrugs of the shoulders and walking with a slight limp (he once played the part of a limping, shoulder-shrugging detective.) When the young woman he loves appears to love another, he withdraws and assumes the new role of "rejected lover," mumbling appropriate expressions of noble resignation. In the words of his friend, Dr. Strange, Sir Charles does not go out of a room; he "makes an exit," usually with an appropriate exit line.

Physically, Sir Charles is an extremely handsome man. A touch of gray at his temples gives him a kind of added distinction. He looks like what he is—a gentleman first and an actor second—but it is a very close second.

Sir Bartholomew Strange, ("Tollie"), a kindly, middle-aged gray-haired Harley Street doctor. He is a well-known specialist in nervous disorders. In addition to his office and home in London he has a large home, Melfort Abbey, in Yorkshire and within its grounds he has established a sanatorium for his special patients. A lifelong friend of Sir Charles, he is surprised and amused that Charles's current "role" (that of the retired seaman) has lasted a full two years. Dr. Strange would have predicted a maximum "six month run" for that show. According to the local people near his home in Yorkshire, Dr. Strange is very well thought of there.

Violet Milray, Sir Charles Cartwright's secretary/housekeeper. She is a tall and exceedingly ugly woman, but extremely efficient, as if spontaneously generated from a dynamo.

Angela Sutcliffe, a well-known stage actress, no longer young, but with a strong hold on the public and celebrated for her wit and charm.

Cynthia Dacres, a tall woman, with a figure perfectly disciplined to the demands of the moment. She is the owner of Ambrosine Ltd., an expensive dressmaker's shop in Bond Street. A sample of her style of conversation:

> "My dear, it wasn't possible. I mean, things either are possible or they're not. This wasn't. It was simply penetrating."

That was the new word just now—everything was "penetrating."

Captain Freddie Dacres, the husband of Cynthia Dacres, a horse racing enthusiast about whom there have been disreputable rumors—nothing overt, but, somehow, at mention of Freddie Dacres people's eyebrows go up a little. He speaks in a high, clipped voice—a little, red, foxy man with a short mustache and slightly shifty eyes. He is also a heavy drinker.

Hermione Lytton Gore, while "making inquiries," has occasion to have a cocktail with Freddie Dacres in the downstairs club of his expensive apartment block in London. His thoughts of the moment:

> Freddie Dacres smiled indulgently. He liked a young and pretty girl. Not, perhaps, as much as he liked some other things, but well enough.

Possibly the above is intended as a subtle suggestion that Freddie prefers men; it is also possible that he simply prefers liquor.

Anthony Astor (Muriel Wills), a tall, thin young woman with a receding chin, very badly waved, fair hair and a pince-nez. Her voice is high and undistinguished. She is a successful playwright who uses the masculine pseudonym Anthony Astor. During the party at Crow's Nest, Lady Mary Lytton Gore is shocked to learn who she is, because to her Miss Wills looks exactly like an inefficient nursery governess. Another character observes, however, that Miss Wills has very keen eyes, and he forms the impression that she is probably as keenly observant of human nature as Mr. Satterthwaite is.

Reverend Stephen Babbington, the rector of Loomouth for the past seventeen years, a man of sixty-odd, with kind, faded eyes and a disarming, diffident manner. He dies of nicotine poisoning early in the story.

Margaret Babbington, a big, untidy woman who looks full of energy and is likely to be free from petty-mindedness. She often advises Sir Charles on gardening subjects, and during the party at Crow's Nest she speaks earnestly to him on the subject of manure. The Babbingtons have had four sons, one of them deceased and the others living in various outposts of the Empire.

Lady Mary Lytton Gore, an impoverished gentlewoman, widowed at an early age with a child of three. She lives in Loomouth in a small house named Rose Cottage with one maid and her daughter, now a young lady of about twenty. She is a close friend of the Babbingtons who arrived at the village at about the same time. She loves her daughter very much "but is a little alarmed by her." She is worried about her daughter's future and would like her to marry Sir Charles, despite his being more than twice her daughter's age, since he has already "sown his oats" and is probably ready to settle down. She wishes that her daughter had more friends her own age and she disapproves of Oliver Manders, although she considers him to be a good person basically, but with an unfortunate background. Mostly she feels that he is unkind and she does not want a husband like that for her daughter.

Lady Mary's own marriage was unhappy. Her parents had opposed it; the man had a bad reputation, but "like all girls," she was attracted to men with bad reputations. She later admitted that her parents had been right. For this reason she hopes that her daughter will make a better match.

Hermione Lytton Gore ("Egg"), Lady Mary's daughter. She is attracted to Oliver Manders and they think very much alike. Both are very "modern" in the 1930s sense—they despise money and capitalism and Oliver, in fact, is a Communist and was on one occasion extremely rude to Reverend Babbington, making "a rather ill-bred attack on Christianity" in his presence, according to Lady Mary. Egg is very much the kind of young intellectual person who prevailed at that time in both Western Europe and America. Although attracted to Oliver, Egg is in love with Sir Charles, who is at least twice her age.

Egg is bright, energetic, creative and determined—just like all of Agatha Christie's "bright young women" of this period—Tuppence Beresford, Anne Beddingfeld, Lady Eileen Brent (Bundle), Emily Trefusis and Lady Frances Derwent (Frankie.) She is modern and outspoken and sometimes shocks her elders, as she does Mr. Satterthwaite with her comment that "men ought to have affairs—it shows they're not queer or anything," and her remarks about the Church's being "all a mess."

Egg proves to be an excellent sleuth, too, and clever at obtaining confidences. Her scene with one of Mrs. Dacres's clothing models is first rate. First she visits Mrs. Dacres, pretending to have suddenly come into money and wanting to purchase a whole new, expensive wardrobe (fact: it is now September and Egg's bank balance, which must carry her through December, is exactly fifteen pounds twelve shillings.) Then she waits for one of the models to go out for lunch, approaching her in the street with a hastily fabricated story about being a fledgling journalist writing an "inside story" about the fashion business, and within half an hour she knows everything about Mr. and Mrs. Dacres. Whenever the model suggests something like "of course I'm not one to gossip," Egg hastily puts in "Of course not. Do go on!"

Oliver Manders, a very handsome young man of about twenty-five. He has a bitterly hostile attitude towards society in general and its entrenched institutions. As mentioned earlier, he professes to be a Communist, but in fact he is working in the City with an uncle's company and "wants to get rich," this fact being a disappointment to the even more youthfully idealistic Egg. He is moody and sullen most of the time. He says he "wants to chuck it all and be a journalist" but so far this has not happened. Since childhood he has felt rejected because of having been born illegitimately.

Holgate, Sir Charles Cartwright's chauffeur

Temple, Sir Charles Cartwright's smart and obviously feminine housemaid

Dr. MacDougal, the principal doctor in Loomouth, who examines Reverend Babbington after his death, declaring that there is nothing to suggest that his death was not from natural causes.

Mr. Baker, Dr. Strange's regular butler who has been sent away on a paid holiday to a resort near Brighton because of recent poor health

John Ellis, Dr. Strange's temporary replacement butler, who disappears mysteriously early on the morning following the doctor's death.

Dr. Davis, a local doctor in the neighborhood of Melfort Abbey who examines Dr. Strange's body

Superintendent Crossfield, the police officer in charge of the case of Dr. Strange's murder

Colonel Johnson, Superintendent Crossfield's superior. NOTE: Hercule Poirot will be a houseguest of Colonel Johnson in 1937 for the Christmas season in *A Holiday for Murder*. In that novel the name of the county will be given as Middleshire (a fictitious county) and the general area will be referred to as "the Midlands." But in *Murder in Three Acts,* the name of the county in which Dr. Strange lives is clearly stated as Yorkshire. Yorkshire is a large county divided into three parts known as "Ridings," a linguistic descendant of the older term "Thridings." The "West Riding" is in fact part of the English "Midlands," a region noted for numerous densely populated, drab, industrial cities.

Gladys Lyndon, Dr. Strange's efficient secretary

Martha Leckie, Dr. Strange's cook of fifteen years at Melfort Abbey, extremely loquacious but an accurate observer and reporter

Beatrice Church, upper housemaid of thirteen years at Melfort Abbey; she has a ghoulish relish for the tragedy and looks down on tradespeople, including successful ones such as Mrs. Dacres

Doris Cocker, under housemaid at Melfort Abbey, inclined to oversleep in the morning

Victoria Ball, parlormaid at Melfort Abbey, who is inclined to be impertinent, according to Mrs. Leckie

Violet Bassington, kitchenmaid at Melfort Abbey

Lord and Lady Eden; Sir Jocelyn and Lady Cambell, four additional dinner guests of Dr. Strange on the day of his death

A Matron at Dr. Strange's Sanatorium in Yorkshire

Margaret de Rushbridger, age about forty, a special "nerve patient" at Dr. Strange's sanatorium

The Lodgekeeper at the home of Dr. Strange in Yorkshire, a slow-witted man of middle age

Robin, Edward, Lloyd and Stephen, adult children of the Babbingtons, (Robin is deceased.) Egg Lytton Gore had "had a pash" for Robin before he died abroad in a colonial uprising.

Old Mrs. Manders, grandmother of Oliver Manders. She lives at Dunboyne, not far from Loomouth on the road to Plymouth, in Devon.

A Monumental American Woman, an important clothing customer of Cynthia Dacres.

Doris Sims, one of Cynthia Dacres's dress models

Mrs. Milray, the invalid mother of Violet Milray, Sir Charles's secretary/housekeeper

A Man Dressed in Shabby Clothes, who carries a handwritten message from "a loony lady at the sanatorium" to be telegraphed at once to London

A Small Boy who, in exchange for a two-shilling tip, sends the above telegram

Murder in Three Acts (1935)

French into English

Chapter 3

sirop—any sweet liqueur such as "sirop de cassis" (black currant liqueur, a favorite drink of Hercule Poirot)

Chapter 6

demoiselle—young lady
la jeunesse—youth
Maman, joue avec moi.—Mama, play with me.
Amuse-toi avec ta balle, Marcelle.—Go and play with your ball, Marcelle.
Je m'amuse—I'm enjoying myself

Chapter 16

au courant—in the know, up to date
Ah, mais c'est magnifique, ça!—Magnificent!
quelle idée—what an idea!
les femmes—women

Chapter 17

chien de chasse—hunting dog
parfaitement—perfectly

Chapter 18

objets d'art—art objects

Chapter 23

Quelle historie—What nonsense. (Correct spelling: *Quelle histoire*.)
Là, là!—Expression of disgust, such as "Ugh!"
Voilà—There you are.
malheur—oops!
Ah, quelle horreur—What a disgusting thing!
qu'est-ce qu'il y a?—What's wrong? What's happening?

Chapter 25

Mille tonnerres!—Oh my God!

Chapter 26

Quelle idée!—Such an idea!
Ah, c'est ça.—Yes, that's it.
nom de théâtre—stage name
C'est comme ça?—So it's like that? or So that's how it is?
Enfin, moi.—Well, anyway, it's me. (Poirot is answering Miss Milray who is surprised to see him, and she says "You!" He says "Me" but isn't sure if he should say "I" instead, in English, so he reverts to French, "enfin, moi." which he knows to be correct.

Chapter 27

canaille—scoundrel

Comments

Every Christie detective novel is unique, and *Murder in Three Acts* is unique in two ways. First of all, although it is an Hercule Poirot novel, Poirot remains somewhat in the background. He relaxes comfortably in his suite at the Ritz Hotel in London while three amateur sleuths run around England finding out things, guessing at things and bringing all of their new information to him now and then for his comments. He likes it that way, and so do they. In fact, his "intrusion" into the case is not particularly welcomed by the three amateurs who consider the case to be "their show."

The three amateurs all have strong personalities and it is amusing to observe their different approaches to detecting. Egg (Lady Hermione Lytton Gore) uses methods similar to those of Lady Frances Derwent (Frankie,) Lady Eileen Brent (Bundle,) and Emily Trefusis, all heroines of earlier Christie novels. She finds ways of ingratiating herself to whomever she happens to be questioning, often using lies and flattery if appropriate and necessary. Mr. Satterthwaite is completely different. He easily gains the confidence of the more conservative, genteel types, encouraging them to reveal themselves and to reminisce, and then he gently turns the conversation in the direction of his inquiry. Sir Charles Cartwright relies on his fame as an actor and has no difficulty in extracting information from anyone who is awestruck by celebrity, even police officers whose wives are theatre fans.

The second uniqueness in *Murder in Three Acts* is that it is very difficult for anyone to imagine—and to discover—a motive for any of the three murders. There aren't even what one could call "likely suspects" since apparently nobody who could possibly be the murderer seems to benefit from any of the deaths. A butler flees the scene of the second murder, arousing suspicion, but he cannot be connected with the first murder.

The characters in *Murder in Three Acts* are nicely characterized and quite individual. They are not stereotypes, that is to say. Hermione (Egg) is a young girl of unusual intellect. Sir Charles, the stage actor, is an amusing specimen who "acts" every minute of his life and is not aware of how obvious this is to observers. Mr. Satterthwaite is entirely unique. Just as Sir Charles is the consummate actor, even in real life, Mr. Satterthwaite is the consummate spectator, even in real life.

Along with these rather eccentric types are the more conventional but equally appealing characters: Lady Mary who, because of her own past mistakes with men, hopes with all her heart that her daughter will not make the same mistakes. She is a gentle, loving mother, that in itself rather unique in Agatha Christie's novels. She knows that her daughter has been deprived of companions of her own age, but a part of her rejoices in the prospect of the girl's making a marriage with an older man who may be less likely to disappoint her in the future than a younger man might.

Cynthia Dacres is a kind of caricature of the shallow thinker who fills her conversation with buzz words to cover up the fact that it has very little "content."

Egg's investigations in London are very amusing. The scene in Mrs. Dacres's dress shop, Ambrosine, Ltd. is a superb example of Christie humor. As Egg is seated in an ultra-modern armchair, which is faintly reminiscent of a dentist's chair, she watches as models pass before her, endeavoring to appear as though fifty or sixty pounds for a dress is "a mere bagatelle," as Mrs. Dacres "does her stuff":

"Now, do you like this? Those shoulder knots—rather amusing, don't you think? And the waistline's rather penetrating. I shouldn't have the red-lead color, though; I should have it in the new color—Español—most attractive—like mustard with a dash of cayenne in it. How do you like Vin Ordinaire? Rather absurd, isn't it? Quite penetrating and ridiculous. Clothes simply must not be serious nowadays."

"It's very difficult to decide," said Egg. "You see"—she became confidential—"I've never been able to afford any clothes before. We were always so dreadfully poor. I remembered how simply marvelous you looked that night at Crow's Nest, and I thought 'Now that I've got money to spend, I shall go to Mrs. Dacres and ask her to advise me.' I did admire you so much that night." [Note: Pure lies, all of this; Egg despised Cynthia Dacres and referred to her in conversation as "that woman with green hair." And as to money, Egg is nearly broke.]

"My dear, how charming of you. I simply adore dressing a young girl. It's so important that girls shouldn't look raw, if you know what I mean."

"Nothing raw about you," thought Egg ungratefully. "Cooked to a turn, you are."

"You've got so much personality," continued Mrs. Dacres. "You mustn't have anything at all ordinary. Your clothes must be simple, and penetrating, and just faintly risable. You understand? Do you want several things?"

"I thought about four evening frocks, and a couple of day things, and a sports suit or two—that sort of thing."

The honey of Mrs. Dacres' manner became sweeter. It was fortunate that she did not know that at that moment Egg's bank balance was exactly fifteen pounds, twelve shillings, and that the said balance had got to last her until December.

(...)

"Now, this Patou model would be perfect for you. Look at that perfectly useless and ridiculous frill; it makes the whole thing adorable. Young without being tiresome..."

But she was interrupted by a monumental American, evidently a valued client...

And here the interview—which has been a waste of time in terms of gathering useful information relative to the murder case—ends. But it provides Egg with an opportunity of accosting one of the models as she leaves for lunch, and at that point Egg becomes a "young journalist writing an inside story about the fashion business," and learns everything about Mr. and Mrs. Dacres from her.

The world of theatre is mildly ridiculed in this novel—mostly through the almost pathetically, blindly self-centered actor, Sir Charles, but also through the playwright, Muriel Wills who, unlike the witty, sophisticated and articulate characters she creates in her plays, is frumpy and dumpy, wears pince nez and limp clothes and is shy and retreating, "expressing herself much better in writing than in conversation." Agatha Christie is known to have felt that she, too, was much more articulate in writing than in conversation and she hated cocktail parties and their frivolous chatter.

In *The Boomerang Clue* we were treated to the exceedingly unpleasant "religious practice" of Reverend Thomas Jones, witnessing his incessant judgmental preaching at his unfortunate—and perfectly normal and natural—son Bobby who eventually wonders "how much longer he can stick it." In *Murder in Three Acts* both Egg and Oliver Manders, two of the more advanced thinkers among the characters, give a good scolding about people who profess religion but who have no idea of its true spirit or purpose. Egg believes in God and in the spirit of Christianity but laughs at the superficial trappings of established churches, and Oliver admires people who stand up for their beliefs when surrounded by hypocrites. For a conventionally educated woman of the late Victorian period (Christie was born in 1890) these ideas are rather advanced.

Death in the Air (1935)

(Alternate Title: *Death in the Clouds*)

SETTING

The story takes place in September and October of 1934. In Christie's novels, it is rare for the specific year to be mentioned directly, but in this case there is a humorous remark about two archeologists whose thoughts are so thoroughly fixed upon events and conditions five thousand years ago that nineteen hundred and thirty-four A. D. would have been non-existent to them; therefore we know that the year is 1934. The action begins at Le Bourget Aerodrome outside Paris where passengers board a plane bound for Croydon Aerodrome outside London.

The crime takes place in one of the two cabins of the "Prometheus," a small passenger airliner which is probably a typical passenger plane of the period. A Rough Plan of the rear car or cabin of the plane is shown—there are eighteen seats available but on this trip only eleven are in use. There is another "front car" with a similar capacity, possibly for second-class passengers, since the maid of one of the first-class passengers has her seat there. The crime is discovered shortly before the plane lands at Croydon.

A police inquiry takes place at Croydon Aerodrome. Thereafter, the settings include many places in London: Hercule Poirot's flat, one or two restaurants including The Monseigneur and The Corner House; homes of several characters—a luxury apartment in Grosvenor Square, the more humble residence of one of the airline stewards in London, a pub called the Crown and Feathers in the suburb of Croydon, the office of a London dentist, the home and office of a Harley Street doctor, and a hairdressing establishment called Antoine's. There is a scene in the bedroom of an English aristocrat and his wife at their country house, Horbury Chase, in Sussex, and also a scene out in the grounds of the estate, which includes a farm.

Equally important are several settings in Paris: the shop of an antique dealer in the Rue St. Honoré, a private home comprising several floors in the Rue Joliette, the Paris office of Universal Airways in the Boulevard des Capucines and several restaurants. A short scene takes place in a speeding taxicab in Paris.

Interiors are not generally described unless they are important to an understanding of the personality of the occupants of the homes or apartments. The London apartment of a detective storywriter is humorously described as a complete shambles in chaos (probably a tongue-in-cheek reference to Christie's own special place where she did her writing). The private apartment of the murder victim in Paris is described as being crowded with heavy old-fashioned furniture but devoid of personal touches such as photographs and other mementos. At the estate of the English aristocrat in Sussex there are references to horses and dogs, and the fragrances of damp foliage and earth.

There are references to several French resorts and resort towns popular with British vacationers at that time; these include Deauville, Paris-Plage and Wimereux on the English Channel coast and Juan-les-Pins, Antibes and Nice on the Riviera. Two or three of the passengers on the plane are returning to England from vacations in Le Pinet, a fictitious resort located in the area of Juan-les-Pins and Antibes. No action takes place in any of these places, however.

Two references are made to the Great Depression of the 1930s: the antique dealer in Paris mentions that he quoted his "American price" for an item—adding that his "American prices" are now lower than formerly because "they have had the depression there." In a conversation with Hercule Poirot, an English countess states that there are "no more millionaires," to which Poirot replies that of course there are: someone who had three million dollars a few years ago now has only two million, but it is "still adequate."

Drug use among the upper classes and among film and stage actors had been mentioned in several earlier Christie novels; in *Death in the Air*, the ex-actress wife of an English aristocrat is a cocaine addict and a gambling addict as well.

Major advances in communication and transportation have taken place since the writing of *The Mysterious Affair at Styles* in 1916. In that novel the country home of a wealthy family not far from London had no telephone or electricity and the use of automobiles was very limited, pony carts still being in daily use, and aviation was primitive. In *Death in the Air*, written in 1934, it is now possible for well-heeled passengers to travel by scheduled airplane flights—there are at least two daily flights between Paris and London—and it is possible to make long distance telephone calls between Europe and America. Furthermore, it is even possible to send images of photographs via telephone lines. In this novel, Poirot makes a phone call in Paris to an orphanage in Québec, speaks to a person there and, later that day, receives a photo image by telephone from that distant place.

As to automobiles, in one scene Hercule Poirot urges the greatest speed to a Paris taxi driver who then darts in and out of heavy traffic at forty miles per hour, frightening Poirot's co-passenger.

STORY

It is September of 1934. A small passenger plane leaves Le Bourget Aerodrome, outside

Paris, bound for London and carrying eleven passengers in one cabin and ten passengers in another. In the first cabin one of the passengers, known as Madame Giselle, is murdered. A cabin steward discovers her death just before the plane lands at Croydon Aerodrome outside London. A mark on her neck suggests that she has been stung by a wasp, but a native dart is later found on the floor near her seat. It is shown that it was the dart that introduced the poison, the venom of a deadly snake, into the victim.

The murder victim had been a "character" well known to the upper classes of England and France. She was a discreet money lender and her method of ensuring repayment of her loans was to gather private information about her clients and to threaten blackmail if they did not repay their debts to her.

One of the other ten passengers riding in Madame Giselle's cabin must have committed the murder. They are a French archeologist and his adult son; two English aristocrats, Countess Cicely Horbury and the Honorable Venetia Kerr; a young London dentist, a London hairdresser's assistant, a medical doctor, a businessman, a detective story writer, and the private investigator Hercule Poirot.

Hercule Poirot works closely with Inspector Japp of Scotland Yard, along with Monsieur Fournier of the French police, in the unmasking of the killer.

CHARACTERS

Hercule Poirot, the retired Belgian private investigator. In this novel, we are not surprised to learn that he experiences airsickness as well as seasickness. His eccentricities are not particularly apparent in this book, although "order and method" and use of the "little gray cells" continue to be important. His appreciation of well-prepared food is as apparent as ever and he even treats Inspector Japp and a French colleague, Monsieur Fournier of the Paris Sûreté, to a meal at his apartment, perhaps prepared by himself, although this is not stated. In this novel he shows himself to be quite a competent cupid as well, orchestrating—or at least facilitating—the unions of two deserving couples.

Marie Angélique Morisot, known to the public as **"Madame Giselle,"** the murder victim. Known in France and England as a "character," she is an ugly, pock-marked middle aged woman whose business is lending money in secret—and with complete discretion—to upper-class and professional people who find themselves short of funds and needing to borrow "discreetly." Security for Madame Giselle's loans takes the form of embarrassing information about the borrowers, which Madame gathers through a network of informants. If the borrower does not repay the debt, the embarrassing information is given to the authorities, the deceived wife or husband or other appropriate person.

Madame Giselle has accumulated a considerable fortune and nearly all of it is willed to her daughter, whom she has not seen since shortly after the child's birth.

Despite the apparent ruthlessness of Madame Giselle—she accepts no excuses and no amount of tears or pleading ever releases anyone from their debts to her—she is scrupulously discreet and honest and never uses the "embarrassing information" to extort money not already owed to her. Her loyal servant Élise—who has worked for her for more than twenty years—is instructed to burn all of Madame Giselle's business papers if ever she should die or disappear suddenly, in order to protect her clients.

Madame Giselle dies aboard the "Prometheus"—instantly upon receiving a puncture from an exotic dart coated with the venom of a poisonous snake—the dart apparently ejected by means of a native blow-pipe found hidden behind the seat of one of the passengers on the aircraft.

Élise Grandier, Madame Giselle's loyal and confidential maid of many years, who obediently destroys her mistress's papers but cooperates with the police, revealing the existence of an heir to Madame Giselle's fortune.

Georges, the aging *concierge* at the home of Madame Giselle in the Rue Joliette, Paris. His vision is poor and he is annoyed by questions about a certain young woman who visited Madame Giselle the evening before the air flight to England and Madame's death. When shown a typically blurred newspaper photograph of Cicely Horbury in a bathing suit, however, the quality of his vision allows him to notice that she is a good looker.

Jane Grey, a hairdresser's assistant at Antoine's in London, one of the passengers in the cabin in which the crime takes place and, therefore, a suspect. Poirot finds her to be "pretty" when he notices her on the airplane at the beginning of the story, but he also feels enough respect for her intelligence and competence to ask for her assistance in the investigation of the murder. At one point, he even hires her to be his secretary and to accompany him to Paris as part of the investigation. Competence and good looks do not prevent Jane from being a suspect, however, as she is the right age to be the daughter of Madame

Giselle *and* she was raised as an orphan. In this novel, Poirot takes several of the suspects into his confidence and encourages them to believe that they are assisting him when, in reality, he is also studying them and their psychology. Jane is one of these.

Jane is strongly attracted to the handsome blue-eyed and suntanned young dentist, Norman Gale, whom she met at Le Pinet and who is also a passenger on the plane on the day of the murder. In addition, the inquest and subsequent investigation bring her into contact with a charming young French archeologist, Jean Dupont, to whom she feels a second attraction.

Countess Cicely Horbury, (stage name: Cicely Bland; birth name: Martha Jebb) A young stage actress whose beauty and charms dazzled Count Stephen Horbury enough to achieve marriage and a title for her. And money, of course. But after about three years, she became thoroughly fed up with "the county life" so cherished by her husband. She is strictly a city woman—she loves upper class social contacts, trips to the Riviera, losing as much money as possible at the roulette tables, smoking cartons of cigarettes—and snorting coke. She is in fact seriously addicted to cocaine and to gambling, has run up enormous gambling debts, has borrowed large sums of money from the notorious Madame Giselle, and her husband now refuses to cover her debts. Lord Horbury would love to have a divorce but Lady Horbury will not hear of that, since her husband's title was all she had married him for in the first place. And money, of course. She has an actor boyfriend with whom she allows herself to be seen—and even photographed—basking in the sun in bathing suits in the South of France.

Lady Horbury is a typical "aristocrat by marriage" who throws her weight about and demands special treatment by the police because of her social position.

Count Stephen Horbury, the unfortunate husband of Lady Horbury. He loves tradition, the old family home, country life, horses, his favorite spaniel, the smell of damp earth and probably even the smell of manure. He loves visiting the farm, chatting with the old farmer and his wife, and wishes he had married a sensible "county type" woman like Venetia Kerr instead of the self-indulgent actress who had besotted him.

The Butler at Horbury Chase in Sussex, the home of Lord and Lady Horbury

Madeleine, Lady Horbury's maid

The Honorable Venetia Kerr, daughter of Lord Cottesmore, who lives at her family home in Horbury, Sussex, a life-long friend and neighbor of Stephen Horbury. She is described in the thoughts of another character as "the horsey, county type." In the thoughts of Lord Horbury, Venetia "looks her best upon a horse."

Norman Gale, age about twenty-seven, a London dentist. He notices Jane Grey at Le Pinet while playing at the roulette table, and is instantly attracted to her. Later he happens to be seated facing her on the plane to England. His thoughts about her at that moment:

> She's pretty—really pretty. She remembers me all right.... She's very attractive when she smiles—no pyorrhoea there—healthy gums and sound teeth.... Damn it, I feel quite excited. Steady, my boy.

And so now we know what male dentists think about when looking at women.

Miss Ross, Mr. Norman Gale's assistant, an attractive young woman with red hair.

Dr. James Bryant, another of the passengers on the plane, a Harley Street specialist in ear and throat disorders who loves music and plays the flute for relaxation. He is a tall, gray-haired man with an authoritative face. He becomes a suspect of the crime when he reveals to Inspector Japp that he is acquainted with a poison specialist.

A Butler at the home of Dr. Bryant

Armand Dupont, a French archeologist, still another passenger aboard the "Prometheus." Inspector Japp observes that, as Monsieur Dupont and his archeologist son had been seated near the murder victim on the plane, they must have noticed something about the crime. Poirot responds, however, that if the two archeologists were having a really absorbing discussion on some archeological subject of great interest to them, the year 1934 A.D. would not even exist for them. And the fact is that Monsieur Dupont and his son had been engaged in an archaeological discussion during the whole trip and had noticed nothing at all about the crime, which was committed no more than four or five feet from them. They had not even noticed the lunch that they had consumed mechanically, and they had forced the steward to await a pause in their discussion before presenting him with a disappointing tip.

Jean Dupont, Armand Dupont's son, also an archeologist. He is a tall, fair young man with a false air of indolence. Jane Grey finds herself as attracted to Jean Dupont as she is to Norman Gale.

Daniel Clancy, another of the passengers on the "Prometheus," a writer of detective novels. He is a little man who loves eating bananas and cannot give a simple yes or no answer to any question, usually answering something like "No ... that is, well, yes but..." or "Yes ... that is, well not exactly, you see ..." etc.

When the crime is discovered—and the murder method made known—Mr. Clancy is positively delighted that it has been committed in this exciting way, in real life and not just in a sensationalistic novel.

> "The arrow poison of the South American Indians," murmured Mr. Clancy deliriously, a happy smile on his face.

During the airplane flight, Mr. Clancy had left his seat once and passed close by the murder victim. His reason for leaving his seat was to check a Continental Bradshaw—a book of railway timetables—in order to create or break the alibi of one of the characters of his current novel.

Hercule Poirot, accompanied by Jane Grey, visits Mr. Clancy at his London flat which is described as a complete shambles with papers strewn about, cardboard files, bananas, bottles of beer, open books, sofa cushions, a trombone, miscellaneous china, etchings, and a bewildering assortment of fountain pens. Mr. Clancy offers chairs to Hercule Poirot and Jane Grey, but the back of one chair is broken and the other has orange juice spilled on it.

Daniel Clancy's mind seems to be as chaotic as his apartment.

Mr. Clancy's Housekeeper, a forbidding-looking elderly woman in black who evidently accepts the chaos in his workroom philosophically.

James Bell Ryder, another passenger on the "Prometheus." He is the managing director of Ellis Vale Cement Company. He had gone to Paris in order to secure a loan but failed. He denies that it was from Madame Giselle that sought the loan.

A Clerk at Mr. Ryder's office

Henry Mitchell, the First Steward aboard the "Prometheus," he is the first to notice that Madame Giselle is unconscious. He worries that he may be thought to have been careless and that he may be blamed for the murder.

Ruth Mitchell, Henry Mitchell's wife, who tells Poirot of her husband,

> "He worries so. I tell him not to bother his head so. Who's to know what reason foreigners have for murdering each other, and if you ask me, I think it's a dirty trick to have done it in a British aeroplane." She finished her sentence with an indignant and patriotic snort. "If you ask me, there's Bolshies at the back of it."

Albert Davis, Second Steward aboard the "Prometheus."

The Daughter of Old Johnson, owner of The Crown and Feathers, a plump, fair-haired girl, the sweetheart of Albert Davis

Inspector James Japp of Scotland Yard. He is apt to jump to conclusions, but over the years he has acquired enormous respect for Hercule Poirot's abilities. In addition to being a jumper to conclusions, he is a rather ignorant generalizer. Among his pronouncements in this novel are some amusing statements about archeologists, who he says are "liars who say some rotten string of beads is five thousand three hundred and twenty-two years old, and who's to say it isn't?" He also comments about detective story writers who get police procedure all wrong. He declares them to be ignorant scribblers of rubbish.

Inspector Japp works very closely with Hercule Poirot in this novel, as he did in their last adventure together, *Thirteen at Dinner*.

Rogers, Inspector Japp's subordinate

A Very Large Blue-clad Policeman, guarding the exit door at Croydon Aerodrome

A Stolid Constable at Croydon Aerodrome during questioning of the passengers

Maître Alexandre Thibault, Madame Giselle's lawyer, a tall, elderly Frenchman with a gray beard who speaks English slowly and precisely with a slight accent. He is in possession of Madame Giselle's Will and it is to him that her daughter presents herself upon learning of her mother's death.

An Aged Clerk at the Office of Maître Thibault

Dr. James Whistler, the police surgeon for the district of Croydon who examines the murder victim and determines the approximate time of her death

Several Journalists attending the inquest

Dr. Henry Winterspoon, an expert on exotic poisons who examines the poisoned dart, reporting that it had been dipped in the venom of the boomslang, a poisonous South African tree snake.

A Square-faced Member of the Inquest Jury who, noting that the blow-pipe was found hidden behind Hercule Poirot's seat on the plane—and being prejudiced against foreigners in general—urges the jury to present a verdict of willful murder against Hercule Poirot.

A Disdainful Waitress with a Gloomy Manner in a London tea shop who takes Norman Gale and Jane Grey's order with an air of doubt.

An Unnamed Journalist, representing the *Weekly Howl*, who approaches Jane Grey and Norman Gale in the teashop in view of obtaining a story for his paper.

Monsieur Fournier of the Paris Sûreté. The Sûreté is involved because the victim and two of the other passengers on the plane were French. Monsieur Fournier was especially selected by his superior, Monsieur Gilles, because he is fluent in

English. He has "modern" ideas respecting the use of psychology in crime detection, and so he is immediately appreciated by Poirot. He is acquainted with Monsieur Giraud, Poirot's pompous rival from *Murder on the Links,* and Poirot can well imagine the terms in which he has been described by Monsieur Giraud in Paris.

Monsieur Fournier is convinced that there was a "psychological moment" during the voyage when the attention of all the passengers was diverted so that they would not see the murder committed.

Monsieur Gilles, Monsieur Fournier's superior, the chief of the detective force at the Paris Sûreté and an old friend of Hercule Poirot

Monsieur Giraud of the Sûreté in Paris; not a character in the novel but an old adversary of Hercule Poirot referred to in a conversation between Poirot and Monsieur Gilles. He appeared in the 1923 *Murder on the Links.* Monsieur Giraud's methods consisted of all of the modern scientific analyses of tangible clues—while Poirot spoke of the psychology of crime and of the criminal being much more useful in detection. Since their meeting in 1923, Poirot has kept a figure of a foxhound on his mantelpiece, referring to it as "Giraud."

Anne Morisot, the daughter of Madame Giselle, aged about twenty-four or twenty-five. She suddenly appears at the office of her mother's lawyer, Maître Thibault, having been contacted by the mother superior of the orphanage in Quebec where she grew up, and told of her mother's death.

Raymond Barraclough, a well-known stage actor, a good friend and perhaps the lover of Lady Horbury

Monsieur Zeropoulos, a short stout little man with beady black eyes who talks volubly and at great length. He is a Greek antique dealer in the Rue St. Honoré in Paris. The blow-pipe that was found hidden behind one of the passengers' seat on the airplane bore a fragment of a price tag, leading the French police to the Rue St. Honoré.

Jules Perrot, desk clerk at the offices of Universal Airways' office in Paris, a smart-looking dark man behind a highly-polished wooden counter.

A Boy Aged About Fifteen, an employee of Universal Airways

Silas Harper, an American tourist with gray hair, horn-rimmed glasses and a little goatee beard who booked a seat on the "Prometheus" next to Madame Giselle but did not travel aboard the plane that day.

Mr. Ffoulkes, Lord Horbury's solicitor

Andrew Leech, the real name of "Monsieur Antoine," of the London hairdressing establishment employing Jane Grey. Although an ordinary Englishman, he shams a French accent when in the presence of the customers.

Gladys, a co-worker of Jane Grey, who finds dentists "unromantic" and dislikes old women with Pekingeses as much as Jane does.

Mère Angélique, the mother superior at the Institut de Marie, an orphanage in Québec. Mère Angélique evidently reads European newspapers and keeps herself informed. Reading of the death of Marie Morisot (Madame Giselle) and, knowing that Anne Morisot is her daughter and that a substantial inheritance now awaits her, she immediately telegraphs to Anne the news of her mother's death.

The Desk Clerk at a small hotel in Paris

The Concierge at the above hotel

French into English

Note: In this novel there are a father and son referred to as Monsieur Dupont père and Monsieur Dupont fils. "Père" and "fils" (father and son) are the French equivalents of "senior" and "junior."

Chapter 1

rien ne va plus—common phrase used by croupier at roulette table—"no more bets"

Le numéro cinq, rouge, impair, manque—five red odd number lacking

mon estomac—my stomach

Chapter 2 *pardon*—excuse me

Mais enfin! Est-ce que c'est possible?—Good grief! Can this be?

Chapter 3

moi, qui vous parle—I, who speak to you (simply a way to emphasize "*I.*")

Chapter 6

estomac—stomach

chantage—blackmail

Chapter 7

Mon estomac—my stomach

Enchanté—Delighted (to have you accompany me there.)

évidemment—clearly

À propos—By the way

Chapter 8

three *mille* notes—three one-thousand franc notes (a one-thousand franc note was of very small value, no more than about one or two

American dollars.)
Quelle idée!—Such an idea!
Ce n'est pas joli, ça!—That wasn't a nice thing to say!
À demain—See you tomorrow

Chapter 9
estomac—stomach
Évidemment!—Absolutely!
concierge—Caretaker at a French apartment building, usually living in a ground floor apartment, distributing daily mail to the lodgers, relaying messages, generally keeping watch at the entrance and monitoring the building.

Chapter 11
ces messieurs—those gentlemen
omelette aux champignons—mushroom omelet
Sole à la Normande—Sole cooked in the Norman way, probably with a cream-based sauce
concierge—caretaker of building (see above)
mal de mer—seasickness

Chapter 12
Très bien—Very well

Chapter 15
bon!—good!
Épatant—Astounding!
Mon Dieu!—Oh my God!

Chapter 16
chaud-froid—a cold dish consisting of chicken pieces in an aspic prepared from seasoned broth and then chilled
Voilà tout!—That's all it is.
Évidemment!—It certainly is!
Parbleu!—(An expression of impatience with the other speaker.)
Voilà—OK, that's done.
Il est sex appeal?—He's attractive? (Poirot's attempt to use a popular English buzzword)
Comment?—What?
Il faut continuer.—I must keep at it. (Literally: it's necessary to continue.)

Chapter 19
métier—area of expertise, trade
En avant—Forward march!
Écoutez—Listen
Les femmes—Women

Chapter 20
moment psychologique—psychological moment

Chapter 22
Il est sex appeal?—Do you find him attractive?

Chapter 23
Allô—"hello" (when speaking on the telephone)
Au revoir—Good-bye
M(onsieur) le Docteur—Doctor (correct way of addressing a doctor)

Chapter 24
idée fixe—obsession
déjeuner—lunch
Assez bien—She's OK (in answer to the question "Is she pretty?")
Nom d'un nom d'un nom—God damn it! (Strong expression replacing the blasphemous "Nom de Dieu." An expression of extreme feeling, in this case the sudden realization of an important fact heretofore unknown or unnoticed.)

Chapter 25
Parbleu—For God's sake!
Bon Dieu—Good God!
concierge—caretaker (see above)

Chapter 26
C'est ça, n'est-ce pas?—That's right, isn't it?
Ça, c'est très gentil!—That's so nice!

COMMENTS

The characterizations in *Death in the Air* are absolutely Christie's best so far. Everything that is "Agatha Christie" is in this novel. The hilarious portrayal of the banana-eating detective story writer is wonderful, with his banana-eating sleuth, Wilbraham Rice, his appalling "writing room" with its broken, orange-juice-stained chairs and its totally chaotic disarray and his absurd idea of writing the crime into a novel called *The Air Mail Mystery* in which the murderer escapes by parachute and happens to be a snake charmer with easy access to snake venom.

Equally amusing is the portrayal of the "horsey" Venetia Kerr who "looks her best upon a horse" and, in that pose, when asked if she would marry Stephen Horbury if he were free, "looks very straight between her horses ears" and replies. *What* she replies is immaterial—the essential is that she looks very straight between her horse's ears as she says it.

Agatha Christie married an archeologist, Max Mallowan, about four years before writing *Death in the Air*. She had a great life with him and accompanied him to the Near East every year for a long time, doing a lot of her writing there. She must have had a wonderful time including in *Death in the Air* an eccentric detective story writer *and* a pair of archeologists who are so wrapped up in their professional thoughts and conversations that they are not aware of murder being committed four feet from them.

As mentioned in the *Setting* section, since the writing of Christie's first novel *The Mysterious Affair at Styles*, enormous strides had been made in the matters of communication and transportation worldwide and these are documented in Christie's novels. Equally impressive are the strides that have been made by Agatha Christie herself in the wonderful presentation of characters through their expression of attitudes on a wide range of subjects. Jean Dupont's comments on the behaviors of English people abroad, for example; Inspector Japp's comments on detective story writers, whom he describes as "ignorant scribblers," and his comments on archeologists, too, declaring a string of worthless beads to be five thousand three hundred and twenty-two years old, "and who's to say it isn't?"

Christie enthusiasts never tire of rereading her novels primarily because of these memorable personalities, whether the actual mystery plot is very interesting or not. Just meeting these old friends again makes a "good read."

Sometimes the most memorable characters in Christie's detective novels are not the *main* characters. An interesting person in *Death in the Air* is Élise Grandier, the loyal servant of Madame Giselle. Hercule Poirot and Monsieur Fournier question Élise, who has burned all of Madame Giselle's business papers. One of the men makes the mistake of using the phrase "Madame Giselle's victims," in referring to her clients, and Élise has this to say:

> "Victims—victims." Élise spoke with impatience. "You do not understand. Is it necessary to run into debt? To live beyond your means? To run and borrow, and then expect to keep the money as a gift? It is not reasonable, that! Madame was always fair and just. She lent, and she expected repayment. That is only fair. She herself had no debts. Always she paid honorably what she owed. Never, never were there any bills outstanding. And when you say that madame was a hard woman, it is not the truth! Madame was kind. She gave to the Little Sisters of the Poor when they came. She gave money to charitable institutions. When the wife of Georges, the *concierge*, was ill, madame paid for her to go to a hospital in the country."

The above is an excellent example of a unique Christie touch. It does nothing to help solve the mystery—after all, it's just the personal perspective of a very minor character—but it helps to reveal the unique personality of Madame Giselle and presents another memorable Christie character—Élise herself.

If anyone wonders why Agatha Christie has been read and enjoyed around the world by more people than all the rest of the world's detective story writers combined, this must be the reason. Nobody but Agatha Christie combined the *fun* of reading a detective story with the *fun* of making friends with so many delightful, fascinating and memorable characters.

Agatha Christie had a very low opinion of newspapers and reporters, even as far back as her earliest novels. Her dislike for reporters was intensified when, suffering under the stress of her disintegrating first marriage in 1926, she disappeared and her car was found abandoned somewhere. The full, true details of this incident have never been made known but there was plenty of speculation, and some newspapers accused her of shamming amnesia as a publicity stunt to promote her latest book. The whole incident was evidently such a bad memory that Christie makes no reference to it at all in her *Autobiography*. But reporters from that period onwards get very negative portrayals in her books, notably Charles Enderby in the 1931 *Murder at Hazelmoor* and now in *Death in the Air*, in which a large number of reporters attend the inquest.

At the inquest, once the identity of the victim is established, the excited reporters sit with pencils poised. When the lawyer Maître Thibault is questioned, the reporters are not interested, nor are they interested in the questions asked of the two airline stewards, nor of the comments of Dr. Bryant until he says that he is "unfamiliar with that particular poison," at which point they write "Unknown Poison." The reporters write with gusto when a poison expert describes a dart dipped in a preparation of native curare, an arrow poison used by certain tribes. When the expert describes the strength of the poison of the boomslang snake, they write "Extraordinary story. Snake poison in air drama. Deadlier than the cobra."

The reporters have no interest in Hercule Poirot's answers to questions, but when Lady Horbury is called to the witness stand, they write, "Peer's wife gives evidence in air-death mystery" or "...in snake-poison mystery." Those who write for women's papers write, "Lady Horbury wore one of the new collegian hats and fox furs," or "Lady Horbury, who is one of the smartest women in town, wore black with one of the new collegian hats" or "Lady Horbury who before her marriage was Miss Cicely Bland, was smartly dressed in black with one of the new hats." They also comment that Venetia Kerr, the daughter of Lord Cottesmore, "wore a well-cut coat and skirt with one of the new stocks."

The reporters have no more interest in the testimony of Norman Gale, a mere dentist, or of Jane Grey, a mere hairdresser's assistant, or of Daniel Clancy, a mere detective story writer, or of Mr. Ryder, a mere businessman, or Jean and Armand Dupont, mere archeologists, than they have in the testimony of Hercule Poirot, a mere detective.

As the years go on, Agatha Christie incorporates comments, often mildly derisive ones, about fashionable new ideas. Hercule Poirot has used the word "psychology" and the phrase "the psychology of the criminal" since the 1923 *Murder on the Links* and as the years go on, he mentions the natural human "need to talk, to reveal oneself" more and more. But neither Poirot—nor obviously Agatha Christie herself—has ever been very impressed by "psychoanalysis" which was apparently the latest rage in the mid–1930s. In a conversation with Jane Grey, Poirot states that because people love talking about themselves, many a quack is enriched. They tell him how they fell out of the pram at age two, how they pulled their father's beard, and how their mother ate a pear and the juice fell on her orange dress, and then the quack charges them two guineas and they go away, "cured" of insomnia.

For a person of so little formal education, Agatha Christie must have been a woman of incredible observation and perception. Fortunately she was also a genius with her pen.

Death in the Air would be a perfect "first Christie experience."

The A.B.C. Murders (1935)

SETTING

The story takes place from June through October of 1935. It begins in Whitehaven Mansions, a new and ultra-modern apartment building in London in which Hercule Poirot has taken a new flat. He admits that he has chosen this building, at least in part, because of the modern, geometric appearance of its exterior. This will be Poirot's permanent London residence. No details are given of the interior of Poirot's flat but it can be assumed that its décor would be described today as "Art Deco," as it is "ultramodern" in the style of 1935.

The crimes take place in the city of Andover in Hampshire, southwest of London; at Bexhill, a resort town in Sussex on the English Channel south of London; at a modern country house near Churston, a village in Devon not far from Torquay; and in Doncaster, an industrial city in the West Riding of Yorkshire, much further north.

The London locations, in addition to Hercule Poirot's flat, include the offices of Chief Inspector Japp and Inspector Crome of Scotland Yard, a cheap rooming house in the Camden Town district, and one or two restaurants, including the Corner House. Paddington and Euston railway stations are also mentioned.

In Andover the crime takes place in a tiny tobacco and newspaper shop in a poor district. The shop owner, who is the first murder victim, had her living quarters adjoining the shop—a tiny kitchen-parlor combination on the ground floor and two rooms on the upper floor—one being her sparsely furnished bedroom and the other an unused bedroom. There is mention of the Feathers Hotel in the town as well as three pubs: the Seven Stars, the Red Dog and the Three Crowns. The detectives have occasion to visit the home of a poor family living close to the tobacco shop, probably a small terraced house, and it is described as small, dimly lighted and having a tiny sitting room which is overcrowded with a pseudo-Jacobean suite including a sofa. Across the street from the tobacco-newspaper shop is a greengrocer's establishment with more of the produce displayed outside than inside; two short scenes occur there. There are also brief scenes at the homes of two other residents of Andover; one is a small house described as being "as neat and trim as its owner," a bank clerk, and the other is the home of a lower-class couple.

The Bexhill crime takes place at a beach on the sea front; scenes occur at a café, The Ginger Cat, where the murder victim had been employed as a waitress. The café is decorated with orange-checked table cloths and uncomfortable basketwork chairs with orange cushions; the establishment caters mostly to ladies, serving only light meals and no evening meals. A scene also occurs at the home of the murder victim's parents, a new, "minute" bungalow called "Llandudno," one of many recently built by a speculator on the edge of town. The main ground-floor room is called a "living-room" and is probably a combination sitting-dining room; the kitchen is described as "tiny." The house has at least two bedrooms. The area around Bexhill is described as a pleasant resort area popular in summer but relatively quiet at other times. There is a hotel called The Globe in the town.

The Churston crime also occurs out of doors, on a footpath not far from Combeside, a modern residence recently built by the murder victim who was a collector of fine porcelain. It has two large rooms which are filled with his collections but, otherwise, the home is not large. Because the wife of the victim is a terminally-ill cancer patient, an upstairs bedroom (described as being on the "first floor") has been converted to a cheerful sitting room for her. One scene takes place in that room and another takes place in the "long dining room" at breakfast time. Churston Ferrers, ten minutes by train from Paynton, has only a post office and a few antiquated cottages but no shops. It was once isolated but now the area is well developed with large numbers of small bungalows, undoubtedly spoiling to some extent the beauty of the sea coast with its dark green trees, its white stone beaches and the "sapphire blue" sea. There are neighboring beauty spots known as Broadsands and Elbury Cove. Near Torre Station is the Pitt Hotel, mentioned late in the novel because a certain suspect had been staying there at the time of the murder.

The Doncaster crime occurs in a movie theater during the showing of a film; it happens to be the weekend of the annual St. Leger horse race in September and the racecourse is inundated with spectators from all parts of England. One character has a room at a small, old-fashioned inn, the Black Swan, which has no hot running water in the rooms; pitchers of hot water are carried to each room periodically by an employee. The inn has a pub on the ground floor and most of the guests are "tradesmen," or traveling salesmen.

There is no important historical background to the story, other than the world-wide economic depression of the 1930s, which Captain Hastings mentions as the reason for his current return visit to England. Having suffered financially in Argentina, he has left his wife to look after his ranch and has come to England to personally attend to business problems here. There are also one or two references—as there had been in *The Secret Adversary* and *The Secret of Chimneys*—to the sad plight of war veterans having to earn their meager livings as door-to-door salesmen.

Psychology had recently become an extremely popular subject of both serious study and casual talk. In *Death in the Air*, published the same year, it is mentioned that there are psychologists—whom Poirot describes as "quacks"—who encourage patients to recall childhood events in order to be cured of neuroses, and then charge two guineas for this "treatment." In *The A.B.C Murders* psychology plays a far more important role, since the murderer is thought to be a psychopath, and the terms "inferiority complex," "Oedipus complex," "paranoia" and others are bandied about by the detectives, including Poirot. One detective derisively suggests that once the "psychopathic murderer" is caught, he will spend forty-five days in an institution being "treated" and then will be released instead of being incarcerated or executed.

However, the people actively investigating the case include a young Scotland Yard inspector specially chosen by Chief Inspector Japp because of his knowledge of psychology. Poirot feels great respect for him despite a certain arrogance in the young inspector's attitude. An "alienist," that is, a specialist in abnormal psychology, also works closely with the detectives and the local police of the four crime locations.

The parents of one of the victims, a young girl, make a reference to "these modern girls" who are independent and do not expect their social behaviors to be monitored by their parents, staying out late at night if they please.

STORY

Detective Hercule Poirot receives a mysterious letter bearing the signature "A.B.C." In a sarcastic, mocking tone, the writer suggests that a crime will take place in Andover on a certain date in June, and that Poirot will not be able to prevent it. On that date, an old woman, Mrs. Alice Ascher, is murdered in her small tobacco-newspaper shop in a poor neighborhood of that city. On the counter of her shop the police find a copy of the A.B.C. railway guide opened to the Andover page, and no fingerprints are on it. Poirot discusses the letter with the police, who do not take it very seriously, and because the murder victim was an ordinary person, the public takes little interest in the crime.

A few weeks later a second letter informs Poirot that a crime will take place at Bexhill on a certain date. On that date a young woman, Betty Barnard, is strangled on a beach, and under her dead body is found an A.B.C. railway guide opened to the Bexhill page. This causes the police to take the letters seriously. When Poirot receives a letter warning of a crime to take place at Churston, everyone living in Churston whose surname begins with "C" is warned by the police, but not in time to prevent the murder of Sir Carmichael Clarke. Near his body, predictably, is found a copy of an A.B.C. guide opened to the Churston page.

A fourth murder takes place about a month later in Doncaster but Hercule Poirot, assisted by a Scotland Yard inspector and a psychiatrist, succeeds in unmasking the murderer and preventing further killings.

CHARACTERS

Hercule Poirot, the Belgian private investigator with an egg-shaped head and an outlandish moustache. Now considerably aging, he has taken to dyeing his hair to conceal the gray. There will be references in future novels to his "suspiciously black hair." He now lives in an ultra-modern apartment building, Whitehaven Mansions, in London. Ever since the 1923 *Murder on the Links*, Poirot has spoken of "the psychology of the murderer," considering tangible clues to be of secondary importance in the detection of crime and leaving them to the police and other lesser intellects. In *The A.B.C. Murders,* Poirot has the pleasure of working with a police inspector who has respect for and knowledge of psychology, in addition to a psychiatrist. Poirot has a personal interest in this mystery, as the murderer writes to him tauntingly before committing each of his crimes.

Captain Hastings, Poirot's old friend whom we first met in *The Mysterious Affair at Styles,* written in 1916. Having left England in 1923 to live in Argentina, he returns now and then for occasional visits. He now returns to England because the world economic depression has adversely affected his ranch in Argentina and also his business interests in England, which he plans to attend to personally. He has an absolutely conventional and mediocre mind, which Poirot claims to appreciate very much since it causes Hastings to believe exactly what the murderer wishes everyone to believe.

Alexander Bonapart Cust, a middle-aged, mediocre person who was given the names Alexander and Bonapart by a mother expecting her son to "cut a figure" in the world. He has always been mediocre—at school and in life. Slightly wounded in the War, and an epileptic, he suffers from severe headaches and occasional loss of memory.

Chief Inspector James Japp of Scotland Yard, another old acquaintance of Hercule Poirot, and as the years go on, more and more of a friend. Introduced in *The Mysterious Affair at Styles* along with Captain Hastings, Inspector Japp at first worked independently of Hercule Poirot, and then gradually found himself consulting more and more with him. As recently as the 1933 *Thirteen at Dinner,* Chief Inspector Japp, while consulting at every stage with Poirot, repeatedly expressed the view that Poirot enjoyed "making things difficult" and had "very funny ideas." As a matter of fact, he said some rather insulting things to and about Poirot in that novel. In a later novel, the 1935 *Death in the Air,* he showed Poirot much more respect, although his simplistic views and his tendency to jump to conclusions were as apparent as always. In this story, *The A.B.C. Murders,* Chief Inspector Japp at last concedes the importance of psychology—at least in a case in which an apparent serial killer is involved—and manfully steps aside, assigning a younger and more knowledgeable Scotland Yard inspector to the case. Chief Inspector Japp appears briefly in the earlier chapters only.

Inspector Crome of Scotland Yard, who has a working knowledge of psychology. He is in charge of the case and there is never disagreement between him and Hercule Poirot, who feels great respect for him, despite Crome's perhaps youthful and naïve belief that he is the only detective on the case who has very much knowledge. Crome mildly resents Poirot's presence—and the respect that other people show for this "eccentric foreigner,"—but he is polite and correct at all times—much more than Chief Inspector Japp would be.

Chief Constables of the counties of Hampshire, Sussex, Devon and the West Riding of Yorkshire and various lower ranking police officers at the four crime sites, including Inspector Glen and Constable Briggs of Andover, Mr. Wells of the Churston Police, Superintendent Carter of the Sussex Police and Sergeant Jacobs of Scotland Yard

Sir Lionel, the Assistant Commissioner of the C.I.D. (Criminal Investigations Department)

Dr. Kerr, the Police Surgeon in Andover who examines the body of Mrs. Ascher and determines the time of her death, which he attributes to a blow to the back of the head with a heavy, blunt instrument

Dr. Logan of Churston, who looks after the terminally-ill Lady Clarke and who examines the body of Sir Carmichael Clarke after he is murdered

Dr. Thompson, a well-known alienist (a specialist in abnormal psychology), with whom Inspector Crome and Hercule Poirot discuss the psychological aspects of the case

Mrs. Alice Ascher, the first murder victim, a woman of about sixty, who had worked in domestic service until a small legacy from a former employer permitted her to establish a small tobacco and newspaper shop in a poor district of Andover. According to the local authorities, she has always been respectable and hardworking. Mrs. Ascher has had no children and has been separated from her alcoholic, abusive husband for several years, although he has visited her from time to time badgering her for money, which she has given to him in small amounts.

An old wedding photo of Mr. and Mrs. Ascher, found in Mrs. Ascher's bedroom, reveals that she was quite beautiful when young and that her husband was a handsome, soldierly fellow. Hastings comments on the "ravages of time" upon viewing this photo—after seeing the face of Mrs. Ascher's corpse—but Poirot points out that the bones of the head and face have retained their basic beauty.

Tom and Harry, brothers of Mrs. Ascher. Tom was killed in the War; Harry went to South America many years ago and has never been heard from since. Mrs. Ascher has no living relatives other than her niece Mary Drower.

Franz Ascher, the estranged husband of Mrs. Ascher. According to the police, "He drinks and is by way of being a nasty customer—he's threatened her life more than once." Mr. Ascher is never seriously suspected of Mrs. Ascher's murder, partly because friends provide him with an alibi, but mostly because the murder is thought to be the work of a more intelligent, lucid and literate person—one capable of planning the crime in advance and writing in a derisive but grammatically correct way to Hercule Poirot.

Dick Willow, Old Curdie, and George Platt, friends of Franz Ascher who provide him with a plausible alibi, although they are the kind of people the police feel would gladly lie to help a friend.

A Harassed-looking Young Policeman who attempts to keep a crowd from gathering outside the tobacco shop where the Andover crime occurred

A Stout Lady, her **Lank Husband** and a **Hoarse-voiced Shop Boy** in the greengrocer's shop opposite Mrs. Ascher's tobacco shop whom Hastings questions without acquiring very much new information.

A Small, Astonished and Suspicious Boy in the street to whom Hastings makes a present of strawberries and lettuce which he had purchased at the greengrocer's only for the privilege of speaking with its owners

Mr. James Partridge, a bank clerk, possibly the last person who saw Mrs. Ascher alive. He had purchased a packet of pipe tobacco from Mrs. Ascher at approximately 5:30 in the afternoon, shortly before her death. He is a little man who wears a pince-nez and is very dry and spare-looking and extremely precise in all his utterances. He lives in a small house that is as neat and trim as he. He was not a friend of Mrs. Ascher and knew nothing about her personal life, but he had been a regular customer of hers.

Mr. Albert (Bert) Riddell, a platelayer who found nobody at the counter at Mrs. Ascher's shop at 6:00 p.m. on the day of her murder.

Mr. Riddell's Obviously Nervous Wife

Miss Rose, deceased, who lived at a house called The Grange, three miles from Andover. Mrs. Ascher had worked for her as a cook-housekeeper before Miss Rose died, and received a legacy from her, enabling her to establish the small tobacco-newspaper shop.

Mrs. Fowler, a sharp-faced woman and neighbor of Mrs. Ascher. When Hercule Poirot and Captain Hastings visit her she is at once antagonistic, suspecting them of being salesmen, but when Poirot introduces himself as representing the *Evening Flicker* and offers her five pounds for a brief interview, she is most gracious. She confirms the evidence that Mrs. Ascher's husband had been abusive whenever he came near the shop, but she states that Mrs. Ascher herself "could be a real tarter when roused—give as good as she got any day.." and therefore never seriously feared her husband.

Edie, Mrs. Fowler's daughter

The Second Child of Mrs. Fowler, a very dirty child of unspecified sex that needs its nose attending to.

Mary Drower, a niece of Mrs. Ascher, a housemaid at a large country home near Overton, just a few miles from Andover. A very superior, steady young woman, she is a pretty, dark-haired girl with conservative views of marriage, finding it natural that, despite the abusiveness of Mrs. Asher's husband, Mrs. Ascher had provided him with money from time to time, because "well, you see, he was her husband."

The Second Housemaid at the house near Overton

Elizabeth (Betty) Barnard, the second murder victim, age twenty-three, a waitress at the Ginger Cat Café in Bexhill. By all accounts she was a major flirt and saw no reason to deprive herself of the companionship of various young men despite being informally engaged to one in particular.

Donald Fraser, Betty Barnard's fiancé. He has a jealous nature and was known to have had several serious rows with Betty on the subject of her flirtatious behavior with other men.

Colonel Jerome, retired, who discovered the dead body of Betty Barnard during an early morning walk with his dog

Miss Merrion, the manageress of the Ginger Cat where Betty Barnard was employed. She is a very thin woman of forty with wispy orange hair.

Miss Higley, a plump, dark-haired waitress at the Ginger Cat, not a close friend of Betty's and, in fact, regarded by Betty as "common," according to Betty's sister. As a witness, "the buxom Miss Higley was persistently maddening. Every statement she made was repeated and qualified half a dozen times. The net result was meager in the extreme."

Mr. Barnard, Betty's father, a stout, bewildered-looking man of about fifty-five. He had been in the ironmongery business in Kennington and retired two years ago, moving with his family to a new bungalow in Bexhill because he had always meant to live near the sea.

Mrs. Barnard, Betty's mother.

Megan Barnard, Betty Barnard's protective, older sister who works as a typist in London. She is intelligent and well informed, recognizing Poirot's name and cooperating fully with him in the investigation.

Sir Carmichael Clarke, the third murder victim, a well-known throat specialist who retired and then inherited a fortune from a wealthy uncle. His passion was a collection of Chinese pottery and porcelain, and two large rooms of his modern house near a village in Devon are devoted to his collections. Upon his death, his fortune passes to his terminally-ill wife and then to his only brother, Franklin Clarke.

Lady Clarke, Sir Carmichael Clarke's wife, who is suffering from terminal cancer.

Franklin Clarke, Sir Carmichael Clarke's only brother. He has "the resolute competent manner of a man accustomed to meeting with emergencies—a fair-haired man with a sunburnt face." After a few days he is not satisfied with the progress the police are making with the case—he finds Inspector Crome's manner distinctly irritating—and he proposes a kind of special task force—to work under Poirot's orders—composed of the friends and relatives of the murdered people. He even offers to pay each of them—Mary Drower, Megan Barnard, Donald Fraser, Thora Grey and even Hercule Poirot—their accustomed income while involved in the case. Poirot concurs enthusiastically with this suggestion, pointing out that in the course of shared conversations a link among the three murders may be discovered, and indeed one is.

Miss Thora Grey, secretary to Sir Carmichael Clarke.

Deveril, the elderly butler at the home of Sir Carmichael Clarke

Nurse Capstick, a hospital nurse who looks after Lady Clarke

Mr. Hill, who has a strange conversation with Mr. A. B. Cust in the Princess Gardens at Torquay harbor.

Mrs. Marbury, Mr. Cust's landlady in London, who notices that Mr. Cust is feeling poorly on the day of the Doncaster murder.

Bert Marbury, Mrs. Marbury's brother in Canada

Lily Marbury, daughter of Mrs. Marbury, who thought Mr. Cust was going to Cheltenham on the day of the Doncaster murder.

Tom Hartigan, Lily Marbury's boyfriend who saw Mr. Cust at Euston Station that morning—not at Paddington—and so he must not have been going to Cheltenham. [Euston Station serves passengers to northern destinations, including Doncaster.]

George Earlsfield, a barber, the fourth murder victim. He is stabbed to death at the Regal Cinema in Doncaster during the showing of a film.

Mr. Leadbetter, a patron of the Regal Cinema in Doncaster, who discovered the dead body of the fourth murder victim

Roger Emmanuel Downes, a schoolmaster at Highfield School for Boys, who would have been the fourth victim if he had not changed seats during the film at the Regal Cinema

Mr. Geoffrey Parnell and **Sam Baker and his Young Lady**, witnesses who left the Regal Cinema at the same time as Mr. Cust

Mr. Jameson, Commissionaire at the Regal Cinema

Mr. Ball, owner of the Black Swan Inn in Doncaster, who insisted that the reluctant Mary Stroud take her story to the police.

Mary Stroud, a chambermaid at the Black Swan Inn in Doncaster, who carried a pitcher of hot water to Mr. Cust's room, knocked at the door and, receiving no answer, entered the room to find Mr. Cust washing his hands in cold water—water which was clearly stained with blood.

A Couple of Chauffeurs working on cars in the courtyard of the Black Swan Inn, who noticed Mr. Cust leaving the inn in a furtive manner through the courtyard entrance.

Young Lucas, the defense attorney for Mr. Cust

Mr. Strange, an engineer aged about forty, who states that he played dominoes all evening with Mr. Cust when Betty Barnard was killed, thereby providing Mr. Cust with an alibi.

FRENCH INTO ENGLISH

Chapter 1

Quelle horreur!—What a horrible thought!
N'est-ce pas?—Yes, aren't they?
C'est vrai.—That's true.
Pas mal.—Quite a bit.
recherché—out of the ordinary
fine—exceptional, masterful
Pas encore—Not yet

Comment?—What?
Merci—Thank you

Chapter 3
Pardon?—I beg your pardon?
Précisément!—An excellent idea!
intime—private, intimate
À tout à l'heure—See you later or "talk to you later"

Chapter 5
Pauvre femme—Poor woman

Chapter 6
Oui, c'est peut-être la...—Ah, maybe that's the ...
mise en scène—the "stage set" (the officer is explaining what the police found—the body, the cigarette packet, the railway guide, etc. at the scene of the crime.)
Pauvre femme—Poor woman
Parbleu—expression of impatience (Poirot judges Hastings should not need to ask the point of it all)
quelconque—random (a random purchase of just anything)
Cache cache—the children's game "hide and seek"

Chapter 7
Bon soir—Good evening (correctly written *Bonsoir*)

Chapter 8
le type—the type

Chapter 9
Faites attention—Be careful
Pas ça—No, that's not what I mean
pour une femme—from a woman's point of view
Du tout—Not in the least

Chapter 11
À la bonne heure—at last
un peu—rather

Chapter 13
Ça, oui—Yes, that's true
pour le sport—for fun

Chapter 14
Vite—vite—Quickly, quickly
C'est trop tard—It's too late
Mais qu'est-ce que vous faites là?—What on earth are you doing?
Vous éprouvez trop d'émotion—You're too upset
Ah, c'est ingénieux, ça!—Ingenious!
crime intime—private murder

Chapter 15
Vous croyez?—You really think so?
Encore!—Again!

Chapter 17
la chance—luck
inconnu—mystery person
Et alors, je vais à la pêche.—And then I shall go fishing.
Inutile—No need

Chapter 18
Une bonne idée!—An excellent idea!
rapprochement—gathering
enfin—in short
au fond—in depth
chance—mere luck
mise en scène—stage set
Tout de même—In any case

Chapter 19
tout à fait à part—quite independently
Comme ça—Like this
Mais je crois que la blonde l'emporte sur la brunette!—But I think the blonde wins over the brunette.
C'est tout naturel—It's quite natural
dernier cri—the latest fashion

Chapter 20
Du tout—Absolutely false!
bêtises—idiocy (foolish ideas or statements)
Parbleu—Absolutely

Chapter 21
C'est ingénieux. Tout de même c'est bien imaginé, ça.—Very clever. You've got to admit this was well planned.
Mes enfants—kids
ça vient...—it's coming
À vous la parole—You have the floor (it's your turn to speak)
Mieux que ça, mademoiselle—You can do better than that, miss

Chapter 23
petite—dear
mes amis—friends
Rouge—Red
Comment—What?
Du tout!—Not at all!
Rouge—Red

Chapter 31
grand mal and *petit mal*—universal medical terms applying to epilepsy

Mon cher Hastings—My good Hastings
je vous assure—let me assure you

Chapter 32
Voilà!—That's that!
Bon—Good, that's settled.
mon cher M. Clarke—my dear Mr. Clarke
ma foi—for God's sake
mon enfant—my dear
Alors c'est bien, mon enfant—All right, forget about it, dear.
les bêtises—foolish statements
Tout de même—and yet

Chapter 34
Quelle idée—Such an idea!
Passons!—Let's get on with things!
Mais si!—Yes it *does* make sense!
En vérité—The truth is...
Rouge, impair, manque—(expression used in roulette playing: red, odd number, lacking)

Chapter 35
Le sport—fair, good sportsmanship
un cœur magnifique—a wonderful heart
simplement une blague—just a joke
Vive le sport—Let's hear it for the sport (the "sport" of detecting, in this case)

COMMENTS

In *The A.B.C. Murders,* Hercule Poirot is allowed to indulge his interest in and commitment to the psychological aspects of crime and criminals. For many years he has contended that "when one understands the mind of the murderer it is an easy matter to identify him." Captain Hastings and Inspector Japp have no appreciation for psychology, Hastings constantly badgering Poirot to "do something" when Poirot spends his time "using the little grey cells" and Inspector Japp deriding Poirot's "little ideas" and jumping to all obvious conclusions. But in this novel, Inspector Japp steps aside and assigns the case to a younger inspector, one who can apply psychology to crime detection. Hastings, for his part, is present as an observer, usually a puzzled one.

The characters in this novel are not as fully developed as they are in Christie's previous few, except perhaps Alexander Bonapart Cust. Not very much can be said about their individual personalities. We do not know, for example, the profession of Franklin Clarke, Sir Carmichael Clarke's brother, even though he is a major character. One or two of the minor characters are portrayed in a mildly amusing way—the "feline and gingery, orange-haired" manageress of the Ginger Cat, for example—but for the most part the book is relatively humorless and a tone of depressing seriousness pervades it.

Megan Barnard, the sister of one of the murder victims, is an intelligent and assertive young woman whose personality resembles that of Emily Trefusis in *Murder at Hazelmoor* and perhaps that of Hermione (Egg) Lytton Gore of *Murder in Three Acts*. But aside from these one or two memorable people, most of the characters in *The A.B.C. Murders* are rather shadowy.

Readers of the novel in 1935 probably found many of the conversations touching on psychology to be very interesting. On the day when Poirot and Hastings interview the two men whose evidence brackets the time of Mrs. Ascher's murder—the neat and precise Mr. Partridge and the "blustery giant" Mr. Riddell, Poirot says:

"Well, here were two men known to have been in the shop at the requisite time of day. Either of them *might* be the murderer. And there is nothing as yet to show that one or other of them is *not* the murderer."

"That great hulking brute, Riddell, perhaps," I admitted.

"Oh, I am inclined to acquit Riddell off-hand. He was nervous, blustering, obviously uneasy—"

"But surely that just shows—"

"A nature diametrically opposed to that which penned the A.B.C. letter. Conceit and self-confidence are the characteristics that we must look for."

"Some one who throws his weight about?"

"Possibly. But some people, under a nervous and self-effacing manner, conceal a great deal of vanity and self-satisfaction."

"You don't think that little Mr. Partridge—?"

"He is more *le type*. One cannot say more than that. He acts as the writer of the letter would act—goes at once to the police—pushes himself to the fore—enjoys his position."

Murder in Mesopotamia (1936)

SETTING

The year is approximately 1931 (the novel was published in 1936 and probably written in 1935, but the narrator, Amy Leatheran, explains that the events she is relating occurred "four years ago.") We will recall that in the novel *Murder in the Calais Coach,* Poirot happens to be on the train because he is returning home to England from Syria where he had assisted the French government in some kind of scandal or crime. According to the narrator of *Murder in Meso-*

potamia, before returning to England, Poirot made a trip to Baghdad—simply a pleasure trip in order to visit Baghdad for the first time. On his way from there back to Syria he became involved in this murder case at the archeological expedition site. She goes on to explain that, after the murder was solved, Poirot returned to Syria and then took the Orient Express train to England, solving the *Murder in the Calais Coach* on the way. This should explain why, although this novel was published after *Murder in the Calais Coach,* the events in *Murder in Mesopotamia* actually occurred just a short time earlier.

The story takes place at and near an archeological "dig" in Mesopotamia (now called Iraq) where there is a special building called the "-expedition house" consisting of individual bedrooms plus several other rooms for different purposes. There is a dining room, and a "living room" which is really an all-purpose room where people can read, but also containing many of the archeological findings. There is a photography room and an adjoining dark room, an "antika room" where artifacts are stored, and a kitchen and perhaps one or two other rooms. It's important to note that the building is a one-story structure enclosing a large courtyard and that there is just one entrance—an archway which is wide enough to allow an automobile to pass. The archway is locked at night and guarded at all other times.

The individual rooms open onto the courtyard and all of their windows—except the rooms along the south side of the building—also face the courtyard. The windows of the rooms on the south side face the open country, but are barred. Therefore the only entrance to the complex is through the archway. A detailed plan of the building is shown on one page of an early chapter. All of the rooms are entirely functional and quite sparsely furnished. The two bathrooms are especially primitive and in the opinion of the narrator, Nurse Leatheran, can hardly be called "bathrooms" as they have no running water. Old fashioned metal bath tubs are used and buckets of hot water are carried to the rooms by servants.

In addition, there are brief scenes at the archeological dig itself, where excavations are taking place. One or two scenes also occur at a small town, Hassanieh, which because of the clear, dry air of the region is actually visible from the expedition house although it is about thirty minutes away by car on a primitive road. At the beginning of the novel there is a scene in Baghdad, and another at the home of an English family in Alwiyah which must be very close to Baghdad.

The narrator travels from Baghdad to Hassanieh overnight by train, and then by car from there to the expedition site.

Historical Background

One of the outcomes of World War One was that certain areas in the Middle East became "protectorates" of Great Britain and France. From 1918 until about 1946 France was the ruling force in Lebanon and Syria, while Great Britain was the ruling force in Palestine, Jordan and Mesopotamia (now called Iraq.) "Mesopotamia" was specifically the old, traditional name for the area between the Tigris and Euphrates rivers, an exceptionally fertile region in ancient times and a part of the "Fertile Crescent," described by historians as one of the "cradles of civilization." During the period of the British Protectorate of Mesopotamia, American and British archeologists, including Christie's husband Professor Max Mallowan, were responsible for increasing the world's knowledge of the ancient civilizations of that region as well as most of the current knowledge of ancient Egyptian civilization. During the same period, French archeologists studied ancient ruins in Syria and Lebanon.

If you have already read Christie's *Murder in the Calais Coach,* you will recall that Hercule Poirot happened to be on the Orient Express train returning to England "from Syria, where he had assisted the *French* government" in some kind of government scandal. Syria was, of course, a "Protectorate" of France at the time, and that was why it was the "French government" that Poirot assisted.

In *Murder in Mesopotamia* it is the *British* authorities in Baghdad who prevail upon Hercule Poirot to solve the murder of Louise Leidner, since Mesopotamia is a "Protectorate" of Great Britain. This also accounts for the presence in Baghdad of several American and British characters in the story—the American archeologist Eric Leidner and the British Dr. Reilly, Captain Maitland, the Kelseys, the Wrights and of course the narrator, British hospital nurse Amy Leatheran.

Murder in Mesopotamia is the first of Christie's detective novels that are set in the Middle East, but soon there will be two more—*Death on the Nile,* set in Egypt and *Appointment with Death,* set in Jordan. During the 1940s there will be *Death Comes as the End,* set in ancient Egypt, and then in 1951 there will be *They Came to Baghdad,* set in modern-day Iraq. Because Agatha Christie spent six months of every year, from 1930 to 1938, working with her husband at his archeological expedition sites in the Middle East, her descriptions of the settings in these novels are probably authentic and contribute a good deal to the charm of the stories.

STORY

It is 1935 when Dr. Giles Reilly, an English physician living in Baghdad, asks Nurse Amy Leatheran to write an account of a murder and its investigation that took place in 1931 at an archeological expedition in Iraq while she was a participant there. Protesting that she is not a skilled writer, she nevertheless allows herself to be persuaded to write the account, telling her story in the first person.

Mrs. Louise Leidner, the American wife of archeologist Eric Leidner, had married an American named Frederick Bosner in 1918. Accidentally discovering that he was traitor in the pay of the German government, she dutifully reported him to the authorities and he was arrested, tried and condemned to death for treason. He escaped from prison but was later reported killed in a train accident. However, his widow began receiving threatening letters from him whenever she formed a relationship with another man, and the letters threatened that she would be killed if she ever remarried.

There were no threatening letters when Louise met and fell in love with Eric Leidner, however, and the couple married. Recently, however, the letters began arriving again, and then one day, Mrs. Leidner is found dead in her room at the archeological expedition site. For certain reasons it is clear that a member of the expedition must be the killer. These suspects include a priest who is an expert in ancient languages, three other archeologists and several assistants plus the wife of one of the other archeologists.

As Hercule Poirot happens to be visiting Baghdad, the British authorities prevail upon him to solve the mystery of Mrs. Leidner's murder, which he does, but not in time to prevent a second killing.

CHARACTERS

Hercule Poirot, the Belgian private investigator. He has just assisted the French government in Syria with a problem of a scandalous or criminal nature. While on his way to visit Baghdad, he passes through the town of Hassanieh and is approached by Captain Maitland to solve the mystery of a murder at an archeological dig a few miles away.

Amy Leatheran, age thirty-two, an English hospital nurse and the narrator of the story. We meet all of the characters through their conversation in her presence, through remarks made about them by other characters, and through Nurse Leatheran's personal thoughts which we must evaluate within the context of her personality and what we perceive to be her level of intelligence and ability to judge. She is a competent nurse within the schema of Agatha Christie's perceptions of what a nurse is like. Recall that Christie was not fond of nurses in general and her portrayals of them place them on a par with the more intelligent and autocratic of servants. Nurse Leatheran embodies all of the good—and the bad—of being British and, in particular, a British spinster. She responds affirmatively to men who are handsome—practically losing control of herself in her description of the handsome archeologist Richard Cary—and although she recognizes and appreciates beautiful features—shape of forehead, eye color, etc. in good-looking women, she focuses her attention more on the faults in their personalities, wondering how it is that men can be attracted to such "cats." She regards men in general as helpless mice in the claws of cats that are ruled by the instinct to torment.

Being an Englishwoman of mediocre education she is, of course, disgusted by everything that is not English—the roads in Iraq, for example, and "dirt masquerading as picturesqueness" and of course she is suspicious of such upstarts as foreigners and Catholics, not to mention persons of other races. She writes a clear and detailed account of the mystery, however, without distorting anything, and she is honest in admitting the prejudiced nature of her personal comments about the other characters.

As the story goes on, Nurse Leatheran develops enormous respect for Hercule Poirot and eventually comes to think of her relationship with him as like that of a competent nurse to a first-rate surgeon.

Sheila Reilly, aged about twenty-one. Of all the characters, she is the most rudely outspoken. She is intelligent and perceptive and very sure of herself. On the negative side, she is crude and rude. When the murder occurs and the other characters are reluctant to "speak ill of the dead" she openly declares that the dead cannot be harmed by speech and that there is no point in distorting facts. "If anyone deserved to die," Sheila declares, "it was Louise Leidner." In the opinion of Nurse Leatheran, a good share of Sheila's dislike of Louise is attributable to good old-fashioned jealousy, and Sheila's own father concurs with Nurse Leatheran. According to her father, Sheila recognizes the "sex appeal" of Louise Leidner, who is nearly twice her age, and resents the attraction most men feel for her. According to one or two of the other characters, Sheila has a "pash" for one of the young men on the expedition, David Emmott, and she expects all of the young men to "dance attendance" around her. Sheila lives in Baghdad with her father, Dr. Giles Reilly.

Dr. Giles Reilly, a medical doctor in Baghdad who arranges for Nurse Leatheran to join the expedition for the next two months to "look after" Louise Leidner, who is experiencing "irrational fears." Dr. Reilly is introduced at the beginning of the novel, as it is he who asks Nurse Leatheran to write her account of the incident, arguing that because she was "in the thick of things," but was "an outsider," she could write the most objective account of it.

Dr. Reilly meets with Captain Maitland and Hercule Poirot occasionally to discuss the case. He appears to consider himself very knowledgeable of psychology. The original readers of this 1936 novel probably felt more respect for his knowledge than today's readers would, although clearly Agatha Christie intended his ideas to be taken seriously by the reader.

Major and Mrs. Kelsey, an English couple with an infant living near Baghdad, friends of Dr. Reilly. It is Mrs. Kelsey's trip to Baghdad with the new baby that occasions Nurse Leatheran's first trip abroad.

Mr. Perryman, a friend of Mrs. Kelsey who describes the expedition in the presence of Nurse Leatheran, giving a picture of not quite the happy family that it had once been.

The Wrights, another English couple in Baghdad, friends of the Kelseys

Dr. Eric Leidner, an American archeologist of Swedish ancestry. He heads the expedition which is now in its fifth or sixth year. He married his wife two years ago. He is "a middle-aged man with a rather nervous, hesitating manner. There was something gentle and kindly and rather helpless about him," according to Nurse Leatheran in her first impression. He is extremely devoted to his wife and, according to some of the other characters, he expects everyone in the expedition to feel equally devoted to her.

Louise Leidner, a very beautiful woman despite her thirty-nine years. She is the murder victim and the most important character, since her personality is analyzed and judged repeatedly through the appraisals of all of the other characters. She is variously described as "very kind," "very intelligent," "a pathological center stager," "a first class liar," "a vicious man-craving cat" and many other things, depending on who is providing the description. Hercule Poirot, for a long time, has contended that the a major clue to any murder is the personality of the killer, but in this story he seems to feel that it is the personality of the victim that must be understood before the mystery can be solved.

Mrs. Leidner has "fancies," according to her husband—she has visions of a face not attached to a body at her window during the night, and sometimes a hand not attached to an arm; a shadow falling across a floor or wall causes her to scream with fright. She lives in deadly fear for her life, for she has received threatening letters from her former husband, who was supposed to have died in 1918. Dr. Leidner hires Nurse Leatheran to be a companion to his wife in order to make her feel safe.

Joseph Mercado, another archeologist, aged about forty, "a tall, thin, melancholy man, with a sallow complexion and a queer, soft, shapeless-looking beard." He is very nervous and appears to be depressed most of the time. Addiction to an unspecified drug, which he takes through injections, is the cause of his depression and nervousness.

Marie Mercado, Joseph's wife, considerably younger than he, aged about twenty-five, "sort of dark and slinky-looking, if you know what I mean," according to Nurse Leatheran. "Quite nice looking in a kind of way, but rather as though she might have what my mother used to call 'a touch of the tar brush.' She had on a very vivid pullover, and her nails matched it in color. She had a thin, birdlike, eager face with big eyes and rather a tight, suspicious mouth." In another description Nurse Leatheran tells us that Mrs. Mercado is wearing a shade of nail polish that is a "hideous red-orange color." Mrs. Mercado is very "high strung;" in one scene she has a screaming fit.

Marie Mercado is of no use to Poirot in his investigations since, unlike most of the other characters, she is incapable of speaking truthfully about the victim, describing her as all sweetness and love while, as all of the other characters know, Mrs. Mercado thoroughly detested Mrs. Leidner.

William Coleman, a young Englishman aged about twenty-three. Nurse Leatheran wonders if the stereotypical Britishness of this young man can possibly be real. He is "chipper" to the point of being nauseating; he does not enter a room; he "bustles in," chirping "Hallo,'allo,'allo," and talks incessantly. In the presence of Sheila Reilly he stammers and blushes and his conversation becomes slightly more idiotic than it was before, if that's possible. He reminds nurse Leatheran of a large stupid dog wagging its tail and trying to please. He is obviously hopelessly in love with Sheila.

Carl Reiter, age twenty-eight, an American from Chicago who speaks English with no accent (except for the expected slight American accent,) but whose sentence structures suggest a foreign, perhaps German, influence. He is the expedition photographer.

David Emmott, another young American, aged twenty-nine. He is very polite but taciturn, speaking minimally. It is difficult to know what he is thinking.

Father Lavigny, a monk from Carthage who is an expert in translating ancient languages. Certain members of the expedition find Father Lavigny's transcriptions to be a bit "vague."

Richard Cary, an archeologist aged thirty-eight or thirty-nine. His manner towards Louise Leidner is unnaturally formal and there is such tension between them that certain characters suspect that the two are concealing a love affair.

Ann Johnson, another one of the "old timers" of the expedition, having been with Dr. Leidner the longest. She is extremely admiring of and devoted to Dr. Leidner and speaks wistfully of former years when everyone on the dig was happy and everyone had such "fun." According to her, since Dr. Leidner's marriage an atmosphere of tension has developed in the group, because Dr. Leidner must divide his attention between the archeological activities and serving the needs of his "neurotic" wife.

Frederick Bosner, the first husband of Mrs. Leidner, who supposedly died in 1918 but from whom she has received threatening letters.

William Bosner, a younger brother of Frederick, from whom nothing has been heard since 1918, but who is thought to be the possible writer of the threatening letters purporting to be from Frederick.

Abdullah, a little Arab boy whose job consists of washing newly-unearthed pots in the expedition house courtyard. He "sings with a queer, nasal chant" as he works.

Captain Maitland, in charge of the police in Hassanieh. It is he who invites Hercule Poirot to help solve the murder of Mrs. Leidner.

Ibrahim and Mansur, two Arab house boys

An Indian Cook

Jean Berat, the French Consul to Iraq

A Stranger Dressed in European Clothes who is seen peeping into one of the windows of the expedition house and who is later seen speaking with Father Lavigny.

A Foreman to the Arab Expedition Laborers

Rufus Van Aldin, a wealthy American businessman, not a character in this novel but an acquaintance of Dr. Leidner who speaks highly of Hercule Poirot and recommends him to Dr. Leidner. Van Aldin was a character in the 1928 *The Mystery of the Blue Train*.

FRENCH INTO ENGLISH

Note: Hercule Poirot enters this story in Chapter 13. One of the characters is a Catholic priest and one is a British nurse. In England nurses are addressed as "Sister," just as nuns are. Poirot uses the French expressions "ma soeur" and "mon père" consistently (sister, father) to address these two characters.

Chapter 3
allumeuse—a woman who flirts for a devious purpose, as to inspire jealousy elsewhere, or for some other malicious intent

Chapter 13
Pères Blancs—"White Fathers," a religious order so named because of the white robe or habit worn by the priests
passons!—Let's move along, let's get on with things

Chapter 15
Bien!—OK, good!
Tout de même—All the same

Chapter 16
Bien.—All right
Pourquoi pas?—Why not?
Pères Blancs—White Fathers (religious order)

Chapter 17 *Eh bien*—OK

Chapter 18
tête-à-tête—in private and confidential
Eh bien?—Yes, go on...

Chapter 19 *tendresse*—romantic feeling

Chapter 20
Très bien.—Good.
clichés—overused, trite conversation fillers
enfin—or even
Pas plus sérieux que ça?—Nothing more serious than that?
tendresse—romantic feeling
Encore moi—It's me again

mon Dieu!—Good heavens!
Bien!—All right, then.
savoir-faire—literally "know-how," expertise

Chapter 21
mon cher—friend, pal
N'est-ce pas? Isn't it the truth?

Chapter 22
Eh bien—Well then, what about it?
je comprends—I understand

Chapter 24
mon enfant—dear
la pauvre femme—the poor woman!
Sacré nom d'un chien—va!—Euphemism for *Sacré nom de Dieu!* (Holy name of God) a very strong expression of anger or, in this case, exasperation. Roughly as strong as "God damn son of a bitch!" in English. The literal meaning is "holy name of a dog."

Chapter 25
Vous voilà, mon cher—So here you are, my friend!
Mon pauvre collègue—My poor colleague

Chapter 27
Eh bien—Well
Mon ami—Friend
crime passionnel—crime motivated by uncontrolled emotion, most often sexual jealousy
objets d'art—artifacts, art objects
dans son caractère—consistent with his personality

COMMENTS

Murder in Mesopotamia is an especially charming detective novel because of its exotic setting—an archeological dig in Iraq. It is made even more charming by a personable narrator, an English hospital nurse who is fascinated by the entire experience of being in a country so different from England and also by the idea of unearthing the remains of ancient civilizations. The cast of characters is a unique and interesting assortment of people, some of whom are dedicated to the work of the expedition but a couple of whom—specifically the wives of two of the archeologists—are present more or less as companions to their husbands. Additional important characters are a medical doctor and his outspoken daughter who live in Baghdad.

The narrator, hospital nurse Amy Leatheran, is very British and she makes continual judgments (the pitiful state of the "roads" in Iraq, which are not even "roads" by British standards—nothing but rocky trails which become muddy trails when there is rain, and of course the "unsanitary" state of everything). Her portrayals of the characters are also a reflection of her particular points of view. She does not mind making "catty" remarks about one or two of the female characters and she does not mind being rapturous about what she perceives as masculine good looks and masculine good character traits. All of this is effective in a way that would be impossible if Captain Hastings were the narrator, and it is clear that Christie avoided the use of Hastings in this novel for that reason, creating this feminine narrator instead.

As to the detection of the mystery, we have seen in Christie's most recent novels a growing importance of psychology, especially in *The A.B.C. Murders,* and there is even more psychology in *Murder in Mesopotamia*. It is possible that a lot of the "psychobabble" that takes place in this work of light fiction from 1936 is nonsense and that it would be laughable to a modern reader who is knowledgeable of modern psychology. The pronouncements of Dr. Reilly in particular would probably be scoffed at today.

The character portrayals in *Murder in Mesopotamia* are very skillfully done. They are a balance between the impressions of Nurse Leatheran and statements about them made by other characters, and since all of the characters are carefully portrayed, it is possible for the reader to form clear ideas because he can evaluate those statements within the context of those other characters' individual prejudices. We hear, for example, Louise Leidner described by many different people, each in a slightly different way, and then we form our own ideas about her.

It takes some stretching of the imagination to accept certain murder motives in a few of Christie's detective novels. The motive in this particular novel may strike many readers as unsatisfactory. The other characters, however, react naturally to all of the events, and the crime detection performed by Hercule Poirot is ingenious.

Agatha Christie often mentioned receiving letters from her readers pointing out inaccuracies and other faults in her books, such as medical impossibilities respecting poisons, or geographical errors—usually petty things. In the 1935 *Death in the Air* Chief Inspector Japp had commented on the inaccurate portrayals of police procedure that he had read in detective novels, which he said were written by "ignorant scribblers." The detective story writer in that novel, Daniel Clancy, did seem to be an ignorant scribbler, judging from the ridiculous plot he was planning for his next grand opus, *The Air Mail Mystery*. On the subject of the "inaccuracies and faults" of detective novelists, Nurse Leatheran, in *Murder in Mesopotamia,* treats us to this amusing comment:

> Mrs. Leidner went to her room to rest. I settled her as usual and then went to my own room, taking a book with me as I did not feel sleepy. It was about a quarter to one, and a couple of hours passed quite pleasantly. I was reading *Death in a Nursing Home*—really a most exciting story—though I don't think the author knew much about the way nursing homes are run! At any rate I've never known a nursing home like that! I really felt inclined to write to the author and put him right about a few points.

The fact that detective novelist Ngaio Marsh published *The Nursing Home Murder* a year earlier is probably no coincidence. Christie was a great admirer of Ngaio Marsh, however, so the reference to a nursing home as a setting for a detective novel is probably no more than a friendly joke. In any case, these touches of humor regarding detective story writers and their public will find full flowering in Christie's next novel, *Cards on the Table* in the person of detective story writer Ariadne Oliver who will appear now and then in future novels to "assist" Hercule Poirot.

In *Peril at End House,* we noticed that Hercule Poirot, the continental European with typical continental "realist" views, was repeatedly exasperated by English reluctance to speak the truth, substituting clichés for facts. In *Murder in Mesopotamia* he loses patience with Miss Johnson when he asks her for her honest opinion of Mrs. Leidner:

> "That's all very well," began Miss Johnson and stopped.
> "Do not make me the British *clichés*," Poirot begged. "Do not say it is not the cricket or the football, that to speak anything but well of the dead is not done—that—*enfin*—there is loyalty! Loyalty, it is a pestilential thing in crime. Again and again it obscures the truth."

By the time the novel ends, the narrator, Nurse Leatheran has learned that people are multifaceted and that appearances are misleading. She learns, among other things, that Hercule Poirot is a genius, despite the fact that he is a five-foot-five foreigner with a huge mustache and imperfect English, and that even murderers may have virtues. She observes:

> "Somehow, the more I get older, and the more I see of people and sadness and illness and everything, the sorrier I get for everyone. Sometimes, I declare, I don't know what's become of the good strict principles my aunt brought me up with. A very religious woman she was, and most particular. There wasn't one of our neighbors whose faults she didn't know backward and forward."

And so evidently new experiences in life are teaching compassion to Nurse Leatheran and also teaching her that the kind of organized religion she grew up with hadn't very much to do with Christianity. Christie doesn't often make references to religion but when she does, she lets it be known that, in her opinion, a lot of the practice in "organized religion" is flawed, especially the practice of "knowing other people's faults backward and forward" and calling it Christianity.

Cards on the Table (1936)

SETTING

It is October of 1935. Most of the action takes place in London but there are scenes in the western county of Devon and in Wallingford, Berkshire, which is a county just west of London close to Oxford. Agatha Christie and her husband Professor Mallowan purchased a house in Wallingford during the early 1930s and later bought an additional, much larger property, in Devon.

The initial setting is a kind of gallery or exhibition hall called Wessex House, in London, where an exhibition of snuffboxes, a fundraiser for the London hospitals, is taking place.

The décor in at least five residences is given unusually thorough description in this novel, primarily to complement the character portrayals of their occupants. One of these is the luxurious London apartment of the murder victim—a wealthy socialite and art collector. In the apartment there are several expensive and beautifully made cabinets, oriental rugs, Chinese and other art objects, a grand piano and tables and chairs of elegant design and excellent quality. A formal dinner takes place in the dining room and, afterwards, eight people play bridge at tables in two separate rooms, at least one having a fire in the fireplace. The host is fond of "creative" and "atmospheric" lighting which includes "indirect lighting" (a fashion statement of the 1930s,) which gives a soft glow to the two rooms, while small lamps at the card tables, along with the fire light, provide just enough additional light for card playing.

There are two scenes in the somewhat more modest but comfortable home of another character. It is 111 Cheyne Lane in Chelsea, and is a small house of very neat and trim appearance standing in a quiet street. The entrance door is painted black, the brass knocker and handle gleam in the sunlight, and the steps are particularly well whitened. The interior features well-polished furniture, chintz upholstery, numerous silver photograph frames and a beautiful tall jar filled with chrysanthemums.

There is a brief scene in the office of a London physician, at 200 Gloucester Terrace, which is also the doctor's home. The doctor is unmarried and has a cook, a parlormaid and a housekeeper who live in the house.

There is also a scene in a private apartment in Harley Street near the residences and offices of fashionable doctors, but it is not the home of a doctor. It is the home of the eccentric detective story writer Ariadne Oliver and it is ludicrously decorated with outlandish wallpaper (multi-colored and semi-fantastic tropical birds amid jungle foliage), tattered furniture with papers littering every horizontal surface, and apples that have spilled from a paper bag and rolled about on the floor, there to be left until "someone" picks them up, probably the elderly housemaid. Fortunately the meticulous, obsessed-with-neatness Hercule Poirot has no occasion to enter this apartment. It is reminiscent of the chaotic apartment of the detective storywriter Daniel Clancy, whom we met in *Death in the Air*, published about a year earlier.

The residence of another character is located in South Kensington, one of the better districts of London, but the house and furnishings are substandard. When Poirot arrives there, a suspicious housemaid takes his card and leaves him standing outside for a few minutes, where he is disgusted by the spectacle of the unpolished brass door knocker. "Ah! For some brasso and a rag," he murmurs to himself. Once inside the house, he is further disgusted by a rather dark room smelling of stale flowers and unemptied ash trays and filled with silk cushions of exotic colors, all in need of cleaning.

Additional London settings include a shop that sells expensive women's clothing, a small pastry cook's near Harley Street where two characters have tea, and the sitting room in Hercule Poirot's apartment. Poirot's residence is not described but we know that for the past year he has lived in a modern block of flats called Whitehaven Mansions.

A small house called Wendon Cottage in Wallingford, shared by two young women, is the setting for two or three scenes. Outside the house, there is a small old-fashioned garden with Michaelmas daisies and straggling chrysanthemums behind the cottage and, beyond it, a field and the river. The interior of the house is cozy, with a crackling fire and flowers in vases.

There is a scene in the police station in the fictitious small town of Combeacre in Devon where a Scotland Yard detective makes inquiries about past events.

There is no mention of any contemporary historical events or conditions. There is one brief reference to "the new horsy hats" for women, whatever that may mean, perhaps a millinery fashion suggesting "the country look," and "tight poodle curls," a hair fashion for young women. A brief fashion fad of the 1930s were "pajamas" worn by women instead of dresses, actually a sort of early "pant suit." One female character is described as wearing "embroidered crepe de Chine pajamas."

There is one humorous reference to automobile design. The overweight Mrs. Oliver extricates herself with some difficulty from her small two-seater car, the makers of which evidently believed that "only a pair of sylphlike knees" would ever be under the steering wheel.

STORY

It is October of 1935 and Hercule Poirot meets a casual acquaintance, Mr. Shaitana, at a fundraising event for London hospitals. Mr. Shaitana is an odd person whose physical appearance is even more eccentric than Poirot's. The features of his face, especially the eyebrows, suggest Mephistopheles, a legendary devil character of literature. He speaks in a bored, world-weary fashion and is an outrageous snob. While on the subject of "collections" he mentions the strange idea of a collection of "successful murderers." Mr. Shaitana claims to have made the acquaintance of several murderers who have never been accused or convicted, and he comes up with the idea of having a dinner party to "show off his collection" to the master sleuth, Hercule Poirot. Before Poirot has a chance to refuse this invitation, the two of them have set a date for the dinner party. Poirot comments that Mr. Shaitana's hobby of "collecting murderers" may be a dangerous one, but Mr. Shaitana simply laughs "a very Mephistophelian laugh." The dinner party will take place on Friday, October 18.

Poirot goes to the dinner party and meets the following guests: wooden-faced Superintendent Battle of Scotland Yard; handsome, bronzed, fiftyish Colonel Race, and Ariadne Oliver, an outlandishly eccentric detective story writer. There are also four other guests: a successful middle-aged physician, Dr. Roberts; a handsome military man, Major Despard, who has a lot in common with Colonel Race; a young woman of twenty-five, Anne Meredith; and an older lady aged sixty-three, Mrs. Lorrimer. These four people are evidently the "successful murderers" whom the Mephistophelian Mr. Shaitana has "collected."

After dinner, the eight guests play bridge in two adjoining rooms, the four "sleuths" in one room and the four "successful murderers" in the other. At some time during the evening Mr. Shaitana is stabbed through the heart by one of the "successful murderers" while the person is "dummy" during a bridge rubber.

Hercule Poirot and Superintendent Battle solve the mystery.

CHARACTERS

Mr. Shaitana, a wealthy socialite and a connoisseur and collector of art objects. He lives in a luxurious London apartment filled with beautiful furniture, oriental rugs, and art objects from exotic places. He has a reputation for giving fabulous parties to which a large variety of people, including stage and screen celebrities, are invited. Some of his parties are said to be "definitely queer parties," implying that extremely off-beat guests are welcome. There is a cruel streak in his personality, however, and he enjoys making people "squirm" by suggesting that he knows embarrassing things about them.

Mr. Shaitana is not a likeable person, and even the people in the story who accept his invitation to the dinner party have reasons for disliking him. For one thing, he is very effeminate and uses "scent," something that was not done in the 1930s by "normal" men. One of the female characters declares that she has always been "a little afraid" of him. The male characters are, for the most part, disgusted by him. One of his affectations is to mimic the "Mephistopheles" character of literature—a kind of devil character. He even uses makeup to give his eyebrows a "Mephistophelian" appearance, and at one point he "laughs a very Mephistophelian laugh."

Mr. Shaitana is murdered in the course of a dinner and card-playing party at his home after insinuating that some of the guests may have committed murder in the past.

Hercule Poirot, the "retired" Belgian private investigator living in London. He is almost as eccentric—at least in physical appearance—as Mr. Shaitana is, with his egg-shaped head and ostentatious mustache. He is disturbed by Mr. Shaitana's claim that undetected murders can be admirable acts of artistry and that one of his hobbies is a "collection of murderers" which he plans to display to Poirot at a special party arranged for the purpose.

A Lovely Young Thing with Tight Poodle Curls, a young unnamed lady with whom Mr. Shaitana speaks briefly in the presence of Hercule Poirot at a fund-raising event for London Hospitals

A Gray-haired Butler at the home of Mr. Shaitana

Ariadne Oliver, a writer of detective stories, who is a superficial and satirical self-portrait of Agatha Christie herself. Similarities between Mrs. Christie and Mrs. Oliver: they are both very much overweight; they both love apples above all other foods and keep a supply within close reach at all times; they write detective novels featuring an eccentric foreigner (Christie's Poirot is a Belgian who hates cold weather; Oliver's Sven Hjerson is a Finn who breaks the ice on his bath water every morning). Both authors receive volumes of letters from readers pointing out the inaccuracies of details in their books, such as incorrect accounts of police procedures, inaccurate properties of various poisons, spring and fall flowering plants blooming at the same time, geographical impossibilities, etc.

In addition, Mrs. Oliver has eccentricities of her own: ridiculous taste in clothes (high-heeled "city" shoes with country tweeds), constant problems with ever-changing coiffures, and absurd decorating ideas for her home as well as a general lack of organization.

Furthermore, unlike Agatha Christie, Mrs. Oliver is a lousy writer. She cheerfully admits that all of her books are exactly the same, except for the names of the characters. If a book seems to be too short to be called a novel, she simply extends it by adding one or two additional murders, claiming that her readers like "lots of dead bodies." In this story, when a young woman asks if she may bring Mrs. Oliver one of her books for her to autograph, Mrs. Oliver flutes, "Oh, I can do better than that," and she opens a cabinet, extracting a fresh copy of *The Affair of the Second Goldfish*, declaring it to be "not such frightful tripe as the others." She is a "feminist" in the worst sense, claiming that "woman's intuition" rules and that if a woman were at the head of Scotland Yard the country would be much more crime-free. Whenever one of her ideas is met with doubt by a male character, she presents her "how like a man!" look in response.

Superintendent Battle of Scotland Yard, whom we met in *The Secret of Chimneys* (1925)

and *The Seven Dials Mystery* (1929.) He is "squarely built" and his trademark wooden face conceals a thorough and methodical mind, which is more to Hercule Poirot's liking than the mind of Chief Inspector Japp, Poirot's more usual Scotland Yard colleague who jumps to conclusions and accepts easy and obvious solutions that often contradict known facts.

Colonel Race, an adventurer whom we met in the 1924 *The Man in the Brown Suit*. He was Anne Beddingfeld's idea of the "strong, silent men of Rhodesia." Colonel Race is one of the dinner guests and he assists Superintendent Battle marginally in the investigation of one of the murder suspects.

Dr. Roberts, a successful middle-aged physician. He is one of the four guests suspected of murdering Mr. Shaitana. According to Mr. Shaitana, he—like the other three—had committed murder in the past.

Mrs. Lorrimer, a widow aged sixty-three and a first-class bridge player who can recall all of the moves in a bridge game a week after it is played, but who is observant only of things that interest her personally. She is, along with Dr. Roberts, a murder suspect. Poirot finds her to be well informed and thoroughly intelligent, as he discusses the latest plays and books and world politics with her. In his investigation of Mrs. Lorrimer, Superintendent Battle finds nothing incriminating. The worst anyone can say about her is that she "doesn't suffer fools gladly," yet Mr. Shaitana included her in his list of guests who had been "successful murderers" of the past.

Major John Despard, a tall, lean, handsome man, with a small scar on one temple. When introduced to Colonel Race he recognizes an immediate affinity and their conversation soon turns to sporting activities and comparing their experiences on safaris.

Colonel Race, after investigating Major Despard, declares him to be above suspicion, a "Pucka Sahib," which statement leaves Superintendent Battle as unimpressed as it would leave Hercule Poirot. Mr. Shaitana had, after all, included Major Despard in his collection of "successful murderers."

After the murder of Mr. Shaitana, Major Despard does nothing to conceal a hearty dislike for the man.

"He was too well dressed; he wore his hair too long, and he smelled of scent."

Anne Meredith, an attractive young woman of twenty-five who lives with another young lady in Wallingford, not far from London. Left a penniless orphan at the age of eighteen with no training for work of any kind, she has worked as a personal companion or nursery governess for various families for the past few years. According to Mr. Shaitana, she too has committed murder successfully, and she is one of the suspects of *his* murder.

A Divisional Surgeon who examines the body of Mr. Shaitana after the murder

Divisional Inspector Anderson, A Camera Man, A Fingerprint Expert and a Constable who are summoned by Superintendent Battle upon discovery of the death of Mr. Shaitana

Miss Burgess, Dr. Roberts's rather aloof though competent-looking young secretary. She meets Superintendent Battle with a cool gaze and is uninviting and minimal in her responses, but she is no match for the able superintendent who obtains from her all the information he needs about some of Dr. Roberts's past experiences with female patients.

Mrs. Graves, a former patient of Dr. Roberts, who thought he was poisoning her

Mrs. Craddock, a former patient of Dr. Roberts, who died of "fever" in one of the colonies after the death of her husband

Mr. Craddock, husband of the above, who died of anthrax by using a contaminated shaving brush.

Rhoda Dawes, the housemate and close friend of Anne Meredith. According to locals, it is Miss Dawes who "has the money" and owns the house, a cottage in Wallingford, Berkshire.

Mr. Bury, an aging attorney mentioned by Anne Meredith and Rhoda Dawes.

Mr. Pickerigell, the former owner of Wendon Cottage where Rhoda Dawes and Anne Meredith now live.

Mrs. Anstwell, a loquacious charwoman who "does" for Anne Meredith and Rhoda Dawes and who is a useful informant to Superintendent Battle

Mrs. Eldon, a former employer of Anne Meredith, who served as a nurse-governess for two small boys before Mrs. Eldon joined her husband in Palestine

Mrs. Emily Deering, another former employer of Anne Meredith for whom she worked as a companion/gardener. She lives at Marsh Dene, Little Hembury, Devon and is dying of cancer.

Mrs. Benson, still another former employer of Anne Meredith, now deceased, who lived at Combeacre in Devon. Mrs. Benson died when she drank hat paint, which someone had foolishly stored in a medicine bottle without changing the label. She was a rigid type of Christian, a trifle severe toward young people, and "a self-righteous grenadier of a woman, working her companions hard and changing her servants often."

Sergeant O'Connor, called "The Maidservant's Prayer" by his colleagues at Scotland Yard because his good looks make him "irresistible to the fair sex."

Elsie Blatt, late parlormaid to a certain Mrs. Craddock, a patient of Dr. Roberts who died of fever in one of the colonies after her husband died of anthrax. Making use of his good looks, Sergeant O'Connor achieves a date with Elsie and, at a movie theatre, turns the conversation to the deaths of Mr. and Mrs. Craddock—and learns the truth. Elsie is one of many Christie "servant" characters who enjoy "reliving past scandals."

A Stout Woman Carrying Parcels at Debenham's, a London department store

A Uniformed Attendant at Mrs. Oliver's apartment building, who shows Rhoda Dawes to Mrs. Oliver's apartment

The Elderly Maid of Mrs. Oliver

Professor Timothy Luxmore, a botanist who died somewhere in a South American jungle while studying exotic plants with his wife and Major Despard. The official account of his death was that he died of "fever," a story confirmed by loyal natives but contradicted by a disgruntled one, who claimed that Professor Luxmore had been shot.

Mrs. Luxmore, Professor Luxmore's eccentric widow who lives in a poorly-kept house in Kensington. Poirot obtains a bit of truth—and a good deal of distortion of facts—from her on the subject of her husband's death. Poirot later suggests to another character that Mrs. Luxmore is "a romantic woman" and receives this response: "Romantic be damned. She's an out-and-out liar."

Inspector James Japp of Scotland Yard, not a character in this novel but quoted by Superintendent Battle as having often described Poirot as having a "tortuous mind." He is an old friend of Poirot's whom we have met in several novels, most recently but briefly in the 1935 *The A.B.C. Murders.* He had worked most closely with Poirot in the 1933 *Thirteen at Dinner* and the 1935 *Death in the Air.*

Mrs. Luxmore's Maid, who looks at Hercule Poirot with deep disapproval, showing no disposition to admit him into the house, but then does so upon the orders of her employer.

A Sympathetic-looking and Not Too Haughty Damsel, a sales clerk in a store specializing in expensive women's clothing and accessories, who nearly faints when Poirot purchases eighteen pair of the most delicate and expensive women's hose. Only her training in scornfulness prevents her from fainting behind the counter.

Inspector Harper of the Combeacre Police in Devon. Superintendent Battle consults him in the matter of the death of Mrs. Benson, the former employer whom Anne Meredith had "forgotten" to mention to the police.

An Elderly Parlormaid at the home of Mrs. Lorrimer

Dr. Lang, Mrs. Lorrimer's regular doctor who prescribed sleeping medications for her

Dr. Davidson, a divisional surgeon who examines the body of a certain murder victim and determines the cause of death

Constable Turner, who drives Poirot and Battle quickly to Wendon Cottage in Wallingford to visit Anne Meredith and Rhoda Dawes the morning after the second murder.

Stephens, a young red-haired employee of the Chelsea Window Cleaners Association who happened to be washing an upstairs window at a certain house where a certain person died several years ago.

Sir Charles Imphrey, Home Office Handwriting Analyst

Gerald Hemingway, a promising young actor

FRENCH INTO ENGLISH

Chapter 1
en garde—poised (for the fight, as in fencing)
Tout de même—all the same
Mille remerciments—Thank you so very much!

Chapter 2
embonpoint—slight plumpness suggesting good health
vieux jeu—"old hat," out-of-date
foie gras—goose liver paste

Chapter 3
Quel enfantillage!—Such childishness!

Chapter 10
Du tout—du tout—No problem!

Chapter 11
épatant—stunning, amazing
Je crois bien—I should say so!
objets de vertus—delicate art objects
dans son caractère—consistent with his character
Au fond—basically

Chapter 15
Tout de même—still, all the same
fluxion de poitrine—chest cold
amour propre—pride
Malheureusement—Unfortunately

Chapter 19 *Enchanté*—Delighted

Chapter 20
crime passionnel—violent crime (usually murder) committed while in a state of uncontrolled emotion, usually outrage at sexual betrayal

Chapter 21
Quelle femme! Ce pauvre Despard! Ce qu'il a dû souffrir! Quel voyage épouvantable.!—What a woman! That poor Despard! What he must have suffered! What a horrible trip!
C'est ça. C'est ça exactement—That's it. That's exactly right.
Enfin—at last
Eh bien—Well...

Chapter 23
C'est pénible, n'est-ce pas?—It's painful, isn't it?
Pas si bête—not too dumb (Poirot is commenting mentally on the quick thinking of the woman he's speaking to)
piège—trap
à l'avance—in advance
mille remerciments—Thanks so very much

Chapter 24 *Pas du tout*—Not really

Chapter 25
rapprochement—gathering of minds

Chapter 26
Épatant—Astounding
sacré nom d'un petit bonhomme—expression of frustration, not translatable literally
dans son caractère—consistent with one's personality

Chapter 27
Magnifique!—Stupendous!
Je crois bien!—You bet I have!

Chapter 28
Qu'est-ce qu'il y a?—What's happening?
Eh bien—Yes, go on...
Bien—All right
Je vous remercie—Thank you

Chapter 31
C'est fini—It's over
à merveille—perfectly

COMMENTS

In *Cards on the Table* Agatha Christie introduces an amusing new character, Mrs. Ariadne Oliver, a detective story writer superficially modeled after herself. The Mrs. Oliver character had actually been introduced in the 1932 short story collection *Mr. Parker Pyne, Detective,* but in *Cards on the Table* she meets Hercule Poirot for the first time and makes her first appearance in a novel. Similarities between Agatha Christie and the fictional Ariadne Oliver: both women are very much overweight; both women love apples; and both writers have created eccentric foreign sleuths (Mrs. Oliver's foreign sleuth is the Finnish Sven Hjerson.)

Regarding Mrs. Oliver's weight problem, she has difficulty entering and exiting from her small car, and whenever she does, apples invariably roll out of it onto the pavement (this happens in *Cards on the Table* and then later in *Mrs. McGinty's Dead.*) She is careful, in this novel, to choose the strongest-looking basket chair when offered one, "having had several unfortunate experiences with flimsy summer furniture."

But that is where the similarities end.

Christie once accused herself of being "a perfect sausage machine," and cranking out one detective novel after another as though they were all the same. Actually the idea that all of Christie's books are "the same" could not be further from the truth. In one Christie novel we have a lot of contradictory clues and a group of suspects who are unknown to each other. In another book we have practically no clues but a group of fascinating suspects, an examination of whose psychology leads to the solution. In another book the victim is universally detested and there is a whole village full of motivated suspects, all with opportunities and no alibis. In another book we have cast-iron alibis everywhere we look, but there are plenty of motives. In another there seems to be no conceivable motive and yet one of a small number of persons *must* be the killer.

In some books, Hercule Poirot solves the mystery single-handedly with his "assistant" Captain Hastings just being his usual puzzled self. In another book Poirot sits back and allows a small group of amateurs do all of the work, simply giving a little guidance when requested to do so. In one book he is at odds with a Scotland Yard inspector from beginning to end; in another he works closely with Scotland Yard and the mystery is solved that way. In one book it's the psychology of the victim that matters; in another book it's the psychology of the killer. In some books a couple of youthful adventurers suspect a crime when a death was assumed to be an accident and they solve the mystery with no help from the police or anyone else. Every detective novel that Christie produced was *unique*.

Ariadne Oliver, on the other hand, fully and cheerfully admits that all of her books are the same, but that it doesn't really matter because her readers simply want "lots of dead bodies" and nobody realizes—except Poirot, who has suggested it—that the books are really all alike. Her most famous book is *The Body in the Library*, a title that Christie conceived as very silly and stereotypical, but then she had fun with the title later, giving it to one of her own novels in the early 1940s.

The Ariadne Oliver character is clearly not in the same class as the real Agatha Christie. She is just a fun person, a sort of comic relief, and nearly everything she says is silly nonsense, especially her nonsense about "woman's intuition." In this book, during a bridge game, her "woman's intuition" tells her to lead a club, with disastrous results, and then after the murder the same "woman's intuition" tells her who the killer is. "My instincts never lie," she declares. But a few days later suspicion begins to build against another person, and then she denies her former accusation, stating "I never thought it was him. Not for a minute. He's too obvious, somehow."

Christie writes in her *Autobiography* that, at least during the early 1930s, she wrote "just for money." She even states that in those days, if she needed a certain amount of money for something, such as a new roof for the house, she would find out the cost of it, and calculate how much money a novel or a group of short stories would bring—including serial rights—and would then set about writing the book or stories that would bring her that amount of money. Mrs. Oliver also writes just for money, as she explains to Rhoda Dawes, who has just remarked that writing "doesn't seem like work." Mrs. Oliver explains that writing is very hard work indeed, and that sometimes the only thing that keeps her going is her bankbook when she sees how overdrawn she is.

And so Mrs. Oliver fully admits that her writing isn't worth much, and that she does it primarily for money. Agatha Christie never took herself very seriously. Her creation of the Ariadne Oliver character proves this—as well as occasionally having her characters make remarks such as, "Now if this were happening in a book…" In one story a character summarizes some earlier events, and a second character remarks, "Sounds like a thriller by a lady novelist."

Christie had found, right from the beginning of her career, that no matter how hard she tried to be accurate with details, there were always a few "smarty-pants" among her readers who wrote to her pointing out that she had gotten something wrong, such as police procedure. In the 1935 *Death in the Air* Inspector Japp had commented about how unrealistically police officers were treated by what he called "ignorant scribblers"—writers of detective fiction—and in the 1936 *Murder in Mesopotamia*, nurse Amy Leatheran complained that the author of *Death in a Nursing Home* could not have known very much about nursing homes. Christie must have received petty complaints from readers about details such as the season of the story being spring but fall flowers such as chrysanthemums blooming in a garden. Mrs. Oliver voices her wrath on this subject, pointing out that florists have all kinds of flowers at all seasons.

In *Cards on the Table* there are bowls of chrysanthemums and tulips together in Mr. Shaitana's living room and one character, supposedly knowledgeable about flowers, remarks "so early for tulips!" which is a double absurdity. First of all, there can never be tulips and chrysanthemums together because tulips bloom only in spring and chrysanthemums only in fall, and then of course in this story the month is *October*. The tulips would have to be "next year's tulips" to be called "early" in October. This must have been a joke on Christie's part. She must have been thinking, "Let's see how many irate letters from gardening authorities this will bring!"

One last word about the Ariadne Oliver character. It is mentioned above that Mrs. Oliver is a "fun" character existing more or less for comic relief, and as an amusing parody of Agatha Christie herself. That's not entirely true, however, because quite often the Mrs. Oliver character serves a useful purpose. She is able to do things that Poirot is unable to do, either because he is "a foreigner" or simply because he is a man. In *Cards on the Table,* Mrs. Oliver is the one of the four "sleuths" who is chosen to ingratiate herself with young Anne Meredith and she is able to earn the young woman's trust much more easily than it would have been for Colonel Race, Superintendent Battle or Hercule Poirot. In future stories, she will be able to engage in gossip and light banter with other female characters and obtain information that would be inaccessible to Hercule Poirot.

Cards on the Table has an unusually small number of principal characters—just four possible suspects, plus the housemate of one of them. Their personalities are carefully studied and it is information about their past lives—which reveals their psychology—that brings Hercule Poirot to a certainty of who the killer is.

The four suspects are interesting people, but the most memorable character in the book is the hilarious Mrs. Luxmore, the widow of the deceased botanist Dr. Timothy Luxmore. Poirot asks for the truth about the death of her husband in South America and she presents a picture of a passionate love affair between herself and Major Despard, which is pure imagination on her part (the Major later tells Poirot that "she's a damned liar.") Poirot promises that the truth of her husband's death and the "love affair" will never be made public, and then:

> A sweet womanly smile stole over Mrs. Luxmore's face. She raised her hand slightly, so that Poirot, whether he had meant to do so or not, was forced to kiss it. "An unhappy woman thanks you, Monsieur Poirot," she said.
> It was the last word of a persecuted queen to a favored courtier—clearly an exit line. Poirot duly made his exit. Once out in the street, he drew a long breath of fresh air.

During his conversation with Mrs. Luxmore, Poirot had made a subtle but hilarious remark himself, on a subject he enjoys ridiculing: the English habit of referring to "fair play" and "playing the game" and for saying things like "that isn't cricket." Mrs. Luxmore had just told him an absurd story about a passionate love affair she allegedly had with Major Despard in which the two of them had endured noble silence on the subject of their love.

> "Neither of us would admit what was happening," went on Mrs. Luxmore. "John Despard never said anything. He was the soul of honor."
> "But a woman always knows," prompted Poirot.
> "How right you are. Yes, a woman knows. But I never showed him that I knew. We were Major Despard and Mrs. Luxmore to each other right up to the end. We were both determined to play the game." She was silent, lost in admiration of that noble attitude.
> "True," murmured Poirot. "One must play the cricket. As one of your poets so finely says, 'I could not love thee, dear so much, Loved I not cricket more.'"
> "Honor," corrected Mrs. Luxmore with a slight frown.
> "Of course—of course—honor. 'Loved I not honor more.'"

As time goes on Poirot, while not actually French but feeling typical French exasperation with British romanticism and denial of reality, will come out with these derisive gems with increasing regularity. In another scene in *Cards on the Table*, Rhoda Dawes tells Poirot that Major Despard's interest in her and in Anne Meredith is "to protect them" during the investigation. Poirot smiles at this—knowing that sexual attraction is probably at least as important as the Major's "protective" instincts—and Poirot's sly smile causes Rhoda to think to herself:

> "Oh dear, he's going to be French, and it does embarrass me so."

"Going to be French" in this context clearly means "Going to speak reality," for it is the reality of sex that embarrasses her, as it embarrasses most middle-class British characters in Christie's stories. Christie's male British characters stammer and blush whenever anyone suggests they may feel sexual attraction towards a woman, and the men with red hair blush the reddest. As to the women in Christie's stories, their automatic response is usually to say "I don't know what you mean!" Poirot and all other *foreign* characters are invariably puzzled by this.

Although critics have cited *Cards on the Table* as being among Christie's best detective stories, there is one very unsatisfactory aspect of it. Mr. Shaitana is an extremely effeminate, almost grotesque center-stager. He is an incredible snob, his speech is filled with sarcasm, he uses scent and makeup, and he hosts outrageous parties. Some of his parties are definitely "queer parties," as we learn in the first chapter, and it is not unreasonable to understand the word "queer" in one of its special uses—a reference to homosexuals. It is perfectly possible to imagine the existence of such a person in places such as London, New York, Paris or Hollywood at that time. For there to exist an occasional outrageous eccentric who throws exotic parties that attract the likes of movie stars and other shady types is not at all impossible. What *is* impossible is that a group consisting of Hercule Poirot, a Scotland Yard superintendent, two masculine "big game hunters," a nursery governess, an ordinary middle class woman of advanced age, and a Harley street doctor would ever consider being dinner guests of someone like Mr. Shaitana. All four of the murder suspects admit to disliking Mr. Shaitana, especially Major Despard. Why, then, did they accept Mr. Shaitana's dinner invitation?

If Mr. Shaitana's personality were not quite so outrageous it would have been more believable. He could have been, for example, a very conservative type of person with a "mean streak" but still an acceptable social companion to the characters in the book. He could have been a wealthy businessman or an aristocrat who was notable for charitable work and who cultivated a wide circle of friends, including people like those in the novel. He might also harbor a strong moral outrage regarding unpunished criminals, and might host a party for the purpose of frightening some of those people, perhaps even with a plan for exposing them. Such a person would have been a much more believable host to this particular group.

CAUTION: One of the murder suspects in *Cards on the Table*, as well as one of the secondary characters, will reappear in Christie's 1961 novel *The Pale Horse*, and so if you read *The Pale Horse*, or the chapter on that novel in this book, before reading *Cards on the Table*, you will of course know who they are and that will spoil your full enjoyment of *Cards on the Table*. Furthermore, one character in *Cards on the Table* appeared in the 1924 *The Man in the Brown Suit* and that person was a suspect in the earlier story. Reading *Cards on the Table* before *The Man in the Brown Suit* will spoil your full enjoyment of the earlier book as well, so proceed with caution.

Death on the Nile (1937)

Setting

It is approximately October through January, probably in 1935–36, as the novel was first published in 1937. *Part One* of the novel is entitled "England" but this part includes settings in America, England, the island of Majorca, and Jerusalem. The American settings are a luxury apartment overlooking Central Park in New York and the office of a firm of lawyers further downtown. The English settings are a large country house called Wode Hall at the fictitious village of Malton-under-Wode in an unspecified county; a "modish little restaurant" called Chez Ma Tante, in London; and the offices of a law firm which may be in London, although an employee of the firm later gives his home address as a town in Northamptonshire, suggesting that the firm may be there instead.

Wode Hall is a large home recently owned by a titled gentleman who has found it necessary to sell it because of "financial reverses." An American heiress has just purchased it for 60,000 pounds and has also spent 50,000 pounds for modernization and alterations. These sums should be evaluated in light of the fact that one character in the novel has been managing to live on an income of less than two hundred pounds per year and that she has recently purchased a "dilapidated two-seater" automobile for fifteen pounds. She describes the car as "having moods," meaning that though it provides transportation, it is not reliable. The price of a marginally functional used car today may be used to judge the value of 15 pounds in 1935, and the value of the 60,000-pound country mansion judged accordingly. The young heiress also owns a string of pearls worth 50,000 pounds. At one point in the story the pearls are stolen and are seen as a possible motive for murder; their actual value should be understood in evaluating the strength of that murder motive.

Wode Hall itself is not described in detail, but it is portrayed as a large mansion at the edge of an old-world English village. The young American heiress who has just purchased it is effecting changes which, though discreetly hidden from view so as not to detract from the old world appearance of the mansion, are probably resented by the locals and most certainly by the former owner, who declines an invitation to view the changes. A modern swimming pool is planned for one area of the property and consequently the owner plans to have several "old, insanitary cottages" torn down and the inhabitants relocated—to the annoyance of several of them—since the pool would be visible from the old cottages.

The brief scenes in Majorca and Jerusalem take place in hotels and are simply locations in which a few of the characters discuss their plans for visiting Egypt in January.

Part Two of the novel, entitled "Egypt," takes place principally aboard a steamer, the *Karnak*, which carries passengers on a round-trip cruise between the first and second cataracts of the Nile, through the region of Egypt known as Nubia. The Cataract Hotel in Assuan is the starting point for this section which includes descriptions of the island of Elephantine. There is a brief ten-minute train ride for some of the characters from Assuan to Shellal, the point of departure for the steamer. Thereafter, all of the action takes place aboard the steamer which travels from Shellal south to the second cataract and back—a trip requiring several days—and it is during the return trip that the first crime occurs, followed by two more murders on the following day. Hercule Poirot solves the mystery aboard the steamer on the day of the second and third murders.

The ancient Egyptian temple of Abu Simbel is described, as the steamer stops there twice: once during daylight and then again by night upon its northbound return trip.

No important historical events are evoked other than one or two brief references to "the recent slump" in Wall Street (a euphemistic description of the catastrophic Great Depression) and the actions of one American character are motivated by these financial conditions.

In most Christie novels of this period, clothing is described only when it is useful in characterization, or for some other specific reason. In

Thirteen at Dinner, for example, a hat worn at the "outrageous angle" fashionable during the early 1930s hid the side of a woman's face, making her identification by a witness invalid. In Death on the Nile there are numerous descriptions of colors and fabrics worn by the female characters for no reason other than Christie's apparently whimsical interest in them. We read that in one scene Mrs. Allerton is looking distinguished in black lace; in another scene she wears a dress of light grey striped silk. Linnet Doyle is seen once in a simple white dress and pearls, then in a soft shade of apricot linen. One day, Jacqueline de Bellefort wears a wine-colored evening frock, and on another day she looks childish in a blue gingham dress. Mrs. Otterbourne at one point is dressed in a "floating batik material." The "simple" white dress worn by Linnet, by the way, is described by Tim Allerton as "just a length of stuff with a kind of cord round the middle" to which his mother replies, "Yes, darling. A very nice manly description of an eighty-guinea model." Eighty guineas was the equivalent of eighty-four pounds, nearly half of Jacqueline de Bellefort's annual income and more than five times the amount she had paid for her "dilapidated two-seater car."

Third-world poverty is vividly evoked when, in the town of Assuan, a large number of persistent street vendors and child beggars descend upon Hercule Poirot and his companion. Poirot, gesturing impatiently, waves away this "swarm of human flies."

The 1930s' interest in modern psychology—which plays an important part in most of Christie's novels of the period, especially in The A.B.C. Murders and in Murder in Mesopotamia—has a smaller part in Death on the Nile. One of the characters is afflicted with "kleptomania" and that disorder is briefly discussed; it was perhaps one of the "new" psychoses of the period. There is also a character afflicted by alcoholism, and the unhappiness that it causes for the adult daughter of that character is important in her characterization. For alcoholism to be treated as a "sickness" may have been relatively new in the 1930s, as the words "alcoholic" and "alcoholism" do not occur in the story. The character in question is the author of lurid, sensationalistic novels which have fallen out of favor among a fickle reading public, resulting in her depression and a predisposition to alcoholism.

Communism was, during the 1930s, an attractive idea to many young intellectuals of Western Europe and America and there were many, such as the American writer Theodore Dreiser, who joined the Communist Party and promoted its ideology. We noted in Christie's 1935 Murder in Three Acts that a certain young man, Oliver Manders, was a Communist. He was portrayed as being rather naïve and at odds with the world in general due to an unfortunate past, and he was also an unkind person, but he was loved by an intelligent young woman who shared his views—with the exception of his atheism. In Death on the Nile a young man of aristocratic birth and considerable wealth "became a Communist while studying at Oxford." He is seen by some characters as obnoxious and ill-mannered, but by more indulgent, avuncular characters he is regarded as youthful and spirited.

Story

The year is 1935 or 1936 during autumn and early winter. Linnet Ridgeway is a wealthy American heiress who has recently purchased a large country mansion, Wode Hall, at the edge of an old-world village. An impoverished friend, Jacqueline de Bellefort, appeals to Linnet to hire her unemployed fiancé, Simon Doyle, as an estate manager. Linnet hires Simon, and the two soon fall in love and marry. Their honeymoon trip takes them across Europe to Egypt, but the embittered, jealous Jacqueline stalks them every step of the way in efforts to make their lives miserable.

One evening, aboard a Nile steamer, Jacqueline has too much to drink and abuses Simon verbally in the presence of some other travelers. When he ignores her ravings, she fires a pistol at him, wounding him in one leg, and then breaks down in hysterics. A nurse takes her to her cabin, administers a tranquilizer by injection, and remains with her for the night. Another passenger who is a doctor treats Simon's leg wound and keeps him in his own cabin for the night.

The following morning Linnet is found dead in her bed, having been shot at close range in the head while she slept, and a string of valuable pearls is missing from her cabin. Because the most logical suspect, Jacqueline, has a perfect alibi, Hercule Poirot and Colonel Race, who are also on the steamer, search for murder motives among the other passengers, finding several. Soon a second person is killed, apparently having witnessed the first murder and attempted to blackmail the killer, and then a third murder takes place. Hercule Poirot solves the case before another killing can occur.

Characters

Linnet Ridgeway, a twenty-year-old American heiress, daughter of successful businessman

Melhuish Ridgeway and wealthy Anna Hartz, whose fortune passes to her upon her twenty-first birthday or her marriage. She has "money, beauty, good health and brains." Many characters feel that for her to have everything is "unfair." She is not consciously cruel but she is thoughtless and insensitive. Without hesitation, for example, she orders the destruction of a cluster of old cottages bordering her estate, because they "would overlook the new swimming pool." She gives no thought to the feelings of the occupants of the old cottages, who may have lived in them all their lives, pointing out that their new lodgings will be far superior in terms of comfort and "sanitation." Without hesitation she "steals" the fiancé of her closest friend, a girl who has nothing in the world except her beloved fiancé. Hercule Poirot, not normally a person who moralizes, quotes the Bible to Linnet, comparing her to a rich man who took for himself the only animal owned by a poor man.

Linnet rides in a scarlet, chauffeur-driven Rolls Royce, a nauseating sight in the eyes of the residents of the old world village of Malton-under-Wode where she has purchased Wode Hall from an impoverished aristocrat.

During her honeymoon cruise aboard a Nile steamer she is shot to death while asleep in her cabin.

Mr. Burnaby, the landlord of The Three Crowns in Malton-under-Wode who observes that it is "wicked and unfair" for Linnet Ridgeway to have so much while others have so little.

A Lean and Seedy-looking Man, Mr. Burnaby's conversation partner in the pub, who observes:

> "It seems all wrong to me—her looking like that. Money *and* looks—it's too much! If a girl's as rich as that she's no right to be a good-looker as well. And she *is* a good-looker.... Got everything, that girl has. Doesn't seem fair..."

Sir George Wode, the former owner of Wode Hall, who has been unlucky with horses and has found it necessary to sell Wode Hall for "a cool sixty-thousand." Wode Hall had been in his family for generations and he bitterly resents the modernizations its new owner has effected in it.

The Hon. Joanna Southwood, a close friend of Linnet Ridgeway. She is a stylish young woman who uses fashionable conversation fillers such as "too, too divine" and "perfectly marvelous." She frequently complains about being "broke" but she is seen in the most expensive places and goes everywhere in expensive clothes. According to her second cousin Tim Allerton, she achieves this solely with good credit, which she obtains simply by expressing expensive tastes, but clearly there is a source of considerable income in the background.

According to Joanna's cousin, Mrs. Allerton, Joanna is "insincere, affected and essentially superficial."

Linnet Ridgeway's "Ecclesiastical" Butler who announces Jacqueline de Bellefort with the proper mournful intonation.

Jacqueline de Bellefort, the daughter of a womanizing French count and an American heiress who lost all of her money in the Wall Street crash, leaving Jacqueline penniless. Jacqueline and Linnet had studied together at a convent in Paris during adolescence and had become lifelong friends, although Linnet recalls that Jackie's "Latin blood" is responsible for a violent temperament. She once stuck a penknife into someone because that person had been tormenting an animal.

Jacqueline is a small, slender young woman who is passionately in love—according to Poirot, "too much" in love—with Simon Doyle. When her best friend Linnet "steals" Simon from her, she becomes obsessed with revenge.

Marie, Linnet Ridgeway's personal maid, who was engaged to an Englishman working in Egypt until Linnet made inquiries and discovered that he was already married—with children—to an Egyptian woman.

Lord Windlesham, an aristocrat whose family home is Charltonbury, an Elizabethan mansion far more imposing than Wode Hall. He is in love with Linnet and tells himself that he would marry her even if she were poor. He notes with satisfaction, however, that she is *not* poor. When Linnet abandons him for Simon Doyle, Lord Windlesham takes it hard.

Simon Doyle, a tall, handsome young man from a good Devonshire family but unfortunately "a younger son" and therefore not an heir. Though recently employed, he has more recently been let go because the firm is "cutting down." Jacqueline de Bellefort is passionately in love with him, and he with her, although when Poirot overhears a conversation of theirs in a London restaurant, he worries that Jacqueline loves Simon "too much" and that he may simply be one of those men who "let themselves be loved."

When Simon meets Linnet Ridgeway and becomes her estate manager, Linnet falls in love with him and they marry within a month. Together they become the object of Jacqueline's obsessive hatred.

Hercule Poirot, the famous Belgian detective.

Gaston Blondin, the owner of *Chez Ma Tante,* a "modish little restaurant" in London frequented by Poirot. He rarely singles out or pays special attention to customers—even the rich, the beautiful, the notorious and the well-born—letting them wait their turn for a table on crowded evenings, but for "Monsieur Poirot" there is always a table which mysteriously appears in a most favorable position. He shares Poirot's well-known aversion to sea travel, calling seasickness "an unfairness of the good God."

Jules, the maître d'hôtel at *Chez Ma Tante* who, Monsieur Blondin promises, "will compose for Poirot a little meal that will be a poem—positively a poem!"

Mr. Pierce, Linnet Ridgeway's architect, who is supervising the removal of "some insanitary cottages" at the edge of her estate. The old cottages would otherwise overlook the new swimming pool.

Tim Allerton, a tall, thin young man with dark hair and a rather narrow chest. He is popularly supposed "to write," but it is understood among his friends that inquiries as to literary output are not encouraged.

Tim is very much attached to his mother and is a close friend of his mother's cousin, Joanna Southwood, an attachment of which his mother disapproves, as she dislikes Joanna very much.

Mrs. Allerton, Tim Allerton's mother, a good-looking, white-haired woman of fifty. She is very fond of her son and rather possessive, mildly resenting the fact that he does not show her every letter he receives, especially letters from Joanna Southwood. Nevertheless she is a kind person and, of all the characters in the story, the one most respected by Poirot for having accurate perceptions. She is very much interested in people—"all the different types" as she expresses it—even the incredibly snobbish American Miss Van Schuyler who snubs her at first but with whom she succeeds in "breaking the ice" through outrageous name-dropping.

The Devinishes and **"Old Monty,"** friends of the Allertons mentioned in a letter from Joanna Southwood to Tim Allerton. The former are getting divorced and the latter has been "had up" for drunk driving.

Mrs. Leech, a stout woman who claims to have lost a ruby ring at the hotel in Majorca where the Allertons are staying. Tim insists that she must have lost it in the water while swimming, which she shouldn't have been doing anyway, according to Tim, as she is fat and ugly.

Miss Marie Van Schuyler, an aging New York snob who lives in an apartment overlooking Central Park. Hercule Poirot first notices her in the train going from Assuan to Shellal. When Tim suggests to his mother that it will be useless to attempt conversation with this incredible snob, Mrs. Allerton responds:

"Not at all. I shall pave the way by sitting near her and conversing, in low (but penetrating), well-bred tones, about any titled relations and friends I can remember. I think a casual mention of your second cousin, once removed, the Duke of Glasgow, would probably do the trick."

Mrs. Robson, a poor relation of Miss Van Schuyler's. Mrs. Robson is "ever so grateful" to Miss Van Schuyler for offering to take her daughter Cornelia, who suffers a lot from not being a social success, on a trip to exotic Egypt. She hopes that during the trip there will be "no trouble," as she expresses it to Miss Van Schuyler's nurse.

Miss Bowers, a trained hospital nurse and constant companion to Miss Van Schuyler, for whom she has worked for two years. Nurse Bowers assures Mrs. Robson that there will be "no trouble," as she "keeps a good look-out always."

Cornelia Ruth Robson, Miss Van Schuyler's niece, who is as grateful as her mother for the opportunity of traveling abroad for the first time. She is enthusiastic about everything—the historic monuments of ancient Egypt, the beautiful blue Nile, etc.—and she enjoys Dr. Bessner's erudite talk about psychology and archeology. Though rather clumsy and unattractive herself, she feels not envy or jealousy but admiration for Linnet's breathtaking beauty. Despite Cornelia's poverty and mediocre looks, she receives two marriage proposals while aboard the Nile steamer.

Andrew Pennington, a tall, distinguished looking grey-haired man with a keen, clean-shaven American face. He is a lawyer with an office in downtown Manhattan and, as Linnet Ridgeway's American trustee, he is responsible for her finances until she takes control of them personally upon her twenty-first birthday or her marriage. He was an old friend of Linnet's deceased father, Melhuish Ridgeway, and has known Linnet since she was a small child. He becomes very upset upon learning of Linnet's sudden and unexpected marriage because he has been speculating with her money and has taken a major stock market loss.

Pennington carries a large revolver with him in his travels and it is with that firearm that one of the murders is committed.

Sterndale Rockford, Andrew Pennington's business partner

A Smart-looking Stenographer who answers Mr. Pennington's buzzer with commendable promptitude

William Carmichael, the senior partner of Carmichael, Grant & Carmichael, Linnet Ridgeway's British lawyers. Learning in a letter from Linnet that Andrew Pennington has, "by coincidence" turned up in Egypt, Mr. Carmichael suspects that something is "fishy" and sends his nephew to Egypt to investigate "and to act, if necessary."

A Thin, Weedy Youth who works in the offices of Carmichael, Grant and Carmichael.

James Leechdale Fanthorp, William Carmichael's nephew, who reluctantly travels by air to Egypt at his uncle's request to "keep his eyes and ears open" and "to act if necessary." He is a very quiet young man who surprises everyone aboard the *Karnak* by butting into a conversation between Linnet Doyle and Andrew Pennington, congratulating her for her careful business practice of reading documents before signing them.

Solome Otterbourne, a middle-aged British writer of lurid romance novels whose public has begun to find other reading interests. She habitually wears a turban of native material draped around her head. It soon becomes obvious to the passengers aboard the *Karnak* that she is in the advanced stages of alcoholism and certain passengers begin referring to her as "that awful turban woman." On one occasion Poirot stumbles upon her in a state of complete intoxication, and on another occasion he overhears her arguing with her daughter and using the word "ingratitude."

Rosalie Otterbourne, the adult daughter of Solome Otterbourne. She is loyal to her mother but, overburdened by the responsibility of trying to keep her mother away from drink, she has found no personal happiness and has become bitter. She is most often sullen and sulky, and on at least two occasions she expresses great hostility towards Linnet.

Five Watchful Bead Sellers, Two Vendors of Post Cards, Three Sellers of Plaster Scarabs, a Couple of Donkey Boys and Some Detached but Hopeful Infantile Riff-raff—this "human cluster of flies" closes in upon Hercule Poirot and Rosalie Otterbourne in the city of Assuan as they stroll outside the hotel gate.

Signor Guido Richetti, a slightly podgy, middle-aged Italian archeologist who converses with Poirot in French and is intense about archeology. When Linnet accidentally opens a telegram addressed to him he becomes inordinately enraged.

A Nubian Boatman with superior skill in handling a small sailboat

Dr. Carl Bessner, an Austrian medical doctor and psychologist who has a prestigious practice in Vienna. It is fortunate that he is aboard the *Karnak*, as his medical services are required several times in the course of the cruise. He is fond of Cornelia Robson, commenting:

"A very nice maiden, that. She does not look so starved as some of these young women. No, she has the nice curves. She listens too, very intelligently; it is a pleasure to instruct her."

Mr. Ferguson, a tall, dark-haired young man with a thin face and a pugnacious chin. He is a young Communist and on several occasions he gives vent to his hostility towards the capitalist system and its products, in particular the "rich but useless" Linnet Doyle and the snobbish American Miss Van Schuyler.

Louise Bourget, Linnet Doyle's personal maid of two months who accompanies her on the Nile cruise. She has replaced Marie, Linnet's former maid.

Colonel Race, a tall, bronzed man whom Poirot met a year earlier in *Cards on the Table*, a man "of unadvertised goings and comings. He was usually to be found in one of the outposts of Empire where trouble was brewing." True to his British prejudices—which had caused him to remark in *Cards on the Table* that Major John Despard was a "pucka sahib"—a comment belying a British attitude frequently derided by Poirot—he comments that Dr. Carl Bessner is "a kind of Bosche," although his nationality is Austrian, since his native language is German.

Rufus Van Aldin, an American millionaire who was a character in the 1928 *The Mystery of the Blue Train* and who is a friend of Miss Van Schuyler, though not a character in *Death on the Nile*. Despite Miss Van Schuyler's incredible snobbery, she condescends to speak to Hercule Poirot, mentioning that Van Aldin had spoken highly of him, and she even expresses an interest in hearing about some of Poirot's former cases.

The Manager of the *Karnak*

A Steward into whose arms the distraught Louise Bourget falls upon discovering the corpse of Linnet Doyle

Fleetwood, a big, truculent-looking man who is one of the engineers of the *Karnak* and, coincidentally, the man to whom Linnet's former maid Marie had been engaged until Linnet reported that he was already married. He admits that he had a grudge against Linnet for that reason but he denies killing her.

A Second Steward and **A Stewardess**

Lord Dawlish, the true name—and rank—of one of the passengers named above

Captain Hastings, Poirot's "assistant" in several stories. Though not a character in the present story, he is mentioned briefly by Poirot as wearing "the same kind of tie" as one of the passengers—a comment intended to suggest that that passenger is one of the "old school" type.

Chief Inspector Japp of Scotland Yard, a frequent colleague of Poirot when investigating crimes in England, mentioned briefly by Poirot in connection with certain jewel robberies currently under investigation.

French into English

Part One—England

Chapter 5
Sa Majesté, la reine Linette. Linette la blonde!—Her majesty, Queen Linnet, Linnet the Blonde!

Chapter 6
empressement—enthusiasm, warmth
maître d'hôtel—head waiter
Un qui aime et un qui se laisse aimer.—One who loves, and another who lets himself be loved.

Part Two—Egypt

Chapter 1
Tenez—Oh, well...
Bien—Very good!

Chapter 2 À votre santé—Cheers!

Chapter 3 eh bien—well. Écoutez—Listen

Chapter 5
Tiens, c'est drole, ça!—Hmm ... that's rather intriguing
Un qui aime et un qui se laisse aimer—One who loves, and another who lets himself be loved.
Ah, vraiment—Oh, really!

Chapter 6 parbleu—for Heaven's sake

Chapter 8
grande amoureuse—a desirable, passionate woman

Chapter 9 Ma foi—Good heavens!

Chapter 10
les femmes—women
Peut-être—maybe

Chapter 12
Ah! non!—Impossible!
Non d'un nom d'un nom!—Son of a bitch!
Eh bien—Well...
vieux jeu—out of date, old fashioned

C'est l'enfantillage—It's childishness
Eh bien—All right, then
Bien—OK

Chapter 13 mon enfant—dear

Chapter 14 sacré—damn!
Eh bien?—Well, what do you think?

Chapter 15
Très bien—All right
À merveille!—Wonderful!
Bonne nuit—Good night
article de luxe—piece of luxury goods
Nom d'un nom d'un nom!—God damn it!

Chapter 16
crime passionnel—crime, usually murder, committed while in a state of uncontrolled emotion, typically sexual jealousy

Chapter 17
Cherchez la femme—Look for the woman
cherchez—look for
moi qui vous parle—I myself
Ce cher Woolworth—Good old Woolworth's (cheap dime-store goods)
jeune fille—girlish
Cette pauvre Madame Doyle—That poor Mrs. Doyle

Chapter 18
Pauvre petite—You poor dear
La politesse—Politeness, courtesy

Chapter 19 Tiens!—Hmm....!

Chapter 20
cette pauvre petite Rosalie—that poor little Rosalie

Chapter 21 Zut!—Shit!
On ne prend pas les mouches avec le vinaigre—You don't catch flies with vinegar
bon Dieu—good heavens
Qu'est-ce qu'il y a?—What's the matter?

Chapter 22
a mille note—a one-thousand franc note (a bank note of little value, no more than a couple of dollars)
femme de chambre—chamber maid
Les chiffons d'aujourd'hui—the latest fashions

Chapter 23
eh bien—then
Bon Dieu—God

Mais oui—mais oui—Of course it will!
Le roi est mort—vive le roi—The king is dead. Long live the king!
Short rhyme:
La vie est vaine, Un peu d'amour, Un peu de haine, Et puis bonjour—Life is tough, a bit of love, a bit of hate, and then so-long.
La vie est breve, Un peu d'espoir, Un peu de rêve, Et puis bonsoir.—Life is short. A bit of hope, a bit of dreaming, and then it's over.
Tiens—c'est vrai.—Hey, that's right!

Chapter 24 *Mais oui*—Yessir!

Chapter 25 *malaise*—discomfort

Chapter 26
Mais c'est tout.—But that's all.
Mais oui—mais oui!—Yes, of course!

Chapter 27
jeune fille—girl
Mais oui—Of course

Chapter 28
mille franc note—a one thousand franc note (small change)
En vérité—As a matter of fact

Chapter 30
Quel pays sauvage!—Such wild countryside!

COMMENTS

A large number of interesting characters populate *Death on the Nile* and their personalities have unusual complexity for light fiction. Rosalie Otterbourne suffers as the adult child of an alcoholic and struggles to suppress feelings of resentment towards her mother and, in addition, feelings of hate and jealousy towards another character—one who she believes has all of the happiness while she herself has none. The clumsy, socially unsuccessful and physically mediocre Cornelia Robson, though bullied constantly by an insensitive aunt, has so much capacity for enjoying life that she revels in every minute of her experiences despite her aunt's bullying. Mrs. Allerton, though not the kind of mother modern thinkers would accept—she is autocratic and domineering towards her adult son—is perceptive and interested in people of all kinds, and she is compassionate. Linnet Doyle, though clearly egotistical thanks to her beauty, wealth and upbringing, is in no way a cruel person—she is simply spoiled and thoughtless. Jacqueline de Bellefort has only one source of happiness—her beloved fiancé—and when that happiness is destroyed she loses all sense of proportion and becomes obsessed with revenge, though she never stops loving the man who has left her for another woman. As mentioned in the *Setting* section above, one character is a young aristocrat who became a Communist while a student at Oxford. Every character in this novel has a strong individual personality that is memorable.

For the characters alone, this novel would be worth reading even if there were not the exciting murder mystery to solve. The story is especially exciting because the panic-stricken murderer kills a witness to the first murder, then a witness to the second one, in rapid succession, while suspicion points first to one character and then to another.

On the subject of "class," once again we are reminded of Agatha Christie's attitude toward the servant classes as Hercule Poirot comments blithely that the blackmailer, being of "that class," would naturally be put off guard when handed the hush-money because "naturally, that class would count the money."

Poirot has, once again, occasion to be irritated by British denials of reality. Simon Doyle observes that Poirot is "not very encouraging" on the subject of Jacqueline de Bellefort's jealous behaviors and Poirot thinks to himself: "The Anglo Saxon, he takes nothing seriously but playing games! He does not grow up." Poirot will make this same comment the following year in the 1938 *Appointment with Death* when speaking of Colonel Carbury.

Poirot Loses a Client (1937)

(Alternate Titles: *Dumb Witness, Murder at Littlegreen House, Mystery at Littlegreen House*)

SETTING

The action takes place during April through July in 1936, the death of the victim actually taking place on May 1, in the fictitious small town of Market Basing. We know that the year is 1936 because Hercule Poirot notes that year marked on the tombstone of the murder victim. Market Basing was first mentioned in the 1925 *The Secret of Chimneys* as being the nearest market town to the old country estate of Chimneys, and in that novel travelers from London to Market Basing boarded trains at Paddington Station. Therefore it was clear that Market Basing was "somewhere west of London," although the county in which it was located was never named. In *Poirot Loses a Client* Market Basing is clearly stated as being in the county of Berkshire, which is in fact just a few miles west of London.

In this story Hastings and Poirot travel from London to Market Basing more than once by car—Hastings revealing that he has purchased a second-hand Austin—a convertible or more probably a roadster, since Hastings mentions the discomfort of driving in busy London traffic on a hot day "in an open car." Using "The Great West Road," they reach Market Basing in about an hour and a half. "The Great West Road" in 1936 was probably just a two-lane paved road, but it must have been considered to be a modern highway for the time. Market Basing itself is three miles removed from the "modern" Great West Road, and consequently not very much traffic passes through it. It is an "old world town" that clearly had more importance in the past than it has today. Travelers in England find that the country is, in fact, filled with "old world" towns and villages which "were once important." Towns such as Salisbury and Wells, each of which boasts a magnificent medieval cathedral, must have been major centers centuries ago but their populations—and importance—were later far surpassed by industrial cities such as Sheffield and Manchester. Fortunately the "old world" appearance of such places is carefully protected by laws put in place by a population that values the beauty of the countryside and the preservation of history.

In Market Basing, Poirot and Hastings book a couple of rooms at The George Hotel, which is probably actually a small inn. Poirot has occasion to complain of the food served there and even the supremely British Hastings is disgusted by its watery cabbage, dispirited potatoes, tasteless stewed fruit and custard and a doubtful fluid called coffee. On another occasion in this same inn Poirot does a good deal of groaning about the soup.

Poirot's disgust with English cooking—and his delight in finding an occasional excellent little *bistrot* in London, such as *Chez Ma Tante* which is mentioned in *Death on the Nile* the same year, or *La Vieille Grand'Mère*, which will be mentioned in the 1952 *Mrs. McGinty's Dead*,—are frequent sources of humor in Christie's novels. For further remarks on this subject, see the *Comments* section of the present novel.

The house in which the crime occurs, Littlegreen House, is described as an elegant home from the "Georgian" period—that period between about 1720 and 1805 during the reigns of Kings George I, II, III and IV—which produced country homes of graceful proportions and considerable elegance. A house agent, early in the novel, touts the advantages of the house, although another character points out that it's one of those old houses "right on the road." This means that the road passes directly in front of the entrance door of the house, a disadvantage in this modern day of noisy and smoky automobiles. The house is well furnished with fine old furniture, mostly overly ornate Victorian pieces but also some finer examples of Hepplewhite and Chippendale from the earlier period. One room of the house is called the "morning room."

In addition to the scenes at Littlegreen House and The George Hotel, there is an amusing scene in the office of a house agent, in which a young woman employee—evidently a clerk-typist—is absolutely bored with her job and extremely stupid as well, and where a super-salesman type presents Poirot and Hastings with a glowing "realtor's" description of Littlegreen House. He cites the asking price of 2,850 pounds as being "simply a steal," but Hastings later remarks that the house is probably worth only half that amount and that there is probably only one bathroom serving the eight bedrooms. We have here another concrete example of the value of the pound during the 1930s—an eight-bedroom "period house" in excellent condition, in the "country" but not far from London with an asking price of less than three thousand pounds, *and* a knowledgeable person declaring its actual value to be only half that amount.

Other references to money values in the novel are some remarks made by one of the characters who admits that her capital of 30,000 pounds, left to her by her father, can generate an income of "twelve hundred a year." With this income, she states, she could manage "very prettily," although it does not provide the flashy kind of life she craves. Recall that in *Death on the Nile*, published the same year, Jacqueline de Bellefort struggles but manages to survive on less than two hundred pounds annually and purchases a dilapidated but at least marginally serviceable car for fifteen pounds. With all of this in mind, we must realize that the amount of money left by the murder victim in *Poirot Loses a Client*—nearly four hundred thousand pounds—is indeed a fortune.

An entertaining scene takes place outside the town of Market Basing at the home of two eccentric middle-aged sisters. The house, an antiquated cottage, is reached by a circuitous drive over narrow, winding lanes, and is extremely picturesque—so picturesque, in fact, as to appear that it may collapse at any moment. The interior is dim even in the daytime owing to its very small windows, and Hastings remarks that there is probably no plumbing at all. Water is probably drawn by a hand pump, and there is, in Hastings's words, "probably an earth closet in the garden"—undoubtedly what Americans would call an "outhouse."

Slightly more distant from Market Basing—about one mile away—is Morton Manor, the home of Miss Caroline Peabody, and it is succinctly described in the narration as an ugly substantial house of the Victorian period.

In Christie novels, houses built during the "Victorian Period" (about 1830 to 1900) are invariably described as "ugly." Christie's preferred periods in domestic architecture seem to be the earlier Georgian period (the period of Littlegreen House) and the even earlier Queen Anne period. Houses of those periods exhibit simplicity, symmetry and beautiful exterior and interior proportions. During the Victorian period, industrialists made fortunes and spent those fortunes on ostentatious homes designed more for display of wealth than for architectural beauty, and the wealthy industrialists were not known for having much education, refinement, taste or appreciation for art. The homes of Victorian millionaires were often miniature castles, designed to suggest that the occupants were able to live "like kings."

In an early chapter of the 1924 novel *The Man in the Brown Suit*, we may recall that Anne Beddingfeld finds a scrap of paper with the words "Kilmorden Castle" written on it. She assumes that "Kilmorden Castle" is a "great house" somewhere in England, probably the historic home of some aristocratic family, and she consults reference books in order to find it, but it does not appear to exist. The thought then occurs to her that "Kilmorden Castle" may be "one of those castellated abominations." She is referring to "fake castles" built by Victorian millionaires and given names to suggest that they really were castles.

Very soon, in the 1939 novel *Easy to Kill*, we will encounter a modern-day "castellated abomination" in the form of a perfectly good Queen Anne period home to which the current millionaire owner has added stone towers at the corners and other false façades to make the house resemble a castle, and to advertise his wealth and success.

Returning to the matter at hand—the settings in *Poirot Loses a Client*—a minor setting is the office of a firm of lawyers in the neighboring larger town of Cranchester, and in London there are scenes at Poirot's apartment, a "modernistic" (today we would call it "Art Deco") block of flats called Whitehaven Mansions. Poirot has there a collection of books on psychology, one of his interests, and a character is found reading one of those as he awaits an interview. There are also scenes at an apartment in the Chelsea district of London, and one at an apartment in Bayswater. A stylish young woman, Theresa Arundell, lives in the Chelsea apartment, which is furnished expensively in the modern style and features gleaming chromium and thick rugs with geometric designs on them. The Bayswater apartment, occupied by old Wilhelmina Lawson, is so crammed with furniture and odds and ends that one can hardly move about without fear of knocking something over.

Three fictitious London hotels are also named—the Durham, the Wellington and the Coniston. The Wellington is a small inconspicuous hotel of the boarding-house variety in Bayswater; the Coniston is an unsavory place near Euston Railway Station, and the Durham is in the Bloomsbury district.

The historical events of the 1930s play no part in this story. Ladies' fashions play a small part in the characterization of Theresa Arundell and of her cousin Bella Tanios. Bella constantly attempts to copy, at lower cost, the expensive fashions sported by her more stylish and better-looking cousin Theresa. A detail mentioned is the mid-1930s habit of wearing hats "rakishly tilted over the right eye" but which the dowdy, dumpy Bella wears perched on the back of her head or otherwise "incorrectly." Theresa is described as having a face that is heavily made up with freakishly plucked eyebrows, giving her an air of "mocking irony." The description is not so much a comment on her taste but a comment on the makeup fashions of approximately 1936, the "Marlene Dietrich look," so to speak. By this time Agatha Christie was a matron of forty-six years of age and was undoubtedly an amused observer, and no longer a follower, of current fashions. The makeup, coiffures, hats and dresses of the middle 1930s probably disgusted her.

STORY

It is mid–April of 1936 and Easter Sunday is approaching. In the village of Market Basing, Miss Emily Arundell lives in her elegant family home, Littlegreen House, with a companion and just two servants. She is well past seventy, is understandably quite Victorian in her attitudes, and one day she realizes that she is getting old—in fact in a moment of reality she observes to herself, "I *am* old!" She has always intended to leave her considerable fortune equally divided among her only living relatives, two nieces and a nephew, although none of them has ever been entirely satisfactory to her.

At Easter the relatives visit her and remain at Littlegreen House until Wednesday. Habitually suffering from insomnia, Emily is in the habit of rising during the night and strolling about the house in the semi-darkness, enjoying private reminiscences. On Tuesday evening, during one of these strolls, she falls down the stairs but, miraculously, she is only bruised by the fall. Family members suggest that she slipped on a rubber ball that was left at the top of the stairs by her pet terrier, but Emily knows that something quite different—and quite alarming—caused her to fall. She knows that someone in the house deliberately tried to kill her.

In order to deprive her relatives of a reason for killing her, Emily immediately writes a new Will leaving her entire fortune to her companion, leaving nothing to her living relatives, and publicly announcing the fact. Several weeks later, Emily dies, apparently of a liver disorder from which she has been suffering for some time.

Approximately two months later, Hercule Poirot receives a letter from Emily. She had written the letter at the moment that she created her new Will, but being obsessed with neatness and habitually "tucking things away," she had apparently tucked it away and later thought that she had mailed it. A house servant found the letter in a sealed envelope several weeks after Emily's death and, not knowing what else to do with it, she affixed a stamp to it and mailed it. In the letter Emily had expressed fears for her life and appealed to Poirot to assist her.

Poirot and his friend Hastings travel to Market Basing and learn that Emily Arundell died several weeks ago. Since no crime has been suspected by the authorities, Poirot and Hastings investigate the death of Emily Arundell without police assistance and unmask her killer.

CHARACTERS

All of the members of the Arundell family are listed here, including the deceased members, whose names are shown in *italics*. Most of the information about the deceased persons is provided to Poirot and Hastings by the loquacious Miss Caroline Peabody, a local gossip and close friend of the murder victim, Emily Arundell.

General John Laverton Arundell, who died in 1888 and whose service in the army had included the period of the Indian Mutiny of 1857. According to Miss Peabody, General Arundell drank heavily and the family took cartloads of bottles out of the house and buried them at night. Regarding General Arundell's experiences in the army and in India, Miss Peabody explains that she never bothered to listen to the General's boring stories about India. She also states that the General was quite a stupid man, but that brains were unimportant in the military since all one needed to do was to pay attention to one's colonel's wife and to listen respectfully to one's superior officers.

No reference at all is made to General Arundell's wife. The couple had five children:

Matilda Arundell, the eldest child of General Arundell. She taught Sunday school and never married, although she had been sweet on one of the curates.

Emily Harriet Laverton Arundell, the sole survivor of her generation, and the murder victim in the story. She never married. She is described below with the other living family members.

Thomas Arundell who, according to Miss Peabody, was a bit of an old woman—nobody thought he'd ever marry. But there was a sensational murder case. A certain Mrs. Varley, a good-looking woman, was accused of and tried for poisoning her husband, but she was acquitted. Thomas Arundell used to read all the accounts of the trial in the papers, and when the trial was over, he went to London, sought Mrs. Varley out, and married her, shocking the family and the whole town. The family was outraged by Thomas's marriage and refused to receive his wife. Thomas was mortally offended by this, and he and his bride went off to live in the Channel Islands and nobody heard from them again. He outlived his wife by three years. Their two children, Theresa and Charles, are described below. Each of them received a legacy of 30,000 pounds upon his death.

Arabella Biggs, who according to Miss Peabody, was a plain girl with a face like a scone. At the age of forty she married a chemistry professor at Cambridge. The couple produced one daughter, Arabella, the present Bella Tanios, described below.

Agnes Arundell, the youngest of the family and the prettiest. According to Miss Peabody, she was "almost fast," evidently a major flirt, but despite being "the pretty one" she never married.

Emily Harriet Laverton Arundell, the murder victim. She is well over seventy years old, has Victorian notions about everything and is very disappointed in the younger generation. Her only living relatives are two nieces and a nephew—Theresa, Bella and Charles—to whom she plans to leave her fortune of nearly 400,000 pounds, although she disapproves of all three for one reason or another. She disapproves of Theresa because of her modern, party-going, London life style. She is also rather disgusted with the young man Theresa wants to marry, a young doctor who is very serious and quiet. "A poor stick," is how she describes him, recalling more robust gentlemen of her youth, and she wonders why the fast-living Theresa and this quiet, serious young doctor can possibly be attracted to each other. As to Theresa's brother Charles, he is not trustworthy and already has a reputation for minor crimes: forgery, to be exact. For the remaining niece, Bella, Emily has no strong negative feelings, although she has always disapproved of Bella's outrageous affront to the family: Bella married a Greek!

Basically a kind person, Miss Arundell is nevertheless autocratic, demanding, impatient and often downright rude. She has had a series of "companions," each one satisfactory in her own way, but in every case Miss Arundell has become bored after about a year and has taken on a new companion. She bullies her current companion, Wilhelmina Lawson, but at one point she softens and apologizes, telling Minnie that she appreciates her patience. Emily's two servants, a maid of twenty years and a cook of four years, are accustomed to her ways and are devoted to her.

Emily has a frightening accident one night while her family is staying at her home for the Easter holiday: she falls down the stairs and, though she survives miraculously with no broken bones, she is badly shaken and becomes suspicious that the "accident" was actually "caused" by a member of the family. Frightened that a member of the family wants to kill her, she abruptly changes her Will, leaving all of her wealth to her companion, Minnie, and makes the new Will known to her nephew and nieces in order to deprive them of a reason for killing her.

Emily dies about two weeks after making the new Will, apparently of a liver disorder that had afflicted her a year or two earlier but from which she had apparently recovered. Her new Will then becomes public, provoking astonishment in the town of Market Basing, where most people find it extremely unfair to "her own flesh and blood" and suspect that "something is behind it."

Mr. Jones, a grocer at Market Basing whose reaction to Miss Arundell's Will is to declare that blood is thicker than water.

Mrs. Lamphrey, who runs the Market Basing post office, and whose reaction to the Will is that "There's something behind it, depend upon it. You mark my words."

Miss Wilhelmina Lawson ("Minnie"), Emily Arundell's current companion. She claims to be surprised by the terms of Emily's Will, but she is thought by some to have known more about the Will than she admits. She loves children and dislikes Emily's nephew Charles. Everyone is surprised at Emily's having left her home and fortune to Minnie, whom she has known for only about a year.

Although the family—and in fact the whole town—is shocked by Miss Lawson's being the sole beneficiary of Emily Arundell's Will, nobody seriously suspects her of "undue influence" since her personality is that of a non-assertive, somewhat muddle-headed but kindly old lady.

Bella Tanios, one of Emily's two nieces, the daughter of her sister Arabella. Bella committed the outrageous act of marrying a Greek, and to Emily's way of thinking, "Arundells do *not* marry Greeks." She is a dumpy, dowdy sort of woman who is devoted to her children and not much else. She is awkward in society and pathetically attempts to copy—with cheap imitations—the stylish wardrobe of her more sophisticated and better-looking cousin Theresa. Her own money has been unwisely invested by her husband and has been lost. She wishes that Aunt Emily would subsidize an English education for her two children but has not the courage to ask. According to Emily, Bella spoils her children—who never dream of doing what they are told—but she considers Bella to be a good woman.

Dr. Jacob Tanios, the Greek physician who is Bella's husband. Even the most British residents of Market Basing concede that he has very charming manners and is a very kind person as well as a good doctor. If only he were not Greek! And he has a beard!

Mary and Edward Tanios, aged about seven and five, children of Jacob and Bella Tanios. According to Emily Arundell, they are both thoroughly spoiled.

Theresa Arundell, another niece of Emily Arundell, the daughter of her brother Thomas. She is a stylish young woman of about twenty-eight or nine, tall and slender, her jet black hair and dead pale, heavily made-up face giving her the look of an "exaggerated drawing in black and white." Her "freakishly plucked" eyebrows give her "an air of mocking irony."

Theresa belongs to "a young, bright, go-ahead set in London—a set that has freak parties and occasionally ends up in police courts." It is a great surprise to everyone—and especially to Theresa herself—that she is in love with a young doctor, Rex Donaldson, who has none of those attributes himself, even declining to drink a glass of select port—drinking water instead—at Emily Arundell's table. Theresa has already squandered a substantial personal inheritance of her own, since she craves a flashy lifestyle, and wishes her aunt would advance her a sum of money that would make it possible for her future husband to "specialize" rather than endure the dull life of a general practitioner. The following are some of her thoughts about Rex:

> She thought as she had thought once or twice before, how singularly unsuitable it was that she should have fallen in love with Rex Donaldson. Why did these things, these ludicrous and amazing madnesses, happen to one? A profitless question. This had happened to her.
>
> She frowned, wondered at herself. Her crowd had been so gay—so cynical. Love affairs were necessary to life, of course, but why take them seriously? One loved and passed on.
>
> But this feeling of hers for Rex Donaldson was different, it went deeper. She felt instinctively that here there would be no passing on ... her need of him was simple and profound. Everything about him fascinated her. His calmness and detachment, so different from her own hectic, grasping life, the clear, logical coldness of his scientific mind, and something else, imperfectly understood, a secret force in the man masked by his unassuming slightly pedantic manner, but which she nevertheless felt and sensed instinctively.
>
> In Rex Donaldson there was genius—and the fact that his profession was the main preoccupation of his life and that she was only a part—though a necessary part—of existence to him only heightened his attraction for her. She found herself for the first time in her selfish pleasure-loving life content to take second place. The prospect fascinated her. For Rex she would do anything—anything!

Charles Arundell, aged about thirty-two, Theresa's brother and Emily's only nephew. He is "a bad lot" and has already been known to commit forgery, for which he was expelled from Oxford. On Easter Sunday, he is overheard "threatening" Emily Arundell, although he insists he was "only joking." He had asked for a gift of a hundred pounds, which Emily immediately refused, to which he replied that she was setting herself up to be "bumped off" for an inheritance.

Rogers, the butcher in Market Basing to whom Emily delivers a sharp word on the subject of some inferior meat he recently sold her.

Miss Caroline Peabody, who has known Emily Arundell for over fifty years. She is "spherical" in outline. She lives at Morton Manor, a mile from Market Basing. She is a sharp-witted—and sharp-tongued—old lady who provides Poirot and Hastings with a wealth of useful information about the Arundell family, past and present, although the "information" is filled with amusing Victorian judgments.

Dr. Rex Donaldson, described by Caroline Peabody with terms such as "namby-pamby" and "a poor stick." Emily Arundell and Caroline Peabody agree that he has no business thinking of marrying Theresa, since he has no money. He is a fair-haired young man of medium height with a solemn face and pince-nez and a rather colourless appearance with pale blue, slightly protruding eyes. He is fascinated by his studies on the subject of ductless glands and has dreams of specializing. According to Charles Arundell, Rex looks at Theresa "as if she were a specimen." The Victorian Emily Arundell finds him to be "unmanly" when he declines a glass of that manly drink, port wine, and asks for water instead.

Angus, the aging gardener at Littlegreen House, a big, rugged old man who, together with Mr. Purvis's clerk, witnessed the signing of Emily Arundell's latest Will.

Ellen, the elderly house parlourmaid at Littlegreen House who has been with the family for twenty years. It was she who, nearly two months after Emily's death, found Emily's April 17 letter to Hercule Poirot "tucked away" and, not knowing what else to do with it, affixed a stamp to it and mailed it.

The Local Librarian, who does not have the particular books Emily has requested, and substitutes another which she is sure Emily will like.

Julia and Isabel Tripp, two middle-aged, eccentric sisters who live in an antiquated cottage reached from Market Basing along winding country lanes. They are spiritualists and conduct séances. Among their 1936 "eccentricities" is vegetarianism, and Poirot and Hastings narrowly escape being drawn into sharing their simple meal of shredded raw vegetables, dried fruit and brown bread. Today, of course, these ladies would not be regarded as eccentrics. They would probably be teaching courses in spiritualism and vegetarianism at the local community college at the taxpayers' expense. Naturally these eccentrics are not interested in fashionable clothing and one of them is seen in a gingham-patterned dress more appropriate for a child of ten than for a middle aged woman. "Mutton dressed as lamb" is what Miss Peabody calls this.

Though generally regarded by the locals as stupid women without breeding, the Tripp sisters are good friends of Wilhelmina Lawson, and to please her, Emily Arundell agrees to invite them to dinner at Littlegreen House a few days before her death. Although Emily considers psychic phenomena to be ridiculous nonsense, on that occasion the Tripp sisters conduct a séance and they and Miss Lawson witness—in the dim light of approaching evening—a "manifestation" in the form of a greenish ribbon of mist issuing from Emily's mouth and surrounding her head like a halo. A more scientific explanation for this "manifestation" later presents itself.

Mr. Lonsdale, the vicar, who strongly disapproves of psychic phenomena, and is therefore thought by Wilhelmina Lawson to be narrow-minded.

Dr. Grainger, aged about sixty-odd. He has been in Market Basing since 1919—that is, for the past seventeen years, although the waiter at the George Inn, in a conversation with Poirot and Hastings, had said that Dr. Granger had been in Market Basing for forty years. Because of Emily's frequent bouts with insomnia, Dr. Grainger had suggested a sleeping draught for her, which she refused, describing sleeping draughts as something used by the weak—those persons who cannot endure a finger ache or a toothache or an occasional sleepless night. Dr. Grainger declares Emily Arundell's death to be from natural causes.

Mary Fox, a lady whom Emily Arundell met last year at Cheltenham, the daughter of the Canon of Exeter Cathedral.

William Purvis, Esq. of Messrs Purvis, Purvis, Charlesworth and Purvis, Solicitors with offices in Harchester. Mr. Purvis is Emily Arundell's lawyer who tried to dissuade her from making the new Will, judging it to be grossly unfair to her family.

Arthur Hastings, an old friend of Hercule Poirot, who has lived in Argentina since about 1923 but who returns to England for a visit from time to time, as he is doing now. As usual, he is the narrator of the story, except for the early chapters, which occur before he and Poirot become involved in the case. He "assists" Poirot in solving the mystery of Emily Arundell's death. He is extremely British and one of his habits is to be shocked by Poirot's free and creative use of lies in order to obtain facts about his cases. "Really, Poirot!" is a frequent ejaculation of his, and he is always accusing Poirot of "not playing the game," to which Poirot invariably responds that he is solving a murder, not "playing games." One example of "not playing the game" that occurs in this novel is Poirot's "eavesdropping." As Poirot and Hastings leave the apartment of Theresa Arundell, once the door is closed, Poirot listens at the door and hears Theresa shout "You fool!" at her brother. Hastings is shocked by this and it would be typical of him to say, "Really, Poirot, that isn't cricket." Over the years Poirot has gotten absolutely sick and tired of hearing Hastings tell him that he "isn't playing the game."

Fortunately for Poirot—and perhaps for Christie's readers as well—this novel is the last in which Hastings will appear until *Curtain* is published in 1975. Agatha Christie grew tired of the Hastings character and banished him permanently to Argentina in 1937. Although he is closely associated with Poirot by most Christie readers, he actually appears in only eight of the thirty-three Poirot novels, the eighth being *Curtain*.

Hercule Poirot, the famous Belgian detective with an egg-shaped head and a flamboyant mustache. On June 28 he receives a letter that Emily Arundell wrote on April 17, a fact that Poirot finds more interesting than the letter itself and which causes him to take an interest in the case. In this novel he protects himself from draughts while riding in an open car by wearing an overcoat and scarf (it is late June and early July) and endures at least two disgusting meals at a mediocre English country inn. He shocks Hastings even more than usual by inventing convenient lies to explain his interest in the case and to ingratiate himself with some of the characters, since he at first wishes to conceal his suspicion that a murder has been committed.

A Burly, Ox-eyed Fellow, a Market Basing local whom Poirot and Hastings approach for directions to Littlegreen House.

Bob, Emily Arundell's pet wire-haired terrier. He had the bad habit of leaving his ball at the top of the stairs, and so Miss Arundell always kept it safely stored for the night in a certain drawer.

Mr. Gabler, of Messrs Gabler and Stretcher, House Agents in Market Basing. Mr. Gabler provides Poirot with an "Order to View" for Littlegreen House, warning him to make a quick offer as the property is so desirable it is sure to sell immediately to one of two persons who are already interested. He provides Poirot with some background information about the death of Miss Arundell, and about the current owner of the house.

Miss Jenkins, a young, adenoidal woman with a lacklustre eye, a person of incredible stupidity and incompetence, employed by Messrs Gabler and Stretcher as a receptionist. See the final paragraphs of the *Comments* section for the 1953 *Funerals Are Fatal* for a full inventory of "Adenoidal—and Therefore Stupid—Females" in Christie's novels.

Mrs. Samuels, an unfortunate lady who phones the offices of Messrs Gabler and Stretcher while Mr. Gabler is out, and who leaves a telephone number with the incompetent Miss Jenkins who, of course, gets it wrong.

A Waiter in the coffee room at The George Hotel in Market Basing who serves Poirot and Hastings a disgusting meal but provides them with useful facts about Emily Arundell, her family, her companion Miss Lawson, and her notorious new Will.

Dr. Harding, mentioned by the waiter at The George as "not doing much." He is older than Dr. Grainger and perhaps he is semi-retired.

Annie, the cook at Littlegreen House who has been there for four years. She is a large, pleasant-faced woman.

A Decrepit Butler at the home of Miss Caroline Peabody

A Child of Fourteen or Thereabouts, who opens the door to Poirot and Hastings at the cottage of the Tripp sisters

A Pert-looking Maid who opens the door at Miss Lawson's flat in London

The Chemist at Market Basing who sold Mrs. Tanios a strange, new prescription written by Dr. Tanios.

Nurse Carruthers of Market Basing who attended to Emily Arundell during the last days of her life.

George, Poirot's manservant in London, whom we met only once before, in the 1928 *The Mystery of the Blue Train*. He prepares an excellent omelet for Poirot and accurately describes two lady visitors.

A Man of Medium Height and Fair Hair who escorts Bella Tanios's children away from the Wellington Hotel in London.

The Manager of the Coniston Hotel in London

A Porter employed by the Coniston Hotel in London

A Doctor summoned by the Coniston Hotel in London

FRENCH INTO ENGLISH

Chapter 5
Continuez toujours—Keep going (keep on reading)
Jamais de la vie!—No way! (Absolutely not, etc.)
C'est curieux, n'est-ce pas?—That's odd, isn't it?

Chapter 6
vieux jeu—old fashioned, out of date
Parbleu—untranslatable expression of impatience, such as "For Pete's sake!" etc.
C'est dommage—That's a pity

Chapter 8
Brave chien, va!—Good doggie!

Chapter 11
Les demoiselles—The Misses
Comment?—What?

Chapter 12
Pour nous, un bon bifteck—A good steak for us
Au contraire—On the contrary

Chapter 13
Ça ne vous regarde pas—That's none of your business

Chapter 18
Ma foi—My gosh
non, ce n'est pas ça—no, that's not it
Très bien—All right, then

Chapter 19
le diable—the devil

Chapter 21
Oh, là là—Wow!
entre nous—just between you and me
C'est formidable, ça—That was tremendous (a great deal of work)
Le pot au feu—a soup containing two or more different meats (both beef and chicken, for example) cooked together in a seasoned broth, and then the broth is served in bowls and the meats are served on plates.

Chapter 22
Merci—No thank you
empressement—warmth, enthusiasm
C'est épatent—That's terrific (correct spelling: épatant)
Au revoir—Good bye

Chapter 23
Dépêchons-nous—Let's hurry
Du tout, du tout—Not at all

Chapter 24
Carte blanche—complete freedom to act
Au revoir—good bye
C'est drôle, ça—That's funny

Chapter 25
N'est-ce pas?—Yes, isn't it?
En vérité—To tell you the truth...
bien entendu—of course

Chapter 26
Du calme, du calme—Be calm

Chapter 28 *Ma foi*—Say...

COMMENTS

Poirot Loses a Client is not one of Agatha Christie's best known novels. That's easy to understand when we note that several masterpieces had already been written. *The Murder of Roger Ackroyd, Murder in the Calais Coach, Thirteen at Dinner, The A.B.C. Murders, Death in the Air* and *Death on the Nile* were such spectacular successes that those novels alone could have been Christie's only output to date with no lessening of her fame. And the 1939 *And Then There Were None* is just around the corner, ending the decade with what may be her most popular book.

Nevertheless, *Poirot Loses a Client* is a delightful detective story, and like all other Christie novels, it has its own special uniqueness. The special uniqueness, in this case, is that there is no officially-acknowledged crime—the police are not even called into the case, since it is only Hercule Poirot's personal suspicions—aroused by a letter from a lady who died fifty-nine days before Poirot received the letter, apparently of natural causes. Poirot solves this case on his own entirely, his friend Arthur Hastings being, in this story, no more than a conversation partner.

Actually there were two earlier novels in which there was "no official recognition" of foul play, and it was only the suspicions of amateur sleuths that prompted the investigations and led to the solutions. Those were *The Boomerang Clue* and *Murder in Three Acts*, although in the latter novel Poirot did assist the amateurs and then solved the case based on their findings. But in *Poirot Loses a Client,* Poirot himself sets out to solve a murder that only he suspects.

Three different character types which will become Christie "fixtures" in the next decades are present in *Poirot Loses a Client,* and now is a good time to take stock of them.

1. THE BORING RETIRED MILITARY MAN FROM THE COLONIES

In the 1926 *The Murder of Roger Ackroyd* we met Colonel Carter who, at a Mah Jong party at the Sheppard home, bored everyone with stories—some perhaps fabricated—about his experiences in India and China.

In the 1930 *Murder at the Vicarage,* one of the houses in the village of St. Mary Mead had a new occupant, Mrs. Lestrange. Her interior decorating was a dramatic improvement over that of the former owner, an Anglo-Indian colonel, who had filled the house with numerous brass tables and Burmese idols.

In the 1931 *Murder at Hazelmoor,* Major Burnaby was described as a typical retired military man who had no sense of money and made foolish investments repeatedly. Another character in the story was Captain Wyatt who lived with an Indian servant in an overheated cottage and despised all young men except those who listened attentively to his stories about India.

In the 1934 *Murder in the Calais Coach* we met Colonel Arbuthnot, who was presented as a person so ethnocentrically British that "just another damned foreigner" (Hercule Poirot, in fact) was not even worth his glance, and in general he "had no use" for Americans. He used the term "Pukka Sahib" which Poirot ridiculed.

And now, in the 1937 *Poirot Loses a Client,* we are treated to Miss Peabody's portrayal of General John Laverton Arundell. He was a drinker and he was a stupid man, and Miss Peabody goes on to say that "stupidity" doesn't matter much in the army—you just suck up to your superior officer and that's how you succeed in the military. She also mentions that she had never bothered to listen to General Arundell's "boring India stories."

In a couple of years, we will meet Major Horton who, in the 1939 *Easy to Kill,* will bore Luke Fitzwilliam with "the usual India stories of fakirs and rope and mango tricks." In the 1940 *The Patriotic Murders,* Colonel Abercrombie will have no occasion to bore anyone with India stories, but he will turn his chair in order not to be forced to behold the disgusting spectacle of the obviously foreign Hercule Poirot while waiting to see the dentist. In the 1941 *Evil Under the Sun* there will be Major Barry whom, at the Jolly Roger Hotel, the other guests will learn to divert from his boring India stories by interrupting with new subjects of conversation. In the 1941 *N or M?* there will be Major Bletchley, who will bore everyone at the Sans Souci guesthouse with his experiences on the North West Frontier. In the 1948 *There Is a Tide* there will be Major Porter whose description of the Indian rope trick will consume three quarters of an hour. In the 1950 *A Murder Is Announced*, Colonel Easterbrook will force a book about India on the unfortunate Miss Blacklock, and Miss Hinchliffe will liken *his* description of the Indian rope trick to mass hypnotism. In the 1964 *A Caribbean Mystery* there will be Major Palgrave who will bore everyone at the Golden Palm Hotel with Africa stories, and only kindly Miss Marple, who understands that Major Palgrave is a lonely old man, will listen to his stories patiently and murmur expressions such as "How interesting. Please do go on."

It is clear that, right from the beginning, Agatha Christie was not impressed by colonial military types despite the importance of Britain's empire. For one thing, it is the military types who exhibit the most obnoxiously negative attitudes toward foreigners, and Agatha Christie's father was an American. From her earliest childhood she must have heard negative comments about foreigners—and about Americans—from a lot of people, but she knew that her American father was a perfectly fine person. In other words she was aware, from an early age, of the silliness of ethnocentricity, although in her earliest novels, her portrayals of Central Europeans are hardly flattering. (See the *Comments* section for the 1922 *The Secret Adversary* and the 1925 *The Secret of Chimneys*.)

In any case, the "boring old Anglo-Indian colonel" will frequently add a touch of humor, usually in the person of a minor character in Christie novels.

2. THE VILLAGE GOSSIP

It was in *The Murder of Roger Ackroyd* (1926) that Christie first introduced this type of character in the amusing person of Caroline Sheppard. Just a few years later, in *Murder at the Vicarage* (1930) several village gossips, including Miss Jane Marple, play major roles, Christie later writing in her *Autobiography* that it was the Caroline Sheppard character who may have inspired her to create Miss Marple. In *Murder at Hazelmoor*, there are two gossips of the first order—the sensible, perceptive Caroline Percehouse and the pathologically motor-mouthed Amelia Curtis. "It's almost a disease the way that woman talks," declares Mrs. Willett, another character.

Now, in the 1937 *Poirot Loses a Client* we have a hilarious experience with Caroline Peabody, although she is not actually a villager, living about a mile from Market Basing.

The "village gossip" will play increasingly important roles in Christie's novels once she reintroduces Miss Jane Marple in 1942 with *The Body in the Library* and in ten subsequent Miss Marple novels during the next three decades. It may be noteworthy that three of the above-referenced "busy bodies" are named "Caroline."

3. THE AGING PERSON WHO IS UNHAPPY ABOUT THE YOUNGER GENERATION

In Christie's first novel, the 1920 *The Mysterious Affair at Styles*, Emily Inglethorpe is not a particularly unkind person, but she is known to expect "something in return" for her generosity. She holds her two sons and a poor relation more or less hostage as they await her death so that they can inherit. She marries a man of whom they do not approve and they fear she may leave to him all of her fortune, which in fact she does. Meanwhile she provides adequately but not generously for her sons. Emily dies.

In the 1923 *Murder on the Links,* Paul Renauld is unhappy about a love affair between his son Jack and a certain young woman, and during an altercation between the father and son on that subject, Jack tells his father, "When you're dead I will do as I please." Paul dies.

In the 1926 *The Murder of Roger Ackroyd*, Roger Ackroyd is not happy with his stepson Ralph Paton's "wild, London lifestyle" and is especially annoyed about Ralph's plans to marry a girl of the servant class. Ralph has good reason to think he will be disinherited on that score alone. Roger dies.

In the 1931 *Murder at Hazelmoor* Miss Caroline Percehouse is clearly displeased with her nephew Ronald Garfield who "sucks up" to her outrageously in efforts to remain her heir. She would feel more respect for him if he would "stand up to her" once in a while. Fortunately she does not die; in failing health for years, she has come to the old-world village of Sittaford "to die" but the fresh air of Devon has revived her health and she may now live for several more years, to the chagrin of her inheritance-awaiting nephew.

Now in the 1937 *Poirot Loses a Client* there is another "Emily" who is just plain disgusted with the younger generation and disinherits them all when she suspects that one of them may be plotting to murder her. Like Miss Percehouse in *Murder at Hazelmoor* she is impatient with subservient people who "grovel," as does her current companion Minnie Lawson. She wishes that Minnie would "stand up to her more." Emily dies.

There will soon be another disgusted "aging parent"—Simeon Lee—in the 1938 *A Holiday for Murder*. He will be disappointed in the younger generation because they lack spirit, independence and assertiveness and he will wish that they would "stand up to him" more, just as Caroline Percehouse and Emily Arundell do. And there will be several more of these discontented parents in future years, notably Rex Fortescue in the 1953 *A Pocket Full of Rye* and old Luther Crackenthorpe in the 1957 *What Mrs. McGillicuddy Saw*. In two of these three future novels, the parent will die.

On the subject of parent-child relationships, it is time to have another look at Christie's portrayal of parents in general and mothers in particular. In *Poirot Loses a Client*, Bella Tanios is portrayed as a dumpy, dowdy, simple-minded woman who is devoted to her children, hardly a flattering description of a conscientious parent. All through the years, Christie has largely avoided mothers and quite often the mothers who do occur in her books are negative characters. In *Poirot Loses a Client*, we learn something about Emily Arundell's family—her deceased siblings and her *father*—but nothing is said about her mother. The bright, enthusiastic young people who populate the earliest novels usually do not seem to have "parents" at all, and when they do, they are usually lovable but muddleheaded *fathers*, not mothers. For example:

In *The Secret of Chimneys* and *The Seven Dials Mystery*, Bundle Brent has a lovable fuddy-duddy for a father but no mother. Evidently her mother is dead, and she is never mentioned.

In *The Boomerang Clue*, Frankie Derwent has a lovable fuddy-duddy for a father but no mother. Evidently her mother is dead, and she is never mentioned.

In *The Man in the Brown Suit*, Anne Beddingfeld has a lovable fuddy-duddy for a father but no mother. Evidently her mother is dead, and she is never mentioned.

In *The Secret Adversary*, Tuppence has a lovable but old-fashioned fuddy-duddy of a father but no mother. Evidently her mother is dead, and she is never mentioned. Tommy Beresford's parents are both dead, although there is an estranged uncle in the background, who became estranged when Tommy refused to allow himself to be adopted by the uncle, telling him, "I'm all my mother's got." The estranged uncle is, fortunately, a rich fuddy-duddy who eventually reconciles with Tommy.

In *Murder on the Links,* Jack Renauld does have two living—and loving—parents, although his father strongly objects to his marriage plans. Then his father dies.

In *The Mystery of the Blue Train*, Ruth Kettering has a loving father but no mother. Evidently her mother is dead, and she is never mentioned. In that same novel, teen-aged Lenox Tamplin despises and is ashamed of her manipulative, social-climbing, gigolo-keeping mother, the Viscountess Rosalie Tamplin. Technically her current husband is not a "gigolo," but he is penniless, very handsome and twenty years younger than she, so what would *you* call him?

In *Murder at the Vicarage*, Lettice Protheroe has a vicious father whom the whole village detests, and an adulterous mother. The vicious father dies.

In *Murder at Hazelmoor,* the parents of Emily Trefusis are not mentioned at all, nor are her fiancé James Pearson's. They are probably conveniently dead, and they are never mentioned. In that novel, Ronald Garfield also has no parents; he lives for the day when he will inherit a fortune from his bullying aunt, Caroline Percehouse. There is, however, a good mother-daughter relationship in this novel—*a first, and a rarity in Christie*—that of Mrs. Willett and her daughter Violet.

In *Peril at End House,* Magdala Buckley's parents are both dead and the quality of her relationship with them is not discussed, nor are they ever even mentioned. She is known to have had an unusually close relationship with her grandfather, who is remembered as "Old Nick" while she herself is known as "Young Nick." There is no mention of her grandmother, of course.

In *Thirteen at Dinner,* Lord Edgware is an abominable person who is detested—and feared—by his daughter Geraldine Marsh. Her mother may be dead, having run away from her wicked husband when Geraldine was a baby, but in any case Geraldine has grown up motherless. Lord Edgware dies.

In *Murder in Three Acts,* Hermione Lytton Gore is a modern girl whom her mother finds perplexing and, although their relationship is not a dysfunctional one, it is a distant one and Hermione largely ignores her mother.

In *The A.B.C. Murders* the parents of murder victim Betty Barnard are portrayed as simple, ordinary loving parents, something rare in a Christie novel.

In *Murder in Mesopotamia,* we again have a motherless young woman, Sheila Reilly, an outspoken, rather cynical young woman. Her father, Dr. Reilly, finds her immature but feels affection for her and does not oppress her or attempt to control her. As to her mother—dead, of course, and never mentioned.

In *Death on the Nile* we have Linnet Ridgeway who remembers her father Meluish Ridgeway with fondness but we hear nothing about her mother. Both are dead, of course, as are the parents of her friend Jacqueline de Bellefort, although Jacqueline's mother is favored with a brief mention: she lost all her money in the Wall Street crash.

Now, in *Poirot Loses a Client,* as mentioned above, we learn a good deal about Emily Arundell's *father*, but nothing about her *mother*, who is not even mentioned. Poirot, at the local churchyard, does locate both her parents' tombstones, but Miss Peabody does not comment about her *mother*—only about her *father*. The only mother among the younger generation is the "dumpy, dowdy and boring" Bella Tanios.

In Christie's next novel, *Appointment with Death*, we will meet her all-time worst mother, diagnosed as a "mental sadist" by a character who is an eminent psychologist. She inflicts emotional pain on her children simply for the pleasure of doing so and even creates new opportunities for hurting them when the ordinary, daily opportunities lose their interest. Fortunately, she dies.

In the future there will be additional Christie female characters who, if both of their parents are dead, they will recall their *fathers* with fondness but they will not recall their *mothers* at all, or at least their memories of their mothers will not be mentioned. And in the few cases in which their mothers are living, their relationships with their mothers will usually be remote and often unpleasant ones.

But by 1965 Christie (who will then be age seventy-five) will have changed her mind about mothers in general. They will become important guardians of their daughters' welfare, chiefly in the matter of male contacts, and it will truly be an unfortunate young woman who does not have a mother to guide her in her contacts with men! We will encounter Miss Jane Marple, whom we will have already met in the 1930 *Murder at the Vicarage*, in two novels during the 1940s, four novels during the 1950s, and two more novels in the early 1960s before we learn, in the 1965 *At Bertram's Hotel*, that she was one of those lucky girls whose parents had "nipped in the bud" a love affair that she had once had with an "unsuitable young man" whom she had met again, much later in life, only to realize how right her parents had been. See the *Comments* section for the 1965 *At Bertram's Hotel* for remarks about that startling new development.

It is clear, from a reading of Agatha Christie's *Autobiography*, that she enjoyed a closer relationship with her charming, witty father than with her rather scatterbrained mother. Her father enjoyed horseracing and played the piano beautifully. Her mother flitted from one religious sect to another, dragging her unfortunate children from church to church. She was also obsessed with following every new nutrition fad, at one point ordering eggs at every meal, and at another point ordering fish at every meal until her husband intervened and demanded sensible meals for the family. One good thing that came of her mother's religious activities: Agatha learned at an early age that there can be a lot of silliness in organized religion, especially in the way one sect bickers with another, and so she was tolerant of all religious beliefs, though probably not a particularly religious person herself. Her second husband, with whom she enjoyed a permanent and happy marriage, was a Catholic and Christie probably found it easy to disregard any criticism that may have come her way from anti–Catholic acquaintances.

In the matter of parent-child relationships, Christie herself could not have been a very interested parent. When her first husband announced his desire for a divorce, she made a weak effort to dissuade him, mentioning that their daughter Rosalind actually preferred him to her ("She thinks of you as the parent, not me.") And as the years went on, Christie cannot have had a very close relationship with Rosalind, because when Rosalind announced her engagement in 1941, she asked her mother, "Do you want to be at the wedding?" Christie was shocked by the question and responded, "Of course I want to be at the wedding." If a daughter needs to ask her mother if she "wants" to come to her wedding, the relationship between the mother and daughter cannot be a very close one. Christie must have done some serious thinking on this subject after being "shocked" by her daughter's question.

There can be little doubt that, on the subject of mother-child relationships, Agatha Christie was unusually lacking in understanding and interest. She obviously did not like children as a rule, and children are rarely seen in her books. The only children mentioned in all of her novels this far are two raucous, immature younger sisters of Bundle Brent in *The Secret of Chimneys,* aged about ten and twelve but behaving more like four-year-olds; the seven-year-old son of Henry and Sylvia Bassington-ffrench in *The Boomerang Clue;* a disgustingly stupid and filthy child of unspecified gender, a neighbor of Mrs. Ascher in *The A.B.C. Murders;* the ten-year-old son of a gardener in *Peril at End House* who wishes the murder victim had had her throat cut instead of simply being shot, because he once saw pigs being killed and "liked it;" a work-shirking child named Abdullah employed by the archeological expedition in *Murder in Mesopotamia;* a group of child beggars who are described as "a swarm of human flies" in *Death on the Nile;* and now the evidently "spoiled" children of Bella and Jacob Tanios in *Poirot Loses a Client,* only one of whom appears in the story, and only briefly, as she interrupts a conversation of her mother. There had also been, in *Murder in Three Acts,* a bored French child who told her mother she "had nothing to do" and was told by the annoyed mother to go and play with her ball. Evidently to Christie, children—and most mothers—were nuisances that were best avoided, in her life and in her writing, (that is, until the 1965 *At Bertram's Hotel*, in which mothers acquire a whole new importance for Christie.)

In addition to all of the above, in *Poirot Loses a Client* we are again reminded of Agatha Christie's attitude toward servants: that they are "actively happy and appreciated," as she remarked in her *Autobiography*, and Hastings describes the housemaid Ellen as "a pleasant-faced woman of between fifty and sixty, clearly the old-fashioned type of servant seldom seen nowadays." It was in exactly those terms that he described Dorcas, a housemaid in *The Mysterious Affair at Styles*, written about twenty years earlier. For further remarks about "servants" in Christie novels, see the *Comments* section for the chapter on that earlier novel.

Finally, it can be noted that Christie's attitude toward nurses was not a very affirmative one. In this novel, the housemaid Ellen characterizes a certain hospital nurse as "a stuck-up young thing, all starched collars and cuffs, wanting tea made at all hours." Housemaids in several Christie novels make similar remarks about nurses, especially their demands for "trays to be brought up" and "cups of tea at all hours." Nurses are usually portrayed as "know-it-alls" who punctuate their pronouncements by snorting and adjusting their cuffs. Nurse Leatheran, the narrator in *Murder in Mesopotamia*, has all the narrow-mindedness and self-righteousness that Christie evidently attributes to nurses in general, although she soon learns to trust and respect that funny little "foreigner" Hercule Poirot. In the end she admits that she has learned a good deal about life and people from this new experience and that the straight and narrow "Christian" upbringing she received from an aunt may have been a bit wanting. In the 1940 *Sad Cypress*, there will be two know-it-all nurses who will click their tongues and smile to each other about the silly optimism of a naïve young doctor who does not have "their experience."

It is possible that Christie's experiences as a "nurse" during World War One, and her contacts with nurses at that time, were responsible for her negative attitude towards them.

A minor point of interest in *Poirot Loses a Client* is that Christie, for the first time, begins to comment on the beauty of English flower gardens in specific ways. The garden at Littlegreen House, at this season, is displaying tall lupines and delphinium, with their blue and purple flower spikes, together with bright red poppies, certainly a beautiful sight. The English style perennial border, a mixture of flowering plants specially selected for their colors, height, and blooming period to give a gradually-changing display of color all through the season, but giving the impression of being natural and unplanned, has been admired for generations. Hercule Poirot, with his obsession for neatness, symmetry and "disciplined nature" naturally prefers the look of the formal parks and gardens of France and Belgium with their neat rows of identical trees and flower beds planted in geometric patterns, but even *he* will admit—in the 1940 *The Patriotic Murders*—that there is something uniquely beautiful about the English idea of flower gardening and there will be two male characters in that story who will be expert flower gardeners.

Christie will invoke English enthusiasm for, and expertise in, flower gardening from time to time in future stories, sometimes humorously. In the 1939 *Easy to Kill*, there is an old lady—a minor character—who has only three occasions to speak in the whole story. On all three occasions she speaks of nothing but flower gardening. In the 1942 *The Body in the Library*, the story opens with the words, "Mrs. Bantry was dreaming..." Dolly Bantry, a friend of Miss Jane Marple, is having a beautiful dream about her sweet peas taking a "first" at the flower show. A bit later in the story, when Miss Marple suggests that a certain young man may be a murderer, Dolly objects. "I know his mother! Her herbaceous borders make me green with envy, and she's frightfully generous with cuttings!" Still later, when it occurs to her and to Miss Marple that it is possible that Mrs. Bantry's husband may have had a "relationship" with a young girl, Mrs. Bantry attempts to console herself with the words, "Well, after all, I have the garden."

Another aspect of the British culture that receives a noteworthy mention in *Poirot Loses a Client* is English cooking, which has had a bad reputation for generations. Hercule Poirot has always suffered from it, but from time to time he discovers a little *bistrot* in London where the food is wonderful and the cook is, of course, French. In this novel, even his supremely British friend Captain Hastings complains of the food at their inn in Market Basing and of course Poirot does a good deal of groaning about it. In future novels, in small ways, Christie will pay tribute to the superiority of *foreign* cooks. There will be, for example, the Central European cook Mitzi in the 1950 *A Murder Is Announced* who will make a superb cake called "Delicious Death," and who will become enraged when someone uses her omelet pan for frying onions: "Now it will have to be washed and never, never do I wash my omelet pan!" she will scream. In the 1955 *Hickory, Dickory, Death* a London youth hostel, despite its higher-than-usual rates for students, will have a permanent waiting list largely because of its excellent meals, thanks to its Italian cook. In the 1954 *So Many Steps to Death* every meal consumed by the British protagonist in Morocco will be described as excellent. To be fair, it should be mentioned that, from time to time, there will also be English cooks whom other characters will describe as "excellent cooks" although the meals and individual dishes that they prepare will rarely be specified. It is true that in the 1953 *Funerals Are Fatal* the young English cook Marjorie will prepare an excellent chocolate soufflé, but Marjorie will be despised by the housekeeper and butler because she does not represent, to them, "good service," despite her cooking skills.

The dichotomy of "excellent English flower gardening" vs. "bad English cooking" will be beautifully expressed through the personality of Miss Jane Marple, the Christie sleuth who was introduced in the 1930 *Murder at the Vicarage*, and who will soon reappear in the 1942 *The Body in the Library* and then with increasing regularity over the next three decades. Miss Marple will be a devoted flower gardener, and she will suffer immeasurably as she grows older and her old friend Dr. Haydock forbids her to bend and stoop, making flower gardening impossible for her. We will note, however, that Miss Marple will *never* enter her own kitchen to cook a meal for herself or for anyone else. She will *always* have somebody to do her cooking for her. That's because she is *a true English lady*. If Christie had characterized Miss Marple as an excellent, interested cook, she simply would not have made sense as *a true English lady*. On one occasion—in the 1976 *Sleeping Murder* (written during the 1940s but withheld from publication until after Christie's death)—Miss Marple will *claim* to have lost her recipes for baked apple pudding and gingerbread, but this will be a *lie* concocted in order to obtain the address of the person who allegedly gave her the recipes long ago. And as late as 1969, in *Hallowe'en Party*, a young widow who was "left very badly off" by her husband when he died, and who works "part-time" as a secretary, will have a cook and a cleaning lady despite her low-income status. Obviously, to Christie there was something lowly about cooking. Cooking in Christie stories is *always* performed by a person of "the servant class"—or by a foreigner, such as our very eccentric foreign friend Hercule Poirot who, in addition to having an appreciation for excellent cooking, is an excellent cook himself. In *Poirot Loses a Client* Hastings "narrowly avoids a disquisition on cooking" when Poirot begins to speak of *le pot au feu* during one of their bad meals at The George, and in the 1952 *Mrs. McGinty's Dead,* Poirot will teach a young Englishwoman how to make an omelet.

Appointment with Death (1938)

SETTING

This novel was first published in 1938, but assigning a specific year to its action is impossible. Agatha Christie did not usually mention any particular year in her novels, although she did mention, in *Death in the Air,* that to one of the characters, the archeologist Monsieur Dupont, the year 1934 would not really exist because he was so accustomed to thinking about events that took place thousands of years ago. Therefore we can state that that story takes place in 1934. In *Poirot Loses a Client* the year 1936 is shown on the tombstone of the murder victim as the year of her death. But most often, Christie does not specify an exact year for the action.

In *Appointment with Death,* no year is mentioned but there are references to three earlier Christie novels, *Murder in the Calais Coach, The A.B.C. Murders* and *Cards on the Table. Cards on the Table,* the most recent of the three, was published in 1936 and so, logically, the action of *Appointment with Death* must take place no earlier than 1935 or 1936. However, at the end of the story there is an "Epilogue" in which certain characters of the story are reunited "five years later," that is, no earlier than 1940, which is impossible, since the first readers of the novel read it in 1938! Christie, of course, never expected her books to be remembered, let alone written about and subjected to this kind of scrutiny seventy years later, and so she saw no reason to be careful about the chronology of events among them. After all, she considered them to be nothing but light fiction, books to be enjoyed for a short time and then promptly forgotten. As a matter of fact, she forgot about many of them herself as the years went on. During the 1960s she confessed that she had no recollection at all of writing the 1932 *Peril at End House,* nor did she remember how, why or when she wrote the 1930 *Murder at the Vicarage.*

In any case, in *Appointment with Death* we are certainly at some time during the 1930s and there are a couple of references to current "regimes" in which human life is not highly valued, clearly references to Bolshevist Russia and Nazi Germany. There is also a reference, by one of the characters, to the extreme difficulty of getting any kind of work when one has "no training," since there are "people with qualifications but who are out of work," a reference to the catastrophic world-wide Depression of the 1930s.

To review a bit of the history of the "Near East," (now most often called "The Middle East,") one of the terms of the Treaty of Versailles (1918) was that France and Britain would have "spheres of influence" in lands that had formerly been part of the old Ottoman Empire. Specifically, Palestine, Jordan and Mesopotamia became "mandates" or "protectorates" of Britain while Syria and Lebanon became "mandates" or "protectorates" of France. The independent state of Israel, of course, did not come into being until much later—after World War II, in fact.

All of the action in this novel takes place in Palestine and Jordan, both British protectorates, and so the person in charge of "clearing up the facts of the case" is Colonel Carbury, who is responsible to the British government.

The story begins in Jerusalem, in Palestine, at the Solomon Hotel. Most of the characters are tourists who travel into Jordan (then called Transjordan) to Amman and to the ruins of the ancient city of Petra, located in a desolate region of rocky cliffs. It is there among the ruins, in a kind of semi-permanent campsite for tourists, consisting of tents as well as ancient cave dwellings fitted for sleeping, that the murder takes place. As the tourists travel to this exotic place they pass through ancient Jericho and have lunch there. The action extends over a period of about a week and a half.

Both France and Britain were enthusiastic supporters of archeological studies in the region during the period of their protectorates and Agatha Christie herself became fascinated by the ever-increasing discoveries and knowledge that these studies revealed. Her second husband, Professor Max Mallowan, was an eminent archeologist and she accompanied him on his expeditions each year during the 1930s until 1938. She was able to describe "the rose-red city of Petra," therefore, from her own experience.

It has been noted that in Christie's novels of the 1930s, the relatively new science known as "psychology" plays an important part, more in some novels than in others, of course. In *Appointment with Death,* one character is a well-known French psychologist, another is a young medical doctor with a strong interest in psychology, and there is of course Hercule Poirot who has infinite respect for the true science of psychology and considerable understanding of it. It is possible that the "psychoanalyses" provided by these characters were more acceptable to readers during the 1930s than they can be today. There is a good deal of discussion about the "psychology" of the murder victim and the members of her family, and Christie must have felt quite confident that these conversations could have taken place in real life among informed people. Therefore she must have had a strong interest in the subject and informed herself a good deal. There had been, in some earlier Christie novels, some rather unflattering remarks about certain doctors earning quite a good living by encouraging patients to lie on sofas and talk about their memories of childhood trivial events, and then being "cured" of neuroses. One could conclude from those remarks that Christie was not very impressed with "the science of psychology" and, in the earlier years, it is possible that she was not, but clearly by 1938 she understood that modern psychology was something worthwhile and a true science. She uses the term "schizophrenia" in this novel for the first time and one of the characters is described as being a "mental sadist."

Of much less importance, but a source of humor in the novel, are some remarks made by two of the characters about certain contemporary conditions. One character remarks that "many *quite* well brought up young girls of *good* family belong to these dreadful Communists!" During the 1930s, communism appealed to considerable numbers of young intellectuals of Western Europe and America as well, and we have already met two Christie characters who are "young Communists"—Oliver Manders in the 1935 *Murder in Three Acts,* and Mr. Ferguson in the 1937 *Death on the Nile.* The person in *Appointment with Death* who remarks about those "dreadful Communists" is a twittering, harmless old governess, Miss Amabel Pierce.

There are even more amusing remarks made by the politician Lady Westholme on subjects such as nutrition for the working classes, sanitation in all parts of the Empire, prostitution in Argentina, and other subjects of special interest to her.

An interesting remark is made on the subject of women and their abilities. Sarah King, a young woman who has just finished medical studies and has qualified as a physician, is extremely annoyed by the intellectually mediocre Miss Pierce who remarks about Lady Westholme, "I'm always so *glad* when a woman accomplishes something!" to which Sarah replies ferociously

"Why?" To Sarah, Miss Pierce's statement implies that for a woman to "accomplish anything" is something unusual which merits special citation—an insult to womanhood. To Sarah, one should be "glad" when *anyone*—male or female—accomplishes something. In 1938 this was, of course, an idea that was three or four decades ahead of its time, and for it to be presented in "light fiction" was remarkable. Obviously in some quarters, the women's liberation movement had already begun.

Story

In some year during the 1930s a group of assorted travelers are visiting Palestine and Jordan. These include a young British medical doctor, Sarah King; a well-known French psychologist, Dr. Gerard; an overbearing British politician, Lady Westholme; a retired British governess, Miss Amabel Pierce, and a strange American family, the Boyntons. The family consists of the widowed, obese, cruel and controlling Mrs. Boynton, a married step-son and his wife, two additional adult step-children and one natural daughter who is the youngest. Sarah King and Dr. Gerard soon become friends and observe with amazement and disgust the emotional cruelty that Mrs. Boynton practices, apparently for the pleasure of inflicting pain, on her child and step-children. She has brought them up to shun all contacts with people outside the family. Sarah attempts to draw two of the step-children out of their "prison" and to become social companions to them, but she fails.

At a campsite designed for tourists among the ruins of an ancient city in Jordan, Mrs. Boynton dies in a chair that is positioned in a shady spot while the rest of her family and the other tourists are away on a brief walking tour. Later, Dr. Gerard notices that a syringe in his tent is not in its usual place and that a quantity of a certain lethal drug is missing. Suspecting foul play in the matter of Mrs. Boynton's death, he notifies the authorities of his suspicion, and Colonel Carbury, who is in charge of police in the region, asks a guest of his, the famous detective Hercule Poirot, to assist in the investigation. Poirot promises to solve the case within twenty-four hours, which he of course does.

Characters

Hercule Poirot, the famous Belgian private investigator with an egg-shaped head, an outlandish mustache and, for the last few years, "suspiciously black hair." He is enjoying a holiday in the Middle East, first in Palestine and then in Jordan, and he is asked to assist in a case of possible murder.

Colonel Carbury of the British military establishment, who is in charge of operations in Amman, Jordan. At the moment, he has a possible murder case on his hands. "I'm a tidy man," he often says of himself. Clearly he cannot be referring to his physical appearance, since Colonel Carbury's tie is usually under his left ear, his socks are wrinkled, and his coat is stained and torn. Poirot recognizes the inner neatness of Colonel Carbury's mind, however.

Colonel Carbury is fully aware of Hercule Poirot's special talents and his history of successes in crime detection. Their mutual friend, Colonel Race, has written to Colonel Carbury about Poirot's amazing work in the matter of the Shaitana murder in London (the subject of the 1936 *Cards on the Table*.) Colonel Carbury feels an almost child-like appreciation for Poirot's meticulous procedures. He loves reading detective stories and at one point, he asks Poirot to write a list of significant facts, the way detectives do in books. Poirot complies, and Colonel Carbury responds delightedly, as if Poirot were actually writing a mystery story and not solving a mystery:

> "Capital! Just the thing! You've made it difficult—and seemingly irrelevant—absolutely the authentic touch!... Splendid! I don't get it at all!"

Afterwards, as he is leaving, Poirot murmurs to himself, "Incredible! The English never grow up!"

Colonel Race, the mutual friend who provides Hercule Poirot with a letter of introduction to Colonel Carbury. He is reputed to be in the secret service and is often found in some remote outpost of the British Empire, usually when trouble is brewing. We met him in the 1924 *The Man in the Brown Suit,* the 1936 *Cards on the Table* and, most recently, in the 1937 *Death on the Nile*. He is not a character in *Appointment with Death*, however.

Sarah King, M.B., a young Englishwoman who has just qualified as a physician and is enjoying a relaxing tour of the Middle East before settling in to serious work. She is intelligent and assertive, and she is disgusted by the way the Boynton family allows their vicious, autocratic mother to bully and manipulate them. She tries to help them by encouraging them to "break away" from their mother and to enjoy acquaintances and experiences outside the family circle, but she fails at this and feels sadness and pity for them.

She is a feminist and reacts vigorously when another character suggests that for a woman to "accomplish something" is a remarkable feat.

Dr. Theodore Gerard, a well-known French psychologist who is interested in the pathologies exhibited by the Boynton family. It is he who first has reason to suspect foul play in the matter of Mrs. Boynton's death.

Mrs. Elmer Boynton, an American widow who practices systematic emotional cruelty upon her child and stepchildren, evidently simply for the gratification of inflicting pain. A former prison wardress, she is psychologically well equipped for her self-appointed task of destroying the egos of those in her care.

Lennox Boynton, the eldest stepson of Mrs. Boynton. Upon his mother's advice, he married Nadine and, naturally, they made their home with Mrs. Boynton who would hear of no other plan. Lennox is the most pathetic of the Boynton family, having given up any desire for freedom. According to his sister Carol, he goes around in a kind of day-dream and hardly ever speaks. His wife Nadine tries to convince him that he can break away from his mother's domination if he really wants to, and if he will just try. But Lennox has been dominated for too long and even his will to be free has been destroyed.

Nadine Boynton, who made the mistake of marrying into the Boynton family. She alone is unaffected by her mother-in-law's spell.

Raymond Boynton, Mrs. Boynton's younger stepson, a young man in his early twenties. Sarah's first impression, as she speaks to him in the train on the way to Jerusalem, is that of a nice, pathetically eager schoolboy.

Carol Boynton, Mrs. Boynton's stepdaughter. She resembles Raymond very much and some people observe that they could be twins. Unlike their older brother Lennox, Carol and Raymond have not lost their desire for freedom. They speak of killing their stepmother and Hercule Poirot overhears one line of that conversation:

"You do see, don't you, that she's got to be killed?"

Ginevra Boynton, the only member of the Boynton family who is actually Mrs. Boynton's biological child. She is frail and, according to Dr. Gerard, she is approaching schizophrenia. She has delusions of being a royal personage imprisoned by enemies.

Jefferson Cope, a pleasant middle-aged American of a strictly conventional type. He has a slow, pleasant, somewhat monotonous voice. Mr. Cope knew Nadine Boynton before she married Lennox Boynton, and he is well acquainted with the family. Nevertheless, in conversations with Dr. Gerard, he exhibits a failure to grasp the full force of evil that permeates Mrs. Boynton's being, minimizing her control over her family and simply describing it as "a bit heavy handed."

Lady Westholme, a member of Parliament who is among the other visitors to Jerusalem and Petra. A totally humorless person herself, she provides a good deal of comic relief in this otherwise grief-ridden story. She had met her husband, a simple-minded peer whose only interests in life were hunting, shooting and fishing, on an ocean voyage. She pushed her husband into politics, but eventually realizing that he had no interest or talent for politics, she ran for office and became an M.P. herself. She is much respected and almost universally disliked. She will flare her nostrils and lecture on any one of her interests at a moment's notice. These include Agriculture, Housing, Slum Clearance, Family Life and Welfare Work amongst Women, and Prostitution in Argentina. She lives entirely in tweeds and stout brogues, breeds dogs, and bullies the villagers. During her travels in Palestine and Jordan in this story she lectures the hotel manager about better hotel management, she argues with Castle Tours about the size of the car that was promised for the trip to Petra and, with the help of a reliable guidebook, regularly contradicts the tour guide's explanations of the sights.

A similar lady politician has already appeared in an earlier Christie novel. It was Marcia, Marchioness of Caterham in the 1929 *The Seven Dials Mystery*, who had the ridiculous idea that Bundle Brent could be the foremost political hostess in England, provided she married suitably.

Miss Amabel Pierce, an elderly ex-governess who reads novels with titles such as *The Love Quest*. She is enjoying a trip abroad made possible by a recent legacy. Although she proves to be thoroughly unobservant and suggestible, she makes one very important observation and dutifully reports it to Hercule Poirot.

A Voluble Dragoman who escorts the Boynton family on their trip out of Jerusalem.

Mahmoud, a Fat Dragoman, the guide who escorts Sarah, Dr. Gerard, Lady Westholme and Miss Pierce on their one-week tour to Petra, manfully enduring Lady Westholme's guidebook-based contradictions.

Strange Wild-faced Men who surround the touring car as it enters Ma'an, as the party finally approaches the rock stronghold of Petra.

Numerous Bedouin Servants

A Native Servant wearing Breeches Much Patched who escorts Sarah to her tent in the camp at Petra

Abdul, the native servant who is dispatched to tell Mrs. Boynton that dinner is being served, but who finds her to be unresponsive.

French into English

Part One

Chapter 2
La maman—the mom
La famille Boynton—The Boynton family

Chapter 3
Le Matin—"The Morning" (name of a French-language newspaper such as "The Morning News," etc.)

Chapter 4
Une dompteuse—feminine form of "*un dompteur*," an animal tamer, such as a lion tamer (*un dompteur de lions*), here applied to Mrs. Boynton as a person who destroys natural instincts or impulses in her children

Chapter 9
Tout de même—All the same
Pardon—Excuse me

Chapter 10
métier—trade or "professional calling"

Part Two

Chapter 1 *Pardon?*—I beg your pardon?

Chapter 3
tendresse—romantic feeling
planté là—standing as if "planted" there

Chapter 4
Du tout!—Nonsense! (Sarah King has just pretended not to know what Poirot is talking about and he is letting her know that he isn't fooled.)
Eh bien—Well...
Famille Boynton—Boynton family
la Maman—the mom
hein?—Eh? (Isn't that true?)
un bon moment—a moment of good feeling
Continuez—Go on (continue)

Chapter 8 *pardon*—excuse me

Chapter 11
soigné—well-dressed, well-groomed

quelle horreur de femme!—what a horrible woman!
une dompteuse—feminine form of *un dompteur*, a tamer of animals
la pauvre Ginevra—poor Ginevra
la Maman—the mom

Chapter 12
Nous allons changer tout ça!—We're going to change all that!

Chapter 14 *Mais oui*—of course

Chapter 15
la famille Boynton—the Boynton family
Tout simplement—Quite simply
Comment?—What? (What's that you're saying?)
Eh bien—And so...

Chapter 16
Ah ça, non!—Absolutely not!

Chapter 17
Je suis entièrement de votre avis—I agree with you entirely

Chapter 18
mesdames et messieurs—ladies and gentlemen
mes amis—friends

Epilogue
mes hommages—congratulations
eh bien—so...
la famille Boynton—the Boynton family

Comments

The murder victim in *Appointment with Death* is such an evil figure that she almost seems to deserve her fate as much as the victim in *Murder in the Calais Coach*. In that earlier novel, the murder victim had been a known criminal who had kidnapped and then murdered a child, causing the deaths of four additional innocent people. In *Appointment with Death,* the murder of Mrs. Boynton liberates four innocent young people from her emotional cruelty.

The plight of these four young people is carefully studied from a psychological standpoint by three knowledgeable characters—a psychiatrist, a medical doctor and Hercule Poirot. This is the Christie novel in which the serious study of psychology plays the greatest role to date. It is possible that the discussions of psychology that take place among these characters could not occur today, almost seventy years after the novel was written, but the original readers in 1938 must have found them fascinating and believable.

As mentioned in the chapter on *Murder in Mesopotamia,* Agatha Christie, though probably not an especially religious person herself, was impatient with the idea of various "sects" interminably quarreling with one another. This was undoubtedly a legacy of her mother's bouncing around from one sect to another during Christie's childhood. Here in *Appointment with Death* there is a brief but interesting summary of those thoughts during a conversation between Sarah King and Dr. Gerard.

> "Are you a Christian, Mademoiselle?"
> Sarah said slowly:
> "I don't know. I used to think that I wasn't anything. But now—I'm not sure. I feel—oh, I feel that if I could sweep all this away—" she made a violent gesture—"all the buildings and the sects and the fierce squabbling churches—that—that I might see Christ's quiet figure riding into Jerusalem on a donkey—and believe in him."

This conversation typifies the tone of *Appointment with Death,* a very serious and rather sad story. Well-plotted and populated with thoughtfully-drawn characters, it is not very much "fun" to read, in the sense that some of Christie's earlier books are. Still, there are occasions to "laugh out loud," thanks to the presence of the hilarious Lady Westholme, who offers the only comic relief in the book.

To some critics the ending of this novel is disappointing. It is a weak ending, to be sure, and the Epilogue, in which we find that several marriages have occurred among the characters, seems a bit silly, but perhaps a "trite, happy ending" is all that could save this otherwise gloomy, depressing story.

One small point: in *Appointment with Death* there is a discussion between Mr. Jefferson Cope, a friend of the Boynton family, and the French psychologist, Dr. Gerard. They are discussing the very "close" Boynton family and the doctor notes that all of Mrs. Boynton's family are dependent on her financially. Mr. Cope explains:

> "That is so. And she's encouraged them to live at home and not go out and look for jobs. Well, maybe that's all right; there's plenty of money. They don't need to take jobs but I think for the male sex, anyway, work's a good tonic..."

"Work's a good tonic..."

This is the very first time in any Agatha Christie novel that any character has suggested that there is anything *meritorious* about work for its own sake. As noted in the chapter on *The Mysterious Affair at Styles,* in her *Autobiography* Christie made a point of saying that she had never understood why anybody worked when he did not have to, and she asked point blank "Why does anybody think there's something *meritorious* about working?" Not only did she feel there was nothing *meritorious* about work, in her books we are told that people who actually *work* for their livings are far beneath those who do not have to work. If your father worked and earned and saved, he is to be despised, but now that you have inherited what your father worked and earned and saved, you needn't dirty yourself by working yourself. You have been "born" into money, and so you are a gentleman, unlike your ungentlemanly father. It's rather sickening, from an American point of view, but it was part of Agatha Christie's schema. In a novel published the following year, *Easy to Kill,* there will be a man who keeps an antique shop. Another character will hasten to explain to the detective that he must not think ill of the man for keeping the shop, since "he is actually a gentleman," and not one of those lowly "tradespeople." In the 1940 *Sad Cypress,* a male character who expects to inherit a fortune from an aunt, who provides him with an income in the meantime so that he needn't work, will actually admit that he "preserves his self-respect by having a job."

But no more of this, as these issues will turn up in the chapters on those other novels. It is mentioned here simply because it is "something new" for Christie.

A Holiday for Murder (1938)

(Alternate Titles: *Murder for Christmas* and *Hercule Poirot's Christmas*)

SETTING

It is late December—specifically December 22 through 28—and the year is probably 1937, since the novel was published in 1938. Because one of the characters is a Spaniard, there are a few references to the Spanish Civil War, which began in 1936 and ended in March of 1939. This conflict was a revolt by the Spanish landowners and the military leaders against a newly formed Republic, dating only from 1931, which had replaced—through a quiet revolution—the old monarchy, sending the royal family into exile. The 1936 revolt against the new Republic was led by General Francisco Franco and would probably not have succeeded if Britain and France had supplied arms to the forces loyal to the Republic, but both countries were reluctant to provoke war and practiced an "appeasement" policy which was much discredited later. Hitler and Mussolini supplied arms to Franco's forces and the revolt succeeded, ending the Spanish Republic in 1939 and replacing it with a military dictatorship that lasted until General Franco's death in 1975.

A point of interest is that, in the 1935 *Murder in Three Acts,* Dr. Strange died at his home at some unspecified place in the county of Yorkshire. The person in charge of that case was Colonel Johnson, who was the Chief Constable of the county. In *A Holiday for Murder,* Hercule Poirot spends the Christmas holiday at the home of Colonel Johnson, who makes one or two references to the earlier case. If you have not yet read *Murder in Three Acts,* be warned that the remarks made by Colonel Johnson in *A Holiday for Murder* may give away the solution to *Murder in Three Acts,* so please enjoy the earlier novel first if you have not already done so.

The home of Colonel Johnson lacks central heating, and Hercule Poirot expresses his usual aversion to the English climate, noting that Colonel Johnson's fireplace provides scorching heat for one's feet but does nothing to prevent cold drafts throughout the room. One female character uses a "little screen of papier maché" to shield her face from the fire when visiting her grandfather in his room at Gorston Hall, which also lacks central heating; the rooms are heated individually by fireplaces.

Although in *Murder in Three Acts* Colonel Johnson was the Chief Constable of the County—and the county specified was Yorkshire—in *A Holiday for Murder* the name of the county is changed to a fictitious one: "Middleshire." It is an appropriate name for the county, as a portion of Yorkshire and several neighboring counties make up a region known as "The Midlands," an area known for grim, overcrowded industrial cities that developed in the early industrial period. Manchester, Mansfield, Sheffield, Nottingham, and Doncaster are only a few of these grimy, inhospitable towns which during Victorian times were the settings for the pitiful working conditions described by Dickens in his novel *Hard Times* and where the earliest organized labor movements began. "The Black Country" was a term that is associated with "The Industrial Midlands."

In *A Holiday for Murder,* however, the major setting is not one of the cities but a large, comfortable country home called Gorston Hall, within walking distance of the town of Longdale, near Addlesfield. There is a brief scene at the office of Colonel Johnson, which may be in Addlesfield, perhaps a fictitious renaming of Doncaster.

A member of the family, who has returned to the home for the first time in twenty years, refers to Gorston Hall as "an ugly old mansion" and just a while later as "a mausoleum." In more objective terms the house is described as "a large solidly built house with no special architectural pretensions." It is a comfortable home, however, with a big blue and gold drawing-room and perhaps another, smaller drawing room. There is a small study, a music room containing a piano, a ballroom with a parquet floor containing a "gramophone"—an old term for phonograph—and of course a dining room. Scenes take place in all of these rooms. Naturally there are also kitchen quarters and probably other ground floor rooms.

A large bedroom on the "first floor" (the upper floor) is the scene of the crime. It is furnished in flamboyant, old fashioned styles—heavy brocaded wallpaper, rich leather armchairs and large vases embossed with dragons. Everything in the room is magnificent, costly and solid. One of the chairs is a big "grandfather chair" and there is a large wood-burning fireplace which is in use during the season, as the house has no central heating. The room has two windows facing the front drive and the only door leading into the room is from the hallway. One of the two telephones in the house is in this room. These facts are important in the solution of the crime.

Outside the house is a series of tubs containing soil and used by the lady of the house as settings for miniature gardens, her hobby.

Although a large family once occupied the home, currently there are only three residents—a very old man who keeps to his room on the "first floor"—and the old man's son and daughter-in-law. There are also eight house servants plus a male nurse-attendant who is also referred to as the "valet." The eight house servants are an aging butler, a young footman, a cook, a kitchenmaid, three housemaids and a so-called "between-maid." There is also a gardener whose living quarters are not in the house proper; perhaps there is a lodge or cottage in which he lives. The gardener is the father of the young footman.

The earliest scenes in the novel take place in various unspecified locations in England, as the members of the Lee family discuss their plans for spending the Christmas holiday with their father at Gorston Hall. One of these conversations takes place at the home of one of the family members in a town called Westeringham; another scene takes place in a third-class compartment of a crowded train as it leaves London, probably from Euston Station. The scene is briefly but vividly described as follows:

> "Overhead a dim fog clouded the station. Large engines hissed superbly, throwing off clouds of steam into the cold raw air. Everything was dirty and smoke-grimed. Stephen thought with revulsion:
> "What a foul country—what a foul city!"

The aforementioned Stephen has spent all of his life in South Africa and this is his first visit to England. In these dreary surroundings he feels a pang of homesickness for sunshine, blue skies, blue flowers borne on vines that cover every little shanty. In his thoughts he compares that pleasant scene with the station in London, which he perceives as nothing but dirt, grime and endless, incessant crowds, hurrying around like busy ants running about their anthill.

Story

Aging Simeon Lee, who in his youth was a diamond prospector and later became rich by inventing a special tool used in diamond mining, lives as a semi-invalid in a comfortable mansion in the Industrial Midlands with his middle-aged son Alfred and his daughter-in-law Lydia. Simeon has two other married sons: George, who is a mediocre politician and David, a moderately successful painter. Simeon's remaining son Harry is the "black sheep in the family" and has not been seen in years. Simeon's only daughter married a Spanish artist long ago and she has recently died, leaving a daughter who was raised in Spain and whom the family has never met.

It is just a few days before Christmas in 1937 and Simeon invites his whole family, including the estranged "black sheep" Harry and his granddaughter Pilar Estravados to his home, Gorston Hall, for Christmas. On Christmas Eve he instructs his manservant to bring the whole family up to his room for the express purpose of insulting each of them in each other's presence. It is an ugly scene after which one of his daughters-in-law tells him that she is afraid. "Of me?" he asks. "No," she replies. "Afraid *for* you."

Later that evening Simeon is brutally murdered in his room just after the family has dinner. The room is locked and it is necessary for the family to break in, finding that the windows are also locked. Simeon's throat has been cut and he lies dead in a pool of blood.

Hercule Poirot happens to be a Christmas guest of an old friend, Colonel Johnson, who is the chief constable of the county and in charge of the case. Hercule Poirot, of course, solves the mystery.

Characters

Hercule Poirot, the Belgian private investigator who is spending the Christmas holidays with an old friend, Colonel Johnson, at his home in the English Midlands. He wishes that Colonel Johnson's home had modern central heating instead of fireplaces, which provide scorching heat for one's feet without preventing cold drafts around one's neck.

Poirot has always been annoyed with what he sees as British childishness and sentimentality. In *Appointment with Death,* he had occasion to remark, "Incredible. The English never grow up," when Colonel Carbury, the man actually in charge of solving the mystery of Mrs. Boynton's death, treated the investigation as if it were a detective novel and cheered Poirot on with remarks such as "Capital! You've got me stumped!" In *A Holiday for Murder,* it is again an officer of the police that Poirot loses patience with. Colonel Johnson suggests that Christmas time is not a time when crimes occur because there is "peace and good will all round," but Poirot, that Continental realist, disagrees. He affirms that all of that "peace and goodwill" to which lip service is routinely paid at Christmas is nothing but hypocrisy practiced "for the season" and that it puts people under a strain—it makes people try to act lovingly towards each other when they do not feel love, creating tension and actually making crime more likely.

Colonel Johnson, the Chief Constable of the County of Middleshire, whom we met in *Murder in Three Acts.* Poirot is spending the Christmas holiday with him at his home, and it is there that they have the above discussion about holiday spirit and hypocrisy.

Mr. Sugden, Superintendent of the Local Police who possesses the only mustache in England that Poirot admires almost as much as his own. He is described as a handsome, tall and broad-shouldered man who moves with a sense of his own importance.

Simeon Lee, a successful diamond prospector in his youth, and later a successful inventor and millionaire. He is now a semi-invalid confined to his bedroom. His only pleasures in life seem to be fingering some uncut diamonds that were the first he ever discovered, ("My beauties," as he calls them) and insulting his offspring with remarks such as

"You're not worth a penny piece, any of you! I'm sick of you all! You're not *men!* You're weaklings—a set of namby-pamby weaklings—Pilar's worth any two of you put together! I'll swear to Heaven I've got a better son somewhere in the world than any of you even if you are born the right side of the blanket! I tell you I'm sick of the sight of you all! Get out!"

This charming individual will be found later in his locked room with his throat cut, lying in a pool of blood, and the tears shed by his family upon his demise will be negligible.

Adelaide Lee, (deceased) Simeon Lee's late wife. She "died of a broken heart," according to her devoted son David, because of her husband's incessant infidelities, which she "endured for years without complaint." David's wife Hilda has occasion, however, to contradict that notion, explaining to Hercule Poirot that Adelaide complained incessantly and laid the whole burden of her unhappiness on the shoulders of her innocent son.

Alfred Lee, a squarely built man of middle-age with a gentle face and mild brown eyes. He is the only one of Simeon's sons who has remained with the family business and who continues to live with his father in the family home. He overlooks all of Simeon's tyrannical behaviors and obeys all of Simeon's orders. For his part, Simeon would feel more respect for Alfred if he would "stand up to him" once in a while.

Lydia Lee, Alfred Lee's wife, for whom Simeon feels more respect than for Alfred. She feels that Simeon, although he is generous with them in a monetary sense, treats them as slaves and that Alfred should demand some independence from his father.

George Lee, another of Simeon's sons who is a mediocre politician. He often uses the word "duty" and he is indeed as "dutiful" a son to Simeon as Alfred is, *and* is equally repugnant to Simeon because of it. In a conversation with Lydia, Simeon refers to George as "A poor stick. Nothing but a gasbag!" In a conversation with Pilar Estravados, Simeon calls George "A stick! A stuffed codfish! A pompous windbag with no brains and no guts..."

Magdalene Lee, George's wife, aged about twenty-one. According to Simeon, George picked her up at a mannequin parade. She had said her father was a retired naval officer, but Simeon has always suspected that the retired naval officer with whom she lived was actually her lover. Her chief interest in life is her clothes, for which she accumulates large piles of bills.

David Lee, Simeon's youngest son, for whom he feels no more love than for his other sons. In Simeon's opinion, David is "unmanly," a "namby pamby" who has pursued the "tomfoolery" of music and art. David is an artist who earns a meager living through his painting but knows that he cannot be considered a success. Still, he provides for himself and his wife and would like to forget that his father exists. He hates his father, in fact, because of the way his father treated his mother.

Hilda Lee, David's intelligent and sympathetic wife who would like to see her husband "forgive and forget." When David and Hilda receive the invitation to spend Christmas at Gorston Hall, she believes—or hopes—that it is a truly generous gesture on the part of her father-in-law to make amends, and so she prevails upon David to accept the invitation. Once she experiences Simeon Lee's hateful outburst in the presence of the whole family, however, she realizes that she was mistaken.

Henry (Harry) Lee, the only one of Simeon's sons who is not married. He has lived abroad—here and there—for the past twenty years, having forged his father's name to a check for several hundred pounds and left a note saying "an office life is not for me." He has outraged Alfred, from time to time, by writing to his father asking for money, and receiving it.

Stephen Farr, the son of Ebenezer Farr, Simeon Lee's prospecting partner during their youthful days. He has lived all his life in Africa. Pilar Estravados notices him in the train as it chugs out of the station in London, and these are her thoughts:

> That was a handsome man standing in the corridor... Pilar thought he was very handsome. She liked his deeply bronzed face and his high bridged nose and his square shoulders. More quickly than any English girl, Pilar had seen that the man admired her. She had not looked at him once directly, but she knew perfectly how often he had looked at her and exactly how he had looked.
> She registered the facts without much interest or emotion. She came from a country where men looked at women as a matter of course and did not disguise the fact unduly. She wondered if he was an Englishman and decided that he was not.
> "He is too alive, too real, to be English," Pilar decided.

Ebenezer Farr (deceased), Stephen's father, Simeon Lee's old prospecting partner.

Pilar Estravados, the object of Stephen Farr's admiration in the train leaving London for the "dreary midlands of England." She is Simeon Lee's only grandchild, the daughter of Jennifer, who married a Spanish artist and left England forever. Jennifer has just died and Simeon has invited Pilar to make her home at Gorston Hall.

Sydney Horbury, Simeon Lee's male nurse attendant or "valet," as he is also called. Everyone notes with distaste that he creeps around like a cat. He has an alibi for the time Simeon was killed: he was at the movies with a girlfriend, Doris Buckle. He also has good references.

Edward Tressilian, the aging butler at Gorston Hall, who has been with the family for forty years.

Walter Champion, the footman at Gorston Hall, young and inexperienced, who sometimes actually passes the gravy before the vegetables. Or is it the vegetables before the gravy? (Doesn't matter much, does it, since the food is English?) He is the son of the gardener.

Emily Reeves, the Cook at Gorston Hall

Queenie Jones, the Kitchenmaid at Gorston Hall

Gladys Spent, Grace Bent, Beatrice Moscombe, and **Joan Kench**, housemaids at Gorston Hall

Doris Buckle, a young lady employed at the local dairy shop, who was enjoying an evening at the movies with Sydney Horbury at the moment that Simeon Lee's throat was being cut.

Major West and the **Hon. Jasper Finch**, respectable people who were former employers of Sidney Horbury

Colonel Johnson's Manservant who announces a phone call from Superintendent Sugden

A Constable at Gorston Hall who opens the door to Hercule Poirot and Colonel Johnson when they arrive

A Doctor who is examining Simeon Lee's body when Poirot and Colonel Johnson arrive at Gorston Hall

Mr. Charlton of Charlton, Hodgkins & Brace, Simeon Lee's attorney who has the dubious pleasure of reading the Will to the family after the inquest. He hastens to leave the premises before the inevitable family bickering that always follows the reading of a Will.

A Militant-looking Grey-haired Lady in Pilar Estravados's railway compartment who, despite the cold air of the December day, had opened the window. Pilar closed it the moment the lady departed for "first lunch."

FRENCH INTO ENGLISH

(Parts One and Two contain no French words or expressions)

PART 3

Chapter 5
pour le bon motif, c'est entendu—for a good cause, of course
malaise—discomfort, anxiety

Chapter 6 *Très bien*—All right, then.

Chapter 7 *tout de même*—nevertheless

Chapter 8
conseil de famille—family council

Chapter 11
Jolie mannequin, la petite. Elle se pose tout naturellement. Elle a les yeux dures—This girl is a great model—she looks quite life-like. Her eyes look menacing. (implying a conscious effort at making an effect)
Elle joue très bien la comédie, cette petite—This girl's a damned good actress
Mais oui—Yes, it has

Chapter 13
Les femmes—Women
Dieu merci—Thank God!

PART 4

Chapter 1
C'est bien imaginé, ça!—That's a clever idea!

Chapter 2
Mon cher collègue—Good friend and colleague

Chapter 4 *Sapristi!*—Holy shit!

PART 5

Chapter 2
Pardon?—I beg your pardon?

Chapter 3
la toilette—good grooming, the art of dressing attractively

Chapter 4
Eh bien?—Well?

PART 6

Chapter 2 *les jeux d'enfants*—kids' games

Chapter 4
Madre de Dios—(Spanish) Mother of God!

PART 7

Chapter 6 *Pour moi*—As for me...

Comments

A Holiday for Murder has two things in common with its immediate predecessor, *Appointment with Death*: an oppressive, unloving parent and a rather weak, contrived solution. Both have interesting, psychologically complex characters, however, and both make fascinating reading.

After meeting the detestable Mrs. Elmer Boynton in *Appointment with Death*, old Simeon Lee almost seems to be a swell guy, despite his cruel tongue. The worst that can actually be said of him is that he is one of those exceptional "high achievers" who expect their children to be the same, but they are not, and so he is disappointed in them. Of course he treats his adult children abominably, but he secretly wishes that they would "stand up to him" once in a while, just as he wished that his wife had stood up to him during her lifetime.

Of Simeon's four sons, there is only one who actually hates his father: David Lee. David had been an unusually sensitive child who grew up feeling that his father's adulterous conduct had hurt his mother, who had "borne her grief without complaint." Actually the truth, as revealed by David's wife Hilda, is that David's mother never shut up about it and sobbed incessantly, dumping all of her problems on her innocent, sensitive son. In other words, she was one of those whiners who make their problems the problems of their nearest and dearest.

Two of Simeon's sons—Alfred and George—are exactly what Simeon accuses them of being: they are mediocre people who "suck up" to their father because he provides them with a generous income and because one day they will inherit his fortune. Alfred's own wife faults him for not standing up to his father and we know that even Simeon wishes that Alfred would "talk back" once in a while and demand some independence. George is a mediocre politician who married a mediocre woman who has no interests except her wardrobe and who probably married him only for status. As to Harry, he has always been an irresponsible leech who stole money from his father and then, despite "abandoning" the family, never hesitated to write to his father and ask for handouts whenever his irresponsible behaviors landed him in trouble.

And so, unlike the innocent victims of Mrs. Boynton's perverted manipulations in *Appointment with Death*, the sons of Simeon Lee have plenty of faults of their own. Alfred has a wife who is probably a better wife than he deserves, and David is lucky to have a wife who understands his feelings and tries very hard to help him put old problems into the past and to live for the present and future.

All of this does not necessarily make an excellent detective novel, of course. Hercule Poirot enjoys himself wallowing in the psychology of all of these people and he pretends to be arriving at "the truth" through the use of his little gray cells. But the fact is, when he "reveals all" we wonder how he has discovered the truth, other than by just plain guessing. We also wonder, since there is absolutely no evidence—let alone proof—upon which to base an arrest and bring a conviction, why the murderer so freely admits the deed. For serious readers of detective stories, *A Holiday for Murder* is no better than *Appointment with Death*, but for Agatha Christie fans, it's a fun read.

In addition to "wallowing in the psychology" of the Lee family, in this story Hercule Poirot has another occasion to react negatively to "British sentimentality," in this case British failure to recognize the hypocrisy that is systematically practiced at holiday time. Colonel Johnson thinks that with all the holiday spirit at Christmas time—"Peace, goodwill—and all that kind of thing. Good will all round..." murder is not likely to happen, to which Poirot replies that all of that "good will all round" is nothing but "hypocrisy practiced for the season." It puts people under a strain, he contends, and actually makes crime more likely. A minute later, of course, Colonel Johnson receives the news of Simeon Lee's murder.

There is not much humor in *A Holiday for Murder*, although Agatha Christie's silly attempts to show "cultural differences" between Britons and Spaniards are rather amusing. Christie appears to have acquired all of her "knowledge" of Spanish culture from the opera stage. Stephen Farr's thoughts about Pilar Estravados, when he sees her in the train in the first chapter of the book, are downright hilarious:

> And then, suddenly, he caught his breath, looking into a carriage. This girl was different. Black hair, rich creamy pallor—eyes with the depth and darkness of night in them. The sad proud eyes of the South.... It was all wrong that this girl should be sitting in this train among these dull drab looking people—all wrong that she should be going into the dreary midlands of England. She should have been on a balcony, a rose between her lips, a piece of black lace and heat and the smell of blood—the smell of the bull-ring—in the air.... She should be somewhere splendid, not squeezed into the corner of a third class carriage....

Pilar's observations about the cultural differences between Britons and Spaniards are equally hilarious and simplistic:

"...I like to see people get angry. I like it very much. But here in England they do not get angry like they do in Spain. In Spain they take out their knives and they curse and shout. In England they do nothing, just get very red in the face and shut up their mouths tight."

Despite these almost grotesquely oversimplified cultural stereotypings, it is gratifying to be reminded that Christie was at least aware that British outlooks were not the only ones possible. Way back in 1923 a French servant woman, in *Murder on the Links,* observed that the English are apt to do the most unaccountable things, like going out walking in the early morning chill. In *The Mystery of the Blue Train* Derek Kettering's French mistress Mirelle observes, "You are extraordinary, you English," when he is shocked and offended by the thought that his wife may be as adulterous as he is. Poirot never ceases to be amazed by British naïveté in the matter of "fair play," British reluctance to acknowledge the existence of sex, British refusal to enter the kitchen and learn to turn ordinary foods into delicious culinary experiences, etc. Pilar Estravados is just another in a series of foreign observers and commentators on British silliness. Regarding British "fair play," Poirot tosses this remark to Colonel Johnson on the subject of poison, as they discuss the murder of Dr. Strange, who died of nicotine poisoning in *Murder in Three Acts:* "There was a time when you would have considered all poisoning un–English. A device of foreigners! Unsportsmanlike!"

Poirot has always contended that, if encouraged to talk, people will eventually reveal the truth, often unknowingly, and quite often without being asked direct questions. In *A Holiday for Murder* for the first time he uses the expression "Father Confessor" to describe himself, after one character seeks him out to reveal some new information, and then another character does the same. This idea will be repeated in future novels, most obviously during the 1950s when, in *Funerals Are Fatal* he will take a seat in the summer house of a large property and, one by one, nearly all of the suspects will visit him there uninvited and "spill their guts."

Easy to Kill (1939)

(Alternate Title: *Murder Is Easy)*

SETTING

It is June of 1938 or 1939. The opening scene takes place in a train traveling to London from one of the ports, probably Southampton, since one of the main characters has just arrived from the Far East and is traveling from the port city to London in the special "boat train." It is also conceivable that he is traveling from *Dover* to London, since there were also "boat trains" carrying passengers who had arrived by ferry from France to Dover, and it is possible that the character has made a stop in France first. The only importance of all of this is that the main setting for the novel is a fictitious village called Wychwood-under-Ashe, and this village is close to the railway line connecting the port with London. If the port is Southampton, then Wychwood-under-Ashe can be assumed to be in the county of Hampshire, which is southwest of London. But if the port is Dover, then the village of Wychwood must be in the county of Kent, just southeast of London. To add to this intriguing confusion, the port in question may even be *Plymouth* in the more distant, southwestern county of Devon! In any case, we do know that Wychwood is just thirty-five miles from London.

The London scenes take place at the home of the protagonist's best friend; no description of the home is provided, but since he is a single man he undoubtedly lives in a flat.

The bulk of the story, however, takes place in the aforementioned Wychwood-under-Ashe, a village having two inns (The Seven Stars and The Bells and Motley, this last having just three guest bedrooms) and a village green with a duck pond. In addition to the usual "haphazard" cottages and other buildings typical of old-world villages, there is a much more prominent house called Wych Hall, dating from the Queen Anne period, which is now a library/museum. Attached to this large old house is a recently-constructed addition, which is actually a small house in itself. In this little house lives an old woman who is the last survivor of the family that once owned the larger house. Her family had become impoverished and had to sell the house, but fortunately a wealthy local benefactor saved it from the sad fate of possible demolition by purchasing it and making it into a well-maintained "library/museum," and building onto it the little house for the old woman to live in.

The "museum" collection is not very impressive, consisting of some Roman pottery and coins, some South Sea curiosities, a Malay headdress, various Indian gods "presented by Major Horton," together with a large and malevolent-looking Buddha and a case of doubtful-looking Egyptian beads. The building has three stories, and it should be noted that one of the murder victims falls from one of its "second story" windows, which from the American point of view would be called "third story" windows.

In addition to this "library-museum" and the two inns, there is a tobacco-and-newspaper shop, a new antique shop, and a church and vicarage. There is no description of the church but, if the village is typical, the church probably dates from the Middle Ages and is a stone building in Norman French style.

There is also a large, white, modern building, "austere and irrelevant to the cheerful haphazardness of the rest of the place," which is the local Institute and Lads' Club.

About half a mile outside the village proper is a much grander residence, also dating from the Queen Anne period, but which has been altered by its current owner. It is in fact one of the "castellated abominations" mentioned by Christie in two earlier novels. Stone towers and false façades have been added to make it look like a miniature castle in order to satisfy the owner's need for ostentatious display of wealth and status. The name of this house is Wych Manor and several scenes take place within its walls and grounds. An impressive new iron gate guards the main entrance to the grounds and a similar one, between pillars surmounted by large stone pineapples, guards a side entrance. The interior of the house is comfortably furnished but is not described in very much detail. One of the ground floor rooms is the library, which has "French windows," that is, windows whose sills are close to the floor and which swing on hinges, thus allowing persons to enter and leave the house through them. One character actually leaves the house at midnight through one of the library windows.

The following description of Wych Manor is provided as the protagonist arrives there by automobile from the village:

> He found the gates easily; they were of new and elaborate wrought iron. He drove in, caught a gleam of red brick through the trees, and turned a corner of the drive to be stupefied by the appalling and incongruous castellated mass that greeted his eyes.... While he was contemplating the nightmare, the sun went in. He became suddenly conscious of the overlying menace of Ashe Ridge. There was a sudden sharp gust of wind, blowing back the leaves of the trees....

"Ashe Ridge" is a geographic feature that plays an atmospheric role in the story, evidently a rocky outcropping that causes intermittent sudden gusts of turbulent wind whenever an otherwise mild breeze occurs.

Just outside Wychwood is a place known as "The Witches' Meadow" with which some ancient legends of witchcraft are associated.

No historical events of the late 1930s are mentioned in the novel, but we know that the British Empire was still extensive and the sleuth happens to be a British police officer returning home to England from his post in the "Mayang Straits," presumably somewhere in the area of Singapore. Another character refers to a nephew who is currently a young police officer in Palestine, which was a British protectorate from 1918 until after World War II. The British protectorates of Mesopotamia and Palestine were settings for two previous Christie detective novels, the 1936 *Murder in Mesopotamia* and the 1938 *Appointment with Death*.

Trivia such as clothing fashions of the period play no role at all, although the following may be noted. In America and in Europe as well, it was not until the mid–1950s that adult males willingly wore "shorts" for any purpose other than certain sports, such as tennis or hiking, and of course there were "bathing trunks" for use at the beach. But "shorts" worn in public in towns and cities were considered to be feminine attire, or else "kids' pants." Little boys wore "short pants" until about age eight or nine, then graduated to "long pants," in which they remained forever, no matter how intensely hot a summer day might be. An adult male might allow himself to be seen shirtless while mowing his lawn during a heat wave, but his pants were long pants, never shorts. After about 1955 such innovations as "Bermuda shorts" made their way into men's casual summer wardrobes but even in the early 1960s those were not allowed in the dining rooms of the typical Midwestern university unless accompanied by long stockings. Adult males were not expected to exhibit their hairy legs at any time or place except in sporting activities.

At one point in the story three "strangers from London" arrive at the village of Wychwood and take rooms at one of the inns. One is a young woman "without eyebrows" and another is "a man in shorts." As to the eyebrowless female, a late 1930s feminine fashion statement was to have severely plucked eyebrows and false ones penciled thinly in unnatural formations. Christie mentions a character in another novel as having "freakishly plucked eyebrows." The "eyebrowless woman" in *Easy to Kill* is evidently at the forefront of fashion, and the "man in shorts" is undoubtedly a major nonconformist and probably gay. He also wears "a lovely plum-coloured silk shirt," and the third person in the group is a man "wearing a lavender suit." These are friends of the eccentric owner of the local antique shop—an effeminate young man who, according to local gossip, participates in witchcraft. The date of arrival of these three eccentrics from London—June 21, which is Midsummer Eve—suggests that there will be "gay doings" tonight out at the Witches' Meadow. See the *Appendix* for a discussion of the words "queer" and "gay" in Christie's novels.

These remarks are made simply to underscore the "shocking" appearance that these people would have made in an English village of the late 1930s. During that period, "normal" men did *not* wear shorts, even in the summer.

Two makes of automobile are mentioned in the novel. A wealthy resident of Wychwood owns at least two cars: one is a large, chauffeur-driven Rolls and the other is a two-seater of unspecified make. The narrator's best friend, who lives in London, mentions that he owns a "Ford V-8."

On the subject of money values, it should be mentioned again that the value of British pounds and American dollars was much higher seven decades ago than it is today. One character in *Easy to Kill* works as a private secretary to a millionaire for the salary of six pounds weekly. We may recall that in the 1937 *Death on the Nile*, Jacqueline de Bellefort's annual income of just under two hundred pounds allowed her to purchase an unreliable but somewhat functional car for fifteen pounds.

Story

It is June of 1938 or 1939 and Luke Fitzwilliam has just retired from his job as a police officer in a fictitious, remote outpost of the Empire and has returned to England. In the boat train he chats with an amiable old lady, Miss Lavinia Fullerton, who lives in the village of Wychwood, thirty-five miles from London. Miss Fullerton is on her way to visit Scotland Yard to report three recent murders in Wychwood, and to warn of a fourth murder that is soon to take place—that of Dr. Humbleby. Luke smiles to himself about this silly old lady's fantasies and wonders if Scotland Yard has a special department just to deal with ladies like her.

The next day, however, he reads in the newspaper about a certain Lavinia Fullerton of Wychwood who was run down by a hit-and-run driver the evening before and killed. Then, about a week later, he reads in the paper about a certain Dr. Humbleby of Wychwood who died "suddenly at his residence." Luke wonders if Miss Fullerton had been right in her prediction of Dr. Humbleby's death, and if she may have been murdered in London to silence her.

Posing as a historian writing a book about village witchcraft practices, Luke visits Wychwood and pursues a private investigation of his own. There he befriends Bridget Conway, the secretary of a millionaire, and the couple investigates the matter as a team. There have in fact been a number of recent deaths, but all of them appear to have been accidental and unrelated. Luke and Bridget discover the truth just in time to prevent Bridget's own untimely death.

Characters

Luke Fitzwilliam, a retired British police officer from a remote outpost of the Empire who returns home to England to find himself involved in the unraveling of a murder mystery in a village not far from London. He is not physically described and his age is never stated, but he must be relatively young, since he is interesting to twenty-eight-year-old Bridget Conway, another main character.

Jimmy Lorrimer, Luke's best friend. He has a cousin in the village of Wychwood—Bridget Conway—and achieves her cooperation in welcoming Luke to Wychwood and introducing him as a writer.

A Gloomy-looking Porter at Fenny Clayton Junction, where Luke gets off the train to read the newspaper about a horse racing event as his train proceeds without him.

A Gentleman of Military Aspect Smoking a Cigar sitting alone in a smoking compartment of a train

A Tired-looking, Genteel-looking Young Woman, Possibly a Nursery Governess traveling with an **Active-looking Small Boy of About Three**, seen in another compartment of the train.

Aunt Mildred, Luke's aunt who allowed him to keep a grass snake when he was a child, "decidedly a good one as aunts go." When Luke notices that an elderly woman sitting alone in a compartment of the train reminds him of his Aunt Mildred, he chooses to sit in that compartment rather than with the military gent or the governess and the active child.

Miss Lavinia Fullerton, the aforementioned elderly lady in the train. Luke, who is a "man of many aunts," correctly predicts that this elderly lady does not intend to travel to London in silence. She tells him of her purpose in going to London: to inform Scotland Yard of three recent murders in her village and of the most certain and imminent occurrence of a fourth. She even provides names of the three victims and that of the future victim. Soon after leaving the train in London she is run over and killed by a car while crossing Whitehall, and the driver of the car does not stop.

Wonky Pooh, Miss Fullerton's orange Persian cat whose ear is infected.

John Reed, the local constable in Wychwood who, in Miss Fullerton's opinion, is a very civil-spoken, pleasant man who is used to dealing with people who've drunk too much, or have exceeded the speed limits, or who haven't taken out a dog license, but who would not be quite the person to deal with anything serious—like *murder.*

Amy Gibbs, an inefficient and insolent housemaid who provided unsatisfactory service at several houses in Wychwood and then died of oxalic acid poisoning—drinking hat paint "by accident" instead of a cough preparation that was in a similar bottle. Or was it suicide? There is speculation that she might have been pregnant. She had a regular boyfriend and was also flirtatious with other men.

Jim Harvey, Amy Gibbs's boyfriend, a handsome young auto mechanic.

Miss Church, Amy's unpleasant aunt whose sharp nose, shifty eyes and voluble tongue all alike fill Luke with nausea. She provides information about Amy's character and habits.

Henry (Harry) Carter, the owner of The Seven Stars, "that nasty little pub down by the river," (description provided by Bridget Conway.) He fell—or was pushed—off a footbridge and drowned in the river. The vicar describes him as "a dissenter." Lord Easterfield calls him a "socialistic drunkard." According to the more articulate and precise young Dr. Thomas, Carter "ill-treated his wife, bullied his daughter, was quarrelsome and abusive, and had had a row with most people in the place." It is widely believed that his wife and daughter are glad to be rid of him.

Mrs. Carter, the wife of Mr. Carter for whom her husband's death was a "merciful release" according to Mrs. Pierce.

Lucy Carter, the pretty daughter of Henry Carter who works as a barmaid at The Seven Stars. According to Mrs. Pierce, Mr. Abbot, the solicitor, takes a fancy to her.

Tommy Pierce, a nasty adolescent with a cruel streak who enjoyed cutting up wasps and twisting the arms of the smaller boys. He did odd work for several residents of Wychwood but was never satisfactory. Lord Easterfield fired him when he caught him doing comical imitations of His Lordship for the entertainment of the two undergardeners. But later Lord Easterfield procured another job for Tommy—washing windows at the library/museum. Poor Tommy fell to his death from an upper-story window. Or was he pushed? For one thing, while working at the office of the lawyer Mr. Abbot, Tommy had read a confidential letter from a young lady to Mr. Abbot.

Mrs. Pierce, Tommy's mother, and the mother of "six other little blessings," in the words of Luke Fitzwilliam. According to her, Tommy was "just high spirited" and "never meant no harm," and he was so good at imitations and, really, "in a lawyer's office a confidential letter shouldn't be just lying around, now should it?"

Two Undergardeners at Wych Manor who were great fans of Tommy Pierce, Imitator Extraordinaire

Dr. John Humbleby, the older doctor in the village who Miss Fullerton had predicted would be "the next to die" and who really did die—of acute septicemia. He had had a bad row with Lord Easterfield on the subject of the water supply and was also known to be disliked by Dr. Thomas, his much younger partner.

Jessie Rose Humbleby, the widow of Dr. Humbleby who tells Luke that the world is "a very wicked place."

Rose Humbleby, Dr. and Mrs. Humbleby's pretty daughter with whom young Dr. Thomas is in love. Dr. Humbleby had objected to this attachment, and then he died.

Bridget Conway, the twenty-eight-year-old cousin of Luke's friend Jim Lorrimer and a pseudo-cousin of Luke. She was jilted by Johnnie Cornish who left her for a fat, middle-aged woman with a North Country accent and an income of 30,000 pounds. Bridget is therefore embittered and quite willing to sacrifice love in her life for the security of a future marriage to her wealthy employer, Lord Easterfield. Her family had been the former owners of Wych Manor, the large home currently owned by His Lordship.

Johnnie Cornish, the aforementioned ex-fiancé of Bridget Conway and current husband of the fat, rich North Country woman.

Lord Gordon Easterfield, a "self-made man" whose favorite topic of discussion—in fact practically his *only* topic of discussion—is himself and his success. He owns several weekly newspapers whose mission he takes very seriously:

> "You wouldn't believe what I've got on my shoulders," said Lord Easterfield. "I take a personal interest in each one of my publications. I consider that I'm responsible for molding the public mind. Next week millions of people will be thinking and feeling just exactly what I've intended to make them feel and think. That's a very solemn thought. That means responsibility. Well, I don't mind responsibility."

To which his secretary-fiancée replies: "You're a great man, Gordon. Have some more tea."

Luke Fitzwilliam, once he becomes well acquainted with Bridget Conway, confronts her on the subject of her planned marriage to Lord Easterfield, asking her why she would consider marrying this old bore. Bridget, who is embittered because a fiancé in the past left her for a fat North-Country woman with money, replies:

> "Because as his secretary I get six pounds a week, and as his wife I shall get a hundred thousand settled on me, a jewel case full of pearls and diamonds, a handsome allowance, and various perquisites of the married state."

Mrs. Anstruther, an aunt of Bridget Conway who also lives at Wych Manor. Her only interest in life is flower gardening and she speaks only three times in the whole novel—all three times on a gardening subject. On the day after Luke's arrival at Wych Manor, Mrs. Anstruther treats him to an interrogation as to what kind of flowers he had in his garden in the Mayang Straits, followed by a lecture on which flowers would have done well there.

The Butler at Ashe Manor

Rivers, Lord Easterfield's chauffeur, who offends His Lordship by taking a girl joyriding in His Lordship's Rolls. Lord Easterfield fires Rivers instantly, saying he won't have drunkenness, immorality and impertinence on his estate. Rivers, who has had quite enough drink to loosen his tongue, responds:

> "You won't have this and you won't have that, you old buzzard! Your estate! Think we don't all know your father kept a boot shop down here? Makes us laugh ourselves sick, it does, seeing you strutting about as cock of the walk! What are you, I'd like to know? You're no better than I am, that's what you are!"

Rivers dies that same day—a large ornamental stone pineapple falls off the wall near the back gate onto Rivers's drunken, immoral and impertinent head.

Mr. Abbot, the local solicitor, who had fired bratty little Tommy Pierce for reading a private letter in his office. He describes Tommy as a good-for-nothing, prying, meddlesome jackanapes. In another conversation he describes Dr. Humbleby as being absolutely pigheaded and a diehard of the worst description. Did Mr. Abbot dislike both of these individuals enough to murder them?

Dr. Geoffrey Thomas, the young partner of Dr. Humbleby who felt intimidated by the older man's popularity. According to the vicar, Dr. Thomas's mood and general spirit improved greatly upon the death of Dr. Humbleby.

Rev. Alfred Wake, the "rector" or "vicar" (both terms are used) of Wychwood-under-Ashe. He provides useful information about most of the residents of Wychwood. Despite being a clergyman, he has surprisingly modern ideas about psychology, describing Tommy Pierce's bullying behaviors as simply childish and immature.

Giles, the sexton of the parish church who the vicar promises will provide Luke with a list of all recent deaths in the town

Mr. Hobbs, the churchwarden, who had been the butt of one of Tommy Pierce's more popular and successful imitations

Mr. Ellswprthy, a strange young man who owns the new antique shop in Wychwood. There are local rumors that he dabbles in witchcraft. Occasionally he hosts rather strange visitors from London.

A Man with Shorts, Spectacles and a Lovely Plum-colored Silk Shirt; a Fat Man in a Lavender Suit; and a Female with No Eyebrows Dressed in a Peplum, three of Mr. Ellsworthy's friends from London who visit him in Wychwood on June 21, that is on "Midsummer Eve," a special day for witches and their fans.

Major Horton, referred to by most of the people in Wychwood as "Major Horton and His Bulldogs." He is rarely seen without them and rarely turns his attention fully away from them, no matter how interesting the conversation. The villagers unanimously agree that he was miserable while his wife was alive. The major was very fond of his wife, however, and he praises the institution of marriage in the highest terms, stating that a wife keeps a man up to the mark. Just like being in the army, in fact.

Like all ex-military types in Christie novels, Major Horton loves to bore people to death with stories about India. In this story, as soon as he learns that Luke has been in the Far East, he accosts Luke, starts a conversation about the Empire, and Luke only escapes ten minutes later, after enduring the usual histories of fakirs and rope and mango tricks that are dear to the retired Anglo-Indian.

Lydia Horton, Major Horton's recently-deceased wife. Although Major Horton speaks of her in glowing terms, Bridget insists that she was an extremely disagreeable woman who henpecked her husband and never scrupled to underline publicly the fact that it was *she* who had the money. Bridget wonders why Major Horton never took a hatchet to her.

Augustus, Nero and Nelly, Major Horton's bulldogs, who brightened up at once upon the death of Mrs. Horton, according to Bridget Conway. Major Horton is rarely seen without them.

Mrs. Rose, Old Bell, and That Child of the Elkinses and Poor Old Ben Stanbury, persons cited by the vicar as having died recently in Wychwood-under-Ashe.

Miss Honoria Waynflete, a very genteel lady in her late fifties who works two days a week at Wych Hall, the library/museum which was once her family home. The generous Lord Easterfield rescued her family home when it was about to be demolished or sold and converted to flats, and made it into the local library/museum that it is today. He even built a new addition onto it in the form of a little house for Miss Waynflete to live in. Miss Waynflete was once engaged to Lord Easterfield but her family considered him to be beneath her.

"Cook," the servant who was with Miss Waynflete when it was discovered that Amy Gibbs had died in her locked bedroom.

Emily, a small clumsy-looking girl with pronounced adenoids, who asks, "If you bleese, biss, did you bean the frilled billow cases?" Emily is Miss Waynflete's maid.

Old Colonel Waynflete, Honoria Waynflete's father, who died many years ago, but who is well remembered by Lord Easterfield, according to whom the Colonel was very conservative whereas his daughter Honoria was "a radical, very earnest—all for abolishing class distinctions."

Mr. Jones, the bank manager who assists Luke in opening a local checking account. He admires Lord Easterfield very much, describing him as a handsome local benefactor who has contributed a good deal to the welfare of young boys, offering them advantages that he never had himself.

A Clerk at the office of Mr. Jones

Hetty Jones, Mr. Jones's giggling daughter who is present at a tennis party at Wych Manor

An Ancient Laborer who follows Luke out of the Seven Stars and shows Luke the little bridge where Harry Carter had fallen into the water and "drownded."

Sir William Ossington, a.k.a. "Billy Bones," an influential friend of Luke's at Scotland Yard with whom he confers on the subject of the hit-and-run death of Miss Fullerton and other matters.

Officer Bonner, the London police officer in charge of the case of Miss Fullerton's death

Mr. Satcherverell, the coroner in the case of Miss Fullerton's death

Superintendent Battle, the wooden-faced Scotland Yard officer who is sent to Wychwood-under-Ashe by Sir William after Luke explains all of the known facts. His role in the story is very small and he does no investigating at all, for it is Luke Fitzwilliam himself who solves the case on the very day that Superintendent Battle arrives.

We have met Superintendent Battle in three earlier novels, first in the 1925 *The Secret of Chimneys,* then in the 1929 *The Seven Dials Mystery,* and finally in the 1936 *Cards on the Table.* He will make his final appearance in the 1944 *Towards Zero.* His smallest role is in the present story, in which he is introduced in a very late chapter.

COMMENTS

In *Easy to Kill,* several themes and character types that have developed over the years in Christie detective novels are again in evidence. The "boring ex-colonial military man," first introduced in *The Murder of Roger Ackroyd* and then repeated in several later novels is here in the person of "Major Horton And His Bulldogs." The prim village spinster, introduced in *The Murder of Roger Ackroyd,* and then multiplied in *Murder at the Vicarage,* is here in Lavinia Fullerton and Honoria Waynflete. The self-made-man who never lets anyone forget his humble origins, introduced first in *The Murder of Roger Ackroyd* as Roger Ackroyd himself, then repeated as Sir Oswald Coote in *The Seven Dials Mystery,* is here in the person of Lord Easterfield.

Agatha Christie detested newspaper reporters and newspapers in general. The unscrupulous reporter Charles Enderby in *Murder at Hazelmoor* was a touch of humor and there are nearly always negative references to newspaper reporting in general in Christie novels of every period. An outstanding scene that comes to mind is the inquest scene in *Death in the Air.* In *Easy to Kill,* the self-made millionaire Lord Easterfield owns several of "those nasty little weekly papers" and boasts of his responsibility to "shape public opinion."

For some reason, Agatha Christie did not like hospital nurses, and they are always portrayed as smug "know-it-alls" in her books. In *Easy to Kill* Major Horton describes two hospital nurses who attended to his ailing wife as "about as sympathetic as a brace of grandfather clocks. 'The patient this' and 'the patient that.' Can't stand hospital nurses. So smug."

British fondness for—and expertise in—flower gardening is a rather late development in Christie's writing. It is mentioned first, and only briefly, in a description of a perennial garden in the 1937 *Poirot Loses a Client.* In *Easy to Kill,* it is expressed in the amusing minor character, Mrs. Anstruther, who has only three occasions to speak in the story, each time on a gardening subject.

Psychology had always been a subject of importance to Hercule Poirot, even as early as the 1923 *Murder on the Links*, but it was in the mid–1930s that Christie's novels began to incorporate serious discussions that included terms such as *schizophrenia, inferiority complex* and others. In the 1935 *Death in the Air*, Hercule Poirot treated psychoanalysis with mild disparagement, stating that people's natural need to talk about themselves has enriched numerous "quacks," but in every novel since then there have been serious discussions about psychology and it has been treated as a true science. In *Easy to Kill* there is talk, mainly by young Dr. Thomas, about "homicidal maniacs" and he lends Luke Fitzwilliam a book entitled *Inferiority and Crime*.

Christie's negative attitude toward children is again expressed in this novel. The bratty adolescent Tommy Pierce was a bully who pinched and twisted the arms of smaller boys and liked to cut up wasps. His mother was saddened by his death, of course, but as Luke Fitzwilliam sarcastically remarks later, she has "six other little blessings to console her." She is, of course, a low-class person, which explains why she has had eight pregnancies (another child had died in toddlerhood.) Christie clearly regarded the "lower classes" as having too many children for their own good, and in the 1952 *Mrs. McGinty's Dead,* Poirot will have some negative thoughts about the "haphazard fecundity" of a certain poor family. In another story, a few years later, a woman of the "lower classes" will express great pride in the fact that she is one of eleven siblings.

On the subject of "class," Christie again reminds us that persons of true breeding "have" money but they never "earn" it. Lord Easterfield is the prime example of the ungentlemanly "earner of money," but there is also a comment by Miss Honoria Waynflete about Mr. Ellsworthy, who runs the new antique shop. She makes a special point of telling Luke Fitzwilliam that, although Mr. Ellsworthy operates the antique business, he is actually a "gentleman." People who "keep shops" in Christie novels are never quite respectable, since their need to earn money shouts of their unfortunate origin of not having been "born into money." Christie herself, of course, was "born into money." Her father inherited capital investments, which generated sufficient interest income to support his family. He never did a lick of work, to Christie's great satisfaction, and she also pointed out in her *Autobiography* that she never understood why some people thought that there was anything "meritorious" about work for its own sake. The satisfaction of supporting oneself—of pulling one's own weight—was alien to Christie's schema.

A new element in "the Christie schema" is introduced in *Easy to Kill:* the idea that education is not as important as many people think it is. Luke Fitzwilliam voices that view when he says to Mr. Jones, the banker, that "education is too highly rated nowadays." Hercule Poirot's old friend, Mr. Goby, whom we first met in the 1928 *The Mystery of the Blue Train,* will have a good deal to say about the uselessness of education for the working classes in the 1953 *Funerals Are Fatal.* Over the next decades Christie will repeat this idea—that education is not worth much—whenever a character suggests that "environment and education" are important in a person's upbringing. To Christie, it is biological breeding that matters, not environment and education. She will ridicule, in the 1952 *Murder with Mirrors,* the idea of "reforming" juvenile delinquents by changing their environment, and she will preach against adoption of children in the 1958 *Ordeal by Innocence.*

In the 1949 *Crooked House,* there will be the Leonides family, known for its "unscrupulousness" and the de Haviland family, known for its "ruthlessness." The "unscrupulousness" of the Leonides family is, fortunately, tempered with "kindliness." But a descendent of both families *might* inherit the "unscrupulousness" of the Leonides blood line and the "ruthlessness" of the de Haviland blood line *without* the tempering effect of "kindliness," and a murderer might be the result. For full details of this nonsense, read the *Comments* section for *Crooked House,* or better still, read the novel.

Christie often puts the phrase "that class" or "the servant class" into the mouths of her sympathetic characters, including Hercule Poirot and Miss Marple. Poirot knows, for example, that "that class" cannot be "rushed" during questioning. During questioning, of course, "that class" usually exhibits "pleasurable excitement" or "ghoulish enjoyment" about the murder or "morbid curiosity" about the details of the crime. They get these negative qualities, of course, by being born into the "servant class." It's in their blood. And there are often reminders that "good servants" are no longer to be found. In this novel Miss Waynflete remembers Amy Gibbs as not a very good servant, adding that there are hardly any good servants nowadays.

In her *Autobiography,* which she wrote during the 1960s, Christie states that, during her childhood, "servants were actively happy and appreciated." She noted with displeasure—even as early as 1916 when writing *The Mysterious Affair at Styles*—that "good servants" were fast disappearing, and for some reason it never occurred to her that there was a good reason for it: servants were NOT "actively happy and appreciated." They were servants simply because there were no other employment opportunities for them. Therefore it is not surprising that she was displeased with modern trends to improve the education of the masses. Education prepares people for employment that does *not* consist of polishing other people's brass doorknockers and putting up with their insults.

And Then There Were None (1939)

(Alternate Titles: *Ten Little Niggers* and *Ten Little Indians*)

SETTING

The story takes place in August of 1938 or 1939. As the story opens there are brief scenes in which individual travelers make their way towards an island off the south coast of Devon; three or four scenes take place in train compartments and two are in automobiles. The "scenes" are actually the thoughts of the individual travelers—mostly recollections of their pasts and their private thoughts about their reasons for going to the island. The large city of Exeter, in Devon, is named as a place where one of the railway passengers changes trains.

From the fictitious town of Oakbridge in south Devon, the characters travel in small groups by taxi to the tiny fictitious fishing village of Sticklehaven (which has a little inn called The Seven Stars) and then by motorboat to Indian Island, which is located one mile from shore in the English Channel. It is a tiny, rocky island, uninhabited except for a large, modern, luxurious home built just a few years earlier by an American millionaire and then sold to the present owner. Access to the island is by boat from Sticklehaven and during stormy weather access to the island is impossible. There is no telephone in the house, of course, and electricity is produced by a generator which is probably powered by some liquid fuel. Mail and perishable provisions are brought to the island by motorboat daily.

The house consists of a ground floor, a bedroom floor and an attic above for storage and for servants' quarters. The ground floor rooms include the kitchen and pantry, a dining room with French windows, a drawing room, a smoking room and perhaps others. There are also verandas on at least two sides of the exterior. Detailed descriptions of the décor are sparse but suggest extreme simplicity in a tasteful "modern" style, such as the large dining room table which is circular. The bedroom of one guest has walls painted in a soft, pale color and there is a modern adjoining bathroom in light blue tile. A point noted by the guests is that, because of the modern construction of the house, there are none of the "hiding places" that would be more likely in a house of earlier vintage:

> If this had been an old house, with creaking wood, and dark shadows, and heavily paneled walls, there might have been an eerie feeling. But this house was the essence of modernity. There were no dark corners—no possible sliding panels—it was flooded with electric light—everything was new and bright and shining. There was nothing hidden in this house, nothing concealed. It had no atmosphere about it. Somehow, that was the most frightening thing of all...

Once the characters arrive at Indian Island, it remains the permanent setting for the story. Although the island is not a remote one—the south coast of Devon is clearly visible one mile to the north—it is a frightening place since communication with the mainland is impossible unless a boat comes to the island from the mainland. A couple of days and nights of stormy weather contribute to the frightening atmosphere.

No important contemporary historical events or conditions are mentioned in the novel, although there are one or two references to the fighting that took place in France during World War I. At one point in the story a group of characters mention a few current events, including "the latest appearance of the Loch Ness Monster," which was apparently in the news at the time. Two makes of automobile are named—a Morris, driven by a doctor and a Dalmain, driven by a young man. The Morris was a low-priced car but the Dalmain—which may be a fictitious make—is described as an expensive, fast and sporty car which must have cost "hundreds and hundreds."

STORY

It is August of 1938 or 1939. As the story begins, eight unmarried individuals—two women and six men—and a married couple arrive at Indian Island, a tiny, rocky island one mile off the southern coast of Devon in the English Channel. Their reasons for going to the island vary. The married couple is a butler and cook who have been hired temporarily by the owner, Mr. Owen, who has communicated with them only by letter. One of the women is a young school games mistress who has been hired as a temporary secretary for the owner's wife, Mrs. Owen. The other woman is an elderly spinster who received a mysterious letter of invitation—bearing a scarcely-legible signature, the writer claiming to have met her a couple of years earlier—and offering her a free summer holiday at their "new guest house" on Indian Island.

As to the men, one is an adventurer of the "soldier of fortune" type with a reputation for "having a quick mind in a tight place." He has been offered a hundred guineas in cash—in advance—to go to the island as a "guest" and he is warned to expect some kind of "action." Another is a middle-aged physician who had received a request from Mr. Owen to spend a week "observing" Mrs. Owen, who appears to be having a nervous problem. Another man is an ex-policeman who is given a list of the names of the guests and paid a substantial sum to "be on hand" to observe the group for a reason that is not clearly explained. The other men—a retired army general, a young playboy and a judge—have received invitation letters of similar vagueness, purporting to be from friends and acquaintances, or simply from "friends of friends."

There is just one house on Indian Island, a beautiful but starkly modern house that is practically brand new. The guests are informed by the two servants that their hosts will be delayed and that they are to make themselves comfortable and enjoy a pleasant dinner. After dinner, while they are gathered in the drawing room, a frightening voice makes an announcement. The Voice accuses every person in the house of committing a murder in the past for which he or she was never punished. The names of the victims and alleged murderers, and even the dates of the alleged crimes, are given. The "Voice" is actually a record being played on an old-fashioned record player—the type with a large trumpet—in the next room, and the servant woman had placed the record on the record player in obedience to written instructions from her employer.

Everyone is shocked and angered and they begin to discuss plans for leaving Indian Island at the first opportunity. Communication between the island and the mainland takes place only by a motorboat that comes each morning to bring supplies—except during bad weather. These discussions are brutally interrupted when one of the guests, the young playboy, dies instantly of cyanide poisoning upon tossing down a glass of whiskey. Later in the evening, the guests notice that a group of ten Indian figurines in the center of the round dining room table now consists of just nine figures.

In the morning it is discovered that the servant woman has died in her sleep from unknown causes, and the group of Indian figurines now numbers just eight. One by one the guests die, and it is clear that one of the terrified guests is the murderer, since a thorough search of the house and the island proves that there are no other people on the island.

Any further comment at this point would reveal the ending.

CHARACTERS

Lawrence John Wargrave (Mr. Justice Wargrave), a retired judge who receives a vague letter from a friend, Lady Constance Culmington, inviting him to Indian Island to "bask in the sun" with friends. Despite not having seen Lady Culmington for seven or eight years, Justice Wargrave goes to Indian Island. Once there, he is much appreciated, as he has the presence of mind to call the group of terrified guests together for rational discussions of events at times when panic would otherwise consume the group.

He is accused by The Voice of having "killed" Edward Seton by using his personal persuasiveness to sway a jury against the man on trial despite the jury's obvious belief in his innocence.

Llewellen (for the Crown) and Matthews (for the Defense), lawyers in the Seton case.

Vera Elizabeth Claythorne, a games mistress at a third-class school who would like a better position but knows that she is lucky to have *any* job with children, considering the fact that a child once in her care had drowned. An employment agency surprised her with a pleasant proposition: a temporary post as a secretary on a secluded island off the coast of Devon in August. What could be nicer?

The Voice accuses Vera of killing a child, Cyril Hamilton, in 1935. Fact: Vera was in love with Cyril's uncle, Hugo Hamilton, who would have inherited a fortune if Cyril had been a girl. But if Cyril were to die while too young to inherit ... and he was, after all, not a nice child.

Cyril Ogilvie Hamilton, a "horrid, whiny, spoilt little brat" who often pestered Vera with "Why can't I swim out to the rock, Miss Claythorne?" "The rock" was much too far from shore for a child his age to reach safely, but Vera decided to allow Cyril to swim to the rock "when Mummy isn't looking, and then you'll be able to wave to her from the rock, won't that be nice?" And so Cyril drowned as Vera swam slowly towards him in a show of a rescue effort.

Hugo Hamilton, Cyril's young uncle who became rich after Cyril died but who never spoke to Vera again. He must have suspected that Vera had deliberately caused Cyril's death, but nobody else had suspected it, not even Cyril's mother.

Emily Brent, a sixty-five-year-old spinster who has *always* pleased God. Always! She knows exactly what God wants and she has never, *never* sinned. She reads the Bible daily and quotes it at people whenever an occasion arises. She goes to Indian Island, having received a letter from a former acquaintance inviting her for a free holiday in August, although she only vaguely remembers the acquaintance—someone she met two or three years earlier at a resort.

The Voice accuses Miss Brent of bringing about the death of a former housemaid, Beatrice Taylor in 1931. What nonsense! Beatrice had become what one calls "in trouble," and when Emily learned of this, she would not keep her one hour longer under her roof. Not content with one sin on her soul, the abandoned creature committed a still graver sin. She took her own life. Naturally, Emily has nothing for which to reproach herself, since it was Beatrice's own sin that drove her to suicide.

Captain Philip Lombard, an adventurer—a "soldier of fortune" whose past actions had not always been quite legal but who was known to be "a good man in a tight spot." He is broke and is glad to have been offered a hundred guineas for only a week's work on Indian Island, being fully warned that he should expect "trouble" there.

The Voice accuses Captain Lombard of bringing about the death of twenty-one east African natives in 1932. Fact: he, along with two partners and the twenty-one natives, were lost in the wilderness and the food supply was dangerously low. He and the two partners took the food supplies, set off on their own, and eventually found their way back to civilization, but the natives were left to certain death by starvation. But after all, says the Captain, "Self-preservation's a man's first duty. And natives don't mind dying, you know. They don't feel about is as Europeans do."

Isaac Morris, "a shady little creature" and a dope peddler whose "client" provides Lombard with his hundred-guinea, one-week "job" at Indian Island.

General John Gordon Macarthur, a retired military officer. A letter from Mr. Owen names a couple of Macarthur's old cronies, saying that they will be at Indian Island and would enjoy seeing him again and chatting about the old days. General Macarthur looks forward to seeing a couple of old friends again.

During the worst days of fighting in France—during the Great War—Macarthur had learned that his wife was having an affair with a young soldier under his command, a certain Arthur Richmond. At Indian Island, The Voice accuses General Macarthur of deliberately causing Arthur Richmond's death by sending him on a reconnaissance mission in which the chances of survival were negligible. Macarthur knew that Richmond's death would simply be viewed as "just another unfortunate war blunder."

Leslie Macarthur, General Macarthur's wife who had a love affair with Arthur Richmond.

Young Armitage, another young subordinate of General Macarthur who may have known that Macarthur deliberately sent Richmond into harm's way and who perhaps had "talked."

Spoof Leggard and Johnny Dyer, the two old cronies of General Macarthur mentioned by Mr. Owen in his letter.

Old Tom Brent, a crony of General Macarthur and an uncle of Emily Brent

Edward George Armstrong, a successful Harley Street surgeon. Fifteen years earlier he had developed a drinking problem, but he has pulled himself out of it, fortunately.

The Voice accuses Dr. Armstrong of causing the death of Louisa Mary Clees in 1925. Fact: Dr. Armstrong was intoxicated while performing surgery. He bungled the surgery and the patient died. The Sister in attendance knew, but she was loyal to him and had held her tongue. Or had she?

Anthony Marston, a virile young man and a creature of sensation and of action—not much of a thinker and certainly not a person with a conscience. He received a wire from a pal, Badger Berkeley, suggesting that he spend a week with "friends" at Indian Island for fun and thrills. Badger is good at finding rich friends and Tony has nothing better to do.

The Voice accuses Tony of murdering John and Lucy Combes the previous year. Fact: John and Lucy were children who darted out of a cottage and into the road while Tony was speeding through a village near Cambridge. His car struck and killed them both. Anthony feels no guilt, of course, as it was "just an accident" and not his fault. He had received a fine and his driver's license had been suspended briefly.

Badger Berkeley, the aforementioned pal of Tony Marston

Several Young Women who look admiringly at handsome Tony when he stops at a village pub for a drink while on his way to Devon.

Several Old Men and Errand Boys who jump for safety as Tony speeds away from the pub in his Super Sport Dalmain. The Errand Boys admire the Dalmain.

William Henry Blore, an ex-C.I.D. man who receives a letter from the mysterious Mr. Owen—along with a substantial fee and list of guests invited to Indian Island—to go to the island and "keep his eyes open" for trouble.

At the island, The Voice accuses Blore of bringing about the death of James Stephen Landor in 1928. Fact: the criminal element had bribed Blore to give false testimony at Landor's trial and Landor, though innocent, was sent to prison where he soon died.

An Elderly Seafaring Gentleman with a Bleary Eye, riding in the train with Blore, who predicts stormy weather in the area of Indian Island for the next few days

Porters and Taxicab Drivers at Oakbridge railway station

Fred Narracot, who owns a motorboat with which he ferries passengers to and from Indian Island and takes mail, newspapers and groceries as ordered to the house on the island each morning. He remembers the "wild parties" that used to take place there when the rich American who built the house still owned it. He's puzzled by the odd assortment of people who are invited to the island by the new owner, Mr. Owen. A stern-looking old woman? A younger woman without much style or class? An assortment of men who look rather "common" except for the flashy young fellow who arrives at Sticklehaven in the fabulous Super Sport Dalmain.

Thomas and Ethel Rogers, the husband and wife servant team at the house on Indian Island. They were offered their position as temporary servants by the current owner, Mr. Owen, by letter and had never met him personally.

The Voice accuses Mr. and Mrs. Rogers of bringing about the death of Jennifer Brady in 1929. Fact: Mr. and Mrs. Rogers had been in service with Miss Brady, an invalid who needed to inhale a dose of amyl nitrite whenever she had an attack of a certain cardiac ailment. One evening a storm caused the telephone to be out of order and when Miss Brady had an attack, Mr. Rogers went out "as quickly as he could" to fetch the doctor, but the doctor arrived too late. Miss Brady died and there was no way for anyone to know if the Rogers had given her the dose of amyl nitrite. Mr. and Mrs. Rogers then received a tidy legacy.

Sir Thomas Legge, Assistant Commissioner at Scotland Yard

Inspector Maine of Scotland Yard

COMMENTS

And Then There Were None is probably Agatha Christie's best known murder mystery. It is incredibly suspenseful and baffling and the ending is shocking. The book is a unique masterpiece.

It is scarcely possible to comment further on this book without hinting at its ending. The characterizations are as good as those in other Christie novels of the period, but it is the sequence of events and the mounting suspense and bafflement that make it a memorable—or better stated, an *unforgettable*—experience.

As usual with Christie's detective novels of the late 1930s there are numerous references to psychology. The subject of "homicidal maniacs" is brought up in a conversation, and the private thoughts of one character include the phrase "repressed during childhood" as she thinks about one of the other characters.

One of the characters describes himself as having a contradictory set of passions: a strong, lifelong desire to kill, along with an equally strong, lifelong belief in justice and in the idea that the innocent must not be harmed. These "passions" are presented as explanations for his choice of career.

Regarding children and Agatha Christie's attitude towards them, the one child of importance mentioned in the book is repeatedly described in a character's thoughts as "a horrid, whiny, spoilt little brat." For a discussion of Christie's generally negative portrayals of children in her writing, see the *Comments* section for the 1942 *The Body in the Library*.

Regarding the money values mentioned in *And Then There Were None*, the games mistress who goes to the island in order to take a job as secretary to the lady of the house receives five pounds in cash "for expenses." Five pounds was evidently enough for train and taxi fares from London to the south coast of Devon, and for any new clothing that she would have required for the trip. One character receives a hundred guineas (one hundred five pounds) in cash—in advance—as an incentive to place himself in a "dangerous" situation on Indian Island—a sum that he does not hesitate to accept in exchange for placing himself in harm's way. A fabulous automobile which provokes the admiration of young men and small boys is assumed to have cost "hundreds and hundreds" by a minor character. Recall that in *Easy to Kill,* which was also published in 1939, the secretary to a millionaire earned six pounds weekly. These comments are intended to remind the reader of the high value of the British pound in the late 1930s as compared with its value today.

Two different characters voice Agatha Christie's conviction that "to be born into money" is much better than "to earn money." An old sailor, who operates a motorboat service to the island, remembers the kinds of parties that used to take place on the island when it was owned by a wealthy American. He is surprised by the present, strange assortment of somewhat ordinary people who are going to the island. His thoughts:

> There was only one satisfactory passenger in the boat. The last gentleman, the one who had arrived in the car (and what a car! A car such as had never been seen in Sticklehaven before. Must have cost hundreds and hundreds, a car like that.) He was the right kind. Born to money, he was. If the party had been all like him, he'd understand it…

The driver of the car which "must have cost hundreds and hundreds" is an irresponsible young man whose main concern seems to be whether or not the hosts at Indian Island will be generous with drinks. His thoughts:

> "Hope they'd do one well in drinks. Never knew with these fellows who'd made their money and weren't born to it."

Evidently it has been his experience that people who have worked hard and earned their money are careful spenders when entertaining.

SUMMARY FOR THE 1930S

Agatha Christie's Belgian private investigator Hercule Poirot, created in approximately 1915 or 1916 for her first detective novel, *The Mysterious Affair at Styles* (published in 1920) appeared in four more novels during the 1920s and in twelve of her seventeen detective novels published during the 1930s. Miss Jane Marple, created in 1930 for *Murder at the Vicarage,* did not reappear at all during the 1930s except in a group of short stories. The 1930s were definitely the "Golden Age of Hercule Poirot."

Christie's skill with characterization reached its full maturity with the 1933 *Thirteen at Dinner,* and remained outstanding from that point onwards.

The treatment of psychology as a true science, in Christie's detective novels, begins approximately with the 1935 *The A.B.C. Murders* and characterizes all of her novels for the rest of the decade, and to a somewhat lesser degree in all future decades of her career. Christie will always be aware, however, of popular misconceptions about psychology and from time to time there will be characters with "half baked" ideas about psychology who will be a source of humor in her future novels. The school headmistress Miss Amphrey in the 1944 *Towards Zero* comes to mind, as well Colonel Easterbrook in the 1950 *A Murder Is Announced,* Colin McNabb in the 1955 *Hickory, Dickory, Death,* and Miss Rowan in the 1959 *Cat Among the Pigeons.*

British ethnocentricity, expressed in early Christie novels in the form of stereotypical, mostly negative, characterizations of most foreign characters, is now expressed only by the servant class, which continues to be "suspicious of foreigners," and by the aging military types such as the "retired Anglo-Indian colonels" who bore the other characters with their stories about India and the glories of the Empire. Anti-Semitic remarks that dotted the pages of early novels are absent by the late 1930s and will never again appear in Christie's writing. The most offensive ones in the earliest novels had in fact been edited out of the American editions.

Disparaging comments about British hypocrisy in sexual and other matters—coming in the 1920s from characters such as the cynical, gold-digging French mistress of Derek Kettering in *The Mystery of the Blue Train,* now flow freely from scientific minds such as that of Dr. Gerard in *Appointment with Death* and, of course, endlessly from the extremely continental Hercule Poirot.

When Christie wrote *The Mysterious Affair at Styles,* she was a young woman of about twenty-five. When she completed *And Then There Were None* in 1939 she was a mature woman of forty-nine, nearly ten years into her second marriage and a person with a much richer cultural experience. Gradually Hercule Poirot, portrayed as an intensely "eccentric" foreigner in the earliest novels, has become "Papa Poirot," the man who understands psychology, sees facts for what they are, detests hypocrisy and scoffs at foolish optimism. Twice in novels of the 1930s he comments that the British "labor under the false notion that theirs is a free country." He has become a voice of common sense and reason and is no longer just a clown with a streak of genius for solving mysteries.

Although the Hastings character is well known to all Christie fans, it may be a surprise to some readers that Hastings appeared only eight times in the thirty-three novels that feature Hercule Poirot—three times in the 1920s, four times during the 1930s, and then once during the 1970s. Those eight appearances were:

The Mysterious Affair at Styles (1920); *Murder on the Links* (1923); *The Big Four* (1927); *Peril at End House* (1932); *Thirteen at Dinner* (1933); *The A.B.C. Murders* (1935); *Poirot Loses a Client* (1937); *Curtain* (1975).

The Scotland Yard inspector most often associated with Hercule Poirot is, of course, Inspector James Japp, but his appearances, too, are rarer in the Poirot novels than most readers probably realize. He appeared in just seven of the Poirot novels:

The Mysterious Affair at Styles (1920); *The Big Four* (1927); *Peril at End House* (1932); *Thirteen at Dinner* (1933); *Death in the Air* (1935); *The A.B.C. Murders* (1935); *The Patriotic Murders* (1940).

Although Inspector Japp was introduced in *The Mysterious Affair at Styles,* his interactions with Hercule Poirot were minimal in that story and the two men did not work together in any way. Japp's appearances were also minimal in *The Big Four, Peril at End House,* and *The A.B.C. Murders.* Only in *Thirteen at Dinner, Death in the Air* and *The Patriotic Murders* can Inspector Japp be thought of as a major character with whom Hercule Poirot interacted frequently, and he never appeared in a novel again after 1940.

As to Hercule Poirot himself, Christie featured him less frequently during the remaining decades of her career. He appears in just six of the thirteen novels she published during the 1940s, five of the twelve novels published during the 1950s, three of the nine novels published in the 1960s, and two of the six novels published in the 1970s.

A person who had never read an Agatha Christie detective novel, and wished for a "good Christie experience" for his first one, might be advised to make his selection from Christie's novels of the 1930s. Good choices for that person would be *Peril at End House, Thirteen at Dinner, Death in the Air,* and *Death on the Nile. And Then There Were None* might be suggested as a fourth or fifth Christie experience. After that, all the rest of Christie's remaining novels should be read in chronological order.

Sad Cypress (1940)

SETTING

The story takes place in July and August of 1939 with a murder trial taking place in October. The setting is the fictitious village of Maidensford in Berkshire, a county just a few miles west of London. Maidensford has an inn called the King's Arms—which is described as being clean and serving good meals—and also a baker's, a dairy and a grocery, and a café called The Blue Tit. On the edge of the village is an impressive country estate called Hunterbury. The grounds of Hunterbury are probably surrounded by hedges or walls, for there is a lodge occupied by the lodgekeeper and his daughter. See the *Appendix* for an explanation of the term "lodge."

The main house is not described in very much detail except that it is very large and for that reason will be difficult to sell despite the fact that it has been thoroughly updated with gas and electric lighting. "Thoroughly updated" evidently does not necessarily include central heating, as all of the rooms derive their heat individually from fireplaces. There is a ground-floor room called the "morning room" where a murder by poisoning takes place, and a library with a massive writing table. There is a scene in the kitchen and pantry of this large home, and one or two scenes in an upstairs bedroom. The décor of these rooms is not described but we learn that in the drawing room there is a large "secretaire" desk—a "somewhat flamboyant piece of inlaid marquetry" and some chairs in the same style.

No contemporary historical events or conditions are mentioned, although the actor Clark Gable is named as starring in a current film about "one of those millionaire blokes who neglected his wife, and then she pretended she'd done the dirty on him." The character describing this movie uses the expression "at the movies" rather than the expression "at the pictures" which was more usual in British speech in earlier times, and at least one other character also uses the expression "the movies" in this novel.

Women's clothing, hairstyles and makeup are not mentioned at all except for the habitual black dress of an old housekeeper.

In earlier novels, Christie's characters often used the derogatory ethnic word "Bosche" in referring to Germans. As recently as 1937, in *Death on the Nile,* Colonel Race describes the Austrian Dr. Bessner as "a kind of Bosche." In *Sad Cypress,* there are no derogatory references to Germans or to Germany. Two young girls of the household are said to have spent a year or two in Germany "being finished," which must have been a bit unusual, as upper-middle class English girls were routinely sent to France for that purpose, French being the far more important language on an international level than German. In two earlier novels, Christie had described Germans as "slurping their soup" as they ate, and the characterizations of Germans in general had never been flattering, although all of these "characterizations" were expressed through comments made by other characters, never by an unseen narrator voicing the thoughts of the author.

Most sources state 1940 as the earliest copyright date for the novel, but some state it as being 1939. In any case, Britain was clearly headed for war with Germany as the novel was being written, both Austria and Czechoslovakia having been annexed to Germany in 1938, and Poland being invaded and defeated in September of 1939. The fall of France, Belgium, the Netherlands and Norway took place in 1940 and the Battle of Britain was just around the corner. The mood in England at the beginning of World War II was one of extreme depression and fear, as both France and Britain had practiced a policy of "appeasement" towards Germany in a failed effort to avoid war, and neither country was prepared for an invasion. Christie's avoidance of derogatory references to Germans may be attributable to caution, as there was no certainty that Germany would be defeated.

There is an amusing reference to the British Royal Family. Hercule Poirot has become very skilled at ingratiating himself with persons likely to resist his questions. Knowing that the reactionary housekeeper at Hunterbury is a close follower of all Royal activities, Poirot pretends to be interested in discussing with her the problem of "finding a suitable husband for the young Princess." That Princess was, of course, the future Queen Elizabeth who was a teenager at the time. As usual, Poirot is successful and soon has the housekeeper eating out of his hand.

Two automobile makes are mentioned: the "Ford Ten," which is probably an English-made Ford, much smaller than the American Ford of the time. There is also a "smooth Daimler," a luxury model.

The speed of "modern" air travel makes it possible for two witnesses to be brought to England from distant New Zealand in time for the trial.

There are references to honeysuckle and roses blooming, as the story takes place during summer, and the general beauty of summer greenery contributes to atmosphere, as one character wanders through a wooded area and enjoys the sunlight filtering through the trees.

Story

It is summer of 1939. Elinor Carlisle and Roddy Welman are cousins who have been close friends since early childhood. They are not actually blood relatives—Elinor is the niece of aging Laura Welman while Roddy is the nephew of old Mrs. Welman's long-deceased husband. Their friendship is deep rooted and as they have grown into adulthood they have both felt that they would be happy as a married couple one day, although Elinor is not sure that Roddy cares for her as much as she does for him.

One day Elinor receives an anonymous letter signed "Well Wisher." Written in an illiterate style, suggesting a low level of education in the writer, the letter warns that a certain person has been "sucking up" to Mrs. Welman and that Mrs. Welman may make *her* her sole heir, and deprive Elinor and Roddy of what is "rightly theirs." Though Elinor and Roddy are disgusted by the letter, they begin to worry that Mrs. Welman may in fact be planning to leave her considerable fortune to young Mary Gerrard, the daughter of the lodgekeeper at Hunterbury, Mrs. Welman's gracious estate. The pair visits their aunt, finding that Mary Gerrard has indeed ingratiated herself with Mrs. Welman. Furthermore, Roddy instantly falls hopelessly in love with Mary despite years of an informal engagement to Elinor.

Mrs. Welman suffers a severe stroke (the last of many) and a few days later she dies, just before she is able to speak with her lawyer in the matter of making provisions in her Will for Mary. Elinor inherits Hunterbury and all of Mrs. Welman's fortune.

Soon Mary Gerrard dies of a poison that has been put into her tea or some sandwiches that she ate. Elinor Carlisle is arrested, tried and condemned to hang for the murders of both Mrs. Welman and Mary Gerrard.

The reader learns all of these facts at the beginning of the book, but the story actually begins when Hercule Poirot is summoned to the village by the local doctor, who believes that Elinor is innocent. The doctor begs Poirot to find evidence that will cast at least some doubt about Elinor's guilt. From that point onwards, Hercule Poirot conducts a private investigation which, of course, leads to the truth.

Characters

Laura Welman, a wealthy, aging, childless widow. She is in declining health and is bedridden at her beautiful old home, Hunterbury. She is being cared for by a private duty nurse, the local district nurse, and by young Mary Gerrard, the daughter of the lodgekeeper. Mrs. Welman has shown unusual interest in this young girl, providing her with a deluxe education, including two years on the Continent at a finishing school.

Mrs. Welman is also very fond of her niece and nephew, Elinor Carlisle and Roddy Welman, and has always hoped that they would marry and live together at Hunterbury one day. But she has always given the rather Victorian advice to Elinor to avoid showing too much love to a man. Men do not like devotion, she affirms. They feel it as possessiveness.

Henry Welman, Laura Welman's husband who died young of double pneumonia, leaving Laura a very young and childless widow. He was "comfortably off" when he married Laura, but she had been an heiress and was very wealthy in her own right.

Elinor Katharine Carlisle, Laura Welman's only living blood relative, who lives in London. Both of her parents are dead. During childhood she had spent many summers with her cousin, Roddy, at Hunterbury and had been led to believe that she and Roddy would inherit Aunt Laura's estate and wealth upon her death. Just exactly *who* would inherit—Elinor or Roddy—was not important, because the two of them have always planned to marry one day.

Although Elinor loves Roddy with all her heart, she is careful not to express this strong love, having been advised by older females in the family—including Aunt Laura—that a man should never be "too sure" that he is loved.

Roderick (Roddy) Welman, Laura Welman's nephew—that is to say, the son of her husband's brother and therefore a "nephew by marriage." On the subject of "not showing too much love for a man," Roddy is apparently fascinated by Elinor's not showing too much love for him.

> "You're adorable, Elinor," he tells her. "That little air of yours—aloof—untouchable—*la Princesse Lointaine*. It's that quality of yours that made me love you..."

Despite these charming remarks, the moment Roddy lays eyes on Mary Gerrard he falls in love with her and forgets Elinor completely.

Mary Gerrard, the beautiful daughter of the lodgekeeper at Hunterbury, and therefore a girl of the "lower classes" but who has a level of education and sophistication "far above her class" thanks to the special attention paid to her by Mrs. Welman. Most of the people in the village find it unfitting for a girl of her class to have "risen out of it," including her father, who is the most strident, but also a young working class man in the village who had hoped to marry her, the old housekeeper at Hunterbury, and even Elinor and Roddy themselves.

Mary is grateful to Mrs. Welman for all she has done for her and understands that she will be "provided for" in some way that will help her to train for some kind of work. She does not encourage Roddy's attentions, reminding him that he is engaged to Elinor. Mary dies of a poison that was put into her tea or some sandwiches.

Effraim Gerrard, the lodgekeeper and Mary's aging father who resents her "fine airs and graces," which he perceives to be inappropriate for a girl of their class. He has, in fact, never liked Mary very much, ever since she was a small child.

Eliza Gerrard, Effraim Gerrard's deceased wife, Mary's mother

Eileen O'Brien, a private duty nurse who, along with others, cares for Laura Welman in the last weeks of her life. She is Irish, cheerful and talkative, and when she talks, you could "cut her brogue with a knife," according to Elinor.

Jessie Hopkins, the district nurse who visits Mrs. Welman and several other patients in the neighborhood daily. She has a reputation for being a major gossip.

Peter Lord, the young doctor who finds Mrs. Welman to have died of "natural causes." He is a young man of thirty-two with sandy hair, a pleasantly ugly freckled face and a remarkably square jaw. His eyes are a keen piercing light blue.

Those of us who have read all of Agatha Christie's novels know that a man with a "pleasantly ugly" face can do no wrong. It's the handsome ones who *may* be bad guys, although they may not be. Tommy Beresford *(The Secret Adversary)* and Bill Eversleigh *(The Secret of Chimneys* and *The Seven Dials Mystery)* were both "pleasantly ugly," and in the 1966 *Third Girl*, Dr. Stillingfleet will be "attractively ugly." The "pleasantly ugly" men also blush profusely whenever anyone suggests that they may have noticed the good looks of a female. In this story, when Mrs. Welman asks what he thinks of her niece Elinor, Dr. Lord goes "suddenly scarlet ... his very eyebrows blushed..." He obviously feels a strong attraction to Elinor and it is he who, after Elinor's trial and conviction, appeals to Hercule Poirot to reinvestigate the case.

When asked why he does not plan to specialize, as most young doctors seem to want to do, Dr. Lord replies that he enjoys working with the ordinary illnesses and will be content to remain a country doctor for the rest of his life, until he grows old and a younger man comes to the village with "fresh new ideas," and older villagers resist the younger man and say "Oh, but old Dr. Lord has been here for so long and he's so kind..." etc.

The dichotomy of the "older, more experienced doctor" vs. the "younger, more up-to-date doctor" has already occurred in several of Christie's novels, most recently in *Easy to Kill* in which old Dr. Humbleby and young Dr. Thomas do not get along because the older doctor is popular despite the younger doctor's being better qualified. Here, in *Sad Cypress,* the old housekeeper, Mrs. Bishop, expresses the view that old Dr. Ransome is preferable to young Dr. Lord, because he "has been here *many* years!"

Jim Partington and his Sisters, friends of Roddy and Elinor. Their mother had gone out to the Riviera, had fallen for a handsome Italian, and left every penny to him. Her children were unable to upset the Will. These facts are mentioned by Roddy to Elinor as evidence that a speedy visit to Aunt Laura might not be a bad idea, in view of the suggestions made in the anonymous letter that Elinor received.

Emma Bishop, the housekeeper at Hunterbury, who has been in service there for eighteen years. She is a very conservative type who is suspicious of the very foreign-appearing Hercule Poirot, but he has become expert in turning such people's special prejudices to his advantage. The following scene is a superb touch of Christie humor, as Hercule Poirot melts the armor of the foreigner-despising Emma Bishop:

> In the awesome majesty of Mrs. Bishop's black-clad presence Hercule Poirot sat humbly insignificant.
> The thawing of Mrs. Bishop was no easy matter. For Mrs. Bishop, a lady of conservative habits and views, strongly disapproved of foreigners. And a foreigner most indubitably Hercule Poirot was. Her responses were frosty and she eyed him with disfavor and suspicion.
> Hercule Poirot was persuasive. He was adroit. But charm he never so wisely, Mrs. Bishop remained aloof and implacable.
> Hercule Poirot played his last card. He recounted with naïve pride a recent visit of his to Sandringham. He spoke with admiration of the graciousness and delightful simplicity and kindness of Royalty. [Note: Sandringham is a large estate in the county of Norfolk, owned by the Royal Family and used as a vacation spot at certain times of the year.]
> Mrs. Bishop, who followed daily in the court circular the exact movements of Royalty, was overborne. After all, if They had sent for Mr. Poirot—Well, naturally, that made All the Difference. Foreigner or no foreigner, who was she, Emma Bishop, to hold back where Royalty had led the way?
> Presently she and M. Poirot were engaged in pleasant conversation on a really interesting theme—no less than the selection of a suitable future husband for the Princess.
> Having finally exhausted all possible candidates as Not Good Enough, the talk reverted to less exalted circles.

Thereafter, Poirot has Mrs. Bishop eating out of his hand.

Sir Lewis Rycroft, who died in 1917 in the Great War, and who was a good friend of Mrs. Welman. He was a good enough friend, in fact, to warrant his photograph's being kept in a locked drawer in Mrs. Welman's bedroom forever. Sir Lewis's wife had been in an asylum for several years before he went off to war.

Ted Bigland, the son of a local farmer who works in Henderson's Garage down the road, a "fair young giant." He was in love with Mary Gerrard but felt that all of her schooling placed her above him.

Rufus Bigland, Ted Bigland's father, a farmer.

Old Mrs. Caldecott and Eliza Ryken, patients of District Nurse Hopkins

Mr. Seddon of Seddon, Blatherwick & Seddon, Mrs. Welman's lawyer, who had tried unsuccessfully to persuade her to make a Will many times, only to hear her say, "I don't expect to die just yet." Not an outstanding lawyer, he seems to be fond of those trite phrases "highly irregular," and "most improper." Poirot explains that he is working in the interests of Elinor Carlisle, at the request of Dr. Lord.

> Mr. Seddon's eyebrows rose very high. "Indeed! That seems to me very irregular—very irregular. The arrangements for Miss Carlisle's defense are entirely in our hands. I really do not think we need any outside assistance in this case."
> Poirot asked, "Is that because your client's innocence will be so easily proved?"
> Mr. Seddon winced. Then he became wrathful in a dry legal fashion. "That," he said, "is a most improper question. Most improper."

Mary Riley, Mary Gerrard's aunt in New Zealand, and her only living relative, her mother's sister. Mary Gerrard makes a Will leaving everything to her Aunt Mary.

Sir George Kerr, the former local M.P. who has died recently

Major Somervell, the current M.P., who purchases Hunterbury from Elinor Carlisle for 12,500 pounds.

Mr. Abbott, the grocer who sells Elinor Carlisle two pots of fish paste

Horlick, the tall, good-looking undergardener at Hunterbury who notices a certain automobile parked near the house on the day that Mary Gerrard dies. Like the other servants, he had hoped that Hunterbury would remain with the family after the death of Mrs. Welman, and he hopes to remain there himself as gardener for the new owner, Major Somervell.

Mrs. Parkinson, Old Nellie, and That Poor Creature Who's Not All There at Ivy Cottage, people in the village among whom Nurse Hopkins plans to distribute Mrs. Welman's clothing.

Dr. Ransome, young Dr. Lord's predecessor, preferred by the crusty housekeeper, Mrs. Bishop.

Colonel Randolph and Mrs. Dacres, examples of people who had left their fortunes to strangers instead of to their own flesh and blood

Chief Inspector Marsden of Scotland Yard, who assures Hercule Poirot of Elinor Carlisle's guilt

A Couple of Giggling Girls, servants of young Dr. Lord

Dr. Alan Garcia, a distinguished analyst who analyzes the contents of Mary Gerrard's stomach after her death, finding morphine

Inspector Brill, the officer who finds the poison label on the floor in the kitchen at Hunterbury the day that Mary Gerrard dies

Emily Biggs and Roger Wade, confectioners' assistants who witness the signing of Mary Gerrard's Will

Alfred James Wargrave, a rose grower from Emsworth, Berkshire, a neighboring town, and an expert witness

James Arthur Littledale, a chemist with the wholesale chemists Jenkins and Hale who is familiar with poison labels

Amelia Mary Sedley, of Bonaba, Auckland, New Zealand, an acquaintance of a certain Mary Draper, whose maiden name was Mary Riley

Edward John Marshall, of Deptford, New Zealand, another acquaintance of the above-named Mary Draper

Sir Samuel Attenbury, representing the Crown in the trial of Elinor Carlisle

Sir Edwin Bulmer, attorney for the defense of Elinor Carlisle. Sir Edwin is known as "the forlorn hope man."

FRENCH INTO ENGLISH

Note: Very little French occurs in this novel. Hercule Poirot's first appearance is in Chapter 8. He refrains from using French in nearly all of his conversation.

Chapter 1
La Princesse Lointaine—The Distant Princess

Chapter 8
eh bien—well...
Mon Dieu—Good heavens
C'est difficile—It's difficult

Chapter 10
tête à tête—private one-on-one conversation

Chapter 16
mon cher—my friend
Eh bien—well...

Chapter 18
comme ça—just like that

Chapter 26
Mon cher—My friend
C'est l'enfantillage—That was childishness

COMMENTS

Sad Cypress has an interesting and unique structure, as it begins with a Prologue in which a murder trial is about to begin and we read the thoughts of the accused woman as the prosecuting attorney introduces the case against her. After this short Prologue we wonder if she is guilty or innocent. Then we read about all of the events that led to her arrest and indictment and we see that there is good reason to believe that she is guilty. Finally, Hercule Poirot comes into the story, much later than usual—almost half way through the novel, in fact—and he has the same impression of her guilt that we have. He works his way through the evidence and listens for himself to what everyone has to say—paying special attention to their lies—and finally he knows the truth.

Hercule Poirot has a special problem in this novel: he must interact with people in an English village with no "proper Englishman" to pave the way. In *The Murder of Roger Ackroyd*, Dr. Sheppard introduced him to everyone in the village, and that made him accepted, since Dr. Sheppard was a respected member of the community. In *Poirot Loses a Client*, the fact that Poirot had his "very British friend Hastings" with him most of the time made conversations with the villagers in that novel possible. But in *Sad Cypress*, although Poirot is introduced by young Dr. Lord, he encounters unusual resistance from the "English village" cast. He finds it necessary to go to great lengths to ingratiate himself with them, even pretending to be interested in the British Royal Family and who the future Queen's husband should be. Agatha Christie later commented that Poirot "did not belong" in *Sad Cypress*. She was probably right, and a character such as Miss Marple might have been a better choice for a sleuth, her "Nosy Parker" personality being right at home with the other village gossips. Miss Marple had been introduced ten years earlier in *Murder at the Vicarage*, but she must not have interested

Christie or her readers very much. With the exception of a group of short stories published a couple of years after *Murder at the Vicarage,* Christie never featured Miss Marple again in that decade, allowing Poirot to dominate the 1930s with no fewer than twelve appearances in novels.

Sad Cypress, though clearly one of Agatha Christie's *detective* novels, and one of her best, is also a rather serious story about love relationships, something that may not appeal very much to a reader who is interested only in reading an interesting detective story. As early as the late 1920s Christie evidently wished to write more "serious" literature and with some effort managed to prevail upon her English publisher to accept a "straight" novel, publishing it in 1930 under the pseudonym Mary Westmacott. She wrote a total of six "straight" novels under that name, keeping its true identity a secret even from friends for at least fifteen years. In all of them, love relationships seem to be the main issues, and some critics have described them as "women's fiction."

Christie's desire to make a study of love relationships is something that shows itself in *Sad Cypress* more than in any previous detective novel, and it will occur rather often in her detective novels of the 1940s, making them a bit tedious to certain readers. *There Is a Tide, Murder After Hours* and *Remembered Death* come to mind as the best examples of "not very typical Agatha Christie detective stories" because they are actually stories about love relationships more than they are "detective stories."

Christie herself may have been somewhat uncomfortable with the "love" aspect of *Sad Cypress,* and perhaps even a bit embarrassed by it, as in the following conversation between Mrs. Welman and her niece, Elinor:

> Elinor said gravely, "I care for Roddy enough and not too much."
> Mrs. Welman nodded approval. "I think, then, you'll be happy. Roddy needs love—but he doesn't like violent emotion. He'd shy off from possessiveness."
> Elinor said with feeling, "You know Roddy very well!"
> Mrs. Welman said, "If Roddy cares for you just a *little* more than you care for him—well, that's all to the good."
> Elinor said sharply, "Aunt Agatha's Advice Column. '*Keep your boy friend guessing! Don't let him be too sure of you!*'"

It can be no accident that Christie chose the name "Agatha" for that amusing line. She seems to be, in a way, laughing at herself for creating this "love" element in the story, although without an understanding of the love relationship, it would be difficult to establish the strong murder motive that the situation requires.

It was mentioned, in the *Comments* section of *Appointment with Death,* that a certain character introduced, for the first time in a Christie detective novel, the notion that "working for a living might just be something *meritorious.*" (Christie wrote, during the 1960s in her *Autobiography,* that the notion of work's being *meritorious* was a silly idea.) Actually the character in that novel calls work "a good tonic for the male sex" even if it is not necessary for the man to earn a living. In *Sad Cypress,* Roddy Welman has occasion to say that he "maintains his self respect" by working even though his rich aunt provides him with handouts to save him the trouble, and he expects to share in the inheritance of a fortune one day. Obviously the idea that work might actually be a good thing for people must have been something that bothered Christie, at least a little, since it has begun to creep into her characters' thinking, even in minor ways. But that old German proverb *Die Arbeit macht das Leben züss* (Work makes life sweet) must have been something that Christie would not have understood.

Agatha Christie began to "preach" against education for the lower classes in the 1939 *Easy to Kill* with a character who comments, "Education is too highly rated nowadays." In *Sad Cypress,* several characters are annoyed by the fact that a girl of the "lower classes" has been given an education that she should not have had. During a conversation in which Elinor and Roddy discuss Mary Gerrard and her father's resentment of her "fine airs and graces," Roddy makes the statement that giving someone education is often "cruelty, not kindness." The housekeeper at Hunterbury, Mrs. Bishop, would concur wholeheartedly with these statements, and she regards Mary as very much "above herself" as a result of her education. A variety of characters voice these opinions and we can take them as simply part of their characterization, if we like, or else we can feel that Agatha Christie is "preaching" at us on the subject. In her later novels she will make a point of downgrading the idea of education for the lower classes, especially when education is promoted as a deterrent to crime. It is known that Christie loved the idea of a "servant class" which was "actively happy and appreciated," as she stated in her *Autobiography,* and that she saw the demise of the "servant class" as a great misfortune for society. Nothing wipes out a "servant class" more effectively than education. If Christie had been an American in the 1850s she probably would have said, "Slaves are actively happy and appreciated" and that freeing them would be "cruelty, not kindness."

Naturally, Christie again reminds us, through the words of one or two characters, that the quality of servants has diminished. In this story it is Nurse Hopkins who affirms that servant girls can't do a decent day's work nowadays, but nurses themselves always take a beating in Agatha Christie's stories. Old Effraim, Mary Gerrard's father, says that nurses are "full of cheerfulness over other people's troubles," and Mrs. Welman is annoyed by all nurses because they always seem to think you'd like a nice cup of tea at five in the morning. Nurses in Christie novels are invariably pessimists, too, and are surprised whenever a patient recovers. In this story, when Mrs. Welman dies, one nurse remarks to the other that "the doctor will be surprised," and the other replies, with a tinge of disapproval, "He's always so *hopeful* about his cases." The other nurse then says, "Ah, he's young! He hasn't our experience."

Although there is not very much humor in *Sad Cypress,* there is the hilarious scene, mentioned above, in which Hercule Poirot ingratiates himself with the ultra-conservative housekeeper Mrs. Bishop by pretending to care about the "important subject" of choosing a proper husband for the future Queen of England. Mrs. Bishop follows every movement of the Royal Family. Christie, although she loved the idea of keeping "the servant class" well in its place without education, was not particularly impressed by the aristocratic class, which was *above* her. In other words, the idea of a "class system" was a good one, as long as she was a member of one of the upper ones. Aristocrats in all of her novels are most often silly old, harmless, good-natured fuddy-duddies. Their more intelligent offspring, such as Lady Eileen Brent *(The Secret of Chimneys* and *The Seven Dials Mystery)* and Lady Frances Derwent *(The Boomerang Clue)* happily associate with non-aristocrats and even marry them, with the full approval of their fuddy-duddy fathers (they never have mothers, of course, who might object. For a discussion of the relative absence of mothers in Christie's stories, see the *Comments* section for the 1937 *Poirot Loses a Client.)*

It is well known, of course, that Agatha Christie became Dame Agatha—first by being married to a man who received a knighthood because of his achievements in archeology, and then later for her own achievements as a writer of internationally recognized merit. She very happily accepted this expression of recognition from the monarchy, and was extremely honored to have tea with Her Majesty in connection with it. But she laughed up her sleeve at the aristocracy and at all people who were impressed with it for its own sake, and her satirical portrayal of Mrs. Bishop's devotion to The Royal Family in *Sad Cypress* is ample proof of that. Christie had expressed the same idea in the 1934 *The Boomerang Clue* when Lady Frances Derwent fooled her father's lawyer into believing that he had been impersonated by "The young duke of ... oh, but that would be telling..." whereupon the lawyer instantly forgave the impersonator. And she told Bobby that her father's lawyer "eats out of my hand. Very useful things, titles."

Again the subject of money values must be introduced because in 1939 they had nothing in common with today's values. In this novel, Mrs. Welman has a "fortune" of 200,000 pounds (the equivalent of several million pounds today) and after her death, Elinor Carlisle settles upon the servants the following generous sums:

> Five hundred pounds to the housekeeper, who has been in her position for eighteen years;
> Fifty pounds each to two of the maids, probably because they also have been with the family a long time;
> Twenty-five pounds to the head gardener, an old man with years of service
> Five pounds each to the rest of the servants

We may judge the value of the pound in 1939 by the fact that in the 1939 *Easy to Kill,* the private secretary to a wealthy businessman earns six pounds weekly, and in the 1946 *Murder After Hours,* a sales assistant in a Bond Street women's dress shop earns four pounds a week. In the 1948 *There Is a Tide,* a second gardener at a home in a fairly isolated village would be paid three pounds weekly. In the 1940 *The Patriotic Murders,* the fiancé of a dental assistant boasts about his "great new job" paying ten pounds a week and, therefore, his girl can "chuck her job and start shopping for her trousseau."

Considering the number of servants working at Hunterbury, it is safe to assume that the estate is a very large one; yet when Elinor Carlisle sells it to the current M.P. the price is just 12,500 pounds, even though it is "thoroughly modernized" with gas and electric lighting.

Psychology had been an important subject touched upon in Agatha Christie's novels since about 1935 but it has a very small role in *Sad Cypress,* except for a couple of remarks made by young Dr. Lord about the human face being a "mask" hiding emotions.

In *Sad Cypress* Christie introduces for the first time the idea of *euthanasia* in the conversations of a couple of the characters, although the word is not actually used. Mrs. Welman suggests to Dr. Lord that he might be well advised to "finish her off out of mercy," to which he replies that he does not relish the idea of being hanged, although he jokingly suggests that if she were to leave him her fortune, he might risk it. Elinor Carlisle and Roddy Welman also discuss the idea briefly, in a conversation about their Aunt Laura after she has suffered a second stroke, Elinor expressing the view that people ought to be "set free—if they themselves really want it" and Roddy pointing out that if people were allowed to put their aging relatives "out of their pain," some might kill even their healthy relations, human nature being what it is.

The Patriotic Murders (1940)

(Alternate Titles: *An Overdose of Death* and *One, Two, Buckle My Shoe*)

Setting

It is spring and summer of 1939 or 1940. No particular months are mentioned, but early in the story Hercule Poirot notices a bird building its nest outside his window—therefore it is spring—and as the weeks pass, there are eventual references to night scented stocks, Russell lupines and sweet Williams, all summer-flowering plants, as well as roses. Most of the action takes place in London, although there are scenes at a country residence near the fictitious town of Exsham in the county of Kent, just southeast of London, and two scenes at a residence in the town of Hertford, about thirty miles north of London.

The principal London setting is a house in Queen Charlotte Street, which is the home and professional office of a dentist and his partner. The only entrance and exit to the house is through the front door. The ground floor contains a waiting room for patients and probably other rooms for utility purposes. The next floor (the first floor in European terms) has the surgery and office of the dentist's partner; the second floor is the same size and layout as the first floor and is the surgery and office of the principal dentist (a murder victim dies here). On the third and fourth floors is the residence of the dentist and his sister; these two floors are described as a "maisonette." In addition to the stairways, there is a small elevator, operated by a page boy, serving all of the floors. There is also a basement which once had a rear entrance, but the entrance is now closed. The geography of this house has some importance, as the murder occurs in the second floor surgery and the elevator and stairs are both used by several characters in their movements. At least two different characters relate having seen, unobserved themselves, other characters as they watched from landings above.

If the house has central heating, it was installed in the building more recently than its original construction, as there is a fireplace even in the second-floor dental surgery.

Other London settings include Hercule Poirot's flat in Whitehaven Mansions, a modern block of luxury flats. The flat is not described but we know from previous novels that the décor is ultra modern, for that is Poirot's taste. There are scenes at a luxury home of a financier, called the Gothic House, described as a well known feature on Chelsea Embankment. The exterior is not described but the interior is "luxurious with an expensive simplicity." On the "first floor" (second floor in American terms) is a large library overlooking the river. On the lower floor, off the hall, is a small room where one brief scene takes place.

A block of flats called King Leopold Mansions, near Battersea Park, is another London setting just a short walk from the Gothic House. The apartment there is decorated in modern, but not especially expensive, style. The living-room is smartly furnished in an up-to-date style featuring a good deal of chrome and some large, square-looking easy chairs upholstered in a pale fawn geometric fabric. The bedroom in this apartment is also in a modern style with a rose-pink color scheme. Within the apartment is a small lumber and box room containing a large, metal chest for fur storage—it is in this sealed chest that a rotting corpse is discovered.

Other London settings include Logan's Corner House, a restaurant where Poirot meets with a young couple for a conversation, and Regent's Park where Poirot enjoys the spectacle of nursemaids being courted by their boyfriends while children sail toy boats in a pond.

There is a scene at a small house at Ealing, evidently a suburb of London, as Poirot arrives there by subway, exiting at Ealing Broadway station. The house is a five minute walk from the subway station, and its address is 88 Castelgardens Road. It is a small, semi-detached house and the neatness of the front garden draws an admiring nod from Hercule Poirot, as both the house and the garden are "admirably symmetrical."

A further London setting is the Holborn Palace Hotel, where Poirot makes a surprise, unwelcome visit to a suspect during his breakfast, and two scenes occur at the Glengowrie Court Hotel.

In the course of the story Poirot spends a couple of days as a houseguest at a home near the town of Exsham in the county of Kent, just southeast of London. This is a second home to the financier who lives at the Gothic House in London, and Hercule Poirot notes the same expensive simplicity within it that he had appreciated at the Gothic House. On this estate there is also a small, rustic cottage.

As to the settings in Hertfordshire, one is a small country cottage near Hertford which is not described at all; there is also a scene in a "derelict tea shop" in a nearby village.

The novel was written and published just after the beginning of World War II. Germany had annexed Austria and Czechoslovakia in 1938, and it was in September of 1939 that Poland was invaded and quickly defeated. If the action of the novel takes place in the summer of 1939, then the Polish invasion has not yet taken place, but if it is the summer of 1940, Poland, Belgium, the Netherlands, Norway and France have already fallen to the Nazis. There is no direct mention of the War and its fighting and invasions, but in a conversation between Poirot and his dentist there is a negative reference to Mussolini and Hitler. Both the dentist and Chief Inspector Japp cite a certain financier—another character in the novel—as being important to the stability of the present government and who is constantly being threatened by subversive elements and, therefore, requiring police protection. It is stated that several groups—including "the Reds"—would like to see him "put out of the way" and there are references to Nazi-like organizations within England itself. One character, a young man who is engaged to the dentist's secretary-assistant, is a member of one of these arm-band-wearing organizations.

Political difficulties for the British in India are also mentioned, and there are references to espionage activities in various places in Europe, including a fictitious country called Herjoslovakia, perhaps the same place as "Herzoslovakia" which played a part in *The Secret of Chimneys* fifteen years earlier. At one point in the story an Indian student in London fires a shot at a financier and the Prime Minister as they are leaving the P.M.'s residence in Downing Street.

The conflicting ideologies of these troubled times are expressed by at least five or six characters in the novel: a conservative dentist, a conservative financier, an ex-secret service man, and a Scotland Yard inspector, all representing the stability of the present government, and two young idealists who represent the "subversive" element, plus a wealthy young woman who is in love with one of the young idealists but who does not mind being one of the probable heirs of a fabulously wealthy financier. There is talk of "a few deaths of insignificant people" not being very important if their deaths assist in the maintenance of national stability, but Hercule Poirot is steadfast in his disapproval of the murder of innocents.

With all of this depressing international unrest as a background to the novel, it may seem petty to mention more frivolous contemporary backgrounds, but here goes. There are several references to radio—at King Leopold Mansions, for example, several tenants have radios and a police officer says that probably all of the tenants were listening to them when a murder took place and, therefore, would not have heard anything out of the way. Chief Inspector Japp mentions that Scotland Yard has published descriptions of a missing woman, and "even pulled in the B.B.C." in efforts to find her, the first reference in a Christie novel to that radio broadcasting company. The word "radio" occurs several times in *The Patriotic Murders*, for some reason, instead of the usual British term "wireless," but this may be true only of the American editions.

A female character mentions that she had a conversation with another woman about the new Ginger Rogers-Fred Astaire movie, one of a series of popular musicals of the 1930s. As to clothing fashion, a wealthy young woman at one point wears a Schiaparelli model in Regent's Park and her mother, in another scene, is described as being very smartly dressed, with a hat clinging to an eyebrow in the midst of a very *soignée* coiffure.

These are minor points, of course. A young boy, employed as a page at the dental office where the crime takes place, is an avid reader of "cheap detective fiction" and is currently enjoying *Murder at 11:45*, which he says is "an American novel, a real corker, all about gunmen." He is equally enthusiastic about luxury automobiles, and mentions that one patient arrived at the dentist's office in a Daimler, and another in a Rolls, both luxury makes. Later, there is a reference to a car of unnamed make:

> It was a car of sporting build—one of those cars from which it is necessary to wriggle from under the wheel in sections.

As usual, there are a few references to money values in 1939–1940. An ordinary undergardener is said to earn a weekly salary of two pounds, fifteen shillings (or perhaps a bit less, according to his employer). A dental assistant's boyfriend makes a special trip to the dentist's office to tell her about his "marvelous new job" which pays ten pounds weekly. He has no particular education or skills and a salary of ten pounds weekly is indeed very good for a person of his class. We recall that in a novel written about a year earlier, *Easy to Kill,* the efficient secretary of a millionaire earned six pounds a week.

Story

On a spring day in 1939 or 1940, Hercule Poirot makes his twice-annual visit to his dentist. Later that afternoon, Inspector Japp of Scotland Yard visits Poirot at his flat to tell him that Mr. Morley, the dentist, committed suicide in his surgery no more than an hour after Poirot's appointment. Having noted Poirot's name in the appointment book, Inspector Japp feels that Poirot may be interested, and indeed he is. During Poirot's appointment, Mr. Morley had been in the best of spirits. The dentist's sister, who shares his lodgings above the dental practice, had also stated that he had been his usual self earlier that morning, and so no suicide motive can be imagined.

Scotland Yard is not normally involved in suicide cases, but in this case Alistair Blunt, a wealthy financier and an important person in the British economy, was also a patient of Mr. Morley's that morning, and there have been threats against Mr. Blunt by numerous groups, including "the Reds" and a Nazi organization. Scotland Yard keeps a close watch over Mr. Blunt because of his importance to the stability of the government. As Inspector Japp expresses it, "In this country we look after people like Mr. Blunt."

An investigation of all of the people who were at the dental office that morning leads to a maze of interrelationships, the discovery that one of Mr. Morley's patients died in his hotel room a few hours after his appointment, and that another of that day's patients disappeared the same afternoon, her rotting corpse being found in a trunk several weeks later.

Hercule Poirot works his way through this maze and reveals a solution that is stunning in its simplicity.

Characters

Hercule Poirot, the Belgian private investigator with the egg-shaped head and flamboyant mustache. Although he frequently points out that "there is only one Hercule Poirot, he is unique," he is a mere mortal when it comes to visiting the dentist. His foreign appearance causes him, in this novel, to be treated as an insect by at least one very British character and two very American ones.

Mr. Henry Morley, Hercule Poirot's dentist. An hour after Poirot's dental treatment he is found lying on the floor of his surgery with a bullet hole in his temple. Did he commit suicide? His fingerprints, and no others, are found on the revolver lying on the floor near his hand. He seems to be a person without problems in his life, according to his devoted sister.

Georgina Morley, Henry Morley's devoted sister. She is convinced her brother did *not* commit suicide, as there is no conceivable reason for him to have done so.

Gladys Nevill, Mr. Morley's highly-satisfactory secretary-assistant who has worked for him for three years. Like most girls (at least in Agatha Christie's novels) she is attracted to the wrong kind of men. Gladys has a boyfriend who cannot hold a job and she refuses to give him up, despite the urgings of her concerned employer.

Frank Carter, Gladys Nevill's "unsuitable" suitor.

Alfred Biggs, the pageboy who has worked for Mr. Morley and Mr. Reilly for two weeks and has managed to do everything wrong. Among his shortcomings is his inability to pronounce the patients' names. One by one he shows Mr. Perrer, Colonel Arrowbumby, Mrs. Soap and Miss Some Berry Seal (Mr. Poirot, Colonel Abercrombie, Mrs. Soames and Miss Sainsbury-Seale) among others into the dental surgery on the day of Mr. Morley's death. He loves to read detective novels and thrillers and is currently reading "a real corker—an American novel all about gunmen." Despite Alfred's difficulty with names and his unfortunate taste in literature, he provides reliable accounts of the morning's activities at the dental office.

Mabelle Sainsbury-Seale, a patient of Mr. Morley who arrives at the office just as Poirot is leaving. She disappears that evening from the Glengowrie Court Hotel, leaving her clothing and luggage behind. A month later her body is found, with the face disfigured beyond recognition, hidden in a fur-storage chest at the apartment of a friend.

Mr. Reilly, Mr. Morley's dental partner who, in Georgina Morley's opinion, is unsatisfactory—and drinks too much. She does not specify in what way he is "unsatisfactory" except to remark that alcoholic breath does not inspire confidence while one is in the dentist's chair.

Mr. Amberiotis, described by Mr. Raikes as "that fat foreigner," and by Frank Carter as "an oily fat bloke." Mr. Amberiotis was another dental patient of Mr. Morley. A few hours later he died in his hotel room of an overdose of the anesthetic he had received by injection at the dentist's office. Was it an accidental overdose or did the dentist murder him deliberately? Mr. Amberiotis owns a small, struggling hotel in Greece but he is also known to have been a small-time blackmailer and had dabbled in espionage. Some people might have had a motive for killing him, but would a perfectly ordinary dentist like Mr. Morley have a motive?

Little Dimitri, someone who will benefit from Mr. Amberiotis's new "gold mine" and his benevolent nature

The Good Constantopopolous who, struggling with his little restaurant, will have pleasant surprises thanks to the benevolent nature of Mr. Amberiotis and his new "gold mine." What can this new "gold mine" be? Perhaps a new opportunity for blackmail?

Mrs. Bolitho, a tall, commanding female with a deep voice, staying at the Glengowrie Court Hotel, who urges Miss Sainsbury-Seale to keep her dental appointment even though her tooth has stopped aching.

Mr. Samuel Rotherstein, a member of a board of directors who notices something odd in Alistair Blunt's manner during the meeting.

Alistair Blunt, an extremely important financier, one of the most powerful men in England. He is in fact so important to the stability of the present Government that Scotland Yard keeps itself apprised of all of his movements, as there have been threats against his life from both the Communists and the Nazis, and it is exactly for those reasons that Scotland Yard is brought into the case of Mr. Morley's death. Alistair had visited Mr. Morley's dental practice on the day that Mr. Morley died.

Rebecca Sanseverato, Alistair Blunt's deceased wife, for whom he had functioned as "prince consort" until her untimely death.

Colonel Abercrombie, a dental patient of Mr. Reilly. In the waiting room at the dental office, the Colonel looks at Poirot

> "...with an air of one considering some noxious insect. It was not so much his gun he looked as though he wished he had with him, as his Flit spray."

The Colonel then snatches up the *Times,* turns his chair so as to avoid seeing Poirot, and settles down to read it.

[**Note:** Flit spray was a popular insecticide widely marketed during the 1930s. A hilarious scene in an old Laurel and Hardy comedy film shows Stan Laurel battling with a single fly, which is buzzing around and landing repeatedly on an elaborate wedding cake. Stan thoroughly saturates the fly—and the cake—with Flit spray.]

Howard Raikes, a young American of about thirty and easily the most unpleasant character in the story. He was yet another patient at the dental office—with an appointment with Mr. Reilly—but he left the office without keeping the appointment. Poirot visits Mr. Raikes at his hotel early one morning, at breakfast time. It is an extremely unpleasant interview in which Mr. Raikes accuses Poirot of being Alistair Blunt's "private dick" and then decries the capitalist system and established institutions in general. He ends his tirades with this statement about Alistair Blunt:

> "He's an obstruction in the way of progress and he's got to be removed. There's no room in the world today for men like Blunt..."

Unbelievably, Alistair Blunt's own niece is in love with Howard Raikes and is thrilled and inspired by his ideas.

Chief Inspector James Japp of Scotland Yard, whom we met in Christie's first novel, the 1920 *The Mysterious Affair at Styles* and then in several subsequent stories. It is in *The Patriotic Murders* that he makes his final appearance with Hercule Poirot, although there will be numerous references to him by Poirot in future novels. His chief qualities are a tendency to jump to conclusions and to accept easy solutions even in the face of contradictory evidence. In earlier novels he felt little respect for Hercule Poirot but over the years his attitude has changed. In this novel he works closely with Poirot for the first time since the 1935 *Death in the Air*. Still, as usual he prefers an easy solution and constantly accuses Poirot of "making things difficult" by pointing out facts that contradict the easy solution. "So there you are. It's a clear case," he often says, only to have the "clear case" disproved later. When that happens, he finds it necessary to "eat humble pie" and say things like, "Poirot, you're the goods!" In this novel, Japp visits Poirot at his flat specifically to apologize and to tell Poirot that he was right in believing that Mr. Morley was murdered.

A Constable who opens the door at the dental surgery for Poirot and Japp when they arrive

A Man with a Camera who photographs the corpse of Mr. Morley

Miss Kirby, a dental patient who had an appointment with Mr. Morley at 12:30 p.m. and who left in an irate manner when not called by the dentist by 1:15 p.m.

A Divisional Surgeon who examines Mr. Morley's body

Faithful George, Hercule Poirot's manservant whom we have known since *The Mystery of the Blue Train* but whose appearances, so far, have been rare. Poirot explains the entire problem to George, hoping to benefit from George's insights, but George offers only the following pronouncement:

> "It strikes me, that you will have to find another dentist to attend to your teeth in the future, sir."
> Hercule Poirot said, "You surpass yourself, George."

We know that George is a good cook, because in a previous novel he prepared an excellent omelet for Poirot's consumption. In all other respects, however, he is absolutely British. During Poirot's explanation of the case, his only remarks are "Quite so, quite so" and, when Mr. Amberiotis is mentioned, he says, "These foreigners, sir..."

Gladys Nevill's Aunt in Somerset who did *not* suffer a stroke and was surprised to see Gladys when she arrived unexpectedly

Mrs. Soames, a patient of Mr. Morley who, earlier in the day, had visited him about her new plate.

Betty Heath, a nine-year-old dental patient of Mr. Reilly who was seen earlier in the morning.

Mrs. Heath, Betty Heath's mother who brought her to her dental appointment.

Lady Grant, whose dental appointment with Mr. Morley was just before Hercule Poirot's.

Jane Olivera, Alistair Blunt's niece by marriage. She is in love with Howard Raikes, the American idealist who detests Blunt and all he stands for, and Jane shares his ideas. But despite her espousal of these "modern ideas"—and her belief that what is needed is "a new heaven and a new earth,"—she wears a "Schiaparelli creation" to walk in Regent's Park with Howard, and she does not object to being one of the future heirs of Uncle Alistair's fortune.

On one occasion, Poirot introduces the subject of Jane's friends. Her response:

> "I haven't got any friends. Only a silly crowd I drink and dance and talk inane catchwords with! Howard's the only *real* person I've ever come up against."

Julia Olivera, Jane's mother, a plump middle aged woman who is a sister-in-law to Alistair Blunt. She does *not* like Hercule Poirot. During a visit to Blunt at his home in Kent, Mrs. Olivera ignores Poirot entirely, but at one point she cannot help noticing him as he enters the room.

> Mrs. Olivera was playing patience.
> She looked up as Poirot entered, surveyed him with the cold look she might have bestowed upon a black beetle, and murmured distantly, "Red knave on black queen."

Mr. Barnes, a dental patient of Mr. Reilly whose appointment was at noon. He is retired from the Home Office and has a complex, cloak-and-dagger explanation for Mr. Morley's death which does not impress Hercule Poirot.

A Maid at the home of Mr. Barnes

Mrs. Harrison, the Manageress of the Glengowrie Court Hotel, who reports the disappearance of Miss Sainsbury-Seale

Mrs. Adams, a friend of Mabelle Sainsbury-Seale who had known her in India but who has not seen her since her return to England

Emma, Mr. and Miss Morley's Cook, a devoted and trusted servant

Agnes Fletcher, a house-parlormaid of Mr. and Miss Morley who accompanies Miss Morley when she moves to the country after her brother's death. Several weeks after the death of Mr. Morley, Agnes writes a letter to Hercule Poirot begging him to visit her in Hertfordshire, as she has important new information to give to him. She is terrified of being mixed up with the police, as her parents have always been "very particular..."

A Porter at King Leopold Mansions who discovers a rotting corpse in a fur-storage trunk. It was he who, reading of Miss Sainsbury-Seale's disappearance, remembered her as a guest of Mrs. Sylvia Chapman

Sylvia Chapman, a friend of Mabelle Sainsbury-Seale who lives in King Leopold Mansions, not far from Alistair Blunt's London home, the Gothic House. She once let it drop to her friend Mrs. Merton that her husband was in the Secret Service...

Albert Chapman, allegedly a commercial traveler, the husband of Sylvia Chapman. Is he really in the Secret Service? Nellie, a maid at King Leopold Mansions, believes he was just a "gay deceiver."

Sergeant Beddoes, a young police officer who attends to the matter of Miss Sainsbury-Seale's body being found in Mrs. Chapman's flat. According to Chief Inspector Japp, he's a bit too "educated."

Nellie, a day maid at King Leopold Mansions who "did" for Mrs. Chapman

Mrs. Merton of King Leopold Mansions, said to be Mrs. Chapman's best friend in the Mansions. It is from her that Poirot learns about the "true" profession of Mrs. Chapman's husband.

A Divisional Surgeon who examined the body of Mabelle Sainsbury-Seale and pointed out that the disfigurement of her face occurred *after* she had died.

Mr. Leatheran, Mr. Morley's successor at the dental office

Ram Lal, a Hindu student living in London, and a friend of Howard Raikes, who fires a shot at the Prime Minister and Alistair Blunt as they are leaving 10 Downing Street.

Mr. Selby, Alistair Blunt's secretary, a tall, limp young man with an accomplished social manner.

Helen Montressor, a "poor relation" to Alistair Blunt whom he generously allows to occupy a small cottage, rent free, on his country estate in Kent

Head Gardener MacAlister at Alistair Blunt's estate in Kent who recently hired a new undergardener

An Unnamed New Undergardener at Alistair Blunt's estate in Kent. Poirot recognizes him at once.

Archerton, a member of parliament who, according to Alistair Blunt, is always critical of the established order

Joseph Aarons, a theatrical agent and friend of Poirot, who consults with him occasionally. We met him first in *Murder on the Links,* seventeen years ago.

FRENCH INTO ENGLISH

Chapter 1
distrait—inattentive
hein?—aren't you? (*hein?* at the end of a statement is the equivalent of "n'est-ce pas?")

Chapter 2
Eh bien?—Well?
Eh bien, mon vieux—Well, friend...
Eh bien—Okay, then...
Mon cher—Friend
enfin—well, actually...
C'était ça—That's what it was!
ce pauvre Morley—poor old Morley
cherchez la femme—find the woman
ce pauvre M. Morley—that poor Mr. Morley

Chapter 3
Bonjour, mon ami—Good morning, friend
mon cher—friend

Chapter 4 *mon ami*—friend

Chapter 5
Pardon?—Excuse me?
mon ami—friend

Mais oui—You bet I am...
Vraiment—Really
Allô?—Hello
soignée—carefully arranged
C'est ridicule—It's ridiculous

Chapter 7
Jeunesse—Youth
Bonjour, mademoiselle—Good morning, miss
pardon—excuse me
mon ami—friend
amende honorable—courteous apology

Chapter 8
da capo—back to the beginning (an Italian musical term here used facetiously)

Chapter 9 *pardon*—excuse me

COMMENTS

The story in *The Patriotic Murders* appears to be extremely complicated while we are reading it, but the solution shows that the murders, for which there are very substantial motives, were planned with great simplicity. What makes the story seem complicated is the large number and variety of characters whose relationships with each other seem unlikely but which make sense once we understand the solution.

The novel's immediate predecessor, *Sad Cypress,* caused us to be immersed in a love story, whether we were interested in it or not. We are immersed, in *The Patriotic Murders,* in a good deal of talk about contemporary thoughts on the complex subject of conservatism versus "new ideas," some of the new ideas being revolutionary and idealistic. Anger and bitterness among some segments of society, particularly the youthful segment, play a part. There are no direct references to World War II, which is in its beginning stages, but the uneasy fear inspired by events on the Continent permeates the story's atmosphere and there is a good deal of talk by and about "subversive" types of people.

Perhaps the most interesting character in the novel is Jane Olivera, a wealthy young woman who expects to inherit still more wealth, but who frankly admits that she has no friends; she has only a silly crowd with whom she drinks and dances and talks inane catchwords. When she encounters the "angry young man" Howard Raikes he is, to her, the only *real* person she has ever come up against. He has "half-baked" radical ideas which appeal to her in her youthfulness and she falls in love with him for that reason. Their relationship is reminiscent of the one between Egg Lytton Gore and Oliver Manders in the 1935 *Murder in Three Acts*. In both cases the young men are rude and boorish.

The remaining characters in *The Patriotic Murders* are rather forgettable, although three of them provide a bit of humor. The pageboy at the dental office, Alfred Biggs, is an amusing diversion with his mispronunciations and his descriptions of the patients. He may remind you of Albert, the "small lift boy" in the 1922 *The Secret Adversary*. Mabelle Sainsbury-Seale is also amusing in her scatterbrained way, and the jovial Dr. Reilly has a few lines that bring a chuckle. But these people are only encountered once or twice each.

As we have seen in other novels, Christie is not above laughing at herself and the kind of books that she writes. In addition to the reference to Alfred Biggs's "low taste in literature" (thrillers), there is a comment by Chief Inspector Japp that the case is beginning to resemble "a thriller by a lady novelist."

Again we encounter one of Christie's stock characters—the Anglo-Indian colonel, who is usually portrayed as the club bore (or the village bore) and who is always very anti-foreign. In this book the Anglo-Indian colonel is Colonel Abercrombie, but he has no role at all except to glare at the very foreign Hercule Poirot and to give the impression that he would like to exterminate him with insect spray. His attitude is like that of Colonel Arbuthnot in *Murder in the Calais Coach* who, upon entering the dining car and noticing Poirot, instantly turned his glance elsewhere, thinking "Just another damned foreigner."

A few of Christie's recent new "themes" are present in *The Patriotic Murders*. Education is again said to be not as valuable as it is cut out to be. The dentist Mr. Morley states that the stupid pageboy Alfred Biggs is proof that modern education is not much good. Chief Inspector Japp complains mildly about the "fancy new education" of Sergeant Beddoes, although in *The A.B.C. Murders,* we recall that he manfully stepped aside for the far more educated, and younger, Inspector Crome whose understanding of modern psychology was needed in that particular case.

The special importance of flower gardening in English life, a relatively recent addition to Agatha Christie's repertoire of themes—first introduced just three years earlier in *Poirot Loses a Client*—is expressed here in the personalities of two male characters. The ex-secret-service agent Mr. Barnes and the supremely important financier Alistair Blunt both speak proudly and knowledgeably about their flower gardens. Even Hercule Poirot—whose general attitude toward nature is that it should be "disciplined" in the manner of formal French-style parks and gardens with identical trees planted in perfect rows and bedding flowers planted in symmetrical beds—is struck by the beauty of English-style herbaceous borders which, through careful planning, appear "natural."

At the house in Kent, there is a beautiful system of gardens which, although in the informal English style, Poirot finds admirable. On the evening of his arrival, Poirot happily notices the smell of night-scented stocks in the air, and the next morning he goes out into the gardens:

> The herbaceous borders were in full beauty and though Poirot himself leaned to a more orderly type of flower arrangement—a neat arrangement of beds of scarlet geraniums such as are seen at Ostend—he nevertheless realized that here was the perfection of the English garden spirit.

Later that day Poirot's host, a gardening enthusiast as well as a very rich financier, speaks glowingly of his sweet Williams, and of the marvelous colors of his Russell lupines.

As the years go on, English flower gardens—and enthusiastic gardeners—will play even stronger roles, sometimes in humorous ways. We recall that in the 1939 *Easy to Kill* there was an amusing female character who spoke only three times, each time on some gardening subject. In the opening scene in the 1942 *The Body in the Library*, Mrs. Bantry, a flower gardening enthusiast, awakens one morning from a beautiful dream in which her sweet peas "had taken a first at the flower show." An hour or two later, during a conversation with Miss Marple about a certain young man who *may* be the murderer in the story, Mrs. Bantry will instantly absolve him from suspicion, stating that she knows the young man's mother, Selina Blake, who has marvelous herbaceous borders and who is "frightfully generous with cuttings."

Still later, Mrs. Bantry and Miss Marple begin to fear that the police may suspect Mrs. Bantry's husband of the murder, since it was in the Bantrys' library that the body of a young girl was discovered. The police may even suspect that Colonel Bantry was having an affair with the young girl. Mrs. Bantry's reaction to this idea:

> "As though Arthur could have anything to do with it!"
> Miss Marple was silent. Mrs. Bantry turned on her accusingly. "And don't tell me about some frightful old man who kept his housemaid. Arthur isn't like that."
> "No, no, of course not."
> "No, but he really isn't. He's just, sometimes, a

little bit silly about pretty girls who come to tennis. You know, rather fatuous and avuncular. There's no harm in it. And why shouldn't he? After all," finished Mrs. Bantry rather obscurely, "I've got the garden."

Hercule Poirot has always been a voice of "realism" in the midst of British characters who are plagued with "romanticism" in their thinking. In this novel he listens indulgently but pityingly to a young girl who feels sure that she can "reform" her boyfriend. He has heard that argument, the same blithe belief in the redeeming power of a woman's love, many times.

By now Poirot has also had just about enough of being described with adjectives such as "odd," "peculiar," and "strange." He had had quite enough of that long ago from his friend Chief Inspector Japp in particular. In this novel, as usual, Japp has a theory about the case which disregards and even contradicts several cold facts, and so Poirot objects to the theory. Another character states, "You're an odd sort of person." Poirot responds:

> "I am very odd. That is to say, I am methodical, orderly and logical—and I do not like distorting facts to support a theory. That, I find, *is* unusual!"

As usual, there is a mother-daughter relationship which is not a good one. Jane Olivera's mother does not want her to associate with Howard Raikes—the man Jane describes as "the only real person I had ever run up against." Her mother takes her from America to England in an effort to separate the lovers. She fails, of course.

Evil Under the Sun (1941)

SETTING

The story takes place in August of some year immediately preceding the fall of France to the Germans, which took place in the summer of 1940. The mention in the story of Margaret Mitchell's novel *Gone with the Wind* places the action of the story no earlier than 1936, and 1939 is the latest year in which casual vacationing at an English Channel resort would be likely, considering the fact that the Battle of Britain began the following year. Therefore we may think of the story as taking place in about 1937 or 1938.

The setting is tiny "Smuggler's Island" off the southern coast of Devon near the fictitious village of Leathercombe Bay which is populated mainly by fishermen. The nearest town of any size is the fictitious resort town of St. Loo.

In the 1932 novel *Peril at End House,* the setting is also the town of St. Loo, but it is stated to be in Cornwall, a small county occupying the western peninsula of southern England. In that novel Colonel Weston is a local police constable, and he reappears in *Evil Under the Sun* and even has a brief conversation with Poirot about the earlier case. Therefore it is the same town of St. Loo, although now the town is clearly stated to be in Devon, the county just east of Cornwall. Christie must have forgotten that, in the earlier novel, she had placed the town in Cornwall. She later admitted in her *Autobiography* that her memories of books written between 1929 and 1932 were vague. The southern coasts of both counties are similar and are known for vacation resorts, and the name "St. Loo" is believable as a place name in either county since both have real towns and villages with "Loo-" as part of their names.

"Cornwall and Devon" are actually often spoken of in just those terms, being right next to each other, and the southern coasts of both counties have been described as "The English Riviera," having the warmest summer weather in England. British sun-seekers have long flocked to that coast in summer for sun and warmth in their otherwise rather cool, rainy country. But even in this story there is one day of steady rain and mist during which the vacationers must remain indoors the whole day.

The county of Devon was a favorite area of Agatha Christie. She spent her childhood in Torquay, a resort town on the south coast of Devon, and during the late 1930s she and her husband purchased a large Georgian-period home called Greenway House in Devon not far from Torquay. They had already purchased a smaller, Queen Anne period home—Winterbrook House—in Wallingford, Berkshire, much closer to London. Winterbrook House was right in the town of Wallingford, which had easy and quick access by car and railway to London. Greenway House, in Devon, was much larger and had beautiful geography surrounding it. It was Christie's favorite home.

A special feature of Devon consists of two areas of quite beautiful but desolate wasteland known for centuries as "the moors." In north Devon is an area called Exmoor and, in the south, there is the larger area known as "Dartmoor." The very mention of "Dartmoor" evokes romantic images of wild desolation, roaming packs of wolves, danger and loneliness. The frightening story, *The Hound of the Baskervilles,* takes place there, and because of the isolation of Dartmoor, the notorious Dartmoor Prison was built there long ago and has been a source of inspiration for stories of escaped convicts and murders. The setting for the 1931 *Murder at Hazelmoor* is the picturesque, isolated village of Sittaford on the edge of Dartmoor, and a slightly larger settlement six miles distant, Exhampton.

The fictitious "Smuggler's Island," as the story goes, was purchased in the late 1700s by an eccentric ex-seaman who built a large, comfortable home upon it. His heirs did not appreciate the isolated location of the house and allowed it to suffer neglect for several generations until 1922, when the island was purchased by someone interested in creating a resort for vacationers. The old house was expanded and modernized until the year of our story, 1937 or 1938, by which time it has become a comfortable and exclusive resort hotel called "The Jolly Roger." The tiny island is very close to the mainland and a modern concrete causeway has been built connecting the island to it. The causeway can be used by both pedestrians and automobiles, but because it is covered with water during high tide, the hotel garage is located on the mainland. The island and mainland are in fact so near to each other that most hotel guests use small rowboats when needing to get to the mainland. A gate on the causeway warns that the island is private and "only for hotel guests."

The island is very small and it is possible for moderately athletic persons to row all the way around it in about an hour despite the constant eastbound current on the south coast. On the mainland, in the tiny village of Leathercombe Bay, there is a small shop catering to the needs of visitors. Inside, along one wall is a kind of lending library, but most of the books are at least ten years old, although there is a copy of Margaret Mitchell's *Gone with the Wind*, which was no more a year or two old at the time. The inquest takes place at a place named The Red Bull, evidently a pub or inn of some kind in the village.

The Jolly Roger Hotel has electricity, but there is no telephone and at least one character goes to the mainland—in fact all the way to St. Loo—to make some private telephone calls, as there are only one or two telephones in Leathercombe Bay itself and neither is located in a private place. The guest bedrooms at the Jolly Roger are, of course, on the upper floor. The ground floor has a dining room, a billiard room, and a bar in addition to the lobby.

A few of the hotel guests have automobiles that are parked in the hotel parking garage on the mainland, but the only automobile make mentioned in the book is a Sunbeam, owned by the character Horace Blatt.

Geographic features of the tiny island include a grassy elevated plateau, from which there is a steep descent among cliffs to the small coves and beaches below. From the upper floor of the hotel, an outside staircase or ladder leads down to the ground from which a steep footpath leads further down to a rocky beach for swimming. This is used by nature lovers who enjoy an "early morning dip" before breakfast, although the main bathing beach is more conveniently located right in front of the hotel.

There are scenes in the hotel rooms, in the dining room of the hotel and in the lobby, as well as many scenes on the bathing beach and among the rocky cliffs adjoining it, into which small niches with seats have been carved for the benefit of the guests. Hercule Poirot has one or two occasions to "eavesdrop" upon conversations taking place among these rustic, secluded places.

At some distance from the main beach fronting the hotel are several coves not visible from the hotel or its beach. One of these, on the western side, is picturesquely called "Pixy Cove" and has its own small beach. Among the rocks is a narrow opening leading to "Pixy Cave" which, though known to fishermen of past generations, has been forgotten by the locals due to the fact that the island has been in private hands and carefully protected from intruders for about twenty-five years. Pixy Cove and its tiny beach are popular with the hotel guests in the afternoons at tea time for picnics, since there is sun at that time, but in the mornings it is generally deserted, since it is in the shade of the cliffs. Pixy Cove is easily reached by rowboat from the hotel beach, but it is more quickly reached by a footpath over the island and then down an iron ladder attached to the cliffside. This ladder is intimidating to persons who have a fear of heights but is easy sport for more athletic types, especially younger people. Pixy Cove—and Pixy Cave—play an important role in the story.

Although we are now on the eve of World War II, there is no mention of current events other than one remark by a character who states that "one would not aspire to be either Mussolini or Princess Elizabeth" at the moment. Hercule Poirot has occasion to express his distaste for the modern custom of showing so much flesh on the beach. He compares the spectacle of this "exposed flesh" to cuts of meat on a butcher's slab, and speaks nostalgically of former times when "an exposed ankle or a shapely calf" was sufficient to arouse sexual interest, and modest clothing kept a woman's beauty mysterious. His observations may at first seem irrelevant to the story but, upon reading the story, we will see that they assist him in solving the murder.

Clothing fashions of the times are not mentioned very much in the story, although one of the characters is a successful dressmaker whose London shop is in Brook Street, and who expresses one or two judgments about the other female characters' taste—or lack thereof—in color and line.

Story

It is August of 1937 or 1938 and Hercule Poirot, the famous Belgian private investigator, is enjoying a holiday at a resort hotel, The Jolly Roger, located on tiny Smuggler's Island off Leathercombe Bay on the south coast of Devon.

Among the other guests are two couples, the young Redferns and the slightly-older Marshalls. Arlena Marshall is a beautiful former stage actress whose husband is a conservative gentleman with an adolescent daughter from an earlier marriage. Patrick Redfern is a spectacular specimen of athletic young manhood. Arlena and Patrick flirt outrageously with each other, oblivious to the feelings of their respective spouses, and everyone at the hotel is amazed by their behavior. Even Hercule Poirot, the sophisticated Continental European who has rarely been known to "moralize," lectures Patrick on his behavior. Everyone feels a storm gathering.

Arlena's dead body is soon discovered on a tiny beach near a secluded cave not far from the hotel. She has been strangled by someone with powerful hands. There is no shortage of suspects, of course. There is her cuckolded husband, the wife of her lover, her resentful step-daughter, a fanatical parson, and an athletic spinster, to name just a few. Inside the cave near Arlena's corpse the police find a cache of smuggled heroin as well.

Hercule Poirot solves this mystery with his usual skill.

Characters

Hercule Poirot, the Belgian detective with the egg-shaped head and flamboyant mustache. As has been his custom for the last few years, it is the psychology of the murder victim that interests Poirot the most—and which eventually leads to the solution of the crime.

Mrs. Gardener, whose constant chatter can only be compared, in our experience, with that of Mrs. Amelia Curtis in the 1931 *Murder at Hazelmoor*, who provoked the following comment from another character: "It's almost a disease the way that woman talks." Mrs. Gardener has an unbelievable capacity for incessant chatter, and she ends every paragraph with, "Isn't that so, Odell?" or "Isn't that just what I said, Odell?" or "And I'm sure my husband agrees, don't you Odell?" to which he answers "Yes, darling," as if on cue. Of her many monologues, the following is memorable and typical for its "relevance" to the general conversation. Captain Marshall has just finished a swim, and has announced to the group, "Pretty good in the sea this morning. Unfortunately I've got a lot of work to do. Must go and get on with it." Mrs. Gardener responds:

> "Why, if that isn't too bad, Captain Marshall. On a beautiful day like this, too. My, wasn't yesterday too terrible? I said to Mr. Gardener that if the weather was going to continue like that, we'd just have to leave. It's so melancholy, you know, with the mist right up around the island. Gives you a kind of ghostly feeling, but then I've always been very susceptible to atmosphere ever since I was a child. Sometimes, you know, I'd feel I just had to scream and scream. And that, of course, was very trying to my parents. But my mother was a lovely woman and she said to my father, 'Sinclair, if the child feels like that, we must let her do it. Screaming is her way of expressing herself.' And of course my father agreed. He was devoted to my mother and just did everything she said. They were a perfectly lovely couple, as I'm sure Mr. Gardener will agree. They were a very remarkable couple, weren't they, Odell?"
>
> "Yes, darling." said Mr. Gardener.

Mr. Odell Gardener, the poor wretch who is married to the pathologically loquacious Mrs. Gardener. On the rare occasions when he is not in the presence of his wife, he shows surprising intelligence. Hercule Poirot, in an effort to gather impressions from as many people as possible of the personality of the murder victim, asks Mr. Gardener what he thought of Arlena Marshall. Mr. Gardener proves to be the only character in the story whose impression of her is exactly the same as Poirot's: that she was not very bright.

Irene Gardener, the Gardeners' adult daughter. She is not a character in the story, but Mrs. Gardener mentions her in some comments.

Emily Brewster, an amiable, athletic British spinster of indeterminate age, a tough athletic woman with grizzled hair and a pleasant weatherbeaten face. We first meet her on the beach at the Jolly Roger. The sound of her conversation with Mrs. Gardener is likened to that of "a sheepdog whose short stentorian barks interrupt the ceaseless yapping of a Pomeranian."

Mr. Kelso at Cooks, who arranged the Gardeners' entire itinerary and was *most* helpful in every way.

Rosamund Darnley, a sophisticated and successful businesswoman from London, the owner of an exclusive dressmaking establishment, Rose Mond, in Brook Street. Hercule Poirot is personally very fond of her, admitting that he admires her as much as any woman he has ever met.

Cornelia Robson, not a character in this story but a passenger aboard the *Karnak* in the 1937 *Death on the Nile*, and a friend of the Gardeners, as Mrs. Gardener explains,

> "You see, M. Poirot, I'd heard a lot about you from Cornelia Robson who was at Badenhof in May when Mr. Gardener and I were there. And of course Cornelia told us all about that business in Egypt when Linnet Ridgeway was killed. She said you were wonderful and I've always been simply crazy to meet you, haven't I, Odell?"
>
> "Yes, darling."

Major Barry, yet another in a long series of "boring Anglo-Indian ex-military men" we have met in Christie novels. This one has "protruberant, boiled gooseberry eyes." Poirot describes him briefly as "Major Barry, Retired Indian Army. An admirer of women. A teller of long and boring stories."

Reverend Stephen Lane, a clergyman whose pronouncements on "the presence of evil" sound almost fanatical.

Christine Redfern, an ash blonde with very fair skin. She is pretty in a "negative" way, with small, dainty hands and feet. Despite her "rather anaemic prettiness," Poirot considers her to have "plenty of resolution, courage and good sense."

Patrick Redfern, who is young, attractive to women, a magnificent swimmer, a good tennis player and an accomplished dancer. He does not disguise his attraction to Arlena Marshall, telling the authorities after her death that his feelings for her were nothing but an infatuation.

Arlena Stuart (Arlena Marshall), a stage actress who has been retired for a year and a half. She has been married to Kenneth Marshall for four years, but that has not prevented her from welcoming the attentions of other men, including Old Sir Roger Erskine who died just three years ago, leaving her every penny of his 50,000-pound bank account.

When Arlena makes her first appearance in the story, her arrival on the beach has "all the importance of a stage entrance." Depending on who is describing her, she is either an immoral homewrecker or simply a woman of low intelligence who invites exploitation by men. All agree that she is a stunningly beautiful woman.

Captain Kenneth Marshall, Arlena Stuart's husband of four years. According to his old friend, Rosamund Darnley, he has a penchant for making unfortunate marriages. His first wife had been accused and tried, though acquitted, of murdering her former husband. Kenneth is a conservative thinker in the matter of divorce and refuses to discuss that subject, despite his wife's extramarital behaviors.

Linda Marshall, the fifteen-year-old daughter of Kenneth Marshall, and daughter of the woman who had been tried and acquitted for the murder of her first husband. She bitterly resents her stepmother Arlena and wishes that she would die. She wishes that she had a stepmother who treated her as a real human being—someone like Rosamund Darnley.

Ruth Marshall, Kenneth's first wife and Linda's natural mother. She died when Linda was a baby. She was tried for murdering her first husband, but was acquitted.

The Cowan Boys and the Young Mastermans, athletic youngsters who are guests at the Jolly Roger who run up and down the ladder leading to Pixy Cove, enjoying the sport of it, although most people, including the athletic Miss Brewster "would funk it."

A Gal Out in Simla, recalled by the boring Anglo-Indian army man, Major Barry, during a discussion of Arlena Marshall's behavior.

Two Young Men, Little More Than Boys, who are attracted to, but ignored by, Arlena Stuart when she notices handsome Patrick Redfern on the beach.

Lady Codrington, who had divorced her husband, citing Arlena Stuart.

Old Sir Roger Erskine, one of Arlena Stuart's conquests. He left her his fortune of 50,000 pounds one year after she married Kenneth Marshall.

The Rylands, friends of Arlena who told her about Smuggler's Island and the Jolly Roger Hotel

Arthur Hastings, an old friend of Hercule Poirot, whom we have met in earlier novels. Not a character in this novel, he makes a brief appearance in Hercule Poirot's thoughts.

Horace Blatt, another one of the guests at the Jolly Roger Hotel who loves to be "the life of the party," although he finds the other guests a bit cool towards him. His idea of a good time is talking about his success in his hardware business.

Inspector Colgate, the local police officer who is called to Smuggler's Island upon the discovery of Arlena's death. Hercule Poirot likes his rugged face, his shrewd eyes, and his slow unhurried manner.

Constable Hawkes, who stays with Arlena's body when, after the medical examination, the authorities leave the murder site.

Dr. Neasdon, the police surgeon who examines Arlena's body and determines the time of her death. He also identifies the white powder that is later found in a box hidden inside Pixy Cave.

Chief Constable Weston (Colonel Weston) of the local police, Inspector Colgate's superior. He met Hercule Poirot several years ago in the 1932 *Peril at End House.*

Mrs. Castle, the owner and proprietor of The Jolly Roger Hotel who is "always most particular."

Jolly Roger Hotel Staff:

Gladys Narracott, a chambermaid who provides valuable, accurate information to the investigators.

Elsie, another chambermaid

Two Additional Chambermaids

Henry At The Bar, the cocktail host, a Jolly Roger institution of many years

George, who attends to the bathing beach, costumes and floats

William, the hotel gardener and "boots"

Albert, the Head Waiter

Three Additional Waiters under the supervision of Albert

A Cook and Two Helpers

A Girl in the Bureau Downstairs

Barkett, Markett & Applegood, Arlena Stuart's solicitors in Bedford Square, London

J.N., the writer of a recent letter to Arlena Stuart which appears to suggest that she has recently paid him (or her) a considerable sum of money

Heald, a person at police headquarters (presumably a man, since he is referred to only by his surname) who determines the length of time it must have taken one of the suspects to type certain letters

A Police Constable who is at Pixy Cove when Poirot and others visit it for a second time on the day of the crime.

Sergeant Phillips, a plain clothes officer who examines the beach at Pixy Cove for clues

P. C. Flint, a police officer who determines the length of time it would take to reach Pixy Cove from the Jolly Roger hotel by walking overland and using the iron ladder

Alice Corrigan and Nellie Parsons, who were recently strangled to death in separate incidents in Surrey. Neither of their cases was ever solved.

A Couple Who Come to Have Lunch at the Jolly Roger on the day of the murder but are turned away because "there has been an accident."

FRENCH INTO ENGLISH

Chapter 1
Merci, Mademoiselle—No, thank you, Miss.
eh bien—well, then
Parbleu—Heavens!
C'est possible—Possibly

Chapter 2 *mon cher*—my good friend

Chapter 3
Les femmes—Women
Eh bien—But then...

Chapter 4
Ah, ça, jamais...par example—No way in hell!

Chapter 5
Tout de même, mon Colonel—All the same, Colonel
crime passionnel—a murder committed while under the influence of strong emotion, usually sexual jealousy
Mais oui—Absolutely

Chapter 6 *Mon cher*—My good friend

Chapter 7
bien entendu—of course
pardon—excuse me

Chapter 8
Les femmes!—Women!
C'est possible—That's possible
C'est fantastique!—It doesn't make sense!
Pour l'amour de Dieu!—For Pete's sake!

Chapter 9
très moutarde—pretty spicy
Crime passionnel—(see Chapter 5, above)

Chapter 12
La haute Mode—High fashion

COMMENTS

The Patriotic Murders, the immediate predecessor of *Evil Under the Sun,* was characterized by an extremely complicated story and multiple relationships among a very large number of characters. The complexity of the story itself—and the constant revelations of new facts—hold the reader's attention, as well as the questions of "how and why" the murders took place. On the other hand, the characters were relatively uninteresting in themselves, with just one or two exceptions.

In *Evil Under the Sun* the story is extremely simple, as it was in *A Holiday for Murder* and *Appointment with Death*. In all three of these novels there is a person who is strongly disliked, or even hated, by several people and when that person is murdered, several people fall under suspicion. In *Evil Under the Sun,* the characters are unusually interesting and the way in which the murderer planned the crime is unique. But the story itself is extremely simple.

One of the more interesting characters is Rosamund Darnley who has brains, charm and a warm heart. Hercule Poirot admits that he admires her as much as he as ever admired any woman. She is independent and successful in a business of her own—she owns a fine dressmaking establishment in Brook Street. If we remember Cynthia Dacres, a character in the 1935 *Murder in Three Acts,* who was a dressmaker with her shop in Bond Street, there is no similarity between the two. Mrs. Dacres was nothing but a fashion statement personified, with her constant use of the word "penetrating" and her asinine comments such as "women's clothes must be absolutely absurd—look at those perfectly useless shoulder knots, darling, aren't they just too penetrating..." There is none of this silly babble in the thoughts or speech of Rosamund Darnley. She is concerned for the happiness of her old friend Kenneth Marshall and especially for Kenneth's teenage daughter who is suffering because of a non-caring stepmother.

It was at approximately this time in Christie's life that her own daughter, Rosalind, announced that she was engaged and asked Christie, "Do you want to be at the wedding?" The question shocked Christie, who responded, "Of course I want to be at the wedding," and then Christie must have done some deep thinking about the quality of her mothering during Rosalind's childhood and youth, if her daughter could feel so distant that she would ask if her mother "wanted" to be at her wedding. The character Linda Marshall has a famous actress for a stepmother, who ignores her. She wishes that Rosamund Darnley were her stepmother instead, because Rosamund "treats her like an actual human being." Christie may have wondered if her daughter Rosalind had wished for a mother who "treated her like an actual human being." In all of Christie's early novels, there is never a close relationship between a mother and a daughter, and this is the third example of an adolescent girl in a Christie novel who resents a stepmother. (The first was Lettice Protheroe in *Murder at the Vicarage,* and the second was Geraldine Marsh in *Thirteen at Dinner.*) The difference between those young ladies and Linda Marshall is that they also detested their fathers whereas Linda loves her father, Kenneth, and feels that her life—and his—would be much better if he had a wife like Rosamund.

Another side to Rosamund's personality is a shadow of doubt regarding the depth of her own happiness. She feels gratified and proud of her achievements in her business but the fact that she has never married seems to bother her a little, as though somehow there is something missing in her life. She deliberately fences with Poirot, in a friendly way, on this subject, trying to provoke him into delivering a pronouncement on the value of family life, but he refuses to be drawn in and to play judge.

Other memorable characters in *Evil Under the Sun* include the unforgettable Mrs. Gardener, with her hilarious monologues and silent husband. Like Mrs. Amelia Curtis in *Murder at Hazelmoor,* she is a goodhearted person but pathologically motor-mouthed. Both women have husbands who tolerate them benignly.

Then there is Emily Brewster, a commonsense British spinster who has a voice like a man and a golf handicap of four, and who rows boats around the island every day for fun.

No Christie novel would be complete without a boring Anglo-Indian ex-army man. We have seen several of those since the 1926 *The Murder of Roger Ackroyd,* and Major Barry is the best one so far. The guests at the Jolly Roger Hotel have learned how to redirect the conversation whenever Major Barry shows signs of embarking on one of his dreaded India stories, which is practically every time he opens his mouth.

The "self-made man" is never safe in a Christie novel; in this one there is Horace Blatt whom everybody shuns because his favorite subject of conversation is Horace Blatt!

The more important characters, of course, are the two married couples, the Redferns and the Marshalls, four completely different personalities, but it's not very easy to know exactly what they are like because everyone's comments about them are different. Miss Brewster says that Patrick Redfern is a "fool," someone else calls him a "philandering husband;" still another character says he's a simple kind of guy who loves his wife and is *not* a philanderer. Depending on who is speaking, Arlena Marshall is either a "home wrecker," or simply "not very bright." Most people pity Christine Redfern but Poirot says, "She has something Arlena Marshall does not have—brains." And as the story draws to its end, we find that more than one of these people have qualities we never suspected.

The subject of divorce gets a brief treatment in this novel when Kenneth Marshall refuses to consider divorcing his wife and condemns the "modern" trend of easy divorce, affirming that people should live by their decisions.

None of the characters appears to be a drug user, but the prevalence of drugs during that period is mentioned again—as it has been mentioned in several of Christie's books since *The Murder of Roger Ackroyd* (1926). The police find a cache of smuggled heroin in Pixy Cave and wonder if it can have something to do with the murder of Arlena Marshall.

As we already know, whenever The Press is mentioned by Agatha Christie, it is a negative mention. As Kenneth Marshall leaves The Red Bull, where the preliminary inquest has taken place, he meets a crowd of staring and finger-pointing villagers and reporters with ceaselessly-clicking cameras. One reporter snaps a picture of Kenneth and Rosamund walking together, and Rosamund turns to Kenneth and murmurs, "*Captain Marshall and a friend leaving The Red Bull after the inquest.*"

Just a detail here—we recall that Poirot's friend Hastings was always scandalized whenever Poirot made so bold as to search a woman's room, to find and read her private letters, rifle through her lingerie drawer for clues, etc. All of this was "not playing the game," and made Hastings blush and babble things like "Really, Poirot!" In *Evil Under the Sun*, Poirot and two officers go through Arlena Marshall's bedroom. Poirot searches Arlena Marshall's underwear drawer without provoking any outrage among the officers, since they are busy reading her private letters! But, of course, she was already dead, so perhaps that made All the Difference.

Another small point: That phrase "I don't know what you mean!" which seems to be popular with Christie's Britons, whenever they are asked something about their sex lives, occurs twice in the speech of the alleged philanderer Patrick Redfern. He first uses it when his wife asks him "Did you know that woman was going to be here?" It's quite a simple, grammatically correct question and free of erudite vocabulary, but Redfern's answer is "I don't know what you mean." To this Christine replies, "I think you do."

The same day, Poirot is lecturing Redfern on his behavior:

"*Les femmes*." Poirot leaned back and closed his eyes. "I know something of them. They are capable of complicating life unbearably. And the English, they conduct their affairs indescribably. If it was necessary for you to come here, M. Redfern, why, in the name of Heaven, did you bring your wife?"

Patrick Redfern said angrily: "I don't know what you mean."

Hercule Poirot said calmly: "You know perfectly."

Poirot's statement, "And the English, they conduct their affairs indescribably," is not a new idea in Christie. In the 1923 *Murder on the Links* an old French servant woman had complained that a certain Englishman was conducting an extramarital affair "with no reticence, no discretion. *Style anglais*, no doubt." This caused Hastings to "bound indignantly in his seat." How dare this common French servant woman suggest that English people are anything but honorable in all matters? We may also recall that in the 1928 *The Mystery of the Blue Train*, Derek Kettering's French mistress Mirelle had said "You are extraordinary, you English!" when he was outraged by her suggestion that his wife was just as adulterous as he.

Regarding the "English personality," certain Americans and persons from "other colonies" have already remarked in Christie novels that the English are a bit "reserved" when dealing with strangers. The South Africans, Mrs. Willett and her daughter Violet, in the 1931 *Murder at Hazelmoor*, were seen by the villagers at Sittaford as "far too matey," constantly exhorting the neighbors to "drop in at any time." Then in the 1932 *Peril at End House* the Australians, Mr. and Mrs. Croft, are described as "oppressively friendly" by Nick Buckley. In *Evil Under the Sun*, it is the Americans, Mr. and Mrs. Gardener who find English people to be "rather cool" at first:

"If there is a fault about the British it is that they're inclined to be a bit stand-offish until they've known you a couple of years. After that nobody could be nicer. Mr. Kelso said that interesting people came here and I see he was right. There's you, M. Poirot and Miss Darnley. Oh! I was just tickled to death when I found out who you were, wasn't I, Odell?"

"You were, darling."

Evil Under the Sun has all of Agatha Christie's best qualities, and it is very typical. It would be a good choice as a "first Christie" to read.

N or M? (1941)

SETTING

It is late winter or early spring through summer of 1940. The story begins in a small flat somewhere in London. After a brief scene at King's Cross railway station in London, the remainder of the story takes place primarily at a fictitious resort town called Leahampton, presumably on the southern coast of England. Since no county is specified and no particular geographical features are mentioned, except some flat areas away from the coast where enemy planes would be able to land, it is impossible to specify the county in which Leahampton is located, but it is probably Devon or Hampshire, which are both famous for their seaside resorts.

Leahampton is large enough to be well served by railway; it is described as "a budding Bournemouth or Torquay." Those two cities had been long established as summer resorts on the English Channel, and so the comparison suggests that Leahampton is on its way to becoming another popular resort center on the south coast of England. Nearly all of the action takes place within a boarding house—a substantial red brick building—called Sans Souci. There are also scenes at a large modern home built about sixteen years ago just outside of Leahampton, also on the coast, with its own access to the coastline. The name of this house is Smugglers' Rest and it is described as having an ultra modern kitchen and modern bathrooms "with all the modern gadgets."

The owner of the house explains that it was built during the 1920s by a German working for the German government, and was equipped with at least two secret rooms containing wireless transmitters and large concealed gasoline tanks in the garage. There are also other features that would be useful to the enemy in case of an invasion: a cave for concealment of weapons and personnel and a secluded cove where a motor boat could be landed in secret.

Near the end of the story one of the characters travels by train to a place called Yarrow, then walks five miles across country to a village called Leatherbarrow where a dental surgeon has an office. A brief scene takes place in that office.

All of the real events of spring and summer of 1940 related to World War II are backgrounds to the story. As the story begins, certain characters mention that Germany has already invaded Belgium, that the evacuation of Dunkerque has taken place, and that "things are looking bad for France." As the story progresses, France falls to Germany—this took place during the summer of 1940. The story ends a few weeks after this.

The term "fifth column" was coined during the Spanish Civil War (1936–1939) by General Francisco Franco, who once said that he had four columns of troops outside the city of Madrid and a "fifth column" of people working for his cause inside the city. The term then came into use to refer to spy networks within countries whose work was to facilitate an invasion by disrupting government, industries, communications etc. The "fifth column" spy networks were generally thought to be populated largely by treasonous citizens of the country itself. In his book *The Second World War*, Winston Churchill affirmed that "there was no fifth column in Britain." Nevertheless, in Christie's novel *N or M?*, there is a "fifth column" at work in England, and its leaders are known to be British subjects. The title of the book refers to two people, N being a man and M being a woman, who are thought to be the leaders of this "fifth column." The task of the two main characters, Tommy and Tuppence Beresford, is the unmasking of one or both of these people, who are thought to be living at the Sans Souci boarding house in Leahampton.

Because of the importance of the War in the novel, no other contemporary events or conditions are mentioned. Two female characters spend a good deal of time knitting "Balaclava helmets" for soldiers with khaki colored wool. The adult son of the two main characters is in the Royal Air Force; their daughter is engaged in some kind of message coding work. Most of the conversations are a mixture of fact and surmise about the war and how long it may last (one character believes it will last two months longer at the most, while another affirms that it will go on for six more years.) British unpreparedness for war and Germany's efficiency in making war are also important subjects of conversation. By the end of 1940 all of Continental Europe except the Soviet Union had either surrendered to or was engaged in treaties with Germany, with Great Britain being the only Western European country still at war with her. Bombings of London and other British cities had begun, and one of the characters living at Leahampton is a young mother with a baby who has left London to escape the danger of the bombardments. A male character has sent his wife and children to Wales for safety.

Minor comments about everyday wartime conditions include a reference to margarine being used instead of scarce butter and a rose garden having been converted to a potato patch to supplement rationed food.

One of the few references to automobiles in the story is that a young male character drives a "racy looking" car.

Although a trivial detail, the following may interest readers who are not old enough to remember "celluloid." In the story someone buys a "celluloid duck" for the child Betty Sprot to float in her bath. Celluloid was an early plastic. A major component of it was natural cellulose, hence its name. It was used in the manufacture of cheap toys and other items but its life span was short, as it was fragile and tended to crack and break upon aging. Celluloid became obsolete for all uses with the advancement of modern plastics technology.

Story

It is late winter or early spring of 1940 and Tommy and Tuppence Beresford, whom we met in the 1922 *The Secret Adversary*, are now in their mid-forties and have two grown children, twins Derek and Deborah. Derek is in the Royal Air Force and Deborah works in a "coding department" of the Government, but Tommy and Tuppence are considered to be "too old" for war work and are extremely depressed about it.

One day a "Mr. Grant," (a younger colleague of their old friend "Mr. Carter") approaches Tommy with an important new task: the unmasking of two British "fifth column" traitors who are working to facilitate the imminent German invasion of Britain. Their code names are "N" and "M," and they are thought to be living at the Sans Souci guest house in the seaside resort town of Leahampton.

Tommy is forbidden to tell his wife Tuppence about the assignment, and a story is fabricated about his going to Scotland to do "rather dull but important war-related clerical work" there. Tommy goes Scotland and then is immediately sent to Leahampton, where he is astonished to find Tuppence, who has already been there for two or three days, registered at the Sans Souci guest house as the widowed Mrs. Blenkensop!

"Mr. Carter" had warned "Mr. Grant" not to try to keep Tuppence out of things, considering Tuppence's detective instincts. After having a good laugh, "Mr. Grant" says to Tommy, "Tell your wife I eat dirt" and he consents to husband and wife working together.

Working independently and conferring at intervals, through a series of dangerous and exciting adventures, the couple succeeds in unmasking both "N" and "M."

Characters

Tommy and Tuppence Beresford, a British couple who were featured in the 1922 *The Secret Adversary* when "their united ages would certainly not have totalled forty-five." Tommy is now forty-six and Tuppence, being a woman, is of course ageless. The Government evidently considers them to be "too old" for useful patriotic work, though they long to serve their war-threatened nation as they once did, hunting for master criminals and living with danger. Their wish is fulfilled in this novel as they unmask two "fifth column" British traitors.

Deborah Beresford, daughter of the above couple, who is employed with the government in some kind of "coding" work—very secret, of course.

Derek Beresford, twin brother of Deborah. He is in the Royal Air Force.

Lord Easthampton, a.k.a. "Mr. Carter," who provided Tommy and Tuppence with their exciting assignment in *The Secret Adversary*. Now aging and ailing, he lives in Scotland and spends his time fishing. But he remembers Tommy and Tuppence and recommends them to "Mr. Grant" for an assignment.

"Mr. Grant," a younger version of "Mr. Carter," of the Home Office. He presents an important assignment for Tommy (but nothing for Tuppence.) Little does he know of Tuppence's cunning, for she finds a way to be a part of the action.

Maureen, an aging neighbor of the Beresfords.

Farquhar, Tommy Beresford's predecessor in the current assignment of tracking down "M" and "N," fifth-column spies working for Germany. He was "accidentally" run down by a truck but lived long enough to say "N or M Song Susie."

N and M, code names for two spies—British subjects working for the Nazi cause in England. N is a man and M is a woman. They are thought to be living at Leahampton, a resort town on the southern coast of England.

Mrs. Perenna, proprietress of the boarding house Sans Souci in Leahampton. She is "a rather untidy looking, middle-aged woman with a large mop of fiercely curling black hair, some vaguely applied makeup and a determined smile showing a lot of very white teeth."

Sheila Perenna, a beautiful young woman, the daughter of Mrs. Perenna. She harbors bitter feelings about patriotism and war and is in love with a young German refugee.

Miss Meadowes, deceased. She is the "aunt" of the new resident of Sans Souci, "Mr. Meadowes," alias Tommy Beresford

Beatrice, an "almost imbecile looking, adenoidal maid" at Sans Souci

Martha, another maid working at Sans Souci

Mrs. O'Rourke, a large, cheerful Irishwoman and resident of Sans Souci. Tommy Beresford's first impression:

> A terrifying mountain of a woman with beady eyes and a moustache gave him a beaming smile.

Major Bletchley, a resident of Sans Souci who treats Tommy, on the evening of his arrival, to "a long and extremely boring account of Major Bletchley's experiences on the North West Frontier." Major Bletchley is the obligatory "boring old ex-military man." He is so stereotypically "the boring old ex-military Englishman" that Tuppence at one point wonders if he can be real.

Carl von Deinem, a handsome, young German chemist, a refugee who left behind two brothers in concentration camps in Germany. His father was killed by the Nazis and his mother died of a broken heart. Depending on who is talking, Carl is either a "good" German or a "bad" German. He's a "good" German if we consider him to have come to England to escape from a vicious dictatorship. He's a "bad" German if we consider him to be a traitor to his native country. When Carl tells Tuppence about his family, Tuppence thinks, "The way he says that—as though he had learned it by heart." Perhaps Carl really is a "good" German in that he is in England working for Germany.

Miss Minton, another resident of Sans Souci, an elderly lady. She wears pale sky-blue jumpers, and chains or bead necklaces. Her skirts are tweedy and have "a depressed droop at the back." She is an expert and constant knitter, and is certain that the War cannot last more than another two months, as Hitler is suffering "from a *disease*—absolutely fatal—he'll be raving mad by August!"

Alfred and Elizabeth Caley, a middle-aged British couple living at Sans Souci. Mrs. Caley is negligible, as her only role and goal in life seem to be waiting on her demanding, hypochondriac husband. Tommy and Tuppence wonder if Mrs. Caley, like Major Bletchley, can be real. As Tuppence expresses it, "I mean there can't be many women *quite* as idiotic as she seems."

As to Mr. Cayley, he's a man of very strong opinions and deep knowledge about Germany, on which subject he enjoys expounding while in the presence of any interested listener.

Millicent Sprot, a young mother who has come from London to Leahampton to protect herself and her baby girl from the danger of the London bombings. According to Tuppence, she has boiled gooseberry eyes and a slightly vacant face. It was at her husband's insistence that she came to Leahampton with her child, and she is clearly bored here, often repeating, "I'm sure it must be safe to return to London."

Betty Sprot, Mrs. Sprot's little girl, just under three years old and still not speaking very intelligibly. She loves being read to and has a double collection of nursery rhyme books—a set of old, dirty ones and clean new copies provided by her modern, hygienic mama.

Arthur Sprot, Mrs. Sprot's husband who has remained in London to work.

"Mrs. Blenkensop," Tuppence's alias for the duration of her stay at Sans Souci. She is "a widow who is devoted to three sons by her first marriage."

Douglas Hill, Raymond Hill, and Cyril Hill, "Mrs. Blenkensop's" three grown sons by her first marriage. As Tuppence explains to Tommy, Blenkensop is such an unusual name that the existence of three young Blenkensops in the armed forces would be quite a simple matter to disprove. So much better to have invented a "first marriage" to a man named Hill, for there are three full pages of Hills in the London telephone directory.

Commander Haydock, the current owner of a fine, modern house, Smugglers' Rest, not very far from Sans Souci. He purchased it after finally convincing the authorities that the original builder and owner of the house was a German agent. The house has all the modern gadgets of modern houses, plus special features such as hidden wireless rooms that were clearly intended by the original owner for use in fifth-column work.

The Secretary at the Golf Clubhouse

Patrick Maguire, the deceased husband of Mrs. Perenna and father of Sheila. He was active in the Irish rebellion and was executed as a traitor.

Mr. Faraday, a fictional gentleman to whom Tuppence places a telephone call

Vanda Polonska, a strange, foreign-looking woman who lurks mysteriously about Sans Souci, explaining her presence by asking first for one person, then for another.

Mr. Rosenstein and Mrs. Gottlieb, two people Vanda Polonska asks about before confessing, "I make mistake."

Mr. Hahn, the original owner and builder of Smugglers' Rest, correctly suspected by Commander Haydock of being a German spy.

A New Chief Constable, who was smart enough to listen to Commander Haydock in the matter of Mr. Hahn, and who launched a successful investigation resulting in Mr. Hahn's arrest.

Albert Batt, the "small lift boy" in the 1922 *The Secret Adversary* who assisted Tommy and

Tuppence in that adventure, then later became their only servant when they established the International Detective Agency. He is now married and a parent, and the proud owner of The Duck and Dog, a pub in south London. Summoned to Leahampton by Tuppence, he assists them in their new adventures. Albert's wife and children are safely tucked away in Wales, although he notes that there have been bombings even there.

A Tradesman's Boy with a Bicycle at St. Lucian's, across the road from Sans Souci

A Maid at St. Lucian's

Mr. Robbins, who noticed a little girl in a green gingham dress walking with a strange-looking lady.

"Ready Rita," Tuppence's nickname for Rita Vandemeyer, a character in *The Secret Adversary* whom Albert Batt recollects during a conversation with Tuppence

Appledore, a manservant of Commander Haydock and an unusually skilled table waiter, in fact, almost "foreign" in his table-waiting expertise

Mr. Walters and Dr. Curtis, two passersby who walk with Tommy from Smugglers' Rest to Sans Souci just before he disappears into thin air.

Anthony (Tony) Marsden, a tall, handsome young man who works in the same "coding" office as Deborah Beresford

Aunt Gracie in Cornwall, with whom Tuppence tells Deborah and Derek she is staying because of her deteriorating health.

Charles, a friend of Deborah Beresford who visits Cornwall and learns—and reports to Deborah—that Tuppence is *not* staying with Aunt Gracie.

Mrs. Rowley, Deborah Beresford's landlady who cannot imagine who could have taken a framed photograph of Tuppence from Deborah's room

Gladys, a maid at Mrs. Rowley's house, who also cannot imagine who could have taken the photograph of Tuppence

Selina, a cousin of Miss Minton who compares her sufferings with those of Aunt Gracie in Cornwall

A Good-looking Young Man in a Car who meets Tuppence at Yarrow railway station

A Competent-looking Middle Aged Woman who assists Tuppence with her nurse disguise

"Freda Elton of Sheffield," Tuppence's false name when she is disguised as a nurse

Dr. Binion, a dental surgeon at Yarrow

Anna, an elderly woman with a stolid peasant face—"not an English face"—who admits Tuppence to the office of Dr. Binion

COMMENTS

If you have not yet read the 1922 *The Secret Adversary*, it would be a good idea to read that novel before reading *N or M?*, because you will then be familiar with the two main characters, Tommy and Tuppence Beresford, and with their friend Albert Batt. You may also consider reading the 1929 collection of short stories, *Partners in Crime*, which stars Tommy and Tuppence as the owners of a fledgling detective agency. You will enjoy *N or M?* more if you are already familiar with these personalities.

The Secret Adversary had for its background the recently-ended First World War, the post-war unemployment and impoverishment of Britain, and the general fear of Bolshevism and revolution. Otherwise the story was fanciful and filled with light-hearted characterizations of stereotypical dangerous criminal types of an imagined kind. *N or M?* is much more serious and much more somber, as it takes place amid the reality of the Second World War and the very real menace of a possibly successful German invasion and conquest of Britain.

There are a couple of amusing characters in *N or M?*. Among them are an elderly couple, Mr. and Mrs. Cayley. Mrs. Cayley's purpose in life seems to be to look after her hypochondriac husband who claims to know all about Germany and can talk on that subject for two hours at a stretch without interruption. There is an obese Irishwoman with a "beard and mustache" who frightens Tuppence with her size and sinister smile. With these exceptions, however, the characters in *N or M?* offer little humor and the atmosphere of the book is quite grim.

One character, Sheila Perenna, is cynical and angry about the idea of "patriotism" because her father had been killed while fighting for the Irish cause. She considers his death to have been unnecessary and futile. She is in love with a German refugee and is criticized for it.

There are comments by British characters suggesting that the German refugee Carl von Deinem is a "good German," since he chose to leave the war-mongering German dictatorship and establish himself in England, a free country wishing for peace. But other British characters present the view that "good Germans" remain in Germany, patriotically serving their country, and that Carl is one of the "rats" who betrayed his native land. Still others suspect him of being loyal to Germany and of coming to England to work as a spy in Germany's service. There is talk of a kind of "honor" in fighting for one's country—a soldier of one nation kills a soldier of another because of the *battle,* but there exists a mutual respect between the enemy fighters. This is contrasted with the "treasonous" conduct of persons of any country who collaborate with the enemy and assist in the defeat of their own country.

Discussions about Carl von Deinem suggest that if he is, in fact, working as a spy for Germany in England, his penalty must be death, but it will at least be an "honorable" death since his work was in the patriotic service of his country. The British traitors who are known as "M" and "N" are "dishonorable," since their work is in the service of the enemy.

Several references are made to the general lack of preparedness for war under which Britain had labored while foolishly pursuing—along with France—an "appeasement" policy with respect to Germany and her threats. There are comments about the efficiency of the German war machine, and the superiority of German air power. There are also outraged comments about German soldiers machine gunning innocent civilians, and a comment that "the Nazi creed is a *youth* creed," when someone doubts that one of the younger characters could be an enemy collaborator.

Some of Sheila Perenna's apparently unpatriotic pronouncements are attributed to "the natural rebelliousness of youth." Regarding youth, the Beresfords explain to each other why they feel differently now than they did during the First World War: "When you're young you don't see the pity and the waste of war." They are as committed to their present task as they were to their tasks during the earlier war, but they are definitely not "having fun" this time around.

The Body in the Library (1942)

SETTING

The story takes place in and near the fictitious village of St. Mary Mead and at a luxury hotel in the fictitious resort town of Danemouth on the south coast of England. There is a real resort town named Bournemouth on the coast of the county of Hampshire, and it can be deduced that Danemouth is modeled after Bournemouth.

Christie introduced the village of St. Mary Mead in the 1928 novel *The Mystery of the Blue Train.* There was no mention of the county in which the village was located, but Paddington Station was the London railway station serving passengers to that area, and therefore the village must have been somewhere west of London. Two other novels of the period named the neighboring town of Market Basing as also being served by Paddington Station, but again no county was mentioned. In the 1930 *Murder at the Vicarage,* St. Mary Mead is located in the fictitious county of Downshire.

Then, in 1937, Market Basing was the setting for *Poirot Loses a Client* and in that novel the real county of Berkshire was stated as being the location of Market Basing. A road leading out of that town was marked "Much Benham Road," suggesting that Much Benham was a neighboring town. Much Benham is the nearest market town to St. Mary Mead; therefore it can be assumed that all three of these places are in the real county of Berkshire.

For *The Body in the Library,* Christie places St. Mary Mead in a new fictitious county, Radfordshire, and the neighboring county is the fictitious coastal county of "Glenshire." In Glenshire is the fictitious coastal resort town of Danemouth, which can be thought of as a fictional Bournemouth. These changes are necessary in order to place St. Mary Mead within "half an hour's drive" of the coastal resort of Danemouth for reasons that are made clear as one reads the story.

There is no detailed description of St. Mary Mead, although the pub known as The Blue Boar, which was mentioned in the 1930 *Murder at the Vicarage,* is still prospering. The vicar and his wife, Leonard and Griselda Clement, continue to live there as well as Miss Marple, Mrs. Price-Ridley, Miss Hartnell and Miss Wetherby, all of whom we met in the 1930 *Murder at the Vicarage.* There is a brief reference to Old Hall, the finest and most elaborate house in the village, which was the home of the murder victim in the earlier novel. In addition, we visit two homes that were not mentioned earlier—a large mansion called Gossington Hall, located about a mile and a half from the village—and a new, smaller house called Chatsworth. Gossington Hall is a fine residence staffed with numerous servants, including a butler, a cook and several housemaids and gardeners. Chatsworth is very negatively described as "all modern conveniences enclosed in a hideous shell of half timbering and sham Tudor." Recently built by a man named Booker, the villagers refer to the house as "Mr. Booker's New House." It is located about a quarter mile from the village proper, on the road leading to Gossington Hall.

Gossington Hall—and the vicarage with which we are familiar from having read *Murder at the Vicarage*—both have French windows on the ground floor and characters use these windows to enter and leave the houses from time to time. At Gossington Hall, where the murder victim is found lying on the hearthrug in the library, a library window is found to have been forced open and evidently used by the murderer to enter the house. In one scene, Miss Marple leaves her own cottage "through the French windows of her drawing room," goes to the vicarage next door, and taps on the window of the vicarage drawing room to gain admittance.

At Danemouth, the setting is a large, modern luxury hotel called The Majestic, which caters to well-to-do vacationers. The grounds include tennis courts and there is a tennis pro employed to work with the guests on their skills; this man is also a "dance pro" and part of his job is to be a dancing partner for female guests who lack dancing partners. There is a ballroom and a live dance orchestra. A female employee is "bridge and dance hostess." Her job is to perform exhibition dances at certain hours with the "dance pro" and to serve as a dance partner for male guests as well as to match the guests for bridge games. The Majestic is clearly a much more deluxe establishment than the resort hotel, The Jolly Roger, which we encountered in *Evil Under the Sun* a year or two earlier.

American readers must remember that whenever there are references to a "first floor" in Christie novels, it is *always* the "second floor" that is meant, because the ground floor of any building in Europe is called the "ground floor" and the floor above that one is the "first floor." At the Majestic Hotel, all of the guest rooms are located on the upper floor ("first floor") and there is also a "dingy corridor" leading to some less desirable rooms having no view of the sea. These rooms are used by the staff, including the servants and other employees, and are furnished with cast-off, older furniture formerly used in the more desirable, "guest rooms." It is possible to enter and leave these "staff rooms" by a small staircase and a terrace at the side of the hotel unseen by anyone at the main front entrance of the hotel.

The story takes place in late September, probably in 1939. There are references to the film industry and, in particular, to the actress Vivien Leigh who was evidently "discovered" and then became the famous female star of *Gone with the Wind*. She was selected for the part in January of 1939. This is important because in *The Body in the Library* a starry-eyed teenage girl hopes to be "discovered" in a similar way, and so the action in the story can take place no earlier than 1939. However, the action cannot take place very much later than that because of the ominous events of World War II. France fell to Germany in the summer of 1940 and then Germany began to attack Britain by air. Under those conditions there would have been no pleasant vacationing at seaside resorts in Britain. Therefore it is wise for readers to imagine the story as taking place in 1939.

There is a reference to the difficulty of finding work because of economic conditions. The character who is the "dance and tennis pro" explains that, despite a "public school education," he would be lucky to find a job as reception clerk in a hotel. He in fact did have a job as a salesman in a plumbing establishment, selling "superb peach and lemon colored porcelain baths," but he was fired for incompetence. Since he is a good tennis player and dancer, he has this current position, which he considers to be equally degrading. See the entry "Public School" in the *Appendix*.

The "Minoan Fourteen," a make of automobile which is undoubtedly fictitious, is described as "the year's popular cheap car," and there are no fewer than eight identical Minoan Fourteens parked in the Majestic Hotel parking lot on one particular day.

The village of St. Mary Mead experiences considerable excitement when it is rumored that a "film star" has moved into "Mr. Booker's New House," but this interest soon dies when it is learned that the occupant is only a minor person involved in designing sets for films. Only the proprietor of The Blue Boar continues to be enthusiastic about this new resident, as he often hosts parties for London friends who patronize the Blue Boar regularly. Regarding these parties, the village spinsters are scandalized by their noise and tone, as they supposedly feature drunkenness, nudity and sex. We must take these comments with a grain of salt because, in the course of the story, the dead body of a fully-clothed young woman is found in the library at Gossington Hall and, within an hour, the imaginative village gossips declare that the body was naked.

STORY

On a bright September morning in 1939 a housemaid at Gossington Hall, a large mansion near the village of St. Mary Mead, discovers the corpse of a young woman lying on the hearth rug in the library. She awakens her employers, Colonel and Mrs. Bantry, with the news and they are at first disbelieving. Mrs. Bantry's disbelief soon changes to pleasurable excitement and she phones her friend, Jane Marple, at the unheard-of hour of 7:45 a.m., begging her to come to Gossington Hall at once, since she is "so good at bodies."

Miss Marple has a reputation for having special abilities in crime solving.

The victim had been a dance hostess at a luxury hotel in the nearby resort of Danemouth. Soon the murder of a second young girl is discovered. Miss Marple solves the mystery of both killings by laying a trap that prevents a third murder and catches the murderer in the act.

CHARACTERS

Dolly Bantry, the lady of the house at Gossington Hall, a large residence about a mile and a half from the village of St. Mary Mead. She is an old friend of Miss Jane Marple, a resident of the village. Mrs. Bantry is an enthusiastic flower gardener and, as the story begins, she is having a beautiful dream about her sweet peas taking a First at the flower show. When the body of a young girl is found in her library, she "puts on a good face," according to her husband, and appears not to be upset. Actually, she's thrilled about this exciting new experience—until the entire village begins to suspect that her husband and the young girl had been having a "relationship."

Colonel Arthur Bantry, Mrs. Bantry's husband, who is stunned by the discovery of a body in his library. He affirms and reaffirms that he has never laid eyes on the girl in his life. Nobody except his wife and Miss Marple believe him, however, and as time goes on, he is shunned by everyone in the village.

Mary, the First Housemaid at Gossington Hall, who discovers the body in the library while opening the curtains there on a beautiful September morning.

Second Housemaid at Gossington Hall

Mrs. Eccles, the cook, or possibly the housekeeper, who soothes the hysterical housemaid Mary

Lorrimer, the butler at Gossington Hall

Leonard Clement, the vicar of St. Mary Mead, whom we met in the 1930 *Murder at the Vicarage*. In Mrs. Bantry's dream about the flower show, it is the vicar, dressed in his cassock and surplice, who is giving out the prizes—in church.

Griselda Clement, the vicar's wife who, in the above dream, wanders past the vicar dressed in a bathing suit, "but, as is the blessed habit of dreams, this fact did not arouse the disapproval of the parish in the way it would assuredly have done in real life." We also met Griselda in the 1930 *Murder at the Vicarage*.

David Clement, the baby boy of the Clements who is currently learning to crawl.

Police Constable Palk, who is the first police officer to hear of the crime.

Mrs. Palk, the wife of Constable Palk, who when told by her husband that Colonel Bantry doesn't know the dead girl from Adam, asks, "Then what was she doing in 'is library?"

Inspector Slack, a police officer from Much Benham, whom we met in the 1930 *Murder at the Vicarage*. He is "an energetic man who belied his name and who accompanied his bustling manner with a good deal of disregard for the feelings of anyone he did not consider important."

Colonel Melchett, the Chief Constable of the County of Radfordshire and Inspector Slack's superior. He is "an irascible-looking man with a habit of tugging at his short red mustache." He is a friend of the Bantrys, and Inspector Slack feels that Colonel Melchett is shielding them, tacitly accusing him of favoring his own class, and it's possible that he is.

Jane Marple, an elderly spinster living in St. Mary Mead, who solved the mystery in *Murder at the Vicarage* several years earlier and then solved many more mysteries in *The Tuesday Club Murders*, a group of short stories. She has developed a reputation for cleverness, but she denies this with great humility. She affirms over and over again that "the world is a very wicked place" and that it is foolish to believe anything anyone says until one verifies the facts personally. She solves most mysteries not by "woman's intuition," which she considers to be silly notion, but by what she describes as "specialized knowledge of village life," and she often recalls people and events of whom she is "reminded" by certain aspects of a case. As soon as she sees the body of the girl in the Bantrys' library, Mrs. Bantry asks, "Well, doesn't it remind you of something?" And of course, it does.

Raymond West, Miss Marple's nephew who "writes clever books." He has no part in this story, except in the thoughts of Miss Marple when her telephone rings at the unheard-of hour of seven forty-five a.m.

Muswell, the Bantrys' chauffeur, who fetches Miss Marple at the request of Mrs. Bantry on the morning of the murder.

Dr. Haydock, the doctor at St. Mary Mead, and also the police surgeon, whom we met in *Murder at the Vicarage*. He is a big, broad-shouldered man. Occasionally he finds that the police are apt to try to "bend" medical evidence in the interest of finding an easy solution to a crime, but he refuses to cooperate with them on that subject.

Two Plainclothes Men, One with a Camera, who study the evidence at the scene of the crime

Mrs. Chetty's Youngest, Edie, who bit her nails and liked "cheap finery" and of whom the murder victim reminds Miss Marple

Basil Blake, who lives in "Mr. Booker's new house," a quarter of a mile from St. Mary Mead proper. Mrs. Bantry is a friend of his mother, and affirms, "He was an adorable baby in his bath." The adorable baby, however, has grown up to be a rather rude young man.

Selina Blake, the mother of Basil Blake and a friend of Mrs. Bantry. She has herbaceous borders that make Mrs. Bantry green with envy, and she is "frightfully generous with cuttings." Therefore, according to Mrs. Bantry, her son cannot be guilty of the crime.

Old Mrs. Berry, a day woman who "does for" Basil Blake and who reported to Miss Marple the condition of his home after one of his parties.

The Landlord of the Blue Boar, who is very happy to have Basil Blake living in the village, as his frequent parties result in increased revenues at the pub.

Dinah Lee, Basil Blake's girlfriend, a platinum blonde with a temperament

Rosenberg, a "filthy brute of a Central European" who pawed Dinah about at last night's party, to Basil's disgust.

A Black-haired Spanish Girl who was occupying Basil's attention while he was getting drunk at the above party

Simmons, a police officer who examined the library window at Gossington Hall, declaring the break-in to be an "amateur job."

Mrs. Saunders, age thirty-six, dark hair, blue eyes, and missing a week ago, one of four women recently reported missing. According to the police, "everyone but her husband knows she's gone off with a commercial man from Leeds."

Mrs. Barnard, age sixty-five, another of the four women reported missing

Pamela Reeves, age sixteen, brown hair in pigtails, five feet five inches tall, reported missing. She was last seen with friends at a Girl Guides rally.

Ruby Keene, age eighteen, five feet four inches tall, platinum blonde, reported missing from the Majestic Hotel in Danemouth where she was a dancer. Her dead body is found in the library at Gossington Hall. She was about to be "adopted" by a fatherly guest at the hotel, Mr. Conway Jefferson, a fact that was resented by Conway's daughter-in-law and son-in-law. They describe her as a "garden variety gold-digger."

Mr. Prestcott, the manager of the Majestic Hotel, who is understandably upset about the murder of Ruby Keene, but who seems more upset about its potential effect on the hotel.

Josephine ("Josie") Turner, the bridge and dance hostess at the Majestic Hotel. It was Josie who brought her cousin Ruby to the Majestic to dance in her place after she had twisted her ankle, and it is she who identifies the body found in the Bantrys' library as that of Ruby.

One of Josie's qualities is an unusual ability to "smooth over differences" between people. As "bridge hostess" at the hotel, she is able to successfully match strangers for card games, and as "dance hostess" she provides unaccompanied males with a dance partner. She is popular with the hotel guests.

Raymond Starr, the handsome "dance and tennis pro" at the Majestic Hotel, "a fine-looking specimen, tall, lithe and good-looking, with very white teeth in a deeply bronzed face. He was dark and graceful. He had a pleasant, friendly manner and was very popular in the hotel." Raymond explains that, as a result of his public school education, his only job qualifications are the ability to teach tennis and ballroom dancing.

Conway Jefferson, a wealthy, elderly man who lost his wife, son and daughter—and the use of his legs—in a tragic airplane accident eight years ago. His two children's spouses survived and he has treated them as his own children ever since, providing them with a home and living expenses, because of the grief all three of them have shared.

Mr. Jefferson had formed a fatherly attachment to Ruby Keene and was about to adopt her before she was murdered.

Margaret Jefferson, Conway Jefferson's wife, who was killed in the airplane accident eight years ago.

Rosamund Gaskell, Conway Jefferson's daughter, also killed in the plane accident

Mark Gaskell, Conway Jefferson's son-in-law. A poor man when he married Rosamund Jefferson, he benefited from Conway's generosity early in his marriage, but he is a gambler who has squandered all of his wife's money and he is now entirely dependent on Conway. He is a murder suspect because a settlement by Conway Jefferson upon Ruby Keene would have deprived him of a substantial inheritance.

Frank Jefferson, Conway Jefferson's only son, who died in the airplane accident eight years ago. Although not a dishonest man, he was not very talented in finance and had made poor investments with the money he received from his father upon his marriage. His widow, Adelaide, is now impoverished and dependent on her father-in-law's continued generosity.

Adelaide Jefferson, Frank Jefferson's widow, who has a nine-year-old son by an earlier marriage. For eight years she and her son have lived under Conway Jefferson's roof, but she has grown "weary of grief." She would like to remarry but fears that her "independence" might be viewed by Conway as "abandonment." Like her brother-in-law Mark, she is a murder suspect, and for the same reason.

Mike Carmody, Adelaide Jefferson's first husband, who died shortly after they were married, before their son Peter was born

Peter Carmody, Adelaide Jefferson's nine-year-old son. He is a bright, cheerful child who is delighted with the excitement of the murder case, as he is a reader of detective stories and even has autographs from Dorothy Sayers, Agatha Christie, Dickson Carr and H. C. Bailey! A cute kid. He collects clues, or better stated, "souvenirs" of the case. In a match box he has the tip of a fingernail of Ruby Keene—the murder victim—and a segment of a shoelace used by George Bartlett, which Peter snipped off and has kept as a souvenir "just in case George turns out to be the murderer."

George Bartlett, a young guest at the Majestic Hotel who was the last person to see Ruby Keene alive, but who denies any knowledge of her disappearance. His car is later found burned in a nearby quarry, with the incinerated corpse of a female inside.

Miss Wetherby, Miss Hartnell, and Mrs. Price-Ridley, three ladies with time on their hands and other people's private lives on their minds. Mrs. Price-Ridley is a rich and dictatorial widow; the others are garden-variety British spinsters. We met them in the 1930 *Murder at the Vicarage* and they are still alive and well and living in St. Mary Mead. Within hours—or even minutes—of the discovery of the body in the Bantrys' library, they decide that the murdered girl must have been Arthur Bantry's mistress.

Clara, Mrs. Price-Ridley's little maid and "informant." Her current "information" includes the falsehood that the body of the girl found in Colonel Bantry's library was naked.

The Fishmonger who, owing to his advantageous geographical position within the village, always knows where everyone is

The Fishmonger's Young Man, who told Clara, Mrs. Price-Ridley's maid, that "he'd never have believed it of Colonel Bantry—not with him handing round the plate on Sundays and all."

Superintendent Harper, of the Glenshire police. He is involved in the investigation, along with Colonel Melchett and Inspector Slack of the Radfordshire police, because the murder victim Ruby Keene lived and worked in Danemouth, which is in Glenshire. Of the three police officers, Superintendent Harper is the kindest, and the most modern and intelligent, somewhat resembling Inspector Narracott whom we met in the 1931 *Murder at Hazelmoor*. He tends to be soothing with Mr. Prestcott, the hotel manager, while Colonel Melchett tends to be brutally blunt.

Superintendent Harper also recognizes his own limitations and the special abilities of other people. He solicits the aid of both Miss Marple and Sir Henry Clithering in probing the minds of certain characters because he knows they can be more effective than he. The brutally blunt Colonel Melchett and the downright rudely disrespectful Inspector Slack would have failed in these cases, and neither would have admitted that special abilities are to be found in other persons.

The Night Porter at the Majestic Hotel who had no information to offer about Ruby Keene's disappearance or about George Bartlett's activities of the evening

The Barman at the Majestic Hotel, who saw George Bartlett looking melancholy, but cannot remember quite when

Edwards, Conway Jefferson's valet, who provides Sir Henry Clithering with special insights about everyone in the Jefferson family

Sir Henry Clithering, a retired Scotland Yard officer and an old friend of Miss Marple and of Conway Jefferson. He is called to Danemouth by Conway Jefferson in order to work "on his own, as if an amateur" to find the murderer of Ruby Keene. It is he who recommends Miss Marple to Conway and, of course, it is she who solves the mystery.

Sergeant Higgins, a subordinate of Superintendent Harper, who is in charge of the disappearance of George Bartlett's car

Lil, the writer of a letter found in Ruby Keene's handbag. She is a friend of Ruby's and works at the Palais de Danse in south London

Mr. Findeison, Young Reg, May, Barney, Old Grouser and Ada, people mentioned in the letter written by Lil to Ruby Keene

A Laborer who noticed "glare as from fire" near a quarry and reported it to the police

Mr. Harbottle, his Sister and their Maidservant, people of whom Miss Marple is reminded by the present case. Mr. Harbottle's sister had gone away for a few weeks and when she returned she found the maidservant "quite above herself, sitting in the drawing room and not wearing her cap and apron." After delivering a reprimand to the maidservant, Miss Harbottle herself was dismissed from her brother's home and found herself living in quite uncomfortable lodgings.

Mr. Badger the Chemist, his Wife, and the

Young Lady Who Worked in the Cosmetics Section, additional people of whom Miss Marple is reminded. Mr. Badger was "quite taken" by the Young Lady and gave her a valuable piece of jewelry, then was outraged to learn (thanks to his wife's investigation of the matter) that she had pawned it and given the money to her boyfriend to gamble with.

Jessie Golden, the Baker's Daughter, whom Miss Marple compares with Josephine Turner. She was a nursery governess who married the son of the house.

Mr. Cargill, the builder, of whom Miss Marple is reminded by Mark Gaskell. He bluffed a lot of people into having things done to their houses they never meant to do, and then overcharged them for it.

King Cophetua and the Beggar Maid, an old story recalled by Miss Marple in comparison with the relationship between Conway Jefferson and Ruby Keene

Briggs, the head gardener at Old Hall in St. Mary Mead who kept the place better with three men and a boy than it had once been kept by six men. Like Sir Henry, he is retired now but does occasional "jobbing." He always knew when someone wasn't working.

Hugo McLean, an old friend—and a longtime suitor—of Adelaide Jefferson. He was near Danemouth at the time of the crime. Adelaide has an alibi for the time of the murder but Hugo does not. Ruby Keene's death restored Adelaide's chances of an inheritance and, since Hugo hopes to marry her, he had a motive for the murder.

Dr. Metcalf, who explains the state of Conway Jefferson's health. Dr. Metcalf is one of the best-known physicians in Danemouth; his presence in the sickroom has an invariably cheering effect, although he explains that Conway Jefferson's health, due to a weak heart, is precarious, and that "any sudden shock might cause him to 'pop off.'"

The Elder Brother of Raymond Starr who is doing well in New York in the publishing business

An Old Colonel at a Hotel on the Riviera who insulted Raymond Starr by referring to him repeatedly—and loudly—as "the gigolo."

Mrs. Partridge and Alice, yet two more "village parallels" from Miss Marple's repertoire. Alice always twitched her nose when she was about to cheat with the tradesmen's accounts, holding back a shilling or two and saying it could go on next week's. Mrs. Partridge also twitched her nose and that was why Miss Marple was so against her being sent to do the Red Cross collections. She succeeded in embezzling seventy-five pounds before she was caught.

Florence Small, Jessie Davis, Beatrice Henniker, Mary Price and Lilian Ridgeway, all young friends of the missing girl Pamela Reeves, whose body was found burned in the car at the quarry. All agree that Pamela told them that she was planning to go to Woolworth's in Danemouth after the Girl Guide rally, and then home afterwards. But during their interviews with the police, which Miss Marple is allowed to observe, Miss Marple senses that Florence knows something more, and she succeeds in extracting that information from her.

A Constable at the police station in Danemouth who interviews the above five young ladies in the presence of Miss Marple.

A Film Producer Just Back from Hollywood who proposed a "screen test" to a certain starry-eyed young lady

Mr. Hamsteiter, the "boss" of the above Film Producer

The Most Influential Parishioner Who Didn't Like Children, and who visited Griselda Clement just as Miss Marple was leaving the vicarage

The Vicarage Maid, who announced the arrival of The Most Influential Parishioner

Old Sims, Basil Blake's family lawyer

Anderson, one of Colonel Bantry's tenant farmers, who is going to have a new roof on his house, as the old one can no longer be patched

Thompson, a man chosen in place of Colonel Bantry, for unexplained reasons, to chair the meeting of the Radfordshire Council Meeting

The Duffs, who must cancel the dinner to which Colonel Bantry is invited because "Cook is ill."

The Naylors, who are only too pleased to learn that Colonel Bantry does not feel up to visiting them as scheduled

A Stout, Perspiring Man seen dancing with Josie Turner in the Majestic Hotel ballroom

An Anemic-looking Girl with Adenoids, Dull Brown Hair and an Expensive and Unbecoming Dress seen dancing with Raymond Starr in the Majestic Hotel ballroom

Watson, a character from the Sherlock Holmes stories, the "sidekick" of Holmes. Sir Henry Clithering compares his relationship to Miss Marple with Watson's to Holmes.

COMMENTS

The Miss Marple character was created in 1930 for *Murder at the Vicarage* and the character reappeared a couple of years later in a group of short stories entitled *The Tuesday Club Mur-*

ders. For some reason Christie chose to wait a decade before starring Miss Marple in another book. It is in *The Body in the Library* that Miss Marple makes this reappearance.

A large number of interesting characters populate *The Body in the Library,* and one of them is refreshingly new. It is Conway Jefferson, who is old and wealthy but who actually *likes* young people. In most Christie stories, the older generation invariably dislikes the younger one—not only the younger generation in general but especially the young people of the family. Most often the older person holds the purse strings and threatens to "disinherit" the young people unless they "suck up," which they bitterly resent. Conway Jefferson is completely different. He generously divides his fortune between his two children upon their marriages so that they can enjoy their "inheritances" while they are still young enough to be able to. In two future Christie novels we will encounter similar characters. In the 1948 *There Is a Tide* there will be generous Gordon Cloade, and in the 1949 *Crooked House* we will encounter generous Aristide Leonides.

An interesting assortment of law enforcement officers is another feature of *The Body in the Library.* There is Colonel Melchett, who is very conservative, somewhat narrow-minded, and brutally abrupt. There is Inspector Slack, who is energetic, rude and insulting. There is Superintendent Harper, who is gentle, courteous, and respectful of the abilities of others. There is the retired Sir Henry Clithering, who was known for his ability to quickly grasp and sum up the facts in a case. He is a friend of Miss Marple and he brings her into the case more or less officially.

In many of the earlier Christie novels the police were just plain failures. Hercule Poirot, in particular, although he has always paid lip service to the "excellent British police force," usually found himself at odds with Inspector Japp, although it must be admitted that over the years they became more and more "partners" and less the "adversaries" that they had been at first. Still, the police got rather poor treatment by Agatha Christie in her earlier stories, and evidently other detective story writers treated them even worse.

We have in *The Body in the Library* a knowledgeable expert in detective stories in the person of nine-year-old Peter Carmody, who declares that "making fun of the police in detective stories is old fashioned." Peter is the first child character whom Agatha Christie portrays in a completely affirmative way. He is bright, articulate and intelligent, and he has autographs of several detective story writers, including the famous Agatha Christie! His mother, Adelaide Jefferson, is portrayed as being not only a devoted mother but also as an attractive and intelligent person. Both of these are firsts in Christie. There have been very few children in Christie's books to date, and they have all been rather negative characters, except perhaps the cute toddler Betty Sprot in *N or M?,* and the unhappy fifteen-year-old Linda Marshall in *Evil Under the Sun.*

In the 1939 *And Then There Were None* there was a child who had drowned. He was described as "a horrid, whiny, spoilt little brat." The same year, in *Easy to Kill,* we heard of a mean adolescent boy who enjoyed cutting up wasps and twisting smaller boys' arms. In the 1937 *Poirot Loses a Client* there was a young mother, Bella Tanios, whom everybody described as dull, dowdy, dumpy, unfashionable and "devoted to her children." The children were described by more than one character as being "thoroughly spoiled." In the 1935 *The A.B.C. Murders* there was a "filthy child of undetermined gender that needed its nose attended to." Its mother was a disgusting woman "of the lower classes" who expected to be paid for answering Hercule Poirot's questions. In the 1932 *Peril at End House,* there was a ten-year-old boy who wished the murder victim had had her throat cut instead of simply being shot. He once saw pigs being killed and liked it. Of course he was, like the filthy, snotty-nosed child in *The A.B.C. Murders,* a child of working class parents, so what can one expect? Aside from these, there had been no children at all in Christie's detective novels, unless we count Lady Eileen Brent's two younger sisters, Daisy and Dulcie in the 1925 *The Secret of Chimneys,* aged ten and twelve but acting like five-year-olds, and the seven-year-old son of Henry and Sylvia Bassington-ffrench in the 1934 *The Boomerang Clue,* who was not even described.

In the future there will be some more nasty little brats. In the 1946 *Murder After Hours* a naughty little boy will craftily obtain mummy's permission to manufacture nitroglycerin, and in the 1949 *Crooked House* an exceptionally naughty little girl will do some things that are even worse. In the 1952 *Mrs. McGinty's Dead* two rotten little brats will torture a cat in Ariadne Oliver's presence and sass their mother in Hercule Poirot's. In the 1956 *Dead Man's Folly* a greedy little girl will sell secrets about her murdered older sister to Hercule Poirot for five shillings. It will not be until the 1957 *What Mrs. McGillicuddy Saw* that we will encounter any more *likeable* children in a Christie novel: fourteen-year-old Alexander Eastley and his school chum James Stoddart-West who, like Peter Carmody, will have fun looking for clues and will provide us with a few chuckles. There will be some cute kids in the 1963 *The Clocks,* some pleasant teenagers in the 1969 *Hallowe'en Party* and some more pleasant teenagers in the 1974 *Postern of Fate.*

There are a couple of interesting comments from characters in *The Body in the Library* on the subject of "masculinity." Basil Blake, who is involved in the film industry, remarks that Colonel Bantry had always treated him as being "artistic and effeminate." The "dance and tennis pro," Raymond Starr, is rather despised by Colonel Melchett because of the "graceful way he walks, that swing from the hips." When he learns that the man's original name was Ramón—he had had a Spanish or Latin American mother—Melchett says to himself, "That explains that swing from the hips." It may be more Christie's perception than actual reality, or there may be some reality in the idea that there is an English prejudice against men who exhibit "artistic" tendencies. There has been only one Englishman, so far in a Christie novel, who had any interest in music or art. It was David Lee in *A Holiday for Murder,* who tried to succeed as a painter and also played the piano—and was despised for it by his macho, diamond-prospecting father who had lived in the wilds and fathered legions of illegitimate children—a *real* man, in other words.

Artists in Agatha Christie novels have always been—so far—second or third class citizens, banished by (or escaping from) their otherwise respectable families to unsavory places like France or Spain. In *Murder in Retrospect,* which will come a year after *The Body in the Library,* the father of Amyas Crale will "die of shock" when his only son "blossoms into being a painter." In Christie novels, English girls who marry artists are never heard from again, although their offspring—like Pilar Estravados in *A Holiday for Murder*—sometimes return to the family to make trouble.

Writers, too, seem to be somewhat disreputable types in the Christie world. Miss Marple describes her nephew Raymond West as "a writer, and therefore erratic, although early rising was not one of his eccentricities." In Christie's first novel, *The Mysterious Affair at Styles,* Lawrence Cavendish, though qualifying as a medical doctor, preferred to spend his time writing poetry, which his brother John ridiculed. In *Murder at Hazelmoor,* Martin Dering was a "moderately successful novelist" of whom Emily Trefusis stated: "Women talk about sex in corners with him. Real men hate him." In *Death on the Nile,* Tim Allerton was said to be a writer, although "it was understood among his friends that inquiries as to literary output were not encouraged," and of course Solome Otterbourne, in that same book, was a writer of vulgar trash and a pathetic alcoholic.

On the subject of "masculinity in the Christie world," there is an amusing scene in *The Body in the Library* in which Colonel Bantry is very angry about something a younger man has done. Colonel Bantry soon learns, however, that the young man had had "quite a bit to drink," and then his attitude softens towards the man, exhibiting "the Englishman's sympathy for alcoholic excess." It is doubtful, however, that Colonel Bantry would have "softened" in his attitude towards a *woman* who had gotten wasted and then done something stupid.

One final comment on a trivial subject in a discussion already plagued with triviality. Agatha Christie clearly had definite tastes in domestic architecture: If a *new* house is built, it should be *modern*. It should not be "pretending" to be something from another period. She has spoken of "castellated abominations"—usually houses built during the Victorian period by industrialists seeking to exhibit their wealth by building houses that resembled castles or châteaux from remote periods. Christie herself purchased two genuine period homes—a house from the Queen Anne period in Wallingford, Berkshire, close to London, and a much larger home built during the Georgian period, in the county of Devon. She appreciated the fine architecture of those periods but had no use for new buildings masquerading as "period pieces." As early as the 1924 *The Man in the Brown Suit,* there was a reference to "castellated abominations," and in the 1939 *Easy to Kill,* the self-made millionaire owner of several trashy weekly newspapers had purchased a Queen Anne period home and then altered it with fake stone turrets to make it look like a medieval castle, truly a "castellated abomination." In *The Body in the Library* there is a house near St. Mary Mead called Chatsworth, and the villagers refer to it as "Mr. Booker's new house" (Mr. Booker had built it.) It is described as "all modern conveniences enclosed in a hideous shell of half timbering and sham Tudor."

There is also a touch of humor in *The Body in the Library* regarding the British enthusiasm for flower gardening. Please see the *Comments* sections for the 1937 *Poirot Loses a Client* and the 1940 *The Patriotic Murders* for further discussions of that subject if it interests you.

The Moving Finger (1942)

(Alternate Title: *The Case of the Moving Finger*)

Setting

It is Spring of 1940 or 1941, but there are no references to current events, other than the possibility that the narrator, who is recuperating from injuries received in a flying accident, may have had the accident in the course of war action.

The setting is the fictitious village of Lymstock. No county is mentioned, but Lymstock is probably located in Devon, as the town is described as being close to "the moor," a reference to an area of wasteland called Dartmoor, in south Devon. There is a scene at the office of a physician in London and also a scene at a dressmaker's establishment in London. Aside from this, all of the action takes place in Lymstock, which is described as a very small, unimportant place in modern times but which was an important town at the time of the Norman Conquest in the eleventh century. Lymstock is served by railway but the station, for unknown reasons, is located half a mile from the village. There is a reference to the larger nearby town of Exhampton, further evidence that the story takes place in the county of Devon, since Exhampton is a major setting in the 1931 *Murder Hazelmoor,* and in that story Devon is clearly the county. Lymstock is further described as a place where everyone knows everyone else's business and where gossip is usually rampant.

Within the town there is a brief scene at a bakery, one or two scenes at the police station, a scene at the "Women's Institute" (described as "an ugly gabled building") and several scenes outside, in the High Street and also in the road leading to the railway station. Most scenes, however, take place in various private homes.

The narrator and his sister are renting a substantial home called Little Furze in Lymstock. The owner of Little Furze is an elderly woman whose investment income has diminished and who therefore finds it necessary to let the house to strangers while she lives in furnished rooms kept in Lymstock by a former servant woman. The house is not described in detail but there is a "little study" with windows facing the back of the property. There is a cook-housekeeper who lives in the home and a girl who comes in daily; there is also a gardener.

A scene takes place in a house called Prior's Lodge which, along with its owner, is described thus:

> Mr. Pye was an extremely ladylike plump little man, devoted to his *petit point* chairs, his Dresden shepherdesses and his collection of period furniture. He lived at Prior's Lodge in the grounds of which were the ruins of the old Priory dissolved at the Reformation.
> It was hardly a man's house. The curtains and cushions were of pastel shades in the most expensive silks.
> Mr. Pye's small plump hands quivered with excitement as he described and exhibited his treasures, and his voice rose to a falsetto squeak as he narrated the exciting circumstances in which he had brought his Italian bedstead home from Verona.

Mr. Pye describes the inhabitants of Lymstock in negative terms:

> "The dear good people down here, you know, so painfully bucolic—not to say *provincial*. Vandals—absolute vandals! And the insides of their houses—it would make you weep, dear lady, I assure you it would make you weep."

The servant staff at Prior's Lodge consists of a husband and wife; it is the husband who does the cooking and the wife is, among other things, the housekeeper and parlor maid.

Several scenes take place at the home of a lawyer and his family; this house has a "morning room" facing the front. Two murders take place in this home—one in an upstairs bedroom and one in the lower hall; the body of the second victim is concealed in a rarely used cupboard under the stairway. The house has a "second floor," (from the American point of view, a "third floor") in which there is "the old nursery" with a window facing the road. At this house there is a cook and one housemaid.

One or two scenes take place at the vicarage, "an attractive old house with a big, shabby, comfortable drawing room with faded rose cretonne." Servants at this home are not mentioned.

Story

It is spring of 1940 or 1941. Jerry Burton, a pilot, has been injured in a flying accident and is ordered by his London doctor to spend several months recuperating "away from cares and responsibilities," ideally in a country village where he can rest and enjoy peace and quiet. He and his sister Joanna rent a comfortable home called Little Furze in the village of Lymstock in Devon, near Dartmoor.

They soon receive an ugly anonymous letter

consisting of words cut from the pages of a book and pasted on a sheet of paper. The writer of the letter insinuates that Jerry and Joanna are not brother and sister at all but are unmarried lovers.

The local doctor, who visits Jerry at Little Furze on a regular basis to monitor his recuperation, explains that such anonymous letters have been received by large numbers of people in Lymstock, always accusing the recipients of sexual misdeeds.

Soon the wife of a local attorney commits suicide, having received a letter suggesting that one of their two sons is not the son of her husband. A few days later, a housemaid is murdered in their home.

The local police accomplish nothing in their investigations, but the wife of the vicar appeals to an old friend, Miss Jane Marple of St. Mary Mead, to come to Lymstock to solve the mysteries, which she does with her usual skill.

Characters

Jerry Burton, a young pilot who has suffered a serious flying accident, potentially forcing him to remain on his back for the rest of his life. Fortunately, in the words of his London doctor, he has the "constitution of an elephant," for he mends quickly in the "peaceful atmosphere" of a country village. In addition to the murder case and the mystery of the anonymous letters, Jerry becomes personally interested in the welfare of a young woman—Megan Hunter—who is plagued by low self-esteem. Jerry Burton is the narrator of the story.

Joanna Burton, Jerry's sister. She shares her brother's interest in the "neglected stepdaughter"—Megan Hunter—and pursues a new love interest in Lymstock: Dr. Owen Griffith.

Marcus Kent, Jerry Burton's London doctor, who prescribes a few months of rest in the country.

Emily Barton, the elderly owner of Little Furze, the house in Lymstock that Jerry and Joanna rent for the duration of his convalescence. She is, in Jerry's words, "the perfect spinster of village tradition."

Old Mrs. Barton, the tyrannical mother of Emily Barton, who died some years ago.

Edith Barton, Emily Barton's sister who died of influenza

Minnie Barton, Emily's sister who had an operation but did not recover

Mable Barton, Emily's sister who died of a stroke

Faithful Florence, Emily Barton's former parlourmaid who now has furnished rooms to let in Lymstock and is providing Miss Barton with a pair of them. She is "a tall, raw-boned, fierce-looking woman."

Partridge, Emily Barton's current housekeeper who has agreed to stay on at Little Furze while Jerry and Joanna Burton are living there.

Beatrice, the "daily" girl who helped Partridge at Little Furze until she received an anonymous letter accusing her of a sexual relationship with Jerry Burton

Richard Symmington, the lawyer in Lymstock, and the uninterested step-father of Megan Hunter.

Mona Symmington, Richard Symmington's wife. She divorced her first husband early in their marriage and settled with her baby daughter in Lymstock "to forget," then married the only eligible bachelor in the village. She is "a small anemic woman, fadedly pretty, who talked in a thin melancholy voice of servant difficulties and her health." Like her husband Richard, she is a source of annoyance to Jerry and Joanna because she appears not to like her daughter.

Brian Symmington and **Colin Symmington**, sons of Richard and Mona. Their parents appear to be much more interested in them than in Mrs. Symmington's daughter Megan.

Megan Hunter, the twenty-year-old daughter of Mona Symmington by a previous marriage. She is tall, ungainly, awkward and "young for her age." That is, she is childish and, though out of school, appears to have no adult interests, no friends, no hobbies and no interest in the future.

Captain Hunter, Mrs. Symmington's first husband and Megan's natural father. He is said to have been a blackmailer.

Rose, the cook at the Symmington home, a plump pudding-face woman of forty.

Agnes Woddell, a housemaid at the Symmington home. She is murdered and her body is hidden in a cupboard beneath the stairway. She had been planning to visit Partridge, the housekeeper at Little Furze, to ask for advice about something important, but she never kept the appointment.

Dr. Owen Griffith, the doctor in Lymstock who visits Jerry Burton each week to monitor the progress of his recovery. It is from Griffith that Jerry learns that other people in Lymstock have received anonymous letters. Griffith himself has received one accusing him of sexual acts with his female patients.

Aimee Griffith, Owen Griffith's sister who keeps house for him. She is a handsome woman in a masculine weather-beaten way, with a deep voice. She is also a feminist and resents the fact that her parents gladly financed her brother's medical studies but would never have countenanced doing the same for her, since she was female. Nevertheless, she enjoys village life and is active in all village activities—the Girl Guides, etc.

Reverend Caleb Dane Calthrop, the vicar of Lymstock. He is a scholarly, absentminded fuddy-duddy who constantly quotes from Latin whether anyone listening understands it or not. According to Jerry, "Dane Calthrop was perhaps a being more remote from everyday life than anyone I have ever met. His existence was in his books and in his study."

Maud Dane Calthrop, the wife of Rev. Dane Calthrop. She seldom gives advice and never interferes, yet she represents to the uneasy consciences of the village "the Deity personified." Mrs. Dane Calthrop takes her position of "wife of the vicar" very seriously and feels that she should know what everyone in the village is thinking. She is also the only person in the village who feels pity for the writer of the anonymous letters, describing the writer as "someone who has been racked with some terrible unhappiness."

Miss Ginch, Mr. Symington's former clerk-typist. Anonymous letters written to her and to Mr. Symington accused them of having illicit relations, a ridiculous notion, since she is "forty at least, with pince-nez and teeth like a rabbit." As a result of the letter, she changes jobs and now works for the local house agents. Jerry senses, however, that despite Miss Ginch's apparent annoyance and embarrassment about the letters, she is rather thrilled by the thought that someone attributes "illicit relations" to her.

Beatrice's Friend at the Garage, who also received an anonymous letter accusing Beatrice of sexual acts with Jerry Burton, and who believed it.

That Awful Old Bore Colonel Appleby, who bemoans the fact that there are no decent-looking girls in Lymstock, "except that governess girl of the Symingtons. She's worth looking at."

A Very Old Man on a Stool Writing Slowly and Laboriously at the office of Mr. Symington

A Small, Cheeky-looking Boy at the same office

Elsie Holland, the nursery governess at the Symington home, who takes care of their sons but ignores their daughter. Jerry Burton is bowled over by her physical beauty but disappointed in her speech.

Mr. Pye, "an extremely ladylike plump little man, devoted to his *petit point* chairs, his Dresden shepherdesses and his collection of period furniture." He considers the residents of Lymstock to be Philistines and he values art and good taste above everything else. He is also a gossip who tells Jerry and Joanna all about everyone in the village.

According to Miss Emily Barton, Mr. Pye has "strange visitors" to his home, possibly because he has traveled so much. [Note: Christie is undoubtedly suggesting that Mr. Pye is gay—he is repeatedly described as extremely effeminate—and this reference to "strange visitors," made by the Victorian Miss Barton, is reminiscent of the "strange visitors" received by the effeminate, and probably gay, Mr. Ellsworthy in the 1939 *Easy to Kill*.]

Mr. and Mrs. Prescott, Mr. Pye's house servants

The Coroner, who declares that the person responsible for writing the anonymous letters was "morally guilty of murder" in the matter of Mrs. Symington's suicide

Superintendent Nash, "tall, soldierly, with quiet reflective eyes and a straightforward, unassuming manner." Nash considers it a certainty that the anonymous letters are being written by a middle-aged woman, probably a spinster, basing this on past experience with similar cases.

Inspector Graves, a police officer from London with experience in anonymous letter cases

Jennifer Clark, the barmaid at the Three Crowns pub who is yet another person who receives an anonymous letter

The Bank Manager, still another recipient of an anonymous letter

That Milliner Woman, who wrote anonymous letters, a few years ago, which were similar to the present ones

A Schoolgirl in Northumberland, an example of an anonymous letter writer who was easily caught

Old Adams, the gardener at Little Furze

The Schoolmistress who, according to the gentle Miss Emily Barton, "is a most unpleasant young woman. Quite a *Red*, I'm afraid."

Constable Bert Rundle, who guards the front door at the Symington home after Agnes Woddell is found murdered there

Young Rendell from the Fish Shop, Agnes's boyfriend, who had a row with her over the anonymous letters

The District Nurse, who has an alibi for both murders

Mrs. Emory, a "daily woman" who works at Little Furze

Dora, over at Combe Acre, who successfully fended off "one of those narsty tramps who sell those little printed poems, by locking herself in the bathroom until the mistress returned"

Sir Henry Lushington, who was with Mr. Symmington all afternoon on the day of Agnes Woddell's death

Dr. Moresby, who together with Dr. Griffith, performs the post mortem on Agnes Woddell

Mrs. Cleat, the "local witch" who is at first suspected of writing the anonymous letters

Miss Jane Marple, a friend of Maud Dane Calthrop, who comes to Lymstock at her request to lend a hand in the solving of the mystery. We met Miss Marple in the 1930 *Murder at the Vicarage* and the 1942 *The Body in the Library*. In those stories she was a major character, but in *The Moving Finger* she is introduced very late in the story.

Edith, a former maid of Miss Marple, "such a nice little maid, and so willing, but sometimes just a *little* slow to take in things"—like Agnes Woddell

The Sister-in law of a Niece of Miss Marple's Cousin, who had a great deal of annoyance and trouble over some anonymous letters

Mary Grey, a.k.a. "Mirotin," Joanna Burton's dressmaker in London who transforms Megan Hunter into an attractive woman

A Stout Woman who was Enamored of a Skin-tight Powder-blue Evening Dress, with whom Mary Grey was being firm when Jerry Burton and Megan Hunter arrived

Antoine, Joanna's hairdresser who creates a new coiffure for Megan Hunter.

A Woman in a Farmhouse Having a Baby, whom Owen Griffith brings through the delivery safely, with Joanna's inexpert help

Paul, a former boyfriend of Joanna, from whom she receives a letter

Sergeant Parkins at the police station in Lymstock who, together with Superintendent Nash, identifies the writer of at least one of the anonymous letters

Mildmay of Exhampton, a lawyer recommended by Richard Symmington to the person accused of writing one of the letters

The Grocer's Wife, who "always thought the person accused of writing the letters had a queer look..."

Sir Jasper Harrington-West, a deceased friend of Mrs. Dane Calthrop, and among whose estate papers a certain murder weapon was found

COMMENTS

The Moving Finger may present a problem to American readers because the American edition differs considerably from the English edition in ways that may cause confusion. First of all, the English edition is divided into fifteen chapters, most of which are subdivided into numbered sections. The American edition is considerably shorter, consisting of eight rather long chapters, and some characters from the English edition are omitted in the American one.

In the American edition, the character "Mrs. Cleat" is mentioned for the first time in Chapter Three, in this paragraph:

> I was silent, for I had had a shock. The community was so small. Unconsciously I had visualized the writer of the letters as a Mrs. Cleat or her like, some spiteful, cunning half-wit.

There is no previous mention of a "Mrs. Cleat," and a reader may wonder "Who is this Mrs. Cleat?" Later in the story, the name "Mrs. Cleat" occurs again, and Joanna Burton explains that she is the "local witch," but how Joanna came to know this is not explained.

The English edition of the novel includes several characters that are not in the American one. One of these is Mrs. Baker, the mother of the housemaid Beatrice. It is in a conversation with Mrs. Baker that Jerry Burton learns, in the English edition, about the villagers' suspicions that "the local witch, Mrs. Cleat" is the writer of the anonymous letters.

There is also a statement by Jerry Burton that he intends to pay a visit to the local bakery to complain about "the currant loaf." No currant loaf had been previously mentioned, and a reader might wonder "What's this about a currant loaf?"

It is possible that Christie shortened the novel at the request of the American publishers, omitting the Mrs. Baker character but forgetting that it was she who had made Jerry aware of Mrs. Cleat, and omitting a previous conversation about an unsatisfactory currant loaf. There are other minor differences between the English and American editions. Mr. Pye's home is called Prior's End in the English Edition but Prior's Lodge in the American one. The housekeeper at Little Furze is called Mary Partridge in the English edition, and is consistently referred to as "Mary," but in the American edition she is consistently called "Partridge" and the name "Mary" is never mentioned.

In any case, the American reader should be aware that if at times there is confusion about how a piece of knowledge came to a character, it is possible that the American edition lacks the background event, the conversation, or even the character that provided it.

The Moving Finger may not appeal to certain readers because of the personalities of the narrator, Jerry Burton, and of his sister Joanna. They are judgmental about people and often sarcastic in their conversations with each other. One of Burton's habits is to compare people, especially Megan Hunter, to animals. He compares her to a horse, then a dog, then a stricken gazelle, then a hungry bird. He compares the face of the vicar's wife to that of a greyhound and her tread to that of an elephant. Certain readers may find this rather tiresome, and the personality of Jerry's sister Joanna is almost as unattractive as his.

Jerry's scene in the High Street, in which he is "bowled over" by the "incredible beauty" of Elsie Holland—only to be turned off instantly by the sound of her voice seems rather silly and pointless. His action of taking Megan Hunter to London to be "transformed" by a dressmaker and a hairdresser—and then "falling in love with his creation" and proudly showing off his "possession" at a restaurant—may strike some readers as a very insulting statement about what brings a young girl to adulthood and also about what love is. Furthermore, this silly act has nothing to do with the mystery.

In one scene Jerry and Joanna together "assist" Megan on her journey into womanhood by offering her her first cocktail. A fashionable new dress, a fashionable new coiffure, a cocktail glass in her hand and, voilà—she's grown up and lovable and happy. It is difficult to imagine that Christie was not embarrassed by this nonsense.

There are a number of interesting characters in *The Moving Finger,* to be sure, such as Aimee Griffith who makes some strong statements about a woman's right to build a career for herself. But quite a few of the characters are unpleasant ones and there is practically no humor at all. When Jerry and his sister Joanna have occasions to laugh, it is usually derisive laughter at the expense of a character who is beneath them socially, such as Elsie Holland who is "nothing but a nursery governess" or Rose, who is "one of those servants."

The effeminate Mr. Pye is a particularly unpleasant character, gleefully enjoying the sensation of the murder in Lymstock, but bemoaning the fact that it's just the sordid murder of "a little serving girl." The vicar is a very negative example of a clergyman, with his Latin quotations and general aloofness from the real world.

Finally, although Miss Marple solves the mystery, she is a minor character who is introduced practically at the end of the book, and there are not the usual interesting conversations between her and the other characters. In fact, she is in only two short scenes.

In this book, Christie attempted to "deal with" the problem of a young person who has low self-esteem because of neglectful, unaffectionate parents. She might better have treated this subject, if she wanted to, in one of her "straight" novels that she published under the pseudonym Mary Westmacott. It is possible that her own relationship with her daughter caused her to be interested in poor mother-daughter relationships in her writing. It would have been better, however, if she had not introduced this weighty subject in a "light fiction" murder mystery and then dealt with it so poorly.

For these reasons, *The Moving Finger* cannot be recommended as a "first Christie experience."

CAUTION: Two characters in *The Moving Finger* will reappear in Christie's 1961 novel *The Pale Horse.* If you have not yet read *The Pale Horse,* you are advised not to read the chapter on that novel, as it will eliminate two possible suspects and prevent your full enjoyment of *The Moving Finger.*

Murder in Retrospect (1943)

(Alternate Title: *Five Little Pigs*)

SETTING

Some sources give the publication year of *Murder in Retrospect* as 1943, but the earliest copyright year is 1941, and so we may place the action of the story in that year. It is late springtime when the story begins, as there are references to white lilac and Darwin tulips in bloom.

Although the "present year" is 1941, we soon move back sixteen years to 1925 when a woman was found guilty of the murder of her husband and sentenced to life in prison. The crime occurred in September of that year. The 1925 settings are two large, adjoining country estates in south Devon on the English Channel coast. The names of the estates are Alderbury, where the crime takes place, and Handcross Manor. Both are substantial homes.

At the time of the crime (1925) Alderbury, which has been in the Crale family for generations, is occupied by the current heir, a successful and wealthy painter, along with his wife and five-year-old daughter, and his wife's adolescent sister plus a governess, a nurse and three servants. Handcross Manor is occupied by a middle-aged gentleman whose interest in affluence is minimal. He lives the life of a simple country squire dabbling in botanical hobbies; there are probably one or two servants in his house but they are not mentioned.

In the present year (1941) Alderbury has become a hostel for students but Handcross Manor is still occupied by the aging country squire who continues to live a simple, solitary life.

Although the two large estates adjoin each other, the houses themselves are in fact about a mile and a half apart. Both properties have coastlines on the English Channel, and an inlet known as "The Creek" separates them; it has the appearance of a narrow river but is in fact part of the sea. It is narrow enough to be easily crossed by an average swimmer and there are rowboats that members of both families use to cross it. The houses are three miles apart by road, since the road curves inland.

At Alderbury there is a veranda from which it is possible to hear conversations taking place inside one room of the house when windows are open. Near the seacoast on the property there is a unique area enclosed by artificial "battlements" known as "The Battery Garden" with miniature cannons contributing to the fanciful idea. The artist sometimes uses this enclosed garden for painting, and it is there, while painting on a beautiful September afternoon, that he dies.

The 1941 settings include several offices and residences in London, because a few of the characters now live there. One residence is an apartment overlooking Regent's Park. Another is the luxurious home of a peer and his wife in Brook Street; the interior of this home is described as being furnished expensively but with no particular taste. At this home there are a butler and a footman and certainly other servants. One residence is a one-room "flatlet" where an aging governess lives in poverty. The room is described as "bedroom, sitting-room, dining-room and, by judicious use of the gas ring, kitchen, with a kind of cubbyhole attached to it containing a quarter-length bath and the usual offices."

The residence of Hercule Poirot is the setting for the opening scene, but there is no description of the apartment. Since we have no reason to believe that Hercule Poirot has moved, we can assume that he still lives in the modern London apartment building known as Whitehaven Mansions, where he has lived since the 1935 *The A.B.C. Murders*.

In addition to the London residences, the 1941 settings include the offices of at least two law firms. There is a scene in which Hercule Poirot and Ex-Superintendent Hale have a conversation, but whether this takes place at the home of the retired policeman or at an office somewhere in Devon or in London is not specified. Poirot travels to the county of Essex, just east of London, to interview one old gentleman at his home.

There are no references to any current events in the novel despite the fact that the bombing of Britain by Germany must be taking place. The only social development playing a role is the relatively easy acceptance of divorce in 1941 as compared with 1925; one or two characters comment that "today, a wife would divorce her husband for such causes, but sixteen years ago things were different." There is also one character—an old woman—who is steadfast in her Victorian traditional thinking, but who is enough of a feminist to affirm a woman's right to divorce when the husband has been adulterous.

Automobiles are not mentioned at all in the novel, and current clothing fashions are not either. On the first page of the novel the clothing of a young woman is described only to characterize her as a wealthy young woman with a good figure and good taste.

STORY

It is springtime in 1941 when Hercule Poirot receives a visit from a sophisticated young woman of twenty-one, Carla Lemarchant. She immediately explains that her original name was Caroline Crale, and she explains the purpose of her visit.

Sixteen years ago, when she was five years old, someone poisoned her father, the artist Amyas Crale. Her mother, Caroline Crale, was tried and convicted of the murder and sent to prison for life. Before dying in prison, she wrote a letter to be given to her daughter upon reaching the age of twenty-one. In the letter she swore to her daughter that she was innocent of the crime. Carla feels that she has good reason to believe her mother, and she appeals to Hercule Poirot to investigate this sixteen-year-old case and to prove, if possible, that her mother was indeed innocent.

After convincing himself that Carla will accept "the truth" even if it is an unwelcome truth, Poirot enthusiastically embarks on this investigation and, as always, he succeeds.

CHARACTERS

Hercule Poirot, the Belgian private investigator with the flamboyant mustache and egg-shaped head. In this story, Poirot uses very little

French and speaks correct English at all times, not using his "fractured English" direct translations of French which had characterized his speech in earlier stories. There are no references to his obsessions with neatness and symmetry, his aversion to the cold and to boats and ships, and there is no reference to his sophisticated palate. He does, however, on one or two occasions, take advantage of his "foreignness," as when speaking with Philip Blake, a person who Poirot feels must be flattered and allowed to feel intellectually superior.

> He was at his most foreign today. He was out to be despised but patronized.

Since Poirot is investigating a crime that occurred in the distant past, he has no interactions with police authorities in this story other than to question one officer who had remembered the old case.

Poirot, as we know, does not hesitate to use lies in order to ingratiate himself with certain kinds of characters in view of obtaining their cooperation. In this story he sticks to the truth—that he is a detective investigating a sixteen-year-old murder case—when interviewing two intelligent women who, he perceives, would not be fooled by a concocted story. But for the benefit of another woman and two men, he fabricates a false explanation for his interest in the case, knowing that if they knew that he was re-investigating the old case, they would refuse to cooperate.

Carla Lemarchant, (a.k.a. Caroline Crale the Younger), who writes to Hercule Poirot, requesting an interview. She engages Hercule Poirot to investigate a murder that took place sixteen years ago, hopefully to establish the fact of her mother's innocence.

Caroline Crale (deceased), mother of Carla Lemarchant. Originally Caroline Spalding, she had married Amyas Crale, a talented and well-known painter. She was arrested, tried and convicted of poisoning her husband when their daughter was five years old. What kind of woman was she? Five different people who knew her give five different answers to that question. Philip Blake describes her as a selfish shrew who made her husband's life a hell on earth with her jealousy, and who finally murdered him. Philip's brother Meredith describes her as a gentle creature who "forgave and forgave" her husband for his infidelities, and who was driven to murder by an insensitive husband who allowed his mistress to torment her. The aging governess of Caroline's younger sister describes her as a devoted wife who was entirely justified in committing murder. The "other woman," Elsa Greer, describes her as an evil woman who stood in the way of her husband's happiness when she could have released him from marriage in order to allow him to find contentment with another woman. Her younger sister Angela is the only person with memories of the crime who has ever believed that Caroline was innocent.

At the time of the murder trial, there was never any doubt—on either side—about her guilt. Even the defense attorneys admitted that "leniency in sentencing" was all they could hope for.

Amyas Crale, the father of Carla Lemarchant, who was poisoned sixteen years ago. What kind of man was he? The defense attorneys at the trial of Caroline Crale made a weak case in favor of suicide, but nobody—even they—ever believed that. Amyas Crale "loved the lusts of the flesh and enjoyed them." He was the last person on earth who would have committed suicide. His best friend, Philip Blake, affirms that although Amyas had plenty of affairs with women, the only woman he ever loved was his wife, and in any case, his art always came first, and Caroline should have understood that. According to Meredith, Amyas treated his wife abominably. According to the old governess, Cecilia Williams, he was irresponsible and cruel to his wife with his constant womanizing, and furthermore, he was not even a good painter. Naturally, Elsa Greer describes him as a wonderful man who deserved happiness but was murdered by a jealous wife. Caroline's younger sister Angela insists that Amyas and Caroline were devoted to each other and she agrees with Philip that Caroline was the only woman who ever mattered to Amyas.

A Nice Fat Farmer's Wife, whom Carla Lemarchant faintly remembers taking care of her before she left England for Canada when she was just five years old.

Uncle Simon and Aunt Louise in Montreal, who gave Caroline Crale's daughter the name Carla Lemarchant and raised her, never speaking to her of her real parents or of the murder.

John Rattery, Carla Lemarchant's fiancé

Sir Montague Depleach, attorney for the defense in the trial of Caroline Crale, who did his best to make a case for suicide, but failed to impress the jury with that notion.

Old Mayhew, now deceased, the senior partner of the firm who briefed Sir Montague for the defense

Elsa Greer, (Now Lady Dittisham), the daughter of a Yorkshire manufacturer. Amyas Crale was painting her portrait when she revealed to Caroline that Amyas was going to leave Caroline for her. She is negatively described, by everyone who remembers the murder and the trial, as a self-indulgent young girl who had no morals whatsoever. At the trial, the judge did not like her, the jury did not like her, and the attorneys on both sides did not like her either.

Cecilia Williams, who was governess to Caroline Crale's younger sister, Angela Warren. Her testimony at the trial was clear and unbiased. Although she felt that Caroline was absolutely justified in murdering her husband, Miss Williams was truthful and made no effort to refute or minimize the damning evidence against Caroline.

Humphrey Rudolph, the prosecuting attorney at the trial, now deceased. His job was very easy, as all evidence pointed to the guilt of Caroline Crale.

Quentin Fogg, a junior partner in Humphrey Rudolph's firm, who remembers Caroline Crale and who admired her, saying "She was never defeated because she never gave battle."

Philip Blake, Amyas Crale's best friend since childhood. According to some characters, he is a "nasty money-grubbing little brute" who went "into the City." According to his brother Meredith, he always resented Caroline because her marriage to Amyas interfered with his friendship with Amyas. Meredith describes Philip as "a mass of prejudices."

Meredith Blake, the older brother of Philip. While Philip has been a stockbroker living in London for years, Meredith inherited the family home in Devon, Handcross Manor, and lives there still. At the time of the murder and earlier, his hobby had been growing and studying medicinal herbs. It was from his laboratory that the poison used to kill Amyas Crale was stolen and he has suffered remorse ever since. He was once in love with Caroline, before she married Amyas Crale. Unlike his brother Philip, he has always been content with the life of an impoverished country squire.

Angela Warren, the younger half-sister of Caroline Crale. About fifteen years old at the time of the murder, she is now a successful and well-known archeologist. When she was a toddler, her older half-sister Caroline, in a fit of sibling jealousy, threw a heavy paperweight at her. The incident permanently disfigured one side of her face and destroyed the vision in one eye. Despite the incident, Angela forgave her sister long ago and has never borne any rancor towards her. But at the trial, the prosecuting attorney made the most of the incident, citing it as evidence of Caroline's "uncontrollable temper."

Old Avis, the judge at the trial, now deceased. Like the jury, he disliked Elsa Greer and felt that Caroline had been very much wronged. He saw her killing of Amyas Crale as the result of provocation and commuted her sentence to penal servitude for life.

George Mayhew, a young member of the firm of criminal lawyers that briefed the defending attorney. He was just nineteen years old at the time of the trial and remembers little about it.

Caleb Johnathan, a retired member of the Crale family's regular firm of solicitors. He provides Hercule Poirot with his most valuable insights on the subject of the Crale family.

Mr. Edmunds, the managing clerk of the Mayhew firm, who speaks with a "Scottish burr." He had taken a strong interest in the case and has definite opinions about everyone involved.

Richard Crale and Enoch Crale, Amyas Crale's father and grandfather. According to Mr. Johnathan, Richard Crale "died of the shock" when his son Amyas blossomed into being "a painter, of all things in the world." Both of his children had disappointed him: Amyas became a painter and Diana married a man who "wasn't a gentleman."

Mrs. Richard Crale, Amyas Crale's mother, who was "cram full of ideas—more ideas than sense," according to Mr. Johnathan. She played the harp and "enjoyed poor health and looked very picturesque on her sofa."

Diana Crale, Amyas Crale's sister who disappointed her father by marrying a man who was "not a gentleman."

Ex-Superintendent Hale, who remembers the case well and provides Hercule Poirot with the names of everyone involved.

Inspector Conway, whom Dr. Faussett phoned about the death of Amyas Crale

Dr. Andrew Faussett, who was summoned to Alderbury by the Crale family when Amyas was found dead

A Sergeant and a Police Surgeon who went to Alderbury along with Dr. Faussett

Colonel Frere, the chief constable who put the matter of Amyas Crale's murder into the hands of Superintendent Hale

A Nurse employed by the Crale family to attend to the five-year-old Caroline, daughter of Amyas and Caroline Crale

Lady Tressilian, the godmother of Caroline Crale. The nurse and young Caroline were visiting her in London on the day of the murder and so were not at home.

Lady Mary Lytton Gore, a friend of the Crale family. From her Hercule Poirot receives a letter of recommendation to facilitate his acceptance by Philip and Meredith Blake. Poirot first met her in the 1935 *Murder in Three Acts*.

Admiral Cronshaw, another person who provides Poirot with a letter of recommendation

A Middle-aged Butler at the home of Lord and Lady Dittisham in London

A Footman at the above home in London

Lord Dittisham, the current (and third) husband of Elsa Greer. He has enjoyed some success as a poet.

FRENCH INTO ENGLISH

Note: Hercule Poirot uses very little French in this novel. A few of the expressions below do not even occur in his conversation; they are part of the narrative text.

Chapter 1
Tout de même—Just the same...
En avant—Forward march!
En arrière—Backward

Chapter 2
mon cher—my friend

Chapter 5
succès d'estime—considerable success

Chapter 6
femme formidable—a woman to be reckoned with, an exceptional woman
The *bon dieu*—God

COMMENTS

Agatha Christie's characterization in *Murder in Retrospect* is outstandingly thorough and subtle. Five important characters present five differing portrayals of a murder victim and of the alleged murderer. Each of these people is also described by the others, and so as readers we are treated to a very rich experience in character development. Since the murder occurred sixteen years before Hercule Poirot's investigation of it, there is no action; there are only conversations from which Poirot and the reader form impressions of the suspects and draw conclusions. The mystery itself is fascinating and the solution is logical.

This is a novel to be read slowly and thoughtfully. It would not be a very good "first Christie experience" because it lacks humor and "sparkle" that make other Christie novels more fun to read. It should be postponed and read as perhaps a "fifth or sixth" Christie experience. It is certainly one of her best creations.

There are a few "favorite Christie issues and character types" that occur in *Murder in Retrospect*. In *The Body in the Library* there was an aging man who, unlike most "aging persons" in Christie's novels, was actually fond of the younger generation, enjoying the presence of young people, and behaving generously towards his children. That was Conway Jefferson, and he was very unusual. Most "aging persons" in Christie novels are antagonistic towards the younger generation, as we have seen.

In *Murder in Retrospect,* the older generation of two neighboring families finds the whole younger generation to be insufferable. Richard Crale, the father of Amyas and Diana, was disgusted with his children. Diana married a man who was "not a gentleman" and, according to one character, he "died of the shock" when his son Amyas blossomed into being a painter. The neighboring family, the Blakes, produced two sons who did not share their traditional attitudes. One son had no interest in country living and went to London to "make money." The other son actually preferred studying animal life to killing it!

As to a young Englishman's "disappointing" his family by "blossoming into an artist," it has already been observed that men with artistic leanings are generally unwelcome in the usual cast of Christie's more conservative characters (see the *Comments* section for *The Body in the Library.)*

Agatha Christie, in her *Autobiography,* made some interesting and amusing observations about "feminine behavior" in the late Victorian period. One favored "feminine behavior" was for a woman to make the most of illness, to faint often, and to be weak and delicate, spending entire days propped on pillows on a sofa, being "attended to." In *Murder in Retrospect* we have one of those women in the person of Amyas Crale's "artistic" mother who "enjoyed poor health." It may be that the fashionableness of being "physically weak and delicate" during the Victorian period corresponds roughly with the fashionableness, a few years ago, of being neurotic and having an "analyst," if one was an affluent suburban woman. To be free of neuroses was, apparently, to be boring.

Conservative Christie characters are usually very anti-foreign, at least in the earliest novels, and we have had plenty of experience with ex-military types such as Colonel Arbuthnot in *Murder in the Calais Coach* who ignores Poirot, sensing at once that he is "just another damned foreigner." Colonel Abercrombie in *The Patriotic Murders,* upon beholding Hercule Poirot in the dentist's waiting room, appeared to wish he had with him his insect spray. The very foreign Poirot is, in fact, likened to an insect by three different characters in that book.

In *Murder in Retrospect* one character, Philip Blake, is "too much of an Englishman to take the pretensions of a foreigner seriously." Christie understood that there was deep-rooted anti-foreign sentiment in English society and she obviously despised it more and more as the years went on.

Feminism has been an issue in Christie novels since at least as early as the 1938 *Appointment with Death,* in which Sarah King, a medical doctor, expressed anger when anyone found it "unusual" for a woman to accomplish something in a profession. In the 1941 *Evil Under the Sun,* Rosamund Darnley was a successful businesswoman and "a woman admired as much as any other" by Hercule Poirot. In *The Moving Finger,* Aimee Griffith made strong statements about her parents who "would not think of" paying the fees for her to study medicine, while they willingly financed her brother's medical studies. In *Murder in Retrospect,* Cecilia Williams makes equally strong statements about the equality of the sexes. Although an uncompromising Victorian woman on the subject of "the immorality of Men," she is modern in her view of divorce when it is a case of a married woman who is repeatedly insulted by a philandering husband. Though believing that Caroline Crale was absolutely justified in murdering her husband, she was scrupulously honest at the trial and did not minimize the damning evidence against the accused woman.

The whole subject of adultery, and a spouse's reaction to it, is an interesting issue in *Murder in Retrospect* and an important subject in the understanding of the psychology of both the victim and the alleged killer.

The issue of "healthy neglect" being a part of the "good parenting" ideas of the 1940s was touched upon briefly by Griselda Clement who, in the 1942 *The Body in the Library,* read all the latest books on good parenting and did her best (unsuccessfully) to neglect her adored toddler. In *Murder in Retrospect* the governess, Cecilia Williams, delivers quite a long monologue on the subject, affirming that mothers in particular are apt to smother their children—especially when there is only one child—with too much supervision. In both of these novels the subject of parenting is irrelevant to the story, of course. Christie simply felt like lecturing on the subject. If the subject of Christie's views on parenting interests you, see the *Summary for the 1940s,* the *Summary for the 1950s,* and the *Comments* sections for *At Bertram's Hotel* and *Nemesis.*

A matter of passing interest may be the original British title of the book: *Five Little Pigs.* Early in the novel, as Poirot is told of the five witnesses to the crime, he is reminded of the nursery rhyme that begins "This little pig went to market..."

Philip Blake is "the little pig who went to market." He is a successful stockbroker.

Meredith Blake is "the little pig who stayed home." He inherited the family home and remained there for the rest of his life, contented with the life of an impoverished country squire.

Elsa Greer is "the little pig who had roast beef." She went through two husbands and is now the wife of a third, each time increasing her affluence and raising her social position.

Cecilia Williams is "the little pig who had none." She has always been a penniless—and loveless—governess.

Angela Warren is "the little pig who cried wee-wee-wee." She had good reason to "cry," having been permanently disfigured, and blinded in one eye, by an impulsive act of sibling jealousy committed by her older half-sister, although she has never borne any rancor and has achieved more success in life than any of the other four "little pigs."

Note: A word about the name "Amyas"

A character in the novel comments on the name "Amyas," which Amyas Crale's father thought ridiculous. The name was given to the child by his "artistic mother who enjoyed bad health and played the harp." She admired the writings of Charles Kingsley, a minor Victorian poet and novelist. "Amyas" is the name of a character in his 1855 novel *Westward Ho!,* a historical novel set in the Elizabethan period.

In a future Christie novel, the 1953 *A Pocket Full of Rye,* a mother who is fond of reading Alfred Tennyson's long romantic poem *The Idylls of the King* will name her two sons Lancelot and Percival after characters in the poem.

Towards Zero (1944)

(Alternate Title: *Come and Be Hanged*)

Setting

Although first published in 1944, and probably written that year or the preceding year, the action in *Towards Zero* cannot take place during the Second World War. Two of the characters, a husband and wife, accept an invitation from friends to make a yachting trip with them from England to Norway during June. Norway fell to Nazi Germany in 1940 and, even if it had not, there would certainly be no recreational boating in the North Sea during wartime. If we absolutely must place the story in a specific year, then it must be some year in the late 1930s before war became a serious threat to England. It might make just as much sense to disregard this matter, and to fantasize that the story takes place in a mythical 1944 which is free of war.

The above is of little importance, since there are no references whatsoever to current events, fashions, etc. There is no reference to the War or even wartime conditions such as rationing, etc. in the novel. The only "current interest" or "trendy subject" mentioned in the book is the continued popular interest in psychology which was also exploited in certain films of the period, notably Alfred Hitchcock's 1945 "Spellbound." There is in the novel a headmistress at a school who is enthusiastic about "psychology" but who has no real knowledge or understanding of it and who blunders her way through a faulty "use" of psychology in an effort to identify a kleptomaniac among the students. She incorrectly identifies the culprit as the daughter of Superintendent Battle of Scotland Yard, who declares "that woman is a fool" and immediately removes his daughter from the school. He comments that, while there is indeed a true science of psychology, the "half-baked" notions exhibited by the school headmistress have nothing to do with it. In one or two conversations, Superintendent Battle mentions his friend Hercule Poirot as having a true understanding of the subject, although Poirot is not a character in the story.

After preliminary scenes in various places—in London, in Maidstone (a good-size real city in the county of Kent) and in at least one unnamed place, the action settles at a private home at the fictitious village of Salt Creek near the fictitious town of Saltington. These can be presumed to be on the southern coast of either Cornwall or Devon in southwestern England. There is a mention of the nearby town of St. Loo which, in the 1932 *Peril at End House*, was presented as being in Cornwall but which Christie placed in Devon for the 1941 *Evil Under the Sun*. Whether St. Loo is in Cornwall or Devon is not very important, however, since both counties have similar coastlines on the English channel which are dotted with resort centers, this being England's warmest and sunniest region, long known as "the English Riviera." In the British edition of the book there is evidently a map of the area, but for some reason the American edition omits it.

The private home where the murder takes place is picturesquely named Gull's Point. The age and construction period of the home are not stated but it is the large, comfortable home of a wealthy family and it is probably from the Georgian period, a favorite architectural period for Christie. From her bedroom, the aging owner of the home, Lady Tressilian, has an unfortunately clear view of a neighboring resort hotel called Easterhead Bay, a modern construction not to her taste. She comments:

> "I am glad," said Lady Tressilian, closing her eyes, "that Matthew never saw that vulgar building. The coastline was *quite* unspoilt in his time."

For the past two or three decades the coastline in this area has blossomed with resorts filled with newly-built hotels, and in some cases large private homes have been converted to hotels for vacationers. We recall that that was the case with the Jolly Roger Hotel in *Evil Under the Sun*.

In the village of Salt Creek there is an older, much more traditional hotel called the Balmoral Court where one of the characters has a room. The hotel is described as having all of the old-fashioned comforts, including bathtubs with mahogany surrounds, excellent service and meals, and a recently-installed lift (elevator).

The large home called Gull's Point has several family bedrooms on the "first floor," ("second floor," from the American point of view) and there is a floor above that which has a "lumber room," a servants' bathroom and at least four or five servants' bedrooms. The police have occasion to inspect these servants' rooms and the bathroom and to comment on the personalities of the various servants as evidenced by their possessions and their personal housekeeping habits. The butler, for example, has a few pieces of old, good quality but cracked porcelain; the cook's room is immaculately tidy; the kitchen maid's is disorderly, etc. The "lumber room" might be called the "attic" by Americans and contains the usual clutter of cast-off furniture, etc.

Family bedrooms and guestrooms on the floor below are mentioned in a similar way and offer a few clues about the personalities of their occupants. The ground floor of the house is not described in detail but there are French windows in a few of the rooms and there is a study, a library, a drawing room, a dining room as well as the kitchen and pantry and no doubt other rooms. The front entrance to the house is visible from an upper hall and a servant passing along the upper hall has occasion to notice the departure of one character through that entrance.

The house is built on the edge of a cliff and the west and south surfaces of the building are almost flush with it. The garden is on the east side of the house and the front of the house faces the north. These details will be important to the reader, as certain characters have their rooms facing the west with views of the sea only, while others have their views facing the east. The east bedrooms overlook the garden and the Easterhead Bay Hotel mentioned above.

There is an early scene in a nursing home or hospital in an unspecified location. There is also an early scene at the home of Superintendent Battle in London and then a brief scene at Meadway, a school for girls at Maidstone in Kent. The drawing room of the school headmistress is decorated in a way that expresses the personality of headmistress herself:

> Her room was representative of the spirit of Meadway. Everything was of a cool oatmeal color—there were big jars of daffodils and bowls of tulips and hyacinths. One or two good copies of the antique Greek, two pieces of advanced modern sculpture, two Italian primitives on the walls.

Another early scene takes place at the home of a married couple; it is probably a modern home, since it has a glassed-in veranda.

With the above exceptions, rooms are not described in detail in this novel except for a few mentions of minor details. The library at Gull's Point, for example, contains a "massive Victorian table," and the drawing room has a wireless and a gramophone (radio and record player) both of which are used in the course of one scene or another. Dance music is played on the "gramophone" and a couple of characters dance to it, and one person asks an older gentleman if he likes jazz, to which he politely but untruthfully replies in the affirmative.

One of the final scenes takes place in a motor boat in the inlet known as Salt Creek; the boat is large enough to accommodate at least half a dozen people.

The story begins in London in mid-November and ends the following September, with most of the action taking place at Gull's Point during that final month.

Two automobile makes are mentioned: Old Mr. Treves owns a "smooth running Daimler," which is driven by a chauffeur, and Mary Aldin picks up Thomas Royde at the Saltington railway station in a Ford.

STORY

The story opens on a November evening at the London club of a group of lawyers who are discussing a recent murder trial. One of the oldest and most respected members of the club, Mr. Treves, mentions that in detective novels the story always seems to begin in the wrong place—with the murder. He contends that a murder is not the beginning of a story—it is logically the "end" of a story, since a murder is generally carefully planned well in advance. These remarks do not make a very strong impression on anyone in the room and, as Mr. Treves leaves the club to go home, there are comments suggesting that "the old boy is getting older." However, Mr. Treves's remarks are a foreshadowing of the story we are about to read.

In January we meet Andrew McWhirter, who is recuperating in a nursing home after attempting suicide. A young nurse scolds him for his suicide attempt, telling him that one day he may be very important to someone. This is a second foreshadowing of events to come.

In March we meet Superintendent Battle at breakfast with his wife. The couple has just received a letter from the headmistress of the boarding school where their youngest daughter Sylvia is enrolled. It appears that their daughter has been stealing. Superintendent Battle goes to the school and, finding the headmistress to be a "fool," he immediately withdraws Sylvia from the school. This is a third foreshadowing of future events.

In April we meet Nevile Strange and his wife Kay, as they discuss plans for the summer and fall. Nevile suggests that they visit his aunt and former guardian, Lady Tressilian at her home, Gull's Point, in September, which is when his ex-wife Audrey is usually there. Kay considers this idea to be preposterous but she reluctantly agrees to it.

In September the guests at Gull's point consist of Nevile and Kay Strange, Nevile's ex-wife Audrey Strange, and an old suitor of Audrey's, Thomas Royde. The atmosphere is extremely tense. Audrey is silent most of the time, Kay is sarcastic most of the time, Nevile is miserable all of the time and Lady Tressilian finds the whole situation to be insufferable.

One evening Nevile has a row with Lady Tressilian and goes off to a neighboring hotel to play billiards with a friend, returning well after midnight. In the morning, Lady Tressilian is found dead in her room. She has been brutally murdered, apparently having been struck with a golf club which is lying on the floor with blood and hairs on it. In Nevile's room there is a suit he had worn the evening before, and there is blood on one of the cuffs. The police cannot believe that Nevile, "despite being an athlete," could have been so stupid as to leave such "obliging clues." They feel certain that he is being framed for the murder.

Inspector James Leach, a nephew of Superintendent Battle, is in charge of the case. Both the uncle and the nephew work together to solve the case.

Characters

A Group of Lawyers at their Club Discussing the Lamorne Case

Old Depleach, the prosecuting attorney in the Lamorne Case.

Young Arthur, who made the most of that servant girl's evidence in the Lamorne Case

Bentmore, who summed up in the Lamorne Case

Mr. Treves, the oldest and most respected member of the above group who seems not to be very interested in the Lamorne Case and who, instead, makes a seemingly irrelevant remark when asked his opinion—something about detective novels beginning at the wrong place—the murder. They should begin, according to Old Mr. Treves, long before that, when the murder is first conceived and planned by the murderer. Poor old Treves! An acute brain, but "anno domini tells in the end," say his friends after he leaves.

A Solicitous Butler-Valet at the home of Mr. Treves

Andrew MacWhirter, whose determined honesty cost him his job (he had refused to lie to the authorities about his boss's driving) and his chances of ever finding another. His wife then left him for a "more successful" man. Then he had a job doing heavy work and damaged his insides, and the doctor told him he'd never be strong again. Then he began to drink. Best to end it all by throwing himself off a cliff. Curse these interfering do-gooders—that pair of officious sweethearts who saw him at the cliff edge and summoned help. And here he was in a hospital being scolded by a young twit of a nurse!

Herbert Clay, MacWhirter's former employer who fired him and made sure he would never have another job.

The Doctor who told Andrew he'd never be strong again

Mona MacWhirter, Andrew's ex-wife who left him for a man who *did* have a job

Those Officious Sweethearts who chose to have a tryst on that rainy night, of all times, near Andrew's chosen suicide site.

A Nurse in Charge of the Ward who tells Andrew that suicide is "just wrong. Someday you may accomplish something terribly important."

The Murderer who methodically writes down the murder plan—complete with alternative courses of action—and then, with a smile, destroys the written record of the plan, retaining it only mentally.

Superintendent Battle of Scotland Yard, an old friend of ours, who is having breakfast at home with his wife, when an unpleasant letter arrives from the headmistress of his daughter's school. As we already know, Battle never expresses any emotion, nor does his face ever register any expression. His face, in fact, has the aspect of a face carved out of wood: solid and durable and, in some way, impressive.

From prior experiences with Superintendent Battle (*The Secret of Chimneys, The Seven Dials Mystery, Cards on the Table,* and very briefly in *Easy to Kill*) we also know that his qualities include patience and persistent determination and a way of giving a suspect plenty of rope with which to hang himself.

Battle has all the respect in the world for the true science of psychology and its practitioners, but not for amateurs with "half-baked ideas" about it who go around doing damage with their ideas.

Mary Battle, Superintendent Battle's tearful wife who is the first to read the letter from the headmistress

Sylvia Battle, the Battles' youngest daughter, age sixteen, who attends school in Maidstone, in Kent. According to the headmistress at her school, Sylvia has been guilty of numerous thefts.

Miss Amphrey, the headmistress of Meadway, an enthusiastic practitioner of "psychology." First suspecting Sylvia, then staring at Sylvia repeatedly and finally submitting Sylvia to a series of word association tests, she has successfully obtained a confession from her. According to Superintendent Battle, Miss Amphrey is a fool and her notions of psychology and its practice are nonsense. Furthermore, his daughter is no thief!

One or Two Girls in the Passage at Meadway who stand politely but whose eyes are full of curiosity about Superintendent Battle's interview with Miss Amphrey

Olive Parsons, another girl in the passage with rather fuzzy, fair hair, very pink cheeks, a spot on her chin, blue eyes far apart and a smug expression on her face—probably the *real* culprit in the matter of the thefts at Meadway

Nevile Strange, a handsome young man of thirty-three. He is an excellent swimmer, tennis player and all-around athlete. He has plenty of money, a beautiful young wife, a comfortable home and expectations of a 50,000-pound inheritance. He believes that it would be a fine idea for his ex-wife and his present wife to meet and to become friends, an idea which his present wife finds preposterous.

Kay Strange, formerly Kay Mortimer, age twenty-three, Nevile's beautiful young wife of a year and a half. Lady Tressilian dislikes Kay very much, referring to her as "that scarlet-toed creature."

Shirty, a friend of Kay's who has a yacht and has invited the Stranges to take a pleasure cruise to Norway in June

Lady Camilla Tressilian, well past seventy, Nevile's wealthy aunt and former guardian. Learning that Nevile's ex-wife Audrey seems to have no objection to being at Gull's Point at the same time that Nevile and his current wife are there, she says to her devoted maid, "I'm an old woman. Nothing makes sense any more. The sooner I'm out of this world the better. I don't understand anything or anyone in it."

Lady Tressilian is brutally murdered one night in her room, struck in the forehead by a blunt object.

Sir Matthew Tressilian, Lady Tressilian's late husband who was a judge. He had come to Gull's Point with his wife thirty years ago. Ten years ago, he drowned when the dinghy he was sailing capsized almost in front of his wife's eyes.

Mary Aldin, age thirty-six, Lady Tressilian's intelligent and well-read companion.

Audrey Strange, Nevile's first wife. She is described by Nevile's current wife as "...anemic and washed up—as a dish rag. No life or go in her!" To other characters she has a delicate, moth-like beauty and looks her best in the moonlight. Audrey suffered a mental breakdown after her divorce from Nevile, but she has apparently recovered.

The Howes (Leonard, his Current Wife and his Ex-Wife,) all of whom are the best of friends

Edward (Ted) Latimer, age twenty-five, Kay Strange's handsome, former suitor. Alas, he is poor, and so Kay naturally married Nevile instead. What else could the poor girl do? Lady Tressilian does not like him, and refers to him as "that very theatrical-looking young man who is always hanging around Kay."

Mrs. Royde at the Rectory, who helped Audrey to cope with a nervous breakdown after the break-up of her marriage

The Darlingtons at Esbank, with whom Audrey stays during early May

Jane Barrett, Lady Tressilian's elderly devoted maid, described by Lady Tressilian as "The comfort of my life! A grim old battleax, absolutely devoted. She's been with me for years." Each night before retiring, Barrett drinks an infusion of senna pods. On the night of Lady Tressilian's murder, someone mixes a sleep-inducing drug into the infusion to ensure that Barrett will not respond if summoned by Lady Tressilian's bell.

Thomas Royde, a.k.a. "True Thomas," an old friend and former suitor of Audrey. He is a planter in Malaya and now returns to England for a visit after an absence of nearly eight years, hoping that Audrey, who is now divorced, will marry him at last.

A Deft-fingered Malayan No. 1 Boy who attends to Thomas Royde's packing for the trip.

Allen Drake, Thomas Royde's business partner in Malaya

Adrian Royde, Thomas's brother who died in an auto accident a few years ago

Mrs. Mackay of the Marine Hotel, which is unfortunately being pulled down and replaced with an all-new hotel for tourists. She knew all of Mr. Treves's needs.

Mr. and Mrs. Rogers, proprietors of the Balmoral Court Hotel in Salt Creek, an old fashioned place that is in line with Mr. Treves's tastes and needs. Mrs. Rogers is an excellent cook.

Rufus Lord, the former employer of Mr. and Mrs. Rogers

Lord Mounthead, a friend of Rufus Lord, who had the best dinners in London thanks to his cook, the above Mrs. Rogers.

Young Merrick, age nineteen, an even better tennis player than Nevile Strange

Inspector James Leach (Jim), nephew of Superintendent Battle, who lives at Saltington. He is in charge of the investigation of Lady Tressilian's murder

A Porter at the railway station in Saltington

Hurstall, the aged butler at Gull's Point who feels the tension in the house as much as anyone and is "all on edge."

Mrs. Spicer, the cook at Gull's Point, who has become "jumpy" because of the tense atmosphere in the house

Mary Aldin's Father who had been a helpless invalid for some years before his death

Mrs. Lucan who is occupying the ground-floor rooms at the Balmoral Court Hotel that were supposed to be reserved for Mr. Treves

A Former Maid of Lady Tressilian who enjoyed swimming in Salt Creek but was nearly swept out to sea by the strong current on one occasion

Old Bouncer, a dog that bit Audrey Strange's ear during her childhood

Dr. Lazenby, the police surgeon of the district. He diagnoses the cause of Mr. Treves's death and also examines the body of Lady Tressilian when she dies

Joe, the porter at the Balmoral Court Hotel who declares that the lift was *not* out of order on the preceding evening

The Kitchenmaid at Gull's Point who bursts into tears and gives notice because of the atmosphere of tension and unrest in the house

Alice Bentham, the gooseberry-eyed housemaid who screams and drops a crockery-laden tray upon finding Lady Tressilian dead in her bed "with a great hole in her head and blood everywhere."

Emma Wales, another housemaid at Gull's Point

Major Robert Mitchell, the Chief Constable of the district who assigns the case to young Inspector James Leach and permits James's uncle, Superintendent Battle, to participate in the investigations

Sir Edgar Cotton, Superintendent Battle's superior at Scotland Yard

Detective Sergeant Jones, who tests the golf club for fingerprints and takes the fingerprints of everyone in the household

Mr. Trelawny of Askwith & Trelawny, Lady Tressilian's solicitors. He is a tall, distinguished-looking man with a keen dark eye. He reveals the terms of Lady Tressilian's Will.

Williams, a police officer who examines all of the bedrooms at Gull's Point

Hercule Poirot, the famous Belgian private investigator. Not a character in this story, he is nevertheless an inspiration to Superintendent Battle who notices something in a bedroom that would have annoyed Poirot. Battle admires Hercule Poirot's true understanding—and application—of psychology in murder cases.

Will and George Barnes, who operate "the ferry"—a rowing boat that makes regular trips across Salt Creek for the convenience of local residents and vacationers

Mrs. Beddoes, a fat North-Country lady staying at the Easterhead Bay Hotel, and a friend of Ted Latimer. She was with him in one of the little writing rooms at a particular time one evening

Lord Cornelly, a rich and eccentric peer who values honesty

Diana Brinton, age thirteen, who is staying at the Easterhead Bay Hotel with her family, and who becomes a new friend of Andrew Mac-Whirter

Don, Diana Brinton's wire haired terrier who enjoys rolling around on dead fish at the beach

A Girl in Charge of the 24-Hour Cleaners

A Chambermaid at the Easterhead Bay Hotel who tells Andrew MacWhirter all about the murder of Lady Tressilian

COMMENTS

There is something unique about each of Agatha Christie's detective novels, despite Christie's self-deprecating statement that she was "a regular sausage machine," cranking out book after book and implying that they were all similar to each other.

Sometimes the crime seems to have no motive. Sometimes there are plenty of motives but no suspect without an alibi. Sometimes there seems to be no suspect. Sometimes there are more than one murder and all have something in common. Sometimes there are more than one murder and they appear to have nothing in common at all. As to solutions, we have only to recall *Murder in the Calais Coach, The Murder of Roger Ackroyd, And Then There Were None, Thirteen at Dinner,* and several others if we want to cite extremely original, unique dénouements. Sometimes the crime is planned with extreme simplicity; at other times the planning is very complex.

The uniqueness of *Towards Zero* is hinted at in the Prologue, when Old Mr. Treves states that a detective story should *end* with the murder, not *begin* with it. You must read the novel in order to appreciate this particular point.

Christie's skillful characterization reached a level that can only be described as magnificent in her last novel, *Murder in Retrospect.* Not only were the characters beautifully and subtly portrayed, each one was a unique personality and also a new kind of character for Christie.

The characterization in *Towards Zero* is also very good, and Christie uses some of the same techniques in presenting the characters that she used in *Murder in Retrospect,* presenting each important character through the conversations *and the thoughts* of other characters. However, there is not very much "uniqueness" in the characters in *Towards Zero.* Most of them are repetitions of characters we have already met in recent Christie novels.

For example, Nevile Strange—the handsome, athletic young man—is practically a rubber stamp of Patrick Redfern in *Evil Under the Sun.* Audrey Strange, her frail, moth-like beauty being overshadowed by the dramatic beauty of another woman, is very similar to Christine Redfern in that same novel. Kay Strange is a flamboyantly beautiful woman similar to Arlena Stuart, again from the novel *Evil Under the Sun.* Her views on marriage and divorce are exactly the same as those of Elsa Greer in *Murder in Retrospect.*

Lady Tressilian is one of a long line of aging autocrats who are disgusted with the younger generation. Emily Arundell, the victim in *Poirot*

Loses a Client, was another and of course so was Simeon Lee in *A Holiday for Murder,* not to mention Roger Ackroyd in *The Murder of Roger Ackroyd.* "Devoted companions" and "devoted housemaids" and "aging butlers" such as Mary Aldin, Jane Barrett and Hurstwell populate most of Agatha Christie's stories. It is true that Mary Aldin is "a cut above the average companion," according to Lady Tressilian. But most of the characters in *Towards Zero* are copies of people we have seen before in Christie's books. If *Towards Zero* is memorable, it is not because of the characters but because of the unique murder plan.

Just a few comments on aspects that some readers may find irritating in *Towards Zero:* There is a good deal of generalization by several characters, even including Superintendent Battle. Old Mr. Treves makes sexist generalizations about women and both Lady Tressilian and Mary Aldin make sexist generalizations about men. Superintendent Battle judges a young man's character by his looks alone. There is the usual negative portrayal of the "know-it-all" hospital nurse. Specific details:

Mary Aldin's generalization about "men," which she makes *in a conversation with a man:*

> "I don't think he wanted to break up his marriage—I'm sure he didn't. But the girl was absolutely determined. She wouldn't rest until she'd got him to leave his wife—and what's a man to do under those circumstances? It flatters him, of course."

Lady Tressilian's generalization about "men," which she also makes in a conversation *with a man:*

> "Nevile, like most men, is usually anxious to avoid any kind of embarrassment or possible unpleasantness."

Lady Tressillan makes the following "men" statement to Mary Aldin:

> "Nevile, like all men, believes what he wants to believe!"

In a conversation with Mr. Treves, Lady Tressilian says:

> "You don't understand Audrey. She was violently in love with Nevile. Too much so, perhaps. After he left her for this girl (although I don't blame him entirely—the girl pursued him everywhere and you know what men are!) she never wanted to see him again."

During that same conversation, Mr. Treves says to Lady Tressilian:

> "It has been my experience that women possess little or no pride where love affairs are concerned. Pride is a quality often on their lips, but not apparent in their actions."

On the subject of judging a person by his physical appearance, there is Superintendent Battle's judgment of Ted Latimer which he bases entirely on the young man's looks, and in a minor scene Mary Aldin meets Andrew MacWhirter and decides that "he does not look like a friend of Audrey's." What do Audrey Strange's friends—or anyone's friends, for that matter, "look like?"

As to Christie's well-known negative attitude toward nurses, the young nurse who attends to Andrew MacWhirter, "smiles in a gentle, superior way." Nothing can penetrate "her nurse's armor of indulgent indifference. He was a patient, not a man." Andrew says to her, "You nurses. You *nurses!* You're inhuman, that's what you are!" Her reply: "We know what's best for you, you see." When he explains his suicide effort, the nurse "made a little clicking noise with her tongue. It indicated abstract sympathy." But the worst is yet to come. When Andrew tells the nurse that he may attempt suicide again, she shakes her head decidedly:

> "Oh, no," she said. "You won't kill yourself now."
> "Why not?"
> "They never do."

Andrew is, to the nurse, not an individual person. He's a member of a class: "They."

Death Comes as the End (1945)

SETTING

The year is approximately 2000 B.C. and the story takes place at the estate of a wealthy family on the West bank of the Nile at Thebes in Egypt. The owner of the estate is a "Ka Priest." In an Author's Note at the beginning of the book, Christie explains that a Ka Priest is a person to whom property has been bequeathed in exchange for a promise to maintain the tomb of the testator and to provide offerings on certain feast days for the repose of the deceased's soul.

A large family lives in the main house of the estate. They are a widowed father and his aged mother, his two married sons and their wives, an adolescent son, a widowed daughter and her child, plus a "poor relation" and numerous slaves. The house has a "living room," bedrooms and a "women's quarters" at the back of the house. There are smaller buildings for specific purposes—one just for weaving, for example, and evidently there is one just for cooking and baking.

The peacefully flowing Nile River is visible from the house and there are scenes near and on its banks, including one or two scenes with boats and barges of the period. The geography includes a rocky cliff near the tomb of the testator and a dangerous footpath along the edge of the cliff where two characters meet their death by being thrown from it.

Everyday items such as foods eaten by ancient Egyptians receive occasional mention; there are roasted ducks and other birds, triangular loaves of bread, and there is "wine from Syria," plus cakes with honey. All of this can be assumed to be authentic since Christie researched the subject as far as it was possible for her at the time.

There is mention of a past "Golden Age," during which all of Egypt had been united, and the characters hope that in the future Egypt will once again be united and powerful, but at the present time there is disunity and suspicion of people "from the North."

Story

We are in Egypt in approximately 2000 B.C. The protagonist, Renisenb, a recently widowed young mother, returns to her family estate with her four-year-old daughter to live. Her father, Imhotep, is away on business when she arrives, but he soon returns home with something new: a beautiful young concubine, Nofret. The family attempts to make Nofret feel welcome among them, but she soon shows herself to be an arrogant woman who throws her weight around and insults individual members of the family whenever she can.

Soon Imhotep goes away on another business trip and, in his absence, Renisenb's two sisters-in-law spar frequently with Nofret and, finally, one of them slaps Nofret in a fit of anger. Nofret writes a letter to Imhotep to complain of the family's treatment of her, and the angry Imhotep responds with a letter stating that he has disinherited everyone in the family in order to punish them for their mistreatment of his concubine.

Soon the body of Nofret is found at the bottom of a cliff. Everyone in the family fears that someone in the family murdered her, but they pretend to believe that her death was an accident. Imhotep returns from his trip and accepts the "fact" of her accidental death, but soon one of Renisenb's sisters-in-law falls to her death in the same place in which the concubine died. Before dying, she utters the name "Nofret."

The family fears that Nofret has come back from the dead to avenge herself on them, but the wise old matriarch Esa recognizes this as silly superstition and realizes that someone in the family is the killer. Three more murders occur, but the murderer dies while in the act of attempting still a sixth killing.

Characters

Imhotep, the widowed patriarch of the family, a Ka-Priest who received his property in exchange for the service of maintaining the tomb of "The Great Noble Meriptah." He controls his family by refusing to grant any measure of authority to any of his sons, forcing them to work for him and to follow all of his orders.

Ashayet, Imhotep's deceased wife, to whom Imhotep appeals—through a prayerful message sent to the Underworld—for protection against the wrathful Nofret

Yahmose, Imhotep's eldest son, who is conservative and respectful of his father's wishes and who is reluctant to "stand up to" his father and assert independence and demand "partnership."

Satipy, wife of Yahmose, a loudmouthed shrew who picks on her husband constantly, telling him that *she* is a better man than *he* is. She experiences a major personality change, however, after the first murder occurs.

Sobek, the second son of Imhotep, Yahmose's handsome younger brother who is an impulsive risk taker and is angered by his father's refusal to trust his business decisions. He would stand up to his father if it were not for the wisdom of his wife

Kait, wife of Sobek, who seems to be interested in nothing but her children, listens to her husband with half an ear and replies mechanically with platitudes such as "Yes, that is right, Sobek. You are so wise." But when her husband gives an indication that he is about to commit a foolish act of defiance towards his father, Kait snaps out some intelligent wisdom and surprises him.

Little Ankh, baby daughter of Kait and Sobek who is just learning to walk

Several Unnamed Children of Kait and Sobek, one of whom makes the mistake of getting in Nofret's way one day

Renisenb, Imhotep's widowed daughter, and the protagonist in the story. She loved her husband very much and misses him, but resolves to let the past die and to live for the present. She soon feels stifled among the women of the household with their petty bickering and rivalries.

Khay, deceased husband of Renisenb, a handsome man and a good husband and father who died young

Teti, four-year-old daughter of Renisenb who plays with a toy wooden hippopotamus that once belonged to Renisenb. You pull a string and its mouth opens.

Ipy, youngest son of Imhotep, a spoiled, mouthy, sixteen-year-old brat

Esa, the matriarch of the family, mother of Imhotep and grandmother of Yahmose, Sobek, Renisenb and Ipy. She walks with a stick and her vision is nearly gone, but her mind is as acute as ever. She is enjoying the last years of her life by remaining pleasantly detached from the foolishness of the younger generations, laughing to herself about them, and enjoying delicious foods. She takes a serious interest in the murders, however, when it becomes obvious that a member of the household is the killer.

Henet, a poor relation for whom Imhotep provides a home. She nauseates the whole family with her incessant reminders of her "selfless devotion" for which, she says, nobody is grateful, while she sows seeds of discord in the family and sucks up to Imhotep, who is blind to her tricks.

Hori, Imhotep's man of business and affairs for whom Imhotep feels great respect

Nofret, a woman from the North and Imhotep's concubine. She usually wears a cruel, catlike, self-satisfied smile on her face and she is insolent and insulting. She falls to her death from a high cliff, poor thing.

Kameni, a nephew of Imhotep and a scribe in his employ. He's a good-looking fellow who "sings a good love song."

Yaii, a woman to whom some land on the estate is rented

Ipi and Montu, expensive embalmers; "too expensive for a mere concubine," according to the frugal Imhotep

Numerous Child and Adult Slaves

COMMENTS

Each of Agatha Christie's detective novels is "unique" in one way or another. *Death Comes as the End* must be the most unique of all, and it certainly is a delightful change of pace. It is an interesting and even amusing story, certainly more amusing than its author intended it to be, since most of the laughs come when the Ancient Egyptian characters exhibit attitudes that are typical of early-twentieth-century Britons. The most amusing line is uttered by Renisenb who has a "crush" on the handsome scribe Kameni. Someone smiles slyly and says to her, "He sings a good love song, doesn't he?" to which Renisenb indignantly replies, "I don't know what you mean!" If Hercule Poirot were present in that scene he would undoubtedly have remarked, "How charmingly British of Mademoiselle Renisenb—to her, sex is 'not quite nice.'"

Other amusing tidbits include the attitude of Imhotep's family towards Hori, Kameni and Nofret. These three characters are "from the North," and the family notes that "We really don't know anything about them!" Possibly they have no connections at all! Tut tut!

On the subject of "connections," it was evidently even more important in ancient Egypt to have influential friends than it was in Christie's England. When Imhotep's family decides to send a message to the Underworld through the priest Mersu, Father Mersu points out that it needs stronger measures than a message to the mere concubine Nofret. Henet says:

> "Now your mother, Ashayet, was a great lady. Her mother's brother was the Nomarch and her brother was Chief Butler to the Vizier of Thebes. If it's once brought to *her* knowledge, she'll see to it that a mere concubine isn't allowed to destroy her own children! Oh yes, we'll get justice done."

So even *dead* V.I.P.'s are good to have in your circle of acquaintances.

A few of the characters are somewhat recognizable Christie "fixtures." There is the aging patriarch who thinks nobody but he can run the family business efficiently. There are three sons—the eldest being conservative and reluctant to take risks; the middle one is an impatient, impulsive, heavy-drinking, womanizing risk taker; the youngest is a spoiled brat indulged by the father and resented by his brothers.

There is an assertive wife who thinks her husband should stand up to his father, like Lydia Lee in *A Holiday for Murder* who wishes her husband Alfred would stand up to his father, Simeon Lee. There is a "stupid, devoted mother," like Bella Tanios in *Poirot Loses a Client*. There is an intelligent young woman who resents being classified as "nothing but a woman," like Sarah King in *Appointment with Death*. At least two of the young men are sexy guys with sparkling white teeth and broad shoulders like Raymond Starr (*The Body in the Library*), Nevile Strange and Ted Latimer (*Towards Zero*) and Patrick Redfern (*Evil Under the Sun*) and many others. There's an aging matriarch who despises the younger generation for one reason or another, as do Emily Arundell in *Poirot Loses a Client*, Simeon Lee in *A Holiday for Murder* and Camilla Tressilian in *Towards Zero*. In fact, practically the whole story could have taken place in early twentieth-century England with only some name changes. Christie "admits" in her Author's Note that "Both place and time are incidental to the story. Any other place at any other time would have served as well." Christie evidently believed that she knew enough about universal human nature and behaviors to make these statements, and to portray ancient Egyptians as if they were rubber stamps of early-twentieth-century upper-middle-class Britons.

If we are keeping track of the sexist attitudes of Christie's characters, we must not disregard the generalizations that various characters make about "men" and "women:"

Kait, the wife of Sobek who is more devoted to her children than anything else, does not seem to be mourning for her dead husband Sobek, and she explains to Renisenb:

> "...What love and respect should I have for a man like that? And what are men anyway? They are necessary to breed children, that is all. But the strength of the race is in the women. It is *we*, Renisenb, who hand down to our children all that is ours. As for men, let them breed and die early..."

Here are some comments from Esa, the aging matriarch:

> "My son is a fool and always has been," said Esa. "All men like flattery—and Henet applies flattery as lavishly as unguents are applied at a banquet..."
> "Women work roundabout—and they learn (if they are not born with the knowledge) to play on the weaknesses of men."

Christie had contended, in her *Autobiography*, that women of the Victorian generation, while officially without power or authority, usually got their way because they fully understood the weaknesses of men and exploited that knowledge. Evidently ancient Egyptian women, according to Christie, were just as smart as Victorian women were.

The following is a comment by Imhotep upon being warned that "Henet sometimes makes trouble with her tongue."

> "Pah! Nonsense! All women do!"

There is an interesting observation by Renisenb on the relationship between mothers and daughters. Watching her young daughter playing, Renisenb thinks to herself:

> "She is *me*—and she is Khay..."
> Then Teti looked up, and seeing her mother, she smiled. It was a grave, friendly smile, with confidence in it and pleasure.
> Renisenb thought: "No, she is not me and she is not Khay—she is *herself*. She is Teti. She is alone, as I am alone, as we are all alone. If there is love between us we shall be friends all our life—but if there is not love she will grow up and we shall be strangers. She is Teti and I am Renisenb."

And so we know that Christie understood, by this time in her life, that a mother and a daughter can be strangers to each other if there has not been love between them. She may have learned this from personal experience.

In the *Comments* section for the chapter on *Poirot Loses a Client,* there is an inventory of Christie female characters who have good relationships with their fathers but whose mothers are never mentioned and who are dead. A few of those are Lady Eileen Brent, Lady Frances Derwent, Tuppence Cowley Beresford, Anne Beddingfeld, Ruth Kettering, Magdala Buckley, Sheila Reilly, and Linnet Ridgeway. To this list we may now add Renisenb in *Death Comes as the End,* yet another young woman who enjoys a good father-daughter relationship but whose past relationship with her deceased mother is never mentioned.

Remembered Death (1945)

(Alternate Title: *Sparkling Cyanide*)

SETTING

Remembered Death was first published in 1945 and the action can be assumed to take place in approximately that year. There are no direct references to the Second World War, although one of the characters is rumored to have some connection with the arms industry and there are hints of sabotage to that industry in England.

The story begins in November of one year and ends in November of the following year. Most of the action takes place in London and at two adjoining country estates in the county of Sussex, south of London.

Several scenes take place at the fictitious Kidderminster House, the home of a wealthy and politically influential family, near Hyde Park. The only servant mentioned in that home is "a pontifical butler" but of course there must be several servants. Of more importance are scenes at the London home of a successful businessman, the husband of the first murder victim. The house is referred to as "the house in Elvaston Square," and consists of at least four floors with a drawing room and a study on the "first floor" ("second floor" from the American point of view) and with two additional floors above. The bedroom of one of the important characters is on the uppermost floor. At that residence there is a cook and a parlourmaid.

The Sussex homes are a Queen Anne period home called Fairhaven and a Georgian period home called Little Priors, which is on a twelve-acre property. The nearest market town to these properties is eight miles away, but there is a nearby village called Marlingham. Servants at these two homes are not mentioned except for Hawkins, the gardener at Little Priors. The London businessman mentioned above purchases Little Priors early in the story and his secretary makes redecorating decisions, resulting in a freshly painted and furnished interior which is not described but which is probably in modern but conservative taste. The house called Fairhaven is not described at all.

The most important London setting is a luxurious restaurant, the Luxembourg, where two murders take place. The restaurant has a French headwaiter, who is well known to the clientele, and several other French and Italian waiters. The restaurant has cabaret type entertainment including a "Negro orchestra," exhibition dancers and vaudeville-type one-man acts. After the first murder occurs there, a couple of the socially prominent characters mention that, although they would like to avoid the place because of its association with the crime, "one is constantly being invited there" and so it cannot be avoided.

A minor London setting is a small restaurant where a police officer interviews a witness. Another interview takes place at a home in Cadogan Square.

One of the characters appears to be an American with a shady background, perhaps a gangster, who has spent time in prison. He speaks correct British English but in one scene, when frightened and angered, he uses the term "bumped off" (killed) and threatens (or perhaps simply warns) a young woman with these menacing words: "You don't want your lovely face carved up, do you?... It doesn't only happen in books and films. It happens in real life, too." There is an additional American character, Morales, who is interviewed at his room at the Ritz Hotel. His speech is thoroughly that of the stereotypical American gangster we remember from early sound films. American gangster films of the 1930s and 1940s were just as popular among the British public as they were in America and Christie must have seen a few of them, in addition to reading American crime novels as well.

Incidentally, in 1962 this author wrote a letter to Agatha Christie asking her if there were any American mystery writers that she enjoyed. She wrote that she liked the Mr. and Mrs. North stories by Frances and Richard Lockridge. Those books were filled with American underworld slang. Other American writers that she mentioned were Elizabeth Daly, Craig Rice and Hilda Lawrence. She declared *Death of a Doll* by Hilda Lawrence to be one of the best detective stories ever written. As a bonus, in her letter she also mentioned her favorite British detective story writers: Margery Allingham, Ngaio Marsh, Michael Gilbert and possibly one or two others, but she did *not* mention Dorothy Sayers, which was surprising, since that author was very much respected at the time.

Story

We are in approximately 1945. The narration of the story begins "in the middle" so to speak. We read the thoughts of several characters who were present at a birthday party six months ago when Rosemary Barton "committed suicide" by drinking a glass of champagne laced with potassium cyanide, dying instantly. She had been recovering from an episode of influenza and the particular strain of flu prevailing that year was known to cause depression. Now, six months later, Rosemary's husband George has received two anonymous letters claiming that Rosemary did not commit suicide but was murdered. If that is true, the murderer must have been one of the people who were seated at the table in the restaurant where Rosemary died.

George shows the anonymous letters to Rosemary's younger sister, Iris Marle, who has been living in the Barton home for some time. From that point onwards we read the thoughts of Iris and of George, as well as those of the other people who had been guests at the restaurant. These are Anthony Brown, Ruth Lessing, and Sandra and Stephen Farraday. There had been a total of just seven people at the table that evening. An eighth invited guest, George's friend Colonel Race, had been unable to attend.

George and Iris do not know whether the claim in the anonymous letters is truth or just a spiteful act of malice. But both of them do a great deal of thinking about Rosemary and her life in an effort to discover who might have had a motive for her murder. For several chapters we read their thoughts about her, and we also read the thoughts of several other people about her.

The following November, George Barton

arranges a dinner party at the same restaurant where Rosemary died, inviting all of the guests who were present at the earlier party. His plan is to "lay a trap" for the murderer. At this second dinner party another person dies, in exactly the same way that Rosemary had died.

Colonel Race assists the police in solving this mystery.

CHARACTERS

Rosemary Barton, a young woman aged about twenty-three, recently married to George Barton. She died during her birthday party at a restaurant by drinking a glass of champagne laced with potassium cyanide. "Suicide while in depression after influenza" was the coroner's rather weak verdict. Through the thoughts of her sister Iris, her husband George, and numerous other characters we learn what kind of person Rosemary was and why several people may have wished for her to die. She is generally seen as a flighty young woman of little intellect.

Iris Marle, Rosemary's sister who is six years younger. When Rosemary died, all of her money—a considerable fortune—came to Iris in trust per the terms of their Uncle Paul's Will.

George Barton, Rosemary's husband. Considerably older than Rosemary, he was surprised when she accepted his marriage proposal and fully expected that, because of their age difference, there would be "snags," that is, love affairs, and he told himself that he would accept such "incidents." But when he found hard evidence of a love affair between Rosemary and another man, "his blood had sung in his ears."

Ruth Lessing, George Barton's devoted secretary of several years, who detested Rosemary and could not believe it when George married such a selfish, thoughtless young woman.

Paul Bennett, called "Uncle Paul" by Rosemary and Iris. He was not an uncle at all but a former suitor of their mother. He left his fortune to Rosemary and then to her sister Iris.

Viola Marle, the mother of Rosemary and Iris. She died when Iris was seventeen and Rosemary was twenty-three.

Hector Marle, Rosemary and Iris's father, who died when Iris was five and Rosemary was eleven. He drank.

Gloria King, Maisie Atwell and Jean Raymond, a few of Rosemary's close friends

The Marle Family's Solicitor, a courtly old gentleman with a shining bald head and unexpectedly shrewd eyes.

Lucilla Drake, remembered by Iris as Aunt Lucilla, an amiable, elderly sheep with little will of her own. A half sister of Hector Marle, Iris and Rosemary's father, she is in impoverished circumstances owing to the financial claims of her son Victor, the "black sheep of the Marle family." Upon Rosemary's death, Lucilla is invited to come and live in the Barton home to act as Iris's chaperon and to introduce her to "society."

Lucilla Drake will hear no evil about her beloved son Victor who is, by all accounts, an absolutely irresponsible rotter.

> Her son had turned out an anxiety, a source of grief and a constant financial drain—but never a disappointment. Mrs. Drake refused to recognize anything in her son Victor except an amiable weakness of character. Victor was too trusting—too easily led astray by bad companions because of his own belief in them. Victor was unlucky. Victor was deceived. Victor was swindled. He was the cat's-paw of wicked men who exploited his innocence. The pleasant, rather silly sheep's face hardened into obstinacy when criticism of Victor was to the fore. She knew her own son. He was a dear boy, full of high spirits, and his so-called friends took advantage of him.

Victor Drake, the irresponsible son of Mrs. Lucilla Drake. Whenever he cables to his mother asking for money, George Barton sends a smaller sum than asked for, and it usually satisfies him—until his next crisis. At one point George puts Victor on a ship bound for South America, instructing his secretary Ruth Lessing to accompany Victor to the pier at Tilbury and not to put the money into his hand until he is on board.

Stephen Farraday, a man of humble origins who, through sheer effort and determination, succeeded academically and became a Member of Parliament. He then deliberately cultivated an acquaintance with the Kidderminster family in order to marry one of their daughters for no reason but to have the right political connection. Then he fell madly—although briefly—in love with Rosemary Barton, and their affair threatened to ruin both his marriage and his career.

Stephen Farraday's Father, a small builder who married "above his class" and was bothered by it

Stephen Farraday's Mother, an alcoholic who married "beneath her class."

Sandra Farraday (formerly Lady Alexandra Hayle), the youngest and least attractive daughter of Lord and Lady Kidderminster, who married Stephen Farraday and provided him with good political connections. No fool, she knew the day Rosemary Barton became Stephen's mistress. "She knew the scent the creature used..."

Lord Kidderminster, the head of a great political family who, "with his little imperial, his tall distinguished figure, was known by sight everywhere."

Lady Victoria Kidderminster, his wife. "Lady Kidderminster's large rocking-horse face was familiar on public platforms and on committees all over England."

MacTavish, Sandra Farraday's Scotch terrier

Colonel Race, whom we first met in the 1924 *The Man in the Brown Suit* and whom Anne Beddingfeld admired as "just her ideal of the strong silent men of Rhodesia." He reappeared in two more novels, first in *Cards on the Table* and then, more prominently, in *Death on the Nile*. He is now over sixty years old but still the tall, erect, military figure with the tanned face, closely cropped iron-grey hair and shrewd dark eyes that he was in years past. He is an out-of-door man, "essentially of the empire builder type." He has spent most of his life abroad.

Anthony Browne, one of Rosemary Barton's male friends, a rather shadowy figure who is thought to be in the arms business. Rosemary one day learned a guilty secret about Anthony, and he warned her not to bring the subject up again, unless she wanted "to have her face carved up" or "to be bumped off."

Lord Dewsbury, chairman of United Arms Ltd., with whom Anthony Browne had scraped an acquaintance.

Dr. Wylie and Dr. Gaskell, two of Lucilla Drake's doctors

Cranford, the grocer at Marlingham in Sussex

Hawkins, the Gardener at Little Priors, in Sussex

Rosemary's Regular Doctor, who in response to George Barton's questions several months after Rosemary's death, assured him that Rosemary had *not* been suicidal. He had been away from England at the time of Rosemary's death, and it was a younger doctor who had mentioned that the strain of influenza afflicting Rosemary had been known to produce depression. But Rosemary's Regular Doctor, when returning to England and learning of her "suicide," was very surprised about it.

Charles, "the notorious and popular headwaiter" at the Luxembourg, an institution known by the patrons for many years. He poured the champagne on the day Rosemary died.

Giuseppe Balsano, the smiling, middle-aged Italian waiter who served the dinner on the day Rosemary died—and again a year later when another person died. He has worked at the Luxembourg for twelve years, has a wife and three children and a good reputation. He has "a rather monkey-like intelligent face."

Pierre, Charles's sixteen-year-old nephew and an apprentice waiter at the Luxembourg, "one of six harried underlings"

Monsieur Robert, a patron at the Luxembourg who was in a hurry for his sauce when Pierre retrieved Iris's handbag from the floor and replaced it on the table

Pedro Morales, in the words of Inspector Kemp, "a nasty piece of goods from Mexico—even the whites of his eyes are yellow…" He was at another table at the Luxembourg on the evening of the second death.

Christine Shannon, in the words of Inspector Kemp, "a blond lovely." She was Pedro Morales's date on the evening of the second death, and the pair was seated at a small table nearby. Inspector Kemp and Colonel Race interview her at her flat. Miss Shannon surprises Kemp and Race by proving to be an unusually keen and shrewd observer.

The Hon. Patricia Brice-Woodworth, a young London socialite who was seated with her fiancé at another small table near the one where someone died. Unlike Christine Shannon, she observed nothing about the people at the neighboring table, except that Sandra Farraday was wearing a Schiaparelli model.

General Lord Woodworth, father of Patricia Brice-Woodworth, who has no intention of allowing his daughter to be questioned about a murder case without a solicitor present—until he recognizes his old friend, "Johnny" Race.

Gerald Tollington, a young man who is engaged to Patricia Brice-Woodworth, and who was seated with her on the evening of the second crime. The police do not bother to interview him, knowing that he probably only had eyes for Patricia that evening.

Three Men and Three Girls Dancing, A Man Who Could Make Noises and Lenny and Flo, entertainers at the Luxembourg on the evening of the second crime

Mr. Goldstein, the owner of the Luxembourg, who is very kind and fair. He gives the waiter Giuseppe a week off so that people will not harass him with questions about the murder at the restaurant

Alexander Ogilvie, George Barton's agent in Buenos Aires, "a sober, hard-headed Scotsman" who provides him with useful information about the activities of Victor Drake.

Mrs. Pound, the cook at the Barton residence at Elvaston Square. Though she had the misfortune of being slightly deaf, and had a tendency to over pepper the soup, and her pastry was sometimes a little heavy, she was "an excellent woman." She had been with George ever since George married, and she made no fuss about moving to the country when George bought the house in Sussex, unlike the parlourmaid Betty who gave notice rather than move to the country.

Betty Archdale, a good-looking parlourmaid at Elvaston Square who gave notice rather than remain with George, Iris and Lucilla when they moved temporarily to Little Priors in Sussex, "in the dead of the country and not even a bus route!" When informed by Lucilla that her carelessness would have to be mentioned in her reference (she had once broken six wine glasses all at the same time), Betty told Lucilla "kind of sarcastic like" that at any rate she'd find a place "where people didn't get bumped off!"

Mrs. Rees-Talbot, a lively near-brunette of forty-nine, an old friend of Colonel Race and the current employer of Betty Archdale. She provides Race with the name of the variety of cherries commonly used in making cherry jam.

Superintendent Battle of Scotland Yard, not a character in the story but the mentor of the much younger Chief Inspector Kemp, who emulates him.

Chief Inspector Kemp of Scotland Yard, who is in charge of investigating the second murder. Although not normally involved in simple murder cases, Scotland Yard is involved in this case because of the "Kidderminster Connection."—the presence of Stephen and Sandra Farraday at the table where the murder took place.

Adams, the police officer who had handled the case when Rosemary Barton died a year earlier

Sergeant Pollack, who announces to Kemp the arrival of a Miss Chloe West at his office

Chloe West, a young actress who is at the moment "resting" (that is to say, out of work). Having learned of the second murder at the Luxembourg, she brings a fascinating and important story to the attention of Chief Inspector Kemp.

A Uniformed Man from Chief Inspector Kemp's Office, who is present at the private interview granted by Stephen Farraday

A Telephone Girl at George Barton's office whom Ruth Lessing fired for having the impertinence of imitating her and George for the entertainment of the other telephone girls

A Pontifical Butler at Kidderminster House who shows Chief Inspector Kemp into the room where the Kidderminster clan is assembled.

A Little Page at Claridge's who announces to Anthony Browne the arrival of Colonel Race

Colonel Pusey, a former acquaintance of Lucilla Drake.

Monkey Coleman, an American acquaintance of Anthony Browne whom he notices, but avoids, at the Luxembourg on the evening of the second murder.

Evans, the new parlourmaid at Elvaston Square, who has replaced Betty Archdale

Mrs. Marsham, whose letter Lucilla Drake is looking for when Race, Kemp and an unknown man arrive in search of Iris.

Canon Westbury, the clergyman who conducts the second victim's funeral service

COMMENTS

Remembered Death is a masterpiece of subtle and complex characterization, as was the 1943 *Murder in Retrospect*. In the earlier novel, Christie presented fascinating characterizations through the spoken and written words—heard and read by Hercule Poirot—of five different people with five different points of view. The result was a superb experience in character development, which would have been impossible in a story told in the first person by a narrator.

Of course, those five people in *Murder in Retrospect* could have been lying to Poirot—both verbally and in their written accounts of the case. It was necessary for Poirot to listen and read with extreme care and judgment in order to see the truth emerge from statements that might have been laced with falsehood or, at least, exaggeration and inaccuracy.

In *Remembered Death* we read not the spoken and written words of witnesses to the crime, but the actual *thoughts* of the people involved. Their thoughts may not be complete truth, of course, but they are their own true beliefs—of that we are sure. When Iris Marle thinks about the letter she found in the pocket of Rosemary's dressing gown, we know that the letter exists and that Iris found it. There is no need for us to guess whether she is telling the truth about it, because she is not *talking* about it—she is *thinking* about it. We learn about Rosemary—and about the other characters—through the true thoughts and recollections of the other characters, and the characters themselves are a varied and interesting group of people.

Noteworthy is the way in which Christie presents "politicians" in this novel. We have observed, ever since the 1924 *The Man in the Brown Suit*, that Agatha Christie did not have much respect for, or interest in, politicians in general. Most often they appear in her stories as ridiculous characters, intensely serious about themselves and their own importance, but boring to everyone else. Sir Eustace Pedlar in *The Man in the Brown Suit* is a lazy, irresponsible Member of Parliament who resents his secretary's determination to make him work. In *The Secret of Chimneys* and *The*

Seven Dials Mystery, George Lomax of the Foreign Office is a ridiculous figure and Lady Eileen Brent's Aunt Marcia, the Marchioness of Caterham, whose house "smelled of sealing wax, bird seed and slightly decayed flowers," is even more ridiculous with her talk of Lady Eileen's potentially becoming the "foremost political hostess in England, provided she marries suitably." In *Appointment with Death* Lady Westholme, another Member of Parliament, is the ultimate ridiculous politician and she was apparently modeled after a real-life lady MP whom Winston Churchill himself disliked very much. In *A Holiday for Murder,* George Lee is an MP who is despised by his father for being "A poor stick! A gas bag! A stuffed codfish! A pompous windbag with no brains and no guts!" who speaks of nothing but "duty" and has married a mindless bimbo twenty years younger who thinks of nothing but her clothes. It is impossible for us to feel the slightest respect for any of these politicians.

In *Remembered Death,* the Member of Parliament Stephen Farraday, his wife Sandra, and Sandra's parents Lord and Lady Kidderminster are given much more realistic treatment. Rather than being the butt of light-hearted ridicule, they are real people with differing personalities, and private lives filled with emotional conflicts. The Kidderminsters have the usual, expected concern about the "family background" of any potential son-in-law, but they realistically set that aside and accept Stephen as Sandra's husband since, according to Lord Kidderminster, Stephen has great promise and Lady Kidderminster knows that Sandra is not particularly attractive and is lucky to have inspired Stephen's interest. And they both know that Sandra has determination. When they begin to fear that their daughter may be a murderess, they have a very serious discussion—or rather, a dispute—about how to approach the matter, Lord Kidderminster stubbornly clinging to "honor" but Lady Kidderminster declaring honor to be "rubbish" when one's own daughter is in danger.

Stephen Farraday is a fascinating character, having risen from humble origins and succeeded in life and a career through "sheer will and determination." His mad infatuation with a mindless but beautiful young woman—and his later realization of the full madness of that infatuation—are an interesting story in themselves. The personality of Sandra Farraday, who loves her husband "with medieval intensity" is another fascinating portrayal. These "political" characters are not the usual "comic relief" that we have seen in earlier Christie novels.

On the subject of Sandra Farraday, Christie uses an interesting technique in the characterization, dwelling on the theme of Sandra's "medieval" personality, and placing that idea into the thoughts of several characters as they think and speak about her.

Anthony Browne, in a conversation with Iris Marle, first uses the word "medieval" in connection with Sandra:

> "Sandra, on the other hand, has a narrow medieval mind, is capable of fanatical devotion, and is courageous to the point of recklessness."

Later, when Inspector Kemp visits Kidderminster House, we have this pen portrait of Sandra:

> She was wearing a dress of some soft dark red material, and sitting as she was, with the light from the long narrow window behind her, she reminded Kemp of a stained glass figure he had once seen in a cathedral abroad. The long oval of her face and the slight angularity of her shoulders helped the illusion. Saint Somebody-or-other, they had told him—but Lady Alexandra Farraday was no saint—not by a long way. And yet some of these old saints had been funny people from his point of view, not kindly ordinary decent Christian folk, but intolerant, fanatical, cruel to themselves and others.

A few minutes later, during a discussion of the second murder, Lord Kidderminster says to Sandra:

> "*You* thought it was suicide, didn't you, Sandra, my dear?"
> The Gothic figure bowed its head slightly.

Anthony Browne has another conversation with Iris Marle on the subject of Sandra:

> "I can't believe either Ruth or Sandra would do such a thing."
> "You think too highly of people. Sandra is the kind of Gothic creature who would have burned her enemies at the stake in the Middle Ages..."

Then still later, in a conversation with Colonel Race, Chief Inspector Kemp tells him that he suspects Sandra Farraday of the murder.

> "So that's your bet," said Race. "Reasons?"
> "You shall have 'em. I'd say she's the type that's madly jealous. And autocratic, too. Like that queen in history—Eleanor of Something, that followed the clue to Fair Rosamund's bower and offered her the choice of a dagger or a cup of poison."

The subject of motherhood in Christie's novels of the early 1940s has been an interesting one, especially as her portrayal of "devoted mothers" has changed a bit since Bella Tanios, in the 1937 *Poirot Loses a Client* was described as "dumpy, dowdy, and devoted to her children." There are three kinds of mothers in *Remembered Death.*

There is the incompetent, devoted mother of a rotter who "can do no wrong," Lucilla Drake. There is the protective mother of a possible murderess, Lady Victoria Kidderminster, who would expect her husband to "pull any amount of strings" to prevent even a guilty daughter from being punished for crime. But the most interesting, though extremely brief, picture of a certain kind of motherhood, is this pen portrait of Viola Marle, the mother of Rosemary and Iris:

> Viola Marle had always been a somewhat remote mother, preoccupied mainly with her own health, relegating her children to nurses, governesses, schools, but invariably charming to them in those brief moments when she came across them.

Viola Marle was, in fact, exactly the kind of mother that Agatha Christie was: a remote one, who relegated her daughter to nurses, governesses and schools. And she was probably charming to her daughter in those brief moments when she came across her.

In *Death Comes as the End,* the protagonist Renisenb wisely noted that a mother and a daughter can be strangers to each other if there has been no love between them. This preoccupation with "motherhood" all began, for Christie, when her daughter Rosalind shocked her in 1941 by asking her if she was interested in attending her wedding. There must have been a good deal of soul-searching on Christie's part as a result.

Although *Remembered Death* is a rather somber book, there is a bit of humor in the person of Lucilla Drake and what is described as her "discursive" style of speaking—that is, her tendency to chatter on and on, bouncing from one subject to the next without regard for her listener's interest, somewhat like the hilarious Mrs. Gardener in *Evil Under the Sun* or the equally hilarious Amelia Curtis in *Murder at Hazelmoor.* Lucilla Drake is a much more pathetic creature, however, having been burdened late in life with the unexpected birth of a child when she was nearly forty, and the child growing up to be a substantially worthless person whose faults she cannot force herself to face.

As to this "worthless child," he is Victor Drake, one in a long line of "black sheep in the family" presented by Christie over the years. Most often these "black sheep" begin their disgraceful careers by forging a check "while at Oxford." Those who do not forge checks "while at Oxford" forge them "while at Cambridge." In *Poirot Loses a Client*, Charles Arundell forged his checks at Oxford. In *The Man in the Brown Suit,* John Eardsley "had been wild at Cambridge—his father had paid his debts more than once." Ronald Marsh (*Thirteen at Dinner*) and Ralph Paton (*The Murder of Roger Ackroyd*) were both extravagant and self-indulgent young men who ran up debts; check forging is not mentioned in their résumés, but could have been.

Victor Drake forged a check at Oxford but, as his mother explains, that wasn't for money—it was more for fun, since he had talent in drawing and so, naturally, it would have seemed quite a good joke for him to copy another person's handwriting, wouldn't it? In the 1948 *There Is a Tide,* another "black sheep"—a cousin of Frances Cloade—will forge a check at Oxford.

Murder After Hours (1946)

(Alternate Title: *The Hollow*)

Setting

Murder After Hours was first published in 1946 and the action can be thought of as taking place that year or perhaps a year earlier. Current events play no role in the story. There are only two references to "current interests." In a conversation about people who commit suicide by putting their heads into gas ovens, one character jestingly asks "what will they do in the 'all electric houses' of the future?" Evidently there was, at the time, speculation that electricity would one day replace all other forms of energy for homes. The other "current interest" reference is a statement by a police officer that he enjoys the film performances of Deanna Durbin and Hedy Lamarr. Durbin was a young singer who played in youth-oriented musicals and Hedy Lamarr was a beautiful brunette who played light romantic roles.

The London settings include two residences, a restaurant called "The Berkeley," a women's dress shop in Bond Street, and a hospital called St. Christopher's. One residence is that of a Harley Street physician whose family home occupies the upper floors of his office building. In one scene the doctor is delayed between patients while, upstairs in the family dining room, his wife and two children wait for him to come up for lunch. We may recall that the dentist, Mr. Morley in *The Patriotic Murders,* had his residence above his surgery in Queen Charlotte Street, a similar arrangement. The doctor's family has a French governess for his two children, aged nine and twelve; the only servants mentioned are a cook and a housemaid.

Another London residence is the studio of a sculptress in the Chelsea district.

The main setting is a large country estate called The Hollow near the fictitious market town of Market Depleach in the fictitious county of Wieldshire. It is suggested that this county is somewhere south of London—perhaps it is modeled after Sussex, since there is a reference to London's Waterloo railway station as being the one serving that area of England for trains from London. The home is not described in very much detail, although it is grand enough to have a "flower room," and the property is large enough to have a swimming pool with an adjoining "Pavilion," plus attractive herbaceous borders, a kitchen garden and other garden features, including a wooded area. The property also includes a farm, which is probably kept by tenant farmers, and the lady of the house goes to the farm on the day of the murder to fetch freshly-laid eggs. As the story takes place in September, dahlia and chrysanthemum are two of the flowering plants mentioned.

Very near to The Hollow are two newer, much smaller houses which were built by "competing builders" before the National Trust "stepped in and prevented further development in the interests of preserving the beauty of the English countryside." These two houses are described as "cottages," and one is in a square modern style obviously appealing, at least in its exterior styling, to its owner, Hercule Poirot. The other is one of those "hideous sham Tudor" houses much disliked by Agatha Christie (see the *Comments* section for *The Body in the Library.)* Both of these cottages are just a few steps away from the pavilion and swimming pool of The Hollow, if one follows a path through a wooded area, although the official road leading to the main entrance of The Hollow is much longer.

Servants at The Hollow include an aging butler, a cook and kitchen maid and at least one or two housemaids.

Another "setting," which we never actually visit, but which is an important subject of conversation and thought—a good deal of it wistful and nostalgic—is a country estate called Ainswick. Considerably older and larger than The Hollow, it must be located somewhere west of London, since two characters discuss going there from London by train from Paddington Station.

There are also one or two brief scenes at a private home in the real town of Bexhill, a resort town in Sussex on the English Channel coast, which had been the setting for one of the crimes in *The A.B.C. Murders.* Why Christie took the trouble to create the fictitious county of "Wieldshire," placing it in more or less the location of the real county of Sussex and then actually naming the real town of Bexhill as a setting is a bit puzzling. It would have made more sense just to call the county by its real name, since a real town within it is named.

Several scenes in the novel feature automobiles and at least three different makes, one possibly being a fictitious make, are mentioned. The Harley Street doctor owns a car of unspecified make which, because it is not in daily use, is garaged at some distance and must be "ordered" when needed. In the story, the doctor and his wife use the car to drive to The Hollow to visit friends for the weekend. Another character drives a Delage, an expensive, streamlined, high-performance sport model from France. There is mention of a "rented Daimler" being worth the expense because of special circumstances, and in the thoughts of one character, she remembers "the family Daimler" owned by her uncle when she was a child. The Daimler was also a luxury make. A "cheap car" called the Ventnor 10 is mentioned because the owner of the sporty Delage is followed through the countryside by someone driving a Ventnor 10. She attempts to outpace the other car but is unable to, and so she correctly concludes that the Ventnor 10 is one of many specially-equipped ordinary-looking, unmarked cars used by the police.

For the benefit of readers interested in monitoring the value of British currency during the period, in *Murder After Hours* a female character, having no skills or education qualifying her for a better-paying job, works as a saleslady in an expensive Bond Street dress shop at four pounds per week. At one point in the story a male character, who has inherited wealth and does not need to work, pays three hundred forty-two pounds for an engagement ring. How any ring, however jewel encrusted, can be worth eighty-five times the weekly salary of a working woman is somewhat incredible, but there it is. The widow of the murdered man purchases a black dress for mourning for twelve guineas (twelve pounds and twelve shillings.)

"Cellophane," spelled with the capital "C" is mentioned once in the novel. It was a new product at the time and was the first packaging material that claimed to guarantee an air-tight seal to protect the freshness of the food products within. Full-page advertisements in *Life Magazine* during the 1940s promoted that quality and urged consumers to purchase food products that were packaged with Cellophane.

Story

It is September of approximately 1945. John Christow is a brilliant Harley Street physician who is searching for a cure for an illness known as Ridgeway's Disease. Although he has grown weary of his private practice, which seems to be dominated by rich hypochondriac women, he functions very well in the practice and his passion for finding the cure for Ridgeway's Disease sustains his interest. He has two children and a boring wife, Gerda, who is devoted to him. He also has a mistress who is a woman of superior intellect—she is Henrietta Savernake, a successful sculptress.

Henry and Lucy Angkatell, who have a gracious home called The Hollow somewhere south of London, host a weekend gathering to which the Christows, Henrietta and a few other guests are invited. These include Edward Angkatell, who is a pleasant but dull person and a long-time suitor of Henrietta; a young man who is a distant relative of Lucy Angkatell; and a "poor relation" of the Angkatells, Midge Hardcastle.

On the first evening of the weekend, the group experiences a surprise visit from screen actress Veronica Cray, who happens to be renting a neighboring cottage and "has run out of matches." John was once in love with her and almost married her, but he left her for Gerda because Veronica expected him to chuck his medical career and follow her to Hollywood.

After obtaining some boxes of matches, Veronica insists that John walk back with her to her cottage since they have "so much to talk about." John does not return to The Hollow until 3:00 a.m., and it is clear that the couple made love during the hours that they spent at her cottage.

The following morning, John is shot to death outside the house beside the swimming pool, and several members of the household are shocked to see his wife Gerda standing over his body with a pistol in her hand. However, it is soon determined that the bullet that killed John Christow was from another gun. Gerda's story is that she saw John lying beside the pool and picked up the gun for reasons that she cannot explain.

Hercule Poirot, who lives in a second neighboring cottage, solves this mystery in which the police make no progress.

Characters

Lady Angkatell (Lucy), a rather eccentric middle-aged woman whose chief characteristics are discursive speech and surrealistic thought processes. That is to say, she bounces from one subject to another in a way that might be described as "scatty," but there always seems to be truth in everything she says. The police officer in charge of the case at one point wonders if such people can really exist, and Hercule Poirot suspects that there is much more intelligence in Lucy Angkatell than meets the eye (or ear.) In the opening scene she rises at an unreasonably early hour and simply walks into one of her guests' room and begins speaking. After thoroughly rousing the person from sleep, she sets a tea kettle on the gas ring in the bathroom, and returns to bed—and to sleep—destroying the tea kettle. Servants routinely replace burned teakettles from a large supply of new ones kept in the pantry.

Lord Angkatell (Henry), Lucy's husband. He was a High Commissioner when Hercule Poirot was last in Baghdad, evidently at the time of the action in *Murder in Mesopotamia*, which was in 1931. He was also once the governor of "the Hollowene Islands," a fictitious outpost of the British Empire. He has a large collection of neatly displayed and catalogued firearms. He wisely keeps his bedroom door locked to prevent the unwanted entry of his wife at early hours of the morning.

Midge Hardcastle, a young cousin of Lucy Angkatell who grew up in a grim north country manufacturing town. Her mother was an Angkatell, but she was fonder of her father. Midge is a penniless, "poor relation" of Lucy, who would gladly provide a home and even an allowance for her at The Hollow, but Midge is determined to be independent.

Midge has always been in love with Edward Angkatell but Edward has never noticed her.

John Christow, a brilliant medical doctor with a prestigious Harley Street practice, although his practice—consisting largely of catering to the whims of wealthy, hypochondriac women—would have worn him down were it not for his dedication to finding a cure for "Ridgeway's Disease."

Fifteen years ago John jilted a woman he was about to marry, Veronica Cray, a well-known screen actress who had expected him to give up his medical career and go to Hollywood with her. He had immediately married his wife Gerda simply to have a wife as unlike Veronica as possible. But ever since, he has wondered if it was a strength or a weakness of character that caused him to do that. During a chance encounter with Veronica in the story that question will be answered.

John's mistress, Henrietta Savernake, is a

woman of intelligence and curiosity with talents of her own—she is a successful sculptress. With her, John can unburden himself of frustrations with his work and find an interested listener, unlike his low-functioning, devoted but dull wife Gerda. John admits to himself, however, that he could not imagine having Henrietta for a wife, because he would expect the same devotion and subservience of her as he expects of Gerda, and if she were to be like Gerda he could not love her!

Gerda Christow, John's devoted, maddeningly selfless wife. She is a person of below-average intellectual functioning. Someone shoots and kills John Christow at The Hollow, and his wife Gerda is found standing over his dying body, holding a revolver.

Terence Christow, the twelve-year-old son of John and Gerda Christow. He is a very bright child with a strong interest in the natural sciences.

Zena Christow, Terence Christow's nine-year-old sister

Henrietta Savernake, a talented sculptress and John Christow's mistress. She lives at her studio in the Chelsea district of London. To John, she is everything that his wife Gerda is not. She is an independent thinker and she has passion for her work, just as John has for his. She is vibrant and in love with life.

David Angkatell, a seventeen-year-old distant relative of the Angkatells who, because of the laws of inheritance, will one day inherit Ainswick, Edward Angkatell's home. David is a sulky, moody youngster of considerable intellect who shares his generation's disapproval of most traditional British values—the Empire, for example, and the inequality of the social classes. During the weekend at The Hollow he spends most of his time being in a bad mood. To the amusement of Lucy Angkatell, at dinner on the first evening, the crafty Henrietta "brings David out of his shell" by expressing an opinion about modern art music. This gives David the opportunity of saying rudely "That's because you don't know the slightest thing about it," and then embarking on a lecture on the subject.

Edward Angkatell, a "first cousin once removed" of Lucy Angkatell, who inherited her family's beautiful home, Ainswick, because he is a male. He enjoys his quiet life of a "country squire" and the master of Ainswick, but he is not a rich man, and he has no great intellect or ambition. He has always been in love with Henrietta Savernake, but she has always refused his marriage proposals. Midge Hardcastle has always been in love with Edward, but he has never noticed her.

Hercule Poirot, the Belgian private investigator with the egg-shaped head and flamboyant mustache. He happens to own Resthaven, one of two newly-constructed cottages that abut the property of The Hollow. The Angkatells invite him to The Hollow for lunch on the day of the murder, and he arrives just in time to witness the ugly spectacle of Gerda Christow standing over her dying husband with a revolver in her hand.

Although Poirot has purchased Resthaven, a modern cottage in the country, he does not like country life. "Trees," he says, "have an untidy habit of shedding their leaves." The only things he likes about Resthaven are the modern, perfectly square design of the building, and the kitchen garden that has been planted in neat rows by his gardener, Victor.

Gudgeon, the butler at The Hollow, who is seen carrying a firearm on the day John Christow is murdered

Simons, a housemaid at The Hollow

Mrs. Medway, the cook at The Hollow who, on the afternoon of the murder, exhibits great sensitivity by serving a dessert which is *not* a family favorite.

Doris Emmott, the kitchenmaid at The Hollow who provides important information to Inspector Grange and then receives a scolding from Gudgeon, the butler, for not obtaining his permission first.

Doris Sanders, Henrietta's model for a piece of sculpture. Henrietta had been looking for a model to begin the new piece and, while riding in a bus in London one day, was startled to see a young girl—Doris Sanders—who had exactly the right face—"a foreshortened childish face, half parted lips, and eyes—lovely, vacant, blind eyes."

Doris has a trivial, spiteful mind and chatters incessantly. Unfortunately her personality makes its way into Henrietta's sculpture without the artist's realizing it.

Mrs. Crabtree (Old Mother Crabtree), the only patient John Christow is truly interested in. She has Ridgeway's Disease and cheerfully encourages John to experiment with treatments for her.

Mrs. Forrester of Park Lane Court, Mrs. Pearstock from Tottenham, and A Patient with No Real Problem, patients of John Christow on the morning that he and Gerda go to The Hollow for the weekend.

Veronica Cray, a film actress of a slightly more intellectual type than the run-of-the-mill Hollywood star. She was engaged to John Christow fifteen years ago and expected him to chuck his medical career and follow her to Hollywood. Now, she happens to be staying in a weekend cottage called Dovecotes, next door to The Hollow.

Radley, a physician with whom John Christow wanted to work at the time of his engagement to Veronica Cray.

Beryl Collier (Collie), John Christow's secretary, "a plain girl, but damned efficient," according to John's thoughts.

Lewis, a housemaid at the Christow home

Cook at the Christow home

"Mademoiselle," the unnamed French governess at the Christow home who looks after the two children during their parents' absence when they go to The Hollow. Gerda Christow worries that the children may not be obedient to her, as "French governesses seem to have so little authority."

Scobell, a physician for whom John Christow feels little respect

Neil, a better physician than Scobell, in John Christow's opinion

Nicholson Minor, a school chum of Terence Christow, with whom he plans to make nitroglycerin in the shrubbery of the Minor home, with Mummy's approval. (He had said to his mother, "Nicholson Minor and I are going to make nitroglycerin in their shrubbery next week," to which Gerda had replied, "That's nice, dear.")

Old Uncle Geoffrey, Midge Hardcastle's uncle who owned Ainswick during her childhood and made her and her friends welcome there at holiday times.

Tremlet, the old head gardener at Ainswick during Midge's childhood, who explained why Edward, and not Lucy, would one day inherit Ainswick.

Albert, a garage mechanic who looks after Henrietta Savernake's car, a powerful and sporty Delage

Cholmondeley-Marjoribanks, a squirrel with a broken paw that Edward and Henrietta nursed back to health during their childhood days at Ainswick

Old Mrs. Bondy, the housekeeper at Ainswick who knew that the squirrel would run up the chimney one day

Ygdrasil, an ancient oak tree at Ainswick fondly recalled by Henrietta; also the name of a fanciful tree she is in the habit of "doodling."

Victor, Poirot's Belgian gardener at Resthaven, his cottage near The Hollow. Victor has created a vegetable garden, the neat rows of which satisfy Poirot's need for symmetry in an otherwise chaotic, asymmetrical landscape.

Françoise, Victor's wife and Poirot's excellent cook

Inspector Grange, a "large heavily built man with a down-drooping pessimistic mustache."

Teddy, one of Inspector Grange's young sons. He will soon be receiving a Meccano set for Christmas.

Sergeant Combes, who is assisting Inspector Grange. Because of his good looks he is given the task of questioning the servant staff at the Christow home in Harley Street since servant girls, unlike higher-class Englishwomen, respond best to sex (according to Christie). Sergeant O'Connor, whom we met in the 1936 *Cards on the Table,* was given similar tasks. Because of his good looks he was called "The Maidservant's Prayer" by his colleagues.

Chief Constable of Wieldshire, Grange's superior and, in Grange's opinion, "a fussy despot and a tuft-hunter."

A Retired Military Man with a Distinguished Career

The Wife of the Retired Military Man who surprised the world by shooting her husband

The Careys, friends of the Angkatells whose luncheon engagement Lucy must cancel because of the murder

Madame Alfrege, the rude, unpleasant owner of the dress shop where Midge Hardcastle labors five and a half days per week at four pounds weekly.

Midge Hardcastle's Father, whose family business was destined to decline and fail, not because of any shortcoming of his but simply because of "the march of time." He died when Midge was eighteen and she remembers him with affection.

Midge Hardcastle's Mother, an Angkatell, who died when Midge was thirteen and whom she remembers only vaguely.

Elsie Patterson, a sister of Gerda Christow, who invites her to her home in Bexhill to live for a time after John's death.

Mr. Mears, the gardener at The Hollow

Mrs. Mears, his wife, who held her baby in a curious way because she was left-handed

A Spaniel belonging to Mr. and Mrs. Mears. Henrietta Savernake "borrows" the spaniel and takes it for a walk in order to have a pretext for visiting Hercule Poirot at his cottage.

A Dark Saleswoman at Madame Alfrege's dress shop.

Two Platinum Blonde Little Minxes, A Stout and Bewildered Customer, A Woman with a Fretful Voice and An Opulent-looking Woman with a Pekingese, customers at Madame Alfrege's, when Edward Angkatell visits Midge Hardcastle there one day

A Discreet Salesman at a jewelry shop in Bond Street

David Angkatell's Mother, who was "insane" in the 1940s sense. Probably she was simply mentally ill, but Inspector Grange suggests at one point that David may have inherited her "insanity."

FRENCH INTO ENGLISH

Note: Although the Belgian detective Hercule Poirot is featured in this novel, he uses very little of the French language.

Chapter 11
Quel beau paysage!—What beautiful scenery!
Je suis un peu snob—I'm a bit of a snob
Une originale!—Quite a personality!
Enfin—Good grief
spirituel—witty, amusing

Chapter 13
crise de nerfs—nervous breakdown

Chapter 19 *mon ami*—my friend

Chapter 29
C'est formidable!—Stupendous!

COMMENTS

Murder After Hours is not likely to be a favorite detective novel among very many of Christie's fans. The "murder mystery" aspect seems to take a rather distant "back seat" to other themes—the relationships between the main characters, their hopes and dreams, and their frustrations. It is true that a murder takes place and that the local police are called in to investigate it. It is also true that Hercule Poirot is involved in the case, but only because he is a neighbor of the owners of the home which is the setting for the murder. There is very little "detection" to speak of. A man is shot and killed, a woman is seen holding a gun while he lies dying, the bullet that killed him is not from that gun but from another, and the other gun is later found with fingerprints on it which cannot be identified. The police are left helpless and Hercule Poirot arrives at the solution only by a lucky guess—and perhaps by the apparent illegitimacy of the "clues." There are not many elements of a good detective story in this novel.

Readers of this novel are treated, instead, to some very interesting, complex and contradictory characters who are portrayed with great skill.

A mediocre country squire wastes his life in the hopes of marrying a woman whose intellect and artistic talents are far above his and he is too mediocre to understand why she continually refuses his proposals. Meanwhile he hardly notices another woman who loves him dearly and who would make him a perfect wife.

A brilliant but egotistical physician, whose passion for his work comes before any woman, has a wife and a mistress—the wife exasperates him because of the very qualities for which he married her—devotion and subservience—and the mistress exasperates him by refusing to be like his wife.

A talented, successful sculptress lives her life to the full and enjoys every moment of it. She loves a man who she knows cannot possibly love her as much, or in the same way, and she accepts this, not simply with resignation but with fullness and even enjoyment of that reality.

A woman survives on a degrading, four-pound-a-week job in a dress shop rather than sponge off rich relations who would gladly provide her with a comfortable home and living. She feels bitterness about the gulf that separates the "leisured" from the "working" and feels more in common with a sulky teenager with "socialistic" ideas than with her rich relations. She loves a man who is too stupid to recognize the fact that she would make him an excellent wife and she lives in a constant state of deep sadness.

It may have been a mistake for Christie to write *Murder After Hours* as one of her detective novels. The murder of John Christow could have been changed to an accidental death, the "murder mystery" aspect could have been omitted entirely, and the result would have been an interesting psychological novel to be published under the Mary Westmacott pseudonym that Christie had occasionally used since 1930 for her six non-detective novels. Fans of detective fiction who expect an exciting murder mystery may be disappointed or even bored by the extensive characterizations and by a good many of the events in this novel which contribute nothing to the detection of the crime.

In *Murder After Hours* we are reminded, once again, of Agatha Christie's belief, cited in her *Autobiography*, that servants were "actively happy and appreciated," much more than people who worked as shop assistants and the like. The butler Gudgeon, for example, is praised by Lucy Angkatell in the highest terms ("We depend on Gudgeon for everything,") and the Angkatells' cook, Mrs. Medway is warmly congratulated for her "sensitivity" in not serving a favorite dessert to the family after the murder. Meanwhile Midge Hardcastle endures daily insults from surly customers, and from her boss, in the dress shop where she is employed—insults with which the

Angkatell family would not dream of assailing their servants. Christie was quite sincere in her belief that all of those servants were totally content with their lives. She seemed to be oblivious to the fact that, by 1945, servants were leaving domestic service in massive numbers and taking other jobs even if their "masters" did not dare to be insulting to them. There had been a shortage of domestic servants since as far back as *The Mysterious Affair at Styles,* written in 1916, for the very reason that people hate being domestic servants. Christie must not have understood anything about that.

A final point on the subject of servants: in addition to being "actively happy and appreciated," females of the servant class, being of a lower order of humanity and therefore more animalistic than regular British folks, gladly respond to sex—at least in the Christie schema. Therefore handsome Sergeant Combes is sent to interview the servants at the Christow home in London, just as Sergeant O'Connor, "the Maidservant's Prayer," was sent to interview the servant girl Elsie Blatt in *Cards on the Table.* In *Murder at the Vicarage,* the crafty Miss Marple had sent handsome Lawrence Redding to speak to the female servants at Old Hall, knowing that they would respond to his good looks and reveal more information to him than they would have to the police. In the 1950 *A Murder Is Announced,* Miss Marple will note the "manly proportions and handsome face" of Detective Inspector Craddock, and will assure him that he will have no difficulty in extracting from the waitress Myrna Harris all of the facts that she had been reluctant to reveal at an earlier interview.

In *Murder After Hours,* we are once again presented with "motherless" characters. Midge Hardcastle's mother is a distant memory to her, having died when Midge was thirteen (cause of death not important enough to mention) but her dearly loved father survived until she was eighteen—and Midge has warm memories of him, of course. The charming Lucy Angkatell is, conveniently, not a mother. David Angkatell's mother was "insane," whatever that means. (As late as the 1940s "insanity" in the family was still a serious subject in popular literature and of course in movies, in which people who were in love were afraid to marry if there was "insanity" in their family history because they might produce "insane" children. In at least one film made during the 1940s a woman nobly deprives herself of marriage to a man she loves because there is "insanity" in her family history.)

Unfortunately Christie creates another stupid, incompetent, but "devoted" mother in the person of Gerda Christow. She is dumpy and dowdy, just as Bella Tanios was in the 1937 *Poirot Loses a Client.* She disappoints her twelve-year-old son by not being interested in chemistry and, especially, by not knowing that the manufacture of nitroglycerin is inappropriate as a childhood play activity. Gerda barely functions as a housewife with a couple of servants to supervise.

We know that Christie created an amusing character, the detective storywriter Ariadne Oliver, giving to that character some of her own superficial qualities. Both Agatha Christie and Ariadne Oliver are overweight, apple-munching writers of light fiction whose public never tires of their eccentric foreign sleuths, and both agree that writing is "hard work." The major difference between the two is that Mrs. Oliver is a lousy writer whose books are all the same except for the names of the characters, a fact she cheerfully admits, while Christie's books are all unique in one way or another. (See the *Comments* and *Characters* sections for *Cards on the Table.*)

Remarks that Christie makes in her *Autobiography* about the inspirations, challenges and frustrations of a writer cause one to feel that she was creating in Henrietta Savernake, in *Murder After Hours,* a truer pen-portrait of herself *as a creator* than she created in the comical Ariadne Oliver character. In Henrietta's conversation with Edward Angkatell about her "success" as a sculptress, she speaks of her work in roughly the same terms that Christie used in speaking of her writing. Henrietta tells Edward that sculpting is something that "gets *at* you." Christie wrote in her *Autobiography* that creating plots and characters were something that "got *at* her" and that there were plenty of frustrations until the book she was working on was finally finished. Then, for a time, there was relief—until the next inspiration came, and then the frustrations and challenges began anew.

In the discussion of the 1945 *Remembered Death* it was noted that, in that novel, Christie treated politicians in a much more serious way than she had previously. In her earlier novels, politicians were secondary characters, usually ridiculous people who simply provided comic relief, but in *Remembered Death,* Stephen Farraday and his wife Sandra and her family are given serious portrayals as complex individuals. Now, in *Murder After Hours* a medical doctor with complex, sometimes contradictory emotions is a central figure for the first time. Doctors in earlier Christie novels were usually Harley Street stereotypes or else country general practitioners without very much individuality, and they were always minor characters. In *Murder in Retrospect* a painter was given serious consideration as an interesting, complex character, and now in *Murder After Hours* another artist, a sculptress, is portrayed with even more complexity. Christie's skill in characterization continues to advance.

An unusual and pleasant aspect of *Murder After Hours* is the frequent evocation of the beauty of nature, especially in the fall season, to which several characters respond enthusiastically and, sometimes, with nostalgia. There are numerous poetic evocations of "leaves turning from gold to brown" and "the strong autumn sunlight," notably in the thoughts of Henrietta Savernake as she drives through the countryside from London to The Hollow. The following passage is worth quoting, as Midge Hardcastle imagines Edward Angkatell at his home:

> Edward at Ainswick—Midge half closed her eyes, picturing it. He would sit, she thought, in the library, on the west side of the house. There was a magnolia that almost covered one window and which filled the room with a golden green light in the afternoons. Through the other window you looked out on the lawn and a tall Wellingtonia stood up like a sentinel. And to the right was the big copper beech.
> Oh, Ainswick—Ainswick—
> She could smell the soft air that drifted in from the magnolia which would still, in September, have some great, white, sweet-smelling, waxy flowers on it—And the pine cones on the fire—and a faintly musty smell from the kind of book that Edward was sure to be reading. He would be sitting in the saddleback chair, and occasionally, perhaps, his eyes would go from the book to the fire, and he would think, just for a minute, of Henrietta—

There Is a Tide (1948)

(Alternate Title: *Taken at the Flood*)

SETTING

The story begins with a conversation taking place at a London club during an air raid in October 1944. A recent bombing and the consequent death of several members of a household are the subjects of the conversation. The story then moves to the early spring of 1946, to a small village somewhere southeast of London. Of far more importance than the physical settings, however, are the post-war conditions in England, to which there are constant references. These range from the daily nuisance of food rationing to the much more serious problems of older people being put into desperate financial difficulties by increased taxation and reduced incomes and, more importantly, a spirit of depression, a feeling of "things being unsettled," and the difficulty of readjusting to civilian life after combat duties for returning military personnel.

There are at least three or four references to "ration cards" or "ration books" in the novel. A hotel employee, knowing that a guest plans to stay a few days, asks for his "ration book." There are references to housewives standing in line at the confectioners' in order to get cake made from rationed sugar and butter, and standing in line for fish and other common items. At one home the cook manages to produce relatively tasty meals and is thus mildly suspected of having black market connections; one housewife is rumored to slip the fisherman an extra ten shillings every second week in exchange for favored treatment in the matter of rationing. Food rationing in post-war England continued until at least the early 1950s. American readers who are old enough to remember the earliest days of television will recall the endless appeals for Americans to send "Care Packages" to Europe. One clip that was shown repeatedly was of a British housewife being sold "one week's ration" of lamb chops—a portion that struck most American viewers as approximately one average serving.

The protagonist, Lynn Marchmont, who has served for three or four years in the Wrens, now returns to her home to find her mother in tears because of debts that have accumulated not because of extravagant spending but for such necessities as a roof repair, the replacement of a worn-out kitchen boiler and a new main water line. Reduced income, increased taxation, War Damage Insurance coupons to pay, all of these conspire against a tired old woman of sixty-two who, during the war, worked fourteen hours a day cleaning and cooking for evacuees from London who had been placed in her home.

A retired military man living poorly on a meager fixed income finds it necessary to sell one of his few valuable possessions—the rug in his sitting room—in order to make ends meet, and despite his lifetime of honorable behavior, he is tempted to commit an illegal act in order to have some badly needed cash. An elderly doctor who is tired and ready to retire cannot afford to and so must continue to work indefinitely.

There are references to "increased wages" being responsible for small businesses having to let employees go and reduce the quality of their service. An expensive block of service flats in London, for example, now has just one doorman instead of two, and meals are no longer sent up to rooms, except breakfasts. A police officer complains that a local laundry has been unable to serve his family for a month. Included in a discussion of the bridesmaids' dresses for a wedding is speculation about whether enough fabric to make them can be gotten with their combined clothing ration allowances.

In addition to the above problems characterizing post-war England, there are references to the War's having "unsettled" everything and everybody. There is "ill will" everywhere, according to the protagonist. It has become a ritual to criticize the Government.

Most interesting of all is the idea of the returning "war heroes" who find themselves "changed." The protagonist, Lynn Marchmont, spent the entire War abroad in the Wrens, leading a life of danger and excitement. She returns to her home in a quiet village and finds life there insufferably stifling and boring, and her fiancé of seven years an unsatisfactory companion to her. During the fighting, she had longed to be at home again, but now that she is at home, she feels out of place and unsettled. She frequently loses patience with her mother who dwells on subjects Lynn now considers trivial, such as the selection of bridesmaids for her wedding, or the problem of getting fabric to make dresses for the bridesmaids. She resents being called "my girl" by her mother and she resents being expected to keep her mother informed of her whereabouts—after all, she has been fighting in a foreign war, living with danger and being responsible for herself for years. Now that she is at home again she must deal with her mother being "worried" about her simply if she is out in the village after dark.

In a conversation with Hercule Poirot, Lynn makes these remarks:

> "I've changed. I've been away for three—four years. Now I've come back I'm not the same person who went away. That's the tragedy everywhere. People coming home changed, having to readjust themselves. You can't go away and lead a different kind of life and not change!"

Considering the importance of the "post-war" atmosphere of the setting, it seems almost trivial to comment on the actual physical settings of the novel, but for those readers who are interested, the story takes place primarily in a fictitious village called Warmsley Vale, in the fictitious county of Oastshire. There is no reference to what part of England Oastshire is in, except that at one point in the story, a person boards a train to London at Warmsley Heath (a settlement next to Warmsley Vale) and arrives in London at Victoria Station. Victoria Station serves travelers from London to Canterbury and the Channel port cities of Dover and Folkstone, and travelers to France needing to cross the English Channel to Calais always boarded their trains at Victoria Station. Therefore Oastshire must be modeled after the real county of Kent, in which the above towns are located.

Warmsley Vale is described as having been, in the past, a market town but which has degenerated to a mere village, as it is no longer on a main road. It has an impressive church of the dominant Church of England sect, and there is also a much less pretentious Roman Catholic church in which one brief scene occurs. There are two inns—The Stag and The Bells and Motley. The Stag has a room with a fireplace marked "For Residents Only" and a "Coffee Room" where meals are served. On one day a placard states that a dinner consisting of Windsor Soup, Vienna Steak and Potatoes and Steamed Pudding will be served in the Coffee Room promptly at 7:00 p.m. An irate elderly woman residing at the inn ridicules the "Vienna Steak" as being nothing but chopped horsemeat.

A guest room at the Stag, in which a murder takes place, contains a writing-table, a chest of drawers and an upright wardrobe of good old-fashioned mahogany, a large brass double bed, a basin with hot and cold water, a few chairs, an old-fashioned Victorian grate, and a heavy marble mantelpiece.

Several homes in the village of Warmsley Vale serve as settings; in general they are comfortable but somewhat shabby older houses. One is occupied by a doctor and his wife—the dining room of this home, described as shabby and rather ugly is the setting for a family gathering; a cluttered drawing room in this home is the setting of another brief scene. A stately Georgian-period home is occupied by a lawyer and his wife. The pleasant drawing room of this home has windows opening onto a walled garden with pear trees.

There is also a larger, much more modern and luxurious home, called Furrowbank, which was built by the brother of the above-mentioned lawyer and doctor, and which is now occupied by the brother's young widow and her brother. It is described as being expensively and tastefully decorated but with nothing to suggest the personalities of its present occupants, who have lived there only a short time.

Not far from Warmsley Vale is a much more recent settlement called Warmsley Heath. It is a center for golfing enthusiasts and features a couple of golf courses and a few modern hotels. It is served by a main road and by the railway line. Its existence is more or less resented by the residents of the older, more picturesquely traditional Warmsley Vale.

The young widow who lives at Furrowbank with her brother also rents a luxurious "service flat" in London's Mayfair district, in a block called "Shepherd's Court." Service since the war has declined, as meals are no longer sent up to the rooms, except for breakfast. The rooms are expensively furnished in a modern décor with superbly appointed bathrooms that gleam with tiles and chromium.

As most of the story takes place in the springtime, there are numerous mentions of flowers appropriate to the season—daffodils which have just finished blooming, early tulips, then lilac, rhododendron, viburnum and peach trees in bloom.

A trivial point on the subject of money values: several sums of money are mentioned in the novel. Frances Cloade asks Rosaleen Cloade for 10,000 pounds to get her husband out of financial difficulty; Adela Marchmont asks for, and obtains, 500 pounds; Katherine Cloade asks for and obtains 250 pounds; and "Enoch Arden" attempts to extort 10,000 pounds from David Hunter and Rosaleen Cloade. In order to understand the value of these sums in 1946, it is useful to note that Adela Marchmont, after solving her financial problems with the 500 pounds she obtains from Rosaleen, speaks of hiring a second gardener for her home. She points out that the second gardener would only have to be paid three pounds a week, and that they could grow more vegetables. Her daughter objects to the idea, stating that with three pounds a week they could buy a lot more vegetables than a second gardener would produce. In *Murder After Hours,* published two years earlier, a woman working as a salesperson in a London dress shop earned four pounds a week; in the 1939 *Easy to Kill,* a private secretary to a wealthy businessman earned six pounds a week. These amounts may be used to judge the values of the larger sums mentioned in the novel.

Story

The story concerns the Cloade family of Warmsley Vale, a village somewhere southeast of London. Jeremy Cloade is a competent and successful partner in a firm of lawyers, his brother Lionel is a practicing physician and his older brother Gordon has become extremely rich in business. Gordon has always been generous with his family and provided them with gifts of money and assurances that they may ask for financial help at any time. Although everyone in the family works and nobody is what could be termed a "parasite," there has always been the comforting knowledge that there was money in the background. The family members also know that they are all named as beneficiaries in his Will.

Gordon surprises the family, however, by suddenly marrying a beautiful young widow, Rosaleen Underhay, whom he met on an ocean voyage. Upon arrival in England the couple goes to stay at Gordon's London home. It is 1944 and World War Two is still raging. A day or two after Gordon and his young wife arrive, an enemy bombardment destroys Gordon's home, killing him and his three servants. His young wife and her brother are unharmed.

Gordon's marriage to Rosaleen invalidated his former Will and made her his sole heir. He would undoubtedly have written a new Will that included his relatives, if he had had time to do so. With the death of Gordon, the Cloade family has lost their benefactor and each member of the family falls into financial desperation.

A rumor circulates, however, that there is reason to believe that Rosaleen's first husband, Robert Underhay, is still alive. He was reported dead some years ago, but if he is in fact alive, Rosaleen's marriage to Gordon Cloade is invalid and, of course, so is her claim to his property and fortune. One day, a stranger calling himself "Enoch Arden" arrives at the village and takes a room at the local inn. He writes to Rosaleen's surly brother, David Hunter, asking him to pay him a visit at the inn to discuss "Robert Underhay." He tells David that he has it in his power to prove that Robert Underhay is still alive or, alternatively, not to prove it. If David Hunter pays him 10,000 pounds, Underhay will remain dead and Rosaleen's right of inheritance to Gordon Cloade's fortune will remain unquestioned. If David does not cooperate, however, the Cloade family will be glad to pay Arden to produce a living Robert Underhay.

A few days later, "Enoch Arden" is found dead in his room at the inn, apparently having been struck in the head with a heavy object. Hercule Poirot, who has already been contacted by two members of the Cloade family in the matter of Robert Underhay, solves the mystery.

Characters

Major George Douglas Porter, late of the Indian Army and a member of a London club. He is known as the "club bore," and as he drones on with his boring stories about India, nobody listens or encourages him to continue with them, a fact to which he is of course oblivious. A younger member of the club, Mr. Mellon, explains to Hercule Poirot that the club in general is a crashing collection of old bores, but that Major Porter is the worst. His description of the Indian rope trick takes three quarters of an hour, and he knows everybody whose mother ever passed through Poona.

Young Mr. Mellon, a friend of Hercule Poirot and a member of the same club as Major Porter.

Hercule Poirot, the famous Belgian private investigator with the egg-shaped head and flamboyant mustache. His foreign eccentricities are not as apparent in this story as they have been in the past.

George, Hercule Poirot's manservant, the meticulous accuracy of whose descriptions has always pleased Poirot. In this story he accurately describes Mrs. Lionel Cloade as "untidy and somewhat artistic in appearance."

Gordon Cloade, an extremely wealthy man, and a very generous one with respect to his relations. He has always encouraged them to rely on him for financial assistance of any kind, and assured them that they will be his heirs. Upon Gordon's unexpected marriage, his 1940 Will was nullified and he did not have time to write a new Will that would have provided for his family. He was killed in a bomb blast shortly after returning to London with his bride, and she became his sole heir.

Rosaleen Cloade, formerly Rosaleen Underhay, Gordon Cloade's young bride, who is now his very wealthy widow. A farm girl from Ireland, she had been a mediocre actress in a mediocre company and met Robert Underhay in Capetown. Robert was reported killed one day, and Rosaleen then met and married Gordon Cloade. Rosaleen is a beautiful young girl with "the most enormous eyes—dark blue and what they call put in with a smutty finger."

Rosaleen feels guilty about inheriting Gordon Cloade's fortune which, but for her, would have been divided among the Cloade family, but her brother David Hunter does his best to assure her that the Cloades had no claim on Gordon's wealth.

A Parlormaid at Furrowbank, the home of Gordon Cloade, occupied now only by his widow Rosaleen and her brother David Hunter

Frederick Game, Elizabeth Game, and **Eileen Corrigan,** Gordon Cloade's three servants who died along with him in the blast that destroyed his London home.

Robert Underhay, Rosaleen Cloade's first husband. He was reported to have died somewhere in Africa (she had married him in Cape-town.) Realizing that marrying Rosaleen had been a mistake—she was bored with their life in the African wilderness—and unable to countenance giving her a divorce—he was a Catholic—he once hinted to his friend Major Porter that he might "find another way to give her independence," that is, to disappear and to be reported dead, and then to change his identity.

David Hunter, Rosaleen Cloade's protective brother, a surly young man who dislikes the Cloade family, regarding them as spongers.

Jeremy Cloade, the elder brother of Gordon Cloade, a senior partner in a firm of solicitors. Like all of the Cloades, Jeremy has relied on Gordon for financial assistance when needed.

When Gordon dies, Jeremy falls into financial desperation because he has been speculating with trust funds in his law firm and has lost a good deal of the firm's money. He would have asked Gordon for money to cover his embezzlement, if Gordon had not died. He feels more shame than he has ever felt in his life when it becomes necessary to reveal all of this to his wife.

Frances Cloade, Jeremy Cloade's wife. She was born and bred "in an atmosphere of financial instability" and has no interest in money. Jeremy had rescued her slightly-crooked father, a breeder of horses, from bankruptcy and possibly a prison term, and then Frances married Jeremy. Jeremy has never been sure if she married him for love or simply as repayment for rescuing her father.

Lord Edward Trenton, Frances Cloade's father, a breeder of horses and a bit of a crook. Through special exertions, his solicitor rescued him from a fate worse than bankruptcy, and then became his son-in-law.

Charles Trenton, a cousin of Frances Cloade, who was even more crooked than her father and was "hustled off to the colonies."

Gerald Trenton, another cousin of Frances and another "black sheep" of the family. We know that Christie's black sheep usually begin their blacksheepness by forging checks while at either Oxford or Cambridge. This one forged his at Oxford.

Edna, a small, intelligent-looking but adenoidal maid, age fifteen, at the Jeremy Cloade home.

Antony Cloade, son of Jeremy and Frances. He died while fighting in the recent war.

Dr. Lionel Cloade, brother of Jeremy and Gordon. He is tired of work and wishes that he could retire, but he must continue to work indefinitely because he has lost his benefactor, Gordon Cloade, who would have supported Lionel and his wife, allowing him to write a book about medicinal herbs throughout history. He suffers from an illness and has become addicted to a costly drug for pain relief.

Katherine Cloade ("Aunt Kathy"), a "comic relief" character whose visit to Hercule Poirot in the Prologue is memorable. Although married to a doctor, she asks "Science? What can it do?" She is a spiritualist and regularly consults mediums, the cards, the Ouija board and anything else known to have spiritualistic importance. According to her niece, Lynn Marchmont, Katherine's "capacity for muddling the simplest issues amounted practically to genius."

Madame Elvary, a medium whom Katherine Cloade often consults

Adela Marchmont, a sister-in-law of Gordon Cloade and the widowed mother of Lynn Marchmont, the protagonist. Like the rest of the Cloades, she has grown dependent on Gordon and continues to live in her family home, White House, which is large and expensive to maintain. She is now in financial desperation, is overdrawn at the bank and has received threats from at least one creditor.

Lynn Marchmont, the protagonist, a young woman who has just been demobbed from the Wrens. Expecting to be happy to be at home again after four years fighting abroad, she finds that she is not the same Lynn Marchmont who left Warmsley Vale a few years ago. After experiencing the excitement of war and foreign places—the smell of dust and garlic and danger—she finds Warmsley Vale to be oppressively dull, provincial, narrow and lifeless. What is more, Lynn finds her fiancé of seven years, Rowley Cloade, to be nearly as dull, provincial, narrow and lifeless as the rest of the village. The thought of marrying Rowley now frightens her, as does her puzzling new attraction to David Hunter.

Rowland Cloade (Rowley), a young farmer, and the nephew of Gordon Cloade. He has been engaged to Lynn Marchmont for seven years. While she was abroad fighting in the Wrens, Rowley stayed at home and worked the farm.

Maurice Cloade, deceased, a brother of Gordon, Lionel and Jeremy. He was Rowley Cloade's father.

Johnny Vavasour, Rowley Cloade's farming business partner who died in the War.

Mary Lewis, a housewife in the village who is rumored to slip the fisherman an extra ten shillings every second week for special treatment in the matter of rationing

Old Mullard, the head gardener at Furrowbank

Edwards, the second gardener at Furrowbank, who saw David Hunter there at 7:30 p.m. on the evening of the murder

"Enoch Arden," a bearded, suntanned man with a knapsack who takes a room at The Stag and then receives a visit from David Hunter one evening. He is murdered a few days later in his room.

Beatrice Lippincott, the barmaid-receptionist at The Stag whose curiosity prompts her to eavesdrop on a conversation between Enoch Arden and David Hunter.

Lily, an adenoidal girl with a giggle, who works at The Stag

Marjorie Macrae, Adela Marchmont's best friend who would feel very hurt if her daughter Joan were not chosen to be one of Lynn Marchmont's bridesmaids.

Joan Macrae, Marjorie's daughter, who is loathed by Lynn Marchmont

Gladys Aitkin, who discovers the dead body of Enoch Arden in Room #5 at The Stag.

Superintendent Spence of the Oastshire Police. He is well acquainted with all of the Cloade family, and is slightly acquainted with Hercule Poirot, having heard about him for many years through his friend Chief Inspector Japp of Scotland Yard. Superintendent Spence is in charge of the case but welcomes the assistance of Hercule Poirot, who appears on the scene, having read of the murder of Enoch Arden in the newspapers.

Sergeant Graves, Superintendent Spence's assistant who conceals his excellent French accent from his superior in order not to anger him.

A Resplendent Person in Uniform at Shepherd's Court who cooperates with Superintendent Spence in the matter of Rosaleen Cloade's and David Hunter's movements on the day of the murder

Mr. Gaythorne, a criminal lawyer David Hunter plans to engage

Mr. Pebmarsh, the coroner

A Jury of Nine Local Worthies, the Coroner's Jury, who return a verdict of willful murder against David Hunter

Constable Peacock and Sergeant Vane, police officers who were summoned to The Stag upon discovery of the body

The Police Surgeon, who examined the body of Enoch Arden and established the time of death. He was not entirely satisfied with the alleged murder weapon.

Chief Inspector Japp of Scotland Yard, not a character in the novel but an old friend of ours, and of both Hercule Poirot and Superintendent Spence, to whom he has often described Poirot's "tortuous mind."

Mrs. Leadbetter (Canon Leadbetter's Widow), a monumental woman with iron-gray hair, a flourishing mustache and a deep, awe-inspiring voice. She detests all foreigners and dislikes the behaviors and the hair and clothing fashions of young girls. She saw a young woman in an orange headscarf coming out of, and then re-entering, Enoch Arden's room on the evening of his death.

The Landlady at Major Porter's Flat, who reported that Major Porter had been in a state of anxiety and depression for several days before his death

Jimmy Pierce, a villager who was kicked out of The Stag for being quarrelsome after drinking too much. He saw "a tart from London wearing an orange headscarf" in a telephone booth outside the post office on the evening of Enoch Arden's murder.

Brigadier Conroy, who knew David Hunter well during the war years and who, when hearing of David's arrest, comes to Warmsley Vale to offer whatever assistance he can.

French into English

Note: As has been the case in several other recent Christie novels, Hercule Poirot uses very little French in *There Is a Tide*. The expression *Cherchez la femme* occurs twice in the conversation of two British police officers.

Prologue

Chapter 2 *chère madame*—dear lady

Book One

Chapter 16
cherchez la femme—find the woman

Book Two

Chapter 1 *eh bien*—well, then

Chapter 5
mon ami—friend
mon cher—friend
Eh bien—Well, OK then
ma foi—Goodness!

Chapter 6
C'est un beau paysage—It's beautiful countryside
Bon Dieu—Good grief!

Chapter 7
Cherchez la femme—Find the woman

Chapter 10 *au fond*—fundamentally

Chapter 11 *mon cher*—my friend

Chapter 12 *C'est épatant*—It's astonishing

Chapter 16 *Eh bien*—Well?

Comments

There Is a Tide is rather unique in that current conditions of everyday life in England—specifically the conditions of 1946—are detailed and made an important aspect of the story. As readers, we are immersed in the depressing conditions of post-war England. Christie paints a picture of a society that has been hurt not only by the War itself but by conflicting ideas about the handling of post-war conditions. There is "ill will" everywhere, unrest, and dissatisfaction about the new directions that government and society are taking. In no other murder mystery does Christie bring current events and conditions so vividly into the story.

The murder mystery is, in itself, a fascinating one and there is even a touch of humor early in the story. Katherine Cloade, better known as "Aunt Kathie," with her swinging, clanking necklaces, her nonsense about "spirit guidance" and her reliance on cards and the Ouija board, even for advice on financial investments, visits Hercule Poirot at his London flat. The following is a part of their conversation:

> "Do you believe in the reality of the spirit world, M. Poirot?
> "I am a good Catholic," said Poirot cautiously.
> "Blind! The Church is blind—prejudiced, foolish—not welcoming the reality and beauty of the world that lies behind this one."
> "At twelve o'clock," said Hercule Poirot, "I have an important appointment."
> It was a well-timed remark. Mrs. Cloade leaned forward.
> "I must come to the point at once. Would it be possible for you, M. Poirot, to find a missing person?"
> Poirot's eyebrows rose.
> "It might be possible—yes," he replied cautiously. "But the police, my dear Mrs. Cloade, could do so a great deal more easily than I could. They have all the necessary machinery."
> Mrs. Cloade waved away the police as she had waved away the Catholic Church.
> "No, M. Poirot—it is to you I have been guided—by those beyond the veil. Now listen. My brother Gordon married some weeks before his

death, a young widow—a Mrs. Underhay. Her first husband (poor child, such a grief to her) was reported dead in Africa. A mysterious country—Africa."

"A mysterious continent," Poirot corrected her. "Possibly. What part—"

She swept on.

"Central Africa. The home of voodoo, of the zombie—"

"The zombie is in the West Indies."

Mrs. Cloade swept on.

"—of black magic—of strange and secret practices—a country where a man could disappear and never be heard of again."

"Possibly, possibly," said Poirot. "But the same is true of Piccadilly Circus."

Mrs. Cloade waved away Piccadilly Circus.

And the conversation goes on to include a detailed account of the miraculous revelations of the Ouija board which had convinced Mrs. Cloade that Robert Underhay was still alive and that she must consult no other person but the famous Hercule Poirot to find him.

There are a number of very interesting characters in *There Is a Tide,* and they are portrayed with all of Christie's usual skill. A scene between Jeremy and Frances Cloade, in which he reveals to his beloved wife the truth of his shameful behavior in the matter of embezzlement—and her plucky reaction to it—is just as memorable as the hilarious interview Poirot has with Mrs. Lionel Cloade. The portrayal of Lynn Marchmont and her frustration with the changes that have taken place within her, which make it impossible for her to feel happy in her native village, is fascinating, and so is her fiancé Rowley Cloade's reaction to her statements about her changed self.

In the 1945 *Remembered Death,* Christie for the first time portrayed a politician—Stephen Farraday—as a person with complex strengths and weaknesses and human passions and failings. His wife Sandra and her politically-involved family, the Kidderminsters, were given equally thoughtful treatment. Formerly, politicians in Christie novels had been ridiculous, pompous, comic figures such as George Lomax in *The Secret of Chimneys* and *The Seven Dials Mystery,* and Lady Westholme in *Appointment with Death.* Then, in *Murder After Hours,* Christie created, for the first time, an interesting, complex character who was a medical doctor, John Christow. In her earlier novels, doctors had been more or less stereotypical secondary characters.

In earlier Christie novels, lawyers also had been nothing more than secondary characters. They were usually dried-up old men sitting in stuffy offices and were described jokingly as having "very lawyerlike chins" or "very lawyerlike noses." Christie evidently was no fonder of lawyers than of politicians, at least in her early years. We recall old Mr. Spragge in *The Boomerang Clue* who loved royalty and ate out of Lady Frances Derwent's hand. (See the *Comments* section of the chapter on that novel).

In *There Is a Tide,* we have the first Christie lawyer who is portrayed as a person with complex motivations, feelings and failings. It is Jeremy Cloade who is confronted with the ominous task of confessing to his wife that he has been an embezzler, and there is a touching reference to his, and his wife's, feelings as they learned of the death of their only son on the battlefield of the War.

Christie had, as early as *The Secret Adversary,* commented on the difficulty of returning servicemen after war to find a place in society again, although in that earlier period it was mostly a matter of finding employment in an England afflicted by terrific unemployment and an economy in ruins. In *There Is a Tide* there is the contention that some of the best fighters in a war are, sometimes, the worst kind of people in civilian life—people who are fearless and, therefore, dangerous and not trustworthy; people who can be counted on in wartime not to lose their nerve, to embark with gusto on dangerous missions, but who in civilian life might embark with equal gusto on dangerous acts of criminal behavior.

Superintendent Spence, in a conversation with Hercule Poirot, has these comments about David Hunter and men like him:

"I know his type," said the superintendent thoughtfully. "It's a type that's done well during the war. Any amount of physical courage. Audacity and a reckless disregard of personal safety. The sort that will face any odds. It's the kind that is likely to win the V.C.—though, mind you, it's often a posthumous one. Yes, in wartime, a man like that is a hero. But in peace—well, in peace such men usually end up in prison. They like excitement and they can't run straight, and they don't give a damn for society—And finally they've no regard for human life."

It is possible that this idea has some merit, or it may simply have been a personal fantasy of Christie's. In any case, Christie will reintroduce the idea in several future novels. In the 1951 *They Came to Baghdad,* Edward Goring will explain that he was successful in the Royal Air Force during the war because "you didn't have to be brainy in the air force," but now he is bored by his office job and is not very good at it. In the 1953 *A Pocket Full of Rye,* Patricia Fortescue will describe her first husband Don, who was a fighter pilot during the war, and she will express the view that it was just as well that he died, since he probably would not have been able to adjust to civilian life. In the 1956 *Dead Man's Folly*, Old Merdell will describe Mrs. Folliat's younger son James as a similar type of character. He was a wastrel in civilian life, but during the war he "was given a chance to be a hero" and redeemed himself, so to speak. In the 1957 *What Mrs. McGillicuddy Saw,* there will be Bryan Eastley who was a fighter pilot and a hero during the war but cannot find a place for himself in civilian life. Finally, in the 1965 *At Bertram's Hotel* there will be Michael Gorman who won medals for bravery during the war but who is nothing but a hotel doorman today.

Another interesting "Christie idea" that is developed in this novel is that service in war provides "direction" to soldiers who, once they return to civilian life, find that they have lost the ability to be *self-directing*. The protagonist Lynn Marchmont finds that, in addition to finding life in her village narrow and boring, after her experiences abroad in the war, she feels that she is "drifting" with no sense of purpose. While in the military service, all decisions had been made for her. The "weight of individual decision" had been lifted from her. She fears the spiritual danger of having learned how much easier life is if one ceases to think.

Religion never plays a very important role in Agatha Christie's detective novels, and it can be assumed that if Christie was a religious person herself, she practiced religion in a quiet, private way. Christie's mother bounced around from one religious sect to another, taking her children with her, and at an early age Christie probably formed the idea that differences between sects were unimportant and that disputes between them were futile and silly. There are occasional clergymen in her books, and generally they are either pale, stereotypical secondary characters, or else they are unpleasant, judgmental and self-righteous, or else they are simply ineffectual. Characters who are "strongly religious" are usually "strongly self-righteous and judgmental" and their idea of Christian virtue seems to be equated with sexual abstinence and nothing else, except perhaps finding faults in other people.

For example, there is Leonard Clement, the vicar in *Murder at the Vicarage* who allows the spinsters of the village to gather at the vicarage once a week to sip tea and to engage in as much character assassination as possible. As a clergyman he evidently has no Christianizing effect on these women. There is Rev. Thomas Jones in *The Boomerang Clue* who badgers his son with criticism every minute of the day. There is Rev. Dane Calthrop in *The Moving Finger* who is totally book-ridden and laces his speech with so many quotations in incomprehensible Latin that nobody has listened to him for years. There is Rev. Stephen Lane in *Evil Under the Sun* who is frankly mentally ill. The Bible-reading and Bible-quoting Emily Brent in *And Then There Were None* feels no guilt about anything she has ever done. She drove a housemaid to suicide by firing her for being pregnant but unmarried, but her conscience is clear because it was the girl's "sin" that drove her to the "even more grievous sin" of suicide.

In fact, there are no characters—at least this far in the long parade of Christie detective novels—who are religious in any kind of sincere, constructive way. In *There Is a Tide,* however, a guilt-ridden young girl who is Catholic enters a Catholic church to pray and to confess her sins. Hercule Poirot happens to be in the church and speaks to her in a way that is consoling and nonjudgmental, reminding her that "we are all sinners." Christie probably felt more respect for the practices and teachings of the Catholic faith than for those of the predominant Church of England, and it may be recalled that her second husband, the archeologist Max Mallowan, was a practicing Catholic. Early in the story, Poirot tells Katherine Cloade that he is "a good Catholic," but in all the years we have known him, he has never been a prude, or self-righteous or judgmental about anything except serious sins, such as murder. He has often repeated that he "does not approve of murder." On one occasion he does lecture a man for bringing his wife and mistress together at a seaside resort and allowing the mistress to torment the wife—it is Patrick Redfern in *Evil Under the Sun*. On another occasion, in *Death on the Nile*, he compares Linnet Doyle to a rich man in the Bible who took for himself the only animal belonging to a poor man. But otherwise, Poirot practices his religion privately and he does not moralize, keeping his nose out of other people's business except for the purpose of gathering facts about a murder case.

In contrast to the sincerely religious young woman who is consoled by Poirot in *There Is a Tide,* there is an extremely unpleasant old woman, Mrs. Leadbetter, the widow of an Anglican clergyman. She insults Hercule Poirot by telling him, "You're a foreigner. In my opinion, you should all go back." She then fills the air with tirades touching on the "immoral behavior" of young girls today (they are "man mad," she says) and they wear filthy make-up, they don't wear proper hats—even in church—and they have "ugly" permanently waved hair, they wear slacks and shorts, etc. All of this is unsolicited monologue, of course, to which Poirot politely listens.

What is interesting, of course, is that this angry, judgmental, self-righteous old woman is the widow of a clergyman.

It should be noted, however, that in most of Christie's novels, wives of clergymen are usually much more pleasant people than Mrs. Leadbetter. The wife of the Latin-quoting vicar in *The Moving Finger*, Mrs. Dane Calthrop, is a woman of great intelligence—and compassion—and Griselda, the young wife of Reverend Clement in *Murder at the Vicarage* and *The Body in the Library*, is a kindly person with a sense of humor. The wife of Reverend Babbington in *Murder in Three Acts* is meekness personified and keeps to her flower garden. Bunch Harmon, the wife of the vicar in *A Murder Is Announced*, is cheerful and incurably happy.

Note: A word about "Enoch Arden"

The Victorian poet Alfred Tennyson was one of the few people in history—perhaps the only one—who got rich by writing and publishing poetry. He did this by writing sentimental verses that appealed to people of that period. One of his most sentimental creations was his 1854 *Enoch Arden*, a poem about a married man with three children who, having lost his job because of an accident, took a job on a ship in order to provide for his family. As a result of a shipwreck, Arden was stranded on an island for ten years. His wife, hearing nothing from him, assumed that he was dead and married Arden's best friend, having a child with him. After ten years, Arden was rescued and returned to England. Finding his wife remarried, he nobly concealed his identity and watched as his best friend stood father to his children and husband to his wife.

This poem was widely known and admired by literate Britons for a long time. In *There Is a Tide*, Robert Underhay imagines himself as a kind of "Enoch Arden" nobly stepping aside to allow his wife to remarry.

Crooked House (1949)

SETTING

The story takes place immediately after the end of World War Two. Most sources give 1949 as the publication year, but the earliest copyright year was 1948; therefore Christie wrote the book no later than that year. Christie mentioned in her *Autobiography* that *Crooked House* was a special favorite of hers and that she had "saved it up for a long time." That may mean that she planned the story and characters several years earlier or simply that she wrote it as early as 1946 and waited three years to have it published.

In any case we may assume that the story takes place in the fall of 1945 or 1946 because two characters have just returned to England after being released from the armed forces in which they had served during the Second World War. There is a reference to another character's having been a "conscientious objector" and having been given other war related work to do at home. A sixteen-year-old child makes a reference to bombs falling in the suburban London setting of their home during the War, and a certain family is said to have lost their home due to enemy bombing. There is also a passing reference to a large pair of iron gates at the entrance to the property of a large home, the gates having been "requisitioned" during the war because of the dire need for iron in any form.

Unlike *There Is a Tide,* published just one year earlier, in *Crooked House* post-war conditions play no role in the story at all and there is not even a reference to such everyday annoyances as food rationing or increased taxation. There is one comical reference, however, to clothing rationing: a female character admits that there is a man at a garage near Shaftesbury Avenue who sells her "clothing coupons" illegally. In *There Is a Tide,* the setting is, in fact, so dominated by the "post-war world" that the physical settings are of little importance. In *Crooked House*, the house referred to by the title dominates everything and nearly all of the action takes place within it.

The title of *Crooked House* is actually a whimsical reference by one of its occupants to "Three Gables," a mansion located in Swinly Dean, described by the narrator as "the well-known outer suburb of London which boasts three excellent golf courses for the city financier." We may need to stretch the imagination in order to accommodate the fact that one of the characters, having experienced an injury, is taken by ambulance to "Market Basing General Hospital." If this is a reference to the town of "Market Basing" mentioned in several earlier Christie detective novels—located in Berkshire in *Poirot Loses a Client* but in two different fictitious counties in other stories—then we can assume that Swinly Dean is an "outer suburb" near or in Berkshire. Berkshire is just west of London.

Three Gables was built in approximately 1900 by Aristide Leonides, a businessman, as a gift for his first wife. It is a huge mansion styled to look like a picturesque English cottage that has "grown overnight like a mushroom." One character comments that Eleven Gables would have been a more appropriate name for it. Although originally built as a single-family home, the mansion was modified twice—once in 1937 or 1938, and once again during World War II—in order to allow three separate families to have self-contained living quarters within. The entire ground floor is now occupied by Philip Leonides, one of Aristide's middle-aged sons, and his wife Magda and their three children. The floor above (the "first floor" in English terminology) is divided into two apartments, one occupied by old Aristide and his young wife Brenda and several servants. The other upper-floor apartment is occupied by Aristide's son Roger and his wife Clemency. The drawing rooms of the three "living units" are interestingly described and are, of course, an expression of the individual personalities of the occupants.

Although old Aristide and his young wife Brenda have a cook, a valet-attendant and two housemaids, Roger and Clemency have no servants at all because Clemency, who is a scientist, favors a simple, Spartan life and is repulsed by money, materialism and luxury. Philip and Magda have only an old "nannie" who has become a housekeeper to them, and occasional day help. They have difficulty in retaining servants because of Magda's moods. She is a temperamental stage actress who once threw a breakfast tray at a maid while in a furor about a bad review of one of her performances.

Philip Leonides is an intellectual type who writes books and articles about obscure periods in history. Their drawing room is more an expression of his actress wife's personality than of his. It is filled with furniture covered in heavy brocade and, on every available table and on the walls there are photographs and pictures of actors, dancers and stage scenes and designs, as well as masses of flowers in vases. Clemency Leonides, the wife of Philip's brother Roger, dislikes the room intensely, describing it as "just a stage set. A background for Magda to play her scenes against."

The bookish Philip has a library of his own, a big room full of books. "It smelt of the mustiness of old books and just a little of beeswax."

The upper-floor apartment belonging to Roger and Clemency Leonides is an expression of Clemency's "scientist's" mind. The walls are painted white—"not an ivory or a pale cream which is what one usually means when one says 'white' in house decoration." There are no ornaments and hardly any furniture—only mere utilitarian necessities. Their kitchen is "bare and spotlessly clean."

Clemency's husband Roger has a special room of his own, which is completely different. A roll top desk is untidily covered with papers, old pipes and tobacco ash; there are big shabby easy chairs and Persian rugs on the floor. Old framed photographs of school groups, cricket groups, and military groups plus a few paintings adorn the walls. It strikes the protagonist as "an intensely personal room," unlike the rest of Roger and Clemency's apartment.

The drawing room in the upper-floor apartment of old Aristide Leonides and his young wife Brenda is a comfortable room furnished with "colored cretonnes and striped silk curtains."

The descriptions of rooms in Agatha Christie's stories are always interesting expressions of their occupants' personalities.

In addition to the three living units of Three Gables, there is a former nursery which is now used as a schoolroom for the two younger children of Philip and Magda Leonides. It is a large room reached by a corridor and a short flight of stairs within the living quarters of Aristide and Brenda Leonides. There is also a floor above the living quarters consisting of dusty attics containing, among other things, water pressure cisterns.

On the grounds of Three Gables are a couple of disused outbuildings; one is an old kennel and the other is a storage building for gardening equipment and lawn furniture. There is nothing particularly interesting about the gardens, however. Because the season is late autumn there are occasional references to chrysanthemums and leafless trees.

There is only one reference to an automobile make, the "Ford 10," probably an "English Ford" made in Britain for the home market, a smaller car than the American Ford of that time. The narrator drives a small two-seater of unnamed make.

The "Three Gables" setting completely dominates the novel and there are only brief scenes elsewhere—at the office of an assistant commissioner of Scotland Yard, who happens to be the narrator's father, and at a couple of London restaurants, Shepheard's and Mario's. There is one reference to the London department store Debenham's.

STORY

Aristide Leonides, a wealthy Greek restaurateur, married an Englishwoman and built a fantastic—or better stated, fanciful—mansion for her, naming it Three Gables. The couple produced eight children, but Aristide's wife died shortly after the birth of the youngest child. Today, just two of Aristide's children are still living. They are his middle-aged son Philip, an historian who writes books, and Roger, an incompetent businessman. Philip's wife Magda is a stage actress whose career frequently takes her away from London, and the home of Roger and his scientist wife Clemency was destroyed during the war. Therefore Three Gables has been converted to three separate living units and all three families have lived harmoniously within its walls for several years.

Aristide is now eighty-four years old and married to a very young woman, Brenda, who is fifty years his junior. He suffers from an illness that requires a daily injection of insulin, which Brenda is in the habit of administering, and he uses eserine for glaucoma. One day he dies suddenly, and it is soon discovered that someone tampered with the insulin vials, filling one with eserine. Upon being injected with the eserine, Aristide dies almost instantly.

It is clear that the poisoning was deliberate, and that someone in the household must be the murderer. It is nearly impossible, however, to imagine anyone in the house having a motive because Aristide has always been generous with his family and everyone has always been fond of him. The police make very little progress in the case because, although they discover some plausible motives among the family members, they cannot find evidence to implicate one particular person. The identity of the murderer is revealed in a very unusual way after three more deaths occur.

CHARACTERS

Charles Hayward, age thirty-five, who returns to England at the close of the Second World War during which he has been serving in the East. During the early days of the War he had worked with the Special Branch of Scotland Yard. He is in love with Sophia Leonides whom he met a couple of years earlier in Egypt. Charles is the son of a Scotland Yard assistant commissioner and, when Aristide Leonides dies, his father encourages him to help solve the mystery.

Sophia Leonides, age about twenty-four at the close of the War. During the war she held a fairly high position at the Foreign Office in Cairo, a considerable accomplishment for a person of her age. Like the rest of her family, she hopes that the person who killed her grandfather is "the right person," that is, Brenda Leonides, her grandfather's young wife. Because if Brenda is not the killer, someone in the family must be.

Aristide Leonides, grandfather of Sophia and of two other children, Sophia's younger brother and sister. In 1884, Aristide had arrived in London, a penniless immigrant. Starting with a small restaurant, he succeeded well in business and before long was a millionaire. Always kind and generous towards his family, he is nevertheless murdered by one of them.

Marcia Leonides (deceased), formerly Marcia de Haviland, Aristide's first wife, an Englishwoman. She died of pneumonia in 1905.

Brenda Leonides, Aristide's young wife of ten years, now aged thirty-four. According to the police, Brenda is the person most likely to have murdered Aristide, and everyone in the family sincerely hopes that they are right.

Brenda is a very simple woman—she had been a waitress in one of Aristide's restaurants when she met him—and her needs are easily fulfilled by shopping trips, movies and simple reading. The family was shocked when Aristide married her ten years ago, but apparently their marriage has been a happy one, as Aristide has always made her feel "special" and she evidently has made him happy.

Philip Leonides, Sophia's father, an intellectual person who writes unprofitable books about history. His generous father made a large settlement on him several years ago, allowing Philip to enjoy himself among his books. Surprisingly, he appears to enjoy a very happy marriage with an unbelievably self-centered actress.

Magda Leonides, Philip's wife and Sophia's mother. She is an incredibly self-centered, rather mediocre stage actress. She does not enter a room, she "makes an entrance," and when she leaves a room, it is always with an appropriate "exit line."

Eustace Leonides, Sophia's younger brother, age sixteen. He was afflicted with infantile paralysis a few years ago and continues to walk with stiffness. He is a handsome boy and very intelligent but rather scornful and ill-tempered. Sophia has found him "moody and odd" since his bout with the illness.

Josephine Leonides, Sophia's younger sister, age eleven or twelve. An extremely ugly child, she is intelligent and articulate. She enjoys reading murder mysteries and provides a good deal of useful information to Charles about family activities, as she is also a major snoop. During the investigations, Josephine has more than one occasion to declare "The police are stupid," and at one point she tells Charles, "It's about time for another murder. It always happens that way in books."

Roger Leonides, the eldest son of Aristide, Philip's older brother. Although he has absolutely no business ability, he was given control of Associated Catering by his father and has, through incompetence, brought it close to ruin. A very emotional person, in an irresponsible outburst he accuses Brenda Leonides of the murder of his father.

Clemency Leonides, Roger's wife, a research scientist. She is as different from Roger as Magda is from her husband Philip. She has absolutely no interest in money, comforts and luxuries. According to Sophia, Clemency's idea of a meal is lettuce, tomatoes and raw carrot, and if Roger did not get a square meal in the City every day, he would starve. For his part, Roger thinks that Clemency is the most wonderful wife a man could have, and she is just as devoted to him as he is to her.

Sir Arthur Hayward, father of Charles Hayward and an Assistant Commissioner of Scotland Yard

Chief Inspector Taverner, the police officer in charge of the case

Detective Sergeant Lamb, Chief Inspector Taverner's assistant

Edith de Haviland, a sister of Marcia de Haviland, Aristide's first wife. Upon Marcia's death in 1905 she came to Three Gables to look after Marcia's children. In her own words, "I couldn't leave them to be brought up by a dago." She still lives at Three Gables and looks after Sophia's younger brother and sister.

Electra and Joyce Leonides, two deceased daughters of Aristide Leonides

Laurence Brown, tutor to Philip and Magda's children, Eustace and Josephine. He was hired by Aristide to educate Eustace at home because of his illness. He is an excellent teacher with a special talent for bringing otherwise dull subjects to life for his pupils, but he is a very nervous person. A very sensitive person, he was a conscientious objector during the war and that was how he came to be hired as a tutor. He is mildly suspected of having an affair with Aristide's young wife Brenda.

Janet Rowe ("Nannie"), who had been Nannie to all of the Leonides children and later became cook-housekeeper to the Philip Leonides family. She is convinced that the Communists—or if not the Communists, the Catholics—are behind the murder of Aristide Leonides.

Mr. Gaitskill, Aristide Leonides's attorney of many years who is enormously offended upon learning that Aristide entrusted his rewritten Will to an old friend for safekeeping instead of to Mr. Gaitskill

Johnson, Aristide Leonides' valet-attendant

Terry, Brenda Leonides' former Irish boyfriend who, according to her, left her pregnant and then went abroad. But it turned out that she wasn't pregnant after all.

Gladys, a housemaid of Philip and Magda Leonides who gave notice after Magda, while in a furor over a bad review of one of her performances, hurled a breakfast tray at her.

Janet Woolmer, a parlourmaid who witnessed the signing of Aristide Leonides's Will

A Doctor who suspected foul play in the matter of Aristide Leonides's death and refused to sign a death certificate

A Shorthand Writer at the office of Sir Arthur Hayward

Constance Kent, a girl who murdered her baby brother

Richard, Clemency's former husband with whom she was extremely happy despite his poverty. Like Clemency, he was a scientist.

Ralph Alstir, a friend of Magda Leonides who will see to Josephine's enrollment at a Swiss school

Mr. Agrodopolous, an old friend of Aristide Leonides whom he had helped during their youth. It was to him, and not to his lawyer Mr. Gaitskill, that Aristide sent his Will for safekeeping.

Mr. Agrodopolous's Son, who was to guard Aristide's Will in the event that his father died before Aristide Leonides

Dr. Gray, who is acquainted with Magda Leonides and attends to Josephine at the hospital

Old Carberry, a judge with a reputation for being righteous about illicit love

Eagles and Humphrey Kerr, the probable defense attorneys for any person who is arrested in the case

A Plainclothes Man at Three Gables after the second death

Evans, the Leonides' chauffeur

A Photographer and Two Other Men at Three Gables after the second death

COMMENTS

The dénouement of *Crooked House* is stunning and unforgettable. Since the police fail to solve the case, there is not very much interesting detection to enjoy, but the book is extremely pleasant reading because of a cast of interesting, skillfully portrayed characters—and because the ending is a shocker.

The older generation in Christie's novels is quite often portrayed as tyrannical and antagonistic towards the younger generation. In 1942, however, Christie created for *The Body in the Library,* a new kind of wealthy older person—Conway Jefferson. Jefferson had always been kind and generous towards his family and had even settled large sums of money on them while they were young so that they would not have to wait for him to die in order to benefit from his wealth. In *There Is a Tide,* Gordon Cloade was a similar character. Now, in *Crooked House* we have a third wealthy parent who exhibits kindliness and generosity to all of his family, but he is nevertheless a victim of murder. Neither the family nor the police can imagine any motive for Aristide Leonides' murder except the possibility that his young wife may have wished to hasten his death in order to marry a younger man, but even this is doubtful, as nearly everyone in the family agrees.

Except for the pleasant experience of reading about some very interesting characters, and of course for the astonishing ending, there is nothing particularly remarkable about *Crooked House.*

There is one aspect of the book that some readers may dislike, and that is Christie's conviction that character traits are inherited by blood and are not the product of education and environment. She said of the painter Amyas Crale in *Murder in Retrospect,* for example, that he had "inherited" his artistic instincts from his "artistic" mother who had written poetry and played the harp. Another explanation might be that his mother valued art, encouraged her son in his pursuit of it, and allowed him to pursue it without interference. In *Crooked House,* there are one or two serious discussions about the de Haviland family being "ruthless" and the Leonides family being "unscrupulous." Someone remarks that the "unscrupulousness" of the Leonides family was "tempered with kindliness." There is a suggestion that a person of a future generation produced by a combination of these two "bloodlines" might inherit both the "unscrupulousness" and the "ruthlessness" but not the "tempering effect of kindliness." Discussions of this kind may be a source of irritation to certain readers.

Christie was quite convinced that character traits are inherited through blood and that education and environment are powerless to change these inherited traits. In several future novels she will "lecture" on this subject, most stridently in the 1952 *Murder with Mirrors* and the 1958 *Ordeal by Innocence.*

It may be interesting to note that, at the time, there was serious discussion in some circles about the above subject in America as well. A best-selling novel by William March, *The Bad Seed,* appeared in 1954 and it was soon successfully dramatized by Maxwell Anderson, enjoying an enormous success on the stage and in a 1956 filming. The theme of the story was the notion that evil proclivities can be passed through blood from one generation to the next and, even if not to the next, possibly to a third generation. Environment has no power in shaping the character of the person who unfortunately inherits the "bad seed," nor does that person have any ability to apply moral judgments, since that person is without a "normal conscience." The Catholic Church in America placed the film on its "C" list—"Morally Condemned"—for that reason.

There is also, in *Crooked House,* the suggestion that a murderer is a person who has not attained full adulthood—who retains the aggressive instincts that cause some children to, for example, do harm to their younger siblings because of jealously. Allegedly, normal maturation into adulthood brings a kind of "moral sense" which "puts the brakes" on aggressive behavioral tendencies. Doctor Haydock, as early as the 1930 *Murder at the Vicarage,* describes criminals as being victims of "glandular dysfunction," an idea which is ridiculed by Inspector Slack and Colonel Melchett. In the 1933 *Thirteen at Dinner* a secretary who keeps herself abreast of "new thought" repeats Dr. Haydock's idea of "glandular dysfunction" in criminals, and this is ridiculed by Hercule Poirot and Inspector Japp. We now have a further "scientific explanation" of criminal behavior, this time related to normal vs. abnormal maturation.

The reader's personal perspectives on these subjects may affect his or her enjoyment of *Crooked House.*

SUMMARY FOR THE 1940S

Agatha Christie began writing non-detective fiction rather early in her career, publishing a "straight novel" in 1930 under the pseudonym Mary Westmacott. It seems apparent that she wished to become a more "serious" author and not just a writer of "light fiction." She published a total of six "straight" novels under the Mary Westmacott pseudonym over three decades. They were not very much liked by her publishers and most critics were not very impressed, although during the 1940s, *Absent in the Spring* was published and that novel was her best effort in this vein.

Christie's desire to branch out into more serious writing is quite obvious in her detective stories of the 1940s, especially in *The Moving Finger, Murder in Retrospect, Remembered Death, Murder After Hours,* and *There Is a Tide.* In these novels the characterization, and especially the relationships between the characters, is done with a much more serious hand than in most of her other detective novels. At least one of them—

Murder After Hours—probably should not have been a detective story at all but a novel about interpersonal relationships and how they are affected by one person and then by the death of that person. *There Is a Tide,* also, would have made a good novel about the psychological effects of war and its aftermath on families and the "murder mystery" aspect of the story could have been omitted.

Christie's detective novels of the 1940s, especially those mentioned above, generally lack the sparkle, humor and light-heartedness of her earlier books. It may be worth repeating that Agatha Christie, like all people, matured as she grew older, and her writing ability also matured. The major change, which came about gradually, was an increasing ability to create life-like characters with complex personalities. The physical descriptions of faces—the line of the jaw, the shape of the forehead—have not changed very much. Christie still uses the term "a determined chin," as if the part of the brain that was responsible for the quality of determination were somehow located in that part of the anatomy. But we now learn about the characters in much better ways than by descriptions of their faces and the shapes of their skulls. As far back as the 1936 *Murder in Mesopotamia* Christie was creating character portrayals entirely through the words of the people who knew those characters. Hercule Poirot had to solve that mystery by learning as much as he could about the victim, whom he had never known, and Christie managed to bring all of that learning to him through the various points of view of everyone at the expedition site. The point in that story was, of course, that *the psychology of the victim* was what mattered, but it was in that novel that Christie must have discovered how much more effectively a character can be portrayed if the ideas of various people can be used to create the characterization. The person need not even be in the story at all—it may be a person who has been dead for sixteen years, as was the case of Caroline and Amyas Crale in *Murder in Retrospect.* In that novel, Poirot relied on what everyone *said* or *wrote* about those two people and the events surrounding the crime. Then, in *Remembered Death,* Christie put the reader right into the *thoughts* of a variety of people. The reader learned about Stephen Farraday, for example, through his own thoughts about himself and through his wife's own thoughts about him, and not just by what people *chose to say* about him or what he *chose to tell others* about himself. This kind of characterization was even more skillfully utilized in *Murder After Hours,* as the reader is carried through the thoughts and memories of Midge Hardcastle, Henrietta Savernake, Edward Angkatell, John Christow and Gerda Christow. None of this ever occurred in Christie's novels before 1940.

Not only are the characters now portrayed with much more clarity, being a sum of various points of view, but they are now much more complex and sometimes contradictory. The self-revelation that Lynn Marchmont experiences in the 1948 *There Is a Tide* would never have occurred in an earlier Christie novel, at least not before about 1943. The sadness of Midge Hardcastle and the frustration of Gerda Christow in *Murder After Hours* could not have been expressed, either.

Characters now sometimes find themselves surprised by their own reactions to events and puzzled by their feelings towards others. Outstandingly memorable characters from the 1940s are Lynn Marchmont and Jeremy and Frances Cloade (*There Is a Tide*); Henrietta Savernake, John Christow and Midge Hardcastle (*Murder After Hours*); Stephen and Sandra Farraday (*Remembered Death*); Caroline Crale and Angela Warren (*Murder in Retrospect,*) and Elinor Carlisle (*Sad Cypress.*) No Christie character portrayals from the 1920s or 1930s approach these for subtlety.

The 1940s also seem to be a decade of serious thought for Christie on a variety of subjects. Psychology was clearly of very much interest to her between about 1935 and 1940 and, although it does not actually disappear from the novels of the 1940s, it is often disregarded or only referred to in passing, but it will reappear vigorously during the 1950s. The subjects of love, marriage, and marital loyalty and infidelity occupy Christie's thoughts a good deal more now. Beginning with *Sad Cypress,* Christie's first novel of the decade, we are immersed in a love story whether we want that experience or not, as Elinor Carlisle realizes with sadness and bitterness that Roddy Welman, whom she has loved for years, suddenly loves another woman. If we remember anything about the book a year after reading it, it is that aspect of the story and probably not the murder and its solution at all. When one recalls *Murder After Hours* a year after reading it, one may not even remember who it was who killed John Christow. Much more lasting may be one's memories of Midge Hardcastle's deep sadness, her nostalgic longings for Edward Angkatell and for Ainswick; Gerda Christow's frustrated mind racing around in circles about what to do about the mutton joint that's getting cold on the dinner table; Henrietta Savernake's selfless devotion to John; Edward's pathetic misconceptions about Henrietta's refusal to marry him; John's dissatisfaction with his marriage together with his knowledge that divorce and remarriage to another woman would not be a solution, since the problem is within himself.

The subject of "parenting" was clearly on Christie's mind all through the 1940s. In *Evil Under the Sun* we experience an adolescent girl's resentment of a non-caring step-mother. In *The Moving Finger* we experience the chronic depression of a twenty-year-old girl/woman whose existence her mother and stepfather would like to forget. In *The Body in the Library* there is a reference, albeit a comic one, to modern parenting books which advise as much "neglect" as possible for toddlers and in *Murder in Retrospect* the aging governess, Cecilia Williams delivers a long lecture on the bad effects of "overattention" to children. In *Crooked House,* the narrator Charles Hayward declares that "more children suffer from interference than from non-interference" from their parents and Clemency Leonides makes the following interesting statement:

> "I think, when your children have grown up, that you should cut away from them, efface yourself, slink away, force them to forget you."

Finally, yet another comment on the usual absence of mother-daughter relationships in Christie's detective novels. Recall that in *Murder After Hours* no adult has any memories of his or her mother, although Midge Hardcastle remembers her father with fondness. In *There Is a Tide,* the only mother of an adult woman is Adela Marchmont for whom her daughter Lynn feels affection but with whom there is no longer any mutual understanding. Adela continues to badger Lynn with trivia such as bridesmaid dresses and urges her to select for one of her bridesmaids a girl she loathes simply because the girl's mother is a friend of Adela's. In *Crooked House,* all of Aristide Leonides's children were brought up by their Aunt Edith since their mother died in 1905 when the youngest was a baby and none of the children remembers that mother. As to her grandchildren Sophia, Eustace and Josephine, they have no mother at all. Magda Leonides is a self-absorbed clown of a stage actress who has probably never thought of her children as anything but just three more faces in the audience.

For further remarks on the subject of the absence of mother-daughter relationships in Christie's novels, see the *Comments* section for the 1937 *Poirot Loses a Client.*

A Murder Is Announced (1950)

SETTING

It is October of approximately 1947 or 1948, as there are one or two characters aged about twenty-five who are said to have been born in 1922. The fictitious village of Chipping Cleghorn is the main setting, but there are one or two scenes at a luxury hotel, the Spa Hotel in Medenham Wells, not far away. The county is the fictitious Middleshire. This was also the name of the county in which Gorston Hall was located in the 1938 *A Holiday for Murder.* In that novel "Middleshire" was stated as being located in the Industrial Midlands of England, perhaps modeled after Lancashire or the West Riding of Yorkshire. One scene takes place at an aging castle in Scotland, the home of a dying, wealthy widow.

It is possible to imagine the "Middleshire" in *A Murder Is Announced* to be the same county as the "Middleshire" in *A Holiday for Murder,* since no particular geographic features in the novel prevent that assumption. However, not far away from Chipping Cleghorn is the town of "Milchester," in which one character is studying to be a dispenser and another is studying engineering. These characters travel to and from Milchester each day by regular bus service. In other novels featuring Miss Marple, Milchester is in the same area as St. Mary Mead, which has generally been located "somewhere west of London." In one novel Berkshire is suggested as its county, and in other novels the fictitious counties of Downshire and Radfordshire are specified. None of this has very much importance since nothing in the present story suggests that Chipping Cleghorn is anything but a typical English village that could be located anywhere in England.

Christie was not particularly careful about geographic consistency from one novel to the next. Of course she never suspected that, decades later, her writings would be subjected to scrutiny of any kind. She certainly never suspected that one day there would be beautifully bound sets of "The Complete Works of Agatha Christie" and books written about her and her writings. She considered her detective novels to be nothing but "light fiction" to be read for fun and then soon forgotten. We know that she placed the town of St. Loo in the county of Cornwall in one novel, and then in Devon in a later one.

Chipping Cleghorn has a butcher, a baker, a grocer, an antique shop, two tea shops and numerous cottages which were formerly lived in by agricultural laborers but have been improved and are now occupied by elderly spinsters and retired couples. There is also a church and vicarage. The antique shop is strategically located next door to the Blue Bird Tea Room so that motorists stopping for "a nice cup of tea and the somewhat euphemistically named 'Homemade Cakes' of a bright saffron color" may be tempted by Mr. Elliot's judiciously planned shop window. There is an establishment called The Red Cow, which may be the second tea shop referred to. An important scene takes place in The Blue Bird Tea Room and Café. There is a railway station in the village as well.

A mildly amusing description of The Blue Bird Tea Room is provided when Miss Marple follows another character inside:

> Miss Marple subsided gratefully onto the rather angular little blue painted armchair which the Bluebird affected.... A sulky-looking girl in a pink overall with a flight of bluebirds down the front of it took their order for coffee and cakes with a yawn and an air of weary patience.... Dora Bunner stretched out her hand and bit abstractedly into a lurid salmon-colored cake.

Negative portrayals of tea shops and their employees are routine in Christie novels, however, and not necessarily a comment on current conditions. We recall that in one of the final chapters of the 1934 *The Boomerang Clue*, "for the first time in the history of the Orient Café, one of its waitresses hurried..." and in the 1935 *Death in the Air*, two characters have tea in a London tea shop:

> ...a disdainful waitress with a gloomy manner took their order with an air of doubt as of one who might say, "Don't blame me if you're disappointed. They say we serve teas here, but I never heard of it."

Several homes in the village are settings for action and conversations, one being the vicarage. The vicarage drawing room reminds one of the police officers of his own Cumberland home, with faded chintz, big shabby armchairs, and flowers strewn about. The vicar and his wife have two children and no servants except for a woman who comes to clean twice a week. The general absence of live-in servants in post–War England is apparent.

Another house, called The Boulders, was formerly a row of three small attached cottages that have been "thrown into one." This is the home of two older women who keep chickens and pigs and do farming in a small way. There must be a small orchard on the property, as in one scene one of the ladies is picking apples. They have no help except for a woman who comes to clean the house on certain days.

The main setting, however, is a house called Little Paddocks. What was formerly a typical Victorian "double drawing room"—two small rooms with an archway between—is now a single larger room with a fireplace at each end. There are also a dining room, a study, and kitchen and scullery on the ground floor. The bedrooms are upstairs and evidently the only toilet is upstairs also, since one character comments that, at a recent birthday party in the house, "everybody went to the loo (the toilet)" and so everyone had an opportunity of entering one of the upstairs bedrooms unobserved and placing there a bottle of poisoned aspirin tablets.

Little Paddocks has central heating which uses coke.

> "You've got your central heating on," said Miss Hinchliffe. She said it accusingly. "Very early."

This is a reference to fuel shortages and rationing in post–War England and the practice of postponing the use of any central heating until the use of fireplaces to warm individual rooms was no longer practical.

The household at Little Paddocks consists of five adults and one live-in maid. There is also a woman who comes to clean five mornings a week. The live-in maid is a refugee from Central Europe who is bitter about her degrading position (in her native country she had earned a university degree in economics.) The whole household finds it necessary to "handle her with kid gloves" lest she bolt.

The occupants of another home are a retired Anglo-Indian colonel and his wife. They have a woman who comes to clean on certain days, but the colonel's wife is otherwise on her own. An elderly woman and her grown son are privileged to have a live-in maid who also cooks, but the mother has to be careful not to offend the maid, lest she take a dislike to them and "give notice." The mother admonishes her son for reading *The Daily Worker* when the maid is present, as it offends her.

This same lady later tells a police officer that when her family lived in India they had no fewer than eighteen servants, and it does not seem to occur to her that the reason her family was able to have eighteen servants was the abject poverty of India, with its millions of people on the edge of starvation and, therefore, "eager to serve."

At a large estate called Dayas Hall the result of several years of labor shortages in the matter of gardening is apparent. Couch grass, groundsel, bindweed and other garden pests show "every sign of vigorous growth." An aging gardener explains to a police officer that a place of this size needs three men and a boy to maintain it, but he is now forced to work alone with only a young woman as a helper.

All of this "shortage of domestic help" is seen by the characters in the story as an expression of "hard times." It does not occur to them that if there is a shortage of domestic help, it can only be that large numbers of people who were formerly condemned to the indignity of domestic service now have better employment opportunities.

Christie brought "post–War" conditions into her 1948 *There Is a Tide* in a big way. In *A Murder Is Announced,* there is not much of the spirit of depression and "unsettledness" that is spoken of in the earlier book. Instead, the daily nuisances of rationing and black marketeering are treated simply as background. There is a good deal of illegal "bartering" between families, for example. A family with a large vegetable garden trades vegetable marrows (squash) for honey produced by another family. Horsemeat is still in use and is probably not rationed, but such luxuries as butter, cream, sugar, chocolate, raisins and certainly choice meats are. The vicar's wife explains to a police officer why Miss Hinchliffe denied being at Little Paddocks on a certain day:

> "Thursday is the day one of the farms round here makes butter. They let anybody they like have a bit. It's usually Miss Hinchliffe who collects it. She's very much in with all the farmers—because of her pigs, I think. But it's all a bit hush-hush, you know; a kind of local scheme of barter. One person gets butter and sends along cucumbers, or something like that—and a little something when a pig's killed…"

At one point someone refers to "a tin of butter that we got from America" that can be used in a special cake. She also suggests using "some of those raisins we were saving for Christmas" in the cake. It is now early November. Someone offers a box of chocolates as a birthday gift and this provokes amused comments about the black market.

Clothing is rationed, too, and the working class women of the village are said to be willing to trade some of their "clothing coupons" for a used winter coat in good condition. This provides the former owner of the coat with more than her allotment of coupons and thus to be able to get a new, more stylish coat more often. Recall that in Christie's previous novel, *Crooked House,* Magda Leonides regularly purchased illegal clothing coupons from a man at a garage near Shaftesbury Avenue in London, but that was the only reference to rationing of any kind in that novel.

As mentioned above, heating fuel was rationed and at Little Paddocks the lady of the house explains that she is only able to get her allotment of coal by proving that she has no other fuel for cooking.

In the story there is suspicion, by the police and others, that certain people are not necessarily who they say they are. This leads to a discussion of another post–War condition: identity theft. Large numbers of people were killed, displaced or otherwise disappeared during the War. Many of the "otherwise disappeared" category resurfaced after the War with new identities stolen from people who were in fact killed. Furthermore, society has changed. In large cities it had always been common and accepted that one did not know much about one's neighbors, but in villages one knew everyone's families for generations. In the present (1947–1948), many of the residents of the village have only lived there for a few years and what they claim about their pasts—and their families—must be taken at face value. Therefore the police, in this investigation, find it necessary to look into the backgrounds of several of the villagers, even a retired Anglo-Indian colonel, who must be investigated to make sure he is not another person. In the story there are, in fact, no fewer than three characters who are concealing their true identities.

The story begins with an aborted, violent murder plot, and this leads certain characters to comment that crime has been on the increase since the War. One opinion is that "it's from the pictures," that is, the influence of films about gangsters, but another person opines that the rise in crime is attributable to the large number of "foreigners" who have come to live in England since the War. This person automatically suspects the foreign cook at Little Paddocks of having been in collusion with the foreign intruder and, furthermore, of being a Communist. Another person expresses the view that it is deserters from the armed forces, "desperate men roaming the countryside" who are committing the crimes.

There is a mention of a storage depository in London having been blitzed, and the consequent loss of all of one character's mementos, including photographs. The police are unable, therefore, to establish the identity of a person through old photographs.

At one point in the story a group of people listen to the evening news on the radio, and that gives rise to a discussion of the horrors of atomic warfare, Russia (which one person considers to be a menace to civilization) and radioactivity.

Automobiles are in daily use, of course, but the only character who is known to own one is

Miss Hinchliffe of The Boulders. It is a small car of unspecified make. A police officer makes a train journey to Scotland to interview a wealthy, dying woman. Her elderly chauffeur meets him at the station in an "old fashioned Daimler" and drives him to the "gray-walled keep," an aging castle in the highlands.

As the villagers read the "Personals" column of *The Gazette* they note that one family is offering their 1935 Daimler automobile for sale, and that a lady who is going abroad wishes to sell her two-piece navy suiting without mentioning the size or price. She will probably exchange it for some clothing coupons (an illegal act) and the "buyer" will alter it to fit.

Story

It is October 29 of 1947 or 1948 and the residents of the village of Chipping Cleghorn read in the local weekly paper, among the "Personal" ads:

> "A murder is announced and will take place on Friday, October 29th, at Little Paddocks, at 6:30 p.m. Friends please accept this, the only intimation."

Everyone in the village reads the local paper and all are astounded by this strange announcement. All assume that it is some kind of prank, or perhaps an invitation for a sort of "murder game" entertainment. The residents of Little Paddocks itself are as surprised by the announcement as everyone else.

At 6:15 p.m., curious villagers begin dropping in at Little Paddocks and, promptly at 6:30, the lights go out and a man with a flashlight enters the room and shouts "Stick 'em up." Everyone is thrilled by this entertaining spectacle, but then immediately three shots are fired and the man falls into the room. When the lights are restored, it is discovered that the man is dead, the flashlight and a revolver are lying on the floor near him, and the lady of the house is bleeding from one side of her face.

The police are disposed to close the case as "attempted murder, then suicide or accident," since nobody but the intruder has died. However, Miss Marple, who has been staying at a hotel in a nearby resort where the "intruder" was a receptionist, takes an interest in the case. She is convinced of two things: the young man did not have the personality of a murderer, and furthermore, there is no proof that it was he who fired the gun, since in the darkness the only thing that could have been visible to the people in the room was the flashlight.

Miss Marple and Inspector Craddock of the local police work together to solve this exciting mystery, in which two more murders occur.

Characters

Johnnie Butt, a little boy employed by Mr. Totman, the stationer, to deliver periodicals to the residents of Chipping Cleghorn on his bicycle every morning except Sunday

Mr. and Mrs. Butt, Johnnie's parents. According to Mrs. Harmon, the vicar's wife, Mr. Butt, "who never went to church and used to be practically the local atheist, comes every Sunday now on purpose" just to hear Reverend Harmon preach.

Mrs. Butt does housework for the Easterbrooks and the Harmons. She shares with Mrs. Harmon the fact that Colonel Easterbrook has a revolver in his collar drawer.

Mr. Totman, the stationer in the High Street of Chipping Cleghorn who supplies all of the periodicals requested by the villagers

Colonel Archie Easterbrook, a retired Anglo-Indian colonel. He is interested in psychology and provides an "interesting" psychological explanation for the crime. He is also one in a long line of "boring old Anglo-Indian colonels" in Christie's stories. One character in the story tries desperately *not* to have to read a book about India that the Colonel insists on lending to her, and another character likens his description of the Indian rope trick to "mass hypnotism."

Laura Easterbrook, who is thirty years younger than her husband, the Colonel. Through the "practical application" of psychology, (flattery, in other words), she convinces her reluctant husband that they absolutely *must* go to Little Paddocks in response to the announcement in the *Gazette*. She tells him that his expertise in police procedure will be necessary in order to make the "murder game" a success.

Mrs. Swettenham, who lives with her son Edmund in a cottage in Chipping Cleghorn. She wears a wig and reads *The Times* daily and the *Gazette* each Friday. She scolds her son for reading *The Daily Worker* in the presence of Mrs. Finch, their cook. Mrs. Finch does not like it! "If she takes a dislike to us and won't come, who else could we get?"

Edmund Swettenham, Mrs. Swettenham's son, who feels that his political views have nothing to do with Mrs. Finch. He is writing a book and he is in love with Phillipa Haymes, who lives at Little Paddocks as a lodger and works as a gardener at Dayas Hall.

Miss Hinchliffe, a tall, rather masculine, robust middle-aged woman who, with her friend Miss Murgatroyd, raises pigs and chickens at the Boulders, three antiquated cottages that have been thrown into one. She has a weatherbeaten countenance, a stentorian voice and a man's haircut. She was in the A.R.P. during the War and had an awfully good time. Her main interest in going to Little Paddocks on the evening of the "announcement" is to be offered a drink.

Miss Murgatroyd, Miss Hinchliffe's housemate-companion. She has a round, good-natured face and, in the opinion of Miss Hinchliffe, "gray fluff" for brains. After working her "gray fluff" considerably, she remembers something "extraordinary" about the incident at Little Paddocks.

Mrs. Finch, the cook-parlourmaid at the Swettenham home who dislikes *The Daily Worker* and late breakfasts. She is "a grim-looking female in an aged velvet beret."

Miss Letitia Blacklock, the owner of Little Paddocks, a medium-size early Victorian house in Chipping Cleghorn. She is as surprised as anyone in the village by the strange announcement in *The Gazette* about a murder being planned for Friday evening in her home.

Miss Blacklock had been, for many years, the "private secretary" to a financier, Randall Goedler. Actually she had much more business acumen than Goedler had, and skillfully guided him, over the years, in many business decisions—to his unquestioned benefit. His reward to her: he left his vast fortune to his frail, delicate wife for the duration of her life (which nobody expected to last very long) and then to Miss Blacklock. He died about ten years ago and Mrs. Goedler is now in the last weeks of her life. Miss Blacklock will soon be an immensely wealthy woman.

Miss Dora Bunner, age sixty-four, an old friend of Letitia Blacklock. Dora's life had not been a success. She never married, had to earn her own living, and never mastered anything or succeeded at anything. She lives at Little Paddocks as a companion and helper to Miss Blacklock.

Rev. Julian Harmon, the amiable vicar of Chipping Cleghorn. He loves reading murder mysteries and his most recent sermon was much better than usual because, finding a murder mystery in his study as he was about to compose the sermon, he became so engrossed in the book that he had to sketch the sermon out "quickly, without the usual scholarly twists and bits and learned references," according to his wife.

Diana Harmon ("Bunch") the cheerful, loquacious wife of Rev. Harmon. The roundness of her face and form is responsible for her nickname. She is unaffected and honest. On the evening of the "announced murder" she is the only one of the guests who does not pretend to be there for some other reason. Bunch's most noteworthy trait is her incurable happiness.

Susan and Edward, Rev. Julian and Diana Harmon's two children

Tiglath-Pileser, the Harmons' cat, who shows Miss Marple how the lights were caused to go out on the evening of the incident at Little Paddocks

Julia Simmons, a young woman of about twenty-five, a distant cousin to Letitia Blacklock. At the request of Julia's mother, Letitia's second cousin, both Julia and her brother Patrick live at Little Paddocks as paying guests. They are both studying at Milchester, which is fifty minutes away by bus. Letitia has welcomed them into her home and she enjoys their company. Julia is studying to be a dispenser.

Patrick Simmons, Julia's brother, who is studying for an engineering degree at the University of Milchester. He is a tall, handsome young man. As noted above, he and his sister live at Little Paddocks as paying guests. They have been there for about two months.

Phillipa Haymes, a young widow with an eight-year-old son. Her husband was killed in the War. She works as a gardener at a large house in the neighborhood, and is more or less a "lodger" at Little Paddocks. She is strongly disliked by the cook at Little Paddocks, a Central European refugee, who describes her as haughty and "a Nazi."

Ronald Haymes, Phillipa Haymes's husband who was killed in the War

Harry Haymes, Phillipa Haymes's eight-year-old son who is away at school

Mitzi, the "foreign help" at little Paddocks, a war refugee from somewhere in Central Europe. She is an excellent cook but tends to scream at the slightest provocation. She feels degraded by her lowly position—in her native country she had earned a university degree in economics. Both the family and the police suspect that she is a habitual liar.

Mitzi makes a special cake that the family finds absolutely delectable, and which Patrick Simmons has dubbed "Delicious Death."

Evans, the man who lit the central heating at Little Paddocks. There is no mention of his position; perhaps he does gardening work for Letitia Blacklock. He is only mentioned one time.

Old Man Ashe, the surly old gardener at Dayas Hall, one in a long line of surly, lazy old gardeners in Christie novels.

George Rydesdale, the Chief Constable of

Middleshire, Detective Inspector Craddock's superior. He is in the habit of listening rather than talking. Then, in his unemotional voice, he gives a brief order and the order is obeyed.

Detective Inspector Dermot Eric Craddock, of the Middleshire Police. He is officially in charge of the case. The godson of Sir Henry Clithering, he has brains, imagination, and the self-discipline to go slow, to check and examine each fact and to keep an open mind until the very end of a case.

Although we are not favored with a physical description of Inspector Craddock, we can deduce that he is a good-looking man thanks to the following remarks of Miss Marple's. Miss Marple believes that Myrna Harris, a waitress at the Spa Hotel, is concealing something that she knows about Rudy Scherz. She explains to Inspector Craddock:

> "Yes, she's worried. Afraid she might have to give evidence or something like that. But I expect"—her candid blue eyes swept over the manly proportions and handsome face of Detective Inspector Craddock with truly feminine Victorian appreciation—"that you will be able to persuade her to tell you all she knows."

This is not the first time that Miss Marple has suggested that a good-looking man make use of his looks when information is needed from a woman. In the 1930 *Murder at the Vicarage* she exploited Lawrence Redding's good looks in the same way.

Constable Legge, who took the call from Little Paddocks about the hold-up and the death of Rudi Scherz and "...acted very well, with promptitude and presence of mind."

Rudi Scherz who, until he died at Little Paddocks at 6:30 p.m. on October 29, was employed as a receptionist at the Spa Hotel in Medenham Wells.

Sergeant Fletcher, Detective Inspector Craddock's assistant. He is the first to interview the household at Little Paddocks.

Sir Henry Clithering, a tall, distinguished-looking, elderly man. He is an ex-commissioner of Scotland Yard, Dermot Craddock's godfather, and an old friend and admirer of Miss Jane Marple. Sir Henry has great respect for village-dwelling "old pussies" because of their detective instincts.

An Adenoidal Blonde at the office of *The Gazette* who accepts unquestioningly all advertisements to be placed in *The Gazette,* even ones announcing murders.

Miss Jane Marple, whom we first met in the 1930 *Murder at the Vicarage,* and then in two subsequent novels. She is now about twenty years older and suffers from rheumatism. Her old friend Sir Henry Clithering is overcome with joy at learning that she is involved in the case:

> "Ye gods and little fishes," said Sir Henry, "can it be? George, it's my own particular, one and only, four-starred pussy. The super-pussy of all old pussies. And she has managed somehow to be at Medenham Wells, instead of peacefully at home in St. Mary Mead, just at the right time to be mixed up in a murder. Once more a murder is announced—for the benefit and enjoyment of Miss Marple."

Mr. Rowlandson, the manager of the Spa Hotel, a tall, florid man with a hearty manner. He had suspected Rudi Scherz of cheating the hotel guests in small ways—adding spurious charges to their bills, mainly, and then pocketing the excess amount that they paid.

Myrna Harris, a waitress at the Spa Hotel who was a friend of Rudi Scherz. She is a pretty girl with "a glorious head of red hair and a pert nose." She is also—as are all "servant class people" in Christie stories—"deeply conscious of the indignity of being interviewed by the police" and is alarmed by and wary of questions. Miss Marple notices that Myrna is upset and distrait, and realizes that she may be concealing some important information about Rudi Scherz. She encourages Detective Inspector Craddock to question Myrna a second time, and on that occasion Myrna discloses a very important fact.

Elinor Simmons, a second cousin of Letitia Blacklock and the mother of Patrick and Julia. She lives at Cannes, in the south of France.

Mrs. Huggins from the Village who does housework at Little Paddocks five mornings a week.

Jim Huggins, her husband

Ned Barker, a villager who thinks the increase in violent crime in England has come from "people going to the pictures too much."

Tom Riley, a villager who thinks the increase in crime comes from letting foreigners run about loose in England. He suspects Mitzi, the cook at Little Paddocks, of being "a Communist or worse."

Florrie, the daughter of Old Bellamy, who says Miss Blacklock's pearls are just "costume jewelry" and not the real thing.

Mrs. Lucas, the owner of Dayas Hall who resents the police coming and questioning Phillipa Haymes while she is working instead of waiting till they can question her "on her own time." She is a habitual complainer.

Mrs. Mopp, who does housework at The Boulders and who is, unlike most of the cleaning ladies in the village, not a talker.

Mr. and Mrs. Raymond West, Miss Marple's nephew and his wife. Raymond is a successful writer of "clever books" but Miss Marple has never been impressed with his books or his ideas. She describes Raymond and his wife:

> "Yes, the dear boy has been so successful with his clever books. The last one was a Book Society choice—quite the worst one he has written, actually, but I do think that is so often the case, don't you? The dear boy insisted on paying all my expenses. And his dear wife is making a name for herself, too, as an artist. Mostly jugs of dying flowers and broken combs on windowsills. I never dare tell her, but I still admire Blair Leighton and Alma-Tadema. Oh, but I'm chattering..."

Jim Kelly, a notorious swindler Detective Inspector Craddock had helped to put behind bars not long ago. He had the same "shifty eye" that Miss Marple said she had noticed about Rudi Scherz.

Randall Goedler, who died in 1938. He was an immensely successful financier and investor. A good deal of his success—perhaps even most of it—was attributable to the decisions of his "secretary" Letitia Blacklock, who actually had more business sense than he had, and who steered him away from bad risks and toward good ones many times. For this he was eternally grateful.

Belle Goedler, Randall Goedler's wife, to whom he was devoted. Always a delicate and sickly woman, she has survived nine or ten years after his death, but she is now near death herself at her castle in Scotland and has no more than a few weeks to live. When she dies her fortune will go to Letitia Blacklock—provided that Letitia is still living.

Sonia Stamfordis, the estranged sister of Randall Goedler who enraged her brother by marrying Dmitri Stamfordis, whom Randall regarded as "a crook." She went abroad with her husband, only writing to her brother's wife one time—to announce the birth of twins. Randall and Belle never heard from her again.

Dmitri Stamfordis, the disreputable husband of Randall Goedler's sister Sonia

"Pip and Emma," twins born to Sonia and Dmitri Stamfordis in 1922, eighteen months after their marriage. They were thus named because they were born just after noon, that is, "in the P.M." Whether they are still alive or not, nobody knows. In fact the only evidence of their existence is the single letter that Sonia Stamfordis wrote to her brother's wife, Belle. But if they do in fact exist, they have an ample motive for the murder of Miss Letitia Blacklock, as they will then inherit Randall Goedler's fortune when their Aunt Belle dies.

Charlotte Blacklock, the invalid sister of Letitia who died of consumption just before the Second World War.

Mr. Elliot, the owner of the antique shop next door to the Blue Bird Tea Room and Café.

Julia, a waitress at the Blue Bird Tea Room and Café who objects to being called "a Peculiar," as she has always been "a good Church of England."

A Parlourmaid in the past who was no good at all at waiting at table, who mixed up the kitchen knives with the dining room ones and whose cap was never straight. Miss Marple kept her because she was so pleasant to have about the house and because she said things "straight out." She eventually married a Baptist minister and they had five children.

Florrie, of whom the above plain-speaking former parlourmaid of Miss Marple had said, "She sits down just like a married woman." The fact is that Florrie was pregnant, having been "taken in by the gentlemanly appearance of the hairdresser's assistant." Miss Marple had a little talk with him and the couple had a very nice wedding and settled down quite happily.

A Gentlemanly Assistant at the Hairdresser's who married Florrie after a little talk with Miss Marple.

Nurse Ellerton, one of Miss Marple's "village parallels." She committed "mercy killings" twice, both times inheriting large sums of money from her patients.

A Young Man on the Liner, another of Miss Marple's "village parallels." He stole things and told his mother he had bought them abroad. Then he murdered his mother in order to prevent her from giving him away.

Mrs. Cray at the Wool Shop, who was devoted to her son and spoiled him, of course.

Joan Croft, one Miss Marple's "village parallels." She used to stalk about smoking a cigar or a pipe, making quite a strange spectacle in the village. But one day there was a bank holdup and Joan happened to be in the bank. She knocked the man down and took his revolver, and was later congratulated for her courage by the Bench. Miss Marple is reminded of Joan by Miss Hinchliffe, a rather masculine type who had the time of her life during the War in the A.R.P.

That Girl at St. Jean des Collines who felt cut off from the world because her husband was a forger

Major Vaughan at the Larches and **Colonel Wright at Simla Lodge,** Anglo-Indian colonels whose lives were without incident

Mr. Hodgson, the bank manager who married a woman young enough to be his daughter.

He had met her on a cruise, and she had lied to him about her past.

Mrs. Wotherspoon who drew her own old-age pension as well as that of Mrs. Bartlett, who had died some years earlier

The Elderly Chauffeur of Mrs. Belle Goedler
The Elderly Butler of Mrs. Belle Goedler
Sister McClelland, a nurse who cares for old Mrs. Goedler

Mr. Beddingfeld, Letitia Blacklock's lawyer
A Dying Parishioner out at Lock Hamlet
A Child Needing to Get to Hospital At Once
Old Doctor Blacklock, the father of Letitia and Charlotte, who was an old fashioned tyrant

Mr. Curtiss, the Wesleyan Minister, who refused to have his child wear a dental plate, affirming that it was God's will if the child's teeth stuck out. When it was pointed out that he shaved and trimmed his hair despite God's causing his hair and beard to grow, he said that that was entirely different. "So like a man!" comments Miss Marple.

Constable Edwards, who is an expert in shorthand writing

Dr. Adolf Koch who operated a special clinic in Berne, Switzerland

COMMENTS

A Murder Is Announced, the first of Christie's detective novels to be published in the 1950s, must have been very well received by her fans, especially by those who may have been disappointed by *Remembered Death, Murder After Hours* and *There Is a Tide*. The tone of those three novels is rather serious and all three might have made interesting non-detective novels because of the complex personalities of the characters. Christie seemed to be attempting to write "more serious" fiction with those efforts and, to her fans who had enjoyed the more light-hearted touch of her earlier detective novels, the recent ones may have seemed a bit dull. In the 1949 *Crooked House* there seems to be a return to the "good old Christie" detective novel, and there certainly is that return in *A Murder Is Announced*.

The superbly thorough characterization for which *Murder in Retrospect, Remembered Death, Murder After Hours* and *There Is a Tide* are remarkable is notably absent in *A Murder Is Announced*. Some major characters are hardly developed at all, such as Julia Simmons and Patrick Simmons, for example. They are not even physically described except for a comment or two that Julia has hazel eyes and a steady gaze, and Patrick is "tall and handsome." Phillipa Haymes's only personality traits seem to be devotion to her son and a very reserved demeanor. We learn that Letitia Blacklock was devoted to her invalid sister and that she showed unusual business acumen while working for Randall Goedler, but otherwise her personality is not developed. And we know nothing of the private thoughts of any of these characters. Nevertheless, they are among the main characters in the story.

Developed in more detail is the personality of Dora Bunner—through her own revelations to Miss Marple, and through the thoughts of Letitia Blacklock. Miss Hinchliffe is an amusing character with her aggressively masculine personality, and so is her scatty housemate, Miss Murgatroyd. Mitzi, the foreign cook at Little Paddocks provides a good deal of humor with her "foreign" eccentricities: unreasoning fear of the police (probably learned through gruesome experiences on the Continent during the War), her bitter resentment of her reduced position in society, and her intensity on the subject of seriously good cooking and baking.

But excellent characterization is not a distinguishing quality of this novel. What is memorable about the novel is the mystery itself—and its detection. An excellent working relationship exists between Miss Marple and Inspector Craddock and his associates and all of them need to work very hard. Finding a motive for the first "attempted murder"—a shooting—is difficult enough, and the second death—a poisoning—appears to be an accidental result of a second murder attempt. The third killing—a strangling—is, of course no accident. This story is exciting and beautifully plotted and several clues are provided—clues that careful readers should not miss.

In the 1948 *There Is a Tide*, Christie made "post–War England" such an important feature of the story that some readers may remember that aspect of the book more than the murder mystery itself. They may, in fact, remember it less as a detective story and more as the story of a woman's problems in readjusting to rural life in England after serving in the armed forces in wartime. In *A Murder Is Announced* the frequent references to the post–War conditions of food rationing, fuel rationing, clothing rationing and black marketeering are an interesting part of the background, but not an essential one and certainly not a distraction.

A Murder Is Announced is a "must-read" and would make an excellent "first Christie experience."

They Came to Baghdad (1951)

Setting

The year is 1950 and nearly all of the action takes place in Iraq, which is no longer the "British protectorate" that it was during the years between the two world wars, when it was the setting for the 1936 *Murder in Mesopotamia*. Preliminary scenes include one at the office of an internationally important New York banker and several scenes in London. These include two guest suites and the dining room at the Savoy Hotel, a private home in a "quiet, rather dingy square" in Kensington, a London nursing home, a jewelry shop and a florist's in Bond Street and an exclusive tailor's in Savile Row. There are also scenes at the office of a London businessman, at an employment agency and in the fictitious Fitz James Gardens, a tiny triangular park "in the shadow of a tall warehouse."

The protagonist, a young Englishwoman, makes an airplane trip from London to Baghdad. There is a stop for rest in Tripolitania in North Africa, and an overnight stop at Cairo. While in Cairo the young woman makes a brief excursion to visit some pyramids in the area, and then she finally arrives in Baghdad. She makes a railway trip to Basrah, and later an automobile trip to Damascus in Syria and then back again by plane to Baghdad. The airliner that carries her from London to Cairo is described as holding from twenty to thirty people, including crew members, and is probably an up-to-date craft for the period. Of course it is a propeller-driven plane as there are as yet no jet airliners. The only make of automobile mentioned in the book is the Standard, which may be a fictitious make.

Agatha Christie married an archeologist in 1930 and accompanied him to the Middle East on his expeditions every year until 1938, and then again from 1948 through the mid–1950s. The couple maintained a home in Baghdad and Christie came to know the city very well. Her colorful descriptions of the streets, the noise, dust and general squalor, the markets, the hotels and everything else can be assumed to be authentic for the period.

The story, however, has little to do with Iraq or Syria. Any country in the world—except the United States or the Soviet Union—could have been the setting, for it is not the physical setting but the international situation that matters. We are in the early days of the Cold War and the two superpowers, The United States and The Soviet Union, are suspicious and fearful of each other. Baghdad is simply the site of a scheduled meeting of the heads of the United States and the Soviet Union along with three individuals—one American and two British—who have important documentation about a secret organization that is bent on disrupting peace efforts worldwide.

Story

It is 1950 and the two Superpowers, The United States and The Soviet Union, representing opposing ideologies, exist in constant fear and distrust of each other. Despite this, both countries have made efforts to approach each other with the goal of friendship and mutual understanding—or at least mutual tolerance—because both powers know that a Third World War would be a disaster. But whenever it appears that the two superpowers seem to be moving toward peaceful negotiations, there is an unexplained breakdown in communications and understandings. There appears to be a well-organized, nameless, subversive organization whose goal is to achieve supreme power by fostering a Third World War which will destroy both Superpowers, leaving the organization alone to rule the world—or what is left of it. Twenty-eight brilliant young scientists, engineers and otherwise talented people have vanished from their native countries and money has also been disappearing. People and money do not normally "vanish." It is clear that these people and the money are going *somewhere*.

The existence of a well-run, secret organization—complete with underground laboratories staffed by talented scientists from every country in the world—seems to be such a fantastic idea that the few people who have heard about it cannot take it seriously. However, there are three individuals who have documented proof of its existence and of its plans. A meeting of these three important people, and of the heads of state of both superpowers, is scheduled to take place in Baghdad for discussions of the matter.

Into this exciting and dangerous situation stumbles Victoria Jones, a mediocre London shorthand typist who has just been fired for entertaining the office staff by imitating the boss's wife on company time. While eating her lunch in a park, she meets a charming young man who introduces himself only as "Edward," and she immediately falls in love with him. As Edward leaves, he tells Victoria that he is about to leave for Baghdad, where he works for an organization called The Olive Branch.

Victoria finds a way to follow her beloved "Edward" to Baghdad, and from that point onwards she has the most exciting adventures imaginable, playing an important role in the destruction of the "secret organization."

Characters

Captain Crosbie, whom we meet on Page One of the story. His official identity is that of an employee of an oil company in Baghdad, but he is actually an important agent of the British government and one of a small group of people who are charged with preventing a sinister organization from leading the world to another war.

Mr. Dakin, of the Iraqi Iranian Oil Company. He is a friend of Captain Crosbie and the head of the small group to which Crosbie belongs.

Henry Carmichael, a.k.a. "Fakir" Carmichael. Through his travels and adventures in remote regions of the Middle East and Asia, he has stumbled upon a fantastic organization. The headquarters of this organization, located in a remote area of China or Tibet, includes secret underground laboratories. The goal of the organization is to foster world-wide destruction through war, and then later to rule the world—or what is left of it. Carmichael has recently returned to that secret place and plans to bring back proof of the existence of the organization.

Sir Rupert Crofton Lee, a world traveler, a writer of travel books, and a great authority on the interior of China. He is one of only two people who believed Henry Carmichael's fantastic stories—the other being Mr. Dakin—and Sir Rupert has verified Carmichael's claims.

Otto Morganthal, the head of the New York firm of Morganthal, Brown and Shipperke, international bankers

Anna Scheele, Mr. Morganthal's personal secretary. She has knowledge and documentation of the financial aspects of the secret organization, and she is one of the three people who are scheduled to meet in Baghdad.

Miss Wygate, another secretary in Mr. Morganthal's office who can attend to things during Anna Scheele's three-week absence.

Mr. Cornwall, who will attend to the Ascher Merger during Anna Scheele's absence.

Elsie, Anna Scheele's sister, who lives at 17 Elmsleigh Gardens in Kensington, London. She is about to have an internal operation and wishes her sister to be near her.

An Elderly Woman with a Suspicious Face who opens the door at the home of Anna Scheele's sister Elsie

Victoria Jones, a young, inefficient shorthand typist who works in London. That is, when she is not out of a job. Currently she is out of a job because of some impromptu entertainment she has provided in the form of an imitation of the boss's wife for the benefit of the other three typists and the office boy while in the supposed safety of the boss's absence.

It is Victoria's ability to "lie with fluency, ease and artistic fervour" that is largely responsible for her survival in this tale of danger and international intrigue. Learning that an archeologist in Iraq is expecting a young female anthropologist, Victoria successfully poses as the anthropologist, promising herself to look up the word at the first opportunity if there is such a thing as a dictionary at the archeological dig.

Mr. Greenholtz of Greenholtz, Simmon & Lederbetter of Graysholme Street, London. He is (or was until recently) Victoria Jones's employer

Mrs. Greenholtz, who is the subject of Victoria's imitation for the entertainment of the office staff.

Three Other Typists and an Office Boy who are very much entertained by Victoria's "performance" until interrupted by the unexpected return of Mr. Greenholtz

Edward Goring, a handsome young man whom Victoria Jones meets while eating lunch one day in FitzJames Gardens. During the Second World War he was a fighter pilot. He works for an organization in Baghdad known as The Olive Branch, which seeks to bring together young people of different cultures through shared reading and discussion of translated works of English authors. Edward suspects that there is something "bogus" about The Olive Branch.

Victoria falls in love with this young man within five or ten minutes of meeting him, and follows him to Baghdad in order to be near him.

A Little Dark Man who follows Anna Scheele around London in a taxi

An Agitated Woman with Parcels to whom the taxi driver had been singularly blind a moment or two before picking up The Little Dark Man mentioned above

A Smartly Dressed Young Woman who follows Anna Scheele into two shops in Bond Street

A Fair, Rather Vacant-looking Young Man who rides with the Smartly Dressed Young Woman in a grey Standard which is following Anna Scheele's taxi

Mr. Bolford, of Bolford & Avery's in Savile Row, who takes an order from Anna Scheele for a tailored suit and comments negatively on the decline in the quality of British goods in recent years.

They Came to Baghdad (1951)

Louisa, a short, plump woman who searches Anna Scheele's room at the Savoy, finding nothing

The Maître d'Hôtel at the Savoy Hotel who inquires affectionately after the health of Otto Morganthal

Miss Spencer of St. Guildric's Agency, who habitually assists Victoria in finding a new position whenever she gets sacked, which is quite often.

A Lady with Two Little Girls wanting a governess-nurse for a passage to Australia

Dr. Pauncefoot Jones, a famous archeologist who is presently excavating the ancient city of Murik at Tell Aswad, one hundred twenty miles from Baghdad. He is a small rotund man with a semi-bald head and a twinkling eye. He welcomes Victoria, swallowing hook-line-and-sinker her nonsense about being the anthropologist he has been expecting. Fortunately Victoria's name somewhat resembles the name of the real anthropologist, Veronica—or is it Venetia? The world-renowned archeologist cannot quite remember. Details!

Mrs. Pauncefoot Jones, Dr. Pauncefoot Jones's wife

Mrs. Hamilton Clipp, a loquacious American lady who broke her arm as she fell on some steps in Westminster Abbey. She is flying to Baghdad and needs a traveling companion because the broken arm makes everything so awkward for her. She is "a short bird-like sharp-eyed little woman." Like Mrs. Gardener in the 1941 *Evil Under the Sun,* Mrs. Hamilton Clipp is a non-stop talker and a "typical" American traveler.

Mr. Hamilton Clipp, the husband of Mrs. Hamilton Clipp. He is a very tall, thin, grey-haired American with slow, deliberate speech and a kindly aspect.

Lady Cynthia Bradbury, who has recently left England for East Africa. The unscrupulous Victoria Jones takes advantage of her absence from England by writing for herself a glowing recommendation, signed by Lady Bradbury, on Ritz Hotel stationery.

The Bishop of Llangow, a.k.a. The Bishop of Languao, a spurious uncle of Victoria's whose "recommendation" Victoria forges on stationery from a hotel known to cater to higher clergy and country gentlewomen. At first he is the fictitious "Bishop of Llangow," but when Mrs. Cardew Trench observes, "Nonsense, there's no such person," he becomes "Bishop of Languao, a colonial bishop in the Pacific Archipelago." Mrs. Cardew Trench knows nothing of colonial bishops.

Mr. Burgeon in American Express who will get the necessary visas for Victoria's trip to Baghdad

Abdul Suleiman of the Marsh Arabs, the boatman who brings Henry Carmichael, in disguise, to Basrah.

Two Men Carrying a Portable Cinema in the desert

A Shopkeeper in Basrah where *ferwahs* are sold

A Customer wearing green around his fez, indicating that he is a Hajji who has been to Mecca

Salah Hassan, the owner of the shop in Basrah

Mr. Walter Williams of Messrs Cross and Company, Importers and Shipping Agents, the alias Henry Carmichael would have used if he had succeeded in changing into a new disguise at the shop where *ferwahs* were sold

Richard Baker, an archeologist and friend of Dr. Pauncefoot Jones. He had known Henry Carmichael while at Eton. Baker had been nicknamed "Owl" at school because of his unusually large and solid pair of spectacles.

Gerald Clayton, the British Consul General at Basrah. He is a quiet grey haired man with a thoughtful face.

Rosa Clayton, Gerald Clayton's wife, a woman with a buoyant personality and abounding vitality.

Robert Hall, of Achilles Works, Enfield. He is a stoutish Englishman with a grey moustache who carries a revolver and who, in the waiting room of the British Consulate at Basrah, attempts to shoot Henry Carmichael.

A Tired-looking Man, a Man Who Looked Like an Iraqi Clerk, and an Elderly Persian in Flowing, Snowy Robes, other people in the waiting room at the British Consulate in Basrah when Henry Carmichael's life is threatened

Archie Gaunt, a friend of the Claytons in Kuwait who will put Richard Baker up during his stay there

A Man in a Loud Check Coat who, during a short stop in Tripolitania, takes a fancy to Victoria and tells her at some length all about the manufacture of lead pencils.

Mrs. Kitchin and Her Two Small Children with whom Victoria has the pleasure of visiting some pyramids near Cairo

Young Mr. Shrivenham of the British Embassy in Baghdad who has the task of greeting Sir Rupert Crofton Lee at the airport and escorting him to the Embassy and, later, to the Tio Hotel

Lansdowne, Rice and Best, important people at the British Embassy in Baghdad who are either absent or otherwise indisposed when Sir Rupert arrives

A Servant at the British Embassy in Baghdad who offers to unpack for Sir Rupert

Marcus Tio, the owner of the Tio Hotel in Baghdad. He claims to know "everyone in Baghdad." However, when asked about Dr. Rathbone, he replies, "I do not know. He does not stay at the Tio."

Mr. Harrison who should have greeted Mrs. Hamilton Clipp at the airport

Mrs. Cardew Trench, "one of those weatherbeaten Englishwomen of indeterminate age who can always be found in any foreign city."

Professor Kalzman and Mr. and Mrs. McIntyre, friends of Marcus Tio

Mr. Betoun Evans, the English advisor at the Museum in Baghdad

Dr. Rathbone, an imposing-looking elderly man of about 60, with a high-domed forehead and white hair. "Benevolence, kindliness and charm were the most apparent qualities of his personality. A producer of plays would have cast him without hesitation for the role of the great philanthropist." He is the director of The Olive Branch.

Catherine, a volunteer at The Olive Branch in Baghdad. She is a Syrian girl from Damascus. Working together at The Olive Branch, Catherine and Victoria develop a hearty dislike for each other.

A Good-looking Dark Girl seen speaking with Catherine at The Olive Branch

A Dark-haired Man in a Mauve Pinstripe Suit and **A Man in a Police Officer's Uniform** who search Victoria's room while Henry Carmichael is hidden there

Paul Tio, a medical doctor who happens to be a brother of Marcus Tio

A Man Called Harrison from Kirkuk and **A Nurse Who Works at the Jewish Hospital in Baghdad**, other guests whose rooms are on the same floor of the Tio Hotel as Victoria's

Michael Rakounian and Isaac Nahoum, two members of the Olive Branch who have a fight despite all the peace, understanding and brotherhood that are preached there. Isaac gets a cut lip out of it.

Miss Ankoumian, a plain but competent-looking young woman who provides Victoria with a cream shampoo—and a surprise

An Arab who brings Victoria a meal while she is held captive

A Couple of Women, One Holding a Baby, who giggle and watch as the Arab brings food to Victoria's prison

Abdul, the driver of Richard Baker's car

A Foreman at the Tell Aswad

Veronica, a.k.a. Venetia, Dr. Pauncefoot Jones's anthropologist niece, whom he is expecting. Since he is too much of an archeologist to remember whether her name is Veronica or Venetia, it is no surprise that when Victoria turns up he accepts her as the anthropologist, despite the fact that she does not even know the meaning of the word.

Emerson at Cambridge who wrote to Dr. Pauncefoot Jones about Veronica, a.k.a Venetia

Lawrence, not a character in the novel but a reference to E. T. Lawrence (1888–1935) an Englishman who, as a student, toured Syria on foot as part of his work on his thesis on the Crusades. Later he promoted Arab self-rule and was discouraged by the terms of the Treaty of Versailles which, among other things, created the French and British protectorates of Syria and Mesopotamia. Later, as Winston Churchill's advisor, he was able to help achieve some measure of self-rule for Arabs. His life was the subject of a 1962 film, *Lawrence of Arabia*.

In the novel, during a conversation between Richard Baker and Victoria, Baker expresses doubt that any Englishman has ever been able to pass as an Arab. Victoria suggests "Lawrence?" to which Baker replies "I don't think Lawrence ever passed as an Arab." He goes on to say that, on the other hand, Henry Carmichael *could* "pass as an Arab."

Elizabeth Canning, a former associate of Dr. Pauncefoot Jones, and of whom Victoria reminds him with her preposterous story of having been kept prisoner

Two Frenchmen Interested in Archeology who visit Tell Aswad one day. One of them becomes ill and needs to rest in the camp. While there, he makes a thorough search of Richard Baker's room.

A Startled Minion ordered by Marcus Tio to procure a taxi

Abdullah, a servant in the office of Mr. Dakin

Grete Harden, a Danish hotel masseuse who may be Anna Scheele in disguise

A Thin, Dark Frenchwoman who dresses Victoria—and then herself—as nuns with a purpose

A Tall, Dark Man in European Dress, the driver of the car that takes two nuns from Baghdad to Damascus

A Prosperous-looking Iraqi Businessman and **A Young English Doctor** at the aerodrome in Damascus awaiting a connecting flight to Baghdad

A Tall Dark Young Woman in a B.O.A.C. Uniform at the Abbassid Hotel in Damascus who escorts Grete Harden to the B.O.A.C. office because of some difficulty about her ticket.

A Fair Young Man who is Victoria's gaoler aboard the plane from Damascus to Baghdad

Sybil Muirfield, whom Dr. Pauncefoot Jones really felt he could trust

Dr. Alan Breck of the Harwell Atomic Institute

Sheikh Hussein el Ziyara, a holy man and poet and all-around V.I.P.

COMMENTS

They Came to Baghdad is an enormously amusing, entertaining novel. It's an adventure story similar to *The Secret Adversary* and *The Man in the Brown Suit.* No more believable or realistic than those stories, it's just as much fun to read. If you liked the personality of Anne Beddingfeld in *The Man in the Brown Suit,* you will like Victoria Jones.

This book must have been welcomed by Christie fans when it was first published in 1951. It is doubtful that very many people remembered her lighthearted adventure novels of the 1920s, but the few who did were probably even more enthusiastic. Several of Christie's detective novels of the 1940s had been a bit heavy for "light fiction." *They Came To Baghdad* is a frank return to light-heartedness in Christie's writing.

Among the most amusing characters in *They Came to Baghdad* are the non-stop talker Mrs. Hamilton Clipp, who resembles Mrs. Gardener from *Evil Under the Sun,* and Dr. Pauncefoot Jones, the absent-minded archeologist who seriously believes that Victoria—who doesn't even know the meaning of the word "anthropologist"—*is* one. Christie must have done a lot of smiling as she wrote this novel, and there are plenty of "archeologist" jokes in the book, which must have been great fun for Christie's husband, the archeologist Max Mallowan. The first is a scene in the waiting room at the British Consulate in Basrah. The archeologist Richard Baker is sitting among five or six other people.

> There were several people already in the waiting room. Richard hardly glanced at them. He was, in any case, seldom interested by members of the human race. A fragment of antique pottery was always more exciting to him than a mere human being born somewhere in the twentieth century A.D....He allowed his thoughts to dwell pleasantly on some aspects of the Mari letters and the movements of the Benjaminite tribes in 1750 B.C.

At one point in the story Victoria, who has been posing as the niece of Dr. Pauncefoot Jones, realizes that she may soon have to meet him personally. Her boyfriend Edward asks:

"But suppose you and old Pussyfoot Jones come face to face?"

"Pauncefoot. I don't think that is likely. As far as I can make out once archaeologists start to dig, they go on digging like mad, and don't stop."

"Rather like terriers. I say, there's a lot in what you say..."

In a conversation about Victoria, the Claytons make these remarks:

> "She's not an archaeological type," said Mrs. Clayton. "They're usually earnest girls with spectacles—and very often damp hands."
>
> "My dear, you can't generalize in that way."
>
> "—And intellectual and all that. This girl is an amiable nitwit with a lot of common sense. Quite different."

Victoria's personality makes this novel a lot of fun. *They Came to Baghdad* is a must-read and a probable re-read. Victoria's imitation of her boss's wife early in the story, which gets her fired from her job, is hilarious and so is her scene at The Olive Branch in Baghdad, in which she spars with a surly girl from Damascus. "Here we spit on the English," says the Syrian girl, to which Victoria replies, "If you start spitting on me you may get a surprise."

Mrs. McGinty's Dead (1952)

(Alternate Title: *Blood Will Tell*)

SETTING

The story takes place in the spring of 1950 or 1951, although the murder being investigated occurred on the preceding November 22. After a brief scene at a small London restaurant called *La Vieille Grand'mère* and a longer scene at Hercule Poirot's modern London flat, the rest of the story takes place in a village called Broadhinny. Not far from Broadhinny is a larger town called Kilchester where two or three scenes occur at a real estate office, at a café called The Blue Cat, at the police station and at the railway station. There is no indication of where Broadhinny and Kilchester are located within England. There is, however, a "Superintendent Spence" who is presented as being an old friend of Hercule Poirot. The only previous mention of a "Superintendent Spence" in a Christie novel was Superintendent Spence of the Oastshire Police in the 1948 *There Is a Tide,* but there was no mention of a town called Kilchester in that novel.

Assuming that it is the same "Superintendent

Spence" character, and recalling that the fictitious county of Oastshire was probably modeled after the real county of Kent, which is southeast of London and has a long coastline on the English Channel and the Strait of Dover, we may safely place Broadhinny and Kilchester in that area.

Broadhinny is a small village that has lately become residential. It has good bus and train service to Kilchester and Cullenquay, which is a large summer resort eight miles away. The village is so small that it does not even have an inn, although there is a pub called The Three Ducks. A "guest house" of sorts exists—it is a private home with extra bedrooms which the owners rent to paying guests at the rate of seven guineas (seven pounds and seven shillings) weekly for room and board. This is a rather exorbitant rate when one considers that a London shorthand-typist in a Christie novel published a year earlier was earning just three pounds and a few shillings weekly, and especially when one notes the general discomfort and atrocious meals that prevail at this "guest house." There is a combination post office and general store, and a "co-op" from which bread is delivered to homes in the village, but no other businesses are mentioned.

The residents of Broadhinny all live in private homes. The grandest of these, Holmeleigh, is a large, square, modern building of "glazed concrete" and its interior is described as being expensively and tastefully decorated but without personality, rather like the home of Gordon Cloade in *There Is a Tide*. In this home live a wealthy man, who has political ambitions, and his young wife along with several servants. The remaining homes are older houses, described as cottages, and they are not described in much detail, although one of them is overcrowded with cheap travel souvenirs. The general shortage of domestic servants, mentioned in all of Christie's most recent novels, is also mentioned in *Mrs. McGinty's Dead*. The couple who own the "guest house" have no servants at all except for a very unreliable woman who comes once or twice a week to clean. As a matter of fact, the murder victim in the story was an old woman who did housework in several homes in the village, typically two mornings or two afternoons per week and sometimes just one half-day per week. When she died several families felt the loss of her service.

Some of the other "post–War conditions" that were described in the 1950 *A Murder Is Announced* are also mentioned in *Mrs. McGinty's Dead*, but less prominently. One of the families has a foreign girl working as a maid. There is only one mention of food rationing, and only because a character happens to take a telephone message and writes a telephone number on her "coupon book." There is also one mention of a school building having been destroyed by bombs during the war; this to explain why records about a certain character are unavailable. We may recall that in *A Murder Is Announced* a storage building had been destroyed during the War, causing a character to lose all of her mementos and old family photographs. In that story, there was a foreign refugee who worked as a cook for one family, and there had been several references to food and clothing rationing. In *Mrs. McGinty's Dead* there are a few references to the nuisance of "government forms" to fill out, and quite a negative remark is made about the new National Health Insurance:

> "...nowadays even if you've got a chilblain you run to the doctor with it so as to get your money's worth out of the National Health. Too much of this Health business we've got. Never did you any good thinking how bad you feel."

Since Christie herself was a member of the upper middle class, it was only natural that she should have a negative attitude toward the socialistic practice of government funding of medical care for the entire population. Negative remarks about the National Health Insurance will pop up again in the 1957 *What Mrs. McGillicuddy Saw* and perhaps one or two other novels, but not very often.

There is a reference to the post–War housing shortage: despite the fact that a murder occurred in Mrs. McGinty's cottage, a working-class family was glad to move into it because, before that, they had to live with the husband's family "with only a back sitting room and sleeping on two chairs."

One "post–War" condition, however, is extremely important—just as important as it was in *A Murder Is Announced*. It is the changes of personal identity that have been made possible because of deaths and disappearances of so many people during the war. In the village of Broadhinny, there is in fact only one family that clearly has its family roots in the village. The other characters are all "recent arrivals" and there may be secrets in the past lives of each one of them. As a matter of fact, when Poirot begins his investigation in this village, his first conclusion is that Broadhinny consists exclusively of "nice people." Poirot regards that fact as a potential murder motive in itself, since "nice people" are often fearful that "something not nice" in their past—or in their family—may come to light, and they may commit murder in order to silence a person who might spread unpleasant truths. As a matter of fact, it is exactly for that reason that Mrs. McGinty died.

Several automobiles are mentioned as being owned by characters in the story. A wealthy man owns a large Rolls Bentley and his wife has a car of unspecified make of her own. A doctor and his wife each have separate cars. One automobile in the novel is referred to as a "station wagon" but its make is not mentioned. There is one reference to Betty Grable, a popular American movie star of the period. "Electric blue" is a color mentioned in the novel: a young woman wears "an electric blue jumper suit." This color had also been mentioned in *They Came to Baghdad* of the preceding year; it was perhaps a color fad or fashion of that time, although Christie had used the term "electric blue" as early as 1922 in describing the eye color of a character in *The Secret Adversary*.

To clarify one minor point for the benefit of persons unfamiliar with the history of telephone communications: "automatic" telephoning was not yet universal in the early 1950s. That is to say, some rural areas of both England and the United States continued to have telephone systems that relied on live operators. One lifted the receiver and heard an operator's voice asking "Number please?" There was no dial on the telephone. "Dial telephones" were in use in the larger cities much earlier, of course, and as the years went on, more and more rural systems also converted to these new "automatic" dialing systems. This is important because, at one point in the story, Superintendent Spence explains that it is not possible to trace a phone call since "the telephones are automatic in this area," meaning that no live operator was involved in making the connection.

Story

It is spring of 1950 or 1951, and Hercule Poirot is returning home to his London flat after a delicious dinner at a little *bistrot* he has recently discovered. Alas, the pleasure of dining seems to be all that is left in life for him to enjoy. He finds retirement boring and it has been a long time since he has had an interesting case to absorb his thoughts. Arriving home, he finds an old friend, Superintendent Spence of the Kilchester police awaiting him. Superintendent Spence himself is about to retire, but he is embarking on one more case that promises to occupy his full attention.

It is Superintendent Spence's most recent case that worries him, however. A certain James Bentley has been found guilty and is awaiting execution for the murder of his landlady, Ms. McGinty, who was a cleaning lady for several families in the village of Broadhinny. James apparently killed Mrs. McGinty when she surprised him in the act of stealing money from her cottage. All of the evidence was against him and he made a bad impression on the jury, and in fact it was Superintendent Spence who had gathered most of the damning evidence against Bentley. But Superintendent Spence feels that Bentley simply does not have the right personality to be a murderer. In a word, he is not "cocky," and "most murderers are cocky," according to Spence. Bentley is profoundly depressed and does not seem to care whether he is executed or not. Spence appeals to Hercule Poirot to go to Broadhinny and to re-investigate the case, hopefully finding some evidence that casts doubt on Bentley's guilt. Poirot gladly complies with Spence's request.

In Broadhinny, Poirot's first impression is that it is a community of "nice people." He soon learns that Ms. McGinty, though hard working and honest, was a bit of a snoop. He reasons that the only motive anyone would have for killing a woman like her would be that she had "snooped" and discovered a guilty secret in the life of one of these "nice people." He decides to throw his usual discretion to the winds. He boldly announces himself as a detective and he announces publicly that the "rich relations" of James Bentley have hired him to prove his innocence, and that he already knows who the real killer of Mrs. McGinty is. When someone tries to push Poirot into the path of a fast-approaching train, Poirot knows he is on the right track. Unfortunately, the panic he inspires in the killer results in a second murder, but the solution of that crime is very easy, and so the killer is caught.

Characters

Hercule Poirot, the eccentric Belgian private investigator, who now lives primarily for gastronomic pleasures. As the story begins he comes out of the *Vieille Grand'mère,* a little restaurant in Soho where he has enjoyed a superb meal.

> His eyes held a reflective sleepy pleasure. The *escargots de la Vieille Grand'mère* had been delicious. A real find, this dingy little restaurant. Hercule Poirot curled his tongue round his lips. Drawing his handkerchief from his pocket, he dabbed his luxuriant moustaches...
> "Alas," murmured Poirot to his moustaches, "that one can only eat three times a day..."

In this story Poirot suffers as he has never suffered before, as he is forced to stay at the "guesthouse" of John and Maureen Summerhayes in the village of Broadhinny. (See the remarks, below, about Maureen Summerhayes and her "cooking.")

Captain Hastings, Hercule Poirot's dearest old friend, whom we have not met since the 1937 *Poirot Loses a Client* and whom we will not meet again until the 1975 *Curtain*. He does not appear in this story, but he appears in Poirot's fond memories.

George, Hercule Poirot's very British manservant. Poirot appreciates George's ability to describe unexpected visitors with unerring accuracy.

Superintendent Spence of the Kilchester Police, whose face "was a typical countryman's face, unexpressive, self-contained, with shrewd but honest eyes. It was the face of a man with definite standards who would never be bothered by doubts of himself or by doubts of what constituted right and wrong."

Superintendent Spence has never—in his experience—seen an innocent man hanged for something he didn't do. But he is afraid that that is about to happen in the case of James Bentley.

Mrs. McGinty, who was murdered in her cottage in Broadhinny a few months ago. For the past seven years Mrs. McGinty had done housework for several families in the village—one morning a week here, two mornings there, an afternoon or two a week at another house. Everyone was satisfied with Mrs. McGinty's work because she was regular and conscientious. But more than one of the villagers describe her as a bit of a gossip and even a snoop.

Mrs. McGinty's Husband. He died seven years ago of pneumonia.

James Bentley, Mrs. McGinty's lodger who was accused of murdering her and stealing thirty pounds that she had hidden under her bedroom floor. Although Superintendent Spence had gathered most of the evidence that had convicted James Bentley, he cannot believe that Bentley is guilty. According to Spence, Bentley is not "cocky" as most murderers are, in his experience.

James Bentley's Father, a doctor who died when James was nine years old.

James Bentley's Mother, a possessive mother who "looked after her son..."

Mr. Larkin, the baker in Broadhinny, who was responsible for the discovery of Mrs. McGinty's murder. Calling with bread in the morning and getting no response, he summoned a neighbor, Mrs. Elliot, who actually found the body.

Mrs. Elliot, Mrs. McGinty's next door neighbor, who "fairly screamed the house down" upon finding Mrs. McGinty dead in her sitting room.

Young Graybrook, James Bentley's defense attorney. Allotted to Bentley under the Poor Persons Defence Act, he was thoroughly conscientious and put up the best show he could.

Old Stanisdale, the judge at James Bentley's trial. He was scrupulously fair and unbiased.

Maureen Summerhayes, unquestionably the worst cook in England, which is saying a lot. On Hercule Poirot's first day at Long Meadows, as he is suffering in its drafty sitting room, Maureen asks if he would mind if she sliced the beans in the sitting room, as the smell in the kitchen is "too frightful." As she is slicing the beans she notices:

"I say, these beans look a bit black. We store them, you know, in crocks, salted down. But these seem to have gone wrong. I'm afraid they won't be very nice."

Then Maureen proceeds to cut her finger.

"Oo, I'm bleeding over the beans. Not too good as we've got to have them for lunch. Still it won't matter really because they'll go into boiling water. Things are always all right if you boil them, aren't they? Even tins."

"I think," said Hercule Poirot quietly, "that I shall not be in for lunch."

Toward the end of the story Poirot will teach Maureen Summerhayes how to make an omelet. In a later novel, the 1959 *Cat Among the Pigeons*, we will learn that omelet making continues to be her only cooking skill.

Major Johnnie Summerhayes, the husband of England's—and therefore the world's—worst cook. His home maintenance skills match his wife's cooking skills. That's because he lived in India all his life and there were servants to do all of the work. Long Meadows has a window in the drawing room that cannot be closed, and the entrance door opens whenever there is a gust of wind.

The Summerhayes Children, number, names and genders not specified. According to Maureen, the big, drafty house is "fun for the children in the holidays—lots of room to run wild in..."

Flyn and Cormic, the Summerhayes' Irish wolfhounds

Piggy, the Summerhayes' pig

Old Colonel Summerhayes, Johnnie Summerhayes's father. According to Dr. Rendell, he was "a regular tartar, proud as the devil."

An Old Lady Upstairs at Long Meadows.

Bessie Burch, Mrs. McGinty's married niece who lives in the village of Cullavon, three miles from Broadhinny. She inherited Mrs. McGinty's total savings of two hundred thirty pounds.

Joe Burch, Bessie's husband, a painter who works in the home decorating business.

The Burch Children, five in number, ages and genders not specified

Guy Carpenter of the Works, the richest man in Broadhinny. His home is called Holmeleigh and is ultra modern—square and with a glazed concrete exterior. Because the Carpenters are rich, Mrs. McGinty, who did housework for them on Fridays, charged them two shillings per hour (her usual rate was a shilling and ten pence, which is twopence less.) Carpenter has political ambitions; therefore he is careful to maintain good relations with the press. He is polite to Hercule Poirot because he at first thinks that Poirot is a reporter from *The Sunday Companion,* and Poirot does not undeceive him.

Mrs. Eve Carpenter, formerly Eve Selkirk. She has been married to Guy Carpenter for just a few months. She is scared to death by Poirot's interest in the McGinty murder and, even more, by his interest in a *second* murder, for which she tries to pay her servants to provide her with an alibi. Later she tries to pay Hercule Poirot to "protect" her from the police.

An Imperturbable Manservant at the Carpenter home who refuses admittance to Hercule Poirot, suspecting him of being a salesman.

Mr. and Mrs. Croft, servants of the Carpenters, from whom Mrs. Carpenter attempts to purchase an alibi. She is puzzled and angry when they refuse, and even angrier when they report her to the police for approaching them on the subject.

Mr. Scuttle of Messrs Breather and Scuttle, House Agents, former employers of James Bentley. It is his opinion that James Bentley wouldn't have "had the guts" to commit murder—unless he was "barmy."

Maude Williams, a typist at Breather and Scuttle and a friend of James Bentley. As a matter of fact, she is the only person in the story who liked Bentley. She is eager to assist Poirot in finding the real murderer of Mrs. McGinty because she believes in James Bentley's innocence.

Amy, the other secretary in the Breather & Scuttle office, who thought James Bentley was "a drip."

Mr. and Mrs. Kiddle, the current occupants of Mrs. McGinty's cottage. Mr. Kiddle is a plasterer and Mrs. Kiddle is a housewife whose scullery is dirty and whose kitchen is even dirtier. She proudly shows Hercule Poirot the place where Mrs. McGinty was found dead five months earlier.

Ernie, a Sibling of Ernie and an Infant Sibling of Ernie, children of the Kiddles. When Hercule Poirot arrives at the cottage, Ernie is beating on the door with a tin plate. When his mother tells him to stop, he replies "Shan't," and continues his behavior. Later Mrs. Oliver will find two of the children torturing a cat.

Mrs. Sweetiman, the lady who keeps the post office. Poirot correctly predicts that Mrs. Sweetiman will be his most useful source of information about the population of Broadhinny *and* the source of the most important clue in the mystery.

Edna, a girl "with untidy hair and a cold in the head" who is Mrs. Sweetiman's assistant. On the subject of the second murder, Edna has an important piece of information to share with the police.

Reg, Edna's regular boyfriend, of whom her father approves.

Charlie Masters, a farm laborer who is married but whom Edna has been seeing. She had a rendez-vous with Charlie one evening at a turn in the road. While waiting for Charlie, Edna saw someone go into a certain house where a murder took place the same evening.

Edna's Father, a.k.a. "Dad" who will "skin her alive" when he learns of her nocturnal tryst with Charlie Masters.

Albert (Bert) Hayling, a local police constable in whom Edna refuses to confide

Mrs. Laura Upward, one of the ladies for whom Mrs. McGinty had worked, "a vigorous looking woman of sixty odd with iron grey hair and a determined chin." She spends most of her time sitting in a wheeled chair and being waited on by her son Robin and a housemaid. She keeps her son tied to her apron strings. Mrs. Sweetiman suspects that Mrs. Upward can get around more easily than she pretends.

Robin Upward, a young playwright who is currently dramatizing one of Mrs. Ariadne Oliver's novels, and making major changes in the personalities of the characters, to Mrs. Oliver's great annoyance.

Robin calls his mother "Madre" and the two of them smile sickeningly to each other and call each other "darling." Poirot does not comment on their relationship, but the spectacle they create together causes Poirot "to frown" on one occasion.

Janet Groom, an aging housemaid at Laburnums, the Upward home. She is "...a faithful old maid, but it's all she can manage just to do a little simple cooking."

Janet Groom's Niece, with whom Janet goes to live after a tragedy occurs in the Upward home

Dr. Rendell, a large cheerful man of forty. He is the only resident of Broadhinny who has ever heard of Hercule Poirot. He is an articulate, friendly man who does not mind sharing facts and opinions with Poirot on a variety of subjects, including "the commercial life" to which he believes the medical profession has descended thanks to the new National Health Insurance.

> "Don't run away with the idea that I heal the sick. I'm just a glorified form filler and signer of certificates."

Shelagh Rendell, Dr. Rendell's wife, aged about thirty. She is scared to death of Poirot and his presence in Broadhinny, and at one point she accuses him of using the murder case of Mrs. McGinty simply as a "pretext" for being there to delve into other matters. Poirot has no idea of what those "other matters" can be, but it becomes clear to him that Shelagh Rendell must have some kind of guilty secret.

Mrs. Scott, the Rendells' housekeeper who is too old to get down on her knees to scrub floors

Mr. Wetherby of Hunter's Close, another house in Broadhinny. He is a very unfriendly person and his stepdaughter appears to hate him.

Mrs. Wetherby, an "invalid" of the type who "enjoys poor health." She "lives in the past a lot," according to her daughter. Her sitting room is cluttered with souvenirs of the past, and Mrs. Wetherby spends most of her time reclining comfortably on a sofa—when other people are at home. But on one occasion she finds sufficient strength to visit Mrs. Sweetiman at the post office "to purchase wool and knitting needles"—and to learn of the latest developments in Hercule Poirot's investigations. Afterwards,

> Mrs. Wetherby walked back home from the post office with a gait surprisingly spry in one habitually reported to be an invalid.
> Only when she had entered the front door did she once more shuffle feebly into the drawing room and collapse on the sofa.

Deirdre Henderson, the brow-beaten daughter of Mrs. Wetherby and stepdaughter of Mr. Wetherby. She is completely under her mother's thumb and hates her stepfather.

Ben, a fat, old Sealyham owned by Deirdre Henderson

Frieda, the "foreign help" at the Wetherby home

Mr. Benson at the chemist's shop next door to the Burches, in Cullavon, three miles from Broadhinny. He has a telephone and gladly takes messages for Mr. and Mrs. Burch, who do not have one.

Mrs. McGinty's Sister-in-law, who has died

Mrs. Birdlip, a friend of Mrs. McGinty who has also died

Eva Kane and Mr. and Mrs. Craig; Janice Courtland, her Perverted Fiend of a Husband and her Young Lover; **Little Lily Gamboll** who Murdered her Aunt, and **Vera Blake** who Had a Succession of Criminal Husbands, subjects of a lurid article that appeared in *The Sunday Companion* a few days before Mrs. McGinty died last November

Pamela Horsefall, the journalist who wrote the lurid, romantic article last November for *The Sunday Companion*. Hercule Poirot visits her at the offices of that newspaper in London. She sits astride chairs, waves cigarettes as she speaks, lets out neighing sounds like a horse when amused, and says to Poirot, "My dear man, no point in accuracy." She is, in fact, the latest in a string of obnoxious newspaper reporters in Christie's novels, and the best one so far.

Ariadne Oliver, a detective story writer superficially modeled after Agatha Christie herself. Her first appearance in a novel was in the 1936 *Cards on the Table*, although she had appeared earlier in short stories. She and Hercule Poirot have not seen each other since then.

Like Agatha Christie, Ariadne Oliver is euphemistically described as "a large woman" (she's fat) and she loves apples. The front of her dress is usually littered with bits of apple that have fallen from her lips. Her first act in this story is to toss an apple core through an open window of her car and it hits Hercule Poirot in the head. As she exits (with difficulty, "as a volcano erupting") from her small car, a bag of apples tears and apples go rolling down the hill away from the car.

Like Agatha Christie, Ariadne Oliver has created an eccentric foreign sleuth and her readers never tire of him, although she is fed up with him as, by this time in Christie's career, she is fed up with Poirot.

The similarities between Mrs. Oliver and Agatha Christie end there, however, for Mrs. Oliver is a thoroughly stupid woman who believes that "a woman's intuition" is all that is needed in crime solving. She is also a lousy writer who cheerfully admits that all of her books are the same except for the names of the characters.

In this story, Mrs. Oliver struggles with a young playwright who is changing all of her characters in an effort to create "good theatre," undoubtedly a reference to Agatha Christie's own struggles with playwrights in the dramatizations of her stories.

Mr. Shaitana, the murder victim in the 1936 *Cards on the Table,* in which Mrs. Oliver and Hercule Poirot met for the first time.

Inspector Traill who was in charge of the Craig case

A Big Burly Army Sergeant who saves Hercule Poirot's life by catching him just as he is about to fall into the path of an approaching train at the station in Kilchester

The Man Who Was Testing the Electric Meter at the Carpenter home. He was actually an undercover police officer

Cecil Leech, an actor currently in the Little Rep at Cullenquay. Robin Upward hopes he will play the part of Eric in his new play

Denis Callory, another actor Robin Upward hopes will act in his new play

Jean Bellows, an actress who hopes to play Ingrid in Robin Upward's play

Mrs. "Carstairs" or **"Carlisle"** whom Maude Williams visited in Broadhinny a few months ago

Somebody Called Michael and **Somebody Called Peter** at the theatre in Cullenquay, effeminate theatre types who are friends of Robin Upward

Alex Roscoff who fooled Mrs. Upward, but only for a short time

Sergeant Fletcher, one of Superintendent Spence's men

FRENCH INTO ENGLISH

Chapter 1
Vieille Grand'mère—Old Grandmother (the name of a restaurant where Poirot dines)
escargots de la Vieille Grand'mère—Old Grandmother's Snails, probably a specialty of the house
croissants—crescent rolls
Déjeuner—lunch
Le Diner—dinner
ce cher Hastings—good old Hastings
Ce cher cher ami!—That dear old friend!
Cache Cache—A child's game (Hide and Seek)
Le Boulanger—A child's game (The Baker Man)

Chapter 2
Eh bien—Well...
Bien—All right then.

Chapter 3
Eh bien—OK
Mon cher Spence—My good friend Spence
cher ami—friend

Chapter 4
Enfin, c'est insupportable!—My God, this is insufferable!
Nom d'un nom d'un nom!—God damn son of a bitch! (Note: This English translation is not excessively strong. Poirot is absolutely disgusted and angered by the situation in this context.)
Voici, Madame—Here you are, ma'am.

Chapter 8
Eh bien—OK
Oh là là—Good grief!

Chapter 9 *empressement*—warmth

Chapter 10
embonpoint—healthy plumpness
Au revoir—Good-bye

Chapter 11
Mon cher—Friend
mon ami—friend

Chapter 13 *Voilà!*—Here you are!

Chapter 14 *Pardon*—Excuse me.

Chapter 15 *Bon Dieu*—Goodness

Chapter 18
Précisément—Precisely
Ma foi—For Heaven's sake...
Ça se voit!—That's obvious!

Chapter 22
Eh bien—Well...
chic—stylish
comme il faut—appropriate

Chapter 24
mon cher—my good friend
cher ami—friend
secret de Polichinelle—fool's secret

Chapter 25 *Mais oui*—Of course

Epilogue
Bon Dieu—My God!
Mon cher—Friend
Mon Dieu!—My God!

COMMENTS

Mrs. McGinty's Dead is a very good Christie detective story but it would not be a very good "first Christie experience." First published in 1952, this is Hercule Poirot's *twenty-fourth* appearance in a novel, and as Christie wrote it, she must have assumed that most of her readers were already familiar with his personality traits *and* were fond of him despite his eccentricities and perhaps even *because* of them. His obsession with neatness, his need for delicious food and especially his highly developed sense of self-worth are very strongly expressed in this novel—so much so that a reader not already familiar with the character would probably not be fond of him at all. His statements beginning with the likes of "I, the great, the unique, the supreme master of detection, etc. etc." may be a bit disgusting to readers who have not experienced Poirot in his more humble moods. The reader is advised to choose a few of the earlier novels in order to become familiar with Hercule Poirot before sampling this one.

Every Christie detective novel has a particular uniqueness. The uniqueness of *Mrs. McGinty's Dead* is Poirot's approach to the detection. He is not "discreet," he is not "diplomatic." He does not try to flatter people in order to achieve their cooperation, nor does he pretend *not* to be a detective in order to make people feel safe in his presence. Early in the story, he decides that it is the psychology of the *murderer* and not the psychology of the *victim* that matters, since the victim in this case is without psychological complexity. He deduces that Mrs. McGinty must have been killed in order to silence her on some subject. Because everyone in the little village of Broadhinny is a member of that class of people known as "nice people," someone in the village must have had a guilty secret of which Mrs. McGinty had become aware and which she was threatening to make public.

Therefore, Poirot brazenly announces to the whole village—privately to as many individuals as possible, and also publicly at a party—that the man who was convicted of Mrs. McGinty's murder is innocent and that Poirot knows who the real killer is. His strategy is to inspire fear and panic in the murderer and to "provoke a reaction." When someone tries to murder *him*, he knows he is on the right track. Unfortunately the murderer commits a second crime as result of the panic that Poirot inspires, but the second crime is easily solved and the murderer of both victims is unmasked.

Psychology had been a subject of interest to Agatha Christie since her earliest writings, and in the 1938 *Appointment with Death* there was a psychological study of the disastrous effects of a cruel mother on her child and stepchildren. In *Mrs. McGinty's Dead* there are at least three unhealthy mother-child relationships.

There is James Bentley, whose mother kept him close to her and did not approve of his having female friends.

There is Deirdre Henderson, who is described as being a case of "arrested development" —a child with the body of an adult, who is psychologically manipulated by her egocentric mother who "enjoys poor health."

There is Robin Upward whose relationship with his mother is sickeningly affectionate. The things they say to each other cause Hercule Poirot to "frown" and to "wince." One of Mrs. Upward's statements is that Robin is "as good as any daughter" to her. Robin is an effeminate, swishy, limp-wristed creature who is right at home with other like-minded young men in the repertory theater company of a neighboring resort town. As noted in the *Comments* section of the 1937 *Poirot Loses a Client*, mothers of adult children are rare in Christie novels, and when they do appear, they are most often negative characters. The worst was Mrs. Boynton in *Appointment with Death*, but the three mothers in *Mrs. McGinty's Dead* are also destructive characters, although in milder ways.

At a party at the Upward home, several characters have a conversation on the subjects of "mothers," "adoption," and "breeding." The "wise" characters advance the ideas that breeding matters, (one person states "blood does tell"), and that adoption is a bad thing in general. Agatha Christie made it quite clear in her *Autobiography* that she did not like the idea of adoption and that, in her opinion, personality traits are inherited from one's natural parents and environmental forces are powerless to modify those traits. She introduced those subjects rather clumsily in *Crooked House* in 1949, and now in *Mrs. McGinty's Dead* she hammers away at them again. In her next novel, *Murder with Mirrors*, she will preach against the idea of "reforming" juvenile delinquents through environmental changes and, later, in *Ordeal by Innocence* she will preach strongly against adoption.

Christie was clearly annoyed by the increasing democratization of society, the increasing educational opportunities for the masses, and the decreasing importance of inherited social rank everywhere, the National Health Insurance and other forms of "creeping socialism." She was certainly annoyed by the diminishing size of the "servant class" in England. Furthermore, during the early 1940s, when she realized that her relationship with her grown daughter was a remote and distant one, she began rationalizing—finding reasons to exculpate herself for not having "bothered very much" about her daughter during her childhood. A convenient theory may have been that her daughter's personality was predetermined by her blood inheritance and whether she had a close relationship with her mother during childhood or not would not have mattered much. If "blood" matters more than "environment," then one need not feel responsible for guiding one's children safely and sanely through childhood—or failing to do so.

It would have been better if Christie had kept her comments on all of these subjects out of her detective novels. She could have expressed them in the "other" novels that she published under the pseudonym Mary Westmacott. All of the above constitute a second reason for which *Mrs. McGinty's Dead* cannot be recommended as a "first Christie experience." Not only may the conversations about environment and breeding strike some readers as distasteful, they are not very typical of Christie's best writing and, in any case, they are unrelated to the story.

As usual, Christie expresses her general dislike for children in this novel by presenting—for no apparent reason except for the pleasure of doing so—two disgusting children. In one scene, one of the children is banging a tin plate against the door of his parents' cottage and when his mother tells him to stop it, he tells his mother "Shan't!" and continues his behavior. In a later scene both children are found to be gleefully torturing a cat. As to the children's family, they are of course "low class" people. Their scullery is dirty and their kitchen is even dirtier, and they have lots of "brats." Hercule Poirot's thoughts on this family:

> Poirot looked round him. Hard to visualize that this rampant stronghold of haphazard fecundity was once the well scrubbed domain of an elderly woman who was houseproud.

It may also be noteworthy that, although we learn that John and Maureen Summerhayes have children, we are not told their names, ages or sexes or even how many there are, despite the fact that we are told the names of their two dogs and even their pig. The children are, of course, conveniently "away at school, where they belong."

We may recall that in the 1932 *Peril at End House,* ten-year-old Alfred Wilson wishes the murder victim had had her throat cut instead of just being shot, because he had once seen pigs being killed and liked it. In the 1935 *The A.B.C. Murders* there is a filthy child of unknown sex that needed "its" nose attended to. In the 1939 *And Then There Were None,* Cyril Hamilton was "a whiny, spoilt little brat." The two Leonides children in the 1949 *Crooked House* are unpleasant youngsters, especially Josephine who listens at doors and says that "the police are stupid." In the 1939 *Easy to Kill,* Tommy Pierce bullies younger boys and enjoys cutting wasps in half. In the 1937 *Poirot Loses a Client,* Mary and Edward Tanios are described as "spoiled." The only really pleasant children ever to appear in Christie novels so far (and we are now discussing her forty-second detective novel) have been the toddler Betty Sprot in the 1941 *N or M?* and nine-year-old Peter Carmody in the 1942 *The Body in the Library.*

All of the above "negatives" should be sufficient reason for a *new* Christie reader seeking a pleasant reading experience to avoid *Mrs. McGinty's Dead.* However, an *experienced* Christie reader, one who is already well acquainted with Hercule Poirot and his eccentricities—in particular his need for delicious meals and his obsession with neatness and orderliness—will find his experience at the Summerhayes's "guest house" absolutely hilarious.

Seasoned Christie readers who are already aware of Christie's feelings of animosity towards the Press will also be highly amused by Hercule Poirot's interview with the journalist, Pamela Horsefall. As we know, Christie had a very low opinion of newspaper reporters and always portrayed them negatively. The most memorable reporter/liar so far has been Charles Enderby in the 1931 *Murder at Hazelmoor* but there have been scores of negative references to The Press in Christie's novels all through the years, notably in the inquest scene of the 1935 *Death in the Air.* In *Mrs. McGinty's Dead* we have a repulsive journalist in the person of Pamela Horsefall who sits astride chairs, waves cigarettes as she speaks, "lets out neighing sounds like a horse" and says to Poirot, "My dear man. No point in accuracy."

One final comment on a trivial though interesting subject: money. We must keep in mind that even as late as *Mrs. McGinty's Dead* (1952) the value of British currency was far greater than its value in more recent years. The murder victim had two hundred pounds in a savings account, plus thirty pounds hidden in her cottage. If these sums seem to be very small, remember that as a cleaning woman she earned one shilling and ten pence per hour (two shillings per hour at the home of the one wealthy family in the village). At this rate, if she worked forty hours per week, she earned three pounds twelve shillings *per week,* or about 186 pounds *annually* if she worked every week in the year. To her, then, savings amounting to 230 pounds was a substantial sum and considerably more than a year's wages.

Murder with Mirrors (1952)

(Alternate Title: *They Do It with Mirrors*)

Setting

It is the warm season in 1951 or 1952. There are only two physical settings. The opening scene takes place in a deluxe suite of an expensive London hotel, which is not named. Thereafter, all of the action takes place somewhere in the country at an enormous Victorian-era mansion which has been converted to a kind of rehabilitation home for juvenile delinquents. There is no indication at all of the location of this home within England. However, since the mansion was built by "a successful iron master" during Victorian times, it is most likely located in the Industrial Midlands, probably in Lancashire, Nottinghamshire or Yorkshire. Nearby is a fictitious market town called Market Kimble, which has a railway station.

The main building of the home for juvenile offenders consists of a preposterously huge Victorian mansion named Stonygates. As noted above, it was built by a successful industrialist, one of those Victorian millionaires who built "castles" to live in for the purpose of displaying their wealth. Originally the house had no fewer than fourteen "living rooms," that is, drawing rooms or sitting rooms—whatever you care to call them. A later generation (in approximately 1920) added ten bathrooms and electricity for lighting. The person who performed this updating was careful, however, not to alter any of the exterior or interior architecture, regarding the house as a "period piece." One of the young men in the novel jokingly refers to the "period" of the house as being "Best Victorian Lavatory." Another character in the story describes it as a kind of temple to Plutocracy. The architecture appears to be "Gothic revival," probably featuring pointed arches for doors and windows, stained glass and even gargoyles at the eaves. By now, only a small, central portion of the house is maintained as living quarters for the family. The west and east wings have been thoroughly modernized with offices, classrooms, etc. for the juvenile home and there is a complete theater within the building for the purpose of giving a "theater experience" to the young juvenile offenders. The boys write and perform their own plays, designing and building sets and scenery, etc., all as part of their therapy.

The property includes a complex system of gardens featuring an artificial lake, but all of the grounds have been neglected since the war, although the "kitchen garden" is well maintained since it has a utility value.

As it is now about 1951, the electric wiring that was installed in approximately 1920 "when electric light was a novelty," has become inadequate and in one scene a fuse blows when someone turns on a lamp.

A part of the ground floor is illustrated in a drawing presented at the beginning of the novel as an aid to the reader in solving the mystery. The rooms that are shown include the library, the kitchen and a "great hall" in which there is a fireplace, a grand piano and sofas, chairs and tables appropriate to a drawing room. Off the "great hall" is a small study having two windows giving onto a terrace at the back of the house. This terrace runs along the back of the house and there are dining room windows and also a window of a ground floor guestroom giving onto it. The guestroom has a connecting bathroom. It is in this guestroom that a murder takes place.

There is just one reference to World War Two: one of the female characters had been sent to live with relatives in America during the War in order to be safe from bombing and to have the certainty of growing up in a country that was not a fascist dictatorship in the event Britain was successfully invaded and defeated. Otherwise, current and recent history play no role in *Murder with Mirrors,* although there is a brief comment about the attitude of the police officer in charge of the case towards Russia and Russians in general, as he thinks about Alex and Stephen Restarick, whose mother had been Russian:

> A twister with brains—that's how he would sum up Alex Restarick. Cleverer than his brother. Mother had been a Russian or so he had heard. "Russians" to Inspector Curry were what "Bony" had been in the early days of the nineteenth century and what "the Huns" had been in the early twentieth century. Anything to do with Russia was bad in inspector Curry's opinion...

["Bony" refers to Britain's old arch-enemy Napoleon Bonaparte and "the Huns" were the Germans. Now "the enemy" is Russia, as it has been ever since the Bolshevist Revolution and, especially now, with the Cold War and the threat of nuclear war.]

Dominating the background to the story, however, are certain "ideas" that must have been currently fashionable conversation topics in the early 1950s. These include arguments for and against the notion that "environment" is important in shaping the personalities and character traits in people. A more traditional viewpoint still held in certain quarters was that character traits and personality were "inherited"—that is to say, not learned but acquired through "blood." Christie herself clearly held the latter viewpoint, and so arguments in favor of that point of view punctuate the conversations of several of the "more sensible" characters: the police, for example, and our old friend, Miss Jane Marple, as well as an American character who has common sense.

A couple of trivial points: two automobile makes are named. One is "a rather elderly Ford V-8," probably dating from the 1930s, and the other is "a new gleaming two seater Rolls Bentley," a luxury sport model. In the opening scene a rich American woman tries on a "Lanvanelli creation" appraisingly and comments to her friend, "My dear, have you seen what Christian Dior is trying to make us wear in the way of skirts?"

Story

It is approximately 1951 or 1952 and Miss Jane Marple is visiting an old friend at an expensive London hotel. It is Ruth Van Rydock, an American with whom Miss Marple attended school in Italy about fifty years ago when both were in their teens. Ruth is worried about her sister, Carrie Louise, whom she has just visited at her huge Victorian mansion, Stonygates, in the English Midlands. Over the years, Carrie Louise has had three marriages, each time to a "crank," in Ruth's words. The first "crank" believed in education for the lower classes and made the mansion into a school for poor children. The second "crank" was obsessed with art and the theater. Carrie Louise's current "crank" husband is Lewis Serrocold, who has turned Stonygates into a reformatory for juvenile delinquents. During her visit to Stonygates, Ruth formed the strong impression that "something was wrong there," but she was unable to put her finger on what that could be. She begs her friend Jane Marple to visit Carrie Louise and try to find out what, if anything, is wrong at Stonygates.

At Stonygates Miss Marple renews her friendship with Carrie Louise and meets her middle-aged daughter, an adopted grand-daughter, two adopted sons, the teaching staff and even some of the "cases." One of the cases is a strange young man, Edgar Lawson, who takes Miss Marple into his confidence and reveals to her that he is the son of Winston Churchill, although a day or two earlier he had told other people that he was the son of Lord Montgomery.

After dinner on the first day of Miss Marple's stay at Stonygates, while the family is assembled in the great room, Edgar Lawson makes a dramatic entrance and begins to accuse Lewis Serrocold of being his father and of persecuting him. Lewis takes Edgar into his study and closes the door, but the family continues to hear Edgar's absurd ravings, which become even more intense, and then they hear several gunshots fired. The door to the study is locked but eventually someone finds a key. Inside, they find Lewis comforting a pathetically sobbing, regretful Edgar. Lewis explains that Edgar's behavior was some kind of "acting out" related to his neurosis and that he never meant any harm to Lewis. However, at the moment that the family's attention was focused on the scene in Lewis's study, someone entered the bedroom of a guest, Christian Gulbrandsen, and shot him to death.

The police are summoned at once, but it is Miss Marple who solves the mystery of the death of Christian Gulbrandsen.

Characters

Jane Marple, an English spinster well past sixty, from the village of St. Mary Mead. She solves mysteries by always thinking the worst of people (the worst is so often the truth!), never believing anything anyone says until she has confirmed the facts personally, and by being reminded of people in her village past. She never travels without her bird glasses (so useful in bird watching and in acquiring facts about neighbors). But even when *not* using her bird glasses, "her long distance sight was good (as many of her neighbours knew to their cost in the village of St. Mary Mead...)"

Raymond West, Jane Marple's nephew. He makes a lot of money by writing "clever books" and is most generous with his Aunt Jane. He is not a character in this story but he is referred to by Miss Marple in conversations.

Ruth Van Rydock, an American woman practically the same age as Miss Marple, although one would never guess it. Miss Marple looks every day her age but Ruth has retained a girlish figure. She has had a succession of husbands, each one of them rich. In fact, she proudly states that she has always married for money, unlike "poor Carrie Louise," her sister, who has always married idealists, or "cranks" as Ruth prefers to call them. Ruth and her sister Carrie Louise were at school in Italy fifty years ago, and there they met Jane Marple and became lifelong friends with her.

Julius, one of Ruth's many past husbands,

whom she urged to sell out of Amalgamated Cereals before the crash came.

Stephanie, Ruth's personal maid of thirty years. She is the only woman who knows what Ruth really looks like.

Caroline Louise Serrocold (Carrie Louise), Ruth's sister. Unlike her practical sister, who made sure she married a succession of rich men, Carrie Louise has always lived "out of the world" and married idealists, which Ruth calls "cranks," sharing their enthusiasm for whatever their dreams happened to be.

Not one to "make a fuss," Carrie Louise is nevertheless accustomed to "fusses" being made over her by devoted family members and servants.

Lewis Serrocold, Carrie Louise's current husband. He has made Stoneygates into a reformatory for juvenile delinquents.

Eric Gulbrandsen, Carrie Louise's first husband, a Swede or a Norwegian (Ruth is not sure which), who was more than thirty years older than Carrie Louise. He was a widower with three grown sons, at least one of whom was older than Carrie Louise herself. He was a wealthy philanthropist who was devoted to the education of the lower classes and he converted his vast Victorian mansion, Stonygates, into a school for poor children. When he died, Carrie Louise inherited Stonygates.

Christian Gulbrandsen, the eldest of Eric's three sons. He is two years older than Carrie Louise although she is his legal stepmother. He is a big, heavy-featured man, with a slow methodical way of talking. A very wealthy man, he is the primary trustee of the Gulbrandsen Trust. During a visit to Stonygates, he is murdered in a ground-floor guest room.

Pippa, a little girl aged two, whom Eric and Carrie Louise adopted when they found that they were unable to conceive a child themselves. Pippa was pretty and bright and grew up to marry an Italian marchese, but then died in childbirth.

Guido, Marchese di San Severiano, Pippa's husband who, according to Ruth, would never have married Pippa if she had not been rich.

Mildred Strete, née Gulbrandsen, born to Carrie Louise shortly after she and her husband adopted Pippa. Determined to treat both the natural child and the adopted child equally, Carrie Louise inadvertently favored Pippa and neglected Mildred who, as a result, grew up resentful of her adopted sister. Mildred inherited the looks of the Gulbrandsen family who, though worthy people, were very homely. She married a clergyman with whom she lived in the South of England for many years. Recently widowed, she has returned to Stonygates to live.

Mildred is a bitter woman who has always resented her mother for favoring her adoptive sister Pippa. She detests Pippa's daughter Gina and openly accuses her of trying to poison Carrie Louise, citing the fact that Gina is "Italian" and "Italians are poisoners." She openly accuses Gina's husband of being the murderer of Christian Gulbrandsen and she accuses Gina of lying in order to protect him, stating, "Of course she would lie to protect him. She's a Catholic." Mildred is a mass of prejudices, in fact, and her own mother describes her as having been "born to be unhappy."

Gina Hudd, the daughter of Pippa, who died while giving birth to her. She was adopted by Carrie Louise and brought from Italy to Stonygates to be raised. During the War she was sent to America for safety and lived with her Aunt Ruth. There, she met and married Wally Hudd, an American ex-marine, with whom she now lives at Stonygates. She helps with the theatrical productions.

Gina is a beautiful young woman and she enjoys being admired by men. Despite being truly in love with her husband, she enjoys the flirtations of Alex and Stephen Restarick, Carrie Louise's two adopted sons.

Walter Hudd, Gina's young American husband. He is one of the few people at Stonygates who have very much common sense and he feels completely out of place there. He is an ex-marine with "a good war record."

Canon Strete, "a nice man but given to colds in the head," according to Ruth Van Rydock. He was a scholarly antiquarian about ten or fifteen years older than Mildred when they married in 1934. He died recently.

Johnnie Restarick, the second of three "cranks" that Carrie Louise married, according to her sister Ruth. His "cause" was art and theatre. He installed ten new bathrooms at Stonygates but carefully preserved the architecture of the house, calling it "a real period piece." When he married Carrie Louise he had two little boys from a previous marriage. Unable to resist feminine charms of any kind, he soon became involved with a "Dreadful Yugoslavian Woman," in the words of Ruth, and divorced Carrie Louise to marry her. Then he died in an automobile accident and Carrie Louise adopted his two sons.

Johnnie Restarick's First Wife, a Russian dancer, and the mother of Alexis and Stephen, Johnnie's two sons

Alexis Restarick (Alex), the elder of Johnnie Restarick's two sons. Miss Marple's first impression is that he is "a handsome young man and one who bore upon him the authority and good humour of success." He lives in London and is said to be writing a new ballet. His conversation is witty and flippant, even to the police. He is in love with Gina and would like her to divorce Wally Hudd and marry him.

Stephen Restarick, Alex's younger and "more handsome" brother. He runs the dramatic branch of the home for juvenile delinquents. Like Alex, he is in love with Gina Hudd.

That Dreadful Yugoslavian Woman for whom Johnnie Restarick left Carrie Louise. In a fit of rage she drove their car over a cliff somewhere on the Continent and both were killed.

A Kindly Fellow Passenger who assists Miss Marple with her suitcase at Market Kimble station

An Announcer with a Booming Voice and **A Porter** at Market Kimble railway station

Edgar Lawson, one of the "cases" at Stonygates. He is not sure who his real father is—he tells Miss Marple that it is Winston Churchill, but he tells Wally Hudd that it is Lord Montgomery. In the course of the story he accuses Lewis Serrocold of being his father.

Juliet Bellever (Jolly), the housekeeper at Stonygates. She is "a gaunt elderly lady with an arrogant nose and a short haircut, who wears stout, well cut tweeds." Though technically a "servant," Miss Bellever behaves more like a doting parent toward Carrie Louise.

A Commissionaire at the gate of Stonygates, standing on duty in a military fashion.

Fräulein Schweich and her Boots, a teacher in Italy fondly recalled by Miss Marple and Carrie Louise

Young Dr. Maverick, a psychiatrist with a superior smile, whose conversation, consisting almost entirely of the jargon of his trade, is practically unintelligible to Miss Marple. Dr. Maverick smiles in his superior way and makes statements such as "We're all a little mad," and "We're all mental cases," causing Inspector Curry to murmur to another officer that psychiatrists give him a pain in the neck.

Two Spectacled Young Men who are teachers at the institute

Mr. Baumgarten and Mr. Lacy, occupational therapists

Mr. Birnbaum, a physical therapist

Ernie Gregg, one of the "patients" at the institute. He is an expert at lock picking and claims that the dormitory locks are no match for his skills, but according to his pals, Ernie is simply a braggart.

Arthur Jenkins, another one of the "patients" at the institute. His specialty is "the cosh" and he shares technical knowledge on that subject with Gina.

Don, another "patient" at the institute, and a friend of Ernie and Arthur.

Sir John Stillwell, Dr. Maverick's old chief

Miss Moncrief, one of Miss Marple's "village parallels" of whom she is reminded by Mildred Strete.

Dr. Galbraith, Bishop of Cromer, one of the four trustees of the Gulbrandsen Trust, an old man with a sweet smile and thick white hair.

Mr. Gilfoy, another one of the four trustees of the Gulbrandsen Trust, and an eminent lawyer

Inspector Curry, who is in charge of the investigations. He has a pleasant voice and manner and looks quiet and serious and just a little apologetic.

A Police Photographer and a Police Surgeon

Sergeant Lake, Inspector Curry's Assistant

Superintendent Blacker, Inspector Curry's superior, who tells him about Miss Marple's special abilities.

Dr. Gunter of Market Kimble, the Serrocold family physician

Katherine Elsworth, Pippa's mother who was hanged for poisoning her husband, although some people doubted her guilt

Police Constable Dodgett, who clocks the time it would take Alex Restarick to leave his car, commit the crime, and return to his car.

Johnnie Backhouse, another of Miss Marple's "village parallels." "I seen you last night," had been Johnnie Backhouse's unpleasant taunt to all he thought it might affect. It had been a surprisingly successful remark. So many people, Miss Marple reflected, have been in places where they are anxious not to be seen! Ernie Gregg reminds Miss Marple of Johnnie Backhouse.

Leonard Wylie, another "village parallel." Edgar Lawson reminds Miss Marple of Leonard.

COMMENTS

Murder with Mirrors is a lot of fun to read and our old friend Miss Marple, who is in rare form, is in the story right from the beginning.

An important feature of the story is the conflict between the "idealists"—who are madly enthusiastic about the new theories of environment and its importance in shaping personality and character traits—and the "realists-traditionalists"—those who believe that environment is powerless to change whatever traits are "inherited." It is clear that Christie favored the idea expressed by the phrase "blood will tell," although in this story one of the most negative characters, Mildred Strete, seems to be the strongest proponent of that idea. So far as she is concerned, Gina Hudd is a murderess because her *grandmother* had been one, and *furthermore* it must be she who is poisoning Carrie Louise, because Gina is "Italian" and Italians are known to be poisoners! Although Mildred's statements are intended to be taken within the context of a frustrated, narrow-minded old woman whose life has been unsatisfactory in many ways, Christie obviously believed that inheritance through blood was more important than environment.

Agatha Christie was clearly aware that there are cultural differences among nationalities, but she did not believe that those differences were attributable to learning and environment. If Italians, for example, are less afraid to "show their emotions" than English people are, then they must have inherited that "trait" through blood. They do not "learn" that behavior from their families and friends and the culture in which they grow up. And so if an Italian infant is adopted by a British family and raised among English people, the child's "Italian blood" will cause him or her to have that trait of "free expression of emotion" even though he or she has never lived among Italian people. In one scene in *Murder with Mirrors,* Gina Hudd wonders if she is "more upset than anyone else in the house" because she is Italian, and Miss Marple smilingly assures her that her Italian blood is responsible for allowing her to "express herself more freely." According to another character, Alex Restarick, Gina is "cruel" because she is "Italian." He tells another character that Gina "gets under Edgar Lawson's skin..."

> "...because she's a woman—and a beautiful woman, and because she thinks he's funny! She's half Italian, you know, and the Italians have that unconscious vein of cruelty. They've no compassion for anyone who's old or ugly, or peculiar in any way. They point with their fingers and jeer..."

Fact: Gina was born in Italy to Italian-English parents, but she was brought to England as an infant and raised there exclusively among English people. Nevertheless, wise old Miss Marple contends that her "Italian blood..."

In the 1938 *Appointment with Death,* a world-renowned French psychologist, Dr. Gerard, teases the young Englishwoman Sarah King, a medical doctor, about the "fact" that she is, despite all her modern sophistication, still "English," and therefore retains the "racial" feeling that sex is "not quite nice." And so even Christie's most learned characters attribute cultural differences to "race and blood" and not to environment or learning.

In *Murder with Mirrors* there is an amusing scene in which a psychiatrist "smiles in a superior way" several times as he assures a police officer that "we are all mad" and "we are all mental cases," causing the officer to remark that psychiatrists give him a pain in the neck. The whole concept of "rehabilitating" juvenile delinquents through environmental change is very much scoffed at in this book, several characters pointing out that lots of people grow up in nasty environments but still manage to develop into responsible, neurosis-free adults. However, Carrie Louise makes a good case for her husband's efforts:

> "We meant to do so much for these boys.... We did do something. Some of them have done wonderfully well. Several of them are in really responsible positions. A few slid back—that can't be helped. Modern civilised conditions are so complex—too complex for some simple and undeveloped natures..."

The subject of "environment" versus "inherited traits" was a very popular one in the early 1950s. See the *Comments* section for the 1949 novel *Crooked House* for some remarks about William March's novel, *The Bad Seed.*

The characters in *Murder with Mirrors,* though perhaps not developed with the thoroughness that characterized some of Christie's novels of the 1940s, are a colorful, varied lot. Some of the more memorable ones are the plain-speaking, common sense American Wally Hudd who scratches his head and wonders how all these people at Stonygates can be so stupid; frail, "out of this world" Carrie Louise who never "makes a fuss" but is accustomed to having others make a fuss over her; the supercilious, sophisticated Alex Restarick; the born-to-be-unhappy Mildred Strete; the tyrannical "servant," Juliet Bellever; the angelic-faced Cockney brat Ernie Gregg; the neurotic Edgar Lawson; and the sensible Gina who laughs at the whole "family" at Stonygates but enjoys herself thoroughly among them.

A Pocket Full of Rye (1953)

SETTING

It is November of 1952. The principal settings are a business office in London, Amalgamated Investments, owned by Mr. Rex Fortescue, and Mr. Fortescue's home, Yewtree Lodge, which is located in a fictitious suburb, Baydon Heath, just north of London. Minor settings include the office of a small firm of solicitors in Baydon Heath; that of a larger firm of solicitors in London; a private sanatorium near London and Miss Marple's cottage in the fictitious village of St. Mary Mead, which is located somewhere west of London, probably in the county of Berkshire.

The offices of Amalgamated Investments include a front office where three or four typists work, an inner office and an inner waiting room "where the more important clients were allowed to sit;" an anteroom occupied by Mr. Fortescue's private secretary, and Mr. Fortescue's private office.

Baydon Heath is a recent development of expensive, comfortable homes for financiers whose offices are in "the City." Three golf courses serve the affluent population of Baydon Heath, and there is at least one pub, The Three Pigeons. There is also at least one hotel, the Golf Hotel, described by an elderly female character as "a wicked nest of profiteers. Drinking and card playing all the evening." Baydon Heath is just twenty minutes by train from central London and commuting by automobile is also convenient, as traffic is light on the road connecting Baydon Heath with London.

A police officer arriving for the first time at Yewtree Lodge has these thoughts:

> Call it a lodge, indeed! Yewtree Lodge! The affectation of these rich people! The house was what he, Inspector Neele, would call a mansion. He knew what a lodge was. He'd been brought up in one! The lodge at the gates of Hartington Park, that vast unwieldy Palladian house with its twenty-nine bedrooms which had now been taken over by the National Trust. The lodge had been small and attractive from the outside, and had been damp, uncomfortable and devoid of anything but the most primitive form of sanitation within. Fortunately, these facts had been accepted as quite proper and fitting by Inspector Neele's parents. They had no rent to pay and nothing whatever to do except open and shut the gates when required, and there were always plenty of rabbits and an occasional pheasant or so for the pot. Mrs. Neele had never discovered the pleasure of electric irons, slow combustion stoves, airing cupboards, hot and cold water from taps, and the switching on of light by a mere flick of a finger. In winter, the Neeles had an oil lamp and in summer they went to bed when it got dark. They were a healthy family and a happy one, all thoroughly behind the times.

American readers are reminded of the fact that the "first floor" of any building in Europe is actually the "second floor" in American terms. In this story the term "first floor" occurs repeatedly to refer to the bedroom floor of Yewtree Lodge, and an elderly woman, the sister-in-law of Rex Fortescue, lives apart from the family in a small apartment on the "second floor" ("third floor" in American terms.)

There is not very much description of the interior of Yewtree Lodge, but we learn that there is a clearly-marked "Smoking Room" on the ground floor, in addition to a library where afternoon tea is served and where a murder occurs. Being a relatively recent construction, the house has central heating but a fire is lit in the fireplace of the library in one scene.

Although it is now 1952, post-War rationing of certain goods is still in force, and there are a couple of references to "black market nylons" worn by the stylish private secretary of Mr. Fortescue and plenty of "black market butter" being available at his table.

In most of Christie's novels since the late 1940s there have been references to the shortage of domestic help in England. There is a particularly interesting one in *A Pocket Full of Rye,* as Inspector Neele notices that the housekeeper, Mary Dove, appears to be a more educated woman than a housekeeper usually is. Mary explains to him that being a housekeeper is "…the perfect racket. People will pay anything—*anything*—to be spared domestic worries." Mary works only for the very rich and she never stays in any one position for more than a year and a half. She is very well paid.

Regarding automobiles, there is one reference to a "Rolls Bentley sports model coupé." The only reference to current events in the novel is a newspaper story about the discovery of uranium fields somewhere in Africa. Two young men—the husband of one female character, and the brother of another—are said to have been killed in World War Two. One died at Dunkirk and the other was a fighter pilot.

STORY

On a November morning in 1952, Mr. Rex Fortescue experiences a sudden choking fit at his London office and is rushed to a hospital, where he dies within minutes. It is soon learned that he died of a slow-acting poison, taxine, which must have been consumed several hours earlier, probably with breakfast at his home, Yewtree Lodge, in the suburb of Baydon Heath. Inspector Neele, who is in charge of the case, goes to Mr. Fortescue's home at once, meeting the housekeeper and other servants, and learning about the family members. There is Mr. Fortescue's son Percival, who works in the family business, and there is an unmarried daughter, Elaine. There is also another son, Lancelot, who is the "family black sheep" and who lives in Africa with his wife. Finally there is Adele, Rex Fortescue's beautiful young wife, who has a handsome young friend named Vivian Dubois with whom she spends most afternoons "playing golf."

Adele is the most likely murder suspect, since she inherits a fortune upon her husband's death, but some astounding events occur within the next twenty-four hours. A telegram from Lancelot arrives announcing that he plans to arrive at Yewtree Lodge the following day at tea time. This infuriates his brother Percival, who has always despised Lancelot. As announced, Lance arrives the following day and he partakes of afternoon tea in the library with his sister Elaine, his sister-in-law Jennifer and his beautiful new step-mother, Adele. Later that afternoon, Adele is found dead, still seated in the library, with a half-eaten scone in one hand and some tea still in her cup. Traces of potassium cyanide are found in the cup. Then, late in the evening, the body of a housemaid at Yewtree Lodge is found in the rear yard near the clotheslines. She was strangled with a thin garment that the murderer evidently took from the clothesline, and there is a clothespin clipped to her nose.

Miss Jane Marple reads of the "Triple Tragedy at Yewtree Lodge" in the newspapers and she is at once saddened and infuriated. The housemaid who was strangled was Gladys Martin, whom Miss Marple had trained for domestic service a few years earlier. The wicked gesture of clipping the clothespin to Gladys's nose, a despicable act of mockery, causes Miss Marple to set aside her knitting and board the very next train to Baydon Heath with the determination to bring this particularly wicked murderer to justice.

Miss Marple is welcomed by Inspector Neele, who has heard of her special abilities through colleagues in the police force, and the two of them work closely together, successfully identifying the murderer.

CHARACTERS

Miss Somers, an incompetent typist at Amalgamated Investments who cannot even make tea properly. "Oh, dear, I *did* think it was boiling *this* time," she has occasion to say—not once but *twice*.

Miss Griffith, the efficient head typist at Amalgamated Investments, a grey-haired martinet who has been there for sixteen years. She has occasion to say sharply, "Water not boiling *again*, Somers!"—not once but *twice*.

Miss Griffith presents some preliminary information about the Fortescue family to Inspector Neele. She is most enthusiastic about Lancelot Fortescue because he has recently married a young woman with a title. Miss Griffith is much impressed by the aristocracy.

Miss Bell and Miss Chase, other typists in the office of Amalgamated Investments

Irene Grosvenor, Rex Fortescue's glamorous platinum blonde private secretary, who wears an expensively cut little black suit and whose shapely legs are encased in the very best and most expensive black-market nylons. She does not enter or leave a room—she "sails in and out."

The Office Boy who is dispatched to find a doctor—any doctor—anywhere!

Rex Fortescue, a financier whose business practices are similar to those of Aristide Leonides in the 1949 *Crooked House*. One police officer describes him as a "twister." That is, he is always careful to remain within the law, but just barely. He is unscrupulous and many of his dealings might be described as "shady." He has one firm of "reputable" lawyers who handle some of his legal needs, and another firm of lawyers who handle his "other" needs.

Mr. Fortescue dies of taxine poisoning early in the story.

Elvira Fortescue, Rex Fortescue's first wife who died many years ago. She loved reading Tennyson's *The Idylls of the King* and that was why she named her two sons Lancelot and Percival.

Adele Fortescue, Rex Fortescue's beautiful young wife who allegedly married Rex only for his money. According to Mary Dove, the housekeeper:

"Mrs. Fortescue, Adele—was his second wife and about thirty years younger than he was. He came across her at Brighton. She was a manicurist on the look-out for big money. She is very good looking—a real sexy piece, if you know what I mean."

Vivian Edward Dubois, a tall, handsome and charming "friend" of Adele Fortescue who was careful, when writing to her, never to suggest intimacy in their relationship.

Dr. Isaacs of Bethnel Green, a doctor who responds to the frantic pleas of the staff at Amalgamated Investments, on the morning of Rex Fortescue's sudden illness

Sir Edwin Sandeman of Harley Street, a second doctor who arrives at Amalgamated Investments on the morning of Rex Fortescue's sudden illness

Inspector Neele, the son of poor lodgekeepers who is in charge of the case. He scoffs at the humble-sounding name "Yewtree Lodge" that was given to a rich man's luxury mansion, because he knows what a real lodge is. He grew up in one!

Inspector Neele has heard of Jane Marple's special abilities and welcomes her as a colleague in the investigations.

Professor Robert Bernsdorff, a.k.a. Dr. Bernsdorff, a personal friend of Inspector Neele, who informs him that the poison that killed Rex Fortescue was taxine, derived from the berries and needles of the common yew tree.

Percival Fortescue, dubbed "Percy Prim" by a certain police officer, and called "Val" by his wife and "Mr. Val" by the butler. He is a neat fair man of thirty odd, with pale hair and eyelashes and a slightly pedantic way of speech. He is the dutiful, elder son of Rex Fortescue and a partner in the family firm. He is "mean" with money and even goes over the household accounts with Miss Dove, the housekeeper, questioning each and every expenditure.

Jennifer Fortescue, referred to as "Mrs. Percival," or "Mrs. Val" by the servants. She is Percival Fortescue's wife. She is bored with life at Yewtree Lodge and only enjoys shopping and going to movies.

Lancelot Fortescue, Rex Fortescue's younger son and the "black sheep" of the family. You guessed it, he once forged a check, but not at Oxford or Cambridge as check forgers normally do in Christie books. This one forged his check while working with the family firm. His father kicked him out of the firm and he went to Africa to live. We are not favored with a physical description of him, but when Inspector Neele questions Miss Griffith about him, at the office of Amalgamated Investments, she becomes somewhat inarticulate and stammers, "Well, we're all fond of Mr. Lance." Therefore he must be good looking.

Recently Lance has apparently returned to his father's good graces because of a major dispute between his father and his brother Percival.

Patricia Fortescue, Lance Fortescue's wife, whom he met and married in East Africa. The daughter of an Irish peer, she is twice widowed. Her first husband died in the war and the second one shot himself. Her second husband was a "scoundrel" but, because he had a title, in the opinion of Rex Fortescue, Lance has "married well" whereas his other son Percival married an ordinary hospital nurse.

Don, Pat Fortescue's first husband. He was a fighter pilot who died in the Battle of Britain. Pat explains to Miss Marple that Don was wonderful in the war. He had all the qualities that were needed and wanted in a war, but peace would not have suited him. He had a kind of "arrogant insubordination" and wouldn't have fit in or settled down, and so it was actually a good thing that he was killed in the war.

Lord Frederick Anstice, a.k.a. "Freddie," one of those "racehorse persons," who got into trouble with the Jockey Club and blew his brains out just before an inquiry by the Stewards into the running of one of his horses. He was Pat Fortescue's second husband.

If Freddie's problems in sporting circles sound familiar, we learned of a similar person in the 1948 *There Is a Tide*. In that novel, Frances Cloade's father, Lord Edward Trenton, had been a dishonest breeder of horses.

Elaine Fortescue, Rex Fortescue's daughter, the younger sister of Lancelot and Percival. The housekeeper Mary Dove speaks more fondly of her than of the rest of the Fortescue family, describing her as "one of those great schoolgirls who never grow up. She plays games quite well, and runs Guides and Brownies and all that sort of thing."

Gerald Wright, a young teacher who is Elaine Fortescue's fiancé. He has communistic ideas and despises crooked capitalists like Rex Fortescue.

Miss Ramsbottom, a.k.a. "Aunt Effie," the sister of Elvira Fortescue, Rex's deceased wife. She is a religious fanatic who is well over seventy and who keeps to her room on the top floor of Yewtree Lodge, refusing even to take meals with Rex Fortescue's sinful family. She is playing patience when Inspector Neele visits her in her room with the news of Rex's death. Her only reaction to learning that Rex has died is to say, "Struck down at last in his arrogance and sinful pride. Well, it had to come."

Inspector Neele goes on to say,

"It seems possible that he may have been poisoned—"
The inspector paused to observe the effect he had made.
He did not seem to have made any. Miss Ramsbottom merely murmured "Red seven on black eight. Now I can move up the King."

Miss Marple, who is not particularly scrupulous in her methods, ingratiates herself with Miss Ramsbottom by feigning an interest in the "foreign missions." Miss Ramsbottom then offers her the use of an adjoining bedroom rather than obligating her to go and stay at the Golf Hotel, "that nest of profiteers."

Mary Dove, the housekeeper at Yewtree Lodge with the "Mona Lisa" smile. She is expensive but worth it. Taking advantage of the shortage of domestic help, she is an expensive housekeeper who works only for the rich, staying in one household no more than a year and half and then moving on. As housekeepers go, she is extremely candid in her statements to the police about the family, declaring to Inspector Neele that "They're all quite odious."

Crump, the butler at Yewtree Lodge who drinks. Miss Dove keeps him on primarily because his wife is an excellent cook.

Mrs. Crump, the devoted, excellent cook at Yewtree Lodge. By the time the police arrive at Yewtree Lodge, they know that the poison that killed Rex Fortescue must have been consumed with his breakfast. Mrs. Crump does not take kindly to that suggestion and threatens at least one officer with her rolling pin.

In an effort to learn as much as possible about Gladys Martin's behaviors at Yewtree Lodge, Miss Marple ingratiates herself with Mrs. Crump by complimenting her on the lightness of her pastry, explaining to Inspector Neele, "the way to a cook's heart is through her pastry."

Gladys Martin, the parlourmaid, "or waitress as they like to be called nowadays," at Yewtree Lodge. The housekeeper Mary Dove describes her as "quite a decent sort of girl but very nearly half-witted. The adenoidal type." Gladys is found strangled outside near the clotheslines, with a clothespin clipped to her nose.

Albert Evans, a.k.a. "Bert," Gladys Martin's boyfriend who writes postcards to her from various places.

Ellen Curtis, the elderly housemaid at Yewtree Lodge.

Detective-Constable Waite, Inspector Neele's assistant who notes that Amalgamated Investments is a "classy joint" and that some of the people there—Miss Grosvenor and Rex Fortescue—have "ritzy names."

Sergeant Hay, who accompanies Inspector Neele to Yewtree Lodge on his first visit there, and works with him on the investigation.

An Assistant Commissioner, Inspector Neele's superior

Mr. Billingsley of Billingsley, Horsethorpe & Walters, Rex Fortescue's "reputable" lawyers. He is "an urbane man whose discretion is concealed habitually by a misleadingly forthcoming manner." He explains to Inspector Neele the pitiful state of the financial affairs at Amalgamated Investments.

Jane Marple, an elderly spinster from the village of St. Mary Mead. She has a personal interest in this case because one of the murder victims was a parlourmaid whom Miss Marple had trained for domestic service. Miss Marple's principal method in crime solving is "never to believe anything anyone says until verifying the facts personally," because "the worst is usually the truth, human nature being what it is."

Young Fred who delivered fish in St. Mary Mead and always had a pleasant word for the girls, although he didn't mean anything by it. Gladys Martin had a crush on him.

Mr. Ansell of Ansell & Worrall's, solicitors in the High Street of Baydon Heath. He drew up Adele Fortescue's Will.

Dr. Mary Peters, the missionary who last occupied the room next to Miss Ramsbottom's at Yewtree Lodge

MacKenzie, whom Rex Fortescue allegedly once swindled in the matter of the Blackbird Mine, and whom Fortescue may even have killed

Helen MacKenzie, the widow of the above-named MacKenzie who vowed revenge against Rex Fortescue and raised her two children in that spirit of vengefulness. She is now sixty-three years old and a "voluntary" patient at the Pinewood Private Sanatorium.

Donald MacKenzie, the MacKenzies' son who died at Dunkirk

Ruby MacKenzie, the MacKenzies' daughter whom Helen MacKenzie has disowned

Dr. Crosbie, Helen MacKenzie's doctor at the Pinewood Private Sanatorium

Mrs. Emmett, the bank manager's wife who was condemned to a life of loneliness and so took every advantage of her few opportunities to talk. She is Miss Marple's "village parallel" for Jennifer Fortescue.

Miss Trefussis James, who fractured her knee when she was seventy-five. Miss Marple reminds Jennifer Fortescue of her.

Mrs. Latimer, another of Miss Marple's "village parallels." She was efficient and ran everything, and it was several years before they discovered ... oh, but Miss Marple mustn't gossip. Miss Dove reminds Miss Marple of her.

Young Ellis, yet another "village parallel," of whom Miss Marple is reminded by Gerald Wright. He married Marion Bates, the rich ironmonger's daughter, for money.

Mrs. Hardcastle, a hard-faced woman who becomes Percival Fortescue's personal secretary after the death of Rex Fortescue, replacing the glamorous and expensive Miss Grosvenor. She has excellent skills and is very reasonable in her terms.

Sir Henry Clithering, formerly of Scotland Yard, now retired. He is a great friend and admirer of Miss Jane Marple

Kitty, Miss Marple's current housemaid, another trainee from St. Faith's Orphanage

COMMENTS

A Pocket Full of Rye would be a great "first Christie experience" because it's absolutely typical, fun Christie reading. Miss Marple, the elderly lady from the village of St. Mary Mead who solves mysteries through "specialized knowledge," is the sleuth. Her "specialized knowledge" is simply a lifetime of experience with many different types of people right in her own village—people of whom she is "reminded" by others. Furthermore, she has learned that "the world is a very wicked place" and it is unwise to ever believe anything that one is told until verifying it personally. The novel is "vintage" Christie—not one of her more memorable or outstanding novels but certainly as entertaining and pleasant to read as any.

If there is a "uniqueness" in this Christie novel it is Miss Marple's motivation. In most of her previous appearances she has always been drawn into the story by the appeal of a friend, or simply "happened" to be in the vicinity where a crime took place. In the 1930 *Murder at the Vicarage*, of course, she actually lived in the village where the murder occurred, and was personally acquainted with everyone in the village, including the murderer and the victim. In the 1942 *The Body in the Library* she was a good friend of the family in whose house the body of a murder victim was found. In the 1943 *The Moving Finger* the wife of the vicar in another village where a crime took place happened to be a friend of Miss Marple's, and that lady appealed to Miss Marple to come and solve the mystery. In the 1950 *A Murder Is Announced*, Miss Marple happened to be staying in a hotel and it was the receptionist at that hotel who was killed in a neighboring village.

But in *A Pocket Full of Rye* the crime—a triple murder no less—takes place in a wealthy London suburb and, reading the headlines about the "Triple Tragedy at Yewtree Lodge" Miss Marple is outraged. One of the victims is a housemaid whom Miss Marple had trained for domestic service. The housemaid had apparently been hanging clothes on a line to dry and the killer strangled her and then, in a cruel, cynical, final mocking gesture, clipped a clothespin to her nose and left her there. Setting aside her knitting, Miss Marple boards the very next train to Baydon Heath and worms her way into the Fortescue household with one intention: to see to it that this particularly wicked murderer is unmasked and punished.

Miss Marple has occasion to complain that, as the years go on, criminals do not seem to be punished as adequately as they were in earlier times, a sentiment that is shared by her colleague, Inspector Neele:

"This is a wicked murderer, Inspector Neele, and the wicked should not go unpunished."

In the 1948 *There Is a Tide* Christie introduced the idea—whether simply a personal fantasy of her own or something based on tangible evidence is unclear—that people who have been "useful" in wartime are often not nearly so useful in peacetime. She seemed to believe that the fearlessness and daring that make heroes of certain soldiers are the very qualities that make those men "antisocial" and unable to adjust to civilian life in peacetime. In *A Pocket Full of Rye,* Patricia Fortescue's first husband is so described, Patricia explaining that it was perhaps a good thing that her husband was killed in the war because he "would not have fit in" in peacetime. Christie had reintroduced this idea in the person of Edward Goring in the 1951 *They Came to Baghdad,* and she will reintroduce it in three future novels: the 1956 *Dead Man's Folly,* the 1957 *What Mrs. McGillicuddy Saw,* and the 1965 *At Bertram's Hotel.*

The Mary Dove character is something new in Christie's stock of characters: the person who takes advantage of the growing shortage of domestic help and is able to create a lucrative career for herself as an efficient—and therefore expensive—housekeeper. This kind of character will reappear in the 1957 *What Mrs. McGillicuddy Saw* in the person of Lucy Eyelesbarrow. The idea may be just another Christie fantasy, a product of her own strange belief that domestic servants, when they do good work, are "actively happy and appreciated," as she affirmed in her *Autobiography.*

Funerals Are Fatal (1953)

(Alternate Title: *After the Funeral*)

Setting

It is autumn of 1952 or 1953. Action takes place at two substantial country houses in the north of England, at a cottage in a small village in Berkshire a few miles west of London, and at three London residences plus a vacant house in London's Cardigan Street.

Of these, the most important setting is an enormous Victorian mansion called Enderby. We learn that Enderby is "in the north of England" and that the nearest important town is the fictitious Matchfield. The name of the county is not mentioned, but it is probably Yorkshire, since a female character, instead of taking a train, drives to Enderby from her own home which is stated to be in Yorkshire. On the way, her car breaks down and must be towed to a place called Cathstone. Cathstone is described as being "on the edge of the moorland," a desolate but beautiful expanse of wasteland in Yorkshire which was the setting for Emily Brontë's *Wuthering Heights*.

Yorkshire is England's largest county and is divided into three sections called "ridings," the term being a linguistic descendant from the older term "thriding," or "third." The moorlands are located in the North Riding. The West Riding is part of the "Industrial Midlands" of England which also include the industrial counties of Nottinghamshire, Lancashire and others.

Since Christie does not favor us with the exact county in which Enderby is located, we may place it either in the West Riding of Yorkshire or perhaps in Nottinghamshire, but no further from the moorlands than those.

Enderby is described by one young female character as "...hideous. An almost indecent temple to wealth." We may recall that in the 1952 *Murder with Mirrors* the enormous mansion called Stonygates was negatively described as "a kind of temple to Plutocracy." Both Stonygates and Enderby are in the north of England, and both are described as Victorian Gothic in design. Stonygates, built by a successful ironmonger in the middle of the nineteenth century, had been converted into a special school, early in the twentieth century, with only a small central portion of the house maintained as living quarters for the family. In *Funerals Are Fatal*, Enderby, built by another Victorian businessman, has continued to be occupied by his eldest son along with three servants. The aging butler remembers "happier" times when there were younger people and children at Enderby. The elderly house-maid has been in service there for a mere twenty years. The young, excellent cook complains bitterly about the inconveniently large, antiquated kitchen, although we learn that the vast coal-fired cooking stove stands unused, as a modern gas range has supplanted it.

The "eldest son" mentioned above has recently died, and the story actually begins on the day of his funeral. In the course of the story the property will be offered for sale and nobody will be surprised that there are no prospective buyers who are interested in using it as a residence, since even wealthy residents would find it impossible to assemble a staff of servants adequate for its maintenance, the dwindling supply of servants in England now having been apparent for some years.

The only parties expressing an interest in Enderby are the Y.W.C.A and "The Jefferson Trust" which is looking for a building to house its "collection," whatever that may be.

We learn that there is a "Green Drawing Room" and a "White Boudoir" on the ground floor of the mansion. In the Green Drawing Room is a "green malachite table," and on the table is an arrangement of wax flowers under a protective glass dome, evidently a common Victorian decoration. Both the flower arrangement and the table will have significance in the novel. The dining room and library are two other rooms that are mentioned.

The exterior grounds of Enderby are appropriately large for this vast mansion, and there must be at least two "lodges," as we are told that the aging butler had always supposed that upon retirement he would live in "the North Lodge" which would be modernized and made comfortable for him. (See the *Appendix* for an explanation of the term "lodge.") There is also a small summerhouse on the property where a scene late in the story takes place.

A much smaller but still substantial home called Stansfield Grange is another setting. It is a Georgian period home which has suffered neglect in recent years because of the increasing poverty of its owners. They are a middle aged to elderly couple with no live-in servants at all. A local woman does daily housework but returns to her own home each evening to be with her husband. Yorkshire is specifically stated as the county in which Stansfield Grange is located, and the nearest town with a railway station is the fictitious Bayham Campton. The lady of the house drives to Bayham Campton to meet a visitor at the station in "a dilapidated car of almost fabulous antiquity" which she and her husband have never had enough money to replace. The starter of the car often fails and, as the lady expresses it, "sometimes it has to be wound," meaning "cranked." Of possible interest to automotive history buffs is the fact that electric starting motors for cars, although introduced as early as about 1920, were at first unreliable enough to warrant the continued inclusion of cranks as standard equipment "to be used in the event of a starting motor failure." The Ford Motor Company included these cranks for its Ford and Mercury models as late as 1948, and European makes probably continued them even longer. Therefore this car of "almost fabulous antiquity" may not be quite as old as suggested.

Stansfield Grange is not described in very much detail, except for the fact that it is badly in need of paint and that the garden has been neglected for many years. Being a Georgian period home, it must have been built at some time during the eighteenth century and is probably about a century older than Enderby. There is a brief reference to its single telephone, which is "in the style of fifty-odd years ago," and located in a drafty passage behind the stairs.

Another setting is a cottage in the small fictitious village of Lytchett St. Mary in the county of Berkshire. There are three market towns within walking distance of Lytchett St. Mary, two being named Market Keynes and Cholsey. Cholsey has the nearest railway station to the village and Reading is just a short distance further away. At Reading there is a lending library to which one character goes by bus from the village one day to exchange books. These details are mentioned in order to show that there are several possible means of arrival at the village—by train to Cholsey, or by train to Reading and then by bus, and there is also the possibility of driving a car to any one of three neighboring towns and then walking to the village. Therefore it would be easy for someone to go to the village without arousing very much notice. The occupants of the cottage are "connoisseurs" of painting and so it is filled with framed paintings—some purchased at sales for low prices, others painted by one of the ladies living there, and still others by her deceased husband. The furniture is, substantially, worthless junk.

A murder takes place in the cottage in Lytchett St. Mary, and the inquest is held in a place called "the village hall." After the inquest certain characters take lunch at an inn called The King's Arms.

In London we visit the residence of Hercule Poirot, which continues to be described as very modern "with not a single curved line" in the furnishings and décor. It is clearly the same flat in Whitehaven Mansions in which Poirot established himself in the 1935 *The A.B.C. Murders*.

The characters include two young couples who live in flats in London. One of the couples is quite poor and lives in "a tiny flat with a cramped sitting room." The other couple is nearly as poor; they live in a flat in the Chelsea district and are stage actors. A lawyer visits this second couple on the morning after one of their parties, finding the flat to be littered with bottles and glasses and cigarette ends.

Regarding the couple mentioned above who live in the "tiny flat with a cramped sitting room," the young wife hopes to establish a cosmetics business with her inheritance, and there is a scene in a vacant building in London's Cardigan Street where she is found measuring floor space and walls for the future business. During a conversation about her plans, there is a reference to Elizabeth Arden and Helena Rubinstein, two cosmetics businesses that had already been successfully established by women.

As has been the case with most of Christie's recent detective novels, there are constant negative references to the shortage of domestic servants, and constant complaints by upper middle-class characters that the "lower classes" are no longer motivated by loyalty. (See the *Comments* section for further discussion of this subject.) There are also the usual references to recent increases in taxation and, in this story, even Hercule Poirot complains of it.

There are just two brief references to continued rationing of foods and black marketeering. One character notes with approval the lavish way in which a housekeeper dispenses her employer's tea and sugar ration, and a cook mentions having "saved up" six eggs to make a soufflé for which she also obtained some black-market cream. Another character, the former owner of a tea shop, explains that it was the wartime rationing of supplies that caused it to go bankrupt—a "war casualty" as she calls it.

STORY

It is autumn of 1952 or 1953 and Richard Abernethie, age sixty-eight, has just died, apparently of a long-term illness. His doctor had suggested that he might live perhaps two more years, or three at the most. His sudden death was somewhat of a surprise, given the doctor's prognosis, but nobody, including the doctor, was unduly surprised by it.

After the funeral, the family attorney, Mr. Entwhistle, reads the Will to the family, most of whom listen respectfully. Richard's youngest sister, Cora Lansquenet, has always been somewhat low-functioning mentally. She would have been described as "slow" or perhaps even "retarded" in earlier decades. She interrupts with childish remarks such as "Did he leave anything to me?" and when learning that he did, she flutes "Good! I shall go to Capri." The family tolerates Cora's childish chatter as they always have.

But suddenly Cora shocks the family by saying, "Still it's been hushed up very nicely, hasn't it? I think you're all quite right. It should be kept strictly in the family." When Mr. Entwhistle asks what she means, Cora tilts her head to one side and asks, "Well, he *was* murdered, wasn't he?"

The shocked family expresses its displeasure with this outburst and Cora apologizes. But later that day everyone in the family wonders if Cora's remark was just another one of her silly, childish outbursts, or if it had actually been an "unwelcome truth." All her life Cora had had a way of blurting out "unwelcome truths." On one occasion during childhood, for example, she had declared that a certain housemaid "was growing so fat she could hardly get close to the kitchen table. Why does her stomach stick out like that?" The unwelcome truth was that the unmarried maid was pregnant.

The family does not have long to speculate, however, because Cora is brutally murdered in her cottage the following day. Mr. Entwhistle, who feels a deep affection for the Abernethie family, does his best to prove to himself that nobody in the family could have murdered Cora, but he finds that none of their alibis can be verified. As the local police make no progress in the case, Mr. Entwhistle appeals to his friend Hercule Poirot to solve the mystery, and of course Poirot succeeds.

CHARACTERS

Old Lanscombe, the aging butler at Enderby. He is fondly described in the thoughts of Mr. Entwhistle as "loyal and selfless, a good, old-fashioned servant."

Janet, the elderly, live-in housemaid at Enderby. She is just as loyal and selfless, and therefore as good an old-fashioned servant, as Lanscombe.

Marjorie, the young (age twenty-seven) but excellent cook at Enderby. She has none of the good, old-fashioned selflessness and loyalty of "good servants," and is a source of irritation to the old butler, Lanscombe, who feels that she has no dignity and no proper appreciation for his position of authority. She frequently calls the house "a proper old mausoleum" and complains of the immense area of the kitchen, scullery and larder, saying that it's "a day's walk to get round them all."

Marjorie has been at Enderby for just two years and only stays because the money is good, *and* because Mr. Abernethie appreciates her cooking, which is excellent. When Hercule Poirot arrives at Enderby, she immediately recognizes in him "a kindred spirit" because of his appreciation for her cooking.

Mrs. Jacks, the lady who comes in daily—or when needed—to do cleaning and other housework at Enderby.

The Canon, who "read the service beautiful," Mrs. Jacks thought, at Richard Abernethie's funeral

Mr. Entwhistle, the Abernethie family solicitor. It is Mr. Entwhistle who approaches Hercule Poirot to solve the mystery of Cora's murder.

Richard Abernethie, the eldest of seven siblings who outlived all but two. As the eldest, he inherited the vast wealth of his father, Cornelius Abernethie, who had amassed a fortune in Victorian times making corn plasters and related footcare products. Richard would have left the family fortune to his beloved son Mortimer if the latter had not died so tragically and unexpectedly.

Mortimer Abernethie, Richard's only child, a strong, healthy, young man who was suddenly struck by infantile paralysis and died recently.

Helen Abernethie, age about fifty-one or fifty-two, the widow of Richard's brother Leo. Helen and Leo never had any children. Although Helen keeps a small flat in London, her principal residence is a villa in Cyprus.

Timothy Abernethie, Richard's only surviving brother. He is an "invalid" who rarely leaves his bedroom at Stansfield Grange, his neglected Georgian-period home in Yorkshire. He is a constant complainer, one of those Christie characters who "enjoy poor health."

Maude Abernethie, Timothy's wife who waits on him hand and foot.

Mrs. Jones, who comes in daily to do housework for Timothy and Maude Abernethie and who is not fooled by Timothy's "invalidism."

Cora Lansquenet, Richard Abernethie's youngest sibling, born when their mother was nearly fifty. She is clearly a person of subnormal intelligence. She married an artist, Pierre Lansquenet, and the family's reaction to her marriage was so negative that she went away with her husband to France and never communicated with the family again.

After the funeral, Cora shocks the family with the suggestion that her brother Richard was murdered. The following day she herself is brutally murdered in her cottage in Berkshire.

Pierre Lansquenet, Cora's husband. He was a painter, but not a very good one.

George Crossfield, Richard Abernethie's only nephew, a young lawyer who works with a not-very-reputable firm. His father was said to be a not-very-reputable stockbroker. His mother was Richard Abernethie's eldest sister.

Rosamund Shane, one of Richard Abernethie's two nieces. She is a beautiful but mediocre stage actress with a bit of the "impishness" of Cora Lansquenet in her personality. She loves her actor husband very much, despite his infidelities, and is more interested in the success of his career than the success of her own. She is very happy to have her inheritance because it means that her husband can now produce his own plays.

Michael Shane, Rosamund's husband. He is very handsome and a talented actor as well.

Sorrel Dainton, an actress who is currently occupying the extramarital attentions of Michael Shane

Susan Banks, Richard Abernethie's other niece. Cora Lansquenet made Susan her sole heir for the simple reason that she had heard that the family had not approved of Susan's husband, and so she recognized in Susan a "kindred spirit."

Susan has a flair for business and a good deal of energy. With her inheritance she plans to establish her own cosmetics manufacturing firm in Cardigan Street, with a special laboratory for her husband Gregory to work in.

Gregory Banks, Susan's husband, of whom the Abernethie family had not approved because of his lowly position as a "chemist's assistant."

Mollie, a housemaid at Enderby when Cora was a child. Cora noted with great enthusiasm that Mollie was getting so fat that she could hardly get up close to the kitchen table. "Why does her stomach stick out like that?"

The Second Gardener, who was responsible for the change in Mollie's figure. The family had a talk with him and arranged for him to make an honest woman of her, and even provided him with a cottage in which to do it.

Dr. Barton, who prescribed sleeping pills for Timothy Abernethie

Mr. Entwhistle's Sister, who keeps house for him and watches over his health.

James Parrott, the present second partner of Bollard, Entwhistle, Entwhistle and Bollard, who receives a telephone call from the police at Lytchett St. Mary about Cora Lansquenet's murder.

Miss Gilchrist, Cora Lansquenet's "housekeeper/companion" although the "housekeeper" segment of the title is distasteful to her, for she considers herself to be a *lady*. She once owned a tea shop called "The Willow Tree," where all of the china was willow pattern. The rationing of supplies during the war caused the shop to go bankrupt. Since then Miss Gilchrist has survived as a "housekeeper/companion." It is Miss Gilchrist who discovers the brutal murder of Cora Lansquenet.

Inspector Morton of the Berkshire County Police, who is in charge of the case of Cora Lansquenet's murder.

Mrs. Panter from the Village who came to Cora Lansquenet's cottage twice weekly to do the "rough" housework.

Mrs. Lake Down the Lane, with whom Inspector Morton arranges for Miss Gilchrist to spend the night after she discovers the murder of Cora Lansquenet.

Young Lloyd, a lawyer who works with Bollard, Entwhistle, Entwhistle & Bollard. He attends Cora Lansquenet's inquest as a representative of the family.

Gaymarck and **Frogg II**, two racehorses that George Crossfield had backed on the day of Cora Lansquenet's murder.

An Adenoidal Maid who recently left Stansfield Grange to go and work for a family that kept dogs just because she liked "little doggies."

Hercule Poirot, the Belgian private investigator. In this story, Poirot makes good use of his "foreignness." He arranges with Helen Abernethie to invite the whole family to Enderby under the pretense that Poirot (alias Monsieur Pontarlier) has purchased Enderby to be used as a home for war refugees. He is present as the family bickers about who shall have the Spode dessert service and the Boule cabinet and the malachite table, pretending to have minimal understanding of English, but listening and observing very carefully.

Dr. Larraby, Richard Abernethie's doctor

A Nun in Lytchett St. Mary, Berkshire, who is collecting for an orphanage

Alexander Guthrie, an elderly art critic who visits Cora Lansquenet's cottage while Susan Banks is there. He finds nothing of value among the paintings Cora had purchased at various sales, noting that although keen on painting, Cora really knew very little about it.

"John and Mary," newlyweds who sent a piece of wedding cake to Miss Gilchrist

Joan, a friend of Susan Banks, who once sent her a post card signed only "Joan" when Susan had no fewer than eight friends named Joan

A Boy who talks with Susan about her car on the day of the inquest in Lytchett St. Mary, and who had seen her there once before.

Old Mr. Cole, the owner of a chemist's shop, and Gregory Banks's employer. He had once threatened, "If this happens again…."

Miss Gilchrist's Doctor who is summoned by Susan Banks because of Miss Gilchrist's sudden and violent illness

Mr. Goby, a private investigator with a large staff who can find out anything about anybody. We met him in the 1928 *The Mystery of the Blue Train*, as he provided a service to Rufus Van Aldin in the matter of his son-in-law's adulterous conduct. In the present story, Hercule Poirot employs him to gather all pertinent facts about every member of the Abernethie family. His trademark mannerism is never to look a person directly in the eye, focusing instead on some random object in the room.

We will meet Mr. Goby again in the 1966 *Third Girl*, the 1969 *Hallowe'en Party*, and in the 1972 *Elephants Can Remember*. Christie used this somewhat "magical" character whenever Hercule Poirot needed information that he was unable to obtain by ordinary means.

"Monsieur Pontarlier of U.N.A.R.C.O.," the alias used by Hercule Poirot for his first encounter with the Abernethie family

The Vicar who visited Richard Abernethie the day before he died

Some Nuns who called at Enderby for a subscription the day before Richard died

A Man Selling Brushes and Saucepans who called at the back door of Enderby the day before Richard died, and who was very persistent

A Nun collecting for a charity at Stansfield Grange in Yorkshire

A Vacuous-Faced Young Man with Spectacles, a house agent at the property in Cardigan Street where Susan Banks plans to open a shop

Dr. Penrith at Forsdyke House, who has information about Gregory Banks

Jackie Lygo, whom Rosamund must visit in London regarding the revival of a certain play

Superintendent Parwell from Matchfield who is summoned when someone coshes Helen Abernethie on the head

The Mother Superior of a Convent near Lytchett St. Mary who reports some interesting information about goings-on in Cora Lansquenet's cottage on the day of Richard Abernethie's funeral

A Dumbfounded Telegraph Boy who receives a one-pound tip from Hercule Poirot

FRENCH INTO ENGLISH

Chapter 7
mon cher—my good friend
Eh bien—well...

Chapter 12
Enfin—anyway
Ça se peut—That's possible
Mon ami—friend
C'est magnifique!—Wonderful! (Poirot is speaking sarcastically)
Bon dieu—For God's sake
Il ne manquait que ça!—Just what we needed! (sarcasm again intended)

Chapter 13
sirop de cassis—black currant liqueur, a favorite drink of Poirot's

Chapter 14
bêtise—an act of foolishness (implying that Cora meant no malice but was just being her usual "foolish" self)
pardon!—oops!
Entendu—Naturally...

Chapter 18
la toilette—grooming, dressing, etc.

Chapter 19
Femme formidable—a woman to be reckoned with (a strong, assertive woman)
Pardon—I beg your pardon? (Poirot is pretending not to understand, having been playing the part of a "foreigner" without much understanding of English)

Chapter 21
Eh bien?—Well then...
mon ami—my friend
Ma foi!—Good grief!
C'était une blague!—That wasn't real! (That is, the earlier errand he had asked Entwhistle to run was not real. Poirot had made that up for the benefit of the person he knew to be listening on the telephone extension.)
mon vieux—my friend
largesse—generosity (in this case, a generous amount of money offered)
Petit déjeuner—Breakfast

Chapter 23
mon cher—my friend

COMMENTS

Funerals Are Fatal is a delight to read. It's "vintage Christie" and would be a great "first Christie experience" for any reader. There are a large number of interesting characters whose personalities are quite individual, and there are at least three "character types" reappearing in *Funerals Are Fatal* that we have noted in earlier Christie novels. They are important enough to merit special headings.

THE WOMAN WHO LOVES A MAN MORE THAN HE LOVES HER

This character type has already appeared four times in Christie detective novels. They are Theresa Arundell in the 1937 *Poirot Loses a Client*, Elinor Carlisle in the 1940 *Sad Cypress*, Sandra Farraday in the 1945 *Remembered Death*, and Henrietta Savernake in the 1946 *Murder After Hours*. In *Funerals Are Fatal* we have two more examples. First, there is Rosamund Shane, who loves her actor husband despite his sexual infidelities and who wishes for his success in his acting career more than for success in her own career. Then there is Susan Banks, who hopes to establish a cosmetics manufacturing company which will provide her husband with a chance to "prove himself" by having his own laboratory to work in.

After a conversation with Rosamund Shane on the subject of her marriage, Poirot has these thoughts:

> He thought how strange it was that both Richard Abernethie's nieces should have fallen deeply in love with men who were incapable of returning that love. And yet Rosamund was unusually beautiful and Susan was attractive and full of sex appeal. Susan needed and clung to the illusion that Gregory loved her. Rosamund, clear-sighted, had no illusions at all, but knew what she wanted.

THE SPURIOUS INVALID

Timothy Abernethie is clearly much stronger and in much better health than he pretends to be. His wife appears to need someone to look after and cheerfully waits on him hand and foot, but Mrs. Jones, their cleaning lady, is not fooled by his alleged "invalidism." One or two false invalids—both females—appeared in the 1952 *Mrs. McGinty's Dead*. Mrs. Wetherby certainly is one and the lady at the post office, Mrs. Sweetiman, suspects that Mrs. Upward is another. All three of these characters are described as people who "enjoy poor health." In the 1943 *Murder in Retrospect*, we may recall, the "artistic" mother of Amyas Crale had "enjoyed bad health," and in Hercule Poirot's final adventure, *Curtain*, there will be Barbara Franklin.

THE ADENOIDAL—AND THEREFORE STUPID—FEMALE

In the 1937 *Poirot Loses a Client* we met the incredibly stupid and incompetent Miss Jenkins, who worked at the office of the house agents Messrs Gabler and Stretcher. She was "a young adenoidal woman with a lackluster eye" who could not listen to and correctly repeat a telephone number.

In the 1939 *Easy to Kill* we met Emily, a small clumsy-looking girl with pronounced adenoids, Miss Waynflete's maid, who asked, "If you blease, biss, did you bean the frilled billow cases?"

In the 1941 *N or M?*, we met Beatrice, "an almost imbecile looking, adenoidal maid" at the Sans Souci guest house.

In the 1948 *There Is a Tide* we met Edna, "a small, intelligent-looking but adenoidal maid, age fifteen" at the home of Jeremy and Frances Cloade. In that same novel we met Lily, "an adenoidal girl with a giggle," who worked behind the bar at The Stag Inn.

In the 1950 *A Murder Is Announced*, the police wonder how it can be that the Chipping Cleghorn *Gazette* accepted an advertisement announcing a murder. They learn that the person taking the advertisements there is "an adenoidal blonde."

In the 1953 *A Pocket Full of Rye* one of the murder victims, Gladys Martin, was described as "quite a decent sort of girl but very nearly half-witted. The adenoidal type."

Now in the 1953 *Funerals Are Fatal* we learn that "an adenoidal maid" recently left Stansfield Grange and took a post with another family simply because the other family had dogs and "she liked little doggies."

"Adenoidal" people, of course, had always been notorious for seemingly low intelligence. It is doubtful whether the chronic 35-decibel conductive hearing loss that invariably accompanies enlarged adenoids was, before 1953, recognized as being a major cause of delayed cognitive development in children. Ear plugs produce a similar hearing reduction, and so adenoidal children may as well be wearing ear plugs in their ears twenty-four hours a day. Put permanent ear plugs into *your* children's ears and see how smart they never get. Send them to school that way and let them "drift" through their early school experiences in a pleasantly muted, non-stimulating, world. Meanwhile, feel free to enjoy—if you are able to—the ridicule that ignorant Aunt Agatha heaps on these low-class, adenoidal-and-therefore-stupid girls.

The world of the theater receives somewhat more affirmative treatment in *Funerals Are Fatal* than Christie accorded it in the 1952 *Mrs. McGinty's Dead* with the swishy, limp-wristed Robin Upward and his effeminate theatre friends. Michael Shane is a talented actor and his self-admitted "ham actress" wife Rosamund wishes for his success more than anything else. However, Rosamund makes some amusing remarks about a new play that is "filled with modern ideas":

> "...there's the most wonderful chance of a play. Michael's got an option on it. It's a most wonder-

ful part for him and even a small part for me, too. It's about one of these young criminals, you know, that are really saints—it's absolutely full of the latest modern ideas."

The lawyer Mr. Entwhistle, the false invalid Timothy Abernethie, the aging butler Lanscombe, and the aging private investigator Mr. Goby are the strident, discontented voices of tradition in *Funerals Are Fatal*. From them we learn that:

> The servant class is no longer motivated by loyalty, resulting in "a very sad world" for people who have been accustomed to being waited upon by servants who were eager to please.
> People who are willing to cook and do housework are "worth their weight in gold" since they are so scarce.
> The servant class—or what is left of it—expects be paid adequately and to be appreciated.
> Manufactured goods are now defective in both materials and workmanship.
> Employees now work "to time"—that is, they expect their workday to end at certain hour.
> Employees now have "useless" education which simply "gives them ideas" and causes them "to think" needlessly.
> In the past, women did not marry men who worked behind shop counters, but nowadays they marry *anybody!*
> Lawlessness has been on the rise since the war and is largely attributable to foreigners and returning servicemen, and the police do nothing about it.
> Taxation has diminished everyone's income.

Several of the above items are summed up in the following tirades of the crotchety "spurious invalid," Timothy Abernethie:

> "This country's full of gangsters nowadays,—thugs—left over from the war! Going about killing defenseless women. Nobody's got the guts to put these things down—to take a strong hand. What's the country coming to, I'd like to know? What's the damned country coming to?
> "It all began with that damned Labour Government," said Timothy. "Sending the whole Country to blazes. And the Government we've got now is no better. Mealy mouthed milk and water socialists! Look at the state *we're* in! Can't get a decent gardener, can't get servants—poor Maude here has to work herself to a shadow messing about in the kitchen."
> (.....)
> "Fool of a daily woman only left me a lumpy macaroni cheese for supper. I had to go down to the kitchen and warm it up *myself*—and make myself a cup of tea—to say nothing of stoking the boiler. I might have had a heart attack—but does that class of woman care? Not she. With any decent feelings she'd have come back that evening and looked after me properly. No loyalty any more in the lower classes..."

So Many Steps to Death (1954)

(Alternate Title: *Destination Unknown*)

SETTING

It is autumn of 1953 or 1954. Preliminary scenes take place in the offices of a "secret service" agent in London, at London's Heathrow Airport, aboard a plane bound for Paris which lands instead at the northern French town of Beauvais, and then aboard a bus bound for Paris. There is a scene at Orly Airport in Paris, and then a plane trip to Casablanca.

Settings in Casablanca include a room in a modern hotel, the business district surrounding the hotel, and a hospital. The protagonist travels by train from Casablanca to Fez, experiences the picturesque old-world quarter of that city, and then travels by plane and automobile to an undisclosed location in a mountainous region somewhere in Africa where the remainder of the action takes place at a clandestine colony of scientists.

More important than the physical settings is the historical background to the story: the Cold War of the early 1950s. There are constant references to "the Iron Curtain," radioactivity, the threat of nuclear war, and communism. There is a derisive comment about "witch hunts" in America, a reference to the exaggerated fear of communism in America at the time. The terms "the other side" (the Soviet Union and the other "Iron Curtain" countries) and "fellow travelers," (communist sympathizers) occur constantly. A new device, the Geiger counter, plays a role. Modern science and the fear that science and scientists may be abused for evil purposes are the most important themes of the story.

STORY

It is 1953 or 1954 and scientists have been disappearing from the United States, Britain, France and all western countries. It is suspected that some of them are "communist sympathizers" who have gone "behind the Iron Curtain" to work for communist causes, but there is also suspicion that some of the scientists have been kidnapped and taken there against their will. The latest disappearance has been that of the American scientist Thomas Betterton. His British wife,

Olive, claims to have no idea of his whereabouts. She is about to make holiday trip to Casablanca and there is reason to suspect that she has agreed with agents of "the other side" to be taken to her husband. The British authorities, therefore, are watching her movements in hopes of being led to the mysterious place to which the scientists are disappearing.

Hilary Craven is a young Englishwoman who is in the depths of personal depression. Her husband has left her for another woman, her baby daughter has died a painful death from meningitis, and Hilary feels that she has nothing to live for. A trip to sunny, exotic Morocco fails to restore her will to live, and so while in Casablanca she decides to end her life. She goes to several pharmacies in order to purchase enough sleeping tablets to poison herself. Later, in her hotel room, just as she is about to swallow them, a man enters her room and casually states, "I shouldn't do it if I were you." He introduces himself as Jessop and he explains that he saw her buying sleeping tablets at one pharmacy and then another, and then followed her to the hotel. He explains his interest in her by telling her about the disappearing scientists, and about Thomas Betterton and his wife Olive. The fact is that the plane in which Olive was traveling crash landed at Casablanca, and Olive now lies dying in a hospital. She is expected to live no more than a day or two.

Because Hilary and Olive resemble each other closely—both have flaming red hair and their passport descriptions are nearly identical—Jessop proposes that Hilary take Olive's place and follow her travel itinerary. It is supposed that agents "from the other side" are planning to meet Olive somewhere in Fez or Marrakesh and to take her to the "destination unknown." Jessop adds that, if Hilary agrees to the plan, it may result in her death. But it will be a death in the service of her country and, as deaths go, a much more "interesting" death than suicide by poison.

After no more than a couple of seconds of hesitation, Hilary says, "Yes, why not?" A day or two later, Olive Betterton dies and it is reported that Hilary Craven died in a plane accident in Casablanca. She receives a crash course in the life of Olive Betterton and embarks on an exciting journey which leads her to a secret colony of scientists somewhere in the Atlas mountains and to her "husband," Thomas Betterton.

CHARACTERS

Thomas Charles Betterton, a young American physicist who made the startling discovery of ZE Fission. According to his wife Olive, he had very little interest in politics. His work was his life. He is the latest of several brilliant scientists worldwide who have simply vanished.

Elsa Betterton, Thomas Betterton's first wife, the daughter of Professor Mannheim with whom her husband worked in America. She was a brilliant scientist herself. She died about eighteen months ago.

Olive Betterton, Thomas Betterton's current wife, whom he married six months ago. She is a tall woman, about twenty-seven years of age. The most noticeable thing about her is a most magnificent head of auburn red hair.

Jessop of the Secret Service. He has the pale complexion that comes from living most of the day in artificial light—a man of desks and files. It would be difficult to guess his age, as he looks neither old nor young.

Colonel Wharton, a colleague of Jessop in the Secret Service. He is dark with a small military moustache. There is about him an alert nervous energy.

Professor Mannheim, a scientist who escaped from Nazi-occupied Poland during the Second World War and fled with his wife and daughter to America.

Dr. Evans and his Wife, casual friends of the Bettertons, with whom they played bridge.

Walter Griffiths, an American lawyer friend of Thomas Betterton who visited the Bettertons at their London home not long before Thomas disappeared.

Dr. Mark Lucas, a research chemist from Germany who emigrated to the United States and knew Thomas Betteron there. He ran across the Bettertons at a London restaurant just before Thomas disappeared.

Carol Speeder, another American friend of Thomas Betterton, with whom he lunched at the Dorset Hotel just a few days before he left for Paris.

Major Boris Glydr, a Polish gentleman who was a cousin of Thomas Betterton's first wife Elsa.

Major Glydr's Mother, who was Professor Mannheim's only sister

Hilary Craven, a young Englishwoman. She is in the depths of depression, having recently lost her husband to another woman and her only child to a painful death from meningitis. Just as she is about to commit suicide by swallowing an overdose of sleeping pills, Jessop appeals to her to accept a dangerous mission which may result in a more interesting kind of death—one that may serve her country.

Nigel Craven, Hilary's ex-husband who left her for another woman

Brenda Craven, Hilary's baby daughter who struggled with painful meningitis and then died.

An Air Hostess with a Nursery Governess Voice who cheerfully announces that, because of foggy conditions in the Paris region, Hilary's plane will land instead at Beauvais

A Harassed Clerk at Orly Airport who places Hilary Craven on a later flight to Casablanca than the one originally scheduled for her.

A French Doctor, a Nurse, and a Nun at the hospital in Casablanca where Olive Betterton dies.

Mrs. Calvin Baker, an energetic and loquacious American tourist. Hilary meets her for the first time at the Hotel Saint-Louis in Casablanca, "a small, plump, middle-aged woman with well-blued white hair." She is a stereotypical American traveler who complains of unsanitary conditions everywhere and talks incessantly.

> No one could have mistaken Mrs. Calvin Baker for anything but a travelling American, comfortably off, with an inexhaustible thirst for precise information on every subject under the sun.

Mrs. Calvin Baker's personality closely resembles that of Mrs. Hamilton Clipp, whom we met in the 1951 *They Came to Baghdad.* That lady, also, was an American traveler who was disgusted by the lack of sanitation in the Arab countries.

Miss Hetherington, an English spinster traveling in Morocco, and another person Hilary Craven meets at the Hotel Saint-Louis.

> In an uncomfortable Empire type chair, Miss Hetherington who again could not have been mistaken for anything but travelling English, was knitting one of those melancholy shapeless looking garments that English ladies of middle age always seem to be knitting. Miss Hetherington was tall and thin with a scraggy neck, badly arranged hair, and a general expression of moral disapprovement of the Universe.

One of Miss Hetherington's complaints is that in foreign countries the English no longer receive favored treatment.

Mademoiselle Jeanne Maricot, a Frenchwoman whom Hilary observes in the formal salon at the Hotel Saint-Louis.

A Frenchman looking like a prosperous businessman who left the salon "with a look of lingering regret at Mademoiselle Jeanne Maricot."

A Sympathetic Hotel Manager at the Hotel Saint-Louis in Casablanca

Monsieur Henri Laurier, a Frenchman sitting opposite Hilary in the train to Fez. He is well informed and Hilary enjoys a charming conversation with him. He surprises Hilary by asking if there has been snow in England this year.

A Somewhat Disapproving-looking Nun and **Two Moorish Ladies** who share the railway compartment with Hilary Craven and Monsieur Laurier

Porters at the railway station in Fez

Monsieur Aristides, an old man Hilary notices at the Hotel Palais Jamail in Fez.

> An elderly man, very yellow of face, with a little goatee beard. She noticed him because of the extreme deference paid to him by the staff. Plates were whisked away and placed for him at the mere raising of his head. The slightest turn of an eyebrow brought a waiter rushing to his table.

A German sitting alone at a large table in the dining room at the Palais Jamail

A Middle-aged Swede with a Fair, Very Beautiful Girl at the Palais Jamail. They are a wealthy businessman from Sweden and his film star mistress.

An English Family with Two Children, A Good-looking Frenchman, and **Three French Families** at the Palais Jamail in Fez

Andrew Peters, an American with a broad, friendly grin, one of Hilary's "fellow travellers" to the "destination unknown." He is a research chemist with some idealistic enthusiasm for a world in which all people are equal, as he expresses it:

> "Individual happiness does not matter," said Peters seriously. "There must be the happiness of *all*, the brotherhood of the spirit! The workers, free and united, owning the means of production, free of the warmongers, of the greedy, insatiable men who keep everything in their own hands. Science is for *all*, and must not be held jealously by one power or the other."

Torquil Ericsson, another of Hilary's "fellow travellers." He is a brilliant young Norwegian—or perhaps Danish—physicist. On the subject of science, he agrees with Andrew Peters, but he also has ideas of his own:

> "So!" said Ericsson appreciatively, "you are right. The scientists must be the masters. They must control and rule. They and they alone are the Supermen. It is only the Supermen who matter. The slaves must be well treated, but they *are* slaves."

Dr. Barron, a French bacteriologist who has no interest in politics. During a conversation with Hilary and Andrew on the subject of "freedom," Dr. Barron interrupts with

> "Freedom from fools," he said bitterly. "That is what *I* want! That is what my work needs. Freedom from incessant, pettifogging economies! Freedom from all the nagging restrictions that hamper one's work!"

Helga Needheim, a German endocrinologist. Whereas Andrew Peters speaks as though he were a socialist or a communist, Helga seems to have Fascist ideas.

> "Christianity has made fools of women," she said. "Such a worship of weakness, such snivelling humiliation! Pagan women had strength. They rejoiced and conquered! And in order to conquer, no discomfort is unbearable. Nothing is too much to suffer."

An Airplane Pilot
A Berber Chauffeur
A Couple of Giggling Berber Women
A White-robed Figure with a Black, Smiling Face who opens the gate at the compound and admits the "fellow travellers."
Paul Van Heidem, a big handsome man who is fluent in several languages. He greets the group of "fellow travellers," speaking to each in his or her own language.
Miss Jennsen at the Registry, a thin spectacled girl
Dr. Hertz of Vienna, a plastic surgeon
A Woman Who Looks Like a Strict Nursery Governess who presides over the Registry. Her nationality is Swiss.
Dr. Schwartz, a female medical doctor who gives Hilary a complete physical examination
Dr. Rubec, a psychologist who submits Hilary to some basic psychological testing to determine her personality type.
Mademoiselle La Roche, who presides at the dress department of the Unit. She is a Frenchwoman with experience in women's clothing.
A Native Girl with a Shining Dark Face, Mademoiselle La Roche's assistant
Dr. Nielson, the Deputy Director who is the administrative head of the Unit, a big florid man with an urbane manner.
Stenographers at Dr. Nielson's office
The Director of the Unit, who addresses the community on one occasion. His concluding words:

> "This Unit is a gathering place for the Power of all the world. You come here from all parts of the globe, bringing with you your creative scientific knowledge. And with you, you bring *Youth!* No one here is over forty-five. When the day comes, we shall create a Trust. The Brains Trust of Science. And we shall administer world affairs. We shall issue our orders to Capitalists and Kings and Armies and Industries. We shall give the World the *Pax Scientifica.*"

Simon Murchison, who works in the same laboratory as Thomas Betterton at the Unit. He is "a thin, anæmic-looking young man of about twenty-six."
Bianca Murchison, Simon's Italian-born wife. She has studied economics and commercial law. She is at the Unit only as a wife to Simon Murchison and finds the Unit to be somewhat boring for wives.
A Magnificent-looking Native in White Robes who operates a lift at the Unit
Monsieur Leblanc, a French official who conducts an investigation in Morocco to find the "fellow travellers" who disappeared when their plane was destroyed while en route to Marakesh.
Monsieur Leblanc's Orderly
A Native in White Local Dress who found a pink pearl
Mohammed, who would like nothing better than to own a gas station in Chicago
The Master, who owns the Unit and is its financial benefactor
A Woman Who Was a Good Listener and who Married Hilary's Uncle George
A French Minister, The American Ambassador, The British Consul, A Member of Parliament, The Chief of Police and Two Members of a Former Royal Commission

FRENCH INTO ENGLISH

Note: Although this novel does not feature the private investigator Hercule Poirot, a considerable number of French expressions occur in the conversation of minor characters since a good deal of the action takes place in France and in Morocco.

Chapter 1
bateau mouche—an open touring boat in Paris, one of many. It is a popular tourist activity in Paris since many of the most interesting buildings in Paris are close to the River Seine and best seen from the river, for example, the Eiffel Tower, the Cathedral of Notre–Dame, the Conciergerie, the old buildings of the Île Saint-Louis, the Louvre, not to mention historic bridges such as the 17th Century Pont-Neuf and the beautiful Pont Alexandre III.

Chapter 3
Enfin—In a word…
Après tout—After all
Mauvaise affaire!—Bad news

Chapter 4
C'est la fin!—The end is near! (The woman is about to die.)

Chapter 5
Tant pis pour Pierre. Il est vraiment insupportable! Mais le petit Jules, lui il est bien gentil.

Et son père est très bien placé dans les affaires. Enfin, je me décide!"—To hell with Pierre. He's really insufferable. But Jules is awfully nice. And his dad is right up there in business. All right, my mind is made up!
figurez-vous—get this
Ah, mais oui—Yes, certainly

Chapter 6
n'est-ce pas, Madame?—aren't you, ma'am?
conforts modernes—modern conveniences
Ce monsieur-là—That gentleman over there
"Le long des lauriers roses, Rêvant de douces choses."—Along the row of pink-flowered laurels, Dreaming of pretty things...
"Où sont" the message began, then something which she could not decipher, and finally she made out the words *D'antan."* This is a famous line from a poem, *Ballade des Dames du Temps Jadis* by the medieval French lyric poet François Villon. The complete line is *"Où sont les neiges d'antan?"* which means "Where are the snows of yesteryear?" The word "snow" had occurred in the last words of the dying Olive Betterton, and Monsieur Laurier makes a reference to "snow" when speaking with Hilary Craven in the train. Christie evidently felt that her readers would all be familiar with Villon's poem, or at least that one line, which recurs at the end of each stanza. The line is well known by French speakers and is often used in nostalgic evocations, even in popular songs. In any case, it is the word "snow" that is the important clue.
Mille pardons, Madame—I'm so terribly sorry, ma'am.
"Mais viens, donc, Bobo. Qu'est-ce que tu fais? Dépêche-toi!"—Come on, Bobo. What are you doing? Hurry up!
"Laisse ta balle, chérie, on va déjeuner."—Put away your ball, darling. It's lunchtime.

Chapter 7
à jour—out in the open
Mes hommages, Madame—My compliments, Ma'am.

Chapter 8
Toujours des retards insupportables—Always these insufferable delays!

Chapter 11
Enchanté de faire votre connaissance, mon cher docteur—I'm very pleased to meet you, doctor.

Chapter 12
vendeuse—saleslady

haute couture—fine clothing for women
la toilette—grooming, dressing
tailleur—a tailored suit or dress
Entre nous—just between you and me
Boche—a negative ethnic reference to a German person

Chapter 13
raison d'être—life blood

Chapter 14
Ça se peut—That's possible
mon cher—my friend
Pas moi!—Not according to me!
là-bas—over there (that is, "on the other side")
religieuse—nun
le docteur Barron—Dr. Barron
Allô? Qu'est-ce qu'il y a?—Hello? What's up?
Mon cher collègue—esteemed colleague
Enfin, c'est colossal!—Frankly, it's stupendous
Voilà, mon capitaine—There you are, Captain

Chapter 15
entre nous—just between you and me

Chapter 17
Mon cher—My friend
S'il vous plaît, Madame—Please, ma'am

Chapter 18
Asseyez-vous, chère Madame—Please sit down, ma'am.
bien entendu—of course
Chère Madame—Dear lady (the comma after *chère* in the text is incorrect.)

Chapter 19
perdu—lost
Mais—c'est colossal! C'est fantastique! Enfin—c'est formidable!—Terms of increasing strength such as "That's stupendous, it's amazingly stupendous, it's absolutely phenomenal!

Chapter 20
Du tout, M. le Ministre—Absolutely not, Mr. Minister
ce cher Aristides—dear old Aristides
Mon cher—My friend
entourage—the assembly, the group
mon Dieu—My God
impasse—deadlock

COMMENTS

So Many Steps to Death, first published in 1954, bears a superficial resemblance to the 1951 *They Came to Baghdad* in that there is a mysterious "organization" with some apparently sinister goal, and in both novels a young Englishwoman finds herself unexpectedly involved in its unmasking. But the "organizations" in the two stories are completely different. In *They Came to Baghdad* the "organization" had for its goal the disruption of peace between the two Great Powers, and the fostering of a Third World War which would leave the "organization" in control of the world—or what was left of it—after the War. In other words, right from the beginning of the story, the goal of the "organization" is known to be an evil one.

In *So Many Steps to Death,* the purpose of the "organization" is *not* known. All that is known is that scientists of several Western nations—and of every political persuasion—have been disappearing. We learn as we read the story that the "organization" is simply a place where science is free to flourish, unhampered by material, monetary and political constraints—a paradise for true scientists. One of the scientists in the story, the French bacteriologist Dr. Barron, expresses this when he says that the only freedom he is interested in is "freedom from fools."

So Many Steps to Death may strike some readers as being very dated, with all of its references to the Cold War, the communist witch hunts in McCarthy-era America, the "Iron Curtain" and so on. However, the idea of a "paradise for scientists" is an intriguing one that may have some relevance in the modern world. The environmentalists of today, for example, undoubtedly wish that they could direct decisions about preservation of the environment. Instead, they must deal with governments that are often controlled by selfish economic interests. Cancer and AIDS researchers must continually plead for charitable contributions in order to find cures for those diseases despite fabulous wealth and prosperity in America and elsewhere. And ever since the atomic bomb was used at the end of World War Two, scientists have deplored the use of science and technology by governments for destructive purposes.

They Came to Baghdad was a very lighthearted thriller filled with "fun" characters. The heroine, Victoria Jones, was a poor-to-mediocre Cockney typist who got herself fired for imitating the boss's wife on company time and then set off for Baghdad in search of "the man she loved"—a man she had only just met and spoken to for no more than ten minutes, and whom she knew only as "Edward." Victoria's adventures in Iraq were a combination of danger and fun, and along the way we met a lot of amusing characters—Marcus Tio of the Tio Hotel who described everyone as "very nice man" or "very nice lady," a muddleheaded, forgetful archeologist, and others. By comparison, *So Many Steps to Death* is a much more serious and practically humorless book.

There is in *So Many Steps to Death* some interesting "documentation" about a changing British view of the foreign world, or perhaps Agatha Christie's own changing view of the world. The stereotypical "British person traveling abroad" is represented by Miss Hetherington, who complains that British travelers are no longer favored in foreign places as they once were. Like British travelers of the past, she continues to view foreign people—and foreign ideas—with suspicion. She comments negatively, for example, on the fact that French families have their children at the table participating in the full course meal instead of only being given "milk and biscuits, as children should," and that the French parents even allow their children to drink wine! Hilary Craven notes, however, that those French children appear to be very healthy because of it. Both women also note that the French children seem to be "very fond of their papa," which may be a statement suggesting that the French are more affectionate parents than British ones are, and that French children therefore respond with more affection for their parents than British children do. Hilary also notes that American travelers are extremely friendly and congenial whereas British travelers are apt to remain aloof and superior and, therefore, friendless when abroad.

There was probably a realization, beginning in the 1950s, that British people in the past had felt quite superior in practically every way to people of other nationalities, *and* that they really hadn't very good reasons for feeling that way. For one thing, Britain's position in the world began to decline at the beginning of the twentieth century. Its living standard during the second half of the nineteenth century was the highest in the world, since it was the most industrialized country in the world *and* it possessed a vast empire to exploit. By 1950 Britain's empire was substantially gone, its industries were antiquated by world standards, and its living standard, if not actually declining, was being outpaced by rising living standards nearly everywhere else.

Christie noted in her *Autobiography* that around the turn of the century Britain's high standard of living made it possible for any British family, if they owned a home, to get out of debt by renting out their home and going abroad to live for a while. The money one could get for renting one's home allowed one to live adequately at a "not too expensive hotel" in France for the duration and to actually improve one's financial position. Christie's own family went to live in France for a year or two while she was a child for that very reason. But by the early 1950s that was no longer possible.

So Many Steps to Death is a very interesting book but it cannot be recommended as a "first Christie experience," as it is quite atypical. Make this book one of your later Christie reads.

Hickory, Dickory, Death (1955)

(Alternate Title: *Hickory, Dickory, Dock*)

SETTING

It is late spring of 1954 or 1955. The entire story takes place in London, primarily at an international youth hostel or "boarding house" located at 26 Hickory Road. Brief scenes also occur at "Hick's," a shop in the neighborhood that sells sporting and camping goods; a neighborhood pub called The Queen's Necklace; an open-air restaurant in Regent's Park, a sandwich bar, Hercule Poirot's apartment, an office in New Scotland Yard, and a beauty salon called Sabrina Fair in the Mayfair district.

The youth hostel at 26 Hickory Road, which is the main setting, is actually two connected houses that have been thrown into one by the removal of some dividing walls on the basement and ground levels. The result is that there is a very large common room and an extra-large dining room shared by all the residents, while the upper floors remain separate and are served by separate staircases. The bedrooms of the male residents are in one section and those of the females are in the other. There must be at least two upper floors in each section, and some of the walls in the upper floors are new constructions whose purpose is the creation of a larger number of smaller bedrooms than had originally existed. Some of the bedrooms have their windows facing the street while others face a rear yard. The total number of people living in the house is somewhere between fifteen and twenty and several nationalities are represented: English, French, Dutch, West African, Egyptian, Turkish, Indian, American, Jamaican and perhaps others as well. Most of the residents are university students. There is a resident manager who has a self-contained apartment of her own, and there is also a private sitting room maintained by the owner who does not live in the house but often visits. Two cleaning women come to the house regularly, and an Italian married couple provide the meals and the waiting at table.

The "postwar period" appears to have ended, as there are none of the references to the postwar conditions of food rationing, clothing rationing and black marketeering that were noted in most of Christie's recent novels since the 1948 *There Is a Tide*. At the youth hostel there are one or two conversations between the manager and the proprietor about the cost of groceries, but we learn that the hostel manages to provide especially appetizing and plentiful meals thanks to good management, smart grocery shopping and an excellent Italian cook. At one meal the group enjoys an excellent *minestrone* followed by a dish of spaghetti and meatballs and then a chocolate "pudding." [The word "pudding" is in quotation marks because it is probably not a "pudding" in the American sense. In England the word is used in a more general sense and is often simply a synonym for the word "dessert." The "chocolate pudding" referred to is probably a kind of baked, cake-like treat that is spooned into bowls and served warm. Recall that in the 1950 *A Murder Is Announced*, chocolate was rationed and one character offered a box of "black-market" chocolates as a birthday gift. The ability of the cook at a student hostel to produce a "chocolate pudding" as a dessert for a large number of people is, therefore, a firm statement that the days of post–War food rationing are indeed history.]

We are, however, clearly in the "Cold War" period, which was first introduced in Christie's 1951 novel *They Came to Baghdad*. Among the young people living at 26 Hickory Road is at least one "card-carrying Communist" and one or two others are said to have ties with "subversive" organizations. There are two or three references to the "Communist witch hunts" in America. In addition, there is at least one reference to racism in America, which in itself may be a reference to the beginnings of the Civil Rights movement in America and the consequent publicity in Europe on the subject of American racism. At one point in the story, an American girl is threatening to leave the hostel and the proprietor, the Greek Mrs. Nicoletis, suspects that it is because of the black residents who live there. She instructs the manager, Mrs. Hubbard, to question the girl about her reasons.

"And if it is these coloured students, these Indians, these Negresses—then they can all go, you understand? The colour bar, it means everything to these Americans—and for me it is the Americans that matter—as for these coloured ones—Scram!"

She made a dramatic gesture.

"Not while I'm in charge," said Mrs. Hubbard coldly. "And anyway, you're wrong. There's no feeling of that sort here amongst the students, and Sally certainly isn't like that. She and Mr. Akibombo have lunch together quite often, and nobody could be blacker than he is."

"Then it is Communists—you know what the Americans are about Communists. Nigel Chapman now—he is a Communist."

"I doubt it."

"Yes, yes. You should have heard what he was saying the other evening."

Another character has this comment about Sally Finch and Americans in general:

> "That is her American way of thought. They are all the same, these Americans, nervous, apprehensive, suspecting every kind of foolish thing! Look at the fools they make of themselves with their witch hunts, their hysterical spy mania, their obsession over communism. Sally Finch is typical."

In addition to these references to American racism and fear of communism, the apparently increasing problem of jewel and drug smuggling may be considered to be a "historical background" to this novel. In the 1935 *Death in the Air*, we may recall that Chief Inspector Japp of Scotland Yard happened to be at Croydon Aerodrome investigating a drug smuggling case when the airplane bearing Hercule Poirot—and a murder victim—landed there. In the 1941 *Evil Under the Sun*, we recall that one of the characters was a drug smuggler, working on the southern coast of Devon, who received the goods from small boats sailing across the English Channel from France. Now, in *Hickory, Dickory, Death* there appears to be a smuggling operation in which drugs and diamonds are brought into England by unsuspecting travelers, and one or more of the people living at 26 Hickory Road appear to be involved.

A small point that may be of interest to readers who are less than about fifty years old: the use of fountain pens, bottles of ink and in particular the brand of ink named "Quink." We have been using ball point pens so routinely over the past several decades that few of us remember that, although introduced during the 1940s, ball point pens were extremely unreliable during their early years and did not come into general everyday use until about 1960. Before that, high school and college students never relied on ball point pens for things as important as note-taking and, especially, exam writing, because they could "go dry" without warning. Fountain pens were reliable and they were the norm for student use at least as late as about 1961 or 1962. They were a nuisance, of course. You had to fill your pen from an inkbottle in the morning. If you were lucky, and the weather was not too warm, the ink would not leak out into your shirt pocket in the course of the day. Ink stains were permanent, of course. Students often filled their pens at their lockers during passing time, and the floors in the hallways of all schools were permanently spattered with stains from bottles of ink that had fallen and broken.

If you rode in an airplane and you had foolishly placed a partially filled fountain pen in your shirt pocket beforehand, the change in atmospheric pressure in the plane usually caused the air space in the pen to expand and to force ink out of the pen and into your pocket.

"Quink" was a popular brand of ink, and "Carter's" was another. The arrival of "ink cartridge" pens around 1958 was a Godsend—you just slipped a clean new cartridge inside the pen and screwed the point back on and you had a fresh ink supply lasting several days with no ink spills. The only good thing about "those good old days" is that they were gone by about 1961 or 1962 when the first "Bic" pens and their wonderful reliability—and low prices—arrived. The first mention of a ball point pen in a Christie novel will be in the 1957 *What Mrs. McGillicuddy Saw*. Mrs. McGillicuddy will be the proud owner of one of these modern wonders.

In *Hickory, Dickory, Death*, one of the characters uses green ink routinely in his work and a certain character sabotages the study notes of a student by pouring green ink over them. Another character mentions the brand of ink named "Quink." There were several colors of ink available; black, red, green, blue-black, blue and there were certain females who favored an absurd color of Quink called "peacock blue."

STORY

It is spring of approximately 1954 or 1955. Hercule Poirot is shocked to find three errors in a letter that his efficient secretary, Miss Lemon, has just typed. This is so uncharacteristic of Miss Lemon that Poirot asks her if she is unwell. The embarrassed Miss Lemon admits that she has been distrait for some time because of concern for her sister, the widowed Mrs. Hubbard. Mrs. Hubbard has, for the past few months, been the manager of a London hostel for university students and other young people at 26 Hickory Road. At the hostel there have been some strange events—a series petty thefts and a couple of acts of minor sabotage which seem to suggest the presence in the hostel of a person who is perhaps mentally ill and even dangerous.

Poirot offers his services to assist in the solution of this somewhat minor mystery, but soon one of the young women living at the hostel dies, apparently of an overdose of a sleeping preparation. Suicide cannot be imagined, however, because she had that very day accepted a marriage proposal from a young man at the hostel and was in the best of spirits. Soon two more deaths occur. Inspector Sharpe and Hercule Poirot solve the mystery together.

CHARACTERS

Hercule Poirot, the Belgian private investigator who, now that crumpets are baked square as well as round, no longer has anything to complain of. We are again reminded of his "suspiciously black hair" and the "moustache of ferocious proportions" which he twirls contentedly. He continues to be intensely interested in psychology, and in this story he speaks of the psychology of each of the young people living at 26 Hickory Road.

Miss Felicity Lemon, Hercule Poirot's efficient secretary. She makes her first novel appearance in *Hickory, Dickory, Death,* although Christie had introduced her years earlier in short stories. Until the present story, evidently Miss Lemon had *never* made a typing error. She is the perfect secretary and is in fact "almost machinelike."

Mrs. Hubbard, Miss Lemon's sister. She is the manager of a hostel for international students in London and is eminently suited to the position, as she has lived in the East and, according to her sister Miss Lemon, "she understands racial differences and people's susceptibilities."

Mr. Hubbard, Mrs. Hubbard's deceased husband. He had been in the rubber business in Singapore for many years.

Mrs. Nicoletis, the owner of the student hostel in Hickory Road, and the owner of several other youth hostels and related enterprises. She is Greek and emotionally volatile. She is also a closet drinker.

Patricia Lane, a student of archeology. Her mother's engagement ring is stolen at the hostel. A plain-looking young woman and a very serious student, she is not Hercule Poirot's idea of an attractive female.

Valerie Hobhouse, a resident at 26 Hickory Road, but not a student. She "moves with that insolent effortless grace that is common to those who have been professional mannequins." She is a buyer for the Sabrina Fair beauty parlor and travels to Paris about once a month to purchase ladies' accessories for resale at Sabrina Fair.

Leonard ("Len") Bateson, a big, friendly young man with fiery red hair and a cockney accent. He is a medical student, and at the hostel someone steals his stethoscope.

Leonard Bateson's "Insane" Father

Mr. Gopal Ram, who is from India. He smiles at everything, and his reaction to the recent rash of thefts at the hostel is to smile and to say "material possessions do not matter."

Colin McNabb, a young doctor who is doing a post graduate course in psychiatry. He fancies himself an expert in modern psychology and habitually smiles and waves his pipe as he expounds on that subject. When Celia Austin confesses to the thefts, Colin finds her to be such an interesting case that he promises to look after her and, within twenty-four hours, even proposes marriage to her.

Sally Finch, an American girl studying English literature on a Fulbright scholarship. She is "an attractive girl with a mop of red hair and eyes that are bright and intelligent." She is the most attractive girl living at 26 Hickory Road. The thief steals an evening shoe from her.

Nigel Chapman, a history student specializing in the Bronze Age and the Medieval Period, plus Italian. He likes stirring people up and making them angry, and is flippant and sarcastic while being questioned by the police. Some of the people living at the hostel resent his spiteful tongue, but Patricia Lane, the "earnest girl in spectacles" who is studying archeology, is protective of him, almost as a mother would be.

Mr. Akibombo, a very black man from West Africa who smiles all the time and nods his curled black head. His favorite sentence is "Please, I do not understand." According to Celia Austin, he's "frightfully nice." Nothing is stolen from him, but one evening he takes bicarbonate of soda for indigestion and becomes ill from it. He takes it upon himself to have the remains of the powder in the box analyzed, with intriguing results.

Elizabeth Johnston, a black student from Jamaica. She has "the best brain of anyone" at 26 Hickory Road, according to Hercule Poirot. She is studying law and has a rather irritating way of speaking to people. If someone makes a rash statement, she says things like "I'm afraid that is not borne out by the facts. It has been well established by statistics that..."

Nothing is stolen from Elizabeth, but someone sabotages several months' worth of her study notes by pouring green ink over them.

Celia Austin, a dispenser at St. Catherine's Hospital. She also lives at 26 Hickory Road. She is described by most people as "a bit slow on the uptake." She confesses to most of the thefts, is forgiven by all and is taken on as "an interesting case" by the self-styled psychiatrist Colin McNabb, which may have been her plan all along! Colin even proposes marriage to her. What more could a girl want? So why does she commit suicide that same evening?

Celia Austin's Elderly Aunt in Yorkshire

Jean Tomlinson, a physiotherapist at St. Catherine's Hospital. She is not very well liked at the hostel because she is a bit self-righteous. According to Mrs. Hubbard, she is also a "snoop." She is "a young woman of twenty-seven with fair hair, regular features and a rather pursed-up mouth."

Mildred Carey, the senior dispenser at St. Catherine's Hospital who is a friend of Jean Tomlinson

Another Female Dispenser at St. Catherine's Hospital

Miss Baltrout, the explorer who once presented a lecture with transparencies to the students at 26 Hickory Road.

Mrs. Biggs, the cleaning lady who does the top floor bedrooms at 26 Hickory Road

Maria, the Italian cook at 26 Hickory Road. She is largely responsible for the popularity and success of the hostel, as her cooking is first-rate. She threatens to hit a policeman with her rolling pin but her husband, Geronimo, strongly advises her against it.

Geronimo, Maria's husband who waits at table and performs other duties at the hostel. He is "small and active."

A Cleaning Woman who is Deaf

Mr. Chandra Lal, a student from India in whose room the police find some subversive pamphlets.

Miss Reinjeer, who is from the Netherlands

Miss Rysdorff, whose bracelet is stolen

Mr. Ahmed Ali, an Egyptian who is "frightfully political." The police find some naughty pictures and literature in his room while searching it.

Geneviève Maricaud, a young Frenchwoman studying English in London. Her powder compact is stolen.

René Halle, a young Frenchman learning English, and a friend of Geneviève.

Two Turkish Students who took up residence at 26 Hickory Road about a week ago and who understand very little English

William Robinson, a West Indian student who was wanted by the Sheffield police for living on the earnings of a prostitute. He spent a few days at 26 Hickory Road some months ago.

Montagu Jones, a notorious young Communist agitator who came to 26 Hickory Road under a false name a few months ago. He was wanted by the police "to assist" in the matter of the murder of Alice Combe, a publican's wife, near Cambridge.

Inspector Sharpe, who is in charge of the case. He is "a big comfortable looking man with a deceptively mild manner" who "questions Mrs. Hubbard in a soft apologetic voice." Inspector Sharpe became acquainted with Hercule Poirot some years ago in the course of his investigation of "that business down at Cray's Hill," which may refer to a Christie short story (Inspector Sharpe has never appeared in a Christie novel before.)

Sergeant Cobb and **Sergeant Bell**, Inspector Sharpe's assistants.

A Constable Standing in the Hall at 26 Hickory Road

The Proprietor of Hick's, a shop near Hickory Road where sporting goods are sold. He sells a rucksack to Hercule Poirot as a gift for a spurious sporting nephew.

Dr. Coles, who examines the body of Celia Austin

Three Senior Pharmacists at St. Catherine's Hospital

The Lab Attendant at the Dispensary

An Old Woman who scrubs the floor at the Dispensary

Police Constable Bott who, while "swinging magnificently down his beat," is alerted to a lady in distress who soon dies

Sir Arthur Stanley, a famous research chemist who has recently died.

Lady Stanley, Sir Arthur's wife who died two and a half years ago

Rasputin, not a character in the story but a person who is referred to briefly. He was a historical figure of importance in the Russian Revolution. Allegedly a monk but more accurately described as a "faith healer," he was a close friend of the superstitious Empress Alexandra Fyodorovna and of her husband, Czar Nicholas II, having "cured" their only son of hemophilia. Several attempts to assassinate him, including poisoning by cyanide, failed.

An Exquisite Creature in Salmon Pink at the Sabrina Fair beauty salon.

An Equally Lovely but Slightly Older Creature at Sabrina Fair

Mrs. Lucas, the proprietor of Sabrina Fair, "a superb and resplendent Duchess"

Detective Constable McCrae, who searches a certain room at Sabrina Fair

Police Constable Nye, who takes notes as Nigel Chapman speaks at Inspector Sharpe's office.

Old Mr. Endicott, Sir Arthur Stanley's solicitor and an old friend of Hercule Poirot, who had cleared up "that nasty Abernethy business" for him some years ago. This may be a somewhat inaccurate reference to the 1953 *Funerals Are Fatal*, in which a solicitor named "Mr. Entwhistle" had appealed to Hercule Poirot to solve the mystery of a murder in the "Abernethie" family.

Countess Vera Rossakoff, not a character in the story, but an old acquaintance of Hercule Poirot who appears in his thoughts as he interviews Patricia Lane. The Countess was the only woman Poirot had ever been in love with. She was a jewel thief in an early Christie short story and then reappeared as secretary to a master criminal in the 1927 *The Big Four*, then appeared again in a later short story.

FRENCH INTO ENGLISH

Chapter 5
mais oui—certainly
autres temps, autres mœurs—different times, different customs
bon Dieu—for Heaven's sake
Ma foi—Good grief!
Mon Dieu—Oh my God!

Chapter 6
Comment donc? C'est cette petite qui m'a volé mon compact? Ah, par example! J'irais à la police. Je ne supporterais pas une pareille..."—What's this? It was that girl who stole my compact? Damn! I'd go to the police, I wouldn't tolerate such...
Mais il faut qu'elle me le rende, ce compact,"—But she's got to give that compact back to me
Viens, René, nous serons en retard—Come on, René, we'll be late
sans rancune—without a grudge

Chapter 7
poverina—poor little thing (Italian)

Chapter 8
le five o'clock—Poirot's name for afternoon tea. It was in *Mrs. McGinty's Dead* that we first learned of Poirot's aversion for afternoon tea in England because it spoils one's appetite for that major event, dinner.
mon cher—my friend
enfant terrible—an outspoken, rude child
bon Dieu—Goodness!

Chapter 13 *mon ami*—my friend

Chapter 14
Écoutez, mon cher—Listen, my friend

Mais vous êtes très bien ici—Well, you certainly must be very comfortable here

Chapter 16
Moi, je n'aime pas les flics—I don't like cops *pour ça*—for that reason

Chapter 21 *Bon Dieu!*—Oh my God!

Chapter 23 *Très bien*—Very good

COMMENTS

Hickory, Dickory, Death is an enjoyable book mostly because of the youthful and varied cast of characters. These include an enthusiastic though somewhat naïve student of psychology, a warm-hearted and generous though hot-tempered medical student, and a sarcastic, flippant history student. There are an American Fulbright scholar, a smug, self-righteous physical therapist, a brilliant law student from Jamaica, a "very political" Egyptian, and a student from India who smiles and says "material things do not matter." There are an "earnest girl with spectacles" who is studying archeology and playing "mother" to the flippant history student; an intellectually mediocre hospital dispenser who is in love with the handsome young self-styled "psychiatrist;" and a sophisticated young lady who is a buyer for an expensive fashion salon. There are a smiling curly-headed black man from West Africa who continually pleads, "Please, I do not understand," and young people from the Netherlands, France, Turkey and other places. All of this is presided over by a level-headed, middle-aged Englishwoman who likes young people and understands cultural differences, and by an emotionally unstable, closet-drinking Greek hostel owner, plus an Italian couple who prepare and serve especially tasty meals for all of the above. For the interpersonal relationships of this motley crew alone the book is absolutely delightful.

As a detective novel, however, *Hickory, Dickory, Death* has probably never been much admired. Hercule Poirot seems to arrive at "the truth" through a series of lucky guesses rather than any kind of intelligent deduction. At one point a police officer says to Poirot:

> "Really, Poirot! In the Middle Ages you would certainly have been burnt at the stake. How you can possibly know the things you do!"

And it is true that Poirot cannot possibly have "known" any of the things he has just suggested, and he doesn't even have very good reasons for suspecting them.

Christie had always presented British ethnocentrism as a negative aspect of the British culture and placed anti-foreign feelings into the minds of the less intelligent, poorly-educated characters, notably servants and military types or narrow-minded village dwellers. We recall the butler Lanscombe in the 1953 *Funerals Are Fatal* bemoaning the fact that there were "foreigners at Enderby." Lanscombe, of course, was nearly ninety years old. The cook at Enderby was a bright, twenty-seven-year-old Englishwoman who was an excellent cook and welcomed the "foreign" Hercule Poirot into her kitchen because she recognized in him a "kindred spirit" who knew what good cooking was all about.

In *Hickory, Dickory, Death* Christie comes right out and says it: foreigners are the only people who really know anything about cooking, and the Italian couple who prepare and serve meals at 26 Hickory Road are largely responsible for the success of the hostel despite its higher-than-average rates for students. In the 1950 *A Murder Is Announced*, of course, the eccentric Central European cook Mitzi was an excellent cook and baker, too, and in the 1954 *So Many Steps to Death*, restaurant meals at Casablanca and Fez had been described as "excellent."

Foreigners are also perfectly acceptable human beings in general, Christie seems to be saying, as she gathers a group of mixed nationalities at the international student hostel and portrays Elizabeth Johnston, a black law student from Jamaica, as having "the best brain of anyone" in the house. She also throws a few well-deserved darts at American racism in the words of one or two of the characters, and makes sure that the sensible Mrs. Hubbard refuses to cooperate with Mrs. Nicoletis in the matter of sending black students away from the hostel in order to accommodate a potentially racist attitude in an American resident.

There is no doubt that Christie grew up with a totally racist, white-supremacist attitude. That was natural, since she was born white and upper-middle class in 1890. In her early novels she did not hesitate to use physical traits such as eye color, hair color, skin tone, shape of forehead, shape of chin and nose in order to characterize such traits as honesty and trustworthiness in her characters. Blue eyes, in particular, were very important in men, and eyes must never be "too close together." If within the Caucasian race itself it is possible to distinguish the "better" people from the others just by the shape of their heads, the color of their eyes, and the distance between them, naturally all the rest of the races on the planet simply do not count. The "sinister, Magyar" countenances of the scoundrels in early novels such as *The Secret of Chimneys* (1925) are no longer mentioned in Christie's books, and anti–Semitic slurs disappeared in her books during the late 1930s. Now, in *Hickory, Dickory, Death,* people of black races finally qualify as fully human. Even the conservative Miss Lemon, Hercule Poirot's hideous and efficient secretary, volunteers the comment that

> "Half the nurses in our hospitals seem to be black nowadays, and I understand much pleasanter and more attentive than the English ones."

Despite this considerable "growth" on Christie's part, she will always cling to the notion that character traits are inherited. An otherwise intelligent young woman in the story affirms that "gambling is a thing you are born with" and another character fears that the "murderous instinct" of someone's father may be inherited by that person. Another character fears the thought of marriage because his father is "insane" and therefore he may transmit "insanity" to any children he might father. In the 1964 *A Caribbean Mystery,* Christie will change her mind about the notion of "inherited insanity," allowing one of her intelligent characters to state, "nobody believes that anymore," but she will never stop harping on the "fact" that personality traits are the result of blood inheritance and never the product of environment, education, and "upbringing."

There is no reason why *Hickory, Dickory, Death* should not be a "first Christie experience." Not one of Christie's best in terms of detection, it's as good as any of her novels as a pleasant reading experience with interesting characters.

Dead Man's Folly (1956)

SETTING

The story takes place in late summer and early fall and, since the novel was first published in 1956, the year of the action could be as late as 1955 or 1956. However, toward the end of the story, the detective story writer Ariadne Oliver is said to have based one of her books on the events in the case, and that Hercule Poirot read the book "three years later." If we must account for those three years, then the story must have taken place at least three years *before* 1955 or 1956. In any case, no historical events or conditions in the story prevent its taking place as early as 1952. The only historical references are a couple of remarks about Communism, the large numbers of foreigners who have settled in England since the end of World War Two, and specifically the increasing number of foreign students visiting England in the summer.

Although the "Cold War" and the general fear of nuclear war that characterized the 1950s are not specifically mentioned in the novel, there is one character—young Alec Legge—who has suffered a nervous breakdown apparently because of his frustration about "the times we live in" and the apparent apathy of society in the face of it. He is one of those deep thinkers who, because of intense feelings about large issues, cannot allow himself to enjoy small pleasures. "With two destructive world wars already having plagued the twentieth century, and the third and final World War apparently just around the corner with atomic bombs destroying civilization and two superpowers constantly at odds with each other, how can these stupid villagers waste their time and thoughts on this silly fête with its silly 'guess the weight of the cake' games and its silly fake Gypsy fortune teller and its 'murder game'?" he seems to be asking.

With the exception of one or two scenes at the apartment of Hercule Poirot in London, the entire story takes place in the county of Devon at a large country estate called Nasse House near the fictitious village of Nassecombe. Hercule Poirot travels there by train from London's Paddington Station and the distance by train is stated to be exactly two-hundred twelve miles and the trip takes three and a half hours. These specifics are made possible by the fact that Christie modeled Nasse House after Greenway House, the large Georgian period mansion in Devon that she and her second husband purchased in 1939. The Nasse House estate is a large property including a Georgian period mansion that was built in 1790 to replace a large Tudor period house that burned down in approximately 1700. The property includes a farm where a tenant family lives in a cottage. There is also a boathouse on the river, described as a "picturesque thatched affair" jutting out over the water, and this was also modeled after the boathouse at Greenway House.

In addition, the Nasse House property includes a lodge which no longer functions as a "lodge"—a cottage for the gatekeeper to live in—but which has been modernized and made more comfortable as a rental property. The former owner of Nasse House, an elderly woman impoverished by taxation, "death duties" and a diminishing income, has been forced to sell the property but lives on in the lodge thanks to the kindness of the current owners who have modernized it and made it available to her. In a future novel, the 1962 *The Mirror Crack'd,* Mrs. Bantry, whom we met in the 1942 *The Body in the Library,* will enjoy a similar situation. Now widowed, she will have sold her former home, Gossington Hall but stayed on in the modernized lodge. For further discussion about the term "lodge," see the *Appendix.*

The local residents are very gratified that, unlike many large country homes in England, Nasse House continues to be used as a family residence. By now, most large English country homes are being sold and either demolished to make way for building land or they are being converted to hotels, schools, youth hostels, hospitals, and other institutions. A neighboring estate, Hoodown Park, has in fact been converted to a youth hostel that takes in about one hundred young travelers each night, mostly foreign students.

The increasing presence of foreigners in England is a feature of this story, as it has been in a couple of Christie novels since the 1950 *A Murder Is Announced,* in which several minor characters comment on the increase in crime in England, attributing it to the "foreigners" who have come to England since the war. In that story, we recall that the first murder victim happens to be a young man from Switzerland, and he dies in a house in which the cook is a Central European refugee. In the 1955 *Hickory, Dickory, Death,* a London youth hostel serving mostly foreign students, and owned by a foreign woman, is the setting. In *Dead Man's Folly,* the large youth hostel next door to Nasse House caters mostly to foreign students touring England on a budget. When the crime takes place, a local police officer who is said to have an "ingrained prejudice against foreigners" finds it convenient to assume that one of the foreign students from the hostel has committed the crime.

The property of Nasse House is situated on the fictitious River Helm and also enjoys views of the picturesque moor country known as Dartmoor. At the point where the river empties into the English Channel there is a town aptly named Helmmouth. There are no detailed descriptions of Nasse House; it is simply described as "a gracious house, beautifully proportioned" and that the white exterior has a special beauty against its setting of green forested hills.

In general, homes of the Georgian period are characterized by simplicity of design, symmetry and sensible exterior and interior proportions. One reason for the widespread appreciation for Georgian domestic architecture is that the architecture of the period immediately following it—the Victorian period—has been very much disliked in more modern times. It was characterized by excessive ornamentation and a good many fanciful, pretentious features such as pseudo-Gothic pointed arches, stained and leaded glass to suggest medieval church windows, false battlements suggesting castle walls, and even gargoyles. Interiors featured ostentatious, grandiose, spiraling stairways, ridiculous numbers of useless rooms ("the green morning room, the white morning room, the blue morning room, the green drawing room, the white drawing room, the blue drawing room," etc.) Such homes were most often built by wealthy Victorian industrialists and were designed more for the purpose of displaying their wealth than for creating buildings with any kind of architectural beauty or even commonsense comfort. Examples of such "Victorian monstrosities" are to be found in *Murder with Mirrors, Funerals Are Fatal* and *What Mrs. McGillicuddy Saw*. The local residents of Nassecombe who are grateful that Nasse House has not been converted to a hostel or some other institution are not particularly distressed by the fact that the neighboring estate, Hoodown Park, has been converted to a youth hostel, since it is "Victorian" and, therefore, not nearly so worthy as a piece of architecture.

One make of automobile is mentioned: Hercule Poirot is met at the tiny railway station in Nassecombe—where he is the only passenger alighting at the station—by an elderly chauffeur driving a "large Humber saloon car." The chauffeur drives along several miles of narrow, twisting lanes between tall hedges, a characteristic of the county of Devon.

A minor point: the term "I.Q." must have been a new buzzword in the middle 1950s. In a conversation between two police officers on the subject of one character's intelligence, one of the officers states, "Got a low I.Q., I reckon," to which the other officer retorts:

> "Don't bring out these newfangled terms like a parrot. I don't care if she's got a high I.Q. or a low I.Q. All I care about is, is she the sort of woman who'd think it funny, or desirable, or necessary, to put a cord round a girl's neck and strangle her?"

We are again reminded of the diminishing size of the "servant class" in England, as we have been in nearly every Christie novel since the end of World War Two. In *Dead Man's Folly*, the very large Nasse House is owned by a wealthy couple, but there is no housekeeper. The secretary of the homeowner serves as a kind of "secretary-cum-housekeeper."

There is also a conversation about today's gardeners. The former head gardener at Nasse House had lived alone in the rather primitive lodge for thirty years without complaint, but the current head gardener is different, as Mrs. Folliat explains to Poirot:

> "We've got quite a young man now as head gardener, with a young wife—and these young women must have electric irons and modern cookers [stoves] and television and all that. One must go with the times—"

In other words, the "servant class"—such as it is—now expects such eccentricities as marriage. Butlers, cooks, housekeepers, maids and gardeners in the past evidently were content ("actively happy and appreciated," according to Christie in her *Autobiography*) to lead lives without marriage or sex. But today gardeners expect to be able to have wives, and the wives expect modern conveniences within reason.

Incidentally, this is the first mention of television in a Christie novel. Television was introduced in the United States in approximately 1948 and by 1955 virtually every American family owned a television set. Western Europe was about ten years behind the United States in the matter of television use, so perhaps it was a bit unusual for a gardener's wife in England to expect to own a television as early as 1955.

Evidently sex in parked cars was a relatively new development in England in the 1950s, or at least in Christie's consciousness. The local police officer, Police Constable Robert Hoskins, who is a rather provincial type with "an ingrained prejudice against foreigners," is said to spend a good deal of time peeking into parked cars in search of "sexual goings on" which he enjoys talking about while off duty at the local pub. Hoskins explains to Inspector Bland:

> "That's why I say it was a foreigner," continued Hoskins. "One of those that stop up't the Hostel at Hoodown, likely as not. There's some queer ones among them—and a lot of goings on. Be surprised, you would, at what I've seen 'em doing in the bushes and the woods! Every bit as bad as what goes on in parked cars along the Common."

Police Constable Hoskins was by this time an absolute specialist on the subject of sexual "goings on." They formed a large portion of his conversation when off duty and having his pint in the Bull and Bear.

Story

The story begins in late summer some time between about 1952 and 1956. A fête is about to take place at Nasse House, a large estate in Devon. The proceeds of the fête are to benefit some local cause, and detective story writer Ariadne Oliver is hired to create a murder game entertainment instead of the more usual treasure hunt. There are to be clues leading to a certain location where a "murder victim" will be found.

As she plans this complex game, Mrs. Oliver senses that one or more people are succeeding in causing changes in Mrs. Oliver's decisions. The person she has chosen to play the victim is changed, and so is the location of the murder site as well as other details, but it is never quite clear who the person is who is causing the changes to be made. Mrs. Oliver suspects that something is fishy and telephones her friend Hercule Poirot, asking him to come down to Devon and have a look at things.

Poirot, who has no interesting cases occupying his attention at the moment, travels to Devon and spends a day with Mrs. Oliver at Nasse House, meeting the owners of the house, wealthy Sir George and Lady Stubbs, and several of their guests. He confesses to Mrs. Oliver that he can find nothing amiss.

On the morning of the fête, however, Lady Stubbs receives a telegram from a cousin announcing that he will be visiting Nasse House that afternoon and she is very much alarmed, explaining vaguely that her cousin "does bad things." That afternoon, when the fête is in full swing, with participants numbering in the hundreds, Lady Stubbs disappears. Mrs. Oliver takes Poirot to the boat house, which is the location for the murder victim in the game to be discovered, and there they find teenaged Marlene Tucker dead. Marlene was to play the part of the murder victim in the game, but someone strangled her with the rope that was supposed to be just a prop for the game.

The police do their best to solve the mystery of Marlene's murder and Lady Stubbs's disappearance, but it is Hercule Poirot who solves the mystery.

Characters

Miss Felicity Lemon, Hercule Poirot's hideous, efficient secretary. As we recall from her description in the previous Poirot novel *Hickory, Dickory, Death*, she is the perfect secretary—almost machinelike, in fact.

Hercule Poirot, the famous Belgian private investigator with the egg-shaped head, a flamboyant moustache and an obsession for neatness. He becomes involved in this case even before the murder occurs. He is invited to Nasse House by his friend, Mrs. Ariadne Oliver, who suspects that "something is wrong" and that foul play may occur there.

Mrs. Ariadne Oliver, the famous detective novelist whom we met in two previous novels. Like Agatha Christie herself, she is fat, loves eating apples and much prefers writing to speaking. Unlike Christie, she is a lousy writer whose books are all the same except for the names of the characters, but she claims that that does not matter since the only things her readers demand are "plenty of bodies." In this story, she is hired by a wealthy family to plan a "murder game" as an entertainment for an annual charity fête. As she explains to Poirot:

> "Actually," said Mrs. Oliver ruefully, "it's all much harder to arrange than you'd think. Because you've got to allow for real people being quite intelligent, and in my books they needn't be."

A Telephone Operator with a suspicious voice who assists with Mrs. Oliver's telephone call from Nassecombe, Devon to Hercule Poirot's flat in London.

A Porter at the railway station in Nassecombe who does not carry Hercule Poirot's suitcase because he is busy in a baggage compartment

Mitchell, the Stubbs's uniformed chauffeur of Olympian aloofness who meets Hercule Poirot at Nassecombe's tiny railway station in the family's large Humber saloon car.

A Dutch Girl and An Italian Girl perspiring and carrying heavy rucksacks on their backs. Mitchell, the chauffeur mentioned above, obtains Poirot's permission to give them a lift for a short distance.

Hendon, the Stubbs's tall, black-haired butler

Sir George Stubbs, the wealthy new owner of Nasse House. He has no actual title; he was christened "Sir George" by his parents. According to Ariadne Oliver, he is "Rich and plebeian and frightfully stupid outside business, I should think, but probably dead sharp in it."

Sir George is another in a long line of Christie "self made men" who have money but no education, culture or taste.

Lady Stubbs (Hattie), Sir George's young wife. Originally from the West Indies, she is beautiful but extremely stupid, even "half-witted" in the opinion of several people.

Michael Weyman, a handsome young architect who is employed by Sir George Stubbs for certain improvements and additions to Nasse House. He feels frustrated by Sir George's silly ideas about repairing the Folly instead of rebuilding it in a more sensible place, and about building a tennis pavilion styled as a kind of Chinese pagoda simply because Lady Stubbs fancies herself in Chinese "coolie" hats.

Miss Amanda Brewis, Sir George Stubbs's devoted secretary who, Poirot believes, is in love with Sir George. She is a sort of secretary-housekeeper who runs things and writes letters—very grim and efficient. Miss Brewis clearly does not like Hattie Stubbs, at one point describing her as a sly, scheming, clever cat.

Alec Legge, a young "atom scientist," according to Mrs. Ariadne Oliver. He is an intensely serious person who has allowed his "worry about these times we live in" to cause him a nervous breakdown. The constant threat of nuclear war and the East-West rivalry are some of the things that plague him. Upon his doctor's advice, he and his wife have come to Nassecombe and rented a cottage for three months so that he can enjoy rest and relaxation. So far the "country" experience does not seem to be doing him very much good. Upon meeting Hercule Poirot he immediately criticizes the fête because, to him, it is so trivial.

> "Why can't people have some *sense?* Why can't they think? Think of the mess the whole world has got itself into. Don't they realise that the inhabitants of the globe are busy committing suicide?"

Peggy Legge, Alec's wife, "an attractive freckled redhead." Like her husband, she is very intelligent and has a university education. She is becoming weary of her husband's "moods" and there are rumors that she is falling in love with Michael Weyman, whom she had actually known before marrying her husband Alec. At the fête she plays the part of Madame Zuleika, the fortune teller.

Captain Jim Warburton, the agent—perhaps a kind of glorified secretary—of the politically active Mastertons.

Wilfrid Masterton, the local Member of Parliament and a friend of Sir George Stubbs and Mrs. Folliat

Connie Masterton, Wilfred Masterton's wife, "a somewhat monumental woman who reminded Poirot faintly of a bloodhound. She had a full underhung jaw and large, mournful, slightly bloodshot eyes." Mrs. Masterton is an assertive, effective organizer and is largely responsible for the planning and direction of the fête.

Amy Folliat, the last of the Folliats. She lost her husband and both of her sons in the war, and then taxation, death duties and a diminishing income forced her to sell the family home, Nasse House. She continues to live "at home," however, for she rents the lodge of her former home from its current owner, Sir George Stubbs.

Old Squire Folliat, Amy Folliat's father-in-law, deceased for many years.

Major Folliat, Old Squire Folliat's son and Amy Folliat's husband. He cared for nothing but horses—and the bottle.

Henry Folliat, Amy Folliat's elder son

James Folliat, Amy Folliat's younger son, who according to Amy was killed in the Commandos, but Old Merdell offers a slightly expanded description of him:

> "...but Mr. James, he caused her a lot of trouble. Debts and women it were, and then, tu, he were real wild in his temper. Born one of they as can't go straight. But the war suited him, as yu might say—give him his chance. Ah! There's many who can't go straight in peace who dies bravely in war."

Marlene Tucker, a fourteen-year-old granddaughter of Old Merdell, who lives with her parents and two younger siblings in a cottage on the farm at Nasse House. She plays the part of the murder victim in the murder game at the fête. Unfortunately she is actually murdered—strangled with the rope that was supposed to be only a prop in the game. She is (or *was*) an unattractive youngster who compensated for her failure to interest the boys by paying too much attention to other people's private lives.

Old Merdell, a very old man (age ninety-three) with rheumy eyes, the father of Mrs. Tucker, and the grandfather of Marlene. He operates a ferry across the river Helm, and it is he who provides Hercule Poirot with information about Mrs. Folliat's father, husband and two sons. A few days later, he falls into the river and drowns, having had a bit too much to drink. Or is he pushed into the river?

Jim Tucker, Marlene's father, who works at Peterson's farm and lives in a cottage on the Nasse House estate with his wife and two remaining children. He is a large, red-faced man with a pacific expression.

Mrs. Tucker, Marlene's mother and the daughter of "Old Merdell." She is a thin, hatchet-faced woman with stringy blond hair and a sharp nose. She shares Police Constable Hoskins's ingrained prejudice against foreigners and believes that one of the foreign students from the nearby youth hostel murdered her daughter.

Gary Tucker, Marlene Tucker's younger brother

Marylin Tucker, Marlene Tucker's younger

sister who is fat and mischievous. As Poirot leaves the Tuckers' cottage after interviewing her parents, Marylin calls to him from the shadow of the cottage wall, and provides him with some information about Marlene that her parents were not aware of, in exchange for five shillings.

Miss Bird, Marylin's teacher who says it's no good Marylin's trying for the grammar school

Mr. Benson at the Golf Club who was so kind about the extra putters for the clock golf

Betsey Trotwood, an unforgettable character in Dickens's *David Copperfield*. David, wandering through the countryside, first encounters her as she is shooing donkeys out of her flower garden. Kind Aunt Betsey takes David in and cares for him, her first act of care being a thorough washing. She is mentioned in a conversation in the story.

Merdell, the former head gardener at Nasse House who lived in the lodge for thirty years. He was Old Merdell's eldest son and therefore the eldest brother of Mrs. Tucker. He was the eldest of eleven children, in fact.

The Current Head Gardener at Nasse House whose young wife expects such niceties as electric irons, modern stoves and television

Étienne de Sousa, a cousin, or perhaps a second cousin, of Lady Stubbs from the West Indies. He arrives in a launch from his yacht, which is moored at Helmmouth, on the afternoon of the fête but finds that his cousin has disappeared. He is a very dark young man, faultlessly attired in yachting costume. One of the police officers working on the case, Police Constable Hoskins, would like nothing better than for the murderer of Marlene Tucker to be Étienne de Sousa, since he is a foreigner, but no evidence can be found against him.

Marylin Gale, a minor film star who opens the fête at Nasse House.

Pamela and Edward from Tiverton, Dorothy and her Husband, Mr. and Mrs. Knapper and Their Daughter Lucy, Muriel and Reggie, and Edward's Boy Roger, all friends of Mrs. Folliat who attend the fête and are greeted by her as though she were still the mistress of Nasse House.

Madame Zuleika, a.k.a. Peggy Legge, the fortune teller at the fête

A Determined Woman at the fête who makes Poirot pay sixpence to guess the weight of a cake

A Fat Motherly Woman presiding at the Hoopla stall

Violet, a little girl to whom Poirot gives a Kewpie doll he has won in some game at the fête

Violet's Mother

A Young Man Wearing a Turtle Shirt who, stepping backwards to take a better aim at a coconut at the fête, cannons into Hercule Poirot and scowls. The young man, still wearing his turtle shirt, makes an unexplained appearance at the Folly on the day after the fête.

A Determined Old Lady at the Fancy Goods stall who tries to sell Poirot a plastic collar box

An Old Gentleman of Military Aspect who is fast asleep on a garden seat near the tennis court

A Young Man in Shorts with a Prominent Adam's Apple, Freckles and a Yorkshire Accent who is the first to discover the second clue in the murder game.

Two Young Women Touring the Grounds of Nasse House who complain of not enough flowers and too many trees

Detective Inspector Bland, who is in charge of the case of Marlene Tucker's death and Lady Stubbs's disappearance. He is usually at odds with Police Constable Hoskins who persists in believing that a foreigner must be responsible for everything.

Police Constable Robert Hoskins, a local man with a gossipy wife. He is just as gossipy as she and enjoys talking about the sexual goings-on that he has observed in parked cars and in the bushes around the youth hostel. He has an ingrained prejudice against foreigners and is sure a foreigner is responsible for the death of Marlene Tucker and the disappearance of Lady Stubbs.

Sergeant Frank Cottrill, a brisk young man with a good opinion of himself, who always manages to annoy his superior officer. Inspector Bland much prefers the rural wisdom of Hoskins to the smart know-all attitude of Frank Cottrill.

Sergeant Cottrill attends to the removal of the body after the medical examination, and then interviews Lady Stubbs's maid.

Sergeant Farrell and Police Constable Lorimer, other police officers assisting in the case. They search the grounds in an attempt to find some trace of Lady Stubbs.

Hodgson, who is scheduled to come and discuss with Sir George the electrification of the milking sheds on the farm.

Superintendent Baldwin of the Helmmouth Police Station, with whom Inspector Bland examines a "black sodden mass" which proves to be the Chinese coolie style hat that Lady Stubbs had worn on the day of the fête.

Otterweight, an ex-coastguard man whom Superintendent Baldwin consults about tides and currents.

Policewoman Alice Jones, an excellent swimmer, who assists in a police experiment near the boathouse at Nasse House

Major Merrall, Detective Inspector Bland's

superior and the Chief Constable of the County of Devon

Arthur Hastings, an old friend of Hercule Poirot whom we have not met since the 1937 *Poirot Loses a Client.* He is not a character in this story, but Poirot recalls with fondness that Hastings often provided him with ideas, just as Mrs. Ariadne Oliver does in the present story.

A Girl of the Underground Criminal World in Trieste

French into English

Chapter 1
Du tout!—Absolutely not!
Magnifique!—Magnificent!
Grazie—(Italian) Thank you
Très bien, chère Madame—Very well, dear lady
chef d'œuvres—masterpieces

Chapter 4 *Pardon*—Forgive me

Chapter 6 *Voilà*—Here

Chapter 9 *espèce de gala*—a sort of party

Chapter 11 *mon cher*—my friend

Chapter 12
Les femmes—Women
femme formidable—a woman to be reckoned with

Chapter 13 *Eh bien*—Well, now...

Chapter 16 *Mais oui*—Certainly

Chapter 17 *Épatant*—Tremendous!

Comments

Dead Man's Folly, like all of Christie's detective novels, has something unique. The uniqueness in this case is that Hercule Poirot arrives on the scene before any crime is committed, having been summoned there by his friend Ariadne Oliver because she "has a feeling" that something is wrong.

The case is particularly difficult to solve because nobody can imagine any motive for the killing of a teenage girl. Hercule Poirot, however, is a much more careful listener than the police are and he solves the case not by dwelling on tangible clues or by disproving lies or alibis, but by listening and remembering details. He compares the solution of this crime to the correct assembling of the pieces in a jigsaw puzzle. In Christie's previous detective novel, *Hickory, Dickory, Death,* Poirot did some wild guessing and that was the only way he "solved" the mystery. Christie essentially admitted that fact when, in one of the final chapters, one character told Poirot that in the Middle Ages he would have been burned as a witch for the way he was able to "know" the solution. In *Dead Man's Folly,* that is not the case. Everything that Poirot makes use of in solving the mystery is plainly expressed in the course of the story and a reader using Poirot's method of piecing facts together should be able to solve it as well.

There is one annoying aspect of the book that has never occurred before in a Christie detective novel. At least two or three of the characters are unrealistically free in their comments about other characters in the presence of Hercule Poirot, who is a perfect stranger to them. A devoted secretary may be jealous of her boss's wife, or she may simply dislike or even hate her, but she does not normally verbalize those feelings in private conversations with outsiders, least of all with her employer's houseguests. In this story, the secretary Amanda Brewis, despite the fact that Hercule Poirot is a houseguest whom she has never met before, and for no reason at all, expresses to Poirot that her employer's wife is "a sly, scheming, clever cat" and is much more intelligent than she pretends to be.

If a murder had taken place and Poirot or the police were pressing members of a household to reveal private feelings or perceptions about other people in the household, they would explain the reasons for their questions and perhaps—and only perhaps—they would be made aware of certain private perceptions. In this case, however, no murder has taken place (yet!), and Miss Brewis's comments to Hercule Poirot are frankly uncalled for and inappropriate. If Poirot had gone to Sir George and reported Miss Brewis's comments about Lady Stubbs, Miss Brewis would probably have been fired on the spot. Miss Brewis has no reason at all for feeling that Poirot would keep his lips sealed on the subject of her comments.

Another person in the story who speaks negatively to Poirot about other characters is Old Merdell, the man who operates the ferry across the River Helm. He knows nothing at all about Hercule Poirot, other than the fact that Poirot is a houseguest at Nasse House, but he volunteers facts and perceptions about the Folliat family that he would not dare to offer if he thought there was a chance Poirot would report his words to Amy Folliat.

Without being asked, Mrs. Masterton tells Poirot that she thinks there is something "fishy" about Jim Harburton. She also tells him that Sir George is not really "Sir George." Yet this woman, who is the wife of a Member of Parliament, is described as having more political acumen than her husband! A younger sister of the fourteen-year-old murder victim volunteers facts about her sister in private to Poirot apparently without fear that the word will get round to her parents and that she may find herself in deep trouble because of it. When Poirot offers her five shillings in exchange for more facts, she provides more facts.

All of these "facts" and "opinions" that are volunteered to Poirot are important to him in solving the case, but they could have—and should have—come to him in more believable ways. This may be the first suggestion that Christie's decline as a writer is approaching.

In general, the characters in *Dead Man's Folly* are not particularly interesting or memorable, and the characterizations are sketchy. The only character who is very interesting or unique is Alec Legge. He has had a nervous breakdown and his doctor has advised him to retreat to the country for rest and relaxation. The reason for his "nervous breakdown" is not some personal or family problem such as worry about employment or money, or any problem with interpersonal relationships. He is simply a very intelligent man, a scientist and a deep thinker, who sees the direction the modern world is taking and is intensely alarmed and angered by it. From his remark "Don't people see that the inhabitants of the planet are committing suicide?" we can deduce that he is upset by the fact that, ever since the end of World War Two, the world seems to be headed towards a third—and final—war. Every year seems bring faster and better warplanes, more sophisticated weapons, and bigger and more destructive bombs. Alec is not worried about himself, or about his family, or about his job, or about England or about democracy. He is worried about The World. He uses the term "apathy" to describe the atmosphere not only in England but everywhere. He has a very intelligent wife but even she seems to be telling him "Why worry about it? There's nothing anyone can do about it."

These "worldwide" worries came into existence during the 1950s as a result of fear of nuclear warfare. In earlier times, the people of one nation may have "worried" about the evil intentions and power of a rival nation, but there was probably never a feeling that there was anything "wrong" about weapons and war in general.

One's country needed weapons for defense because another country might attack. Wars occurred because there were "aggressor nations" that attacked their neighbors. But in the 1950s all the talk about nuclear war and the futility of it—all the talk about "anti-ballistics missiles" and "anti-anti-ballistics missile missiles" and "anti-anti-anti-ballistics missile missile missiles" showed thinking people that all of this increasingly destructive weaponry was going nowhere but to hell. Politicians and governments seemed to be ignorant and helpless to end the madness. The only people who seemed to see the madness for what it was were the scientists themselves—those who were technically responsible for the advancement of weaponry but had no control over the use of weapons. Alec Legge is one of the sensitive, frustrated scientists who see the madness of the modern world and are bitterly angry about the apathy of populations that allow the madness to go on.

In the 1954 thriller *So Many Steps to Death*, Christie introduced the idea of scientists in every country who were frustrated by lack of money for research, or by government meddling, or by government exploitation of scientific advancement and discovery, etc. In that story there is a kind of "Pax Scientifica" mentioned as a possibility if scientists, rather than dictators and capitalists and communists, can be in control of the world. Under the "Pax Scientifica" there would be scientific advancements only for benign purposes. Alec Legge would have been one of the enthusiastic—or shall we say idealistic—young men who would gladly put patriotism aside in the interest of a "world community" in which there would be no politics, no national rivalry and no threats of war. Since that seems to be impossible, Alec is terribly unhappy.

Alec Legge is probably the only character in *Dead Man's Folly* who is likely to be remembered after one reads the novel. With the exception of the amusingly silly detective story writer Ariadne Oliver, with her silly hairdos and silly clothes and silly remarks about her awful books, there is no humor in this book. The novel is probably not often favored with re-readings by Christie fans, but it is not an unpleasant reading experience.

Christie puts some amusing personal opinions about young people's clothing tastes into the words and thoughts of Hercule Poirot and other characters. When she wrote *Dead Man's Folly*, she was about sixty-five years old, but even as early as the 1948 *There Is a Tide* she has Poirot agreeing with the wife of Canon Leadbetter on the subject of shorts for women, when Mrs. Leadbetter comments that most young women would not wear shorts if they realized how they looked in them from behind. In *Dead Man's Folly* there are negative comments about young men wearing shirts with fanciful printed designs on them (one young man wears a shirt with a variety of turtles and other reptiles crawling all over it) and another young man actually wears shorts! And two girl hikers wear shorts, exposing red thighs and "having no idea of how to dress in a way that is attractive to the opposite sex," in Hercule Poirot's opinion.

Once again we are reminded of Agatha Christie's negative attitude towards the "self-made man," that is, a man who has worked all his life and, through his own efforts, has *become* rich rather than having been *born* rich. Invariably such men are portrayed by Christie as crude, rough, uneducated and lacking in appreciation of the finer things in life, and they believe that money can buy anything. In chronological order, they have been:

Julius P. Hersheimer in the 1922 *The Secret Adversary*. Technically it was his father, and not he, who became rich in the American oil business, but Julius clearly was brought up to believe that money can buy anything. He suggests that, "if there is such a thing as graft in England," he has plenty of money to get his cousin Jane out of any legal problems that may be facing her. At a later point in the story, he points a gun at a certain scoundrel and threatens to kill him. The scoundrel points out that if Julius commits murder he will hang, but Julius laughs and says, "You're forgetting the dollars!" and explains that instead of imprisonment or death, his penalty will be to spend a few months in a psychiatric hospital being "cured" and then to be released. Because of his money, of course.

The next is Roger Ackroyd in the 1926 *The Murder of Roger Ackroyd*. The narrator of that novel, a country doctor, tells us that Roger became rich "through the manufacture of (I think) wagon wheels." In other words, he got rich by manufacturing something too trivial to remember.

In the 1927 *The Big Four* we have a particularly nasty American millionaire, Abe Ryland, allegedly the richest man in the world who is also one of four "master criminals."

In the 1928 *The Mystery of the Blue Train* there is Rufus Van Aldin, the second richest man in the world (an American, of course.) He buys his daughter's love by giving her a set of fabulously expensive and historic rubies (once worn by Catherine the Great, no less) and then tries to throw a hundred thousand pounds at his son-in-law in exchange for not contesting his daughter's petition for divorce.

In the 1929 *The Seven Dials Mystery* there is Sir Oswald Coote who got rich in the steel business. He shows off his wealth by renting the largest and most ostentatious homes in England that he can find. In the story he is renting Chimneys, the ancestral home of Lord Caterham. Lord Caterham's daughter, Lady Eileen Brent, regards Sir Oswald as "a stupid man to whom a hundred pleasures and appreciations, which her father enjoys, are unknown."

In the 1937 *Death on the Nile,* Meluish Ridgeway was an American millionaire who ruined several other men in business through his ruthless, unscrupulous business practices. His daughter Linnet is a selfish young woman who buys a historic mansion in England and proceeds to ruin it with modernizations, including an outdoor swimming pool, and then has three cottages torn down because they would have views of the swimming pool, without regard for the wishes or feelings of the occupants of the cottages. She is thoroughly detested locally. Intelligent, beautiful, rich and thoroughly spoiled, she then steals the fiancé of her best friend, Jacqueline de Bellefort, a poor girl who has nothing in life except the beloved fiancé.

In the 1938 *A Holiday for Murder* we have Simeon Lee, a shriveled-up old man who got rich first by prospecting for diamonds and then by inventing a special tool for use in diamond mining. He torments his offspring by telling them that he probably has hundreds of illegitimate children around the world, every one of them worth more than his legitimate children. His Christmas gift to them is to gather them all together into his room for no other purpose but to insult each one of them in each other's presence, and then to tell them all to get out of his sight.

In the 1939 *Easy to Kill* we have the obnoxious Gordon Easterfield who got rich through the ownership of several trashy weekly newspapers and feels that he has a major responsibility in the shaping of public opinion through his publications. His favorite topic of conversation is Gordon Easterfield. For the purpose of displaying his wealth and importance, he purchased a perfectly fine Queen Anne period home, Wych Manor, and then added false façades and stone towers to make it look like a castle. A visitor to Wych Manor is "stupefied by the appalling and incongruous castellated mass" of the house.

In the 1941 *Evil Under the Sun* we have Horace Blatt whose idea of a good time is talking about himself and his successful hardware business.

In the 1949 *Crooked House* we have Aristide Leonides who became rich through a number of different businesses and enterprises that were always "just inside the law." He is described by the police as a "twister;" never doing anything that was technically illegal, but always figuring out ways to "get around the law." He built, in approximately 1900, a ridiculous mansion, Three Gables. A police officer's first impression of Three Gables is that it should have been named "Eleven Gables" and that it looks like a picturesque cottage swollen all out of proportion, as if it had "grown like a mushroom overnight."

In the 1952 *Murder with Mirrors,* the setting is a preposterously huge Victorian Gothic mansion called Stonygates. It was built by a rich Victorian ironmonger and, originally, the house had "no fewer than fourteen living rooms." A character in the story describes it as "a kind of temple to Plutocracy."

In the 1953 *A Pocket Full of Rye*, Rex Fortescue is another "twister"—the owner of an investment firm, many of whose business dealings have been just short of illegal.

In the 1953 *Funerals Are Fatal,* a Victorian businessman, Cornelius Abernethie, had gotten rich by making corn plasters and other foot-care products. He built a huge Victorian Gothic mansion called Enderby, which is described by one character as "...hideous. An almost indecent temple to wealth."

Now, in the 1956 *Dead Man's Folly* we have Sir George Stubbs, who is described by at least one character as "a self-made man and a complete vulgarian."

In Christie's next novel, the 1957 *What Mrs. McGillicuddy Saw,* there will be the Victorian millionaire Josiah Crackenthorpe, who made a fortune by manufacturing biscuits and relishes and built an ugly Victorian mansion, Rutherford Hall, in 1884. Finally, in the 1976 *Sleeping Murder* (which Christie wrote during the 1940s intending it to be published after her death) there will be Jackie Afflick, a self-made man who owns a fleet of touring busses, drives a garish daffodil-yellow sports car and boasts about his wife's titled relatives.

Christie also reminds us, once again, that the "lower classes" consist primarily of over-productive, semi-animal creatures. In *Dead Man's Folly,* Marlene Tucker's farming parents have produced nine children, and her mother is proud to declare that she herself is one of eleven siblings. In the 1952 *Mrs. McGinty's Dead,* Mr. and Mrs. Kiddle have a new baby plus two bratty older children who torture cats, and Hercule Poirot finds it difficult to believe that this "filthy stronghold of haphazard fecundity was just a short time ago the spotless home of the house-proud Mrs. McGinty." In the 1939 *Easy to Kill* the mother of the bratty pre-teen Tommy Pierce—who liked cutting up wasps and twisting little boys' arms, and then fell to his death while washing upper-story windows at the local library—is able, according to our amateur sleuth and narrator Luke Fitzwilliam, to console herself with "six other little blessings."

Large families are not always the product of the ignorant poor in Christie novels, however. After all, the self-made millionaire in the 1953 *Funerals Are Fatal,* Cornelius Abernethie, who got rich by manufacturing corn plasters and other foot-care products, found time to father seven children. And lest we forget, in the 1949 *Crooked House,* the Greek restaurateur Aristide Leonides fathered eight children. But then, both of these men were "self-made men," so what else could one expect? No doubt they "inherited," through blood, their "haphazard fecundity," and probably the same was true of Simeon Lee, in the 1938 *A Holiday for Murder,* who got rich prospecting for diamonds and fathered legions of illegitimate children (or so he claimed).

In the discussion of the 1948 *There Is a Tide* it was mentioned that Christie had introduced, in that novel, the idea that men who serve well in war time are often not very good citizens in peacetime. They are people who are fearless and, therefore, untrustworthy in civilian life—people who can be counted on in wartime not to lose their nerve, to embark with gusto on dangerous missions, but who in civilian life might embark with equal gusto on dangerous acts of criminal behavior. In that novel it is David Hunter who is described by a police officer as that kind of person, and the protagonist, Lynn Marchmont, recognizes David to be "a type she had known often in service"—the type of man who is worth his weight in gold while in a tight spot but whom one couldn't depend on when out of the firing line—"men who made their own laws and flouted the universe."

Christie reintroduced this idea in several subsequent novels. In the 1951 *They Came to Baghdad,* Edward Goring had enjoyed success in the Royal Air Force during the war, but now that he must work in an office in the city, he is bored and, frankly, not very competent. He explains that "you didn't have to be brainy to do well in the air force." In the 1953 *A Pocket Full of Rye,* Patricia Fortescue describes her first husband Don, who was a fighter pilot during the war and who was killed in action, in similar terms. She believes that, though a hero in wartime, he could not have functioned in the post-war civilian society, and so it was just as well that he was killed. Now, in the 1956 *Dead Man's Folly,* Old Merdell describes Amy Folliat's younger son James as having been more or less a wastrel before the war, but the war "gave him a chance" and he redeemed himself by dying for his country. In the 1957 *What Mrs. McGillicuddy Saw* there will be Bryan Eastley, a Squadron Leader in the Royal Air Force during the war who will find it difficult to adjust to the tameness of civilian life afterwards. And in the 1965 *At Bertram's Hotel* there will be Michael Gorman who won several medals during the war but who can find nothing to do in civilian life except to be a hotel doorman.

What Mrs. McGillicuddy Saw (1957)

(Alternate Titles: *4:50 from Paddington* and *Murder, She Said!*)

Setting

The story takes place in December and January of approximately 1956–1957. Specifically the action begins on December 20 and ends about five weeks later. There are two brief scenes in Paris. One is at the Préfecture de Police in Paris where an English police officer visits a French colleague to discuss certain aspects of the case, and the other is at a theatre where the police question the director of a ballet company. There is a brief scene at a home in Ceylon (now known as Sri Lanka.) There are also several London settings, including the English policeman's office at New Scotland Yard, the flat of an unmarried man, the office and the home of a wealthy businessman, the office of an attorney, and Paddington Railway Station. There are scenes at the railway stations in the fictitious towns of Brackhampton, about forty minutes by train from Paddington, and Milchester, an hour and a quarter further west along the same line.

The novel features Miss Jane Marple as the sleuth. Miss Marple has always resided in a village called St. Mary Mead, and the nearest city of importance to it is the fictitious Milchester, nine miles distant. The name of the county in which St. Mary Mead is located varies from story to story. The fictitious "Downshire" is given as the county in one novel; the fictitious "Radfordshire" is named in another. In still another, we must assume that St. Mary Mead is in the real county of Berkshire, since it is near Market Basing, and that town is stated to be in Berkshire in still another novel.

In *What Mrs. McGillicuddy Saw*, we must assume that Christie has placed Milchester and St. Mary Mead considerably further west in England than in the previous stories. In the opening chapter Mrs. McGillicuddy, a friend of Miss Marple, travels by train from London's Paddington Station to Milchester and the trip takes nearly two hours. Mrs. McGillicuddy falls asleep just a few minutes after the train leaves Paddington, awakening thirty-five minutes later to witness a murder taking place in another train which is running alongside at the same speed in the same direction. An hour and five minutes later, the lady alights from the train at Milchester Station. From these facts we must deduce that Milchester must be located not in Berkshire but in some county further west, perhaps Gloucestershire. The train then continues westward to its eventual terminus at Cardiff in Wales.

The major setting, however, is a large, ugly Victorian mansion called Rutherford Hall, which was built in 1884 by a successful industrialist. When first built, it was on the outskirts of the fictitious Brackhampton, then a rather small town, but over the years Brackhampton has grown and a new railway line has been built. The owner and builder of Rutherford Hall, who died in 1928, had refused to sell any of the property surrounding the house, and so the town gradually grew up around it, with the railway line actually encircling about half of the property. This fact is important because at the beginning of the story, a few minutes before a passenger train reaches Brackhampton, a murder takes place in one of the cars of the train, and for certain reasons Miss Marple deduces that the body of the victim must have been thrown from the train as it was traveling along the edge of the Rutherford Hall property.

On the subject of passenger cars in English trains, it is important to understand what Miss Marple and Mrs. McGillicuddy mean when they use the term "corridor car." The usual European passenger car is divided into compartments seating six to eight passengers each. A narrow corridor runs along the length of the car on one side, and each compartment has a door, usually a sliding one, through which passengers may leave the compartment and walk along the corridor to go to the rest room at the end of the car, or to pass into another car en route to the dining car. Conductors and ticket collectors also walk through the corridor, stopping at each compartment to collect tickets, etc. However, certain English trains also had "non-corridor cars." These cars were also divided into compartments, but there was no corridor. Instead, each compartment had a door that opened directly to the outside of the train. One entered the compartment directly from the station platform, and once the train was in motion, it was impossible for anyone to leave the compartment. It was also impossible, of course, for train personnel such as conductors to enter compartments while the train was in motion. Ticket collecting, etc. therefore always took place while the train was standing in a station.

These facts are important because the murder that Mrs. McGillicuddy witnesses takes place in a compartment of a "non-corridor" car. The murderer knew, therefore, that there was no chance of a conductor or another passenger entering the compartment or witnessing the crime, since there was no corridor, and the murderer also knew that he could throw the body from the train through the compartment door with nobody else on the train seeing it. The murderer could not predict, however, that at the moment he was committing the crime, another train might be running alongside in the same direction and at the same speed, and that a person in the second train might see the crime taking place through the windows.

We know that Christie despised the domestic architecture favored by wealthy industrialists of the Victorian period, and so it is no surprise that Rutherford Hall is negatively described. It is one of those "castellated abominations" built by Victorian millionaires as advertisements of their wealth, and its appearance is that of a kind of miniature Windsor Castle. Both the house and the property have been neglected for some years. The interior of the house is described simply as "a vast and uncomfortable mansion." The kitchen is enormous, with a vast kitchen range standing cold and neglected, an Aga standing beside it. [Note: Aga is the brand name of a modern, deluxe cooking range made in England.]

Although Rutherford Hall is vast, only the current owner, a man in his seventies, and his daughter, an unmarried woman in her late thirties, live there. They have no live-in servants. A woman comes in five mornings a week, and another woman comes in three afternoons a week to do heavy cleaning. The daughter of the old man does a good deal of the housework herself.

The house, built in 1884, replaced a much older house dating from Elizabethan times which was demolished in order to build the present one. But there are numerous outbuildings surviving from the earlier period, all very much neglected and in various stages of disrepair and ruin. These include the gardener's cottage, old pigsties, stables and a "Long Barn" which, according to the present owner, dates from Elizabethan times, although other characters dispute this claim. In the "Long Barn" is stored a large collection of statues and other artworks purchased in Italy and elsewhere by the present owner. One of these artworks is a Greco–Roman sarcophagus in which the body of a murdered woman is discovered.

Although the grounds of Rutherford Hall are extensive, they are practically surrounded by the city of Brackhampton, which has grown enormously over the past twenty years. Views through the windows of the house appear to be views of the open countryside, but when the windows are open during warm weather, the city traffic is clearly audible, as are the rumblings of frequent trains passing along the railway line that encircles half of the property.

There are no current events mentioned in the story, but there are a few amusing details reflecting contemporary thoughts and interests. When the elderly lady riding in the train reports having seen a murder in another train running alongside, the police are reluctant to believe her, and one officer comments to another:

"Whether she's barmy or not, I don't know, but she sticks to her story. As far as all that goes, I dare say it's just make believe—sort of thing old ladies do make up, like seeing flying saucers at the bottom of the garden, and Russian agents in the lending library…"

The term "UFO" was coined during the 1940s or 1950s and we may recall a steady stream of Grade-B science fiction films during that period which featured invaders from other planets arriving in flying saucers. The witness to the crime had just done her Christmas shopping in London, and one of the gifts is a "space gun" for a child relative. Two adolescent boys in the story are avid readers of "space fiction." The reference to "Russian agents" is a reference to the Cold War and its hysteria about Communist infiltration. Jet airplanes are mentioned for the first time in a Christie novel; a new airport has been established near St. Mary Mead and jet planes "breaking the sound barrier" fly overhead, on one occasion causing two panes of glass in Miss Marple's greenhouse to shatter.

When this novel was first published, capital punishment had not yet been abolished in Britain, but there was evidently discussion in progress on that subject. At the end of the novel, when the murderer (represented below by "X") is unmasked, Miss Marple comments:

"Everything X did was bold and audacious and cruel and greedy, and I am really very, very glad," finished Miss Marple, looking as fierce as a fluffy old lady can look, "that they haven't abolished capital punishment yet because I do feel that if there is anyone who ought to hang, it's X."

The term "ball point pen" occurs for the first time in a Christie novel; Mrs. McGillicuddy is the proud owner of one of these convenient new luxuries. We may recall that in the 1955 *Hickory, Dickory, Death* the students living at the youth hostel in London routinely used fountain pens, and a bottle of ink of a certain color figures prominently in the story.

Several makes of automobile are mentioned in the story: a "big hired Daimler" which takes the Crackenthorpe family to and from the inquest; a small MG car owned by a male character, and a Humber Hawk owned by another. One wealthy family owns a Mercedes Benz and a Rolls-Royce. The doctor in the story drives "a battered Austin," a low priced and very popular make.

The subject of taxation is never far away in Christie's post–World War Two novels. The following cynical remark is made by the elderly owner of Rutherford Hall to his son Cedric who will one day inherit Rutherford Hall:

> "Taxation! Don't talk to me of those robbers. A miserable pauper, that's what I am. And it's going to get worse, not better. You wait, my boy," he addressed Cedric, "when you get this place ten to one the Socialists will have it off you and turn it into a Welfare Center or something. And take all your income to keep it up with!"

The shortage of domestic labor—and actually just about any "labor" since the end of the Second World War—is another theme that is rarely absent in Christie's post-war novels. At the beginning of the novel there are one or two references to the diminished number of porters available to carry luggage for passengers at railway stations. The "severe shortage" of domestic servants in England, in this story, results in a lucrative career for one of the main characters. Lucy Eyelesbarrow, a degreed mathematician, passes up a poorly remunerated academic career and successfully "exploits shortage" by developing a unique career as a professional domestic servant, hiring herself out at very high rates for short periods of two to four weeks. She is similar to the housekeeper Mary Dove in the 1953 *A Pocket Full of Rye* who "worked only for the very rich." Mary Dove, however, was a housekeeper who supervised a hired staff but was able to "fill in" if a staff member left unexpectedly. Lucy Eyelesbarrow actually does all the work herself. She cooks and serves meals, polishes silver, attends to old people, cleans up dog messes, runs the vacuum cleaner and, in fact, does everything herself with efficiency.

Story

It is December 20 of approximately 1956. Mrs. Elspeth McGillicuddy, from Scotland, has taken an overnight train to London and spent a long, grueling day shopping for Christmas gifts at various department stores. It is now late afternoon and she is aboard a train destined for Milchester, in the west of England. She plans to spend a few days visiting her friend Jane Marple who lives in the village of St. Mary Mead near Milchester. After a brief nap in her compartment, she awakens at about 5:30 p.m. and notes that it has grown quite dark. Alongside the train there is another train running at the same speed in the same direction. As she looks through the window of her compartment into a lighted compartment of the other train, she sees the back of a tall man who is strangling a young woman with his hands. The face of the woman turns purple, her tongue protrudes from her mouth and, after a few seconds, her body goes limp. A second or two later, one train gains speed and the other slows down, and the second train vanishes from sight.

Mrs. McGillicuddy reports this incident to a conductor, who appears not to believe her. She tells her friend Miss Marple about it and the ladies report the incident to the local police in St. Mary Mead. The police there are well acquainted with Miss Marple and are in the habit of taking her statements seriously, but a few days later they inform her that full inquiries have been made and no body of any murder victim has been found, despite a thorough scrutiny of the train and the railway line.

Miss Marple is certain that a murder has been committed. She studies maps, local gazetteers and railway timetables, and she determines that when the murder was committed the train must have been running along the property line of a large estate called Rutherford Hall. She deduces that the body of the victim must have been thrown from the train into the property itself. Making use of the fact that there is a severe shortage of domestic labor everywhere, she arranges for a friend to take a job as a housemaid at Rutherford Hall and to "snoop." In the course of her "snooping," her friend finds, in one of the outbuildings, the decaying corpse of a woman. The police then have no choice but to open a murder investigation, but it is of course Miss Marple who solves the mystery.

Characters

Mrs. Elspeth McGillicuddy, an elderly lady from Scotland who witnesses a murder being committed in a train running alongside hers on the evening of December 20. Miss Marple believes her story because Elspeth is the kind of woman who finds it very hard to make herself believe that anything at all extraordinary or out of the way could happen. She is *not* suggestible.

A Porter at Paddington Railway Station, London

A Stern Uniformed Guardian at the gate to No. 3 platform at Paddington Station

Margaret, Robby, Jean and Hector, relatives

of Mrs. McGillicuddy for whom she has purchased Christmas gifts in London, specifically face towels, a space gun, a toy rabbit and a pullover respectively.

A Tall, Dark Man Wearing a Heavy Coat, strangling a woman in a train running alongside Mrs. McGillicuddy's train.

A Woman Wearing a Fur Coat, aged between thirty and thirty-five being strangled in a train by a tall, dark man wearing a heavy coat.

A Ticket Collector on the train who does not believe that Mrs. McGillicuddy saw a murder being committed.

A Porter at Brackhampton Railway Station to whom Mrs. McGillicuddy gives a written message to be given to the stationmaster

A Porter at Milchester Railway Station

A Taxi Driver who meets Mrs. McGillicuddy at Milchester and drives her to Miss Marple's cottage in St. Mary Mead, nine miles distant

An Elderly Maid who opens the door at Miss Marple's cottage

Miss Jane Marple, who has a good deal of experience in solving murders. We met her first in the 1930 *Murder at the Vicarage,* and then in five subsequent novels, most recently in the 1953 *A Pocket Full of Rye.* She is now eighty-nine years old.

A Little Girl with a Teddy Bear, A Fat Man who was Asleep, and Several Amused Railway Passengers, characters in an anecdote related by Miss Marple

Dr. Haydock, who has forbidden Miss Marple to bend or stoop, thus making gardening impossible for her. Dr. Haydock is another old friend of Miss Marple's—and of ours—having first appeared in the 1930 *Murder at the Vicarage.*

Old Edwards, an old gardener in St. Mary Mead who is "so opinionated" and lazy, drinking lots of cups of tea and doing very little work

Sergeant Cornish at the St. Mary Mead police station who listens to Mrs. McGillicuddy's story of the murder in the train and judges it to have credibility.

Roderick, Mrs. McGillicuddy's son in Ceylon whom she plans to visit and who is sure to remember Miss Marple, who once assisted him in the matter of some money that was disappearing from a school locker

Sir Henry Clithering, long retired from Scotland Yard, and a good friend—and an appreciator—of Miss Marple. It was he who introduced Miss Marple and recommended her to the police in two previous novels: the 1942 *The Body in the Library,* and the 1950 *A Murder Is Announced.*

Inspector Craddock of New Scotland Yard, Sir Henry Clithering's nephew and godson. He had worked with Miss Marple in the matter of the murders at Little Paddocks in the 1950 *A Murder Is Announced.* He is a fair-haired, good-looking man who is always courteous—almost apologetic—when interviewing persons connected with a criminal matter. Inspector Craddock is also one of Scotland Yard's better-educated officers and he speaks French fluently, a skill that he will find useful in this story.

The Assistant Commissioner of New Scotland Yard, Inspector Craddock's superior, who has heard all about Miss Marple from Sir Henry Clithering, and who is eager to hear what Inspector Craddock has to say about her.

A Nicely Spoken, Pleasant Young Man who shows photographs of the murdered woman to Mrs. McGillicuddy in Ceylon

Monsieur Armand Dessin of the Préfecture de Police in Paris. He assists Inspector Craddock in examining cases of missing women in France in an effort to identify the murdered woman. He is a tall, thin, melancholy-looking man.

Detective Sergeant Bob Wetherall whom Inspector Craddock assigns to investigate Martine Crackenthorpe's London address

Inspector Bacon, a local police officer who assists Inspector Craddock of New Scotland Yard. Inspector Bacon is "a big solid man—his expression was that of one utterly disgusted with humanity—especially artists." His attitude toward artists is expressed in the following lines:

> "Cedric—that's the one who lives abroad. Paints!"
> The Inspector invested the word with its full quota of sinister significance.

In a later scene, Inspector Bacon has these additional words about Cedric:

> "Cocky enough for anything," he said. "I don't care for the type, myself. A loose living lot, these artists, and very likely to be mixed up with a disreputable class of women."
> Craddock smiled.
> "I don't like the way he dresses, either," went on Bacon. "No respect—going to an inquest like that. Dirtiest pair of trousers I've seen in a long while. And did you see his tie? Looked as though it was made of colored string. If you ask me, he's the kind that would easily strangle a woman and make no bones about it."

Although not a fan of artists and men who dress incorrectly for inquests, Inspector Bacon is a fatherly type who kindly allows two adolescent boys—Alexander Eastley and James Stoddart-West—to view the body of the dead woman, remarking that "one is only young once."

Sanders, a police constable who assists Inspector Bacon at the Long Barn where the body of a murdered woman is discovered.

The Chief Constable of the County Johnstone, the police surgeon who examines the body in the sarcophagus and judges the death to have taken place three to four weeks earlier.

A Policeman who, like Inspector Bacon, is also a fatherly type who kindly allows Alexander and James into the back of the hall to watch the inquest

A Theatrical Agent, a friend of Inspector Craddock's, who provides no useful information about the French ballet company with which Anna Stravinska toured England before Christmas

Anna Stravinska, a dancer with the Ballet Maritski who disappeared from the company on approximately December 18 while the company was on tour in England

Madame Joliet, who runs the Ballet Maritski and who does not like the police.

Several Dancers with the Ballet Maritski who offer insights into the character of Anna Stravinska, describing her as a person who talked little about herself and, when she did, it was "mostly lies."

Mr. Wimborne, the senior partner of Luther Crackenthorpe's firm of solicitors. He resents the fact that Lucy Eyelesbarrow discovered the body in the sarcophagus, and he resents the fact that the police question the family about the murder. When Emma Crackenthorpe writes to Martine inviting her to Rutherford Hall, Mr. Wimborne resents the fact that he was not informed of Martine's existence. In a word, Mr. Wimborne thinks he owns the Crackenthorpe family.

A Neat Young Woman at Harold Crackenthorpe's London office who speaks in a discreet murmur through a telephone

Miss Ellis, Harold Crackenthorpe's personal secretary, "a streamlined young woman in a well-cut black suit with a notebook." She does not enter and leave rooms; she "glides" in and out of them. She resembles Rex Fortescue's private secretary, Miss Grosvenor, in the 1953 *A Pocket Full of Rye,* who was said to "sail" in and out of rooms.

Mr. Goldie, who had a conference with Harold Crackenthorpe about the Cromartie merger on the morning of December 20.

Lord Forthville, who lunched with Harold Crackenthorpe at the Berkeley on December 20.

Dicky Rogers and the Soho Lot, racketeers who have had dealings with one of the members of the Crackenthorpe family

Sergeant Leakie, who was assigned to a case of thefts from lorries [trucks]

Chick Evans, one of the Dicky Rogers mob with whom Sergeant Leakie saw one of the Crackenthorpe family at a lorry pullover [truck stop] on December 21

William Baker, a ticket collector at Brackhampton Railway Station who remembered clipping a ticket to London for one of Miss Crackenthorpe's brothers late in the evening of December 20.

Dr. Quimper, age forty-four, who has been Luther Crackenthorpe's doctor for the past few years. He is a tall, genial man, with a casual, offhand, cynical manner that his patients find very stimulating.

A Nurse whom Dr. Quimper places at Rutherford Hall the morning after the poisonings

Old Dr. Morris who was Luther Crackenthorpe's doctor for many years before young Dr. Quimper arrived. Dr. Quimper confided to him his suspicion that someone had tried to poison Luther Crackenthorpe at Christmas time, but Dr. Morris derided this suggestion, citing Luther's frequent "billious attacks" attributable to eating too much rich food at holiday times.

Mrs. Josh Simpkins, a patient of Dr. Quimper, who gave birth to a new set of twins to add to a family of eight.

Mr. Josh Simpkins, who was disappointed that twins, and not quads, were born.

Raymond West, Miss Marple's wealthy nephew who writes "clever books," which Miss Marple secretly derides.

David, Raymond West's second son who works with British Railways. He provides Miss Marple with useful information about various trains passing through and stopping at Brackhampton.

Griselda Clement, the wife of the vicar, Leonard Clement, of St. Mary Mead, whom we met in the 1930 *Murder at the Vicarage* and in the 1942 *The Body in the Library*.

Leonard, Griselda and Leonard's son whom we met as a baby just learning to crawl in the 1942 *The Body in the Library*. (In the earlier story his name was David.) He is now about fourteen years old and extremely knowledgeable of maps, kindly lending an especially useful one to Miss Marple.

Faithful Florence, a former maid of Miss Marple's who now lives in a house in Brackhampton. She has furnished rooms for rent and provides Miss Marple with lodgings for the duration of the investigation. Note: In the 1942 *The Moving Finger,* an elderly woman, Miss Emily Barton, had a former parlourmaid to whom she referred as "Faithful Florence" and who had a house with furnished rooms for rent in Lymstock, the setting for that story. Christie probably remembered the name "Faithful Florence" and the idea of "furnished rooms for rent" and thought that she had assigned that former servant to Miss Marple.

A Very Old Gentleman Reading *The Statesman* in the 4:33 to Brackhampton when Miss Marple travels by that train in order to gather information

A Very Attractive Woman on the plane from Iviza to Paris whom Cedric Crackenthorpe met and later spent time with in London.

Lady Adington and Miss Bartlett, with whom Emma Crackenthorpe lunched on December 20

A Taxi Driver who recognizes a photograph of Cedric Crackenthorpe as a fare he had taken to Paddington Station on a certain day.

Lucy Eyelesbarrow, a brilliant young mathematician who chooses to "exploit shortage" and to work as an expensive short-term domestic servant instead of pursuing a poorly-remunerated academic career.

An Admiral of the Fleet, the Provost of an Oxford college, and A Dame of the British Empire, prominent people for whom Lucy Eyelesbarrow has worked and whom she names as references to Inspector Bacon

Dorothy Cartwright, whose account of having seen a murder in a train would not be nearly so credible as Elspeth McGillicuddy's.

Jenkins at the Garage, one of Miss Marple's "village parallels." Alfred Crackenthorpe reminds Miss Marple of him.

Mr. Eade, another of Miss Marple's "village parallels." Harold Crackenthorpe reminds Miss Marple of him.

Geraldine Webb, the "village parallel" of whom Emma Crackenthorpe reminds Miss Marple.

Old Josiah Crackenthorpe, a very rich Victorian businessman who built Rutherford Hall in 1884. He made a vast fortune by producing sweet and savory biscuits, pickles and relishes under the brand name "Crackenthorpe's Fancies." He died in 1928 after writing an unusual Will that deprived his only surviving son of the right to dispose of the family fortune or to sell Rutherford Hall, passing the property and financial holdings to his grandchildren instead.

Mrs. Josiah Crackenthorpe, who died shortly after the birth of her two sons.

Luther Crackenthorpe, aged about seventy-two. He was Josiah Crackenthorpe's elder son who disappointed his father by refusing to go into the family business, preferring to indulge in art collecting and spending a good deal of money on "rather dubious works of art," primarily *objets d'art* from remote periods. His father's Will allows him to live at Rutherford Hall but deprives him of the right to sell the property. The Will also provides him with an income generated by the family fortune but prevents him from touching the capital. He "enjoys poor health" and behaves as an invalid but is in much better health than he pretends to be.

Henry Crackenthorpe, Josiah Crackenthorpe's younger son. He married an actress and then was killed in an automobile accident while driving after drinking too much in 1911.

Emma Crackenthorpe, Luther Crackenthorpe's only surviving daughter, age thirty-seven. She is unmarried and continues to live with her father at Rutherford Hall.

Edmund Crackenthorpe, Luther Crackenthorpe's eldest son, who was killed in the early days of the Second World War. A few days before he died he wrote a letter to his family telling them he intended to marry a French girl named Martine, but the family never heard any more about it ... until just a few weeks ago when Emma received a letter signed "Martine Crackenthorpe."

Cedric Crackenthorpe, Luther Crackenthorpe's unmarried second son. He is a painter and lives on the Spanish Balearic island Iviza (more often spelled Ibiza.) Being the eldest surviving grandson of Josiah Crackenthorpe, (his older brother Edmund died during the war) he stands to inherit Rutherford Hall upon the death of his father Luther.

Alfred Crackenthorpe, another of Luther Crackenthorpe's sons, also unmarried. He has no particular profession but dabbles in "deals," and is on familiar terms with certain unsavory types, including such known racketeers and shady types as "Dicky Rogers and the Soho lot." He is a good-looking man with a thin, dark face and eyes set rather too close together. He lives in London in a cheap furnished flat.

Harold Crackenthorpe, Luther Crackenthorpe's most "respectable" son, a stuffy and conservative businessman with an office in the City. He has a loveless marriage with the daughter of an impoverished earl.

Lady Alice Crackenthorpe, Harold's wife, the daughter of an impoverished earl. She spends most of her time staying with relations or friends when in England, and she spends the winter months in the South of France. Her contact with her husband is minimal and accidental.

Edith Eastley, Luther Crackenthorpe's daughter who died four years ago. She was the wife of Bryan Eastley and the mother of Alexander.

Bryan Eastley, the widower of Edith. He was a Squadron Leader in the Royal Air Force during the Second World War and, since the war, has had difficulty in finding a meaningful existence in civilian life, working without enthusiasm or success in various boring office jobs. Lucy Eyelesbarrow's first impression of Bryan is "an amiable-looking young man of thirty-odd with brown hair, rather plaintive blue eyes and an enormous fair mustache." He is described by Mrs. Kidder as "ever so nice."

Alexander Eastley, Luther Crackenthorpe's only grandchild, aged about fourteen, with fair hair and blue eyes. He is a bright youngster who enjoys science fiction novels.

Mrs. Kidder, who works at Rutherford Hall five mornings a week and who does not mind sharing facts and opinions about the Crackenthorpe family with Lucy Eyelesbarrow.

Mr. Kidder, Mrs. Kidder's husband who does not approve of her going to Rutherford Hall after a corpse is found in the Long Barn and two members of the Crackenthorpe family are murdered.

Mrs. Hart who comes to Rutherford Hall three afternoons a week to do heavy housework

The Manageress at the Registry Office in Brackhampton with whom Lucy Eyelesbarrow is well acquainted. She puts Lucy into contact with Emma Crackenthorpe.

The Kennedys, friends of Emma Crackenthorpe in North Devon who had Lucy Eyelesbarrow with them while they were having a baby and who reported very favorably about her work

Old Hillman, the gardener at Rutherford Hall who only makes a show of working. He is a gossip and shares a good deal of information about the Crackenthorpe family with Lucy.

A Woman Coming Out of a House who tells Lucy that there is a public telephone at the post office

James Stoddart-West, a.k.a. "Stodders," a school chum of Alexander Eastley, who is spending part of the half-term holiday from school with him at Rutherford Hall. He shares Alexander's enthusiasm for space fiction, for Lucy's excellent cooking, and for the hunt for clues in the present murder case. His parents are extremely wealthy and own a William and Mary period home and two luxury automobiles: a Rolls-Royce and a Mercedes-Benz.

Lord Stoddart-West, James's father. He was a British Air Force paratrooper who parachuted into France during the Second World War and later married a Frenchwoman.

Lady Stoddart-West, James's French-born mother. She makes a surprise visit to Rutherford Hall late in the story, bringing an interesting story to the attention of Emma Crackenthorpe.

Mr. and Mrs. Darwin, Harold Crackenthorpe's servants at his London residence

Mrs. Brierly, one of Miss Marple's "village parallels." Afflicted with a serious disease and confined to hospital, she arranged for post cards to be sent to her children from various countries abroad in order to create the impression that she was traveling abroad and not in a hospital.

A Footman and a Kitchen Maid recalled by Cedric Crackenthorpe. They were employed at Rutherford Hall before the War and had a love affair.

FRENCH INTO ENGLISH

Note: Although this is not an Hercule Poirot novel, a few French words and expressions occur in it:

Chapter 14

chef d'orchestre—music director, orchestra conductor
Elle était assez bien, c'est tout.—She was moderately good-looking, that's all.
Ça se peut!—That's possible.
Ah! dans la guerre.—Oh, during the war
Quelle blague!—What a joke!

Chapter 24 *amour propre*—self-esteem

COMMENTS

A unique murder plan and a varied and interesting cast of characters make *What Mrs. McGillicuddy Saw* a pleasure to read and reread. Miss Jane Marple is the "sleuth" in this novel, but she is now eighty-nine years old and unable to move about easily. However, she cleverly directs—from a distance—the detection through a young friend, and she is in constant communication with an amiable young Scotland Yard inspector with whom she worked a few years earlier in another story. It may have been a mistake for Christie to assign to Miss Marple the specific age of eighty-nine for this novel, because she will feature her again in the 1962 *The Mirror Crack'd*, the 1964 *A Caribbean Mystery*, the 1965 *At Bertram's Hotel*, and the 1971 *Nemesis*. Readers who demand chronological consistency will then conclude that Miss Marple is ninety-four, ninety-six, ninety-seven and one hundred three years old respectively in these last novels.

Some of the characters in the story are more

or less repetitions of characters we have met in earlier Christie novels. Harold Crackenthorpe is the stuffy businessman whose expensively furnished London office suggests affluence but who has made poor business decisions and is very nearly going broke. He has a "streamlined" secretary named Miss Ellis. He is similar to Percival Fortescue in *A Pocket Full of Rye*, whose business is going bust, though largely through the recent irrational actions of his father. Percival Fortescue also had an expensively-furnished office and a "streamlined" secretary. Harold's brother Alfred, the "black sheep in the family" may be compared with Lancelot Fortescue in that same earlier novel. Cedric Crackenthorpe is a stereotypical artist who dresses shabbily, often looks unshaven and unclean, and seems to attract women because of it. Old Luther Crackenthorpe is the stereotypical patriarch who resents his children and suspects that they are awaiting his death just for their inheritance and, in the case of one or two of his children, he is correct. All of the above are interesting characters, although not especially unique in Christie.

There is an especially interesting characteristic about Luther Crackenthorpe, however. Like many Christie characters, he despises the "self-made man." Luther's father Josiah founded a business which became extremely successful, and he would have liked his two sons, Luther and Henry, to join the business, but the two sons became "educated" to the point of despising money and material things. Henry died rather young and Luther considered himself to be "a cut above business," a person who, unlike his "vulgarian" father, appreciated art and the finer things in life. He chose to ignore the family business and to travel the world, accumulating "a collection of dubious works of art." Old Josiah took the view that, since Luther was so far "above" the business of making money, there was no reason why he should inherit the wealth that the family business had produced. In his Will he specified that his *grandchildren*, and not his son, should be his heirs. Luther is hypocritical enough to resent his father's Will. Though despising his "vulgarian" father for spending his life making money, Luther fully expected to inherit all that lovely money without ever having earned it.

Luther is also the kind of parent who feels the need to control his children, even after they have become adults. Naturally he resents the fact that he has no financial control over them. He would like to have the power, for example, to disinherit them if they fail to do his bidding, but he has no power to do so. And so Luther is a very bitter old man who insults his adult sons freely and even smiles with satisfaction when one of them dies.

Lucy Eyelesbarrow is an interesting character, also. The idea of "exploiting shortage" and carving a career for oneself as an expensive domestic servant is an intriguing one, although such a thing is probably not possible. If it were, there would certainly be many Lucy Eyelesbarrows in real life. We may recall that in the 1953 *A Pocket Full of Rye* there was the expensive-but-worth-it efficient housekeeper Mary Dove at Yewtree Lodge, the home of the Fortescue family in an expensive London suburb.

Once again Christie promotes her idea that war heroes often have difficulty in adjusting to civilian life afterwards. She introduced this idea in the 1948 *There Is a Tide*, mentioned it again in 1951 *They Came to Baghdad*, the 1953 *A Pocket Full of Rye* and the 1956 *Dead Man's Folly*, and now develops it further in the character of Bryan Eastley. Bryan admits to Lucy that he has never been "trained" for any kind of useful work in civilian life, but a police officer suggests more serious difficulties in this conversation with another officer:

> "Mind you, I did just wonder about that Air Force chap."
> "Bryan Eastley?"
> "Yes. I've run into one or two of his type. They're what you might call adrift in the world—had danger and death and excitement too early in life. Now they find it tame. Tame and unsatisfactory. In a way, we've given them a raw deal. Though I don't really know what we could do about it. But there they are, all past and no future, so to speak. And they're the kind that don't mind taking chances. The ordinary fellow plays safe by instinct, it's not so much morality as prudence. But these fellows aren't afraid—playing safe isn't really in their vocabulary. If Eastley were mixed up with a woman and wanted to kill her—"

And once again we are treated to Christie's negative attitude toward nurses. In every Christie novel in which a hospital nurse spends time in a private home, the domestic servants complain about her demands, usually for cups of tea for the patient at all hours, and trays carried upstairs. In this novel it is Mrs. Kidder who complains:

> "As for them nurses, they never do a hand's turn," said Mrs. Kidder. "All they want is pots and pots of tea made strong. And meals prepared. Wore out, that's what I am."

It is a pleasure to encounter in *What Mrs. McGillicuddy Saw* the Christie rarity of amiable children. Alexander Eastley and his friend James Stoddart-West are engaging kids who are polite, who are enthusiastically appreciative of Lucy's cooking—especially her desserts—and who have a great time looking for clues and, in general, enjoying the excitement of the murder case. Their presence in the household brings to the story some youthfulness and humor that would otherwise be absent. In earlier Christie novels, the only thoroughly amiable youngster had been Peter Carmody in the 1942 *The Body in the Library*.

In the *Comments* section for the 1956 *Dead Man's Folly*, it was mentioned that two or three minor characters had been unrealistically candid in their negative remarks about the Stubbs family. Old Merdell, though he knew nothing about Hercule Poirot other than the fact that he was a houseguest of the Stubbs, made some negative remarks about Mrs. Folliat's family history which had not been solicited by Poirot. Then Miss Brewis, the secretary-cum-housekeeper at the Stubbs home, made some extremely negative remarks to Poirot about Lady Stubbs, again without being asked for an assessment of that person. It was an unrealistic notion that a secretary would feel free to speak in such a way to a houseguest of her employer.

Now, in *What Mrs. McGillicuddy Saw*, both Mrs. Kidder, a daily woman, and the old gardener Hillman, are equally loose with their tongues in the presence of the newly arrived hired help, Lucy. Perhaps, though, it is the fact that Lucy is another "domestic" that allows Mrs. Kidder and Hillman to feel free to speak to Lucy about the family in a negative way.

One other "unsatisfactory" item in this novel is the story that is brought to Emma Crackenthorpe by Lady Stoddart-West towards the end. There is a rather unbelievable coincidence that the reader is expected to accept. For the reader to be asked to accept a few unlikelihoods is fairly common in Christie but this one is a bit too much, especially when one can think of other, more believable ways in which Christie could have dealt with the situation.

Despite these shortcomings, *What Mrs. McGillicuddy Saw* is a good average Christie detective novel and would make a nice "first Christie experience."

Ordeal by Innocence (1958)

Setting

Ordeal by Innocence was first copyrighted in 1958, and first published in the United States early in 1959. We know, then, that the action must take place no later than the fall of 1958. But there are statements by a minor character, a small boy who, "two years earlier when he was just a kid," had spoken of seeing a "Sputnik" in the vicinity of a house where a murder took place. Now that he is two years older and "much more grown up," he realizes that what he saw was a "bubble car" and not a "Sputnik" at all.

"Sputnik" became a household word in the fall of 1957 when the Soviet Union launched the world's first man-made satellite. The child in the story, seeing a tiny automobile of very strange appearance, had thought it was "one of those Sputniks" that were constantly in the news that fall. Christie, while writing this story, must have forgotten that it was just one year earlier, in the fall of 1957, and not in 1956 that the Soviet satellite Sputnik was launched. This is a minor point, of course, but there is one more item of questionable chronology. One of the characters, Mary Durrant, is described as being twenty-seven years old. We know, from the above, that the action takes place in 1958; therefore she must have been born in 1931. But according to the story, she met her future husband, "a dashing young pilot," *during* World War Two and married him just before the war ended. That is hardly possible since she could have been no more than fourteen years old when the war ended in 1945. The problem would not have occurred if Christie had described her as being thirty-one or thirty-two in 1958.

To learn what a "bubble car" was, if the subject interests you, you may run a search on the Internet to find articles on the subject, complete with photographs of "bubble cars." Briefly, the "bubble car" referred to in the story was a tiny automobile designed in Italy in the early 1950s to provide affordable private transportation to Europeans. Several manufacturers in various European countries produced variations of the car, the best known being the Isetta, which was made by BMW in Germany. Few of these tiny cars were sold in America, since affordable, practical transportation had been available to average and even below-average income Americans for a long time, but in Europe the tiny "bubble cars" and other similar mini-cars were a commercial success.

The English version of the "bubble car" had just three wheels—two in front and one in the rear—and was indeed a strange looking vehicle. One entered the car through the single door in the front—yes, the *front*. A small bench seat accommodated the driver and perhaps one small passenger (if neither the driver nor the passenger was very large) and the whole car had a sort of pyramid shape with a wrap-around rear window, giving the driver and passenger the appearance of being inside a "bubble." It was this strange new appearance of the "bubble car" that made the child in the story think he was seeing a "Sputnik."

One of the main characters in *Ordeal by Innocence* owns a "bubble car" and the fact that the small boy reports having seen a "bubble car" parked near the murder house brings that character under suspicion two years after the crime takes place.

The main setting of the story is a large modern house, Sunny Point, which was built during the 1930s and purchased when nearly new by its current owners. It is located in the fictitious town of Drymouth on the southern coast of England. The name of the county is not specified, but it is probably Devon, since the name of at least two fictitious towns in the story—Drymouth and Redquay—suggest the names of such real towns as Plymouth and Torquay, which are located in Devon on the English Channel coast. As we read the story we also learn that, during the war, the owners of Sunny Point created a War Nursery in their home and received about a dozen children from London in order to keep them safe from enemy bombardments. Therefore the location of Sunny Point must be somewhere that was judged reasonably safe from enemy attack, and Devon was such a place, although the large Devonsire town of Exeter was bombed during the War.

More important than the physical settings of the story are the wartime conditions which resulted in the family that has lived at Sunny Point since those days. The wealthy owners of Sunny Point, Mr. and Mrs. Argyle, unable to have children of their own, had adopted an American child just before the war while visiting New York. Then they established a War Nursery at Sunny Point for London children, mostly orphans and slum children. When the war ended most of the children returned to their parents in London, but two boys and two girls remained unclaimed or unwanted. Mr. and Mrs. Argyle adopted them also, resulting in a total of five adopted children, four of whom are now adults, the fifth having recently died while in prison for the murder of Mrs. Argyle.

A few minor details: the words "telly" (television) and "supermarket" occur in *Ordeal by Innocence* for the first time in a Christie novel, and there is a reference to an amateur performance of the then popular *Waiting for Godot*, an absurdist play written in French during the late 1940s by Samuel Beckett, and then translated into English in 1954. These are in addition to the references to "Sputnik" and the "bubble cars" mentioned above.

Story

In the fall of 1958 Arthur Calgary, a geophysicist, returns to England after a two-year expedition to the South Pole. During his absence he has been out of touch with current events in England. Upon his return to England, he learns of a murder that occurred just a couple of days before he left England in 1956. Rachel Argyle was murdered at her home, Sunny Point, in Devon. Her adopted son Jack was arrested, tried and condemned to life in prison for the crime, and he died in prison a few months later. Jack had claimed that, at the time the crime was committed, he was being given a lift in a car driven by a man, but that alibi was never substantiated despite adequate publicity and efforts to find the man who allegedly gave Jack the lift.

The fact is that it was Arthur who had given Jack Argyle the lift, but the same evening he was struck by a car, suffering concussion and briefly losing his short-term memory. A few days later he was judged sufficiently recovered to leave England on his scheduled trip to the South Pole, and so he left. During his expedition he received no news of the murder trial and the search for the only person who could substantiate Jack's alibi.

Thinking that he will be rendering Jack's family a service, he visits the family in Devon with the news that Jack was innocent of the crime. He is astounded to find that the family is *not* pleased with this news. A member of the family explains that, since Jack did not commit the crime, then someone else in the family must have murdered Rachel Argyle. The murderer could not have been an intruder because the house was well secured and there was no evidence of an unauthorized entry of any person. Jack had been clearly indicated as the murderer because he had threatened Mrs. Argyle just a few hours earlier. Furthermore, he had had a history of scrapes with the law.

The police are forced to open a new investigation in light of Calgary's substantiation of Jack Argyle's alibi, but they make no progress, since the family's statements of events surrounding the crime have not changed. Unless the crime can be solved, everyone in the family will forever be suspected, even though all but one are innocent, hence the title, *Ordeal by Innocence*. Arthur Calgary solves the mystery himself, but not in time to prevent two additional murders.

Characters

Dr. Arthur Calgary, a well-known and respected geophysicist who has recently returned from an expedition to the South Pole. Because of his position and reputation, his story about Jack Argyle's alibi is taken seriously. Calgary has a deep sense of the importance of justice and he feels compelled to bring the news of Jack Argyle's innocence to his family.

Arthur's Friends in Redquay, with whom he partakes of lunch and then tea in efforts to procrastinate in the matter of his visit to the Argyle family

The Driver of a Hired Car, who drives Calgary along the crowded coast road and then inland towards a quay beside a river

A Ferryman who rows Calgary across a river towards Sunny Point

Mr. Marshall, the Argyle family attorney who is not sure that the news of Jack Argyle's innocence should be made public

Rachel Argyle, née Rachel Konstam who, after her parents' death in an airplane crash, devoted her inheritance to the continuation of their philanthropic enterprises. Unable to have natural children with her husband Leo, she turned her philanthropic interests toward helping neglected, unwanted or underprivileged children and, with her husband, adopted five such youngsters. But not everyone had affirmative thoughts about Rachel Argyle and her benevolence.

Rudolph Konstam, a very rich man, Rachel's father. He had many philanthropic interests and brought his daughter up to take an interest in these "benevolent schemes." He and his wife died in an airplane crash.

Rudolph Konstam's Wife, a very rich woman in her own right.

Leo Argyle, Rachel Argyle's husband. Like the rest of the family, he had fully believed that his adopted son Jack had been the person who killed Rachel, although Leo does not like using the words *guilt* or *guilty* in connection with Jack. He had shared his wife's view that Jack was a kind of "misfit."

Hester Argyle, the illegitimate daughter of an Irish hospital nurse and an American G.I. Her mother was only too glad to be rid of her and wanted to bury her past and conceal it from her future husband. Hester is the youngest of the Argyles' adopted children, not yet twenty. She had always resented Rachel Argyle's controlling ways and had run away to "be an actress" with a fourth-rate theatre group instead of going to London to study acting as Mrs. Argyle had advised her to. As an actress she was a failure, and she also made a fool of herself by having a brief affair with a married man for whom she cared nothing.

Michael (Micky) Argyle, another of Rachel and Leo Argyle's adopted children. His mother was a woman of low morals who had a succession of live-in boyfriends, whom young Michael had been taught to refer to as "uncles." She was often drunk, and when drunk she abused Michael, although she always forbade the "uncles" to lay a hand on "our little Micky." Michael was taken to Sunny Point during the war to be safe from the bombings in London and he expected to go back to his mother when the war ended, but when contacted by the Argyles, the mother expressed no interest in him and gladly gave him up for adoption by the Argyles in exchange for one hundred pounds.

Jack (Jacko) Argyle, an orphan who was another of the children adopted by Rachel and Leo Argyle when the war ended. He died of pneumonia four months after being sentenced to life in prison for the murder of his stepmother, Rachel Argyle.

Christina (Tina) Argyle, an orphan, the child of a seaman and a prostitute, a "half caste" (biracial) child, another of Rachel and Leo Argyle's adopted children. She lives in the town of Redmyn, not far from Sunny Point, and works at the library there.

Mary Durrant (formerly Mary Argyle), whom the Argyles adopted just before the Second World War, a slum child from New York. Her guardians, a "slatternly aunt and uncle who drank" were glad to be rid of their little niece.

Philip Durrant, Mary's husband who was "a brave and intelligent young man but an absolute fool when it came to business matters ... then he got polio."

Kirsten (Kirsty) Lindstrom, a Norwegian trained nurse and masseuse who came to the Argyle family during the war to look after the refugee children, and then stayed with the family as their housekeeper. She has always been passionately devoted to the entire family, even to Jacko.

Gwenda Vaughan, Leo Argyle's devoted secretary and; since Rachel Argyle's death, his fiancée, although the recent revelation of Jack Argyle's innocence in the matter of Rachel's murder—and the consequent suspicion of guilt which has been thrown upon the entire remaining household—has prevented a public announcement of the engagement. As a matter of fact, Leo thinks it best to postpone their marriage "indefinitely."

Dr. Donald Craig, a young medical doctor who is Hester Argyle's fiancé but who wonders, now that Jack Argyle has been proven innocent of the murder of Rachel Argyle, if the murderer could have been Hester.

Maureen Clegg, Jack Argyle's widow who had no doubts that he was guilty of the crime.

Joe Clegg, Maureen Clegg's current husband, an electrician. He had known Maureen before she married Jack Argyle and had warned her against him.

A Plump Girl with Brown Hair, and a Dark Girl, cinema usherettes who are co-workers of Maureen Clegg

Dr. MacMaster, a retired physician who has known the Argyle family for many years and shares facts and perceptions about the family with Arthur Calgary. He is clearly Agatha Christie's "voice of wisdom" on the subjects of adoption, motherhood, inheritance of character traits and the futility of "advantages and improved environment" in this story.

Major Finney, the Chief Constable of the County. He is Superintendent Huish's superior.

Superintendent Huish, who is in charge of the case.

A Young Man at the police station whose business it is to make the right responses to Major Finney's statements and questions

Sir Reginald, the Director of Public Prosecutions who believes Arthur Calgary's story

A Sixteen-year-old Boy who opens the door at the building where Maureen and Joe Clegg live on the top floor

Cardinal Massilini who wrote to Leo Argyle about some documents from the archives

Porch, an old school chum of Michael Argyle

Mr. Warborough, a sarcastic form master whom Michael and Porch talked about killing, although they never tried to do it.

Master Cyril Green, a young boy who remembers seeing a "bubble car" near Sunny Point on the day of Mrs. Argyle's murder, although two years earlier, when he was "just a kid," he thought it was a Sputnik

Cyril Green's Mother who has difficulty in allowing Cyril to do his own talking

Police Constable Good, who brings Cyril Green to Superintendent Huish to tell his story about the bubble car

A Heavy, Cumbrous Woman, one of many middle aged women who had succumbed to Jack Argyle's charms and given him money

Mrs. Narracott, one of the daily women at Sunny Point

COMMENTS

In her 1949 *Crooked House,* Christie introduced her contention that personality and character traits are not developed by environment or education but are simply inherited from the blood of one's ancestors. We recall one or two discussions in that novel in which the "ruthlessness" of the de Haviland family and the "unscrupulousness tempered with kindliness" of the Leonides family are seriously discussed. A character suggests that a descendent of both of these bloodlines might inherit de Haviland "ruthlessness" and Leonides "unscrupulousness" *without* inheriting the Leonides "kindliness," and then that person might be a murderer. These conversations actually take place among intelligent people.

In her 1952 *Murder with Mirrors,* the subject of inherited traits comes up again in discussions about Gina Hudd, whose biological mother was Italian. Although Gina has spent her entire life, except for perhaps the first year or two, in England with English adoptive parents, wise old Miss Marple assures her that it is because of her "Italian blood" that she is able to express her emotions more freely than the rest of the household, whose blood is English only.

It is in *Ordeal by Innocence* that Agatha Christie delivers a veritable lecture on the subject of blood inheritance. To Christie, education and environment have nothing to do with shaping the personality and character traits of people. In the story, Rachel and Leo Argyle adopt five children. Three "wise" characters in the story—Rachel's husband Leo, the family attorney Mr. Marshall, and the family physician Dr. MacMaster—take turns debunking Rachel's foolish notion that improved environment and "advantages" are of any use to children who bear the "seeds of their ancestors' weaknesses." Furthermore, adoptive parents are at a disadvantage in their relationships with adoptive children, since there is no "blood tie" between them and, therefore, no "instinctive" mutual understanding.

The following two paragraphs occur in the thoughts of Rachel Argyle's widower Leo on the subject of their adoption of the five children (italics added):

> Yes, Leo thought, surely it was a worth while job to take these children, to give them the benefits of a home and love and a father and mother. Rachel, he thought, had had a right to be triumphant. Only it hadn't worked out quite the way it was supposed to do.... *For these children were not the children that he and Rachel would have had. Within them ran none of the blood of Rachel's hard-working thrifty forebears, none of the drive and ambition by which the less reputable members of her family had gained their assured place in society, none of the vague kindliness and integrity of mind that he remembered in his own father and grandfather and grandmother. None of the intellectual brilliance of his grandparents on either side.*
>
> Everything that environment could do was done for them. It could do a great deal, but it could not

do everything. *There had been those seeds of weakness which had brought them to the nursery in the first place, and under stress those seeds might bear flower...*

In a conversation with his son-in-law Philip Durrant, Leo Argyle expounds on the same subject (italics added):

> "It was an article of faith with her that the blood tie didn't matter. *But the blood tie does matter, you know. There is usually something in one's own children, some kink of temperament, some way of feeling that you recognise and can understand without having to put into words. You haven't got that tie with children you adopt. One has no instinctive knowledge of what goes on in their minds. You judge them, of course, by yourself, by your own thoughts and feelings, but it's wise to recognise that those thoughts and feelings may be very widely divergent from theirs."*

All of the remarks made by Leo Argyle about the folly of disregarding "the blood tie" are restated and expanded by the wise old Dr. MacMaster, who was the Argyle family doctor for many years, and by Mr. Marshall, the family solicitor. The following is a statement by wise old Dr. MacMaster during a conversation with Arthur Calgary (italics added):

> "It's interesting in a way, how they all tried to escape. How they fought not to conform to the pattern that she'd arranged for them. Because she did arrange a pattern, and a very good pattern. She wanted to give them a good home, a good education, a good allowance and a good start in the professions that she chose for them. *She wanted to treat them exactly as though they were hers and Leo Argyle's own children. Only of course they weren't hers and Leo Argyle's own children. They had entirely different instincts, feelings, aptitudes and demands...*"

And the pontifications go on and on, all through the book. Christie might have been better advised to deal with this subject in a non-detective novel, publishing it under her Mary Westmacott pseudonym, instead of including the subject in a "light fiction" detective novel. The subject completely dominates the book and the murder mystery aspect takes a very distant back seat. As a matter of fact, as a detective novel it is very poor. The correct solution of the mystery is not "detected" at all. The protagonist Arthur Calgary simply guesses correctly, confronts the murderer with his guess, and obtains a confession.

Characterization in *Ordeal by Innocence*, on the other hand, is excellent and it is, in fact, better in this novel than in all the rest of Christie's detective novels of the 1950s. The characters are interesting and carefully developed, especially Michael Argyle, with his bitter longings for his biological mother and the excitement of London in wartime, and Mary Durrant, with her well-concealed selfishness.

Cat Among the Pigeons (1959)

SETTING

The story can be assumed to take place in the summer of 1959, since there are no current events mentioned which would place the action in a different year, and 1959 is the earliest copyright date of the novel. There is a reference to "an enormous and almost incredibly opulent Cadillac, painted in two tones, raspberry red and azure blue." It was in the mid-to-late 1950s that American cars reached ridiculous sizes and were painted in garish two and three tone color schemes, and the 1959 Cadillac was an especially extravagant example. There are also references to a "majestic Rolls" a "very small Austin of battered age," and a tiny "Morris Minor" car. There is a reference to the American tennis champion Ruth Allen, and in a telephone conversation, a man describes a woman he has just met with the expression "out of this world," an American slang expression that was coined during the 1950s and, for a few years, was used constantly in conversation and even in product commercials: "Tide laundry detergent is 'out of this world,' etc."

Although no real current events play a role in this story, a revolution or *coup d'état* takes place in a tiny fictitious Middle Eastern kingdom called Ramat. It has but one city, also called Ramat. Early in the story there are scenes in this city—at the Royal Palace and at the Ritz Savoy Hotel, and the following amusing description of the hotel is provided:

> It was modestly called the Ritz Savoy and had a grand modernistic façade. It had opened with a flourish three years ago with a Swiss manager, a Viennese chef, and an Italian maître d'hôtel. Everything had been wonderful. The Viennese chef had gone first, then the Swiss manager. Now the Italian head waiter had gone too. The food was still ambitious, but bad, the service abominable and a good deal of the expensive plumbing had gone wrong.

Two important scenes take place in one of the guestrooms of this hotel.

The following is a description of the fictitious city of Ramat:

> The main street was like most main streets in the Middle East. It was a mixture of squalor and magnificence. Banks reared their vast newly built

magnificence. Innumerable small shops presented a collection of cheap plastic goods. Babies' bootees and cheap cigarette lighters were displayed in unlikely juxtaposition. There were sewing machines, and spare parts for cars. Pharmacies displayed flyblown proprietary medicines, and large notices of penicillin in every form and antibiotics galore. In very few of the shops was there anything that you would normally want to buy, except possibly the latest Swiss watches, hundreds of which were displayed crowded into a tiny window. The assortment was so great that even there one would have shrunk from purchase, dazzled by sheer mass.

Bob, still walking in a kind of stupor, jostled by figures in native or European dress, pulled himself together and asked himself again where the hell he was going.

He turned into a native café and ordered lemon tea. As he sipped it, he began, slowly, to come to. The atmosphere of the café was soothing. At a table opposite him an elderly Arab was peacefully clicking through a string of amber beads. Behind him two men played trictrac. It was a good place to sit and think.

There is a scene at the London residence of Hercule Poirot, which has been called Whitehaven Mansions since the 1935 novel *The A.B.C. Murders,* although in *Cat Among the Pigeons* it is called Whitehouse Mansions, probably due to a memory lapse on the part of the author. There is a brief scene at a fictitious London restaurant, *Le Nid Sauvage,* and a further London setting is the office of a Special Branch officer somewhere in the Bloomsbury district.

The principal physical setting is a girls' boarding school called Meadowbank. The school is located near a fictitious small town called Hurst St. Cyprian. There is no indication of where this school and town are located within England, but they cannot be very far from London, as one of the students at Meadowbank boards a train late one morning, travels to London and visits Hercule Poirot, who then escorts her back to Meadowbank by automobile the same afternoon.

Meadowbank is a very fine, up-to-date, expensive and well-run school and has extensive grounds, which include a newly-constructed Sports Pavilion. Scenes take place in the office of the headmistress of the school, in various staff and student bedrooms, and especially in the Sports Pavilion, which is the scene of two murders in the story.

About two hundred students live and study at the school. The teaching staff is rather small; there is one teacher of mathematics, a French teacher, an economics teacher, a teacher of botany and physics, a teacher of English and geography, and a "games mistress," that is, a physical education teacher. An art teacher visits the school two days per week. There is also a matron. There are just two live-in servants, a cook and a housemaid, the other servants being daily women who come in at intervals to do heavy housework. (How just one cook and one housemaid manage to produce three meals a day for a student body of two hundred and a staff of about ten is a mystery. Christie probably had no idea of how much work would be involved in providing daily meals, all cooked from scratch, for that number of people.) An old gardener has one younger man and two boys working with him and the grounds are very well maintained with neat lawns and flower borders. The early-summer blooming delphinium is mentioned as well as later-blooming asters and dahlias.

The high quality of this school is an important feature of the story. Some of the students are daughters of aristocratic families but others are daughters of university professors and other parents who value excellent educational experiences for their children. One student is a princess from Sweden and another is the cousin of the ruler of the fictitious Middle Eastern kingdom, Ramat, mentioned above.

A brief scene takes place in a department store in an unnamed town not far from Meadowbank. There is also a scene at the family home of one of the students. Their home is not described—aside from a mention that the family has a cook and a cook's helper—and the location of the home within England is not specified.

Late in the story, there is a brief scene in the open countryside of Anatolia (the large portion of Turkey located in Asia Minor) where a tour bus breaks down and the passengers converse with each other at the roadside as they await the repairs to be completed. The mother of one of the British students at Meadowbank is among the passengers and she converses with some difficulty in French with a Turkish woman.

Story

It is springtime in 1959 and in the tiny fictitious Middle Eastern kingdom of Ramat a revolution or *coup d'état* is about to occur. The ruler of Ramat, young Prince Ali Yusuf, who was educated in England and has modern, democratic ideas, has built hospitals and schools and housing. He has done "all the things people want," in his country, but he is now forced to ask himself, "Do people want them?" An attempt has been made on his life by subversive elements and he knows that if he remains in the country he will be killed.

The Prince has a cache of precious stones,

which are his personal property. Knowing that if he is killed while fleeing the country the jewels will be stolen, he entrusts them to his close friend and personal pilot, the young Englishman Bob Rawlinson, feeling confident that Bob will find a way to get them safely out of the country. Bob's older sister, Joan Sutcliffe, happens to be visiting Ramat with her daughter and staying at the Ritz Savoy hotel. Bob goes to the hotel, finding that Joan and her daughter are away on a day tour. But because he is well known and trusted at the hotel, he is allowed to enter Joan's room. There, he hides the jewels somewhere among Joan's and her daughter's possessions. Unknown to Bob, there is a witness to his act of concealing the jewels.

Bob and the Prince attempt to fly out of the country that night but their plane crashes and they are both killed.

A few weeks later, the summer term begins at Meadowbank, an excellent girls' boarding school in England. Joan's daughter Jennifer is a student there, and so is Princess Shaista, the cousin and fiancée of Prince Ali Yusuf. The new games mistress, Miss Springer, is shot to death inside the sports pavilion of the school late one night. The police are summoned, and then a second member of the staff is killed, again inside the sports pavilion. Soon a third staff member is murdered in her own room.

One of the students makes a thrilling discovery and travels in secret to London, boldly appearing at the home of Hercule Poirot to tell him about it. Poirot escorts the young lady back to Meadowbank by car and solves the mystery.

CHARACTERS

Miss Eleanor Vansittart, second in command at Meadowbank. She appears to be almost a "rubber stamp" of the headmistress, Miss Bulstrode. Everyone assumes that when Miss Bulstrode retires, Miss Vansittart will be her successor as headmistress of Meadowbank. But Miss Bulstrode does not want her successor to be a "rubber stamp" of herself. She would prefer a successor who moves with the times and who has fresh ideas of her own.

Miss Honoria Bulstrode, headmistress and one of the founders of Meadowbank. She has imagination, she is innovative, she takes risks, and she refuses to follow the set patterns of other schools. The result is Meadowbank, perhaps the finest school of its kind in England. Miss Bulstrode has kindness but she is also firm and assertive.

Miss Chadwick, a.k.a. "Faithful Chaddy," with whom Miss Bulstrode founded Meadowbank. She is the mathematics instructor at the school. She can always be depended upon in a crisis.

Mrs. Arnold, mother of Lydia Arnold

Lydia Arnold, a student at Meadowbank who recently returned from a cruise to the Greek islands

Lady Garnett, a parent who wrote to Miss Bulstrode about art classes

Mrs. Bird, the mother of Pamela Bird. She wants to discuss something with Miss Bulstrode but there is no time for that discussion on opening day

Pamela Bird, a student whose room has been moved to the far wing by the apple tree. A bottle of something sticky broke inside one of her suitcases.

Lady Violet, the mother of one of the students

Hector, Lady Violet's little boy who has such a nice toy airplane with him

A French-speaking Parent, who would like to discuss a certain subject with Miss Bulstrode but cannot, since this is such a busy day for her.

A Parent Who is an Archeologist or Geologist whom Miss Vansittart politely asks "Have you been digging up more interesting things?"

Ann Shapland, Miss Bulstrode's efficient new secretary who can take her pick of secretarial posts. She had been personal assistant to the chief executive of an oil company, and the private secretary to Sir Mervyn Todhunter, renowned alike for his erudition, his irritability and the illegibility of his handwriting. She numbered two Cabinet Ministers and an important Civil Servant among her employers. But on the whole, her work has always lain among men. She wonders how she is going to like being, as she expresses it to herself, completely submerged in women.

Ann never stays very long in any one job because she has an aging mother who has occasional "attacks of forgetfulness" and gets into trouble.

Major Hargreaves, a harassed-looking father who arrives at Meadowbank with his daughter in a battered Austin

Alison Hargreaves, Major Hargreaves's daughter who looks far calmer than he

The Chauffeur of an enormous and almost incredibly opulent raspberry-red and azure-blue Cadillac

An Immense Bearded, Dark-skinned Man Wearing a Flowing Aba, who brings Princess Shaista to Meadowbank in the enormous and almost incredibly opulent vehicle described above.

He may be an uncle of the Princess, but Miss Bulstrode is not sure.

A Parisian Fashion-plate, that is, a stylishly dressed young woman accompanying the Immense Bearded, Dark-skinned Man and the young Princess

Princess Shaista of Ramat, a new student at Meadowbank. Aged only about fifteen, she has far more sophistication than most English girls of her age, although she is not exactly an intellectual type. After Miss Springer is found murdered, Princess Shaista tells the police that she believes enemies plan to kidnap her, thinking she knows where the jewels belonging to her cousin are hidden. The police do not take her seriously but they will be proven wrong.

Denis Rathbone, "faithful Denis," who wishes that Ann Shapland would marry him, although his work takes him to every part of the world.

Old Briggs, the head gardener at Meadowbank. Recently he has managed with just a two boys helping him, but now there is a hard-working, knowledgeable young man to share the work, and Old Briggs grudgingly admits that the younger man does good work.

Adam Goodman, the new gardener at Meadowbank. His presence at Meadowbank is a bit of a surprise to everyone since it is rare to find a young man willing to do hard physical work.

Miss Elspeth Johnson, the matron at Meadowbank. She is devoted to Meadowbank and if the school were to close, her life would end.

Mademoiselle Angèle Blanche, the new French instructor at Meadowbank. Although her credentials and references are good, she does not appear to be a very good teacher, or even an interested one.

Miss Eileen Rich, who teaches English and Geography at Meadowbank. She is passionate about teaching and is an excellent and inspiring teacher.

Miss Rowan, one of the junior instructors at Meadowbank. She teaches economics but also has a degree in psychology.

Miss Blake, another junior instructor at Meadowbank. She teaches botany and physics.

Giuseppe, one of two young Italian gentlemen whom Miss Blake and Miss Rowan came to know while visiting Florence just before the summer term.

Miss Grace Springer, the new games mistress at Meadowbank who is disliked by most of the students and staff. Everyone seems to have something unpleasant to say about her.

Miss Lorrimer, the former games mistress, who according to Miss Rowan and Miss Blake, "was always so friendly and sociable." **NOTE:** The former secretary of the school was named Vera Lorrimer, but there is no family relationship between the two expressed. Christie's assigning of the same surname to two unrelated characters was probably inadvertent.

Mrs. Gerald Hope, who expects to be able to take her daughter Henrietta to the South of France in about five weeks, thinking it will be "a nice break" for her. She is not pleased to hear from Miss Bulstrode that any such idea is quite impossible, for if she does so, Miss Bulstrode will not have Henrietta back.

Henrietta Hope, a "nice, well balanced, intelligent child who deserves a better mother than Mrs. Gerald Hope" in the opinion of Miss Bulstrode.

The Lambeth Child, for whom Miss Bulstrode did wonders, according to Mrs. Gerald Hope

Margaret, a housemaid at Meadowbank

Julia Upjohn, a very intelligent student at Meadowbank who enjoys learning and absolutely loves Miss Rich's lessons in geography and English literature. It is she who brings Hercule Poirot into the investigation, having heard of him through her aunt, Maureen Summerhayes.

Mrs. Upjohn, the mother of Julia Upjohn. During the war she worked in the Secret Service. On the opening day of the summer term at Meadowbank, while in Miss Bulstrode's office, she happens to glance through the window and sees someone she recognizes and whose presence at Meadowbank surprises her. Then she takes a bus trip to Anatolia.

Aunt Isabel, Julia's aunt who could remove her from Meadowbank School after two murders are committed there, but does not.

Lady Veronica Carlton-Sandways, the mother of twin girls who are students at Meadowbank. She is an alcoholic who is carefully watched by her husband and by his cousin Edith. Together, these two custodians see to it that Lady Veronica is sober on Sports Day and other important occasions, but on this opening day she gives them the slip and arrives at Meadowbank quite intoxicated. Fortunately Miss Chadwick maneuvers Lady Veronica out of view and earshot of the other parents.

Major Carlton-Sandways, the father of the above-mentioned twins, who copes fairly well with his wife's drinking

The Twin Daughters of the Carlton-Sandways, students at Meadowbank

Edith, a cousin of Major Carlton-Sandways who assists him in handling Lady Veronica and her drinking problem.

Prince Ali Yusuf, the hereditary ruler of Ramat which, though small, is one of the richest states in the Middle East. He is "dark, with a smooth olive face and large melancholy eyes." The Prince was educated in England and has "Western" ideas for the modernization and democratization of his country. But the population—or at least certain elements of it—do not appreciate what he is trying to do for the country, and the country is on the verge of revolution.

Bob Rawlinson, who is a sandy-haired and freckled friend of Prince Ali Yusuf, having been his schoolmate in England and who is now his personal pilot. The Prince entrusts to Bob a packet of precious jewels worth three quarters of a million pounds, confident that Bob will find a way to convey them safely out of the country as the two of them attempt to escape from Ramat by air.

Achmed Abdullah, the deceased grandfather of Prince Ali Yusuf. He was a terrible tyrant but is remembered as a hero.

Old Achmed, a mechanic at the hangar who caught another man trying to tamper with Prince Ali Yusuf's private plane

A Man caught in the act of tampering with Prince Ali Yusuf's private airplane

An Elderly Arab in a café in Ramat, peacefully clicking through a string of amber beads

Two Men Playing Trictrac in the café in Ramat.

Joan Sutcliffe, Bob Rawlinson's older sister who happens to be visiting Ramat with her daughter on the eve of the Revolution. Bob would like to entrust Prince Ali Yusuf's jewels to her safekeeping, but he knows that she could not possibly keep the secret to herself. He finds a way to hide the jewels among Joan's and her daughter's belongings without their knowledge just before they leave Ramat bound for England.

Henry Sutcliffe, Joan's husband.

Jennifer Sutcliffe, Henry and Joan's daughter who visits Ramat with her mother, and is later enrolled against her wishes at Meadowbank School. Jennifer's primary interest at school is improving her tennis game.

Aunt Rosamund who was influential in getting Jennifer Sutcliffe admitted to Meadowbank School

A Clerk at the Ritz Savoy Hotel in Ramat who knows Bob Rawlinson well, since he is Prince Ali Yusuf's personal pilot, and cheerfully addresses him as "Squadron Leader."

Mr. and Mrs. Hurst from the Oil Company with whom Joan and Jennifer have gone on a picnic when Bob Rawlinson goes to the Ritz Savoy Hotel to speak with Joan.

John Edmundson, the third secretary at the British Embassy in Ramat *before* the revolution. Later he works at the Foreign Office in London. He is a friend of Bob Rawlinson. He provides useful information to Colonel Pikeaway about conditions in Ramat just before the revolution, and discusses the matter of the jewels and how they may have been gotten out of Ramat. He had worked out a code to use on the telephone with Bob (to foil wiretappers) and had received a phone call from Bob arranging to meet later near one of the banks, at which time Bob would have told him what he had done with the jewels. But rioting broke out and prevented that meeting.

An Arab Flicking Lightly with a Feather Duster in the hotel corridor

A Tall, Unhappy-looking Englishman from the British Consulate in Ramat who insists that Joan and Jennifer leave the city at once by airplane, since a revolution is sure to begin that evening. Before they leave, he makes a thorough search of their luggage.

H. E., the British Ambassador to Ramat

A Young Man who taps on Colonel Pikeaway's office door in Bloomsbury to announce John Edmundson

Colonel Ephraim Pikeaway of "Special Branch."

> Behind a desk sat a fat middle-aged man slumped in a chair. He was wearing a crumpled suit, the front of which was smothered in cigar ash. The windows were closed and the atmosphere was almost unbearable.
> "Well?" said the fat man testily, and speaking with half-closed eyes. "What is it now, eh?"
> It was said of colonel Pikeaway that his eyes were always just closing in sleep, or just opening after sleep. It was also said that his name was not Pikeaway and that he was not a Colonel. But some people will say anything!

Colonel Pikeaway makes it his business to find out if Ali Yusuf's jewels are in England and, if so, where they are. Knowing that Prince Ali Yusuf's cousin, Princess Shaista, is enrolled at Meadowbank school, he sends an agent there to keep an eye on things.

Derek O'Connor, a young employee at the office of Colonel Pikeaway who goes to the port at Tilbury when Joan's ship arrives and breaks the news of her brother's death to her.

"Ronnie," another young man who works for Colonel Pikeaway. He is to infiltrate Meadowbank School and to keep an eye open for developments regarding Princess Shaista. "Ronnie" becomes the young gardener who will be known as "Adam Goodman" at Meadowbank.

"Mr. Robinson," who pays a visit to Colonel Pikeaway's office and who represents "certain interests" in the matter of the jewels from Ramat.

Señora Angelica da Toredo, a Spanish dancer occupying the room on one side of Joan and Jennifer Sutcliffe's at the Ritz Savoy Hotel in Ramat

A Schoolteacher who occupies the room on the other side of Joan and Jennifer Sutcliffe's at the Ritz Savoy Hotel

Andrew Ball, of no fixed address, who burglarized the Sutcliffe home, ransacking Joan Sutcliffe's bedroom on a Sunday morning while the family was in church

Old Mrs. Ellis, the cook at the Sutcliffe home who is deaf and heard nothing, and who was preparing the midday meal while the burglary took place

That Half-witted Daughter of the Bardwells who helps Old Mrs. Ellis on Sunday mornings

Miss Laurie who comes to Meadowbank two days a week to teach art and who, on occasions, takes selected students to London to visit picture galleries.

Two Italian Girls and some German Ones, a few foreign students at Meadowbank mentioned in Julia Upjohn's letter to her mother

Margaret Gore-West, a Senior Prefect at Meadowbank

Margaret Gore-West's Mother

Princess Ingrid of Sweden, a student at Meadowbank. According to Margaret Gore-West, she is "rather fun. Very blue eyes, but she wears braces on her teeth."

René Dupont of Bordeaux to whom Angèle Blanche writes a letter

Gloria, a friend of Miss Vansittart to whom she writes a letter

Mademoiselle Geneviève Depuy, the former French teacher who was a better teacher than Mademoiselle Blanche

Lois and Mary, two of "three pleasant gigglers," students at Meadowbank whom Adam Goodman befriends

Mary Vyse, a student who, according to Miss Bulstrode is "…scholarship class—a wonderfully retentive memory. But what a dull girl!"

Lady Valence, the mother of Jane Valence

Jane Valence, who had trouble with her ears and was seen by the doctor at Meadowbank.

Baron Von Eisenger, the father of Hedwig Von Eisenger, who asks that she be given permission to go the Opera on the occasion of Hellstern's taking the role of Isolde.

Hedwig Von Eisenger, a student from Germany at Meadowbank

Vera Lorrimer, Miss Bulstrode's former secretary, who was inferior to Ann Shapland, her current secretary.

Professor Anderson, the father of Meroe Anderson. He requests permission to take his daughter out next week-end, knowing that it is too early in the term for students to be taken out, but he is leaving for Azerbaijan very soon. His request is granted by Miss Bulstrode who is flexible and bends rules for exceptional circumstances.

Meroe Anderson, a student at Meadowbank

Sergeant Green of the Hurst St. Cyprian police who receives the telephone call late at night about the murder of Miss Springer

Detective Inspector Kelsey, who is in charge of the case of the murder of Miss Springer. He is a perceptive man who is always willing to deviate from the course of routine if a remark strikes him as unusual or worth following up. A local man, he is personally acquainted with Miss Bulstrode and feels great respect for her.

Jean, a student at Meadowbank who had an earache on the night that Miss Springer was killed

A Police Photographer, A Police Officer Taking Fingerprints and **A Police Surgeon**

A Press Magnate and personal friend of Miss Bulstrode who uses his influence to play down the publicity in the matter of Miss Springer's murder

The Home Secretary, Two Press Barons, a Bishop and **The Minister of Education,** other influential personal friends of Miss Bulstrode

Chief Constable Stone, Detective Inspector Kelsey's superior

Sergeant Percy Bond, who assists Detective Inspector Kelsey in the questioning of the Meadowbank staff.

Mrs. Gibbons, the cook at Meadowbank, who is hard of hearing and who provides no useful information to the police.

Doris Hogg, a housemaid at Meadowbank whose information to the police is equally useless.

Sergeant Barber, a Young Policeman in Plain Clothes who takes notes during Detective Inspector Kelsey's interview with Adam Goodman

Mrs. Kolinsky, one of a few "questionable characters" hanging about the neighborhood of Meadowbank.

Giselle d'Aubray, a French student at Meadowbank. In her locker in the Sports Pavilion is a copy of Voltaire's *Candide* complete with illustrations.

A Well-dressed Woman with Golden Hair who delivers a new tennis racquet to Jennifer Sutcliffe and takes her old one to be restrung.

Mrs. Campbell ("Aunt Gina"), Jennifer Sutcliffe's godmother, who had asked the Well-Dressed Woman with Golden Hair to deliver the new tennis racquet and to take away the old one.

The Duchess of Welsham, who invites—or rather summons—Miss Bulstrode to dinner one Sunday.

Henry Banks, who will also dine with Miss Bulstrode and the Duchess. He was one of the original backers of Meadowbank School.

A Liveried Chauffeur in a Cadillac, who comes to Meadowbank to take Princess Shaista to London to visit her uncle.

A Well-bred Young Englishman Telephoning from Claridge's who informs Meadowbank School that Princess Shaista has not appeared at the hotel.

Sir Mervyn Todhunter, Ann Shapland's most recent employer

Lady Todhunter, the wife of Sir Mervyn who did not like the attention her husband was paying to Ann

Ann Shapland's Mother who has periods of forgetfulness and must be attended to at all times.

"A Nice Old Pussy" who lives with Ann Shapland's mother and copes most of the time.

Miss Johnson's Sister, whom she is visiting when the second murder takes place

Georges, Hercule Poirot's manservant who, for the very first time, has difficulty in describing a visitor. **Note:** For some reason Christie chose to spell the manservant's name the French way (*Georges*) in this novel, but he is clearly English and most often has been "George" since first introduced in the 1928 *The Mystery of the Blue Train.*

Hercule Poirot, the Belgian private investigator with the egg-shaped head and flamboyant mustache. He is brought into the case by Julia Upjohn who has heard of him through her aunt, Maureen Summerhayes.

Maureen Summerhayes, Julia Upjohn's "Aunt Maureen" who had told Julia about Hercule Poirot. Poirot had had the terrible experience of staying at Johnnie and Maureen Summerhayes's "guest house" in the village of Broadhinny while solving the mystery in the 1952 *Mrs. McGinty's Dead.* Her housekeeping was abominable and her cooking was so bad that no adjective in the English language could describe it. At the end of the story, Poirot taught Maureen how to make an omelet.

The Préfet (Police Chief) in Geneva, an old friend of Hercule Poirot.

A Young Female Police Detective disguised as a domestic servant at Meadowbank.

A Large and Solid-looking Turkish Woman with whom Mrs. Upjohn converses in French while they wait for their bus to be repaired in Anatolia.

Mr. Atkinson from the Consulate in Ankara who arrives at the site of the bus breakdown and explains to Mrs. Upjohn that her immediate return to England is essential.

A Young Woman of about Twenty-five, whom "Mr. Robinson" visits in London. She is "pleasant looking, with a kind of fair, chocolate-box prettiness."

Allen, the olive-skinned, dark-haired young son of the Young Woman of about Twenty-five.

FRENCH INTO ENGLISH

Note: Poirot uses very little French in this novel, and his first appearance is rather late, as he is not introduced until Chapter 17. French expressions occurring in earlier chapters are used by other characters.

Prologue

Très heureuse de vous voir, madame. Ah, je regrette, ce ne serait pas possible, cette après-midi. (Correct spelling: *cet après-midi*) *Mademoiselle Bulstrode est tellement occupée.*—I'm so happy to see you, ma'am. Oh, I'm sorry, that would not be possible this afternoon. Miss Bulstrode is so busy.

assez bien—not bad looking

formidable!—an all-purpose expression used by French speakers when greatly and affirmatively impressed by something.

Enchantée—Delighted to meet you

Chapter 5

Enfin, vous m'ennuiez, mes enfants! (correct spelling: *vous m'ennuyez*)—You kids are getting on my nerves!

Chapter 7 *le sport*—athletics, sports

Chapter 10 *grande dame*—a fine lady

Chapter 11

Lèse-majesté—a personal offence or affront to a sovereign, here used metaphorically to imply that the murder at Meadowbank was a personal insult to a school of such prestige.

Chapter 17

Nom d'un nom d'un nom!—An extremely strong expression, usually used in anger, but here used by Poirot because he is awestruck by the jewels. *Nom d'un nom* is a euphemism for *Nom de Dieu* (God's name) which is considered very strong, and even sacrilegious. A child of even non-religious parents would be corrected for uttering *Nom de Dieu*, just as an American child would be corrected for saying "God damn it."

Il ne manquait que ça!—Just what we need! (sarcasm)

Chapter 18

Les oreilles ennemies nous écoutent.—Enemy ears are listening to us.

Chapter 19 *Bien*—Very good

Chapter 20 *Entre nous*—Just between us

Chapter 21

mal elevée (correct spelling: *mal élevée*)—"badly brought up," a term usually applied to ill-mannered children, here applied to an adult with the meaning of rudeness or coarseness or lacking in good manners

Chapter 22

Combien—garçons—filles—combien?—How many—boys—girls—how many?
Une fille—One girl
Et garçons?—And boys?
Cinq garçons? Très bien!—Five boys? Very good!

Chapter 24 *mon ami*—my friend

COMMENTS

Cat Among the Pigeons is a delightful mystery novel that combines the traditional detective story with a bit of the cloak-and-dagger fun of a Christie adventure story. Readers who are partial to Christie novels in which at least a few "youthful" characters are present are likely to enjoy *Hickory, Dickory, Death* and *Cat Among the Pigeons* equally well. There are plenty of young people in *Cat Among the Pigeons,* although the only youngsters who are main characters are Julia Upjohn and Jennifer Sutcliffe. But both are engaging kids and Julia is instrumental in searching for and finding something very important, and taking it upon herself to travel alone to London to bring Hercule Poirot into the case. A source of laughs, to those who have read the 1952 *Mrs. McGinty's Dead,* are Julia Upjohn's statements about her aunt, Maureen Summerhayes, England's (and therefore the world's) worst cook. In the earlier novel poor Hercule Poirot was forced to take a room at the Summerhayes' "guesthouse" in Broadhinny and to endure Maureen's sickening meals and pitiful housekeeping.

Christie's characterizations reached a peak of thoroughness and sensitivity during the 1940s with *Murder in Retrospect, Remembered Death, Murder After Hours* and *There Is a Tide.* During the 1950s, however, most of her detective novels are memorable more for their action than for their characters. There seems to be a return to more light-hearted detective fiction with lightly-drawn, sometimes stereotypical characters without the substance that was noted in the four novels of the 1940s mentioned above. An exception is the 1958 *Ordeal by Innocence* in which all of the characters in the Argyle family are portrayed with great detail and subtlety. Now, in *Cat Among the Pigeons* there are a very large number of characters, both major and minor, that come to life amazingly well through their own statements and through comments made about them by others. Christie's technique of having several characters in this novel write letters to parents and friends is a clever way of expanding the characterizations.

Characters in *Cat Among the Pigeons* who are remembered long after one reads the book begin with Miss Bulstrode, a co-founder and headmistress of an excellent school. She has vision; she has original ideas; she has assertiveness; she is strict yet flexible. As the headmistress of a school for youngsters she is absolutely admirable in every way. She knows the strengths and weaknesses of every one of the students and treats each one as an individual.

Equally memorable is the enthusiastic Eileen Rich who brings geography and English literature to life and excitement in her classroom. She is a risk taker who welcomes new challenges and fresh ideas. Like Miss Bulstrode, she has vision. She adores teaching and compares it to fishing—you never know what you will pull from the sea in terms of the students' responses to your teaching; therein lies the excitement of teaching, to her.

There is the hard-working and competent games-mistress Grace Springer who, though competent and thorough, takes no particular pleasure in the achievements of her students.

There is the mediocre Mademoiselle Blanche who is clearly bored by both the students and their learning.

There is the psychology-degreed Miss Rowan who accuses the police of having negative attitudes towards psychology when they point out to her that one cannot commit suicide by firing a gun at oneself from a distance of four feet and then cause the gun to vanish into thin air.

Miss Vansittart is an example of the extremely competent though unimaginative and unoriginal thinker who is content to follow in the footsteps of a predecessor. Never conceiving a fresh, new idea, always playing safe with established practices, she is the kind of person who would respond to a new suggestion with those ugly words, "Well, er, but we've never done things *that* way…"

Miss Chadwick ("Faithful Chaddy") is the kind of person who is always there and who always copes and is always competent and reliable, but who is not in the least "brainy" except in her own small corner of academia.

Then there is the super-competent secretary Ann Shapland who has made a point of being so efficient and skilled in her profession that she can pick and choose her jobs, making a point of never becoming attached to one job or place in particular.

There is Miss Johnson, the competent matron who lives for Meadowbank and feels like a fish out of water between terms. If Meadowbank were to fold, her life would end.

There is the world-traveling Mrs. Upjohn, who has worked in the Secret Service and who enjoys touring even primitive countries by common motorbus, cheerfully sitting at the roadside and attempting to converse on any subject with native women in halting French while the bus is being repaired.

The modern-thinking ruler of a fictitious Middle Eastern country, Prince Ali Yusuf is a fun person to imagine, whether such a person is likely to exist or not. His comments about the questionable acceptance of democracy by populations in the Middle East are rather relevant today (2007) as the war in Iraq enters its fifth year with no end in sight, President Bush denying the existence of civil war, and religious factions massacring each other.

Cat Among the Pigeons is a novel that is filled with fun, memorable characters and plenty of action, and it can be considered a "good vintage Christie" to be recommended as a first Christie experience.

SUMMARY FOR THE 1950S

During the 1940s, Agatha Christie seemed to be trying to move away from the "light fiction" detective story and to write her novels in a more serious style, which included extremely thorough characterizations. The characterizations in four of her detective novels of that decade—*Murder in Retrospect, Remembered Death, There Is a Tide* and *Murder After Hours*—are so thorough that one might remember some of the characters long after the stories themselves are forgotten.

The 1950s are characterized by a return to more traditional Christie detective stories with more emphasis on the crime story and less emphasis on character development. Notable exceptions to this are the last two novels of the decade, *Ordeal by Innocence* and *Cat Among the Pigeons*. In both of these novels the characterization is excellent, and in *Cat Among the Pigeons*, even the minor characters are portrayed with such individuality that many of them are memorable. In general, however, Christie's detective novels of the 1950s are not remarkable for characterization. The stories themselves are more exciting than some of the rather somber novels of the 1940s. The two adventure stories, *They Came To Baghdad* and *So Many Steps to Death* are especially exciting; so are *A Murder Is Announced, A Pocket Full of Rye*, and *Hickory, Dickory, Death* with their multiple murders.

One writer has suggested that Christie's "decline" as a writer of detective stories began during the 1950s. It is true that in two of the novels—the 1955 *Hickory, Dickory, Death* and the 1958 *Ordeal by Innocence*—the solution is reached by pure guesswork rather than through carefully plotted detection. As detective novels, they are probably not favorites among connoisseurs. But Christie's novels of the 1950s are just as entertaining and well written as those of her previous decades, and rereading them is just as enjoyable. Christie's "decline" did not really begin until the beginning of the 1960s with *The Pale Horse*.

Christie had always incorporated social developments and "trends" into her stories as background material. Drug abuse among the upper classes, for example, was mentioned as early as the 1926 *The Murder of Roger Ackroyd*. Drug use or drug trafficking play roles in the 1932 *Peril at End House*, the 1933 *Thirteen at Dinner*, the 1936 *Murder in Mesopotamia*, the 1941 *Evil Under the Sun* and the 1955 *Hickory, Dickory, Death*. The increasing prevalence of divorce is well chronicled through Christie's detective novels beginning as early as the 1928 *The Mystery of the Blue Train*.

Beginning with the 1948 *There Is a Tide*, Christie chronicles changing conditions and attitudes in English society, especially the changes that were not welcomed by the upper middle class, of which she herself was clearly a member. And so the demise of the "servant class" in England is portrayed in her novels of the 1950s as a growing "problem," although the former servants who were now finding better ways of earning their livings would hardly have agreed that there was a "problem" at all. In the 1950 *A Murder Is Announced* the only two households in the village of Chipping Cleghorn still lucky enough to have a live-in cook/housemaid must be very careful never to offend their servant, lest she "bolt." They know that if she does "bolt," a hundred other households will compete for her services.

In the 1952 *Mrs. McGinty's Dead,* four different families have "servant problems." Mrs. Upward has a "faithful old servant," Janet Groom, but she is so old that she can now only manage "a little simple cooking." The Rendels' housekeeper, Mrs. Scott, is too old to get down on her knees and scrub floors. The Wetherbys are reduced to employing a foreign girl named Frieda, who they suspect only took her job with them in order to obtain a visa and work permit, and who will probably leave her job as soon as she finds an English husband. The wealthiest residents of the village, the Carpenters, can afford a husband-and-wife pair of servants, the Crofts. But when Mrs. Carpenter attempts to pay the Crofts to lie to the police and provide her with a false alibi, they astound and anger her not only by refusing, but also by reporting her to the police for approaching them on the subject. There appears to be "no more loyalty among the servant class." The title character, Mrs. McGinty, who dies before the story begins, had worked as a cleaning lady two or three mornings or afternoons each week for all four of the above families, and others in the village as well, and she is very much missed.

In the 1953 *A Pocket Full of Rye,* Mary Dove has found a lucrative career as a first-rate, expensive housekeeper, explaining to the investigating officer, "My dear Inspector Neele, this is the perfect racket. People will pay anything—*anything*—to be spared domestic worries." Mary works only for the rich and remains with one household no more than a year and a half, then moves on to another position. She feels no attachment or loyalty to her employers whatsoever. When asked by Inspector Neele her impressions of the Fortescue family, this is her incredible response:

> "They are really all quite odious. The late Mr. Fortescue was the kind of crook who is always careful to play safe. He boasted a great deal of his various smart dealings. He was rude and overbearing in manner and was a definite bully. Mrs. Fortescue, Adele—was his second wife and about thirty years younger than he was. He came across her at Brighton. She was a manicurist on the lookout for big money. She is very good looking—a real sexy piece, if you know what I mean."

Clearly Mary Dove is not your average "loyal, humble, devoted servant" of Christie-past.

In the 1953 *Funerals Are Fatal,* Timothy and Maude Abernethie have just one servant—Mrs. Jones, a married woman who comes in for a few hours daily. Mrs. Jones refuses to stay overnight to look after Timothy when his wife is away, citing the fact that she has a husband of her own to look after. Timothy regards this as an affront, commenting that there is "no longer any loyalty among the lower classes." Mrs. Jones later tells the police that Timothy is not really an "invalid" at all, and that he gets out and about just fine when he really needs something, like tobacco. "Do him good, I thought," she tells the police, "to get about the house and look after himself for once. Might make him see what a lot he gets done for him." At Enderby, a vast Victorian mansion now occupied only by wealthy old Richard Abernethie, there continue to be two "loyal old servants," a housekeeper and a butler who are in their eighties. They resent the intrusion of a twenty-seven-year-old upstart of a cook, Marjorie, who is not their idea of "good service" despite the fact that she is an excellent cook. She lets them know that the only reason she puts up with the antiquated kitchen at Enderby is because Mr. Abernethie appreciates her cooking—and pays her well for it.

In the 1956 *Dead Man's Folly,* the wealthy Sir George Stubbs has a live-in secretary, Amanda Brewis, who finds herself being more of a housekeeper than a secretary, and who comments to Hercule Poirot that nowadays one doesn't find such niceties as cooks and housekeepers.

In the 1957 *What Mrs. McGillicuddy Saw,* Christie creates a rather unlikely character—Lucy Eyelesbarrow, an educated young woman with a degree in mathematics who, instead of choosing an academic career, "exploits shortage" and works as a very expensive short-term domestic servant. Unlike the "expensive housekeeper," Mary Dove, in the 1953 *A Pocket Full of Rye,* Lucy does not "supervise" servants. She *is* the servant, doing all of the cooking and cleaning herself—charging an arm and a leg and refusing to stay in any one place for more than six weeks. Households all over England fight over her.

In the 1958 *Ordeal by Innocence,* the Argyle family has a Norwegian trained nurse who helped them run a shelter for London children during the war and who later stayed on as a housekeeper out of loyalty to the family. Their only other servants are one or two "day women." In this novel, however, the "problem" of a shortage of servants is never mentioned and, in fact, Christie will leave this subject alone in the future for the most part, perhaps finally realizing that the days of domestic servants for all but the wealthiest Britons are gone for good.

"Reduced incomes" for most upper middle class British families is also a "problem" that is thoroughly chronicled by Christie during the 1950s. These "incomes" are, of course, investment incomes, not incomes that come to one as a result of that lowly thing called "work." England's standard of living had actually been declining ever since the end of World War One. By 1950 Britain was just another poverty-afflicted post-war European country receiving Care Packages from America. Her home industries were antiquated and her empire was gone.

Psychology—both the serious study of it and the popular misconceptions about it—had been a feature in most of Christie's books from about 1935 onwards and well into the 1950s. In the 1955 *Hickory, Dickory, Death* there is Colin McNabb's hilarious nonsense about what he calls Celia Austin's "Cinderella complex." But then in the 1958 *Ordeal by Innocence* there is "serious" talk about the real psychoses of several characters, notably Michael Argyle and his life-long obsession about being "unwanted" by his natural mother.

Unfortunately, beginning with the 1949 *Crooked House*, Christie begins to "preach" on a new subject. It is the idea that character traits are inherited through blood, and that they cannot be shaped by training or education. She "preaches" on that subject now and then all through the 1950s, notably (although mildly) in the 1952 *Mrs. McGinty's Dead*. The original British title for that novel is, in fact, *Blood Will Tell*. She "preaches" even more strongly on the subject in the 1952 *Murder with Mirrors*, ridiculing the idea that bad environment has something to do with youngsters' becoming juvenile delinquents, and making a hilariously stupid remark about "Italian blood." In the 1958 *Ordeal by Innocence* her "preaching" reaches its loudest pitch ever. In that novel, Christie seems militantly determined to promote the idea that training and education—that is, "upbringing"—are of little importance in shaping character traits in children. Her idea is that children will be whatever they have inherited by blood from their ancestors. Adopt a baby from slum parents—even a newborn one—and you are in for trouble because that baby has in its blood the "seeds" that put its ancestors into the slums in the first place.

It is probable that Christie felt that she had been a failure as a parent herself, and therefore she embraced every possible excuse she could find to minimize the importance of her poor parenting practices, just as certain obese people welcome any evidence that obesity is the result of one's genetic makeup, and not the result of immoderate consumption of fats, carbs and sugars. Christie hammered away—through her characters—at the notion that it is a child's blood inheritance and *not* his or her parents' child-rearing practices, that determine his or her character. In any case, it seems that those subjects are out of place in light fiction, and Christie's "preaching" on them may destroy, for some readers, some of the pleasure they might have in reading a few of her books of the 1950s. This is especially likely in the case of *Ordeal by Innocence*.

On the plus side, it is always fun, in reading Christie's novels of the 1950s, to notice the changes in English society that she documented during that decade. The references to the post-war realities of food and clothing rationing are interesting as historical facts, as early as the 1948 *There Is a Tide* and as late as the 1953 *Funerals Are Fatal*, although it is in the 1950 *A Murder Is Announced*, that those conditions are most prominently expressed.

It must have been during the 1950s that Britain's reduced position of importance in the world entered the consciousness of Britons, and it was probably not a very pleasant subject for them to think about. During the second half of the nineteenth century, Britain had the highest living standard in the world and possessed a vast empire all around the world. It was said that "The sun never sets on the British Empire." Large numbers of upper- and middle-class Britons routinely vacationed abroad, notably in the resort areas of the Normandy coast of France and along the French Riviera, and all of this was affordable to them because of the difference in living standards between England and France. Any British family finding itself in financial difficulties could usually solve its problem by "going abroad" for a few months and renting out the family home or flat. One could easily live in France—and even more easily in Spain or Italy—on the rent payments one received, *and* pay off one's debts. Accustomed to their ability to purchase the appearance of respect among foreigners everywhere, it was natural for the British to consider themselves to be culturally, as well as financially, superior to the rest of the world.

By 1950 all of that was history. World War One had ruined Britain's pre-eminence in international shipping and trade, the foundation of her economy. Severe unemployment plagued England all through the 1920s and 1930s, and England grew steadily poorer. With the loss of India in 1947, the British Empire effectively ceased to exist. The independence of East African and Middle Eastern countries ended Britain's dominant position in those areas as well. All of this is reflected, sometimes with subtlety, in comments by Christie characters, such as Miss Hetherington in the 1954 *So Many Steps to Death,* who observes that British travelers abroad "no longer receive favored treatment." She also complains of the small "travel allowance" imposed by the British government in an effort to reduce the amount of British wealth—or what was left of it—that trickled out of England whenever the English spent money abroad.

Christie even dares to suggest, during the 1950s, that some "foreigners" may actually have ways and customs that the British might be well-advised to emulate. From the very beginnings, Christie had placed British ethnocentric remarks in the mouths of the less-educated characters, such as servants, and she ridiculed characters such as the ethnocentric Colonel Arbuthnot in *Murder in the Calais Coach,* who did not even bother to look in Hercule Poirot's direction, describing him mentally as "Just another damned foreigner." But during the 1950s, specific aspects of foreign cultures find themselves portrayed in Christie's novels as being worthy of respect.

Miss Hetherington, in the 1954 *So Many Steps to Death,* in her superior British way, makes a critical remark about a pair of French parents at a hotel in Morocco. The parents have their children with them at the dinner table, allowing them to participate in every course of the meal instead of being given "milk and biscuits in their room, as children should"—AND the parents even allow the children to drink wine! A younger British traveler, Hilary Craven, notes with amusement that the French children appear to be very healthy as a result of it. Miss Hetherington also notes that the children seem to be "very fond of their papa," a subtle suggestion that French parents may express more affection towards their children than British parents do, and therefore receive more affection in return.

In the 1959 *Cat Among the Pigeons,* there is an amusing conversation between the headmistress of an excellent girls' school and one of the teachers. The teacher expresses concern that a certain Middle Eastern student wears a bra that enhances—instead of concealing—the development of her bust. The headmistress remarks that the English custom of making a virtue out of social and sexual immaturity in children is a very bad mistake. She also remarks that it might not be a bad idea for English girls to be sent to the Middle East in order to learn "manners." There is clearly the idea, at least in Christie's mind—and for the first time in her writings—that certain aspects of British ways of living are not quite as "superior" as once thought.

English cooking had been a subject of derisive comment even in Christie's earliest novels, but usually by the very foreign—and therefore extremely eccentric—Hercule Poirot, although in the 1937 *Poirot Loses a Client,* even the supremely British Arthur Hastings complains of the food in an English inn. It is in the 1953 *Funerals Are Fatal* that Poirot has, for the first time, an occasion to tell an English cook—a young woman of twenty-seven who is resented by the aging butler and the housekeeper for her "modern" ways—that she is an excellent cook. She, in turn, embraces "foreign and therefore extremely eccentric" Hercule Poirot as a "kindred spirit." We recall that in the 1950 *A Murder Is Announced,* the household at Little Paddocks was very fortunate to have their Central European immigrant cook Mitzi, despite her irrational fears and tantrums, because she was such an excellent cook. We also recall that the London student hostel in the 1955 *Hickory, Dickory, Death* was a financial success with a waiting list, largely because the meals were "appetizing and sufficient," thanks to the Italian couple who prepared and served the meals there. And we learn, in the 1959 *Cat Among the Pigeons,* seven years after the 1952 *Mrs. McGinty's Dead,* that Maureen Summerhayes, who is England's—and therefore the world's—worst cook, still makes "smashing omelettes" as a result of a cooking lesson once given to her by that eccentric foreigner, Hercule Poirot.

The influx of foreigners in England since the end of World War Two is mentioned in several novels, and these foreigners are blamed—mostly by the poorly-educated British characters—for the increase in crime in England. In the 1950 *A Murder Is Announced,* it is a Swiss hotel receptionist who is the first murder victim, and he dies in a house where the cook is a foreigner. Naturally certain villagers blame the foreignness of these characters for the very fact that the crime took place, and at least one character is sure that the cook is a Communist. In the 1955 *Hickory, Dickory, Death* several foreign students live at the youth hostel where a series of thefts and a murder take place. A few months earlier two other foreign residents had been in trouble with the police—one in connection with a murder in Cambridge and another with prostitution in Sheffield. In the 1956 *Dead Man's Folly* several British characters are annoyed by the fact that a neighboring estate has been converted to a youth hostel catering mostly to foreign students visiting England. A police officer comments about the sexual "goings on" at the hostel, and voices the belief that one of "those foreigners" at the hostel must be the person responsible for the murder he is investigating.

As to "Communists," there are plenty of comments—again, by the poorly educated British characters—that Communists are responsible for the crimes in the stories. As early as the 1949 *Crooked House* a cook/nanny affirms that the murder in the household must be the work of "the Communists, or if not, the Catholics." As late as the 1959 *Cat Among the Pigeons* a young princess from the Middle East believes she will be kidnapped, most likely by Communists, since "Communists are very wicked." In the 1954 *So Many Steps to Death* and the 1955 *Hickory, Dickory, Death* there are derisive comments about the Communist "witch hunts" in America and Americans' exaggerated fear of Communism. All of this is, of course, part of the "Cold War" atmosphere of the 1950s. "Sputnik" became a household word overnight when the Soviet Union launched the first man-made satellite in 1957, and Christie uses that word for the first time in a novel in her 1958 *Ordeal by Innocence*. We are told in the 1957 *What Mrs. McGillicuddy Saw* that it is common for old ladies with vivid imaginations to report sightings of U.F.O.'s and discoveries of Communist agents everywhere.

The tension between the United States and the Soviet Union, in fact, is a major background in two novels: the 1951 *They Came to Baghdad* and the 1954 *So Many Steps to Death*. In the first of these, there seems to be a sinister international organization to which money is flowing from every country at an alarming rate, and the purpose of that organization seems to be to destroy efforts for East-West reconciliation in order to incite a Third World War. In the later novel, it is the frustration felt by sincere scientists around the world because of governments' abuse of science—spending money for weapons instead of curing diseases, for example—that causes some scientists to wish for a secret colony of international, apolitical scientists. All of this because of the use of the atomic bomb at the end of World War Two and the constant fear of a future atomic war. In the 1956 *Dead Man's Folly*, a young scientist has a nervous breakdown because of his frustration about the way the world seems to be headed for a final, atomic war and because governments and populations seem to be blind or apathetic about it.

In addition to the presence of these serious, rather somber subjects in Christie's novels of the 1950s, we note a few minor signs of "changing times" during that decade. Television is first mentioned in a Christie novel in the 1956 *Dead Man's Folly*, and it is first referred to as "telly" in the 1958 *Ordeal by Innocence*. In both cases it is working class people who are the owners of the television sets, a sign of rising living standards among the working class. Jet airplanes and "breaking the sound barrier" are mentioned for the first time in the 1957 *What Mrs. McGillicuddy Saw* and in the same novel that modern wonder, the ball point pen, makes its first appearance in Christie.

As to the improvement in living conditions of working class people during the 1950s, it is the middle class that loses a good deal of its accustomed affluence and comfort in order to pay for it. There is increased taxation in order to pay for such modern benefits as the National Health Insurance, which is derided by certain Christie characters, especially doctors.

For all of this documentation of social change in England alone, the Christie novels of the 1950s are a treasure, and a pleasure to read.

The Pale Horse (1961)

SETTING

The story takes place in the fall of approximately 1960 or 1961. The action takes place mostly in London and in the fictitious village of Much Deeping, which is described as being about twenty miles from the real resort city of Bournemouth on the English Channel in the county of Hampshire.

The London settings include a dimly-lighted, narrow street in a run-down neighborhood close to Paddington Railway station on a foggy night. Scenes also occur in a shabby rooming house, a mediocre café, a pharmacy, and the presbytery of a Catholic church, all in this same neighborhood. Other London settings include an Espresso bar and the service flat of the narrator in Chelsea, a fine restaurant called "Fantasie," a small restaurant specializing in seafoods, and a police station. There is also a scene at the London flat of the detective storywriter, Ariadne Oliver, a character who had appeared in three previous Christie novels. Mrs. Oliver's workroom continues to be described as a disorderly room with walls papered in an outlandish pattern of brightly-colored tropical foliage and birds.

There is a scene at an upscale Mayfair florist's shop, Flower Studies, Ltd., satirically described by one character as

"...one of those arty flower places in Mayfair. You know, three dead twigs, a tulip with its petals pinned back and a speckled laurel leaf. Price three guineas."

There is a scene at a house called Carrington Park in one chapter (but Carraway Park in another—carelessness on the part of Christie?) in the fictitious town of Amberley in the county of Surrey. The house was designed more than a century earlier by the well-known, Regency period architect John Nash; it has the appearance of "a near castle of modest proportions," and its dining room is octagonal in shape.

There are two scenes at the threadbare office of a shady, disbarred lawyer in Birmingham, and one or two scenes at a small, newly-built, sparsely-furnished bungalow within a new housing development, Glendower Close, still under construction on the outskirts of Bournemouth. The small bungalow there is the new home of a recently retired pharmacist who has named it "Everest," supposedly as a joke: "ever-rest."

The main setting, however, is the village of Much Deeping where scenes take place at three private residences, the vicarage and an inn called The King's Arms. The scene at The King's Arms is very brief and consists of the narrator of the story entering only to quickly peruse the registration book in search of certain names.

One of the residences, a major setting, is a very old building dating from the fifteenth century (the owners claim that part of the building actually dates from the fourteenth). The building had for many years served as an inn but has recently been converted to a private home, the former bar of the inn now being furnished with "Chippendale and chintz—clearly a woman's sitting room." The stables and outbuildings of the former inn have been made into one large room, a vast library. The old inn's name had been "The Pale Horse" and the current residents have framed the old inn sign, which crudely pictures a white horse with an indistinct rider on it. The sign is displayed on one wall of a dim corridor inside the house. There is a narrow, twisting staircase leading up out of the former bar of the inn.

A second residence in Much Deeping, called Priors Court and the home of a very wealthy invalid and art collector, is filled with expensive works of art from remote periods and distant places, especially China.

No current events play a role in the story, but there are a few references to some social phenomena of the period. The "beatniks" of the late 1950s and early 1960s were young people from middle or upper class families who rejected their class status for reasons not fully explained, other than as a general reaction against the alleged materialism, status consciousness and superficiality of their parents' generation. They expressed their "non-conformity" by bathing infrequently and dressing in a way that was deliberately unflattering, usually in close-fitting black garments. In a way they were the predecessors of the "hippies" of the late 1960s.

The term "Teddy boy" occurs in the speech of a police officer. Adolescent boys of the "juvenile delinquent" type were referred to as "Teddy-boys" in the early 1960s and generally wore black leather jackets.

There are a few references to modern advances in science and technology and the word "computer" is used for the first time in a Christie novel. The computers of the late 1950s and early 1960s were primitive devices compared with modern computers—there were no word processing programs until the late 1970s and the Internet was not yet dreamed of. The computers of those early years were chiefly mechanical devices for storage and retrieval of data.

The term "extrasensory perception" also occurs in the novel; it was a new subject of trendy conversation at the time. In fact the whole subject of "communication without physical contact" is an important subject in the story and such real phenomena as radio and television waves—unknown just a few years earlier—are cited as suggesting the possibility that there may also be other non-physical means of communication, and that witchcraft, long dismissed by educated people as superstition, may actually have a base in reality.

The term "brainwashing," another buzzword of the period, occurs in a vague reference.

STORY

On a late fall evening of approximately 1960 or 1961, in a poor district near Paddington Station in London, an elderly Catholic priest, Father Gorman, is summoned to the bedside of a dying woman who, suffering from a severe fever after an episode of flu, urgently requests a priest, evidently for confession before death. While the priest is with the woman, she dies.

Father Gorman is attacked and killed in a dark, narrow street as he makes his way back to his presbytery. The torn clothing of the priest suggests that the murderer was looking frantically for something. Inside one of Father Gorman's shoes is a scribbled list of surnames. The police surmise that it was this list of names that the killer must have been looking for.

During a conversation with three friends at a restaurant, the narrator Mark Easterbrook learns of an organization called "The Pale Horse" which allegedly arranges "murders for hire." The following day he has occasion to speak with his friend, detective novelist Ariadne Oliver, who is planning to assist with a fête in the village of Much Deeping, and who expresses the hope that her hosts there will not take her to have drinks at that nasty inn called "The Pale Horse." Intrigued by hearing mention of "The Pale Horse" twice in twenty-four hours, Mark looks forward to visiting Much Deeping and having a look at "The Pale Horse" for himself. He finds that it is nothing but an antiquated former inn dating from the fifteenth century, but the occupants—three eccentric women who have converted the building to a residence—are reputed to be witches, and one of the "witches" speaks to Mark in a way that suggests that murders can be committed by extrasensory means.

Although all of this strikes Mark as nonsense, as the story progresses Mark cannot rid himself of the notion that there is something sinister about The Pale Horse. As to the list of names found in Father Gorman's shoe, the police study the records of deaths over the past year and find that everyone whose name was one of those on the list died a natural death. However, the guest register at the only hotel in Much Deeping shows a number of names that can be linked to the names on the list found in Father Gorman's shoe. Mark becomes convinced that the names on the list are murder victims and that their murders were arranged by relatives who visited the "three witches" at The Pale Horse during the past year.

Mark's girlfriend Hermia Redcliffe scoffs at his ideas, and so does his good friend Jim Corrigan, but Mark succeeds in finding an assistant for his investigation and unmasks what is indeed a murder-for-hire organization.

CHARACTERS

Mark Easterbrook, the narrator of the story. He is an historian who is currently working on a book about the Moguls. He seems to be a rather depressed person. He has an intelligent girlfriend, Hermia Redcliffe, who is a teacher and a writer and who he knows "ought to be" a perfect companion to him, although at times it strikes him that she is insufferably dull.

All through the story, Mark is plagued with self-doubt on the subject of his relationship with Hermia, but more importantly on the subject of whether he can seriously believe in all the talk about "witchcraft" at The Pale Horse.

Mark Easterbrook's Sister, who has often accused him of "living in a world of his own," and who always refers to Hermia Redcliffe as "Mark's girl friend" with an intonation of quotation marks about the term, which never fails to annoy him.

Lou Ellis, a "lank blonde," one of two beatnik girls who get into a fight one evening at Luigi's, an Espresso bar in the Chelsea district of London.

Gene Pleydon, the young man who is the subject of the dispute between the two beatnik girls at Luigi's.

Lou Ellis's New Boyfriend, who according to Catherine Corrigan, is "another dud."

Thomasina Ann Tuckerton, a.k.a. "Tommy Tucker," an unfortunate redhead who loses a good bit of her red hair thanks to Lou Ellis one night at Luigi's. She is soon to become a wealthy heiress (she is not yet twenty-one) but she rejects the wealthy status of her family and associates with a group of beatniks and lives in a dingy flat in Chelsea.

Tommy Tucker dies just a few days after the fight with Lou at Luigi's.

Thomas Tuckerton, Esq., Tommy Tucker's late father who left her a fortune to be held in trust until she is twenty-one or married. She dies before either of those events, and so the money goes to her stepmother.

Mrs. Tuckerton, Thomas's widow and Thomasina's stepmother. Thomasina's death before age twenty-one makes her a very rich woman.

A Young Man Named Doug, one of the embarrassed escorts of Tommy Tucker and Lou Ellis when they have a fight in Luigi's Espresso Bar

A Second Young Man, the other embarrassed escort.

Luigi, the proprietor of Luigi's Espresso Bar. He is a slim, Italian-looking fellow with sideburns whose English is pure Cockney.

"Authority Dressed in Blue," a.k.a. A Constable on the Beat who enters Luigi's as the fight between the beatnik girls is going on and utters the regulation words "What's going on here?" whereupon the fight ends.

Rhoda Despard, a cousin of Mark Easterbrook who lives in the village of Much Deeping near Bournemouth. She was a character in the 1936 *Cards on the Table*. Her name was Rhoda Dawes at the time and she was about twenty-five years old. She now has small children who are young enough to be in the care of a nursery governess; therefore we must not ask for absolute chronological consistency, since that would assign her an age of about fifty in this story, which takes place in about 1960.

Major Hugh Despard, Rhoda's husband, whom she met in 1936 in *Cards on the Table*. He has evidently changed his first name, because in the earlier story he was John Despard.

Mrs. Ariadne Oliver, a detective novelist superficially modeled after Agatha Christie herself. This is her fourth appearance in a Christie novel. In this one, she does not eat a single apple, which is extremely uncharacteristic of her, since in the three earlier novels, she was surrounded by apples at all times and every time she stood up or stepped out of her car, apples rolled in all directions. She is a good friend of Mark Easterbrook, the narrator.

Milly, Mrs. Oliver's maid, an efficient dragon who guards her mistress from the onslaughts of the outside world.

Mrs. Gerahty, Father Gorman's housekeeper

Mike Potter, a young boy sent by Mrs. Coppins to fetch Father Gorman

Father Gorman, the elderly Catholic priest at St. Dominic's church near Paddington Station. After hearing a dying woman's confession, he is murdered while on his way back to his presbytery.

Mrs. Coppins, Mrs. Davis's landlady, who complies with Mrs. Davis's urgent appeal and summons Father Gorman

Mr. Coppins, the deceased husband of Mrs. Coppins, who never believed in a woman's intuition

Mrs. Jessie Davis, who died from complications arising from an episode of influenza. It was Mrs. Davis who urgently requested a priest and then died while Father Gorman was with her.

Mr. Archer, the deceased husband of Mrs. Davis. He died many years ago and, according to Mrs. Davis, he was an invalid. His wife then resumed the use of her maiden surname.

An Elderly Man who works in a shoe repair shop and lives in Mrs. Coppins's rooming house. He has no information about Mrs. Davis.

A Young Girl of Twenty-two who lives in Mrs. Coppins's rooming house. She also has no information about Mrs. Davis.

A Doctor who arrives too late to save Mrs. Davis's life.

Tony, the owner of a café called Tony's Place, where Father Gorman drinks his last cup of coffee. He tells the police about an elderly man who entered the café and then left when Father Gorman did, perhaps to follow him.

Three Young Lads of the Teddy-boy Type, in Edwardian Dress who enter Tony's Place noisily just after Father Gorman does.

An Elderly Man who enters Tony's Place quietly, then leaves without ordering.

Dr. Jim Corrigan, a medical doctor and a friend of Mark Easterbrook's from their days at school, although they have seen nothing of each other for the past fifteen years. Currently working as a police surgeon, it is he who examines Father Gorman's body when it is found. When Mark approaches him for assistance in investigating the three witches of The Pale Horse, Jim uses the words "poppycock" and "balderdash."

Divisional Detective Inspector Lejeune, who is in charge of the case of Father Gorman's murder.

Sergeant Pine, Inspector Lejeune's assistant. He learns about the hole in Father Gorman's pocket from the priest's housekeeper, Mrs. Gerahty.

Lady Hesketh-Dubois, Mark Easterbrook's godmother who died recently. She left him his choice of three watercolor paintings from her home. Her surname was among those on the list that was found in Father Gorman's shoe. Was she killed by contract through The Pale Horse?

Edith Binns, Lady Hesketh-Dubois's former maid, who answers the telephone at the home of the deceased when Jim Corrigan telephones.

A Woman who knew Fr. Gorman and who saw him in the street the night he was killed

Mr. Zachariah Osborne, a chemist who saw Fr. Gorman passing his shop in the street, and another man following him. He is an excellent observer and has made a hobby of studying faces for the express purpose of never forgetting them. He is certain that a particular resident of Much Deeping was the man he saw following Father Gorman in the street just before he was killed.

A Young Man in a White Overall making bottles of medicine in Mr. Osborne's chemist's shop

A Young Lady who was working behind the counter at the chemist's shop the night Fr. Gorman was killed

Hermia Redcliffe, Mark Easterbrook's "steady" girlfriend, although he detests the expression "going steady." She is "a handsome young woman of twenty-eight" and an intelligent young teacher who writes articles for the *Journal*. Being the intelligent person that she is, it is no surprise that she finds Mark's suspicions about "death by witchcraft" to be ridiculous.

David Ardingly, a friend of Mark Easterbrook's. He is a lecturer in history at Oxford. Mark and Hermia run into him while he is having dinner with a friend in a restaurant one evening. Although "a remarkably clever young man," David can only find relaxation with girls who are practically half-witted.

Pamela Stirling, a.k.a. "Poppy," David Ardingly's current girlfriend. Poppy is the first character in the story to mention The Pale Horse as being a murder-for-hire organization.

Mr. Soames White, Lady Hesketh-Dubois's solicitor who informs Mark Easterbrook that he has inherited three watercolor paintings of his choice.

A Pale-faced Lad in French Sailor's Trousers who serves an excellent fish soup to Mark Easterbrook and Jim Corrigan in a small restaurant

A Pleasant but Vague Starlet who opens the fête at Much Deeping

Miss Macalister, the Scottish nursery governess of Rhoda and Hugh Despard's children

Michael Brent, who found the buried treasure at the annual fête three years in a row

Lady Brookbank, who wins the pig at the fête, and is embarrassed about it

Catherine Corrigan, a.k.a. "Ginger," a young woman with red hair who is a houseguest of the Despards on the weekend of the fête. She works for London Galleries as a picture restorer. When Mark fails to interest either Jim Corrigan or Hermia Redcliffe in his investigation of The Pale Horse, he appeals to Ginger. Unlike Jim Corrigan and Hermia Redcliffe, Ginger agrees that there is something sinister and dangerous about the three "witches" at The Pale Horse and she becomes his partner in his investigation.

Rev. Dane Calthrop, the vicar of Much Deeping. We met him in the 1942 *The Moving Finger* when he was the vicar of Lymstock. He is still the same old fool of a clergyman with no communication abilities. His only contribution to conversations is to spout quotations in Latin and to smile benignly, oblivious to the fact that nobody in the room understands Latin—or, more probably, simply not caring if nobody in the room understands Latin.

Mrs. Dane Calthrop, the vicar's far more intelligent wife, as she was in *The Moving Finger*. Unlike the other villagers, she refuses to rule out the possibility that there may be something more than just superstition in witchcraft. She agrees with Mark Easterbrook that something evil is going on, and that in some way, the three women living at The Pale Horse are involved. Mark is surprised to hear her speak in a matter-of-fact way about witchcraft.

Mrs. Horsefall who cheats over the bottle of champagne at the fête.

Mrs. Horsefall's Nephew who gets the bottle of champagne because of his aunt's cheating

Old Lugg, the proprietor of the King's Arms in Much Deeping who generously donates twelve dozen bottles of beer for the bottle stall at the fête.

Thyrza Grey, one of the three "witches" who live at The Pale Horse in Much Deeping. She takes Mark on a personal tour of her library and frightens him with her talk about the "death wish."

Sybil Stamfordis, another of the three "witches" who live at The Pale Horse. She is allegedly a medium.

Bella Webb, the third of the three "witches" at The Pale Horse. She is actually a servant of the two other ladies, their cook, but she assists at their séances.

The Curtis Girl, who has her fortune told at the fête, and then tells her boyfriend Tom that he's "not the only pebble on the beach."

Tom, the Curtis Girl's boyfriend, who replies "I'm not telling you what she promised me. Mebbe you wouldn't like it too well, my girl!"

Old Lizzie Parker, who says of the fortune telling at the fête, "'tis all foolishness. Don't you believe none of it…"

Mrs. Cripps, who disagrees with Lizzie Parker:

> "You know, Lizzie, as well as I do, that Miss Stamfordis sees things as others can't see, and Miss Grey knows to a day when there's going to be a death. Never wrong, she is! Fairly gives me the creeps sometimes…"

Mr. Venables, a wealthy resident of Much Deeping who collects artworks from remote periods in history and from distant places. He lives in a house called Priors Court.

Mr. Venables's Italian Cook who prepares an exceptionally delicious lunch for Mr. Venables and his guests.

Mary Delafontaine, a friend of Mrs. Ariadne Oliver who dies. Her name was on the list Father Gorman carried in his shoe on the night of his murder.

Martin Digby, the great-nephew and heir of Lady Hesketh-Dubois. Mark Easterbrook notices his name written in the register of the King's Arms, an indication that Martin has recently visited Much Deeping. Did he pay a visit to The Pale Horse at that time, and did he arrange for Lady Hesketh-Dubois's "death by witchcraft?"

The Driver of that Jaguar who had no liquor in him despite P.C. Ellis's suspicions

Police Constable Ellis, who thought he smelled liquor on the breath of the driver of the Jaguar

The Niece of Lady Hesketh-Dubois who is married and lives in the North of England

The Nephew of Lady Hesketh-Dubois who lives in Canada

A Certain Mr. Sandford who recently died, leaving a much younger wife free to marry another man. Mr. Sandford, a Roman Catholic, had refused to give his wife a divorce. "Sandford" was one of the names on Father Gorman's list.

Sidney Harmondsworth who died recently, having been suspected of being a blackmailer. The name "Harmondsworth" was also among those on Father Gorman's list.

Sir William Dugdale, an eminent Harley Street doctor who attests to Mr. Venables's history of polio.

Mr. Bradley, a disbarred lawyer whose office is in Birmingham.

A Rather Seedy-looking Man in an Alpaca Coat who opens the door to Mark Easterbrook at the home of Mrs. Tuckerton in Surrey

A Doctor who diagnoses bronchopneumonia in a certain patient

The Home Office Psychologist, "a quaint little cock robin of a man, rising up and down on his toes, with eyes twinkling though very thick lenses"

Eileen Brandon, a friend of Poppy's who worked for the same consumer research company that Mrs. Davis did. She left the job because she thought there was "something wrong about it."

Detective Sergeant Lee, who accompanies Divisional Detective-Inspector Lejeune, Mark Easterbrook and Mr. Osborne on a certain visit to a residence in Much Deeping.

COMMENTS

A reader who is intrigued by the subject of witchcraft will probably enjoy reading *The Pale Horse*. As readers, we are not asked to believe in witchcraft, but we *are* forced to read a lot of conversation on the subject, and some of it is rather repetitious. At times it appears that Christie is lecturing on the subject, in fact, almost as she lectured on the subject of "inheritance of character traits" in *Ordeal by Innocence* just a few years earlier. If you feel that the subject of witchcraft is just plain silly, then skip *The Pale Horse*.

Conversations in *The Pale Horse* sometimes seem irrelevant to the story and to character development. In Chapter Four, for example, there is some irrelevant talk about the weather and the route the driver of a car takes to get to a restaurant, and then in the restaurant there is some more irrelevant talk about different performances of *Macbeth* that the characters have seen. The conversation about *Macbeth* does introduce the subject of murder and murderers, but it needn't have been quite so long. As the years go on, repetitiousness in conversations—as well as subjects of conversations that are irrelevant to the story—will occur more and more in Christie's novels. *The Pale Horse* seems to be her first novel in which this is noticeable.

For reasons that are not clear, Christie chose to resurrect Major Despard and Rhoda Dawes, two characters in the 1936 *Cards on the Table,* for this novel, a rather silly idea. It would have been better to create a new couple, since the presence of the Despards in *The Pale Horse* has nothing to do with the earlier book. But since they *are* in *The Pale Horse*, it seems that they ought to be the correct age, since we are now in 1961 and the couple should be twenty-five years older. But they are not presented as a middle-aged couple—they are a young couple with children, and the children are young enough to require a nursery governess. The very presence of the nursery governess in the story is a bit silly, also, since she has only one or two lines to speak and, furthermore, she is included in a social gathering of the family, which would not be characteristic. Governesses, like servants, were not a part of the family—they were employees. As to the "children," they seem to be nowhere when this gathering takes place. We don't even know the number, names and ages of the children, yet Christie places their governess in the room with a group of guests, apparently just to sit and listen. Why did she bother? The Despards' children, if there were any, could have been "grown children living on their own,"—since they are never seen in the story anyway—and the unimportant character of their "governess" dispensed with.

One of the characters, Catherine Corrigan (at first only identified as "Ginger," who becomes a main character about half way through the novel), happens to be a guest of the Despards, but she is never introduced and her relationship to the Despards is never explained. Is she a resident of the village? A guest from London? We are simply told the names of the people in the room—the vicar and his wife, the Despards, Mrs. Oliver, Mark Easterbrook, the nursery governess and "Ginger,"—and then everybody converses. Later we learn that "Ginger" works for the London Galleries and does restoration of old paintings, but never do we know how she happens to be at the Despards' home, and what her relationship is to them.

It should not be necessary for the reader to wonder "Who is this Ginger person, anyway?" It would have been a simple matter to explain her presence in the group—a cousin of Rhoda's from

London, for example, or a niece of Hugh Despard. By the way, for reasons unknown—and probably just Christie's faulty memory—Major Despard's first name was John in *Cards on the Table* but his name is Hugh in *The Pale Horse*.

The personality and behaviors of one character are extremely unrealistic, or at least very puzzling. Pamela Stirling, who is also called "Poppy," is the rather mindless but decorative female companion of a brilliant university lecturer, David Ardingly. At a restaurant table shared by Mark Easterbrook, his girlfriend Hermia Redcliffe, Poppy and David, Poppy mentions The Pale Horse as being a "murder for hire" organization. When questioned further about it by the others, she becomes embarrassed and withdraws from the conversation. A few days later she is absolutely terrified when Mark goes to her workplace, a flower shop, and questions her about it. If she knows that The Pale Horse is a murder-for-hire organization, why does she not report it to the authorities? One is forced to wonder if she is a *part* of the Pale Horse organization, especially a few days later when she consents to seeing Mark again with David and Mark's guest, Ginger, whom Poppy has never met before. Mark's friend Ginger "makes friends with" Poppy and before we know it, Poppy is telling Ginger all about The Pale Horse. Ginger tells Poppy that she wants to murder her boyfriend's wife, and Poppy has no problem at all with that! She actually gives Ginger the name and address of the man in Birmingham to whom one goes to arrange a murder. Just like that, as if Ginger had asked Poppy to recommend a good hairdresser. It just doesn't seem real.

It has always been necessary, in more minor ways, to "suspend disbelief" so to speak while reading Christie's novels, especially the earlier ones in which some incredibly unlikely things happen, and in the later ones in which there are just too many coincidences. In the case of Poppy, it is very difficult to suspend disbelief, and a reader might wonder if Poppy is actually a member of the Pale Horse organization and is laying a trap for Ginger and Mark. But Ginger and Mark suspect no trap, and in fact, there is no trap.

As to coincidences, there are just too many of them in *The Pale Horse*, so many that listing them here would require several pages.

Just a minor point: Christie's belief that personality traits are acquired not through environment or learning but through physical inheritance—in other words, from the blood of one's biological ancestors—mercifully was not mentioned at all in her preceding novel, the 1959 *Cat Among the Pigeons*, although it was the subject of a veritable lecture in the 1958 *Ordeal by Innocence*. It pops up just once in *The Pale Horse* when we learn that Divisional Detective-Inspector Lejeune's habit of using "surprisingly graphic gestures" while speaking came to him through the *blood* he inherited from his seventeenth-century French Huguenot ancestors. It reminds one of Gina Hudd, in the 1952 *Murder with Mirrors* who, although she was brought up by an English family in England, had "Italian blood" in her veins and therefore, according to Miss Marple, found it easier to express her feelings than she would have if her blood had been English only.

In reading *The Pale Horse* one gets the rather sad impression that Agatha Christie feels tired and worn out from years of writing stories and now writes with less enthusiasm and interest. *The Pale Horse* makes a poor contribution to her reputation as a writer of interesting light fiction. In fact it "pales by comparison" with nearly all of the novels she wrote during the previous decades. It is clearly with this novel that Christie's decline as a writer begins.

The Mirror Crack'd (1962)

(Alternate Title: *The Mirror Crack'd from Side to Side*)

SETTING

It is summer of approximately 1962 and our sleuth, Miss Jane Marple, who must now be about ninety-four years old (since her age had been specified as eighty-nine in the 1957 *What Mrs. McGillicuddy Saw*) still lives in her cottage in the village of St. Mary Mead. In earlier novels, the village has been placed in one real county (Berkshire) and in two fictitious ones (Radfordshire and Downshire) but in *The Mirror Crack'd* no county name is specified. We can assume that the village—and two neighboring larger towns, Much Benham and Market Basing—are somewhere west of London in south central England, probably in Berkshire.

Gossington Hall, a large Victorian mansion, was a major setting in the 1942 *The Body in the Library*. It was described as being about a mile and a half from the village of St. Mary Mead. In *The Mirror Crack'd* we should picture it somewhat closer to the village, perhaps no more than a quarter mile away, as in one scene Miss Marple visits her friend Dolly Bantry at the East Lodge of

Gossington Hall and her friend asks her if she had come there on foot. A mile and a half on foot by a ninety-four-year-old woman would be a bit more than one could expect. Miss Marple's old friend Dr. Haydock has forbidden her to do any gardening except some "light pruning" and has even insisted that she have a live-in companion.

In the 1942 *The Body in the Library,* Gossington Hall was the residence of Colonel Arthur Bantry and his wife Dolly. There was a large staff of servants, including a butler, a cook, at least two or three maids and a chauffeur plus one or two gardeners. There was no mention of the Bantrys' having any children. In the present story, which takes place twenty years later, Colonel Bantry has died and his widow Dolly has sold Gossington Hall and the entire property except the East Lodge and about three quarters of an acre. She has modernized the lodge with running water from the water main and such advancements as an indoor bathroom and a modern kitchen addition. Mrs. Bantry now calls the East Lodge her home, is quite comfortable living there, and is very glad to be rid of the huge mansion. We learn now that she has four grown children and nine grandchildren.

The mansion itself has changed hands three or four times since Mrs. Bantry sold it four years ago. First there was a failed attempt to run it as a guesthouse. Then four individuals purchased it and created four roughly divided flats within it, but those people later quarreled and sold it again. Then the Ministry of Health had bought it for "some obscure purpose for which they eventually did not want it," recently selling it to the present owners, a famous but somewhat over-the-hill American film star named Marina Gregg and her husband, who is a successful film director.

Marina Gregg's age is not stated but certain characters guess it at about forty-five, or nearer fifty. One of her early films, *Bird of Passage,* is mentioned, and Marina's co-star in that film had been a very handsome actor named Joel Roberts. It is possible that this is a reference to the real 1932 film *Bird of Paradise* which starred a very handsome actor, Joel McCrea and the exceptionally beautiful actress Dolores del Rio. Marina would have been about twenty years old in 1932, the correct age for the part.

Marina Gregg and her husband have modernized Gossington Hall with the addition of several luxuriously tiled bathrooms on the "first floor." American readers are reminded of the fact that in Britain, as well as elsewhere in Europe, the upper floor of a house, which Americans would call the "second floor," is called the "first floor." In this novel there are numerous references to the "first floor" at Gossington Hall which includes, not only the bedrooms and newly-added bathrooms, but also Marina Gregg's private sitting room and her husband's office. Two ground-floor rooms—the library and study—have been thrown together and made into a large music room with a grand piano in one end and a cluster of sofas, chairs and tables near the other end. "Picture windows" have replaced some of the older windows in the house.

At the top of the main stairway, a large room has been created by the elimination of a guest-room and dressing room, which had formerly occupied the space. This large room is important in the story, as it is where the film star and her husband welcome a number of special guests during a major event—a fête benefiting an ambulance company. It is in this place that one of the special guests dies after drinking a poisoned cocktail.

Although the grounds of Gossington Hall have suffered neglect during the years of vacancy alternating with ownership by persons uninterested in them, the present owners have spared no expense in restoring the grounds and the herbaceous border, which had been Mrs. Bantry's pride and joy. They have added a California-style swimming pool complete with a dressing pavilion. The local people are very impressed by the swimming pool, although one or two of them note that an outdoor swimming pool, while appropriate for the climate of California, is not very sensible in England where there is usually no more than one week in summer during which an outdoor swimming pool can be enjoyed comfortably. The local ladies are most impressed by the luxurious new bathrooms, which feature marble and tile fixtures in beautiful, stylish colors.

The village itself, St. Mary Mead, has also changed a good deal since the 1942 *The Body in the Library.* In Chapter One there is a fascinating description of the village which expresses the changes that have been brought about by modernization over the last decade or so. Although Miss Marple has been featured in several novels since she was first introduced in the 1930 *Murder at the Vicarage,* only in that story and in the 1942 *The Body in the Library* had St. Mary Mead been a major setting. From those stories we may recall Miss Wetherby, Miss Hartnell, Mrs. Price Ridley and the vicar Rev. Leonard Clement and his wife Griselda. Of those people, we learn that Miss Wetherby has died but we hear nothing about Mrs. Price Ridley. We must assume that the Clements no longer live in St. Mary Mead since Griselda is mentioned only as someone from whom Miss Marple continues to receive Christmas cards. Miss Hartnell, however, is still alive and living in the village, "fighting progress to the last gasp." All of the old houses of the village are still there and their exterior appearances have not changed much, except for fresh new paint colors on a few, but the interiors of some have been modernized with new kitchens and additional bathrooms. New arrivals in the village, such as the bank manager and his family who now occupy the cottage formerly owned by Miss Wetherby, have modernized the interiors of the homes but they have allowed the exterior appearances to remain unchanged, since it was the "old world charm" extolled by the real estate people that had attracted them to the houses in the first place.

The village street has changed enormously, however. The fishmonger's shop now has "new super windows behind which refrigerated fish gleam," and in place of the former basket shop is a modern supermarket which Miss Marple and Miss Hartnell find tiring and intimidating with its wire baskets, check-out lanes and unfamiliar products, such as breakfast cereals packaged in inconvenient sizes. Barnes, the grocer, is still there and unchanged, "for which Miss Hartnell and Miss Marple and others daily thank heaven," and the butcher shop is also unchanged.

The most important change to the village, however, is what the old ladies of the village refer to as "the Development." It is a new housing development of nearly-identical semi-detached houses that are said to have all of the modern conveniences within, and which are also said to be very well built, although the walls separating them are thin by the standards of former times and a certain young couple living in one of the houses receives frequent complaints from their neighbors when they play their recorded music too loud.

Regarding the recorded music, there is a reference to a "stereogram" (stereo record player) owned by the young couple mentioned above; the husband enjoys classical music and believes that such works as Tchaikovsky's *1812 Overture* should be played at full volume in order to appreciate their full tone.

Both Miss Marple and her friend Mrs. Bantry make numerous plaintive references to the fact that the days of live-in housemaids are now gone. Even the term "parlourmaid" has become somewhat archaic. A young married woman from the Development comes to Miss Marple's cottage each morning to do housework, and in her speech the word "lounge" has replaced the former term "drawing room," which she regards as quaint and old-fashioned. Miss Marple fondly remembers the days when parlourmaids used a brush and dustpan instead of "a virulent Hoover" with which the lady from the Development fills the cottage with noise each morning. Miss Marple, and Christie herself, evidently both believe that a brush and dustpan are as effective in cleaning carpets as "virulent Hoovers" are, and that a housemaid who opts for the vacuum cleaner is simply being lazy. Christie obviously never did a bit of housework. Recall that in the 1959 *Cat Among the Pigeons* a single cook at a boarding school prepared three meals a day from scratch for a student body of two hundred and a staff of ten. If Christie had ever done any cooking she would have known that that was impossible. In the 1965 *At Bertram's Hotel* Christie will staff the kitchen of a good-sized London hotel with just one cook who will produce breakfast, lunch and dinner for all of the guests and even have time to make "real seedcake" and "real muffins" from scratch for tea every day.

There are no current events mentioned in *The Mirror Crack'd*. The term "Teds" occurs in one reference. The "Teddy boys" of the late 1950s and early 1960s were adolescent boys who sported black leather jackets and were regarded as likely "juvenile delinquents," which some of them undoubtedly were, although most were probably not. Most were simply fad-followers, as were the "beatniks" referred to in Christie's previous novel *The Pale Horse*. There is a nostalgic reference to a past when film actresses were not expected to have a particular body type and were not referred to with terms such as "The Bust" or "The Torso." This is probably a reference to the minor American film star Jayne Mansfield (1933–1967) who was referred to as "The Bust." She had no acting talent, her only assets being her face and her unnaturally large bosom, which certain fans found to be "sexy." She starred in second-rate, Technicolor exploitation films from about 1955 until her death in 1967 in an automobile accident and was soon forgotten.

Christie, in characterizing film stars as far back as the 1933 *Thirteen at Dinner,* had generally portrayed them as self-absorbed individuals who changed spouses often and indulged in addictive drugs. In *The Mirror Crack'd,* Marina Gregg has had a series of at least five different husbands. She, as well as the rest of her household—which includes her husband, her "social secretary" and a young man who is a sort of messenger and household dragon—all use a prescription drug called Calmo which, according to Marina Gregg's private live-in physician, "calms you or it peps you up, makes you feel you could do things which otherwise you might fancy that you couldn't." There are quantities of this substance within easy reach everywhere in the house, and it is a strong dose of Calmo that is the poison used to commit the murder.

Story

It is summer of approximately 1962. Gossington Hall, a large Victorian mansion on the edge of the village of St. Mary Mead, has recently been purchased by an American film actress, Marina Gregg, and her film-director husband, Jason Rudd. Marina, who had suffered a nervous breakdown and had been out of films for a few years, has now recovered and is making her "comeback" at a film studio just a few miles away.

In order to ingratiate themselves with the local population, Marina and her husband allow the grounds of Gossington Hall to be used for a special fête to benefit a local ambulance company. For an extra shilling, one can also be admitted to the house itself for a tour of the interior renovations, and perhaps even catch a glimpse of the famous film star herself.

During the fête a local woman, one of those who are admitted inside the house, suddenly dies while sipping a cocktail, and in the dregs of the cocktail glass are found the remains of a strong prescription drug. No motive can be imagined for the murder of this woman, who was a friendly, civic-minded person, but soon it is learned that the cocktail that the woman drank had actually been poured for Marina Gregg. In the crowded room the woman's own drink had spilled, and Marina offered her her own cocktail as a replacement, as she had not yet drunk from the glass. The question then becomes, "Who tried to murder Marina Gregg?"

Soon arsenic is found in Marina's cup of coffee at the studio canteen, and then a person who recently made a large bank deposit is killed, suggesting that the person was a blackmailer who knew the identity of the killer.

Chief Inspector Craddock again works with Miss Marple and the two of them solve the mystery together.

Characters

Miss Jane Marple, an old lady of ninety-four, living in the village of St. Mary Mead. Her age is not actually stated in the story, but in the 1957 *What Mrs. McGillicuddy Saw* we were specifically told that she was eighty-nine years old. She has considerable experience in solving mysteries, her first case having been *Murder at the Vicarage* in 1930. One of her favorite occupations, flower gardening, is now practically forbidden to her because of her advancing frailty. "Only a little light pruning, and no bending or stooping," orders her old friend, Dr. Haydock. Dr. Haydock has also ordered her to have a live-in companion, an idea to which Miss Marple would not be opposed if only it were someone *other than* Miss Knight!

Colonel Protheroe, Ann Protheroe and Griselda Clement, the Vicar's Wife, people in Miss Marple's past whom she recalls while knitting at her window and enjoying the view of her garden. The Protheroes were characters in the 1930 *Murder at the Vicarage*. Griselda and her husband were also characters in that story and Griselda made a brief appearance in the 1942 *The Body in the Library* along with her baby boy, who is now a grown man with a good job. The Clements no longer live in St. Mary Mead but Miss Marple continues to receive Christmas cards from Griselda.

Old Laycock, an old gardening "jobber" who comes to Miss Marple's cottage three times a week and performs very unsatisfactorily.

Miss Hartnell, one of several village spinsters introduced in the 1930 *Murder at the Vicarage,* and the only one still surviving along with Miss Marple. She "fights progress to the last gasp" and especially dislikes the modern supermarket at the end of the village street.

Cherry Baker, a young married lady from the new "Development." She comes to Miss Marple's cottage to clean every day and to do some cooking. She is a quick and efficient cook and an intelligent girl who takes telephone calls correctly and is quick to spot inaccuracies in the tradesmen's books. Unfortunately she fills Miss Marple's cottage with the noise of "a virulent Hoover" each morning instead of using a brush and dust-pan as maids once did.

Jim Baker, Cherry's husband, "a big good-looking blond giant of a man," who when at home is usually intent on assembling a model construction unit while listening to classical music on the couple's "stereogram" at full volume, to the extreme annoyance of their neighbors. He actively appreciates his wife's good cooking and enjoys doing basic home repairs for Miss Marple.

Michael, Jim Baker's young nephew for whom Jim has bought a construction model set as a Christmas present, although Cherry suspects he actually bought it for himself to play with. Jim explains, "He's not quite old enough for it yet."

Faithful Florence, a former maid of Miss Marple, whom we met in the 1957 *What Mrs. McGillicuddy Saw*. In that novel she was living in her own home in Brackhampton and had extra bedrooms to let. She let a room to Miss Marple during the investigation of the murder at Rutherford Hall. She is not a character in this story but Miss Marple has frequent occasions to think wistfully of her.

Amy, Clara and Alice, other former maids of Miss Marple, just three of many girls from St. Faith's Orphanage whom Miss Marple trained for domestic service and who then went on to better-paid jobs elsewhere.

Miss Knight, Miss Marple's live-in companion, whose services are paid in full by Miss Marple's generous nephew, Raymond West. She is an extremely irritating woman, regularly substituting the pronoun "we" for "you" when addressing Miss Marple, as in the following:

> "Here we are!" she exclaimed with a kind of beaming boisterousness, meant to cheer and enliven the sad twilight of the aged. "I hope *we*'ve had our little snooze?"

Raymond West, Miss Marple's wealthy nephew who writes "clever books." He is always generous with his beloved aunt. In this story he pays to have a live-in companion for Miss Marple.

Mrs. Wesley who sells knitting wool in the village

Emily Waters, one of Miss Marple's "village parallels." Miss Knight reminds Miss Marple of Emily.

Lily Price, a young woman who is looking through a new, unfinished house in the Development with her fiancé in consideration of a possible purchase. Leaning out of an upper-story window to see the view of the river, she loses her balance and nearly falls out of the window.

Harry, Lily Price's fiancé. As she nearly falls out of the window, he does nothing but watch, almost as if he hopes that she *will* fall out of the window!

Heather Badcock, who lives in the Development and sees Miss Marple slip on some loose gravel and fall, and invites her into the house for a cup of tea and a brief rest. She is an enthusiastic, civic-minded, hard working person. Some people find her to be a bit overbearing. Heather dies at Gossington Hall by drinking a poisoned cocktail that was apparently intended to kill Marina Gregg.

Arthur Badcock, Heather Badcock's husband. He is a thin, pale man, rather slow in speech. After Heather dies, Miss Marple suspects that Arthur will not miss her very much.

Dr. Haydock, an old friend of Miss Marple's whom we first met in the 1930 *Murder at the Vicarage*. He is now semi-retired. He admires Miss Marple very much and, although he warns her that at her age she must be careful of falls, and forbids her to bend and stoop in the garden, he has a sense of humor and knows that nothing invigorates Miss Marple more than a good murder to solve.

Charlie Chaplin and Greta Garbo, film stars of the silent era whose names come up in a conversation between Dolly Bantry and Miss Marple. Chaplin was a stage actor and mime whose silent films became instant classics that were regularly shown for decades. He was a also a talented producer and director who resisted sound in films, considering films to be primarily a visual medium, and he continued to produce silent films as late as 1936, several years after sound was developed for films. Garbo was a Swedish film actress who began in silent films and made a successful transition to sound films. She retired in approximately 1940 at the height of her career and famously shunned publicity until her death in 1990.

Marina Gregg, an American film actress aged about fifty who, together with her husband Jason Rudd, has recently purchased Gossington Hall to live in. She is described, by everyone close to her, as emotionally fragile and in constant need of reassurance. She suffered a "nervous breakdown" some years ago and has only recently recovered. She feels certain that her new home, Gossington Hall, will be a permanent home to her, but her husband has experienced her "certainties" before and has doubts about it.

Jason Rudd, a.k.a. "Jinks," Marina Gregg's current and fifth husband. He is a successful film director.

Alison Wilde, a lady Miss Marple once knew, one of her "village parallels." She always saw her own point of view so clearly that she didn't always see how things might appear to, or affect, other people. Heather Badcock reminds Miss Marple of Alison.

Dolly Bantry, an old friend of Miss Marple whom we met in the 1942 *The Body in the Library*. It was in the library of Gossington Hall, Colonel and Mrs. Bantry's home, that the body was found. Four years ago Mrs. Bantry, now widowed, sold Gossington Hall and all of its property except a small parcel of gardening space and the East Lodge, which she modernized and now inhabits.

Colonel Arthur Bantry, Mrs. Bantry's late husband.

Mrs. Meavy, Mrs. Bantry's cleaning lady. It

is she who tells Mrs. Bantry about Miss Marple's fall in the Development

Inch, the original owner of Inch's Taxi Service of St. Mary Mead, who began operations with horse-drawn vehicles many years ago and then gradually converted to automobiles. The business has changed hands a few times but its name has remained Inch's Taxi Service, and when using the service, the ladies of the village continue to describe it as "going in Inch."

Young Inch, who took over the business when the elder Inch was too old to drive.

Mr. Bardwell, who purchased the taxi business from the Inch family some years ago, later re-selling it.

Mr. Roberts, the current owner of Inch's Taxi Service.

Dr. Sandford, Dr. Haydock's younger partner. Dr. Haydock is semi-retired and urges his patients to accept Dr. Sandford, calling him a "first-class man with better qualifications than I have." Nevertheless, Miss Marple prefers her old friend Dr. Haydock, explaining that "The younger doctors are all the same—they take your blood pressure, and whatever's the matter with you, you get some kind of mass-produced variety of new pills..."

Dr. Sandford's Wife who, together with Dr. Sandford, was on the landing at Gossington Hall when Heather Badcock died.

Giuseppe, the Italian butler at Gossington Hall who answers the door "with gratifying promptness" when Mrs. Bantry calls there for tea. He also helps to serve the drinks on the upper landing of Gossington Hall on the day of the fête.

Bianca, Giuseppe's wife

Ella Zielinsky, Marina Gregg's efficient social secretary.

Mr. Sampson, the oldest man in St. Mary Mead, who attends the fête.

Mr. Sampson's Daughter-in-Law, who observes, "Never think this was Gossington Hall, would you, now?"

Hailey Preston, "a willowy young man with long wavy hair." He is Jason Rudd's private secretary.

Councillor Allcock and Mrs. Allcock, two of the guests invited to a special reception on the upper landing in Gossington Hall

A Stout Man in Livery Announcing Guests at Gossington Hall on the day of the fête.

The Vicar of St. Mary Mead. He is not named, but he is certainly not the same man—Leonard Clement—who was the vicar in the 1930 *Murder at the Vicarage*, the 1942 *The Body in the Library*, and the 1957 *What Mrs. McGillicuddy Saw*, because in the present story Miss Marple speaks of receiving Christmas cards from Griselda Clement each year, suggesting that the Clements no longer live in St. Mary Mead. The present vicar is simply described as "a lean ascetic man." Miss Marple has one occasion to telephone him to ask a question, and she addresses him simply as "Vicar."

Old Briggs, who does gardening for Dr. Sandford and his wife. He happened to be clipping something quite close to a window there and overheard Dr. Sandford telephoning to the police station after Heather Badcock died.

Old Briggs's Daughter, whose father told her that he had overheard Dr. Sandford telephoning the police

The Postwoman, whom Old Brigg's Daughter told about Dr. Sandford telephoning to the police, and who then told Mrs. Bantry.

Colonel Clittering, Mrs. Clittering, The High Sheriff, The Mayor and his Wife, Joshua Grice and his Wife from the Lower Farm, A Man with Long Hair and One of Those Funny Beards They Wear Nowadays—Quite Young, and Old General Barnstaple from Much Benham—all local people who were invited to the special reception on the upper landing at Gossington Hall and who were noticed by Mrs. Bantry.

Jim Galbraith of the Press, **Donald McNeil** of the *Much Benham Herald and Argus*, and **Three or Four Other Reporters** who were on the upper landing at Gossington Hall when Heather Badcock swallowed a poisoned drink and died.

Ardwyck Fenn, an American film and television producer who is "quite a big figure in American television." He had been a good friend of Marina Gregg's in America many years ago. At the fête, he is Lola Brewster's escort.

Lola Brewster, an "overblonde, minky kind" of American film actress (Mrs. Bantry's description) who was once married to a man who divorced her to marry Marina Gregg. Inspector Craddock, in the course of his investigations of Lola Brewster, has learned that that divorce was not an amicable one. She once said of Marina, in public,

> "That bitch needn't think she'll get away with it. If I don't shoot her now I'll wait and get her in some other way. I don't care how long I wait, years if need be, but I'll get even with her in the end."

Margot Bence, an arty photographer from London, who had her large camera positioned half-way up the stairs at the private reception in Gossington Hall in order to get "artistic" angle shots of the guests. She happened to snap a photograph of Marina Gregg which showed the "frozen look" on her face that Mrs. Bantry had tried so hard to describe, a look that reminded her of the Lady of Shallot as she saw her reflection in the mirror that "crack'd from side to side."

A Local Photographer, who was also present at the private reception in Gossington Hall

Detective Inspector Frank Cornish, of the local police who is the first police officer to take charge of the case of the murder of Heather Badcock.

Frank Cornish's Wife, who was just as excited about the fête—and the possibility of catching a glimpse of Marina Gregg—as everyone else.

Mary Bain, a widowed neighbor of the Badcocks who has lived in St. Mary Mead for about six months. After Heather Badcock's death, she takes a strong interest in Heather's widower.

Florrie West and **Miss Grundle,** who work in the estate agent's office with Arthur Badcock.

Mrs. Bain's Son, who boards with her, as he works nearby.

Dr. Sims, on whose register Heather Badcock is named, although she has been in excellent health and has never needed to see him

Chief Inspector Dermot Craddock of New Scotland Yard. He is a good-looking "young" man, the godson of Sir Henry Clithering, who retired from Scotland Yard some years ago and is an old friend of Miss Jane Marple. Inspector Craddock was in charge of the murders at Little Paddocks in the 1950 *A Murder Is Announced* and came to appreciate Miss Marple's special talents on that occasion. He then worked closely with her in the case of the murders at Rutherford Hall in the 1957 *What Mrs. McGillicuddy Saw.*

When Scotland Yard is called into the matter of the murder of Heather Badcock—there is an "international aspect" to the case, since the crime took place at Gossington Hall which is owned by Americans—Craddock takes a special interest because he remembers Miss Marple, although he is not sure if she is still alive. He is then assigned to the case since his relationship with Miss Marple will provide him with an "in," according to Craddock's superior.

Arriving in St. Mary Mead, Craddock makes his first stop "headquarters"—that is, Miss Marple's cottage—to her amusement and embarrassment.

The Assistant Commissioner of New Scotland Yard who assigns the case to Chief Inspector Dermot Craddock since he has a personal friend—Miss Marple—who lives in St. Mary Mead.

Detective-Sergeant William Tiddler, a.k.a. **"Tom Tiddler,"** Craddock's assistant in the case. Craddock chooses Tiddler because he is a film fan and that interest may come in useful in this case.

Dr. Maurice Gilchrist, Marina Gregg's personal physician who lives at Gossington Hall.

Sir Henry Clithering, a retired Scotland Yard chief inspector, and Dermot Craddock's godfather. He is not a character in this novel but he is a long-time friend and admirer of Miss Marple and it was he who encouraged Dermot Craddock to take Miss Marple seriously in the 1950 *A Murder Is Announced.*

Two Local Girls from the studio canteen working with drinks at the fête

A Man with Spectacles on a Bicycle who brings to Marina Gregg an envelope containing a threatening letter after the death of Heather Badcock.

Lynette Brown, an actress who would get Marina Gregg's role in the film currently being produced at Hellingforth Studios if Marina were to become ill—or if she were to die.

Johnny Jethroe, Margot Bence's assistant, who has exuberant hair and a pink and white face and is "almost as willowy as Hailey Preston." When Dermot Craddock meets him at Margot's studio, he is at work, wearing slippers and a lilac colored smock. At one point Inspector Cornish refers to him as "Margot Bence's pansy assistant."

Elsie and Jane, two fashion models who are working on a photography shoot with Margot Bence in the gardens of the home of the poet Keats at Hampstead Heath.

Andrew Quilp, with whom Margot Bence studied photography at Reingarden Studios at Seven Springs in America.

Margot Bence's Mother who gave her up for adoption at age five.

Angus and **Rod,** Margot Bence's adoptive brothers.

Isidore Wright, Marina Gregg's third husband, a successful playwright.

Mrs. Hartwell and **The Burnabys,** neighbors of Cherry and Jim Baker in the Development, who often complain when Jim plays classical music on his stereo at full volume.

Gladys Dixon, "a plump girl with a plain face," and a friend of Cherry Baker, who also lives in the Development. She works in the canteen at Hellingforth Studios and, on the day of the fête, helps to serve drinks inside Gossington Hall for the private reception. She notices something strange about the matter of Heather Badcock's spilled drink.

Gladys Dixon's Mother

Gladys Dixon's Fifteen-year-old Sister who receives Detective-Sergeant William (Tom) Tiddler with coldness, explaining that Gladys has gone away for a holiday and that neither she nor their mother knows where.

Alfred, Mrs. Pike's Second Son, one of Miss Marple's "village parallels." She is reminded of him during a conversation with Dermot Craddock about the threatening letters that Marina Gregg has received.

Inspector Craddock's Mother, who died when Dermot Craddock was five years old. He happened to be eating jam roll pudding when he overheard a servant telling his nursery governess that Mrs. Craddock had had an accident and been killed. To this day whenever Craddock sees jam roll pudding, a wave of horror and misery and despair comes over him.

The Lauristons' Parlourmaid, another of Miss Marple's "village parallels." In writing telephone messages she often mixed up her pronouns.

Lady Conway, an elderly, somewhat feeble-minded relative of Miss Knight who would like Miss Knight to join her at the Belgrave Hotel at Llandudno.

Mr. Upshaw, a local businessman who makes frequent trips to America. On a recent trip he learned that another local man was once married to Marina Gregg and went by a different name.

An Elderly Butler newly employed at Gossington Hall

Gerald French, who "had an unfortunate past and was quite a talker." He is one of Miss Marple's "village parallels," and Hailey Preston reminds her of Gerald.

Alfred Beadle, Marina Gregg's first husband.

COMMENTS

The Mirror Crack'd can be a delightful reading experience for Christie fans who are especially fond of the Miss Marple character, and who have already read at least two Miss Marple novels—the 1942 *The Body in the Library* and the 1950 *A Murder Is Announced* in particular. If you have not yet read those two novels, it would be best to do so before reading *The Mirror Crack'd* because you will then appreciate the warm relationship that exists between Inspector Craddock and Miss Marple, the history of Gossington Hall, and Mrs. Bantry's personality. Christie's references in *The Mirror Crack'd* to events and characters in the two earlier novels may be a bit puzzling to readers who have not yet read them. Especially puzzling may be some of the "teasing" remarks that Chief Inspector Craddock makes to Miss Marple upon his first visit to her at her cottage.

The Mirror Crack'd is enjoyable reading but it suffers a good deal from repetitiveness, as did its predecessor, *The Pale Horse*. In general the characterizations are not very deep, and the characterization of the film actress Marina Gregg is very much belabored. We hear about her from many different people—her husband, her doctor, her social secretary, and her husband's secretary, and everybody more or less repeats what everyone else has said about her. If there were different opinions or points of view it might have been interesting but as it is, the discussions become a bit tedious to read.

In *The Pale Horse* the reader is expected, perhaps not to actually believe in witchcraft, but to at least be interested in extended discussions about it. If you find discussions about witchcraft a bit of a bore, then *The Pale Horse* can be a bit of a bore. In the case of *The Mirror Crack'd*, Christie seems to want to tell us all about the neuroses of talented film stars. If you are uninterested in that subject, then you may be a bit impatient with *The Mirror Crack'd* in which the alleged sensitivity and emotional needfulness of "extremely talented" film stars are repeatedly and needlessly expounded upon by a number of characters who simply repeat what the others have already said.

If you have read the 1958 *Ordeal by Innocence*, and have been annoyed by Christie's lectures against the adoption of children, then you will also be annoyed by *The Mirror Crack'd*, in which Christie once again berates the adoption of children and makes some very silly statements about "the mothering instinct." Christie had a very serious problem with the whole subject of "motherhood," and most of her novels beginning with the mid–1940s show evidence of it, although *Ordeal by Innocence* and *The Mirror Crack'd* are the ones in which she is the most tiresome in her "lectures" on that subject.

As already mentioned several times, it is never very unusual for Christie to expect her readers to accept some rather unlikely coincidences. There was a rather ridiculous coincidence—and a completely unnecessary one—in the 1957 *What Mrs. McGillicuddy Saw,* and there were far too many in the 1961 *The Pale Horse*. In *The Mirror Crack'd* there is a coincidence that is just plain unacceptable and it seems to be in the story just to provide the police with a reason for arresting an innocent person. There is nothing in the story that requires either the coincidence or the arrest. As a detective novel, *The Mirror Crack'd* is very poor for that reason; the police, as in *The Pale Horse,* achieve nothing in their "investigations" and Miss Marple "solves" the case with the help of a good deal of luck.

Nevertheless, *The Mirror Crack'd* has charms of its own. Miss Marple's secret outing to "the Development"—a new housing development on the edge of Saint Mary Mead—is one of those. She observes the "brave new world" of nearly-identical houses with their television antennæ, the hostile-looking "Teddy boys" dressed in black leather jackets, and the fifteen-year-old girls with their "exuberant busts." All of this strikes the ninety-four-year-old Miss Marple as "depraved," but within minutes she decides that only the externals are new—the people in the Development are the same as people have always been.

In *The Mirror Crack'd* Christie also introduces something rather new: a young couple, apparently of the "working class," whom she portrays in an affirmative way. Working class people in all fifty-two of her earlier novels were nearly always portrayed negatively. They had far too many children, for one thing. The men were often crude abusers of alcohol, and their wives were often bad housekeepers. In *The Mirror Crack'd,* Cherry and Jim Baker are a working class couple who have pleasant personalities. Jim enjoys assembling models of airplanes and listening to classical music on his stereo phonograph. He knows how to do basic home repairs and there is a reference to his having repaired some bathroom shelves at Miss Marple's cottage. He actively appreciates his wife's good cooking, and Cherry actually *enjoys* cooking, stating that "There's something *to* cooking, something you can get your teeth into." Naturally, there have always been women in England who enjoyed cooking—and especially enjoyed cooking for appreciative husbands. But in the Christie world, cooking has always been a lowly household task that a "lady" would not be expected to know anything about, possibly as low as such unmentionables as cleaning the toilet. Cherry and Jim Baker are "a Christie first," being a working class couple who are also "nice people," despite the fact that Jim uses his hands to fix other peoples' bathroom shelves and Cherry cooks, cleans her house all by herself, *and* cleans other people's houses for money!

But Christie will never stop regretting the demise of the servant class, and through Miss Marple's nostalgic musings about the girls from St. Faith's Orphanage that she "trained" for domestic service, we are reminded of Christie's opinion that the servant class does not need education, and in fact is harmed by it. In the "good old days," she tells us, housemaids were not "educated;" they were "trained." They knew how to wash dishes, polish the silver and the brass, and to make beds the right way. They kept their eyes lowered and their mouths shut. If they "walked out" with young men in the neighborhood, the young men were of their own class—the fishmonger's assistant, or the chauffeur of a neighboring family, or the gardener or his son. They were "devoted" to their masters, like "Faithful Florence," one of Miss Marple's favorite former parlourmaids. They knew that it was not "respectful" to sing the latest popular songs while running the vacuum cleaner. They wore uniforms and even caps, and took care not to be very "attractive," especially in households where there were men or boys. And, at least in Christie's stories, if they "got into trouble," it was always "the fishmonger's assistant, or the chauffeur of a neighboring family, or the gardener or his son" who had participated in the "getting into trouble," never the "gentleman of the house." Perish *that* thought!

Christie also reminds us, once again, that old gardeners are lazy and shiftless. In *The Mirror Crack'd,* the lazy old gardener is Old Laycock. The following is a chronological inventory of "lazy old gardeners" from Christie's novels.

Lazy Old Gardeners in Christie Novels

MacDonald, who in the 1929 *The Seven Dials Mystery* talks back to Lady Coote when she asks him to pick some grapes and to turn a portion of the lawn into a bowling green, but who obeys Lady Eileen Brent when she gives him the same orders.

William Wilson, the gardener at End House in the 1932 *Peril at End House,* who "is stupid and lazy and spends a good deal of time in the shed pretending that he is sharpening shears."

Old Man Ashe, "a sour old man leaning on a spade" in the 1950 *A Murder Is Announced.*

Old Edwards, a gardener in the 1957 *What Mrs. McGillicuddy Saw* who "is so opinionated and lazy, drinking lots of cups of tea and doing very little work."

Old Hillman, the gardener at Rutherford Hall in the same novel, who "only makes a show of working."

Old Briggs, the head gardener at Meadowbank School in the 1959 *Cat Among the Pigeons,* who tells a younger gardener to plant asters in a certain border despite orders from the headmistress to plant dahlias there.

And now we are treated to lazy Old Laycock who, in *The Mirror Crack'd,* promises but does not perform, finds every possible excuse for not working, plants cabbages and Brussels sprouts instead of flowers because *he* considers vegetable gardening to be more important than flower gardening, and plants asters and salvias around roses instead of giving proper care to the roses themselves.

In a future novel, the 1971 *Nemesis,* there will be Old George, who will plant the wrong color of Antirrhinum (snapdragons) despite Miss Marple's explicit instructions. Another character in that novel will describe "old gardeners" as men who claim to know all about gardening but do not, and who drink endless cups of tea and do a bit of light weeding instead of substantial work. In the same novel Miss Marple will visit a village churchyard and converse with "an old man moving in slow motion," who is tidying up the gravesites.

Finally, in the 1976 *Sleeping Murder* (actually written during the 1940s) we will be treated to *two* elderly, lazy, tea-drinking, good-for-nothing gardeners. There will be the ungrammatical Foster who will be recalcitrant about making a path down through a rockery, pointing out that "the forsythia would have to go and the weigela, and them there lilacs." Wise old Miss Marple will have the following conversation about Foster with the young couple who are his employers:

> "Do you find your gardener satisfactory, by the way? I hear that he is considered locally as rather a *scrimshanker*—more talk than work."
> "Talk and tea is his specialty," said Giles. "He has about five cups of tea a day. But he works splendidly when we are looking."

Later in the story we will meet Manning, who is described as follows:

> Manning was a bent, crabbed-looking old man with a rheumy and slightly cunning eye. The pace at which he was raking a path accelerated noticeably as his employers drew near.

Christie's negative attitudes toward "old gardeners" may have had an origin in her own life. She obviously knew nothing about gardening herself—at least in her early years—since during those years she received many letters from readers criticizing her for mentioning vases of "flowers from the garden" that could not have bloomed at the same season, such as bowls in which spring-flowering tulips and autumn-flowering chrysanthemums are combined. Because of her gardening ignorance, she probably made unreasonable demands on her own gardeners—ordering them to plant sun-loving plants in shady spots or shrubs destined to grow wide in inadequate spaces, and then saw the gardeners' fact-based protests as "laziness."

There are just two "old gardeners" in all of Christie's novels who are described in affirmative terms. There is Old Manning in the 1920 *The Mysterious Affair at Styles* (perhaps an ancestor of Old Manning in *Sleeping Murder?*) who lowers his eyes and twists his cap in his hands when spoken to by his employer—now there's a *good* servant—one who knows his place! And there is Old Auguste, the French gardener in the 1923 *Murder on the Links* who responds affirmatively when Hercule Poirot flatters him about his magnificent geraniums.

The Clocks (1963)

SETTING

The story takes place in September of 1962 or 1963. The term "behind the Iron Curtain" is still in use, and one character is first suspected and then known to have left England to live in a certain country within what was then called the "Communist Block." There are one or two minor references to "nuclear disarmament" and "the Bomb," and an important element in the story is the hunting down of an Englishman who is suspected of being a counter spy for a Communist state, although this is secondary to the main "murder mystery" in *The Clocks*.

The principal setting is a fictitious seaside town in Sussex called Crowdean, ten miles from the fictitious port of Portlebury. Sussex is the county on the English Channel directly south of London. Within Crowdean the settings include the office of a secretarial and typewriting service, and a number of private "terraced" homes—that is, houses attached in a row which would be described by Americans as "townhouses" or "row houses." This particular row of houses was built about a century earlier in the shape of a crescent and is named "Wilbraham Crescent." It actually consists of two rows of houses with their back yards adjoining.

The interiors and gardens of several houses in Wilbraham Crescent are briefly described as part of the characterizations of their owners. Most memorable is the dirty and foul-smelling interior of the home occupied by a cat lover and her twelve cats. Another home, that of a successful builder, is expensively and somewhat ostentatiously furnished. One of the homeowners is a serious flower gardener who understands bulb planting in the fall and perennial flowering plants in general, and dismisses annual bedding plants as "amateur stuff." Another homeowner—the eccentric cat lover—neglects her garden entirely. There are an apple tree and a pear tree in one of the gardens, and two mischievous boys living at that home are said to squirt water from a hose at the cats in the neighboring garden and to throw apples at them.

Wilbraham Crescent is described several times with adjectives such as "tidy" and "prim" because of its Victorian architecture. In the following paragraphs the narrator, through his private thoughts, comments not on the physical appearance of the homes, but on the sad demise of "neighbors" and "neighborliness" in the modern world:

> ...Neighbours, I reflected bitterly! There was no doubt about it, neighbours were in short supply in Wilbraham Crescent. What I wanted—what Hardcastle wanted—was some nice gossipy, prying, peering old lady with time on her hands. Always hoping to look out and see something scandalous. The trouble is that that kind of old lady seems to have died out nowadays. They are all sitting grouped together in old ladies' homes with every comfort for the aged, or crowding up hospitals where beds are needed urgently for the really sick. The lame and the halt and the old didn't live in their own houses any more, attended by a faithful domestic or by some half-witted poor relation glad of a good home. It was a serious setback to criminal investigation.
>
> I looked across the road. Why couldn't there be any neighbours there? Why couldn't there be a neat row of houses facing me instead of that great, inhuman-looking concrete block? A kind of human beehive, no doubt, tenanted by worker bees who were out all day and only came back in the evening to wash their smalls or make up their faces and go out to meet their young men. By contrast with the inhumanity of that block of flats, I began almost to have a kindly feeling for the faded Victorian gentility of Wilbraham Crescent.

This "great, inhuman-looking concrete block" must be approximately eight stories high, as the narrator describes a "third story window" as being "about half way up the building." We must recall that a "third story" in England is really a "fourth story" in American terms.

London settings include a rather shabby flat occupied by a woman who describes herself as an "actress" who also works as a "hostess." Other characters suggest that she is more or less a prostitute. There is also a brief scene in a London pub called the "Peacock's Arms," where the above woman is a regular patron.

The remaining London setting is Whitehaven Mansions, a block of luxury flats in which Hercule Poirot has lived since the building was new in 1935. In former novels it has been described as "modern," which means "modern" in the 1935 sense, probably having exterior and interior features that would now be described as "Art Deco." In *The Clocks* the building is now nearly thirty years old, and Hercule Poirot's apartment is being redecorated, causing him to complain of the smell of paint and giving him a reason for making a brief visit to Crowdean in Chapter 28, in which he "reveals all."

In addition to the references to the "Iron Curtain," the "Bomb," nuclear disarmament and spying and counter-spying—all of which contribute to the early 1960s background of the story, the following make smaller but equally interesting contributions. One of the characters is a serious and knowledgeable flower gardener, and he has strong feelings in favor of using composting instead of chemical fertilizers. It was in 1962 that Rachel Carson's book *Silent Spring* appeared, launching the modern environmentalist movement. The book condemned the use of chemical pesticides such as DDT and chlordane, and also the use of chemical fertilizers.

There is in *The Clocks* one reference to the European Common Market and discussions within Britain about joining it. Christie also uses the term "formica" for the first time in a novel. "Formica," a trade name for a plastic laminate surface for kitchen work surfaces and tables, was developed as early as the 1920s and by the 1950s it had become the standard surface for tables and counters in American kitchens. Clearly it has become common enough, even in England, for its name to be used generically and spelled without the capital letter. Formica is mentioned twice in this novel: there is a formica-topped table in the kitchen in one of the houses in Wilbraham Crescent, and there are several formica-topped tables in the Buttercup Café, which is described as living up to its name by being "violently and aggressively yellow. Formica table tops, plastic cushions and cups and saucers were all canary colour."

The style of women's shoes having "stiletto" heels is mentioned, as one of the secretaries at the Cavendish Secretarial and Typewriting Bureau loses a heel from one of her shoes. Regarding typewriting, in one scene a typist makes a mistake and reaches automatically for an eraser. Typewriters with the "correction key" made their first appearance in approximately 1973, ten years after *The Clocks* was written, although as early as 1962 there were rolls of white "cover up" tape that could be used to type over errors, and white correction fluids appeared a short time later. But before about 1962 the traditional eraser was the only way to correct typing errors, and of course "computer word processing" did not come until about 1980.

Explicit and uncensored pornographic prose was common by 1963 and the Cavendish Secretarial and Typewriting Bureau has typing contracts with several authors, including one who writes frank pornography, one or two lines of which are quoted as the typist types them.

Story

It is September 9 of approximately 1963 in the town of Crowdean, which is on the English Channel coast in Sussex. Miss Martindale, the owner of the Cavendish Secretarial and Typewriting Bureau, receives a request by telephone from a certain Miss Pebmarsh for a shorthand typist to visit her home at 3:00 p.m. She specifically requests that the typist be Sheila Webb, whom she has employed in the past and whose work has pleased her. In the event Miss Pebmarsh has not yet returned home from some errands by 3:00 p.m., Sheila is to go into the house, which will not be locked, and to wait in the sitting room, which is to the right as she enters.

Sheila goes to the house at 3:00 p.m. as instructed, and receiving no answer when she rings, she enters the house, finding the dead body of a man on the floor in the sitting room. When Miss Pebmarsh, a teacher of the blind who is blind herself, returns to the house, she is questioned by the police and she denies making the phone call to the Cavendish Bureau. Using her hands to explore the face of the dead man, she declares that he is no person with whom she is acquainted.

The investigation of the crime is made extremely difficult because the man cannot be identified. A business card in his wallet naming a "Mr. Curry" as the representative of an insurance company with an address in a certain town is soon shown to be false, as there is no such insurance company and even no such town. The manufacturing labels of the murder victim's clothing have been removed, as if the murderer was determined that the body would not be identified.

Colin Lamb, a marine biologist by profession but who also works with Special Branch on occasion, is currently investigating a suspected British counter-spy who he has reason to believe lives in the block of houses where the murder of "Mr. Curry" occurred. Detective Inspector Hardcastle invites him to participate in the investigation so that he can, at the same time, conduct his investigation of the neighborhood in search of the counter-spy.

The inquest is delayed for some time because of the delay in identifying the murdered man. Finally, however, a woman from London comes forward and identifies him as her ex-husband, and then the inquest is held. As the inquest ends, one of the young typists from the secretarial bureau asks a policeman at the exit door if she may speak with Detective Inspector Hardcastle, explaining, "something she said couldn't be true." The officer advises her to visit the detective later at his office, but she has no opportunity of doing that because she is soon strangled in a public call box a few steps down the street.

The police make no progress in the case, but Colin Lamb happens to be acquainted with Hercule Poirot. Having heard of Poirot's claim that he is able, simply by sitting in a comfortable chair and using his little grey cells, to solve mysteries, he derisively provides Poirot with written summaries of the entire investigation, as if to say, "Let's see if you can solve this one." Soon Poirot visits Crowdean—not because he needs to examine the scene of the crime or to hunt for clues, but because his apartment in London is being redecorated and he is offended by the smell of paint. On the occasion of his visit to Crowdean, he casually "reveals all" to the astonished Colin.

Characters

Mrs. Packer, who lives at 47 Wilbraham Crescent and who specializes in premonitions of disasters. Perhaps she could have described "at great length afterwards the peculiar foreboding and tremors that had beset her" before the crime at number 19 Wilbraham Crescent occurred. But nobody else could have done so.

Miss Katherine Martindale, the owner of the Cavendish Secretarial and Typewriting Bureau in Palace Street, Crowdean, Sussex. Her employees refer to her as "Sandy Cat," but never in her presence. She is about forty years old and her name Katherine and her reddish hair are responsible for her nickname.

Edna Brent, one of the shorthand typists employed by Miss Martindale. She usually has a mint, a toffee or some other kind of candy in her mouth as she speaks on the telephone.

Sheila Webb, another shorthand typist employed by Miss Martindale for about the past ten months. She is a tall girl with brown curling hair. It is Sheila who discovers the body of the dead man at 19 Wilbraham Crescent.

Maureen West, Janet, and Another Typist employed by the Bureau

Armand Levine, an author of lurid pornographic prose who uses the Cavendish Secretarial and Typewriting Bureau.

Miss Millicent Pebmarsh, a teacher of the blind who is blind herself. She has lived at 19 Wilbraham Crescent since 1950. It is in Miss Pebmarsh's sitting room that the body of a murdered man is discovered.

Professor Purdy, an absent-minded archeologist for whom Sheila Webb types regularly.

Colin Lamb, the narrator of some of the chapters in the novel. His regular profession is that of a marine biologist, but he sometimes works as a kind of Secret Agent for the "Special Branch" of the Government. Currently he is working in that capacity in search of a British counterspy who, he as reason to believe, lives somewhere in Wilbraham Crescent.

Detective Inspector Dick Hardcastle, the officer in charge of the murder case.

A Police Surgeon, a Young Plainclothes Detective, a Police Photographer and a Fingerprint Man

Mrs. Lawton, Sheila Webb's maternal aunt, with whom she has lived since her parents died.

Ann Webb, Sheila Webb's Deceased Mother, who was a schoolteacher

Sheila Webb's Deceased Father

"Mr. R. H. Curry," the murder victim. The name is placed here in quotation marks because the only evidence of his name being R. H. Curry is a business card in his notecase showing that name, and the name and address of an insurance company. The company and its address are soon shown to be nonexistent. The victim is a well-groomed, well-dressed middle aged man, apparently a "gentleman." His clothes are of good quality and there is some suggestion of their being of foreign manufacture, though all labels have been removed. Establishing the true identity of the victim is the primary problem in the story.

Mrs. Curtin, Miss Pebmarsh's cleaning lady. She worries that her son Ernie socializes with undesirable youths, one of whom is a member of a gang.

Ernie Curtin, who worries his mother by going about with gang members.

"That Alf," a gang member who is a pal of Ernie Curtin's

A Young Constable stationed outside Miss Pebmarsh's house

The Driver of a Police Car

Josaiah Bland, referred to by Inspector Hardcastle as "Bland the Builder," who lives at 69 Wilbraham Crescent.

Valerie Bland, Josaiah Bland's wife

Larkin, an Englishman who passed state secrets to a foreign government and was recently caught by the "Special Branch."

Hanbury, Colin Lamb's predecessor in the "Special Branch" who had done a lot of work on the Larkin case. He was run over by a hit-and-run car in London, and nobody got its number—clearly he was killed by the enemy. But in his wallet, or in a pocket, was found a cryptic note showing a crescent or half-moon shape with the number 61 and the letter W. Colin believes there is something about 61 Wilbraham Crescent in Crowdean that is related to the person he is searching for.

Mr. James Waterhouse, who lives at 18 Wilbraham Crescent, next door to the house where the murder took place. He is the Managing Clerk of Gainsford & Swettenham, Solicitors.

Miss Edith Waterhouse, James Waterhouse's sister who, according to Inspector Hardcastle, spends most of her time "running him."

Mrs. Head, the Waterhouses' daily woman, who brings to Miss Waterhouse the rumor that the murdered man was the treasurer or a trustee of the Aaronberg Institute and that there was something wrong in the accounts, and that he came to Miss Pebmarsh to inquire about it, and that she "slipped a piece of wire round his neck and strangled him."

One or Two Reporters whom Miss Waterhouse has turned away, refusing to comment on the murder that took place next door a day earlier.

Mrs. Hemming, the eccentric owner of twelve cats, who lives at 20 Wilbraham Crescent, next door to the house where the murder took place. She is the only neighbor who, when visited the following day by Inspector Hardcastle and Colin Lamb, is unaware of the murder that took place next door. When informed of the event, she appears not to be interested.

Mrs. Ramsay, the mother of two small boys who lives on the other side of Wilbraham Crescent. Her rear garden borders on that of the cat-loving Mrs. Hemming but from her yard the garden of 19 Wilbraham Crescent is also visible. She is fond of her two sons but finds them very tiring when they are at home during the summer, and she looks forward to their return to school in the fall.

Mr. Michael Ramsay, an engineer who travels out of England frequently. Currently he is in Sweden on business.

Ted and Bill, Mr. and Mrs. Ramsay's two sons, aged about nine or ten. Mrs. Hemming refers to them as "those terrible boys" because they throw apples at her cats and squirt water at them with a garden hose, and she complains incessantly about them.

Mr. Angus McNaughton, a retired university professor of mathematics who is devoted to flower gardening and is adamant about the superiority of composting to the use of chemical fertilizers.

Mrs. McNaughton, Mr. McNaughton's wife. She is the only person in Wilbraham Crescent who, when shown the photograph of the dead man, believes she has seen him before, although her husband doubts it, and so do Colin Lamb and Inspector Hardcastle.

Gretel, the Danish housemaid of the McNaughtons who "has no sense of time."

Hercule Poirot, the Belgian private investigator who is now extremely aged. He is brought into the case by Colin Lamb whose father, a retired Scotland Yard inspector, was a good friend of Poirot's. Actually Colin presents Poirot with his own complete written account of the investigations for two reasons: to give poor old Monsieur Poirot something interesting to do and to dare him to make good on his old claim that he can solve mysteries simply by sitting back in a comfortable chair and using his "little grey cells." And Poirot does just that, only traveling to Crowdean at the end of the story to "reveal all" to Inspector Hardcastle and to Colin Lamb—and to escape from the smell of paint, as his apartment in Whitehaven Mansions is being renovated.

Poirot still has the habit of caressing his stupendous moustache and sipping fluids such as hot chocolate or *sirop de cassis* while discussing cases with others.

George, Poirot's manservant who has been with him since the 1928 *The Mystery of the Blue Train.* When Poirot receives guests such as Scotland Yard inspectors, he invariably offers them sweet liqueurs or chocolate but George usually enters at that moment with beer or whiskey, to their obvious delight and to Poirot's amazement.

Sergeant Cray, Inspector Hardcastle's assistant in the case.

Mr. Solomon, the proprietor of "a small, dingy bookshop" in London near the British Museum, in which an official of the "Special Branch"—Colin Lamb's superior—keeps a secret office on the second floor. Mr. Solomon is picturesquely described in Colin Lamb's narrative, which in this paragraph has almost a Dickensian flavor:

> I sidled through the doorway. It was necessary to sidle, since precariously arranged books impinged more and more every day on the passageway from the street. Inside, it was clear that the books owned the shop rather than the other way about. Everywhere they had run wild and taken possession of their habitat, breeding and multiplying and clearly lacking any strong hand to keep them down. The distance between bookshelves was so narrow that you could only get along with great difficulty. There were piles of books perched on every shelf or table. On a stool in a corner, hemmed in by books, was an old man in a pork-pie hat with a large flat face like a stuffed fish. He had the air of one who has given up an unequal struggle. He had attempted to master the books, but the books had obviously succeeded in mastering him.

Students, Elderly Colonels, Clergymen, and Two Students of Opposite Sexes Lost to the World in a Closely Knit Embrace, through whom Colin Lamb steers himself on his way to a door, masked by a curtain, on the second floor of Mr. Solomon's bookshop.

An Elderly Woman with gray hair, spectacles of a particularly old-fashioned kind, a black skirt and a rather unexpected peppermint-striped jumper. It is she who opens the "door masked by a curtain" leading to Colonel Beck's office.

Colonel Beck, Colin Lamb's superior in his Secret Service work.

Pendleton, a British counterspy who was caught. He had an English wife who had no idea he was a counter spy, as well as two other wives—and even two daughters—in other countries, all unknown to each other.

Pendleton's English Wife, his German Wife and Two Daughters, and his Swiss Wife

Colin Lamb's Father, a retired Scotland Yard Inspector. He is not named, but he may be Superintendent Battle whom we have met in four previous novels but not since the 1944 *Towards Zero,* in which only his youngest daughter Sylvia was mentioned.

Various Detective Story Writers, including Mrs. Ariadne Oliver, whom Hercule Poirot is currently studying.

Constable Pierce who, after the inquest, suggests that Edna Brent visit Inspector Hardcastle at police headquarters later in the day instead of interrupting him while he is busy conferring with other officers in the inquest room. Unfortunately she is murdered just a few minutes later.

Miss Felicity Lemon, Hercule Poirot's hideous and efficient secretary whom we first met in the 1955 *Hickory, Dickory, Death* and then, more briefly, in the 1956 *Dead Man's Folly.* She is so efficient and organized that she is "almost a machine."

Mr. Enderby, a well-known international lawyer and a friend of Hercule Poirot's. He makes certain inquiries for Poirot in Canada.

Mrs. Merlina Rival, a.k.a. Flossie Gapp, a lady who describes herself as an "actress/hostess." Seeing the police photograph of the murdered man in a newspaper, she identifies him as Harry Castleton, to whom she was once married.

Harry Castleton, Merlina Rival's ex-husband, who made use of his dignified, gentlemanly appearance in exploiting women.

The Chief Constable of the County of Sussex who orders Dick Hardcastle to take Hercule Poirot seriously

A Very Elderly Chauffeur driving a very old Rolls Royce

Geraldine Mary Alexandra Brown, a child aged ten years and three months, with a broken leg in a cast. Confined to her bedroom in a modern apartment building across from Wilbraham Crescent, she spends a good part of every day peering through a pair of opera glasses at the scene below her third-story window. She proves to be very intelligent and articulate and a keen observer.

Geraldine's Father, who is at work when Colin visits Geraldine.

Geraldine's Deceased Mother

Ingrid, a big, blonde Norwegian girl employed as a cook/housekeeper by Geraldine Brown's father. She speaks very little English.

Dick, Geraldine Brown's cousin who does train spotting with opera glasses

Harry, the porter at the apartment building where Geraldine and her father live

Mrs. Perry, who looks after Geraldine on Ingrid's afternoon off.

Fred, the barman at the Peacock's Arms, a pub where Flossie Gapp is a well-known patron

Two Other Patrons at the Peacock's Arms

FRENCH INTO ENGLISH

NOTE: Hercule Poirot solves the mystery in this novel but he appears in just three chapters—14, 22 and 28.

Chapter 4
femme formidable—a woman to be reckoned with; a woman with assertiveness and a strong character

Chapter 14
remplacement—personnel change (the former cleaning lady is being "replaced" by a different one)
Enfin—Well, after all...
mon cher Colin—my good friend Colin
mon ami—friend
Tout de même—all the same
Enfin—Actually...
Maître!—Masterly!
Ce cher Hastings—Dear old Hastings
Sans blague?—Is this for real? (literally: "no joke?")
Épatant—Astounding
hein?—eh?
Je vous remercie infiniment—Thank you very much

Chapter 28
Une petite surprise, n'est-ce pas?—A bit of a surprise, eh?
Pourquoi pas?—Why not?
Mais oui, mon ami—Oh yes, my friend
haute couture—high fashion women's clothing
mon cher—my friend
Un tas de bêtises—A bunch of nonsense
Eh bien—Well...

COMMENTS

The Clocks is a very pleasant detective novel populated by a number of fairly interesting characters, although characterization is not a strong point of the book. As has been the case with some of Christie's recent novels, there is a bit too much coincidence, and Hercule Poirot again makes some guesses that happen to prove correct. Still, the book is fun to read. Part of the interest in the book are the references to spying and counterspying and the idea of people "defecting" to "the other side," an important and popular subject during the "Cold War" which was still actively raging in the early 1960s.

Among the charms of this novel are the conversations with four amiable children—two brothers aged about nine or ten, a ten-year-old girl, and another boy who is probably about the same age. All four are bright kids who enjoy interacting with adults, although the son of the daily woman, Mrs. Curtin, appears to associate with kids whom his mother suspects of being a bad influence.

There is one incident that is rather unbelievable, however. Colin Lamb, at one point, wishes that the neighborhood of Wilbraham Crescent had a few nosy—and therefore observant—old women who might have seen things worth knowing about on the day of the murder. Just as he is having depressing thoughts about the drab concrete apartment building across the road—which he compares to a kind of human beehive to which worker bees return after their day's work—his attention is caught by the reflection of a shiny object in an upper-story window. It is a little girl looking down at him through a pair of opera glasses. He wonders if this little girl may have seen something on the day of the murder. In order to invent a plausible reason for going up to the apartment, he searches the ground beneath the window and luckily finds an insignificant object—an old fruit knife. He determines that the apartment must be on the third floor, estimates the location of the apartment within that floor, and boldly enters the building, taking the elevator to the third floor.

He knocks at the door of the apartment and is greeted by a Norwegian housemaid who speaks very little English and whose hands and apron bear evidence of flour—she has clearly been interrupted while working on some baking project in the kitchen. Colin manages to make her understand that he wants to see "the child" who lives there and who has "dropped the fruit knife" by accident from her window. He is apparently such a conscientious, helpful soul that he feels he must return the fruit knife to the child *personally*.

If you were a housemaid opening the door to a stranger holding a knife—however dull—and wishing to speak *personally* to the child in the house, what would you do?

It is doubtful that you would do what the Norwegian maid does. She welcomes Colin into the apartment, escorts him to the child's room, says something like "you have a visitor" and returns to the kitchen to refocus her attention on pastry making.

The child, a ten-year-old girl with a broken leg elevated in a cast, has no problem with a strange man, who is holding a knife, being left alone with her *and closing the door* while Ingrid goes back to the kitchen. The two of them have a jolly good conversation, and she tells him all about everything that happens every place in Wilbraham Crescent.

It seems rather doubtful that, even forty years ago, strange men carrying knives were allowed into the bedrooms of ten-year-old girls even by the stupidest of Norwegian housemaids.

But with this exception, the events and conversations in the story are believable and there are a few touches of humor, as in the portrayals of the fanatical cat-lover Mrs. Hemming and the absent-minded archeologist Professor Purdy.

The Clocks would not make a good "first Christie experience" because, although it features Hercule Poirot, and it is he who "solves" the mystery (although with the help of some lucky guessing) his role is very small. There is nothing particularly special or remarkable about this novel and it certainly bears no comparison with Christie's many masterpieces from the 1930s, 1940s and 1950s. Read this one *after* you have read most of her earlier works.

A Caribbean Mystery (1964)

SETTING

The year is approximately 1964, but the season has no importance because the story takes place on the fictitious Caribbean island of St. Honoré where there is a year-round tropical climate. Nearby islands mentioned in the story are Martinique and Tobago, and we can assume that St. Honoré is, like Bermuda and several other Caribbean islands, a British possession. It is ruled by an Administrator from its only town, Jamestown. There is no indication of the size or population of either Jamestown or the island itself, which appears to exist primarily as a vacation spot.

The setting is occasioned by the fact that our old friend Miss Jane Marple (who is indeed very old, since we were told in the 1957 *What Mrs. McGillicuddy Saw* that she was already eighty-nine, and therefore she must now be about ninety-six) has been offered a holiday in the Caribbean by her kind and generous nephew, novelist Raymond West. As usual, Miss Marple encounters murder wherever she goes, although this is her first adventure with crime away from England.

All of the action takes place at a resort hotel called The Golden Palm Hotel (also occasionally referred to as The Golden Palm Tree Hotel). The hotel consists of a main building which houses the kitchen and restaurant and probably other rooms such as a dance hall, since there is dancing every night after dinner. The guests stay in small individual bungalows of various sizes, each having a sitting room, one or more bedrooms and a bathroom but of course no kitchen, since all meals are taken at the main building. The dining room is open on two or three sides to the fresh air.

As Miss Marple has dinner in the dining room one evening, she notes that various nationalities are represented at the hotel: British, Venezuelan, Brazilian, French, Italian and American and perhaps others.

Current events of the middle 1960s are not mentioned in the story at all, although there are comments about one or two social developments. One of those is Agatha Christie's perception that adultery, once regarded as a shameful act that sometimes led to scandal and such crimes as blackmail, is no longer hidden from public view. In fact, in the thoughts of ninety-six-year-old Miss Marple, the adulterers of today seem determined to broadcast their activities and call as much attention to them as possible. Sexual experiences of unmarried young people, too, are now perceived as not sinful but expected and even *required* experiences, as we read in the following lines from a current novel that Miss Marple has been given by her nephew in his efforts to "bring her up to date":

> "Do you mean that you've had no sexual experience at ALL?" demanded the young man incredulously. "At *nineteen?* But you *must.* It's vital."
> The girl hung her head unhappily, her straight greasy hair fell forward over her face.
> "I know," she muttered, "I know."
> He looked at her, stained old jersey, the bare feet, the dirty toenails, the smell of rancid fat.... He wondered why he found her so maddeningly attractive.
> Miss Marple wondered, too! And really! To have sex experience urged on you exactly as though it was an iron tonic! Poor young things...

A third social development mentioned in the novel is the widespread overuse of prescription and other drugs. This had been an important issue in the 1962 *The Mirror Crack'd*. In *A Caribbean Mystery* it is a smaller issue, mentioned only once, but it is described as a general trend not confined to entertainers.

A fourth "social development" that is mentioned once or twice is the abolition of the death penalty in Great Britain and certain people's disgust with modern, lenient penalties for murder. It can be thought of as a "social development" since it was the changed views of the voting public that brought about the new legislation. The use of the term "diminished responsibility" as an excuse for criminal behavior also occurs a couple of conversations.

The general public's relatively new and sophisticated familiarity with precise medical terms is suggested by the terms "coronary thrombosis," "hypertension," and "cerebral hemorrhage" which occur in the speech of non-medical characters in *A Caribbean Mystery*. A rather amusing fact is that Christie uses the term "high blood pressure" and simply "blood pressure" interchangeably throughout the novel, as in the question, "Did Major Palgrave ever mention having blood pressure?" Of course a person without "blood pressure" would not be alive.

The slang term "sleeping around" pops up once in this novel, a first for Christie, and in one scene a crude, lecherous man "leers at" a woman, also a Christie first.

Although there had been suggestions of homosexuality in Christie novels as early as the 1933 *Thirteen at Dinner,* and the word "queer" was used specifically with that meaning in the 1935 *Murder in Three Acts,* no Christie character had ever been actually stated to be homosexual. In *A Caribbean Mystery,* Miss Marple's nephew Raymond West arranges her trip to the West Indies, and he provides a "house sitter" to live in her cottage in St. Mary Mead while she is away. That person is an author friend who Raymond knows will keep the house in perfect order, since "he's very house proud—he's a queer." The term "gay" with a non-pejorative homosexual meaning was still not in the general vocabulary in 1964. Since Raymond West considers this man to be a friend and allows him to inhabit Miss Marple's cottage in her absence, he must be using the word "queer" without contempt.

STORY

It is approximately 1964 and Miss Marple, now about ninety-six years old, has suffered another episode of pneumonia in damp, chilly England. Her generous nephew Raymond West finances a holiday for her in the healthful climate of a small island in the Caribbean, the fictitious island of Saint Honoré.

One of the guests at Miss Marple's hotel is a lonely old man, Major Palgrave, who is the stereotypical "boring old ex-colonial type" that we have met in many Christie stories. Understanding that he is a lonely old man whose best years ended long ago, Miss Marple does not mind sitting with him and listening "with half an ear" to his vast repertoire of boring stories about his past, while she pursues pleasant thoughts of her own.

One day Major Palgrave tells Miss Marple a long, boring story about a man who murdered his wife. He happens to have a picture of the man in his wallet, and he asks, "Want to see a picture of a murderer?" But just as he is about to show the picture to Miss Marple, something or someone that he sees over Miss Marple's shoulder causes him to quickly replace the photo in his wallet and to change the subject.

Major Palgrave dies the next day, apparently due to a combination of high blood pressure and overindulgence in alcohol. Miss Marple wonders if he was actually murdered—perhaps by the person whose picture he was about to show to her. Soon a servant woman at the hotel is stabbed to death outside the hotel, and Miss Marple is sure that the two deaths are related.

Because she is at a disadvantage on this remote Caribbean island without her usual contacts, such as Sir Henry Clithering and Inspector Craddock, to vouch for her and to cause the local authorities to take her seriously, she prevails upon another hotel guest, the rude, cantankerous and insulting—but very rich and therefore respected—Mr. Rafiel. She explains her ideas to him and successfully obtains his assistance. Soon there is a third murder, but Miss Marple and Mr. Rafiel are able to set a trap which prevents a fourth killing and catches the murderer in the act.

CHARACTERS

Major Palgrave, a guest at the Golden Palm Hotel in St. Honoré who tells Miss Marple several interesting (or perhaps boring?) stories, illustrating them with photographs. He is another of Christie's "boring ex-military men." Miss Marple does not mind sitting with him and listening with half an ear, while pursuing her own thoughts, because she understands that he is a lonely old man who craves friends and company.

Major Palgrave dies early in the story, is buried in a church cemetery in St. Honoré and is soon forgotten.

Jane Marple, our old friend from the village of St. Mary Mead, a village spinster and a world-class detective, respected by men of high position at New Scotland Yard. We met her first in the 1930 *Murder at the Vicarage* and then in several subsequent novels and short stories, most recently in the 1962 *The Mirror Crack'd*. She must now be about ninety-six years old, since in the 1957 *What Mrs. McGillicuddy Saw* her age was specifically stated to be eighty-nine.

As we know, in solving murder mysteries, Miss Marple relies heavily on "village parallels"—people in her past of whom she is reminded by people involved in the crime story. We learn in *A Caribbean Mystery* that, like Hercule Poirot, she is not above telling lies if there is no other way to advance in her investigation. In the early Hercule Poirot stories, his friend Hastings was always shocked at the ease with which Poirot lied, and criticized him for it, saying things like, "Really, Poirot. That's not playing the game," or "Really, Poirot, that's not cricket," or just simply, "Really, Poirot!" If Hastings were present in *A Caribbean Mystery,* he would have occasion to say, "Really, Miss Marple!" For Miss Marple invents a spurious nephew and sends a doctor to look for the nephew's non-existent photograph among the personal effects of the dead Major Palgrave. It is true that she later apologizes for her lie, which is something Hercule Poirot has never done. But then, he's a foreigner of course, and foreigners lie as a matter of course. Just ask Hastings.

In *A Caribbean Mystery,* Miss Marple is handicapped by not having any of her colleagues and allies, such as the retired Scotland Yard Inspector, Sir Henry Clithering, to vouch for her abilities. She must earn the respect of old Mr. Rafiel in order to pursue her investigation quickly, as he has money and therefore all the respect of everyone on the island. At first he thinks of Miss Marple as just another silly old spinster with knitting wool for brains, but before long he feels great respect for her.

Raymond West, Miss Marple's always-generous nephew, who writes "clever books" as she calls them. Actually Miss Marple has never been impressed with Raymond's books or his ideas and there is usually a twinkle in her eye as she pays him compliments about them, or listens patiently to his pontifications, but she has always appreciated his generosity. In this story he provides her with a holiday in the Caribbean as she recovers from an episode of pneumonia.

Joan West, Raymond's wife who had insisted on giving money to Miss Marple to purchase suitable clothing for the climate of St. Honoré. She is a mildly successful painter whose paintings Miss Marple described in the 1950 *A Murder Is Announced* as "mostly jugs of dying flowers and broken combs on windowsills."

An Author Friend of Raymond's who lives in Miss Marple's cottage and looks after it while she is in the West Indies. Raymond explains that the friend will look after the house all right, as he's "very house-proud. He's a queer."

Diana Horrocks, another friend of Raymond's, who accompanies Miss Marple as far as Trinidad on the plane flight.

The Sandersons, the former owners of the Golden Palm Hotel in St. Honoré.

Molly Kendal who, with her husband Tim, owns and operates the Golden Palm Hotel. She is "an ingenuous blonde of twenty-odd, always apparently in good spirits" who greets Miss Marple warmly and does everything to make her comfortable.

Tim Kendal, "lean, dark and in his thirties," Molly's husband who worries about their making a success of the Golden Palm Hotel.

Friendly, Smiling West Indian Girls who wait on Miss Marple and the other guests

Old Mr. Rafiel, a rich, cantankerous and insulting but intelligent old man who is a guest at the Golden Palm Hotel. He becomes Miss Marple's ally in the investigation of the murder.

Dr. Graham, a doctor who listens to Miss Marple's suspicions and goes to the authorities, ordering an exhumation of Major Palgrave's body.

Canon Jeremy Prescott, "a round, rubicund

man, breathing geniality," an English clergyman who is a guest at the Golden Palm Hotel. He disapproves of idle gossip, which his sister Joan enjoys, and on several occasions he admonishes her on that subject.

Joan Prescott, the Canon's sister. She is exactly like the "old pussies" in St. Mary Mead whom we met in the 1930 *Murder at the Vicarage* and then in the 1942 *The Body in the Library*. Every single bit of her conversation is gossip, although it does not seem to be malicious gossip. Whenever the Canon is not present, Miss Prescott and Miss Marple put their heads together and discuss everyone at the hotel.

Mrs. Linnett and her Cough Mixture, Young Polegate and his Very Odd Behavior, Georgy Wood's Possibly Spurious Mother, and Joe Arden and his Wife and Their Quarrel, all nostalgically recalled by Miss Marple in the relative boredom of St. Honoré

Harry Western, the guilty party in a murder case in St. Honoré a couple of years ago, mentioned by Major Palgrave in response to Miss Marple's question "Does anything ever happen here, I wonder?"

Harry Western's Wife, who had a lover whom Harry shot.

The Count of Ferrari, Mrs. Western's lover who was shot by her husband.

A Doctor Friend of Major Palgrave who told an interesting story about a married woman who attempted suicide, was rescued just in time by her husband, and then succeeded in doing away with herself just a short time later.

A Doctor Friend of Major Palgrave's Doctor Friend who had heard a very similar story, then recognized a photograph, shown him by the other doctor, as the husband in his own story, although the husbands and wives had different names.

Greg Dyson, an American entomologist who publishes articles about butterflies in *The National Geographic*. He is "a big, boisterous, happy-looking man with an upstanding bush of thick grey hair." He is also a bit of a lecher, and he "leers" at Molly Kendal and "makes passes" at her whenever possible.

Lucky Dyson (née Greatorex), Greg Dyson's wife, apparently also an entomologist. She is "a golden blonde woman" aged about forty, rather loud, and fond of drink. At one point she declares loudly that she'll die if she doesn't have a drink "at once or sooner." Certain people suspect that she is having an affair with Edward Hillingdon.

Gail Dyson, Greg Dyson's first wife who died rather suddenly. The doctor, according to Joan Prescott's sources (people who knew the Dysons, and who later came to St. Honoré and talked about things), "wasn't very satisfied." Greg Dyson married Lucky Greatorex just a month later, having inherited a considerable amount of money from Gail.

Colonel Edward Hillingdon, a botanist and a good friend of Greg Dyson. It is rumored that he is an even better friend of Greg Dyson's wife. He is "dark and lean" and rather quiet.

Evelyn Hillingdon, "a handsome but rather weatherbeaten woman." Despite external appearances which suggest that she and her husband are devoted to each other, Evelyn reveals, in a private conversation with Molly Kendal, that she has a loveless marriage and that she tolerates her husband's relationship with Lucky Dyson in order to keep the family intact for the benefit of her children.

Esther Walters, old Mr. Rafiel's secretary. She tolerates Mr. Rafiel's insulting behaviors because he pays her a much higher salary than she could possibly earn doing the same work for someone else.

Esther Walters's Mother, a widow who lives in Chichester

Arthur Jackson, Mr. Rafiel's valet-attendant, a qualified masseur. He is "a young man, tall and good-looking."

That Girl who was a Conductress on the Market Basing Bus, one of Miss Marple's "village parallels." Molly Kendal reminds Miss Marple of her.

The Headwaiter at the Royal George Hotel in Medchester, Miss Marple's "village parallel" for Tim Kendal.

General Leroy, Captain Flemming, Admiral Wicklow, and Commander Richardson, "village parallels" for Major Palgrave, all indistinguishable from each other with their incessant, boring stories about tigers, lions, and elephants and places like India, Kenya, and China.

Sir George Trollope, Miss Marple's "village parallel" for Greg Dyson. Sir George was always full of jokes.

Mr. Murdoch, another "village parallel" for Greg Dyson. He had a rather bad reputation, but some people said it was just gossip, and Mr. Murdoch himself liked to encourage the rumours!

Marleen at The Three Crowns, Miss Marple's "village parallel" for Lucky Dyson

Lady Caroline Wolfe, a "village parallel" for Evelyn Hillingdon. Lady Caroline committed suicide.

Leslie James, a second "village parallel" for Evelyn Hillingdon. Leslie James was a quiet woman who seldom showed what she felt. She sold her house and left without ever telling anyone where she was going.

Major Harper, a "village parallel" for Edward Hillingdon. He had quietly cut his throat one day, and nobody had ever known why. Miss Marple thought that she did know, but she'd never been quite sure...

That Hulking Swede, a lifeguard at the Golden Palm Hotel beach

Denzil, a spurious nephew of Miss Marple whom she invents as part of her investigation of Major Palgrave's death

Victoria Johnson, a native West Indian woman who works as a chambermaid at the Golden Palm Hotel. She is "a magnificent creature with a torso of black marble such as a sculptor would have enjoyed."

Victoria lives with a man whom she considers to be her current husband and with whom she has had two children. She is stabbed to death one evening in some bushes outside the Golden Palm Hotel.

Big John Ellis, "a big handsome Negro" who is Victoria Johnson's "current husband," though "without ceremony." He is the father of her two children.

Dr. Robertson, the local police doctor who certifies Major Palgraves's death as having been a natural one.

Mr. Daventry, the Administrator of St. Honoré in Jamestown. He is a grave young man of thirty-five who is reluctant to believe Dr. Graham's suspicions about Major Palgrave's death, but who finally agrees to an exhumation of the body.

A Servant at Mr. Daventry's Office

Fernando, the Italian *maître d'hôtel* at the Golden Palm Hotel

Inspector Weston of the St. Honoré police force, "a slender dark man in police uniform." He is in charge of the case of Victoria Johnson's murder.

Señora de Caspearo, a handsome married woman from Venezuela who, while sunning herself on the beach, is always surrounded by attentive men. Her reaction upon beholding old Mr. Rafiel in bathing attire:

> "How ugly are old men! Oh, how they are ugly! They should all be put to death at forty, or perhaps thirty-five would be better. Yes?"

Enrico, one of the Cuban cooks at the Golden Palm Hotel who saw Molly Kendal walk through the kitchen with a knife in her hand and then leave the hotel through the kitchen door.

Sir Henry Clithering, a retired Scotland Yard inspector and an old friend, admirer and ally of Miss Marple. He is not a character in the story but Miss Marple wishes that he were, for he would vouch for her and prevail upon the local authorities to take her suspicions seriously. We have known him since the 1942 *The Body in the Library.*

Chief Inspector Dermot Craddock, another, younger ally of Miss Marple who she wishes were in St. Honoré to vouch for her. We first met him in the 1950 *A Murder Is Announced,* in the course of which he acquired great respect for Miss Marple. In the 1962 *The Mirror Crack'd,* when called to St. Mary Mead to investigate the death of Heather Badcock, Craddock made his first stop "headquarters"—that is, Miss Marple's cottage, to her embarrassment and amusement. Miss Marple feels close enough to Chief Inspector Craddock to refer to him as "Dermot," and to address him as "my dear boy."

Jonas Perry, Miss Marple's "village parallel" for Arthur Jackson. Jonas worked for the St. Mary Mead Town Clerk's office and "was not very satisfactory."

Some French and Italian Children playing on the beach who call upon Canon Prescott to settle their minor disputes, addressing him as *Mon père* (Father).

An Assorted Bag of Gentlemen in Attendance who usually surround the attractive and vivacious Venezuelan lady, Señora de Caspearo

An Uncle of Molly Kendal who, according to Joan Prescott, once removed all of his clothes in Green Park tube station.

An Elderly Clergyman who, according to Miss Marple, also once stripped in public.

The Wife of the Elderly Clergyman who came in a taxi, wrapped her naked husband in a blanket, and took him home.

An Unsuitable Young Man whom Molly Kendal had wanted to marry. Her family prevented the marriage.

The Young and Inexperienced Doctor who attended to the first Mrs. Dyson and was puzzled when she died

COMMENTS

If you enjoy the Miss Marple character, you will like *A Caribbean Mystery* because Miss Marple is present throughout the story and she is in rare form. The exotic setting of a Caribbean island is a nice change, although it is nothing but a setting—the story could have taken place at an English coastal resort just as well.

There is none of the repetitious dialogue in *A Caribbean Mystery* that seemed to afflict two of Christie's recent novels, *The Mirror Crack'd* and *The Pale Horse,* and there are no unacceptable "coincidences" that the reader is expected to accept. Instead, there is fast-moving action and concise dialogue as Miss Marple moves quickly to acquire knowledge about the characters, and to acquire a reliable investigative assistant. She is handicapped in this story by being away from home where her old friend Sir Henry Clithering, formerly of Scotland Yard, could vouch for her and encourage younger police officers to take her ideas seriously.

The characters in *A Caribbean Mystery* are not particularly memorable or individual. However, the relationship between Miss Marple and old Mr. Rafiel is fun to read about, as she earns the respect of this cantankerous and insulting but intelligent old man by boldly telling him the facts as she sees them and appealing to him as an ally in solving the mystery.

One pleasant surprise occurs in the story: Christie had begun to "lecture" her readers several years ago on the subject of "inherited character traits"—most stridently in the 1949 *Crooked House*, the 1952 *Murder with Mirrors*, and the 1958 *Ordeal by Innocence*, and to a lesser degree in a few other novels, whenever a "foolish" character suggested that environment or upbringing were important influences on a person's character. The "wise" characters always affirmed that *everything* in one's personality comes by inheritance through blood. On many occasions "insanity in the family" was cited as a serious issue, and of course the term "insane" was used indiscriminately to include all degrees of mental illness. In *A Caribbean Mystery* we have evidence that Christie became enlightened on the subject, as she allows at least one of her "wise" characters to say of "inherited insanity," "Nobody believes that anymore." When the gossipy sister of a clergyman whispers to her that Molly Kendal's uncle was crazy (he once took off his clothes in a London tube station) Miss Marple hastens to remark that she once knew of an elderly *clergyman* who "suffered from the same disorder."

On a related subject, it has been quite a long time since Christie described the shape of a man's forehead or chin, or the exact distance between his eyes, or the exact shade of blue of his eyes, as evidence of his character. In *A Caribbean Mystery* the Englishmen's faces are not described at all except for a few general adjectives such as "dark" or "good-looking." And at least two "Negro" characters in the story are allowed to have the same kinds of thoughts as "regular" people, and to have the words "beautiful" and "handsome" in their physical descriptions. To be fair to Christie, though, we should recall that as early as 1955, in *Hickory, Dickory, Death*, she had presented at least two black characters very affirmatively. Mr. Akibombo was a very friendly man from Africa, and Elizabeth Johnston, a law student from the West Indies, was described by Hercule Poirot as having "the best brain of anyone at the hostel." Furthermore, Hercule Poirot's secretary Miss Lemon had volunteered the following:

"Half the nurses in our hospitals seem to be black nowadays, and I understand much pleasanter and more attentive than the English ones."

As a "first Christie experience," *A Caribbean Mystery* cannot be recommended because, as usual in her later novels, Christie presents the Miss Marple character as if she is writing only for her loyal fans who already know all about Miss Marple. She presents the usual listing of "village parallels," for example, without explaining their significance in Miss Marple's crime-solving techniques, and she drops the important names Sir Henry Clithering and "Dermot" without explaining who they are, evidently assuming that the reader has read a few Miss Marple stories and is already familiar with them.

But for Christie fans, and especially for Miss Marple fans, *A Caribbean Mystery* is thoroughly enjoyable. It is Christie's best detective novel of the 1960s.

At Bertram's Hotel (1965)

Setting

On August 8, 1963 a sensational train robbery took place in the English county of Buckinghamshire. The Glasgow to London "travelling post office" was stopped by tampered signals and a well-organized gang of fifteen men subdued the train's crew and stole 2.3 million pounds in used one-, five-, and ten-pound notes. That was the equivalent of about forty million pounds in the present year (2007.) No firearms were used in the robbery and the only physical harm to a member of the train crew was some bruising to the train's engineer, who was struck with an iron bar. The police soon discovered the gang's hideout, a farm in Buckinghamshire, and arrested some, but not all, of the fifteen members of the gang. Most of the money was never recovered.

Agatha Christie undoubtedly used this incident, now referred to as The Great Train Robbery, as inspiration for the incident of the train robbery in *At Bertram's Hotel*. In the story a well-organized gang of criminals is said to have committed a number of sensational robberies, and in the course of the story "The Irish Express," a mail train, is halted and robbed of huge amounts of money, without violence.

The story takes place in late October of 1964 or 1965. The principal setting is the fictitious Bertram's Hotel, located in "Pond Street," which is said to be not far from Hyde Park. The telephone number of Bertram's Hotel has a "Mayfair" exchange, suggesting quite an upper-class neighborhood within London. The hotel dates from about 1840 but, unlike other old hotels, it does not seem to have changed very much over the past fifty years or so. Walking into Bertram's Hotel, according to several characters, is like walking into an England of fifty years earlier. There is a pontifical butler presiding over afternoon tea which features silver teapots, real china, and "real" seedcake and muffins. Chambermaids wear uniforms and caps and keep their eyes lowered. Bathrooms are decorated with old-fashioned rose-patterned wallpapers and the guestrooms have none of those annoying modern touches such as in-room televisions. The guests seem to consist mainly of aging aristocrats and aging clergymen. When Miss Marple arrives at Bertram's Hotel, she is delighted with its old-fashioned charms, but she soon begins to suspect that it's nothing but a big theatrical production, and that something fishy must be behind it. So important is the setting of Bertram's Hotel that the hotel itself is almost a character in the story.

Aside from the obvious origin of the idea of the train robbery in the story—The Great Train Robbery of 1963—there are no current events mentioned in the novel. There are no references to the "Cold War," to Communism, the atomic bomb, etc. as there have been in several recent Christie novels. The Beatles, a brand-new rock music group, are mentioned vaguely once by an older person who really has no idea what "Beatles" can be. A powerful sports car called a Mercedes-Otto, driven by a famous racing car driver, makes an appearance and so does an old Oxford Morris sedan driven by an elderly clergyman.

The housekeeper of an elderly clergyman makes a reference to the "Frigidaire," using the brand name instead of the generic term "refrigerator." The British were, and still are to some extent, accustomed to referring generically to any vacuum cleaner as a "Hoover." Americans' habit of using the trade name "Kleenex" to refer generically to any facial tissue is a similar practice.

There are comments from elderly characters that mothers today (1964–1965) do not "protect" their daughters from predatory, unsuitable male companions as they once did, preventing unfortunate marriages *and* illegitimate pregnancies. It is generally known that the older segment of *every* generation has always complained about youth and "modern times" in a similar way. It must be deduced that Christie, now a woman of about seventy-five years of age, is expressing typical "old people's views," and not really accurately reporting "societal trends." She portrays the "old fashioned, conscientious mother" as one who has her daughter's welfare at heart, and she portrays the "modern mothers" as neglectful. Another viewpoint on this subject might be that those "old fashioned" mothers were more interested in their family image than their daughters' happiness, whereas the more modern mothers care less for "image" than their ancestors did, and feel that children should learn to make their own decisions and, if they make mistakes, to learn from them. In any case, Christie's comments—through her elderly characters—about "modern girls and their modern mothers" cannot be taken very seriously as "documentation of British social trends." See the *Comments* section for further remarks on this subject.

STORY

Because Miss Marple enjoyed her holiday on the Caribbean island of St. Honoré so much (in the 1964 *A Caribbean Mystery*), her generous nephew Raymond now offers her another holiday of her choice. Miss Marple requests a pleasant week or two at an expensive old-fashioned hotel in London where she once stayed with an uncle and aunt when she was about fourteen years old. It is Bertram's Hotel in Pond Street.

Arriving at the hotel, Miss Marple is absolutely delighted with the fact that, unlike everything else in recent years, Bertram's Hotel has not changed a bit. There appears to have been no modernization at all. There is even the genteel custom of afternoon tea presided over by a pontifical butler and featuring silver teapots and real muffins. The chambermaids wear caps, keep their eyes lowered, and are respectful. Bertram's Hotel is, in fact, so much like a luxury hotel of fifty or sixty years ago that Miss Marple soon wonders if it can be real. She has the unsettling impression that it is one big theatrical production, and that something unnatural must be behind it. Even the guests seem unnatural. Mostly aging aristocrats, genteel old ladies from the country, and gray-haired clergymen, plus a sprinkling of French and American families who are enchanted with this "real English hotel," Miss Marple wonders if all of *them* are actually real.

Inspector Davy of Scotland Yard, who is investigating a series of recent large-scale robberies, also believes that Bertram's Hotel is, frankly, a fake. He believes that it is a front for some criminal activities related to the robberies, and when he goes to Bertram's to investigate, he becomes a friend of Miss Marple. Soon one of the guests at the hotel, the aging and forgetful Canon Pennyfather, disappears and then the hotel doorman is shot to death outside on a foggy night.

Inspector Davy solves the mystery of the train robberies and Miss Marple assists him in the matter of the disappearing clergyman and the death of the doorman.

CHARACTERS

Michael ("Micky" or "Mick") Gorman, the "commissionaire" (doorman) at Bertram's Hotel. He is described in Chief Inspector Davy's thoughts as "Over six feet. Good-looking chap. A bit run to seed. Ex-Army. Lot of medals—genuine, probably. A bit shifty? Drinks too much."

The American Barman at Bertram's Hotel, who makes the Americans feel at home by providing them with bourbon, rye and every kind of cocktail.

The English Barman at Bertram's Hotel who deals with sherries and Pimm's No. 1, and talks knowledgeably about the runners at Ascot and Newbury with the middle-aged Englishmen who stay at Bertram's during the more serious race meetings.

Henry, the butler at Bertram's Hotel, who presides over afternoon tea, and who is described as "a large and magnificent figure, a ripe fifty, avuncular, sympathetic, and with the courtly manners of that long vanished species: the perfect butler."

Slim Youths who perform the actual work at tea time under Henry's austere direction.

Lady Selina Hazy, a sixty-five-year-old guest at Bertram's Hotel from Leicestershire, and an old friend of Jane Marple. She is in London to visit a Harley Street specialist about her arthritis, and to visit her dentist.

Lady Selina's Second Son, who was stationed at an airfield near St. Mary Mead during the war. Lady Selina had taken a house there for two years in order to be near him, and it was then that she met Jane Marple.

Colonel Derek Luscombe, "...erect, soldierly, race glasses hanging round his neck." He is the incompetent guardian of his niece, young Elvira Blake, an heiress, and one of her three trustees. Despite being one of her trustees, he has evidently never bothered to read the trust—having no idea of how much money she has or who would inherit it if she were to marry or to die.

Miss Jane Marple, whom we met for the first time in the 1930 *Murder at the Vicarage* and whom Christie did not again feature in a novel until the 1942 *The Body in the Library*. Recently, however, Miss Marple has made much more regular appearances, starring in six or seven novels since 1950.

Miss Marple would be about ninety-seven years old, if we were eccentric enough to keep track of her age, having been described as being eighty-nine years old in the 1957 *What Mrs. McGillicuddy Saw*. In this story we are asked, however, to think of her as being about sixty-five years old.

Miss Marple has a reputation for being very good at crime solving, despite having spent nearly all of her long life in a tiny village. She solves crimes by remembering people in her village of whom she is reminded by people who are possible suspects of the crime, referring to her past village acquaintances as "village parallels." She is also an unabashed and unashamed gossip, and sees no reason not to listen attentively to private conversations. She prefers the term "taking an interest" to the cruder term "eavesdropping." In this novel she eavesdrops—excuse me—*takes an interest* in several private conversations—in one of the writing rooms at Bertram's Hotel, in the fourth-floor restaurant at the Army and Navy Store, at a tea enclosure near Chelsea Bridge, and no doubt in other places as well.

Miss Marple is extremely intelligent, and she is perhaps the only one of the guests at Bertram's Hotel who at first senses, and then becomes convinced, that the place is a fake and that something very wrong is going on there. It's "just too good to be true," as she explains. She befriends Chief-Inspector Davy of Scotland Yard who shares her suspicions about Bertram's Hotel.

"The Cook" at Bertram's Hotel who has an old, authentic "receipt" for "real seedcake." As noted in the 1959 *Cat Among the Pigeons*, Christie apparently had no idea of how many people would be needed as "cooks" for a large number of people. In that novel she stated that there was "a cook" at Meadowbank School, and that lady miraculously provided three meals a day, all cooked from scratch, for a student body of two hundred plus the staff. A kitchen staff of at least five or six cooks would be more reasonable in that story, and also in this one. But then, Christie was a "lady" and could not be expected to know details of meal preparation. And so at Bertram's Hotel there is "The Cook."

Two Church Canons, the Dean of Chislehampton, a Bishop, Old Lady Berry, Mrs. Posselthwaite from Somerset, Sybil Kerr, the Dear Bishop of Medmenham, Cicely Longhurst, Archdeacon Abercrombie and many others, all of whom are guests at Bertram's Hotel when Miss Marple arrives there.

Miss Gorringe, the receptionist at Bertram's Hotel. She knows every one of the clientele and, like Royalty, never forgets a face.

Mr. Humfries, the manager—or perhaps the owner—of Bertram's hotel, a man of about fifty with good manners and the presence of a Junior Minister. Chief Inspector Davy suspects that he may be something else.

Raymond West, a wealthy nephew of Miss Marple who writes "clever books," as she expresses it. Despite the cleverness of his books, Miss Marple considers him to be a rather stupid man and always has, ever since his first mention in the 1930 *Murder at the Vicarage,* in which there was usually "a twinkle in her eye as she listened to his talk with a flattering interest," though he has never noticed this. In the 1964 *A Caribbean Mystery,* Raymond had given Miss Marple a modern novel to read in order to "bring her up to date and into the real world of today." Miss Marple's reaction to that was to say to herself, "People like Raymond are so ignorant..."

In defense of Raymond West, he has always been extremely kind and generous towards his old aunt. He and his wife provided her with a beautiful holiday on a Caribbean island in *A Caribbean Mystery,* and they are now paying for her current two-week stay at the expensive Bertram's Hotel in London.

Joan West, Raymond West's wife, who is a painter. In the 1950 *A Murder Is Announced,* Miss Marple had described Joan's paintings as "mostly jugs of dying flowers and broken combs on windowsills."

The Canon of Ely, who was Miss Marple's uncle Thomas and who died many years ago. He and his wife had spent a short time with young Jane Marple at Bertram's Hotel when she was a schoolgirl aged fourteen.

Amy McAllister of Boston, Miss Marple's American friend who recently stayed at Bertram's Hotel with her husband.

That Very Unsuitable Young Man whom Miss Marple wanted to marry when she was very young. Her wise parents nipped the relationship in the bud and young Jane cried herself to sleep for a week. But many years later she ran across him and realized that her parents had been right about him.

Lady Bess Sedgwick, an unlikely guest at Bertram's Hotel.

Bess Sedgwick was a name that almost everyone in England knew. For over thirty years now, Bess Sedgwick had been reported by the Press as doing this or that outrageous or extraordinary thing. For a good part of the war she had been a member of the French Resistance, and was said to have six notches on her gun representing dead Germans. She had flown solo across the Atlantic years ago, had ridden on horseback across Europe and fetched up at Lake Van. She had driven racing cars, had once saved two children from a burning house, had several marriages to her credit and discredit and was said to be the second best-dressed woman in Europe. It was also said that she had successfully smuggled herself aboard a nuclear submarine on its test voyage...(...)...

An Irish Groom, Bess's first husband, although the marriage ceremony may have been faked by the Irish Groom's friends. In any case, Bess's parents rescued her in time and paid the young man off.

Old Coniston, Bess's second husband, thirty years older than she and "quite dotty about her." The marriage didn't last long, but it provided Bess with a daughter. That is, it provided *Old Coniston* with a daughter, because when Bess divorced Old Coniston, it was he who retained the child. Bess was *not* the mothering kind.

Johnny Sedgwick, Bess's third husband, from whom she gained a title. She has retained the title and the name. This marriage didn't last very long either, because Johnny Sedgwick broke his neck steeplechasing.

Ridgway Becker, Bess's fourth husband, the American yacht owner. Bess divorced him three years ago.

Ladislaus Malinowski, a handsome young racing car driver who is rumored to be Bess Sedgwick's current love interest. He is about twenty years younger than she. His appearance at Bertram's Hotel is even more surprising than Bess's.

The Bishop of Westchester, long deceased, whom Miss Marple knew well enough to call "dear Robbie," as she had once cared for him as a child.

A Middle-aged, Uniformed Lift Operator at Bertram's Hotel

Mrs. Carpenter, "a fussy looking middle-aged woman wearing a rather unfortunate flowered violet hat..." who is apparently some relation to Elvira Blake, or to Colonel Luscombe, although no family relationship is ever stated. She escorts Elvira back to England after an extended stay in Italy to be "finished."

Elvira Blake, aged approximately nineteen or twenty, Bess Sedgwick's daughter who has been brought up by relatives of Bess's second husband, "Old Coniston," Elvira's father. She has the outward appearances of a naïve, sheltered young girl but has mastered the art of deceiving her guardians and has succeeded in meeting several "unsuitable young men," including Ladislaus Malinowski, with whom she is in love. She is unaware, of course, that her mother is also in love with studly Ladislaus.

The Contessa Martinelli, a.k.a. "Old Macaroni," who runs a finishing school in Italy where Elvira and her friend Bridget have recently been "finished." Although very strict, she was no match for Elvira and Bridget's careful planning for "successful wickedness."

Mildred Melford, Colonel Luscombe's cousin who lives in Kent. It is planned that Elvira will live with her till she is twenty-one. According to Elvira, she is "fearfully easy to deceive."

Nancy Melford, Mildred's daughter, a girl about the same age as Elvira

Canon Pennyfather, age sixty-three, an unbelievably forgetful clergyman from Chadminster. He would have to be described as prematurely senile, for he does not even remember that he has already had dinner, enters an Indian restaurant and orders a curry dish, all the while wondering why he is not hungry. He mixes up dates, misses a conference in Switzerland where he should have flown *yesterday* but did not, etc. He disappears one evening while staying at Bertram's Hotel and it is about a week before anyone begins to worry about him, since he often meets old friends, goes to stay with them, and "forgets" to phone his housekeeper to tell her of his whereabouts, but thinks he remembers telling her.

Sir Ronald Graves, Assistant Commissioner of Scotland Yard. He presides at a conference of six or seven men in his office on the subject of a recent rash of highly successful robberies: bank hold-ups, snatches of pay-rolls, thefts of consignments of jewels sent through the mail, train robberies, etc.

Chief-Inspector Fred Davy, a.k.a. "Father," who has reason to suspect a connection between Bertram's Hotel and the recent rash of successful large-scale robberies.

Comstock, Superintendent Andrews, and Inspector McNeil, other police officers who are present at the conference with Sir Ronald Graves.

The Harris Crowd, Marks, and Weber, criminals thought to be responsible for the recent rash of large-scale robberies

Rose Sheldon, a chambermaid at Bertram's Hotel who looks after Canon Pennyfather's and Miss Marple's rooms

Parfitt, the former commissionaire at Bertram's Hotel who fell ill and had to leave suddenly, and who was replaced by the current commissionaire, Michael Gorman

Bridget, a friend of Elvira Blake, with whom she spent time in Italy "being finished" at the school operated by "Old Macaroni," that is, the Contessa Martinelli. She participates in Elvira's elaborate plan to raise enough cash to buy an airline ticket to Ireland and to go there for a day. She envies Elvira for *not* having a mother.

Bridget's Mother, who is "quite a pet" but asks so many *questions!* She is exactly the kind of mother of whom Miss Marple would approve, of course, since she carefully screens her daughter's contacts with outsiders, probably for social rank and certainly for wealth status.

Guido, a young Italian who was one of Elvira's clandestine boyfriends while she was in Italy being "finished." He writes letters to her signed "Ginevra," as there is a probability that Elvira's letters are first read by her guardians before being given to her.

Mr. Bollard, the owner of a posh jewelry shop, Bollard & Whitney, in Bond Street, a sort of "family jeweller" to whom Elvira takes her watch to have it repaired and regulated on occasion.

A "Frock-Coated Nobleman," actually just a clerk-assistant at Mr. Bollard's jewelry shop in Bond Street

Miss Marple's Aunt Helen who liked the Army and Navy Stores

Harry Russell, Miss Marple's "village parallel" for Ladislaus Malinowski

Dr. Whittaker of the S.O.A.S., a friend of Canon Pennyfather

Edmunds, another friend of Canon Pennyfather, whom he meets while dining one evening at the Athenæum.

An Elderly Lady aboard the Irish Mail who thought she recognized Canon Pennyfather boarding the train while it was being robbed

An Elderly Cleric with a Thatch of Thick White Hair seen boarding the train in open country while it was being robbed

Mademoiselle, a former governess of Elvira's who now lives at Wimbledon

Richard Egerton, a lawyer and one of Elvira Blake's trustees.

Miss Cordell, Richard Egerton's secretary

Lord Frederick, a.k.a. "Freddie," a dejected-looking client of Richard Egerton, who has "not a leg to stand on." He must raise twelve thousand pounds immediately in order to settle a case out of court.

A Cousin of Elvira Blake's Father, who inherited his title and estate but not his personal property

Mrs. McCrae, Canon Pennyfather's housekeeper who is accustomed to his absent-mindedness and is annoyed, but not immediately alarmed, by his failure to return home at the expected time or even the expected day, or even a day or two later. She eventually reports his disappearance to the police.

Archdeacon Simmons, who is scheduled to come and stay at Canon Pennyfather's home upon the Canon's return from London and Lucerne. It is he who, after several attempts to locate Canon Pennyfather with telephone inquiries to the Canon's friends, finally advises Mrs. McCrae to notify the police.

Canon Pennyfather's Sister, who had not the faintest idea of where her brother might be.

Dr. Weissgarten, a loquacious Hebrew scholar who explained to Archdeacon Simmons that Canon Pennyfather had *not* attended the conference in Lucerne as scheduled.

Inspector Campbell of Scotland Yard who is in charge of the case of the disappearance of Canon Pennyfather.

Alice, an earnest-looking girl assistant at the reception desk at Bertram's Hotel

Colonel Mortimer, a guest at Bertram's Hotel who needs to be reminded that his field glasses are being kept at the desk

Sergeant Wadell, who telephoned Bertram's Hotel and spoke with Miss Gorringe about the disappearance of Canon Pennyfather.

The Honorable Mrs. Saunders of Lyme Regis who has booked Room #17 at Bertram's Hotel from October 23 onwards

The Bishop of Norwich, a guest at Bertram's Hotel who is a friend of Canon Pennyfather

Mrs. Jameson and her Daughters, whom Miss Gorringe saw speaking with Canon Pennyfather before he disappeared

General Radley, another friend of Canon Pennyfather who is staying at Bertram's Hotel. He is nearly deaf and is of no help to Chief-Inspector Davy in finding Canon Pennyfather.

The Marchioness of Barlowe, an example of a "modern" great-grandmother

A Pale Young Man, one of the "slim young men" who run and fetch under the austere orders of Bertram's perfect butler, Henry

Mr. and Mrs. Elmer Cabot, Americans who leave Bertram's Hotel with vast American wardrobe cases and are on their way to Paris

A Porter in a Striped Apron carrying the Cabots' luggage to a taxi

Mrs. Emma Wheeling, a middle-aged woman in a village, in whose house Canon Pennyfather awakens after apparently being struck by a car and suffering concussion

Mr. Wheeling, Emma Wheeling's husband, who carried Canon Pennyfather into their home, having found him lying by the side of the road one evening in their village, Milton St. John.

Dr. Stokes, not really a doctor, because he has been "struck off" for performing illegal abortions, but who is "a good enough doctor" to advise the Wheelings on the subject of concussion, and who tells them to keep Canon Pennyfather in a darkened room for several days.

Mr. Robinson, whom we met in the 1959 *Cat Among the Pigeons.* Chief-Inspector Davy visits him in his "rather shabby office." It is from the mysterious Mr. Robinson, who has some connection with "Special Branch," that Chief-Inspector Davy learns some facts about the Hoffman brothers.

Sonia, Mr. Robinson's secretary

Carlos, a person with whom Mr. Robinson speaks by telephone in a language that may be Turkish, Persian or Armenian, or perhaps none of those

Wilhelm and Robert Hoffman, who have various business interests in Britain and on the Continent

A Middle-aged Lady who is foolish enough to plan to walk from Bertram's Hotel to Chelsea in the fog

Archdeacon Tomlinson from Salisbury who is due to arrive next week at Bertram's Hotel

An Ascetic-looking Middle Aged Man in the lounge of Bertram's Hotel, who is marking corrections in a manuscript

One or Two Married Couples in the lounge of Bertram's Hotel, who have no need to converse with each other

Miss Marple's Grandmother who, many years ago while having tea at the Élysée Hotel in Paris, suddenly realized that she was the only woman in the place wearing a bonnet. She immediately gave all her bonnets away to a theatre company for use in costumes.

Miss Marple's Mother, whose name was Clara

Doctors and Fingerprint Men who come to Bertram's Hotel after a man is shot to death in front of the hotel

A Policeman Writing Unobtrusively as Inspector Davy and Miss Marple converse with another hotel guest at Bertram's Hotel

COMMENTS

At Bertram's Hotel cannot be anyone's "favorite Christie detective novel," although for some reason many readers are fond of it. The only murder in the story occurs near the end, and the "solution" consists of guessing on the part of Miss Marple who admits to the police that they are not likely to bring a successful case against the alleged murderer, since there is no evidence upon which to build a case. Miss Marple's partner in the investigations is Chief-Inspector Davy of Scotland Yard, who is mainly occupied with solving a rash of large-scale robberies, and this aspect of the story is more fully developed than the events leading to the murder.

The book is carelessly and haphazardly written, and it almost seems that Christie was more interested in rambling on and on about recent changes in England and English society than writing an interesting novel. There are many pages of rather dull reminiscences by Miss Marple about her mother's and grandmother's shopping expeditions in London sixty years earlier, for example.

A rather amazing new subject for Christie to "preach" about occurs for the first time in *At Bertram's Hotel*. We may recall that, all through the years, "mothers" have been amazingly and very conveniently absent in Christie novels, especially mothers of adult characters and *especially* mothers of adult *female characters*. See the Comments section of the 1937 *Poirot Loses a Client* for a full discussion of that subject, and for a list of mothers of adult female characters in Christie's detective novels who are "conveniently dead and never mentioned," and whose daughters seem to survive very nicely, and quite happily, without them. For decades it seemed apparent that, to Christie, mothers were nothing but a nuisance to be avoided, and mothering itself was, to Christie, a kind of distasteful "animal instinct," as portrayed in the 1958 *Ordeal by Innocence* and the 1962 *The Mirror Crack'd*. Furthermore, Christie had been "preaching" against the value of "education and environment" beginning with the 1949 *Crooked House* and in several of her novels of the 1950s, most stridently in her 1958 *Ordeal by Innocence*, in which she expressed the view that education and environment are of no value at all in shaping the character traits of children and that, therefore, "parenting" is really of no importance.

Suddenly, now that Christie is seventy-five years old, parents—and especially mothers—become extremely important, and it is indeed the unfortunate girl who is deprived of the expert, conscientious guidance of a mother in the selection of her male companions and future husband. We have known Miss Jane Marple since the 1930 *Murder at the Vicarage*, and we have met her again in approximately eight subsequent novels. Never, not even one time, has Miss Marple spoken of or even thought about her own parents. Suddenly, in *At Bertram's Hotel*, we learn that Miss Marple was rescued by her conscientious parents from an "unsuitable" young man during her youth. She had cried herself to sleep for a week when her parents "nipped the relationship in the bud," but years later she had met the man again and had realized how right her parents had been about him!

In Christie's next few novels there will be repeated reminders that today (the 1960s) there are no longer the "conscientious" mothers of the past who protected their daughters from "unsuitable" male contacts. In particular, see the Comments section for the 1966 *Third Girl* and the Setting section for the 1969 *Hallowe'en Party*.

The characterizations in *At Bertram's Hotel* are lackluster and there are no memorable characters, except perhaps Bess Sedgwick, who is a rather outlandish and unbelievable character. Those characters who *are* believable are uninteresting and forgettable.

Most of the enjoyment of reading Agatha Christie comes either from the excitement of the murder investigation, or the excitement or danger of the action, or from the fascinating characterizations, or from the humor. There are none of these in *At Bertram's Hotel*. Furthermore, even though we have learned that we must accept a rather unacceptable coincidence once in a while in Christie novels (especially in the later novels—the 1961 *The Pale Horse* holding the record for sheer numbers of unacceptable coincidences so far)—there are just too many coincidences in *At Bertram's Hotel*. Some examples:

> In the vast city of London, which is filled with hotels of all kinds, Bess Sedgwick just *happens* to be at Bertram's Hotel at the same time that her estranged daughter is registered there by her guardian.
> Bess Sedgwick's current lover, studly Ladislaus Malinowski, just *happens* to meet Bess's daughter Elvira in Italy, and Elvira falls in love with him.
> Miss Marple, on holiday in the vast city of London, just *happens* to be having lunch on the fourth floor of The Army and Navy Store at the same time that Bess and Ladislaus are also there having lunch.
> A few days later, Miss Marple, still in the vast city of London, just *happens* to stop at a tea enclosure in Hyde Park where Ladislaus Malinowski is having tea with Elvira Blake, Bess's daughter.
> Miss Marple just *happens* to be in a writing room at Bertram's Hotel when Bess Sedgwick has a certain revealing conversation through the open window with the hotel commissionaire Michael Gorman. Bess had thought the room was empty.
> Elvira Blake just *happens* to be in the same writing room at the same time, and the evidently blind Bess Sedgwick does not know that *she* is also in the

room while she is having her incriminating, confidential conversation through the window with Michael Gorman.

Miss Marple just *happens* to be unable to sleep one night and rises from her bed at about three o'clock in the morning. Hearing footsteps in the corridor, she opens her door and sees Canon Pennyfather who just *happens* to be walking along the corridor towards the stairs and then down them.

In addition to these flaws, the book is filled with needlessly long narrations of petty events. In Chapter 11, the narration of Mrs. McCrae's thoughts and actions regarding the disappearance of Canon Pennyfather, her phone call to Bertram's Hotel, and her conversations with Archdeacon Simmons on the subject, occupy all eight pages of the chapter. We learn what Mrs. McCrae had planned to cook for the Canon's dinner and all of the reasons for which she chose that item (Dover sole). We learn of all of her reasons for and against being upset about his disappearance. We learn the content of every telephone call that Archdeacon Simmons makes in futile efforts to locate the Canon. The only outcome of the chapter is that Mrs. McCrae is finally convinced that she must notify the police of the Canon's disappearance. In other words, the chapter just rambles on and on as though it were "padding."

Chapter 12 is equally tedious with a narration of one of Miss Marple's meanderings through London, for no apparent reason other than to provide the short scene in which Miss Marple sees Ladislaus Malinowski in a tea enclosure in Hyde Park with Elvira Blake.

Chapter 10 begins with a tedious paragraph detailing the history of the law firm of which Richard Egerton, a minor character of little importance, is a part.

Christie's 1964 novel *A Caribbean Mystery* was absolutely free of these defects. It is rather amazing that *At Bertram's Hotel*, written just one year later, can be so inferior. It is clear that Christie's decline as a writer, described as "steep and rapid" by one critic, has begun.

This novel cannot be recommended to any reader except a person who especially enjoys the Miss Marple character and who does not mind being dragged through Miss Marple's musings about how much better the world—or at least England—*used* to be.

Third Girl (1966)

SETTING

The story takes place during the end of summer or early fall (since there is one reference to a woman tying up dahlias in her garden) but no other seasonal references are made. The year can be no earlier than approximately 1966, as there are numerous references to the drug culture among youth, and the outlandish clothing sported by some young people, including very long, curling hair for young men and flamboyant clothing featuring bright colors and ruffles which in the past had been reserved for female attire. Most of the action takes place in London, although there are one or two scenes at a house called Crosshedges at the edge of a village named Long Basing. The location of Long Basing is not specified but it cannot be far from London, as the occupant of Crosshedges, a businessman, commutes to London daily; whether he commutes by car or train we do not know.

Long Basing is a minor setting—as noted above only one or two scenes occur there, and both are in just one house in the village—but there is a long, needlessly detailed description of the village. The village has no importance in the story at all, yet its description is nearly three pages long. Another village in the story is described in a similar, though fortunately somewhat briefer, way.

The London settings include the apartment of Hercule Poirot in what we must assume continues to be the building known as Whitehaven Mansions, which was brand-new in 1935 when Poirot moved into it in *The A.B.C. Murders,* and which was remodeled in 1963 in *The Clocks.* Poirot's apartment is not described but we know that all of his furnishings and decorations are square and symmetrical, as he is obsessed with neatness and symmetry.

Another London setting is the apartment of detective storywriter Ariadne Oliver, whom we first met in the 1936 *Cards on the Table.* Her sitting room has always been described as having a wallpaper with brightly-colored tropical birds in a forest. In this story the old wallpaper has been replaced with a multitude of ripe cherries still on their trees, and Mrs. Oliver is having doubts about whether the change represents an improvement.

London itself has undergone some changes, as there are now some ugly skyscrapers sprouting in the neighborhood of St. Paul's Cathedral, and there is a particularly ugly new apartment building, seven or eight stories high, called Borodene Mansions. The flimsiness of this modern construction is illustrated when the numeral 7 of the number 67 falls off the door of an apartment just as Mrs. Oliver arrives there. In a later scene, the building manager shows one of the apartments to Hercule Poirot, explaining that all of the apartments in the building are furnished exactly the same—even the furniture is all the same—except for one wall in the sitting room, which is papered to suit the tenant—as long as the tenant agrees to one of eight wallpaper designs. The manager explains that most of the tenants are working people with no interest in "decorating." They live in Borodene Mansions simply because of its modern comforts—modern kitchens and bathrooms and central heating.

A scene takes place in a rather sinister part of London "between King's Road and the river." The area is filled with alleyways and cul-de-sacs among decrepit warehouses. In this dreary neighborhood a scene takes place at a squalid "artist's studio" reached by a ladder-like flight of rickety steps in what appears to be an abandoned warehouse. As Mrs. Oliver leaves the "studio" she is mugged.

More important than the physical settings in *Third Girl* are the social backgrounds. As it is now 1966, the drug culture is in full swing and several characters—all young people—are said to use drugs with names like "Purple Hearts," "LSD," and "hemp," in addition to tranquillizers, uppers, downers, reefers, and other delights. There is a reference to a couple of hooligan gangs having a fight with "flick knives" in the courtyard of Borodene Mansions one night. And as in most of Christie's recent novels, there is the reminder that "mothers no longer protect their daughters from unsuitable young men" and most girls, nowadays, live apart from their families. As a matter of fact, there are *many* reminders of that "fact" in *Third Girl*. The term "third girl," is explained by the knowledgeable Mrs. Oliver as referring to those living arrangements in which a working girl takes an apartment with a fairly high rent, brings a friend in to share the apartment and the rent, and then advertises in the newspaper for a "third girl" to spread the rental costs over three people. All of this was undoubtedly relatively new in England, although in America young working women—as well as young working men—had been sharing quarters and living away from their parents for several decades. For young unmarried women to be living away from family control is clearly seen by Christie as *not* a nice thing for girls, who ought to be living at home until they are married to "suitable" young men who have earned the approval of the girls' parents.

Christie again reminds us, as she has always done, even in her earliest novels, that girls are *always* attracted to the worst sort of young men. What is different about the young men of 1966 is that they are now "greasy" and "dirty," they have long, curling hair that reaches their shoulders and they wear flamboyant clothing. Regarding the "flamboyant clothing," Mrs. Oliver repeatedly refers to David Baker as "the Peacock."

Drab, shoddily-constructed modern apartment buildings, dirty-looking, outlandishly dressed youth, the drug culture, street crime—these are the important "social backgrounds" of *Third Girl*.

Story

One morning in late summer or early fall of 1966, Hercule Poirot is at breakfast in his apartment when he receives a visit from a young girl dressed in a way that is disgusting to him—that is, in the fashion of 1966. Poirot's manservant George explains that the young lady wants to see Poirot about "a murder that she might have committed." Poirot has George show the young lady in, but as soon as she sees Poirot, she says, "I've changed my mind. I don't want to be rude, but you're too old. Nobody told me you were so old. You're too old." And she leaves without revealing her name or anything else about herself.

Feeling annoyed and extremely hurt by the young woman's statement that he is "too old," Poirot phones his friend Mrs. Oliver who insists that he come to her apartment at once for a cup of chocolate and soothing conversation. There, they discuss the girl, whom Mrs. Oliver remembers as someone to whom she had actually recommended Poirot a few days earlier. A phone call to a friend clarifies the girl's name and some facts about her family.

The young girl is Norma Restarick and she soon disappears. Efforts to find her, in order to gather facts about the "murder that the girl may have committed," lead Poirot to a village not far from London and they lead Mrs. Oliver to a seedy district of abandoned warehouses where she is mugged.

A murder soon occurs in the apartment that Norma shares with two other young women. Hercule Poirot, of course, solves the mystery.

Characters

Hercule Poirot, the Belgian private investigator who, when we met him last in the 1963 *The Clocks,* was writing an analysis of the great writers of detective fiction. In the opening chapter of *Third Girl,* we learn that he has completed this *magnum opus* and is now, frankly, bored. He welcomes this new case in which a young girl "thinks she may have committed a murder."

George, Hercule Poirot's impeccable manservant, who has always been a bit of a snob when callers arrive, using phrases such as "a...er...*gentleman* is asking for you," implying that the caller does not quite qualify. In this story it is "a—a—*young lady*" who is calling. Poirot asks if the young lady is good-looking, and George responds, "In my view, no, sir, but there is no accounting for tastes." The young lady is dressed in the current fashions of 1966, of which we will read detailed descriptions in this story.

Norma Restarick, a young lady who visits Poirot during his breakfast one morning. She has told George that she wishes to see Monsieur Poirot because she believes she may have committed a murder. Later in the story, Dr. Stillingfleet describes Norma as "...full of drugs. I'd say she'd been taking purple hearts, and dream bombs, and probably L.S.D. She's been all hopped up for some time..."

Ariadne Oliver, the celebrated detective story writer whom Poirot met for the first time in the 1936 *Cards on the Table*. The two of them worked together in the 1952 *Mrs. McGinty's Dead* and in the 1956 *Dead Man's Folly*. Mrs. Oliver appeared without Hercule Poirot in the 1961 *The Pale Horse*. They are now together again in *Third Girl*.

Mrs. Oliver's best-known trademark eccentricity, in the first three novels mentioned above, was a great fondness for apples, with which she seemed to be surrounded at all times. In *The Pale Horse* and *Third Girl*, however, apples are not mentioned at all in connection with Mrs. Oliver. A second trademark eccentricity is continual coiffure changes; a third is frightening taste in clothing, and a fourth is the pitiful wallpaper on her sitting room walls. Since the 1936 *Cards on the Table,* and perhaps even earlier in short stories, the paper was one of brightly-colored tropical birds in a forest or jungle. At the beginning of *Third Girl* we learn that Mrs. Oliver has redecorated and the new wallpaper features ripe cherries on their trees, giving one the impression of being in the middle of a cherry orchard.

In the earlier novels, Mrs. Oliver was in the habit of pointing out one particular suspect and declaring that person to be the murderer, citing "woman's intuition" as her unfailing guide to this knowledge. When proven wrong she usually made some statement such as "I never really suspected him (her)."

In this novel, Mrs. Oliver refrains from identifying the murderer and admits confusion all the way to the end when Hercule Poirot finally "reveals all." But she is instrumental in bringing about a good deal of the action. It is she who sends Norma Restarick to Hercule Poirot in the first place; it is she who identifies her to Hercule Poirot; it is she who finds Norma in a café after she "disappears," and leads Poirot to her; it is she who learns of the apparent suicide of Louise Charpentier at Borodene Mansions, and it is she who finds an important link between that woman and someone else in the novel.

Mr. Goby, a kind of "detective's detective," an old friend of Hercule Poirot who has appeared now and then in Hercule Poirot stories since about 1928. He has a staff of agents who can find out anything about anybody. In this novel, Poirot makes use of Mr. Goby to learn about the backgrounds of several characters: David Baker, Claudia Reece-Holland, Frances Cary, and the entire Restarick family.

Mr. Goby's trademark eccentricity is never to make eye contact with the person he is speaking with, addressing an object in the room instead. During his conversation with Hercule Poirot in Chapter 6 of *Third Girl*, he addresses the claw foot of an antique table, the clock on the chimney piece, and an electric radiator at Hercule Poirot's flat. In this scene Christie makes a bit of a slip. It is well known that Poirot has only square, modern furniture and it has been said many times that there is no such thing as a curved line in his flat; therefore there can be no "claw foot of an antique table."

Mr. Goby is described as "a small, shrunken little man, so nondescript as to be practically nonexistent."

Chief-Inspector Neele of Scotland Yard, an old friend of Hercule Poirot, who provides him with information about the Restarick family and the Wedderburn Gallery. **Note:** There has never been a "Chief-Inspector Neele of Scotland Yard" in a previous Poirot story, although there was an "Inspector Neele" in the 1953 Miss Marple novel, *A Pocket Full of Rye*.

Naomi Lorrimer, a friend of Ariadne Oliver. It was at the Lorrimer home that Mrs. Oliver first met Norma Restarick, and it is from Mrs. Lorrimer that Mrs. Oliver obtains certain names in—and a bit of gossip about—the Restarick family for Poirot's use.

Sven Hjerson, the Finnish sleuth in Mrs. Oliver's detective stories. In the Ariadne Oliver character, Agatha Christie parodies herself, and Sven Hjerson is a parody of Hercule Poirot, both being "eccentric foreigners."

Andrew Restarick, Norma Restarick's father who abandoned his wife and their five-year-old daughter Norma and went to Africa for a life of adventure—and profit. He is now back in England, with a new wife, and is finding it difficult to re-establish familial ties with Norma.

Mary Restarick, Andrew Restarick's new wife and Norma Restarick's stepmother. Hercule Poirot sees her for the first time as he arrives at Crosshedges, as she is working in the garden. She and her stepdaughter feel a hearty mutual dislike.

Sir Roderick Horsefield, an uncle of Andrew Restarick by marriage. He is described by Mrs. Oliver as "an uncle of incredible antiquity. Rather deaf. He's frightfully distinguished—strings of letters after his name."

After informing himself—through Mr. Goby—of numerous trivial facts in Sir Roderick's life, Poirot visits him at his home, pretending to be an old acquaintance, and Sir Roderick is completely taken in by this falsehood.

Sonia, Sir Roderick's secretary, described as an "au pair" girl.

Claudia Reece-Holland, one of Norma Restarick's roommates at Borodene Mansions, and Andrew Restarick's secretary.

Emlyn Reece-Holland, Claudia's father, a Member of Parliament.

David Baker, Norma Restarick's boyfriend, of whom her father and stepmother do not approve. Because of his stylishly flamboyant clothes, Mrs. Oliver refers to him repeatedly as "the peacock."

Frances Cary, the second of Norma Restarick's London roommates. She works for an art gallery, arranging exhibitions and art shows in other cities. In a conversation with Claudia Reese-Holland, Frances mentions a party she attended the night before, during which she tried some new pills called "Emerald Dreams."

Lansberger, a portrait painter who was popular about twenty years ago. He painted the portraits of Andrew Restarick and his first wife, Grace.

Colonel Race, Monsieur Giraud of the Sûreté, General Abercromby, and **Air Marshal Sir Edmund Collingsby,** names that Poirot "drops" in order to ingratiate himself with old Sir Roderick Horsefield, as if Poirot had known all of them personally. Actually, he did know Monsieur Giraud a long time ago, finding him a very unpleasant adversary in the 1923 *Murder on the Links*. And of course Colonel Race worked with Poirot twice during the 1930s—in the 1936 *Cards on the Table* and then in the 1937 *Death on the Nile*. We also met him in the 1924 *The Man in the Brown Suit* and the 1945 *Remembered Death*, two novels in which Poirot did not appear.

Captain Henderson, another name "dropped" by Hercule Poirot in his act of ingratiating himself with Sir Roderick. Henderson was a secret agent, and a British traitor, whom Poirot and others supposedly "unmasked" during the Second World War.

Edith, Mrs. Oliver's maid

Several Porters at Borodene Mansions, whom Mr. Goby's agents question about Norma Restarick and her two roommates

Micky, one of the above porters at Borodene Mansions who, when encouraged with glasses of whiskey, provides a good deal of information about goings on at the building and especially in the courtyard.

A Gang of Young Thugs fighting with flick-knives in the courtyard of Borodene Mansions on a recent evening

Simon Restarick, Andrew Restarick's older brother who was more interested in the family business than Andrew ever was. He died about a year ago, leaving no children. His wife had died a couple of years earlier. It was the death of Simon Restarick that ostensibly brought Andrew Restarick back to England and to the family business, to take over the operations.

Louise Birell, the woman for whom Andrew Restarick left his wife and five-year-old daughter several years ago.

Grace Restarick, née Baldwin, Andrew Restarick's first wife, whom he abandoned. She died about three years ago. She had been an "invalid" for the last few years of her life, although some people doubt that she was ever seriously an invalid.

Louise Charpentier, a woman living at 76 Borodene Mansions, on the top floor of the building, who recently committed suicide by throwing herself from her balcony. The understanding among the tenants is that she thought she had cancer. She had never been a very popular tenant of the building, as she was a drinker and often hosted noisy parties.

Two Clumsy Furniture Movers at Borodene Mansions who move Mrs. Charpentier's furniture out of the building.

A Middle-aged Woman with a Mop who opens the door to Mrs. Oliver at 67 Borodene Mansions on a day when all three of the girls are out. She gossips freely with Mrs. Oliver about the three girls who live in the apartment.

The Two Sons of the Above-named Middle-aged Woman with a Mop

A Man in the Street Scurrying and Muttering

Miss Felicity Lemon, Hercule Poirot's "hideous and efficient" secretary, whom we met for the first time in the 1955 *Hickory, Dickory, Death,* in which she had a substantial role. Since then she has appeared only briefly or simply in references.

Peter Cardiff, a young painter whom Mrs. Oliver meets in a dirty artist's studio in a tumble-down district between King's Road and the river.

A Foreigner Who Does Not Speak English and so cannot provide Mrs. Oliver with directions to King's Road

Dr. Stillingfleet, who snatches Norma Restarick from the path of a speeding Jaguar in London. He is "a man of perhaps thirty-odd with red hair and a rather attractively ugly face, the kind of face that is craggy but interesting."

Annie, Dr. Stillingfleet's servant or secretary who prepares a pot of tea for Norma and the doctor

A Policeman Writing in a Notebook in the hospital where Mrs. Oliver wakes up after being "coshed."

A Sister with an air of authority by the door of Mrs. Oliver's hospital room

A Nurse at Mrs. Oliver's bedside

Montgomery and Alanbrooke and Auchinleck, and even Old Moran, old men who are "shooting their mouths off writing their memoirs"

An Eighty-three-Year-Old Gardener at Crosshedges

A Couple of Women Always Dodging About the House Making a Noise with Hoovers at Crosshedges

Lord Mountbryan who, in an anecdote recounted by Poirot's manservant George, "lost his sense" and was taken in by a young masseuse and gave her gifts and money which she proceeded to pass to her "brother" to pay his debts.

James Patrick Restarick, Andrew Restarick's father.

A Junior Attaché of the Herzogovenian Embassy with whom a certain character in the story is seen sitting on a bench in Hyde Park

An Unnamed Uniformed Porter at Borodene Mansions who has only been employed there for a week, and who therefore has no useful information

Joe, another porter at Borodene Mansions who has worked there for some time and who *does* have useful information

Mr. McFarlane, who is "in charge" at Borodene Mansions, evidently the building manager

Mrs. Wilder, who occupied #76 Borodene Mansions before Mrs. Charpentier moved in two years ago

Mr. Travers, who has just moved into #76 Borodene Mansions

A Young Man at Chief-Inspector Neele's office who introduces Hercule Poirot

An Old Aunt of Norma Restarick's—on her mother's side—who was "mildly potty." Norma lived with her after her mother died three years ago. The aunt died of a stroke six months ago.

A Millionaire from Texas buying artworks in London

The Lift Boy at Scotland Yard

Mr. Roscombe, the manager (or perhaps owner) of Wedderburn Gallery. He has a "soft, purring voice."

A Middle-aged Woman at Andrew Restarick's Office who receives Hercule Poirot

Miss Battersby, the retired headmistress of Meadowfield School who remembers all of her students. She is "a tall, distinguished-looking woman with upswept gray hair and an energetic manner."

Eileen, a casual friend of Frances Cary

Mrs. Jacobs, an elderly woman who lives in the flat next door to 67 Borodene Mansions

Sergeant Conolly, the first police officer to arrive at Borodene Mansions when a murder victim is found inside #67.

FRENCH INTO ENGLISH

Chapter 1

pâtisserie—pastry shop

Eh bien?—Well?

Nom d'un nom d'un nom...—God damn! (Poirot is extremely shocked and annoyed by the behavior of the young girl who has just left. The expression *Nom d'un nom d'un nom* is a euphemism for *Nom de Dieu* (Name of God), which is very strong even among the non-religious in French-speaking countries.)

Chapter 2

Sapristi!—Damn it! (Poirot is very much annoyed again) *Sapristi* is a euphemism for *Sacristi*, which is another deliberate use of the "Name of God," literally "Holy Christ!" Poirot would never say *Sacristi* or *Nom de Dieu*, but when extremely annoyed he uses the euphemisms freely.

Bonjour—Good morning

Ah ça, non, par example!—Oh, not that, for God's sake! (Poirot is having a *very* bad day.)

langue de chats—cats' tongue (probably some kind of thin, oval shaped cookies resembling cats' tongues in shape

Chère madame, dear lady

"Plus ça change, plus c'est la même chose,"—A French saying meaning "The more things change, the more they seem to be the same." It's not really appropriate in this context since the wallpaper has only been changed once since 1936, when the tropical bird wallpaper

was first mentioned. What Poirot probably means is that the new wallpaper is just as disgusting as the old one was.
C'est inouï!—It's astounding!
Assez, madame, assez!—Enough, enough!

Chapter 3 *en bloc*—in one piece

Chapter 4
potager—vegetable garden, kitchen garden
enchanté—delighted to meet you

Chapter 6 *C'est difficile*—It's difficult

Chapter 8
Vraiment?—Really?
Eh bien—Well..
Chère madame—Dear lady
Au revoir—Good-bye. (Poirot uses this expression, the usual "friendly" good-bye because he hopes, or expects, to see Norma again. Later, at the end of an unpleasant phone conversation with Mrs. Oliver, he will say *Adieu!* to her, subtly suggesting that he has no wish to see or hear from her again.) *Adieu* is the French way of expressing a "final" good-bye.

Chapter 11
La politesse—courtesy
Les femmes!—Women!

Chapter 13
sirop de cassis—Black currant liqueur, a favorite drink of Poirot's
empressement—warmth, enthusiasm
Enchanté—Delighted to meet you
Enfin—Good grief!

Chapter 14
Chère Madame—Dear lady
tasse de chocolat—cup of chocolate
Nom d'un nom d'un nom!—God damn it!
Mais oui—Yes, I can. (Christie's French here is incorrect. Poirot should have said "*Mais si*." When "yes" is expressed as a contradiction to something, as in this case, the word is *si*, not *oui*. Christie's French was very good, but it was not perfect.
bon Dieu—for God's sake
Adieu, chère madame—Good-bye, dear lady. (Poirot's conversation with Mrs. Oliver has been a frustrating one for him, and his use of *adieu* instead of *au revoir* expresses that. He has no present desire to see or speak with Mrs. Oliver again (at least in the near future.)

Chapter 15
tisane—a hot infusion similar to tea but made with leaves of some plant other than tea. Poirot has always stated that he hates English tea, but he likes *tisanes*. Camomile tea would be described as a *tisane* in French

Chapter 16
C'est fantastique—Another example of Christie's incorrect French. She means for Poirot to be saying something like the English "It's fantastic" or "It's amazing." The correct French expression would be something like *C'est merveilleux, C'est épatant* or *C'est inouï*. The French word *fantastique* simply means "fanciful," as did the English word "fantastic" a century or more ago, before everyday speech gave it its common meaning of "wonderful," etc.

Chapter 18
Les Jeunes—"The young," meaning "young artists"
vraiment!—Really!
avant-garde—ultra modern
C'est moi—Speaking (that is, it is I who am speaking on the telephone.)
Tout de même—All the same
eh bien—well, then

Chapter 19
les femmes—women
carte blanche—full liberty, a free hand

Chapter 20
malade imaginaire—hypochondriac

Chapter 21
Tout de même—All the same
les femmes—women
Quelle déception—How disappointing. (If the phrase "how disappointing" appears not to fit the context, blame Christie's bad French, because that's what *Quelle déception* means. It is not clear what she intends for Poirot to be expressing here. Perhaps it is "confusion."
mon ami—my friend

Chapter 22 *les femmes*—women

Chapter 24
chère madame—dear lady
mon enfant—dear (literally, "my child" but a common way of expressing sympathy or gentleness to a younger person, not necessarily a child)

Chapter 25

sirop de cassis—black currant liqueur
chère madame—dear lady
maquillage—make-up
Enfin—In fact
Mon enfant—Dear (as above, Poirot addresses the young girl with gentleness)
la politique—politics
Madame, un petit moment—Just a moment, madame

COMMENTS

Third Girl would have been a much better detective novel if Christie had written it about ten years earlier. Unfortunately, it is flawed by the defects that characterize most of her last novels—a good deal of repetitiousness and redundancy in dialogue, unacceptable coincidences and, frankly, "padding." There are entire chapters that really need not have been included. One that comes to mind is Chapter 20, in which Poirot pays a visit to the retired headmistress of a school Norma Restarick once attended, simply in order to ask the headmistress her opinion of Norma Restarick's mental health. It is a silly idea, since Norma's mental health could have changed in the last few years and, in any case, the old headmistress's opinion would only be her opinion. The chapter, and the character of the old headmistress, are probably there only as "padding" and could have been omitted. In that chapter there is also a rather superfluous description of the village in which the old lady lives—a perfectly unremarkable English village. In an earlier chapter there is an even longer, superfluous description of another village.

The content of Chapter 19, too, could have been summed up in one sentence, since the chapter consists of nothing but a visit by Hercule Poirot to the office of Andrew Restarick in which he informs Mr. Restarick that he has made no progress in finding Restarick's daughter. Andrew Restarick's conversation in that chapter provides no new information or insights about the Restarick family. One has the impression that the entire chapter was "inserted" after the novel was completed in order to give the book additional length.

Another "superfluous" chapter is Chapter 14 in which Poirot visits Ariadne Oliver and neither has any new information to share with the other. The conversation goes around and around and leads nowhere.

Near the beginning of the story Poirot has two interviews with his old friend Mr. Goby, and one interview would have been sufficient. At the second interview the information Mr. Goby provides to Poirot is not very different from what he has already provided during the first interview and, as one reads it, one wonders if Christie was inadvertently writing the same chapter for a second time. Furthermore, Poirot mysteriously obtains information about a certain character even *before* the first interview with Mr. Goby, causing one to wonder where this information came from. Then in a later chapter Poirot consults with his friend, Chief Inspector Neele, who gives him a good deal of the same information that Mr. Goby has already done, suggesting more useless "padding." It almost seems that Christie wrote *Third Girl* mainly for the purpose of writing about the clothing, hairstyles and drug use among young people in the middle 1960s and that she gave much less thought to the "detective story," sketching it out and piecing it together and then finding it too short to be called a novel, and then "padding" it with long, repetitious conversations and superfluous descriptions wherever possible.

Several characters in *Third Girl* repeat Christie's contention that "modern mothers" do not look after their daughters conscientiously as "better mothers" did in the past—mothers who carefully "screened" their daughters' male contacts, supposedly to "protect" them from unhappy relationships and unhappy marriages. These comments about "good and bad mothers," placed in the conversations of the older characters by a seventy-seven-year-old author, become quite tiresome. All of the talk about the way some young people dressed during the late 1960s—high leather boots, tight, dark-colored pants, long hair on both sexes—may be interesting as historical documentation but it is only documentation of superficial clothing and grooming fashions, and the negative reactions of very old people to the fashions sported by the young.

Hercule Poirot, now extremely aged, complains that young girls no longer try to look attractive to the opposite sex. He began complaining about that as far back as the 1948 *There Is a Tide*, in which he agreed with an old woman's remark that girls would not wear shorts if they knew how they looked in them from behind.

Characterization in *Third Girl* is unremarkable, and there are no particularly memorable or unique characters. The only interesting thing about the novel—and it would only be interesting for a Christie dévoté—is her superficial portrayal of one segment of the "younger generation" in England during the middle and late 1960s—the segment that followed the clothing fads of the times and indulged in recreational drugs, as seen through the eyes of a middle-class Englishwoman who was born in 1890. The novel is a typical product of Christie's decline and should be postponed until all of her earlier novels have been read. Perhaps it should even be postponed "indefinitely."

Endless Night (1967)

SETTING

The story takes place in approximately 1967, but no current events are mentioned and there are none of the comments about clothing fashions or the drug culture that firmly placed the action of Christie's preceding novel, *Third Girl,* in the middle 1960s. The action takes place primarily in a fictitious village called Kingston Bishop, which is located near the edge of an area of "moorland." The specific county of England is not named, but it is evidently the county of Devon. There are "moorlands" in Devon and also in the northern county of Yorkshire, but Christie especially enjoyed placing her stories in Devon since she had grown up in Torquay, a resort on the south coast of Devon.

One or two scenes also take place at Market Chadwell, a larger town not far from the village of Kingston Bishop, and there is a scene at the London home of the working-class mother of the narrator. There is also a scene in Regent's Park in London where a pair of lovers meets for a meal and conversation. Market Chadwell is said to have a "three-star hotel" and a scene takes place at a café there called The Blue Dog. There is a scene at a restaurant or inn called "The George" in another nearby town called Bartington. "The George" is said to have good food, although the characters who dine there are not impressed with their dessert, which is described as "apple tart with a self-conscious piece of phony pastry on top of it."

The principal setting, however, is a piece of land on the edge of the village of Kingston Bishop popularly known as "Gipsy's Acre." The land is said to be an "unlucky" place, since there have been numerous accidents there in the past, including automobile accidents on the dangerously curving road leading to it. On the property an old house called "The Towers" has been allowed to fall into ruin and, at the beginning of the story, the property is for sale. There are vague local superstitions about the property once being inhabited by gypsies who were "run off the land," and who expressed their resentment for this by placing a "curse" on the land. This alleged "curse" is a major factor in the story.

One or two details about "modern life" find their way into this novel. One of them is the increasing popularity of air travel between the continents, as several American characters travel frequently between the United States and England by passenger airliner. As late as the middle 1960s, however, the passenger ships were still carrying full loads of travelers between continents. Air fares were still extremely high, and for the price of a plane ticket to Europe, one could have instead a leisurely and pleasant ocean voyage lasting about six days, with delicious meals and entertainment included, plus the chance of meeting large numbers of interesting people and making new friends. One could also take along any number of suitcases and trunks. Anyone who was not in a hurry and was going to Europe for an extended stay still traveled by ship.

One of the characters in the story does in fact travel from America to England aboard the famous old liner *Queen Mary,* but all of the others travel by air.

STORY

The narrator, Michael Rogers, who is in his early twenties, is an unsettled young working class man from London. He bounces around from one job to another—jobs such as selling encyclopedias and vacuum cleaners, doing horticultural work in a botanical garden, doing fruit picking in summer and driving wealthy people to and from vacation spots in France and Germany.

In a village named Kingston Bishop he notices a piece of land that is for sale, and he has fantasies about a famous architect, Rudolph Santonix, designing and building a home for him there. This is a fantasy, of course, because Michael is poor and is likely to always remain poor.

One day he meets a young American girl in the area of this tract of land, which is known as Gipsy's Acre, and the couple fall in love and become engaged. An old gypsy woman tells their fortunes and warns them to have nothing to do with Gipsy's Acre, as it is "cursed."

Michael does not know it, but his fiancée is a wealthy heiress who surprises him by purchasing Gipsy's Acre as a gift for him. They marry and commission Santonix to design and build a home for them. Once they move into the house, they have the unpleasant experience of someone throwing a stone through a window as if to express to them that they are not welcome.

A mysterious death occurs and then another character disappears. The ending of the story is completely unexpected.

Characters

Rudolf Santonix, a famous, eccentric, expensive and terminally-ill architect. He designs and builds a new house for Michael Rogers and his bride.

Ellie (Funella) Guteman, an extremely wealthy American heiress, age twenty at the beginning of the story, and then twenty-one a short time later. She marries the narrator, Michael Rogers.

A Local Man Clipping a Hedge who tells Michael Rogers about Gipsy's Acre and explains how it got its name: "Some tale or other. It was gipsies' land once, they say, and they were turned off, and they put a curse on it."

Old Geordie, who "got his neck broke" in Gipsy's Acre.

Michael Rogers, the narrator of the story, a young man who describes himself not as lazy but as "unsettled," bouncing around from one job to another. He has worked as a chauffeur, driving wealthy people in luxury cars to various places in England and on the Continent. He has sold encyclopedias and vacuum cleaners and a few other things; has been a waiter in a third-class hotel, a life guard on a summer beach, and has worked in a botanical garden.

Esther Lee, who was given a cottage to live in by Major Phillpot—a reward for having once saved a child from drowning. According to the locals, Mrs. Lee spends more time outside than inside her cottage, however, as she "doesn't like the inside of houses. Them as has got gipsy blood don't." She warns Michael and Ellie to stay away from Gipsy's Acre.

Major Phillpot, the most important person locally, referred to sarcastically in Michael Rogers's thoughts as "God."

Mrs. Phillpot, Major Phillpot's invalid wife.

Gervase Phillpot, an ancestor of Major Phillpot who was allegedly poisoned by his foreign wife, a portrait of whom still hangs in Major Phillpot's home

A Man Working in an Art Shop who surprises Michael Rogers with the high price of a certain painting.

Dmitri Constantine, who commissions Rudolf Santonix to build a new house for him on the French Riviera. He is unhappy with the cost overruns.

A Man and his Wife who hire Michael's cars-for-hire company to chauffeur them to Kingston Bishop in order to attend a sale of antiques in a house recently placed on the market. It is on this occasion that Michael becomes aware of Gipsy's Acre.

An Auctioneer who presides at the auction of The Towers, a.k.a. "Gipsy's Acre."

Whetherby, a competitive builder from Helminster, who attends the auction of The Towers

Dakham and Coombe, lawyers from a Liverpool firm who also attend the auction and bid on the property

An Unknown Professional-looking, Well Dressed Londoner who also bids on the property

A Farmer who attends the auction

Greta Andersen, an "au pair" girl and close friend of Ellie Guteman. She is half Swedish and half German. Ellie's family hired her to teach German to Ellie, but their friendship grew.

"Uncle Frank," a brother-in-law to Ellie's deceased father.

Mrs. Rogers, Michael's mother, with whom he has a rather poor relationship. In Michael's view, his mother has always tried to "alter" him.

Cora van Stuyvesant, Ellie Guteman's widowed stepmother, who has no interest in Ellie except being paid an allowance, although a large sum of money had been settled upon her upon the death of Ellie's father.

Ellie Guteman's Wealthy Grandfather. His vast fortune came to Ellie when her own father died suddenly.

Minnie Thompson, an American oil heiress who ran off with a lifeguard. Her family "bought him off" to get rid of him—for $200,000.

Mr. Crawford, Ellie's "hatchet-faced" English lawyer.

Mrs. Nora Bennington, a friend of Ellie's whom Michael and Ellie accidentally meet while honeymooning in Greece

Andrew Lippincott, called "Uncle Andrew" by Ellie Guteman. He is a lawyer and Ellie's principal guardian and trustee

William R. Pardoe, called "Uncle Reuben" by Ellie Guteman, a cousin of hers

Stanford Lloyd, another of Ellie's trustees, who manages her investments.

A Correct, Slightly Phony-looking Manservant at the home of Major Phillpot

Dr. Shaw, a neighbor of Ellie and Michael Rogers, "an elderly man with a kindly but tired manner."

The Vicar who is "young and earnest."

A Middle-aged Woman with a Bullying Voice who Breeds Corgis, another neighbor of Michael and Ellie

Claudia Hardcastle, a local woman who seems to live for horses. She forms the habit of riding with Ellie from time to time. By the merest of coincidences, she is the half-sister of the architect Rudolf Santonix.

Sergeant Keene, to whom Michael complains about Mrs. Lee

Carson, Ellie and Michael's new manservant, hired to replace their former manservant who left after a short time

Mrs. Carson, wife of Carson, a good cook

Mr. Cressington, an art collector from London

The Presiding Goddess of the George, evidently the head waitress

A Man Digging Peat who noticed a riderless horse on the morning that someone disappeared

The Groom employed by Michael and Ellie Rogers to attend to their horses

A Hiker

A Rosy-faced Woman Taking a Shortcut

An Old Road Man Working with Paving Stones

The Coroner, "a small fussy little man with pince-nez."

COMMENTS

If *Endless Night* received any good reviews upon publication, it can only be that the critics wished to be kind to the great and venerable Agatha Christie who was by then seventy-seven years old and clearly in steep decline as a writer. Christie had been an extremely famous and highly respected writer for a long time, and *Endless Night* is her fifty-eighth detective novel.

Endless Night is a silly story filled with unlikely events and dull characters. A few of the characters are described briefly; others are hardly described at all, and interactions between them are very routine and usually of little importance in the story. The coroner is described simply as "a fussy little man with pince-nez," a silly description since the pince-nez had gone out of use at least two or three decades earlier.

Some of the dialogue in *Endless Night* sounds embarrassingly childish, especially Ellie Guteman's. Equally embarrassing is Christie's attempt to write a story in the first person, and having the narrator be a mediocre young working-class male. The thoughts of this narrator, penned by a seventy-seven-year-old upper-middle-class woman, are not natural.

Clearly this novel is not typical of Agatha Christie and should not be a "first Christie experience" for anyone. It is another unfortunate product of her decline, and a rather embarrassing one.

By the Pricking of My Thumbs (1968)

SETTING

The copyright year for *By the Pricking of My Thumbs* is 1968, and in the story there is a reference to a fictitious "big post office robbery of nineteen sixty-five." Therefore we know that the action takes place between those two years, perhaps in 1967. As there are peonies blooming in a private garden in one scene, the season must be late spring or early summer. There are no current events or even "current trends" mentioned in the story. Unlike the 1966 *Third Girl*, *By the Pricking of My Thumbs* contains no references to current fashions among young people, or comments through Christie's characters about "trendy" behaviors in society.

The only "social development" mentioned in the novel is the sad fate of aging persons who are now often placed in nursing homes instead of being allowed to grow old and die in the familiar surroundings of their family homes among younger people of their own families, or at least attended to by a loyal companion or servant. There had been a reference to that recent development in the 1963 *The Clocks* when the narrator noticed that Wilbraham Crescent was singularly devoid of "neighbors—nosy old women who would have noticed things." (See the *Setting* section for that novel.) In the course of the story, we visit a nursing home for aging ladies, Sunny Ridge. The location of Sunny Ridge within England is not specified but it is probably not far from London.

Christie will reintroduce the subject of living arrangements for aging persons in her 1972 *Elephants Can Remember*.

Sunny Ridge is a setting for certain important events and conversations in the story, but a more important setting is an old Georgian period house two miles from the fictitious village of Sutton Chancellor, which is seven miles from Market Basing. Christie first mentioned the town of Market Basing in the 1925 *The Secret of Chimneys*, and then specified its location, in the 1937 *Poirot Loses a Client*, as being in the county of Berkshire, just a few miles west of London. In *By the Pricking of My Thumbs*, Market Basing is now located in the fictitious county of "Melfordshire," and is reached by train from London's Waterloo Station. Therefore "Melfordshire" must be modeled after either Hampshire or Sussex. Christie was not particularly consistent with geography among her novels.

As to chronological consistency, in this novel there is not much of that either. We learn in *By the Pricking of My Thumbs* that Tommy and Tuppence Beresford have been married for "about thirty years" and that they have grown children who are married. Actually, Tommy and Tuppence married right after their adventures in *The Secret Adversary*, which took place in about 1920 or 1921, and in the 1941 *N or M?* their twin children, Derek and Deborah, were already young adults engaged in war work, although neither was yet married. If we were to insist on chronological consistency, the Beresfords' children must now be at least in their late forties and Tommy and Tuppence must be nearly seventy, and they have been married for nearly fifty years. However, Christie evidently intends for us to imagine them to be approximately in their mid-to late-fifties. The character Albert Batt is married and has three small children; in *The Secret Adversary*, he was about twelve years old, meaning that in 1967 he would be approximately sixty, rather old to be a father of three small children.

The town of Market Basing has a hospital called Market Basing Royal Hospital, and at least two hotels: The Blue Dragon (which is a "two-star" hotel) and the Lamb and Flag which is described as "quieter." The village of Sutton Chancellor is briefly described as having a village shop, a post office and about a dozen small houses or cottages plus six newly-built "Council houses." The church in the village of Sutton Chancellor is favored with an interesting description:

> It was an attractive old church standing in a sizable churchyard with a lone yew tree standing by the church door...(...)...The inside was unattractive. The church was an old one, undoubtedly, but it had had a zealous wash and brushup in Victorian times. Its pitch-pine pews and its flaring red and blue glass windows had ruined any antique charm it had once possessed...

It seems to have been stylish, in the 1960s and earlier, to lay the blame of all "destructive renovation" of medieval buildings at the doorstep of the Victorians. Actually a good many examples of medieval architecture in all parts of Europe were "renovated" in ways that destroyed their original beauty as early as the seventeenth and eighteenth centuries. The magnificent cathedral of Amiens in northern France, as well as Notre Dame in Paris, had nearly all of their medieval stained glass *replaced by clear glass*, thanks to the judgments of higher clergy, during the reigns of Louis XIV and Louis XV in efforts to "modernize" the cathedrals by "bringing more light into them." During the nineteenth century—that is, during the hated "Victorian" period—new stained glass was installed in the windows of Notre Dame in Paris and many other churches, in efforts to restore their medieval authenticity.

The actual truth is that the people of the Enlightenment Period (the eighteenth century) had no use for medieval art and architecture, regarding it as "barbaric." In fact the term "Gothic" came into use during that century to describe medieval architecture because the word "Gothic" was synonymous with "barbarian," originally referring to certain uncivilized tribes of northern Europe during Roman times—the Goths, the Visigoths, the Ostrogoths, etc.

Christie was probably not aware of any of the above facts and followed the usual custom of blaming the Victorians for everything, in this case for putting "flaring red and blue" glass into the windows of medieval churches.

There is also a comment in *By the Pricking of My Thumbs* that the large size of the church in Sutton Chancellor suggests that the village was, in earlier times, a much more important place than it became in later years. That is the case with many towns in Europe. Examples are the relatively unimportant English towns of Salisbury, Wells, and Lincoln, all of which boast magnificent medieval cathedrals, suggesting that they were far more important in medieval times than they became later.

To return to the subject of specific settings in *By the Pricking of My Thumbs,* the Georgian period house near the village of Sutton Chancellor is on a twisting country road at the edge of a canal, and is visible from passenger trains passing by the property. The house has been divided into two living units in an unusual way. Instead of being divided into left and right halves, with each half facing the front, rear and one side, it is divided into a "front half" and a "back half," the ground floor of the back half having originally been the kitchen, scullery and other utility rooms. The ground floor of the front half consists of the more gracious original rooms—drawing room, dining room, etc. with a new kitchen added. The rear half is occupied by a middle-aged couple who pay very low rent; the front half has been unoccupied for some time and is in a state of near ruin.

This house, and a painting of it that was executed about twenty-five years earlier, play an important part in the story.

One final comment: When we last met Tommy and Tuppence Beresford, in the 1941 *N or M?,* they were living in a small "service flat" in London. Their current living quarters are not described at all, but clearly they now live in a private house somewhere away from London, since at one point in the story Tommy "goes to London." We know that the living unit is a house and not a flat, because at one point Tommy goes "upstairs" to one of the bedrooms. These are the only references to their home. We also know that they have an automobile, as Tuppence uses it to travel to Sutton Chancellor and Market Basing in search of a house, pictured in a painting, that she once noticed from a train window.

Story

It is approximately 1967 and Tommy and Prudence ("Tuppence") Beresford, whom we have not met since the 1941 *N or M?*, are now considerably older, and are living comfortably—and in relatively good health—in their own private home somewhere away from London. One day they go to a nursing home to visit Tommy's aging Aunt Ada. This is their last visit with her, because Aunt Ada dies a few weeks later. When Tommy and Tuppence return to the nursing home to gather up Aunt Ada's possessions, they find a painting that they had not noticed earlier. The director of the home explains that a Mrs. Lancaster, who had left the home suddenly at her relatives' insistence a few weeks earlier, had given the painting to Aunt Ada because she had admired it.

Tuppence is frankly bored with her life as it is, after having experienced so many exciting adventures in the past. She imagines something sinister behind Mrs. Lancaster's "sudden" departure from the nursing home, and she feels that she should return the painting to her, since Aunt Ada had owned it for no more than a couple of weeks. Tommy thinks all of this is silly but Tuppence persists. Another thing that intrigues Tuppence is the painting itself. It is of an old house next to a canal, and Tuppence is sure she has seen that house somewhere. After some effort she remembers that she once saw the house from a train window. With absolutely nothing better to do, she sets out in her car one day, determined to find the house, which she does. In the nearby village of Sutton Chancellor, where she asks hundreds of chatty questions about the house and its history, she hears of numerous facts and rumors associated with the house, including rumors about murder. Her nosy questions eventually cause her to be struck by an unknown assailant while she is examining a grave marker in a local cemetery.

Tommy eventually gives in and assists Tuppence in her determination to solve the "mystery" of Mrs. Lancaster and the picture of the house by the canal.

Characters

Thomas ("Tommy") and Prudence ("Tuppence") Beresford, who met during the First World War when Tommy was a soldier and Tuppence was a hospital nurse. Penniless and jobless when the war ended, they were desperate enough to consider running a newspaper ad offering themselves as two young "adventurers, willing to go anywhere and do anything. No *un*reasonable offer refused." In the 1922 *The Secret Adversary* they had all the adventures they could handle. Later they operated as a detective agency in a series of short stories, *Partners in Crime*, published in 1929, and then in the 1941 novel *N or M?* they unmasked two British traitors working for Germany. At that time they had been married for about twenty years and had a set of grown twins, Deborah and Derek.

In all of their adventures, it is Tuppence who generally has the more imagination and Tommy who has the more practical sense. She also has a stronger, less conventional personality than he.

Ada Fanshawe ("Aunt Ada"), age eighty-three, who lives at Sunny Ridge, a nursing home for elderly ladies. She is Tommy's aunt and is a cantankerous, insulting old woman in addition to showing signs of senility. She dies a natural death at Sunny Ridge and is not very much missed.

Great-aunt Primrose, who was a great-aunt of Tuppence's. She was easily as unpleasant as Tommy's Aunt Ada.

Mervyn, a "very charming young man" whom Great-aunt Primrose befriended. He was already wanted by the police for swindling money out of old ladies—twenty five of them, in fact.

Dr. Murray, who looks after the health of the residents of Sunny Ridge.

Dr. Williams, Dr. Murray's new partner

Amy Morgan, whom Aunt Ada outlived, despite the fact that Aunt Ada was said to be the more delicate of the two.

Miss Packard, the manager or matron of Sunny Ridge Nursing Home. She is "a big, sandy-haired woman of about fifty with the air of calm competence about her which Tommy had always admired."

Marlene, an employee at Sunny Ridge

Old Mrs. Carraway, a resident of Sunny Ridge who is in the habit of swallowing small objects, such has her thimble, evidently for attention.

Mrs. Elizabeth Moody, a resident of Sunny Ridge who is senile and cannot remember that she has already had her cup of cocoa.

Nurse Jane, who works at Sunny Ridge

Old Uncle William, the original owner of a small desk that Tommy inherits from Aunt Ada

Tommy's Aunt Caroline, whose death fifteen years ago Aunt Ada seems to have forgotten

Miss Donovan, A young woman with a pince-nez employed at Sunny Ridge

Mrs. Lockett, a resident at Sunny Ridge who declares every day that she is being poisoned in a different way. On the day of Tommy and Tuppence's visit to Aunt Ada, Mrs. Lockett is being poisoned by tainted mushroom soup. According to Miss Packard, Mrs. Lockett simply loves doctors and pretends she is being poisoned in order to occasion a doctor visit.

Mrs. Lancaster, a sweet old lady who seems to be a bit senile. At the beginning of the story, she is a resident of Sunny Ridge Nursing Home, and Tuppence has a short conversation with her in a sitting room. She offers a glass of milk to Tuppence, stating "It's not poisoned today."

Mrs. Lancaster speaks vaguely about "a poor child behind the fireplace." A short time later, Mrs. Lancaster's relatives suddenly take her away from Sunny Ridge, and Tuppence tries to find her. But Mrs. Lancaster and her mysterious "relatives" vanish into thin air. Later, while exploring "the house by the canal," and the village of Sutton Chancellor, Tuppence hears rumors about "a child behind a fireplace."

Two Poor Women with Very Bad Rheumatoid Arthritis, and who are in extreme pain, mentioned by Mrs. Lancaster, who is grateful to be afflicted with no more than a little forgetfulness.

A Girl in a White Overall working at Sunny Ridge, who brings coffee and biscuits to Tuppence in the sitting room

Mr. Rockbury, a lawyer who writes to Tommy Beresford about the disposition of Aunt Ada's Will.

A Young Woman in a Nylon Overall who opens the door to Tommy and Tuppence upon their second visit to Sunny Ridge

Deborah and Derek, twin children of Tommy and Tuppence. They were already young adults in the 1941 *N or M?*. In *By the Pricking of My Thumbs* they are still young (probably in their late twenties) but they are now both married.

Miss O'Keefe, a nurse at Sunny Ridge who seemed to enjoy looking after the cantankerous Aunt Ada until she died. Tommy and Tuppence give Aunt Ada's sable stole to her.

Mrs. Johnson, a relative of Mrs. Lancaster who suddenly takes her away from Sunny Ridge soon after Tommy and Tuppence visit Aunt Ada there.

"Mrs. Blenkensop," the "alias" under which Tuppence worked while unmasking British traitors in the 1941 *N or M?*. There are numerous joking references to that name by Tuppence and Tommy in the present novel.

James Eccles, the lawyer who arranged, with Mrs. Johnson's approval, for Mrs. Lancaster to live at Sunny Ridge.

A Very Nice-looking Young Man who visited Mrs. Lancaster at Sunny Ridge a short time after she began to live there, to ascertain whether or not she was happy there.

Albert Batt, Tommy and Tuppence's only servant. He is married and lives with his wife and several children a short distance from the Beresfords' home. He made his first appearance in the 1922 *The Secret Adversary,* where he was "the small lift boy" at the building in London where Rita Vandemeyer lived. He soon became a colleague of Tommy and Tuppence and appeared in the 1929 series of adventures *Partners in Crime,* and again in the 1941 *N or M?*. He is now middle-aged and "portly."

Milly Batt, Albert Batt's wife

"Mr. Meadowes," the "alias" used by Tommy Beresford in the 1941 *N or M?* while staying at the Sans Souci guest house in Leahampton.

Elizabeth, the Batts' youngest child, who has measles in this story.

Charlie and Jean, the Batts' two other children

Anthea, Tuppence's goddaughter, whom she visited about three years ago at her home somewhere south of London. It was during Tuppence's return trip to London that she noticed "the house by the canal" from a train window.

Jane, Anthea's daughter who received a prize at school.

Anthea's Two Younger Children, who had measles, preventing their mother from attending the ceremony at school where Jane was to receive her prize. It was this situation that occasioned Tuppence's visit to the family. She went to the school so that there would "be someone from the family" as Jane was awarded her prize.

Amos Perry, "a big, elderly man digging slowly and with persistence" at the house by the canal. He lives with his wife in the back half of the house.

Alice Perry, Amos Perry's wife. Tuppence's first impression, upon seeing Mrs. Perry coming out of her house, is that she is a "friendly witch." She happens to be wearing a "steeple hat" at the moment, having just rehearsed the part of a witch for a children's play.

Miss Marchment, a.k.a. Miss Margrave, mentioned by Mrs. Perry when Tuppence asks her about the house in which the Perrys live. She was thought to be an actress.

Nellie Bligh, a.k.a. Gertrude Bligh, a.k.a. Geraldine Bligh, whom Tuppence first meets while she is inside the Sutton Chancellor church arranging flowers, "a middle-aged woman in a tweed coat and skirt."

The Vicar of Sutton Chancellor, a kindly, elderly man.

Major Waters, who writes a letter to the vicar asking if a child named Waters was ever buried in the Sutton Chancellor church cemetery

Julia Waters, the widow of Major Waters and mother of the dead child

A Female Child of Julia Waters, now deceased

The Bradleys, who owned the house by the canal about forty years ago

William Boscowan, the artist who painted the picture of the house by the canal.

Emma Boscowan, née Wing, William Boscowan's widow. She is a sculptress who lives at Hampstead Heath, on the edge of London.

Mrs. Partington, who was particularly irritating at the church meeting.

Mrs. Peake, who, on the subject of flower arranging, will never have the children instructed, saying that instruction robs them of their initiative.

Elizabeth ("Liz") Copleigh, a woman of almost pathological loquacity, who lives in the village of Sutton Chancellor and welcomes all inquiry. She is a godsend to Tuppence, not only because she speaks so freely about everyone, but also because she has no interest in the reasons for Tuppence's apparent curiosity. She provides Tuppence with a room and breakfast in her cottage during Tuppence's brief stay in Sutton Chancellor. The Mrs. Copleigh character bears a strong resemblance to Mrs. Amelia Curtis in the 1931 *Murder at Hazelmoor*. See the *Characters* and *Comments* sections for that novel for details about the Mrs. Curtis character.

George Copleigh, Mrs. Copleigh's husband. Like Mr. Curtis in *Murder at Hazelmoor,* he seldom speaks since he seldom has an opportunity to speak.

Farmer Hart, who rented his farm laborer's cottage to the artist, William Boscowan, while he was painting in Sutton Chancellor, as new cottages for laborers had been recently built by the Council.

Mrs. Charrington, who lived in the house by the canal for a short time with her daughter at the time William Boscowan did the painting of the house.

Lilian Charrington, Mrs. Charrington's daughter who "got into trouble" thanks to her mother's poor supervision.

A Man Who Got Lilian Charrington Into Trouble, identity unknown

Another Artist who recently spent time painting in Sutton Chancellor, not much admired by Mrs. Copleigh, because his pictures were just "funny colours all swirled round. Nothing you could recognize a bit."

Mrs. Badcock's Louise, a local gossip who, according to Mrs. Copleigh, "put it about" that Lilian Charrington had killed her illegitimate baby and then killed herself.

Sir Philip Starke, a former resident of Sutton Chancellor whom Mrs. Copleigh suspected of committing a series of child murders a few years ago. She thinks Sir Philip was "a bit too fond of children." To Tuppence, Sir Philip looks like the subject of an El Greco painting.

Julia Starke, Sir Philip's wife who, according to Mrs. Copleigh, left him suddenly but who, according to Sir Philip, died in 1938.

Sir Philip Starke's Father, a very successful industrialist whose son disappointed him.

A Girl with Spots who receives Tuppence at the office of Messrs Lovebody & Slicker, house agents in Market Basing. She is not very bright.

Mr. Slicker, of Messrs Lovebody & Slicker. He is "a tweed-suited young man in horsy checks."

Mr. Sprig, "an elderly man of apparently despondent disposition" at the office of Messrs. Blodget & Burgess, house agents.

Mrs. Yorke, of Rosetrellis Court for Elderly Ladies at an address in Cumberland. At the home of Miss Bligh, Tuppence notices a letter addressed to Mrs. Yorke.

Robert, a friend of Tommy Beresford who is knowledgeable about painting and works at the New Athenian Galleries in Bond Street. He provides Tommy with information about William Boscowan.

Paul Jaggerowski, a young artist who is said to produce all his works under the influence of drugs. When Tommy tells his friend Robert that he does not like Jaggerowski's paintings, Robert simply says, "Philistine."

A Woman at the reception window of Messrs. Partingdale, Harris, Lockeridge and Partingdale, attorneys in Bloomsbury, with which Mr. Eccles is associated.

Anderson, with whom Tommy Beresford was acquainted some years ago, and whom Tommy recognizes in the street near the office of Partingdale, Harris, Lockeridge and Partingdale, apparently watching or following Mr. Eccles. Anderson is an agent of Ivor Smith.

Ivor Smith, some kind of "Secret Service" person with whom Tommy Beresford has worked in the past, and with whom he confers in the present story about Mr. Eccles.

"Old Bogie Waddock Shooting his Mouth Off at the Conference," Ivor Smith's satirical description of one of his—and Tommy's—old cronies in the "Secret Service."

Reverend Cowley, Tuppence's father, long deceased, whom she recalls as she awakens in the hospital after being struck on the head by an unknown assailant in the cemetery at Sutton Chancellor.

"Prudence Cowley," Tuppence's maiden name. When she awakens in a hospital, suffering from concussion, she briefly experiences loss of memory and gives her name as Prudence Cowley.

A Nurse and **A Sister** at Market Basing Royal Hospital

Happy Hamish and Killer Kate, two criminals to whom Ivor Smith makes a brief reference in the presence of Tommy and Tuppence at their hotel room in Market Basing

An Elderly Woman Polishing Brasses in the church at Sutton Chancellor

COMMENTS

In order to enjoy *By the Pricking of My Thumbs,* the reader must have already read the 1922 *The Secret Adversary* and the 1941 *N or M?,* and thoroughly enjoyed them. If you have read those novels and have enjoyed the Tuppence and Tommy Beresford characters, then you will probably enjoy this story even if the crime and its detection are not very interesting to you. As a detective novel, it is not very exciting, but you will certainly be amused by Tommy and Tuppence's references to their adventures in the earlier stories. If you have not read either of the two earlier novels, it would be best to postpone this one until you do read them.

Several of Christie's novels of the 1960s seem to focus on "issues" or "conditions" that happened to capture her attention at the time, whether they are important to the story or not. In *At Bertram's Hotel* there is a good deal of talk about "the good old days" when there were plenty of servants, everyone knew what *real* muffins and seedcake were, afternoon tea was a daily ritual presided over by an absolutely competent, quasi-ecclesiastical butler, and dish towels came in sensible patterns instead of being covered with pictures of silly things like lobsters. In *Third Girl* the "Christie issues of the moment" seem to be British youth who dress in ways that are disgusting to persons who are in their seventies, and who take drugs and rarely wash; young girls who seem to be attracted to boys who look like girls; and shoddily-constructed modern apartment buildings. In *The Mirror Crack'd,* the Christie "interest of the moment" seems to be the emotional insecurity and generally neurotic nature of talented film actresses. In *The Pale Horse,* it is witchcraft.

In order to enjoy reading the above novels, one needs to be at least somewhat interested in the "Christie interest of the moment," which usually has nothing to do with the story.

In *By the Pricking of My Thumbs,* one needs to be interested in the plight of old people in the modern world, especially at the beginning of the story in which Tommy and Tuppence converse at length about nursing homes for the aged and it is suggested that, "in the good old days," the aging persons—and their families—were better off when the old people were allowed to spend their final years in the familiar surroundings of their own homes or, at least, in the homes of their younger relatives. There are several references to senility in addition to the usual physical ailments common in the aging population.

It seems likely that Christie took a greater-than-usual interest in the history of painting and architecture at approximately the time she wrote this novel. The painting of "the house by the canal" leads Tommy to an art gallery in London where a friend of his points out the characteristics of the painter, William Boscowan, in terms that suggest that Christie may have read about, and studied the paintings of, the American painter Edward Hopper or some similar artist. The descriptions of Boscowan's paintings depicting buildings "devoid of human habitation" can be applied to most of Hopper's paintings. And Christie describes the minor character Sir Philip Starke as having stepped "out of an El Greco canvas." There can be no good reason for this rather bizarre characterization other than the likelihood that Christie "discovered" a momentary interest in El Greco, or perhaps the history of painting in general. It is possible that she traveled to Spain and visited the Prado Museum in Madrid that year, or simply watched a television documentary or acquired a book about El Greco and found herself interested.

As to architecture, Christie seems to have developed a sudden interest in the history of church architecture, also, at this time. In all the years that she had been describing houses in her books—especially Queen Anne, Georgian, and Victorian period houses—she had never bothered to describe a church, despite the facts that England is filled with medieval churches, and that there was always an old church in every village that was a setting of her story. Now, suddenly, she finds it interesting to expound on "faulty Victorian restoration of medieval churches" and she will invoke that subject again in her 1974 *Postern of Fate*.

A clue to this "sudden interest" in medieval church architecture is suggested in one of the later chapters of Christie's *Autobiography*. She mentions that the church in Churston Ferrers, near her home Greenway House in Devon, had a "plain glass east window" that always "gaped at her like a gap in teeth." In a spirit of "benevolence," (or perhaps better stated "benevolent despotism,") Christie wrote a long short story (she does not mention the title) and dedicated the proceeds of the story to the design and installation of a new stained glass window for the "gap" in the east wall of the church. She admits that she knew nothing of stained glass at the time, but she arranged for stained glass experts to submit sketches to her and selected one that she liked because her favorite colors were in it (she mentions mauve and pale green.) She also decided that the subject of the stained glass panel should be "Christ the Good Shepherd" and she argued with the Diocese of Exeter, which firmly stated that east windows in medieval churches *must* have as their subject the Crucifixion. Christie would have none of that and stuck to her determination that if she was going to fund a window for the church, it would be "Christ the Good Shepherd in mauve and pale green" and, naturally, since she was the lady with the money she got her way.

In the course of this temporary interest in medieval churches and their windows, Christie obviously had numerous conversations with knowledgeable people, and probably did a little reading on the subject. She probably picked up some notions about "faulty Victorian restoration" of medieval architecture, in which the "rich but ignorant" Victorians had destroyed the original beauty of medieval churches by installing "flaring red and blue glass" in the windows. It is extremely amusing to note that she then proceeded to "dictate" her own taste and ideas for the design of the new window. It would have made more sense for her to offer to pay for the new window but to leave the decisions about the subject and colors to the experts. Art historians would have made sure that the new "replacement" window was in keeping with the period of the church. As it is, a century from now it will be explained that a "rich but ignorant" woman of the twentieth century who liked mauve and pale green and the idea of "Christ the Good Shepherd" ordered the window "restoration" to be designed *her* way.

In *By the Pricking of My Thumbs,* the conversations and thoughts about certain artists and their styles, and the church architecture, too, may make fairly interesting reading, but of course they have nothing whatever to do with the story, as indeed neither do the problems confronting aging persons and their families.

A trivial point: in Christie's preceding novel, *Endless Night,* she described the coroner as being "a fussy little man with pince-nez." The pince-nez had gone out of use several decades earlier and it is strange that Christie should not have observed that fact personally. In *By the Pricking of My Thumbs,* there are two "young women" who use a pince-nez, a silly notion. For readers unfamiliar with the "pince-nez," it was a style of eyeglasses that lacked the usual wings that go over the ears, and was simply perched on the bridge of the nose. The pince-nez was antiquated as early as the late 1930s, and in films from that period we sometimes see very old people still using them, but by the 1940s the pince-nez was extinct. What could Christie have been thinking? It is true that during the late 1960s there was a fad revival of wire-rimmed glasses and they were called "granny glasses." But there was never a revival of the pince-nez.

The book is not badly written, however, and it is not afflicted with the obvious padding and senseless repetition that mar several recent Christie novels, especially the 1965 *At Bertram's Hotel* and the 1966 *Third Girl*. Recall that in *Third Girl* a certain village was given an exceedingly long, detailed and rather tedious description for no apparent reason. In *By the Pricking of My Thumbs,* the village of Sutton Chancellor is also described, but in a much more sensible—that is to say, brief—manner.

As mentioned above, *By the Pricking of My Thumbs* is primarily for fans of the Tommy and Tuppence characters, who had been featured in only two Christie novels and a book of short stories published much earlier. Christie wrote in a short dedication:

> This book is dedicated to the many readers in this and other countries who write to me asking: "What has happened to Tommy and Tuppence? What are they doing now?"
> My best wishes to you all, and I hope that you will enjoy meeting Tommy and Tuppence again, years older, but with spirit unquenched!

Hallowe'en Party (1969)

SETTING

The story takes place at the end of October and during the first week or two of November in approximately 1968. There is no mention of any current events, but there are some brief references to the clothing and hair styles sported by teen-aged boys at the time—shoulder-length hair and colorful, rather garishly-styled shirts. A fictitious "pop singer" named Eddie Presweight, who sports a beard and probably long hair, is mentioned as being attractive to teen-age girls. As in one or two other recent Christie novels, there is a reference to ESP (extrasensory perception); it was a stylish conversation subject at the time. The terms "Lesbian" and "sex-starved" occur in the speech of a teenager who is probably parroting words and ideas he has heard or read in the media of the time, as he speculates on the subject of who the murderer can be.

Although no current events are mentioned, there is a good deal of conversation about the rising crime rate in Britain, especially murders of children—and sex crimes against children—by mentally ill people who are released from psychiatric facilities for no other reason than overcrowding of the facilities. There is also a negative mention of the recent abolishment of the death penalty in Britain, and of "too much compassion" for young criminals. One character remarks that often "first offenders" are given fines instead of prison terms. The fines are paid by over-indulgent relatives and so there is no actual punishment for the offender. One character, a medical doctor, expresses disgust with the modern tendency to explain—and even to excuse—criminal acts by focusing attention on the alleged mental incapacity of the killer

There is also a good deal of talk about the recent increase of sex crimes and the "carelessness" of modern mothers who do not monitor their daughters' social contacts. This notion that, in the past, conscientious mothers "looked after their grown daughters' interests" whereas the mothers of today do not, has been common in Christie's novels for the past few years, most notably in the 1965 *At Bertram's Hotel* and the 1966 *Third Girl*.

In addition, there are one or two references to drug use among young people. A mother describes a recent party for teenagers in which "peculiar drugs" were a feature.

The primary physical setting in *Hallowe'en Party* is a fictitious village called Woodleigh Common, which one character describes as being about thirty or forty miles from London. A nearby larger town, which has a technical school, is Medchester. No indication is given of the direction from London these places are to be found, and no geographical peculiarity causes them to be imagined in any particular area.

We visit several houses in Woodleigh Common. One of them, called Apple Trees, is a red brick Georgian-style house with a neat beech hedge enclosing it and a pleasant garden showing beyond. It is in this house that the first murder takes place. Three rooms on the ground floor are the settings for different scenes: the drawing room, the dining room and the library. The entrance to the library is visible from the upper landing of the stairway. There is no washroom on the ground floor and one character has occasion to go up the stairs to use the bathroom.

Another house, called Quarry House, is less important than its property which includes a former rock quarry that was transformed just a few years ago by a former owner of the house into a "sunk garden" known as Quarry Woods. A talented landscape architect, who continues to live in the village, created the garden, which is described in detail as consisting of plants carefully selected to appear as if natural to their locations. The garden is open to the public and plays an important role in the story.

In addition to the scenes in the village of Woodleigh Common, there are brief scenes at the London residence of Hercule Poirot, at a restaurant called The Black Boy in a town between Woodleigh Common and London, and at a fictitious beauty spot called Kilterbury Ring which includes tall megalithic stones used by ancient inhabitants in ritual worship.

The middle-aged (or perhaps even elderly, by this time) detective story writer Ariadne Oliver remarks that she is never quite sure of the difference between a pumpkin and a "vegetable marrow" (squash). Pumpkins have never been nearly as common in England as they have always been in America, as pumpkins and their relatives—gourds and certain squashes—were native to the Americas and may have been just making their way into European gardens—and markets—at that time.

A fictitious automobile make, the "Grasshopper Mark Seven," is mentioned as being the most popular car in England. Its silly name is probably a tongue-in-cheek reference by Christie to automobile names such as the Volkswagen "Beetle," the Fiat "Spider," the Hudson "Wasp" and "Hornet" and other zoological names.

Story

It is October 30 of approximately 1968 and detective story writer Ariadne Oliver has been invited to spend a few days with friends, Judith Butler and her adolescent daughter Miranda, at their home in the village of Woodleigh Common. A Hallowe'en party for children aged ten to about sixteen is scheduled for the following day at Apple Trees, a gracious Georgian home in the village, and during the preparations for the party a boastful adolescent girl, Joyce Reynolds, states that she "saw a murder once." The other children jeer at her and the adults scold her for lying, for she has developed a reputation for telling impressive lies about herself in order to make herself important. Nobody believes her and her claim is soon forgotten.

The following day, the party takes place and is a great success. During the party there is a "bobbing for apples" game and a large plastic tub of water is placed in the library for the purpose. At the end of the party, in another room, there is a noisy game called "snapdragon" in which a bowl of raisins is saturated with brandy and ignited. Game participants reach into the flames to pull out handfuls of raisins. Then the party ends and the children leave with their parents.

The adults who remain afterwards to perform "clean up operations" are shocked to find Joyce's dead body in the library. She has been drowned in the tub of water, her head obviously having been held under the water by someone.

The authorities suspect that a stranger with no reasonable motive, aside from possible mental illness, entered the house during the noisy final activity and killed the child. Mrs. Oliver suspects, however, that Joyce may have been killed by someone who felt threatened by her statement of having seen a murder once. She appeals to Hercule Poirot to come to Woodleigh Common to solve the mystery, which he does, but not in time to prevent the murder of a second child and the attempted murder of a third.

CHARACTERS

Ariadne Oliver, the famous detective story writer who first appeared in a Christie novel in the 1936 *Cards on the Table*, although she had appeared in Christie short stories a bit earlier. Her trademark eccentricities include constantly changing coiffures, ridiculous clothes, atrocious interior decorating, and an inordinate fondness for apples (although, surprisingly, her fondness for apples is not mentioned in two of the most recent novels in which she has appeared—*The Pale Horse* and *Third Girl*. Perhaps Christie forgot about the apples obsession while writing those.) But the apple motif returns in *Hallowe'en Party* with a vengeance. A Hallowe'en party takes place at a house called Apple Trees, and a child is deliberately drowned by someone who holds her head in a tub of water used earlier for a "bobbing for apples" game. As a result Mrs. Oliver swears off apples entirely and substitutes munching dates as an oral distraction. It is Mrs. Oliver who brings Hercule Poirot into the case, as she did in *Dead Man's Folly* and, unwittingly, in *Third Girl*.

In the earlier novels, Mrs. Oliver lived in a flat in London's Harley Street—among the fashionable doctors—and for many years her drawing room was papered in a colorful design of jungle plants and brightly colored tropical birds. In the 1966 *Third Girl* Mrs. Oliver finally replaced the thirty-year-old wallpaper with a pattern of cherries ripening on their trees in an orchard. But we learn in *Hallowe'en Party* that she has moved several times and we have no indication of her latest interior decorating atrocities. Perhaps she has been repeatedly evicted for non-payment of rent due to dwindling sales of her books, which would be appropriate, since they are lousy detective novels and "all the same except for the names of the characters" as she cheerfully admitted to Hercule Poirot as far back as the 1936 *Cards on the Table*. Nevertheless, an otherwise intelligent woman, Miss Emlyn, who is the headmistress of a school no less, makes the following charitable though laconic remark about Mrs. Oliver:

> "She writes delightful books. I have met her once or twice."

Judith Butler, whom Ariadne Oliver recently met on a cruise in the Greek Islands. Hercule Poirot and Superintendent Spence agree that Judith is a very attractive woman. In his thoughts, Poirot compares her to Undine, the water spirit, because of her "rather long face and faintly hollow cheeks, and big sea-green eyes fringed with long eyelashes."

Judith is a young widow who was "left very badly off" when her husband was killed in an automobile accident. She works part-time as a secretary. Despite being "left very badly off" and working only part-time as a secretary, she has a cook and a cleaning woman. How this is possible, especially in these modern times of "shortage of domestic servants," is not explained, except perhaps by Christie's late-in-life muddle-headedness.

Judith Butler's Deceased Husband. He was an airline pilot who died in an automobile accident several years ago.

Miranda Butler, Judith's astonishingly adult-speaking twelve-year-old daughter. She spends a good deal of her time watching birds and squirrels in Quarry Woods. She was Joyce Reynolds's best friend. Miranda had a fever on the day of the Hallowe'en Party and so could not attend. Just as Poirot compares Miranda's mother to a "water spirit," he compares Miranda to "a dryad or some elf-like being" when he notices her seated on a fallen tree trunk in Quarry Woods.

Energetic Women, Mostly Mothers plus One or Two Competent Spinsters, bustling about, setting up Mrs. Drake's home for the Hallowe'en party

Joyce Reynolds, a boastful thirteen-year-old girl who, the day before the Hallowe'en party, announced to everyone that she had seen a murder committed once. Nobody believed her, though, because she had a reputation for telling impressive lies about herself in order to "make herself important." On this subject, *everyone* (except her mother) agrees.

Ann Reynolds, Joyce's older sister who once read one of Mrs. Oliver's detective novels, *The Dying Goldfish*. She is an intellectually talented child who, according to one adult in the story, will probably go to university and become a teacher.

Leopold Reynolds, Joyce's eleven-year-old brother. He and his sister Ann agree that Joyce was an incurable liar. Leopold is, like Ann, exceptionally bright, especially in mathematics, and he builds construction models as a hobby.

Mrs. Reynolds, the mother of the Reynolds children. According to Mrs. Oliver, she is "quite a nice woman. Rather stupid, I should think..."

Mr. Reynolds, the father of the Reynolds children, who works in real estate, rather unsuccessfully, according to the well-informed Mrs. Goodbody.

Beatrice Ardley, one of the young girls present on the day of preparations for the party, and who also attended the party. According to Mrs. Oliver, she is "rather smug and superior."

Cathie Johnson, another rather "smug and superior" child, who responded to Joyce's story about having seen a murder by asking, "Then why didn't you go to the police about it?"

Diana and Nan, two other girls at the Hallowe'en party

A Boy of Fifteen and a Girl Little More than Twelve, kissing, sighing and snuggling in the upper-floor hall at Apple Trees

Desmond Holland, age sixteen, who helped with preparations for the party and with the "future husband in the mirror" game during the party. Desmond and his roommate, Nicholas Ransom, study at a technical school in nearby Medchester.

Nicholas Ransom, age eighteen. Desmond and Nicholas, trying very hard to assist Poirot in identifying the killer of Joyce Reynolds, make the following imaginative suggestion:

> "What about the curate?" said Desmond hopefully. "*He* might be a bit off his nut. You know, original sin perhaps, and all that, and the water and the apples and the things and then—look here, I've got a good idea now. Suppose *he* is a bit barmy. Not been here very long. Nobody knows much about him. Supposing it's the snapdragon put it into his head. Hell fire! All those flames going up! Then, you see, he took hold of Joyce and he said, 'Come along with me and I'll show you something.' and he took her to the apple room and he said 'Kneel down.' He said, 'This is a baptism,' and pushed her head in. See? It would all fit. Adam and Eve and the apple and hell fire and the snapdragon and being baptized again to cure you of sin."
> "Perhaps he exposed himself to her first," said Nicholas hopefully. "I mean, there's always got to be a sex background to all these things."
> They both looked with satisfied faces to Poirot.
> "Well," said Poirot, "you've certainly given me something to think about."

Mrs. Rowena Arabella Drake, a middle-aged widow who hosts the Hallowe'en party at her gracious Georgian period home, Apple Trees.

Hugo Edmund Drake, Mrs. Drake's deceased husband, who was struck by polio many years ago and was a "cripple" (Christie's own politically-incorrect term) for many years before he died a year or two ago.

Miss Elizabeth Whittaker, aged about forty, a local schoolteacher who is another of Christie's characters who are described as using a "pince-nez." One of the teen-aged boys shares a theory about Miss Whittaker with Hercule Poirot:

> "Have you any theories yourself?"
> Poirot addressed himself to Nicholas.
> "What, theories as to who did Joyce in?"
> "Yes. I mean something that you might have noticed that could lead you to a suspicion on perhaps purely psychological grounds."
> "Yes, I can see what you mean. There might be something in that."
> "Whittaker for my money," said Desmond, breaking in to Nicholas's absorption in thought.
> "The schoolmistress?" asked Poirot?
> "Yes. Real old spinster, you know. Sex-starved. And all that teaching, bottled up among a lot of women...

Mrs. Hargreaves, the church organist's wife who helped with the preparations for the party

Miss Lee, the doctor's dispenser who also helped with the preparations

Miss Johnson, the organist's sister, who also helped with preparations. (Why her name is Johnson and not Hargreaves is not explained. More Christie muddle-headedness?)

Mrs. Goodbody, who plays the fortune-telling witch at the Hallowe'en party because she has the perfect face for a witch, although a kindly witch. She freely shares her impressions of everyone in the village of Woodleigh Common with Hercule Poirot.

Eddie Presweight, a popular singing star much admired by teenaged girls—not a character in the story, but mentioned by one of the admiring girls at the party

Hercule Poirot, the famous Belgian private investigator with the flamboyant moustache. Although he keeps getting older and older, his self-concept has not changed:

> Many of the evenings were dull now, Hercule Poirot thought. His mind, magnificent as it was (for he had never doubted that fact), required stimulation from outside sources...

Solomon ("Solly") Levy, a friend of Hercule Poirot's who disappoints him by having a nasty cold on the day the two had planned to spend a pleasant evening together reviving their never-ending controversy about the real culprit in the Canning Road Municipal Baths murder.

George, Poirot's impeccable manservant, whom we have known since the 1928 *The Mystery of the Blue Train.*

Superintendent Bert Spence, an old friend of Hercule Poirot, although they have not seen each other since the 1952 *Mrs. McGinty's Dead,* in which Spence appealed to Poirot to reinvestigate a case that had already been tried because he felt that an innocent man had been found guilty and was about to be hanged. Spence is now retired and shares a home with his widowed sister in Woodleigh Common, the village in which the murder takes place.

Elspeth McKay, Superintendent Spence's sister, who has lived in the village of Woodleigh Common for three years. She is a widow with grown children who live in Australia and South Africa. She is able to provide Poirot with insights about most of the people living in the village.

Dr. Ferguson, "a man of sixty, of Scottish extraction, with a brusque manner." He is fed up with psychiatrists and their reports that seem to excuse the behaviors of young criminals.

Rev. Charles Cotterell, the vicar of Woodleigh Common, who was at the Hallowe'en party. "Nice old boy, rather dim" is the assessment of one of the teen-aged boys who helped at the party.

The New Curate, who stammers when he's nervous. The teenaged boys, Desmond Holland and Nicholas Ransom, offer an imaginative theory about the murder of Joyce Reynolds which involves the curate (see above.)

Inspector Tim Raglan of the C.I.D., who "has a very good reputation locally," according to Mrs. Drake.

Mrs. Louise Llewellyn-Smythe, deceased. She had moved to Woodleigh Common several years ago in order to be near her nephew, Hugo Drake.

Olga Seminoff, Mrs. Llewellyn-Smythe's *au pair* girl, to whom she supposedly left her entire fortune, in a codicil to her Will. But the codicil was shown by handwriting experts to be a forgery. When confronted with the prospect of being accused, tried and found guilty of forgery, Olga disappeared.

Olga Seminoff's Father, who was arrested and taken away by the police in her native country, Herzegovina

Olga Seminoff's Mother, who died

Mrs. Minden, who had been Mrs. Llewellyn-Smythe's maid and who now comes to the Butler home to clean. She reported having heard Mrs. Llewellyn-Smythe telling Olga Seminoff to write letters in handwriting resembling her own, and to sign them, as arthritis prevented her from writing without difficulty and she disliked typewritten personal letters to friends.

Charlotte Benfield, a sixteen-year-old shop assistant who was found beaten to death about eighteen months ago

Peter Gordon, who was the prime suspect in the beating death of Charlotte Benfield, but whose alibi was never disproved.

Peter Gordon's Less Reputable Friends who provided him with an alibi.

Thomas Hudd, another possible suspect in the beating death of Charlotte Benfield.

Thomas Hudd's Mother, a "doting mother type." She "didn't encourage girl friends. Kept him as close to her apron strings as she could." She provided her son with an alibi. According to Superintendent Spence, she "would have sworn to kingdom come that he was indoors with her all that evening...."

Lesley Ferrier, who was stabbed in the back not far from the Green Swan pub. He had been conducting an affair with Sandra Griffin, the wife of the pub owner, Harry Griffin. Was Lesley killed by the outraged husband, or by Sandra herself? He was thought to have taken an interest in another woman and to have inspired jealousy in Sandra. His murder was never solved.

Harry Griffin, landlord of The Green Swan

Sandra Griffin, wife of Harry Griffin

Janet White, a schoolteacher who was found strangled on a footpath near Woodleigh Common about two and a half years ago. According to the schoolteacher Miss Whittaker, Janet and her roommate, Nora Ambrose were "oversexed, but in different ways." Janet's murder had never been solved. In a conversation with Hercule Poirot, Desmond Holland and Nicholas Ransom express the belief that Miss White was Lesbian.

Nora Ambrose, a schoolteacher with whom Janet White had shared quarters.

Miss Emlyn, the headmistress of The Elms, an excellent local school. She is competent and helpful to Hercule Poirot, directing him to an important conversation with Miss Whittaker.

Miss Bulstrode, now retired. She was the extremely competent and visionary headmistress of the excellent Meadowbank School in the 1959 *Cat Among the Pigeons*. She is a mutual friend of Miss Emlyn and Hercule Poirot and is fondly remembered by both.

Colonel and Mrs. Weston, the current owners of Quarry House and Quarry Woods. They have no particular interest in the exotic garden, Quarry Woods, which the previous owner had created out of an abandoned quarry, but they benignly tolerate public enjoyment of the garden.

A Thin, Grey-haired Woman who opens the door to Hercule Poirot at Quarry House

Michael Garfield, an extremely talented landscape architect. It was he who designed the unique and beautiful Quarry Woods, a sunk garden featuring plants specially selected and arranged to appear as if natural to their settings. Mrs. Lewellen-Smythe had hired him to execute her own ideas in the creation of the garden, but instead, he had executed his own ideas, skillfully leading Mrs. Lewellen-Smythe to believe that the ideas had been *her*s. The wealthy Mrs. Lewellen-Smythe even built a house for Michael to live in near the garden as a part of his compensation.

Mrs. Perring, Judith Butler's cook

Jeremy Fullerton of Fullerton, Harrison and Leadbetter, the firm of lawyers who looked after Mrs. Llewellyn-Smythe's legal affairs, and also those of her niece, Rowena Drake.

Young Mr. Cole, a law partner of Jeremy Fullerton, who was the first to suspect forgery in the matter of the codicil to Mrs. Llewellyn-Smythe's Will

Miss Miles, Jeremy Fullerton's secretary

Mr. Holden, who is late for his appointment with Jeremy Fullerton and therefore rescheduled

Robert, Jeremy Fullerton's nephew who had been involved in a murder trial. Superintendent Spence had been in charge of the case

James Bentley, the alleged "psychopathic killer" in the 1952 *Mrs. McGinty's Dead*, whom Hercule Poirot proved to be innocent. He is mentioned by retired Superintendent Spence in a conversation with Poirot, as it was he who had asked Poirot to reinvestigate the case after the trial. Bentley had been convicted of murdering his landlady, Mrs. McGinty, and was awaiting execution, but Spence doubted Bentley's guilt, in spite of being the police officer who had gathered most of the evidence against him.

Mr. Waterhouse, an elderly seed merchant in Medchester and the owner of the Grasshopper Mark Seven that ran down and killed Hugo Drake.

An Elderly Gardener at Helpsley Cemetery who is only too eager to put aside his work for a while and chat, at length, with Hercule Poirot about the residents of Woodleigh Common and their history.

An Aunt of the Elderly Gardener's Wife who contracted infantile paralysis while vacationing in Spain

Mrs. Brand, the landlady of Nicholas Ransom and Desmond Holland

A Little Girl Aged Seven who smothered her baby brother and sister to death in their prams

Harriet Leaman, a cleaning lady who witnessed the signing of a codicil to Mrs. Llewellyn-Smythe's Will

James Jenkins, a gardener's helper who also witnessed the signing of a codicil

Mary Doherty, who witnessed the signing of another codicil

Kitty, a child who was said to have fallen into the well at Quarry Woods some years ago

Mr. Goby, an old friend of Hercule Poirot who is a kind of "detective's detective." We first met him in the 1928 *The Mystery of the Blue Train*, and he is still active. His organization extends beyond the borders of Britain, and he provides some useful information to Poirot about Olga Seminoff and her family in central Europe.

Hercule Poirot's Landlady during his brief stay in Woodleigh Common, "a cheerful lady of thirty-odd"

Alfred Richmond, Chief Constable of the County

A Man with a Sharp Legal Face from the public prosecutor's office

Sergeant Goodwin, a local policeman who telephones some important information about Quarry Woods to Elspeth McKay

FRENCH INTO ENGLISH

Note: Hercule Poirot uses very little French in this novel.

Chapter 3
Tout de même—just the same
Eh bien—Oh, well
eau de vie—brandy

Chapter 4 *Eh bien*—Well...

Chapter 5 *mon cher*—my friend

Chapter 11
il y a des ennuis, vous comprenez—there are problems, you understand...
Ça dépend—That depends

Chapter 18 *chemin*—path, route

Chapter 19
chère madame—dear lady
soigné—well groomed

Chapter 20
Ah, ça, non—Not those!
The *tout ensemble*—the over-all appearance
bien placé—comfortably situated

Chapter 27
Translation of the French song quoted by Poirot:
Look, Narcissus,
Look into the water.
Look, Narcissus, at how beautiful you are.
In the whole world there is
Nothing but beauty and youth.
Alas, youth...
Look, Narcissus
Look into the water...

COMMENTS

Hallowe'en Party is a pleasant though unremarkable detective novel, and it is unique in that the two murder victims—and a third intended murder victim—are all children aged thirteen and younger. Hercule Poirot solves the case by deduction and not guessing (which is a bit of a novelty in recent years) and a couple of important clues that the reader should not miss are largely responsible for his success.

Although excellent characterization does not typify Christie's novels of the 1960s, *Hallowe'en Party* contains some charming and clearly portrayed characters, especially some of the youngsters at the Hallowe'en party where the first murder takes place. Poirot's interview with the two teen-aged boys, Desmond and Nicholas, is fun to read and will make you smile. Joyce Reynolds's younger brother Leopold is a cute kid who is smart in science and mathematics, builds mechanical models and does his best to divide his attention between his current model project and Poirot's important questions about his sister's death. The character of Rowena Drake is vividly portrayed through her own speech and actions as well as through comments from other characters. The character of the Central European *au pair* girl Olga Seminoff is clearly portrayed through the thoughts of the lawyer Mr. Fullerton. Mrs. Llewellyn-Smythe comes to life beautifully, even though she is dead, through the many comments of living characters. The personality of the murder victim, young Joyce Reynolds, is perhaps a bit overdone, as no fewer than eight different people characterize her in no uncertain terms as an incurable liar, although the unanimity of these comments is important in leading Poirot to the correct solution of the mystery. Elspeth McKay, Superintendent Spence's widowed sister, is strongly portrayed and somewhat reminiscent of Caroline Sheppard in the 1926 *The Murder of Roger Ackroyd*.

Some of the characterization will strike some readers as a bit silly, however. Poirot's musings about little Miranda Butler as a "wood nymph" and her mother Judith Butler as Undine, the "water spirit," and handsome Michael Garfield as "Narcissus," are a little far-fetched but may intrigue certain readers. Nevertheless, the characterization in *Hallowe'en Party* is probably the best of all of Christie's novels of the 1960s.

Hercule Poirot is lucky, in this case, to have two friends in the village of Woodleigh Common—his old friend Superintendent Spence and Spence's sister, Elspeth McKay—to apprise him of most of the relevant facts about the residents. The last time he was called upon to solve a village crime, in the 1952 *Mrs. McGinty's Dead*, he had no such advantage, although his friend Mrs. Oliver was there to find things out in her nosy-old-lady way and then to pass information on to him.

In *Hallowe'en Party*, Christie's "interest of the moment" seems to be the increased permissiveness in society, "excuses" that are made for criminal behavior based on psychoanalyses of the criminals, and far-too-mild penalties for crime. The problem of mentally-defective persons being released from psychiatric facilities simply because of overcrowding of the facilities seems to be a real one and has provoked comment in America as well in recent years.

In no uncertain terms, Christie reminds us again of her conviction that character traits are inherited through blood and not formed by environment, as Poirot affirms:

> "One must accept facts, and a fact that is expressed by modern biologists ... seems to suggest very strongly that the root of a person's actions lies in his genetic make-up. That a murderer of twenty-four was a murderer in potential at two or three or

four years old. Or of course a mathematician or a musical genius."

As evidence of the above, one character tells of a little girl of seven who deliberately strangled her two younger siblings in their prams. The character concludes that the child was "born rotten inside." Certain knowledgeable persons might suggest, however, that the child may have experienced intense sibling rivalry thanks to asinine behaviors on the part of her parents in the matter of overt affection and attention bestowed on the younger children while being withdrawn from the older one, a common occurrence. Christie does not seem to be aware of such issues.

The repetitiousness of the dialogue in a few of Christie's last novels is not very apparent in *Hallowe'en Party,* which seems to have been more carefully written than a few others. Chapter 11—in which Poirot visits the Quarry Woods, meets Michael Garfield and Miranda Butler, and then later meets Judith Butler at her home—is rather overlong and rambling. Otherwise the novel is nicely written. Not a good choice as a "first Christie experience," it's a good read for fans of Hercule Poirot and Ariadne Oliver.

Summary for the 1960s

The quality of Christie's writing declined during the 1960s and this decade should therefore be avoided by new Christie readers. For serious Christie fans, however, most of the novels of the 1960s are a pleasure to read. If you are already a fan of the Miss Marple character, then *The Mirror Crack'd, A Caribbean Mystery* and *At Bertram's Hotel* will be pleasant reading for you, and if you are partial to Hercule Poirot, you will enjoy *The Clocks, Third Girl* and *Hallowe'en Party.* If you have not met these characters yet, however, you are advised to choose Christie novels from the earlier decades before reading these.

In her novels of the 1960s, Christie dwells a good deal on the changes that have taken place in society, and she clearly views *all* of them as changes for the worse. The phrases "reduced responsibility" and "unfortunate childhood" pop up derisively over and over again in the conversations of doctors, lawyers, and law enforcement people who are disgusted with the excuses that are constantly being made by the defense attorneys and judges in the matter of crime among youth. In at least two or three Christie novels of the 1960s, respected characters in positions of authority suggest that most rapes nowadays are not rapes at all but consensual acts of sex later reported by the young women—at the instigation of their mothers—as rape. And there are constant reminders that the "conscientious" mothers of the past "protected" their daughters from unsuitable young men much more than the "neglectful" mothers of today, who allow their daughters to associate with young men who impregnate them and then depart, or who later prove to be "unsuitable husbands" in one way or another.

If the comments of a woman who was born in 1890 about the directions society was taking during the 1960s do not bore you, then you may enjoy Christie's novels of that period despite their relative paleness as compared with the masterpieces that she produced during the four preceding decades.

The best characterization in Christie's novels of the 1960s is to be found in the 1969 *Hallowe'en Party. A Caribbean Mystery,* however, stands far above the rest in over-all quality and is Christie's only detective novel of the decade that compares favorably with her earlier novels.

Passenger to Frankfurt (1970)

Setting

The reader is asked to imagine this story as taking place just a few years into the future, a fanciful outcome of current political and social trends. The physical settings are much less important than are the current events of the period, since the story is based on Christie's impression of international events and trends, and their imagined causes and potential outcomes.

The opening scene takes place in the passenger waiting room of the airport at Frankfurt, Germany. Subsequent scenes take place in London at the flat of a government agent, which overlooks Green Park and is a ten-minute walk from the American Embassy; in the office of another government agent; inside the American Embassy; and at a concert hall. There is a scene in the cabinet room at 10 Downing Street, the residence of the Prime Minister. Outdoor scenes in London include two incidents in which the protagonist narrowly escapes being deliberately run down by speeding cars and one scene on a pedestrian bridge during a rainy late afternoon rush hour. We have occasion to visit, once again, the stifling, smoke-filled, cigar-ash-littered office of our friend, Colonel Ephraim Pikeaway, the head of "Special Branch" whom we met in the 1959 *Cat Among the Pigeons.*

Outside of London we visit an aging great-aunt of the protagonist at her gracious Georgian-period house, of which she and a nurse and one or two old, loyal servants occupy just a small portion, most of the vast house being covered with dust cloths and cleaned periodically. The location of the house is not specified but it is probably in a county not too distant from London. An important scene takes place at a luxurious private home, a "Stockbroker Tudor" early-twentieth-century home near Godalming in the county of Surrey, just south of London.

Another important scene takes place at a late eighteenth-century "Schloss" (castle) in Bavaria, portions of which have been restored to magnificence. A nearby concert hall is also a setting. There is a scene in an unnamed government office in Paris, and a similar scene takes place in a government office in Germany. Late in the story we visit the residence of an aging, invalid scientist at a venerable old castle in the Scottish moorlands.

As mentioned above, however, it is primarily the social and political atmosphere of the late 1960s that creates the "setting." This atmosphere consists mainly of the world-wide unrest that characterized the period. The Viet Nam War was raging and there were frequent violent anti-war protests in America, especially at universities. The young people of America and Western Europe appeared to be universally opposed to everything about the "establishment," but of course that was an exaggeration. In addition to the war in Viet Nam and the anti-war protests, there were constant conflicts in Africa and the Middle East. There were also, at least in America, racial tensions and riots in several cities beginning in 1966. Along with this, crime in general seemed to be increasing everywhere with senseless vandalism occurring practically every day.

There was incessant talk about traditional values being "irrelevant" and older people were puzzled and shocked by the behaviors of the younger generation. In a word, older citizens—including eighty-year-old Christie herself—watched as the world they knew seemed to be coming apart. It is this "world gone awry" atmosphere that is the primary setting for *Passenger to Frankfurt*, and the reader is asked to imagine the world as it may be just a few years into the future if present developments continue unabated.

For the benefit of readers interested in tracking minor details of modern life as reflected in Christie's writing, in *Passenger to Frankfurt* there are first-time Christie references to automatic electric percolators, rechargeable electric razors, and travelers' checks. There is also a reference to the old woodwind instrument known as the recorder, variations of which had been replaced a couple of centuries earlier by the modern flute, oboe, clarinet, etc. It experienced a mild revival beginning in the late 1950s when an interest in older art music was revived.

Those of us who are old enough to remember the days when businesses began to keep records with early computers appreciate Aunt Matilda's remarks about "those terrible computers that get one's electric light bills all wrong." We remember phoning businesses about incorrect bills and being told things like "Well, the computer says…"

There is also, as there has been in several Christie novels since about 1960, a complaining comment about modern supermarkets by an old woman living in a village, as she speaks with her London nephew about a visit he plans to make her. She complains that the grocery store in her village has turned into a supermarket "six times the size, all rebuilt, baskets and wire trays to carry round and try to fill up with things you don't want, etc…" She asks him to bring her a Camembert cheese and half a Stilton from London, as such delicacies are not stocked at the new supermarket.

Story

It is approximately 1975—a future year, since the book was first published in 1970—and there is unrest everywhere. There are constant riots and student unrest in the major capitals of Europe and America. A British foreign agent, Sir Stafford Nye, is the protagonist. Despite being an agent of British intelligence, he has a cynical view of government and politicians and there is usually a mildly satirical look in his eye and a satirical tone in his voice, as he refuses to take life, his work and especially his colleagues totally seriously. When traveling, even in the course of his work, he affects a bizarre appearance by wearing, instead of a conservative-looking overcoat, a rather flamboyant purply-blue, hooded cape with a red lining.

As the story begins, Stafford Nye is waiting for a plane in the passenger waiting room at the airport in Frankfurt. A beautiful woman approaches him with a story of her life being in danger and that he must help her. He is to allow her to "steal" his cape, passport and boarding pass so that she can use his identity to safely fly to London. In a spirit of adventure, Stafford Nye agrees to this. He "misses" the plane himself and travels to London on a later flight.

In London he experiences two attempts on his life and then is reunited with the woman who, it develops, is an agent of the British government. The Government approaches him with a wild story of a secret, world-wide neo-Fascist organization that is behind all of the world-wide unrest of the moment. He is to infiltrate the organization in order to learn more about it. It is Stafford Nye's well-known satirical and cynical attitude towards the Government and politicians that may make him welcome in the secret organization. The young woman whom he assisted at Frankfurt will be his guide, as she has contacts in the "organization." She is the Countess Renata Zerkowski.

Stafford Nye's adventures lead him to one of the headquarters of the organization, a castle in Bavaria.

Characters

An Authoritative Airline Stewardess who orders passengers to fasten their seat belts because of a period of rough weather soon expected.

Sir Stafford Nye, a British diplomat with a "special" personality. "He had been a disappointment in diplomatic circles. Marked out in early youth by his gifts for great things, he had singularly failed to fulfill his early promise. A peculiar and diabolical sense of humor was wont to afflict him in what should have been his most serious moments."

Sir Stafford's Colleagues in Malaya, dependable but dull people who had "already made up their minds."

Mrs. Nathaniel Edge, the only woman member of the group in Malaya who, despite being well known as having "bees in her bonnet," was no fool when it came down to plain facts. She saw, she listened and she played safe.

Lady Lucy Cleghorn, an old friend of Stafford Nye's, who shares his interest in rare wildflowers, and once traveled to the Balkans in search of them.

Daphne Theodofanous, a.k.a. "Mary Ann," a.k.a. **Countess Renata Zerkowski,** who approaches Stafford Nye in the airport at Frankfurt with a plan that she says will save her life. She later becomes his guide to the secret organization.

Pamela Nye, Sir Stafford Nye's deceased sister, whose face resembled his, and also that of Daphne Theodofanous

Mr. Sidney Cook, a passenger to South Africa

Joan, a little girl in the airport who reaches out for Stafford Nye's stuffed panda

Mother of the above child Joan, "a nice fat woman" going to Australia

Lady Matilda Cleckheaton, Stafford Nye's "Great Aunt Matilda." She plays an unexpectedly important role in the story.

Gordon Chetwynd, a colleague, or perhaps a superior, of Stafford Nye.

Cedric Lazenby, Prime Minister of the United Kingdom and a rather stupid man.

Bascombe, a colleague of Stafford Nye's, who "can be quite fun when he likes."

A Doctor and Some Nurse Creature, the first people Sir Stafford sees when he awakens after having been drugged at the airport in Frankfurt

Some Woman or Other Interested in Studying Archeology, and **A Man who was a Passionate Anti-vivisectionist,** two people with whom Stafford Nye remembers having spoken in the passenger lounge at Frankfurt

Old Leyland, another colleague of Stafford Nye's who "always talks a bit too much."

Gordon Chetwynd's Secretary

Colonel Munro, another colleague of Stafford Nye's, who is worried that Sir Stafford may be "up to something."

Henry Horsham, who is in "security." He has a mustache which he finds useful, as it conceals moments when if finds it difficult to avoid smiling.

Mrs. Worrit, Sir Stafford's housekeeper, a large woman with a rather small brain.

The Gentleman What Called for Sir Stafford's Clothes While He Was Out, a "man from the cleaners" whom the small-brained Mrs. Worrit allowed to search Sir Stafford's room

The Vicar, who is scheduled to have dinner with Aunt Matilda but who "can be put off" in favor of Stafford Nye.

The Organist, who is not a good musician, according to Aunt Matilda

Sybil, a child relative of Sir Stafford Nye for whom he buys a woolly panda at the airport in Frankfurt

Eric Pugh, a friend of Sir Stafford Nye, who gives him a friendly warning not to have "too much fun" with the department.

Mr. Robinson, whom we first met in the 1959 *Cat Among the Pigeons,* and then again in the 1965 *At Bertram's Hotel.* He knows all about money and where it comes from and where it goes, and he is part of British intelligence operations.

Winterton and **Old Cartison,** men in Stafford Nye's department who, according to Eric Pugh, wonder about Stafford Nye's honesty and believe he may be "up to something."

Colonel Ephraim Pikeaway, the head of the

British "Special Branch." We met him, along with Mr. Robinson, in the 1959 *Cat Among the Pigeons*. He has not changed very much, and continues to be "…surrounded as usual by an atmosphere of thick cigar smoke; with his eyes closed, only an occasional blink showed that he was awake and not asleep…"

Colonel Pikeaway's Secretary
Reverend McGill, pastor of the Baptist church around the corner from Colonel Pikeaway's office, whom the Colonel considers to be far more amusing than Sir George Packham, as there is "a splendid touch of hellfire about him."

Sir George Packham, an "undersecretary" or "minister" of the Government who visits Colonel Pikeaway at his office to question him about Stafford Nye's character.

Charleston, Conway and Courtauld, British foreign agents who were later found to be "crooked as sin."

A Magnificent Tenor of Unfortunately Overmagnificent Proportions who, many years ago, permanently spoiled Stafford Nye's appreciation for a certain Wagner opera

Lady Athelhampton, from whom Sir Stafford Nye receives an invitation to donate five guineas for a charity variety performance.

Sir Stafford Nye's Eldest Uncle, the husband of "Great Aunt Matilda" and the father of their two children

Horace, once the groom, then a coachman and finally Aunt Matilda's chauffeur, now aged about eighty

Old Lord Grampion who sold his Turners and even some of his ancestors (*paintings* of his ancestors, that is)

Geoffrey Gouldman who sold his paintings of horses by Stubbs, or something like that

Alexa, a great-great-great-grandmother of Sir Stafford Nye, a Hungarian countess or baroness. His great-great-great-grandfather fell in love with her while at the Embassy in Vienna.

Robert ("Robbie") Shoreham, an old friend of Aunt Matilda, and a famous physicist. His pet project, some years ago, was "Project B," which will have major significance in the present story. He is now an invalid living in the north of Scotland, spending most of his time listening to music, as his speech and walking are impaired.

Mildred ("Milly") Jean Cortman, the wife the American ambassador to Great Britain. She hosts an important dinner party at the Embassy one evening.

Sam Cortman, American Ambassador to Great Britain.

Sir John and Lady Aldborough, Herr von Roken and Frau von Roken, Charles Staggenham, the Minister of Social Security, and Mrs. Staggenham; a Dutchman and his Wife, Signor and Signora Gasparo from Italy, Count Reitner from Germany, Mr. and Mrs. Arbuthnot, An American Businessman, A Professor from One of the Universities in the Middle West; A Married Couple, (the Husband German, the Wife Predominantly, almost aggressively, American), and a Golden-haired Woman who knows all about Countess Renata Zerkowski, all dinner guests at the American Embassy.

Petronella and "**Stephen and his Crowd**," people who cause a disturbance outside the American Embassy in Grosvenor Square on the evening of the dinner party

A Chauffeur who drives Countess Renata Zerkowski's rented luxury car to the house near Godalming in Surrey

A Tall Grenadier of a Parlormaid, who opens the door at the house near Godalming.

Lord Altamount, the owner of the house near Godalming, where Stafford learns about the world-wide, evil organization that he will be asked to infiltrate.

Sir James Kleek, described by Lord Altamount as a "colleague," but actually a servant of his.

The Wife of a Certain Ambassador in Berlin Just Before the War who was moved to tears by one of Hitler's speeches, and then later realized that he had said nothing of substance

Two Manservants in Liveries at the Schloss in Bavaria

The Gräfin Charlotte von Waldsausen, née Charlotte Krapp. She heads a branch of the world-wide, evil organization at an eighteenth-century Schloss in Bavaria.

The Father of Charlotte Krapp, who owned the "vast Krapp yards" in Germany, whatever those were.

Two Middle-aged Women, perhaps High-class Nursing Attendants who assist the somewhat overweight Gräfin Charlotte (a.k.a. "Big Charlotte") to her feet whenever she needs to rise from her chair.

Tall, Fair-haired, Handsome Young Men stationed in the dining room of the Schloss, a kind of bodyguard for "Big Charlotte."

Franz Joseph, the true head of the Bavarian branch of the evil organization, who arrives at the Schloss just as dinner is ending.

Monsieur Grosjean, who presides at an important meeting in Paris.

Signor Vitelli, from Italy, who attends the important meeting in Paris.

Monsieur Poissonier, a member of the French government who is also at the meeting in Paris.

Monsieur Grosjean's Secretary

Monsieur Coin, the French Minister of Home Affairs

The Marshal, who makes a surprise visit at the important meeting in Paris. He is a man whose word had been not only law, but *above* law in France for many past years.

Air Marshal Kenwood, who attends an important meeting in the Cabinet Room at 10 Downing Street, with Prime Minister Cedric Lazenby presiding.

Admiral Philip Blunt, "a large formidable man, who tapped his fingers on the table and bided his time until his moment should come." He can be quite "blunt" in his language, especially when the Prime Minister of the United Kingdom says something stupid.

A Mild Man with an Asiatic Face and a Mongolian Smile at the important meeting in Downing Street

Professor Eckstein, Britain's top scientist, who also attends the Important Meeting in Downing Street.

Dr. Donaldson, Lady Matilda's doctor, who allows himself to be persuaded that Lady Matilda should go to Bavaria "for a cure."

Nurse Amy Leatheran, whom we met in the 1936 *Murder in Mesopotamia,* the action of which took place in 1931. She was the narrator of that story, and soon came to respect, appreciate and admire "that little foreigner, Hercule Poirot," and became his confidante and investigative assistant. Nurse Leatheran is still alive and well and living in England, currently looking after Lady Matilda Cleckheaton, Sir Stafford's great aunt.

Winston Churchill, Prime Minister and Minister of Defense of the United Kingdom during the Second World War, and then Prime Minister again from 1951 to 1955. Not a character in the present story, he is quoted by Colonel Pikeaway as having once said "The news from France is very bad."

Herr Heinrich Spiess Himself, Chancellor of Germany

Dr. Reichardt, a psychiatrist, who is called to the office of the German Chancellor for an important consultation.

"Nanny," perhaps Colonel Pikeaway's secretary or perhaps another employee in his office, one of whose tasks is to use a clothesbrush on the Colonel's suit to remove the habitual layer of cigar ash lying upon it whenever he needs to be made presentable.

Martin B., a government official who brought Adolph Hitler himself to Dr. Reichardt's establishment near Karlsruhe in 1945

Adolph Hitler, Chancellor of Germany from 1933 to 1945, not a character in the story but a person to whom there are numerous references.

A Beautiful Aryan Girl of Good Family whom Adolph Hitler allegedly married in South America after World War Two

A Son Born to Adolph Hitler and the Beautiful Aryan Girl

Anastasia Nikolaëvna, one of the daughters of Czar Nicholas II of Russia, who allegedly escaped when her family was assassinated during the Bolshevist Revolution. She is mentioned during a conversation about the possibility that Adolph Hitler survived World War Two and went to live in South America

An Argentinean Carpenter and a Good-looking Blonde who are, according to Colonel Pikeaway, the true parents of "The Young Siegfried" who claims to be Adolph Hitler's son

Karl Aguileros, the son of the Argentinean Carpenter and the Good-looking Blonde, who inherited his looks from his mother.

Clifford Bent, the son of an Oil King; **Roderick Kitelly,** a young man whose uncle owns a chain of restaurants; and **Jim Brewster,** a young man with beetle brows, who frowns and is perpetually suspicious, all of whom pay a visit to Sir Stafford Nye at his apartment

Lisa What's-her-Name, the Austrian girl, and **Leadenthal,** Professor Shoreham's "assistants," so described by Great Aunt Matilda

Professor John Gottlieb, whom Countess Renata Zerkowski consults on the subject of "Project Benvo."

Squadron Leader Andrews who flies a private airplane, taking Lord Altamount, Henry Horsham, Colonel Munro, Mr. Robinson and Sir James Kleek to Scotland

A Chauffeur in Scotland

Janet, an old Scottish woman of sixty odd, a servant at the home of Professor Shoreham

Miss Neumann, a tall, lean woman between fifty and sixty, Professor Shoreham's secretary

Miss Ellis, who has been Professor Shoreham's nurse for the past two days

Miss Bude, Professor Shoreham's former nurse who left just two days ago

Dr. McCulloch, who looks after the physical health of Professor Shoreham

French and German into English

Note: Although Hercule Poirot is not a character in this novel, several French expressions, and one German one, occur. They are translated below.

Chapter 4
Vous n'êtes pas un pêcheur sérieux. Vous avez des femmes avec vous.—You can't be a very serious fisherman. You have women with you.

Chapters 6 and 9
Ce n'est pas un garçon sérieux—He's not a serious guy

Chapter 10
millefeuille—the pastry known in America as "Napoleon," consisting of a custard-like filling between layers of puff pastry

Chapter 13
les jeunes—young people
Ma foi—Good heavens
Quel blague!—What a joke! (Correctly spelled *Quelle blague!*)
Bon dieu!—My God!

Chapter 15 *Canaille!*—Scoundrels

Chapter 17 *idée fixe*—obsession

Chapter 19
Auf wiedersehen—Good-bye (German)

COMMENTS

Passenger to Frankfurt is a fantasy with the realities of the late 1960s serving as background. Those realities: the Viet Nam War and the anti-War protests at American universities; civil disturbances related to race relations in the United States; the perpetual conflict between Israel and Palestine in the Middle East; increasing, senseless crime in America and Western Europe, including Britain; the widening "generation gap"—the list could go on, but anyone who was an adult by the mid-1960s remembers all of it very well.

Christie wrote an important Introduction to *Passenger to Frankfurt,* which is worth reading carefully, and also worth reviewing once or twice as you move through the novel. You will not be able to enjoy this book if you feel that the book must be believable. It is fantasy, just as science fiction is fantasy.

In a nutshell, the fantasy in *Passenger to Frankfurt* is that the civil disturbances and student protests of the period are carefully controlled by a wealthy, secret neo-Fascist organization bent on creating worldwide anarchy by controlling the minds of the world's youth.

A reader who has become disgusted with government, politicians, scientists (psychiatrists in particular), and who is fed up with violent crime and the excuses that are made for it by lawyers and psychologists, will love *Passenger to Frankfurt.* Are you sick and tired of politicians and their lies? Are you unimpressed with the idea of wealth for its own sake? All of this is soundly trashed by Christie in *Passenger to Frankfurt.* It helps, too, if you have a sense of humor and are not in the habit of taking your work, your friends and yourself too seriously, because the protagonist, Sir Stafford Nye, is a cynical, non-serious type who will accompany you through the story.

Passenger to Frankfurt cannot be recommended as a "first Christie experience" since it is very atypical. A plan might be to read the 1951 *They Came to Baghdad,* the 1954 *So Many Steps to Death* and then *Passenger to Frankfurt* in that order and in rapid succession in order to be in the correct frame of mind for the last one.

Nemesis (1971)

SETTING

Nemesis was first published in 1971 but we are asked to remember the events of the 1964 *A Caribbean Mystery* as having taken place "about a year and a half ago," and so we may place the action of *Nemesis* in about 1966. In the 1957 *What Mrs. McGillicuddy Saw,* the action of which takes place in 1956, Miss Marple's age was specifically stated to be eighty-nine. That would make Miss Marple ninety-nine years old in *Nemesis,* a somewhat unrealistic age. We should probably imagine her to be about seventy-five years old in the present story, since she travels without difficulty in a motor coach, participates in a tour of homes and gardens which lasts for several days, and has a good deal of walking to do.

Regarding geographic consistency, fans of the Miss Marple stories must once again adjust their thinking as to the location of the village of St. Mary Mead. In the past, the village was described as being in the real county of Berkshire in one novel, and in the fictitious counties of Downshire and Radfordshire in at least two other novels, but in any case "somewhere west of London" was the general location for the village. In the present story, we learn that St. Mary Mead is "about twenty-five miles south of London" and that it is near a town called Loomouth, on the English Channel coast, probably in the county of Sussex.

None of this has very much importance, of

course, since the village of St. Mary Mead is not described in the current novel at all, and Miss Marple's home is a setting only in the brief opening scene. Miss Marple does comment, later in the story in answer to a casual question, that St. Mary Mead "has experienced considerable development" in recent years, a subject that was thoroughly treated in the 1962 *The Mirror Crack'd*, in which we learned of the new supermarket, the new housing development, etc.

Early in the story, Miss Marple travels to London and stays briefly at the St. George Hotel, which is described in her thoughts as "quite a modest place" by comparison with the luxurious Bertram's Hotel where she had stayed at her generous nephew's expense a year earlier, in the 1965 *At Bertram's Hotel*. Two scenes take place in London at the office of a small firm of lawyers. The building is somewhat old fashioned and has no elevator.

The main setting for the story is a village called Jocelyn St. Mary, the location of which is not specified. In this village, there is an inn called The Golden Boar, and Miss Marple visits the post office and a wool shop where she gossips with a postal employee and the owner of the wool shop. While staying in the village, Miss Marple is invited to stay for a couple of days at the home of three impoverished, middle-aged sisters. It is a gracious Georgian-period home called The Old Manor House which, though still comfortably furnished, shows signs of considerable neglect due to the poverty of its occupants. Furniture within the house, for example, is of good quality but has not been kept clean and polished. The house is very large but there is no live-in servant, the only servant being a woman who comes each morning to cook and do housework. The grounds of The Old Manor House are also very much neglected for the same reason, a greenhouse and other outbuildings having fallen into complete ruin and areas that were formerly well-planned and maintained lawns and perennial flower gardens now being overrun by weeds.

While visiting the post office, where paperbound novels are sold, Miss Marple notices with distaste the cover of one book picturing a naked woman with bloody scars on her body and a male assailant holding a knife, clearly a semi-pornographic, violence-filled thriller. This is a reference not only to a certain kind of popular literature but also apparently to the recent increase in crimes, including sex crimes, in England. Among the books displayed at the post office is one entitled *Whatever Happened to Baby Jane?*, and this gives rise to a brief conversation between Miss Marple and a postal employee on the subject of crimes against children, although the book was probably a novelization based on the 1963 American film of that title, which was *not* about "crimes against children."

There are numerous references to sex-related crimes in the story, as there have been in several recent Christie novels. In fact, the crime that Miss Marple is asked to investigate is that of a young girl whose brutal murder, several years earlier, had been attributed to her lover, a young man with a history of offences, including sexual ones. On this subject, there are the usual—that is to say, "usual" in recent Christie novels—negative references to young criminals being let off with minimal sentences, "suspended sentences," with the term "diminished responsibility" often being applied to the cases. There are also several references to the crime of rape, and at least two characters express the view that many of the "rapes" currently being reported are probably not really rapes at all. They are consensual sexual acts that are later falsely reported as "rapes" at the encouragement of the "victims'" mothers in order to deny the young women's willing participation in the sexual acts. In Chapter 11, Dr. Wanstead, a psychologist, states:

> "Girls, you must remember, are far more ready to be raped nowadays than they used to be. Their mothers insist, very often, that they should call it rape."

In Chapter 14, the lawyer Mr. Broadribb states:

> "Well, we all know what rape is nowadays. Mum tells the girl she's got to accuse the young man of rape even if the young man hasn't had much chance, with the girl at him all the time to come to the house while Mum's away at work or Dad's gone on holiday. Doesn't stop badgering him until she's forced him to sleep with her. Then, as I say, Mum tells the girl to call it rape."

It may come as a surprise to Christie readers that the above notion of "girls being ready to be raped" was mentioned in a Christie novel written many years earlier. In the 1948 *There Is a Tide*, the protagonist Lynn Marchmont has just returned to England after serving in the Wrens during wartime. Her mother comments:

> "...there have been dreadful things in the papers lately. All these discharged soldiers—they attack girls."

Lynn's response:

> "I expect the girls ask for it."

STORY

It is late spring or early summer of 1966. One

morning Miss Marple notices in the newspaper the death notice of Jason Rafiel. Miss Marple had met Mr. Rafiel about a year and a half earlier while enjoying a pleasant holiday on the Caribbean island of St. Honoré, where she had obtained Mr. Rafiel's help in solving three murders and preventing a fourth. Miss Marple is surprised, about a week later, to receive a letter from Mr. Rafiel's London attorneys asking her to visit them. At their office, the lawyers surprise Miss Marple further by informing her that Mr. Rafiel had instructed them to present Miss Marple with 20,000 pounds if she would consent to accepting "a certain proposition."

Miss Marple deduces that the "proposition" must have something to do with a crime, since it was the solution of a crime that brought her and Mr. Rafiel together a short time ago. She accepts the "proposition," and a few days later she is contacted by Famous Houses and Gardens of Great Britain, a touring organization which explains that Mr. Rafiel has arranged for her a pleasant three-week coach tour of some interesting homes and gardens.

During the tour, the group settles itself at an inn in the village of Jocelyn St. Mary where, to Miss Marple's surprise, she is approached by a local woman with an invitation to stay at their home for a few days. The woman explains that Mr. Rafiel had written to her and her two sisters and asked them to welcome Miss Marple into their home. Clearly it was Mr. Rafiel's wish that Miss Marple be brought into contact with these three women.

At the three ladies' home Miss Marple learns of the murder of a young girl a few years earlier, and of the young man who went to prison as her murderer. He was none other than Michael Rafiel, Jason Rafiel's son. Miss Marple then understands that it is her task to disprove Michael's guilt by unmasking the true killer. A second murder takes place but Miss Marple solves the mystery just in time to prevent her own murder.

CHARACTERS

Miss Jane Marple, an elderly spinster living in the village of St. Mary Mead. In the 1957 *What Mrs. McGillicuddy Saw*, her age was specifically stated to be eighty-nine, but in this story, we are asked to think of her as somewhat younger, as one character describes her age as being "seventy, or nearer eighty." This is Miss Marple's eleventh appearance in a Christie novel. Her principal techniques as a sleuth are a refusal to believe anything anyone says to her until she has personally verified it, and to insist that "the worst is so often true."

In *Nemesis*, Miss Marple is "appointed" to solve an old murder case by old Mr. Rafiel, whom we met in the 1964 *A Caribbean Mystery*, because of her strong belief in justice.

Elizabeth Quantril, not a character in the story, but whose death notice appears in the same newspaper as Mr. Rafiel's.

Jason Rafiel, a very rich, self-made millionaire who happened to be staying at the Golden Palm Hotel on the Caribbean island of Saint-Honoré when Miss Marple was there on a holiday in the 1964 *A Caribbean Mystery*. Mr. Rafiel was a crotchety, insulting old man who got away with his rudeness simply because he was so rich. Nobody escaped Mr. Rafiel's insulting treatment, including Miss Marple. When two deaths occurred on the island, and Miss Marple felt sure that the two deaths were related, she realized that nobody on the island would take her suspicions seriously, regarding her as "just an old lady from England." But since Mr. Rafiel was wealthy—and therefore respected by everyone on the island—Miss Marple appealed to him and successfully obtained his assistance in solving the mystery, earning Mr. Rafiel's respect and admiration.

Jason Rafiel's Wife, who died very young.

Jason Rafiel's Elder Daughter who married but had no children

Jason Rafiel's Younger Daughter who died at age fourteen

Michael Rafiel, Jason Rafiel's son. In the 1964 *A Caribbean Mystery*, nobody had mentioned Michael Rafiel, for good reasons. He has always been a thoroughly unsatisfactory person.

Raymond and Joan West, Miss Marple's nephew and his wife. Raymond is a very successful author of "clever books" and Joan is a somewhat out-of-date painter. They are not characters in this novel but Miss Marple mentions them briefly, as it was they who sent her on her beautiful holiday in the Caribbean to help her recuperate from pneumonia.

Major Palgrave, the murder victim in the 1964 *A Caribbean Mystery*. He was a lonely old ex-soldier whom everyone avoided because he told long, boring stories of his experiences in Africa and other places. He was murdered because he recognized someone on the island whom he knew to be a murderer.

Esther Walters (now Esther Anderson), Mr. Rafiel's private secretary in *A Caribbean Mystery*. She was a widow with a daughter still in school at the time. She tolerated Mr. Rafiel's insulting and unkind treatment of her because she was exceedingly well paid. Her reward for loyal service was a 50,000-pound legacy upon Mr. Rafiel's death. She is now married to a Mr. Edmund Anderson.

Edmund Anderson, the new husband of the former Esther Walters

Arthur Jackson, Mr. Rafiel's nurse-attendant in *A Caribbean Mystery.* Miss Marple had thought of him as "a rather doubtful character." He did not continue to work for Mr. Rafiel when the latter returned to England.

Lord Somebody, who lives in Jersey or Guernsey, for whom Arthur Jackson worked upon Mr. Rafiel's return to England.

Miss Knight, not a character in this story but a live-in companion whom Miss Marple's generous nephew Raymond had insisted on providing for her in the 1962 *The Mirror Crack'd.* Miss Marple could not stand her because she said things like "And how are we feeling today?" to which Miss Marple would acidly reply, "*I* am feeling quite well. I cannot speak for *you!*" Miss Knight monitored Miss Marple's food intake to an oppressive degree, insisted that she follow Dr. Haydock's orders to the letter in the matter of physical activity, and was in general an extremely maddening person. Fortunately, towards the end of the story, a relative of Miss Knight's asked her to come and live in another part of England and Miss Marple enthusiastically bade her farewell.

Cherry Baker, a cheerful young married woman who lived in "The Development," a tract of new houses all looking alike, on the edge of St. Mary Mead in the earlier story *The Mirror Crack'd.* She came to Miss Marple's cottage each morning to do housework. She could not remember to use the term "drawing room," having formed the modern habit of calling that room "the lounge," as most young people had also done by that time. She had the somewhat annoying habit of singing popular songs while operating "a virulent Hoover" instead of quietly using a brush and dustpan as Miss Marple would have preferred, but her work was satisfactory in general. Towards the end of that story, she and her husband moved into the rooms over Miss Marple's kitchen and they have lived there ever since, much to Miss Marple's delight, as Cherry, who is an excellent cook, looks after her and Cherry's husband is handy with repairs and home maintenance.

Jim Baker, Cherry's handsome, blond giant of a husband. He likes assembling model airplanes, listening to recorded classical music at full volume, and eating the scrumptious meals Cherry produces.

Little Gary Hopkins, a local brat whom Miss Marple effectively corrected for torturing a cat on one occasion.

Old George, another in a long line of "lazy, old gardeners" in Christie's novels. This one "works" for Miss Marple, as she is now too old and feeble to attend to her garden herself, but he does it so poorly, and the garden is so unsatisfactory looking, that Miss Marple has repositioned her favorite chair in order *not* to view the garden through the window unless specifically looking through the window with a purpose.

Among Old George's annoying habits is planting the wrong colors of flowers despite Miss Marple's explicit instructions. For further comments on Christie's "lazy old gardeners," see the *Comments* section for the 1962 *The Mirror Crack'd.*

Miss Bartlett, a thick-set woman in a shabby but tough tweed skirt. She engages Miss Marple in some friendly gardening conversation one day outside her cottage.

Mrs. Hastings, a new resident of St. Mary Mead who lives in "one of those new houses at the end of Gibraltar Road." Miss Bartlett is temporarily living with her and helps her with her gardening.

Mr. Broadribb, the senior member of the law firm Broadribb & Schuster in London, Mr. Rafiel's attorneys. At Mr. Broadribb's request, Miss Marple visits him at his office.

Mr. Schuster, Mr. Broadribb's junior partner.

Canon Prescott, who was on holiday on the island of Saint-Honoré when Miss Marple was there in the 1964 *A Caribbean Mystery.* He was fond of children and disliked un–Christian gossip. He lives in the north of England with his unmarried sister.

Joan Prescott, Canon Prescott's sister, who was also at Saint-Honoré in the earlier story. Unlike her brother, she enjoyed gossip and indulged in it with Miss Marple whenever the Canon was out of earshot. She is not a character in this story but Miss Marple writes her a letter asking for the address of Esther Walters, Mr. Rafiel's former private secretary.

George, the taxi driver who is incorrectly addressed as "Edward" by Miss Marple. He works for the local taxicab company, which was originally called "Inch's Taxi Service" but is currently named "Arthur's Car Hire."

Mrs. Sandbourne, the leader of the guided tour of houses and gardens. She is about thirty-five years old.

Mrs. Geraldine Riseley-Porter, a dictatorial old lady, one of four elderly ladies in the tour group.

Miss Joanna Crawford, the niece of the aforementioned loud, dictatorial lady.

Colonel and Mrs. Walker, middle-aged British members of the tour group

Henry and Mamie Butler, middle-aged American members of the tour group. They are somewhat reminiscent of Mr. and Mrs. Gardener in the 1941 *Evil Under the Sun.*

Miss Elizabeth Temple, the retired headmistress of Fallowfield, an excellent school for girls. One of her students was once engaged to Michael Rafiel. Then she died "of love."

A New, Rather Young Headmistress with "Rather Advanced, Progressive Ideas," who is Elizabeth Temple's successor at Fallowfield.

Professor Wanstead, another member of the tour group, who is a pathologist and a psychologist with a special interest in the criminal mind.

Richard Jameson, another member of the tour group, a tall, thin man aged about thirty, with a "highly technical vocabulary." He is an architect, and so when the group tours old houses he provides somewhat overly-detailed explanations of the historic architecture.

Miss Lumley, age approximately seventy, a member of the tour group. She lives in Somerset and complains of the difficulty in getting hardworking, knowledgeable gardeners in recent years.

Miss Bentham, also approximately age seventy, and also a resident of Somerset. She is traveling with her friend, Miss Lumley.

Mr. Caspar, a member of the tour group whose nationality is not known. He speaks with Professor Wanstead in both French and German, his knowledge of English being minimal.

Miss Cooke, a "solidly-built middle-aged lady with blonde hair." She is a member of the tour group and her face is faintly familiar to Miss Marple.

Miss Barrow, a thin, dark-haired middle aged lady who is traveling with Miss Cooke

Emlyn Price, another member of the tour group, a young man who is probably a university student.

A Local Caretaker at a Queen Anne manor house which is on the tour. He is mildly annoyed when the young architect, Richard Jameson, usurps his occupation and explains the architectural details and history to the group.

Holman, a famous landscape architect of the past who designed the garden at the Queen Anne manor house between 1798 and 1800.

Verity Hunt, a young girl who became an orphan when both of her parents were killed in an airplane crash. Clotilde and Anthea Bradbury-Scott, who were friends of the girl's parents, then became her guardians. She was brutally murdered just as she was about to be married.

Mrs. Lavinia Glynne, a childless widow who lives at The Old Manor House in Jocelyn St. Mary with her two sisters, Clotilde and Anthea. It is she who goes to the Golden Boar in the village to invite Miss Marple to their home for a few days upon the suggestion of the recently-deceased Mr. Rafiel.

Old Colonel Bradbury-Scott, an uncle of the Bradbury-Scott sisters and Mrs. Glynne. His wife had died during the birth of their third child, who also died during the birth. His older children both died later—the son died in the war and the married daughter died in Australia. And so he left his home, the Old Manor House, to his nieces Clotilde, Anthea and Lavinia.

Clotilde Bradbury-Scott, the eldest of three sisters. The task of identifying Verity Hunt's body, when it was found six months after she was murdered, fell to Clotilde. She was grief stricken and "never got over it."

Anthea Bradbury-Scott, the youngest of the three sisters, and somewhat "scatty."

The Father of Lavinia, Anthea and Clothilde. He was a major in the Artillery

Janet, a local woman who comes to the Old Manor House each morning to cook and do general housework. She provides Miss Marple with a good deal of information about the Bradbury-Scott sisters and the story of Verity Hunt's murder.

Clotilde Bradbury-Scott's Friends who died in an airplane accident in Spain or Italy. They were the parents of Verity Hunt.

The Princes and the Broads, families whose numerous tombstones Miss Marple notices in the village churchyard.

"Little Melanie," a child whose grave marker in the churchyard Miss Marple notices.

"An Old Man Moving in Slow Motion," who is tidying the graveyard in Jocelyn St. Mary. He provides Miss Marple with a few additional facts about the village of Jocelyn St. Mary. We are thus treated to *two* lazy old gardeners in this novel, the other being Miss Marple's own lazy, tea-drinking, contradictory Old George.

The Police Officer in charge of the murder case against Michael Rafiel. He was "a most reliable detective-superintendent with very good experience in these matters."

An Aunt of Miss Marple who claimed that she could smell when someone was lying

Jack, the Husband of the Lie-sniffing Aunt, who fortunately did not hire the man whose lies his wife smelled

A Young Man whom Jack did not hire, on the advice of his wife who could smell the young man's lies

Nora Broad, a young girl who disappeared about the same time that Verity Hunt was killed, and who was also assumed to be killed, although her body was never found.

Mrs. Blackett, who thought Nora was "in the family way" when she "went off with someone as promised her things..."

Nancy Broad, Nora Broad's mother

A Woman at the reception desk at the hospital in Carristown

Sister Barker, Mr. Reckitt, and **Nurse Edmunds,** personnel at the hospital in Carristown

Sir Henry Clithering, an old friend of Miss Marple's and, coincidentally, of Miss Elizabeth Temple's. Sir Henry had retired from Scotland Yard many years ago. He had become an admirer of Miss Marple even before we first met him in the 1942 *The Body in the Library*. In the 1950 *A Murder Is Announced* he fondly and enthusiastically referred to her as "the super-pussy of all old pussies" and encouraged all younger police officers to take Miss Marple and all of her ideas seriously.

Mr. Courtney, the vicar at Jocelyn St. Mary who conducts a memorial service

Undertakers Suitably Attired, with Proper Mourning Faces

Mrs. Merrypit, the apparent owner of the Merrypit's Wool Shop in Jocelyn St. Mary, who gossips freely with Miss Marple on all subjects

Geoffrey Grant, Bert Williams, Billy Thompson and **Harry Langford,** who were all suspects in the murder of Verity Hunt

"Mrs. Vinegar," Miss Marple's name for a postal employee who has "a rather vinegary face"

Farmer Plummer's Daughter who liked seeing pigs killed

Dr. Stokes, the Coroner

Archdeacon Brabazon, an elderly clergyman in gaiters, "well over seventy," who turned up at the funeral service for Miss Elizabeth Temple in Jocelyn St. Mary.

A Girl Who Was Planting Out Lettuces and who was in the same class in school as Nora Broad. She provides Miss Marple with some facts and opinions about Nora's character.

An Official from the Public Prosecutor's Office

Sir James Lloyd, the Assistant Commissioner of Scotland Yard

Sir Andrew McNeil, the Governor of Manstone Prison

The Home Secretary

Jonathan Birkin, Miss Marple's "village parallel" for Michael Rafiel

Comments

Although not to be recommended as a "first Christie experience," since it lacks the sparkle and humor of so many of Christie's detective novels from earlier decades, *Nemesis* is a must-read for fans of Miss Marple. It would be a good idea to read *The Mirror Crack'd* and *A Caribbean Mystery* just before reading *Nemesis*, since the latter story includes many references to characters and events in the two earlier books. This is especially important to an understanding of the relationships between Miss Marple and Jason Rafiel and between Miss Marple and Cherry Baker.

Like all of Christie's detective novels, *Nemesis* has its own particular uniqueness. In this story, Miss Marple is "summoned from beyond the grave" to solve a murder, but she receives no instruction about the murder. Is it a murder in the distant or recent past? Is it a future murder that she must try to prevent? She successfully answers these questions and solves the case brilliantly, although unfortunately she is unable to prevent another murder from taking place "on her watch."

The repetitiousness of some of Christie's later novels seems to be absent in *Nemesis* and the characterization is unusually interesting for a late novel. The characters are believable and their actions are consistent with their personalities. Certain readers will find the murder motive to be a little far-fetched but, aside from that, the story is well conceived and very well told.

Nemesis is a bit overpopulated by old ladies, which may or may not affect your enjoyment of the book. The only major character who is not an old lady is an old clergyman. If the youthful casts that characterized some of Christie's earlier novels provided you with most of your enjoyment in reading them, then you may not care very much for *Nemesis*. Actually, considering the fact that Christie was about eighty-one years old when she wrote *Nemesis*, it is probably all for the best that she focused on the thoughts and attitudes of aging females instead of trying to imagine, as she did in *Endless Night*, the private musings of young men.

As she has done ever since the late 1940s, Christie again reminds us that environment and "advantages"—as well as conscientious parenting—have little value in shaping the character of any person. If a person is a murderer, he or she was *born* to be one—no ifs, ands or buts. In the case of Michael Rafiel, all of the characters who describe him—and there are several who have occasion to do so—agree unanimously that he was just born bad.

Elephants Can Remember (1972)

SETTING

The year is 1972 and we know that the season is spring because of a brief remark about "bulb flowers, mostly tulips" being in bloom. No current events of the period are mentioned in the story, but the year is established when Mrs. Oliver searches for "last year's address book, the one for 1971."

It should be mentioned here that, unfortunately, Christie was not careful about chronology in this story. At one point in the story, Hercule Poirot visits a cemetery and on a tombstone reads "1952" as being the year of the deaths of three characters, two of whom are parents of the character Celia Ravenscroft. It is repeatedly stated that Celia was "about twelve or fourteen years old" when her parents died, which would make her at least thirty-one years old in 1972, but her age is given as twenty-five or twenty-six. There is also a woman "about fifty years of age" whose daughter, introduced just two pages earlier, was said to be "about thirty-five years of age." If that is true, then the mother was about fifteen years old when she gave birth to her daughter. In any case, the reader is advised to disregard most of the comments by characters on the subject of how many years ago one event or another occurred, and the exact ages of the characters. Of even less importance is Mrs. Oliver's statement that she has known Hercule Poirot "for about twenty years." We know that she met him in the 1936 *Cards on the Table,* thirty-six years earlier.

The dilemma for Christie was that she created several characters who were "elderly" when they first appeared in her stories, having no idea that several decades into the future she would still be using those characters in her writing. Hercule Poirot, for example, was first introduced in the 1920 *The Mysterious Affair at Styles* as a retiree from the Belgian police force. Christie, at the time, had no idea that she would ever write a second detective novel, not to mention sixty-five more, and that Hercule Poirot would be featured in a book that she would write fifty-two years later. Miss Marple was introduced as an "old lady" in the 1930 *Murder at the Vicarage.* Christie unfortunately assigned her the specific age of eighty-nine in the 1957 *What Mrs. McGillicuddy Saw,* and then featured her in several additional novels, including the 1971 *Nemesis.*

There must have been some well-publicized studies about twins at the time, studies that seemed to indicate that, even if separated at birth and brought up under widely different conditions, twin children later showed remarkable similarities in their attitudes, tastes and general personalities. The conclusion was that genetics were a stronger determining factor in a person's personality than previously acknowledged, and Christie was undoubtedly elated to learn of this, as she had been lecturing her readers for several decades on the relative *unimportance* of "good parenting." (For a discussion of this subject, see the *Comments* section for the 1958 *Ordeal by Innocence.*) In *Elephants Can Remember* there are assertions by at least two characters on the subject. "I think we now realize that heredity does more than environment," declares Mrs. Burton-Cox, an overbearing politician who seeks as much knowledge as possible about her potential daughter-in-law's heredity.

The physical settings of *Elephants Can Remember* are unremarkable and relatively unimportant. The opening scene takes place in Ariadne Oliver's apartment in London, which is not described. In earlier novels she had lived "in Harley Street, among the doctors," but we learned in the 1966 *Third Girl* that she had recently moved several times, and we are told at the beginning of the present story that she lives in Eaton Terrace. Soon the setting moves to an unnamed restaurant or club where a literary luncheon takes place, then to Hercule Poirot's apartment, which we know to be in Whitehaven Mansions, an art deco building where he has lived since about 1935, although the forgetful Mrs. Oliver calls it "Whitefriars Mansions." Christie herself had mistakenly referred to it as "Whitehouse Mansions" in the 1959 *Cat Among the Pigeons.*

Scenes take place at various residences in towns and villages that are not described or even named, although the fictitious village of Chipping Bartram, the scene of a tragedy nearly twenty years earlier, becomes an important setting. The village is not described but through dialogue we learn that it has a pub called The George and Flag. The village must be near the seacoast, as a house called Overcliffe, not far from the village, had been the scene of the tragedy referred to, and it is near "cliffs overlooking the sea."

A scene takes place at a residence in the real town of Cheltenham, which is favorably described in these terms:

> Mrs. Oliver looked at Cheltenham with approval. As it happened, she had never been to Cheltenham before. How nice, said Mrs. Oliver to herself, to see some houses that are really like houses, proper houses.

Casting her mind back to youthful days, she remembered that she had known people, or at least her relations, her aunts, had known people who lived at Cheltenham. Retired people usually. Army or Navy. It was the sort of place, she thought, where one would like to come and live if one had spent a good deal of time abroad. It had a feeling of English security, good taste and pleasant chat and conversation.

As to the term "proper houses," Christie dévotés will know at once what is meant by it: "Georgian period" or "Queen Anne period" houses, since those are the only houses of which Christie has ever spoken favorably, aside from expensively and tastefully decorated and furnished *modern* ones.

Hercule Poirot has occasion to visit two characters who live in Geneva in Switzerland, but neither the city nor their homes are described. In general, the settings—both physical and historical—have little importance in *Elephants Can Remember*. In a few of Christie's later novels she makes a point of commenting extensively on the bizarre hair and clothing fashions of young people, and drug use among the young. This was a dominant theme featured in the 1966 *Third Girl*, but in *Elephants Can Remember* there is only the following comment by the elderly Mrs. Oliver about her goddaughter, who is a university lecturer aged about twenty-five:

"—very modern, you know. Goes about with long-haired people in queer clothes. I don't think she takes drugs..."

Since at least as early as the 1963 *The Clocks*, Christie seems to have taken an interest in the living arrangements of the aging population, and that subject is fully treated in the 1968 *By the Pricking of My Thumbs*. (See the *Setting* sections for each of those two novels.) In the course of the present story we visit several aging women who describe their feelings about their current living arrangements. One is a wealthy aristocrat who lives with "a faithful retainer," in a luxurious and probably very expensive complex of apartments described as "homes for the privileged." Another elderly woman, not of the "privileged class" but who had spent her life as a nursery governess, lives contentedly in a "somewhat dilapidated-looking cottage" that is provided for her by "the Council."

Story

It is spring of 1972 and detective story writer Ariadne Oliver reluctantly attends a literary luncheon for the first time. After the meal, a strong-willed, overbearing woman who is a politician of some kind, Mrs. Burton-Cox, steers Mrs. Oliver to a corner settee and tells her that she has an important question. It concerns a goddaughter of Mrs. Oliver's (one of many) whose name is Celia Ravenscroft. Mrs. Burton-Cox's question is "Did her mother kill her father or was it the father who killed the mother?" She explains that her son Desmond and Celia have been discussing marriage, and Mrs. Burton-Cox feels she must know the facts about Celia's parents before approving of the marriage. She hopes that Mrs. Oliver will approach Celia on the subject.

Mrs. Oliver resents this intrusion into private matters and tells Mrs. Burton-Cox that she can do nothing of the kind. Nevertheless, she is intrigued by the question. She contacts Hercule Poirot to discuss it, and the two of them decide to investigate the matter, dividing the investigation between them. Poirot will discuss the deaths of Celia's parents with all of the police authorities who had dealings with it, and Mrs. Oliver will speak with all of her old acquaintances who have memories of the incident, referring to them as "elephants" since elephants are reputed to have long memories.

Poirot and Mrs. Oliver successfully reveal all of the facts surrounding the death of Celia's parents, which they share not with Mrs. Burton-Cox but with the amiable young couple.

Characters

Ariadne Oliver, the detective story writer who made her first appearance in a Christie novel in the 1936 *Cards on the Table*, although she had appeared in short stories before that. Being a fat woman who likes eating apples, she resembles Agatha Christie herself in superficial ways. She also feels awkward in social settings, as Christie was also reported to feel. As to her fondness for apples, she lost her taste for those in her last adventure, the 1969 *Hallowe'en Party*, in which someone murdered a teenager by holding her head under the water in a bucket that had been used earlier for a bobbing-for-apples game. Her "woman's intuition," one of her trademarks in earlier novels, makes no appearance in the present story. As in *Hallowe'en Party* and *Dead Man's Folly*, it is she who draws Hercule Poirot into the story by appealing to him for help.

Maria, a servant of Mrs. Oliver who assists her in her toilette on the day of the literary luncheon.

Edwin Aubyn, a poet with whom Mrs. Oliver converses during the literary luncheon.

Sir Wesley Kent, Mrs. Oliver's other conversation partner during lunch.

Albertina, a foreign friend of Mrs. Oliver who had tried to persuade her to be less self-deprecating.

Maurine Grant, a friend of Mrs. Oliver's who is "great fun" and who is also at the literary luncheon.

Mrs. Burton-Cox, a stranger who approaches Mrs. Oliver rather aggressively at the literary luncheon, after the meal. A widow with a grown son, she has an active and successful political career. She is currently worried about her son's intentions of marrying a young woman of whose family background Mrs. Burton-Cox knows little, except that the girl's parents died in some kind of "suicide pact" tragedy.

Mrs. Burton-Cox's Husband, who refuses to travel without at least two of Mrs. Oliver's books.

Desmond Burton-Cox, Mr. and Mrs. Burton-Cox's son. More specifically, he is the adopted son of Mrs. Burton-Cox who married her current husband after the adoption. He is engaged to Celia Ravenscroft, a goddaughter of Mrs. Oliver.

Celia Ravenscroft, a goddaughter of Mrs. Oliver, one of many. She is about twenty-five years old. It has been some years since Mrs. Oliver has seen her or even thought about her, except when Celia sends her a card at Christmas.

Lady Margaret ("Molly") Ravenscroft, née Margaret Preston Grey. At the age of about thirty-five she died along with her husband—both of gunshot wounds. It appeared to be a murder/suicide, but the police never determined which of the pair did the killing, as blurred fingerprints of both were found on the revolver. As a young girl, Molly had spent time at a *pensionnat* in Paris, where she met Ariadne Oliver, who was of course at the time a young unmarried girl with a different surname.

Margaret Preston Grey's Mother whom Ariadne Oliver had the pleasure of meeting just once, when she came to Paris to visit her daughter at the *pensionnat* where Margaret and Ariadne were living.

Sir Alistair Ravenscroft, Celia Ravenscroft's father who died together with his wife in what was apparently a murder/suicide pact.

Louise, a literary friend of Ariadne Oliver. Seeing her at the literary reception, Mrs. Oliver seizes upon her in order to get free of the overbearing Mrs. Burton-Cox.

Hercule Poirot, the famous Belgian private investigator with the egg-shaped head and flamboyant moustache. He was already an elderly retiree when we first met him in the 1920 *The Mysterious Affair at Styles*. For some years now he has been using artificial coloring for his hair, which is sometimes described as "suspiciously black." Never having suffered from low self-esteem, even when younger, he continues to believe that he is extremely famous, although most of the people he has ever known are now "reposing with suitable memorial stones over them in churchyards."

George, Hercule Poirot's manservant whom we have met from time to time since he was introduced in the 1928 *The Mystery of the Blue Train*.

Miss Sedgwick, Ariadne Oliver's former secretary whom she misses very much.

Miss Livingstone, Ariadne Oliver's current secretary.

Great-aunt Alice, the owner of a very useful book entitled *Enquire Within upon Everything*

Mrs. Matcham, Celia's nursery governess at whom Celia was in the habit of throwing her boots.

Mrs. Matcham's Sister Gracie who died last year of cancer

Mariana Josephine Pontarlier, whose name Mrs. Oliver notices in an old address book. Mrs. Oliver believes she is dead.

Anna Braceby, a friend of Mrs. Oliver's who had lived "in that part of the world," where the tragedy had occurred, another possible "elephant who might remember."

Martha Leghorn at whose wedding Celia had worn an ugly, apricot-colored bridesmaid dress

Edward Ravenscroft, Celia's younger brother who is now a university student in Canada

Superintendent Spence, an old friend of Hercule Poirot's whom we met in the 1952 *Mrs. McGinty's Dead,* and later in the 1969 *Hallowe'en Party*. Hercule Poirot appeals to Superintendent Spence to introduce him to the police officer who was in charge of the Ravenscroft case.

Chief Superintendent Garroway, who was in charge of the Ravenscroft "suicide pact" case. He is "a tall, thin man with a lean, ascetic face, gray hair which left a small round spot like a tonsure so that he had a faint resemblance to an ecclesiastic." He had never been quite satisfied about the Ravenscroft case.

A Canadian Girl who once approached Hercule Poirot to find out the truth about her mother's guilt or innocence of a crime for which she was sent to prison, where she died. Superintendent Spence mentions the case to Poirot but he does not mention the Canadian girl's name. We recall that she was twenty-one-year-old Carla Lemarchant from the 1943 *Murder in Retrospect*.

A Girl Who Said She Had Once Seen a Murder Committed, also referred to by Superintendent Spence but not mentioned by name. She was thirteen-year-old Joyce Reynolds who boasted of having seen a murder, and who was then murdered herself, in the 1969 *Hallowe'en Party.*

Mrs. McGinty, yet another person mentioned by Superintendent Spence. She was the murder victim in the 1952 *Mrs. McGinty's Dead.*

Fred Wizell, the gardener who was working for the Ravenscrofts when they died. He was suspected of the crime by Mrs. Buckle, the Ravenscrofts' cleaning woman.

The Honorable Julia Carstairs, an old friend of Ariadne Oliver who now lives at Hampton Court in an old-age residence for "the privileged." More than seventy years old, she is another of Mrs. Oliver's "elephants who can remember," and she remembers the Ravenscrofts and their death. Her recollections are somewhat more exact than those of old Mrs. Matcham.

Emma, "a faithful retainer" who shares quarters with Julia Carstairs and waits on her

Moira, who looked dreadful in an unbecoming shade of apricot that the bridesmaids wore at the Llewellyns' wedding

Roddy Foster, a cousin of Julia Carstairs who knew the Ravenscrofts in India

Saint Teresa of Ávila, a sixteenth-century Spanish saint mentioned by Molly Ravenscroft to Julia Carstairs when she told of her desire to "start a new life."

Marlene Buckle, a plump woman, aged about thirty-five, who works in the chemist's shop in Chipping Bartram, the village near which the Ravenscrofts died

Mrs. Buckle, Marlene's mother, who was the Ravenscrofts' cleaning woman until about a month before their death. She is now "a thin, energetic woman of about fifty years of age." Yet another "elephant who can remember," her recollections about the Ravenscrofts and their death are quite exact.

Mrs. Buckle's Aunt Emma who came to live with the Buckles, and needed Mrs. Buckle's daily attention. This caused Mrs. Buckle to stop working for the Ravenscrofts about a month before they died.

Mrs. Buckle's Husband who heard, while spending time at the George and Flag, that Mrs. Ravenscroft drank. According to Mrs. Buckle, who was the Ravenscrofts' cleaning lady at the time, that was not true.

A Rather Nasty Sort of Fellow who came to see Mr. Ravenscroft, according to Mrs. Buckle

Mr. Edmunds, Edward Ravenscroft's tutor

A Nephew of the Ravenscrofts who, according to Mrs. Buckle, had been in trouble with the police

"Mrs. Jerryboy," Mrs. Buckle's attempted recollection of the name "Mrs. Jarrow," Molly Ravenscroft's married sister Dorothea ("Dolly") Jarrow. Molly and Dolly were twin sisters.

"Mrs. Jerryboy's Son," who is described by Mrs. Buckle as "shifty."

Miss Felicity Lemon, Hercule Poirot's efficient but hideous secretary, whose first appearance in an Hercule Poirot novel was the 1955 *Hickory, Dickory, Death,* but who had appeared earlier in short stories. Her only role in the present story is to remind Poirot of two appointments and to reschedule a third.

Mademoiselle Rouselle, a.k.a. "Maddy," Celia Ravenscroft's first French governess. Hercule Poirot visits her at her home in Switzerland. Her memories of the Ravenscroft family are clear but she refers Hercule Poirot to Celia's second governess, who was with the Ravenscroft family when Celia's parents died.

Mademoiselle Meauhourat, a.k.a. "Zélie," who became Celia's French governess after Mademoiselle Rouselle returned to Switzerland. Her accounting of the Ravenscroft tragedy will be most enlightening to Hercule Poirot.

Mrs. Rosentelle, Molly Ravenscroft's hairdresser who now lives and works in Cheltenham, where Mrs. Oliver pays her a visit.

Captain Jarrow, husband of Dorothea ("Dolly"), Molly Ravenscroft's twin sister.

Captain and Dorothea Jarrow's Two Children, a girl and a younger boy. The boy was struck by someone and then fell into a pool and drowned. There were conflicting stories about who it was that struck him.

Mr. Fothergill, an "old elephant" provided to Mrs. Oliver by Julia Carstairs for the purpose of recalling events at the time of the tragedy, but who proves unhelpful

Some People Called Marchant who had a child who was killed in India, mentioned by Mr. Fothergill

A Girl at the *pensionnat* in Paris who, Julia Carstairs recalls, was scolded by Mademoiselle Girand for having a picture of a variety actor over her bed

The Father of the Girl at the *pensionnat*. Unknown to Mademoiselle Girand, he was the variety actor in the picture over the girl's bed, a fact which highly amused the girl and her friends.

Mademoiselle Girand, the French mistress at the *pensionnat* who was annoyed to find a picture of a variety actor over the bed of a certain girl.

Monsieur Adolph, the violin master at the

pensionnat who was oblivious to the hero-worship of some of his young female students

A Manservant at the home of Dr. Willoughby who opens the door to Hercule Poirot

Dr. Willoughby the Elder, who had been interested in the case of Dorothea Jarrow. He had a special interest in genetics and the behavioral traits of twins.

Dr. Willoughby the Younger, who was quite a young man when his father was involved with Dorothea Jarrow, but who clearly recalls the case and who shares important facts with Hercule Poirot.

A Woman Who Killed a Friend because she thought she had been commanded by God to destroy the Devil

Mr. Goby, a "detective's detective" whom Hercule Poirot consults from time to time to acquire information. He first appeared in the 1928 *The Mystery of the Blue Train* and has reappeared several times to assist Poirot. He employs a small but excellent and efficient staff and can find out everything about anyone. His trademark eccentricity is never to look directly at the person with whom he is conversing, preferring to direct his gaze at some inanimate object in the room.

Cecil Aldbury, Mrs. Burton-Cox's first husband, who died in an automobile accident four years after they were married. He left a considerable sum of money to a secret mistress of whose existence Mrs. Burton-Cox was unaware.

Kathleen Fenn, Cecil Aldbury's secret mistress. She had a child whom she claimed to be that of Cecil Aldbury.

FRENCH INTO ENGLISH

Chapter 1

une femme formidable—a woman "to be reckoned with," one who is assertive and self-assured
savoir-faire—social sophistication or grace
cause célèbre—a celebrated law case, trial or controversy; one that inspires widespread interest

Chapter 2

chère madame—dear lady
Sirop de cassis—black currant liqueur, a favorite drink of Hercule Poirot's
crème de menthe—a green, mint flavored liqueur, another Poirot favorite
cause célèbre—(see above, Chapter 1)
à la recherche des éléphants—in search of elephants
Bon voyage—enjoy your trip

Chapter 3 *chère madame*—dear lady

Chapter 9

Sirop de Cassis—black currant liqueur
chère madame—dear lady
Qui va à la chasse perd sa place—A French proverb meaning "If you get out of line, you lose your place." Literal translation: "He who goes hunting loses his place."
Mon dieu—Good heavens

Chapter 10

Nom d'un petit bonhomme!—Well, I'll be damned! (Euphemism for the "sacrilegious" expression *Nom de Dieu! (The name of God)* which Poirot never utters

Chapter 13

pensionnat—any boarding school, although the term here refers to a French "finishing school" to which middle and upper-class girls from various countries were sent by their families to acquire fluency in French and other "accomplishments" as well as to have—under close supervision—artistic and musical experiences. Christie herself, as a teenager, spent a year or two in a *pensionnat* in Paris studying piano and voice and trying, unsuccessfully, to improve her French spelling.
Ce n'est pas convenable—It's not nice, it's not "fitting"
Sirop de Cassis—black currant liqueur

Chapter 16 *Chère madame*—dear lady

Chapter 19

pensionnat—(see above, Chapter 13)
Moi, j'aime les enfants—I'm fond of children

Chapter 20

pensionnat—(see above, Chapter 13)

COMMENTS

Elephants Can Remember is quite a pleasant story, although the reader is advised that, as in the case of the 1971 *Nemesis*, most of the characters are aging females and, just as in the earlier story, there is no real "action." There are simply conversations about a crime in the past. Fans of the Hercule Poirot-Ariadne Oliver team will enjoy the book, as both sleuths do quite a bit of investigating, but new Christie readers—especially young readers—may find it quite dull.

There are references to characters in at least three earlier Christie novels—*Murder in Retro-*

spect, Mrs. McGinty's Dead and Hallowe'en Party—but those references are simply interesting reminiscences by Hercule Poirot and are unimportant in the present story. Therefore there is no need to have read them before reading *Elephants Can Remember*, although if one has already read at least two or three of Christie's novels featuring Ariadne Oliver, one's enjoyment of this novel will be enhanced. This is Mrs. Oliver's seventh and final appearance in a Christie novel.

As is the case with all of Christie's novels written during the 1960s and 1970s, this book cannot be recommended as a "first Christie experience" since it is typical of Christie's period of decline rather than of her prime. Beginning Christie readers are advised to choose titles that first appeared before 1960, most of Christie's masterpieces having been produced between about 1930 and 1960.

Postern of Fate (1974)

Setting

The copyright date for *Postern of Fate* is 1973 and there is no reason not to place the action in that year or perhaps in 1972, as no current events mentioned in the story contradict that supposition. In fact there are no current events mentioned in the story at all. As is the case in most of Christie's later novels, we are asked not to be very demanding in the matter of chronological consistency. The two main characters, Tommy and Tuppence Beresford, appear to be an older couple with two grown children and at least three grandchildren, the youngest of whom is just four years old. The three grandchildren mentioned in the book are those of their daughter Deborah, who in the 1941 *N or M?* was about twenty years old and unmarried. That would make her about fifty-one or fifty-two in the present story, somewhat old to be the mother of a four-year-old. Furthermore, two of the grandchildren are said to be twins, but when Deborah visits her parents toward the end of the story, bringing the three children with her, they are aged four, eleven and thirteen, and so there are no "twins." When Christie spoke of "twins," she may have been thinking of Deborah and her twin brother Derek, who were Tommy and Tuppence's own children. Tommy and Tuppence themselves were at least twenty-two years old in the 1922 *The Secret Adversary*, the action of which takes place immediately after the end of the First World War in approximately 1920, and so if we are so eccentric as to expect chronological authenticity, Tommy and Tuppence must now be about seventy-two years old. Probably we are expected to imagine them to be about a decade younger.

In the present story, Tommy and Tuppence live in a newly-acquired but very old house in the fictitious coastal village of Hollowquay, which is aptly named since English localities whose names end in "-quay" are always coastal settlements. The village is described as a summer resort that is crowded in August but much quieter at other times.

Tommy continues to travel to London each day for reasons that are never explained to us, and there are no conversations between Tommy and Tuppence on the subject of his work. Perhaps he is still working for the "Secret Service."

The Beresfords' "new home" is not described in detail but it is a substantial home with a ground floor plus a "first floor" ("second floor" in American terms) probably consisting of just bedrooms and one bathroom and, in addition, a "second floor" ("third floor" in American terms) consisting apparently of one large room that the Beresfords use as a "book room." When they acquired the house they agreed to purchase a large collection of old books that the previous owners were not interested in transporting or disposing of. It is among a large collection of tattered children's books and classic novels that the first clue in the present mystery is discovered.

The house, which is called The Laurels, but which has had a succession of different names since it was built at some time before the First World War, was in somewhat poor condition when the Beresfords acquired it. They have been busy with repairs and updates for the plumbing and electrical service since moving in. There is a garage for their car. A few small outbuildings on the property are in poor condition and contain a few relics left by past generations of homeowners such as dilapidated garden furniture, croquet sets, and antiquated children's toys, in particular a large rocking horse. Among these relics of the past the Beresfords discover other clues to the mystery.

Although there are no "current events" mentioned in the story, there are some references to modern living conditions which include some amusing comments about the frustrations of homeowners on the subject of electrical and plumbing repairs. Tommy Beresford's thoughts on this subject:

> He was used, now, to the general pattern of labor in the building trade, electrical trade, gas employees and others. They came, they showed efficiency, they made optimistic remarks, they went away to fetch something. They didn't come back. One rang

up numbers on the telephone, but they always seemed to be the wrong numbers. If they were the right numbers, the right man was not working at this particular branch of the trade, whatever it was...

In most of Christie's last novels there are occasional negative remarks about the tendency for British society and government to move towards socialism, which Christie clearly did not like. In a conversation between two characters, we read:

> "...you know what life is nowadays. Government, government, you've got to stand it everywhere. In the office, in the home, in the supermarkets, on the television. Private life. That's what we want more of nowadays..."

As early as the 1952 *Mrs. McGinty's Dead* Christie was preaching, through her sympathetic characters, against the National Health Insurance (socialized medicine) and in subsequent novels there are occasional references to government "questions" about such subjects as how many toilets one had in one's home, the kinds of foods one purchased, etc., which certain characters regard as invasions of privacy.

There is also a brief—and negative—reference to the European Common Market which Britain joined after many years of reluctance—the same kind of reluctance that Britain currently (2007) exhibits in the matter of adopting the euro as its currency.

Although the Beresfords' "new" home is the principal setting, there are scenes at a few other homes in the village, as well as one or two scenes in offices in London, but descriptions of these homes and offices are unimportant and usually lacking.

As noted in the *Setting* and *Comments* section for the 1968 *By the Pricking of My Thumbs*, Christie appears to have taken an interest, late in her life, in the history of church architecture and she took the trouble in that novel to make some comments—irrelevant to the story but interesting—about the medieval church in the village of Sutton Chancellor and the poor "restoration" that it had been given by the Victorians. In *Postern of Fate*, the church in Hollowquay suffered the same fate, dating from the twelfth or thirteenth century but having stained-glass windows that were made in the middle of the nineteenth century.

Story

It is late spring or early summer of 1972 or 1973. Tommy and Tuppence Beresford, whom we first met as a young, unmarried couple in the 1922 *The Secret Adversary,* and then as a middle-aged couple in the 1941 *N or M?* and still later as an older couple in the 1968 *By the Pricking of My Thumbs,* are now quite elderly and have recently purchased a somewhat shabby, older home called The Laurels in the village of Hollowquay somewhere on the English Channel coast. Along with the house, they agreed to purchase a large collection of books, which consist primarily of outdated novels and children's books.

In an old copy of Stevenson's *The Black Arrow*, Tuppence is intrigued to find certain words underlined in red in one of the chapters. Puzzling at length over this, she soon realizes that it is not entire words but individual letters that are underlined, and that when written out in sequence, they spell the sentences: "Mary Jordan did not die naturally. It was one of us." The name Alexander Parkinson is written in the inside cover of the book, suggesting that he was the owner of the book.

This provides the imaginative Tuppence with another opportunity to look for and solve a crime in the distant past, as she did in the 1968 *By the Pricking of My Thumbs*. In this case the mystery revolves around a certain Mary Jordan, who lived at The Laurels just before the First World War and was thought by certain locals to be a German spy, but who was in fact a British agent on the trail of a German spy.

Tuppence's investigative activities cause someone to try to murder her, but of course she does not die and, instead, solves this decades-old mystery.

Characters

Thomas ("Tommy") and Prudence (Tuppence) Beresford, whom we first met in the 1922 *The Secret Adversary* and subsequently in a group of short stories and two more novels. They are now an elderly couple living in their "retirement home," a neglected old house badly in need of repairs and updates. Tommy is evidently still active in his "secret service" work, going to meetings in London every day while Tuppence remains at home to deal with plumbers, electricians and other tradesmen. She makes an intriguing discovery while perusing a tattered copy of an old novel and finds herself involved in solving another mystery.

Deborah, Tommy and Tuppence's married daughter. Her married name is not stated, but we know that she has three children, the youngest being a spoiled little four-year-old girl. We met Deborah briefly in the 1941 *N or M?,* when she was a young unmarried adult doing some kind of "coding" work for the government while her parents, unknown to her, were tracking down a British traitor in an English Channel resort town.

Deborah's age is given as "nearly forty," somewhat contradicting the fact that in 1941 she must have been at least twenty and it is now 1972 or 1973. In all of Christie's latest works, we must be flexible on the subject of chronological consistency.

Deborah has a twin brother, Derek, who is not mentioned in the present story but who was in the armed forces in the 1941 story *N or M?*.

Andrew, Deborah's fifteen-year-old son who reads and quotes poetry

Janet, Deborah's eleven-year-old daughter

Rosalie, Deborah's four-year-old daughter who greets her grandmother with "I want my tea."

Albert Batt, the Beresfords' loyal servant who helps with cooking and all other housework. Now a portly, middle-aged widower, he was first introduced as "the small lift boy," probably about eleven years old, at the London flat of the notorious Rita Vandemeyer in the 1922 *The Secret Adversary*. He assisted Tuppence in that story and became the Beresfords' life-long devoted servant. In the 1941 *N or M?* he rescued Tommy from imprisonment by criminals.

Amy Batt, Albert Batt's deceased wife who, according to Albert, made excellent doughnuts but who, according to Tuppence, did not. **Note:** Christie suffers a memory slip in the matter of "Amy's" Christian name. When Albert appeared in the 1941 *N or M?*, we learned that he was married and the father of at least two children, but we were not told the name of his wife. In the 1968 *By the Pricking of My Thumbs*, we learned that his wife's name was Milly and that there were three children still living with them.

Alexander Parkinson, a boy who lived in the Beresfords' present home, now called The Laurels, just before the First World War and whose name is written in a tattered copy of Stevenson's *The Black Arrow*. He died at age fourteen, and according to the Beresfords' cleaning lady, Beatrice, the cause of his death was leukemia, although we will have reason to suspect a more sinister explanation for his death.

Mary Jordan, a young woman who lived at The Laurels as a sort of companion or "au pair girl" to one of the older members of the Parkinson family in approximately 1914. She died shortly before Alexander Parkinson's death, supposedly from poisoning by foxglove leaves which had been "accidentally" mixed with spinach leaves from the garden. Enduring rumors, half a century later, suggest that she was a German spy, but Secret Service friends of Tommy Beresford will contradict that notion. Gwenda, an employee of the post office in Hollowquay, tells Tuppence of her belief that Mary Jordan was a thief, although her "Granny" had affirmed that Mary Jordan was in fact a German spy.

Miss Sanderson, who is in charge of a "white elephant sale" in the village and is delighted with Tuppence's contribution of a disgusting brass lamp that she and Tommy had once foolishly purchased abroad and are now very glad to be rid of.

Hannibal, the Beresfords' Manchester terrier who, after someone attempts to shoot Tuppence in their garden, later helps to identify that person.

"Something That Looked Like a Verger," a person who kept coming out of the church as Tuppence was exploring grave markers in the churchyard.

Underwoods, Overwoods, Parkinsons, Copes, Somers, Chattertons and Griffins, members of various families who are named on grave markers in the churchyard.

Old Isaac Bodlicott, who is commissioned by the Beresfords to make some needed repairs to their "new" home. He is extremely garrulous and his memories of past inhabitants of the neighborhood seem to be unlimited, although it is difficult to know how reliable those memories may be.

Old Isaac may be a bit too "garrulous" on the subject of certain events in the distant past. Tuppence finds his dead body in her garden one day where he has been "coshed," perhaps by a stranger to the vicinity, or perhaps by someone who is *not* a stranger.

Miss Dorothy ("Dodo") Little, whose "surname is misleading, as she is a woman of ample proportions." She is known as "the Parish Pump" because she is so well informed about all things that happen in the parish.

Miss Price-Ridley, "an angular lady with a lot of teeth," a resident of Hollowquay.

Old Mrs. Lupton, an elderly lady who supports herself on two sticks. She remembers "old Mrs. Parkinson, *the* Mrs. Parkinson who lived in the Manor House."

Susan Jordan, an unsatisfactory cook someone remembers when Tuppence casually mentions the name "Jordan" in a conversation.

Mrs. Blackwell, who had been the employer of the unsatisfactory Susan Jordan.

Jane Finn, an important character in the 1922 *The Secret Adversary*, recalled by Tommy Beresford

"An American," to whom Jane Finn is now married, who was also a character in that story

The Waddingtons, a family who lived in The Laurels when it was called "Long Scofield"

The Blackmores, a family who lived in The Laurels before the Waddingtons

The Parkinsons, a family who lived in The Laurels before the Blackmores

Mrs. Griffin, née Winifred Morrison, age ninety-four, who remembers the Parkinsons and some of the events surrounding the deaths of Mary Jordan and Alexander Parkinson.

The District Nurse who was in practice at the time of the Parkinsons, and who is now dead

The Current District Nurse who has only been in Hollowquay for a short time

Elizabeth, the Beresfords' former cleaning lady who frequently found it necessary to ask "Oh, madam, could I speak to you a minute? You see, I've got a problem."

Beatrice, the Beresfords' current cleaning lady who often finds it necessary to approach Tuppence in the same manner

Mrs. Barber, a village resident whom Tuppence visits for what she calls a "coffee morning." Their trivial conversation runs mostly to garden fruits and the dangers of eating seedcake.

Mrs. Bolland, who told Mrs. Barber about Tuppence

An Elderly Woman with Gray Hair, who presides at the post office over the government business of Her Majesty's mails

Gwenda, Beatrice's friend who works at the post office/stationery shop, representing the "household side" of the shop.

Jenny, a friend of Gwenda's who enjoyed the excitement of the Second World War while living in London.

The Parkinsons' Cook who allegedly brought in poisonous foxglove leaves instead of spinach or lettuce for salad, causing the death of Mary Jordan

"Granny," Gwenda's grandmother who told her all about Mary Jordan, the Parkinsons, the foxglove leaves, and "German spies"

The Parkinsons' Old Gardener who was at first blamed for bringing the foxglove leaves into the house

Old Mrs. Atkins who, according to Old Isaac, kept a gun and shot at either side of anyone who approached her house

Mrs. Letherby who, according to Old Isaac, was "nearly had up" for shoplifting, though she was rich

Old Miss Lavinia Shotacomb, a third person whom Old Isaac is eager to tell Tuppence about until Tuppence changes the subject

Mrs. Lottie Jones, the most recent lady of the house at The Laurels. It was from the Jones's that the Beresfords purchased the house and a collection of old books.

The Bassingtons, still another family who once lived at The Laurels

Miss Jenny Lister, a child in the past who, according to Old Isaac, used to ride the rocking horse which is now in ruins inside an equally ruined storage building at The Laurels

Miss Pamela Lister, another child in the past who, according to Old Isaac, enjoyed riding Truelove—a child's four-wheeled vehicle—down the hill towards the monkey puzzle.

Betty Sprot, a child character in the 1941 *N or M?*, whom the Beresfords adopted at the end of that story. She is now grown, lives in East Africa, and is an anthropologist.

Tuppence's Father, a clergyman whom we met briefly at the end of the 1922 *The Secret Adversary*. He is now deceased, of course.

"Mrs. Blenkensop," Tuppence's alias while working with Tommy at the Sans Souci guest house in the 1941 *N or M?*

A Piano Tuner who tunes and admires the Beresfords' fine Erard piano which Tuppence claims they owned while living in London during the Second World War.

Tuppence's Aunt Sarah, who had laurels in her garden

Colonel Atkinson, a.k.a. "Old Moustachio-Monty," an old friend of Tommy's who was in the "secret service" with him. He tells Tommy some facts about certain events connected with The Laurels and Holloquay before and during the First World War.

"That German Chap" and **"That Woman with the Nursery Rhyme Books,"** characters from the 1941 *N or M?* who are mentioned by Colonel Atkinson during a conversation with Tommy

"A Girl on the *Lusitania*" and **"The Enigmatic Mr. Brown,"** two characters in the 1922 *The Secret Adversary* mentioned by Colonel Atkinson in the same conversation. The "Girl on the *Lusitania*" was the aforementioned Jane Finn.

An Uncle of Tuppence's who used to use bay rum from America on his hair

Miss Collodon, a "researcher" employed by Tommy Beresford in London.

"Mutton-Chop," an elderly man and another old "secret service" friend of Tommy's whose real name is not mentioned, and who discusses the pre–World War One events at The Laurels with Tommy

Margery, "Mutton-Chop's" ex-wife whom Tommy never met, as he had missed the wedding. The marriage only survived a year and a half.

"Mutton-Chop's" Sister, with whom he now lives at "Little Pollon."

A Sad, Grizzled Man Sitting in an Office, another friend of Tommy's whose name is not revealed to us. He refers Tommy to Mr. Robinson

The Daughter of the aforementioned Sad, Grizzled Man, who is a god-daughter to Mr. Robinson

A Man of Thirty-five to Forty Years of Age who greets Tommy at the office of Mr. Robinson

Johnson, a nervous-looking young man of about twenty-three employed at the office of Mr. Robinson

Mr. Robinson, whom we first met in the 1959 *Cat Among the Pigeons* and then later in the 1965 *At Bertram's Hotel* and the 1970 *Passenger to Frankfurt*. He continues to be described as "a rather enormous man, of unknown nationality, a man of great weight and many inches, with a very large and yellow face."

An English Officer Who Was Above Suspicion before the First World War. He was nevertheless tried and sentenced for treason.

Franco and Mussolini, fascist dictators of Spain and Italy respectively during the 1930s and 1940s, mentioned by Mr. Robinson in a conversation with Tommy Beresford. Mussolini was hanged by an infuriated mob in Milan towards the end of World War Two but Franco remained the Spanish dictator until his death in 1975.

Jonathan Kane, an English officer who lived at The Laurels between the world wars, another Englishman who was "above suspicion" but who was in fact an enemy agent who promoted Nazism and an alliance with Germany.

Rudyard Kipling, a late-Victorian British writer who is mentioned and praised by Mr. Robinson. The quality of Kipling's writing continues to be recognized but his Victorian attitudes about the British Empire and the "white man's burden" have been unpopular for a long time.

A Chap Who is Coming to See Mr. Robinson in a Few Minutes. He is described by Mr. Robinson as "an awful bore, but he's high up in government circles..."

Dorothy Rogers, who used to be Mrs. Griffin's housemaid and who now only comes to clean for her twice a week.

Mrs. Henderson, who is even older than old Mrs. Griffin, and who lives in Meadowside, an old people's home about twelve to fifteen miles from the village of Hollowquay.

Mrs. Beddingfield, to whom Mrs. Henderson was a nurse-companion when she lived at The Laurels when it was known as "Swallow's Nest."

Rosemary, old Mrs. Griffin's sister

Mrs. Henley, who lives at Apple Tree Lodge, another home for old people

"Deborah's Twins," grandchildren mentioned by Tuppence early in the story, although toward the end of the story, when Deborah arrives at The Laurels for a visit, she brings her three children aged fourteen, eleven and four, and so there are no "twins." This is an example of Christie's carelessness in her last books. Christie may have been thinking of Deborah and her brother Derek, who were twins themselves.

Mr. Durrance, who maintains a photographer's shop in the village and sells film and old photos. He is "a rather tall young man with long flaxen hair and a budding beard."

Mr. Durrance's Father, the original owner of the shop, who was a "hoarder."

An Elderly Woman with Gray Hair and Rather Lackluster Eyes who works in Mr. Durrance's photography shop

Colonel Ephraim Pikeaway, whom we first met in the 1959 *Cat Among the Pigeons,* in which he worked in a stuffy, smoke-filled office in Bloomsbury. We later met him in the 1970 *Passenger to Frankfurt.* He is the head of Britain's "Special Branch." According to Tommy, Colonel Pikeaway "lives in a kind of permanent atmosphere of smoke."

James, the Beresfords' obstinate Sealyham of past years, when they lived in London near Belsize Park

Mrs. Copes, an old woman who looks like a witch and who opens the door to Tommy at the office of Colonel Pikeaway

One or Two Adolescent Boys who "assist the police" in the matter of Old Isaac's death. In other words, who "are suspected and questioned" in the matter

Mrs. Bodlicott, old Isaac Bodlicott's daughter-in-law who, after Isaac's death, visits Tuppence and offers the gardening services of her second son Henry

Henry ("Chuck") Bodlicott, the above-mentioned second son of Mrs. Bodlicott, aged about twelve or thirteen. He is extremely impressed by the stories he has heard about Tommy and Tuppence's past adventures and is eager to assist them in their present investigations.

Clarence, a.k.a. "Clarrie," Henry Bodlicott's chum

Mick, who told Clarence about everything and used to live "up by where the blacksmith used to be"

Tom Gillingham, another of Henry's many adolescent friends

Johnny, Henry's older brother who was not

interested in the stories about past events at The Laurels

Janet, one of ten or twelve boys and girls of assorted ages who are eager to assist Tommy and Tuppence in their investigations. Janet is described as being "intellectually superior" to the rest.

Bert, a tall boy with a squint

A Stout Woman of about Seventy who works at the PPC (the Pensioners' Palace Club, a social center for retirees)

Uncle Ben, an old man with a beard at the PPC who looks to be about a hundred

Uncle Ben's Uncle Len who "knew things"

An Elderly Lady, a Rather Prim One, with Gray Hair and a Lace Fichu, one of several aging people Tuppence meets at the PPC

Maudie, still another aged patron of the PPC. She sings.

Inspector Norris at the police station, with whom Tommy speaks after someone fires a gun at Tuppence, wounding her slightly

Dr. Crossfield, who looks after Tuppence after she receives a gunshot wound

Iris Mullins, "a tall masculine-looking woman in tweed trousers and a Fair Isle pullover." She is sent by old Mrs. Griffin to offer gardening services to the Beresfords after old Isaac's death.

Mrs. Radcliffe, who invites Tuppence to lunch one day.

Angus Crispin, a youngish man in a tweed suit sent by "Mr. Solomon" to assist the Beresfords with gardening

Mrs. Shacklebury, a cleaning lady who works for the Beresfords on certain days

French into English

Note: Although Hercule Poirot is not a character in *Postern of Fate*, four French expressions occur in the novel:

Chapter 3

à point—a cooking term meaning "cooked just right"

Chapter 19

Il faut cultiver son jardin—A French proverb: "One must look after one's own garden."

Chapter 22

Bonnes bouches—compliments, flattering remarks

Chapter 30

La reine le veut.—The queen wills it, or "It's the queen's command."

Comments

Tommy and Tuppence Beresford appeared in only five of Christie's books. They first appeared as a young, unmarried couple in the 1922 *The Secret Adversary* and then as a young married couple in the 1929 short story collection *Partners in Crime*. Christie revived them as a middle-aged couple for the 1941 *N or M?* but evidently gave them no further thought until the late 1960s when readers began asking "Whatever happened to Tommy and Tuppence?" In response, Christie wrote the 1968 *By the Pricking of My Thumbs* in which the Beresfords were portrayed as approximately ten or fifteen years older than they had been in *N or M?*, although it was actually then about twenty-seven years later. It is in *Postern of Fate* that they make their final appearance and they are older still.

For readers who have enjoyed the Tommy and Tuppence characters in the earlier books, *Postern of Fate* can be a pleasant reading experience because of the many references to events and characters in the earlier books. But this novel is not likely to give much reading pleasure to anyone who is not already a "friend" of Tommy and Tuppence. It is filled with meandering and rather pointless, repetitious conversations on trivial subjects that have nothing to do with the story. There are a multitude of inconsequential characters, none of whom is especially interesting or memorable, with the possible exception of old Isaac Bodlicott, who is favored with a long and rather amusing characterization at the beginning of Chapter 10. Chapter 11 is one long orgy of pointless chatter between Tommy and Tuppence and could be omitted entirely from the reading of the novel.

Postern of Fate was the last novel that Christie wrote. Her remaining two works—*Curtain* and *Sleeping Murder*—were written during the 1940s and are much more typical of her better period. Readers who are not special fans of the Beresfords are advised to disregard *Postern of Fate*, which is one of the sad products of her "steep and rapid" decline.

Curtain (1975)

Setting

It is impossible to place the action of *Curtain* in a particular year because Christie wrote the novel during the 1940s, intending that it should be published after her death, whenever that might be. She was therefore careful to avoid all references to current events so that there would be no possibility of assigning a specific year to the action. But since we know that Hercule Poirot worked with Ariadne Oliver to solve the mystery in the 1972 *Elephants Can Remember*, it is logical to place the action of *Curtain* in approximately 1973.

The story takes place at Styles Court, the large country home near the village of Styles St. Mary in the county of Essex, which was the setting of Christie's first published novel, the 1920 *The Mysterious Affair at Styles*, which she actually wrote in approximately 1915–1916. Styles Court had been a large country home occupied by the Cavendish family, and Arthur Hastings had been invited to spend some time there by his friend, John Cavendish. Hercule Poirot was at that time one of several refugees from Belgium being housed in the village of Styles St. Mary, and so Hastings and Poirot were able to renew their old acquaintance. Together they solved the mystery of the death of old Mrs. Inglethorpe, the stepmother of John and Lawrence Cavendish.

Styles Court has been sold and is now being operated as a guest house. The exterior of the house is substantially unchanged, but the interior has been altered with the addition of several bathrooms, and several of the larger bedrooms on the upper floor have been divided in order to create a larger number of smaller guest rooms. Both Hastings and Poirot note with some disappointment that the bathrooms that have been added have been done in a rather cheap, modern way and that, although there is "hot" and cold running water in each bathroom, the "hot" water is lukewarm, the towels are thin, and in general there is none of the luxury that characterized the house in earlier times.

Service at the "guest house" is evidently sufficient, but Poirot and Hastings both complain privately that the meals are rather uninteresting and the coffee is especially bad. Poirot, in particular, complains of the food:

> "…the cooking, it is English at its worst. Those Brussels sprouts so enormous, so hard, that the English like so much. The potatoes boiled and either hard or falling to pieces. The vegetables that taste of water, water, and again water. The complete absence of the salt and pepper in any dish—"

The exterior grounds of Styles are not described in detail, although there is a kind of "summer house" that is rather dilapidated and "spidery."

The entire story takes place at Styles Court except for a brief scene, toward the end, at a place called Eastbourne, where Hastings visits Poirot's old manservant, Georges.

There is a brief mention of the nearby market town of Tadminster, where one female character spends a day shopping. That town had also been mentioned in the 1920 *The Mysterious Affair at Styles*.

Story

Hercule Poirot, now extremely aged and in frail physical health, has returned for a "holiday" to Styles Court in Essex, where he solved his first case in England in 1916. It will be a kind of "family reunion," because he has invited his old friend Arthur Hastings to enjoy some time there, and Hastings's youngest daughter Judith is also staying at Styles in the capacity of secretary to her employer, a scientific researcher.

Poirot confides a second reason for arranging this "family reunion." He is again on the trail of a murderer, but this time he knows who the murderer is! He is certain that another crime will be attempted, and Poirot's aim is to determine who the victim will be, and to act quickly enough to prevent the murder and catch the murderer in the act. Naturally, he does not share the identity of the murderer with Hastings, explaining:

> "Because, *mon cher*, you are still the same old Hastings. You have still the speaking countenance. I do not wish, you see, that you should sit staring at X with your mouth hanging open, your face saying plainly: 'This—this that I am looking at is a murderer.'"

Hastings's task will be to keep his eyes and ears open and to try to identify, in advance, the potential murder victim. Soon there is an "accidental" shooting that results in only a slight wound for one person, and then there is a "suicide" by poisoning, and finally another "suicide" with a revolver. Towards the end of the story, Poirot dies of old age, and Hastings remains mystified about who the murderer can be. But a document written by Poirot before his death, with instructions that it be given to Hastings four months after his death, identifies the murderer.

Characters

Captain Arthur Hastings, an old friend and "side-kick" of Hercule Poirot, whom we first met in the 1920 *The Mysterious Affair at Styles*. He appeared in six additional novels and numerous short stories over the next few years, making his most recent appearance in the 1937 *Poirot Loses* *a Client.* Agatha Christie grew tired of the Hastings character and never featured him again until his—and Poirot's—last case, *Curtain.* As usual, he is the narrator of the story.

"Cinders," the nickname with which Hastings refers to his recently-deceased wife. Her real name was either Bella or Dulcie (Christie herself was confused on that subject). Bella and Dulcie were identical twins, and in *Murder on the Links,* one of the girls impersonated the other for a time. At the end of the story Hastings discovered that he had been calling his future wife by the wrong name. In a later novel he referred to her by the wrong name again, possibly because of a memory slip on Christie's part, but in general he has stuck to referring to her as "Cinderella," which is a name she playfully provided him with on the day they first met on a train in France.

Two Sons and a Daughter Named Grace, three of Hastings's children. They are not characters in the story but are referred to briefly in Hastings's narration. Grace is married and lives with her soldier husband in India. One of the sons is in the navy and the other is married and runs Hastings's ranch in Argentina.

Judith Hastings, Hastings's younger daughter, an important character in the present story. She has always been the child whom Hastings "secretly loved best," and who also had the "best brains" in the family and was therefore encouraged to attend a university and earn a B. Sc. degree. She is secretary to a research physician, Dr. Franklin.

John Cavendish, a character in the 1920 *The Mysterious Affair at Styles,* and an old friend of Hastings who invited him to stay at Styles Court for a short time while Hastings was recovering from battle injuries during World War One. John had qualified as a lawyer but found no need to work, since he had a wealthy stepmother who indulged him with a living allowance. John Cavendish is now dead.

Mary Cavendish, John's wife who lived with him at Styles Court in the shadow of his stepmother, who held the purse strings. Hastings had thought of Mary as a "fascinating, enigmatical creature." She is still alive and lives somewhere in Devon.

Emily Inglethorpe, John Cavendish's stepmother, the murder victim in *The Mysterious Affair at Styles.*

Cynthia Murdoch, a young protégée of Emily Inglethorpe in *The Mysterious Affair at Styles.* She was a beautiful young girl with auburn hair who wept when she learned that Emily had forgotten to provide for her in her Will. Hastings, always susceptible to the charms of beautiful girls—especially weeping ones—immediately proposed to her, which impulsive act sent her into fits of laughter and made her day. Poirot never let Hastings forget that act of foolishness, and thereafter whenever Hastings spoke of an attractive woman—especially of an attractive woman whom Hastings was trying to convince Poirot was "beyond suspicion,"—Poirot would usually ask "Does she have auburn hair?"

Lawrence Cavendish, John Cavendish's younger brother who, though having qualified as a medical doctor, was as averse to working as his brother. Instead, he wrote mediocre verses and accepted a living allowance from his stepmother. At the end of that story he married Cynthia Murdoch and still lives with her and their children in South Africa.

Hercule Poirot, the famous Belgian private investigator. *Curtain* is his last case, and towards the end of the story, he dies, leaving the solution to the mystery written in a document that his lawyers make available to Hastings four months later.

In *Curtain,* Poirot is extremely weak, uses a wheel chair and is physically carried up and down stairways by his current valet-attendant. Though physically feeble, he is mentally as astute as ever.

Colonel George "Toby" Luttrell, the current owner of Styles Court, which he is attempting to run as a guest house along with his wife Daisy.

Daisy Luttrell, Colonel Luttrell's henpecking shrew of a wife who runs the Styles guesthouse with an iron hand, belittles and insults her husband in front of the guests, and affects an Irish brogue, although there is no Irish blood in her.

Dr. John Franklin, Judith Hastings's employer, a research scientist whose passion is the study of tropical diseases.

Barbara Franklin, Dr. Franklin's "semi-invalid" wife. A good many of the characters in the story have a lot to say about her. Sir William Boyd Carrington, who was in love with her before she married Dr. Franklin, thinks the world of her, and so does her husband, but Judith Hastings and Mrs. Franklin's nurse describe her as a self-centered crybaby who talks of nothing but her health to anyone who will listen. According to Nurse Craven, "There isn't much you could teach her about getting her own way. Whatever her ladyship wants happens."

Stephen Norton, a guest at Styles, who is "a grey-haired man, slightly built, who limps and has a boyish, eager face." His hobby is birdwatching.

Sir William Boyd Carrington, another guest at Styles, who has recently inherited a vast, antiquated country house in the neighborhood. He is just the kind of man Hastings has always appreciated: "...good-looking, with a deeply tanned face as though he had led an out-of-door life—the type of man that is becoming more and more rare—an Englishman of the old school, straightforward, fond of out-of-door life, and the kind of man who can command." Hercule Poirot derides these impressions, however, describing Sir William as "an old bore—a windbag—*enfin*—the stuffed shirt!"

Sir William Boyd Carrington's Wife who died in Burma just a short time after they were married

Nurse Craven, a hospital nurse who looks after the "semi-invalid" Mrs. Franklin.

Major Allerton, another guest at Styles, a man to whom Judith Hastings appears to be strongly attracted. Hastings, who knew immediately upon casting his eyes upon Boyd Carrington that he was one of England's most perfect specimens of manhood, makes an equally quick judgment about Major Allerton:

> Major Allerton I instinctively disliked. He was a good-looking man in the early forties, broad-shouldered, bronzed of face, with an easy way of talking, most of what he said holding a double implication. He had the pouches under his eyes that come with a dissipated way of life. I suspected him of racketing around, of gambling, of drinking hard, and of being first and last a womanizer.

In the course of the story, Hastings and his daughter Judith will have at least one major confrontation on the subject of her attraction to Allerton.

Miss Cole, another guest at Styles, "a tall, handsome woman aged about thirty-five."

Georges, Hercule Poirot's manservant, who is not with Poirot at Styles because he is in Eastbourne attending to his father, who is ill. We met "Georges" for the first time in the 1928 *The Mystery of the Blue Train* and he has appeared from time to time, but not every time, at Hercule Poirot's London flat, Whitehaven Mansions. In some stories he is called "George" and in others he has the French version of the name, "Georges," but he is clearly an Englishman, and a social snob. He has been known to pause imperceptibly before using the word "lady" or "gentleman" when announcing visitors at Poirot's home.

Curtiss, Hercule Poirot's temporary valet at Styles. He is, in Hastings's words, "a big man with a bovine rather stupid face." He is also very strong and is able to carry Poirot up and down stairways.

Sir Everard, Sir William Boyd Carrington's old uncle who owned Knatton, the antiquated country home that Boyd Carrington has just inherited.

Dr. Oliver, Mrs. Luttrell's regular doctor

A Nurse who takes care of Mrs. Luttrell during her recovery from a gunshot wound

An Old Woman with Rheumy Eyes and an Unpleasantly Ghoulish Manner who speaks to Hastings after the inquest. She remembers Hastings and the murder that took place at Styles in 1916.

A Housemaid, a "rather stupid-looking girl" at Styles who knocks at a certain bedroom door one morning and receives no answer.

FRENCH INTO ENGLISH

Chapter 1
bien entendu—of course
en famille—as a family
dépêchez-vous—hurry
très bon marché—very economical
À bientôt—See you soon
mon ami—my friend

Chapter 2
mon ami—my friend
très distingué—very distinguished
Les femmes—women
vous êtes encore jeune—you're still young
Enfin—Well,—
mon cher—my good friend
mon ami—friend
Eh bien—Well...
Bien—That's right

Chapter 3
Tout de même—Just the same...
mon cher—my friend
mon ami—my friend
bon Dieu—God
Le mariage—marriage
mon enfant—dear

Chapter 5 *mauvais sujet*—"bad apple"

Chapter 8
le sport—recreation, fun
mon vieux—my friend
Bien!—All right, then!
ma foi—for Pete's sake
mon cher—my friend
Enfin!—All right!
Bien!—All right, then!
enfin—in a word

Chapter 10
"invalid *en chef*"—"resident invalid"

Chapter 12
mon ami—my friend
Eh bien—So...
hein?—do you?

Chapter 13
mon ami—my friend
Tiens—Hey, look at this!

Chapter 14
hein?—isn't that so?
mon ami—my friend
Enfin—Well, after all...

Chapter 15
fluxion de poitrine—chest cold
mon ami—my friend
Eh bien—Well, all right

Chapter 16 *Eh bien*—Well...

Chapter 17
Eh bien, non.—Absolutely not.
Ma foi!—Good grief!
mon Dieu!—for goodness' sake
enfin—anyway
Tout de même—In any case
Cher ami—My dear friend

Postscript
mon ami—my friend
À la fin comme au commencement—In the end just as in the beginning
cher ami—dear friend
L'appétit vient en mangeant—eating makes you hungrier, or eating gives you an appetite
Mon Dieu, non!—Absolutely not!
Mais oui!—Oh yes!
ce pauvre vieux—that poor old fellow
Mais oui—Yes, that's what I said...
Eh bien—Well...
bon Dieu—God

Comments

It is alleged that Christie wrote *Curtain* during the 1940s and intended to have the novel published after her death, whenever that might be. It is Hercule Poirot's final case, and he dies towards the end of the story. If it is true that *Curtain* is a product of the 1940s, it is rather poor by comparison with other Christie novels of that period. The 1940s were Christie's best period in terms of characterization. The characters in *Curtain* are, for the most part, cardboard stereotypes without very much subtlety in their development. As a "detective novel" however, it is extremely unique, although explaining its "uniqueness" would give away the solution.

If it is true that Christie wrote *Curtain* during the 1940s, it is doubtful that she left it alone to be published exactly as she had first written it. Perhaps she re-read it during the late 1960s or early 1970s and "improved it" with a few modern touches. The conversation in Chapter Eleven about "euthanasia—the case for and against it"—strikes one as very unnatural for the 1940s. Of course, the term has been in existence for a very long time, but it was not a "buzzword"—not a "hot topic" of conversation among non-medical people—until the early 1970s, when for a couple of years everyone seemed to be discussing it. It was a topic on television talk shows and there were innumerable articles about it in magazines. Christie probably added the conversation about euthanasia to that chapter as one of her "improvements" before releasing it for publication.

The verbally violent nature of Judith Hastings's treatment of her father in Chapter Twelve, too, is uncharacteristic of Christie's writing during the 1940s. There had always been "old-fashioned" parents in Christie's novels who disapproved of their children's sex lives, but generally the younger people chuckled to themselves and simply ignored their parents' attitudes rather than confronting them aggressively, as Judith Hastings does in *Curtain*. Some of the things she says to her father are rather hurtful and they do not sound like the kinds of things that a Christie character such as Judith would have said to her father during the 1940s. Christie may have altered Judith's conversations with her father in Chapter Twelve during the early 1970s in order to make them sound "modern," which indeed they do.

In any case, *Curtain* should be postponed until one has read all the rest of Hercule Poirot's adventures. That makes thirty-two novels and a large number of short stories that should come first.

Sleeping Murder (1976)

Setting

Unlike the 1975 *Curtain*, in which an aging, wheelchair-bound Hercule Poirot finally dies—requiring us to imagine the action as taking place *after* all of Poirot's previous adventures—*Sleep-*

ing Murder features Miss Jane Marple, and Miss Marple does *not* die in the novel. In fact, she is perfectly healthy and consummately ambulatory (in a late chapter she actually *runs* up a stairway in order to prevent a murder from taking place) and so we are asked to imagine her as a much younger woman than she has been for a very long time.

No current events in the story place the action in any particular decade, but it is reasonable to imagine the story as taking place during the middle 1940s. Toward the end of the story a police officer, upon meeting Miss Marple, makes brief references to events in the 1930 *Murder at the Vicarage,* the 1942 *The Body in the Library* and the 1943 *The Moving Finger* but *no* reference to the 1950 *A Murder Is Announced* or to any later Miss Marple adventure. This tends to confirm the placement of the action in the 1940s. Furthermore, Miss Marple's good friends, Colonel Arthur Bantry and his wife Dolly, are both still living. By the time Mrs. Bantry made her appearance in the 1962 *The Mirror Crack'd,* her husband had died.

Further evidence of the story's taking place in the 1940s is the fact that two elderly sisters adorn the walls of their sitting room with, among other things, framed photographs of "the King in Naval uniform" and "the two young Princesses Elizabeth and Margaret Rose." 1952 was the year of King George VI's death and Queen Elizabeth's coronation, so presumably we are somewhere in time before that year, and perhaps even before the future Queen's marriage year of 1947.

In *Sleeping Murder* we are offered scenes in several different parts of England. In the county of Devon, on the English Channel, we visit two fictitious villages and the three real towns of Plymouth, Exeter and Torquay. We visit an isolated home in England's northernmost county of Northumberland, a mental home in the eastern county of Norfolk, and a residential flat, a hotel and a theater in London.

The primary setting is a fictitious village, Dillmouth, on the south coast of Devon. Dillmouth is described as a charming and old-fashioned little seaside town. It boasts a comfortable hotel called The Royal Clarence which has been in operation for at least twenty years, as one or two of the characters are known to have stayed there nineteen or twenty years earlier. There is also a café or teashop called The Ginger Cat. Brief scenes take place in a needlework shop and at a draper's shop, at the office and home of a conservative lawyer, and at "Calcutta Lodge," the home of a retired real estate agent who once lived in India.

Another house in Dillmouth, however, is the principal setting. It is described as "a small, white Victorian villa," and is now called Hillside, though it had been named St. Catherine's until about twenty years ago. The house is about a hundred years old and has been kept in good condition, although it is somewhat outdated, having just one bathroom and an antiquated kitchen. Recent redecorating has resulted in some drab "mustard-cum-biscuit" wall colors which are not to the new owners' liking. Although there are "six or seven bedrooms" on the upper floor, they are probably somewhat small. The solitary bathroom contains a large bathtub with a "mahogany surround." One of the bedrooms has curved walls—it is evidently a corner "turret" room—and the barred windows suggest that it was once a nursery. The grounds of the house, though somewhat neglected in recent years, are pleasant and once some overgrown shrubs are trimmed or removed, there will be a fine view of the sea from a terrace. The house is an important setting because a murder may have taken place there about twenty years earlier.

The opening scene takes place at the port of Plymouth as one of the main characters, a young married woman, arrives by steamship from her home in New Zealand.

We also visit a house called Galls Hill, in the village of Woodleigh Bolton, about thirty miles inland from Dillmouth and "on the moorland." From this fact, we can know with certainty that Dillmouth is located on the southern coast of Devon, a county which includes an area of romantic, picturesque wasteland known as Dartmoor.

Two other Devonshire towns are settings for brief scenes. In Exeter we visit the office of a businessman, and on the outskirts of Exeter we visit his home, which is a modern, white house built of "snowcrete"—perhaps some form of poured concrete especially formulated in a pure white color instead of the usual gray. It may be the same material as the "glazed concrete" that was used in the construction of a modern house in the 1952 *Mrs. McGinty's Dead.* The final scene of the novel takes place at the Imperial Hotel in the Devonshire coastal resort town of Torquay, where Agatha Christie spent her childhood.

The London settings include the flat of a sophisticated couple—a writer and a painter—in the Chelsea district. The flat has windows overlooking the River Thames. There is also an important scene at a London theatre where Webster's *The Duchess of Malfi* is being presented, and a minor scene at an unnamed hotel in London's Mayfair district.

In the course of the story we visit Miss Jane Marple's cottage in the village of St. Mary Mead, where she has a consultation with her old friend Dr. Haydock. Neither Miss Marple's cottage nor the village is described, but we have been favored many times in other novels with descriptions of the village of St. Mary Mead. Since we are presumably in the late 1940s, the major changes in the village that we noted in the 1962 *The Mirror Crack'd* have not yet occurred. Incidentally, the exact location of St. Mary Mead within England has never been perfectly clear. In the earlier novels there were always strong suggestions that the village was somewhere west of London. In the 1957 *What Mrs. McGillicuddy Saw*, Mrs. McGillicuddy boards a train at London's Paddington Station in order to travel west to Milchester, the nearest town to St. Mary Mead having a railway connection. But in a later novel, the 1971 *Nemesis*, we are told that St. Mary Mead is located "about twenty-five miles south of London," probably in the county of Sussex, and quite close to a fictitious coastal town called Loomouth on the English Channel. It is amusing to note, then, that in *Sleeping Murder* Miss Marple, who wants an excuse to go to Dillmouth in order to help a young couple solve a murder case, induces her old friend Dr. Haydock to prescribe a holiday at a coastal resort "for the sea air." Clearly St. Mary Mead, in *Sleeping Murder*, is now in its accustomed place, in the general area of the county of Berkshire, just a few miles west of London.

In Northumberland we visit an isolated country home, Anstell Manor. It is a Queen Anne period home on a property owned by the family of the present owners for nearly three hundred years, although the Queen Anne period house must have been built in approximately 1700. It is described by the owner as "rather shabby now" due to taxation, which makes upkeep difficult. The property is described as "...a white house, set against a background of bleak hills. A winding drive led up through dense shrubbery..."

In Norfolk we visit Saltmarsh House, a home for mental patients.

In most of Christie's novels there are often references to everyday objects, such as automobiles or clothing styles, or references to popular fads, current films and film stars, etc. but in *Sleeping Murder* there are none of those, except for three automobiles that are mentioned: a "comfortable hired Daimler car," a "small Austin car" and a flamboyant, daffodil-yellow luxury car of unspecified make.

Story

It is approximately 1946 and the season is summer. Gwenda Reed, a recently-married young woman of twenty-one, arrives by ocean liner from New Zealand at the port of Plymouth. Her husband, Giles Reed, must remain in New Zealand for a short time and the two have agreed that Gwenda should travel ahead to England alone and to purchase a house, for they plan to take up residence in England, which is Giles's native land. Giles is not interested in houses and trusts Gwenda to find something suitable that appeals to her.

To her delight, Gwenda finds a house that appeals to her almost immediately, in a village named Dillmouth, not far from Plymouth. While touring the house, at the top of the stairs she experiences a sudden feeling of panic, which she cannot explain. The feeling soon passes, however, and later that day Gwenda happily cables to her husband, "Have bought a house."

A few weeks later, while visiting friends in London, Gwenda is part of a party of six who attend a performance of a classic play, Webster's *The Duchess of Malfi*. When one of the actors speaks the line, "Cover her face, mine eyes dazzle, she died young," Gwenda is seized by irrational terror, screams and runs out of the theater, hails a taxi and returns to her friends' flat. Miss Marple had been one of the party of six at the theater, and she later comforts Gwenda, who explains that the lines spoken by the actor were words that she remembered hearing as a child from a man who was standing over a woman he had just strangled. She had seen this through the banister rails of a stairway above, and somehow she knew that the dead woman's name was Helen. She also tells Miss Marple that, while at her new home in Dillmouth, she has had some strange experiences.

She had expressed to her gardener her wish for some shrubs to be removed and some new steps built from a verandah to the ground. Soon the gardener revealed that there was an old flight of steps that had been planted over, in the exact place where Gwenda wished new steps to be built. In an upstairs bedroom, Gwenda had imagined the room as the future nursery for her children, if she were ever to have any, and she had imagined a wallpaper pattern of red poppies and blue cornflowers for it. A cupboard in the room had been painted shut, and when the decorators succeeded in opening the cupboard, Gwenda was astounded to see that its walls were papered in a poppy-and-cornflower pattern. Finally, Gwenda told her builder that she wanted a doorway opened between the sitting room and dining room. The builder surprised her with the fact that there was actually a doorway there already, which had simply been plastered over at some time in the past.

Miss Marple concludes that a very unusual, though not impossible, coincidence must have occurred. Gwenda must have lived in the house at some time during early childhood and remembered, subconsciously, some of the details. Gwenda had been born in India and was sent to live in New Zealand with relatives as a small child, but unknown to her, she and her father had actually stopped in England and lived in Dillmouth for about a year before Gwenda was sent to New Zealand.

The mystery of the doorway, the steps and the wallpaper is thus adequately explained, but Gwenda worries about the panic she had felt at the top of the stairs when first viewing the house, her irrational reaction to the lines uttered by the actor in the play, and her memory of the woman named "Helen" who had been strangled.

When Gwenda's young husband finally joins her at their new home, they are determined to answer the following questions: Who was "Helen?" Was she murdered? Was she in fact Gwenda's step-mother? If she was murdered, was it her father who killed her? Gwenda and her husband embark on these investigations, but Miss Marple is very worried that they may be treading on dangerous ground, and she advises them to "let sleeping murders lie." Knowing that these bright young people are not likely to take her advice, however, Miss Marple goes to Dillmouth and joins the young couple in their investigations, where another murder takes place and still another is attempted. Of course, Miss Marple solves the mystery.

CHARACTERS

Gwenda Reed, a young woman aged twenty-one who has been married for just three months. She was born in India to English parents, but her mother died when she was just two years old, and so she was sent to New Zealand to be raised by kind relatives. Gwenda's father died a short time later. Gwenda and her young English husband take up residence in England and find themselves involved in a murder that occurred nearly twenty years earlier.

Giles Reed, Gwenda's English husband. We are not favored with a physical description of either Gwenda or Giles, but it is clear from the story and dialogue that they are very fond of each other and that they think very much alike. They share a strong interest in the mystery that Gwenda discovers in their new home in England, and they pursue its investigation with equal enthusiasm.

An Aunt of Giles Reed, from whom he recently inherited some furniture

Mrs. Hengrave, from whom Gwenda and Giles purchase their new home, Hillside. She is "a tall melancholy woman with a cold in the head."

Major Hengrave, Mrs. Hengrave's deceased husband, who had been very fond of Dillmouth, where he had been secretary of the golf club.

Mrs. Cocker, Gwenda Reed's new cook, described as "...a lady of condescending graciousness, inclined to repulse Gwenda's overdemocratic friendliness, but who, once Gwenda had been satisfactorily put in her place, was willing to unbend."

Mrs. Cocker's Niece, who works in a hospital and gets surgical gloves at a reduced price for her aunt to use in washing dishes

Foster, a temperamental jobbing gardener, one in a long line of unsatisfactory, elderly, lazy, tea-drinking, work-shirking gardeners in Christie's novels. (For a discussion of this subject, see the *Comments* section for the 1962 *The Mirror Crack'd*.)

Mr. Sims, the Reeds' builder and decorator.

Taylor, an employee of Mr. Sims

Raymond West, a writer of "clever books" and Jane Marple's generous nephew. He was introduced, along with Miss Marple, in the 1930 *Murder at the Vicarage*. Though generous and kind towards his aunt, he regards her as a "survival" from the Victorian period and very much out of touch with the real world. Miss Marple, in turn, has always treated Raymond with affection and kindness, but secretly regards him as a very ignorant man, and although she uses the expression "clever books" to describe his writing, she considers his books to be trash. In the 1950 *A Murder Is Announced,* Miss Marple mentions that one of his books—"quite his worst"—has been designated as a "Book Society choice." (See her thoughts about Raymond in the *Characters* section of either the 1930 *Murder at the Vicarage,* the 1964 *A Caribbean Mystery* or the 1965 *At Bertram's Hotel.*)

Joan West, Raymond's wife. She is a painter, but not a very good one, according to Aunt Jane. Her style of painting, in fact, is quite "passé" and Miss Marple comments, in the 1950 *A Murder Is Announced,* that Joan's subjects seem to be "mostly jugs of dying flowers and broken combs on windowsills."

Miss Jane Marple, who lives in a village and has a knack for solving murders. Introduced in the 1930 *Murder at the Vicarage,* she is in rare form in this novel, successfully manipulating her old friend Dr. Haydock to prescribe "sea air" so that she can have an excuse for spending some time at Dillmouth assisting—and protecting—Gwenda and Giles Reed. Miss Marple does not hesitate to tell lies in order to make contact with persons who may be useful in her investigation. One amusing lie in this story is her statement that a certain cook, Edith Pagett, once gave her recipes for gingerbread and baked apple pudding which she has unfortunately lost. Fact: Miss Marple never met Edith Pagett in her life, but this little fib obtains for Miss Marple Edith Pagett's current address.

As *Sleeping Murder* was written during the 1940s, we find Miss Marple to be in excellent health and not the very old, semi-ambulatory lady of the 1957 *What Mrs. McGillicuddy Saw* and later stories. As a matter of fact, in a late scene in *Sleeping Murder,* Miss Marple actually runs up a stairway in order to prevent a murder.

An Elderly Artist and a Young Barrister, guests of Raymond and Joan West when they take Miss Marple and Gwenda to the theater, making a party of six.

An Actor in *The Duchess of Malfi* who speaks some words that frighten Gwenda Reed

A Servant at the Wests' home in Chelsea who lets Gwenda into the flat after her frightening experience at the theater

An Elderly Parlourmaid with a Telegram on a Salver at the Wests' home

Helen Spenlove Kennedy, Gwenda's stepmother, her father's second wife. Helen was brought up by her older half-brother, Dr. James Kennedy, at his home in Dillmouth. There had been at least one "undesirable young man" in Helen's life but her half-brother had put an end to that affair. There had also been a young lawyer in Dillmouth, Walter Fane, who had wanted to marry her. She declined his marriage proposal, but later when Walter went to India to take up planting, Helen changed her mind and traveled to India to marry him after all. But, according to the rumor mill, she did not marry him and returned immediately to England, meeting Gwenda's father on the liner and marrying him instead. Then about a year later she vanished. It has been presumed that she ran away with still another man. Or was she murdered?

Major Kelvin James Halliday, Gwenda's father. His first wife died young, when their daughter Gwenda was about two years old, while the family was living in India. He returned to England with his two-year-old daughter, intending to send Gwenda on to New Zealand to be raised by relatives, but on the ship he met and fell in love with Helen Kennedy and married her in London upon arrival in England. The marriage lasted no more than a year, as Helen disappeared one evening, taking a packed suitcase with her. Supposedly she ran away with another man. Major Halliday then sent Gwenda to New Zealand to be raised by relatives, and then he died about a year later at a mental home in Norfolk.

Megan Halliday, Gwenda's natural mother who died in India when Gwenda was two years old

A Man in a White Uniform, A Nannie, and **A Ship Captain with a Beard,** vaguely recalled by Gwenda in her memories of a long ocean voyage when she was about two or three years old.

Miss Alison Danby, a sister of Gwenda's mother who raised Gwenda from the age of three in New Zealand

Evelyn, Miss Marple's "little maid"

The Local Chemist in St. Mary Mead about whom Evelyn relates some juicy local gossip to Miss Marple. But Miss Marple is uninterested, for once, in local gossip, her mind being completely absorbed by the danger to which Gwenda and Giles Reed seem determined to expose themselves

The Vicar's Wife in St. Mary Mead. She is not mentioned by name but she is undoubtedly Griselda Clement, whom we met in the 1930 *Murder at the Vicarage* and in the 1942 *The Body in the Library.*

Dr. Haydock, Miss Marple's doctor of many years who allows her to manipulate him into prescribing "sea air," as she needs an excuse for spending some time in Dillmouth. We have known Dr. Haydock since he was introduced in the 1930 *Murder at the Vicarage.*

Madeleine Smith and Lizzie Borden, past murderers referred to by Dr. Haydock. Neither was ever convicted.

Colonel Arthur Bantry and his Wife Dolly, old friends of Miss Marple's. It was in their library that the body was found in the 1942 *The Body in the Library.*

Esther, the Bantrys' current cook

Mrs. Saunders, the Bantrys' former cook who was an excellent cook but had a mournful voice and always sounded as if she were just going to burst into tears.

Mr. Saunders, Mrs. Saunders's husband. He was the butler while his wife was the cook at the Bantry home. He was fat and lazy and, according to Colonel Bantry, he "watered the whiskey."

Fortunately for Miss Marple, Mr. and Mrs.

Saunders were left a legacy by some former employer and opened a boarding house in Dillmouth, of all places. It is at their boarding house that Miss Marple stays while in Dillmouth.

The Misses Elworthy, who lived at Hillside before the Hengraves did. It was they who gave the house its present name. Hillside had formerly been called St. Catherines, but the Misses Elworthy were very "low church," supported the foreign missions and felt that the name St. Catherines sounded "popish."

Mrs. Findeyson, who owned Hillside/St. Catherines before the Misses Elworthy. She was much admired in the neighborhood and maintained a beautiful garden. She rented her home to Gwenda's parents for a short time—just before Gwenda was sent to New Zealand.

Mr. Penderley of Galbraith & Penderley, house agents. He was not with the firm when Gwenda's parents rented St. Catherines, but he is able to direct Gwenda to a person who may remember.

Old Mr. Galbraith who is retired, is over eighty, and had a stroke last year. He lives at a house called Calcutta Lodge in Dillmouth where a daughter cares for him. Mr. Galbraith remembers Major Halliday, his young wife (Helen) and their baby daughter (Gwenda) well enough to provide some useful information about their stay at St. Catherines.

Miss Galbraith, Old Mr. Galbraith's daughter, "a thin middle-aged woman with suspicious eyes" who receives Gwenda and introduces her to Mr. Galbraith

James Kennedy, M.D., Helen Spenlove Kennedy's older half-brother, a retired physician. Gwenda and Giles visit him at his home, which is a few miles north of Dillmouth on the edge of the moor country. Dr. Kennedy has not heard from his half-sister Helen ever since she left Dillmouth nearly twenty years ago.

Dr. Kennedy's Stepmother, who was the mother of Helen Kennedy. According to Mrs. Fane, she was "a fluffy little thing."

A Venomous-looking Housekeeper at the home of Dr. Kennedy who reluctantly provides tea with toast and jam when Giles and Gwenda pay him a visit.

Jackie Afflick, a successful self-made man who owns a fleet of bright-yellow touring coaches called "Daffodil Coaches, Devon and Dorset Tours." He was the "unsuitable young man" with whom Helen was associated when still very young, and whom her older half-brother, Dr. Kennedy, soon disposed of.

Afflick is very proud of his success in business, and of the social connections he has achieved through marriage, always making a point of introducing his wife as "a cousin of Lord Polterham's," in case anyone is interested.

Dorothy Afflick, Jackie Afflick's wife, who is a cousin of Lord Polterham's, in case anyone is interested. She is "a tall, thin, depressed-looking woman, dressed in rather unexpectedly well-cut clothes."

Walter Fane, a young lawyer who was in love with Helen Kennedy and wanted to marry her. When she refused, he left his father's law firm and went to India to be a tea planter. Eventually he returned to Dillmouth and rejoined the family law firm, where he is now the senior partner. He has never married and still lives with his mother at the family home. His face reminds Gwenda of "a house with all the blinds pulled down."

Mrs. Eleanor Fane, Walter Fane's autocratic, domineering mother.

Dorothy Yarde, a mutual acquaintance of Miss Marple's and Mrs. Fane's who suffers from sciatica

Gerald Fane, Mrs. Fane's eldest son who lives in Singapore where he is in the Far East Bank

Robert Fane, Mrs. Fane's second son, who is in the Army.

Robert Fane's Wife, who is a Roman Catholic, which fact is a source of great annoyance to Robert's mother.

Mrs. Fane's Deceased Husband who was "very Low Church."

Henry, Mrs. Fane's asthmatic spaniel

Louisa, Mrs. Fane's cook who makes excellent scones but is "forgetful, like all of them." And there is no variety in her puddings!

Dr. Lazenby, who was a local doctor at the same time that Dr. Kennedy was in practice in Dillmouth. He was more popular than Dr. Kennedy, according to Foster, the jobbing gardener who remembers.

Lily Kimble, née Abbot, who was the housemaid to the Hallidays when they lived at St. Catherines. When Major Halliday's young wife, Helen, went away one evening, taking a packed suitcase with her, Lily suspected foul play because the "wrong clothes" had been packed. Seeing an advertisement in the newspaper asking for any information about Helen Spenlove Halliday, née Kennedy, she wonders if she should get involved. Her husband advises her to keep out of it.

Jim Kimble, Lily's husband whose conversation is usually limited to uttering an occasional all purpose "Ar."

A Very Charming-looking Old Lady with White Hair, a resident of Saltmarsh House who, sipping a glass of milk, asks Gwenda "Was it your poor child, my dear?" If you have read the 1968 *By the Pricking of My Thumbs,* you may recall that an old woman at a nursing home in that book asked the same question of Tuppence Beresford while sipping a glass of milk. How this line happens to occur in both novels remains a mystery.

A White-uniformed Maid at Saltmarsh House who introduces Giles and Gwenda to Dr. Penrose

Dr. Penrose, the current superintendent at Saltmarsh House who explains the case of Major Halliday's "delusions."

Dr. McGuire, who was the superintendent at Saltmarsh House when Major Halliday died there. He kept Major Halliday's diary as part of the case notes.

Two Young Assistants Engaged with Customers at the art needlework shop in Dillmouth

A Pleasant Woman with Grey Hair in the art needlework shop who sells Miss Marple some pale blue knitting wool and a knitting pattern and who knows nothing about St. Catherines, as she has only lived in Dillmouth for about ten years

An Elderly Assistant at the draper's shop who remembers Mrs. Findeyson, Major Halliday, his young wife and their baby girl

Edith ("Edie") Pagett, who was the Hallidays' cook when they lived at St. Catherines. She is a tall, dark and thin woman with hardly any grey in her hair, though she is about fifty years old. She recalls Major Halliday, his young wife and little "Gwennie." She also has clear memories of everything that happened on the night the young Mrs. Halliday disappeared, and she shares those recollections freely with Giles and Gwenda.

Edith Pagett's Father who had had a farm up behind the hill

Edith Pagett's Mother who, after the death of her husband, sold the farm and bought the little fancy shop at the end of the high street

Mr. Mountford, the local confectioner, who is married to the sister of Edith Pagett

Mrs. Mountford, Mr. Mountford's wife and Edith Pagett's sister

A Waitress at the Ginger Cat café who brings weak coffee

"That Layonee," correctly named "Léonie," a Swiss nurse who was working at St. Catherine's when the Halliday's lived there and who said she "saw something," although her English was so poor that nobody ever quite knew what it was that she "saw."

Thomas, a.k.a. "Thomasina," a cat thought to be a male but which suddenly and unexpectedly gave birth to three kittens. It was the Hallidays' cat, on which the maid had once put a bow from a chocolate box. He (or, rather, *she*) had been a very good mouser.

Miss Narracott who presides at the reception desk at the Royal Clarence Hotel in Dillmouth

Major Richard Erskine, who fell in love with Helen Kennedy aboard the ship on the way to India twenty years ago. He was already married and had two children, however, so the situation was an impossible one. Giles and Gwenda Reed visit Major and Mrs. Erskine at their remote house in Northumberland, and Gwenda finds him to be extremely attractive despite his age.

Janet Erskine, Major Erskine's suspicious, jealous wife.

The Erskines' Two Children. The elder is in the Army and the younger has just finished at Oxford and is going into a publishing firm.

A Man from the Stableyard who moves the Erskines' small Austin car so that Gwenda can maneuver her own car out of their driveway, but not soon enough to prevent Gwenda from overhearing an unpleasant conversation between the Erskines.

Manning, a garrulous gardener, aged seventy-five, whom Miss Marple engages for work on Wednesdays at the Reeds,' as he once worked for the Kennedys and may share useful recollections.

Mrs. Yule who lived up at Niagra, according to Manning. She used to have a yew hedge clipped like a squirrel, which Manning thought silly. "Peacocks is one thing and squirrels is another," he declares.

Colonel Lampard who had lovely beds of begonias.

Young Dr. Brent who now lives at Crosby Lodge, the former home of Dr. Kennedy.

Inspector Last, of the Longford Police Station, to whom the death of Lily Kimble is first reported.

Detective Inspector Primer, who soon becomes the officer in charge of the case. He has heard of Miss Marple and her "special abilities."

The Chief Constable of the County, who leaves the case in the care of Detective Inspector Primer.

Colonel Melrose, who has spoken affirmatively to Detective Inspector Primer on the subject of Miss Marple's special abilities, citing in particular her performance in the matter of the man who was murdered in the St. Mary Mead vicarage (*Murder at the Vicarage,* 1930) and the case in which a body was found in the library of a certain prominent resident of that village several years later (*The Body in the Library,* 1942).

[Note: Christie undoubtedly means to refer to Colonel Melchett, who was a character in each of those novels. There is no Colonel Melrose associated with Miss Marple in any story, although there was a Colonel Melrose in the 1926 Hercule Poirot mystery, *The Murder of Roger Ackroyd*, and another Colonel Melrose in the 1929 *The Seven Dials Mystery*.]

COMMENTS

Sleeping Murder is clearly a product of Agatha Christie's best period in terms of interesting, vivid characterizations. That period was from about 1930 to 1960. Christie is supposed to have written *Sleeping Murder* in the 1940s, intending it to be published after her death, and there is nothing in the novel that contradicts that proposition. The mystery is well conceived and well plotted and the investigation—conducted by an amiable young couple together with Miss Marple, who is in rare form—cannot be faulted in any way.

There are many memorable characters in *Sleeping Murder*. There is the domineering, autocratic Mrs. Fane and her amusing afternoon tea scene with Miss Marple. There is Walter Fane himself whose face reminds Gwenda Reed of "a house with all of its blinds pulled down." There are two old servants—Edith Pagett and Lily Kimble—whose vivid recollections about the night of Helen Halliday's disappearance are fascinating. An amusing and memorable scene occurs at the home of Lily Kimble and her husband Jim in which she patters on and on about the possibility of there being "money in it," that is, in the matter of the advertisement for information about Helen Halliday née Kennedy. There is the "not handsome or tall, but definitely-attractive-to-women" Major Erskine who causes Gwenda Reed to "unconsciously adjust her skirt, tweak a side curl and retouch her lips" despite the fact that *her* husband and *his* wife are both present *and* Eskine is nearly thirty years older than she. There is the rather crude "self-made man" Jackie Afflick who drives a garish bright daffodil-yellow luxury car and boasts about his wife's titled relations, in case anyone is interested.

Fortunately, Christie wrote *Sleeping Murder* before she began her period of "preaching" on such subjects as education for the lower classes (Christie was clearly against it), the *unfortunate* demise of the servant class (which Christie viewed as a definite loss to the world) and, most of all, her favorite topic—the issue of Environment vs. Heredity in the formation of personality and character traits. It is true that Miss Marple has one opportunity in *Sleeping Murder* to say "Blood does tell," citing from her vast repertoire of stories an incident in which a church treasurer who was "morally against gambling in any form," bet all the money from the church Christmas Club on a horse because *his father* had been a gambler. But this is the only instance of such nonsense to appear in *Sleeping Murder*. In order to experience the true depth of Christie's conviction that blood inheritance—genetics, in fact—determines everything about a person's character, by all means don't miss the 1952 *Murder with Mirrors* and the 1958 *Ordeal by Innocence*.

There is no reason why *Sleeping Murder* should not be a good "first Christie experience" since it was written during her prime, and is typical of her best writing. But a better plan might be to read the 1930 *Murder at the Vicarage*, then the 1942 *The Body in the Library*, and then the 1976 *Sleeping Murder*, with the understanding that the action in *Sleeping Murder* takes place during the 1940s. In this way the many references to characters and events in the two earlier novels will make sense and the story will be more fun to read.

SUMMARY FOR THE 1970s

Only six Agatha Christie detective novels were published during the 1970s. The 1975 *Curtain* and the 1976 *Sleeping Murder* were written during the 1940s and their publication was postponed in order to make them Christie's "final published works." They are characteristic of her best period but they cannot be called masterpieces. Hercule Poirot dies in *Curtain*, and so there is no reason to read *Curtain* before you have read all thirty-two of the other novels featuring the Poirot character, most of which are more interesting detective stories anyway. As to *Sleeping Murder*, it is a perfectly good Miss Marple adventure that need not be postponed and could actually be an enjoyable "first Christie experience."

Regarding Christie's other four detective novels of the 1970s, they are strictly for "qualified" readers. The "qualification" for reading and enjoying *Passenger to Frankfurt* is to be cynical about politicians (you must be absolutely fed up with liars in the White House and Congress) and to be willing to immerse yourself in a world that is as unlikely as the world of a science fiction novel. *Passenger to Frankfurt* is really a kind of surrealistic experience, a sort of modern-day "Alice in Wonderland" for adults. It could have been entitled *Stafford Nye and Our Crazy World*.

The full title of the book is *Passenger to Frankfurt: An Extravaganza.*

You are "qualified" to read and enjoy *Nemesis* if you have read most of Christie's earlier Miss Marple novels, including *A Caribbean Mystery* in particular, and if you sincerely like the Miss Marple character. It also helps if you like old people, because in this story nearly everybody is old.

You are "qualified" to read and enjoy *Elephants Can Remember* if you have read at least two or three of the earlier novels that featured Ariadne Oliver and Hercule Poirot working together—and enjoyed their personalities and interactions. You should also be an older person who enjoys reminiscing. *Elephants Can Remember* is likely to bore young readers with its cast of old people and their endless conversations about the past which they feel was superior to the present.

You are "qualified" to read *Postern of Fate* if you have read all of the earlier Tommy and Tuppence stories and enjoyed them and, again, if you are an older person.

"Unqualified" readers are advised to avoid these four books altogether, as there are no fewer than sixty-two other Agatha Christie detective novels that will bring more reading pleasure.

Appendix: British Expressions

Agatha Christie's novels, especially the earliest ones, often contain British terms that may be misleading or unknown to American readers. The following listing may be useful.

APACHE Pronounced "ah-PAHSH," this is a French term, derived from the American name for a certain Indian tribe, but in French it refers to a common criminal or "street thug" of Paris. It occurs in two or three early Christie novels, *The Mystery of the Blue Train* in particular, and in *The Secret of Chimneys*. The term has gone out of use even in France nowadays, but as late as the 1950s tourists in Paris were offered the entertainment of an "apache dance" performed at small nightclubs. A man and woman, dressed as low-life types, danced and treated each other with violence, the man flinging the woman around by her hair and the woman slapping the man's face, etc. But by the 1950s "apache dances for tourists" were a subject of ridicule themselves and were often parodied by comedians.

BAIZE DOOR A "baize door" is a door with one or both sides covered with felt ("baize" is another, older term for "felt") in order to create a measure of soundproofing between rooms. Doors leading to the kitchen in an English house were often "baize doors" so that noises from the kitchen—pots and pans clanging, dishes being washed, voices of cook and kitchenmaid, etc.—would be less audible in other rooms. In at least one Christie novel there is a "baize door" separating the servant's quarters from the rest of the house. In one novel, *Murder at Hazelmoor*, there is a heavy sandbag, which is used as a murder weapon; the fabric with which the bag is made is felt, or "baize." This "sandbag" is actually a long, narrow snakelike bag placed at the bottom of a door to keep cold drafts from entering.

BOOTS The "boots" of a hotel or inn was a person whose job included cleaning boots and shoes that the guests left outside their doors at night. The institution of the "boots" has become antiquated but the term occurs in a few early Christie novels, including *Murder at Hazelmoor* (1931), *The Boomerang Clue* (1934) and *Evil Under the Sun* (1941.) The term does not occur in *The Body in the Library* (1942) but we know that in that novel, the Majestic Hotel must have a "boots" because a nine-year-old boy, collecting clues or "souvenirs" of the investigation, snips the end of a shoe lace from a pair of shoes left outside the door of a man who *may* turn out to be the murderer. The shoes had been left there for the "boots" to clean during the night.

BOSCHE (also spelled *Boche*) This is a term of contempt referring to a German person. It has also been used by the French and may have originated in France. In Christie novels beginning with her first, *The Mysterious Affair at Styles* and at least until the 1954 *So Many Steps to Death* certain characters will use the term when speaking contemptuously of Germans. In the 1937 *Death on the Nile*, Colonel Race states that Dr. Bessner, who is Austrian, is "a kind of Bosche," since his native language is German.

CARS, TRAINS AND OTHER VEHICLES In the early novels cars are often referred to as "motors," and the horn of a car is expressed with the word "Klaxon," a patented auto horn in use at the time, making the old "ooh-gah" sound. The "hood" of the car is usually called "bonnet" in England. "Tire" is usually spelled "tyre," and "wind shield" is "wind screen." Trucks are called "lorries," and trolley cars are "trams." In London the subway system is called "The Tube."

In the past, most European railway passenger cars were divided into compartments with a corridor running along one side of the car. The first-class compartments typically seated six passengers, three seats facing the other three. The second and third class compartments were less comfortable and generally seated eight passengers. In all classes it was possible to open the windows, as there was of course no air conditioning. In England, originally there were first, second and third class "carriages" but at some point the "second class" was phased out and by the time Christie was writing her novels, there were only first and third class. In more recent years American-style "coach" seating has come into use both in Britain and on the Continent, mainly for short-distance lines.

For the reading of one novel, the 1957 *What Mrs. McGillicuddy Saw,* it is important to understand the difference between a "corridor car" and a "non–corridor car." See the *Setting* section for that novel for a discussion of that subject.

British drivers use the term "pull up" meaning "pull over to the curb and park" or simply "to stop." The term is a relic of an older term applied to horse drawn vehicles. One "pulled up" on the reins to make the horse stop.

CHEMIST   A chemist is a pharmacist, and a pharmacy is called a "chemist's shop."

COOKER   A "cooker" is simply a kitchen stove; it is the common British term for that appliance. The term occurs in the 1956 *Dead Man's Folly* and in the 1962 *The Mirror Crack'd,* but the word "range" is also used, as in the 1957 *What Mrs. McGillicuddy Saw* (see the *Setting* section for that novel for a description of the kitchen at Rutherford Hall.)

CURRENCY   Since the late 1960s British currency has been expressed in "pounds" and "pence," with one hundred pence (one hundred pennies) in each pound. This system was created to simplify arithmetic calculations, which were difficult under the older system, which was not based on tens and hundreds.

The older system was: A pound consists of twenty shillings. A shilling consists of twelve pennies (pence).

A "guinea" was a special term used in the valuing of high priced goods and was the equivalent of twenty-one shillings, that is, a pound plus a shilling.

Coins in use before about 1967 were: halfpenny; penny; three pence (pronounced "thrupp'nce"); six pence; one shilling; two shillings; half-crown (two shillings and six pence)

"Two pence" was pronounced "tupp'nce" and an early Christie female character has "Tuppence" for a nickname. A criminal attempting to lure her friend Tommy into a trap sends him a note signed "Twopence," which the criminal assumes is the spelling of her nickname since the pronunciation suggests the monetary expression, thus signaling to Tommy that the note is not really from her.

Bank notes in common use were: tenshilling note; one-pound note; five-pound note; ten-pound note

Slang terms referring to money noted in Christie novels: A fisher (a ten-shilling note); A fiver (a five-pound note); A tenner (a ten-pound note); A bob (a shilling); Two bob (two shillings); Five quid (five pounds); Fifty quid (fifty pounds); etc.

In conversation, expressions such as "two and eight" mean "two shillings and eight pence;" "Three and five" would be "three shillings and five pence," etc.

To be "well into pocket" means "to have plenty of money."

To express "being broke" a Christie character may say "I haven't got a bean," or "I'm out of pocket."

It's extremely important to remember that incredible inflation has taken place since the earliest Christie novels were written. Amounts of money mentioned in these early books have no meaning in present day terms. In the *Setting* or *Comments* sections of the chapters, the amounts of money mentioned in the novel are often cited, along with hints for interpreting their value. For example, in two novels of the 1930s, characters purchase second-hand cars for as little as ten or fifteen pounds; a secretary in a 1939 novel earns six pounds a week. A character in a 1937 novel survives poorly on an annual income of less than 200 pounds; in a 1931 novel a man rents a two story house with three bedrooms for just over two pounds a week. In a 1940 novel, a young man proudly announces that he has a "marvelous new job paying ten pounds a week" and, therefore, his fiancée "can chuck her job as a dental assistant and start shopping for her trousseau." Keep these remarks in mind when evaluating legacies in amounts such as 50,000 pounds which are seen as "fortunes." They were, in fact, fortunes, and quite adequate as murder motives.

DEMOBBED   This is a British slang term for "demobilized," or discharged from military service. It occurs frequently in Christie stories, beginning with the 1922 *The Secret Adversary* in which there is a reference to Tommy Beresford's having been "demobbed" at the end of World War I. In the 1948 *There Is a Tide,* the story begins just after the protagonist, Lynn Marchmont, is "demobbed" from the Wrens at the end of World War II.

DULL   "Boring" or "bored" can both be expressed by "dull." Example: "I'm afraid your brother may be dull living in the village after living in London."

FAG   A younger boy in an English "public school" (see "Public School," below) who was assigned to act as a servant to one of the older boys. The purpose of the practice of "fagging" was to prevent chaos at a school by assigning to the older boys the duty of maintaining discipline among the younger boys. The practice of "fagging" was widespread until the middle of the twentieth century, but declined after about 1960 and was outlawed at most schools during the 1980s because of the harsh physical discipline sometimes inflicted by older boys on younger ones and because of reports of sexual abuse associated with it.

The term "fag" only occurs once in a Christie novel—the 1959 *Cat Among the Pigeons*. In that novel Prince Ali Yusuf, the hereditary ruler of a fictitious Middle Eastern kingdom called Ramat, had been educated at an English "public school" and a young English boy, Bob Rawlinson, had been his "fag." The two are now adult men and good friends, and Rawlinson is the pilot of the prince's private airplane. As a result of Prince Ali Yusuf's English "public school education," he has modern democratic ideas which he is trying unsuccessfully to promote at home in his country.

FIRST FLOOR It may surprise Americans to learn that in most countries—including all of Europe—the "first floor" of a building is *not* the ground floor. It is actually the floor *above* the ground floor, and so the bedrooms in a two-story house in England are on the "first floor." This term is often used in Christie novels, and there are even a few illustrations showing "the first floor" of a house, meaning actually the upper floor consisting of bedrooms, as is the case in *The Mysterious Affair at Styles*. In one novel, a child falls to his death from a "second-story window" while washing windows. In American speech, it is from a third-story window that he falls.

GLARE GLASSES A British term for sunglasses is "glare glasses."

HOUSING In England any dwelling can be referred to as "house" just as in America, but more often the words "cottage" and "bungalow" are used for the smaller houses. The "bungalow" is the smallest individual house, sometimes consisting of just one floor, or perhaps having one or two rooms on an upper floor. A "cottage" is generally a house larger than a "bungalow" and can actually be what Americans would consider to be a full size, substantial home with three or four bedrooms upstairs. "Cottage" would not be applied to a very much larger house, however. Americans are accustomed to using the word "cottage" for a small, lightly constructed building for vacationing and not a permanent residence; in England that is not the case.

In English cities most "houses" are attached to each other in rows and are called "terraced houses." In old villages small houses attached in rows may be referred to as "cottages."

"Flat" is the usual British term for "apartment." The word "apartment" exists in England and can be used for any suite of rooms for any purpose, but the word "flat" continues to be more common when applied to living quarters.

The American term "living room" (which, by the way, is only about a century old even in America, the former term being "parlor") is gaining popularity in England but the usual term continues to be "lounge," and real estate descriptions of houses in England refer to the living room as "lounge." The term "drawing room" has gone out of use but it was still a part of everyday speech in most of Christie's novels through about 1960. It was originally "*withdrawing* room," meaning the room to which the family "withdrew" after the meal while servants cleared the dining room.

In the 1962 *The Mirror Crack'd*, there is an amusing linguistic conflict between old Miss Marple and her young cleaning lady, Cherry Baker. Cherry persists in calling Miss Marple's drawing room "the lounge" despite repeated corrections from Miss Marple. Eventually Cherry settles for a compromise and calls the room "the living room." It is clear that, by 1962, only the oldest people in Britain were still using the term "drawing room."

"Study" and "library" appear to be interchangeable. In at least one Christie novel the murder victim is found in the "study" which some characters later call the "library."

"Boudoir" was a term usually referring to a room reserved for the lady of a large house as a private sitting room, usually, but not always, on an upper floor near her bedroom. It was furnished according to her taste in comfort and was the place she went whenever she wanted privacy—for private conversations or simply to have "time alone." Photo albums and other mementos would usually be kept there. The term comes from the French verb "boudre" meaning "to pout." If a woman was in a bad mood and needed to "have a good cry," it was to the boudoir that she retreated. The term "boudoir" occurs in a few of Christie's earliest stories, notably in *The Mysterious Affair at Styles*, and that room has a special importance in that story.

The man of a large house might also have a "private space" called a "study." There he could smoke without enduring the complaints of the women in the house, and entertain male friends with drinks or strong conversation. Items disgusting to females, such as stuffed heads of animals or paintings of horses and dogs, would be displayed there.

Windows of ground-floor rooms in homes were frequently "French windows," and were often used during warm weather to enter and leave the house. The "French Window" is opened and closed from the center and swings on hinges. Its sill is close enough to the floor to be easily stepped over, even by children. In several Christie novels, characters come into the house "through the window," meaning of course that they simply step into the room from outside over the low threshold of the French window. In the 1952 *Mrs. McGinty's Dead*, Hercule Poirot has the unpleasant experience of staying at a house that is being incompetently run as a guesthouse. The house is in an advanced state of disrepair; the front door will not stay closed, and the owners' dogs are constantly running in and out of the house "through the window" in the sitting room. Clearly that window is a French window.

Screens for windows are not nearly as common in Europe as they are in America, as flying insects do not seem to be as great a problem there, at least in cities.

LODGE A very large country estate in England would typically be surrounded by thick hedges or walls, and the entrance drive would have an impressive iron gate at the road. As this gate might be at a considerable distance from the main house—sometimes a quarter or even half a mile from it—there was typically a "lodge" just inside the large gate. The lodge was a small house or cottage occupied by the "lodge keeper," whose only duties were opening and closing the gate whenever needed. The lodge keeper might be a single man but he might have a wife and even children, all housed in the "lodge."

The term first occurs in the 1924 *The Man in the Brown Suit* in which a gardener and his wife occupy the lodge at Mill house. In the 1926 *The Murder of Roger Ackroyd,* the large estate Femly Park has a lodge which is being rented to a tenant. In the 1929 *The Seven Dials Mystery,* Lady Eileen Brent, who is always in a great hurry, drives her car to the gate and sounds the "Klaxon" furiously (the "Klaxon" was an electrically operated automobile horn that made the old-fashioned "ooh-gah" sound.) In response to her frantic noisemaking, a small child runs out of the lodge and opens the gate; she is the child of the lodge keeper.

In the 1930 *Murder at the Vicarage,* the largest house in St. Mary Mead, "Old Hall," is occupied by the Protheroe family. This large estate has two lodges, evidently because there are two different gates to the estate, and one of the lodges is unoccupied at the moment, although it still has its working telephone. A telephone at the lodge must have been a great convenience to the lodge keeper, as he could then phone the main house to ask whether the gate should be opened to a particular stranger.

In the 1940 *Sad Cypress,* the lodge at the large estate Hunterbury plays an important role because the lodge keeper has a daughter in whom the lady of the large house has taken a special interest. That young woman will be a murder victim and there will be more than the usual passing reference to the "lodge" in that novel.

With the advent of electrically operated gates for large estates, the "lodge keeper" and the lodge itself were no longer necessary and the old lodges often became simply rental houses. In one novel, the 1956 *Dead Man's Folly,* the former lady of the large Nasse House in Devon has been forced to sell the property but the new owners have allowed her to rent the lodge and live there. The lodge has been modernized and made much more comfortable. She is very happy living there since she has ridded herself of the responsibilities and expenses of the huge estate but has not really "left home."

In the 1962 *The Mirror Crack'd*, there is a similar situation. The recently-widowed Dolly Bantry has sold her large mansion Gossington Hall, but she has retained the lodge and a small garden area for herself, modernizing the lodge and making it into a comfortable small home. Like Mrs. Folliat in *Dead Man's Folly,* Mrs. Bantry no longer has the responsibilities of maintaining the large estate but has not really "left home."

See the *Setting* section of the chapter on the 1953 *A Pocket Full of Rye* for some interesting comments by a police inspector on the subject of lodges. In that novel there is a pretentious, new luxury home—actually a mansion—named "Yewtree Lodge," and the inspector, who grew up in a "real" lodge has some amusing remarks on that subject.

MANNEQUIN (also spelled *Manikin*) This

term is most often used in America for a full-size human model used for displaying clothing in store windows but in England it most often applies to *live* clothing models. The term is used this way in at least two Christie novels: the 1928 *The Mystery of the Blue Train* and the 1935 *Murder in Three Acts*.

MEAN This adjective is most often used as a synonym for "miserly" or "stingy" in money matters, rather than as a synonym of "unkind" or "cruel." It is used constantly in the 1957 *What Mrs. McGillicuddy Saw* to describe the miserly Luther Crackenthorpe.

NIGGER This word has been an extremely offensive racial slur since the American Civil War—in America, but not in England. Originally—even in America—the word was simply an English borrowing of the Spanish word "negro" meaning black. It kept that simple meaning in England while, in America, it became a racial slur.

The word occurs occasionally in the speech of Christie characters—earliest in *The Mysterious Affair at Styles* when the parlormaid speaks of a costume party in the past when "Mr. Lawrence was a nigger once," meaning simply that he blackened his face and hands for the costume. In a letter written by Emily Trefusis in *Murder at Hazelmoor* the writer says that she has been "working like the worst kind of nigger," meaning that she has been working very hard. The expression "to work like a nigger" meant "to work very hard," implying "to work as hard as a slave would." In *The Patriotic Murders* the boyfriend of a dental assistant tells her that the dentist "works her like a nigger," meaning that he treats her as a slave.

The original English title of *And Then There Were None* was *Ten Little Niggers* and it provoked no offence or protest in England but the title was changed to *And Then There Were None* for the American edition for obvious reasons. Many years later, however, even in England the term acquired the American-style "racial slur" flavor, and a crowd at a British theatre where *Ten Little Niggers* was playing formed outside to protest the word. The theatre management complied with the protestors' demands and changed the title of the play.

In any case, at no time did Christie ever use the word "nigger" to express contempt for a race.

PAVEMENT VS. SIDEWALK, STREET VS. ROAD The American term "sidewalk" is usually expressed by "pavement" in England. An American mother tells the child to stay on the "sidewalk" and not go into the "street." The British mother tells the child to keep to the "pavement" and not go into the "road."

PUBLIC SCHOOL In most parts of the world, including America, the term "public school" implies a school that is supported by government funding and is attended by students free of charge. In Britain, the term (at least until very recently) referred to expensive boys' schools that were entirely funded by *non–governmental* sources. The only thing "public" about them was that they could be attended by any student who could pay the fees. That is, they were not reserved for students of aristocratic birth. Certain very elite "public schools," in particular Eton and Harrow, supposedly trained intelligent boys for service to the British nation and the Empire. The ineptitude of many British generals during the First World War who had been "educated" in public schools reduced the prestige of public schools in general.

In Christie novels there are innumerable references to "public schools" and "a public school education," and the references are usually derisive ones. Notable is the reference to the "uselessness of a public school education" by the character Raymond Starr in the 1942 *The Body in the Library*. Raymond works as a dance and tennis pro (and "all around gigolo," in his own satirical words) at a prestigious seaside resort hotel. He explains that, as a result of his "public school education," his only marketable skills are teaching tennis and ballroom dancing.

A characteristic of men in Christie novels who have been educated at "public schools" is to regard themselves collectively as a "good old boys" club. They use the term "Pukka Sahib," also spelled "Pucka Sahib" in referring to each other. (See "Pukka Sahib," below.) These men are always portrayed in Christie novels as being suspicious of "foreigners," and, in general, of being quite stupid.

PUKKA SAHIB or PUCKA SAHIB This term was apparently used as an equivalent of "good old boy," and occurs in Christie novels when a man foolishly dismisses from suspicion another man simply because he is "one of the good old boys" for one reason or another. The term was originally used by British soldiers in India with the meaning of "an excellent fellow," and it was used exclusively, of course, in referring to British men.

Men who use the term "pukka sahib" in Christie's novels are always conservative types who mistrust foreigners and, furthermore, who are quite stupid in general. Captain Hastings, for example, is likely to trust certain men simply because they appear to be "good old boys from Harrow or Eton" and to use the term "pukka sahib" to describe them, and to absolve them from suspicion of any wrongdoing. Poirot's reaction will always be to ridicule Hastings for those foolish judgments. In *Murder in the Calais Coach* Colonel Arbuthnot, a British colonial type, tells Poirot and his colleagues of the moment, Monsieur Bouc and Dr. Constantine, that Miss Debenham is a "pukka sahib," thus assuring them that she's "all right." Dr. Constantine later asks the meaning of "pukka sahib" and Poirot explains that it means that Miss Debenham's father and brothers went to the same kind of school as Colonel Arbuthnot. Dr. Constantine says "Oh, then it has nothing to do with the crime," and Poirot responds, "Exactly."

PUSSY or **OLD PUSSY** These are slightly derogatory terms used to refer to "old ladies." Men, and also some younger women, use them in Christie novels to refer to older women in a mildly offensive way, but there is nothing obscene or sexual in their meaning. An "old pussy" is an old lady with time on her hands who probably gossips and expresses judgmental opinions about others, or else is simply outmoded in her thinking. "Old cat" is a synonymous term.

Miss Jane Marple, first introduced in 1930 in *Murder at the Vicarage* but making only rare appearances in early Christie novels (just twice during the 1940s) will become one of Christie's best-known sleuths during the 1950s and 1960s with seven appearances in novels during those decades. Her old friend Sir Henry Clithering, a retired Scotland Yard inspector, uses the term "old pussies" smilingly and even rapturously in describing the special genius of such ladies in solving crimes. In the 1950 *A Murder Is Announced,* Chief Constable Rydesdale receives a letter from Miss Marple and speaks of it to Sir Henry:

> "Authentic letter from an old pussy. Staying at the Royal Spa Hotel. Something she thinks we might like to know in connection with the Chipping Cleghorn business."
>
> "The old pussies," said Sir Henry triumphantly. "What did I tell you? They hear everything. They see everything. And, unlike the famous adage, they speak all evil. What's this particular one got hold of?"

Sir Henry soon learns that it is Jane Marple who wrote the letter. His reaction:

> "Ye gods and little fishes," said Sir Henry, "can it be? George, it's my own particular, one and only, four-starred pussy. The super-pussy of all old pussies. And she has managed somehow to be at Medenham Wells, instead of peacefully at home in St. Mary Mead, just at the right time to be mixed up in a murder. Once more a murder is announced—for the benefit and enjoyment of Miss Marple."

QUEER and **GAY** The word "gay" was not used in general speech to denote "homosexual" until about 1970, although it was probably used among homosexuals themselves much earlier, and in a 1938 comedy film (*Bringing Up Baby*, which starred Katherine Hepburn and Cary Grant), Grant used the word "gay" with its homosexual meaning in one line. In any case, that word in Christie novels *almost never* has a homosexual meaning. If a male character is said to "lead a gay life in London" it simply means that he probably gambles, goes to nightclubs, drinks often, has lots of female friends, and in general is not very serious about work and responsibilities. It does not mean that he is homosexual. In the 1944 *Towards Zero,* a character describes a hotel where he has spent an evening playing billiards as "a gay spot—they keep it up till all hours." He simply means that the hotel is popular with vacationers and that the recreational facilities are used till late at night.

There is just one exception to the above: In the 1939 *Easy to Kill,* there is an effeminate male character, the antique shop owner Mr. Ellsworthy, who is generally thought of as "strange" or "queer" by the residents of the village of Wychwood. One day he receives three outlandishly-dressed guests from London, including a man who wears shorts and a plum-colored shirt and another man who wears a lavender suit, and it is obvious that these men are intended to be seen by the reader as gay. In connection with these men and their host, there is a remark that "there will be gay doings" that night in the village, although the "gay doings" appear to have more to do with witchcraft than sex. See the *Setting* section for *Easy to Kill* if this subject interests you.

The use of the word "queer" to denote "homosexual" is much older and, as early as the 1933 novel *Thirteen at Dinner,* characters use it on occasion to "suggest" homosexuality, as does Lady Edgware in speaking of her husband. In the 1935 *Murder in Three Acts,* Hermione Lytton Gore expresses the view that "men ought to have affairs—it proves they're not queer or anything." This statement shocks her listener, a fussy older man of the Victorian generation; therefore it is assumed that her use of the term—or else her mere introduction of the subject—was a very "modern" thing, at least for females, in the mid–1930s.

RING UP, RING OFF These terms apply to telephone use. The person "rings off" at the end of the conversation (hangs up.) "Ring for the police" means "call the police," and one "rings up" (makes a phone call to) a friend.

STONE People's weight is often expressed by this term, which means "fourteen pounds." A person weighing 140 pounds weighs "ten stone."

VEGETABLE MARROW A "vegetable marrow" is a summer squash, such as zucchini. In the 1926 *The Murder of Roger Ackroyd,* Hercule Poirot attempts briefly to retire to the country and to indulge in a new hobby, the growing of vegetable marrows. There are references to this in one or two subsequent novels as well.

Title and Character Index

Boldfaced page numbers refer to main entries.

Aarons, Joseph 24, 27, 46, 179
Abbot, Mr. 158–59
Abbott, Mr. 170
A.B.C. Murders, The 11, 12, 74, 76, **105–111**, 116, 121, 126, 139, 141–42, 144, 166–167, 180, 198, 205, 225, 265, 277, 316, 360
Abdul (*Appointment with Death*) 148
Abdul (*Murder at Hazelmoor*) 65
Abdul (*They Came to Baghdad*) 256
Abdullah (*Murder in Mesopotamia*) 115, 142
Abdullah (*They Came to Baghdad*) 256
Abdullah, Achmed 319
Abercrombie, Archdeacon 356
Abercrombie, Colonel 139, 176–77, 180, 208
Abercromby, General 363
Abernethie, Cornelius 278, 302
Abernethie, Helen 278
Abernethie, Maude 278, 324
Abernethie, Mortimer 278
Abernethie, Richard 277–78, 324
Abernethie, Timothy 278, 281–82, 324
Achmed, Old 319
Ackroyd, Flora 40–41
Ackroyd, Mrs. Cecil 41, 43
Ackroyd, Roger 39, 40–41, 140, 160, 215, 301
Ada 196
Adams 222
Adams, Carlotta 75–76
Adams, Dr. 22
Adams, Mrs. 178
Adams, Old 202
Adington, Lady 308
Adolph, Monsieur 396
Afflick, Dorothy 412
Afflick, Jackie 302, 412, 414
After the Funeral (see *Funerals Are Fatal*)
Agrodopolous, Mr. 242
Aguileros, Karl 386
Ah Ling 46
Aitkin, Gladys 235
Akibombo, Mr. 289–90, 353
Alanbrooke 364
Albert (*Evil Under the Sun*) 185
Albert (*Remembered Death*) 228
Albertina 395
Aldborough, Sir John and Lady 385

Aldbury, Cecil 397
Aldin, Mary 211, 213, 215
Alexa 385
Alf 345
Alfred 55
Alfrege, Madame 228
Ali, Mr. Ahmed 291
Alice (*At Bertram's Hotel*) 358
Alice (*The Body in the Library*) 197
Alice (*The Mirror Crack'd*) 337
Alice (*The Mystery of the Blue Train*) 50
Alice, Great-aunt 395
Allcock, Councillor 338
Allcock, Mrs. 338
Allen 321
Allerton, Major 406
Allerton, Mrs. 126–28, 131
Allerton, Tim 126–28, 199
Alstir, Ralph 242
Altamount, Lord 385, 386
Alton 77
Amberiotis, Mr. 176, 177–78
Ambrose, Claud 49
Ambrose, Nora 379–80
Amphrey, Miss 166, 212
Amy (*The Mirror Crack'd*) 337
Amy (*Mrs. McGinty's Dead*) 261
Anastasia Nikoläevna 386
Anchoukoff, Boris 38
And Then There Were None 7, 86, 139, **162–166**, 167, 198, 214, 238, 265, 421
Andersen, Greta 368
Anderson (*The Body in the Library*) 197
Anderson (*By the Pricking of My Thumbs*) 373
Anderson, Divisional Inspector 120
Anderson, Edmund 390
Anderson, Esther (formerly Esther Walters) 390
Anderson, Meroe 320
Anderson, Professor 320
Andrassy, Captain 38
Andrenyi, Count 90
Andrenyi, Countess 90
Andrew 400
Andrews, Betsy 45
Andrews, Squadron Leader 386
Andrews, Superintendent 357
Angélique, Mère 102
Angkatell, David 227
Angkatell, Edward 226–27, 230–31, 244
Angkatell, Henry (Lord Angkatell) 226

Angkatell, Lucy (Lady Angkatell) 226, 229–30
Angus (*The Mirror Crack'd*) 339
Angus (*Poirot Loses a Client*) 136
Ankoumian, Miss 256
Anna (*N or M?*) 191
Anna (*The Seven Dials Mystery*) 56
Annette 22
Annie (*The Murder of Roger Ackroyd*) 39, 40, 42
Annie (*The Mysterious Affair at Styles*) 17
Annie (*The Mystery of the Blue Train*) 49
Annie (*Poirot Loses a Client*) 138
Annie (*The Secret Adversary*) 22
Annie (*Third Girl*) 364
Ansell, Mr. 274
Anstice, Lord Frederick ("Freddie") 273
Anstruther, Mrs. 159, 161
Anstwell, Mrs. 120
Anthea 372
Antoine 203
Appleby, Colonel 202
Appleby, Mr. 45
Appledore 191
Appointment with Death 13, 57, 112, 131, 142, **144–149**, 151, 154, 156, 166, 172, 186, 209, 217, 223, 237, 264, 270
Arbuthnot, Colonel 88–89, 139, 180, 208, 326, 422
Arbuthnot, George 83
Arbuthnot, Mr. and Mrs. 385
Archdale, Betty 222
Archer 59, 60–61
Archer, Mr. 330
Archer, Old Mrs. 61
Archerton 179
Arden, Enoch 233, 235, 239
Arden, Joe 351
Arden, Mrs. Joe 351
Ardingly, David 330, 333
Ardley, Beatrice 378
Argyle, Christina (Tina) 313
Argyle, Hester 313
Argyle, Jack (Jacko) 312–14
Argyle, Leo 313–5
Argyle, Michael (Micky) 313–15, 325
Argyle, Rachel 312–14
Aristides, Monsieur 284
Armitage, Young 164
Armstrong, Edward George 164
Arnold, Lydia 317
Arnold, Mrs. 317

Arrichet, Françoise 24, 27, 30
Arthur, Young 212
Arundell, Agnes 134
Arundell, Charles 136, 224
Arundell, Emily Harriet Laverton 134–38, 140, 214, 217
Arundell, General John Laverton 134, 139
Arundell, Matilda 134
Arundell, Theresa 133, 135, 137, 280
Arundell, Thomas 134
Ascher, Franz 108
Ascher, Mrs. Alice 106–08, 142
Ashayet 216–17
Ashe, Old Man 250, 341
Askew, Thomas 83
Astor, Anthony (Muriel Wills) 94
At Bertram's Hotel 13, 142–43, 209, 238, 275, 302, 309, 335, 353–360, 374–76, 382, 384, 388, 402, 410
Athelhampton, Lady 385,
Atkins, Old Mrs. 401
Atkinson, Colonel ("Old Moustachio-Monty") 401
Atkinson, Mr. 321
Attenbury, Sir Samuel 171
Atwell, Maisie 220
Aubyn, Edwin 394
Auchinleck 364
Auguste 24, 27, 30, 342
Augustus 159
Austin, Celia 29–31
Avis, Old 207

Babbington, Edward 95
Babbington, Lloyd 95
Babbington, Margaret 94
Babbington, Reverend Stephen 93–95
Babbington, Robin 95
Babbington, Stephen 95
Backhouse, Johnnie 269
Bacon, Inspector 306–08
Badcock, Arthur 337, 339
Badcock, Heather 337–39, 352
Badcock, Louise 373
Badcock, Mrs. 373
Badger, Mr. 196
Badger, Mrs. 196
Badgworthy, Inspector 37
Baily 17
Bain, Mary 339
Baker, Cherry 336, 339–41, 390, 392, 419
Baker, David 361–63
Baker, Jim 336, 339–41, 390
Baker, Mr. 95
Baker, Mrs. Calvin 284
Baker, Richard 255–57
Baker, Sam 109
Baker, Sam's Young Lady 109
Baker, William 307
Baldwin, Superintendent 298
Ball, Andrew 320
Ball, Mr. 109
Ball, Victoria 95
Balsano, Giuseppe 221
Baltrout, Miss 291
Banks, Gregory 279–80
Banks, Henry 321
Banks, Susan 279–81

Bantry, Colonel Arthur 180, 193–94, 196–97, 199, 334, 337, 408, 411
Bantry, Dolly 143, 180–81, 193–95, 294, 333–35, 337–38, 340, 408, 411, 420
Barber, Mrs. 401
Barber, Sergeant 320
Bardwell, Mr. 338
Barker, Ned 250
Barker, Sister 392
Barlowe, The Marchioness of 358
Barnard, Elizabeth (Betty) 106, 108–09, 141
Barnard, Megan 109, 111
Barnard, Mr. 109
Barnard, Mrs. (*The A.B.C. Murders*) 109
Barnard, Mrs. (*The Body in the Library*) 195
Barnes, Mr. 178, 180
Barnes, Will and George 214
Barney 196
Barnstaple, Old General 338
Barraclough, Raymond 102
Barrett, Jane 213, 215
Barron, Dr. 284, 287
Barrow, Miss 391
Barry, Major 139, 184, 186
Bartlett, George 196
Bartlett, Miss (*Nemesis*) 390
Bartlett, Miss (*What Mrs. McGillicuddy Saw*) 308
Barton, Dr. 279
Barton, Edith 201
Barton, Emily 201, 202, 307
Barton, George 219–22
Barton, Mable 201
Barton, Minnie 201
Barton, Old Mrs. 201
Barton, Rosemary 219–22
Bascombe 384
Bassington, Violet 95
Bassington-ffrench, Henry 83–84
Bassington-ffrench, Roger 82–83
Bassington-ffrench, Sylvia, 83, 142, 198
Bassington-ffrench, Tommy 83
Bassingtons, The 401
Bateman, Rupert ("Pongo") 54
Bateson, Leonard ("Len") 290
Batt, Albert 21–22, 74, 180, 190–91, 370, 372, 400
Batt, Amy 400
Batt, Milly 372
Battersby, Miss 364
Battle, Mary 212
Battle, Superintendent 36, 38, 54–56, 118–21, 123, 160, 210–15, 222, 346
Battle, Sylvia 212, 346
Bauer, John 55
Bauerstein, Dr. 17, 20
Baumgarten, Mr. 269
Beadle, Alfred 340
Beadon, Badger 81–84
Beatrice (*The Moving Finger*) 201–03
Beatrice (*Murder at Hazelmoor*) 65, 68
Beatrice (*N or M?*) 189, 281
Beatrice (*Postern of Fate*) 400–01
Beck, Colonel 346

Becker, Ridgway 356
Beddingfeld, Anne 30–34, 69, 74, 94, 120, 133, 141, 218, 221, 257
Beddingfeld, Mr. 252
Beddingfeld, Professor 30–31
Beddingfield, Mrs. 402
Beddoes, Mrs. 214
Beddoes, Sergeant 178, 180
Bell, Miss 272
Bell, Old 160
Bell, Sergeant 291
Bellever, Juliet (Jolly) 269–70
Bellings, Mrs. 64–66
Bellows, Jean 263
Ben 262
Ben, Uncle 403
Bence, Margot 338–39
Benfield, Charlotte 379
Bennett, Alice 77
Bennett, Paul 220
Bennington, Mrs. Nora 368
Benson, Mr. (*Dead Man's Folly*) 298
Benson, Mr. (*Mrs. McGinty's Dead*) 262
Benson, Mrs. 120–21
Bent, Clifford 386
Bent, Grace 153
Bentham, Alice 214
Bentham, Miss 391
Bentley, James 259–61, 264, 380
Bentmore 212
Berat, Jean 115
Beresford, Deborah 189, 191, 370–72, 398–99, 400, 402
Beresford, Derek 189, 191, 370–72, 398, 400, 402
Beresford, Prudence ("Tuppence") 9, 20–24, 73–74, 94, 141, 188–91, 218, 370–75, 398–99, 400–03, 413, 415, 418
Beresford, Sir William 22
Beresford, Thomas ("Tommy") 9, 20–24, 73, 169, 141, 188–91, 370–75, 398–99, 400–03, 415, 418
Berkeley, Badger 164, 165
Bernsdorff, Professor Robert (a.k.a. Dr. Bernsdorff) 273
Béroldy, Madame 27
Béroldy, Monsieur Arnold 27
Berry, Old Lady 356
Berry, Old Mrs. 195
Bert 403
Bessner, Dr. Carl 129, 167
Best 250
Betterton, Elsa 283
Betterton, Olive 283–84, 286
Betterton, Thomas Charles 282–283, 285
Bex, Monsieur Lucien 27
Bianca 338
Big Four, The 6, 10, 12, 23, 43–47, 51, 57, 73–74, 167, 292, 301
Biggs, Alfred 176, 180
Biggs, Arabella 134
Biggs, Emily 171
Biggs, Mrs. 291
Bigland, Rufus 170
Bigland, Ted 170
Billingsley, Mr. 274
Binion, Dr. 191
Binns, Edith 330

Bird, Miss 298
Bird, Mrs. 317
Bird, Pamela 317
Birdlip, Mrs. 262
Birell, Louise 363
Birkin, Jonathan 392
Birnbaum, Mr. 269
Bishop, Emma 170–73
Black, Mary 42
Blacker, Superintendent 269
Blackett, Mrs. 392
Blacklock, Charlotte 251–52
Blacklock, Miss Letitia 249, 250–52
Blacklock, Old Dr. 252
Blackmores, The 401
Blackwell, Mrs. 400
Blair, The Honorable Mrs. Clarence (Suzanne) 32
Blake, Basil 195, 197, 199
Blake, Elvira 355–57, 359–60
Blake, Meredith 206–07, 209
Blake, Miss 318
Blake, Philip 13, 206–07, 209
Blake, Selina 180, 195
Blake, Vera 262
Blanche, Mademoiselle Angèle 318, 320, 322
Bland, Detective Inspector 295, 298
Bland, Josaiah 345
Bland, Valerie 345
Blatt, Elsie 121, 230
Blatt, Horace 182, 184, 186, 301
Blenkensop, Mrs. 189–90, 372, 401
Bletchley, Major 139, 190
Bligh, Nellie, a.k.a Gertrude Bligh, a.k.a. Geraldine Bligh 373
Blondin, Gaston 127–28
Blood Will Tell see *Mrs. McGinty's Dead*
Blore, William Henry 165
Blunt, Admiral Philip 386
Blunt, Alistair 176–80
Blunt, Major Hector 41
Bob 137
Bodlicott, Henry ("Chuck") 402
Bodlicott, Mrs. 402
Bodlicott, Old Isaac 400, 403
Body in the Library, The 1, 11, 39, 61, 123, 140, 143–44, 165, 180, **192–199**, 203, 208–09, 217, 225, 239, 242, 245, 265, 275, 294, 306–07, 311, 333–34, 336–38, 340, 351–52, 355, 392, 408, 411, 414, 417, 421
Bolford, Mr. 254
Bolitho, Mrs. 177
Bolland, Mrs. 401
Bollard, Mr. 357
Bond, Sergeant Percy 320
Bondy, Old Mrs. 228
Bonner, Officer 160
Boomerang Clue, The 11–12, 80–86, 97, 139, 141–42, 173, 198, 237–38, 246, 417
Borden, Lizzie 411
Borgonneau, Professor 45
Boscowan, Emma 373
Boscowan, William 373–74
Bosner, Frederick 113, 115
Bosner, William 115

Bott, Police Constable 291
Bouc, Monsieur 88–90, 422
Bourget, Louise 129
Bourne, Ursula 42
Bowers, Miss 128
Boyd Carrington, Sir William 405–06
Boynton, Carol 147
Boynton, Ginevra 147
Boynton, Lennox 147
Boynton, Mrs. Elmer 146–69, 154, 264
Boynton, Nadine 147
Boynton, Raymond 147
Brabazon, Archdeacon 392
Braceby, Anna 395
Bradbury, Lady Cynthia 255
Bradbury-Scott, Anthea 391
Bradbury-Scott, Clotilde 391
Bradbury-Scott, Old Colonel 391
Bradley, Mr. 332
Bradleys, The 373
Brand, Mrs. 380
Brandon, Eileen 322
Breck, Dr. Alan 257
Brent, Edna 344, 346
Brent, Emily 86, 164, 238
Brent, Lady Eileen ("Bundle") 36–99, 54–56, 73, 82–84, 94, 96, 141–22, 147, 173, 198, 218, 223, 301, 341, 420
Brent, Michael 331
Brent, Old Tom 164
Brent, Sir Clement Edward Alistair ("Lord Caterham") 37, 55
Brent, Young Dr. 413
Brewis, Miss Amanda 297, 299, 311, 324
Brewster, Emily 183–84, 186
Brewster, Jim 386
Brewster, Lola 338
Brice-Woodworth, The Hon. Patricia 221
Bridget 357
Brierly, Mrs. 309
Briggs 197
Briggs, Constable 107
Briggs, Old (*Cat Among the Pigeons*) 318, 341
Briggs, Old (*The Mirror Crack'd*) 338
Brill, Inspector 171
Brinton, Diana 214
Broad, Nancy 392
Broad, Nora 392
Broadribb, Mr. 388, 390
Bronson, Mr. 46
Brookbank, Lady 331
Brown, Geraldine Mary Alexandra 347
Brown, Laurence 242
Brown, Lynette 339
Brown, Mr. (*The Clocks*) 347
Brown, Mr. (*The Secret Adversary*) 20–23, 401
Browne, Anthony 221–23
Brun, Mademoiselle Geneviève 38
Bryant, Dr. James 100, 104
Buckle, Doris 153
Buckle, Marlene 396
Buckle, Mr. 396
Buckle, Mrs. 396

Buckley, Magdala ("Nick") 69–71, 73–4, 76, 141, 187, 218
Buckley, Maggie 71
Buckley, Mrs. 71
Buckley, The Rev. Giles 71
Bude, Miss 386
Bulmer, Sir Edwin 171
Bulstrode, Miss Honoria 317–18, 320–22, 380
Bunner, Miss Dora 246, 249, 252
Burch, Bessie 260, 262
Burch, Joe 260, 262
Burgeon, Mr. 255
Burgess, Miss 120
Burnaby, Major John 64, 66–68, 139
Burnaby, Mr. 127
Burnabys, The 139
Burton, Jerry 200–04
Burton, Joanna 201, 203–04
Burton-Cox, Desmond 395
Burton-Cox, Mr. 395
Burton-Cox, Mrs. 393–95, 397
Bury, Mr. 120
Butler, Henry and Mamie 391
Butler, Judith 376–77, 379–82
Butler, Miranda 377, 381, 382
Butt, Johnnie 248
Butt, Mr. and Mrs. 248
By the Pricking of My Thumbs 9, **369–375**, 394, 399–400, 403, 413

Cabot, Mr. and Mrs. Elmer 358
Cade, Anthony 36–39, 56, 73
Caldecott, Old Mrs. 170
Caley, Alfred 190
Caley, Elizabeth 190
Calgary, Dr. Arthur 312–15
Callory, Denis 263
Cambell, Lady 95
Cambell, Sir Jocelyn 95
Campbell, Inspector 358
Campbell, Mrs. ("Aunt Gina") 320
Canning, Elizabeth 256
Capstick, Nurse 109
Carberry, Old 242
Carbury, Colonel 131, 145–46, 151
Cardew Trench, Mrs. 255–56
Cardiff, Peter 364
Cards on the Table 12–13, 34, **117–125**, 129, 144, 146, 160, 212, 221, 228, 230, 262, 329, 330, 332–333, 360, 362–63, 377, 393–94
Carey, Mildred 291
Cargill, Mr. 197
Caribbean Mystery, A 8, 13, 61, 139, 293, 309, **348–353**, 354, 356, 360, 382, 387, 389, 390, 392, 410, 415
Carlisle, Elinor Katharine 168–74, 244, 280
Carlos 358
Carlton-Sandways, Lady Veronica 318
Carlton-Sandways, Major 318
Carmichael, Henry 254–256
Carmichael, William 128–129
Carmody, Mike 196
Carmody, Peter 196, 198, 265, 311
Caroline, Aunt 372

Carpenter, Guy 261, 324
Carpenter, Mrs. 356
Carpenter, Mrs. Eve 261, 324
Carraway, Old Mrs. 371
Carrie, Aunt 83
Carroll, Miss 77
Carruthers, Nurse 138
Carson 369
Carson, Mrs. 369
Carstairs, Alan 83
Carstairs, The Honorable Julia 396
Carter, Colonel 41–42, 139
Carter, Frank 176
Carter, Henry (Harry) 158, 160
Carter, Lucy 158
Carter, Mr. A. 21–23, 189
Carter, Mrs. 158
Carter, Superintendent 107
Carthew West Family, The 77
Cartison, Old 384
Carton, Mr. L. B. 31
Cartwright, Dorothy 308
Cartwright, Dr. 38
Cartwright, Sir Charles 92–96
Cary, Frances 362–364
Cary, Richard 113, 115
Case of the Moving Finger, The see *The Moving Finger*
Caspar, Mr. 391
Cassell, Dr. 55
Castle, Mrs. 185
Castleton, Harry 346–47
Cat Among the Pigeons 10, 166, 260, **315–323**, 326–27, 333, 335, 341, 355, 358, 380, 382, 384–85, 393, 402, 419
Catherine 256,
Cavendish, John 15–17, 19, 20, 22, 199, 404–05
Cavendish, Lawrence 15–17, 19, 199, 404–05, 421
Cavendish, Mary 15, 17, 22, 405
Cayman, Mr. Leo 82
Cayman, Mrs. Amelia 82
Chadwick, Miss 317–18, 323
Challenger, Commander George 70, 73, 88,
Champion, Walter 153
Chandra Lal, Mr. 291
Chaplin, Charlie 337
Chapman, Albert 178
Chapman, Nigel 289–91
Chapman, Sylvia 178
Charles (*N or M?*) 191
Charles (*Remembered Death*) 221
Charleston 385
Charlie 372
Charlton, Mr. 153
Charpentier, Louise 362–64
Charrington, Lilian 373
Charrington, Mrs. 373
Chase, Miss 272
Cherubim, Mr. 61
Chetty, Edie 195
Chetwynd, Gordon 384
Chichester, Reverend 32
Chilvers 37
Cholmondeley-Marjoribanks 228
Christow, Gerda 8, 226–28, 230, 244
Christow, John 8, 12, 226–29, 237, 244–45

Christow, Terence 227, 228
Christow, Zena 227
Chudleigh Pratt, Rose 84–85
Church, Beatrice 95
Church, Miss 158
Churchill, Winston 188, 223, 256, 267, 269, 386
Cinderella 26–27, 29–30, 44, 47, 405
Cinders 405
Clancy, Daniel 100–01, 105, 116, 118
Clara (*The Mirror Crack'd*) 337
Clara (*Murder at the Vicarage; The Body in the Library*) 61, 196
Clara (*The Murder of Roger Ackroyd*) 42
Clarence, a.k.a "Clarrie" 402
Clark, Jennifer 202
Clarke, Franklin 109, 111
Clarke, Lady 107, 109
Clarke, Sir Carmichael 106–07, 109, 111
Claude, Mademoiselle 45
Clay, Herbert 212
Claythorne, Vera Elizabeth 163–64
Clayton, Gerald 255, 257
Clayton, Rosa 255, 257
Cleat, Mrs. 203
Cleckheaton, Lady Matilda 384–86
Clegg, Joe 314
Clegg, Maureen 313–14
Cleghorn, Lady Lucy 384
Clement, David 194
Clement, Dennis 59
Clement, Griselda 59, 192, 194, 197, 209, 239, 307, 334, 337–38, 411
Clement, Leonard 307
Clement, Reverend Leonard 59, 62, 192, 194, 238–39, 307, 334, 338
Clithering, Sir Henry 196–98, 250, 274, 306, 339, 349, 350, 352, 353, 392, 422
Clittering, Colonel 338
Clittering, Mrs. 338
Cloade, Antony 234
Cloade, Dr. Lionel 234
Cloade, Frances 224, 233–34, 237, 244, 273, 281
Cloade, Gordon 198, 233–35, 243, 258
Cloade, Jeremy 233–35, 237, 244, 281
Cloade, Katherine ("Aunt Kathy") 13, 233–38
Cloade, Maurice 235
Cloade, Rosaleen (formerly Rosaleen Underhay) 233–34
Cloade, Rowland (Rowley) 235, 237
Clocks, The 199, **342–348**, 360–61, 369, 382, 394
Cobb, Sergeant 291
Cocker, Doris 95
Cocker, Mrs. 410
Codrington, Lady 184
Coin, Monsieur 386
Coker, Mrs. 55
Cole, Miss 406

Cole, Old Mr. 297
Cole, Young Mr. 380
Coleman, Monkey 222
Coleman, William 114
Coles, Dr. 291
Colgate, Inspector 184
Collier, Beryl (Collie) 228
Collingsby, Air Marshal Sir Edmund 363
Collodon, Miss 401
Colonel, The 31
Combeau, Pierre 45
Combes, Sergeant 228, 230
Come and Be Hanged see *Towards Zero*
Comstock 357
Coniston, Old 356–57
Conneau, Georges 27
Conolly, Sergeant 364
Conrad 22
Conroy, Brigadier 236
Constantine, Dmitri 368
Constantine, Dr. 89–90, 422
Constantopolous 177
Conway 385
Conway, Bridget 157–60
Conway, Inspector 207
Conway, Lady 340
Cook, Mr. Sidney 384
Cooke, Miss 391
Coombe 368
Cooper, Mrs. 42
Coote, Lady Maria 54, 341
Coote, Sir Oswald 54, 160, 301
Cope, Mr. Jefferson 147, 149
Copes, Mrs. 402
Copleigh, Elizabeth ("Liz") 373
Copleigh, George 373
Coppins, Mr. 330
Coppins, Mrs. 330
Cordell, Miss 357
Cornelly, Lord 214
Corner, Lady 77
Corner, Sir Montagu 77, 79
Cornish, Detective Inspector Frank 339
Cornish, Johnnie 158
Cornish, Mrs. Frank 339
Cornish, Sergeant 306
Cornwall, Mr. 254
Corrigan, Alice 185
Corrigan, Catherine ("Ginger") 329, 331–33
Corrigan, Dr. Jim 329–31
Corrigan, Eileen 234
Cortman, Mildred Jean ("Milly") 385
Cortman, Sam 385
Cotterell, Rev. Charles 379
Cotton, Sir Edgar 214
Cottrill, Sergeant Frank 298
Courtauld 385
Courtland, Janice 262
Courtney, Mr. 392
Cowley, Archdeacon 22, 374
Crabtree, Mrs. (Old Mother Crabtree) 227
Crackenthorpe, Alfred 308
Crackenthorpe, Cedric 308–10
Crackenthorpe, Edmund 308
Crackenthorpe, Emma 307–09, 311
Crackenthorpe, Harold 307–10

Crackenthorpe, Henry 308
Crackenthorpe, Lady Alice 308
Crackenthorpe, Luther 140, 307–10, 321
Crackenthorpe, Mrs. Josiah 308
Crackenthorpe, Old Josiah 302, 308
Craddock, Detective Inspector Dermot Eric 230, 248, 250–52, 306–07, 336, 338–340, 349, 352
Craddock, Mr. 120–21
Craddock, Mrs. (*Cards on the Table*) 120–21
Craddock, Mrs. (*The Mirror Crack'd*) 340
Craig, Mr. and Mrs. 262
Craig, Dr. Donald 313
Crale, Amyas 199, 205–09, 243–44, 281
Crale, Caroline 205–07, 209, 244
Crale, Diana 207–08
Crale, Enoch 207
Crale, Mrs. Richard 207
Crale, Richard 207–08
Cram, Miss Gladys 60, 74
Cranford 221
Craven, Brenda 284
Craven, Hilary 283–87, 326
Craven, Nigel 283
Craven, Nurse 405–06
Crawford, Miss Joanna 390
Crawford, Mr. 368
Cray, Mrs. 251
Cray, Sergeant 346
Cray, Veronica 226–28
Cressington, Mr. 369
Cripps, Mrs. 331
Crispin, Angus 403
Croft, Joan 251
Croft, Mr. Albert 70, 74, 187
Croft, Mr. and Mrs. 261, 324
Croft, Mrs. Millie 70–71, 74, 187
Crofton Lee, Sir Rupert 254–255
Crome, Inspector 76, 105, 107, 109, 180
Cronshaw, Admiral 208
Crooked House 13, 85, 161, 198, **239–243**, 245, 247, 252, 264–65, 270, 272, 301–02, 314, 325, 327, 353, 359
Crosbie, Captain 254
Crosbie, Dr. 274
Crossfield, Dr. 403
Crossfield, George 278–79
Crossfield, Superintendent 95
Crowther, The Right Honourable Sydney 45
Crump 274
Crump, Mrs. 274
Curdie, Old 108
Curry, Inspector 266, 269
Curry, Mr. R. H. 344–45
Curtain 7, 10, 25, 137, 167, 260, 281, **403–407**, 414
Curtin, Ernie 345, 347
Curtin, Mrs. 345, 347
Curtis, Dr. 191
Curtis, Ellen 274
Curtis Girl, The 331
Curtis, Mr. 65, 373
Curtis, Mrs. Amelia 65, 67–68, 140, 183, 186, 224, 373

Curtiss 406
Curtiss, Mr., the Wesleyan Minister 252
Cust, Alexander Bonapart 107, 109, 111

Dacres, Captain Freddie 94–95, 97
Dacres, Cynthia 94–95, 97, 186
Dacres, Mr. 66
Dacres, Mrs. 171
Dainton, Sorrel 279
Daisy 38, 198
Dakham 368
Dakin, Mr. 254, 256
Dale, Elsie 42
Danby, Miss Alison 411
Dane Calthrop, Maud 202–03, 239, 331
Dane Calthrop, Reverend Caleb 202, 238, 331
Danvers, Mr. 21
Darnley, Rosamund 184, 186–87, 209
Darrell, Claud 46
Darwin, Mr. and Mrs. 309
da Toredo, Señora Angelica 320
d'Aubray, Giselle 320
Daubreuil, Madame 24, 27, 30
Daubreuil, Marthe 24, 27
Daventry, Mr. 352
Daventry, Vera ("Socks") 54, 56
Davidson, Dr. (*The Boomerang Clue*) 84
Davidson, Dr. (*Cards on the Table*) 121
Daviloff, Sonia 46–47
Davis, Albert 101
Davis, Dr. 95
Davis, Jessie 197
Davis, Mrs. Jessie 330, 332
Davis, Nurse 65
Davy, Chief-Inspector Fred ("Father") 354–59
Dawes, Rhoda 120–21, 123–24, 329, 332
Dawlish, Lord 129
Dead Man's Folly 11, 198, 238, 275, **293–302**, 310–11, 324, 326–27, 346, 362, 377, 394, 418, 420,
Deans 45
Death Comes as the End 13, 112, **215–218**, 224
Death in the Air 11, 13, 69, 76, **97–105**, 106–07, 116, 118, 121, 123, 139, 144, 160–61, 167, 177, 246, 265, 289
Death in the Clouds see *Death in the Air*
Death on the Nile 13–14, 34, 112, **125–131**, 132, 139, 141–42, 145–46, 157, 167, 184, 199, 221, 238, 301, 363, 417
de Bellefort, Jacqueline 126–27, 130–32, 141, 157, 301
Debenham, Mary Hermione 88–89, 422
de Caspearo, Señora 352
de Castina, Mrs. 31–32
Deering, Mrs. Emily 120
de Haviland, Edith 242, 245
Delafontaine, Mary 331

de la Roche, Count Armand 49–50, 52
Demiroff, Olga Vassilovna 49
Denzil 352
Depleach, Old 212
Depleach, Sir Montague 206
Depuy, Mademoiselle Geneviève 320
Dering, Martin 64, 66, 199
Dering, Sylvia 64, 66, 67
de Rushbridger, Margaret 95
Derwent, Lady Frances ("Frankie") 81–84, 86, 94, 96, 141, 173, 218, 237
de Sousa, Étienne 298
Despard, Major Hugh 330–33
Despard, Major John 119–21, 124, 129, 330, 332–33
Despard, Rhoda 329, 331–32
Dessin, Monsieur Armand 306
Destination Unknown see *So Many Steps to Death*
Devereux, Ronald ("Ronny") 55
Deveril 109
Devinishes, The 128
Dewsbury, Lord 221
Diana 378
Dick 347
Digby, Martin 331
Digby, Sir Stanley 56
Dimitri 177
Dittisham, Lord 12, 208
Dixon, Gladys 339
Dodgett, Police Constable 269
Doherty, Mary 380
Don (*Murder with Mirrors*) 269
Don (*A Pocket Full of Rye*) 237, 273, 302
Don (*Towards Zero*) 214
Donaldson, Dr. 386
Donaldson, Dr. Rex 136
Donovan, Miss 372
Dora 202
Dorcas 16–18, 143
Dorothy 77
Dortheimer, Mr and Mrs. 76
Dortheimer, Rachel 76
Dove, Mary 271–75, 305, 310, 324
Downes, Roger Emmanuel 109
Doyle, Simon 126–27, 131
Dragomiroff, Princess Natalia 89
Drake, Allen 213
Drake, Hugo Edmund 378–80
Drake, Lucilla 220, 222, 224
Drake, Mrs. Rowena Arabella 378–81
Drake, Victor 220–21, 224
Driver, Miss Jenny 76–77
Drower, Mary 108–09
Dubois, Vivian Edward 272
Dubosc, Lieutenant 88
Duffs, The 197
Dugdale, Sir William 332
Duke, Mr. 65, 68
Dulcibella Kids, The 27
Dulcie 38
Dumb Witness see *Poirot Loses a Client*
Dupont, Armand 100, 102, 105, 144
Dupont, Jean 100, 102, 105
Dupont, René 320

Title and Character Index

Durrance, Mr. 402
Durrant, Mary 311, 313, 315
Durrant, Philip 313, 315
Dutch Pedro 36–37, 39
Dyer, Johnny 164
Dyson, Gail 351–52
Dyson, Greg 351
Dyson, Lucky 351

Eade, Mr. 308
Eagles 242
Eardsley, John 32, 224
Eardsley, Sir Lawrence 32
Earl, William 17
Earlsfield, George 109
Easterbrook, Colonel Archie 139, 166, 248
Easterbrook, Laura 248
Easterbrook, Mark 329–33
Easterfield, Lord Gordon 69, 158–61, 301
Easthampton, Lord ("Mr. Carter") 189
Eastley, Alexander 198, 306, 309–10
Eastley, Bryan 238, 302, 308, 309–10
Eastley, Edith 308
Easy to Kill 69, 133, 139, 143, 149, **155–162**, 166, 170, 172–73, 176, 180, 198–99, 202, 212, 233, 265, 281, 301–02, 422
Eberhard, Herr 56
Eccles, James 372–74
Eccles, Mrs. 194
Eckstein, Professor 386
Eden, Lord and Lady 95
Edge, Mrs. Nathaniel 384
Edgware, Lady (Jane Wilkinson) 75–77, 422
Edgware, Lord 74–77, 141
Edith (*Cat Among the Pigeons*) 318
Edith (*The Moving Finger*) 203
Edith (*Peril at End House*) 71
Edith (*Third Girl*) 363
Edmunds 357
Edmunds, Mr. (*Elephants Can Remember*) 396
Edmunds, Mr. (*Murder in Retrospect*) 207
Edmunds, Nurse 392
Edmundson, John 319
Edna (*Mrs. McGinty's Dead*) 261
Edna (*There Is a Tide*) 234, 281
Edwards (*The Body in the Library*) 196
Edwards (*There Is a Tide*) 235
Edwards, Constable 252
Edwards, Old 306, 341
Egerton, Richard 357, 360
Eileen 364
Eldon, Mrs. 120
Elephants Can Remember 280, 369, **393–398**, 404, 415
Elford, Mr. 84, 86
Elise 37, 39
Elizabeth (*By the Pricking of My Thumbs*) 372
Elizabeth (*Postern of Fate*) 401
Ellen 136, 143
Ellerton, Nurse 251
Elliot, Mr. 251

Elliot, Mrs. 260
Ellis 77
Ellis, Big John 352
Ellis, John 95
Ellis, Lou 329
Ellis, Miss (*Passenger to Frankfurt*) 386
Ellis, Miss (*What Mrs. McGillicuddy Saw*) 307, 310
Ellis, Old Mrs. 320
Ellis, Police Constable 331
Ellis, Young 274
Ellsworthy, Mr. 159, 161, 202, 422
Elmer 65
Elsie (*Evil Under the Sun*) 185
Elsie (*The Mirror Crack'd*) 339
Elsie (*They Came to Baghdad*) 254
Elsworth, Katherine 269
Elton, Freda 191
Elvary, Madame 235
Elworthy, The Misses 412
Emerson at Cambridge 256
Emily (*Easy to Kill*) 160, 281
Emily (*The Man in the Brown Suit*) 31
Emily (*Murder at the Vicarage*) 61
Emlyn, Miss 377, 380
Emma (*Elephants Can Remember*) 396
Emma (*The Patriotic Murders*) 178
Emmett, Mrs. 274
Emmott, David 114–15
Emmott, Doris 227
Emory, Mrs. 202
Enderby, Charles 64–69, 104, 160, 265
Enderby, Mr. 346
Endicott, Old Mr. 291
Endless Night **367–369**, 375, 392
Enrico 352
Entwhistle, Miss 279
Entwhistle, Mr. 277–78, 282, 292
Ericsson, Torquil 284
Erskine, Janet 413
Erskine, Major Richard 413–14
Erskine, Old Sir Roger 184
Esa 216–18
Esther 411
Estravados, Pilar 151–55, 199
Evans (*Crooked House*) 242
Evans (*A Murder Is Announced*) 249
Evans (*Remembered Death*) 222
Evans, Albert ("Bert") 274
Evans, Charles ("Chubby") 50
Evans, Chick 307
Evans, Dr. 283
Evans, Mr. Betoun 256
Evans, Mrs. 283
Evans, Rebecca 64–65
Evans, Robert Henry 64–65
Evelyn 411
Everard, Sir 406
Eversleigh, Bill 36–37, 54–56, 73, 84, 169
Evil Under the Sun 10, 69, 139, **181–187**, 193, 198, 209–10, 214, 217, 224, 238, 245, 255, 257, 289, 301, 323, 391, 417
Eyelesbarrow, Lucy 275, 305, 307–11, 324

Faithful Florence (*The Moving Finger*) 201, 307–08
Faithful Florence (*What Mrs. McGillicuddy Saw*) 307, 337, 341
Fane, Gerald 412
Fane, Mrs. Eleanor 412, 414
Fane, Mrs. Robert 412
Fane, Robert 412
Fane, Walter 411–12, 414
Fanshawe, Ada ("Aunt Ada") 371–72
Fanthorp, James Leechdale 129
Faraday, Mr. 190
Farquhar 189
Farr, Ebenezer 152
Farr, Stephen 152, 154
Farraday, Sandra (formerly Lady Alexandra Hayle) 8, 57, 219–23, 230, 244, 280
Farraday, Stephen 8, 57, 219–20, 222–23, 230, 237, 244
Farrell, Sergeant 298
Faussett, Dr. Andrew 207
Fenn, Ardwyck 338
Fenn, Kathleen 397
Ferguson, Dr. 379
Ferguson, Mr. 129, 146
Fernando 352
Ferrari, The Count of 351
Ferrier, Lesley 379
Ffoulkes, Mr. 102
Finch, Mrs. 248–49
Finch, Sally 289–90
Finch, The Hon. Jasper 153
Findeison, Mr. 196
Findeyson, Mrs. 412–13
Finn, Jane 20–22, 33, 400–01
Finney, Major 314
Fish, Mr. Hiram 38
Fitzwilliam, Luke 139, 157–61, 302
Five Little Pigs see *Murder in Retrospect*
Flavelle, Hippolyte 50
Flavelle, Marie 50
Fleetwood 204
Flemming, Captain 351
Flemming, Mr. Henry 31
Flemming, Mrs. 31, 33
Fletcher, Agnes 178
Fletcher, Sergeant (*McGinty's Dead*) 263
Fletcher, Sergeant (*A Murder Is Announced*) 250
Flint, Police Constable 185
Florrie (recalled by Miss Marple in *A Murder Is Announced*) 251
Florrie (resident of Chipping Cleghorn in *A Murder Is Announced*) 250
Flyn and Cormic 260
Fogg, Quentin 207
Folliat, Amy 238, 295, 297–99, 302, 311, 420
Folliat, Henry 297
Folliat, James 238, 297, 302
Folliat, Major 297
Folliat, Old Squire 297
Forrester, Mrs. 227
Fortescue, Adele 271–72, 274, 324
Fortescue, Elaine 271, 273
Fortescue, Elvira 272–73

Fortescue, Jennifer 273–74
Fortescue, Lancelot 271–73, 310
Fortescue, Patricia 237, 271, 273, 275, 302
Fortescue, Percival 271–74, 310
Fortescue, Rex 13, 140, 270–71, 273–74, 302, 307, 324
Forthville, Lord 307
Foscarelli, Antonio 89
Foster 342, 410, 412
Foster, Roddy 396
Fothergill, Mr. 396
4:50 from Paddington see *What Mrs. McGillicuddy Saw*
Fournier, Monsieur 99, 101–02, 104
Fowler Child of Undetermined Gender 108, 142, 198, 265
Fowler, Edie 108
Fowler, Mrs. 108
Fox, Mary 137
Franco, Francisco 149, 188, 402
Françoise 228
Frank 83
Franklin, Barbara 281, 405–06
Franklin, Dr. John 405
Franz Joseph 385
Fraser, Donald 108–09
Fred (*The Clocks*) 347
Fred (*Murder at Hazelmoor*) 66
Fred, Young 274
Frederick, Lord ("Freddie") 357
Freemantle Freddie 66
French, Gerald 340
Frere, Colonel 207
Frieda 262, 324
Frogg II 279
Fullerton, Jeremy 380–81
Fullerton, Miss Lavinia 157–58, 160
Funerals Are Fatal 9, 12, 19, 137, 144, 155, 161, **275–282**, 292–93, 295, 302, 324–26

Gabler, Mr. 137–38
Gaitskill, Mr. 242
Galbraith, Dr., Bishop of Cromer 269
Galbraith, Jim 338
Galbraith, Miss 412
Galbraith, Old Mr. 412
Gale, Marylin 298
Gale, Norman 100–01, 105
Gamboll, Lily 262
Game, Elizabeth 234
Game, Frederick 234
Ganett, Miss 41
Garbo, Greta 337
Garcia, Dr. Alan 171
Gardener, Irene 183
Gardener, Mr. Odell 183–84, 391
Gardener, Mrs. 183–84, 186–87, 224, 255, 257, 391
Gardner, Jennifer 65–66, 68
Gardner, Robert 65
Garfield, Michael 380–82
Garfield, Ronald 65, 68, 141
Garnett, Lady 317
Garroway, Chief Superintendent 395
Gaskell, Dr. 221
Gaskell, Mark 195, 197
Gaskell, Rosamund 195

Gasparo, Signor and Signora 385
Gaunt, Archie 255
Gaymarck 279
Gaythorne, Mr. 235
Geoffrey, Old Uncle 228
Geordie, Old 368
George (*Evil Under the Sun*) 185
George (Poirot's servant) 50, 138, 178, 234, 260, 321, 346, 361–62, 364, 379, 395, 404, 406
George (taxi driver in *Nemesis*) 390
George, Old (gardener in *Nemesis*) 390–91
Georges 99, 104
Gerahty, Mrs. 330
Gerard, Dr. Theodore 146–47, 149, 166, 270
Geronimo 291
Gerrard, Effraim 169, 172–73
Gerrard, Eliza 169
Gerrard, Mary 168–73
Gibbons, Mrs. 320
Gibbs, Amy 158, 160–61
Gilchrist, Dr. Maurice 339
Gilchrist, Miss 279
Giles 159
Gilfoy, Mr. 269
Gilles, Monsieur 101–02
Gillingham, Tom 402
Ginch, Miss 202
Girand, Mademoiselle 396
Giraud, Monsieur 24–27, 30, 102, 363
Giuseppe (*Cat Among the Pigeons*) 318
Giuseppe (*The Mirror Crack'd*) 338
Gladdie 62
Gladys (*The Boomerang Clue*) 84
Gladys (*Crooked House*) 242
Gladys (*Death in the Air*) 102
Gladys (*N or M?*) 191
Glen, Inspector 107
Gloria 320
Glydr, Major Boris 283
Glynne, Mrs. Lavinia 391
Goby, Mr. 49, 161, 279–80, 282, 362–63, 366, 380, 397
Goedler, Belle 249, 251–52
Goedler, Randall 249, 251
Golden, Jessie 197
Goldie, Mr. 307
Goldstein, Mr. 221
Good, Police Constable 314
Goodbody, Mrs. 378
Goodman, Adam 318–20
Goodwin, Sergeant 380
Gopal Ram, Mr. 290
Gordon, Peter 379
Gore-West, Margaret 320
Goring, Edward 237, 254, 275, 302
Gorman, Father 328, 330–31
Gorman, Michael ("Micky" or "Mick") 238, 302, 355, 357, 359–60
Gorringe, Miss 356, 358
Gottlieb, Professor John 386
Gouldman, Geoffrey 385
Gracie, Aunt 191
Graham, Dr. (*A Caribbean Mystery*) 350

Graham, Dr. (*Peril at End House*) 71
Grainger, Dr. 137–38
Grampion, Old Lord 385
Grandier, Élise 99, 104
Grange, Inspector 227–29
Grant, Geoffrey 392
Grant, Lady 178
Grant, Maurine 395
Grant, Mr. 189
Grant, Robert 45
Graves, Constable 66
Graves, Inspector 202
Graves, Mrs. 120
Graves, Sergeant 235
Graves, Sir Ronald 357
Gray, Dr. 242
Graybrook, Young 260
Green, Master Cyril 314
Green, Sergeant 320
Greenholtz, Mr. 254
Greenholtz, Mrs. 254
Greer, Elsa (Lady Dittisham) 206–09, 214
Gregg, Ernie 269–70
Gregg, Marina 334–40
Gretel 346
Grey, Jane 99–102, 105
Grey, Katherine 49–50, 52, 57
Grey, Mary ("Mirotin") 203
Grey, Miss Thora 109
Grey, Thyrza 331
Grice, Joshua 338
Grice, Mrs. Joshua 338
Griffin, Harry 379
Griffin, Mrs., née Winifred Morrison 401
Griffin, Sandra 379
Griffith, Aimee 201, 204, 209
Griffith, Dr. Owen 201, 203
Griffith, Miss 272–73
Griffiths, Walter 283
Groom, Janet 261, 324
Grosjean, Monsieur 385–86
Grosvenor, Irene 272, 274, 307
Grouser, Old 196
Grünberg, Anita 32
Grundle, Miss 339
Gudgeon 227, 229
Guido 357
Gulbrandsen, Christian 267–68
Gulbrandsen, Eric 268
Gulbrandsen, Pippa 268
Gunter, Dr. 269
Guteman, Funella ("Ellie") 368–69
Guthrie, Alexander 279
Gwenda 401

Hahn, Mr. 190
Hale, Ex-Superintendent 205, 207
Hall, Dr. 22
Hall, Robert 255
Halle, René 291
Halliday, John 45
Halliday, Major Kelvin James 411–13
Halliday, Megan 411
Halliday, Mrs. 45
Hallowe'en Party 144, 199, 280, 359, **375–382**, 394–96, 398
Halsey, Mr. 45
Hamilton Clipp, Mr. 255

Hamilton Clipp, Mrs. 255–57, 284
Hamilton, Cyril Ogilvie 163–64, 265
Hamilton, Hugo 163–64
Hamish, Happy 374
Hammond, Inspector 84
Hamsteiter, Mr. 197
Hanbury 345
Hannibal 400
Harbottle, Miss 196
Harbottle, Mr. 196
Hardcastle, Claudia 368
Hardcastle, Detective Inspector Dick 343–47
Hardcastle, Midge 9, 226–29, 230–31, 244–45
Hardcastle, Mrs. 274
Harden, Grete 256
Harding, Dr. 138
Hardman, Cyrus Bethman 89
Harfield, Mrs. Jane 49–50
Harfield, Mrs. Samuel (Mary Anne) 50
Hargreaves, Alison 317
Hargreaves, Major 317
Hargreaves, Mrs. 378
Harmon, Diana ("Bunch") 239, 248–49
Harmon, Edward 249
Harmon, Rev. Julian 248–49
Harmon, Susan 249
Harmondsworth, Sidney 332
Harper, Inspector 121
Harper, Major 352
Harper, Silas 102
Harper, Superintendent 196, 198
Harrington-West, Sir Jasper 203
Harris, Myrna 230, 250
Harrison, Dr. 50
Harrison, Johnnie 50
Harrison, Mr. 256
Harrison, Mrs. 178
Harrison, Mrs. Polly 50
Harry (*The Clocks*) 347
Harry (*The Mirror Crack'd*) 337
Hart, Farmer 373
Hart, Mrs. 309
Hartigan, Tom 109
Hartley Napiers, The 61
Hartnell, Miss 60, 192, 196, 334–336
Hartwell, Mrs. 339
Harvey, Captain 46
Harvey, Jim 158
Hassan, Salah 255
Hastings, Captain Arthur 4, 5, 12, 16–19, 24–27, 29–30, 41–42, 44–47, 51, 70–71, 73–77, 79–80, 88, 106–08, 111, 116, 122, 129, 132–34, 136–39, 143–44, 166, 171, 184, 187, 260, 299, 326, 350, 404–07, 422
Hastings, Judith 404–07
Hastings, Mrs. 390
Hautet, Monsieur
Hawes, Mr. 27
Hawkes, Constable 185
Hawkins 219, 221
Hawkins, Edward 83
Hay, Sergeant 274
Haydock, Commander 190–91
Haydock, Dr. 58, 61, 144, 194, 243, 306, 334, 336–38, 409, 411

Hayes, Superintendent 42
Hayling, Albert (Bert) 261
Haymes, Harry 249
Haymes, Phillipa 248–50
Haymes, Ronald 249
Hayward, Charles 241–42, 245
Hayward, Sir Arthur 242
Hazy, Lady Selina 355
Head, Mrs. 345
Heald 185
Heath, Betty 178
Heath, Dr. 77
Heath, Mrs. 178
Heavywether, Sir Ernest 18
Hector (*Cat Among the Pigeons*) 317
Hector (*What Mrs. McGillicuddy Saw*) 305
Helen 54
Hemingway, Gerald 121
Hemming, Mrs. 345, 348
Henderson, Captain 363
Henderson, Deirdre 262, 264
Henderson, Mrs. 402
Hendon 296
Henet 217–18
Hengrave, Major 410
Hengrave, Mrs. 410
Henley, Mrs. 402
Henniker, Beatrice 197
Henri, Monsieur 45
Henry (*At Bertram's Hotel*) 355
Henry (*Sleeping Murder*) 412
Henry at the Bar 185
Hercule Poirot's Christmas see *A Holiday for Murder*
Hersheimer, Julius P. 21–22, 301
Hertz, Dr. 285
Hesketh-Dubois, Lady 330–32
Hetherington, Miss 284, 287, 326
Hibbert, Mary 65
Hickory, Dickory, Death 53, 144, 166, **288–293**, 294, 296, 299, 304, 322–23, 325–27, 346, 353, 363, 396
Hickory, Dickory, Dock see *Hickory, Dickory, Death*
Higgins, Sergeant 196
Higley, Miss 108
Hilda 61
Hill, Amy 17
Hill, Cyril 190
Hill, Douglas 190
Hill, Mary 59, 85
Hill, Mr. 109
Hill, Raymond 190
Hillingdon, Colonel Edward 351–52
Hillingdon, Evelyn 351
Hillman, Old 309, 341
Hinchliffe, Miss 139, 246–49, 251–52
Hitler, Adolph 150, 175, 190, 386
Hjerson, Sven 119, 122, 362
Hobbs, Mr. 159
Hobhouse, Valerie 290
Hodgson 298
Hodgson, Mr. 251
Hoffman, Wilhelm and Robert 358
Hogg, Doris 320
Holden, Mr. 380
Holgate 95

Holiday for Murder, A 9, 53, 95, 140, **149–155**, 186, 199, 215, 217–18, 223, 245, 301–02
Holland, Desmond 378–80
Holland, Elsie 202, 204
Hollow, The see *Murder After Hours*
Holman 391
Holmes, Mr. 37
Hope, Henrietta 318
Hope, Mrs. Gerald 318
Hopkins, Jessie 169–71, 173
Hopkins, Little Gary 390
Horace 385
Horbury, Count Stephen (Lord Horbury) 100–03
Horbury, Countess Cicely (Lady Horbury) 99–100, 102, 104
Horbury, Sydney 152–53
Hori 217
Horlick 170
Horrocks, Diana 350
Horsefall, Mrs. 331
Horsefall, Pamela 69, 262, 265
Horsefield, Sir Roderick 363
Horsham, Henry 384, 386
Horton, Lydia 159–60
Horton, Major 139, 155, 159–60
Hoskins, Police Constable Robert 295, 297–98
Howard, Evelyn 16–18, 22, 29
Howell, Mrs. 55
Hubbard, Mr. 290
Hubbard, Mrs. 288–91, 293
Hubbard, Mrs. Caroline Martha 89–90
Hudd, Gina 268–70, 314, 333
Hudd, Mrs. 379
Hudd, Thomas 379
Hudd, Walter 268–70
Huggins, Jim 250
Huggins, Mrs. 250
Huish, Superintendent 314
Humbleby, Dr. John 157–59, 170
Humbleby, Jessie Rose 158
Humbleby, Rose 158
Humfries, Mr. 356
Hunt, Verity 391–92
Hunter, Captain 201
Hunter, David 233–37, 302
Hunter, Megan 201, 203–04
Hurst, Constable 61
Hurst, Mr. and Mrs. 319
Hurstall 213
Hussein el Ziyara, Sheikh 257

Ibrahim 115
Imhotep 216–18
Imphrey, Sir Charles 121
Inch 338
Inch, Young 338
Ingles, Mr. John 44–47
Inglethorpe, Alfred 15–17, 33
Inglethorpe, Emily 15–17, 33, 140, 404–05
Ingrid 347–48
Ingrid, Princess 320
Ipi and Montu 217
Ipy 217
Isaacs, Dr. 272
Isaacstein, Mr. Herman 36–37
Isabel, Aunt 318

Jacks, Mrs. 278
Jackson, Arthur 351, 352, 390
Jacobs, Mrs. 364
Jaggerowski, Paul 373
James (*The Big Four*) 45
James (*Postern of Fate*) 402
James, Leslie 351
James, Mrs. Caroline 32
Jameson, Mr. 109
Jameson, Mrs. 358
Jameson, Richard 391
Jane (*By the Pricking of My Thumbs*) 372
Jane (*The Mirror Crack'd*) 339
Jane, Nurse 371
Janet (an adolescent girl living in the village of Hollowquay in *Postern of Fate*) 403
Janet (*The Clocks*) 344
Janet (*Funerals Are Fatal*) 278
Janet (*Nemesis*) 391
Janet (one of Deborah's children in *Postern of Fate*) 400
Janet (*Passenger to Frankfurt*) 386
Japp, Chief Inspector 16, 22, 41–42, 45–46, 71, 74–77, 79, 99–101, 105–07, 111, 116, 120–21, 123, 129, 167, 175–78, 180–81, 198, 235, 243, 289
Jarrow, Captain 396
Jarrow, Dorothea 396–97
Jarvis 32
Jean (*By the Pricking of My Thumbs*) 372
Jean (*Cat Among the Pigeons*) 320
Jean (*What Mrs. McGillicuddy Saw*) 305
Jeanne 31
Jefferson, Adelaide 195–98
Jefferson, Conway 195–98, 208, 242
Jefferson, Frank 195
Jefferson, Margaret 195
Jenkins 308
Jenkins, Arthur 269
Jenkins, James 380
Jenkins, Miss 137–38, 281
Jennsen, Miss 285
Jenny 401
Jerome, Colonel 108
Jessop 283
Jethroe, Johnny 339
Joan (*Funerals Are Fatal*) 279
Joan (*Passenger to Frankfurt*) 384
Jobson, Mr. 78
Joe (*Third Girl*) 364
Joe (*Towards Zero*) 214
Johnathan, Caleb 207
Johnny 402
Johnson (*Crooked House*) 242
Johnson (*Postern of Fate*) 402
Johnson, Ann 115, 117
Johnson, Cathie 378
Johnson, Colonel 95, 150–51, 153–55
Johnson, Constable 37
Johnson, Miss 378
Johnson, Miss Elspeth 318, 323
Johnson, Mrs. 372
Johnson, Victoria 352
Johnston, Elizabeth 290, 293, 353
Johnstone 307
Joliet, Madame 307

Jones, Bobby 81–86, 97, 173
Jones, Detective Sergeant 214
Jones, Gladys 42
Jones, Hetty 160
Jones, Montagu 291
Jones, Mr. (*Easy to Kill*) 160
Jones, Mr. (*Murder at Hazelmoor*) 66
Jones, Mr. (*Poirot Loses a Client*) 135
Jones, Mrs. 278, 281, 324
Jones, Mrs. Lottie 401
Jones, Policewoman Alice 298
Jones, Queenie 153
Jones, Reverend Thomas 81, 97, 238
Jones, Victoria 253–57, 287
Jordan, Mary 399–401
Jordan, Susan 400
Jules 128
Julia 251
Julius 267

Kait 216, 218
Kalzman, Professor 256
Kameni 217
Kane, Eva 262
Kane, Jonathan 402
Kate, Killer 374
Katie 55
Keene, Ruby 195–97
Keene, Sergeant 369
Kelly, Jim 251
Kelsey, Detective Inspector 320
Kelsey, Major and Mrs. 112, 114
Kelso, Mr. 183, 187
Kemp, Chief Inspector 221–23
Kench, Joan 153
Kendal, Molly 350–53
Kendal, Tim 350
Kennedy, Helen Spenlove 411–14
Kennedy, M.D., James 411–13
Kennedys, The 309
Kent, Captain 45
Kent, Charles 41
Kent, Constance 242
Kent, Marcus 201
Kent, Sir Wesley 395
Kenwood, Air Marshal 386
Kerr, Dr. 107
Kerr, Humphrey 242
Kerr, Sir George 170
Kerr, Sybil 356
Kerr, The Honorable Venetia 99–100, 103–04
Kettering, Derek 12, 49, 155, 166, 187
Kettering, Ruth 12, 49–50, 52, 57, 73, 141, 218
Khay 217–18
Kidder, Mr. 309
Kidder, Mrs. 309–11
Kidderminster, Lady Victoria 220–21, 223–24
Kidderminster, Lord 220–21, 223
Kiddle, Ernie 261, 302
Kiddle, Mr. and Mrs. 261, 302
Kimble, Jim 412, 414
Kimble, Lily, (née Lily Abbot) 412–14
King Victor alias Captain O'Neill 36–38
King, Donald 84

King, Gloria 220
King, M.B., Sarah 145–46, 149, 209, 217, 270
Kipling, Rudyard 402
Kirby, Miss 177
Kirkpatrick, Dorothy 37
Kirkwood, Mr. 66
Kitchin, Mrs. 255
Kitelly, Roderick 386
Kitty (*Hallowe'en Party*) 380
Kitty (*A Pocket full of Rye*) 274)
Kleek, Sir James 385–86
Knight, Miss 336–37, 340, 390
Knighton, Major 49
Koch, Dr. Adolf 252
Kolinsky, Mrs. 320
Konstam, Mrs. Rudolph 313
Konstam, Rudolph 313
Krassnine, Boris Ivanovitch 49

Lacy, Mr. 269
Lake, Mrs. 279
Lake, Sergeant 269
Lamb, Colin 344–48
Lamb, Detective Sergeant 242
Lampard, Colonel 413
Lamphrey, Mrs. 135
Lancaster, Mrs. 371–72
Lane, Patricia 290, 292
Lane, Reverend Stephen 184, 238
Lang, Dr. 121
Langford, Harry 392
Lansberger 363
Lanscombe, Old 278, 282, 293
Lansdowne 255
Lansquenet, Cora 277–80
Lansquenet, Pierre 278
Laon, Félix 45
Larkin 345
Larkin, Mr. 260
La Roche, Mademoiselle 285
Larpent, Miss 64
Larraby, Dr. 279
Last, Inspector 413
Latimer, Edward (Ted) 213–15, 217
Latimer, Mrs. 274
Laurie, Miss 320
Laurier, Monsieur Henri 284, 286
Lavigny, Father 115
Lawrence, E.T. 256
Lawson, Edgar 267, 269–70
Lawson, Miss Wilhelmina ("Minnie") 133, 135–38, 140
Lawton, Mrs. 345
Laycock, Old 336, 341
Lazarus, James 71–73
Lazenby, Cedric 384, 386
Lazenby, Dr. (*Sleeping Murder*) 412
Lazenby, Dr. (*Towards Zero*) 213
Leach, Inspector James (Jim) 212–14
Leadbetter, Mr. 109
Leadbetter, Mrs. 86, 235, 238–39, 300
Leadenthal 386
Leakie, Sergeant 307
Leaman, Harriet 380
Leatheran, Mr. 179
Leatheran, Nurse Amy 86, 111–17, 123, 143, 386
Leblanc, Monsieur 285

Leckie, Martha 95
Lee, Adelaide 152
Lee, Alfred 151–52, 154, 217
Lee, David 151–52, 154, 199
Lee, Detective Sergeant 332
Lee, Dinah 195
Lee, Esther 368–69
Lee, George 151–52, 154, 223
Lee, Henry (Harry) 151–52, 154
Lee, Hilda 152, 154
Lee, Lydia 151–52, 217
Lee, Magdalene 152
Lee, Miss 378
Lee, Simeon 140, 151–54, 215, 217, 301–02
Leech, Andrew 102
Leech, Cecil 263
Leech, Mrs. 128
Leggard, Spoof 164
Legge, Alec 294, 297, 300
Legge, Constable 250
Legge, Peggy 297–98
Legge, Sir Thomas 165
Leghorn, Martha 395
Leidner, Dr. Eric 112–15
Leidner, Louise 112–17
Lejeune, Divisional Detective Inspector 330, 332–33
Lemarchant, Carla 205–06, 395
Lemarchant, Louise 206
Lemarchant, Simon 206
Lemon, Miss Felicity 289–90, 293, 296, 346, 353, 363, 396
Leonides, Aristide 198, 239–43, 245, 272, 301–02
Leonides, Brenda 240–42
Leonides, Clemency 240–42, 245
Leonides, Electra 242
Leonides, Eustace 198, 241–42, 245
Leonides, Josephine 198, 241–42, 245, 265
Leonides, Joyce 242
Leonides, Magda 13, 240–42, 245, 247
Leonides, Marcia (née Marcia de Haviland) 241–42
Leonides, Philip 240–42
Leonides, Roger 240–42
Leonides, Sophia 241–42, 245
Leroy, General 351
Lessing, Ruth 220, 222
Lestrange, Mrs. 58, 60–62, 139
Letherby, Mrs. 401
Leversham, Arthur 45
Levine, Armand 344
Levy, Solomon ("Solly") 379
Lewis 228
Lewis, Mary 235
Leyland, Old 384
Li Chang Yen 45
Lil 196
Lily 235
Lindstrom, Kirsten (Kirsty) 314
Linnett, Mrs. 351
Lionel, Sir 107
Lippincott, Andrew 368
Lippincott, Beatrice 235
Lisa What's-her-Name 386
Lister, Miss Jenny 401
Lister, Miss Pamela 401
Little Ankh 216

Little, Miss Dorothy ("Dodo") 400
Littledale, James Arthur 171
Livingstone, Miss 395
Llangow, The Bishop of (a.k.a. The Bishop of Languao) 255
Llewellen (for the Crown) 163
Llewellyn-Smythe, Mrs. Louise 379–81
Lloyd, Sir James 392
Lloyd, Stanford 368
Lloyd, Young 279
Lockett, Mrs. 372
Logan, Dr. 107
Lois 320
Lolopretjzyl, Baron 37, 38
Lomax, The Honorable George ("Codders") 37, 54–56, 223, 237
Lombard, Captain Philip 164
Longhurst, Cicely 356
Lonsdale, Mr. 137
Lord Edgware Dies see *Thirteen at Dinner*
Lord, Dr. Peter 169–71
Lord, Rufus 213
Lorimer, Police Constable 298
Lorrimer 194
Lorrimer, Jimmy 157–58
Lorrimer, Miss 318
Lorrimer, Mrs. 119–21
Lorrimer, Naomi 362
Lorrimer, Vera 318, 320
Louisa (*Sleeping Murder*) 412
Louisa (*They Came to Baghdad*) 255
Louise 395
Lucan, Mrs. 213
Lucas 32
Lucas, Dr. Mark 283
Lucas, Mrs. (*Hickory, Dickory, Death*) 291
Lucas, Mrs. (*A Murder Is Announced*) 250
Lucas, Young 109
Lugg, Old 331
Luigi 329
Lumley, Miss 391
Lupton, Old Mrs. 400
Luscombe, Colonel Derek 355–57
Lushington, Sir Henry 203
Luttrell, Colonel George ("Toby") 405
Luttrell, Daisy 405–06
Luxmore, Mrs. 121, 124
Luxmore, Professor Timothy 121, 124
Lygo, Jackie 280
Lyndon, Gladys 95
Lytton Gore, Hermione ("Egg") 93–97, 111, 141, 180, 422
Lytton Gore, Lady Mary 94, 208

MacAlister 179
Macalister, Miss 331
MacAllister, Dr. 71
Macarthur, General John Gordon 164
Macarthur, Leslie 164
Macatta, M.P., Mrs. 55–56
MacDonald 54, 341
MacDougal, Dr. 95
Mace, Mr. 17

Mackay, Mrs. 213
MacKenzie 274
MacKenzie, Donald 274
MacKenzie, Helen 274
MacKenzie, Ruby 274
MacMaster, Dr. 314–15
MacQueen, Hector Willard 89–90
Macrae, Joan 235
Macrae, Marjorie 235
MacTavish 221
MacWhirter, Andrew 212, 214–15
MacWhirter, Mona 212
Madeleine 100
Maguire, Patrick 190
Mahmoud 147
Maine, Inspector 165
Maitland, Captain 112–15
Malinowski, Ladislaus 356–57, 359–60
Man in the Brown Suit, The 6, 13, 23, 27, **30–34**, 47, 56–57, 69, 74, 84, 120, 125, 133, 141, 146, 199, 221–22, 224, 257, 363, 420
Manders, Old Mrs. 95
Manders, Oliver 94–95, 97, 126, 145, 180
Manelli, Giuseppe 37
Mannheim, Professor 283
Manning (*Murder at the Vicarage*) 61
Manning (*The Mysterious Affair at Styles*) 17, 342
Manning (*Sleeping Murder*) 342, 413
Mansur 115
Marbury, Bert 109
Marbury, Lily 109
Marbury, Mrs. 109
Marchand 27
Marchese di San Severiano, Guido 268
Marchington, Lord 12, 82–84
Marchment, Miss (a.k.a. Miss Margrave) 372
Marchmont, Adela 233, 235, 245
Marchmont, Lynn 231–32, 235, 237–38, 244, 302, 388, 418
Marcia, Marchioness of Caterham 53, 55–56, 147, 223
Margaret (*Cat Among the Pigeons*) 318
Margaret (*What Mrs. McGillicuddy Saw*) 305
Margery 401
Maria (*Elephants Can Remember*) 394
Maria (*Hickory, Dickory, Death*) 291
Maricaud, Geneviève 291
Maricot, Mademoiselle Jeanne 284
Marie (*Death on the Nile*) 127, 129
Marie (*The Mystery of the Blue Train*) 50
Marjorie 144, 278, 324
Marle, Hector 220
Marle, Iris 219–20, 222–23
Marle, Viola 220, 224
Marleen 351
Marlene 371
Marple, Miss Jane 7, 10, 11, 41, 43, 48, 58–62, 139–40, 142–44,

161, 166, 171–72, 180, 192–99, 201, 203–04, 230, 245–46, 248–52, 267–75, 303–09, 314, 333–42, 348–60, 362, 382, 387–93, 408–15, 419, 422,
Marsden, Anthony (Tony) 191
Marsden, Chief Inspector 171
Marsh, Captain Ronald 76, 224
Marsh, George Alfred St. Vincent *see* Lord Edgware
Marsh, Geraldine 77, 141, 186
Marshal, The 386
Marshall, Arlena *see* Arlena Stuart
Marshall, Captain Kenneth 184, 186–87
Marshall, Edward John 171
Marshall, Linda 184, 186, 198
Marshall, Mr. 313–15
Marshall, Ruth 184
Marsham, Mrs. 222
Marston, Anthony (Tony) 164–65
Martha 189
Martin B. 386
Martin, Bryan 76–77
Martin, Gladys 272, 274, 281
Martin, Miss 45
Martindale, Miss Katherine 344
Martinelli, Contessa ("Old Macaroni") 357
Mary (*The Body in the Library*) 194
Mary (*Cat Among the Pigeons*) 320
Mason, Ada Beatrice 50
Massilini, Cardinal 314
Masterman, Mr. 89
Masters 27
Masters, Charlie 261
Masterton, Connie 297, 300
Masterton, Wilfrid 297
Matcham, Mrs. 395–96
Matthews (for the Defense) 163
Maudie 403
Maureen 189
Maverick, Young Dr. 269
Maxwell, Superintendent 66
May 196
Mayhew, George 207
Mayhew, Old 206
McAllister, Amy 356
McClelland, Sister 252
McCrae, Detective Constable 291
McCrae, Mrs. 358, 360
McCulloch, Dr. 386
McFarlane, Mr. 364
McGill, Reverend 385
McGillicuddy, Mrs. Elspeth 289, 303–06, 308
McGinty, Mrs. 258–62, 264, 302, 324, 380, 396
McGrath, James (Jimmy) 36–37
McGuire, Dr. 413
McIntyre, Mr. and Mrs. 256
McKay, Elspeth 379–81
McLean, Hugo 197
McNabb, Colin 166, 290–91
McNaughton, Mr. Angus 345–46
McNaughton, Mrs. 346
McNeil, Donald 338
McNeil, Inspector 357
McNeil, Sir Andrew 392
Meadowes, Miss 189
Meadowes, Mr. 189, 372

Meadows, Inspector 45
Mears, Mr. 228
Mears, Mrs. 228
Meauhourat, Mademoiselle ("Zélie") 396
Meavy, Mrs. 337
Medway, Mrs. 227, 229
Melanie, Little 391
Melchett, Colonel 58, 61–62, 68, 194, 196, 198–99, 243, 414
Melford, Mildred 357
Melford, Nancy 357
Mellon, Young Mr. 234
Melrose, Colonel (*The Murder of Roger Ackroyd*) 42
Melrose, Colonel (*The Secret of Chimneys* and *The Seven Dials Mystery*) 38, 55
Melrose, Colonel (*Sleeping Murder*) 413
Mercado, Joseph 114
Mercado, Marie 114
Merdell 298
Merdell, Old 238, 297–99, 302, 311
Mere, Alfred 84
Meredith, Anne 119–21, 123–24
Merrall, Major 298
Merrick, Young 213
Merrion, Miss 108
Merrypit, Mrs. 392
Merton, Mrs. 178
Merton, The Dowager Duchess of 77
Merton, The Duke of 76–77
Mervyn 371
Metcalf, Dr. 197
Meyerling 45
Michael 336
Michael, Somebody Called 263
Michel, Pierre (*Murder in the Calais Coach*) 88
Michel, Pierre (*The Mystery of the Blue Train*) 50
Mick 402
Mickey 46
Micky 363
Mildmay of Exhampton 203
Mildred, Aunt 157
Miles, Miss 380
Milly 330
Milray, Mr. Augustus 32
Milray, Mrs. 95
Milray, Violet 94–96
Minden, Mrs. 379
Minks 32
Minor, Nicholson 228
Minton, Miss 190–91
Mirelle 49, 52, 155, 187
Mirror Crack'd from Side to Side, The see The Mirror Crack'd
Mirror Crack'd, The 333–342, 352, 392, 409
Mitchell 296
Mitchell, Henry 101
Mitchell, Major Robert 214
Mitchell, Ruth 101
Mitzi 143, 249–50, 252, 293, 326
Mohammed 285
Moira 396
Mollie 279
Moncrief, Miss 269
Monro, Flossie 46–47

Monsieur le Marquis 49
Montgomery 364
Montressor, Helen 179
Monty, Old 128
Moody, Mrs. Elizabeth 371
Mopp, Mrs. 250
Morales, Pedro 219, 221
Moran, Old 364
Moresby, Dr. 203
Morgan, Amy 371
Morganthal, Otto 254–55
Morisot, Anne 102
Morisot, Marie Angélique ("Madame Giselle") 99, 102
Morley, Georgina 176, 178
Morley, Mr. Henry 176–78, 180, 224
Morris, Isaac 164
Morris, Old Dr. 307
Morseby, Mr. 66
Mortimer, Colonel 358
Morton, Inspector 279
Moscombe, Beatrice 153
Mosgorovsky, Mr. 55–56
Mountbryan, Lord 364
Mountford, Mr. 413
Mountford, Mrs. 413
Mounthead, Lord 213
Moving Finger, The 200–204, 209, 238–39, 243–44, 275, 307, 331, 408
Moxon, Mr. 77
Mrs. McGinty's Dead 12, 69, 85, 122, 132, 144, 161, 198, **257–265**, 281, 292, 302, 321–22, 324–26, 362, 379–81, 395–96, 398–99, 408, 420
Muirfield, Sybil 257
Mullard, Old 235
Mullins, Iris 403
Munro, Colonel 384, 386
Murchison, Bianca 285
Murchison, Simon 285
Murder After Hours 7–9, 11–12, 172, 174, **224–231**, 233, 237, 243–45, 252, 281, 322–323
Murder at Hazelmoor 7, 10, **62–69**, 74, 104, 111, 139–141, 160, 182, 186–87, 196, 199, 224, 265, 373, 417, 421
Murder at Littlegreen House see Poirot Loses a Client
Murder at the Vicarage 7, 10, 41, 43, **57–62**, 68–69, 73–74, 79, 85, 139, 140–42, 144, 160, 166, 172, 186, 192, 194, 196–97, 203, 230, 238–39, 243, 250, 275, 306–07, 334, 336–38, 350–351, 355–356, 359, 393, 408, 410–411, 413, 414, 420, 422
Murder for Christmas see A Holiday for Murder
Murder in Mesopotamia 13, 86, **111–117**, 123, 126, 141–43, 149, 156, 226, 244, 253, 323, 386
Murder in Retrospect 7, 11–13, 199, **204–209**, 214, 222, 230, 243–245, 252, 281, 322–23, 395
Murder in the Calais Coach 13, 82, **86–92**, 111–12, 139, 144, 148, 180, 208, 214, 326, 422
Murder in Three Acts 10, 12, 48, 85, **92–97**, 111, 126, 139, 141–42,

146, 150–51, 155, 180, 186, 208, 239, 349, 421–22
Murder Is Announced, A 9, 19, 139, 144, 166, 230, 239, **245–252**, 258, 275, 281, 288, 293, 294, 306, 323–26, 339–41, 350, 352, 356, 392, 408, 410, 422
Murder Is Easy see *Easy to Kill*
Murder of Roger Ackroyd, The 6, **39–43**, 47, 51, 57, 62, 68–69, 73, 79, 84, 139–40, 160, 171, 186–87, 214–15, 224, 301, 323, 381, 414, 420, 423
Murder on the Links 5, 13, **24–30**, 41, 44, 46–47, 51, 57, 102, 105, 107, 140–41, 155, 161, 167, 179, 187, 342, 363, 405
Murder on the Orient Express see *Murder in the Calais Coach*
Murder, She Said see *What Mrs. McGillicuddy Saw*
Murder with Mirrors 9, 61, 85, 161, 243, 264, **266–270**, 276, 295, 301, 314, 325, 353, 414
Murdoch, Cynthia 16, 17, 27, 45, 405
Murdoch, Mr. 351
Murgatroyd, Miss 249, 252
Murgatroyd, Mr. 55
Murray, Dr. 371
Mussolini, Benito 150, 175, 182, 402
Muswell 194
Mutton-Chop 401
Mysterious Affair at Styles, The 4, 5, 10, **15–20**, 22, 25–26, 29–30, 33, 41, 43, 45, 51–52, 57, 75–76, 80, 98, 104, 107, 140, 143, 149, 162, 166–67, 177, 199, 230, 342, 393, 395, 404–05, 417, 419, 421
Mystery at Littlegreen House see *Poirot Loses a Client*
Mystery of the Blue Train, The 6, 10, 12–13, 39, **48–53**, 57, 73, 92, 115, 129, 138, 141, 155, 161, 166, 178, 187, 192, 279, 301, 321, 323, 346, 379, 380, 395, 397, 406, 417, 421

N or M? 24, 139, **187–192**, 265, 370–72, 398–401, 403
Nadina 31–32
Nahoum, Isaac 256
Nan 378
Nancy 54
Nanny 386
Narracot, Fred 165
Narracott, Gladys 185
Narracott, Inspector 66, 68, 196
Narracott, Miss 413
Narracott, Mrs. 314
Nash, Superintendent 202–03
Naylors, The 197
Neasdon, Dr. 185
Needheim, Helga 284
Neele, Chief-Inspector (*Third Girl*) 362, 366
Neele, Inspector (*A Pocket Full of Rye*) 271–75, 324, 362
Neil 228
Nellie 178
Nellie, Old 171

Nelly 159
Nemesis 209, 309, 342, **387–392**, 393, 397, 409, 415
Nero 159
Neumann, Miss 386
Nevill, Arthur 45
Nevill, Gladys 176
Nicholson, Dr. Jasper 83
Nicholson, Moira 83–84
Nicoletis, Mrs. 288, 290, 292
Nielson, Dr. 285
Nofret 216–17
Norris, Inspector 403
Norton, Stephen 405
Nye, Pamela 384
Nye, Police Constable 291
Nye, Sir Stafford 383–87

Obolovitch, King Nicholas IV 35–36
Obolovitch, Prince Michael 36–38
Obolovitch, Prince Nicholas 38
O'Brien, Eileen 169
O'Connor, Derek 319
O'Connor, Sergeant 121, 228, 230
Ogilvie, Alexander 221
Ohlsson, Greta 90
O'Keefe, Miss 372
Old Bouncer 213
Oliver, Ariadne 12, 117–19, 121–23, 198, 230, 261–62, 293, 296–97, 299–300, 327, 329–30, 331–332, 346, 360–66, 376–78, 381–82, 393–98, 404, 415
Oliver, Dr. 406
Olivera, Jane 178–79, 181
Olivera, Julia 178, 181
Olivier, Madame 44, 45
One, Two, Buckle My Shoe see *The Patriotic Murders*
Ordeal by Innocence 11, 85, 161, 243, 264, **311–315**, 322–25, 327, 332–33, 340, 353, 359, 393, 414
O'Rourke, Mrs. 190
O'Rourke, Terence 56
Osborne, Mr. Zachariah 330, 332
Oscar, Miss 37
Ossington, Sir William ("Billy Bones") 160
Otterbourne, Rosalie 129, 131
Otterbourne, Solome 126, 129, 199
Otterweight 298
Oulard, Denise 27
Oulard, Léonie 27
Overdose of Death, An see *The Patriotic Murders*
Owen, Mr. (*And Then There Were None*) 163–65
Owen, Mr. (*The Boomerang Clue*) 83

Packard, Miss 371–72
Packer, Mrs. 344
Packham, Sir George 385
Pagett, Edith ("Edie") 411, 413–14
Pagett, Guy 31–32
Pagett, Mr. 413
Pagett, Mrs. 413
Pale Horse, The 12, 125, 204, 323, **327–333**, 335, 340–41, 352, 359, 362, 374, 377

Palgrave, Major 139, 349–52, 389
Palk, Mrs. 194
Palk, Police Constable 194
Palmer, Miss Mabel 46
Panter, Mrs. 279
Papapolous, Demetrius 49
Papapolous, Zia 49–50
Pardoe, William R. 368
Parfitt 357
Parker 41
Parker, Amos 66
Parker, Old Lizzie 331
Parkins, Sergeant 203
Parkinson, Alexander 399–401
Parkinson, Mrs. (*Postern of Fate*) 400
Parkinson, Mrs. (*Sad Cypress*) 171
Parkinsons, The 400–01
Parnell, Mr. Geoffrey 109
Parrott, James 279
Parsons, Nellie 185
Parsons, Olive 212
Partington, Jim 170
Partington, Mrs. 373
Partridge 201, 203
Partridge, Mr. James 108, 111
Partridge, Mrs. 197
Parwell, Superintendent 280
Passenger to Frankfurt 8, 10, 13, 24, 57, **382–387**, 402, 414–15
Paton, Captain Ralph 40, 41, 140, 224
Patriotic Murders, The 10–11, 76, 139, 143, 167, 173, **174–181**, 185, 199, 208, 224, 421
Patterson, Elsie 228
Paul 203
Paulovitch, Count Sergius 31
Pauncefoot Jones, Dr. 255–57
Pauncefoot Jones, Mrs. 255
Pavett 49
Paynter, Gerald 45
Paynter, Mr. 45–46
Peabody, Miss Caroline 133–34, 136, 138–40, 142
Peacock, Constable 235
Peake, Mrs. 373
Pearson, Brian 66
Pearson, James 65–67, 141
Pearson, Mary 65
Pearson, Mrs. 44
Pearstock, Mrs. 227
Pebmarsh, Miss Millicent 344–45
Pebmarsh, Mr. 235
Pedlar, M.P., Sir Eustace 31, 33–34, 56, 222
Peel Edgerton, Sir James 22
Penderley, Mr. 412
Pendleton 346
Pennington, Andrew 128–29
Pennyfather, Canon 355, 357–58, 360
Penrith, Dr. 280
Penrose, Dr. 413
Percehouse, Miss Caroline 65, 67–68, 140–41
Perenna, Mrs. 189–90
Perenna, Sheila 189, 191–92
Peril at End House 7, 10, 38, 68, **69–74**, 75–76, 79, 82, 84, 88, 92, 117, 141–42, 144, 167, 181, 185, 187, 198, 210, 265, 323, 341

Perring, Mrs. 380
Perrot, Jules 102
Perry, Alice 372
Perry, Amos 372
Perry, Jonas 352
Perry, Mrs. 347
Perryman, Mr. 114
Peter, Somebody Called 263
Peters, Andrew 284
Peters, Dr. Mary 274
Petronella 385
Pettigrew, Miss 32
Phillips, K.C., Mr. 18
Phillips, Sergeant 185
Phillpot, Gervase 368
Phillpot, Major 368
Phillpot, Mrs. 368
Pickerigell, Mr. 120
Pierce, Constable 346
Pierce, Jimmy 236,
Pierce, Miss Amabel 145–47
Pierce, Mr. 128
Pierce, Mrs. 158
Pierce, Tommy 158–59, 161, 265, 302
Pierre 221
Piggy 260
Pike, Alfred 340
Pikeaway, Colonel Ephraim 319–20, 382, 384–86, 402
Pine, Sergeant 330
Pip and Emma 251
Pirezzio, Antonio 50
Platt, George 108
Pleydon, Gene 329
Pocket Full of Rye, A 13, 86, 140, 209, 237, **270–275**, 281, 302, 305–07, 310, 323–24, 362, 420
Poirot, Achille 46
Poirot, Hercule 4–5, 7, 10, 12–13, 16–18, 22–27, 29–30, 34, 39–47, 49–51, 53, 61–62, 69–71, 73–77, 79–80, 82, 84–90, 92–93, 95–96, 98–102, 104–09, 111–34, 136–41, 143–48, 150–55, 160–61, 166–67, 169–87, 192, 198, 205–10, 214, 217–18, 222–23, 225–29, 232–38, 243–44, 257–65, 277–81, 288–302, 311, 316–18, 321–22, 324, 326, 342–44, 346–48, 350, 353, 359–64, 366, 376–82, 386, 393–98, 404–07, 414–15, 420, 422–23
Poirot Loses a Client 10, 34, 42, 53, 57, **131–144**, 160, 167, 171, 173, 180, 192, 198–99, 217–218, 223–24, 230, 240, 245, 260, 264–65, 280–81, 299, 326, 359, 370
Poissonier, Monsieur 385
Polegate, Young 351
Pollack, Sergeant (*Murder at Hazelmoor*) 66
Pollack, Sergeant (*Remembered Death*) 222
Polonska, Vanda 190
Pontarlier, Mariana Josephine 395
Pontarlier, Monsieur, (a.k.a. Hercule Poirot) 279–80
Porch 314
Porter, Major George Douglas 139, 233–34, 236
Posselthwaite, Mrs. 356

Postern of Fate 199, 375, **398–403**, 415
Potter, Mike 330
Pound, Mr. (*Murder at Hazelmoor*) 65
Pound, Mrs. (*Murder at Hazelmoor*) 65
Pound, Mrs. (*Remembered Death*) 221
Pratt, Mrs. 62
Prescott, Canon Jeremy 350, 352, 390
Prescott, Joan 351–52, 390
Prescott, Mr. and Mrs. 202
Prestcott, Mr. 195–96
Preston Grey, Mrs. 395
Preston, Hailey 338–40
Presweight, Eddie 376, 379
Price Ridley, Mrs. 60–61, 192, 196, 334
Price, Emlyn 391
Price, Lily 337
Price, Mary 197
Price-Ridley, Miss 400
Primer, Detective Inspector 413
Primrose, Great-aunt 371
Pritchard, Alexander 82
Protheroe, Anne 60, 336
Protheroe, Colonel Lucius 58–59, 60, 62, 336, 420
Protheroe, Lettice 60–62, 141, 186
Pugh, Eric 384
Purdy, Professor 345, 348
Purvis, Esq., William 136–37
Pusey, Colonel 222
Pye, Mr. 200, 202–4

Quantril, Elizabeth 389
Quentin, Dr. 45
Quilp, Andrew 339
Quimper, Dr. 307

Race, Colonel 27, 32, 118–20, 123, 126, 129, 146, 167, 219–23, 363, 417
Radcliffe, Mrs. 403
Radley 228
Radley, General 358
Radsky, Countess 56
Rafiel, Jason 350–51, 353, 389, 390–92
Rafiel, Michael 389, 391–92
Raglan, Inspector (*The Murder of Roger Ackroyd*) 42
Raglan, Inspector (*The Seven Dials Mystery*) 55
Raglan, Inspector Tim (*Hallowe'en Party*) 379
Raike, Mrs ("Farmer Raike's Wife") 17
Raikes, Howard 176–9, 181
Rakounian, Michael 256
Ram Lal 179
Ramsay, Bill 345
Ramsay, Mr. Michael 345
Ramsay, Mrs. 345
Ramsay, Ted 345
Ramsbottom, Miss ("Aunt Effie") 86, 273–74
Randolph, Colonel 171
Ransom, Nicholas 378–80
Ransome, Dr. 170–71
Rasputin 291

Ratchett, Samuel Edward 88–89
Rathbone, Denis 318
Rathbone, Dr. 256
Rattery, John 206
Ravenscroft, Celia 393–96
Ravenscroft, Edward 395–96
Ravenscroft, Lady Margaret ("Molly"), née Margaret Preston-Grey 395–96
Ravenscroft, Sir Alistair 395–96
Rawlinson, Bob 317, 319, 419
Rayburn, Harry 32
Raymond, Geoffrey 41
Raymond, Jean 220
Reckitt, Mr. 392
Redcliffe, Hermia 329–31, 333
Redding, Lawrence 60–62, 230, 250
Redfern, Christine 183–84, 186–87, 214
Redfern, Patrick 183–84, 186–87, 214, 217, 238
Reece-Holland, Claudia 362–63
Reece-Holland, Emlyn 363
Reed, Giles 342, 409–13
Reed, Gwenda 409–14
Reed, John 158
Rees-Talbot, Mrs. 222
Reeves 61
Reeves, Emily 153
Reeves, Mr. 32
Reeves, Pamela 195, 197
Reeves, Young 83
Reg 261
Reg, Young 196
Reginald, Sir 314
Reichardt, Dr. 386
Reilly, Dr. Giles 112–14, 116, 141
Reilly, Mr. 176–78, 180
Reilly, Sheila 113–14, 141, 218
Reinjeer, Miss 291
Reiter, Carl 115
Reitner, Count 385
Remembered Death 7, 8, 11, 34, 57, 172, **218–224**, 230, 237, 243–44, 252, 280, 322–23, 363
Renauld, Eloise 24–26
Renauld, Jack 24, 26, 30, 140–41
Renauld, Paul 24–27, 140
Rendell, Dr. 260–62
Rendell, Shelagh, 262
Rendell, Young 202
Renisenb 216–18, 224
Restarick, Alexis (Alex) 266, 268–70
Restarick, Andrew 362–64, 366
Restarick, Grace 363
Restarick, James Patrick 364
Restarick, Johnnie 268–69
Restarick, Mary 363
Restarick, Norma 361–64, 366
Restarick, Simon 363
Restarick, Stephen 266, 268–69
Revel, The Honorable Virginia 36–39, 56, 73
Reynolds, Ann 378
Reynolds, Joyce 377–79, 381, 396
Reynolds, Leopold 378, 381
Reynolds, Mr. 378
Reynolds, Mrs. 378
Rice 255
Rice, Fredericka ("Freddie") 71, 73

438   Title and Character Index

Rich, Miss Eileen 318, 322
Richard 242
Richardson 37
Richardson, Commander 351
Richetti, Signor Guido 129
Richmond, Alfred 380
Richmond, Arthur 164
Riddell, Mr. Albert (Bert) 108, 111
Riddell, Mrs. Albert 108
Ridgeway, Dr. 46
Ridgeway, Lilian 197
Ridgeway, Linnet 126–29, 131, 141, 184, 218, 238, 301
Riley, Mary 170–71
Riley, Tom 250
Riseley-Porter, Mrs. Geraldine 390
Rival, Mrs. Merlina ("Flossie Gapp") 346–47
Rivers 159
Rivington, D.S.O., Colonel H. 83
Rivington, Mrs. 83, 86
Robbins, Mr. 191
Robby 305
Robert (*By the Pricking of My Thumbs*) 373
Robert (*Hallowe'en Party*) 380
Robert, Monsieur 221
Roberts, Dr. (*Cards on the Table*) 119–21
Roberts, Dr. (*Murder at the Vicarage*) 61
Roberts, Mr. 338
Roberts, Mr. and Mrs. 82
Robertson, Dr. 352
Robinson, Mr. 319, 321, 358, 384–86, 402
Robinson, William 291
Robson, Cornelia Ruth 128–9, 131, 184
Robson, Mrs. 128
Rockbury, Mr. 372
Rockford, Sterndale 128
Rod 339
Roderick 306
Rogers (*Death in the Air*) 101
Rogers (*Poirot Loses a Client*) 136
Rogers, Dicky 307–08
Rogers, Dorothy 402
Rogers, Ethel 165
Rogers, Michael 367–69
Rogers, Mr. and Mrs. 213
Rogers, Mrs. 368
Rogers, Thomas 165
Ronnie 319
Rosalie 400
Rosamund, Aunt 319
Roscoff, Alex 263
Roscombe, Mr. 364
Rose (*The Moving Finger*) 201
Rose (*Murder at the Vicarage*) 62
Rose, Miss 108
Rose, Mrs. 160
Rosemary 402
Rosenberg 195
Rosenkraun, Edgar 66
Rosentelle, Mrs. 396
Ross, Donald 77
Ross, Miss 100
Rossakoff, Countess Vera 45, 292
Rotherstein, Mr. Samuel 177
Rouselle, Mademoiselle ("Maddy") 396
Rowan, Miss 166, 318, 322

Rowe, Janet ("Nannie") 242
Rowlandson, Mr. 250
Rowley, Mrs. 191
Royde, Adrian 213
Royde, Mrs. 213
Royde, Thomas ("True Thomas") 211, 213
Roylance, Dr. 22
Rubec, Dr. 285
Rudd, Jason ("Jinks") 336–38
Rudolph, Humphrey 207
Rundle, Constable Bert 202
Russell, Harry 357
Russell, Miss 41, 43, 73
Rycroft, Mr. 65, 67
Rycroft, Sir Lewis 170
Ryder, James Bell 101, 105
Rydesdale, George 249, 422
Ryken, Eliza 170
Ryland, Abe 44–45
Rysdorff, Miss 291

Sad Cypress 143, 149, **167–174**, 179, 244, 280, 420
Sadler, Mrs. 62
Sainsbury-Seale, Maybelle 176–78, 180
Sampson, Mr. 338
Samuels, Mrs. 137
Sandbourne, Mrs. 300
Sandeman, Sir Edwin 272
Sanders 306
Sanders, Doris 227
Sanderson, Miss 400
Sandersons, The 350
Sandford Mrs. 338
Sandford, Dr. 338
Sandford, Mr. 332
Sanseverato, Rebecca 177
Santonix, Rudolf 367, 368
Satcherverell, Mr. 160
Satipy 216
Satterthwaite, Mr. 93–94, 96
Saunders, Mr. (*The Big Four*) 45
Saunders, Mr. (*Sleeping Murder*) 411–412
Saunders, Mrs. (*The Body in the Library*) 195
Saunders, Mrs. (*Sleeping Murder*) 411–412
Saunders, The Honorable Mrs. 358
Savage, John 83–84, 86
Savaronoff, Dr. 46
Savernake, Henrietta 226–28, 230–31, 244, 281
Scheele, Anna 254–56
Scherz, Rudi 250, 251
Schmidt, Hildegarde 90
Schuster, Mr. 390
Schwartz, Dr. 285
Schweich, Fräulein 269
Scobell 228
Scott, Mrs. 262
Scuttle, Mr. 261
Secret Adversary, The 5, 6, 12, 18, 20–24, 29, 33–35, 38, 57, 74, 84, 106, 140–41, 169, 180, 189–91, 237, 257, 259, 301, 370–72, 374, 398–401, 403, 418
Secret of Chimneys, The 6, 10, 13, 23, **34–39**, 47, 53–57, 82, 84, 106, 119, 131, 140–142, 160, 169, 173, 175, 198, 211, 222, 237, 293, 369, 417
Seddon, Mr. 170
Sedgwick, Johnny 356
Sedgwick, Lady Bess 356, 359
Sedgwick, Miss 395
Sedley, Amelia Mary 171
Selby, Mr. 179
Selina 191
Seminoff, Olga 379–81
Serrocold, Caroline Louise (Carrie Louise) 268
Serrocold, Lewis 267, 269
Seton, Michael 69–71, 73
Seton, Sir Matthew 70–71
Seven Dials Mystery, The 6, 10, 12, 23, 36, **53–57**, 82, 84, 120, 141, 147, 160, 169, 173, 212, 237, 301, 341, 414, 420
Shacklebury, Mrs. 403
Shaista, Princess 317–19, 321
Shaitana, Mr. 118–20, 123–24, 146, 262
Shane, Michael 278–79, 281
Shane, Rosamund 278–79, 281
Shannon, Christine 221
Shapland, Ann 317–18, 320–21, 323
Sharpe, Inspector 290–91
Shaw, Dr. 368
Sheldon, Rose 357
Sheppard, Caroline 39–43, 62, 140, 381
Sheppard, Dr. James 39–43, 51, 69, 73, 139, 172
Shirty 213
Shoreham, Robert ("Robbie") 385, 386
Shotacomb, Old Miss Lavinia 401
Shrivenham, Young Mr. 255
Simmons 195
Simmons, Archdeacon
Simmons, Elinor 250
Simmons, Julia 249, 252
Simmons, Mrs. 62
Simmons, Patrick, 249, 252
Simons 227
Simpkins, Mr. Josh 307
Simpkins, Mrs. Josh 307
Sims, Doris 95
Sims, Dr. 339
Sims, Mr. 410
Sims, Old 197
Sittaford Mystery, The see *Murder at Hazelmoor*
Slack, Inspector 61–62, 68, 194, 196, 198, 243
Sleeping Murder 7, 9, 11–12, 144, 302, 342, 403, **407–414**
Slicker, Mr. 373
Small, Florence 197
Smith, Ivor 373–374
Smith, Madeleine 411
So Many Steps to Death 13, 24, 144, **282–288**, 293, 300, 323, 326, 327, 387, 417
Soames White, Mr. 331
Soames, Mrs. 176, 178
Sobek 216–18
Solomon, Mr. 346, 403
Somers, Miss 272
Somervell, Major 170
Sonia (*At Bertram's Hotel*) 358

Sonia (*Third Girl*) 363
Southwood, The Hon. Joanna 127–28
Sparkling Cyanide see *Remembered Death*
Speeder, Carol 283
Spence, Superintendent 235, 237, 257–60, 263, 377, 379–81, 395–96
Spencer, Miss 255
Spent, Gladys 153
Spicer, Mrs. 213
Spiess, Herr Heinrich 386
Spragge, Mr. Frederick 83–84, 86, 237
Sprig, Mr. 373
Springer, Miss Grace 317–18, 320, 322
Sprot, Arthur 190
Sprot, Betty 189–90, 198, 265, 401
Sprot, Millicent 190
Staggenham, Charles 385
Staggenham, Mrs. 385
Stamfordis, Dmitri 251
Stamfordis, Sonia 251
Stamfordis, Sybil 331
Stanbury, Old Ben 160
Stanisdale, Old 260
Stanley, Lady 291
Stanley, Sir Arthur 291
Starke, Julia 373
Starke, Sir Philip 373, 374
Starr, Raymond 195, 197, 199, 217, 421
Stepanov, Count Boris Ivanovitch 21–22
Stephanie 268
Stephen and his Crowd 385
Stephens 121
Stevens 55
Stevens, Mrs. 55
Stillingfleet, Dr. 169, 362, 364
Stillwell, Sir John 269
Stirling, Pamela ("Poppy") 331–33
Stoddart-West, James ("Stodders") 198, 306, 309, 310
Stoddart-West, Lady 309, 311
Stoddart-West, Lord 309
Stokes, Dr. (*At Bertram's Hotel*) 358
Stokes, Dr. (*Nemesis*) 392
Stone, Chief Constable 320
Stone, Dr. 60
Stonor, Gabriel 27, 30
Strange, Audrey 211, 213–15
Strange, Kay 211, 213–14
Strange, Mr. 109
Strange, Nevile 211–14, 217
Strange, Sir Bartholomew ("Tollie") 93–95, 150, 155
Stravinska, Anna 307
Strete, Canon 268
Strete, Mildred, née Gulbrandsen 268–70
Stroud, Mary 109
Stuart, Arlena (Arlena Marshall) 183–87, 214
Stubbs, Hattie (Lady Stubbs) 296–99, 311
Stubbs, Sir George 296–97, 299, 302, 311, 324
Stylptitch, Count 35–37
Sugden, Mr. 151, 153

Suleiman, Abdul 255
Summerhayes, Major Johnnie 260, 265
Summerhayes, Maureen 260, 265, 318, 321–22, 325
Summerhayes, Old Colonel 260
Sutcliffe, Angela 94
Sutcliffe, Henry 319
Sutcliffe, Jennifer 10, 317, 319, 320, 322
Sutcliffe, Joan 10, 317, 319, 320
Sweetiman, Mrs. 261–62, 281
Swettenham, Edmund 248
Swettenham, Mrs. 248
Sybil 384
Symmington, Brian 201
Symmington, Colin 201
Symmington, Mona 201–02
Symmington, Richard 201–03

Taken at the Flood see *There Is a Tide*
Tamplin, The Honorable Lenox 50, 52, 141
Tamplin, Viscountess Rosalie 50, 52, 141
Tanios, Bella 133–35, 138, 141–42, 198, 217, 223, 230
Tanios, Dr. Jacob 135, 138
Tanios, Mary and Edward 135, 198, 265
Taverner, Chief Inspector 242
Teddy 228
Temple 95
Temple, Miss Elizabeth 391–92
Templeton, Edgar 84
Templeton, Mr. 46
Templeton, Mrs. 46
Templeton, Rose Emily 83–84
Ten Little Indians see *And Then There Were None*
Ten Little Niggers see *And Then There Were None*
Teresa of Ávila, Saint 396
Terry 242
Teti 217–18
Theodofanous, Daphne, a.k.a "Mary Ann," a.k.a. Countess Renata Zerkowski 384–86
There Is a Tide 7, 11, 13, 86, 139, 172, 173, 198, 224, **231–239**, 243–45, 247, 252, 257, 258, 273, 275, 281, 288, 300, 302, 310, 322–23, 325, 366, 388, 418
Thesiger, Jimmy 12, 53–56
They Came to Baghdad 12–14, 24, 112, 237, **253–257**, 259, 275, 284, 286–288, 302, 310, 327, 387
They Do It with Mirrors see *Murder with Mirrors*
Thibault, Maître Alexandre 101–02, 104
Third Girl 169, 280, 359, **360–367**, 369, 374–77, 382, 393, 394
Thirteen at Dinner 10, 61, **74–80**, 84, 87–88, 101, 107, 121, 126, 139, 141, 166–67, 186, 214, 224, 243, 323, 335, 349, 422
Thomas, a.k.a. "Thomasina" 413
Thomas, Dr. 82
Thomas, Dr. Geoffrey 158, 161, 170

Thompson 197
Thompson, Billy 392
Thompson, Dr. 107
Thompson, Minnie 368
Three Act Tragedy see *Murder in Three Acts*
Thripp, Mary 42
Tiddler, Detective-Sergeant William ("Tom Tiddler") 339
Tiglath-Pileser 249
Tio, Marcus 256, 287
Tio, Paul 256
Todhunter, Lady 321
Todhunter, Sir Mervyn 317, 321
Tollington, Gerald 221
Tom (*Murder at Hazelmoor*) 66
Tom (*The Pale Horse*) 331
Tomlinson, Archdeacon 358
Tomlinson, Jean 291
Tony 330
Totman, Mr. 248
Towards Zero 10–11, 160, 166, **209–215**, 217, 346, 422
Traill, Inspector 262
Trapp, Mr. Hiram 27
Travers, Mr. 364
Tredwell 38, 54–55
Trefusis, Emily 64–69, 94, 96, 111, 141, 199, 421
Trefussis James, Miss 274
Trelawny, Mr. 214
Tremlet 228
Trenton, Charles 234
Trenton, Gerald 234
Trenton, Lord Edward 234, 273
Tressilian, Edward 153
Tressilian, Lady 207
Tressilian, Lady Camilla 210–11, 213–15, 217
Tressilian, Sir Matthew 213
Trevelyan, R.N., Captain Joseph 63–67
Treves, Dr. 46
Treves, Mr. 211–15
Trevor, Betsey 298
Tripp, Isabel 136–38
Tripp, Julia 136–38
Trollope, Sir George 351
Trotwood, Betsey 298
Tucker, Gary 297
Tucker, Jim 297
Tucker, Marlene 296–98
Tucker, Marylin 207
Tucker, Mrs. 297–98, 332
Tuckerton, Esq., Thomas 329
Tuckerton, Mrs. 329
Tuckerton, Thomasina Ann ("Tommy Tucker") 329
Turner, Constable 121
Turner, Josephine ("Josie") 195, 197

Underhay, Robert 233–34, 237, 239
Upjohn, Julia 318, 321–22
Upjohn, Mrs. 318, 321, 323
Upshaw, Mr. 340
Upward, Mrs. Laura 261, 263–64, 281, 324
Upward, Robin 261, 263, 264, 281

Valence, Jane 320
Valence, Lady 320

Van Aldin, Rufus 49, 52, 115, 129, 279, 301
Vandemeyer, Marguerite (Rita) 21–23, 191, 372, 400
Van Dusen, Mrs. 77
Vane, Sergeant 235
Van Heidem, Paul 285
Van Rydock, Ruth 267–68
Van Schuyler, Miss Marie 128–29
Vansittart, Miss Eleanor 317, 320, 322
van Stuyvesant, Cora 368
Varaga, Queen 35–36
Vaughan, Gwenda 313
Vaughan, Major 251
Vavasour, Johnny 235
Venables, Mr. 331–32
Véroneau, Inez 45
Veronica (a.k.a Venetia) 255–56
Victor 227–28
Vinegar, Mrs. 392
Viner, Old Miss 50
Violet, Lady 317
Vitelli, Signor 385
von Deinem, Carl 190–92
Von Eisenger, Baron 320
Von Eisenger, Hedwig 320
von Roken, Frau 385
von Roken, Herr 385
von Waldsausen, the Gräfin Charlotte, née Charlotte Krapp 385
Vyse, Charles 71
Vyse, Mary 320

Waddingtons, The 401
Waddock, Old Bogie 374
Wade, Elaine 55
Wade, Gerald 54–55
Wade, Roger 171
Wadell, Sergeant 358
Waite, Detective-Constable 274
Wake, Rev. Alfred 159
Wales, Emma 214
Walker, Colonel and Mrs. 391
Walters, Esther 351, 389–90
Walters, Mr. 191
Walton 384
Wanstead, Professor 388, 391
Warborough, Mr. 314
Warburton, Captain Jim 297
Wargrave, Alfred James 171
Wargrave, Lawrence John (Mr. Justice Wargrave) 163
Warren, Angela 207, 209, 244
Warren, Dr. 66
Waterhouse, Miss Edith 345
Waterhouse, Mr. 380
Waterhouse, Mr. James 345
Waters, Emily 337
Waters, Julia 373
Waters, Major 373
Watson, Dr. 25, 197
Waynflete, Miss Honoria 160–61, 281
Waynflete, Old Colonel 160

Webb, Ann 345
Webb, Bella 331
Webb, Geraldine 308
Webb, Mr. 345
Webb, Sheila 344–45
Weissgarten, Dr. 358
Wells, Elizabeth 17
Wells, Mr. (*The A.B.C. Murders*) 107
Wells, Mr. (*The Mysterious Affair at Styles*) 17
Welman, Henry 169
Welman, Laura 168–74
Welman, Roderick (Roddy) 168–70, 172, 174, 244
Welsham, The Duchess of 321
Wesley, Mrs. 337
West, Chloe 222
West, David 307
West, Florrie 339
West, Joan 12, 251, 350, 356, 389, 410, 411
West, Major 153
West, Maureen 344
West, Raymond 12, 61, 194, 251, 267, 307, 337, 348–50, 356, 389, 410, 411
Westbury, Canon 222
Western, Harry 351
Western, Mrs. Harry 351
Westholme, Lady 57, 145–47, 149, 223, 237
Weston, Chief Constable (Colonel Weston) 69, 71, 181, 185
Weston, Colonel and Mrs. 380
Weston, Inspector 352
Wetherall, Detective Sergeant Bob 306
Wetherby, Miss 60, 192, 196, 334–35
Wetherby, Mr. 262
Wetherby, Mrs. 262, 281
Weyman, Michael 297
Whalley, Johnathan 45
Wharton, Colonel 283
What Mrs. McGillicuddy Saw 11, 48, 140, 198, 238, 258, 275, 289, 295, 302, **303–311**, 324, 327, 333, 336–41, 348, 350, 355, 387, 389, 393, 409, 411, 418, 421
Wheeling, Mr. 358
Wheeling, Mrs. Emma 358
Whetherby 368
Whistler, Dr. James 101
White, Janet 379–80
Whitfield, Mr. 71
Whittaker, Dr. 357
Whittaker, Miss Elizabeth 378–80
Whittington, Mr. Edward 21
Why Didn't They Ask Evans? see *The Boomerang Clue*
Wicklow, Admiral 351
Widburn, Mr. Archie 77
Widburn, Mrs. 77

Wilde, Alison 337
Wilder, Mrs. 364
Wilkinson, Jane see Lady Edgware
Willett, Mrs. 64–68, 140–41, 187
Willett, Violet 64–65, 68, 141, 187
William (*Evil Under the Sun*) 185
William (*The Seven Dials Mystery*) 54
William, Old Uncle 372
Williams (*The Seven Dials Mystery*) 55
Williams (*Towards Zero*) 214
Williams, Bert 392
Williams, Cecilia 206–07, 209, 245
Williams, Dr. 371
Williams, Inspector 83, 86
Williams, Maude 261, 263
Williams, Mr. Walter 255
Willis, Sir Abner 38
Willoughby the Elder, Dr. 397
Willoughby the Younger, Dr. 397
Willow, Dick 108
Wilson, Alfred 71, 265
Wilson, Ellen 71
Wilson, Gilmour 46
Wilson, William 71, 341
Wimborne, Mr. 307
Windlesham, Lord 127
Winterspoon, Dr. Henry 101
Winterton 384
Wizell, Fred 396
Woddell, Agnes 201–03
Wode, Sir George 127
Wolfe, Lady Caroline 351
Wonky Pooh 158
Wood, Georgy 351
Woodworth, General Lord 221
Woolmer, Janet 242
Worrit, Mrs. 384
Wotherspoon, Mrs. 252
Wright, Colonel 251
Wright, Gerald 273–74
Wright, Isidore 339
Wright, Mr. and Mrs. 114
Wyatt, Captain 65, 67, 139
Wygate, Miss 254
Wylie, Dr. 221
Wylie, Leonard 269
Wynward, Professor 38

Yahmose 216–17
Yaii 217
Yarde, Dorothy 412
Yardly, Lady 77
Ygdrasil 228
Yorke, Mrs. 373
Yule, Mrs. 413
Yusuf, Prince Ali 316–17, 319, 323, 419

Zerkowski, Countess Renata see Daphne Theodofanous
Zeropoulos, Monsieur 102
Zielinsky, Ella 338

Subject Index

adenoidal females 281
adoption 85, 264, 270, 312–15, 325, 340
adultery 7, 8, 152, 154, 164, 180–81, 183–84, 186, 187, 206, 209, 220, 226–27, 229, 244, 348–49
aging persons 140, 198, 208, 242–43, 308, 310, 343, 369, 371–72, 374, 392, 394, 415
alcohol abuse 126, 129, 131, 199, 290, 292, 297, 313, 318, 363
anti-Semitism 20, 43, 166, 293
archeologists and archeology 3, 6–7, 13, 60, 62, 98–101, 103–05, 112–16, 129, 144–45, 207, 238, 253–57, 287, 345, 348
architecture 58, 132–33, 150, 155–56, 192, 199, 210, 219, 225, 232, 239–40, 266–67, 271, 275, 276–77, 294–95, 297, 301–02, 304, 328, 342–43, 360–61, 367–68, 370, 374–76, 380, 383, 388, 391, 393–94, 408–09, 419–20
aristocracy 11, 49, 53, 55–56, 75–77, 80–82, 84–85, 87, 89–91, 98–100, 126–27, 131, 168, 170–171, 173, 272, 316, 318–19, 354, 394, 408, 412, 414, 421
artists and musicians 199, 206–08, 227, 230–31, 251, 374
automatic percolators 383
automobiles 15, 20, 24, 37, 58, 63, 75, 80–81, 92, 98, 125, 132, 157, 162, 164, 165–66, 168, 175, 182, 188, 193, 211, 225, 240, 247–48, 253, 259, 267, 271, 276, 282, 295, 304–05, 311–12, 315, 354, 364, 367, 371, 376, 382, 409, 417
aviation 4, 69, 81, 87, 98–99, 168, 195, 200–01, 253, 271, 282, 284–85, 304, 309, 313, 317, 327, 367, 377, 383–84

black sheep in the family 136, 151–52, 154, 220, 224, 234, 271, 273, 308, 310
British "fair play" 70, 73, 76, 88, 117, 124, 137, 155, 187, 350

capital punishment 304, 349
central heating in the home 40, 53, 150, 167, 174, 246, 271, 361
children 135, 142–43, 161, 196, 198–99, 261, 265, 287, 309, 310–11, 322, 326, 345, 347–48
clothing fashion and design 75, 77, 87, 92, 94, 97, 104, 118, 125–26, 133, 156–57, 175, 178, 183–84, 186, 259, 267, 300–01, 360–61, 363, 366, 376
Cold War 8, 247, 253, 266, 282, 287–88, 294, 297, 300, 304, 327, 342–43, 347, 354
communism and bolshevism 20, 22–23, 87, 94–95, 101, 126, 129, 131, 145, 175, 177, 242, 247, 273, 282–83, 287–89, 291, 294, 304, 327, 342–43, 354
computers 328, 343, 383
creeping socialism 258, 282, 399
crime in America 21, 44, 75, 87, 89, 175, 186, 219, 301
cultural differences 24–26, 38–39, 117, 124, 131, 143–44, 146, 151–52, 154–55, 180–81, 187, 217–18, 270, 287, 290, 292–93, 326

diminished incomes 200, 231, 235, 282, 294, 297, 325
divorce 73–74, 184, 187, 201, 211–13, 267–68, 335
doctors 169–70, 230, 237
drug abuse 43, 65, 69, 73–74, 84, 98, 100, 187, 289, 323, 335–36, 349, 360–63, 366, 373, 376, 394

education for the lower classes 8, 161, 169, 172–73, 180, 267–68, 282
educators 242, 316–18, 322–23, 364, 378–80
electricity in the home 15, 20, 35, 40, 53, 58, 63, 98, 162, 167, 224, 266, 271, 295, 298
ethnocentrism 18, 23, 38–39, 88–92, 101, 113, 116–17, 129, 135, 164, 166, 167–68, 176–78, 180, 187, 206, 208–09, 235–36, 242, 247, 250, 266, 268, 270, 284, 287, 293–94, 326–27

fascism 145, 175, 177, 188, 191–92, 249
feminism 66, 67, 119, 146, 184, 186, 201–02, 204, 209, 277, 279
film stars and films 69, 74, 76, 167, 175, 193, 224, 226–27, 259, 334–40
flower gardening 118, 123, 143–44, 159–61, 180–81, 194–95, 199, 334, 336, 342–43, 345–46
food and cooking 99, 132, 143–44, 216, 231, 246, 249, 258–60, 265, 274, 278, 288, 291, 293, 316, 321–22, 324, 326, 335–36, 355, 367, 376, 404, 423
foreigners and foreign "eccentricity" 16, 23, 25–26, 30, 38–39, 124, 154–55, 181, 205–06, 249, 252, 288–89, 293–94, 326–27, 346–48
formica 343

genetics v. environment 84–85, 161, 243, 264–65, 266–67, 269–70, 293, 314–15, 325, 333, 353, 381–82, 392–93, 414
gossip 40–41, 43, 60, 62, 65, 67–68, 140, 171, 193, 196, 200, 351, 355, 373

homosexuality 68, 76–77, 94–95, 119, 124, 156–57, 202, 264, 339, 349–350, 376, 379–80, 422–23
housing developments 335
hypocrisy 97, 117, 151, 155, 166, 187

increasing crime 247, 250, 282, 361, 376, 381, 383
inherited wealth v. earned wealth 13, 85, 149, 161, 166, 172, 310
insanity 228–29, 230, 290, 293, 353
Irish home rule 23, 190–91

juvenile delinquency 266–67, 269–70, 328, 335, 341, 345, 361

lawyers 86, 170, 237
lazy old gardeners 341–42
leniency in criminal sentencing 275, 349, 376, 379, 381, 388
love 135–36, 169, 172, 176, 181, 186, 204, 206, 220, 226–27, 229, 244–45, 280–81

masculinity 27, 32, 136, 152, 199, 405–06
military persons 139
money values 5, 67, 81, 125, 132, 157, 162, 165–66, 173, 175–76, 225, 233, 258, 265, 418
motherless characters 141–42, 218, 230, 245
mothers 141–43, 181, 186, 218, 223–24, 230, 245, 264, 340, 354, 359, 366, 376, 388

nature 9, 30, 63, 168, 227, 231
newspaper reporters 6, 68–69, 74, 86, 104–05, 158, 160, 187, 262, 265
nurses 113, 116–17, 143, 160, 173, 215, 310

organic fertilizers 343

parents and parenting 94, 141–43, 186, 204, 209, 245, 287, 314–15, 325, 354, 359, 361, 382, 392
patriotism 175, 188–92
pets 108, 137, 158–60, 213–214, 221, 228, 249, 260, 262, 345, 400, 402, 413

politicians 54–57, 220–223, 237, 384, 386, 414
pornography 291, 344
pregnancy out of wedlock 158, 164, 238, 242, 251, 278–79, 354, 373, 382, 392
psychology 25–26, 75, 100, 102, 105–07, 111, 114, 116, 122, 126, 145, 147–49, 154–55, 159, 161, 165–66, 173, 183, 208, 210, 212, 244, 248, 264, 269–70, 285, 290, 292, 318, 322, 325, 332, 386, 391
public familiarity with precise medical terms 349
public schools 70, 73, 193, 195, 421
pucka sahib 70, 73, 81–82, 88–89, 120, 129, 139, 421–22

racism 38–39, 288–89, 293, 383, 421
radio and television 53, 63, 69, 175, 211, 247, 295, 298, 312, 327–28, 338, 341, 354
railway travel 6, 11–12, 24, 48, 86–87, 92, 125, 151, 155, 157, 162, 188, 232, 253, 271, 277, 282, 303–04, 305, 307, 353–54, 417–418
rationing and black marketeering 15, 188, 231–32, 239, 246–48, 258, 271–72, 277, 288, 325
rechargeable razors 383
recorded music 58, 69, 150, 211, 335–36, 354
religion and clergy 32, 59, 81–82, 85–86, 94–95, 97, 117, 142, 149, 184, 202, 204, 234, 236, 238–39, 249, 251–52, 273, 328, 330–31, 338, 350–52, 357–58, 378–79, 390, 392
sanctimony 59–60, 164, 238–39, 273, 284, 291–92
science 45, 53–54, 56, 188–89, 225, 227, 230, 240, 242, 247, 253, 282–85, 287, 291, 294–95, 297, 300, 311–13, 327, 343–45, 351, 405
self-made men, industrialists, and financiers 158–59, 161, 177, 301–02, 310
servants 8, 15, 17–19, 59, 62, 73–74, 84–85, 104, 121, 131, 143, 150, 161, 169–70, 172–73, 201, 204, 210, 213, 228–30, 246–47, 249–51, 258, 260–62, 264, 271, 273–77, 282, 295, 305, 307–08, 323–25, 335, 341, 354, 374, 377
sex crimes 376, 378, 382, 388
sexism 61–62, 119, 215, 218
sexual morality 39, 238, 295, 348–49, 376, 378–80
snobbery 91, 93, 118, 124, 128–29, 204, 207, 279, 282, 362
socialized medicine 258, 261–62, 264, 327, 399
spiritualism, superstition and witchcraft 64, 136–37, 156–57, 159, 203, 235, 236–37, 328–29, 331–32, 367, 376
spurious invalids 281
supermarkets 335, 383

taxation 231, 239, 277, 282, 294, 297, 305, 327, 409
telephone and telegraph communication 15, 20, 24, 35, 39–40, 53, 58, 63, 98, 150, 162, 182, 259, 262, 277, 423
theater 76–77, 93–94, 96–97, 100, 184, 222, 234, 240–41, 245, 261–64, 266, 268–69, 277–79, 281–82, 307, 312–13, 332, 409, 411
travelers' checks 383

unemployment 4, 5, 20, 80, 191, 193, 237, 325

Victorian feminine behaviors 168–69, 172, 207–08, 218

war and its effects 3–4, 7, 15–16, 20–21, 35, 48, 53, 56–57, 63, 65, 80, 107–08, 112, 149–50, 164, 168, 170, 175, 181, 188–93, 200, 205, 209–10, 218, 231–32, 234–35, 237–39, 242, 244, 246–47, 249, 252–53, 258, 266, 268, 271, 273, 275, 277, 279, 282, 287, 294, 297, 300, 302, 308–10, 312, 325–26, 355
woman's intuition 119, 123, 194, 262, 362
work ethic, the 19, 85, 149, 161, 172
working classes 85, 145, 161, 169, 198, 226, 229, 247, 250, 261, 264, 279, 302, 323–24, 327, 341, 367–68, 390
writers 61, 119, 122–23, 128–29, 199, 251, 261–62, 296, 330, 344, 350, 362, 377, 394
writing and typewriting 289, 304, 327, 343

www.ingramcontent.com/pod-product-compliance
Lightning Source LLC
Chambersburg PA
CBHW080935020526
44116CB00034B/2603